BATMAN
KNIGHTFALL
volume two

KNIGHTQUEST

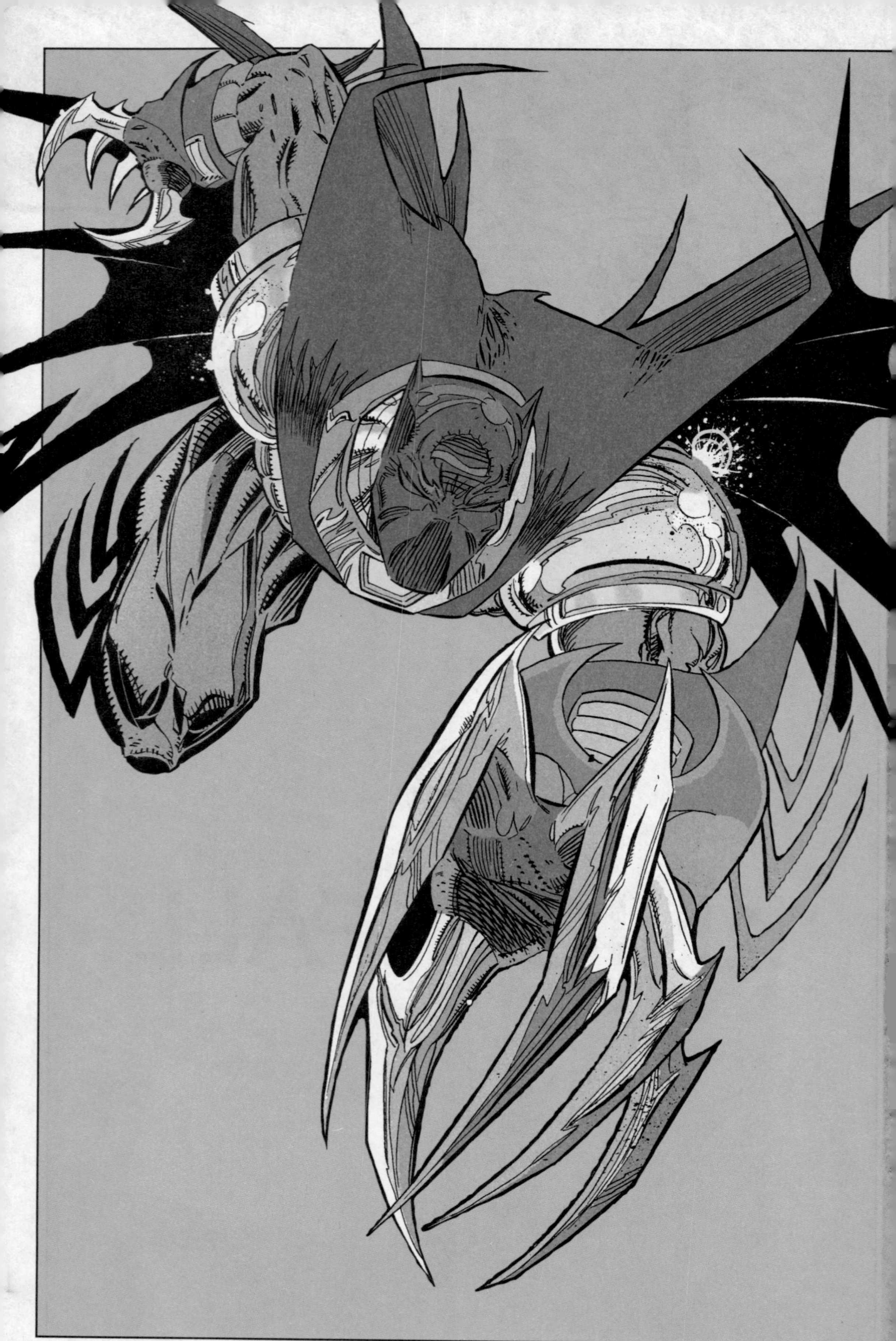

BATMAN

KNIGHTFALL

volume two

KNIGHTQUEST

CHUCK **DIXON** ALAN **GRANT**
DOUG **MOENCH** JO **DUFFY**

writers

GRAHAM **NOLAN** VINCE **GIARRANO**
MIKE **MANLEY** BARRY **KITSON**
JIM **BALENT** BRET **BLEVINS**
TOM **GRUMMETT**

pencillers

SCOTT **HANNA** VINCE **GIARRANO**
MIKE **MANLEY** EDUARDO **BARRETO**
DICK **GIORDANO** BOB **WIACEK**
JOHN **BEATTY** JOSEF **RUBINSTEIN**
FRANK **MCLAUGHLIN** ROBERT R. **SMITH**
RAY **KRYSSING**

inkers

ADRIENNE **ROY**
BUZZ **SETZER**

colorists

JOHN **COSTANZA** TODD **KLEIN**
KEN **BRUZENAK** BOB **PINAHA**
WILLIE **SCHUBERT** ALBERT **DEGUZMAN**

letterers

KELLEY **JONES**

collection cover artist

Batman created by BOB **KANE**

with BILL FINGER

Dennis O'Neil **Scott Peterson** Editors – Original Series
Darren Vincenzo **Jordan Gorfinkel** Assistant Editors – Original Series
Rowena Yow Editor – Collected Edition
Steve Cook Design Director – Books
Robbie Biederman Publication Design

Marie Javins Editor-in-Chief, DC Comics

Daniel Cherry III Senior VP – General Manager
Jim Lee Publisher & Chief Creative Officer
Joen Choe VP – Global Brand & Creative Services
Don Falletti VP – Manufacturing Operations & Workflow Management
Lawrence Ganem VP – Talent Services
Alison Gill Senior VP – Manufacturing & Operations
Nick J. Napolitano VP – Manufacturing Administration & Design
Nancy Spears VP – Revenue

BATMAN: KNIGHTFALL VOLUME TWO

DC Comics, 2900 W. Alameda Avenue, Burbank, CA 91505
Printed by Transcontinental Interweb, Boucherville, QC, Canada. 8/16/21. Eighth Printing.
ISBN: 978-1-4012-3536-9

Library of Congress Cataloging-in-Publication Data

Dixon, Chuck, 1954-
Batman. Knightfall, Volume 2 : knightquest / Chuck Dixon, Alan Grant, Doug Moench, Mary Jo Duffy.
p. cm.
"Originally published in single magazine form in Detective Comics 667-675; Batman: Shadow Of The Bat 19-20, 24-28; Batman 501-508; Catwoman 6-7; Robin 7."
ISBN 978-1-4012-3536-9
1. Graphic novels. I. Grant, Alan, 1949- II. Moench, Doug, 1948- III. Duffy, Jo. IV. Title. V. Title: Knightfall. Volume 2. VI. Title: Knightquest.
PN6728.B36D573 2012
741.5'973–dc23
2012025233

PEFC Certified
This product is from sustainably managed forests and controlled sources
PEFC
PEFC/01-31-106
www.pefc.org

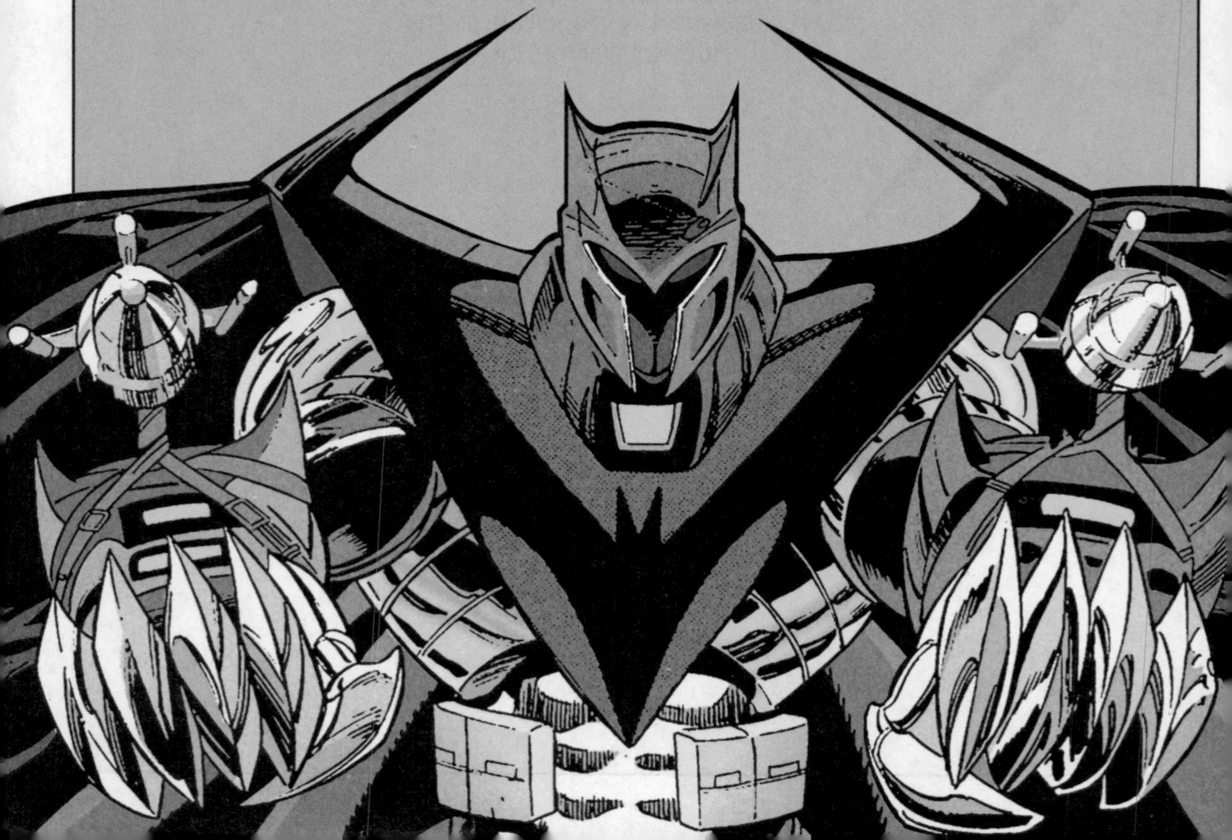

THE STORY SO FAR...

In BATMAN: KNIGHTFALL VOLUME 1, the terrifyingly twisted Bane escaped from Pena Duro prison and immediately journeyed to Gotham to unleash his infinite fury. The hulking lunatic proceeded to free all of Arkham Asylum's many venal villains, creating havoc for an already weary Batman. After methodically taking down Mister Zsasz, Killer Croc, Scarecrow and a number of other crazies, Batman soon reached both his physical and mental breaking point. In an epic showdown with Bane, Batman was thrown off a Gotham skyscraper, and was left heartbroken and paralyzed. While slowly recovering with the help of Robin and the ever-faithful Alfred, Batman, worried for the state of Gotham, appointed Jean Paul Valley (a.k.a. Azreal) to stand in for him. Jean Paul proved to be a ferocious Dark Knight, but his refusal to compromise and his thirst for revenge led him down sinister mental corridors. With a vicious new Batman acting as sentinel of the dark days of Gotham, and with the fearsome Bane still at large, how can Gotham and the true Batman ever recover?

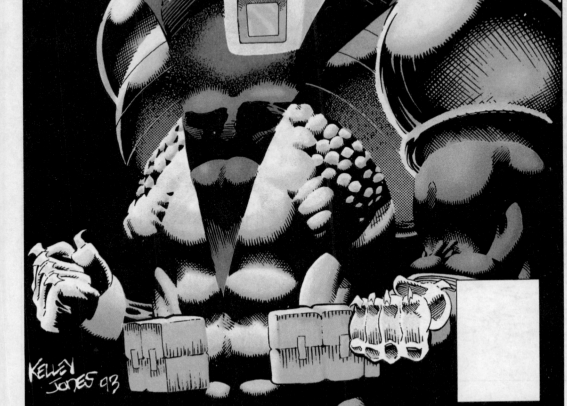

KNIGHTQUEST
THE CRUSADE

DETECTIVE COMICS
FEATURING

BATMAN

DC

DETECTIVE COMICS

667
OCT 93

US$1.25
CAN$1.60
UK 70p

APPROVED BY THE COMICS CODE
AUTHORITY

KELLEY JONES 93

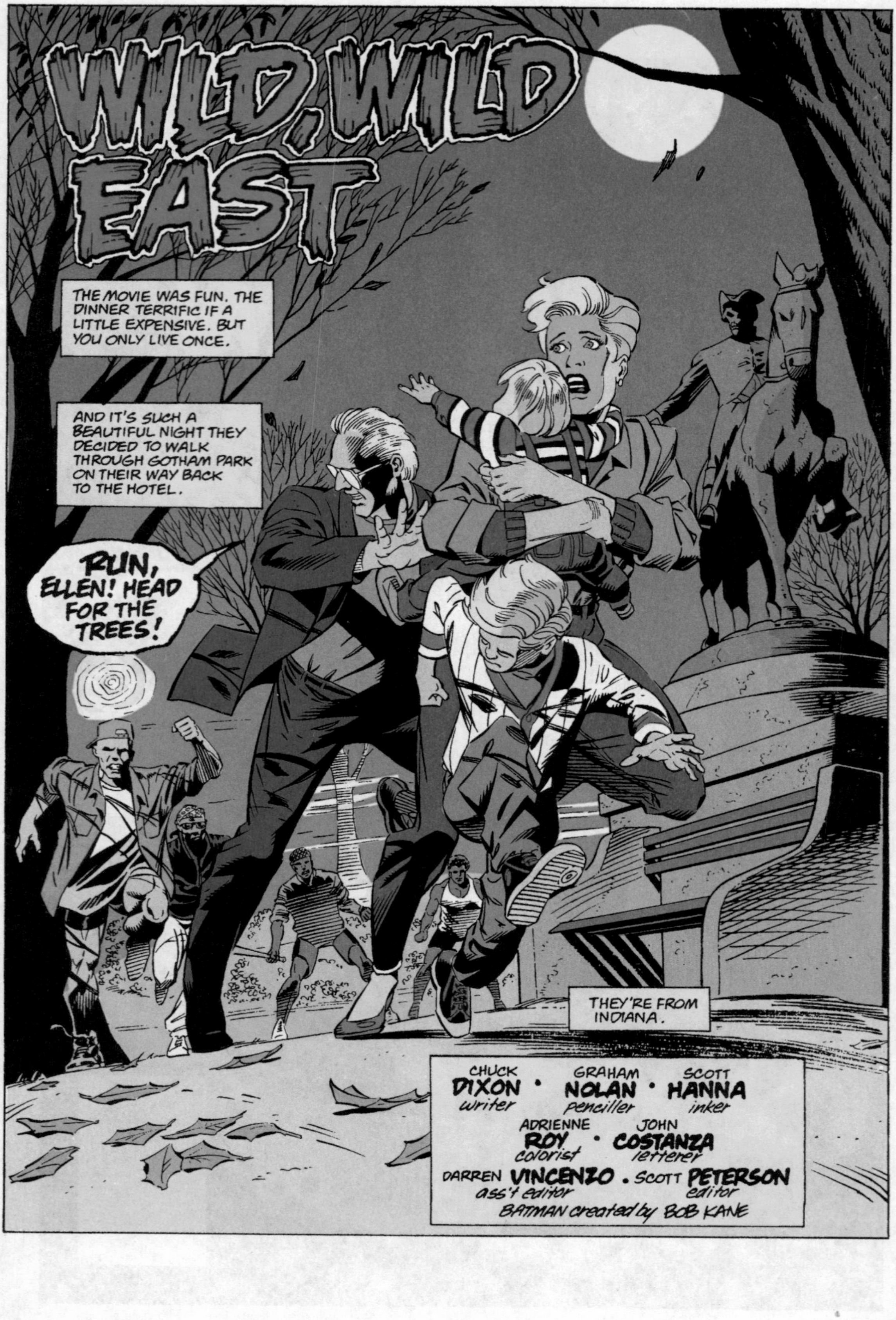
WILD, WILD EAST
THE MOVIE WAS FUN. THE DINNER TERRIFIC IF A LITTLE EXPENSIVE. BUT YOU ONLY LIVE ONCE.
AND IT'S SUCH A BEAUTIFUL NIGHT THEY DECIDED TO WALK THROUGH GOTHAM PARK ON THEIR WAY BACK TO THE HOTEL.
RUN, ELLEN! HEAD FOR THE TREES!
THEY'RE FROM INDIANA.
CHUCK DIXON writer · GRAHAM NOLAN penciller · SCOTT HANNA inker
ADRIENNE ROY colorist · JOHN COSTANZA letterer
DARREN VINCENZO ass't editor · SCOTT PETERSON editor
BATMAN created by BOB KANE

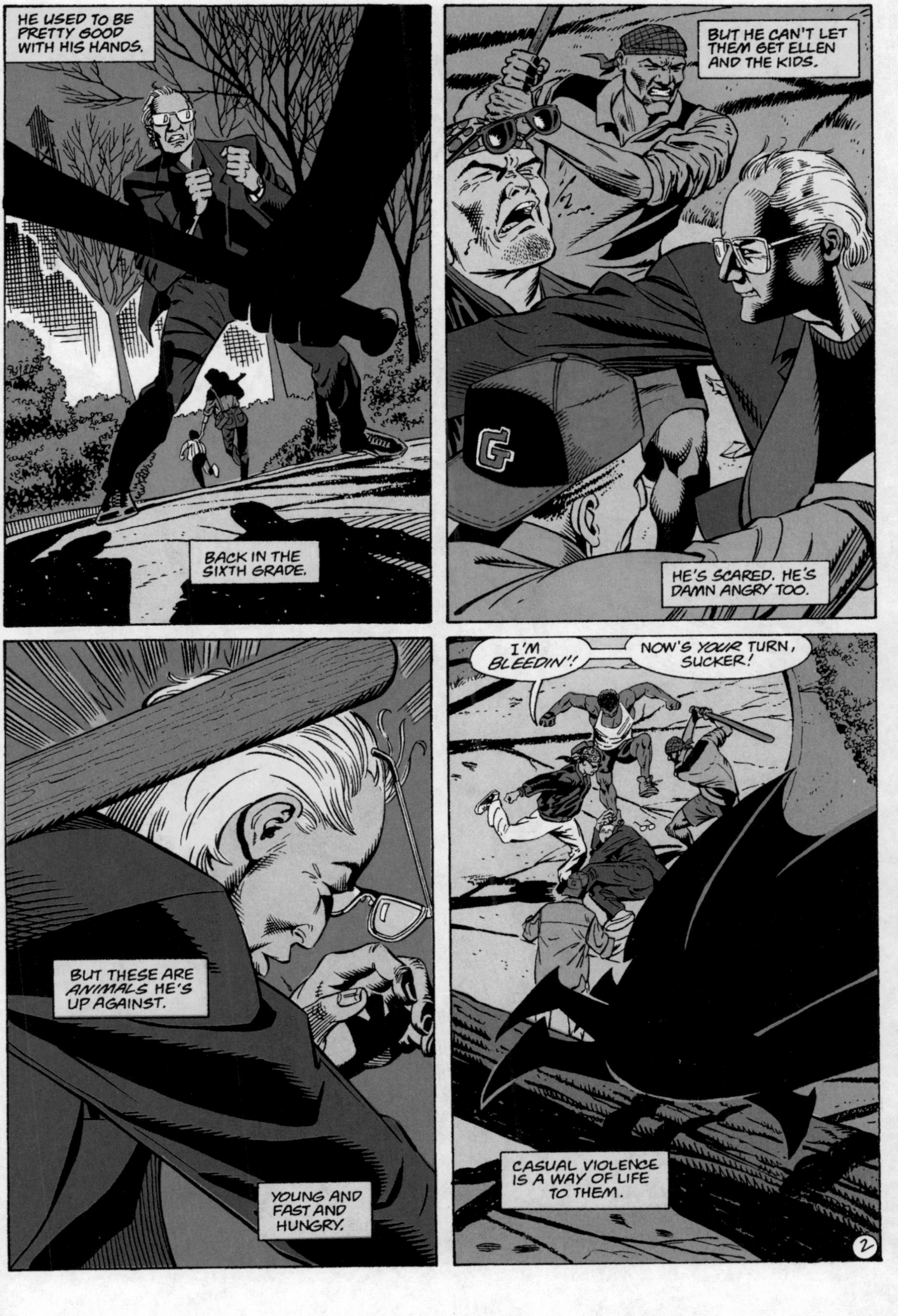
HE USED TO BE PRETTY GOOD WITH HIS HANDS.
BACK IN THE SIXTH GRADE.
BUT HE CAN'T LET THEM GET ELLEN AND THE KIDS.
HE'S SCARED. HE'S DAMN ANGRY TOO.
BUT THESE ARE ANIMALS HE'S UP AGAINST.
YOUNG AND FAST AND HUNGRY.
I'M BLEEDIN'!
NOW'S YOUR TURN, SUCKER!
CASUAL VIOLENCE IS A WAY OF LIFE TO THEM.
2

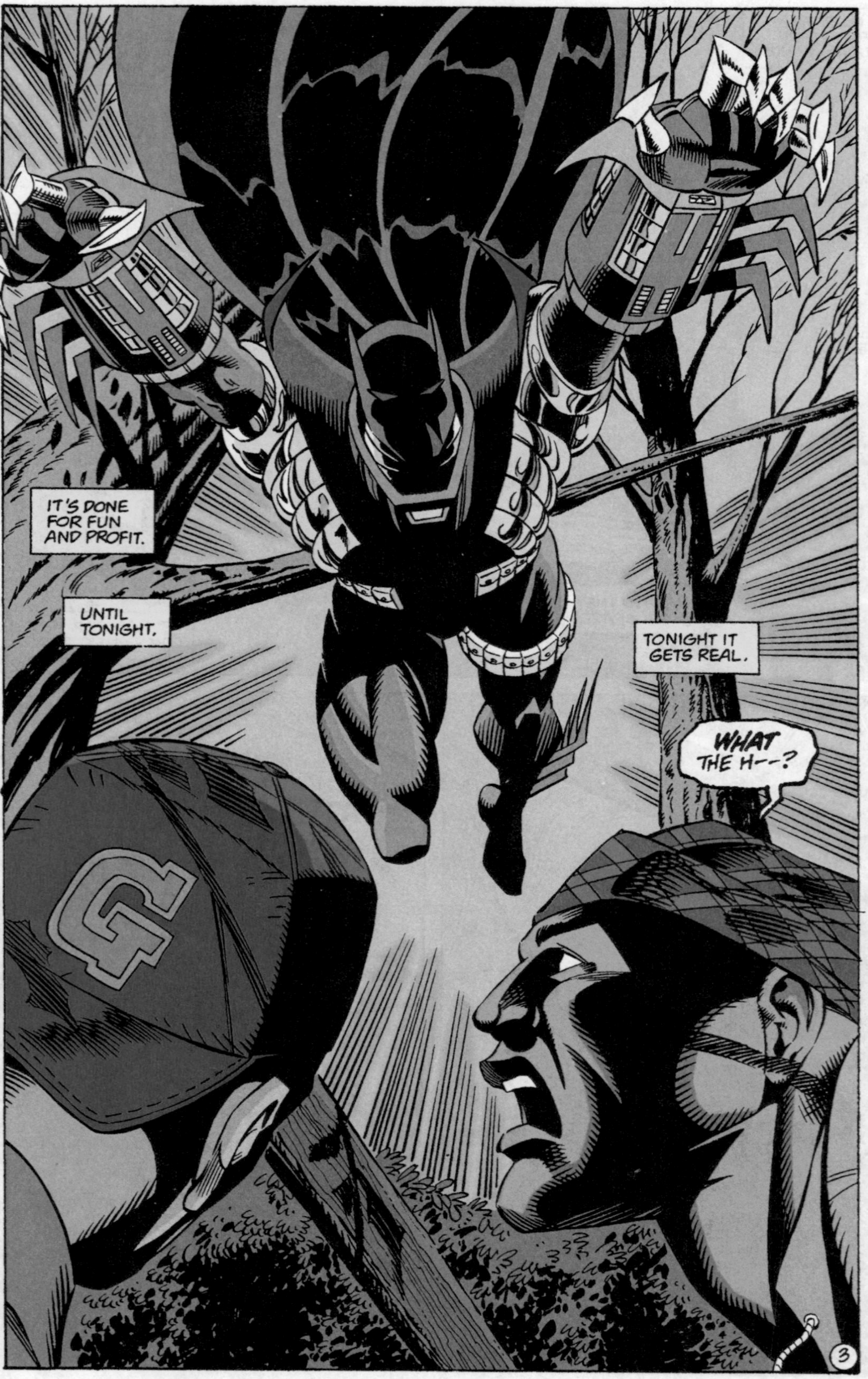
IT'S DONE FOR FUN AND PROFIT.
UNTIL TONIGHT.
TONIGHT IT GETS REAL.
WHAT THE H--?
3

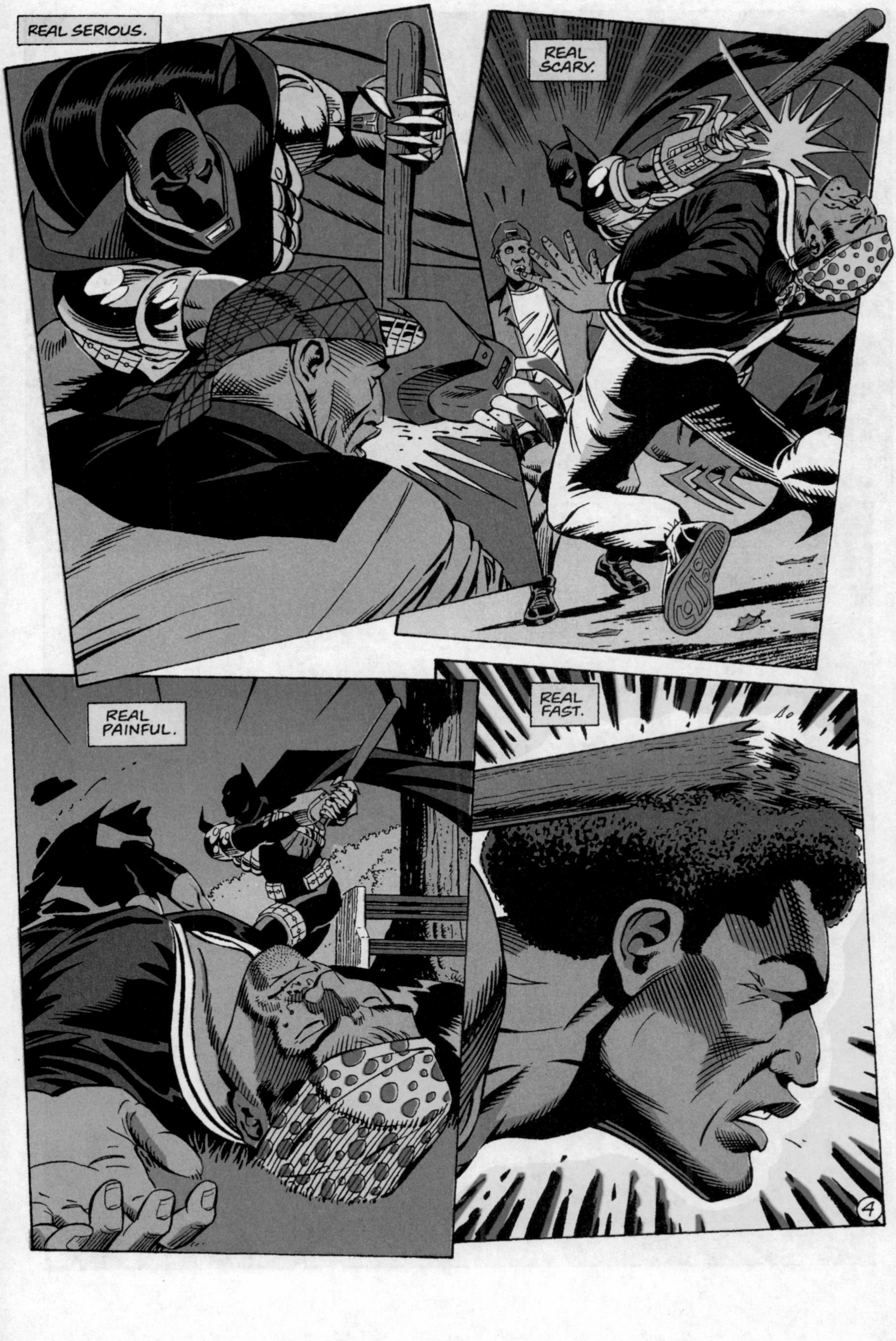
REAL SERIOUS.
REAL SCARY.
REAL PAINFUL.
REAL FAST.
4

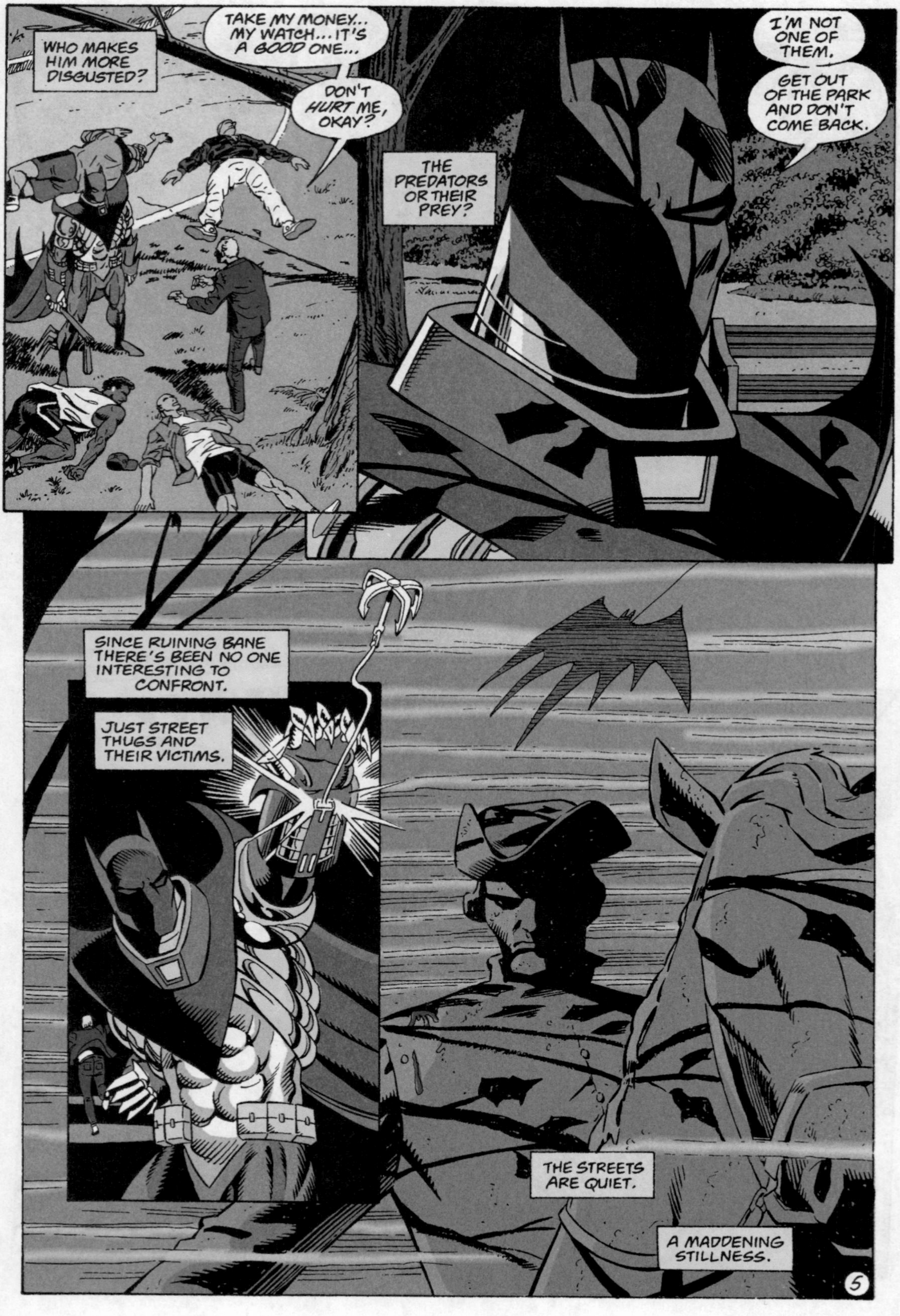
WHO MAKES HIM MORE DISGUSTED?
TAKE MY MONEY... MY WATCH... IT'S A GOOD ONE...
DON'T HURT ME, OKAY?
THE PREDATORS OR THEIR PREY?
I'M NOT ONE OF THEM.
GET OUT OF THE PARK AND DON'T COME BACK.
SINCE RUINING BANE THERE'S BEEN NO ONE INTERESTING TO CONFRONT.
JUST STREET THUGS AND THEIR VICTIMS.
THE STREETS ARE QUIET.
A MADDENING STILLNESS.
5

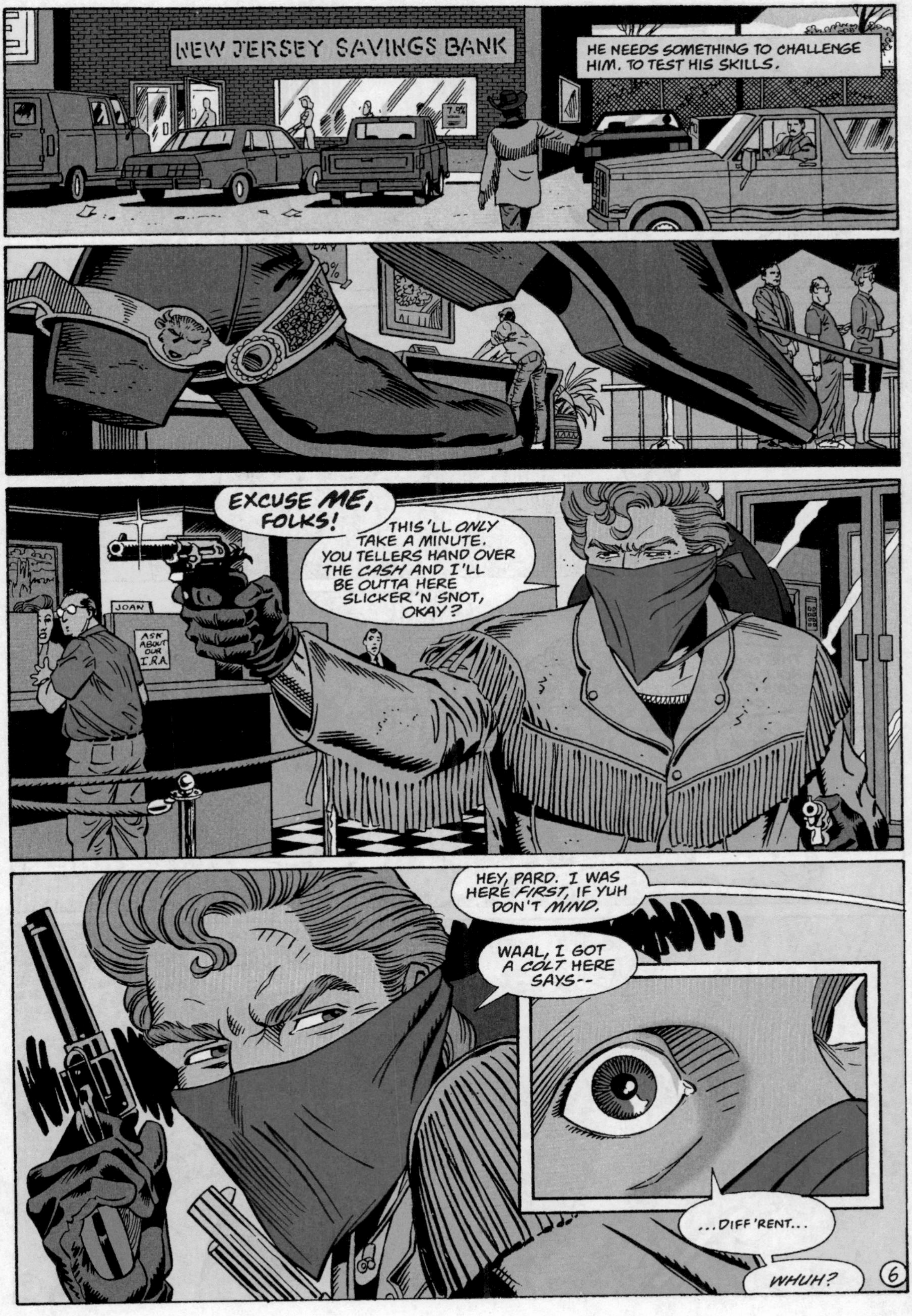
NEW JERSEY SAVINGS BANK
HE NEEDS SOMETHING TO CHALLENGE HIM. TO TEST HIS SKILLS.
EXCUSE ME, FOLKS!
THIS'LL ONLY TAKE A MINUTE. YOU TELLERS HAND OVER THE CASH AND I'LL BE OUTTA HERE SLICKER 'N SNOT, OKAY?
JOAN
ASK ABOUT OUR I.R.A.
HEY, PARD. I WAS HERE FIRST, IF YUH DON'T MIND.
WAAL, I GOT A COLT HERE SAYS--
...DIFF'RENT...
WHUH?
6

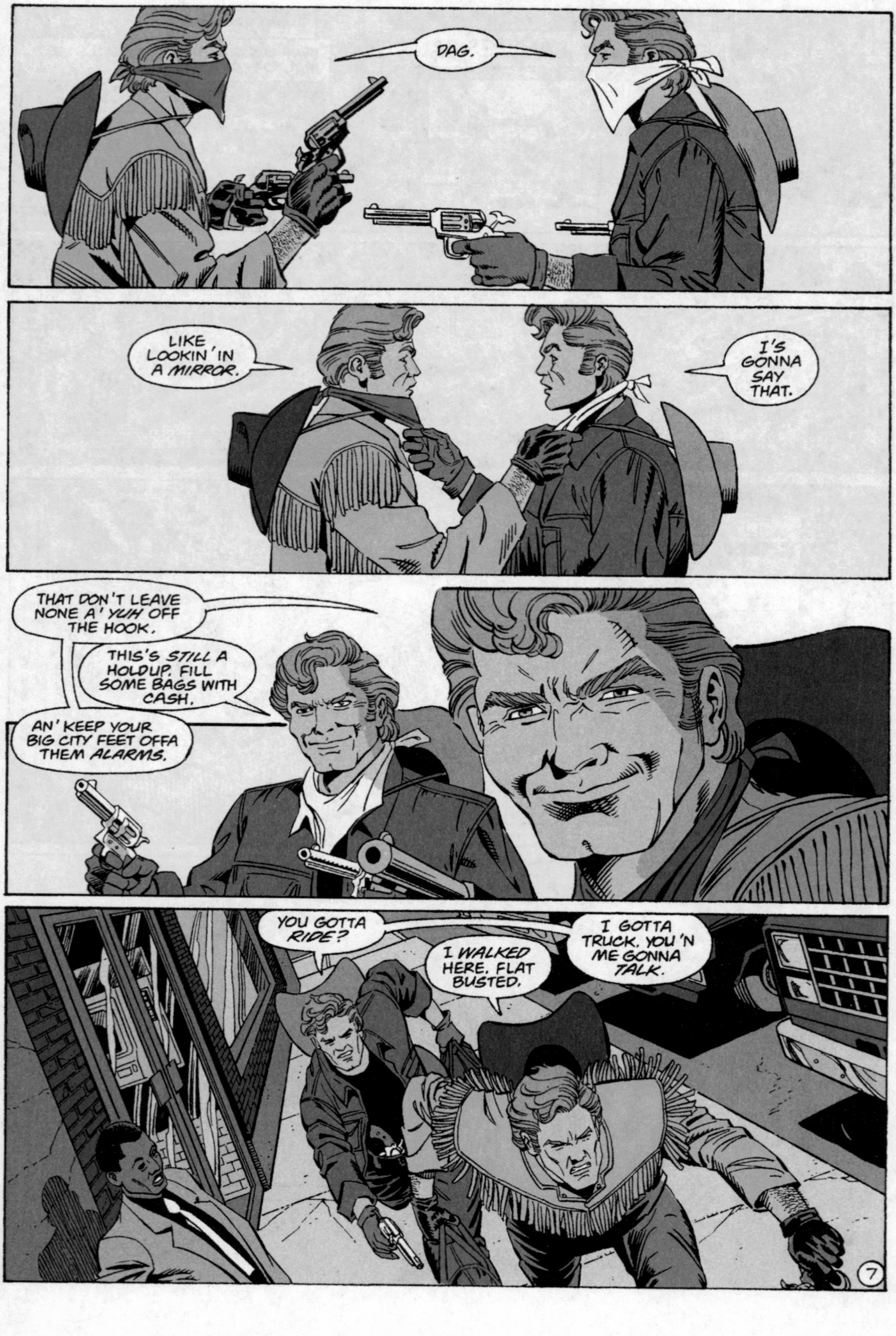

DAG.
LIKE LOOKIN' IN A MIRROR.
I'S GONNA SAY THAT.
THAT DON'T LEAVE NONE A' YUH OFF THE HOOK.
THIS'S STILL A HOLDUP. FILL SOME BAGS WITH CASH.
AN' KEEP YOUR BIG CITY FEET OFFA THEM ALARMS.
YOU GOTTA RIDE?
I WALKED HERE. FLAT BUSTED.
I GOTTA TRUCK. YOU 'N ME GONNA TALK.
7

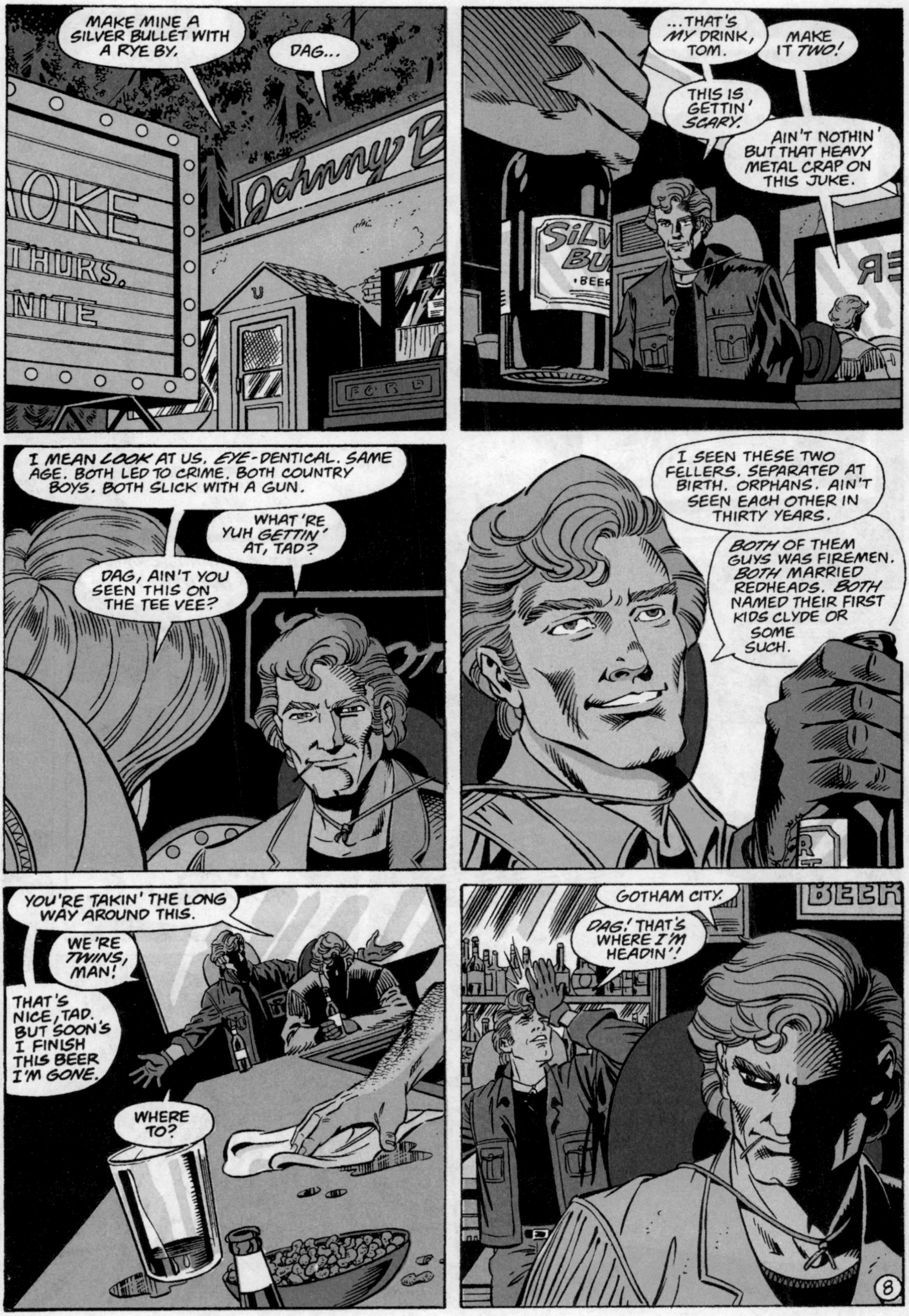
MAKE MINE A SILVER BULLET WITH A RYE BY.
DAG...
...AOKE
THURS.
NITE
Johnny B
...THAT'S MY DRINK, TOM.
MAKE IT TWO!
THIS IS GETTIN' SCARY.
AIN'T NOTHIN' BUT THAT HEAVY METAL CRAP ON THIS JUKE.
I MEAN LOOK AT US. EYE-DENTICAL. SAME AGE. BOTH LED TO CRIME. BOTH COUNTRY BOYS. BOTH SLICK WITH A GUN.
WHAT'RE YUH GETTIN' AT, TAD?
DAG, AIN'T YOU SEEN THIS ON THE TEE VEE?
I SEEN THESE TWO FELLERS. SEPARATED AT BIRTH. ORPHANS. AIN'T SEEN EACH OTHER IN THIRTY YEARS.
BOTH OF THEM GUYS WAS FIREMEN. BOTH MARRIED REDHEADS. BOTH NAMED THEIR FIRST KIDS CLYDE OR SOME SUCH.
YOU'RE TAKIN' THE LONG WAY AROUND THIS.
WE'RE TWINS, MAN!
THAT'S NICE, TAD. BUT SOON'S I FINISH THIS BEER I'M GONE.
WHERE TO?
BEER
GOTHAM CITY.
DAG! THAT'S WHERE I'M HEADIN'!
8

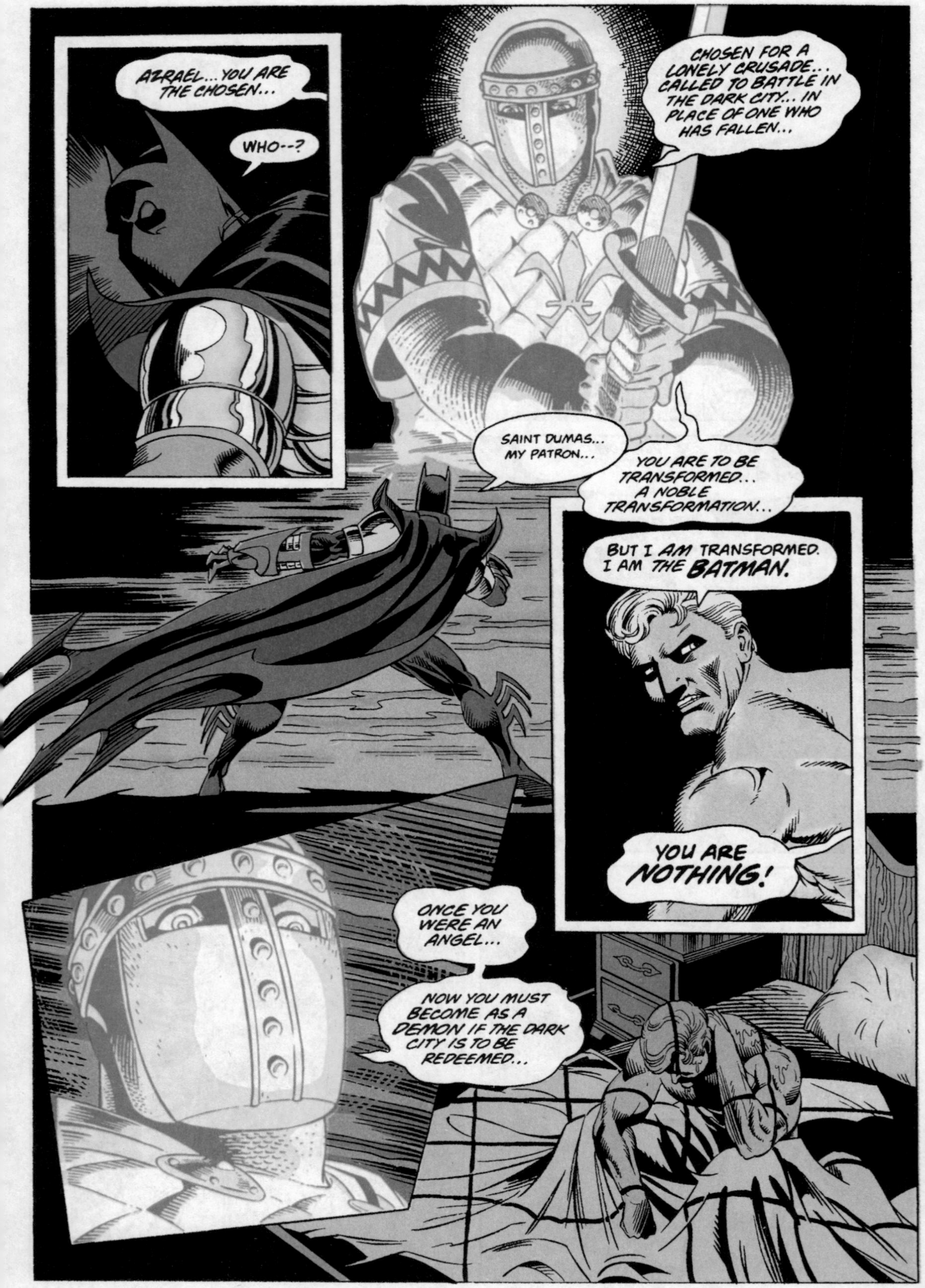
AZRAEL... YOU ARE THE CHOSEN...
WHO--?
CHOSEN FOR A LONELY CRUSADE... CALLED TO BATTLE IN THE DARK CITY... IN PLACE OF ONE WHO HAS FALLEN...
SAINT DUMAS... MY PATRON...
YOU ARE TO BE TRANSFORMED... A NOBLE TRANSFORMATION...
BUT I AM TRANSFORMED. I AM THE BATMAN.
YOU ARE NOTHING!
ONCE YOU WERE AN ANGEL...
NOW YOU MUST BECOME AS A DEMON IF THE DARK CITY IS TO BE REDEEMED...

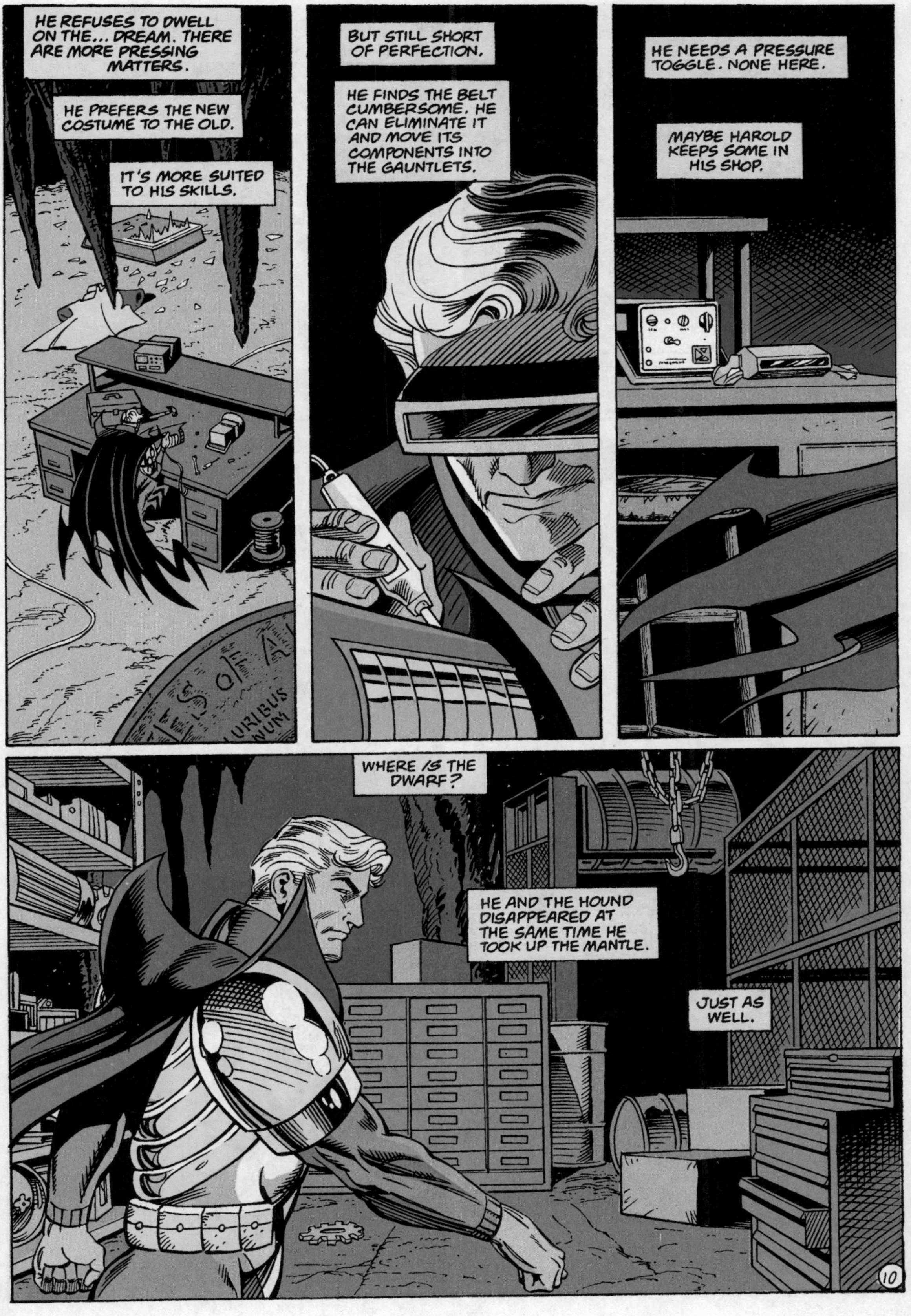
HE REFUSES TO DWELL ON THE... DREAM. THERE ARE MORE PRESSING MATTERS.
HE PREFERS THE NEW COSTUME TO THE OLD.
IT'S MORE SUITED TO HIS SKILLS.
BUT STILL SHORT OF PERFECTION.
HE FINDS THE BELT CUMBERSOME. HE CAN ELIMINATE IT AND MOVE ITS COMPONENTS INTO THE GAUNTLETS.
HE NEEDS A PRESSURE TOGGLE. NONE HERE.
MAYBE HAROLD KEEPS SOME IN HIS SHOP.
WHERE IS THE DWARF?
HE AND THE HOUND DISAPPEARED AT THE SAME TIME HE TOOK UP THE MANTLE.
JUST AS WELL.
10

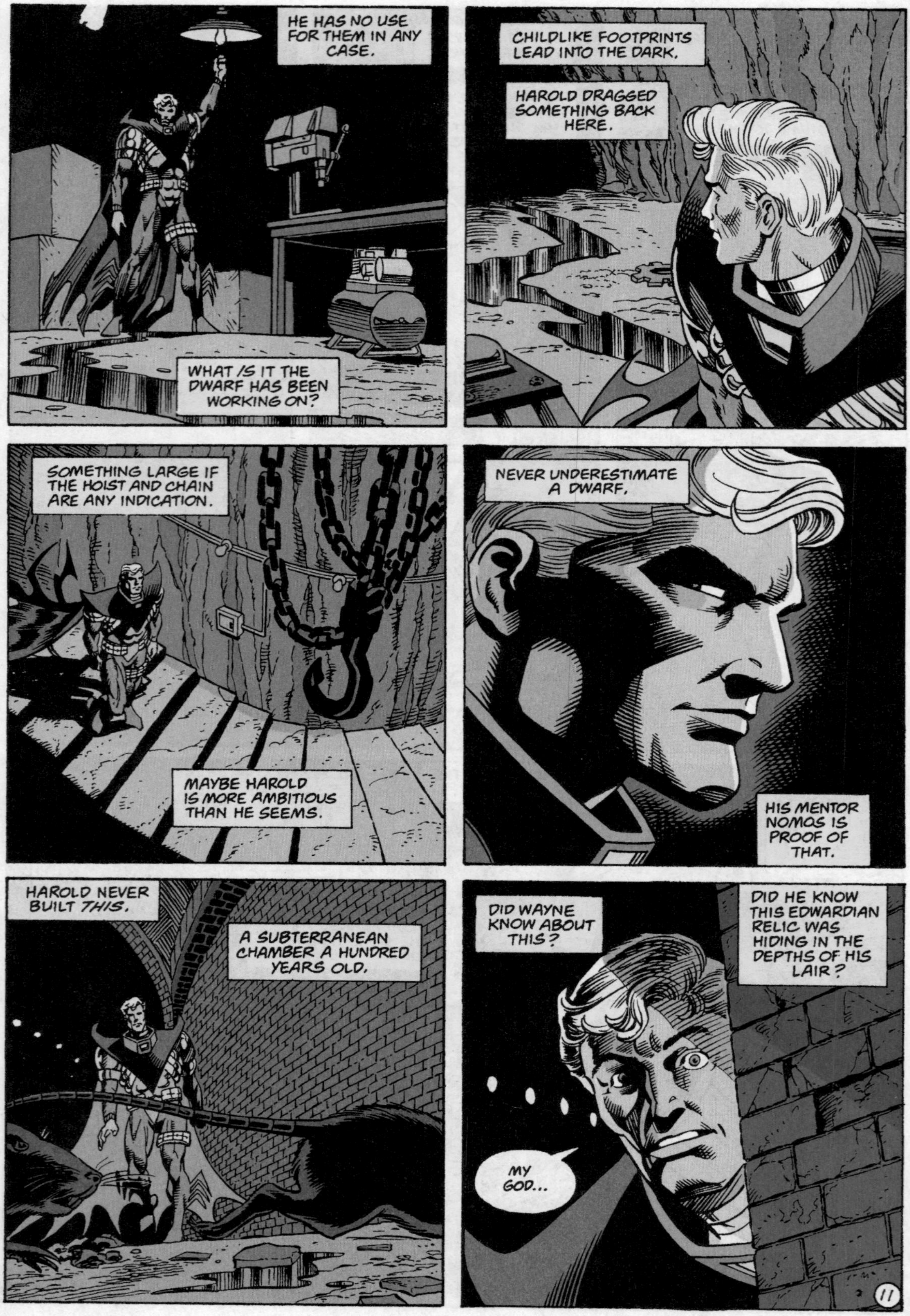
HE HAS NO USE FOR THEM IN ANY CASE.
WHAT IS IT THE DWARF HAS BEEN WORKING ON?
CHILDLIKE FOOTPRINTS LEAD INTO THE DARK.
HAROLD DRAGGED SOMETHING BACK HERE.
SOMETHING LARGE IF THE HOIST AND CHAIN ARE ANY INDICATION.
MAYBE HAROLD IS MORE AMBITIOUS THAN HE SEEMS.
NEVER UNDERESTIMATE A DWARF.
HIS MENTOR NOMOS IS PROOF OF THAT.
HAROLD NEVER BUILT THIS.
A SUBTERRANEAN CHAMBER A HUNDRED YEARS OLD.
DID WAYNE KNOW ABOUT THIS?
DID HE KNOW THIS EDWARDIAN RELIC WAS HIDING IN THE DEPTHS OF HIS LAIR?
MY GOD...
11

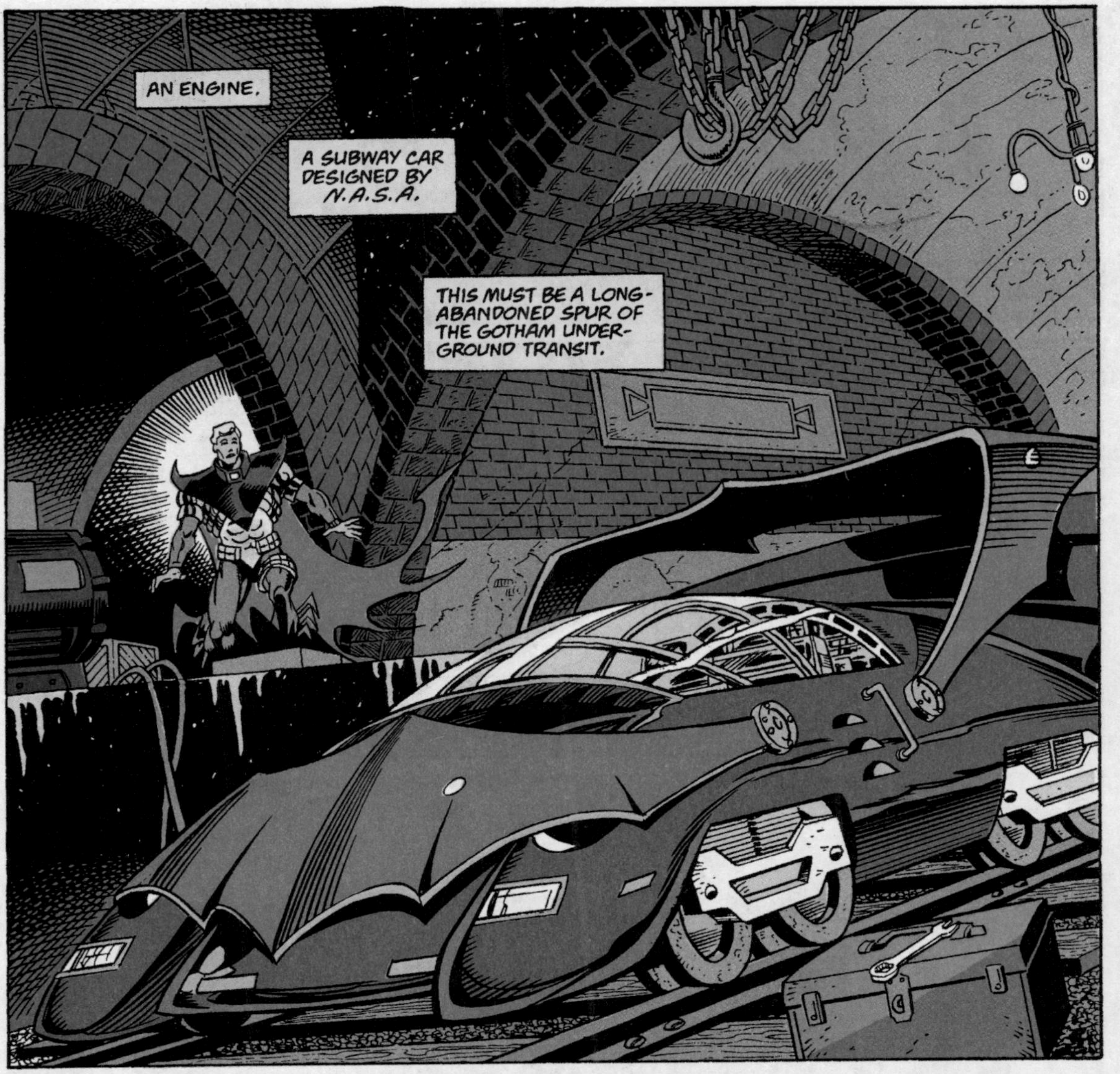
AN ENGINE.
A SUBWAY CAR DESIGNED BY N.A.S.A.
THIS MUST BE A LONG-ABANDONED SPUR OF THE GOTHAM UNDER-GROUND TRANSIT.

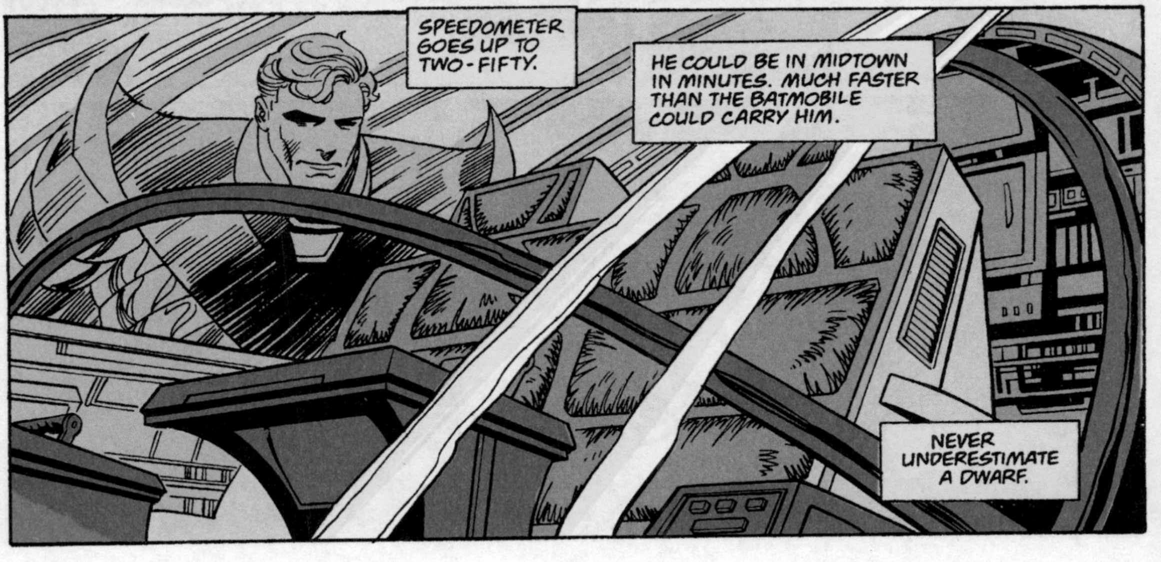
SPEEDOMETER GOES UP TO TWO-FIFTY.
HE COULD BE IN MIDTOWN IN MINUTES. MUCH FASTER THAN THE BATMOBILE COULD CARRY HIM.
NEVER UNDERESTIMATE A DWARF.

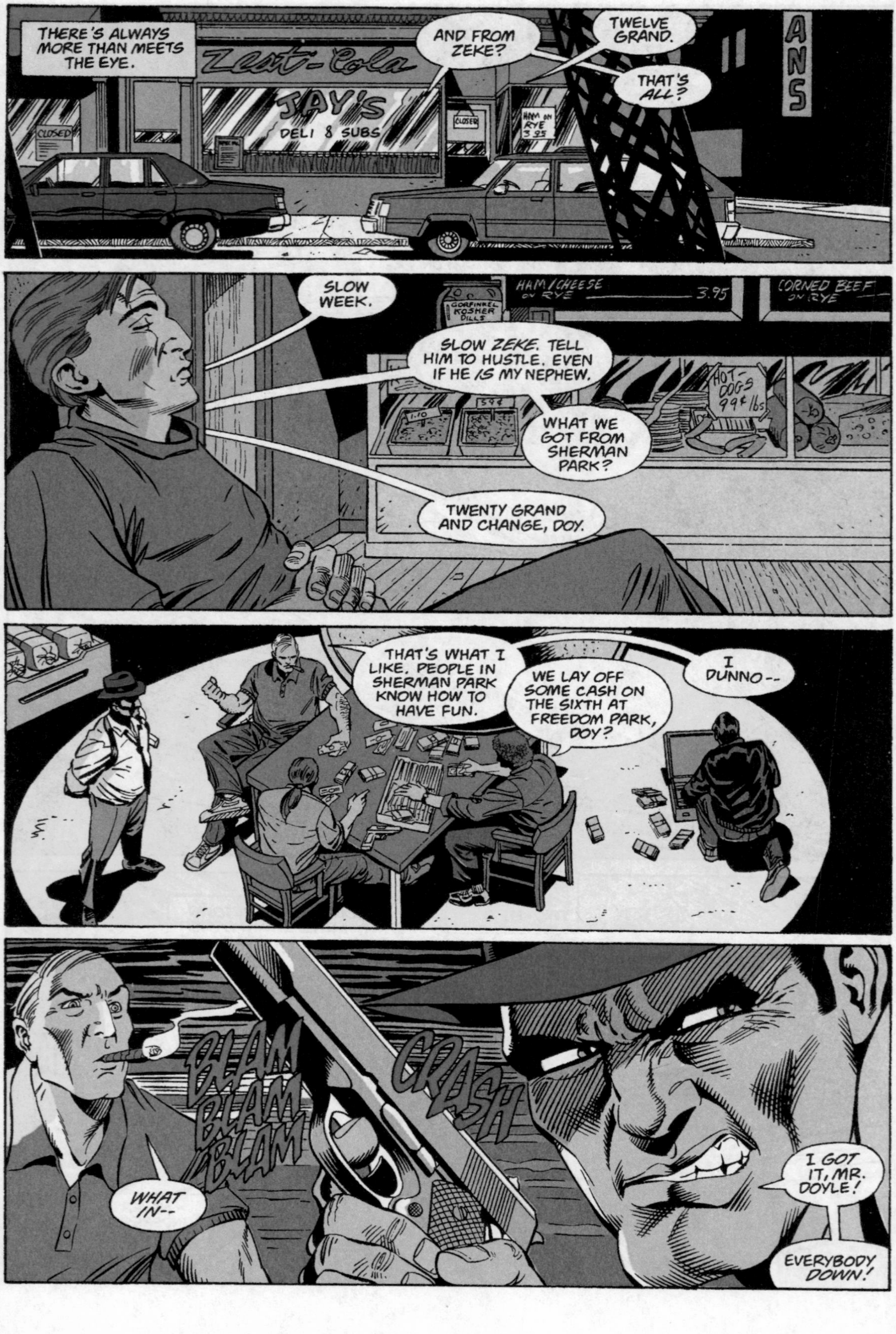
THERE'S ALWAYS MORE THAN MEETS THE EYE.
AND FROM ZEKE?
TWELVE GRAND.
THAT'S ALL?
SLOW WEEK.
SLOW ZEKE. TELL HIM TO HUSTLE. EVEN IF HE IS MY NEPHEW.
WHAT WE GOT FROM SHERMAN PARK?
TWENTY GRAND AND CHANGE, DOY.
THAT'S WHAT I LIKE. PEOPLE IN SHERMAN PARK KNOW HOW TO HAVE FUN.
WE LAY OFF SOME CASH ON THE SIXTH AT FREEDOM PARK, DOY?
I DUNNO--
BLAM BLAM BLAM
CRASH
WHAT IN--
I GOT IT, MR. DOYLE!
EVERYBODY DOWN!

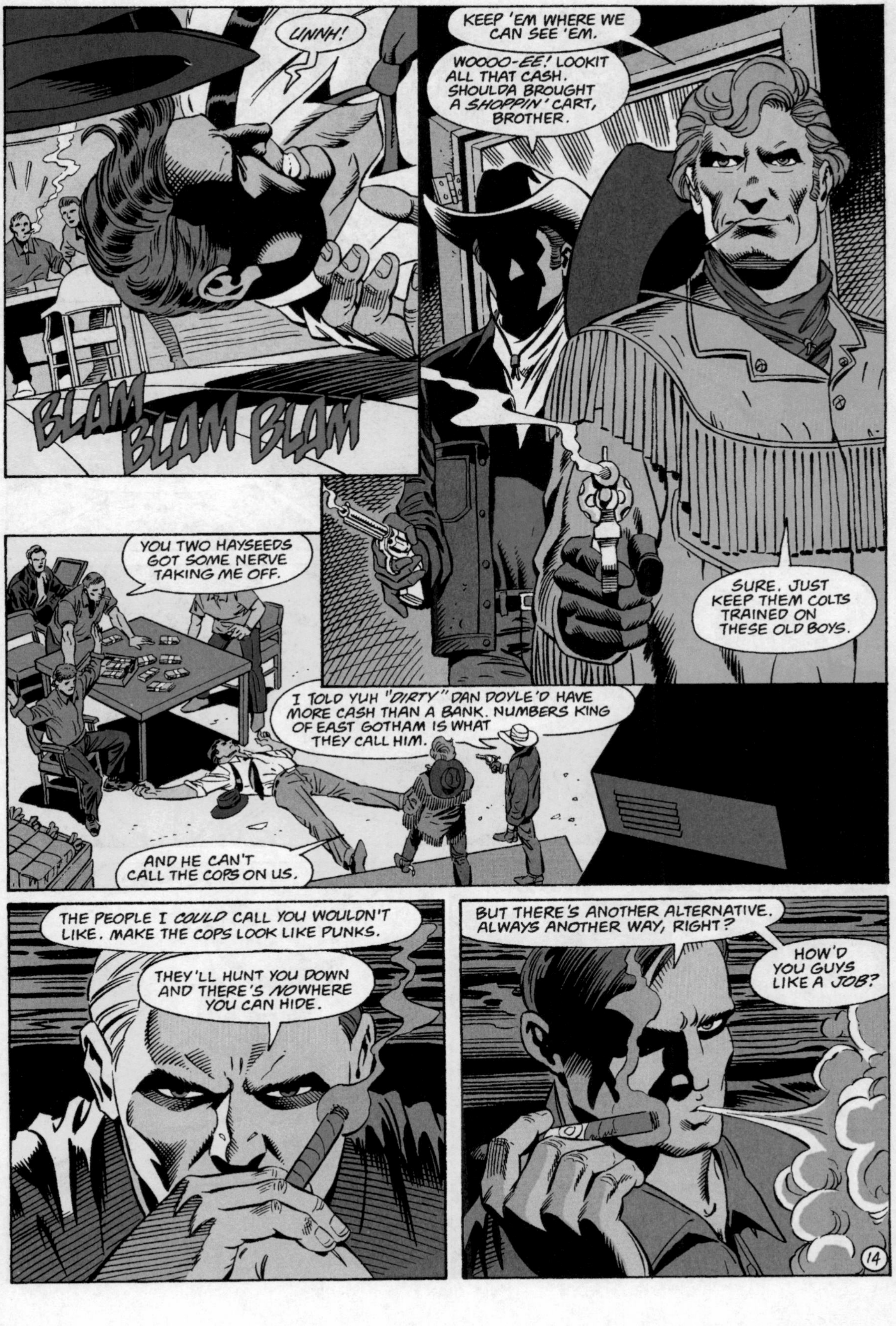
UNNH!
BLAM BLAM BLAM
KEEP 'EM WHERE WE CAN SEE 'EM.
WOOOO-EE! LOOKIT ALL THAT CASH. SHOULDA BROUGHT A SHOPPIN' CART, BROTHER.
SURE. JUST KEEP THEM COLTS TRAINED ON THESE OLD BOYS.
YOU TWO HAYSEEDS GOT SOME NERVE TAKING ME OFF.
I TOLD YUH "DIRTY" DAN DOYLE'D HAVE MORE CASH THAN A BANK. NUMBERS KING OF EAST GOTHAM IS WHAT THEY CALL HIM.
AND HE CAN'T CALL THE COPS ON US.
THE PEOPLE I COULD CALL YOU WOULDN'T LIKE. MAKE THE COPS LOOK LIKE PUNKS.
THEY'LL HUNT YOU DOWN AND THERE'S NOWHERE YOU CAN HIDE.
BUT THERE'S ANOTHER ALTERNATIVE. ALWAYS ANOTHER WAY, RIGHT?
HOW'D YOU GUYS LIKE A JOB?
14

A JOB?

AFTER WE GUNNED TWO OF YOUR BOYS?

WELL, LENNIE AND CLIFF DIDN'T DO SUCH A GOOD JOB STOPPIN' *YOU* GUYS, RIGHT? I SAY GOOD RIDDANCE.

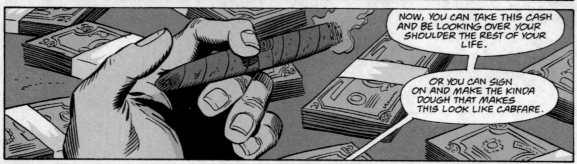

NOW, YOU CAN TAKE THIS CASH AND BE LOOKING OVER YOUR SHOULDER THE REST OF YOUR LIFE.

OR YOU CAN SIGN ON AND MAKE THE KINDA DOUGH THAT MAKES THIS LOOK LIKE CABFARE.

HE'S GOT A POINT.

THIS'S THE BIGTIME ACTION WE CAME TO GOTHAM *LOOKING* FOR.

WE'RE HIRIN' ON, MR. DOYLE.

WHAT IS IT YOU WANT US TO DO?

I GOT SOMETHING THAT'S RIGHT UP YOUR ALLEY, BOYS...

... AN OLD-FASHIONED *GUN* FIGHT.

15

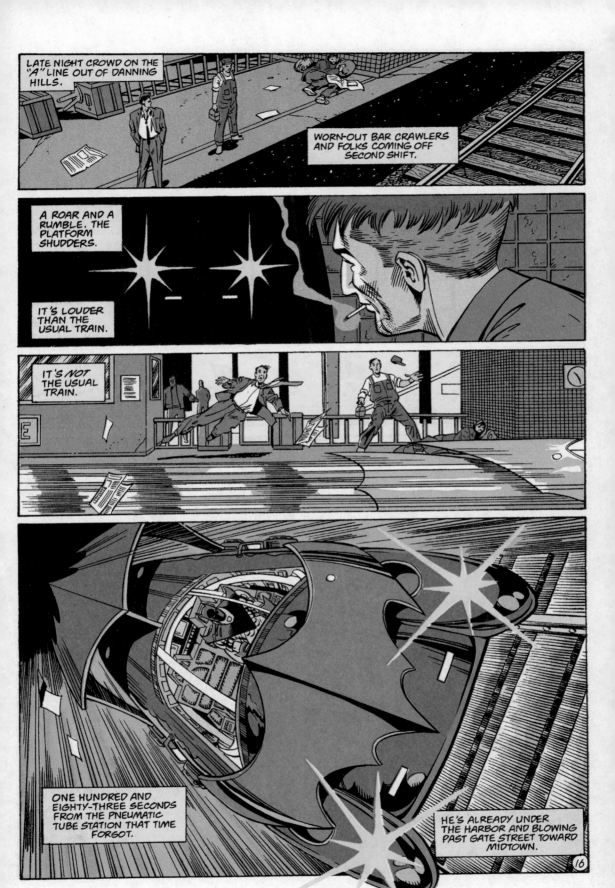

LATE NIGHT CROWD ON THE "A" LINE OUT OF DANNING HILLS.

WORN-OUT BAR CRAWLERS AND FOLKS COMING OFF SECOND SHIFT.

A ROAR AND A RUMBLE. THE PLATFORM SHUDDERS.

IT'S LOUDER THAN THE USUAL TRAIN.

IT'S *NOT* THE USUAL TRAIN.

ONE HUNDRED AND EIGHTY-THREE SECONDS FROM THE PNEUMATIC TUBE STATION THAT TIME FORGOT.

HE'S ALREADY UNDER THE HARBOR AND BLOWING PAST GATE STREET TOWARD MIDTOWN.

16

23

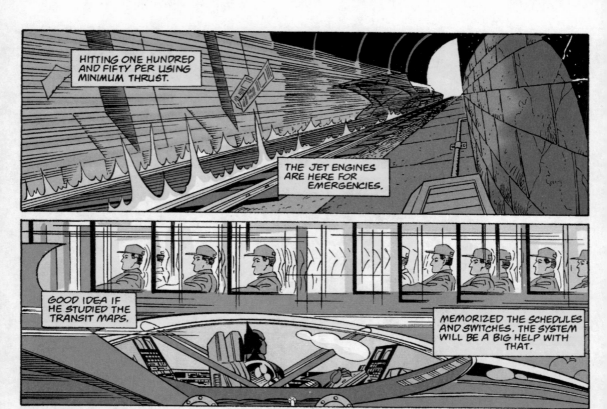

HITTING ONE HUNDRED AND FIFTY PER USING MINIMUM THRUST.

THE JET ENGINES ARE HERE FOR EMERGENCIES.

GOOD IDEA IF HE STUDIED THE TRANSIT MAPS.

MEMORIZED THE SCHEDULES AND SWITCHES. THE SYSTEM WILL BE A BIG HELP WITH THAT.

NOWHERE IN GOTHAM IS OUT OF HIS REACH NOW.

HE LIKES THAT.

TOO BAD ABOUT THE EMPTY SEAT.

WASTE OF VALUABLE SPACE.

17

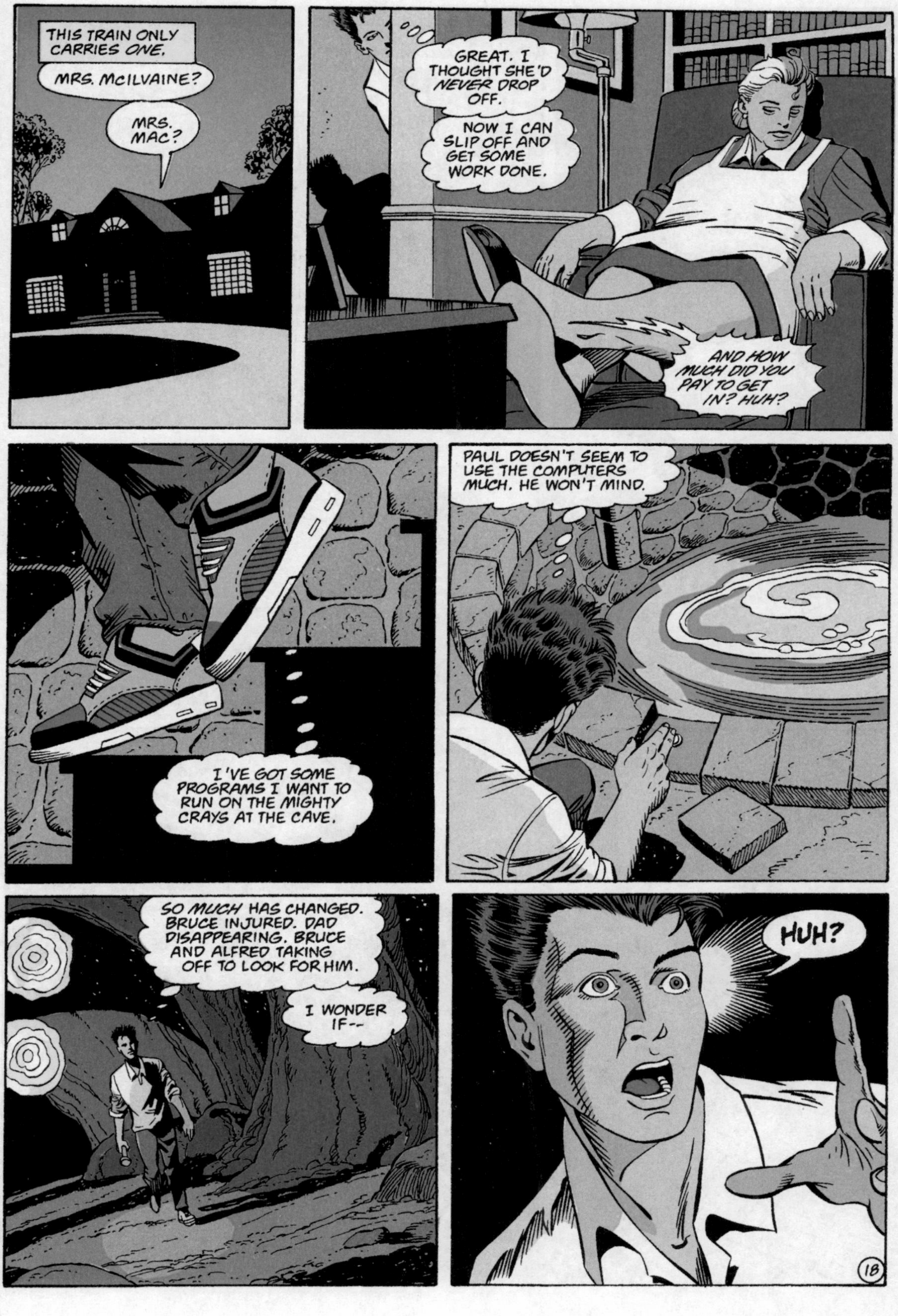
THIS TRAIN ONLY CARRIES ONE.
MRS. McILVAINE?
MRS. MAC?
GREAT. I THOUGHT SHE'D NEVER DROP OFF.
NOW I CAN SLIP OFF AND GET SOME WORK DONE.
AND HOW MUCH DID YOU PAY TO GET IN? HUH?
I'VE GOT SOME PROGRAMS I WANT TO RUN ON THE MIGHTY CRAYS AT THE CAVE.
PAUL DOESN'T SEEM TO USE THE COMPUTERS MUCH. HE WON'T MIND.
SO MUCH HAS CHANGED. BRUCE INJURED. DAD DISAPPEARING. BRUCE AND ALFRED TAKING OFF TO LOOK FOR HIM.
I WONDER IF--
HUH?
18

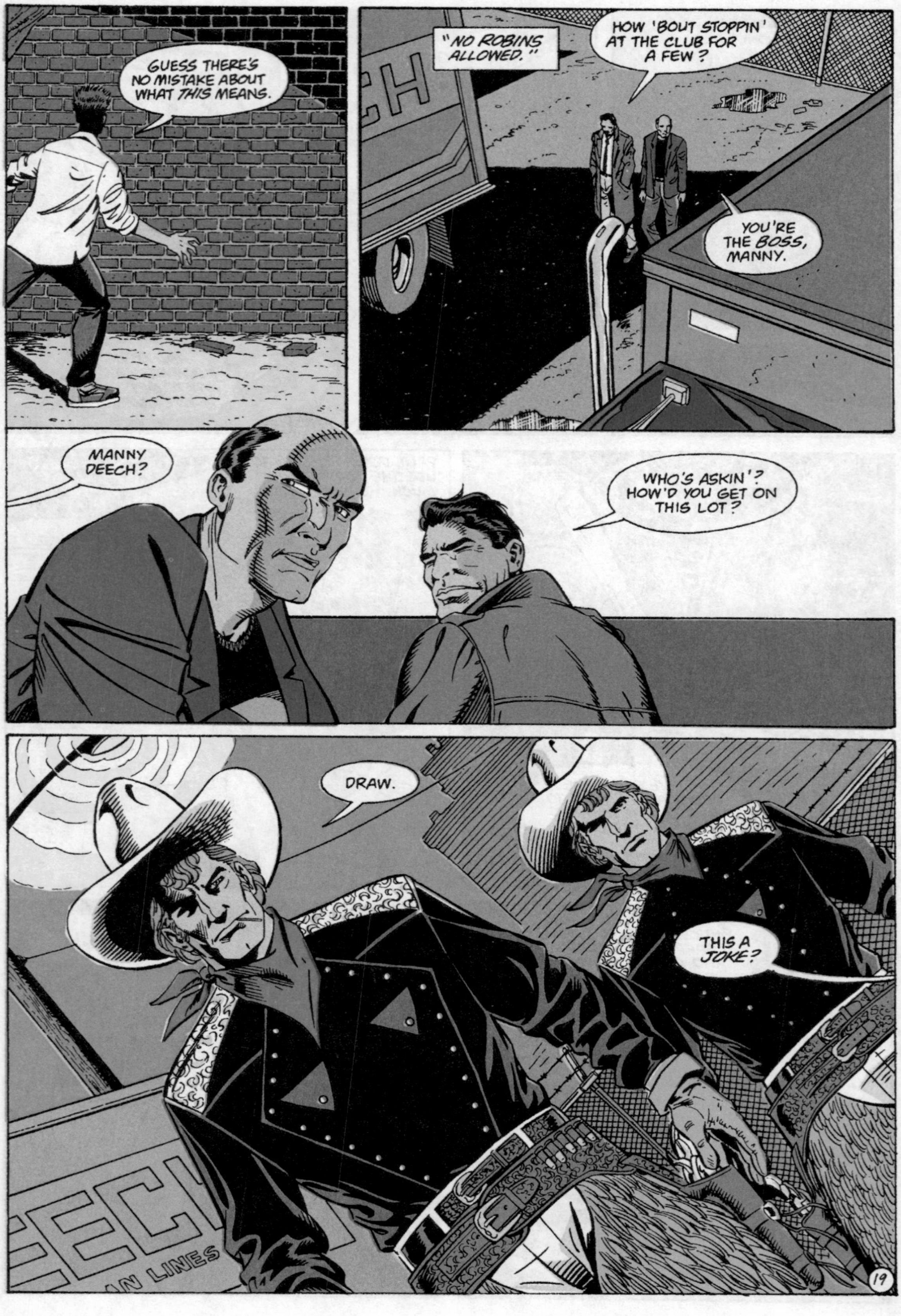
GUESS THERE'S NO MISTAKE ABOUT WHAT THIS MEANS.
"NO ROBINS ALLOWED."
HOW 'BOUT STOPPIN' AT THE CLUB FOR A FEW?
YOU'RE THE BOSS, MANNY.
CH
MANNY DEECH?
WHO'S ASKIN'? HOW'D YOU GET ON THIS LOT?
DRAW.
THIS A JOKE?
EECH
AN LINES
19

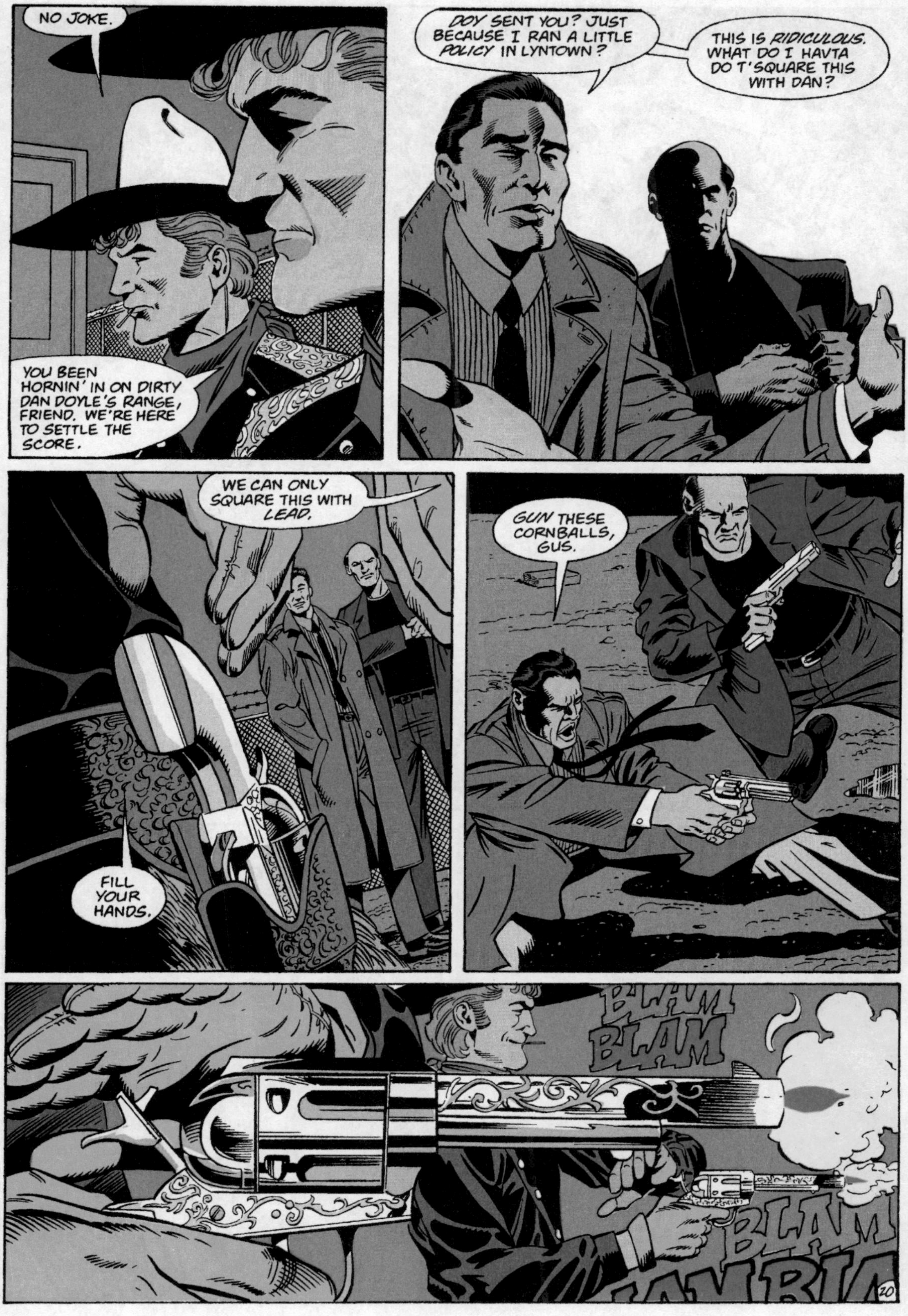
NO JOKE.
YOU BEEN HORNIN' IN ON DIRTY DAN DOYLE'S RANGE, FRIEND. WE'RE HERE TO SETTLE THE SCORE.
DOY SENT YOU? JUST BECAUSE I RAN A LITTLE POLICY IN LYNTOWN?
THIS IS RIDICULOUS. WHAT DO I HAVTA DO T'SQUARE THIS WITH DAN?
WE CAN ONLY SQUARE THIS WITH LEAD.
FILL YOUR HANDS.
GUN THESE CORNBALLS, GUS.
BLAM
BLAM
BLAM
20

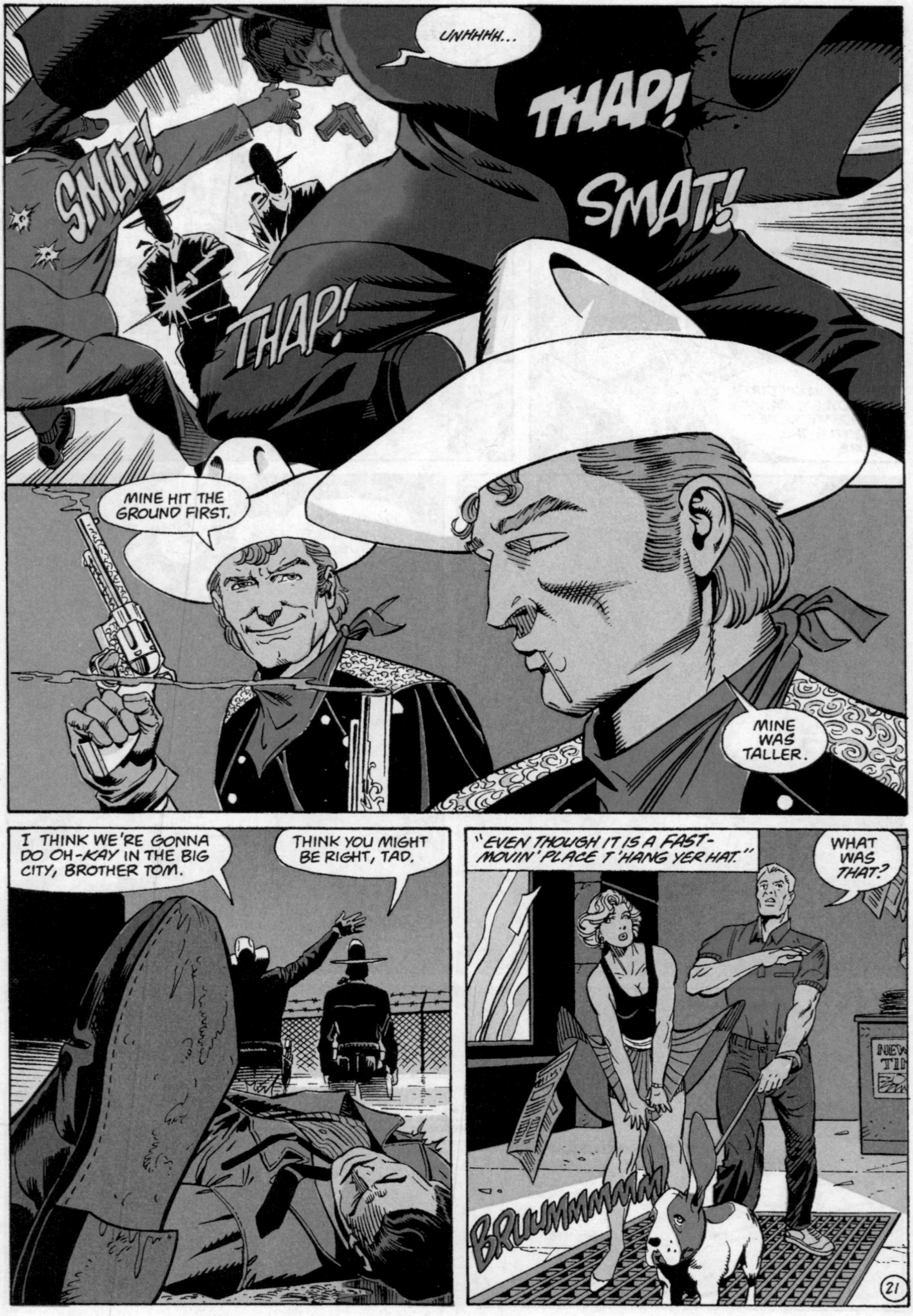
UNHHHH...
THAP!
SMAT!
SMAT!
THAP!
MINE HIT THE GROUND FIRST.
MINE WAS TALLER.
I THINK WE'RE GONNA DO OH-KAY IN THE BIG CITY, BROTHER TOM.
THINK YOU MIGHT BE RIGHT, TAD.
"EVEN THOUGH IT IS A FAST-MOVIN' PLACE T'HANG YER HAT."
WHAT WAS THAT?
BRUUMMMMMM
21

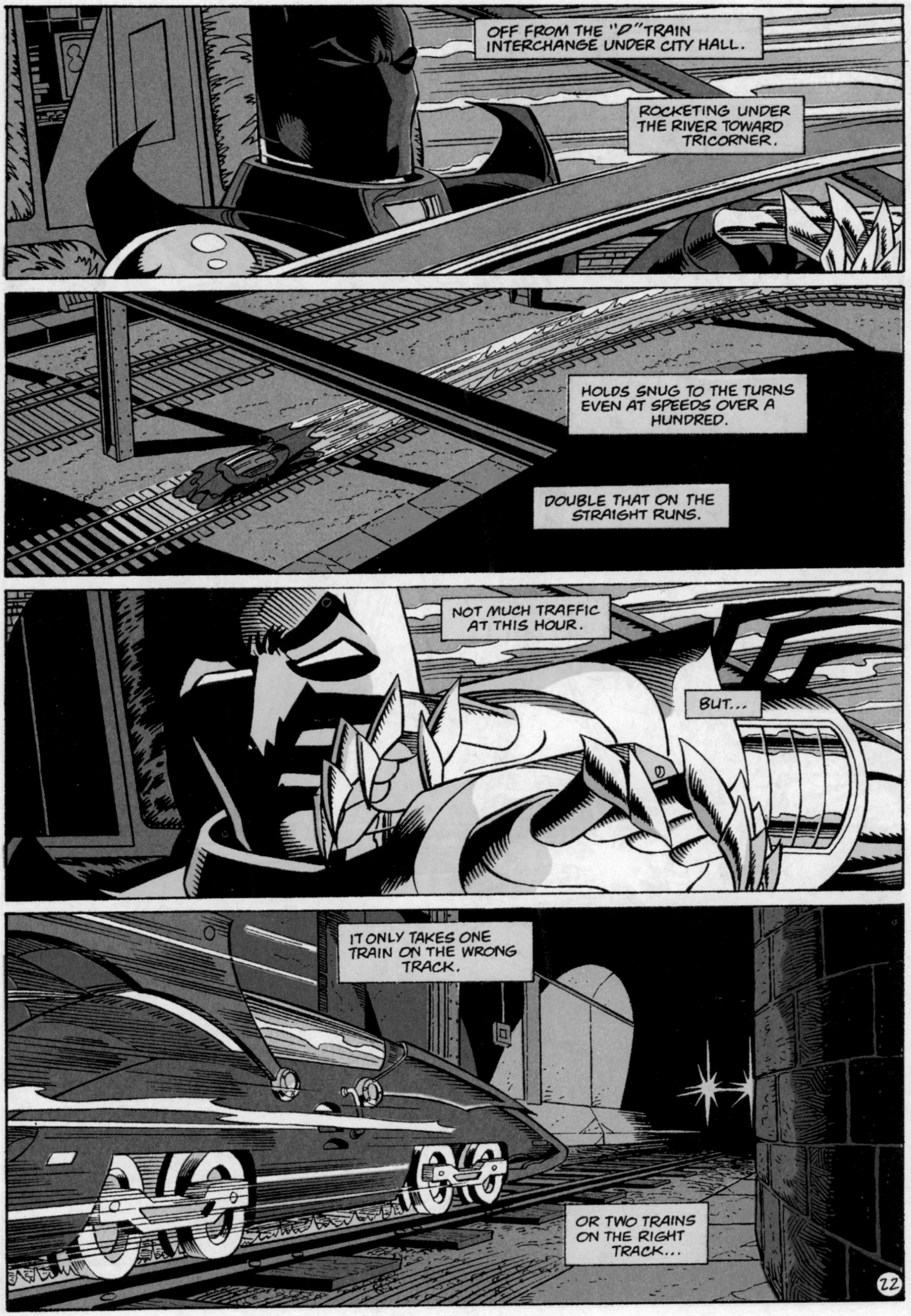

OFF FROM THE "D" TRAIN INTERCHANGE UNDER CITY HALL.
ROCKETING UNDER THE RIVER TOWARD TRICORNER.
HOLDS SNUG TO THE TURNS EVEN AT SPEEDS OVER A HUNDRED.
DOUBLE THAT ON THE STRAIGHT RUNS.
NOT MUCH TRAFFIC AT THIS HOUR.
BUT...
IT ONLY TAKES ONE TRAIN ON THE WRONG TRACK.
OR TWO TRAINS ON THE RIGHT TRACK...
22

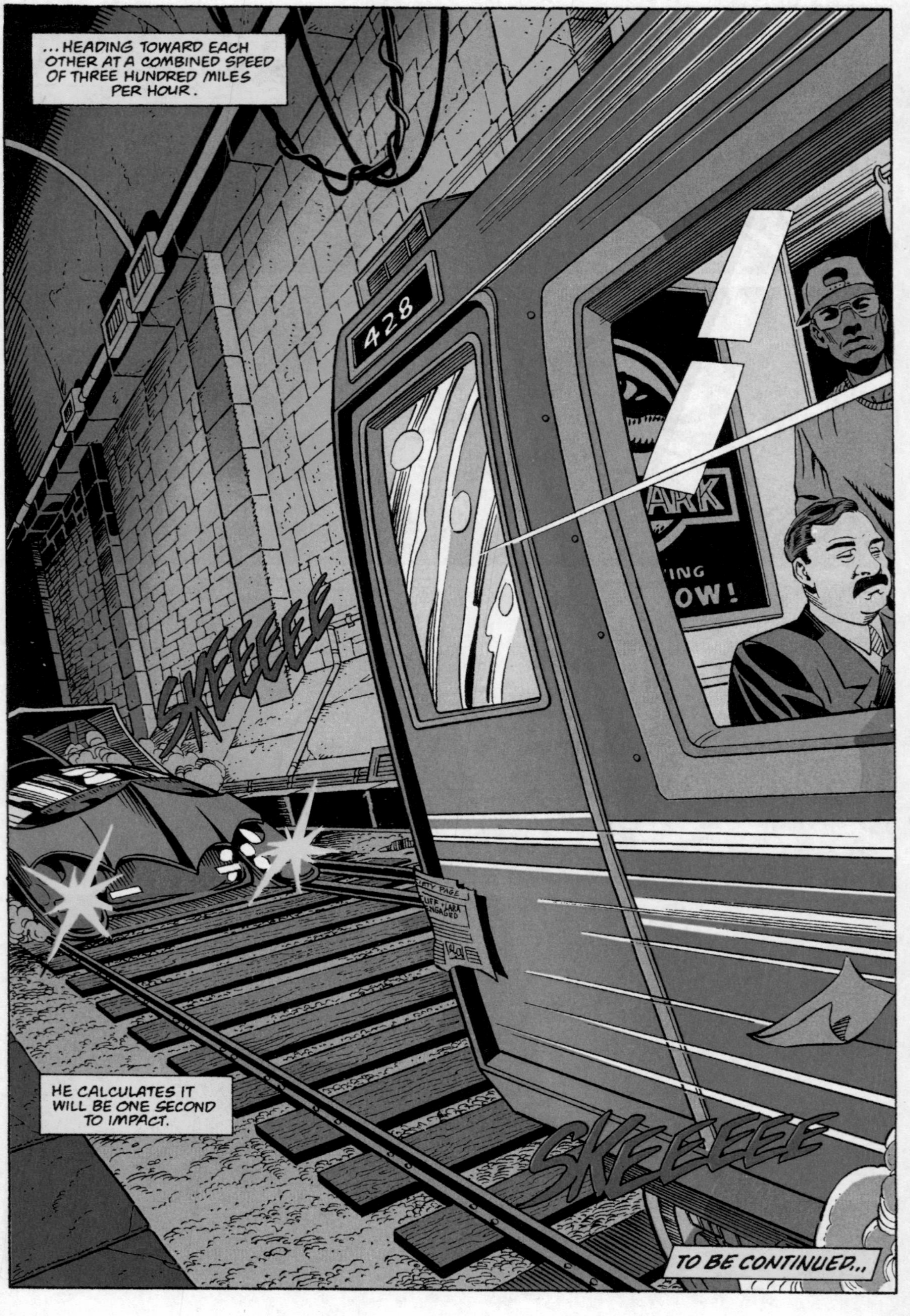
...HEADING TOWARD EACH OTHER AT A COMBINED SPEED OF THREE HUNDRED MILES PER HOUR.
428
SKEEEEE
HE CALCULATES IT WILL BE ONE SECOND TO IMPACT.
SKEEEEE
TO BE CONTINUED...

Cover art by KELLEY JONES

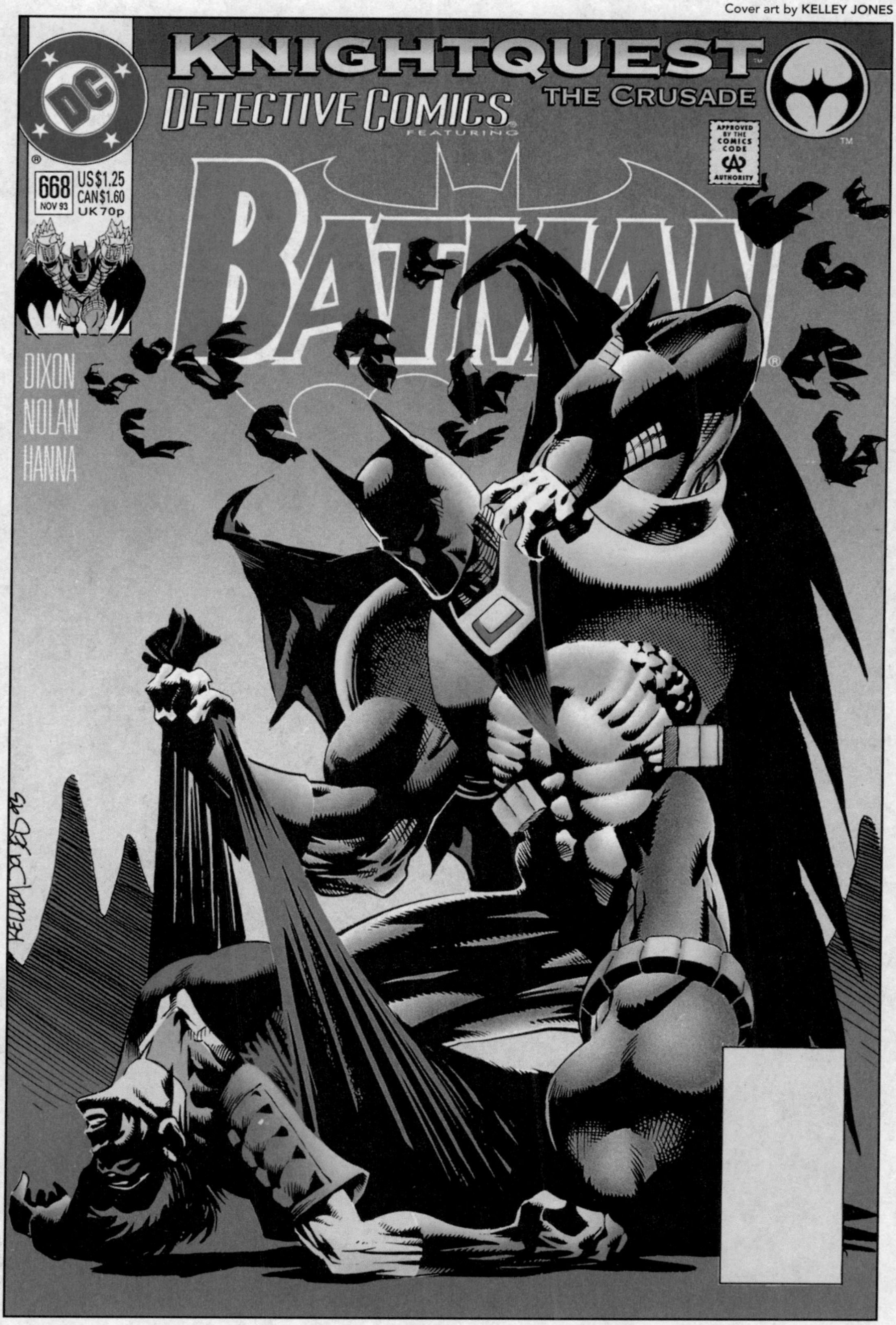

KNIGHTQUEST
DETECTIVE COMICS
THE CRUSADE
FEATURING
BATMAN
668
NOV 93
US$1.25
CAN$1.60
UK70p
APPROVED BY THE COMICS CODE AUTHORITY
DIXON
NOLAN
HANNA

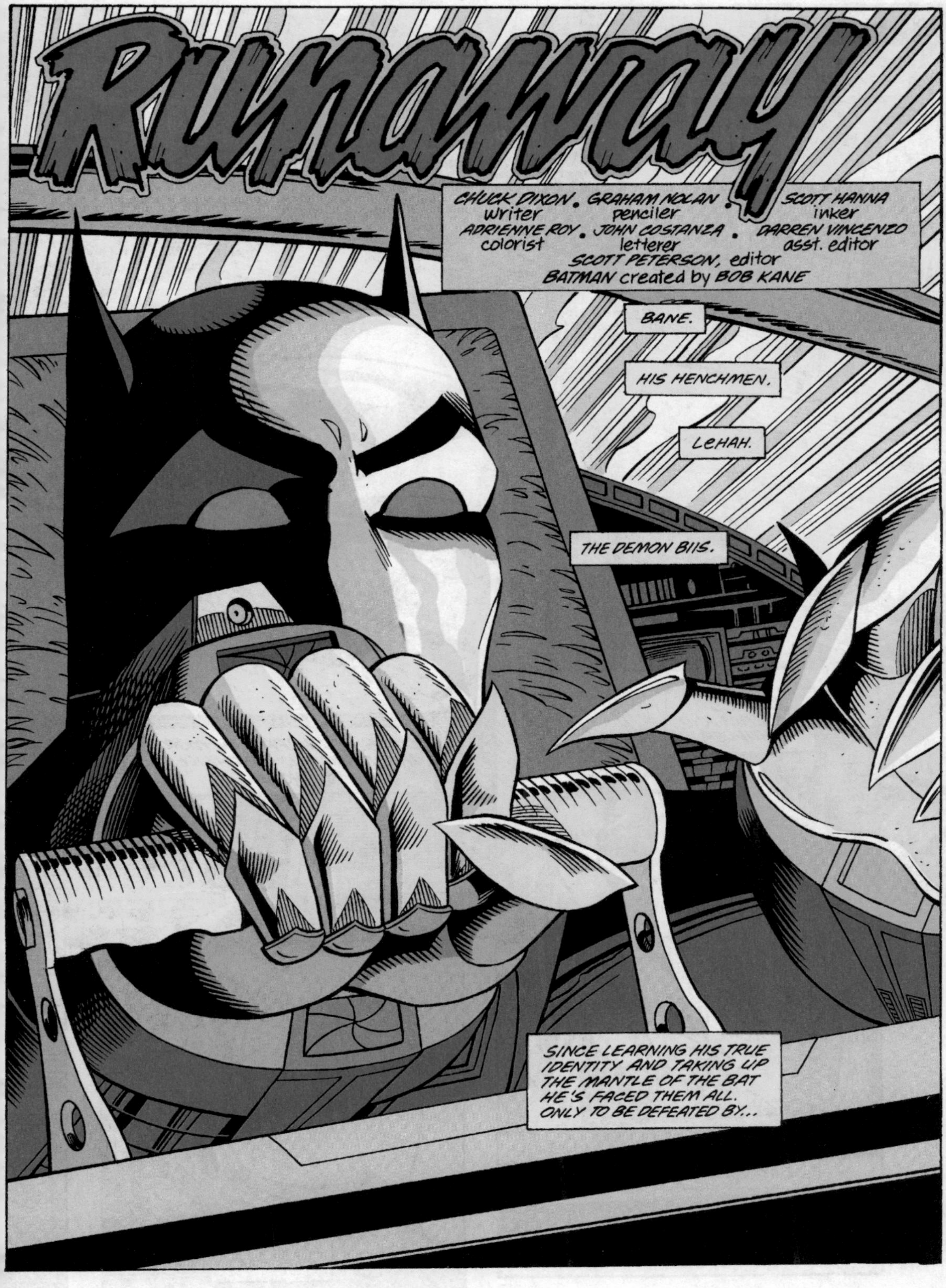
RUNAWAY
CHUCK DIXON • GRAHAM NOLAN • SCOTT HANNA
writer penciler inker
ADRIENNE ROY • JOHN COSTANZA • DARREN VINCENZO
colorist letterer asst. editor
SCOTT PETERSON, editor
BATMAN created by BOB KANE
BANE.
HIS HENCHMEN.
LEHAH.
THE DEMON BIIS.
SINCE LEARNING HIS TRUE IDENTITY AND TAKING UP THE MANTLE OF THE BAT HE'S FACED THEM ALL. ONLY TO BE DEFEATED BY...

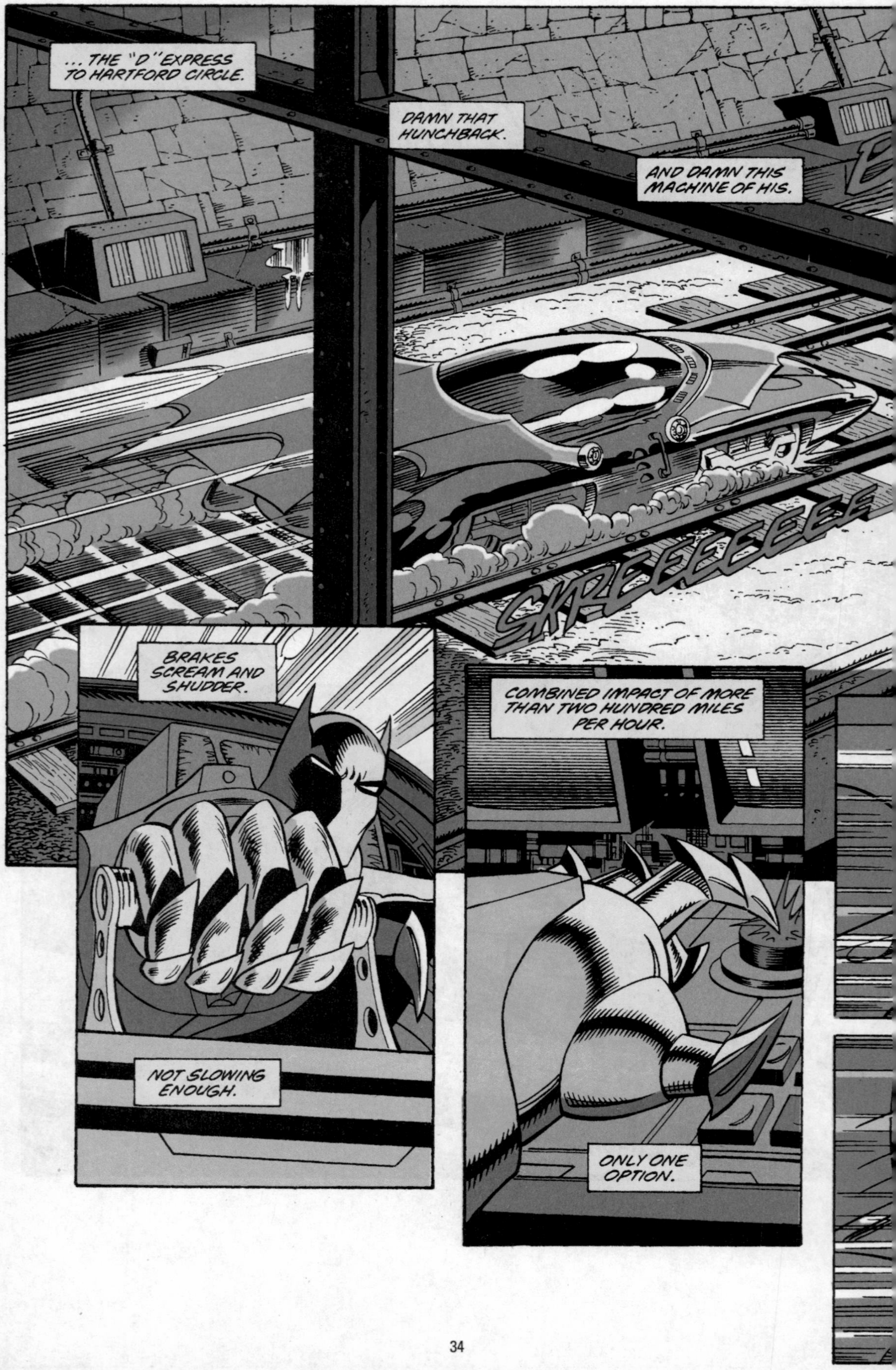

...THE "D" EXPRESS TO HARTFORD CIRCLE.
DAMN THAT HUNCHBACK.
AND DAMN THIS MACHINE OF HIS.
SKREEEEEEEEE
BRAKES SCREAM AND SHUDDER.
NOT SLOWING ENOUGH.
COMBINED IMPACT OF MORE THAN TWO HUNDRED MILES PER HOUR.
ONLY ONE OPTION.

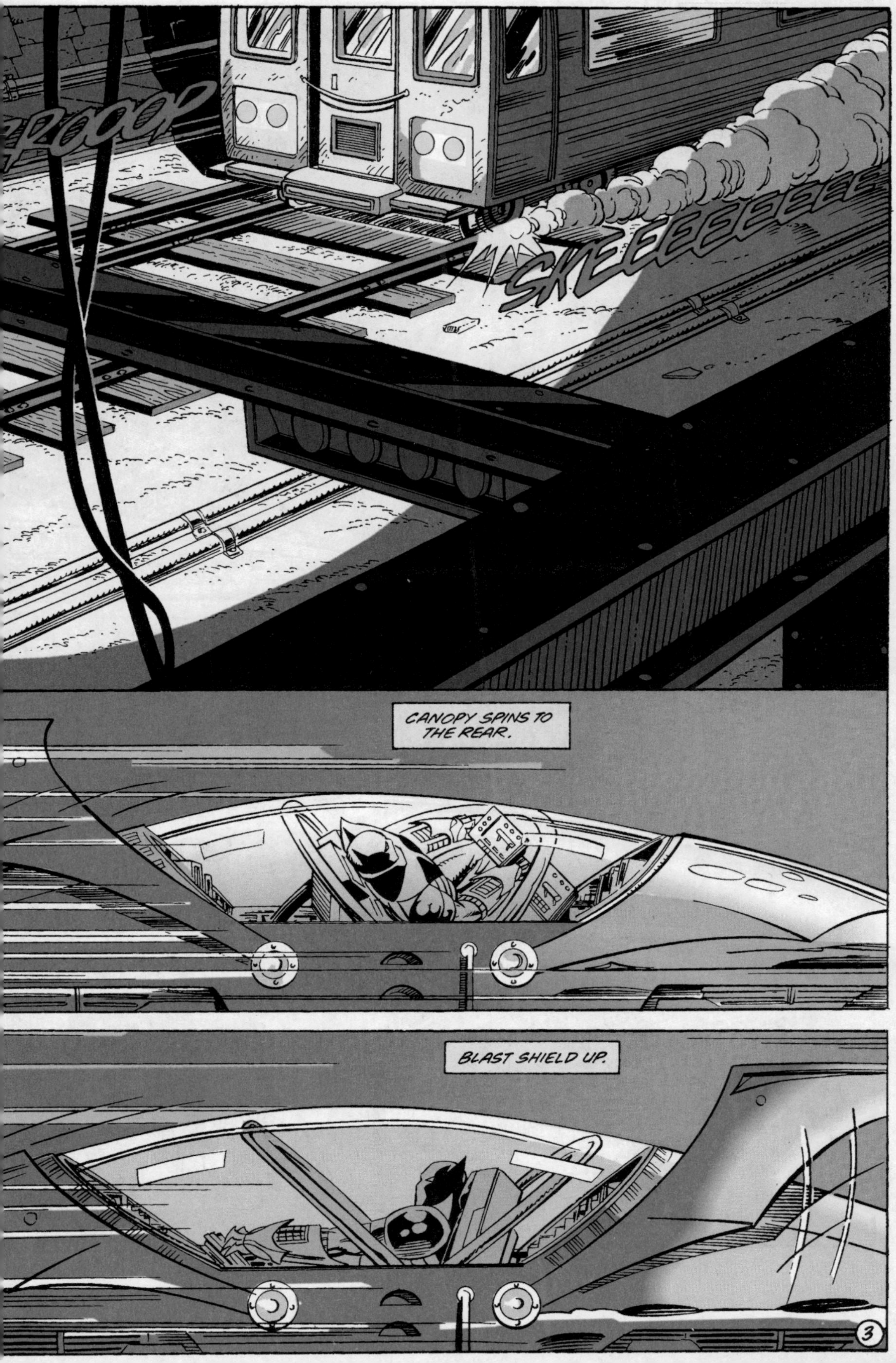

RROOOP
SKEEEEEEEEEE
CANOPY SPINS TO THE REAR.
BLAST SHIELD UP.

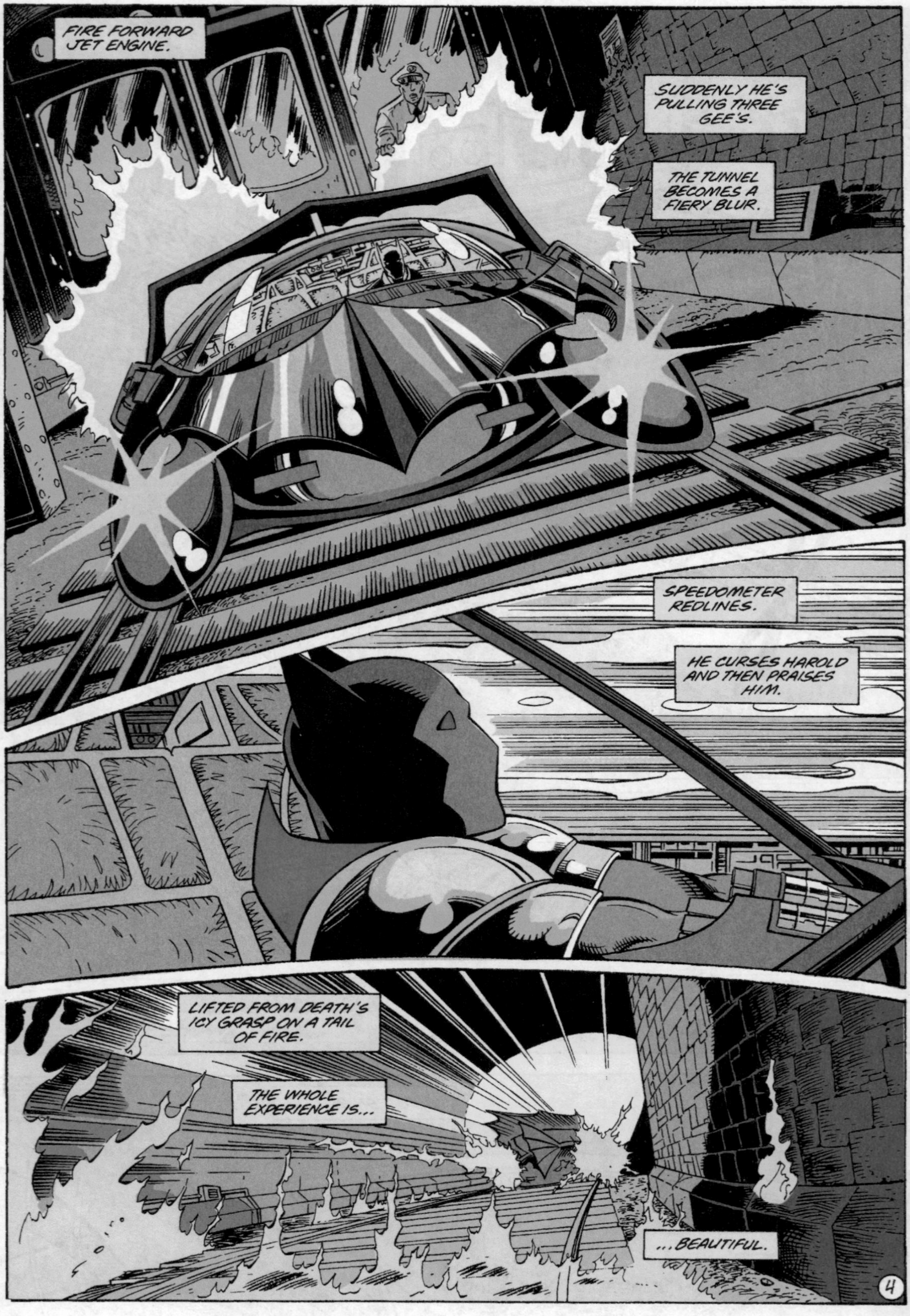
FIRE FORWARD JET ENGINE.
SUDDENLY HE'S PULLING THREE GEE'S.
THE TUNNEL BECOMES A FIERY BLUR.
SPEEDOMETER REDLINES.
HE CURSES HAROLD AND THEN PRAISES HIM.
LIFTED FROM DEATH'S ICY GRASP ON A TAIL OF FIRE.
THE WHOLE EXPERIENCE IS...
...BEAUTIFUL.
4

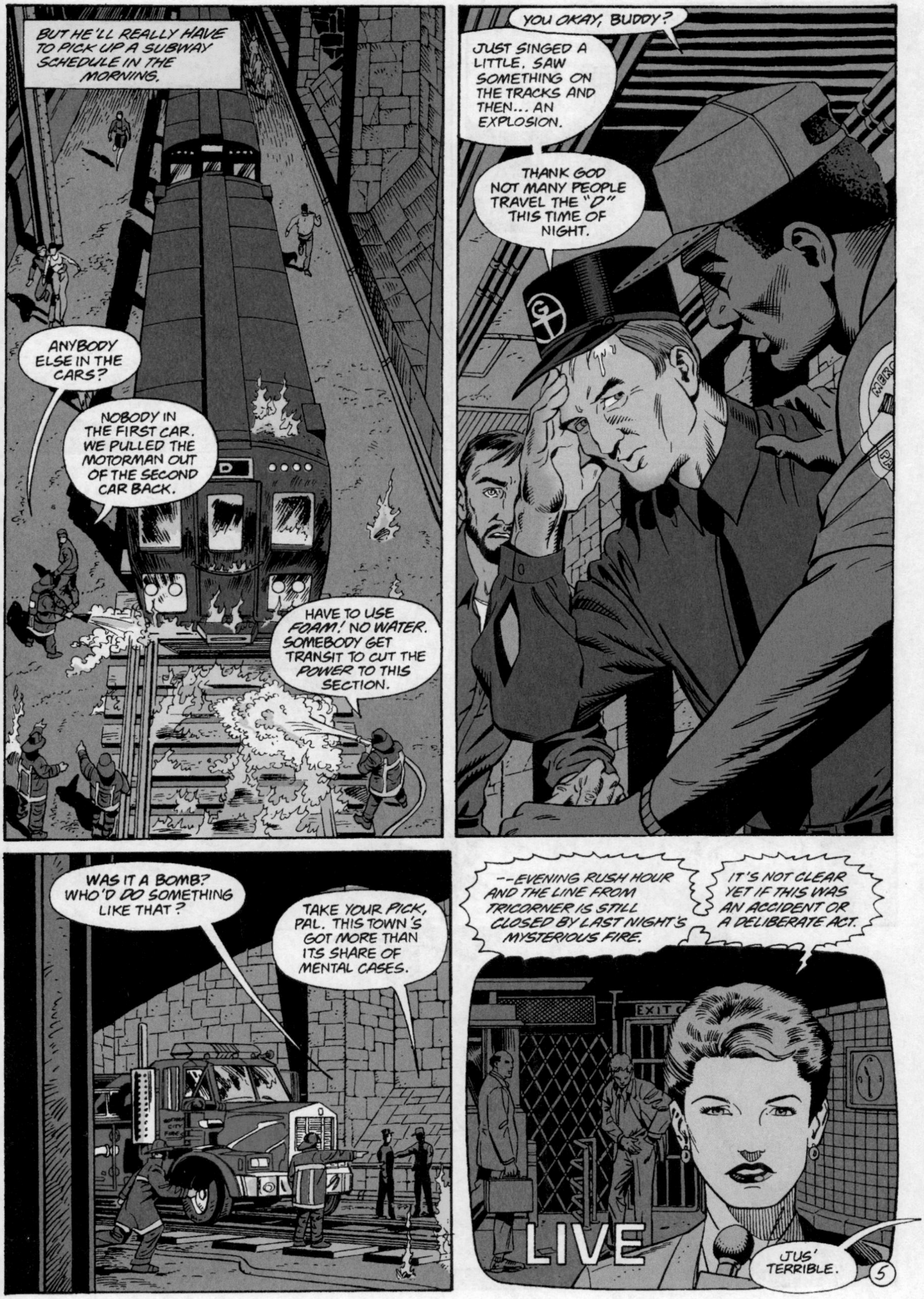
BUT HE'LL REALLY HAVE TO PICK UP A SUBWAY SCHEDULE IN THE MORNING.
ANYBODY ELSE IN THE CARS?
NOBODY IN THE FIRST CAR. WE PULLED THE MOTORMAN OUT OF THE SECOND CAR BACK.
HAVE TO USE FOAM! NO WATER. SOMEBODY GET TRANSIT TO CUT THE POWER TO THIS SECTION.
YOU OKAY, BUDDY?
JUST SINGED A LITTLE. SAW SOMETHING ON THE TRACKS AND THEN... AN EXPLOSION.
THANK GOD NOT MANY PEOPLE TRAVEL THE "D" THIS TIME OF NIGHT.
WAS IT A BOMB? WHO'D DO SOMETHING LIKE THAT?
TAKE YOUR PICK, PAL. THIS TOWN'S GOT MORE THAN ITS SHARE OF MENTAL CASES.
--EVENING RUSH HOUR AND THE LINE FROM TRICORNER IS STILL CLOSED BY LAST NIGHT'S MYSTERIOUS FIRE.
IT'S NOT CLEAR YET IF THIS WAS AN ACCIDENT OR A DELIBERATE ACT.
EXIT
LIVE
JUS' TERRIBLE.
5

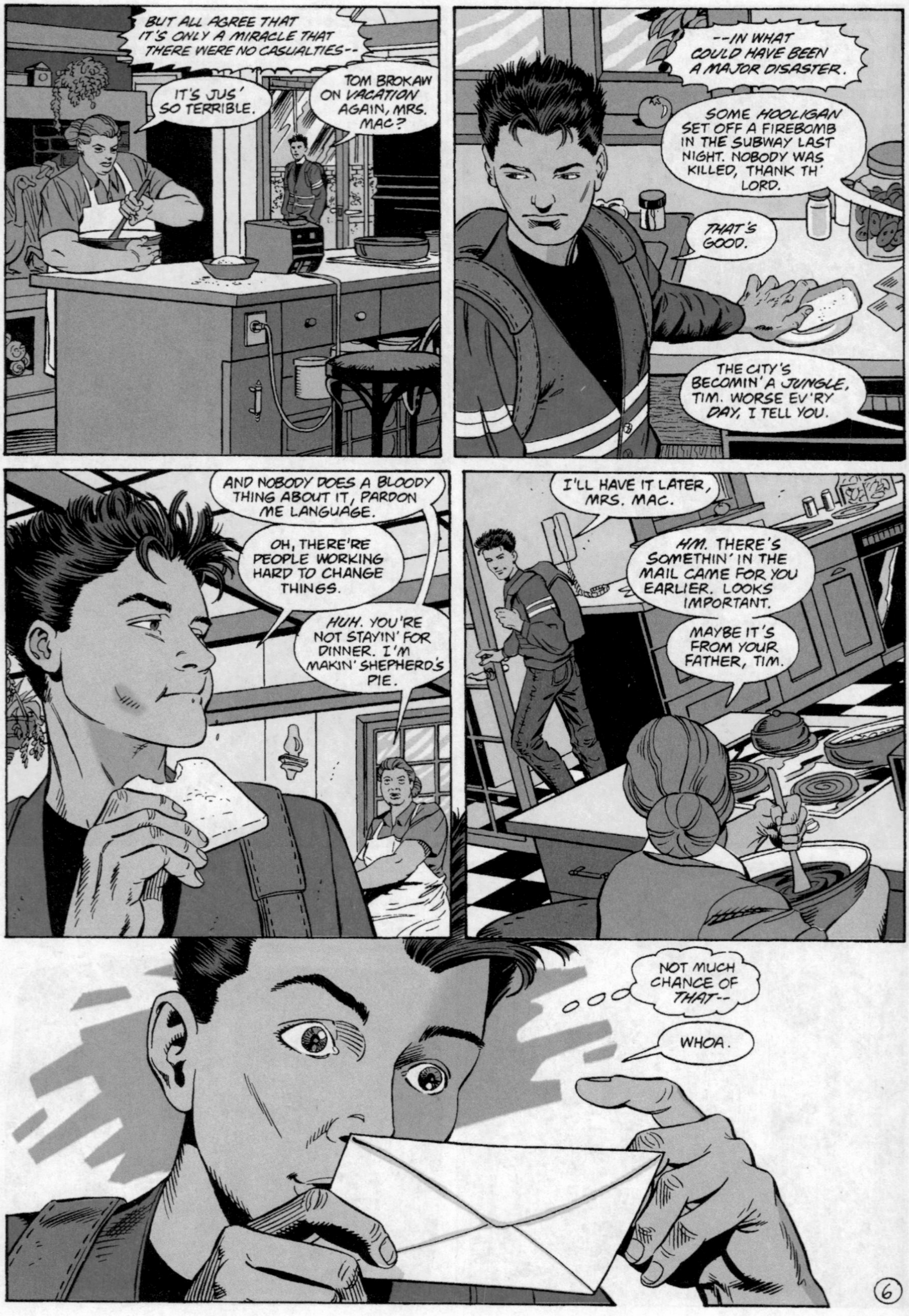
BUT ALL AGREE THAT IT'S ONLY A MIRACLE THAT THERE WERE NO CASUALTIES--
IT'S JUS' SO TERRIBLE.
TOM BROKAW ON VACATION AGAIN, MRS. MAC?
--IN WHAT COULD HAVE BEEN A MAJOR DISASTER.
SOME HOOLIGAN SET OFF A FIREBOMB IN THE SUBWAY LAST NIGHT. NOBODY WAS KILLED, THANK TH' LORD.
THAT'S GOOD.
THE CITY'S BECOMIN' A JUNGLE, TIM. WORSE EV'RY DAY, I TELL YOU.
AND NOBODY DOES A BLOODY THING ABOUT IT, PARDON ME LANGUAGE.
OH, THERE'RE PEOPLE WORKING HARD TO CHANGE THINGS.
HUH. YOU'RE NOT STAYIN' FOR DINNER. I'M MAKIN' SHEPHERD'S PIE.
I'LL HAVE IT LATER, MRS. MAC.
HM. THERE'S SOMETHIN' IN THE MAIL CAME FOR YOU EARLIER. LOOKS IMPORTANT.
MAYBE IT'S FROM YOUR FATHER, TIM.
NOT MUCH CHANCE OF THAT--
WHOA.
6

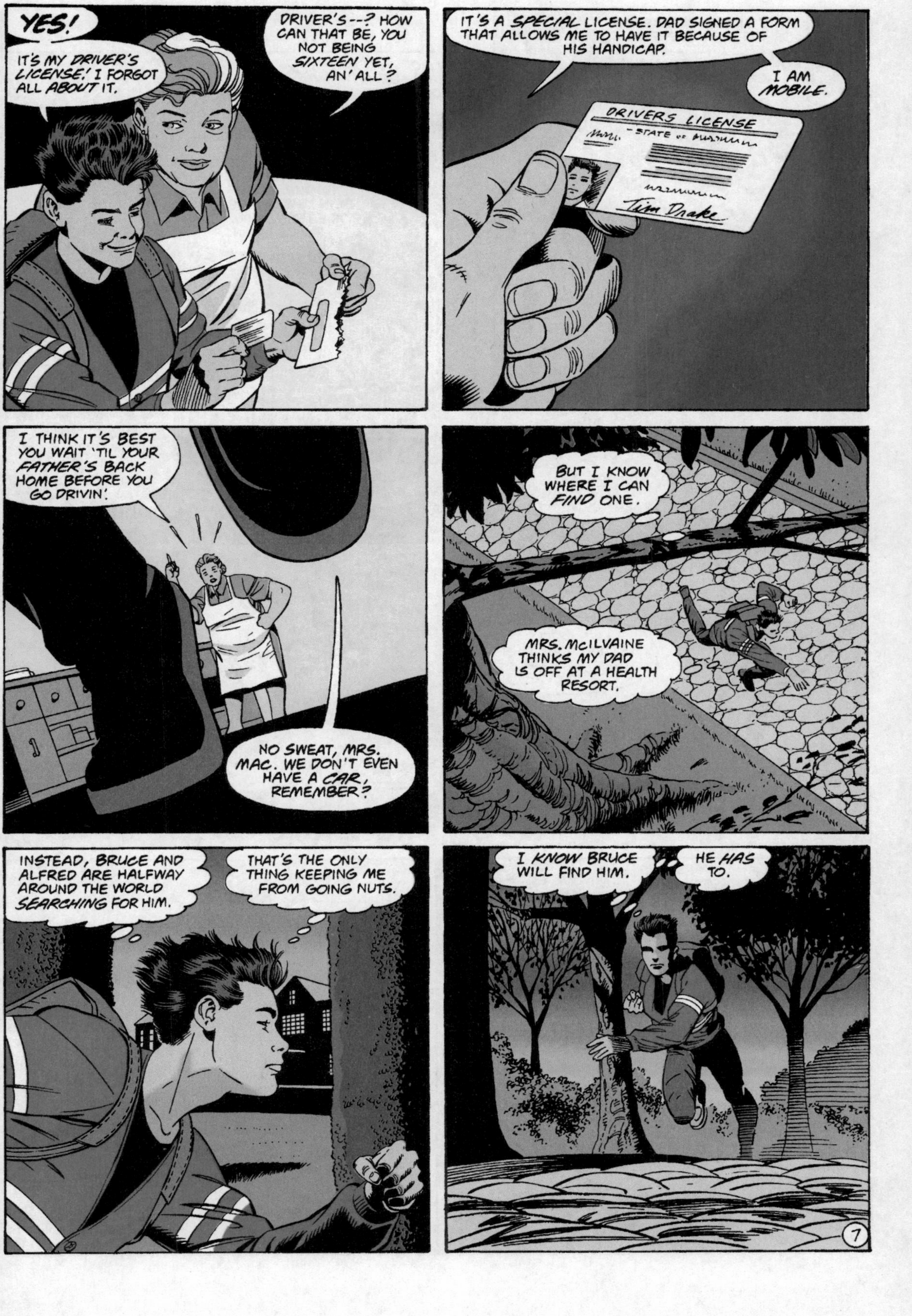
YES!
IT'S MY DRIVER'S LICENSE! I FORGOT ALL ABOUT IT.
DRIVER'S--? HOW CAN THAT BE, YOU NOT BEING SIXTEEN YET, AN' ALL?
IT'S A SPECIAL LICENSE. DAD SIGNED A FORM THAT ALLOWS ME TO HAVE IT BECAUSE OF HIS HANDICAP.
I AM MOBILE.
DRIVERS LICENSE
Tim Drake
I THINK IT'S BEST YOU WAIT 'TIL YOUR FATHER'S BACK HOME BEFORE YOU GO DRIVIN'.
NO SWEAT, MRS. MAC. WE DON'T EVEN HAVE A CAR, REMEMBER?
BUT I KNOW WHERE I CAN FIND ONE.
MRS. McILVAINE THINKS MY DAD IS OFF AT A HEALTH RESORT.
INSTEAD, BRUCE AND ALFRED ARE HALFWAY AROUND THE WORLD SEARCHING FOR HIM.
THAT'S THE ONLY THING KEEPING ME FROM GOING NUTS.
I KNOW BRUCE WILL FIND HIM.
HE HAS TO.
7

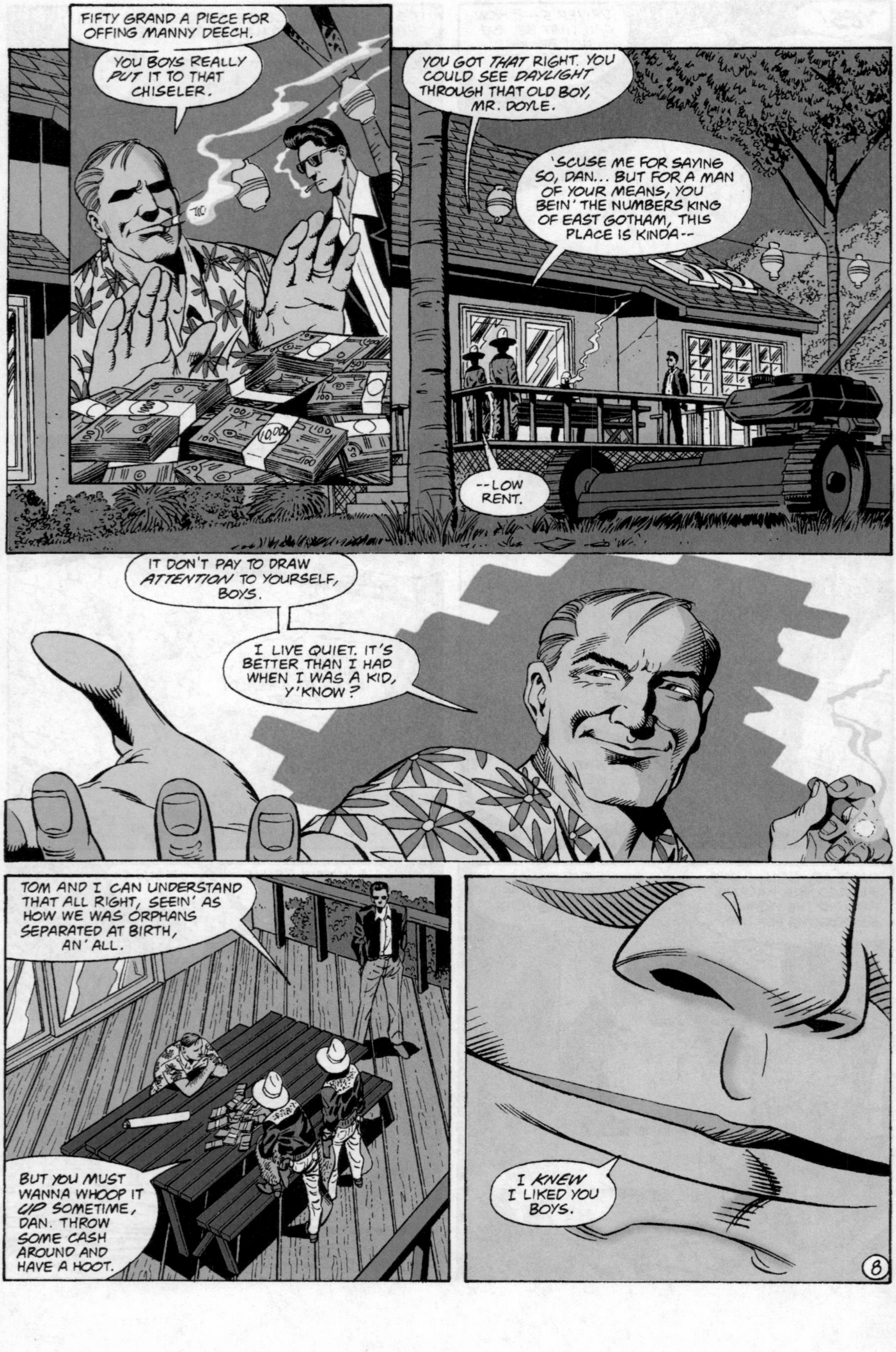
FIFTY GRAND A PIECE FOR OFFING MANNY DEECH.
YOU BOYS REALLY PUT IT TO THAT CHISELER.
YOU GOT THAT RIGHT. YOU COULD SEE DAYLIGHT THROUGH THAT OLD BOY, MR. DOYLE.
'SCUSE ME FOR SAYING SO, DAN... BUT FOR A MAN OF YOUR MEANS, YOU BEIN' THE NUMBERS KING OF EAST GOTHAM, THIS PLACE IS KINDA--
--LOW RENT.
IT DON'T PAY TO DRAW ATTENTION TO YOURSELF, BOYS.
I LIVE QUIET. IT'S BETTER THAN I HAD WHEN I WAS A KID, Y'KNOW?
TOM AND I CAN UNDERSTAND THAT ALL RIGHT, SEEIN' AS HOW WE WAS ORPHANS SEPARATED AT BIRTH, AN' ALL.
BUT YOU MUST WANNA WHOOP IT UP SOMETIME, DAN. THROW SOME CASH AROUND AND HAVE A HOOT.
I KNEW I LIKED YOU BOYS.
8

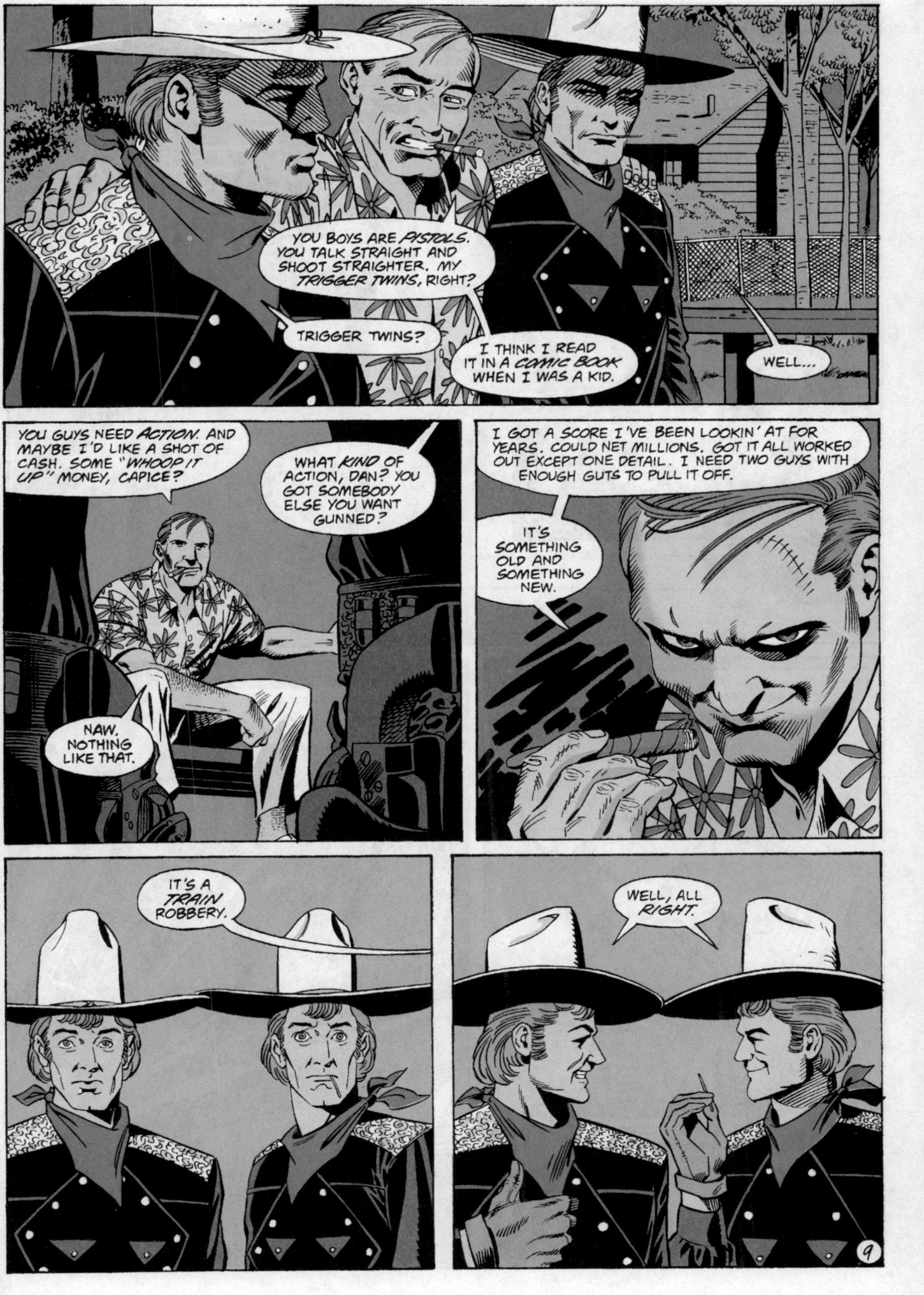
YOU BOYS ARE PISTOLS. YOU TALK STRAIGHT AND SHOOT STRAIGHTER. MY TRIGGER TWINS, RIGHT?
TRIGGER TWINS?
I THINK I READ IT IN A COMIC BOOK WHEN I WAS A KID.
WELL...
YOU GUYS NEED ACTION. AND MAYBE I'D LIKE A SHOT OF CASH. SOME "WHOOP IT UP" MONEY, CAPICE?
WHAT KIND OF ACTION, DAN? YOU GOT SOMEBODY ELSE YOU WANT GUNNED?
NAW. NOTHING LIKE THAT.
I GOT A SCORE I'VE BEEN LOOKIN' AT FOR YEARS. COULD NET MILLIONS. GOT IT ALL WORKED OUT EXCEPT ONE DETAIL. I NEED TWO GUYS WITH ENOUGH GUTS TO PULL IT OFF.
IT'S SOMETHING OLD AND SOMETHING NEW.
IT'S A TRAIN ROBBERY.
WELL, ALL RIGHT.
9

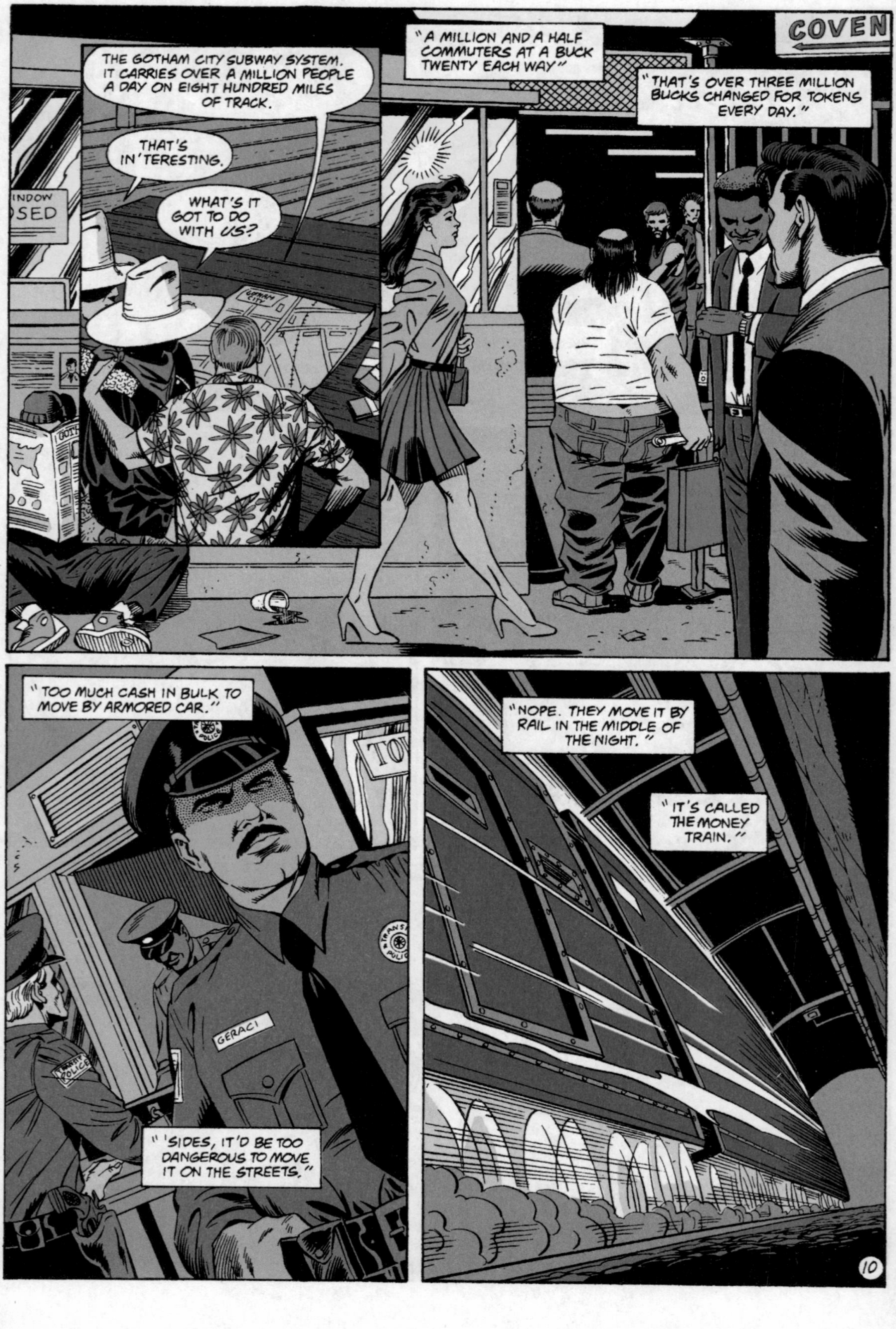
THE GOTHAM CITY SUBWAY SYSTEM. IT CARRIES OVER A MILLION PEOPLE A DAY ON EIGHT HUNDRED MILES OF TRACK.
THAT'S IN'TERESTING.
WHAT'S IT GOT TO DO WITH US?
"A MILLION AND A HALF COMMUTERS AT A BUCK TWENTY EACH WAY"
"THAT'S OVER THREE MILLION BUCKS CHANGED FOR TOKENS EVERY DAY."
COVEN
"TOO MUCH CASH IN BULK TO MOVE BY ARMORED CAR."
GERACI
"'SIDES, IT'D BE TOO DANGEROUS TO MOVE IT ON THE STREETS."
"NOPE. THEY MOVE IT BY RAIL IN THE MIDDLE OF THE NIGHT."
"IT'S CALLED THE MONEY TRAIN."
10

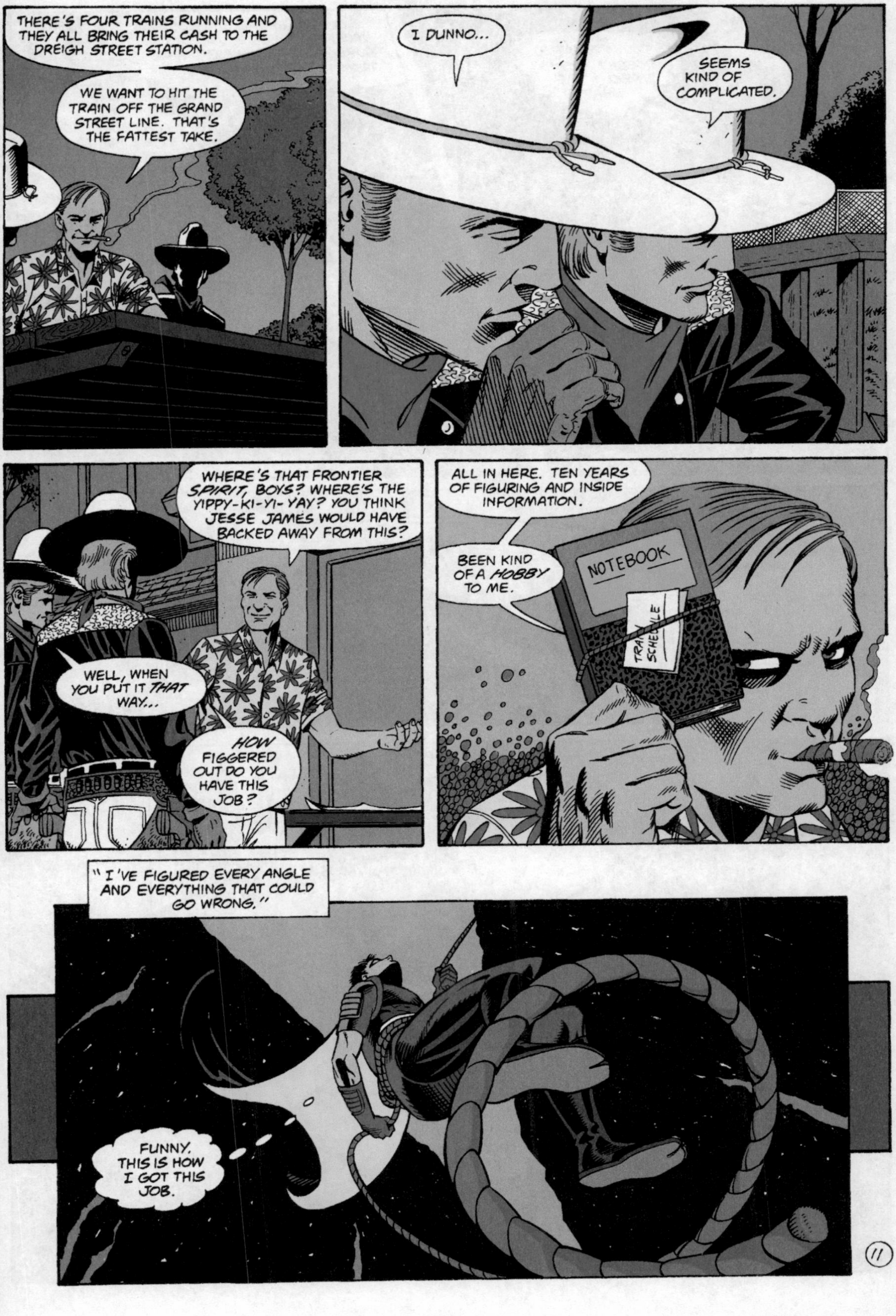
THERE'S FOUR TRAINS RUNNING AND THEY ALL BRING THEIR CASH TO THE DREIGH STREET STATION.
WE WANT TO HIT THE TRAIN OFF THE GRAND STREET LINE. THAT'S THE FATTEST TAKE.
I DUNNO...
SEEMS KIND OF COMPLICATED.
WHERE'S THAT FRONTIER SPIRIT, BOYS? WHERE'S THE YIPPY-KI-YI-YAY? YOU THINK JESSE JAMES WOULD HAVE BACKED AWAY FROM THIS?
WELL, WHEN YOU PUT IT THAT WAY...
HOW FIGGERED OUT DO YOU HAVE THIS JOB?
ALL IN HERE. TEN YEARS OF FIGURING AND INSIDE INFORMATION.
BEEN KIND OF A HOBBY TO ME.
NOTEBOOK
"I'VE FIGURED EVERY ANGLE AND EVERYTHING THAT COULD GO WRONG."
FUNNY. THIS IS HOW I GOT THIS JOB.
11

I FOUND MY OWN WAY INTO THE BATCAVE.

PAUL PROBABLY DOESN'T KNOW ABOUT THIS SHAFT.

HE CLOSED UP THE TUNNEL FROM UNDER MY DAD'S HOUSE. I'M SURE HE SEALED THE ENTRANCE FROM THE WAYNE MANSION.

SOMEBODY HAS TO TELL HIM I'VE GOT AS MUCH RIGHT TO BE HERE AS HE DOES.

MAYBE MORE.

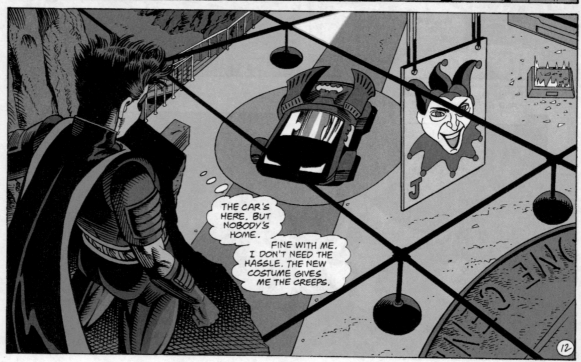

THE CAR'S HERE, BUT NOBODY'S HOME.

FINE WITH ME, I DON'T NEED THE HASSLE. THE NEW COSTUME GIVES ME THE CREEPS.

12

44

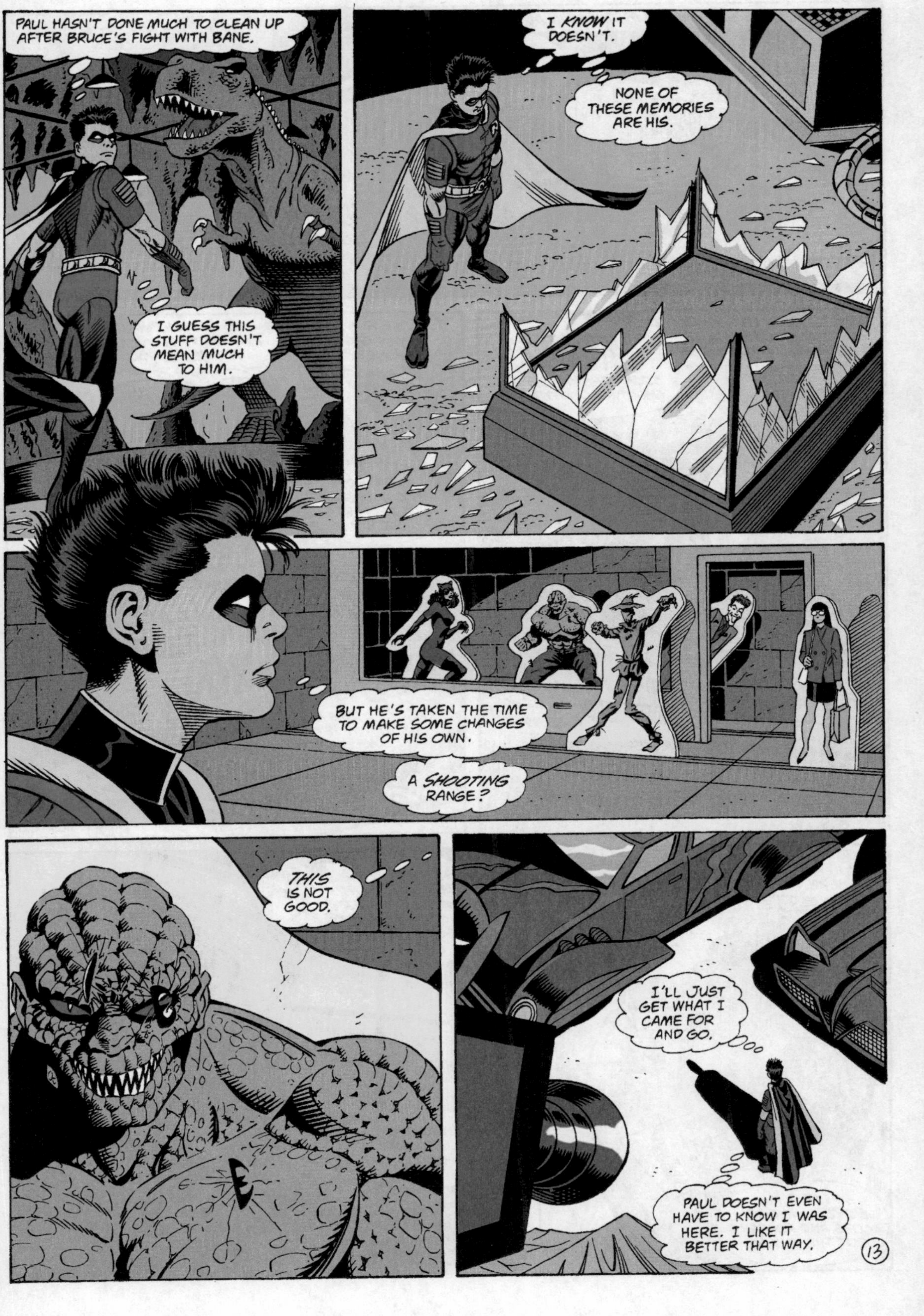
PAUL HASN'T DONE MUCH TO CLEAN UP AFTER BRUCE'S FIGHT WITH BANE.
I GUESS THIS STUFF DOESN'T MEAN MUCH TO HIM.
I KNOW IT DOESN'T.
NONE OF THESE MEMORIES ARE HIS.
BUT HE'S TAKEN THE TIME TO MAKE SOME CHANGES OF HIS OWN.
A SHOOTING RANGE?
THIS IS NOT GOOD.
I'LL JUST GET WHAT I CAME FOR AND GO.
PAUL DOESN'T EVEN HAVE TO KNOW I WAS HERE. I LIKE IT BETTER THAT WAY.
13

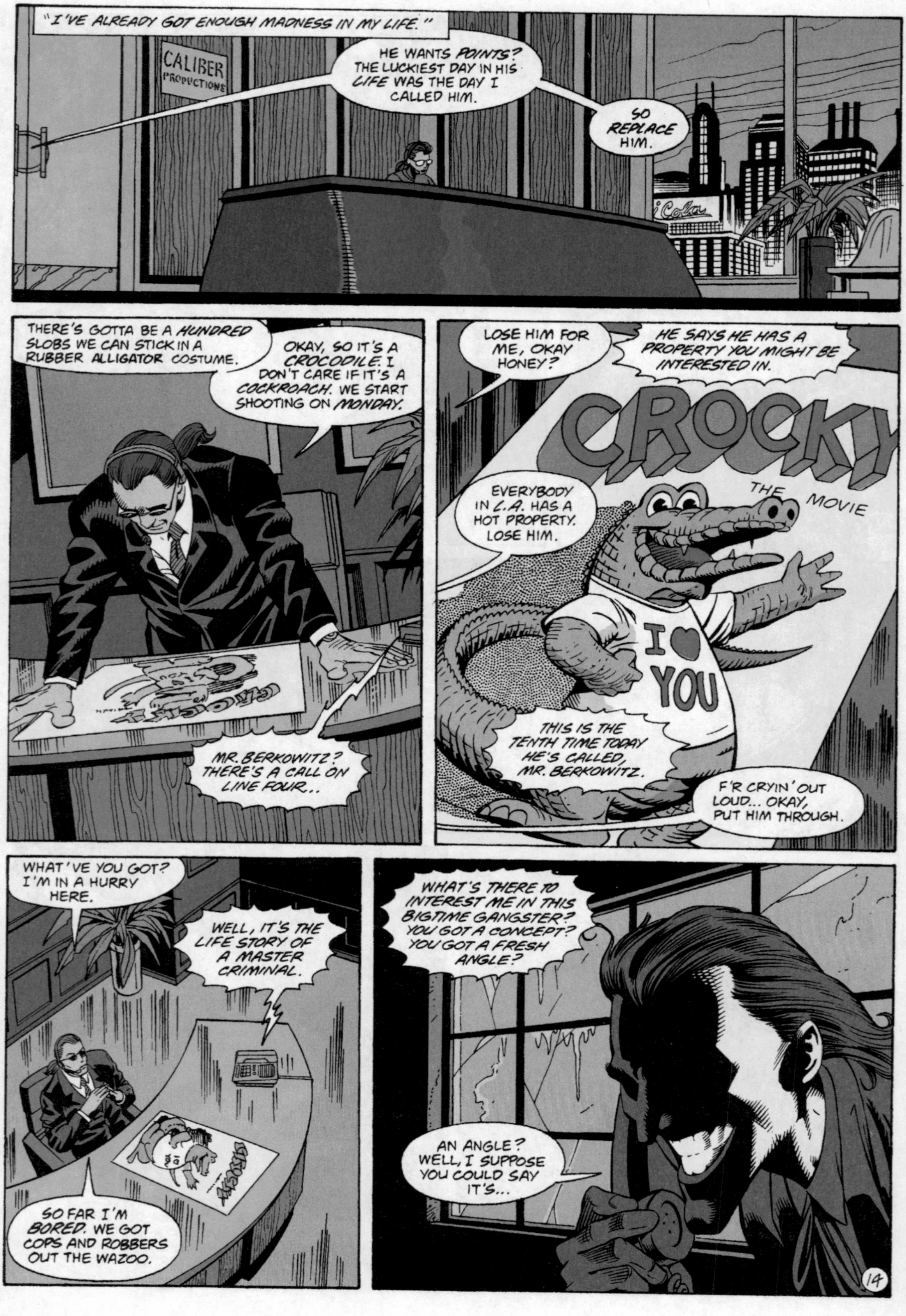
"I'VE ALREADY GOT ENOUGH MADNESS IN MY LIFE."
CALIBER PRODUCTIONS
HE WANTS POINTS? THE LUCKIEST DAY IN HIS LIFE WAS THE DAY I CALLED HIM.
SO REPLACE HIM.
THERE'S GOTTA BE A HUNDRED SLOBS WE CAN STICK IN A RUBBER ALLIGATOR COSTUME.
OKAY, SO IT'S A CROCODILE. I DON'T CARE IF IT'S A COCKROACH. WE START SHOOTING ON MONDAY.
MR. BERKOWITZ? THERE'S A CALL ON LINE FOUR...
LOSE HIM FOR ME, OKAY HONEY?
HE SAYS HE HAS A PROPERTY YOU MIGHT BE INTERESTED IN.
CROCKY THE MOVIE
EVERYBODY IN L.A. HAS A HOT PROPERTY. LOSE HIM.
I ♥ YOU
THIS IS THE TENTH TIME TODAY HE'S CALLED, MR. BERKOWITZ.
F'R CRYIN' OUT LOUD... OKAY, PUT HIM THROUGH.
WHAT'VE YOU GOT? I'M IN A HURRY HERE.
WELL, IT'S THE LIFE STORY OF A MASTER CRIMINAL.
SO FAR I'M BORED. WE GOT COPS AND ROBBERS OUT THE WAZOO.
WHAT'S THERE TO INTEREST ME IN THIS BIGTIME GANGSTER? YOU GOT A CONCEPT? YOU GOT A FRESH ANGLE?
AN ANGLE? WELL, I SUPPOSE YOU COULD SAY IT'S...
14

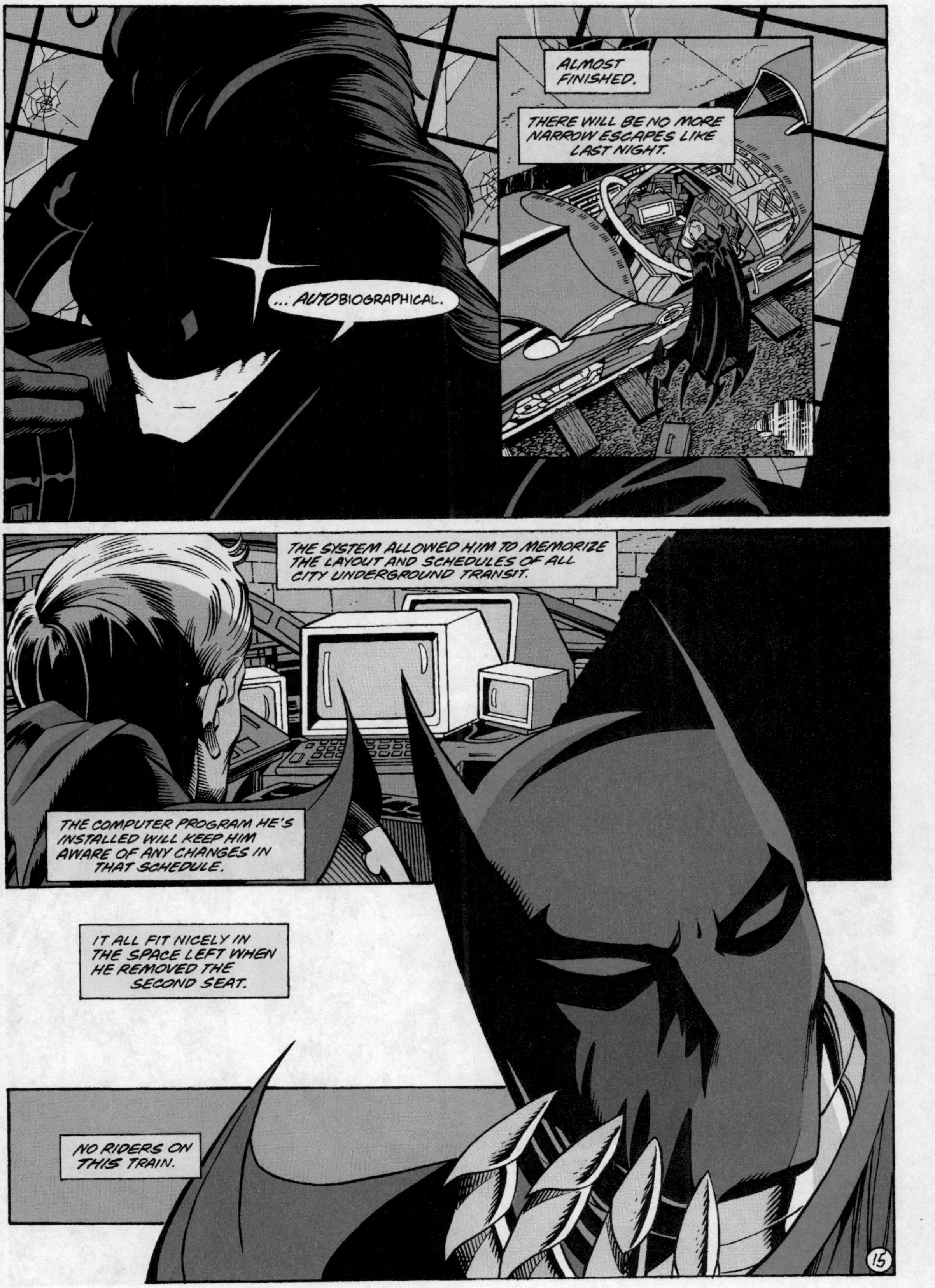
ALMOST FINISHED.
THERE WILL BE NO MORE NARROW ESCAPES LIKE LAST NIGHT.
...AUTOBIOGRAPHICAL.
THE SYSTEM ALLOWED HIM TO MEMORIZE THE LAYOUT AND SCHEDULES OF ALL CITY UNDERGROUND TRANSIT.
THE COMPUTER PROGRAM HE'S INSTALLED WILL KEEP HIM AWARE OF ANY CHANGES IN THAT SCHEDULE.
IT ALL FIT NICELY IN THE SPACE LEFT WHEN HE REMOVED THE SECOND SEAT.
NO RIDERS ON THIS TRAIN.
15

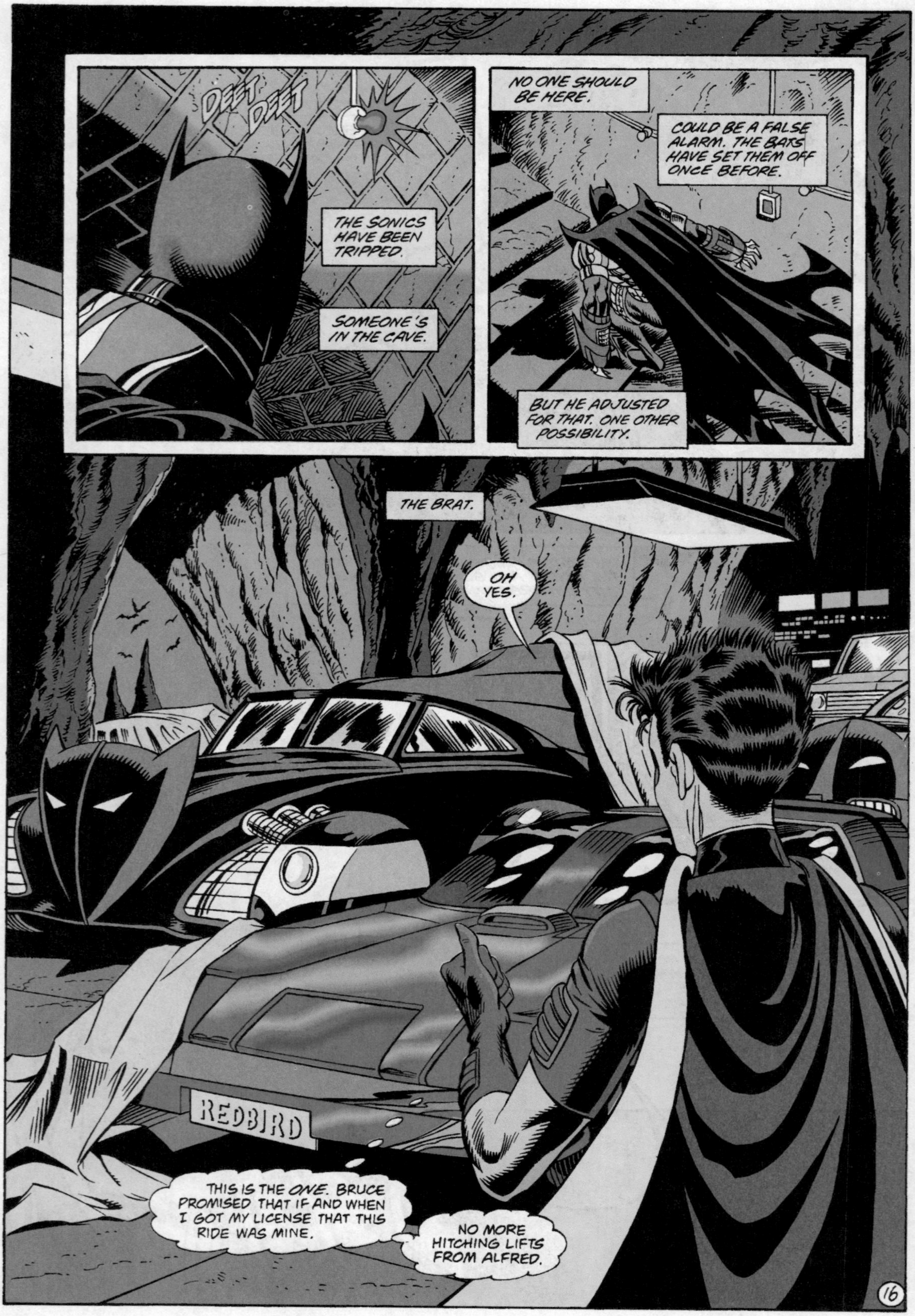
DEET DEET
THE SONICS HAVE BEEN TRIPPED.
SOMEONE'S IN THE CAVE.
NO ONE SHOULD BE HERE.
COULD BE A FALSE ALARM. THE BATS HAVE SET THEM OFF ONCE BEFORE.
BUT HE ADJUSTED FOR THAT. ONE OTHER POSSIBILITY.
THE BRAT.
OH YES.
REDBIRD
THIS IS THE ONE. BRUCE PROMISED THAT IF AND WHEN I GOT MY LICENSE THAT THIS RIDE WAS MINE.
NO MORE HITCHING LIFTS FROM ALFRED.
16

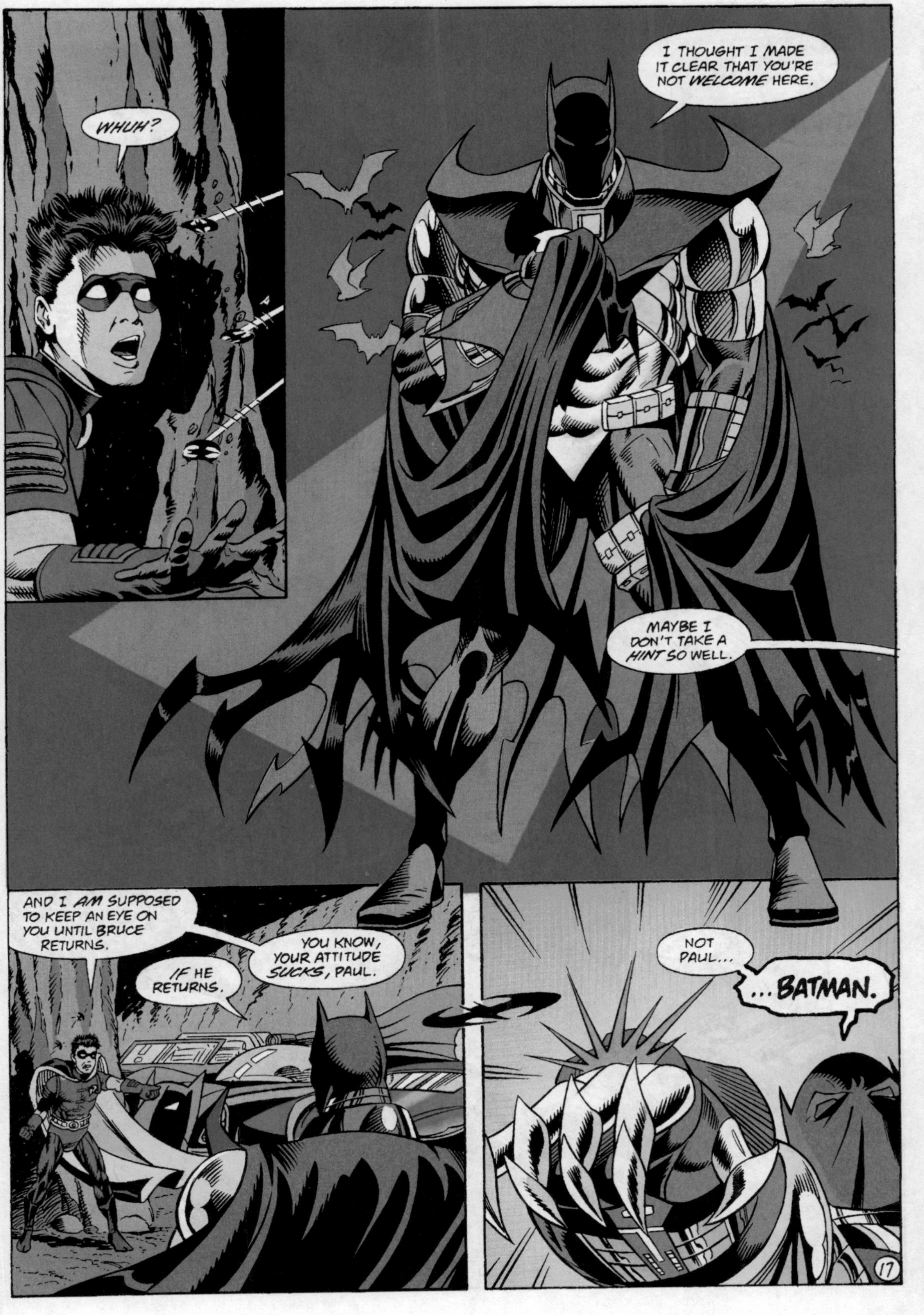
WHUH?
I THOUGHT I MADE IT CLEAR THAT YOU'RE NOT WELCOME HERE.
MAYBE I DON'T TAKE A HINT SO WELL.
AND I AM SUPPOSED TO KEEP AN EYE ON YOU UNTIL BRUCE RETURNS.
IF HE RETURNS.
YOU KNOW, YOUR ATTITUDE SUCKS, PAUL.
NOT PAUL...
...BATMAN.
17

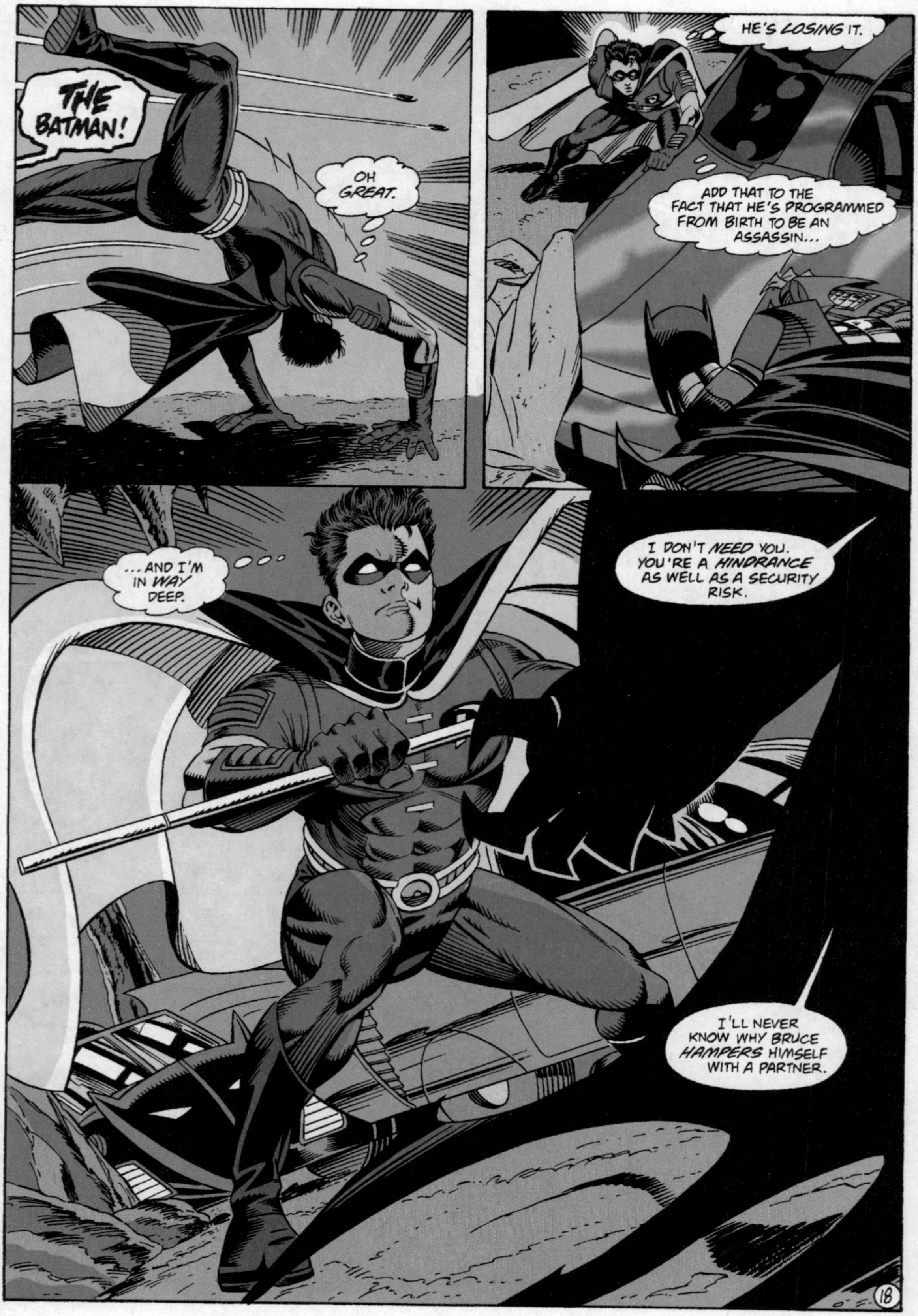
THE BATMAN!
OH GREAT.
HE'S LOSING IT.
ADD THAT TO THE FACT THAT HE'S PROGRAMMED FROM BIRTH TO BE AN ASSASSIN...
...AND I'M IN WAY DEEP.
I DON'T NEED YOU. YOU'RE A HINDRANCE AS WELL AS A SECURITY RISK.
I'LL NEVER KNOW WHY BRUCE HAMPERS HIMSELF WITH A PARTNER.
18

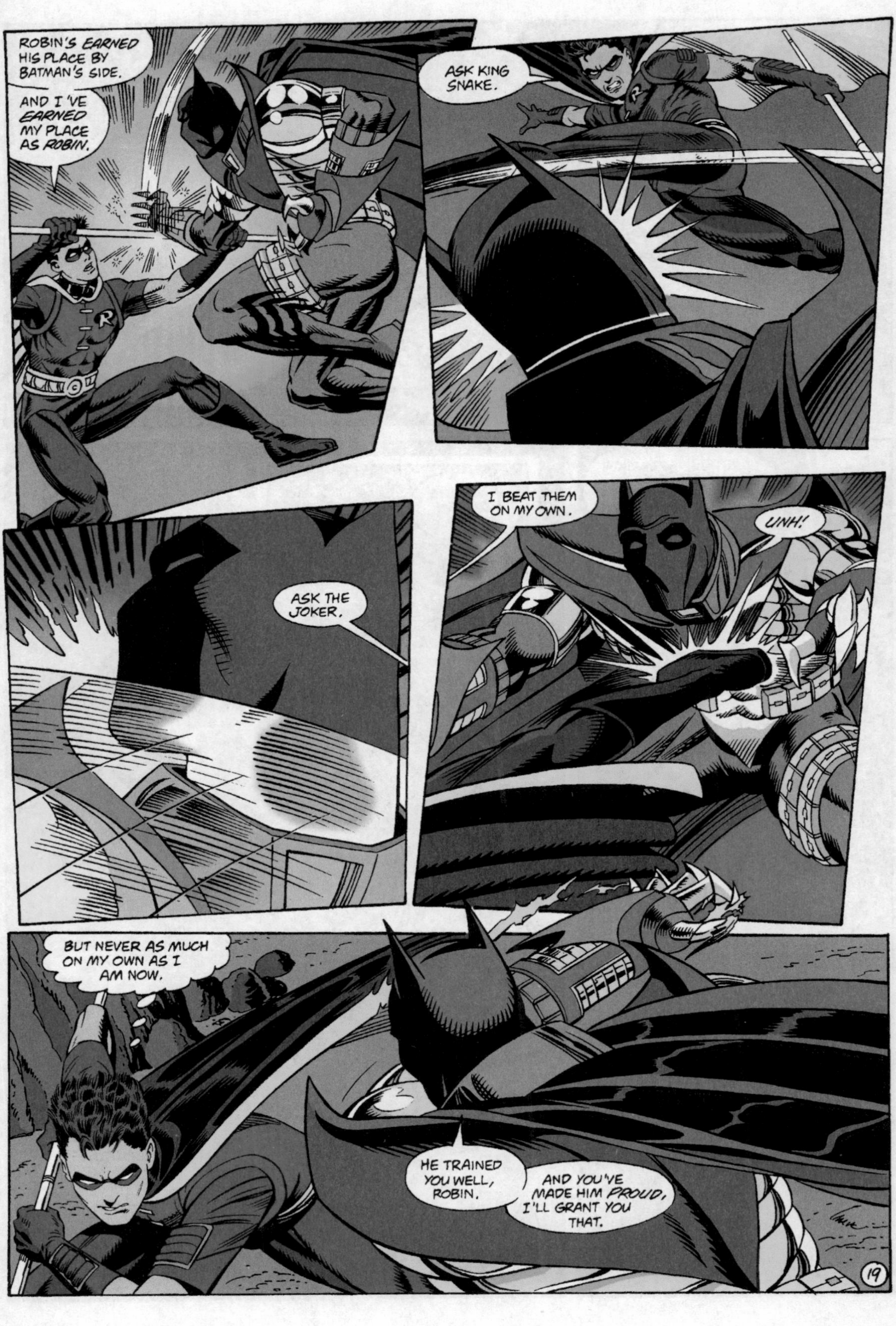
ROBIN'S EARNED HIS PLACE BY BATMAN'S SIDE.
AND I'VE EARNED MY PLACE AS ROBIN.
ASK KING SNAKE.
ASK THE JOKER.
I BEAT THEM ON MY OWN.
UNH!
BUT NEVER AS MUCH ON MY OWN AS I AM NOW.
HE TRAINED YOU WELL, ROBIN.
AND YOU'VE MADE HIM PROUD, I'LL GRANT YOU THAT.
19

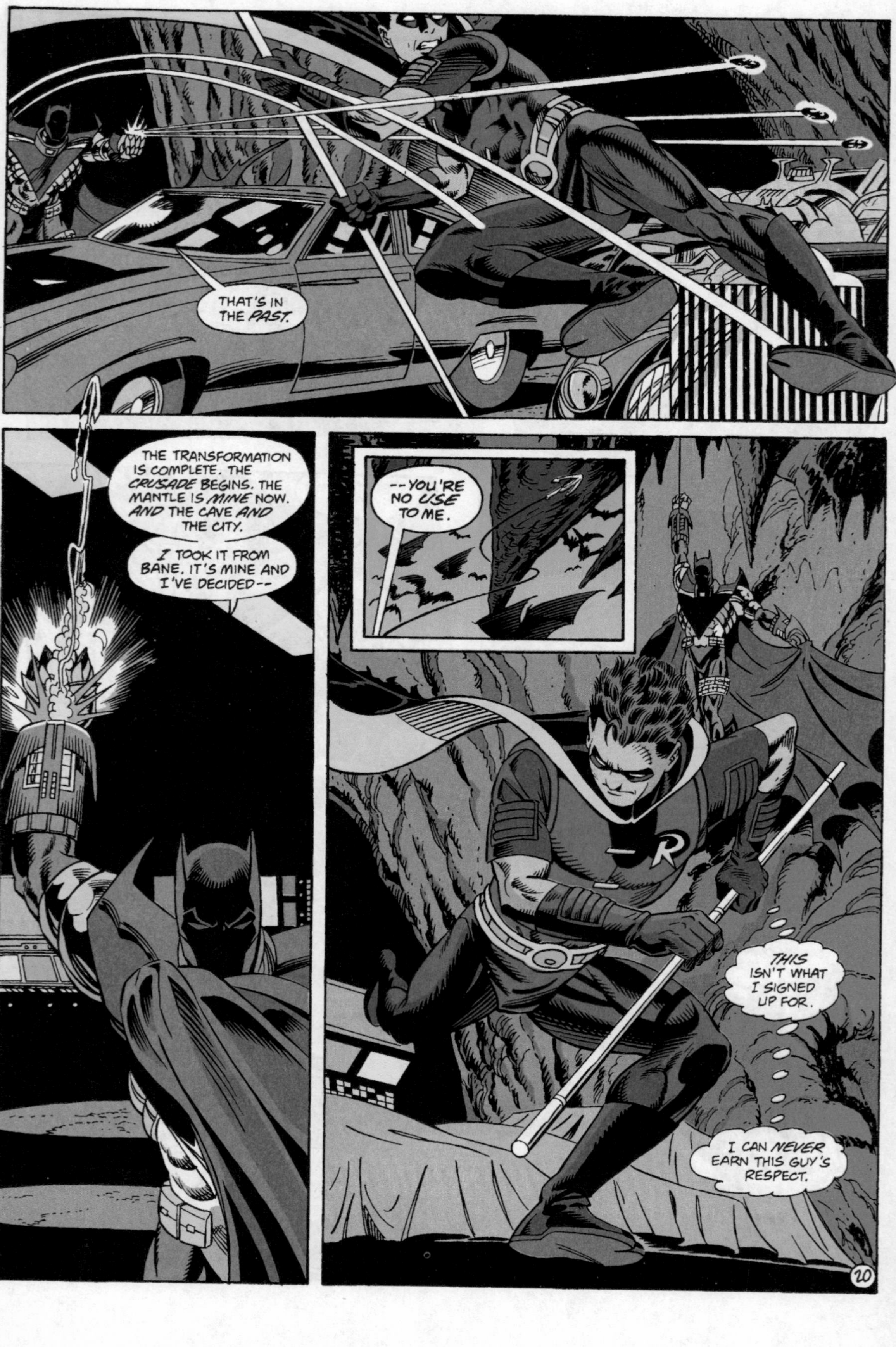
THAT'S IN THE PAST.
THE TRANSFORMATION IS COMPLETE. THE CRUSADE BEGINS. THE MANTLE IS MINE NOW. AND THE CAVE AND THE CITY.
I TOOK IT FROM BANE. IT'S MINE AND I'VE DECIDED--
--YOU'RE NO USE TO ME.
THIS ISN'T WHAT I SIGNED UP FOR.
I CAN NEVER EARN THIS GUY'S RESPECT.
20

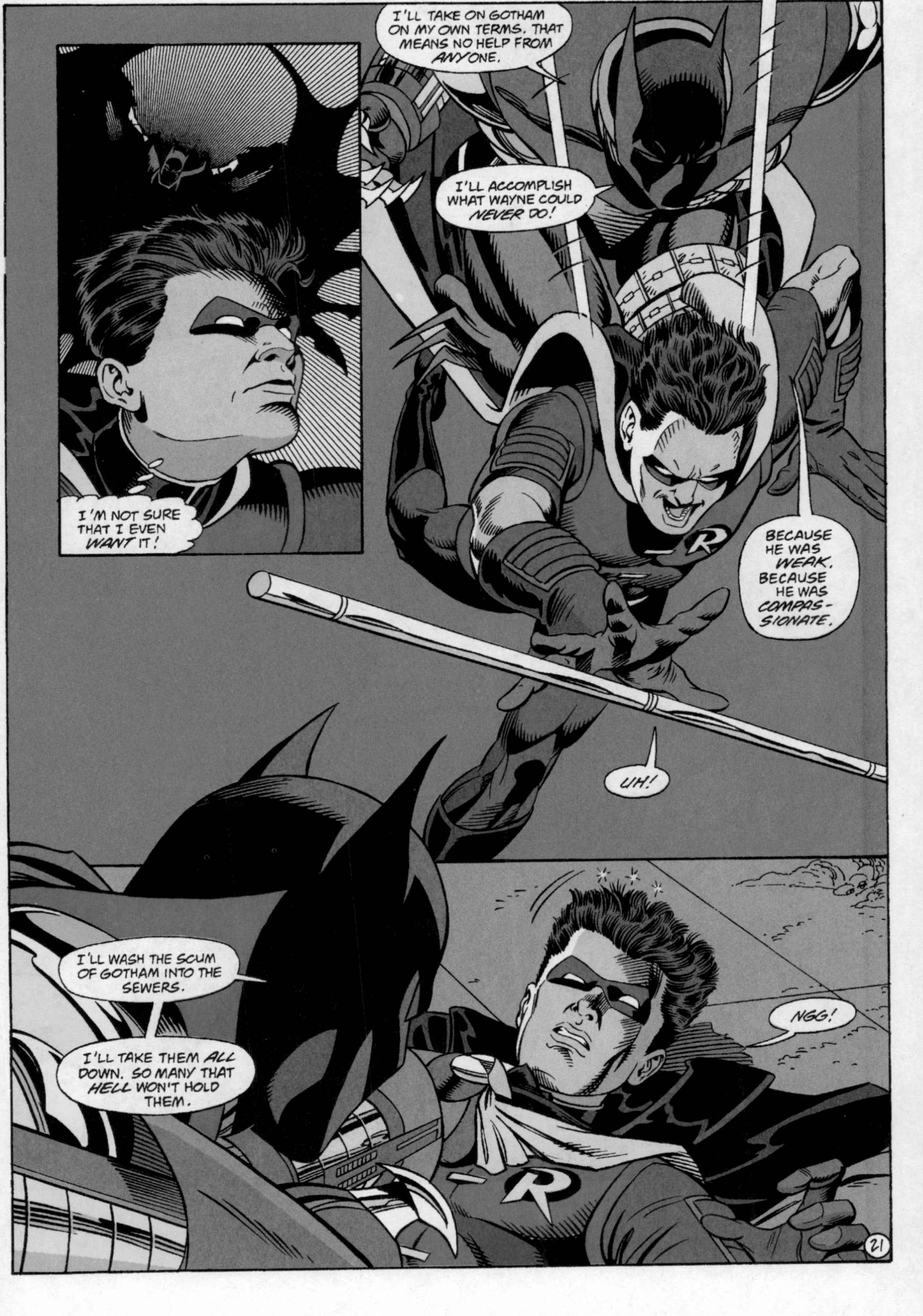
I'M NOT SURE THAT I EVEN WANT IT!
I'LL TAKE ON GOTHAM ON MY OWN TERMS. THAT MEANS NO HELP FROM ANYONE.
I'LL ACCOMPLISH WHAT WAYNE COULD NEVER DO!
BECAUSE HE WAS WEAK. BECAUSE HE WAS COMPAS-SIONATE.
UH!
I'LL WASH THE SCUM OF GOTHAM INTO THE SEWERS.
I'LL TAKE THEM ALL DOWN. SO MANY THAT HELL WON'T HOLD THEM.
NGG!
21

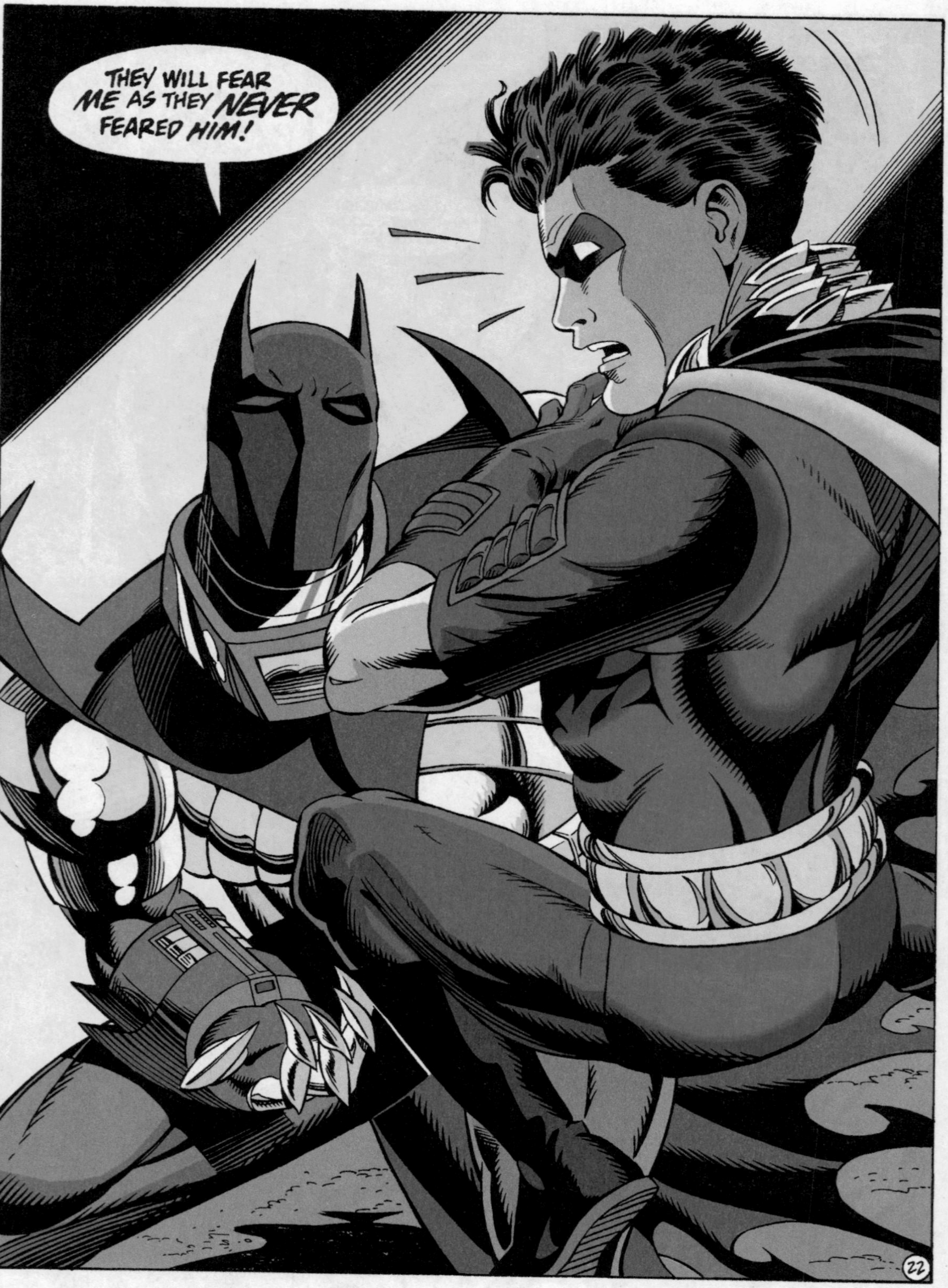
THEY WILL FEAR ME AS THEY NEVER FEARED HIM!
22

Cover art by **BRIAN STELFREEZE**

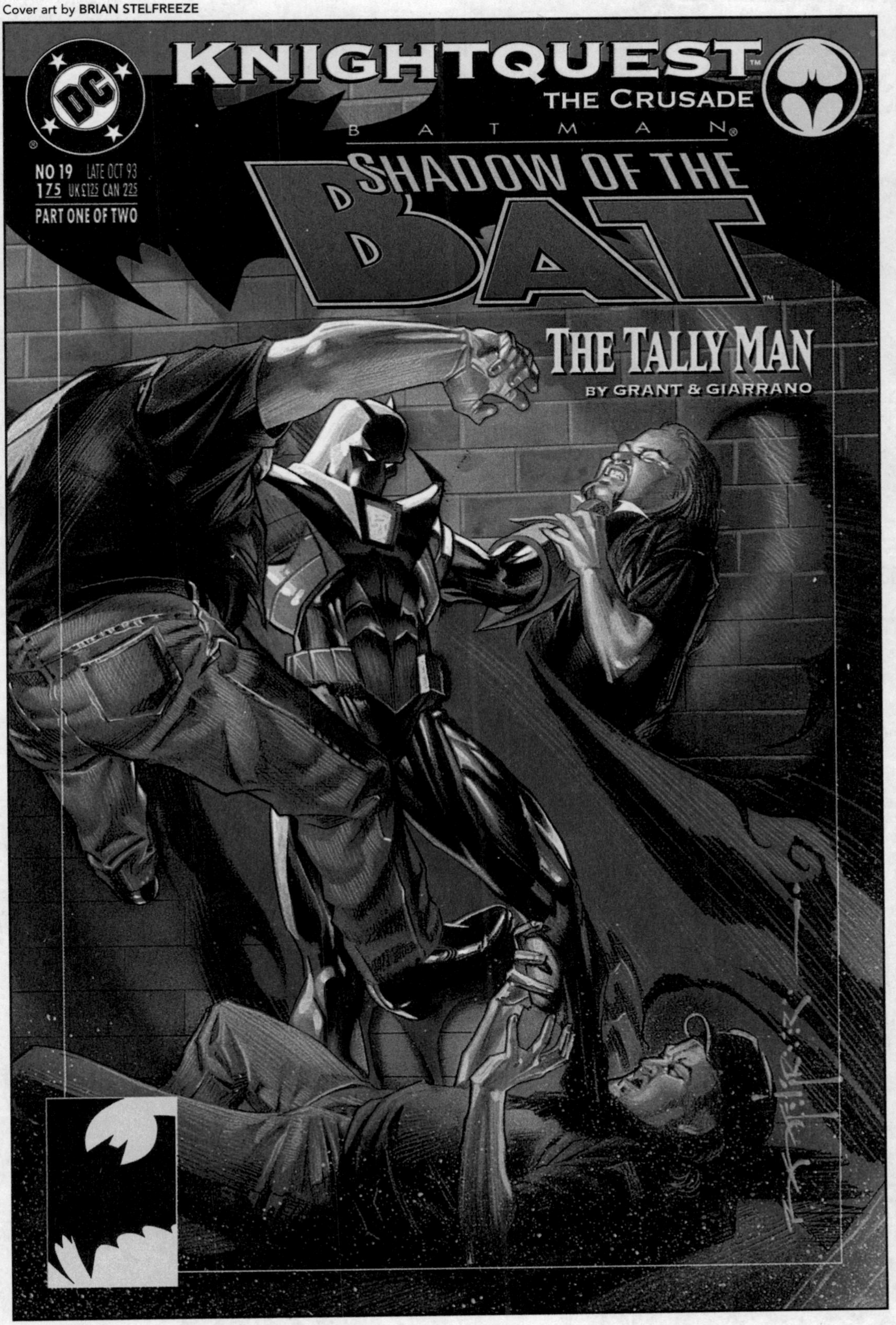
KNIGHTQUEST
THE CRUSADE
BATMAN
SHADOW OF THE BAT
NO 19 LATE OCT 93
1.75 UK £1.25 CAN 2.25
PART ONE OF TWO
THE TALLY MAN
BY GRANT & GIARRANO

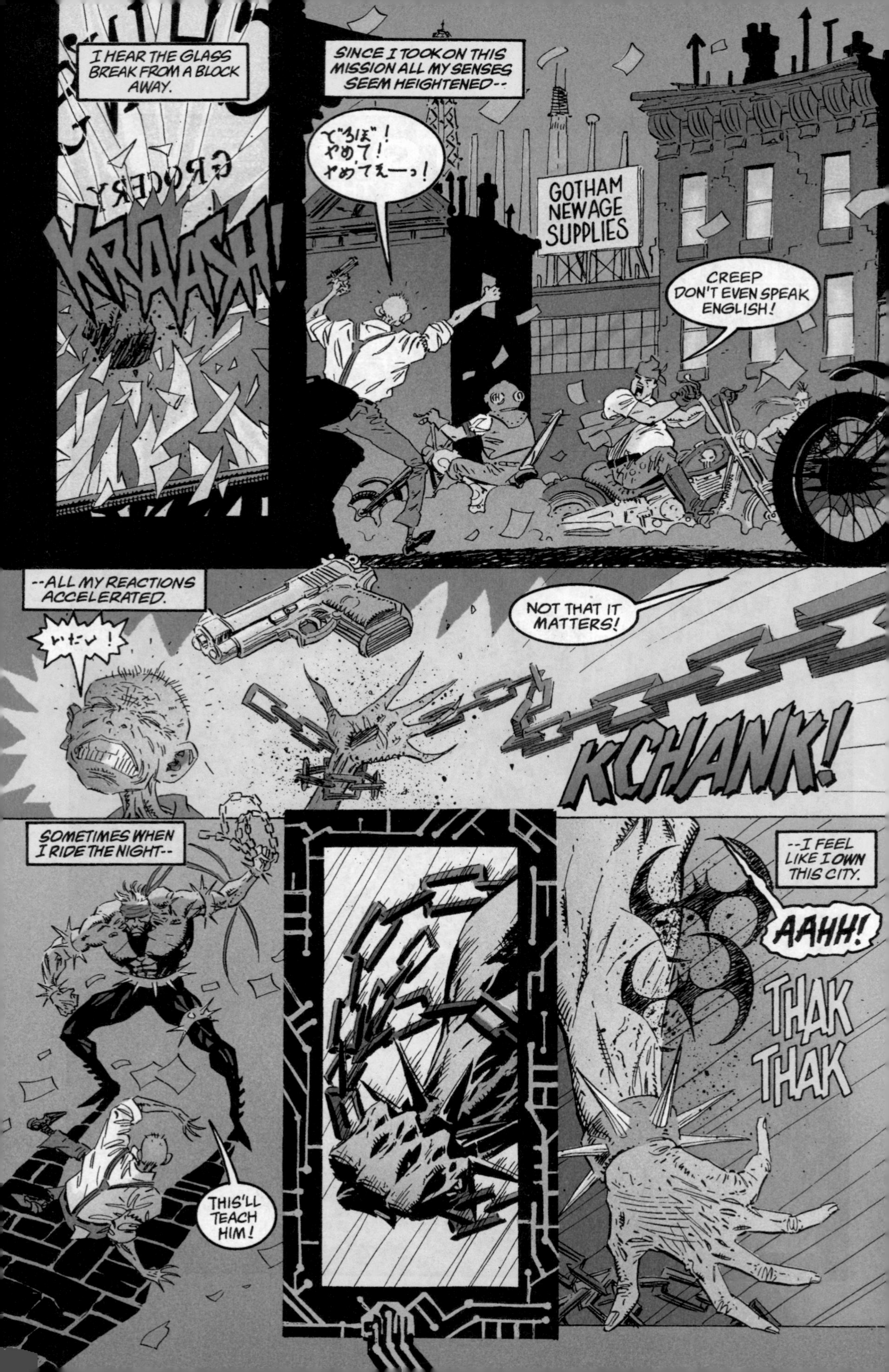

I HEAR THE GLASS BREAK FROM A BLOCK AWAY.
GROCERY
KRASH!
SINCE I TOOK ON THIS MISSION ALL MY SENSES SEEM HEIGHTENED--
でろぼ！
やめて！
やめてえーっ！
GOTHAM NEWAGE SUPPLIES
CREEP DON'T EVEN SPEAK ENGLISH!
--ALL MY REACTIONS ACCELERATED.
いたッ！
NOT THAT IT MATTERS!
KCHANK!
SOMETIMES WHEN I RIDE THE NIGHT--
THIS'LL TEACH HIM!
--I FEEL LIKE I OWN THIS CITY.
AAHH!
THAK THAK

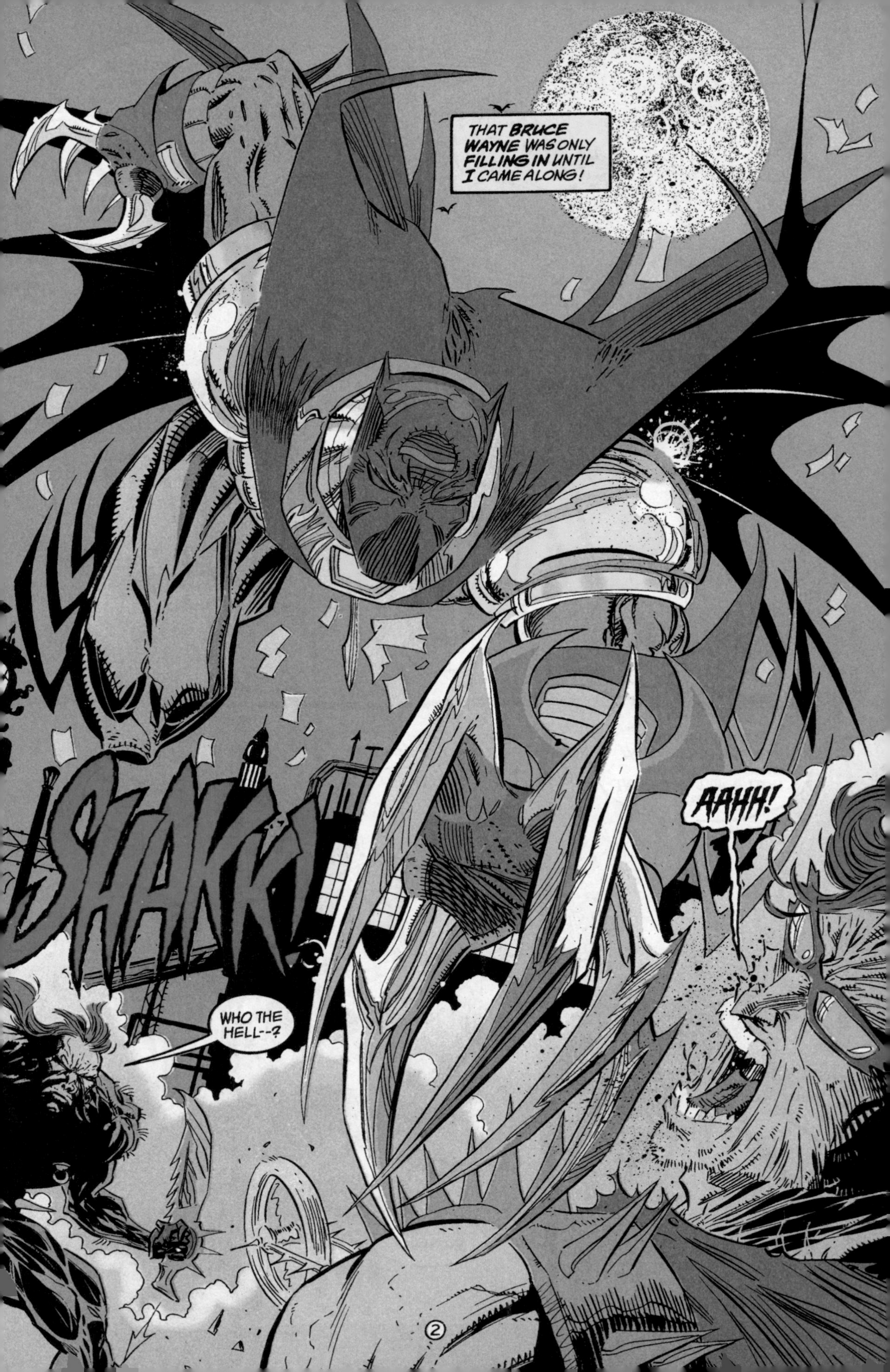
THAT BRUCE WAYNE WAS ONLY FILLING IN UNTIL I CAME ALONG!
SHAKK!
AAHH!
WHO THE HELL--?

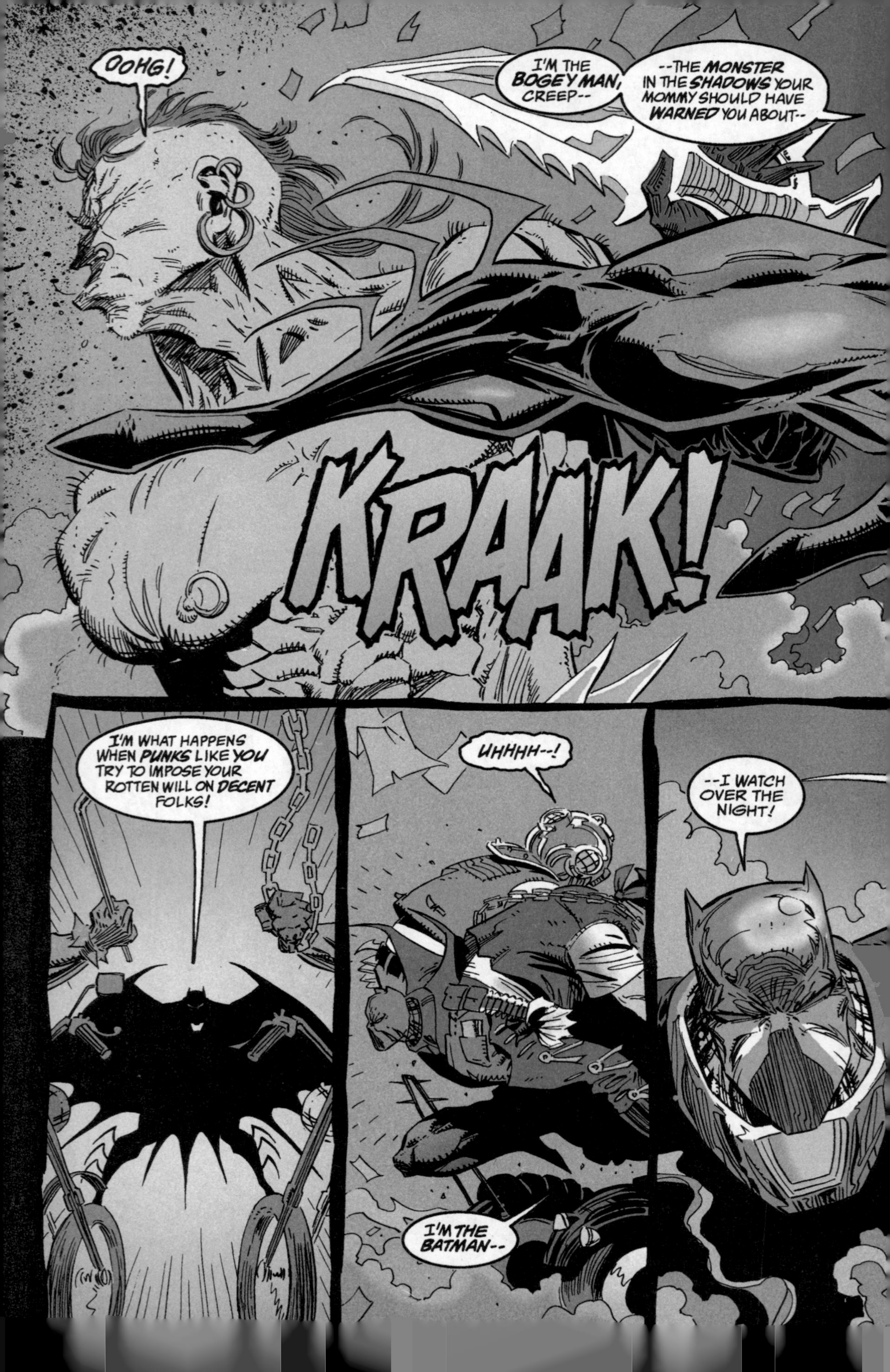
OOHG!
I'M THE BOGEY MAN, CREEP--
--THE MONSTER IN THE SHADOWS YOUR MOMMY SHOULD HAVE WARNED YOU ABOUT--
KRAAK!
I'M WHAT HAPPENS WHEN PUNKS LIKE YOU TRY TO IMPOSE YOUR ROTTEN WILL ON DECENT FOLKS!
UHHHH--!
I'M THE BATMAN--
--I WATCH OVER THE NIGHT!

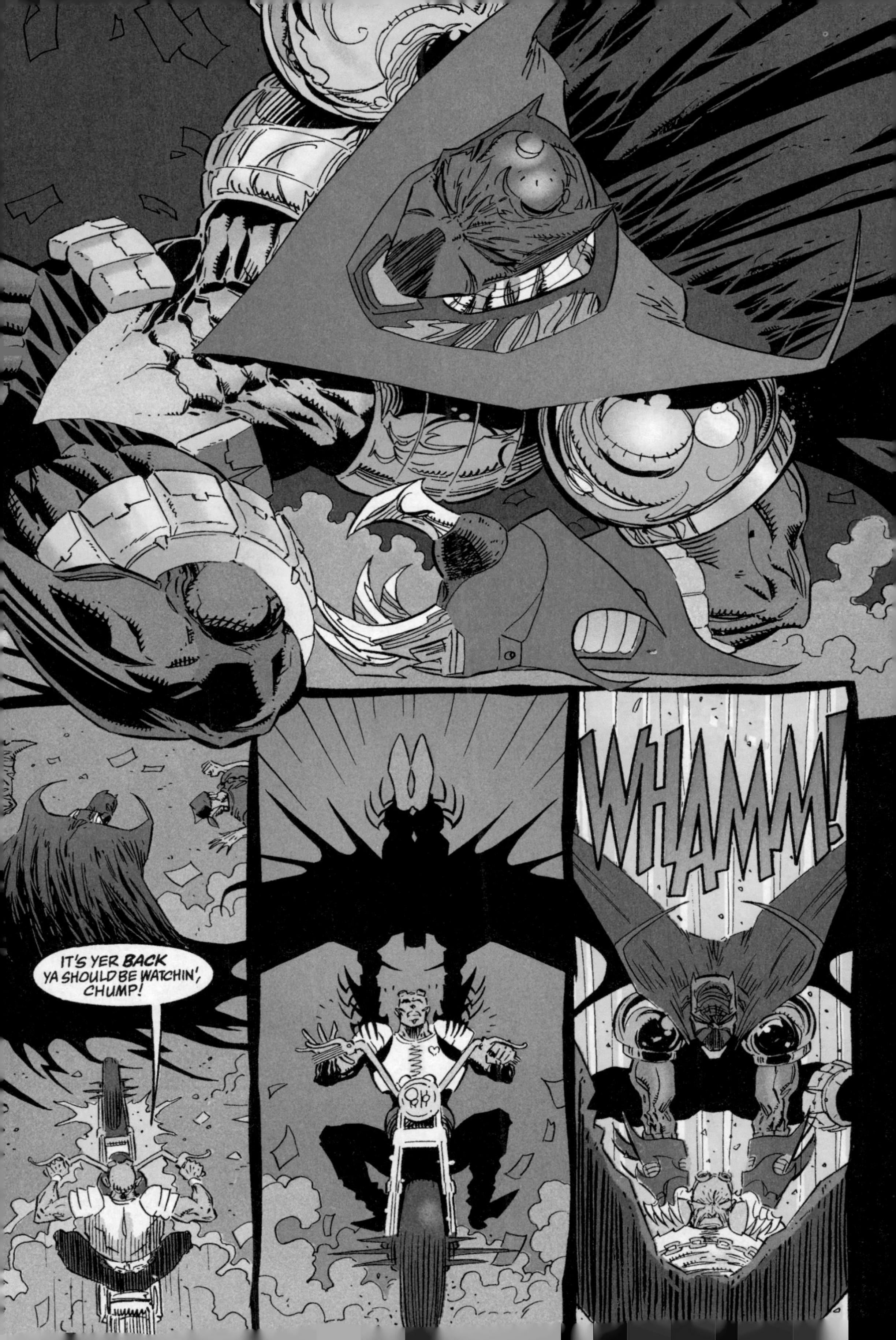
WHAMM!
IT'S YER BACK YA SHOULD BE WATCHIN', CHUMP!

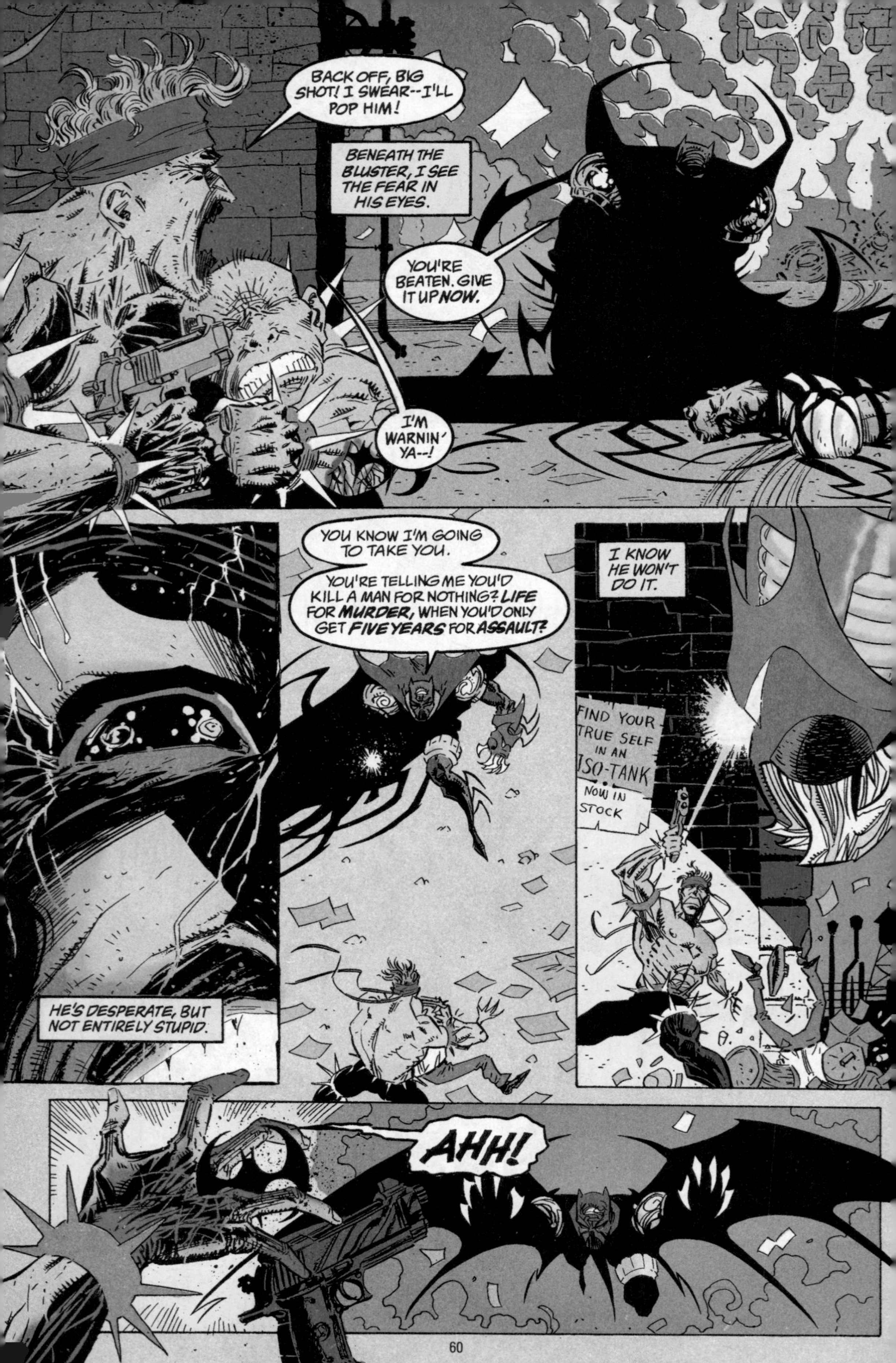
BACK OFF, BIG SHOT! I SWEAR--I'LL POP HIM!
BENEATH THE BLUSTER, I SEE THE FEAR IN HIS EYES.
YOU'RE BEATEN. GIVE IT UP NOW.
I'M WARNIN' YA--!
HE'S DESPERATE, BUT NOT ENTIRELY STUPID.
YOU KNOW I'M GOING TO TAKE YOU.
YOU'RE TELLING ME YOU'D KILL A MAN FOR NOTHING? LIFE FOR MURDER, WHEN YOU'D ONLY GET FIVE YEARS FOR ASSAULT?
I KNOW HE WON'T DO IT.
FIND YOUR TRUE SELF IN AN ISO-TANK
NOW IN STOCK
AHH!

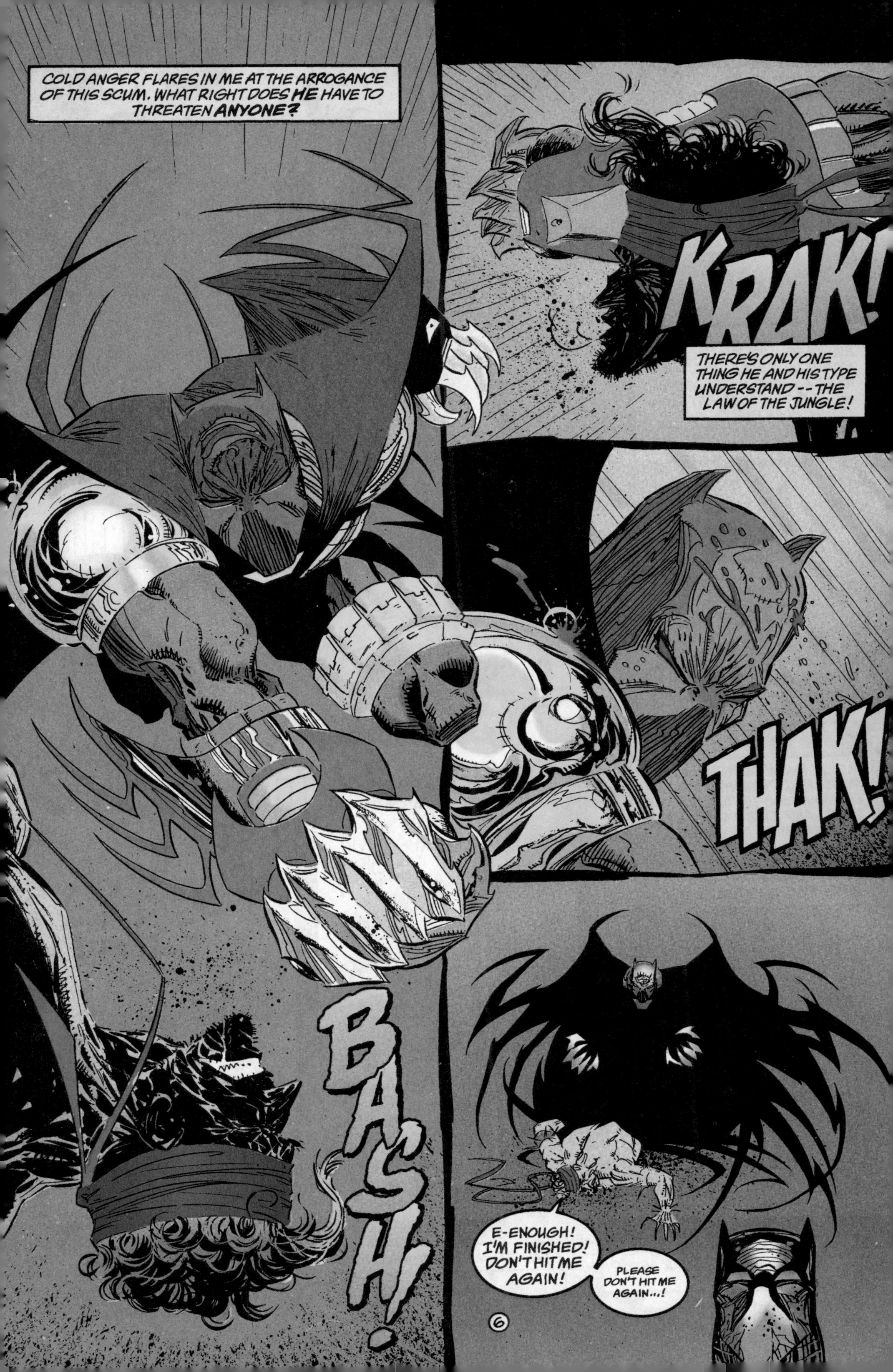
COLD ANGER FLARES IN ME AT THE ARROGANCE OF THIS SCUM. WHAT RIGHT DOES **HE** HAVE TO THREATEN **ANYONE?**
KRAK!
THERE'S ONLY ONE THING HE AND HIS TYPE UNDERSTAND -- THE LAW OF THE JUNGLE!
THAK!
BASH!
E-ENOUGH! I'M FINISHED! DON'T HIT ME AGAIN!
PLEASE DON'T HIT ME AGAIN...!
6

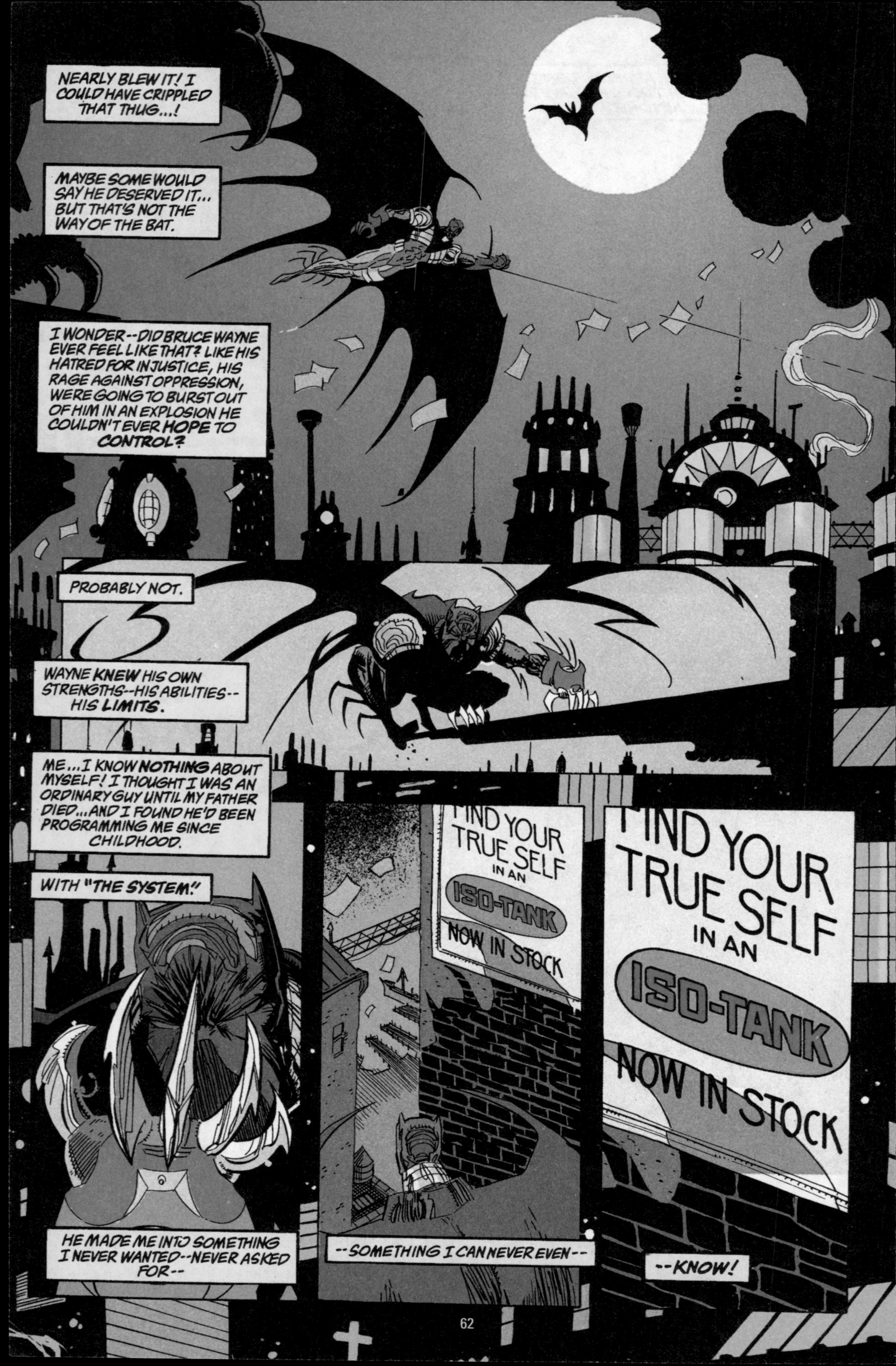
NEARLY BLEW IT! I COULD HAVE CRIPPLED THAT THUG...!
MAYBE SOME WOULD SAY HE DESERVED IT... BUT THAT'S NOT THE WAY OF THE BAT.
I WONDER--DID BRUCE WAYNE EVER FEEL LIKE THAT? LIKE HIS HATRED FOR INJUSTICE, HIS RAGE AGAINST OPPRESSION, WERE GOING TO BURST OUT OF HIM IN AN EXPLOSION HE COULDN'T EVER HOPE TO CONTROL?
PROBABLY NOT.
WAYNE KNEW HIS OWN STRENGTHS--HIS ABILITIES--HIS LIMITS.
ME...I KNOW NOTHING ABOUT MYSELF! I THOUGHT I WAS AN ORDINARY GUY UNTIL MY FATHER DIED...AND I FOUND HE'D BEEN PROGRAMMING ME SINCE CHILDHOOD.
WITH "THE SYSTEM!"
HE MADE ME INTO SOMETHING I NEVER WANTED--NEVER ASKED FOR--
FIND YOUR TRUE SELF IN AN ISO-TANK NOW IN STOCK
--SOMETHING I CAN NEVER EVEN--
FIND YOUR TRUE SELF IN AN ISO-TANK NOW IN STOCK
--KNOW!

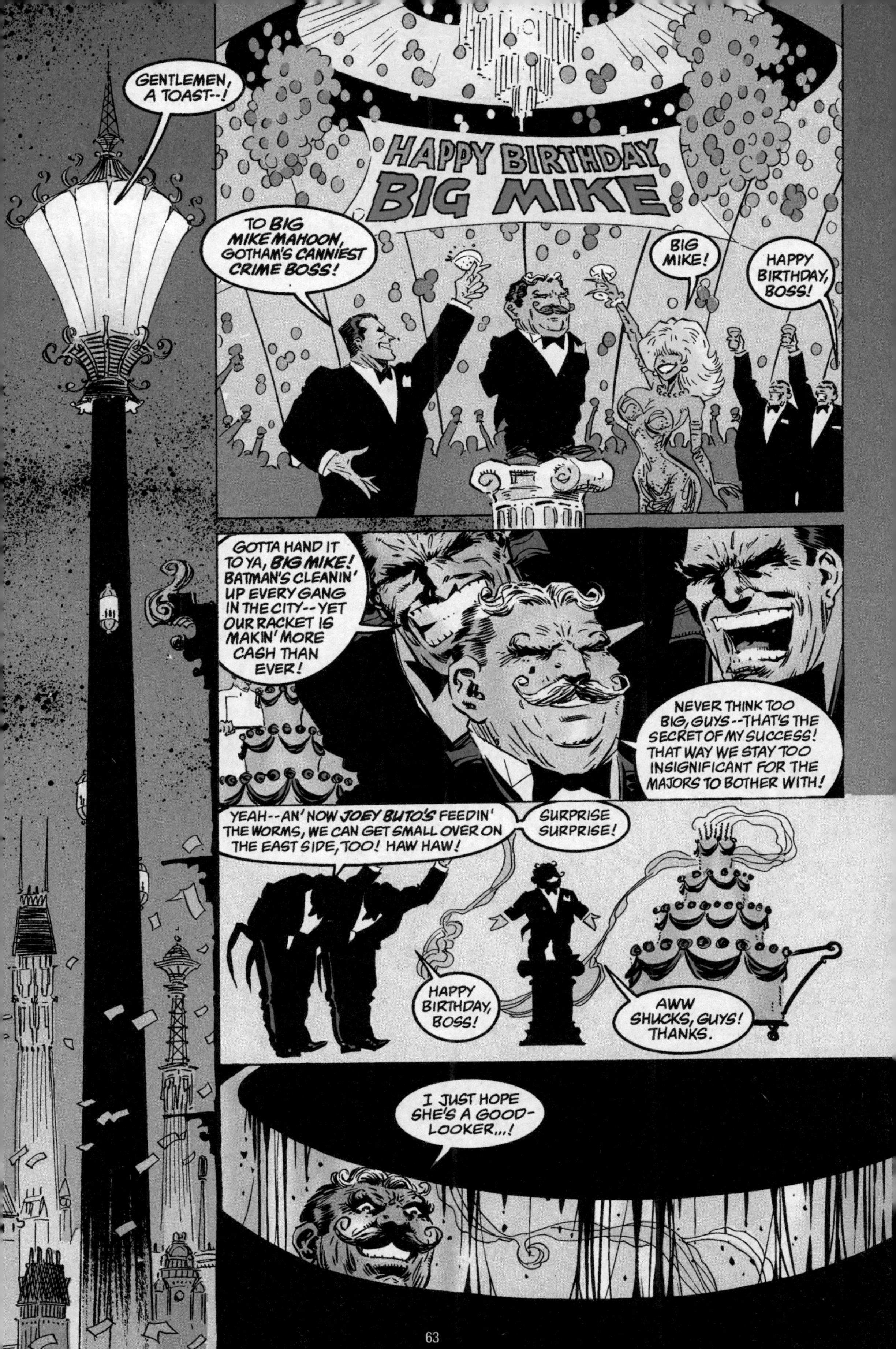
GENTLEMEN, A TOAST--!
HAPPY BIRTHDAY BIG MIKE
TO BIG MIKE MAHOON, GOTHAM'S CANNIEST CRIME BOSS!
BIG MIKE!
HAPPY BIRTHDAY, BOSS!
GOTTA HAND IT TO YA, BIG MIKE! BATMAN'S CLEANIN' UP EVERY GANG IN THE CITY--YET OUR RACKET IS MAKIN' MORE CASH THAN EVER!
NEVER THINK TOO BIG, GUYS--THAT'S THE SECRET OF MY SUCCESS! THAT WAY WE STAY TOO INSIGNIFICANT FOR THE MAJORS TO BOTHER WITH!
YEAH--AN' NOW JOEY BUTO'S FEEDIN' THE WORMS, WE CAN GET SMALL OVER ON THE EAST SIDE, TOO! HAW HAW!
SURPRISE SURPRISE!
HAPPY BIRTHDAY, BOSS!
AWW SHUCKS, GUYS! THANKS.
I JUST HOPE SHE'S A GOOD-LOOKER...!

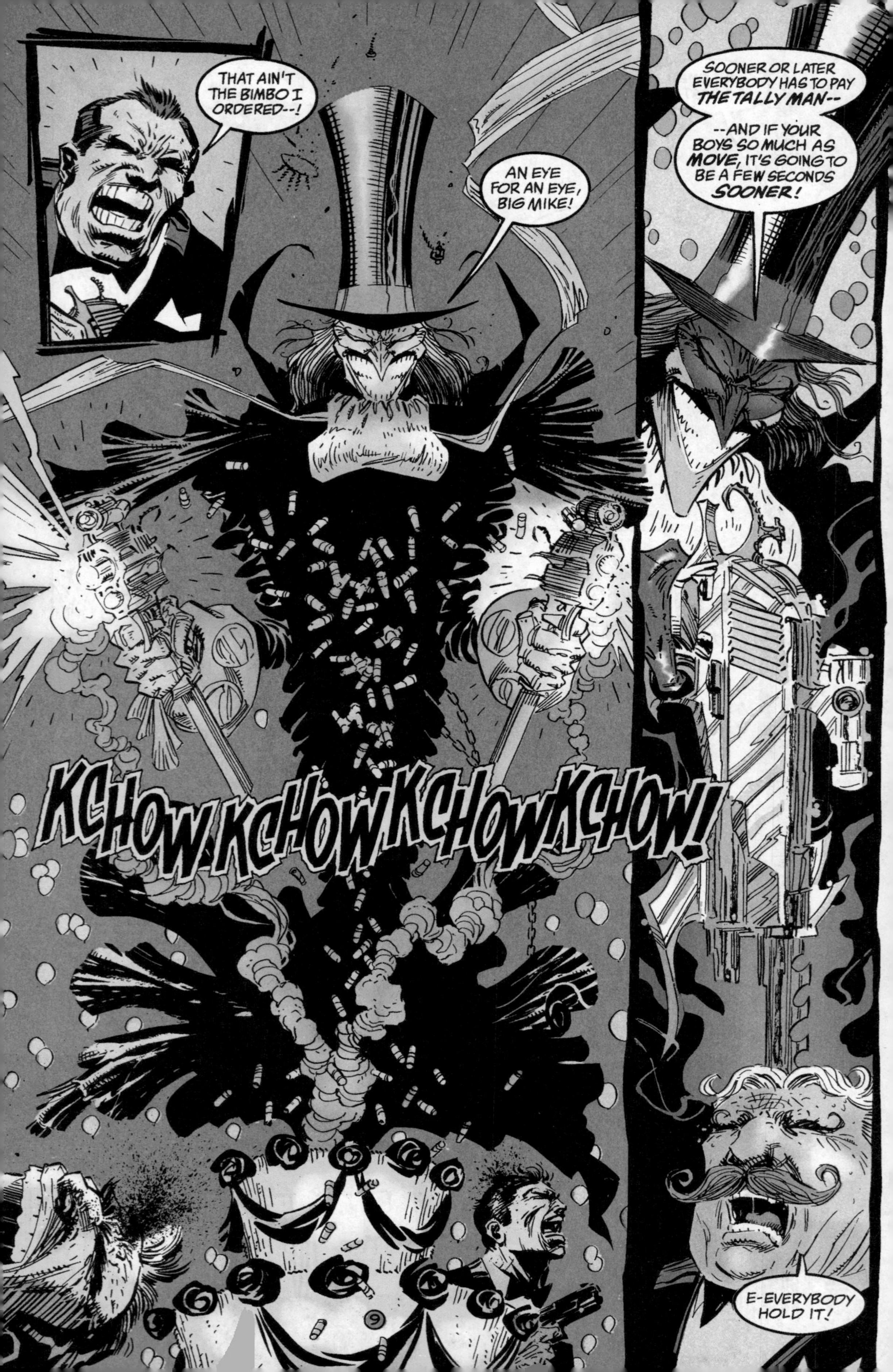
THAT AIN'T THE BIMBO I ORDERED--!
AN EYE FOR AN EYE, BIG MIKE!
SOONER OR LATER EVERYBODY HAS TO PAY THE TALLY MAN--
--AND IF YOUR BOYS SO MUCH AS MOVE, IT'S GOING TO BE A FEW SECONDS SOONER!
KCHOW KCHOW KCHOW KCHOW!
E-EVERYBODY HOLD IT!

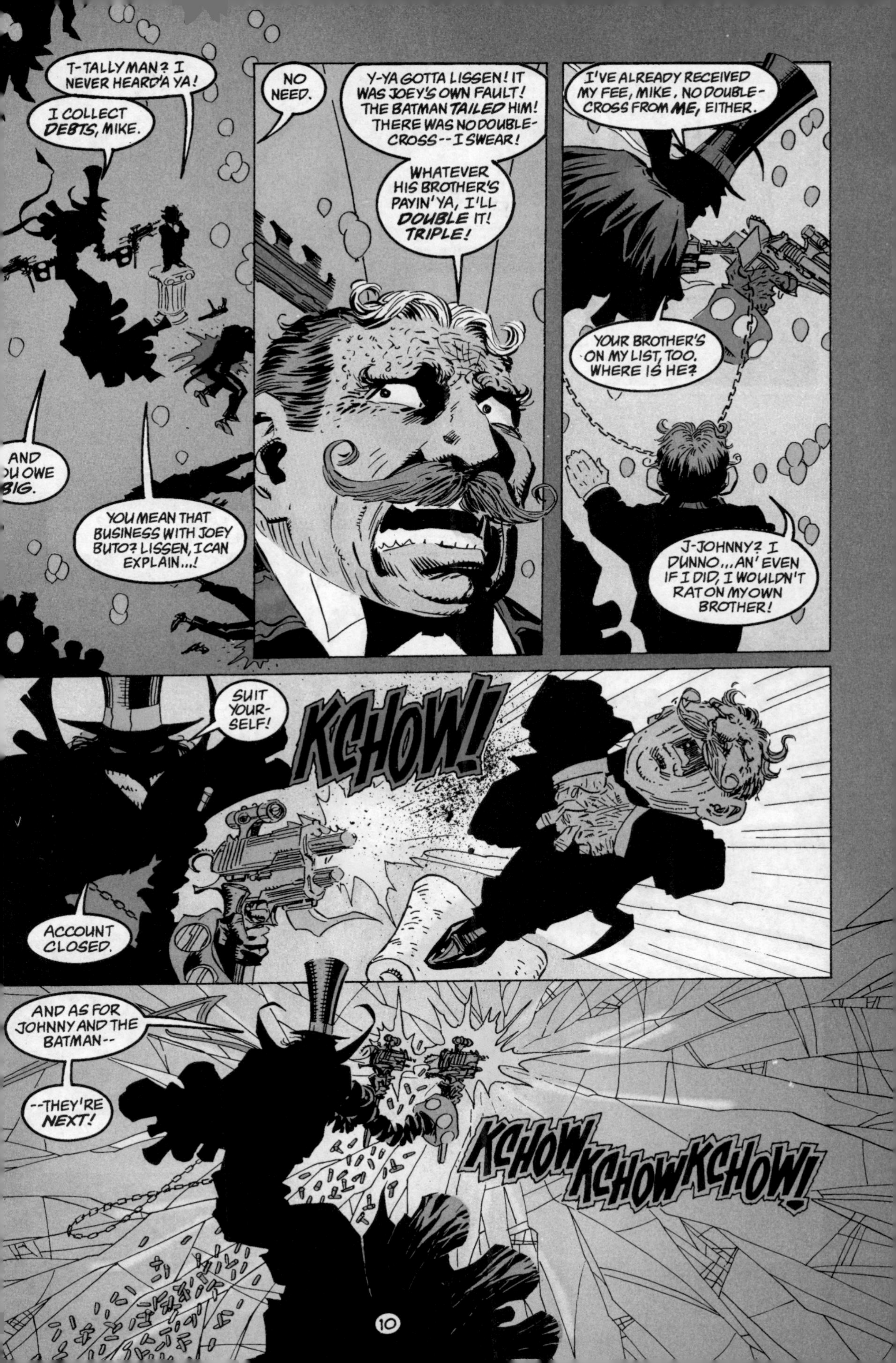

T-TALLY MAN? I NEVER HEARD'A YA!
I COLLECT DEBTS, MIKE.
AND OU OWE BIG.
YOU MEAN THAT BUSINESS WITH JOEY BUTO? LISSEN, I CAN EXPLAIN...!
NO NEED.
Y-YA GOTTA LISSEN! IT WAS JOEY'S OWN FAULT! THE BATMAN TAILED HIM! THERE WAS NO DOUBLE-CROSS--I SWEAR!
WHATEVER HIS BROTHER'S PAYIN' YA, I'LL DOUBLE IT! TRIPLE!
I'VE ALREADY RECEIVED MY FEE, MIKE, NO DOUBLE-CROSS FROM ME, EITHER.
YOUR BROTHER'S ON MY LIST, TOO. WHERE IS HE?
J-JOHNNY? I DUNNO... AN' EVEN IF I DID, I WOULDN'T RAT ON MY OWN BROTHER!
SUIT YOURSELF!
KCHOW!
ACCOUNT CLOSED.
AND AS FOR JOHNNY AND THE BATMAN--
--THEY'RE NEXT!
KCHOW KCHOW KCHOW!

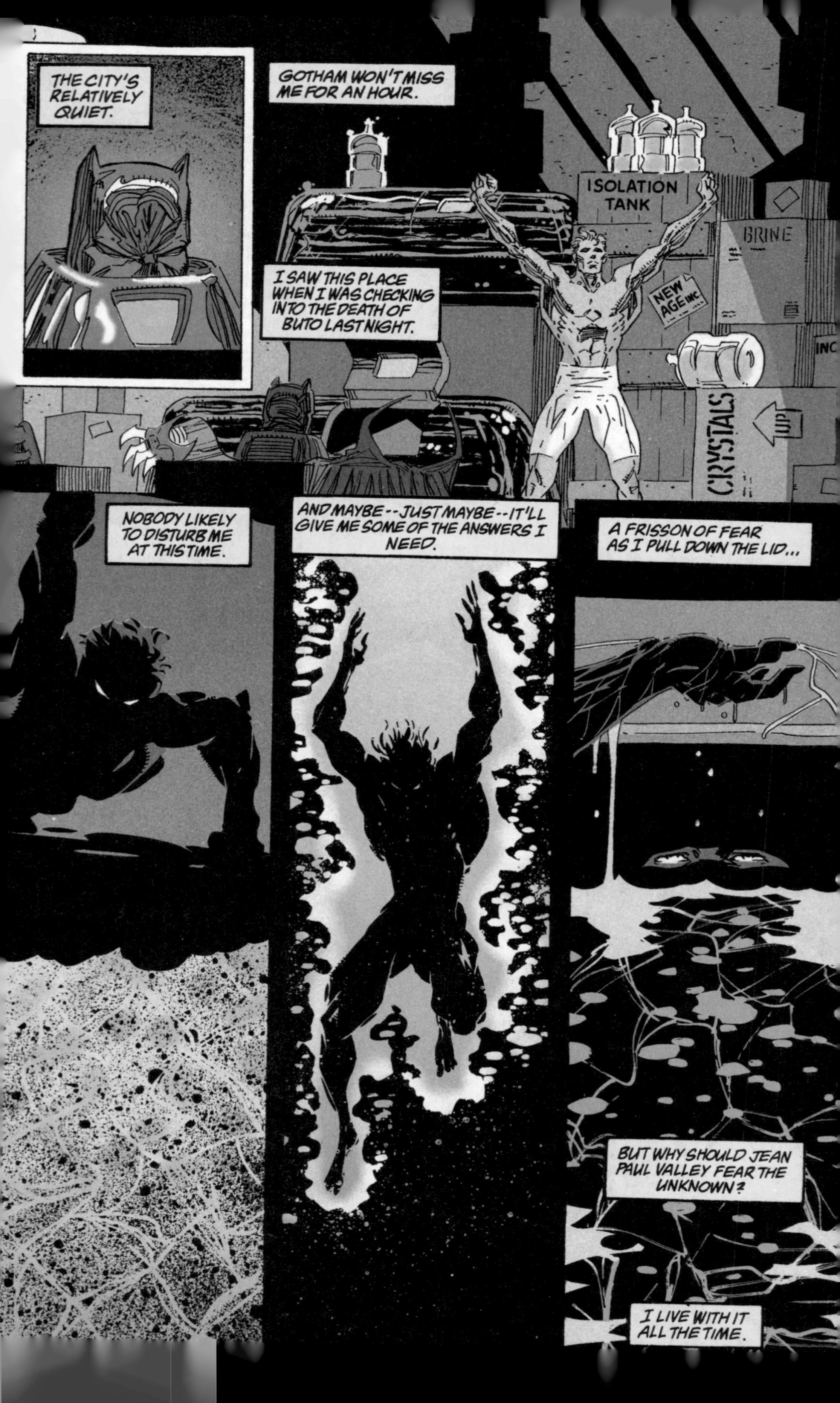
THE CITY'S RELATIVELY QUIET.
GOTHAM WON'T MISS ME FOR AN HOUR.
ISOLATION TANK
BRINE
I SAW THIS PLACE WHEN I WAS CHECKING INTO THE DEATH OF BUTO LAST NIGHT.
NEW AGE INC
CRYSTALS
UP
NOBODY LIKELY TO DISTURB ME AT THIS TIME.
AND MAYBE--JUST MAYBE--IT'LL GIVE ME SOME OF THE ANSWERS I NEED.
A FRISSON OF FEAR AS I PULL DOWN THE LID...
BUT WHY SHOULD JEAN PAUL VALLEY FEAR THE UNKNOWN?
I LIVE WITH IT ALL THE TIME.

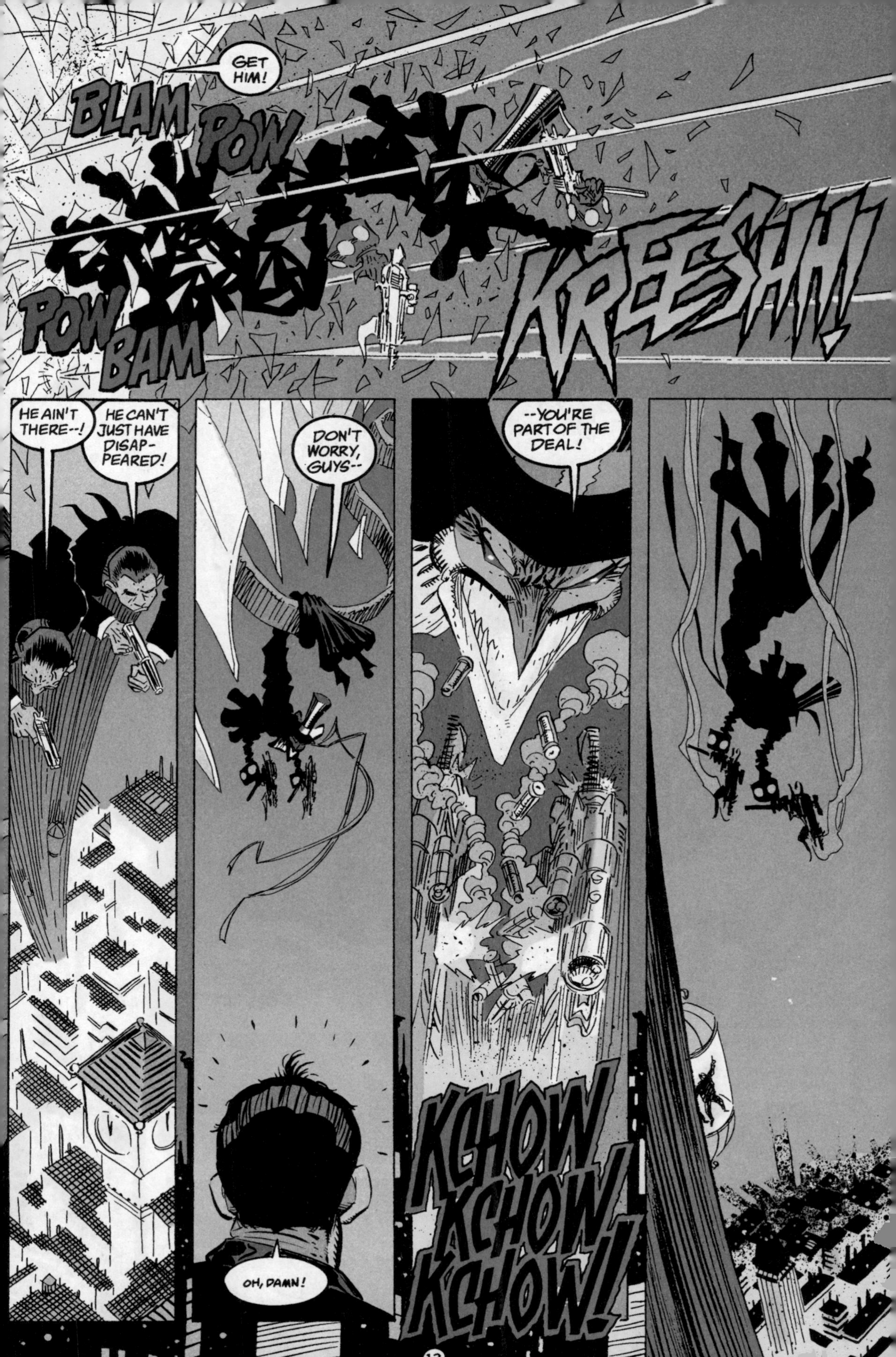
GET HIM!
BLAM
POW
POW
BAM
KREESHH!
HE AIN'T THERE--!
HE CAN'T JUST HAVE DISAP-PEARED!
DON'T WORRY, GUYS--
OH, DAMN!
--YOU'RE PART OF THE DEAL!
KCHOW KCHOW KCHOW!

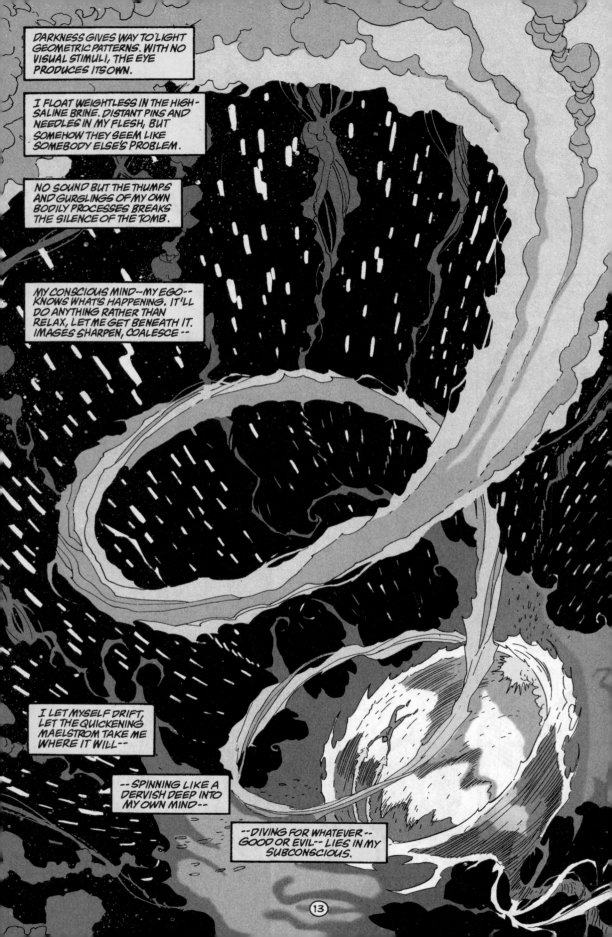

DARKNESS GIVES WAY TO LIGHT GEOMETRIC PATTERNS. WITH NO VISUAL STIMULI, THE EYE PRODUCES ITS OWN.

I FLOAT WEIGHTLESS IN THE HIGH-SALINE BRINE. DISTANT PINS AND NEEDLES IN MY FLESH, BUT SOMEHOW THEY SEEM LIKE SOMEBODY ELSE'S PROBLEM.

NO SOUND BUT THE THUMPS AND GURGLINGS OF MY OWN BODILY PROCESSES BREAKS THE SILENCE OF THE TOMB.

MY CONSCIOUS MIND--MY EGO--KNOWS WHAT'S HAPPENING. IT'LL DO ANYTHING RATHER THAN RELAX, LET ME GET BENEATH IT. IMAGES SHARPEN, COALESCE--

I LET MYSELF DRIFT, LET THE QUICKENING MAELSTROM TAKE ME WHERE IT WILL--

--SPINNING LIKE A DERVISH DEEP INTO MY OWN MIND--

--DIVING FOR WHATEVER -- GOOD OR EVIL-- LIES IN MY SUBCONSCIOUS.

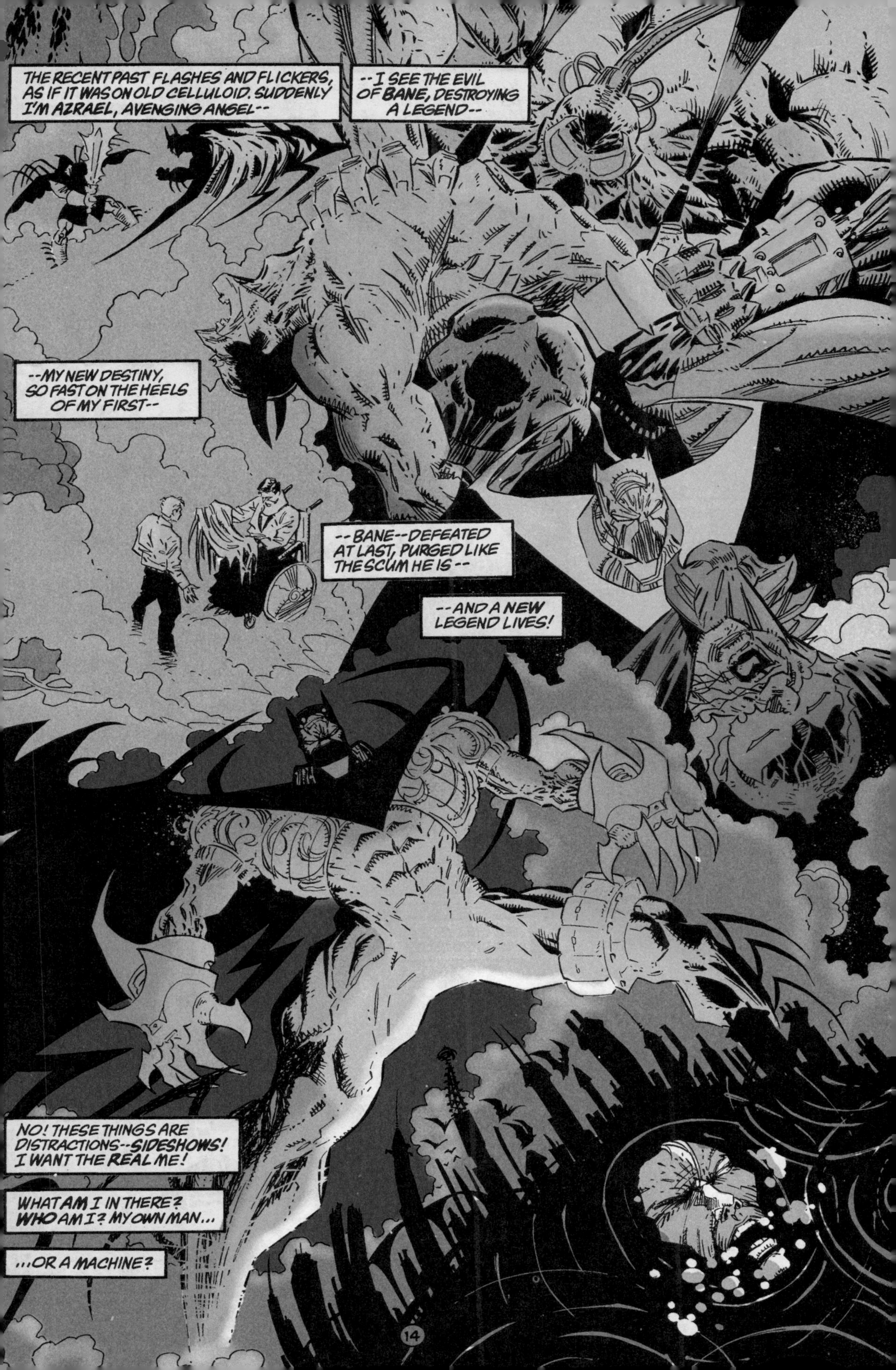
THE RECENT PAST FLASHES AND FLICKERS, AS IF IT WAS ON OLD CELLULOID. SUDDENLY I'M AZRAEL, AVENGING ANGEL--
--I SEE THE EVIL OF BANE, DESTROYING A LEGEND--
--MY NEW DESTINY, SO FAST ON THE HEELS OF MY FIRST--
--BANE--DEFEATED AT LAST, PURGED LIKE THE SCUM HE IS--
--AND A NEW LEGEND LIVES!
NO! THESE THINGS ARE DISTRACTIONS--SIDESHOWS! I WANT THE REAL ME!
WHAT AM I IN THERE? WHO AM I? MY OWN MAN...
...OR A MACHINE?

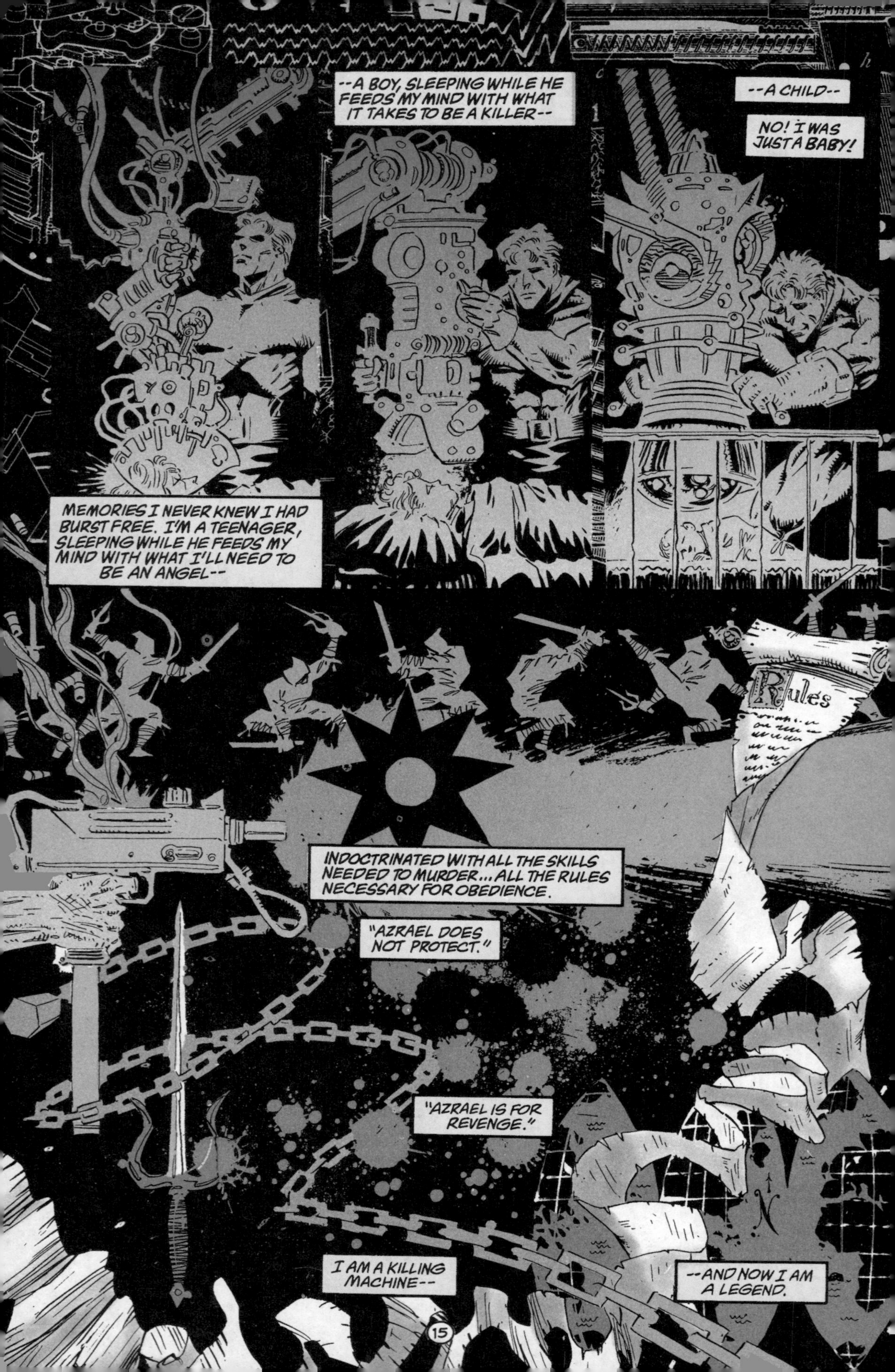
MEMORIES I NEVER KNEW I HAD BURST FREE. I'M A TEENAGER, SLEEPING WHILE HE FEEDS MY MIND WITH WHAT I'LL NEED TO BE AN ANGEL--
--A BOY, SLEEPING WHILE HE FEEDS MY MIND WITH WHAT IT TAKES TO BE A KILLER--
--A CHILD--
NO! I WAS JUST A BABY!
Rules
INDOCTRINATED WITH ALL THE SKILLS NEEDED TO MURDER... ALL THE RULES NECESSARY FOR OBEDIENCE.
"AZRAEL DOES NOT PROTECT."
"AZRAEL IS FOR REVENGE."
I AM A KILLING MACHINE--
--AND NOW I AM A LEGEND.

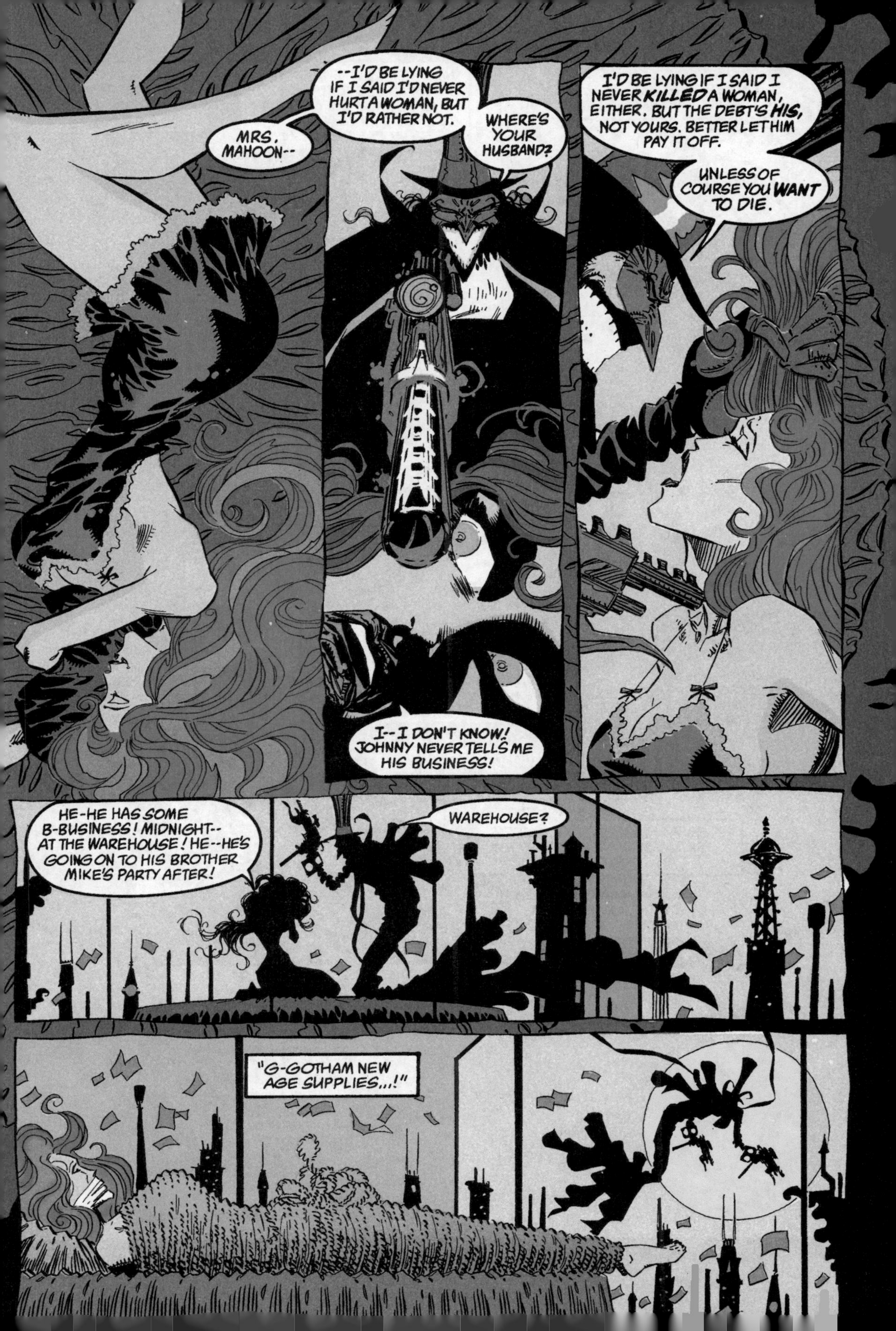
MRS. MAHOON--
--I'D BE LYING IF I SAID I'D NEVER HURT A WOMAN, BUT I'D RATHER NOT.
WHERE'S YOUR HUSBAND?
I--I DON'T KNOW! JOHNNY NEVER TELLS ME HIS BUSINESS!
I'D BE LYING IF I SAID I NEVER KILLED A WOMAN, EITHER. BUT THE DEBT'S HIS, NOT YOURS. BETTER LET HIM PAY IT OFF.
UNLESS OF COURSE YOU WANT TO DIE.
HE-HE HAS SOME B-BUSINESS! MIDNIGHT--AT THE WAREHOUSE! HE--HE'S GOING ON TO HIS BROTHER MIKE'S PARTY AFTER!
WAREHOUSE?
"G-GOTHAM NEW AGE SUPPLIES...!"

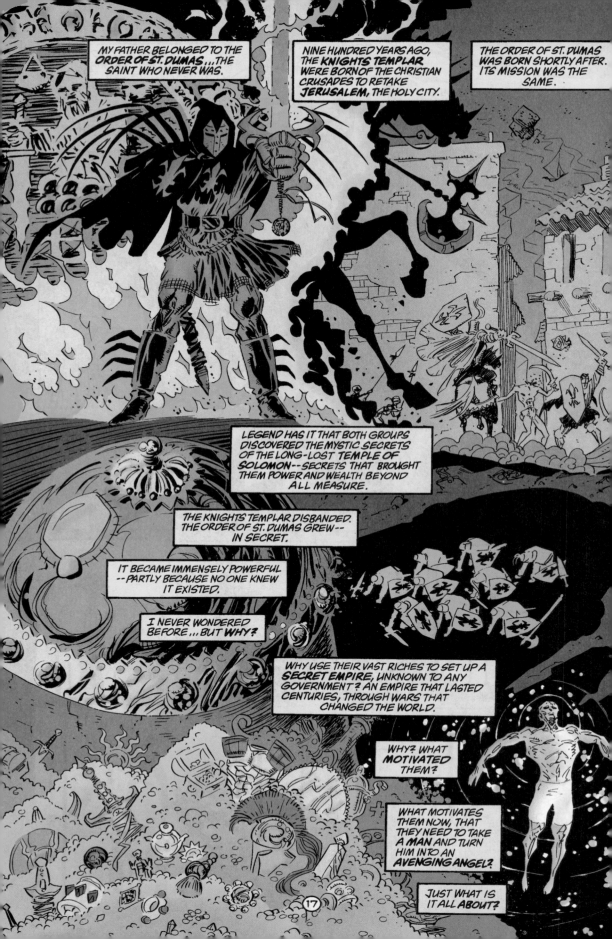

MY FATHER BELONGED TO THE **ORDER OF ST. DUMAS**...THE SAINT WHO NEVER WAS.

NINE HUNDRED YEARS AGO, THE **KNIGHTS TEMPLAR** WERE BORN OF THE CHRISTIAN CRUSADES TO RETAKE **JERUSALEM,** THE HOLY CITY.

THE **ORDER OF ST. DUMAS** WAS BORN SHORTLY AFTER. ITS MISSION WAS THE SAME.

LEGEND HAS IT THAT BOTH GROUPS DISCOVERED THE MYSTIC SECRETS OF THE LONG-LOST **TEMPLE OF SOLOMON** -- SECRETS THAT BROUGHT THEM POWER AND WEALTH BEYOND ALL MEASURE.

THE KNIGHTS TEMPLAR DISBANDED. THE ORDER OF ST. DUMAS GREW -- IN SECRET.

IT BECAME IMMENSELY POWERFUL -- PARTLY BECAUSE NO ONE KNEW IT EXISTED.

I NEVER WONDERED BEFORE...BUT **WHY?**

WHY USE THEIR VAST RICHES TO SET UP A **SECRET EMPIRE,** UNKNOWN TO ANY GOVERNMENT? AN EMPIRE THAT LASTED CENTURIES, THROUGH WARS THAT CHANGED THE WORLD.

WHY? WHAT **MOTIVATED** THEM?

WHAT MOTIVATES THEM NOW, THAT THEY NEED TO TAKE A **MAN** AND TURN HIM INTO AN **AVENGING ANGEL?**

JUST WHAT IS IT ALL **ABOUT?**

17

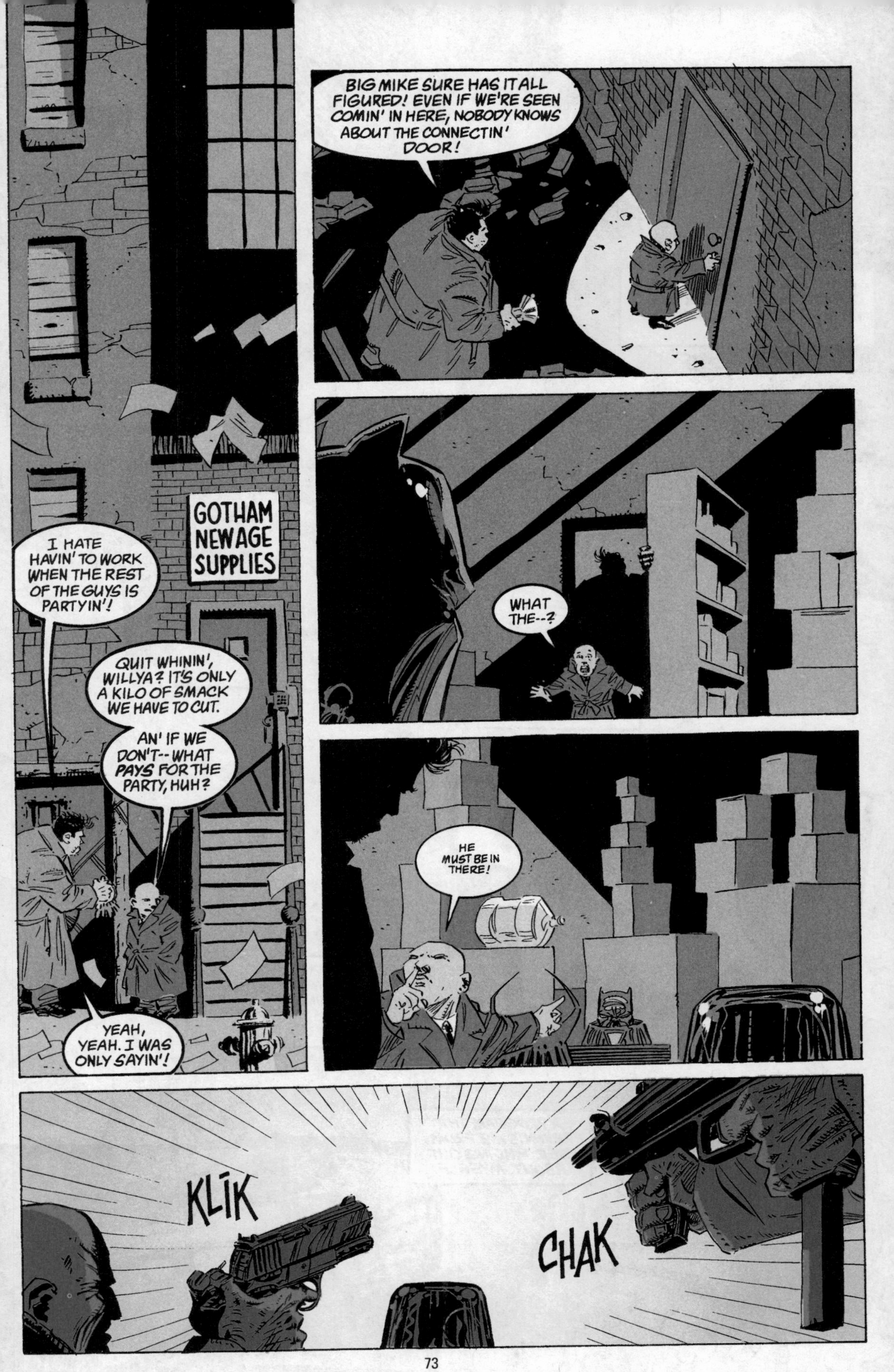
GOTHAM NEWAGE SUPPLIES
I HATE HAVIN' TO WORK WHEN THE REST OF THE GUYS IS PARTYIN'!
QUIT WHININ', WILLYA? IT'S ONLY A KILO OF SMACK WE HAVE TO CUT.
AN' IF WE DON'T--WHAT PAYS FOR THE PARTY, HUH?
YEAH, YEAH. I WAS ONLY SAYIN'!
BIG MIKE SURE HAS IT ALL FIGURED! EVEN IF WE'RE SEEN COMIN' IN HERE, NOBODY KNOWS ABOUT THE CONNECTIN' DOOR!
WHAT THE--?
HE MUST BE IN THERE!
KLIK
CHAK

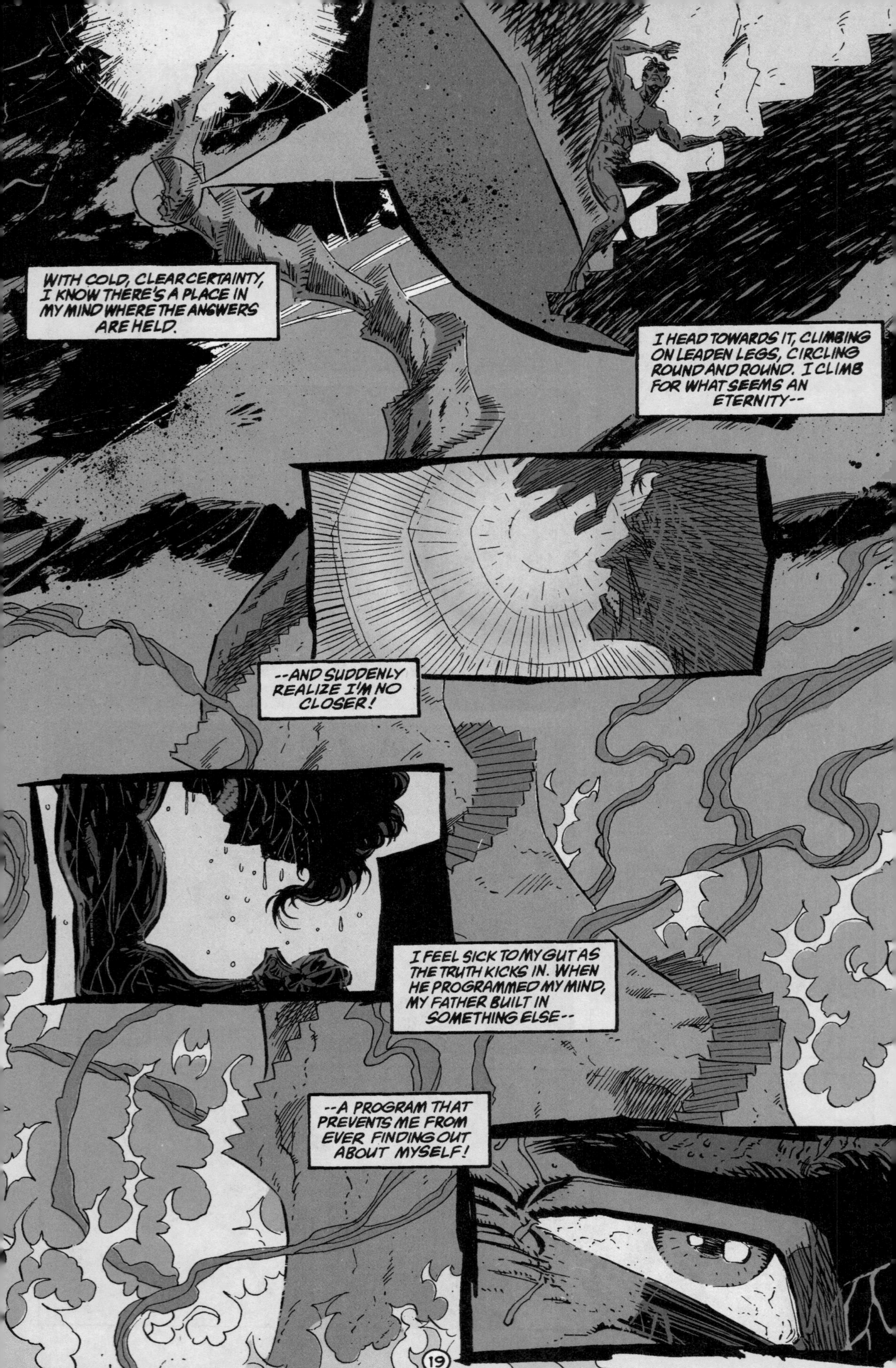
WITH COLD, CLEAR CERTAINTY, I KNOW THERE'S A PLACE IN MY MIND WHERE THE ANSWERS ARE HELD.
I HEAD TOWARDS IT, CLIMBING ON LEADEN LEGS, CIRCLING ROUND AND ROUND. I CLIMB FOR WHAT SEEMS AN ETERNITY--
--AND SUDDENLY REALIZE I'M NO CLOSER!
I FEEL SICK TO MY GUT AS THE TRUTH KICKS IN. WHEN HE PROGRAMMED MY MIND, MY FATHER BUILT IN SOMETHING ELSE--
--A PROGRAM THAT PREVENTS ME FROM EVER FINDING OUT ABOUT MYSELF!

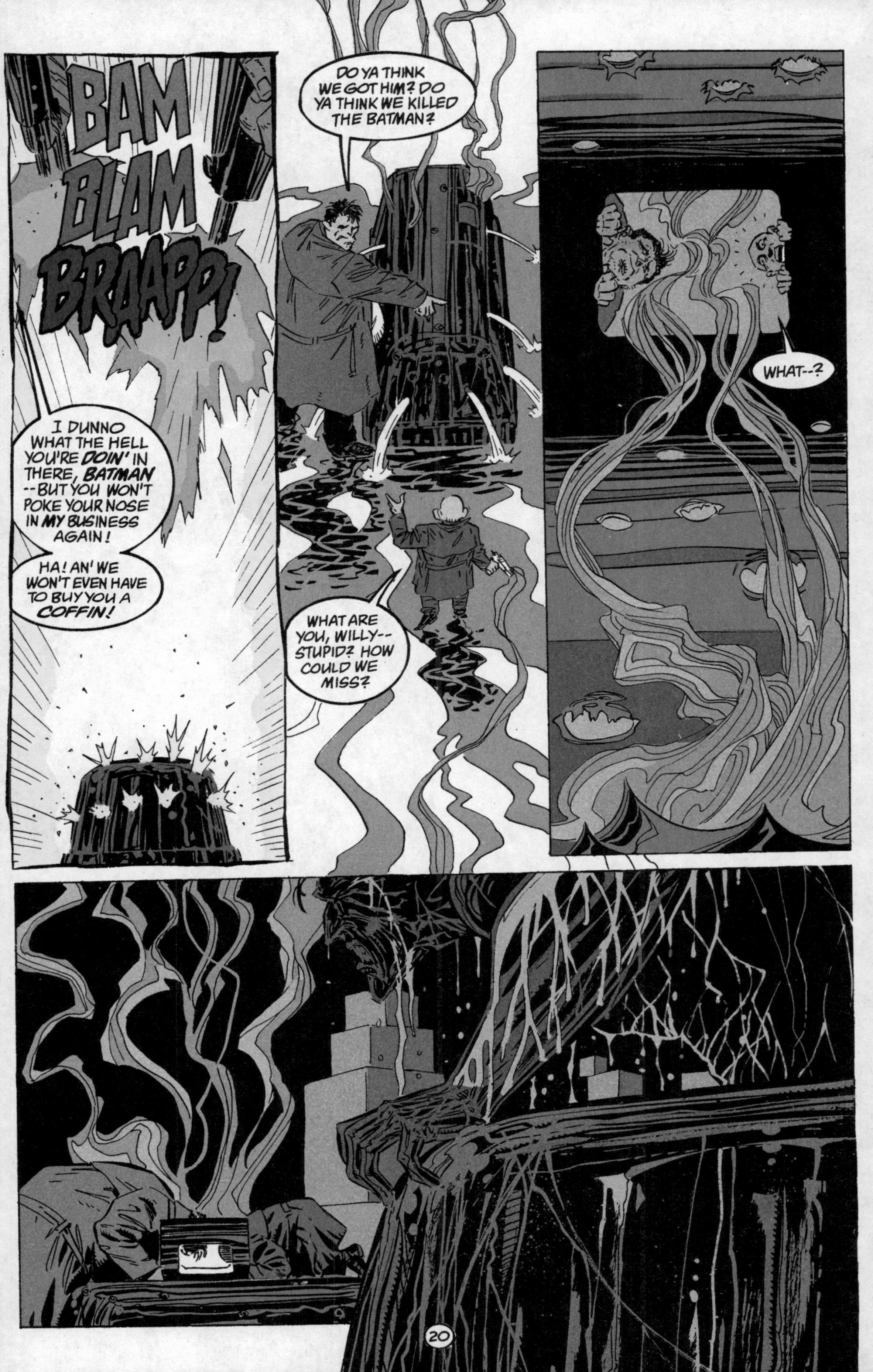
BAM
BLAM
BRAAPP!
I DUNNO WHAT THE HELL YOU'RE DOIN' IN THERE, BATMAN --BUT YOU WON'T POKE YOUR NOSE IN MY BUSINESS AGAIN!
HA! AN' WE WON'T EVEN HAVE TO BUY YOU A COFFIN!
DO YA THINK WE GOT HIM? DO YA THINK WE KILLED THE BATMAN?
WHAT ARE YOU, WILLY-- STUPID? HOW COULD WE MISS?
WHAT--?

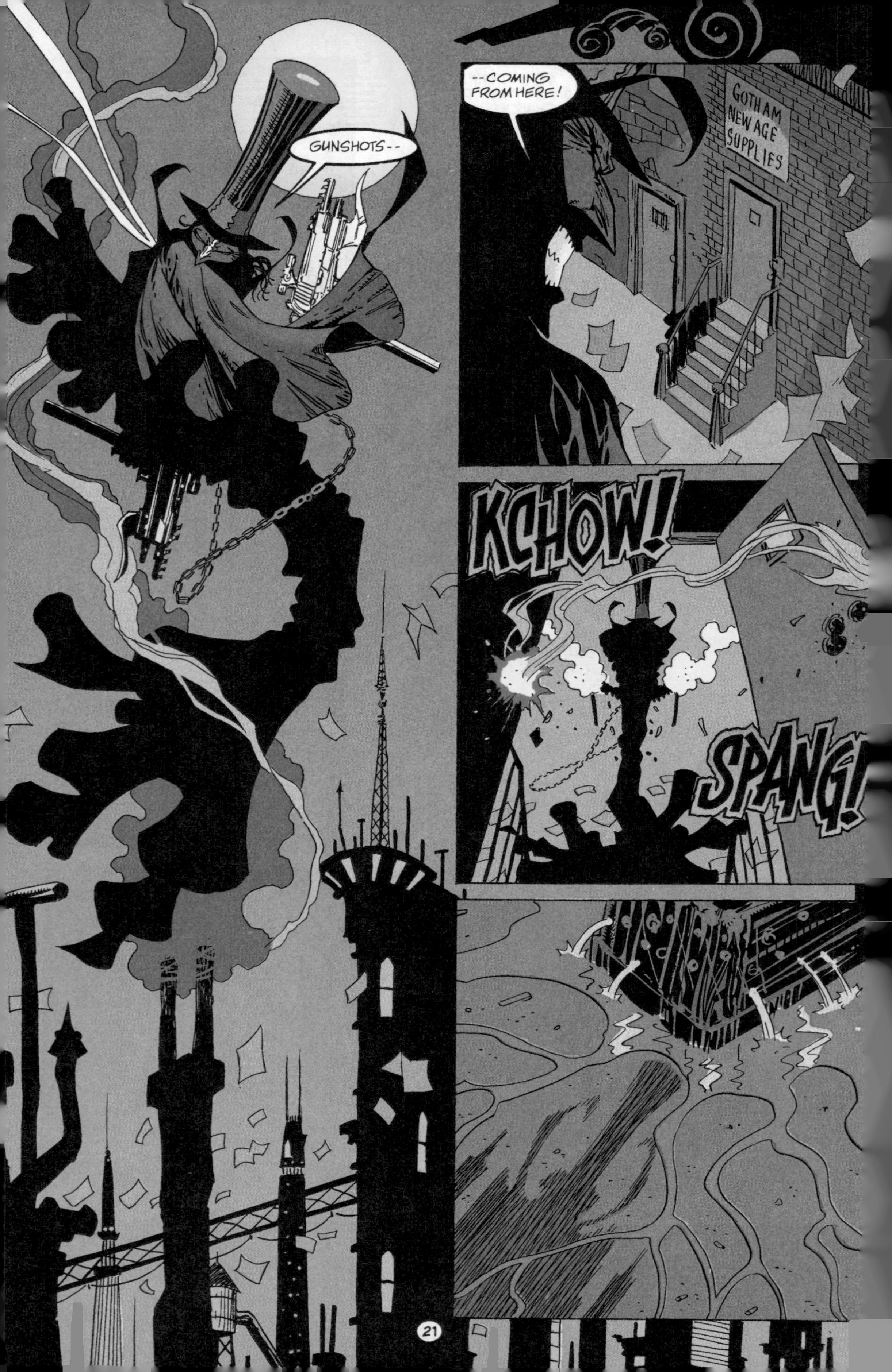
GUNSHOTS--
--COMING FROM HERE!
GOTHAM NEW AGE SUPPLIES
KCHOW!
SPANG!

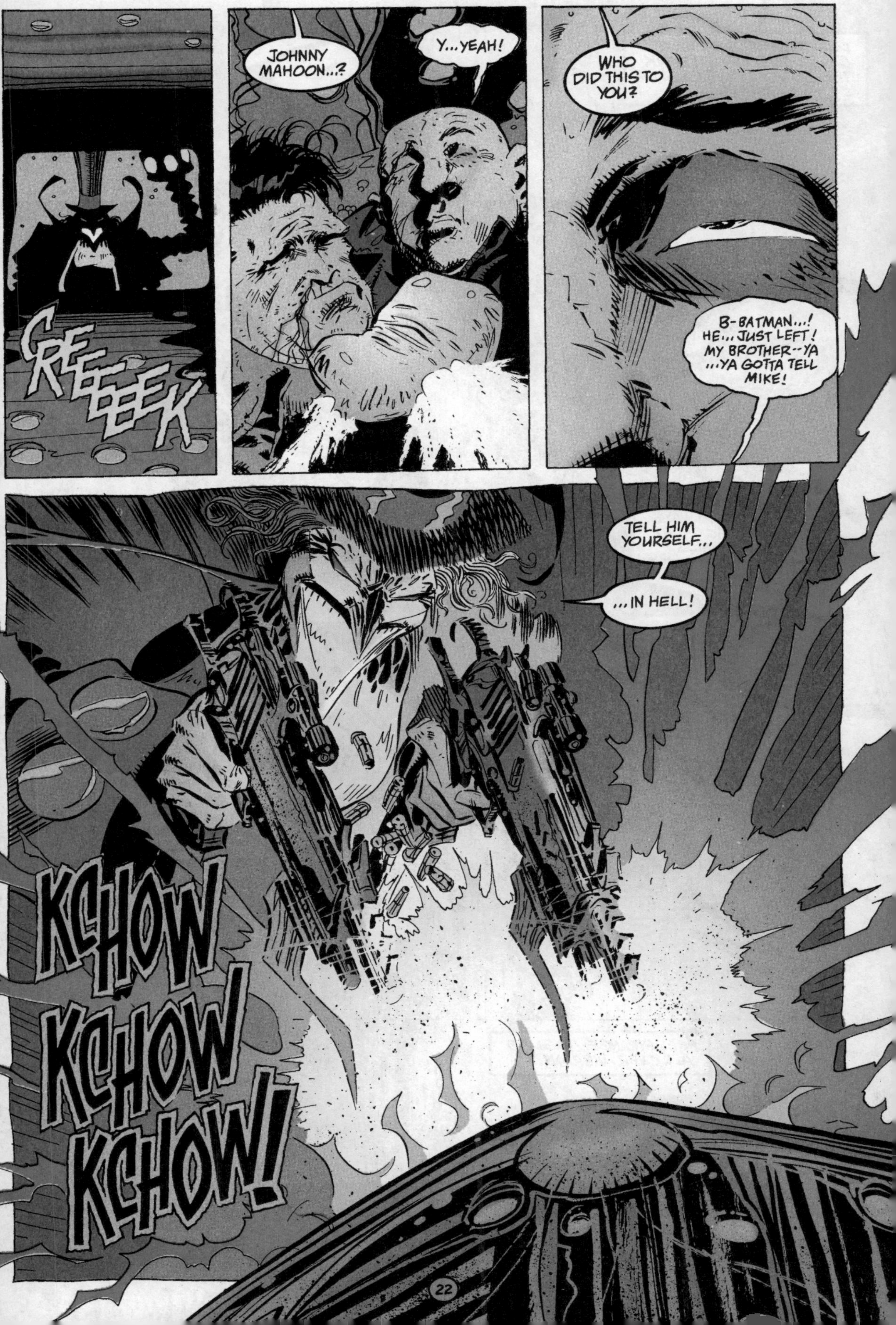
CREEEEEEK
JOHNNY MAHOON...?
Y...YEAH!
WHO DID THIS TO YOU?
B-BATMAN...! HE... JUST LEFT! MY BROTHER--YA ...YA GOTTA TELL MIKE!
TELL HIM YOURSELF...
...IN HELL!
KCHOW
KCHOW
KCHOW!

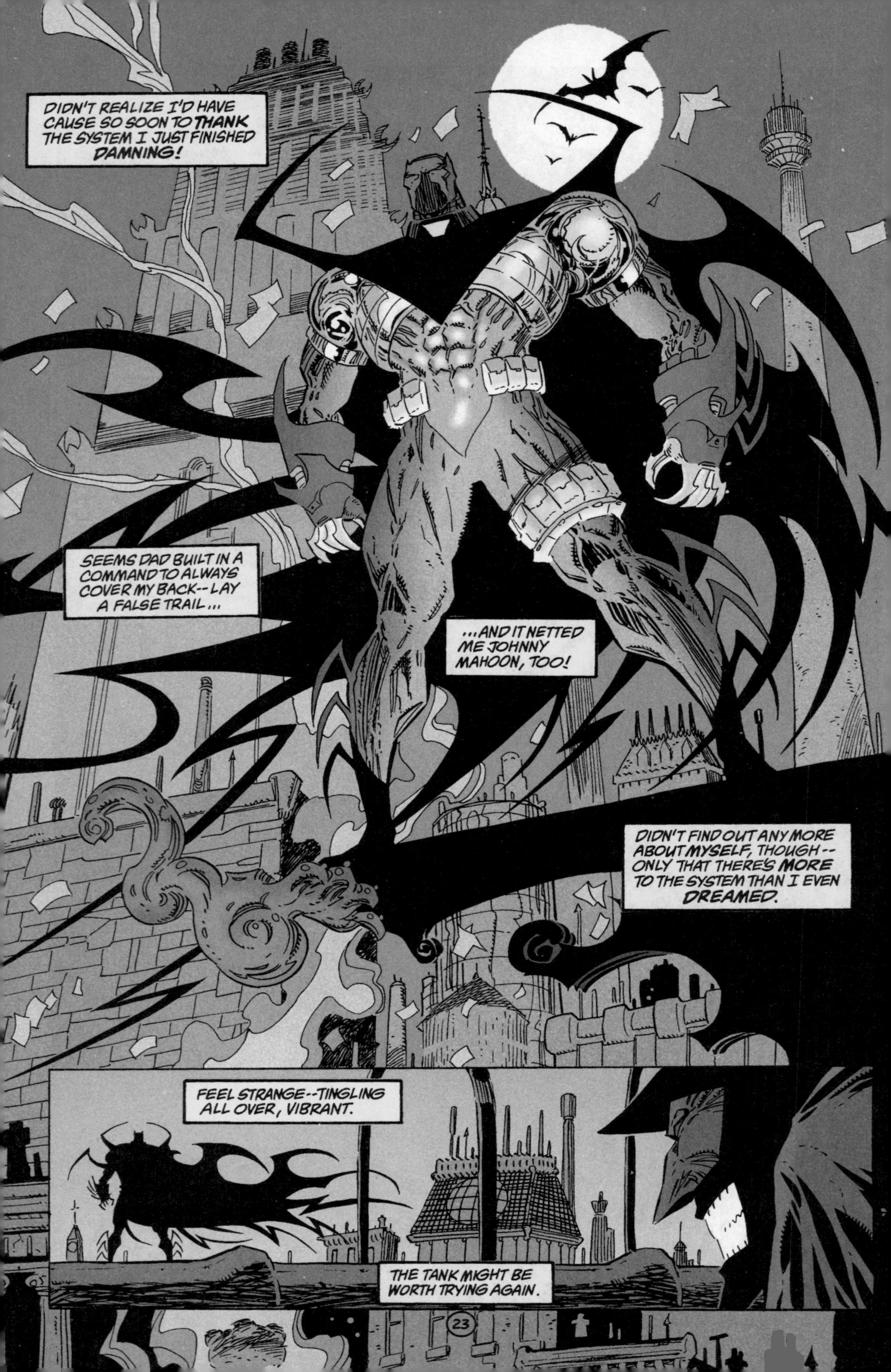
DIDN'T REALIZE I'D HAVE CAUSE SO SOON TO THANK THE SYSTEM I JUST FINISHED DAMNING!
SEEMS DAD BUILT IN A COMMAND TO ALWAYS COVER MY BACK--LAY A FALSE TRAIL...
...AND IT NETTED ME JOHNNY MAHOON, TOO!
DIDN'T FIND OUT ANY MORE ABOUT MYSELF, THOUGH--ONLY THAT THERE'S MORE TO THE SYSTEM THAN I EVEN DREAMED.
FEEL STRANGE--TINGLING ALL OVER, VIBRANT.
THE TANK MIGHT BE WORTH TRYING AGAIN.

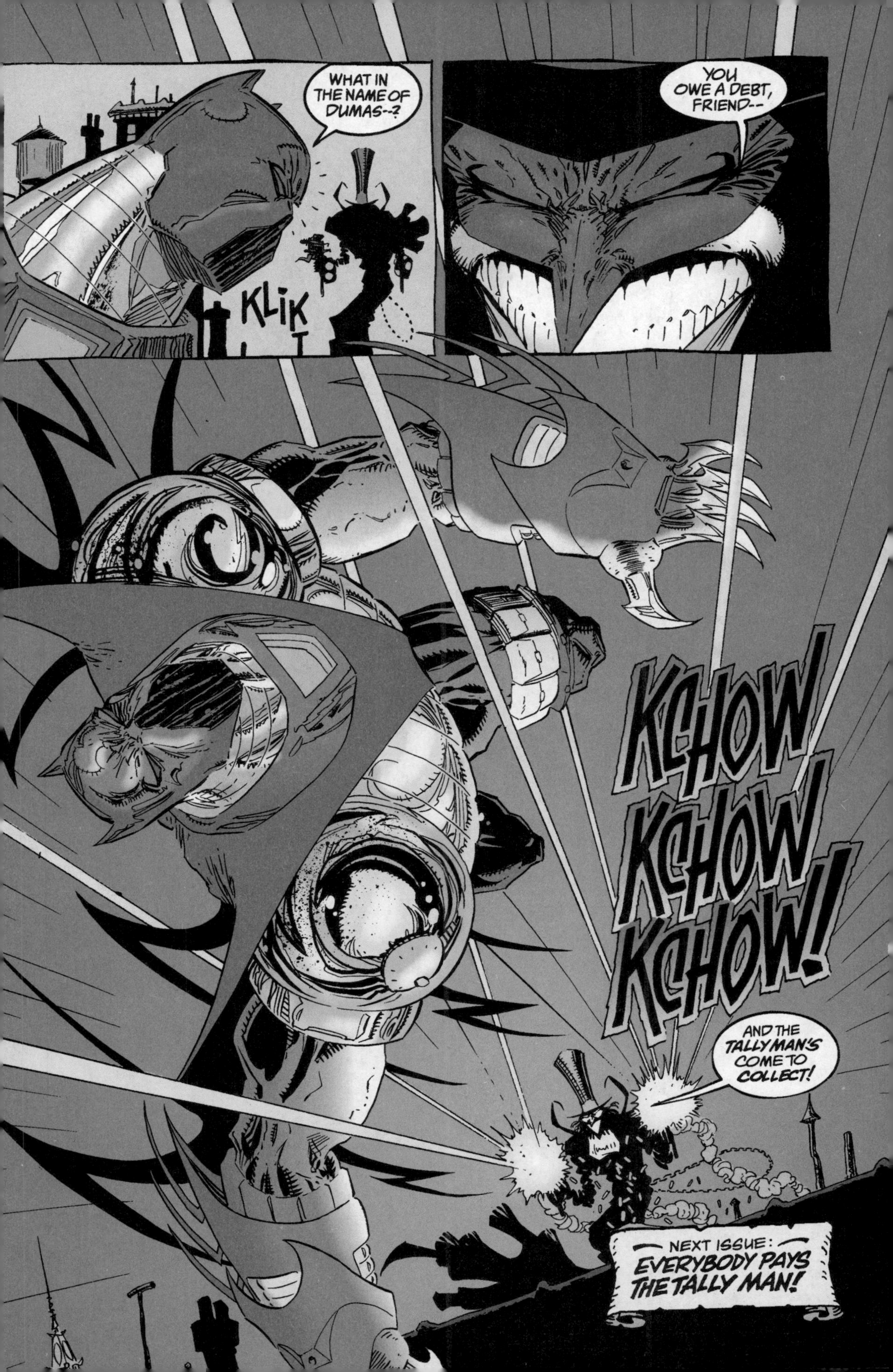
WHAT IN THE NAME OF DUMAS--?
KLIK
YOU OWE A DEBT, FRIEND--
KCHOW KCHOW KCHOW!
AND THE TALLY MAN'S COME TO COLLECT!
NEXT ISSUE: EVERYBODY PAYS THE TALLY MAN!

Cover art by **BRIAN STELFREEZE**

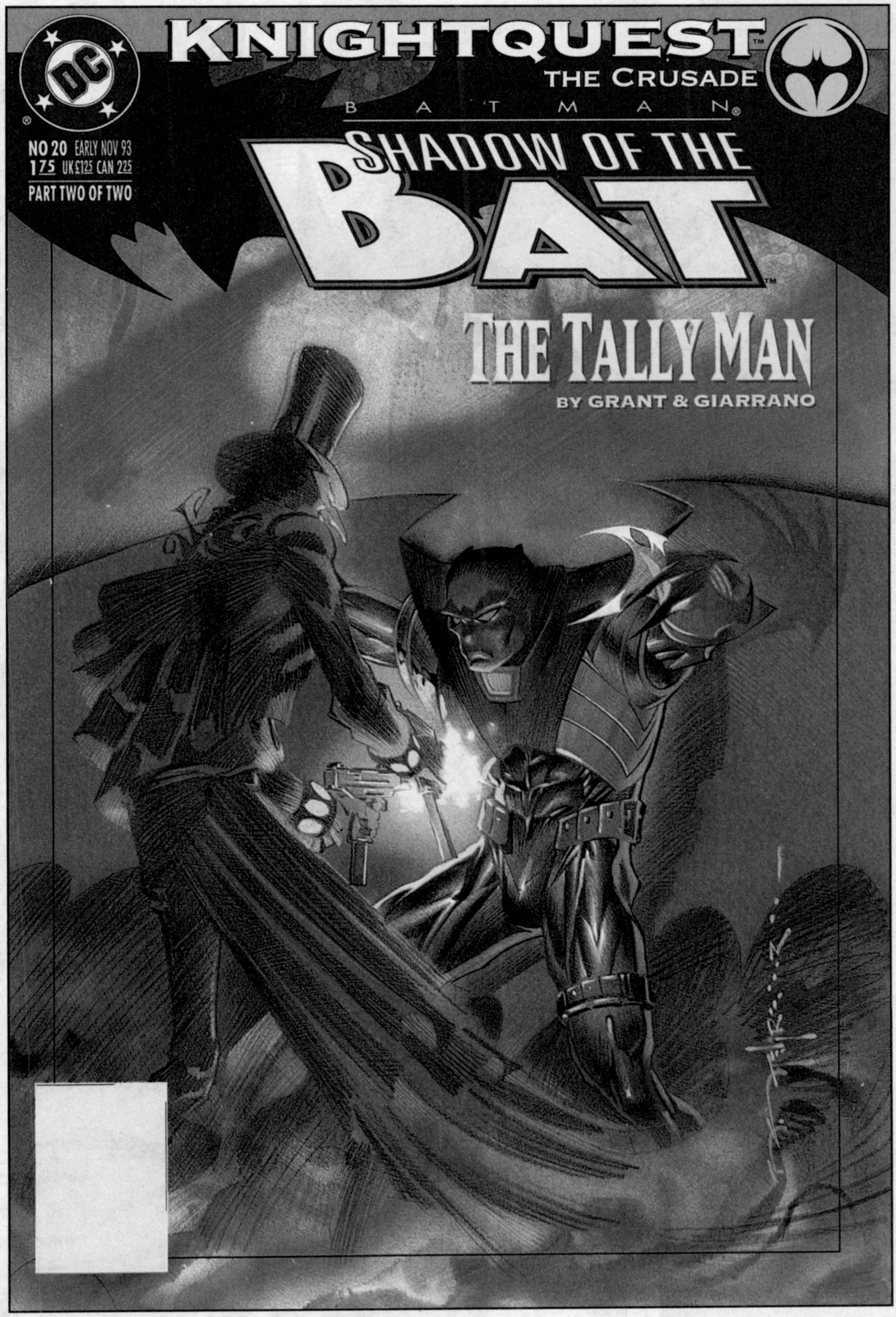
KNIGHTQUEST
THE CRUSADE
BATMAN
SHADOW OF THE BAT
NO 20 EARLY NOV 93
1 75 UK £1 25 CAN 2 25
PART TWO OF TWO
THE TALLY MAN
BY GRANT & GIARRANO

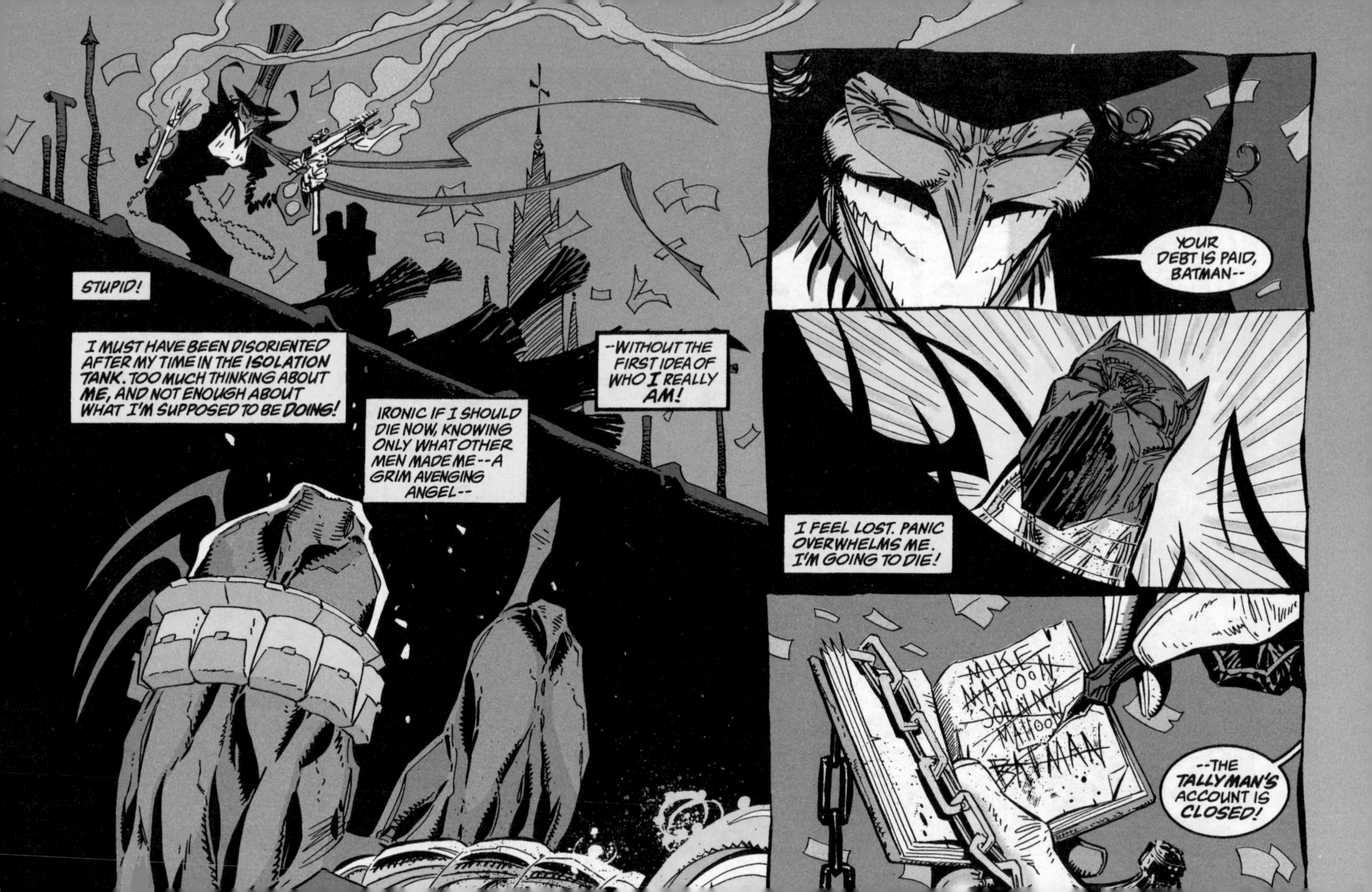
STUPID!
I MUST HAVE BEEN DISORIENTED AFTER MY TIME IN THE ISOLATION TANK. TOO MUCH THINKING ABOUT ME, AND NOT ENOUGH ABOUT WHAT I'M SUPPOSED TO BE DOING!
IRONIC IF I SHOULD DIE NOW, KNOWING ONLY WHAT OTHER MEN MADE ME--A GRIM AVENGING ANGEL--
--WITHOUT THE FIRST IDEA OF WHO I REALLY AM!
YOUR DEBT IS PAID, BATMAN--
I FEEL LOST. PANIC OVERWHELMS ME. I'M GOING TO DIE!
MIKE MAHOON
JOHNNY MAHOON
BATMAN
--THE TALLYMAN'S ACCOUNT IS CLOSED!

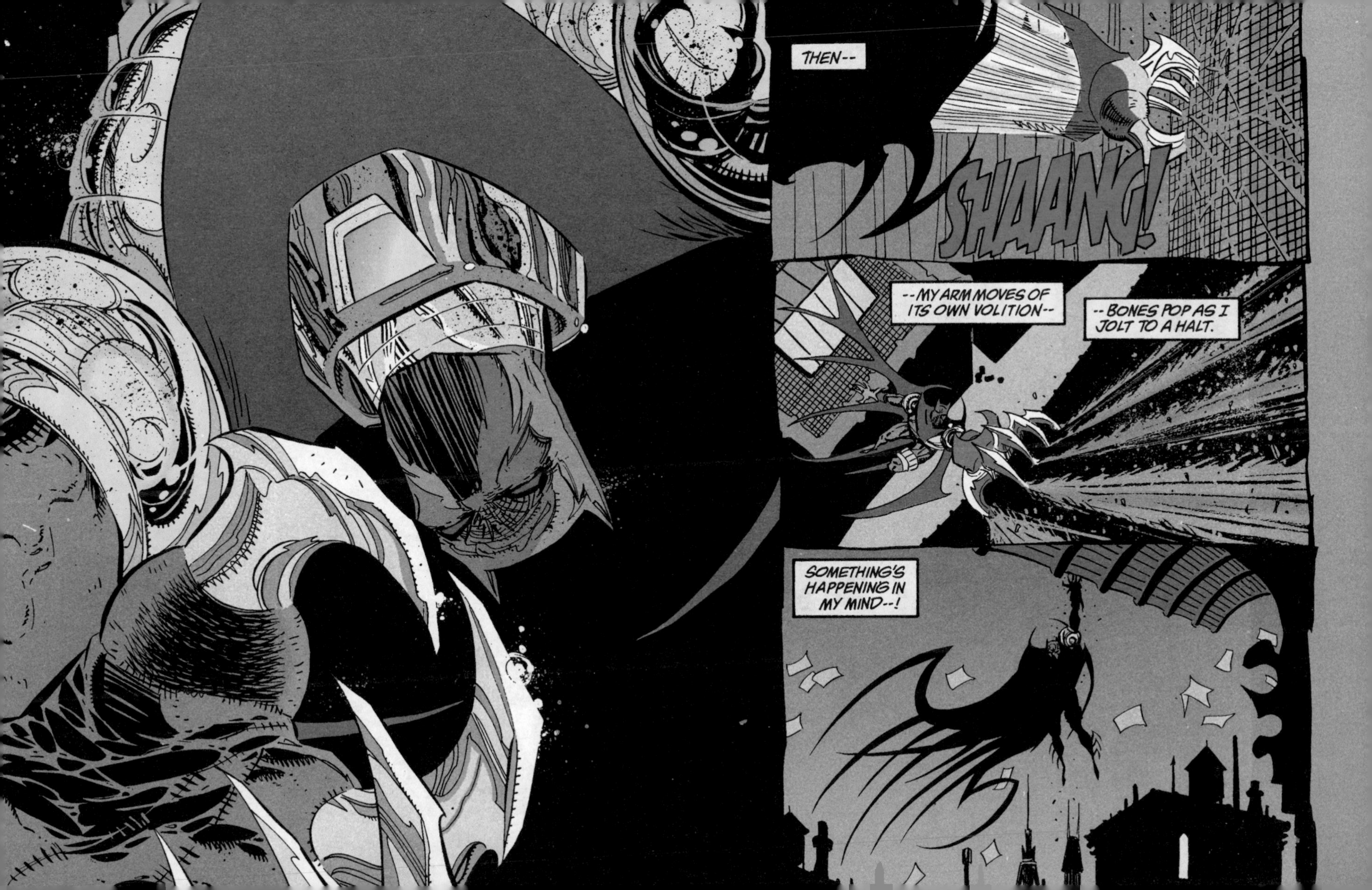
THEN--
SHAANG!
--MY ARM MOVES OF ITS OWN VOLITION--
--BONES POP AS I JOLT TO A HALT.
SOMETHING'S HAPPENING IN MY MIND--!

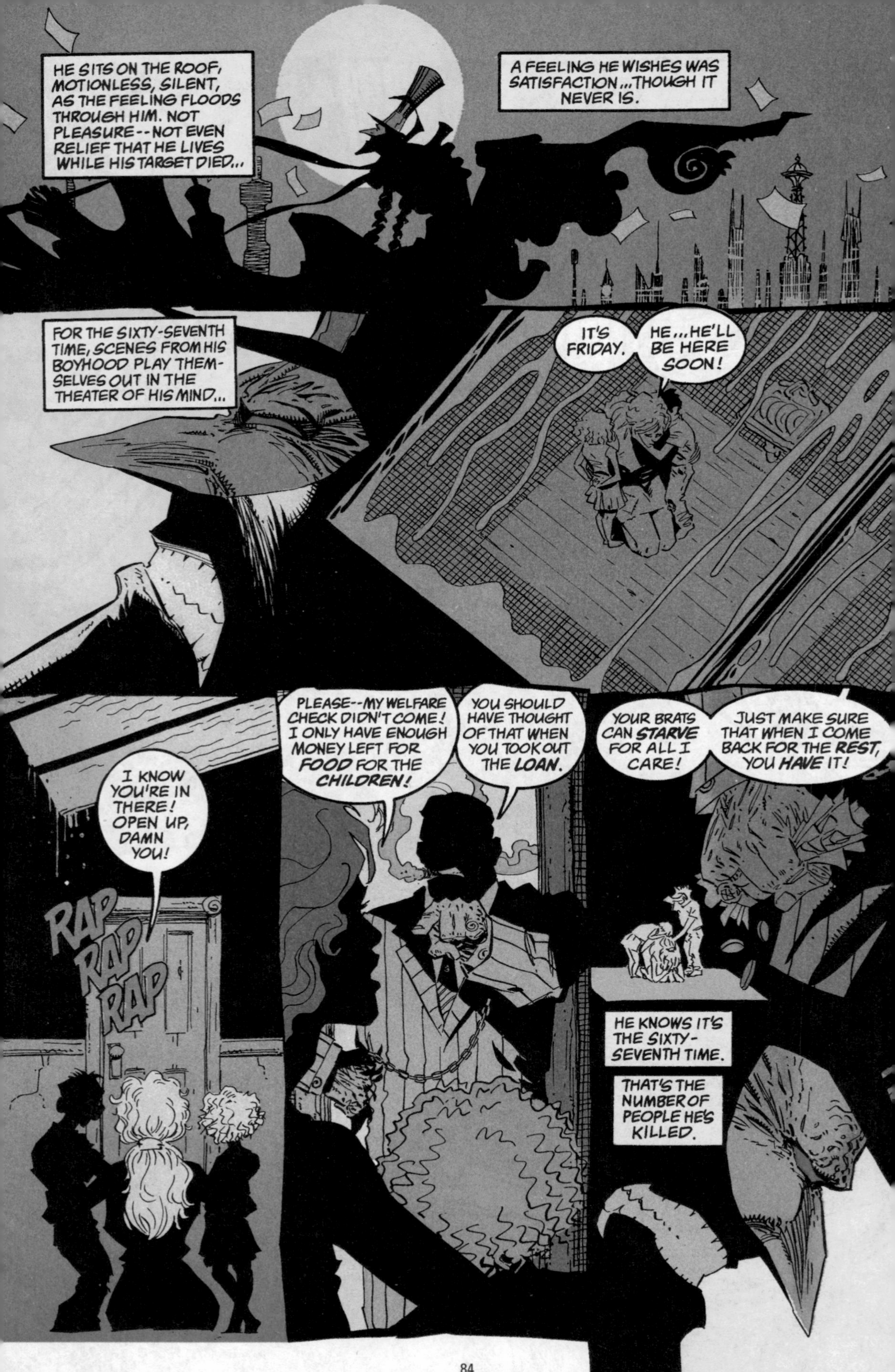

HE SITS ON THE ROOF, MOTIONLESS, SILENT, AS THE FEELING FLOODS THROUGH HIM. NOT PLEASURE--NOT EVEN RELIEF THAT HE LIVES WHILE HIS TARGET DIED...
A FEELING HE WISHES WAS SATISFACTION...THOUGH IT NEVER IS.
FOR THE SIXTY-SEVENTH TIME, SCENES FROM HIS BOYHOOD PLAY THEMSELVES OUT IN THE THEATER OF HIS MIND...
IT'S FRIDAY.
HE...HE'LL BE HERE SOON!
I KNOW YOU'RE IN THERE! OPEN UP, DAMN YOU!
RAP RAP RAP
PLEASE--MY WELFARE CHECK DIDN'T COME! I ONLY HAVE ENOUGH MONEY LEFT FOR FOOD FOR THE CHILDREN!
YOU SHOULD HAVE THOUGHT OF THAT WHEN YOU TOOK OUT THE LOAN.
YOUR BRATS CAN STARVE FOR ALL I CARE!
JUST MAKE SURE THAT WHEN I COME BACK FOR THE REST, YOU HAVE IT!
HE KNOWS IT'S THE SIXTY-SEVENTH TIME.
THAT'S THE NUMBER OF PEOPLE HE'S KILLED.

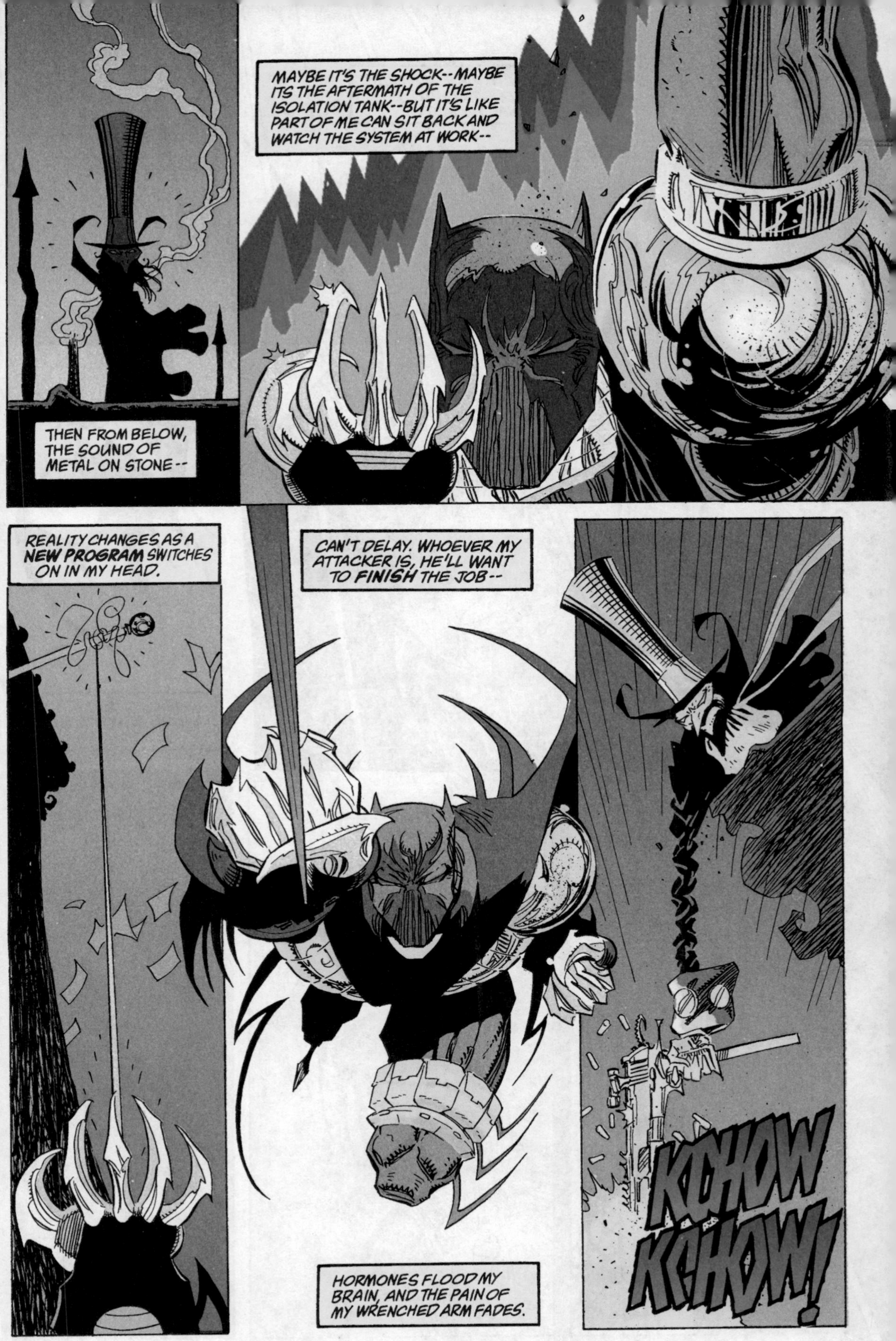
MAYBE IT'S THE SHOCK--MAYBE ITS THE AFTERMATH OF THE ISOLATION TANK--BUT IT'S LIKE PART OF ME CAN SIT BACK AND WATCH THE SYSTEM AT WORK--
THEN FROM BELOW, THE SOUND OF METAL ON STONE--
REALITY CHANGES AS A NEW PROGRAM SWITCHES ON IN MY HEAD.
CAN'T DELAY. WHOEVER MY ATTACKER IS, HE'LL WANT TO FINISH THE JOB--
HORMONES FLOOD MY BRAIN, AND THE PAIN OF MY WRENCHED ARM FADES.
KCHOW
KCHOW!

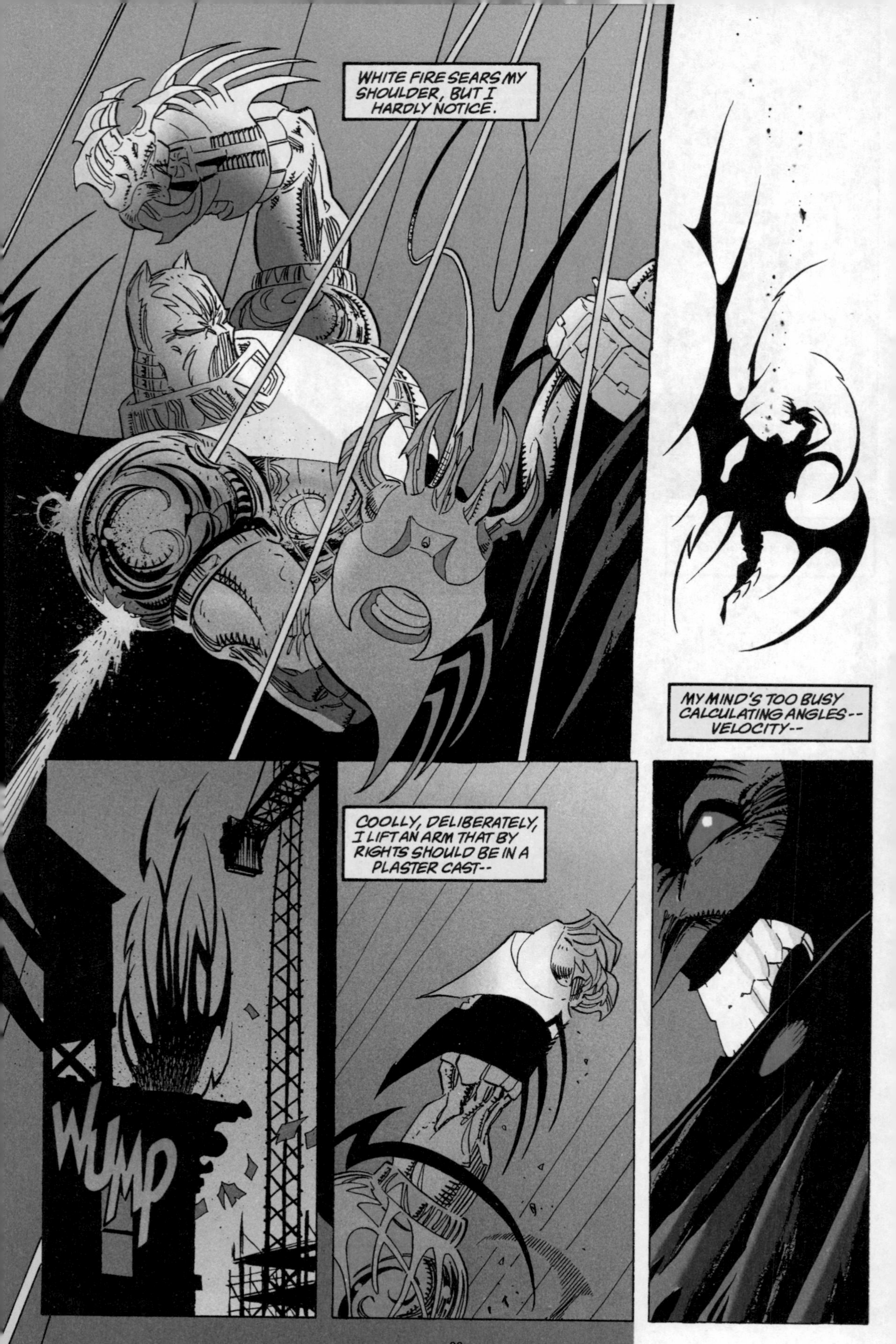
WHITE FIRE SEARS MY SHOULDER, BUT I HARDLY NOTICE.
MY MIND'S TOO BUSY CALCULATING ANGLES-- VELOCITY--
WUMP
COOLLY, DELIBERATELY, I LIFT AN ARM THAT BY RIGHTS SHOULD BE IN A PLASTER CAST--

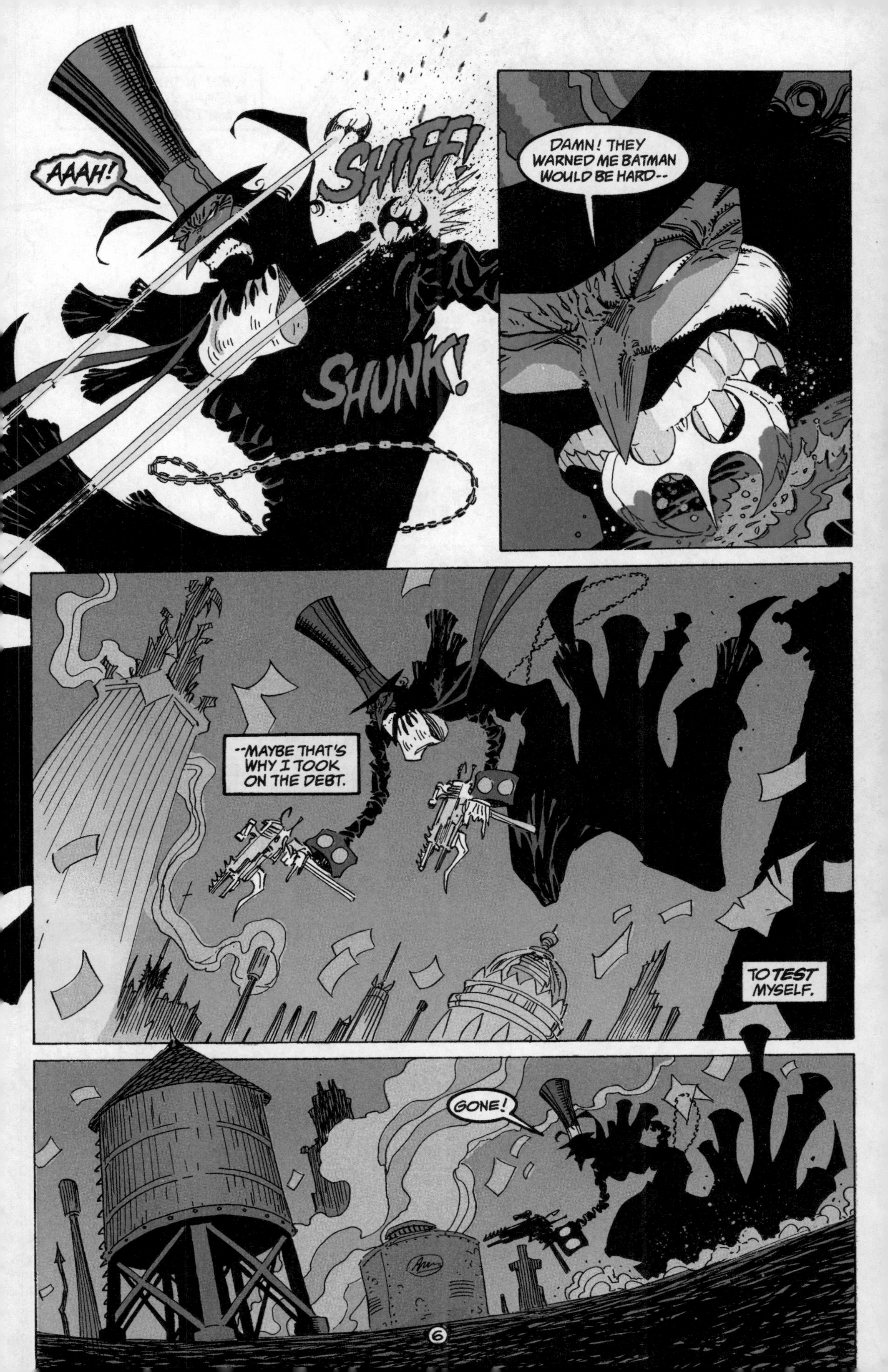
AAAH!
SHIFF!
SHUNK!
DAMN! THEY WARNED ME BATMAN WOULD BE HARD--
--MAYBE THAT'S WHY I TOOK ON THE DEBT.
TO TEST MYSELF.
GONE!

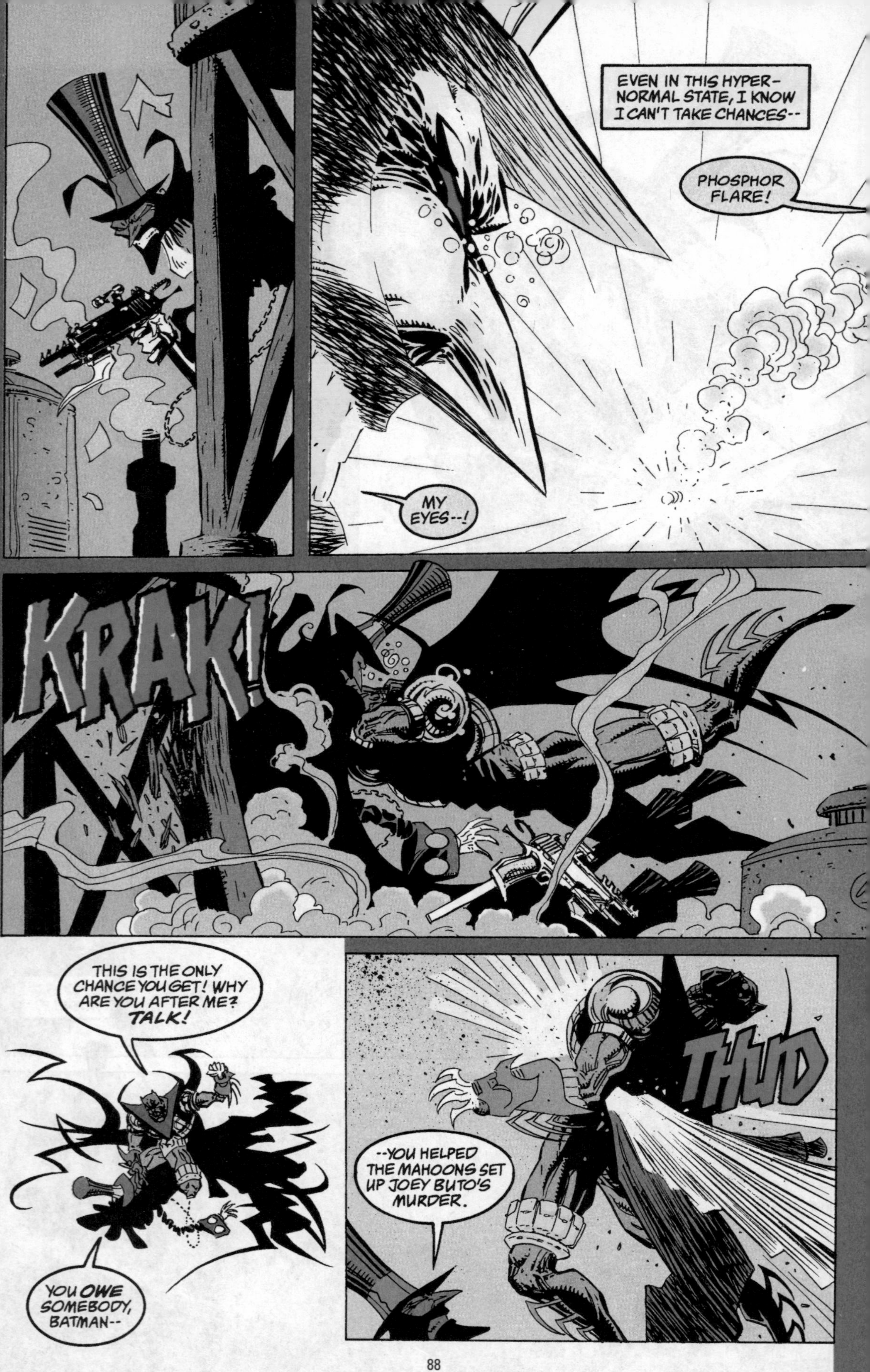
EVEN IN THIS HYPER-NORMAL STATE, I KNOW I CAN'T TAKE CHANCES--
PHOSPHOR FLARE!
MY EYES--!
KRAK!
THIS IS THE ONLY CHANCE YOU GET! WHY ARE YOU AFTER ME? TALK!
YOU OWE SOMEBODY, BATMAN--
THUD
--YOU HELPED THE MAHOONS SET UP JOEY BUTO'S MURDER.

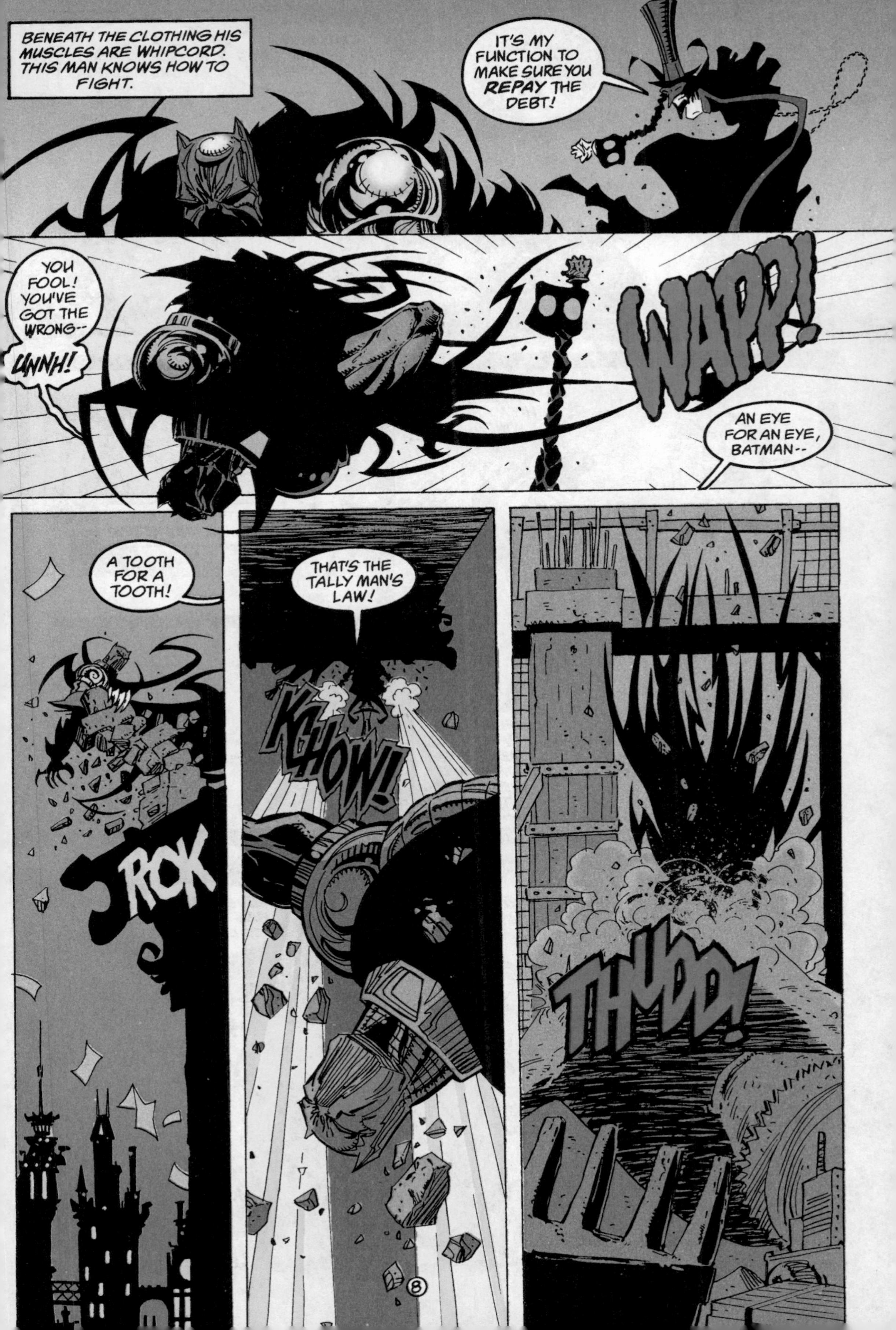
BENEATH THE CLOTHING HIS MUSCLES ARE WHIPCORD. THIS MAN KNOWS HOW TO FIGHT.
IT'S MY FUNCTION TO MAKE SURE YOU REPAY THE DEBT!
YOU FOOL! YOU'VE GOT THE WRONG--
UNNH!
WAPP!
AN EYE FOR AN EYE, BATMAN--
A TOOTH FOR A TOOTH!
ROK
THAT'S THE TALLY MAN'S LAW!
KCHOW!
THUDD!
8

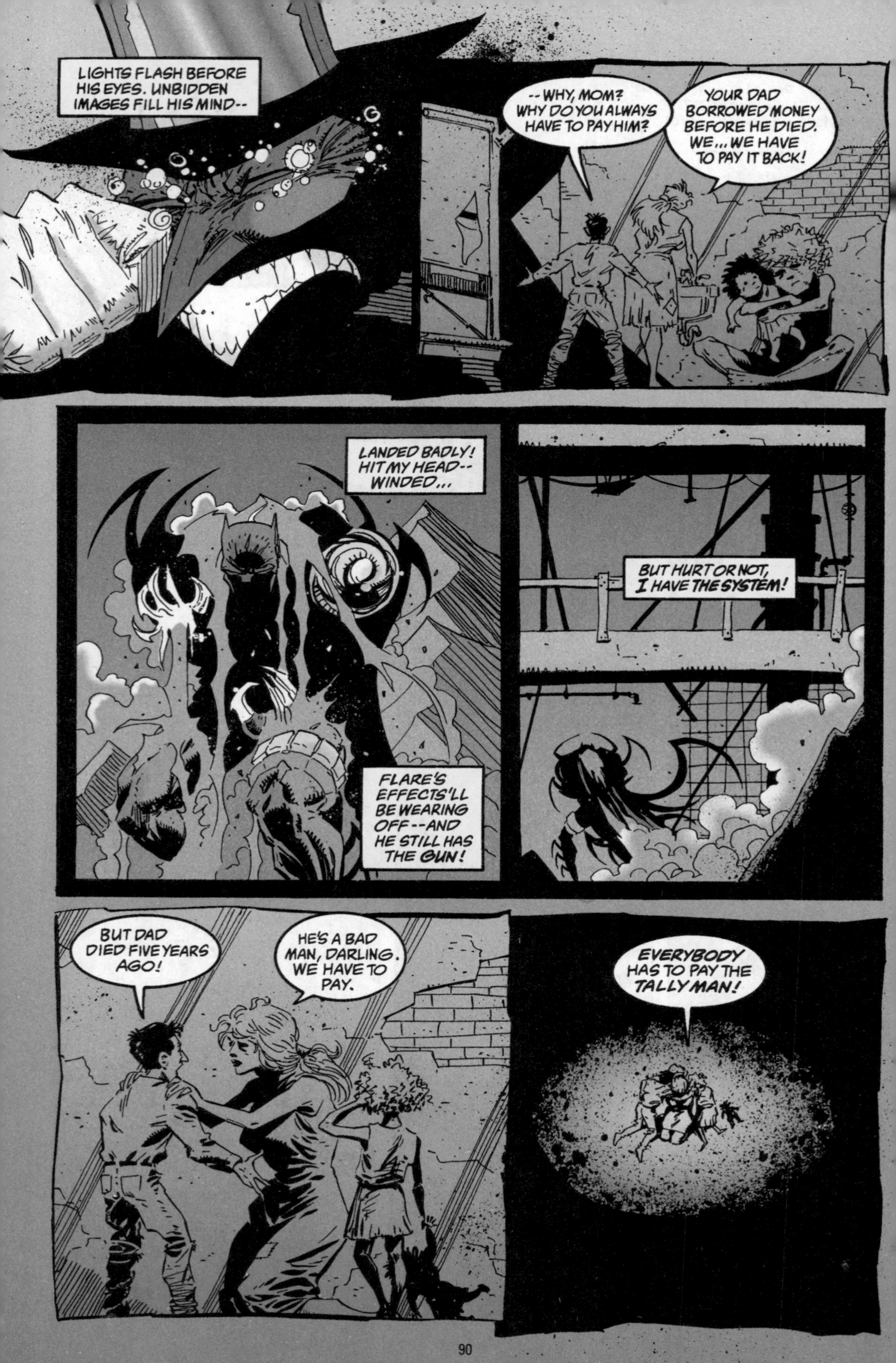
LIGHTS FLASH BEFORE HIS EYES. UNBIDDEN IMAGES FILL HIS MIND--
--WHY, MOM? WHY DO YOU ALWAYS HAVE TO PAY HIM?
YOUR DAD BORROWED MONEY BEFORE HE DIED. WE... WE HAVE TO PAY IT BACK!
LANDED BADLY! HIT MY HEAD-- WINDED...
FLARE'S EFFECTS'LL BE WEARING OFF--AND HE STILL HAS THE GUN!
BUT HURT OR NOT, I HAVE THE SYSTEM!
BUT DAD DIED FIVE YEARS AGO!
HE'S A BAD MAN, DARLING. WE HAVE TO PAY.
EVERYBODY HAS TO PAY THE TALLY MAN!

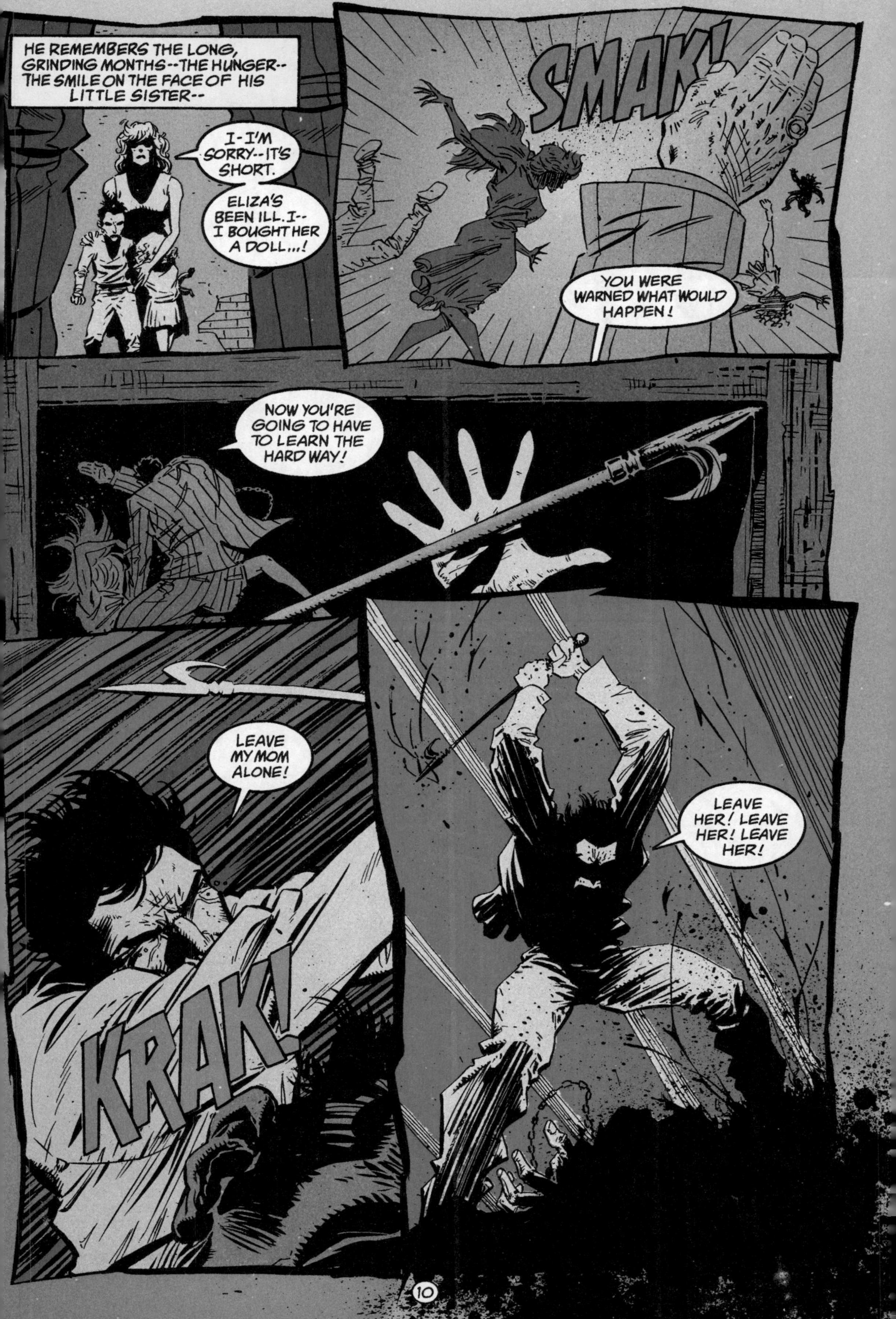
HE REMEMBERS THE LONG, GRINDING MONTHS--THE HUNGER--THE SMILE ON THE FACE OF HIS LITTLE SISTER--
I-I'M SORRY--IT'S SHORT.
ELIZA'S BEEN ILL. I--I BOUGHT HER A DOLL...!
SMAK!
YOU WERE WARNED WHAT WOULD HAPPEN!
NOW YOU'RE GOING TO HAVE TO LEARN THE HARD WAY!
LEAVE MY MOM ALONE!
KRAK!
LEAVE HER! LEAVE HER! LEAVE HER!

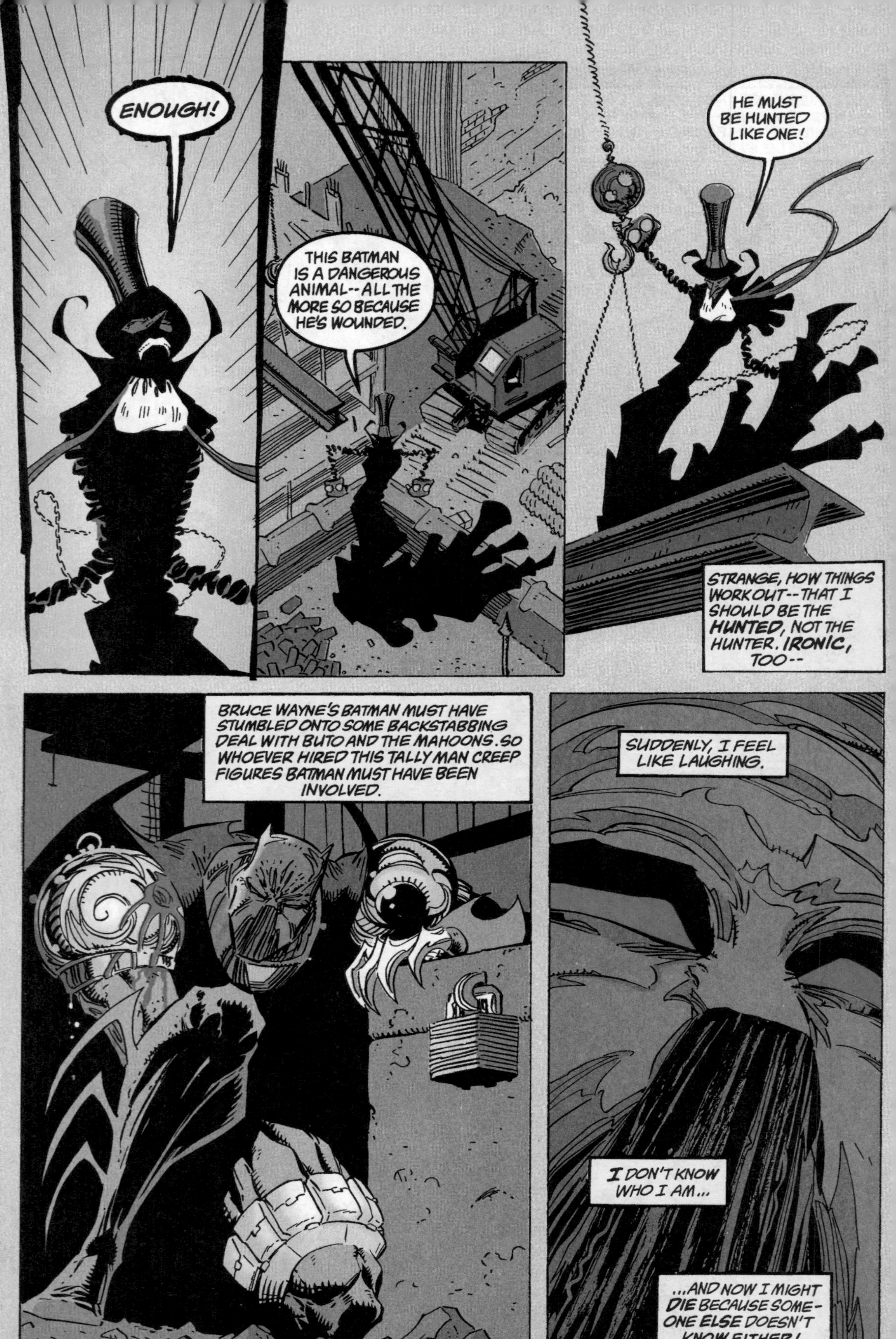
ENOUGH!
THIS BATMAN IS A DANGEROUS ANIMAL--ALL THE MORE SO BECAUSE HE'S WOUNDED.
HE MUST BE HUNTED LIKE ONE!
STRANGE, HOW THINGS WORK OUT--THAT I SHOULD BE THE HUNTED, NOT THE HUNTER. IRONIC, TOO--
BRUCE WAYNE'S BATMAN MUST HAVE STUMBLED ONTO SOME BACKSTABBING DEAL WITH BUTO AND THE MAHOONS. SO WHOEVER HIRED THIS TALLY MAN CREEP FIGURES BATMAN MUST HAVE BEEN INVOLVED.
SUDDENLY, I FEEL LIKE LAUGHING.
I DON'T KNOW WHO I AM...
...AND NOW I MIGHT DIE BECAUSE SOME-ONE ELSE DOESN'T KNOW EITHER!

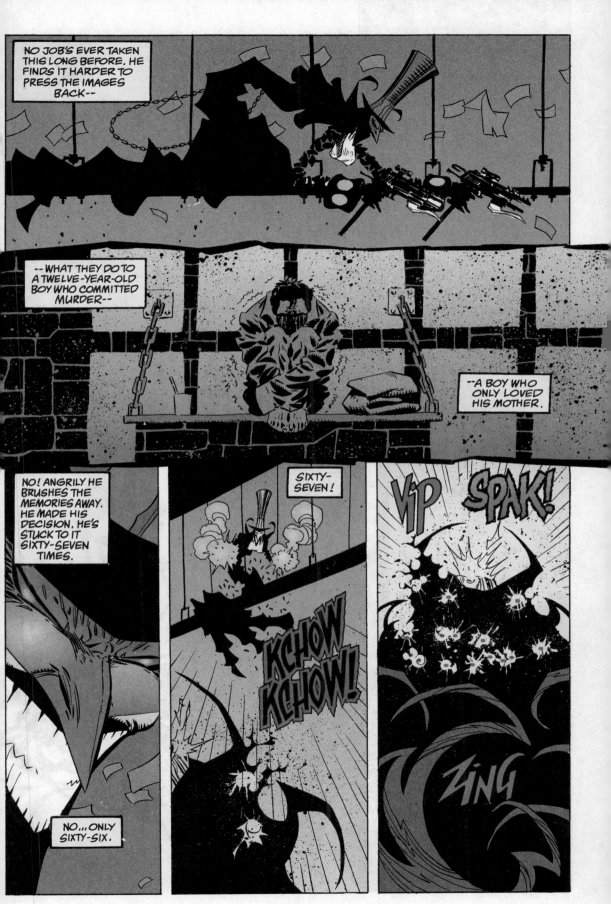

NO JOB'S EVER TAKEN THIS LONG BEFORE. HE FINDS IT HARDER TO PRESS THE IMAGES BACK--

-- WHAT THEY DO TO A TWELVE-YEAR-OLD BOY WHO COMMITTED MURDER--

--A BOY WHO ONLY LOVED HIS MOTHER.

NO! ANGRILY HE BRUSHES THE MEMORIES AWAY. HE MADE HIS DECISION, HE'S STUCK TO IT SIXTY-SEVEN TIMES.

SIXTY-SEVEN!

KCHOW KCHOW!

NO... ONLY SIXTY-SIX.

YIP SPAK!

ZING

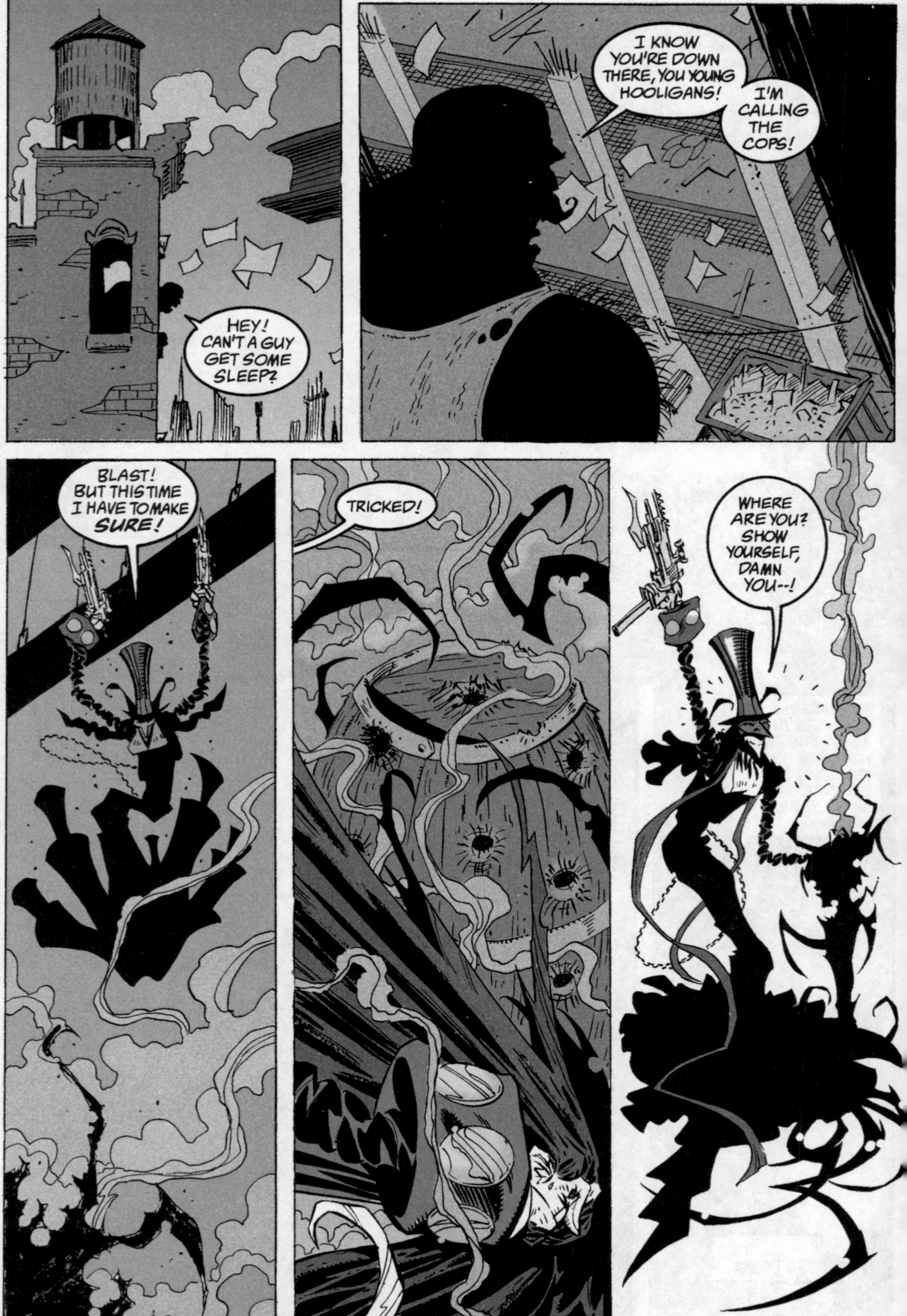
HEY! CAN'T A GUY GET SOME SLEEP?
I KNOW YOU'RE DOWN THERE, YOU YOUNG HOOLIGANS!
I'M CALLING THE COPS!
BLAST! BUT THIS TIME I HAVE TO MAKE SURE!
TRICKED!
WHERE ARE YOU? SHOW YOURSELF, DAMN YOU--!

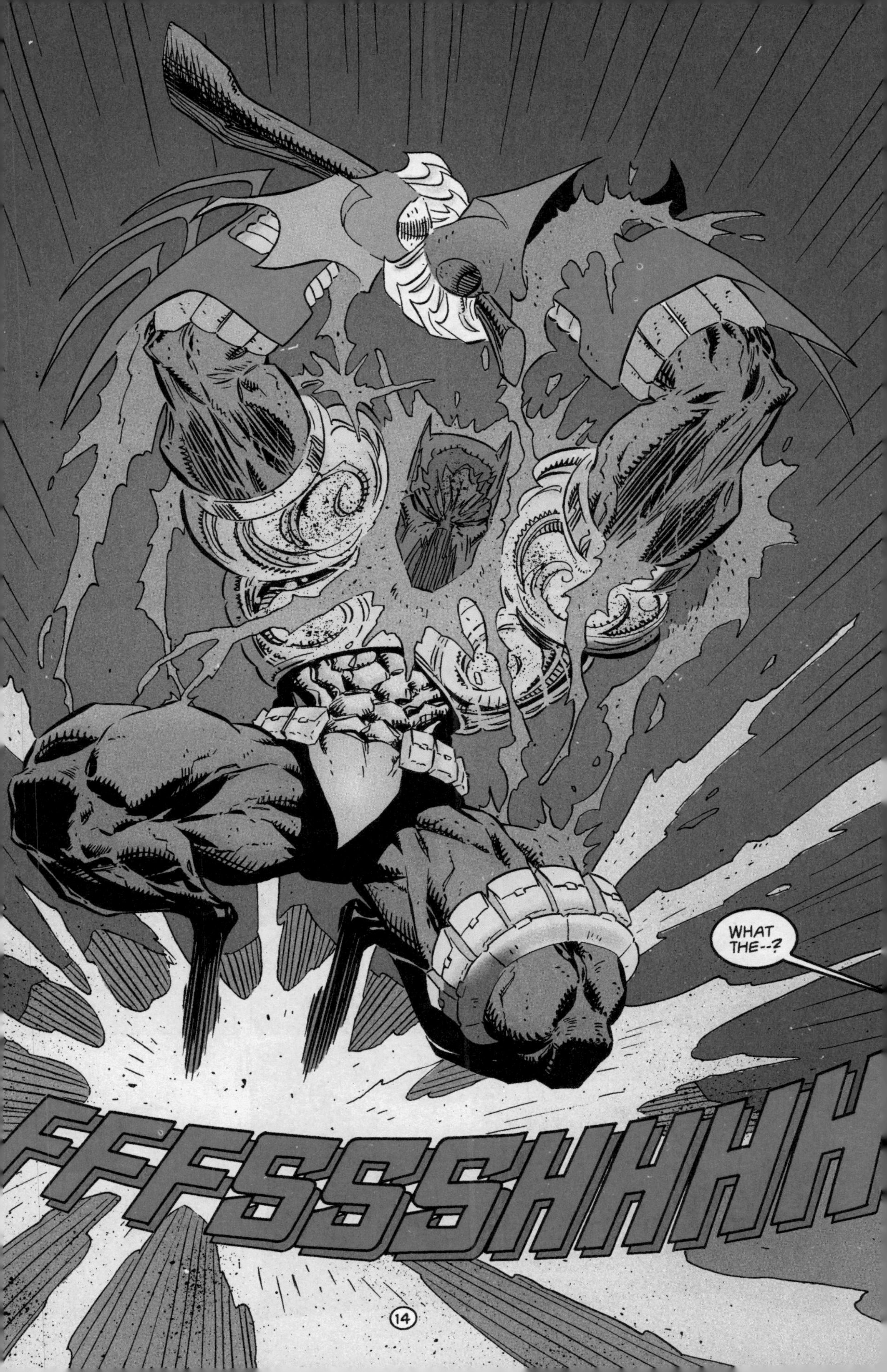
WHAT THE--?
FFSSSHHHH

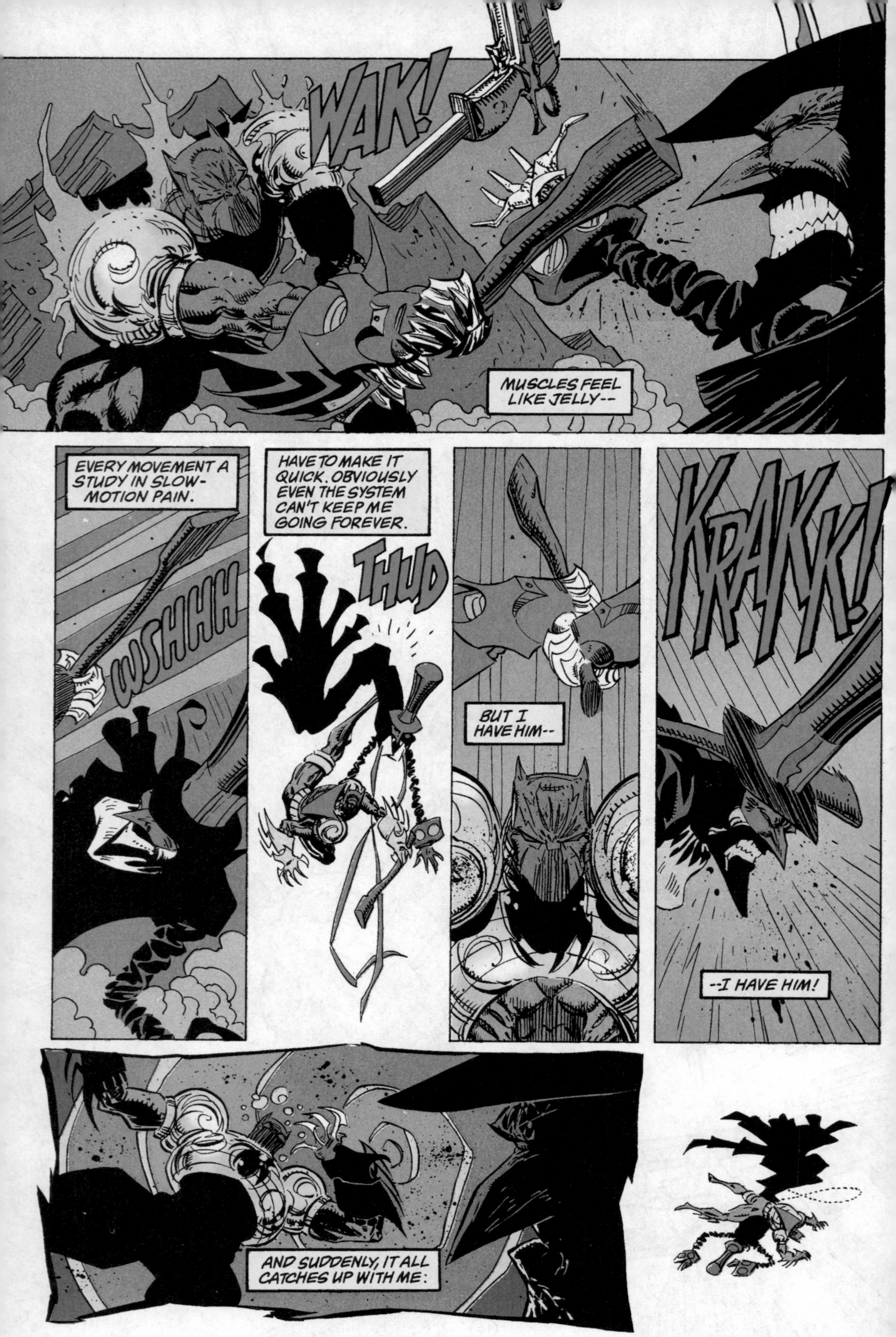
WAK!
MUSCLES FEEL LIKE JELLY--
EVERY MOVEMENT A STUDY IN SLOW-MOTION PAIN.
WSHHH
HAVE TO MAKE IT QUICK. OBVIOUSLY EVEN THE SYSTEM CAN'T KEEP ME GOING FOREVER.
THUD
BUT I HAVE HIM--
KRAKK!
--I HAVE HIM!
AND SUDDENLY, IT ALL CATCHES UP WITH ME:

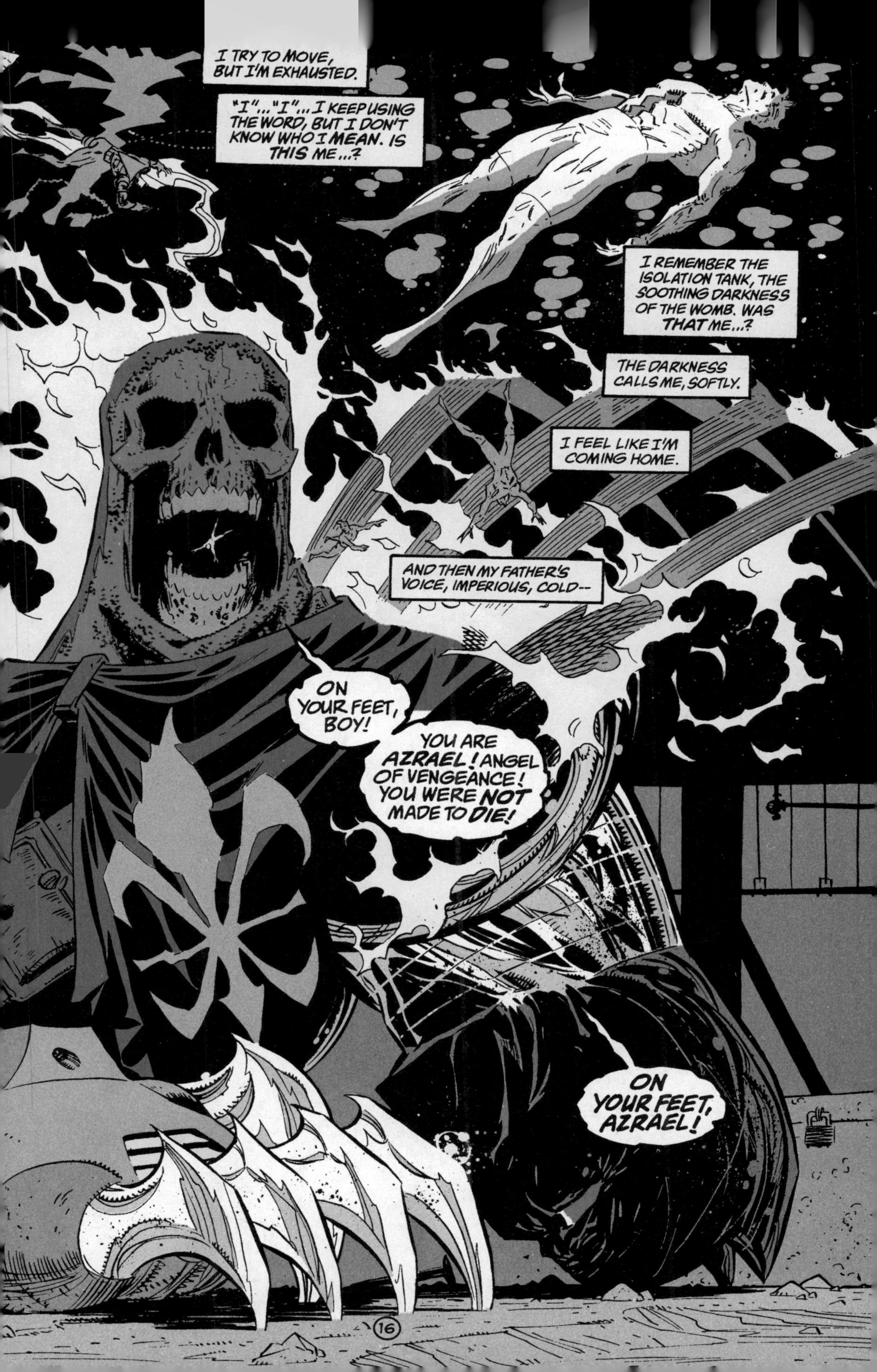
I TRY TO MOVE, BUT I'M EXHAUSTED.
"I"..."I"... I KEEP USING THE WORD, BUT I DON'T KNOW WHO I MEAN. IS THIS ME...?
I REMEMBER THE ISOLATION TANK, THE SOOTHING DARKNESS OF THE WOMB. WAS THAT ME...?
THE DARKNESS CALLS ME, SOFTLY.
I FEEL LIKE I'M COMING HOME.
AND THEN MY FATHER'S VOICE, IMPERIOUS, COLD--
ON YOUR FEET, BOY!
YOU ARE AZRAEL! ANGEL OF VENGEANCE! YOU WERE NOT MADE TO DIE!
ON YOUR FEET, AZRAEL!

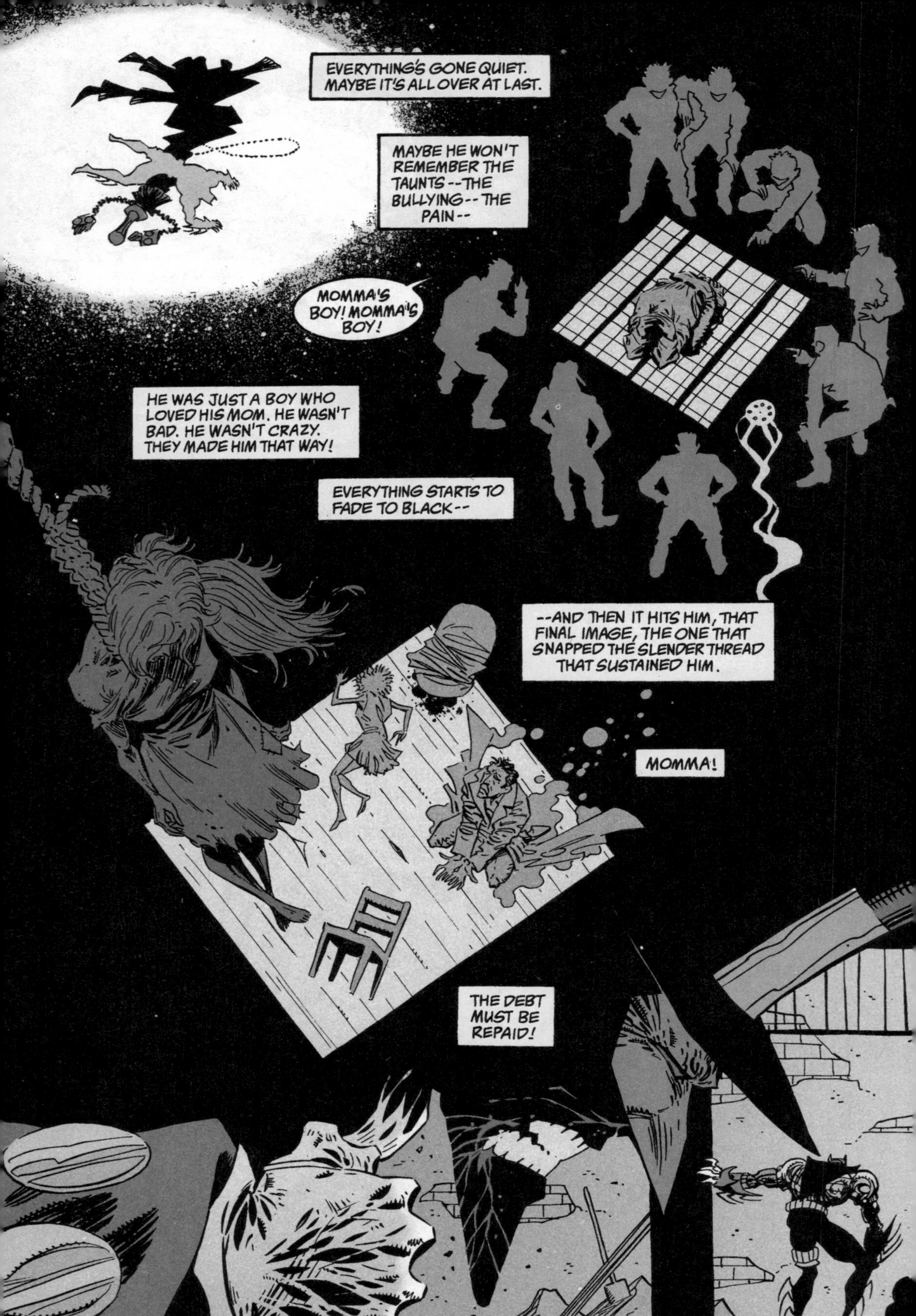
EVERYTHING'S GONE QUIET. MAYBE IT'S ALL OVER AT LAST.
MAYBE HE WON'T REMEMBER THE TAUNTS -- THE BULLYING -- THE PAIN --
MOMMA'S BOY! MOMMA'S BOY!
HE WAS JUST A BOY WHO LOVED HIS MOM. HE WASN'T BAD. HE WASN'T CRAZY. THEY MADE HIM THAT WAY!
EVERYTHING STARTS TO FADE TO BLACK --
-- AND THEN IT HITS HIM, THAT FINAL IMAGE, THE ONE THAT SNAPPED THE SLENDER THREAD THAT SUSTAINED HIM.
MOMMA!
THE DEBT MUST BE REPAID!

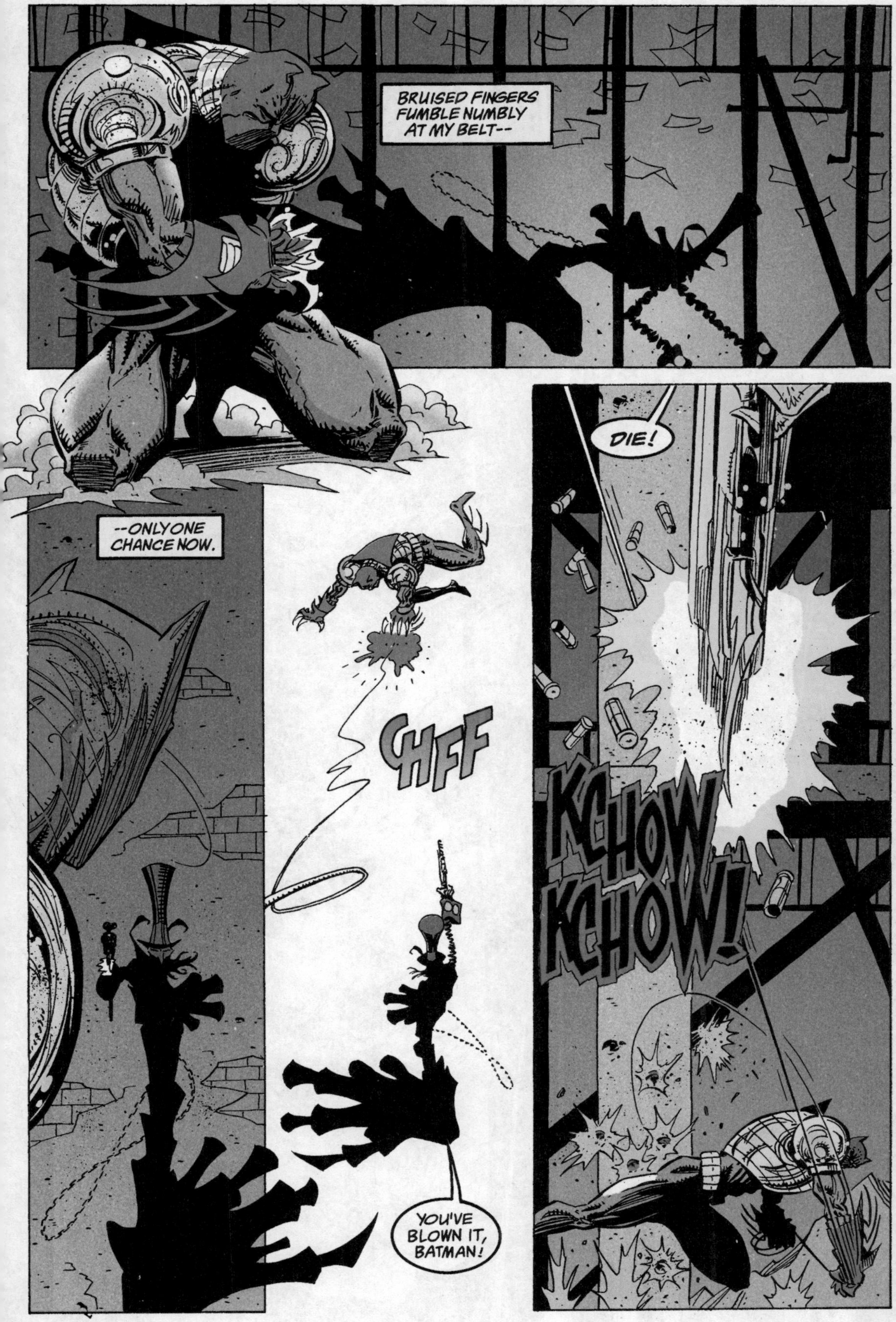
BRUISED FINGERS FUMBLE NUMBLY AT MY BELT--
--ONLY ONE CHANCE NOW.
CHFF
YOU'VE BLOWN IT, BATMAN!
DIE!
KCHOW KCHOW!

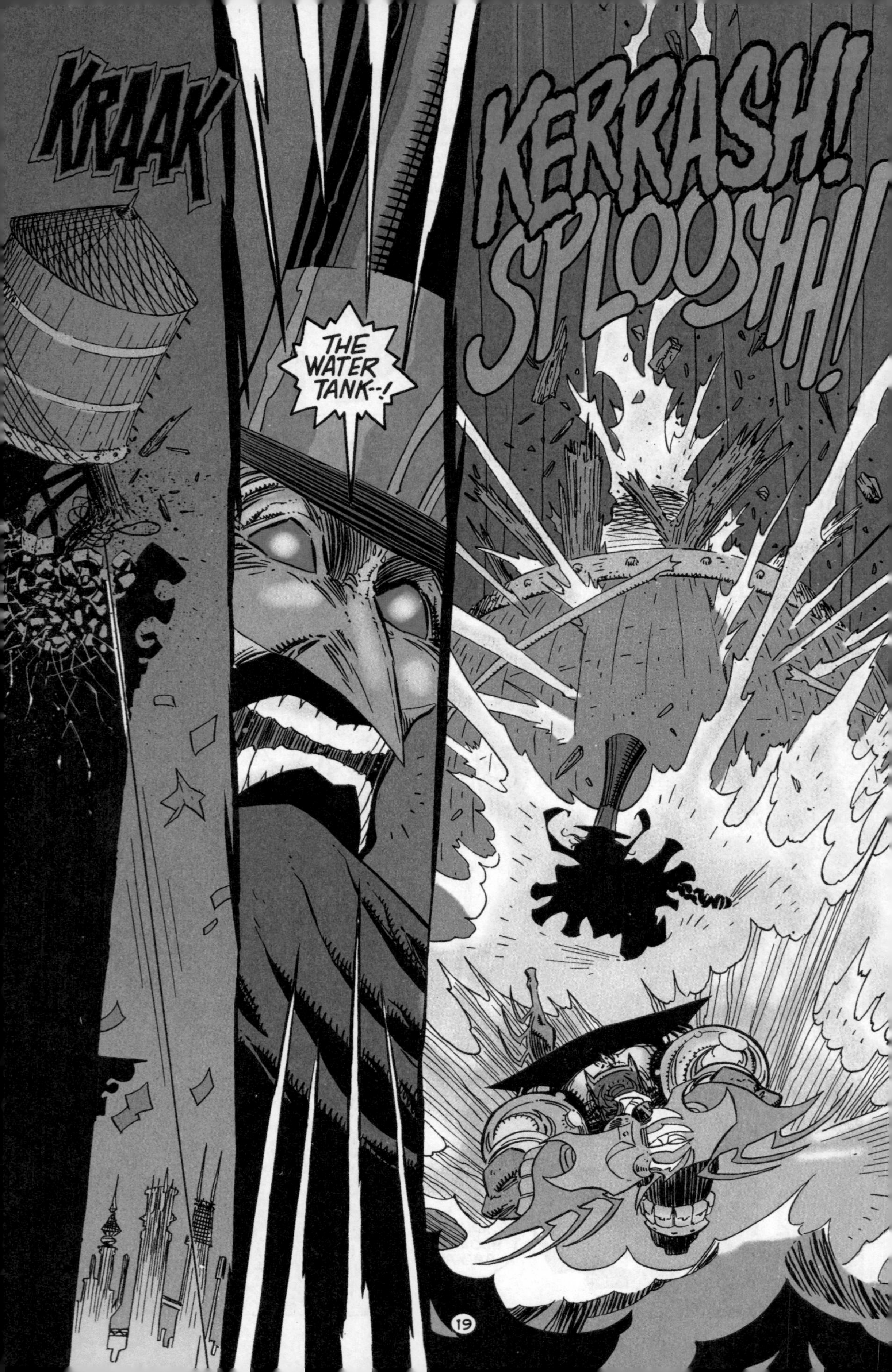
KRAAK
THE WATER TANK--!
KERRASH!
SPLOOSH!!

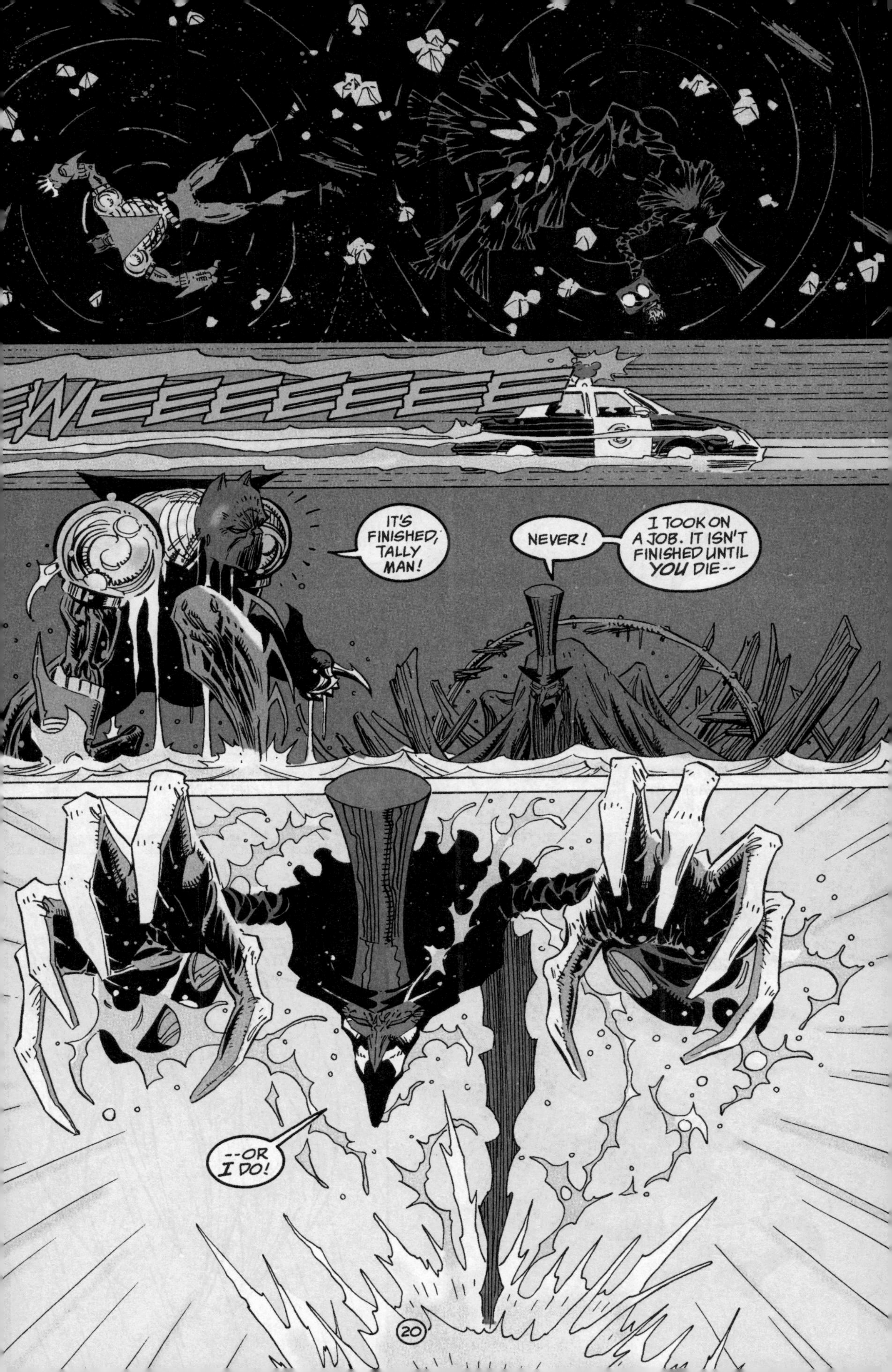

WEEEEEEEE
IT'S FINISHED, TALLY MAN!
NEVER!
I TOOK ON A JOB. IT ISN'T FINISHED UNTIL YOU DIE--
--OR I DO!

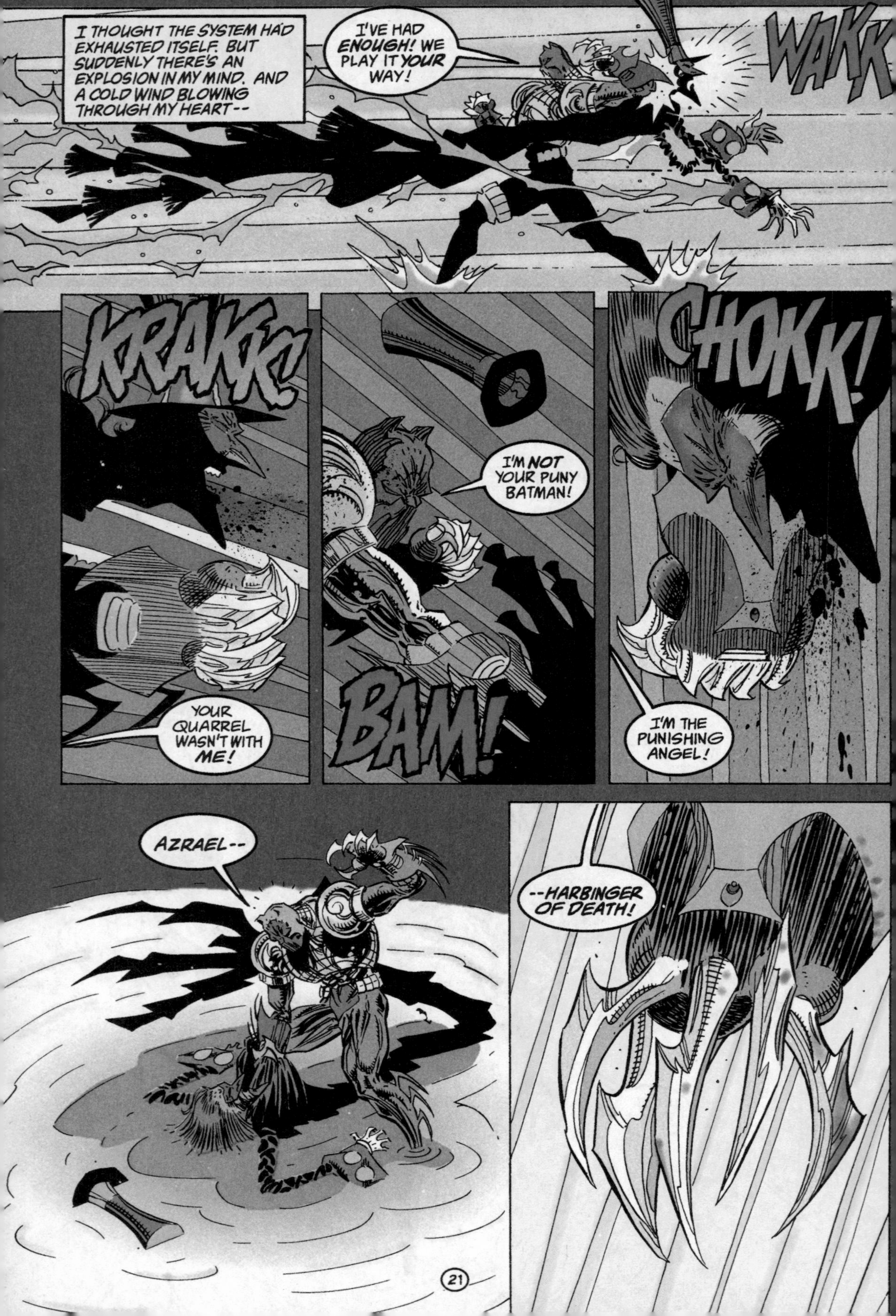
I THOUGHT THE SYSTEM HAD EXHAUSTED ITSELF. BUT SUDDENLY THERE'S AN EXPLOSION IN MY MIND. AND A COLD WIND BLOWING THROUGH MY HEART--
I'VE HAD ENOUGH! WE PLAY IT YOUR WAY!
WAKK
KRAKK!
YOUR QUARREL WASN'T WITH ME!
I'M NOT YOUR PUNY BATMAN!
BAM!
CHOKK!
I'M THE PUNISHING ANGEL!
AZRAEL--
--HARBINGER OF DEATH!

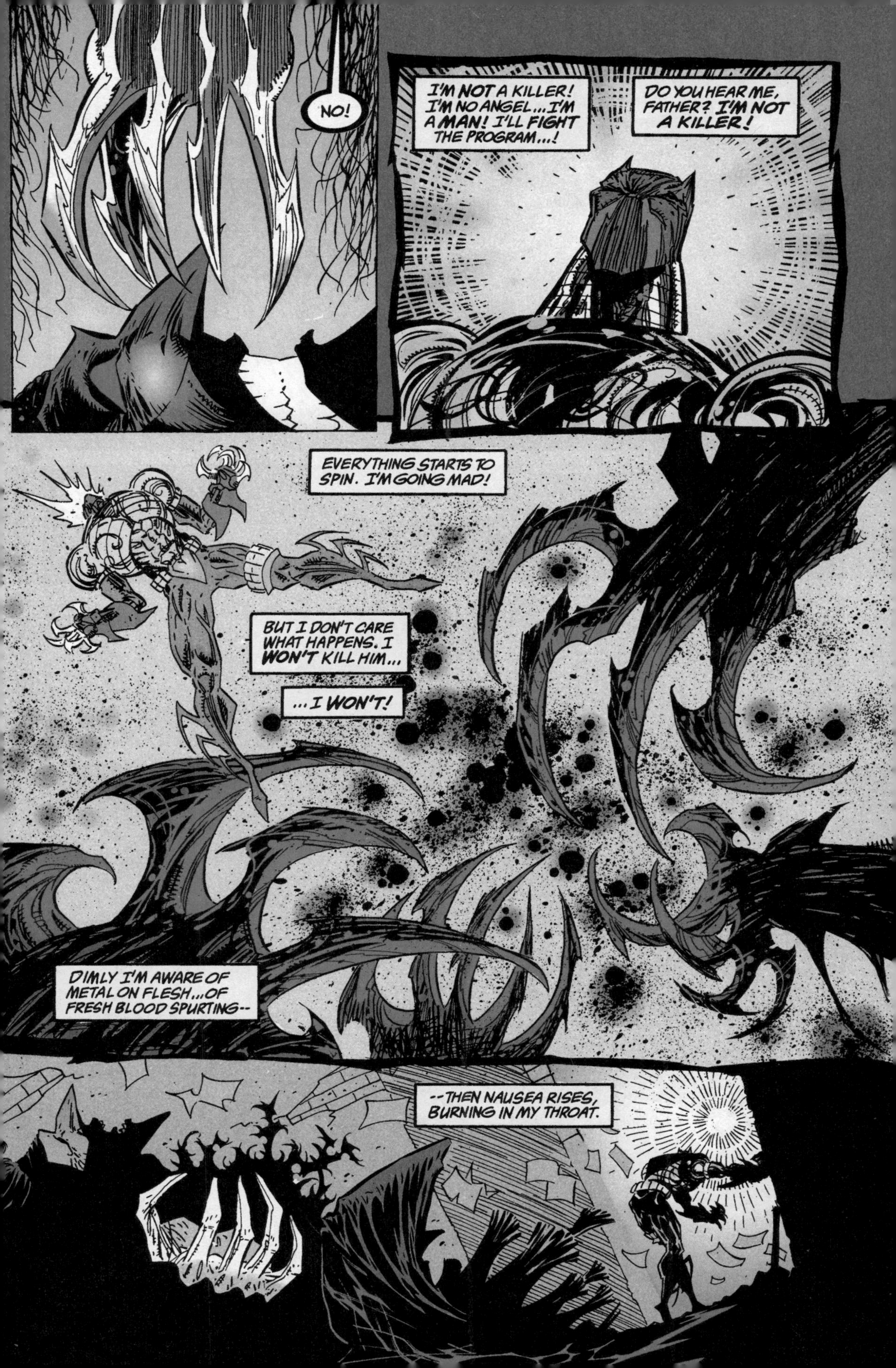
NO!
I'M NOT A KILLER! I'M NO ANGEL... I'M A MAN! I'LL FIGHT THE PROGRAM...!
DO YOU HEAR ME, FATHER? I'M NOT A KILLER!
EVERYTHING STARTS TO SPIN. I'M GOING MAD!
BUT I DON'T CARE WHAT HAPPENS. I WON'T KILL HIM...
...I WON'T!
DIMLY I'M AWARE OF METAL ON FLESH...OF FRESH BLOOD SPURTING--
--THEN NAUSEA RISES, BURNING IN MY THROAT.

THERE--!

CALLER SAID TWO. OTHER ONE MUST'VE GOT AWAY!

ONE'A THESE COSTUMED CREEPS. NOBODY I RECOGNIZE. YOU, KITCH?

NO.

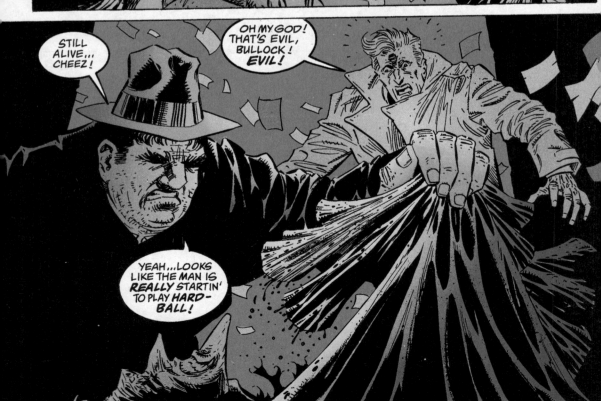

STILL ALIVE... CHEEZ!

OH MY GOD! THAT'S EVIL, BULLOCK! EVIL!

YEAH...LOOKS LIKE THE MAN IS REALLY STARTIN' TO PLAY HARD-BALL!

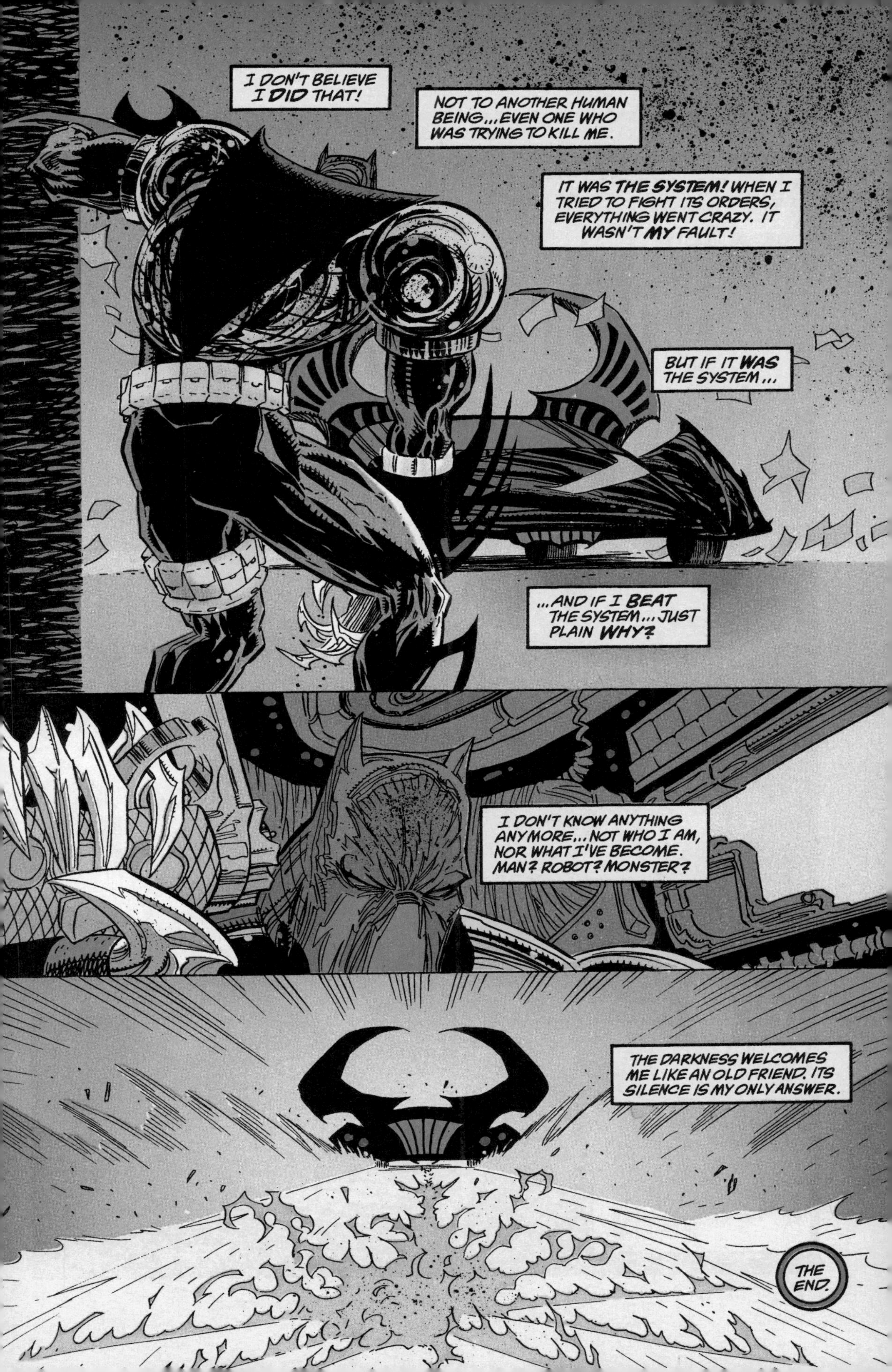
I DON'T BELIEVE I DID THAT!
NOT TO ANOTHER HUMAN BEING... EVEN ONE WHO WAS TRYING TO KILL ME.
IT WAS THE SYSTEM! WHEN I TRIED TO FIGHT ITS ORDERS, EVERYTHING WENT CRAZY. IT WASN'T MY FAULT!
BUT IF IT WAS THE SYSTEM...
...AND IF I BEAT THE SYSTEM... JUST PLAIN WHY?
I DON'T KNOW ANYTHING ANYMORE... NOT WHO I AM, NOR WHAT I'VE BECOME. MAN? ROBOT? MONSTER?
THE DARKNESS WELCOMES ME LIKE AN OLD FRIEND. ITS SILENCE IS MY ONLY ANSWER.
THE END.

Cover art by KELLEY JONES

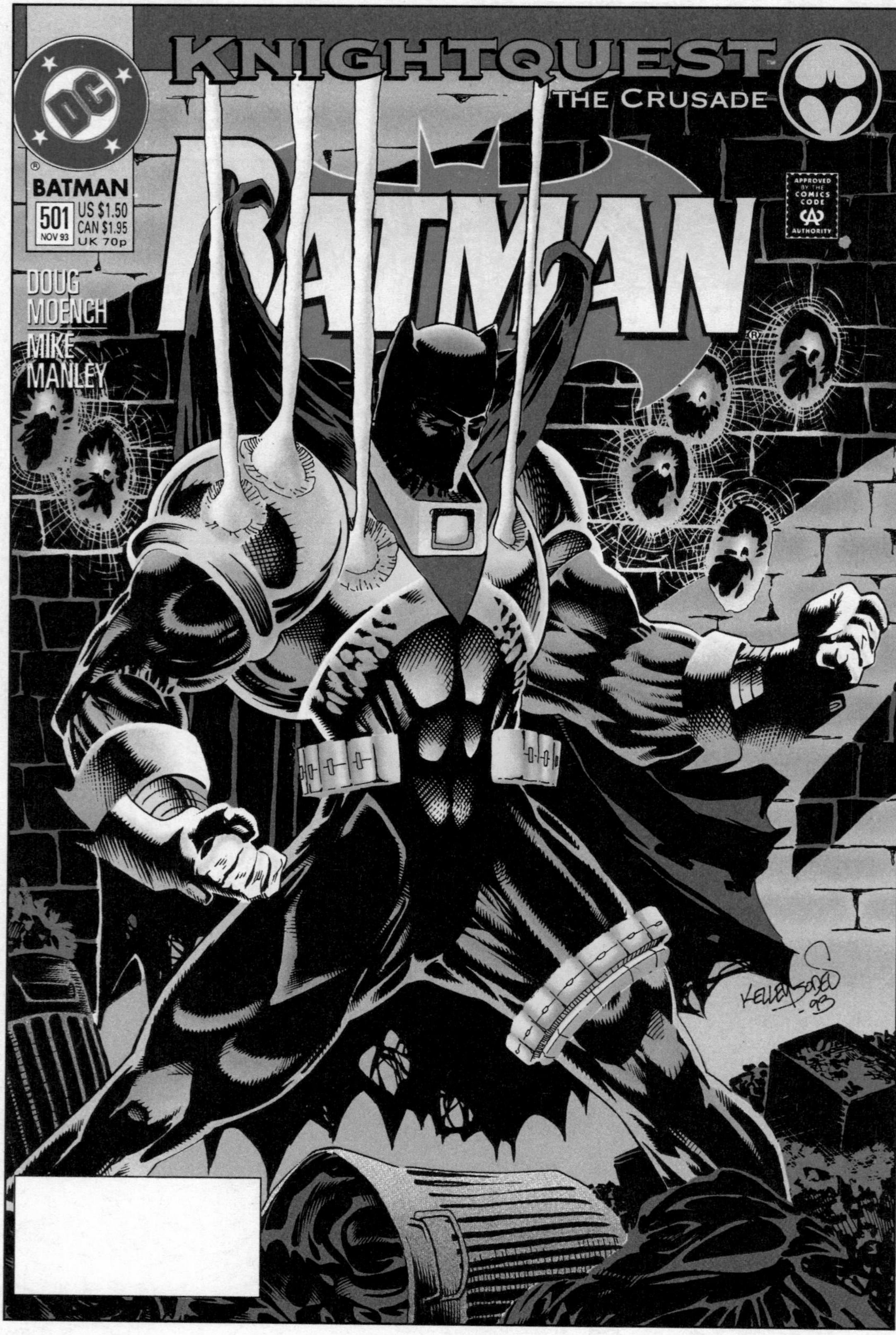
KNIGHTQUEST
THE CRUSADE
DC
BATMAN
501
NOV 93
US $1.50
CAN $1.95
UK 70p
BATMAN
APPROVED BY THE COMICS CODE AUTHORITY
DOUG MOENCH
MIKE MANLEY

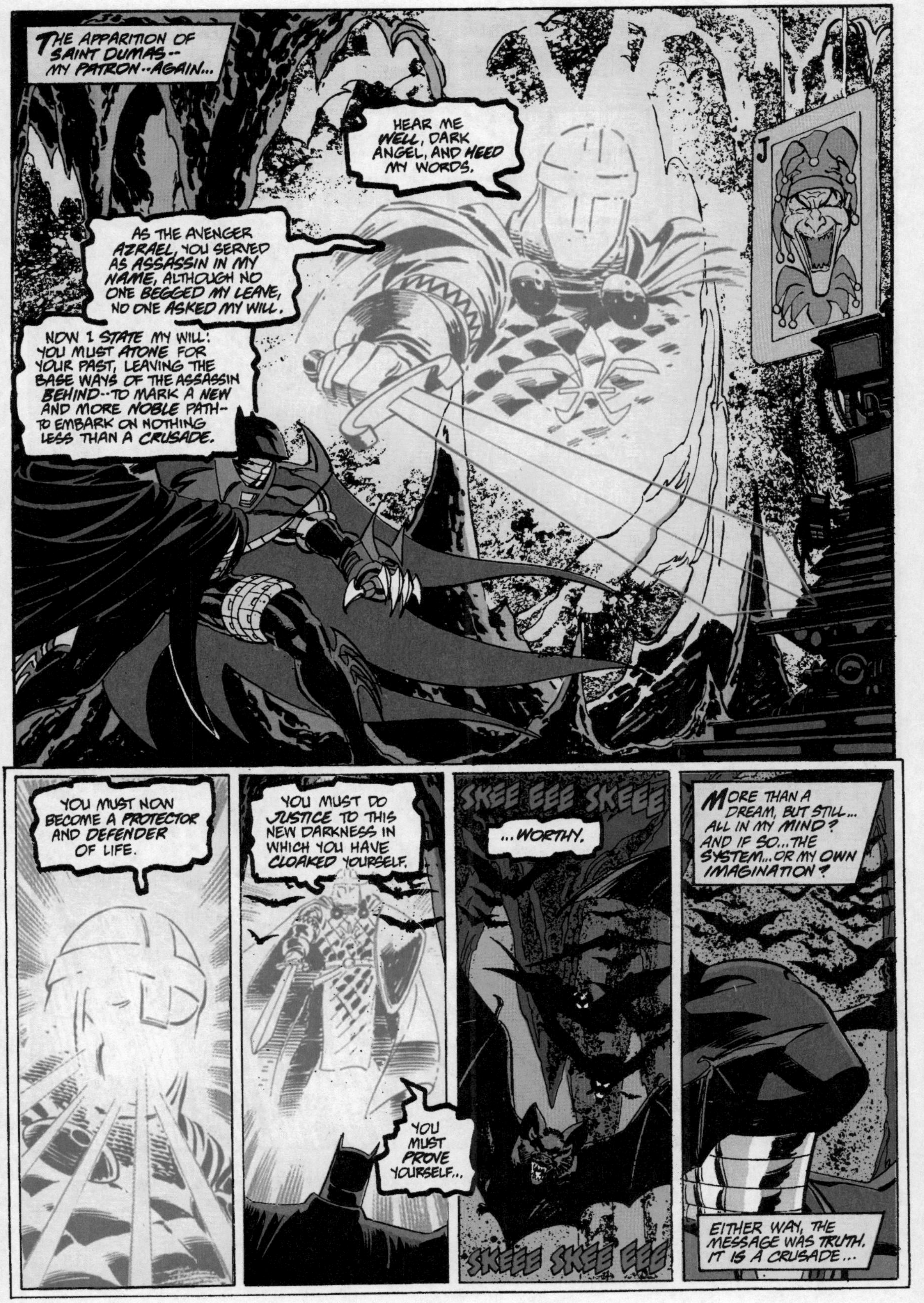
THE APPARITION OF SAINT DUMAS -- MY PATRON -- AGAIN...
HEAR ME WELL, DARK ANGEL, AND HEED MY WORDS.
AS THE AVENGER AZRAEL, YOU SERVED AS ASSASSIN IN MY NAME, ALTHOUGH NO ONE BEGGED MY LEAVE, NO ONE ASKED MY WILL.
NOW I STATE MY WILL: YOU MUST ATONE FOR YOUR PAST, LEAVING THE BASE WAYS OF THE ASSASSIN BEHIND--TO MARK A NEW AND MORE NOBLE PATH--TO EMBARK ON NOTHING LESS THAN A CRUSADE.
YOU MUST NOW BECOME A PROTECTOR AND DEFENDER OF LIFE.
YOU MUST DO JUSTICE TO THIS NEW DARKNESS IN WHICH YOU HAVE CLOAKED YOURSELF.
YOU MUST PROVE YOURSELF...
SKEE EEE SKEEE
...WORTHY.
SKEEE SKEE EEE
MORE THAN A DREAM, BUT STILL... ALL IN MY MIND? AND IF SO... THE SYSTEM... OR MY OWN IMAGINATION?
EITHER WAY, THE MESSAGE WAS TRUTH. IT IS A CRUSADE...

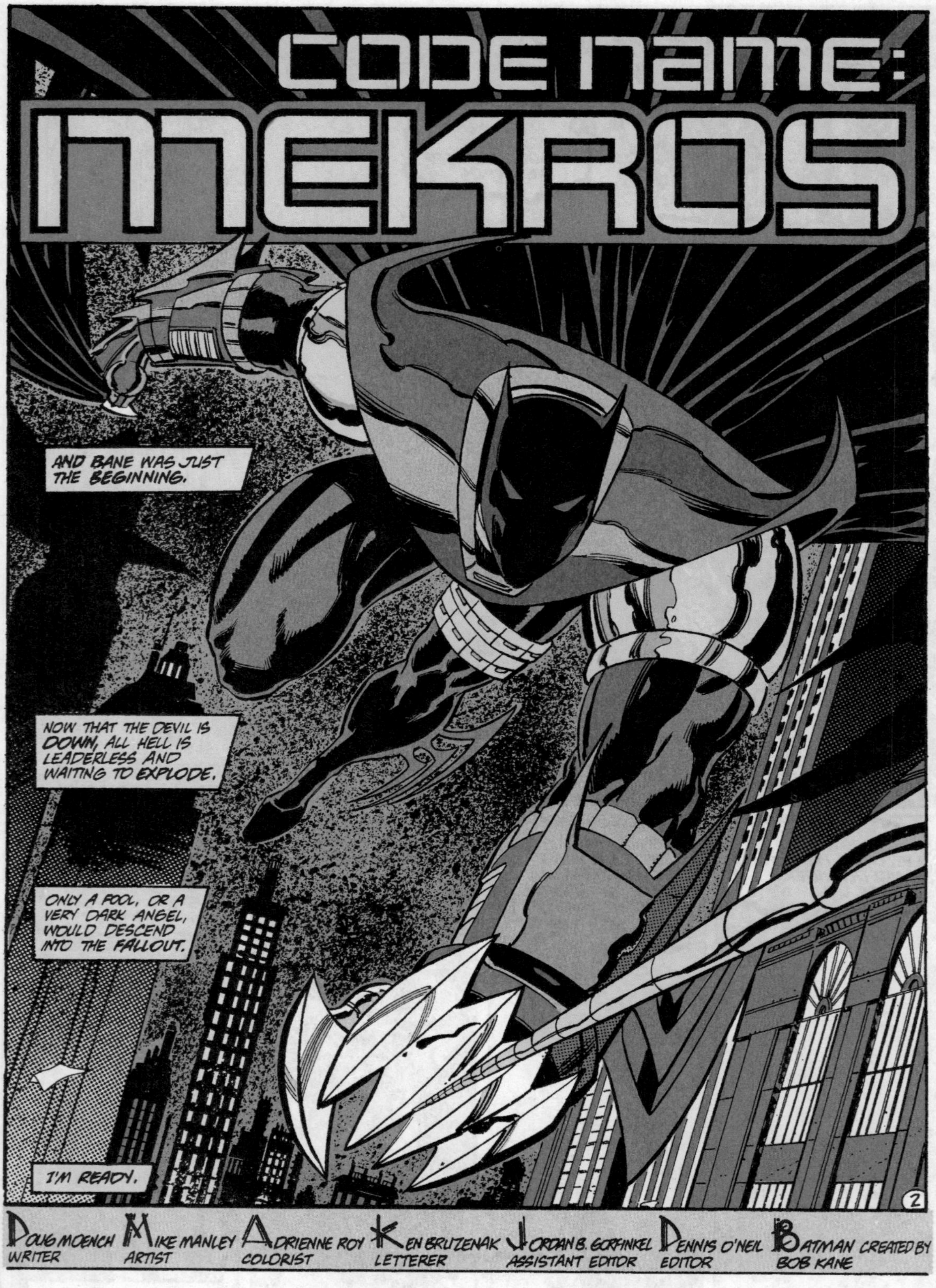

CODE NAME:
NEKROS
AND BANE WAS JUST THE BEGINNING.
NOW THAT THE DEVIL IS DOWN, ALL HELL IS LEADERLESS AND WAITING TO EXPLODE.
ONLY A FOOL, OR A VERY DARK ANGEL, WOULD DESCEND INTO THE FALLOUT.
I'M READY.
2
DOUG MOENCH WRITER
MIKE MANLEY ARTIST
ADRIENNE ROY COLORIST
KEN BRUZENAK LETTERER
JORDAN B. GORFINKEL ASSISTANT EDITOR
DENNIS O'NEIL EDITOR
BATMAN CREATED BY BOB KANE

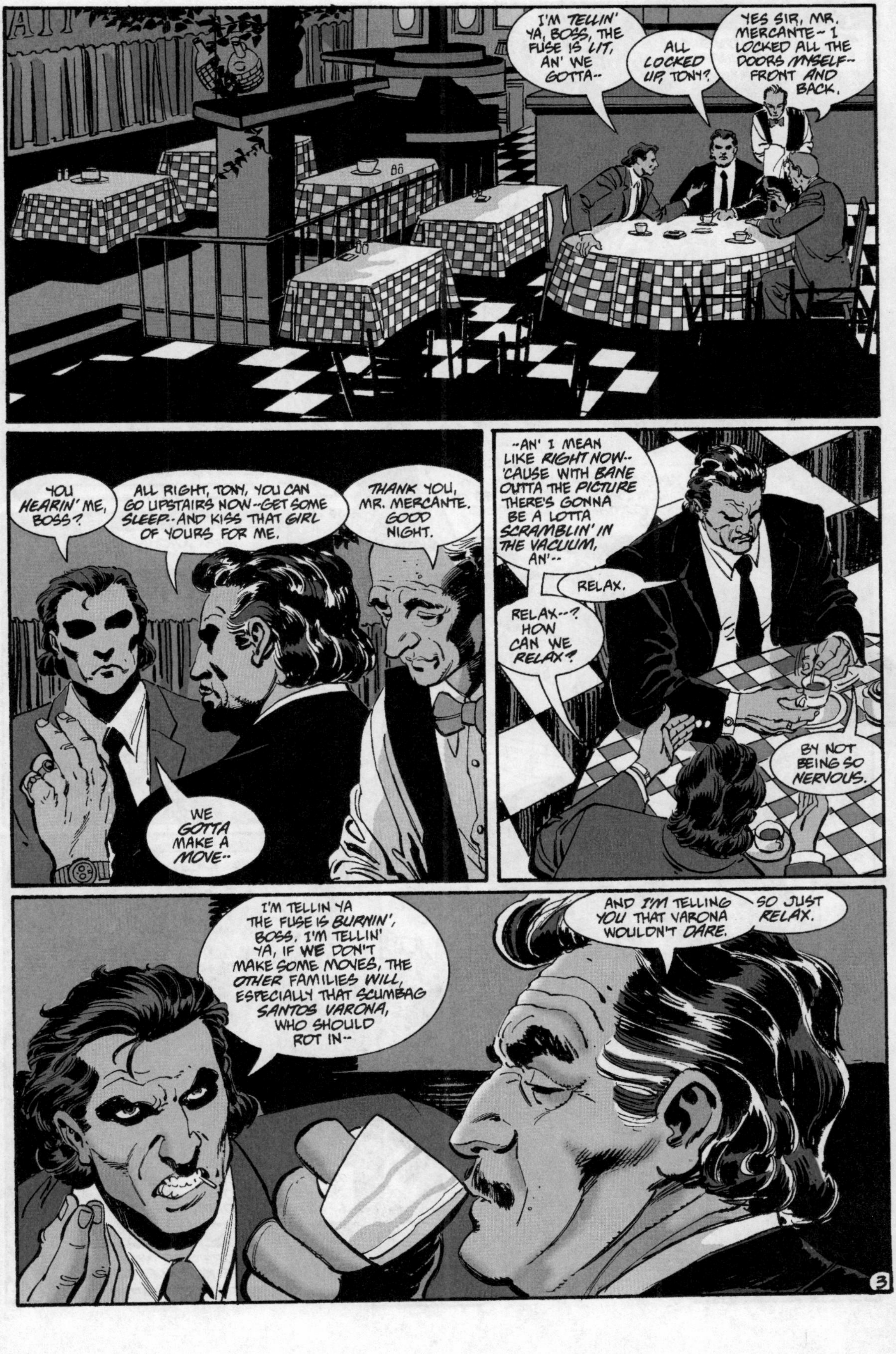
I'M TELLIN' YA, BOSS, THE FUSE IS LIT, AN' WE GOTTA--
ALL LOCKED UP, TONY?
YES SIR, MR. MERCANTE-- I LOCKED ALL THE DOORS MYSELF-- FRONT AND BACK.
YOU HEARIN' ME, BOSS?
ALL RIGHT, TONY, YOU CAN GO UPSTAIRS NOW--GET SOME SLEEP--AND KISS THAT GIRL OF YOURS FOR ME.
THANK YOU, MR. MERCANTE. GOOD NIGHT.
WE GOTTA MAKE A MOVE--
--AN' I MEAN LIKE RIGHT NOW-- 'CAUSE WITH BANE OUTTA THE PICTURE THERE'S GONNA BE A LOTTA SCRAMBLIN' IN THE VACUUM, AN'--
RELAX.
RELAX--? HOW CAN WE RELAX?
BY NOT BEING SO NERVOUS.
I'M TELLIN YA THE FUSE IS BURNIN', BOSS. I'M TELLIN' YA, IF WE DON'T MAKE SOME MOVES, THE OTHER FAMILIES WILL, ESPECIALLY THAT SCUMBAG SANTOS VARONA, WHO SHOULD ROT IN--
AND I'M TELLING YOU THAT VARONA WOULDN'T DARE.
SO JUST RELAX.
3

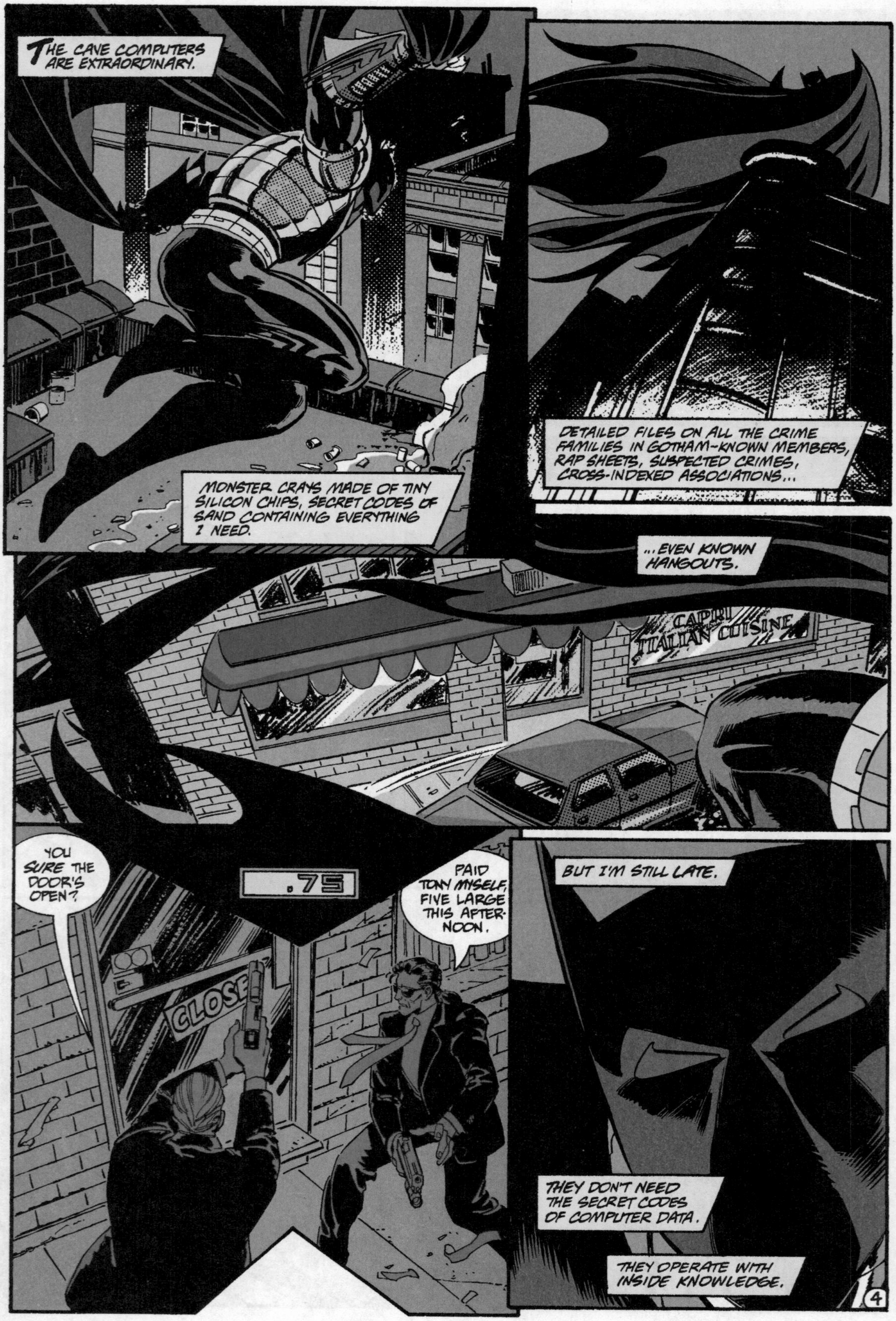
THE CAVE COMPUTERS ARE EXTRAORDINARY.
MONSTER CRAYS MADE OF TINY SILICON CHIPS, SECRET CODES OF SAND CONTAINING EVERYTHING I NEED.
DETAILED FILES ON ALL THE CRIME FAMILIES IN GOTHAM--KNOWN MEMBERS, RAP SHEETS, SUSPECTED CRIMES, CROSS-INDEXED ASSOCIATIONS...
...EVEN KNOWN HANGOUTS.
CAPRI ITALIAN CUISINE
YOU SURE THE DOOR'S OPEN?
.75
PAID TONY MYSELF, FIVE LARGE THIS AFTER-NOON.
CLOSE
BUT I'M STILL LATE.
THEY DON'T NEED THE SECRET CODES OF COMPUTER DATA.
THEY OPERATE WITH INSIDE KNOWLEDGE.
4

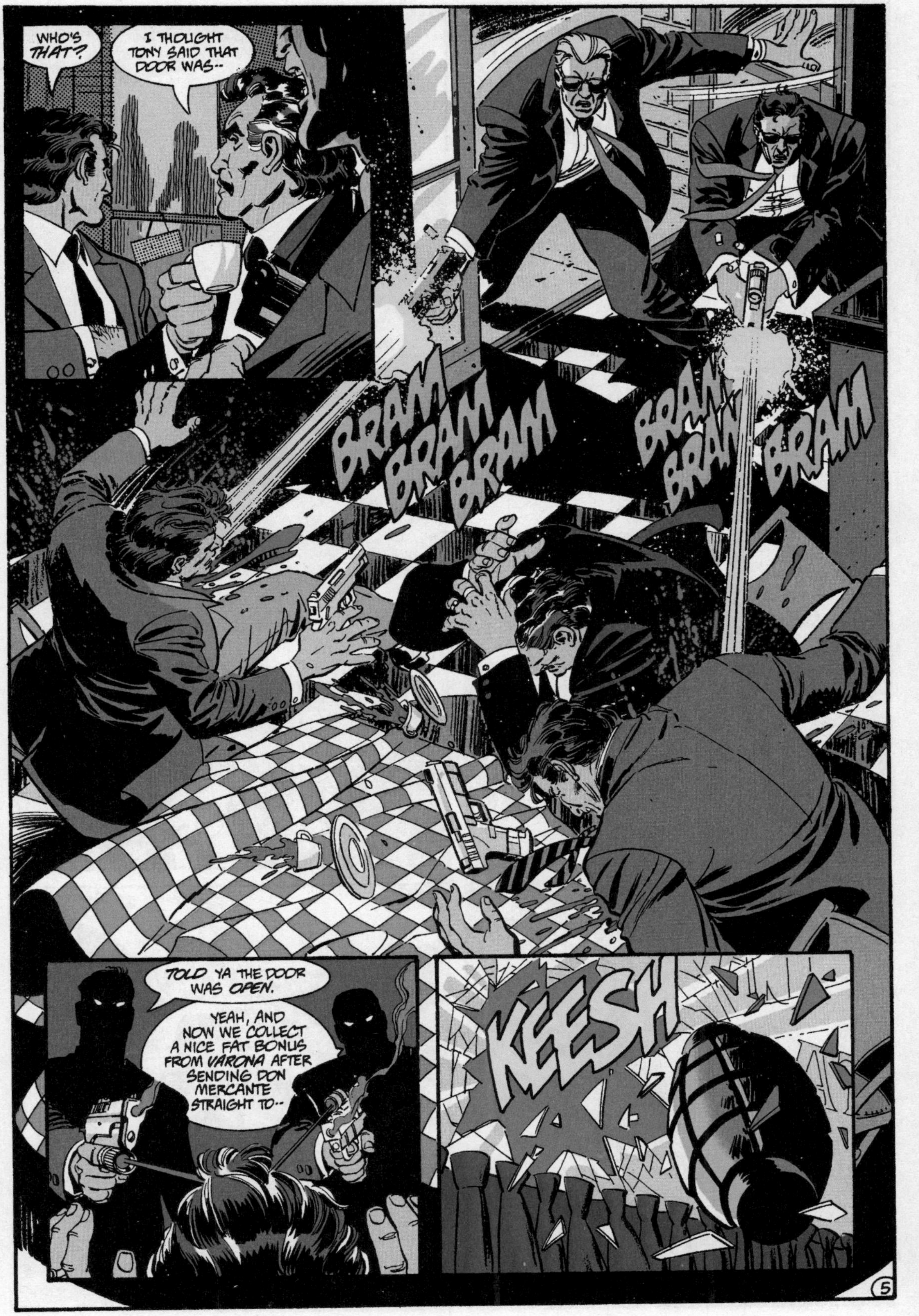

WHO'S THAT?
I THOUGHT TONY SAID THAT DOOR WAS--
BRAM BRAM BRAM
BRAM BRAM BRAM
TOLD YA THE DOOR WAS OPEN.
YEAH, AND NOW WE COLLECT A NICE FAT BONUS FROM VARONA AFTER SENDING DON MERCANTE STRAIGHT TO--
KEESH
5

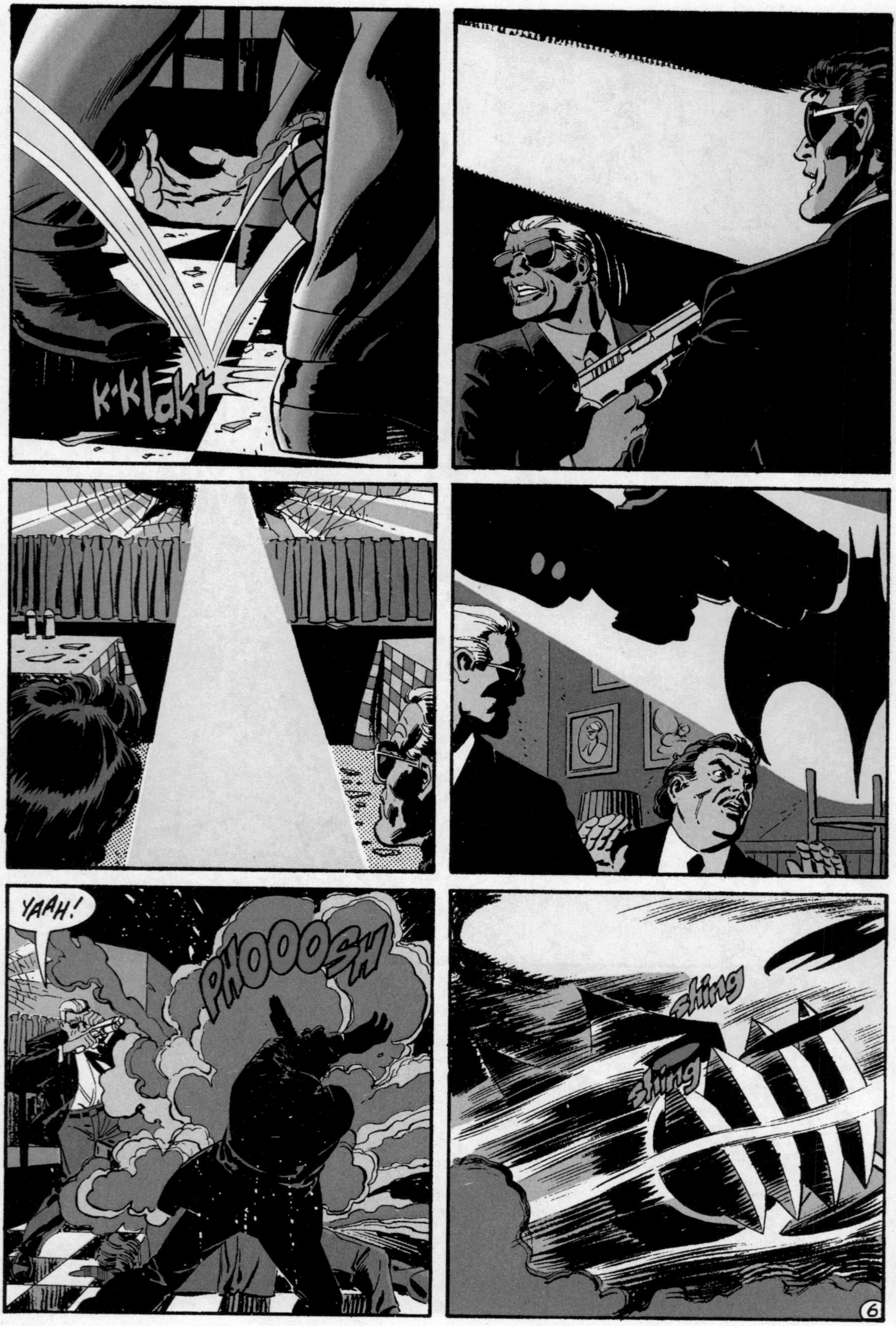
K-KLAKT
YAAH!
PHOOOSH
SHING
SHING
6

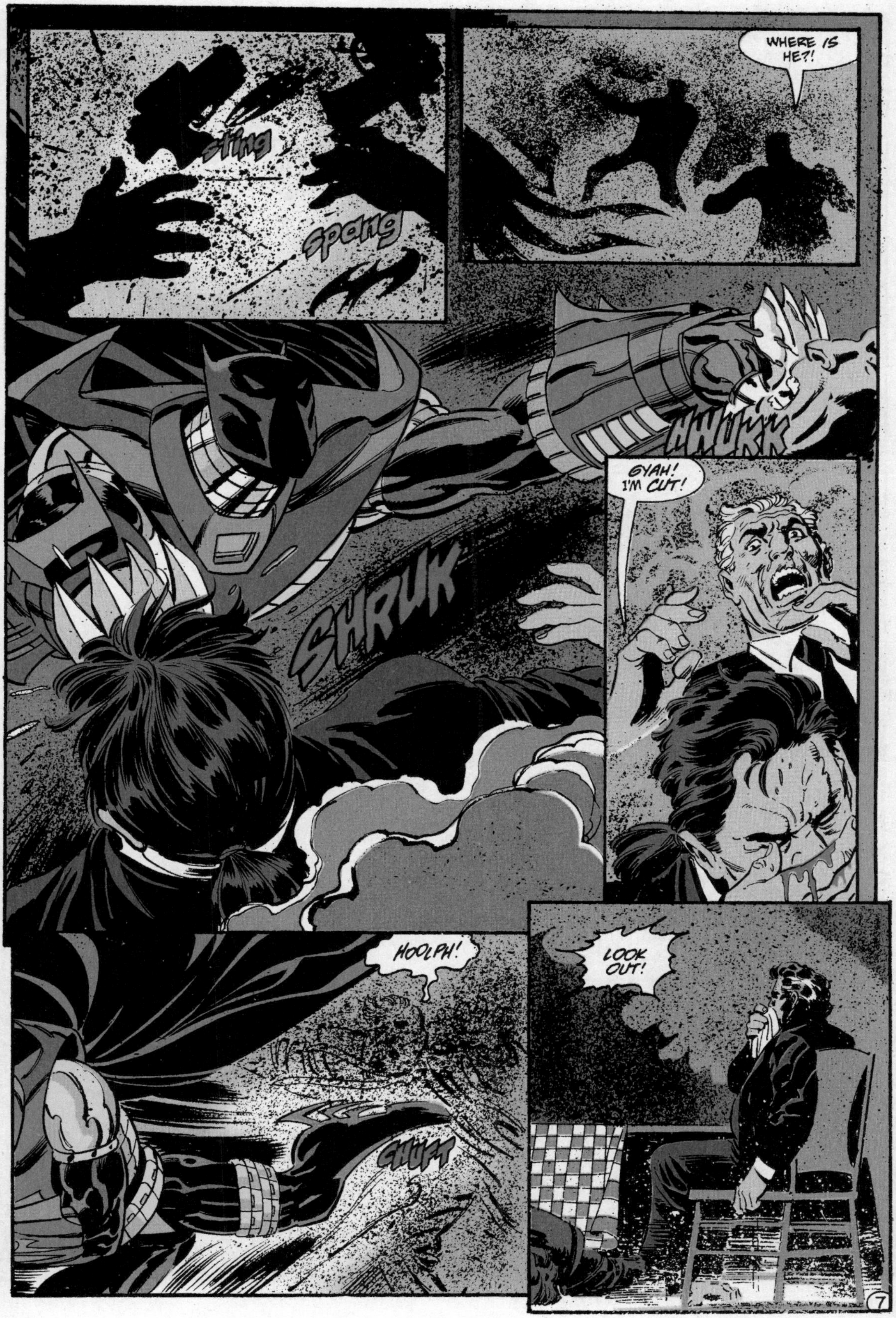
sting
spang
WHERE IS HE?!
HHUKK
SHRUK
GYAH! I'M CUT!
HOOLPH!
CHUFT
LOOK OUT!
7

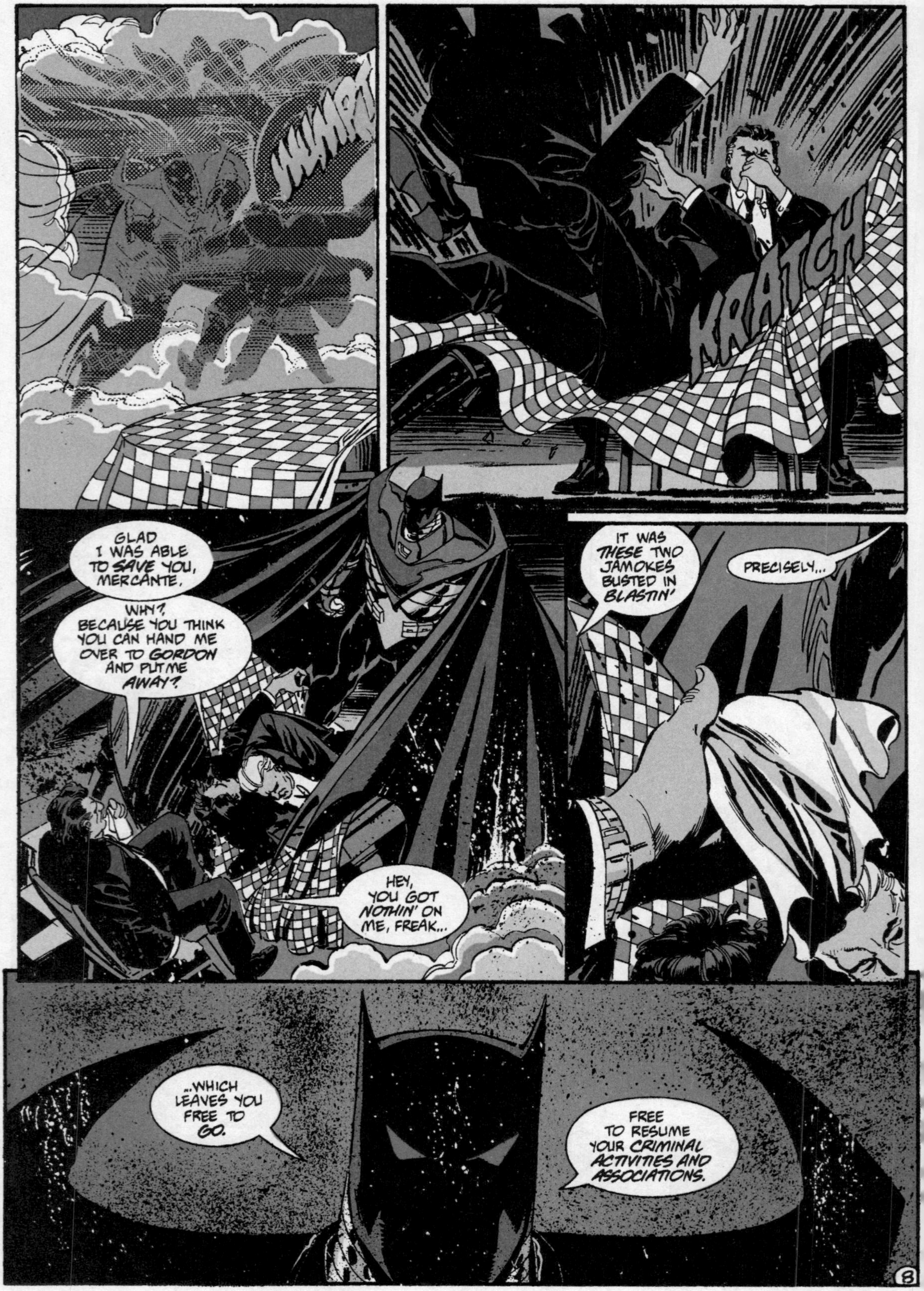
WHUMP!
KRATCH
GLAD I WAS ABLE TO SAVE YOU, MERCANTE.
WHY? BECAUSE YOU THINK YOU CAN HAND ME OVER TO GORDON AND PUT ME AWAY?
HEY, YOU GOT NOTHIN' ON ME, FREAK...
IT WAS THESE TWO JAMOKES BUSTED IN BLASTIN'
PRECISELY...
...WHICH LEAVES YOU FREE TO GO.
FREE TO RESUME YOUR CRIMINAL ACTIVITIES AND ASSOCIATIONS.
8

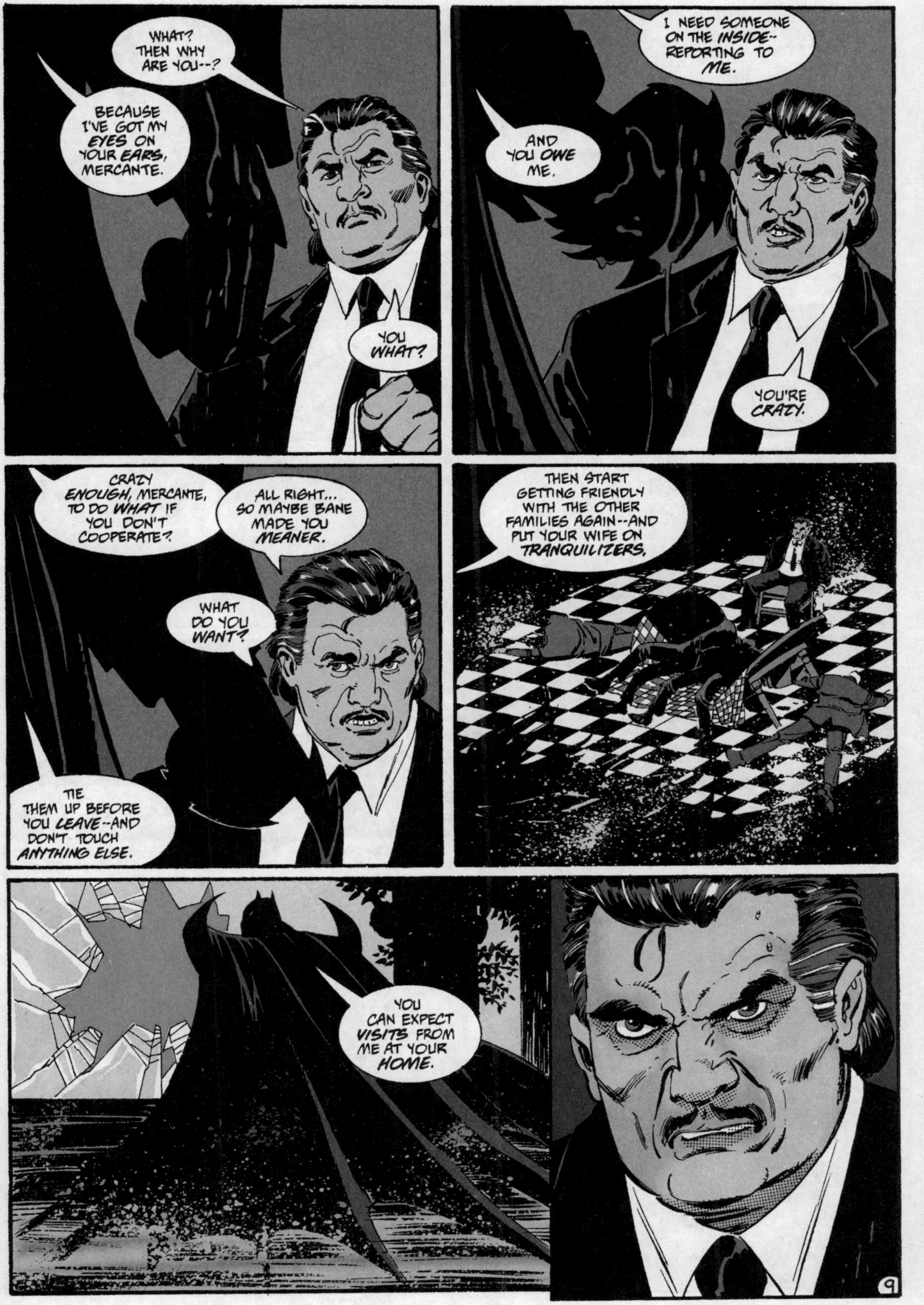
WHAT? THEN WHY ARE YOU--?
BECAUSE I'VE GOT MY EYES ON YOUR EARS, MERCANTE.
YOU WHAT?
I NEED SOMEONE ON THE INSIDE-- REPORTING TO ME.
AND YOU OWE ME.
YOU'RE CRAZY.
CRAZY ENOUGH, MERCANTE, TO DO WHAT IF YOU DON'T COOPERATE?
ALL RIGHT... SO MAYBE BANE MADE YOU MEANER.
WHAT DO YOU WANT?
TIE THEM UP BEFORE YOU LEAVE--AND DON'T TOUCH ANYTHING ELSE.
THEN START GETTING FRIENDLY WITH THE OTHER FAMILIES AGAIN--AND PUT YOUR WIFE ON TRANQUILIZERS.
YOU CAN EXPECT VISITS FROM ME AT YOUR HOME.
9

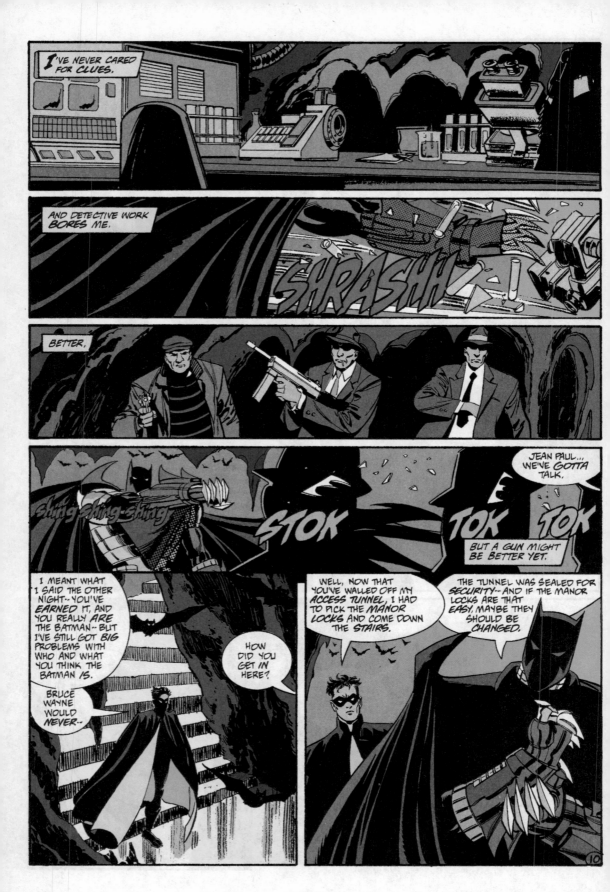

I'VE NEVER CARED FOR CLUES.

AND DETECTIVE WORK BORES ME.

SHRASHH

BETTER.

shing-shing-shing

STOK

TOK TOK

JEAN PAUL... WE'VE GOTTA TALK.

BUT A GUN MIGHT BE BETTER YET.

I MEANT WHAT I SAID THE OTHER NIGHT-- YOU'VE EARNED IT, AND YOU REALLY ARE THE BATMAN-- BUT I'VE STILL GOT BIG PROBLEMS WITH WHO AND WHAT YOU THINK THE BATMAN IS.

BRUCE WAYNE WOULD NEVER--

HOW DID YOU GET IN HERE?

WELL, NOW THAT YOU'VE WALLED OFF MY ACCESS TUNNEL, I HAD TO PICK THE MANOR LOCKS AND COME DOWN THE STAIRS.

THE TUNNEL WAS SEALED FOR SECURITY-- AND IF THE MANOR LOCKS ARE THAT EASY, MAYBE THEY SHOULD BE CHANGED.

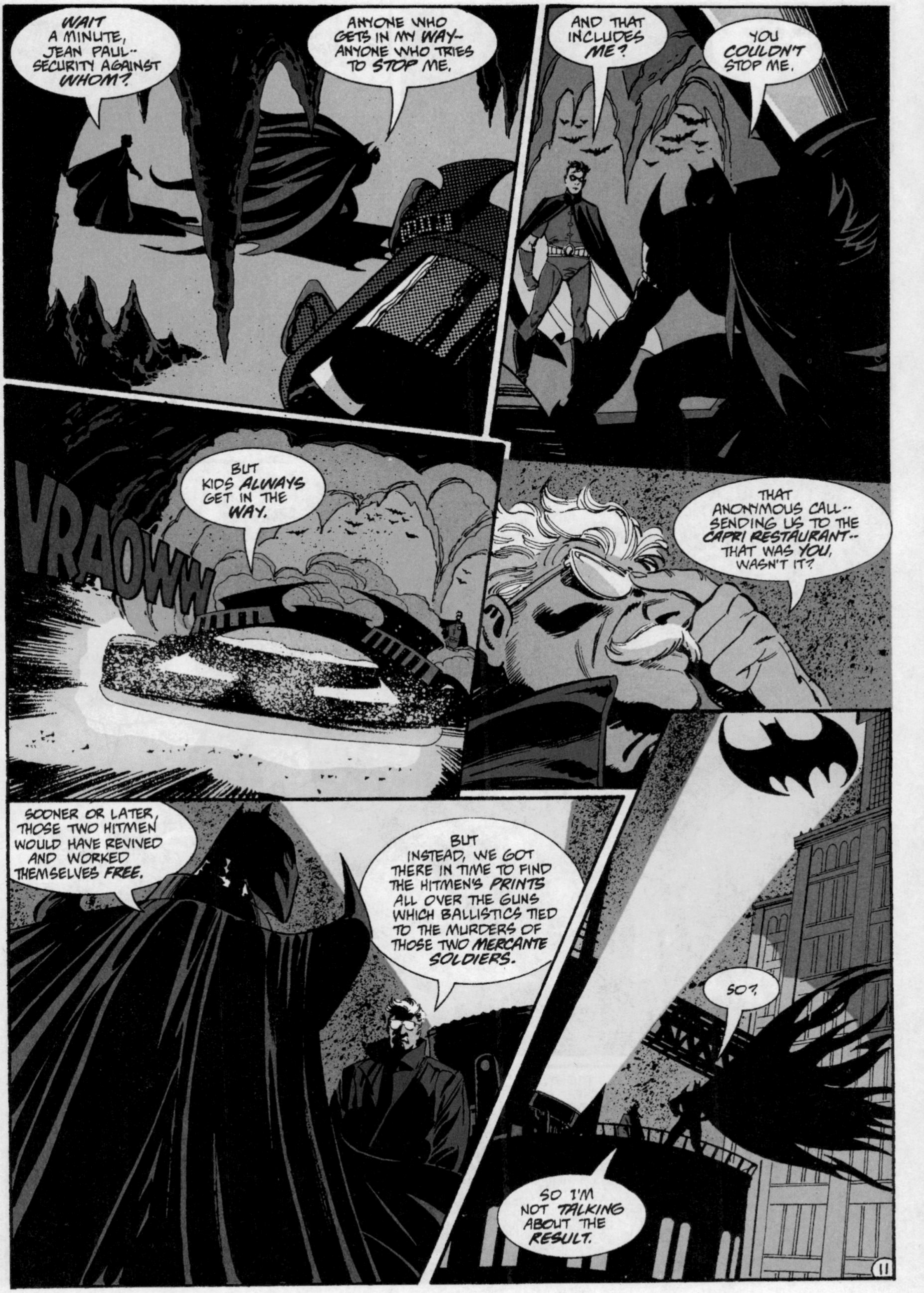
WAIT A MINUTE, JEAN PAUL-- SECURITY AGAINST WHOM?
ANYONE WHO GETS IN MY WAY-- ANYONE WHO TRIES TO STOP ME.
AND THAT INCLUDES ME?
YOU COULDN'T STOP ME.
VRAOWW
BUT KIDS ALWAYS GET IN THE WAY.
THAT ANONYMOUS CALL-- SENDING US TO THE CAPRI RESTAURANT-- THAT WAS YOU, WASN'T IT?
SOONER OR LATER, THOSE TWO HITMEN WOULD HAVE REVIVED AND WORKED THEMSELVES FREE.
BUT INSTEAD, WE GOT THERE IN TIME TO FIND THE HITMEN'S PRINTS ALL OVER THE GUNS WHICH BALLISTICS TIED TO THE MURDERS OF THOSE TWO MERCANTE SOLDIERS.
SO?
SO I'M NOT TALKING ABOUT THE RESULT.
11

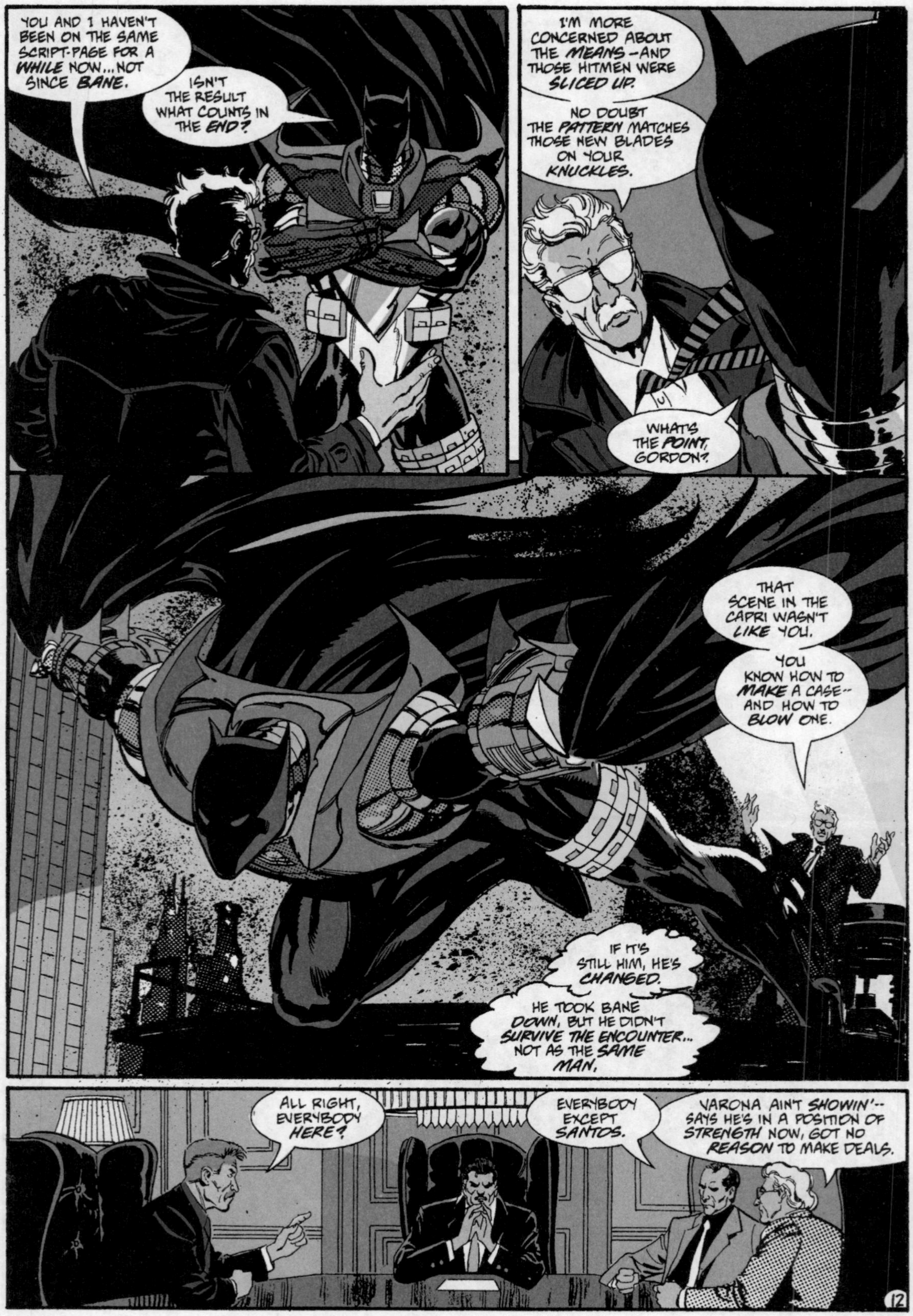
YOU AND I HAVEN'T BEEN ON THE SAME SCRIPT-PAGE FOR A WHILE NOW... NOT SINCE BANE.
ISN'T THE RESULT WHAT COUNTS IN THE END?
I'M MORE CONCERNED ABOUT THE MEANS -- AND THOSE HITMEN WERE SLICED UP.
NO DOUBT THE PATTERN MATCHES THOSE NEW BLADES ON YOUR KNUCKLES.
WHAT'S THE POINT, GORDON?
THAT SCENE IN THE CAPRI WASN'T LIKE YOU.
YOU KNOW HOW TO MAKE A CASE-- AND HOW TO BLOW ONE.
IF IT'S STILL HIM, HE'S CHANGED.
HE TOOK BANE DOWN, BUT HE DIDN'T SURVIVE THE ENCOUNTER... NOT AS THE SAME MAN.
ALL RIGHT, EVERYBODY HERE?
EVERYBODY EXCEPT SANTOS.
VARONA AIN'T SHOWIN'-- SAYS HE'S IN A POSITION OF STRENGTH NOW, GOT NO REASON TO MAKE DEALS.
12

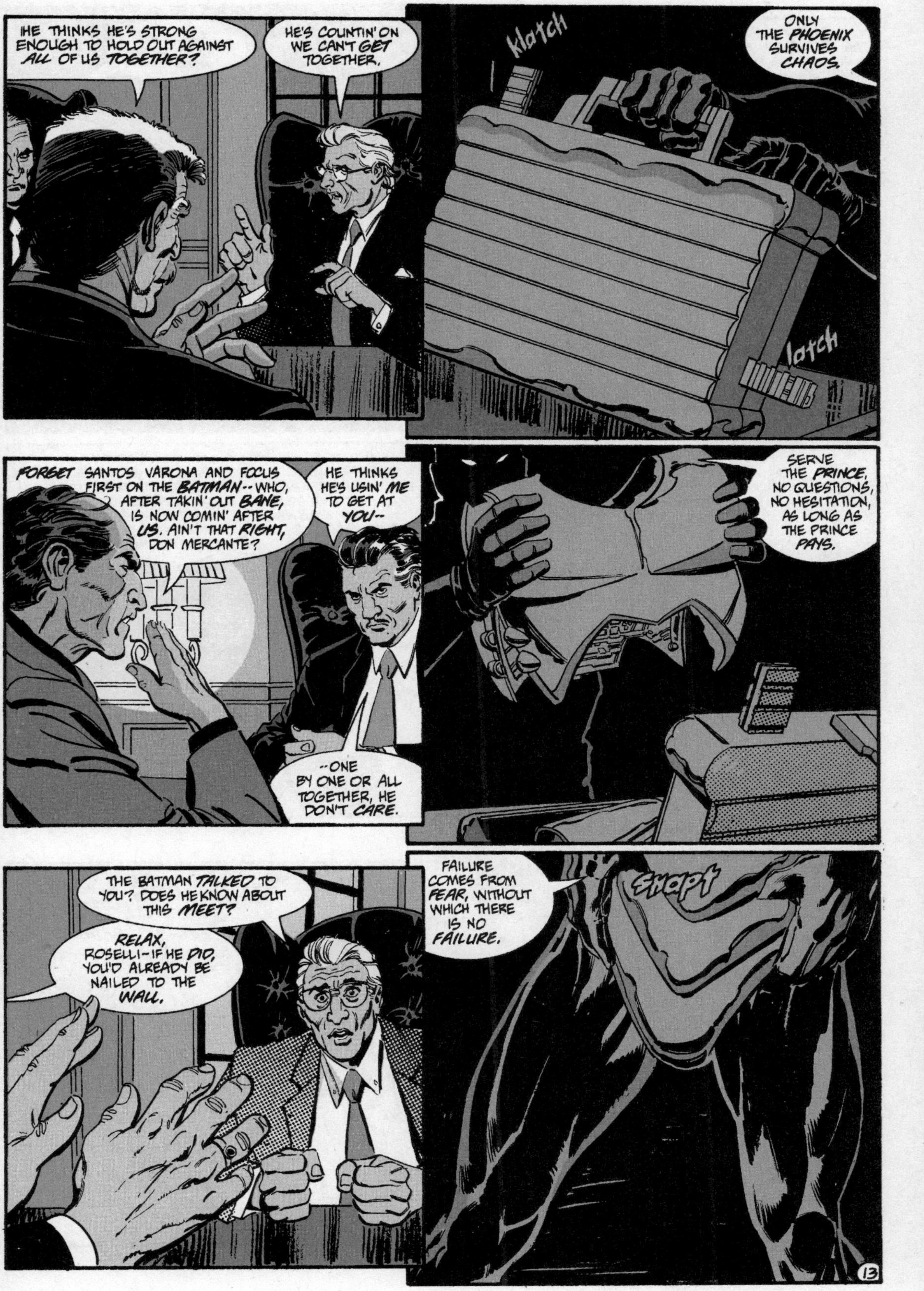
HE THINKS HE'S STRONG ENOUGH TO HOLD OUT AGAINST ALL OF US TOGETHER?
HE'S COUNTIN' ON WE CAN'T GET TOGETHER.
klatch
ONLY THE PHOENIX SURVIVES CHAOS.
latch
FORGET SANTOS VARONA AND FOCUS FIRST ON THE BATMAN--WHO, AFTER TAKIN' OUT BANE, IS NOW COMIN' AFTER US. AIN'T THAT RIGHT, DON MERCANTE?
HE THINKS HE'S USIN' ME TO GET AT YOU--
--ONE BY ONE OR ALL TOGETHER, HE DON'T CARE.
SERVE THE PRINCE, NO QUESTIONS, NO HESITATION, AS LONG AS THE PRINCE PAYS.
THE BATMAN TALKED TO YOU? DOES HE KNOW ABOUT THIS MEET?
RELAX, ROSELLI--IF HE DID, YOU'D ALREADY BE NAILED TO THE WALL.
FAILURE COMES FROM FEAR, WITHOUT WHICH THERE IS NO FAILURE.
snapt
13

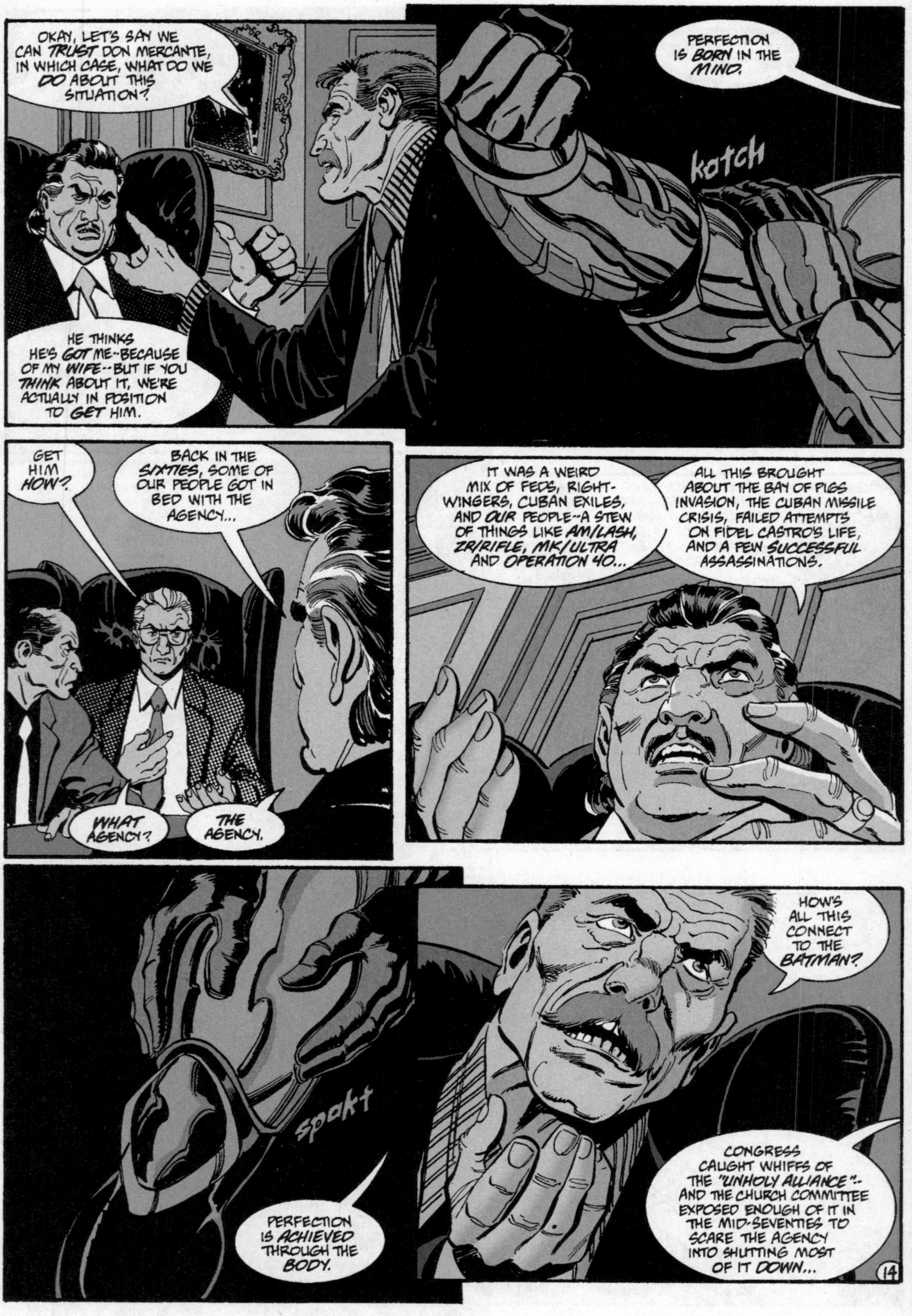
OKAY, LET'S SAY WE CAN TRUST DON MERCANTE, IN WHICH CASE, WHAT DO WE DO ABOUT THIS SITUATION?
HE THINKS HE'S GOT ME--BECAUSE OF MY WIFE--BUT IF YOU THINK ABOUT IT, WE'RE ACTUALLY IN POSITION TO GET HIM.
PERFECTION IS BORN IN THE MIND.
kotch
GET HIM HOW?
BACK IN THE SIXTIES, SOME OF OUR PEOPLE GOT IN BED WITH THE AGENCY...
WHAT AGENCY?
THE AGENCY.
IT WAS A WEIRD MIX OF FEDS, RIGHT-WINGERS, CUBAN EXILES, AND OUR PEOPLE--A STEW OF THINGS LIKE AM/LASH, ZR/RIFLE, MK/ULTRA AND OPERATION 40...
ALL THIS BROUGHT ABOUT THE BAY OF PIGS INVASION, THE CUBAN MISSILE CRISIS, FAILED ATTEMPTS ON FIDEL CASTRO'S LIFE, AND A FEW SUCCESSFUL ASSASSINATIONS.
spakt
PERFECTION IS ACHIEVED THROUGH THE BODY.
HOW'S ALL THIS CONNECT TO THE BATMAN?
CONGRESS CAUGHT WHIFFS OF THE "UNHOLY ALLIANCE"--AND THE CHURCH COMMITTEE EXPOSED ENOUGH OF IT IN THE MID-SEVENTIES TO SCARE THE AGENCY INTO SHUTTING MOST OF IT DOWN...
14

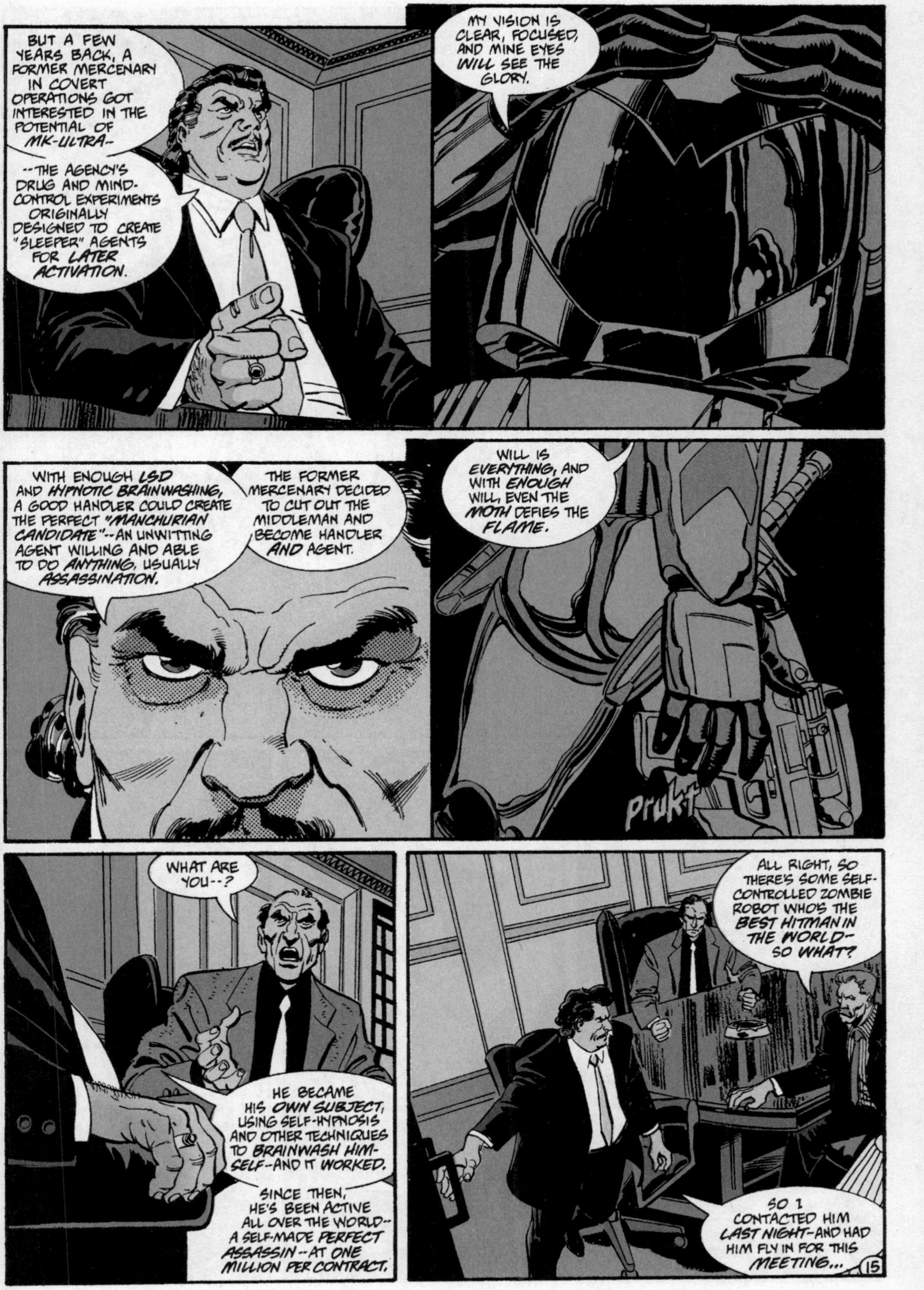

BUT A FEW YEARS BACK, A FORMER MERCENARY IN COVERT OPERATIONS GOT INTERESTED IN THE POTENTIAL OF MK-ULTRA--
--THE AGENCY'S DRUG AND MIND-CONTROL EXPERIMENTS ORIGINALLY DESIGNED TO CREATE "SLEEPER" AGENTS FOR LATER ACTIVATION.
MY VISION IS CLEAR, FOCUSED, AND MINE EYES WILL SEE THE GLORY.
WITH ENOUGH LSD AND HYPNOTIC BRAINWASHING, A GOOD HANDLER COULD CREATE THE PERFECT "MANCHURIAN CANDIDATE"--AN UNWITTING AGENT WILLING AND ABLE TO DO ANYTHING, USUALLY ASSASSINATION.
THE FORMER MERCENARY DECIDED TO CUT OUT THE MIDDLEMAN AND BECOME HANDLER AND AGENT.
WILL IS EVERYTHING, AND WITH ENOUGH WILL, EVEN THE MOTH DEFIES THE FLAME.
Prukt
WHAT ARE YOU--?
HE BECAME HIS OWN SUBJECT, USING SELF-HYPNOSIS AND OTHER TECHNIQUES TO BRAINWASH HIMSELF--AND IT WORKED.
SINCE THEN, HE'S BEEN ACTIVE ALL OVER THE WORLD--A SELF-MADE PERFECT ASSASSIN--AT ONE MILLION PER CONTRACT.
ALL RIGHT, SO THERE'S SOME SELF-CONTROLLED ZOMBIE ROBOT WHO'S THE BEST HITMAN IN THE WORLD--SO WHAT?
SO I CONTACTED HIM LAST NIGHT--AND HAD HIM FLY IN FOR THIS MEETING...
15

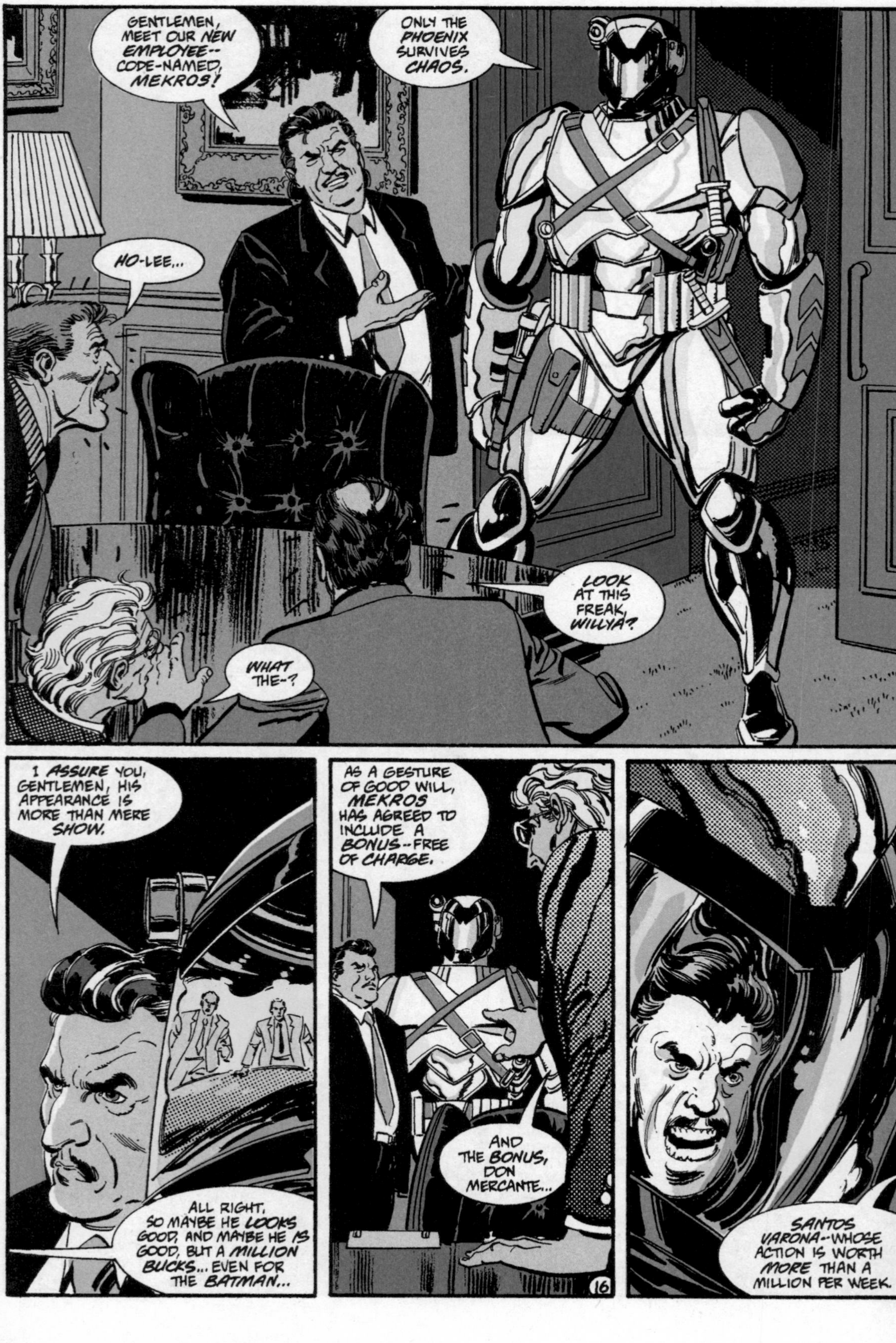
GENTLEMEN, MEET OUR NEW EMPLOYEE-- CODE-NAMED, MEKROS!
ONLY THE PHOENIX SURVIVES CHAOS.
HO-LEE...
LOOK AT THIS FREAK, WILLYA?
WHAT THE-?
I ASSURE YOU, GENTLEMEN, HIS APPEARANCE IS MORE THAN MERE SHOW.
ALL RIGHT, SO MAYBE HE LOOKS GOOD, AND MAYBE HE IS GOOD, BUT A MILLION BUCKS... EVEN FOR THE BATMAN...
AS A GESTURE OF GOOD WILL, MEKROS HAS AGREED TO INCLUDE A BONUS--FREE OF CHARGE.
AND THE BONUS, DON MERCANTE...
16
SANTOS VARONA--WHOSE ACTION IS WORTH MORE THAN A MILLION PER WEEK.

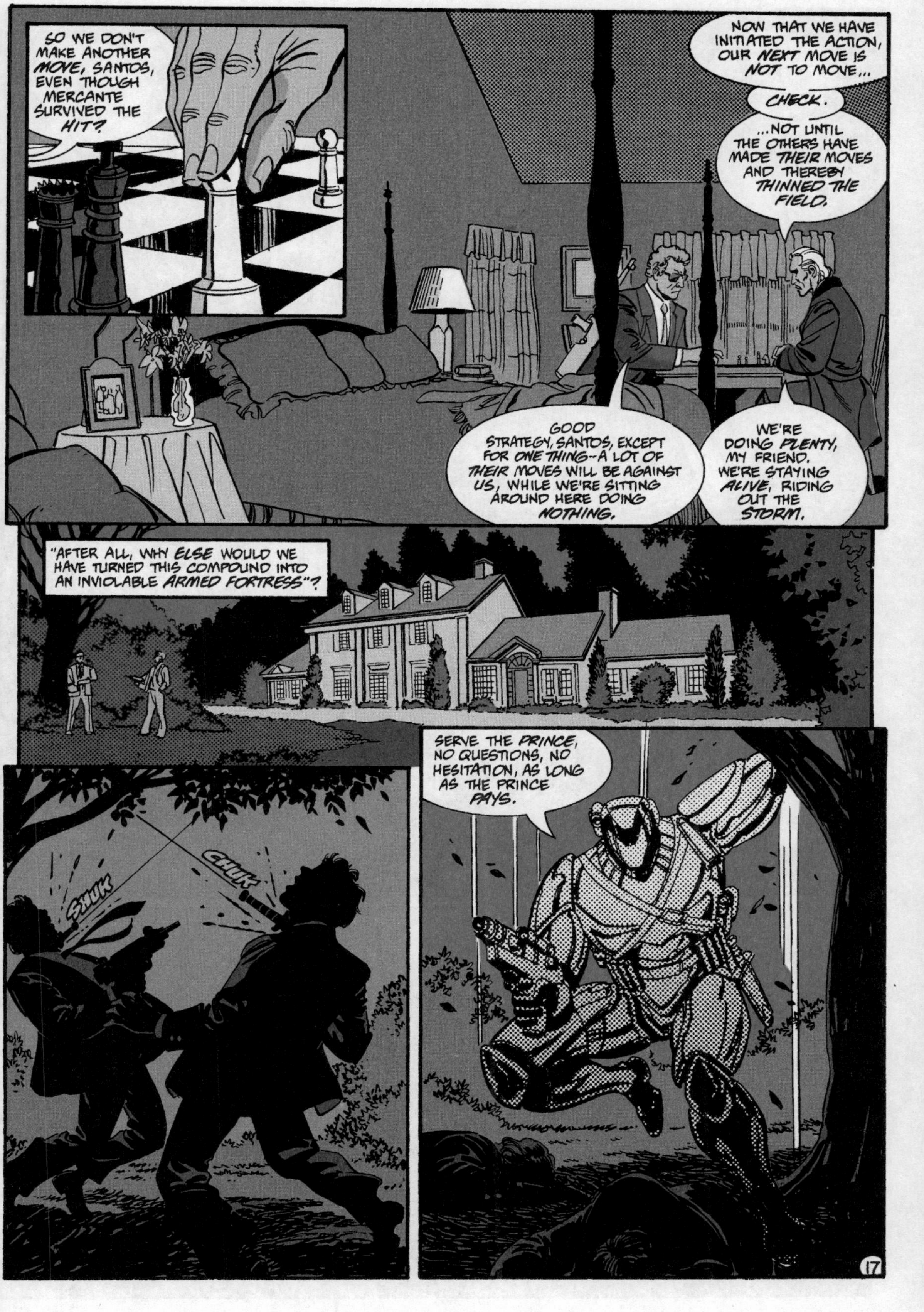
SO WE DON'T MAKE ANOTHER MOVE, SANTOS, EVEN THOUGH MERCANTE SURVIVED THE HIT?
NOW THAT WE HAVE INITIATED THE ACTION, OUR NEXT MOVE IS NOT TO MOVE...
CHECK.
...NOT UNTIL THE OTHERS HAVE MADE THEIR MOVES AND THEREBY THINNED THE FIELD.
GOOD STRATEGY, SANTOS, EXCEPT FOR ONE THING--A LOT OF THEIR MOVES WILL BE AGAINST US, WHILE WE'RE SITTING AROUND HERE DOING NOTHING.
WE'RE DOING PLENTY, MY FRIEND. WE'RE STAYING ALIVE, RIDING OUT THE STORM.
"AFTER ALL, WHY ELSE WOULD WE HAVE TURNED THIS COMPOUND INTO AN INVIOLABLE ARMED FORTRESS"?
SHUK
CHUK
SERVE THE PRINCE, NO QUESTIONS, NO HESITATION, AS LONG AS THE PRINCE PAYS.
17

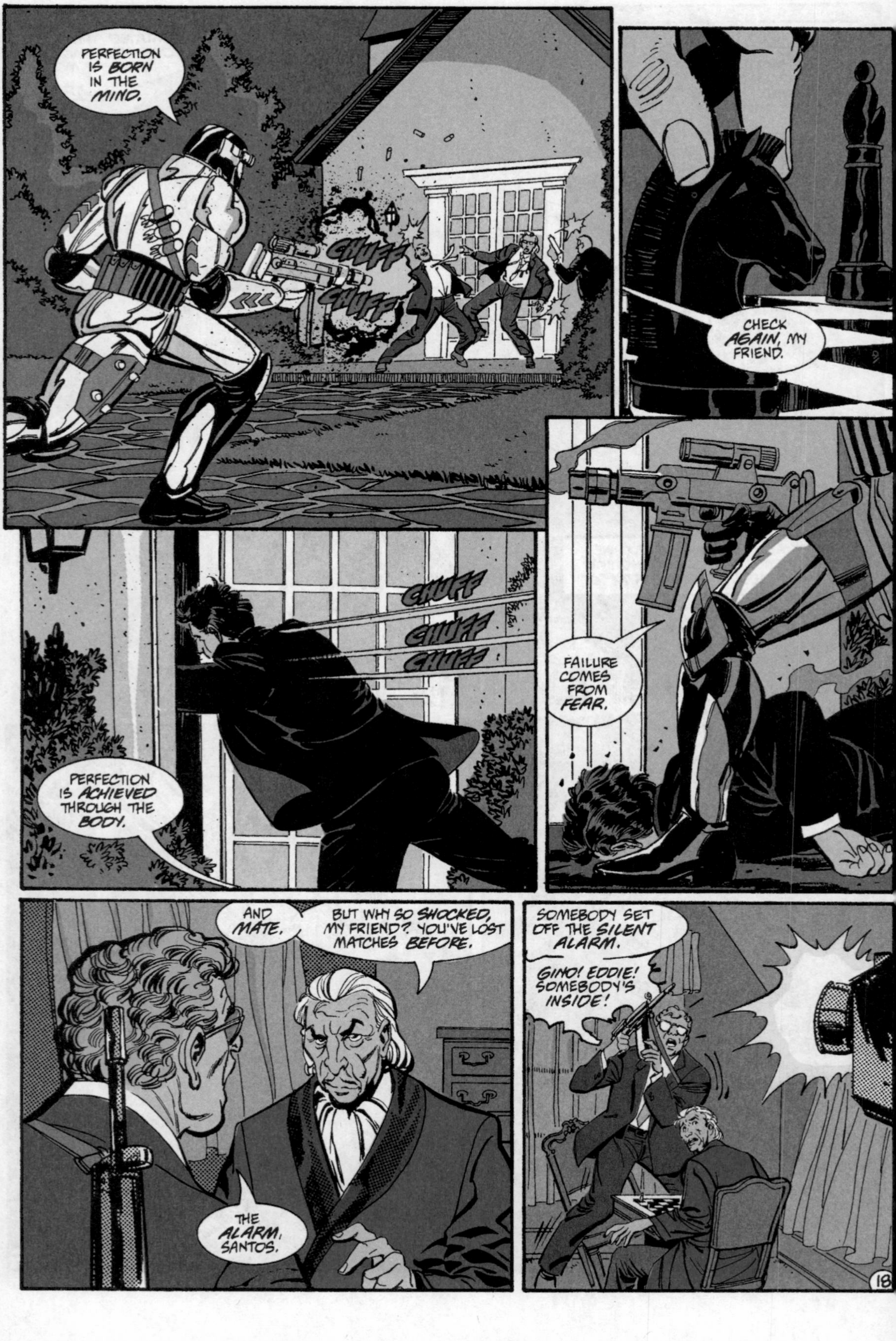
PERFECTION IS BORN IN THE MIND.
CHUFF
CHUFF
CHECK AGAIN, MY FRIEND.
CHUFF
CHUFF
CHUFF
PERFECTION IS ACHIEVED THROUGH THE BODY.
FAILURE COMES FROM FEAR.
AND MATE.
BUT WHY SO SHOCKED, MY FRIEND? YOU'VE LOST MATCHES BEFORE.
THE ALARM, SANTOS.
SOMEBODY SET OFF THE SILENT ALARM.
GINO! EDDIE! SOMEBODY'S INSIDE!
18

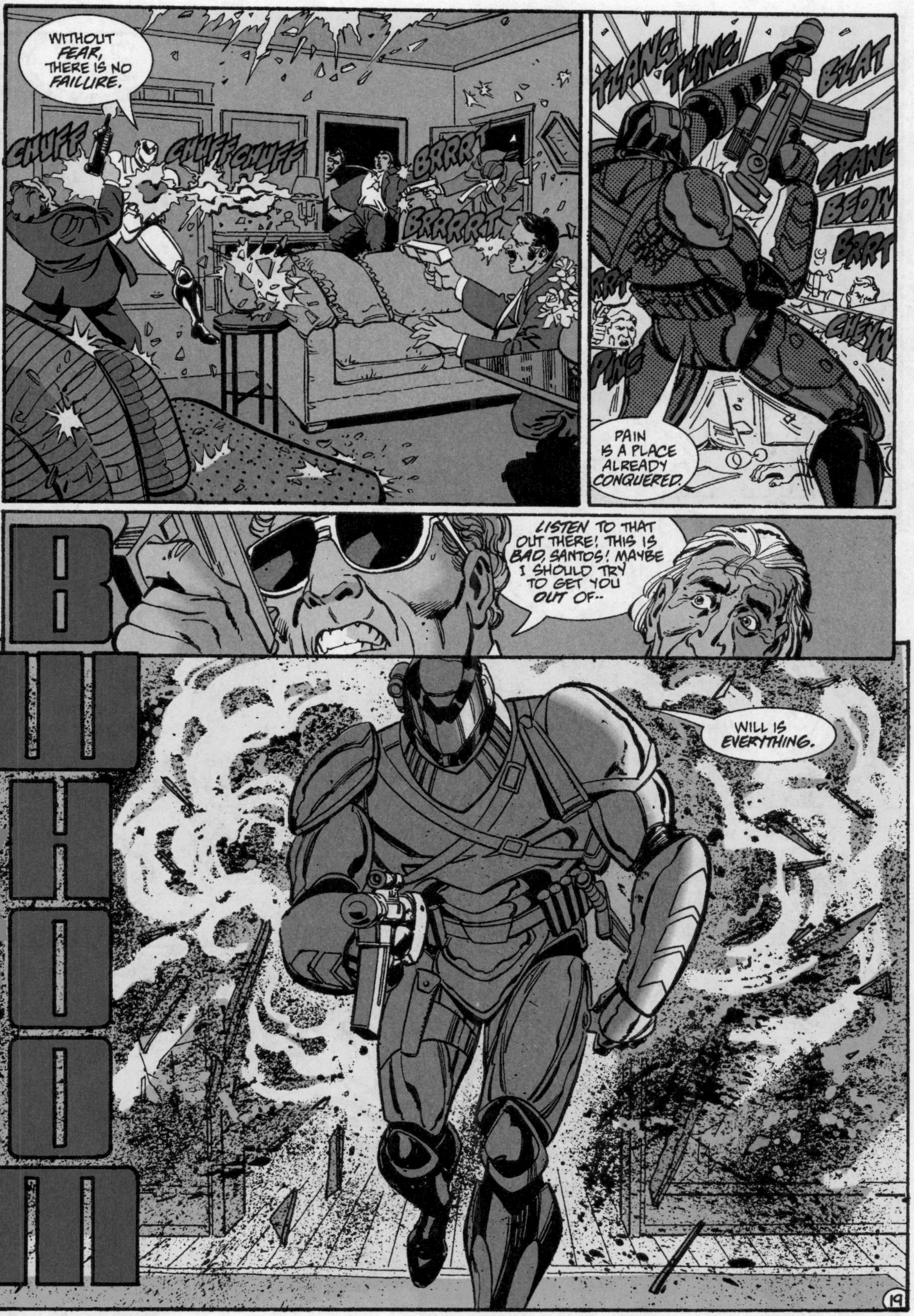

WITHOUT FEAR, THERE IS NO FAILURE.
CHUFF
CHUFF CHUFF CHUFF
BRRRT
BRRRRT
TLANG
TUNG
BLAT
SPANG
BEOW
BRRT
CHEW
PING
PAIN IS A PLACE ALREADY CONQUERED.
LISTEN TO THAT OUT THERE! THIS IS BAD, SANTOS! MAYBE I SHOULD TRY TO GET YOU OUT OF--
BWHOOM
WILL IS EVERYTHING.
19

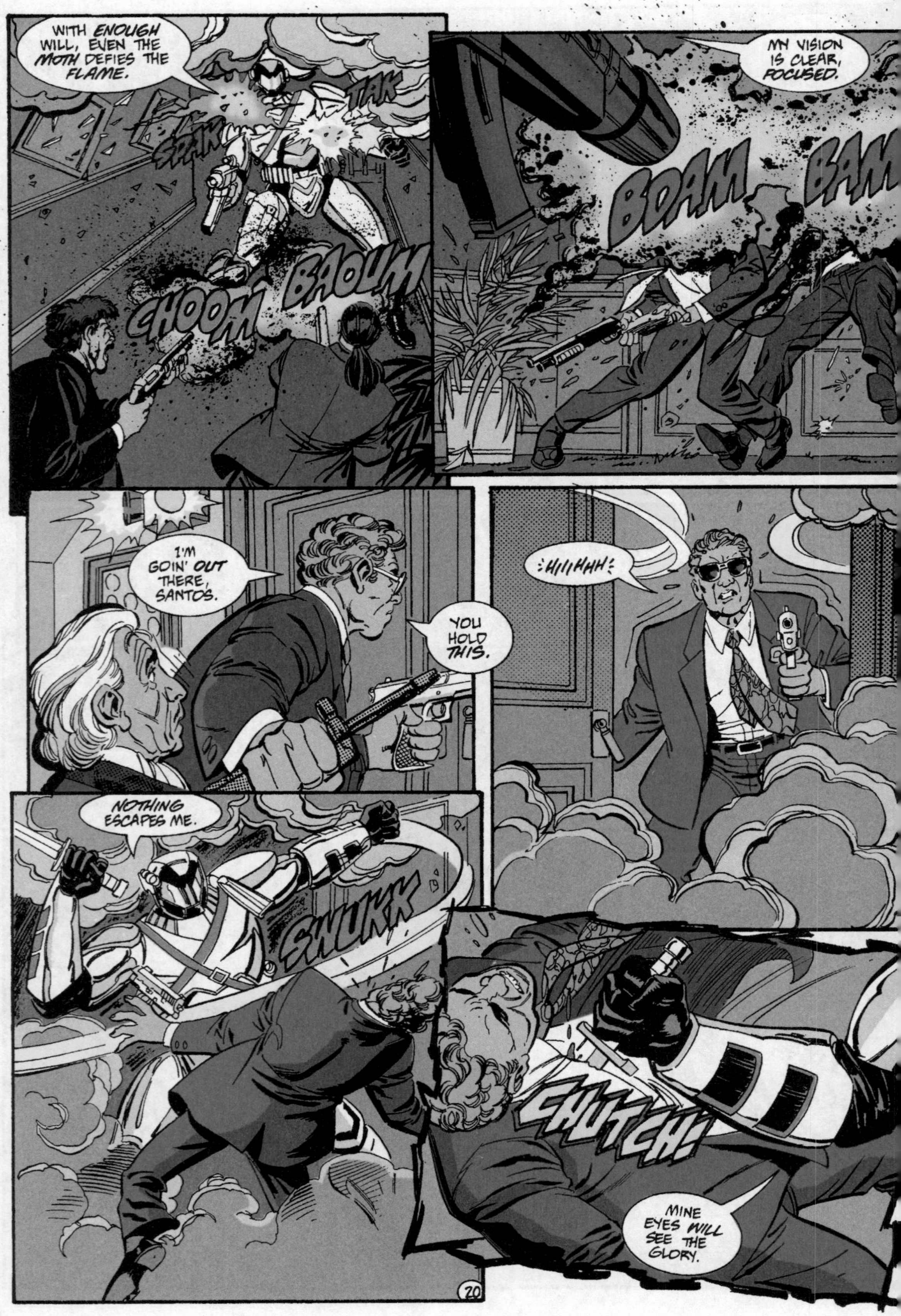
WITH ENOUGH WILL, EVEN THE MOTH DEFIES THE FLAME.
SPAK
TAK
CHOOM
BAOUM
MY VISION IS CLEAR, FOCUSED.
BOAM
BAM
I'M GOIN' OUT THERE, SANTOS.
YOU HOLD THIS.
HIIIHHH!
NOTHING ESCAPES ME.
SNUKK
CHUTCH!
MINE EYES WILL SEE THE GLORY.
20

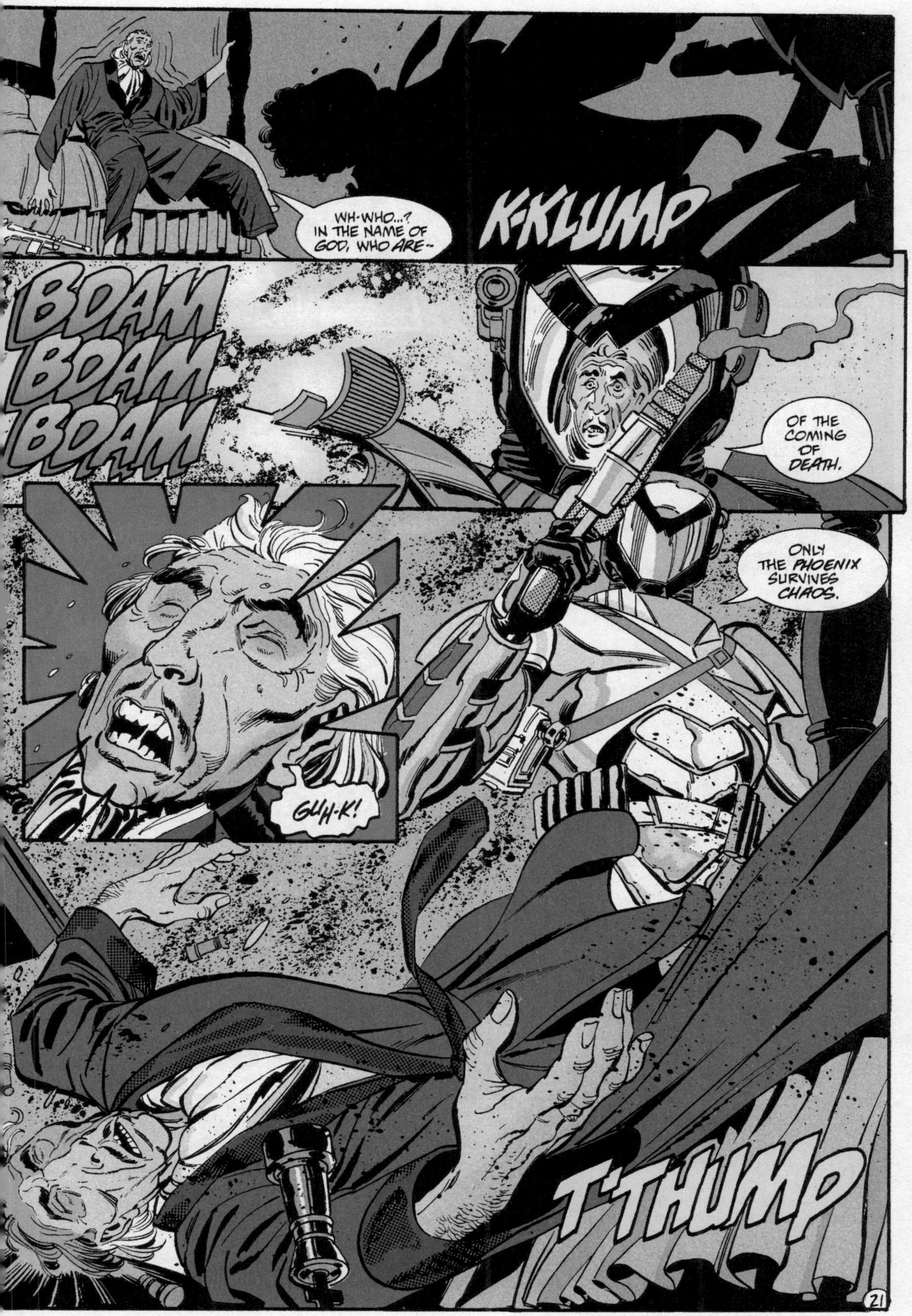
WH-WHO...? IN THE NAME OF GOD, WHO ARE--
K-KLUMP
BDAM BDAM BDAM
OF THE COMING OF DEATH.
ONLY THE PHOENIX SURVIVES CHAOS.
GUH-K!
T'THUMP
21

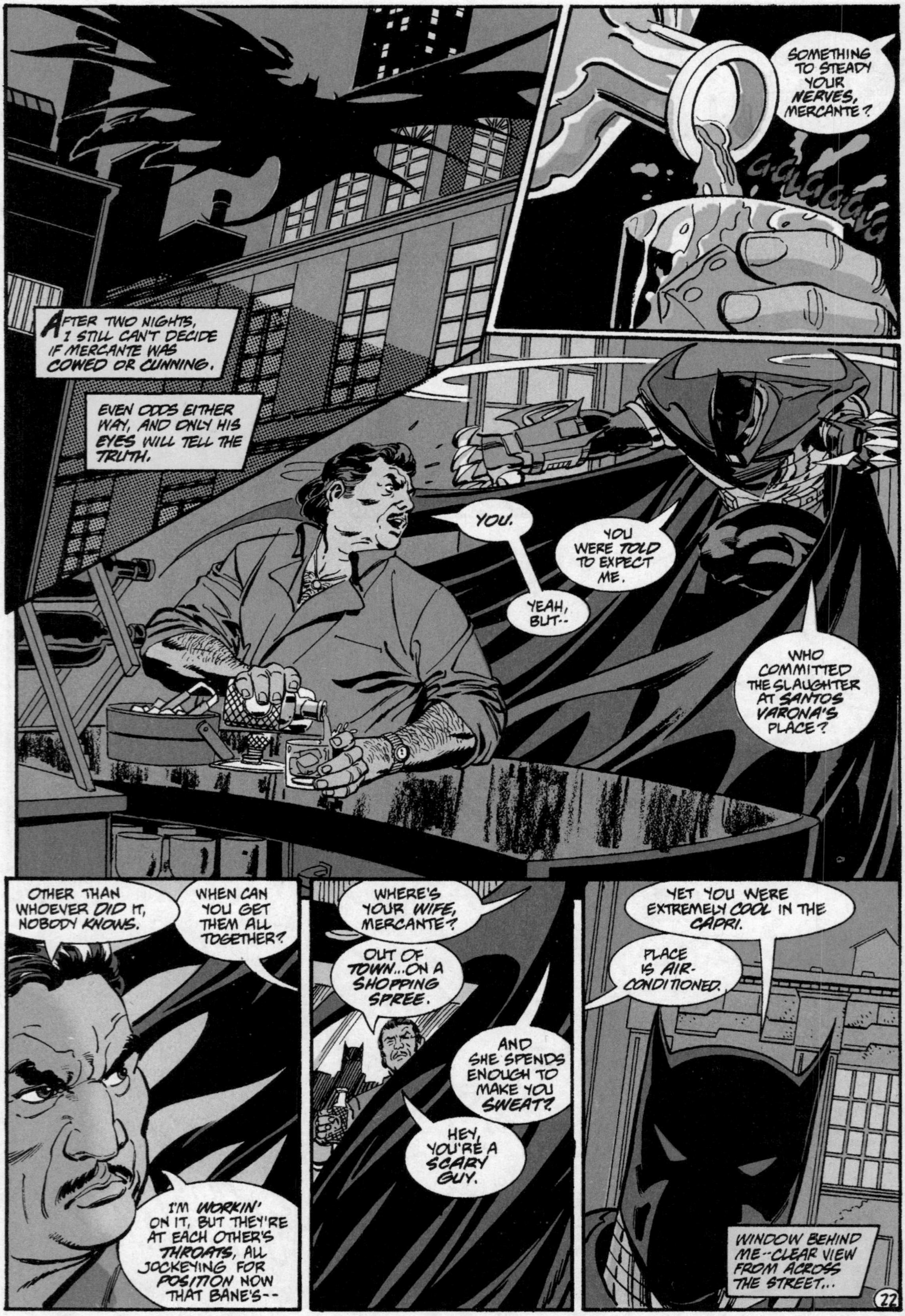
SOMETHING TO STEADY YOUR NERVES, MERCANTE?
GLUGGGGG
AFTER TWO NIGHTS, I STILL CAN'T DECIDE IF MERCANTE WAS COWED OR CUNNING.
EVEN ODDS EITHER WAY, AND ONLY HIS EYES WILL TELL THE TRUTH.
YOU.
YOU WERE TOLD TO EXPECT ME.
YEAH, BUT--
WHO COMMITTED THE SLAUGHTER AT SANTOS VARONA'S PLACE?
OTHER THAN WHOEVER DID IT, NOBODY KNOWS.
WHEN CAN YOU GET THEM ALL TOGETHER?
I'M WORKIN' ON IT, BUT THEY'RE AT EACH OTHER'S THROATS, ALL JOCKEYING FOR POSITION NOW THAT BANE'S--
WHERE'S YOUR WIFE, MERCANTE?
OUT OF TOWN...ON A SHOPPING SPREE.
AND SHE SPENDS ENOUGH TO MAKE YOU SWEAT?
HEY, YOU'RE A SCARY GUY.
YET YOU WERE EXTREMELY COOL IN THE CAPRI.
PLACE IS AIR-CONDITIONED.
WINDOW BEHIND ME--CLEAR VIEW FROM ACROSS THE STREET...
22

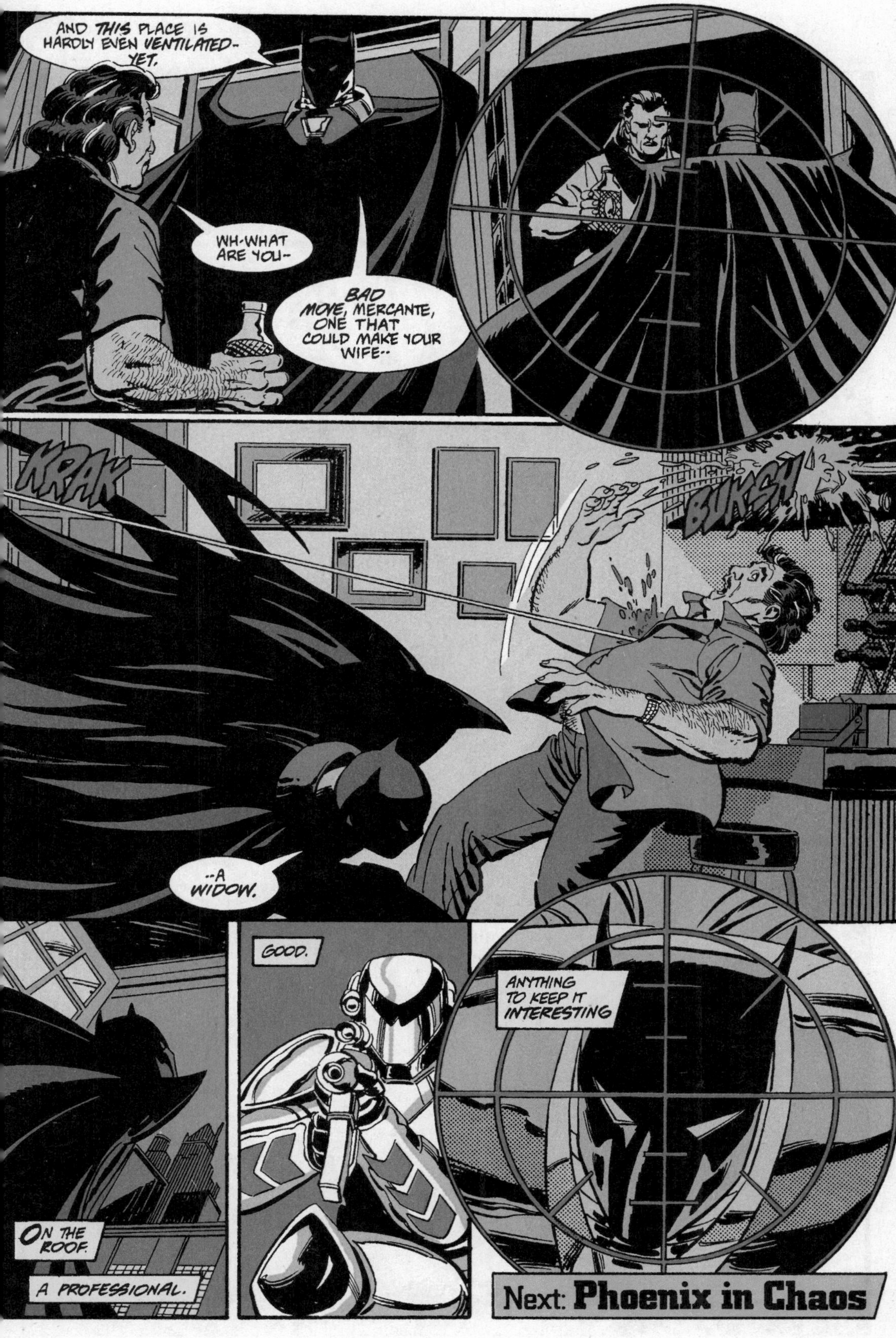
AND THIS PLACE IS HARDLY EVEN VENTILATED-- YET.
WH-WHAT ARE YOU--
BAD MOVE, MERCANTE, ONE THAT COULD MAKE YOUR WIFE--
KRAK
BUKSH
--A WIDOW.
ON THE ROOF.
A PROFESSIONAL.
GOOD.
ANYTHING TO KEEP IT INTERESTING
Next: Phoenix in Chaos

Cover art by KELLEY JONES

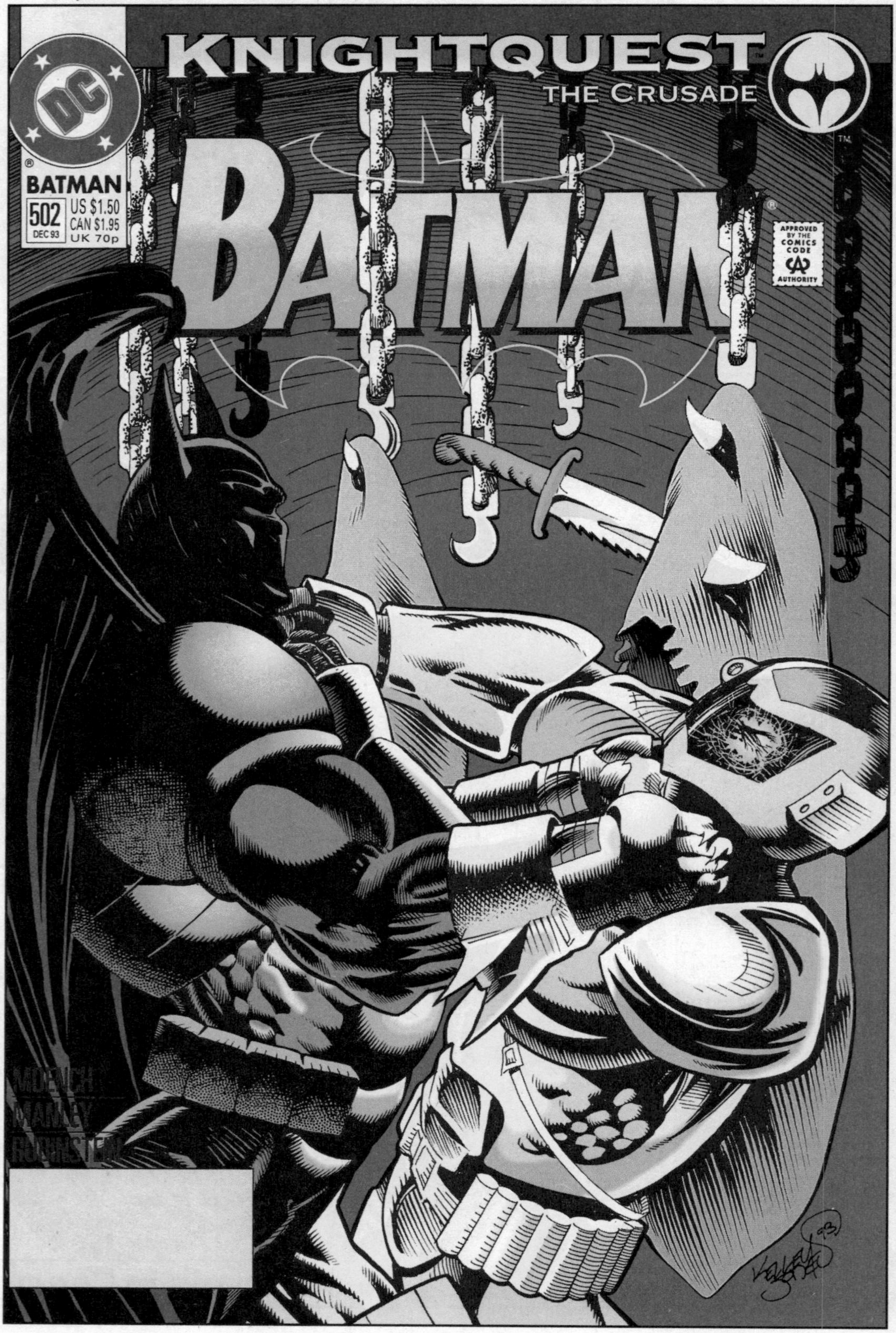
KNIGHTQUEST
THE CRUSADE
BATMAN
502
DEC 93
US $1.50
CAN $1.95
UK 70p
BATMAN
APPROVED BY THE COMICS CODE AUTHORITY
MOENCH
MANLEY
RUBINSTEIN

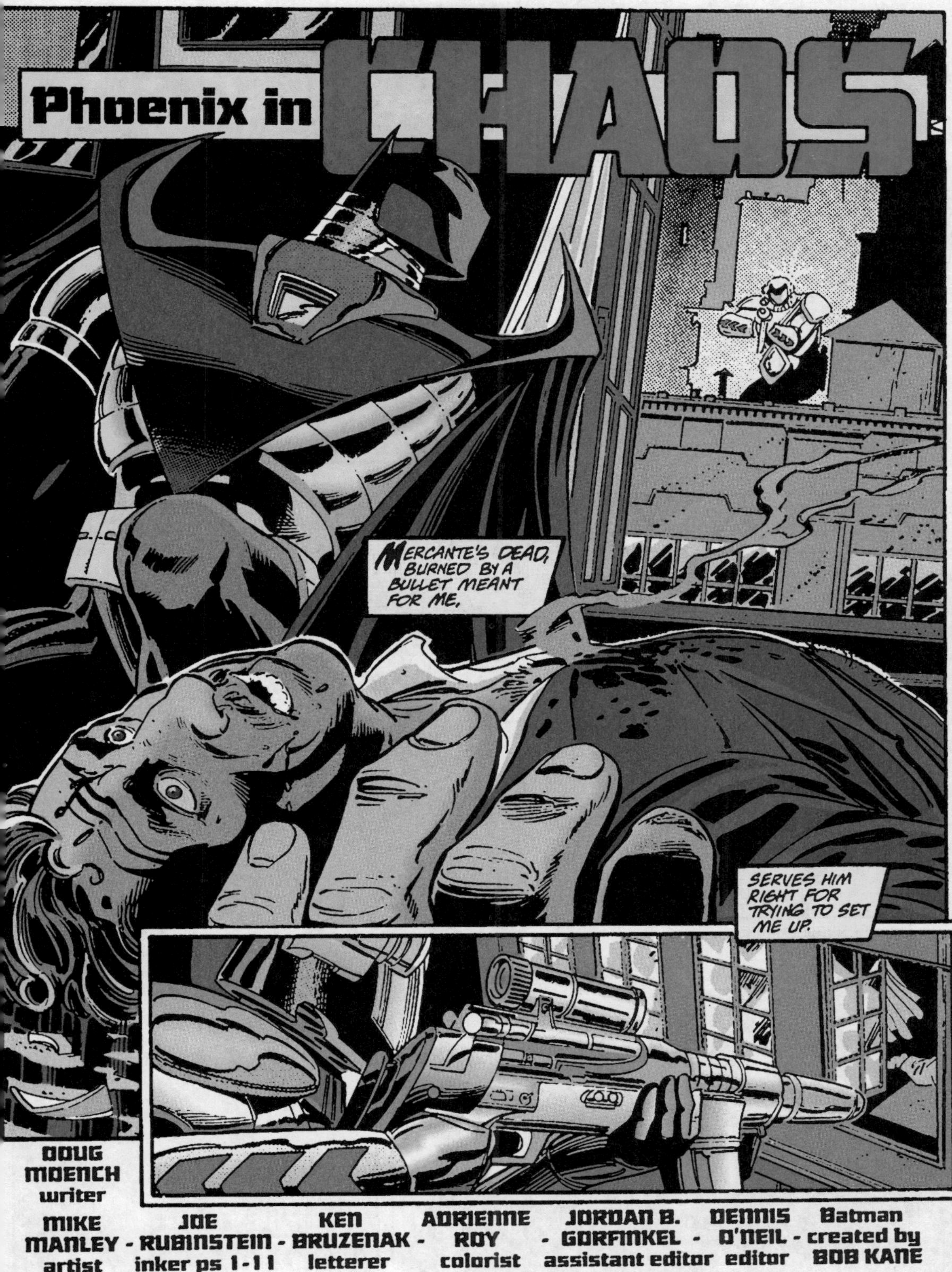
Phoenix in CHAOS
MERCANTE'S DEAD, BURNED BY A BULLET MEANT FOR ME.
SERVES HIM RIGHT FOR TRYING TO SET ME UP.

DOUG MOENCH writer

MIKE MANLEY - artist
JOE RUBINSTEIN - inker ps 1-11
KEN BRUZENAK - letterer
ADRIENNE ROY - colorist
JORDAN B. GORFINKEL - assistant editor
DENNIS O'NEIL - editor
Batman created by BOB KANE

ONLY THE PHOENIX SURVIVES CHAOS.

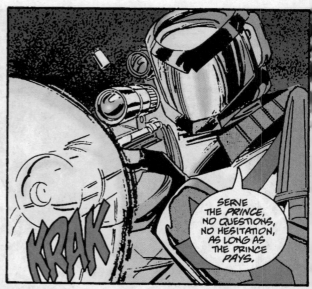

KRAK

SERVE THE PRINCE, NO QUESTIONS, NO HESITATION, AS LONG AS THE PRINCE PAYS.

RIGHT THROUGH THE "HEART."

SP TAK

TIME TO "FALL."

LIGHT...

...OFF.

AND NOW THAT I'M "DEAD"...

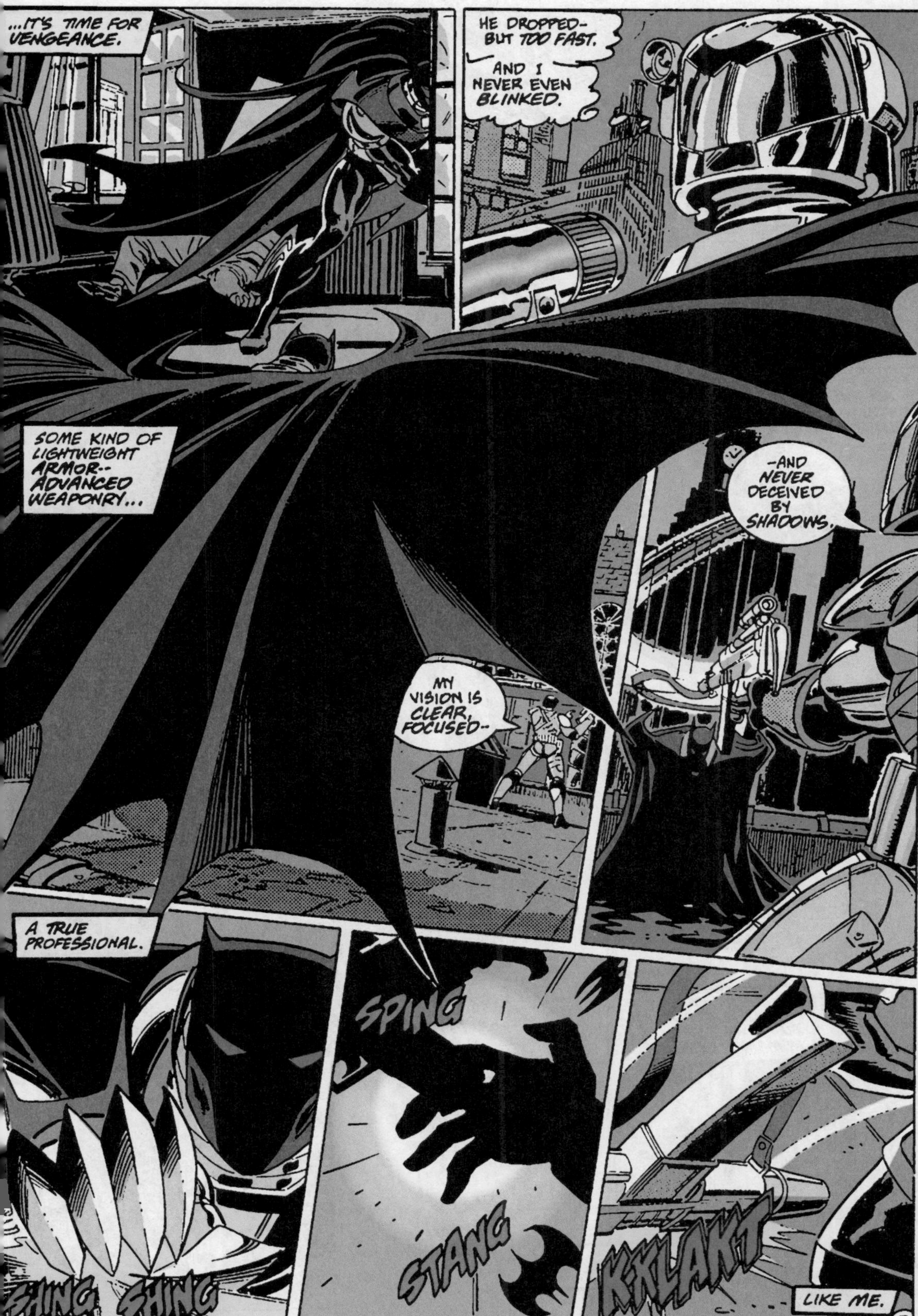
...IT'S TIME FOR VENGEANCE.
HE DROPPED-- BUT TOO FAST.
AND I NEVER EVEN BLINKED.
SOME KIND OF LIGHTWEIGHT ARMOR-- ADVANCED WEAPONRY...
-AND NEVER DECEIVED BY SHADOWS.
MY VISION IS CLEAR, FOCUSED-
A TRUE PROFESSIONAL.
SHING SHING
SPING
STANG
KKLAKT
LIKE ME.
3

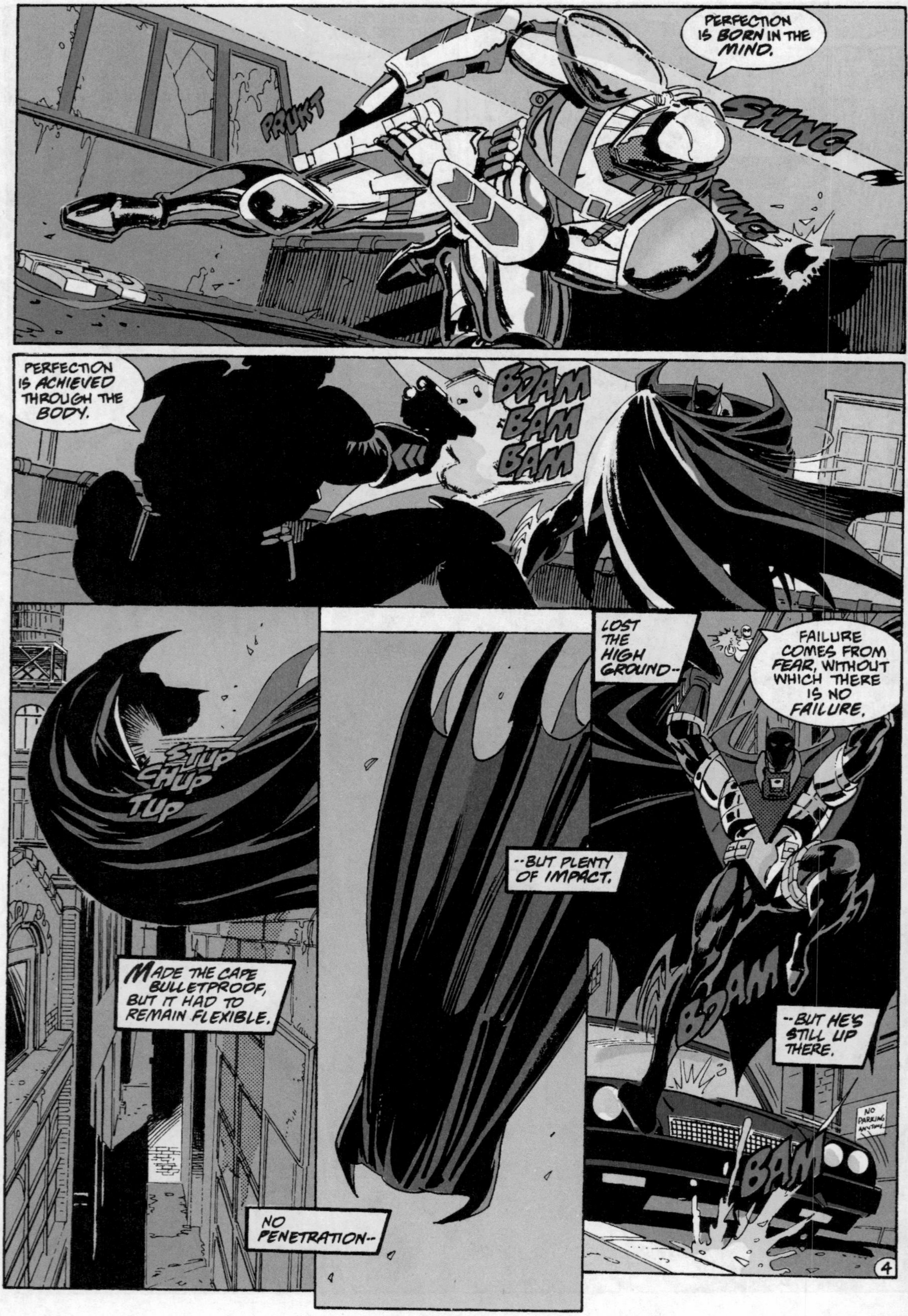
PERFECTION IS BORN IN THE MIND.
PRUKT
SHING
SHING
PERFECTION IS ACHIEVED THROUGH THE BODY.
BDAM BAM BAM
STUP CHUP TUP
MADE THE CAPE BULLETPROOF, BUT IT HAD TO REMAIN FLEXIBLE.
NO PENETRATION--
--BUT PLENTY OF IMPACT.
LOST THE HIGH GROUND--
FAILURE COMES FROM FEAR, WITHOUT WHICH THERE IS NO FAILURE.
BDAM
--BUT HE'S STILL UP THERE.
NO PARKING ANYTIME
BAM
4

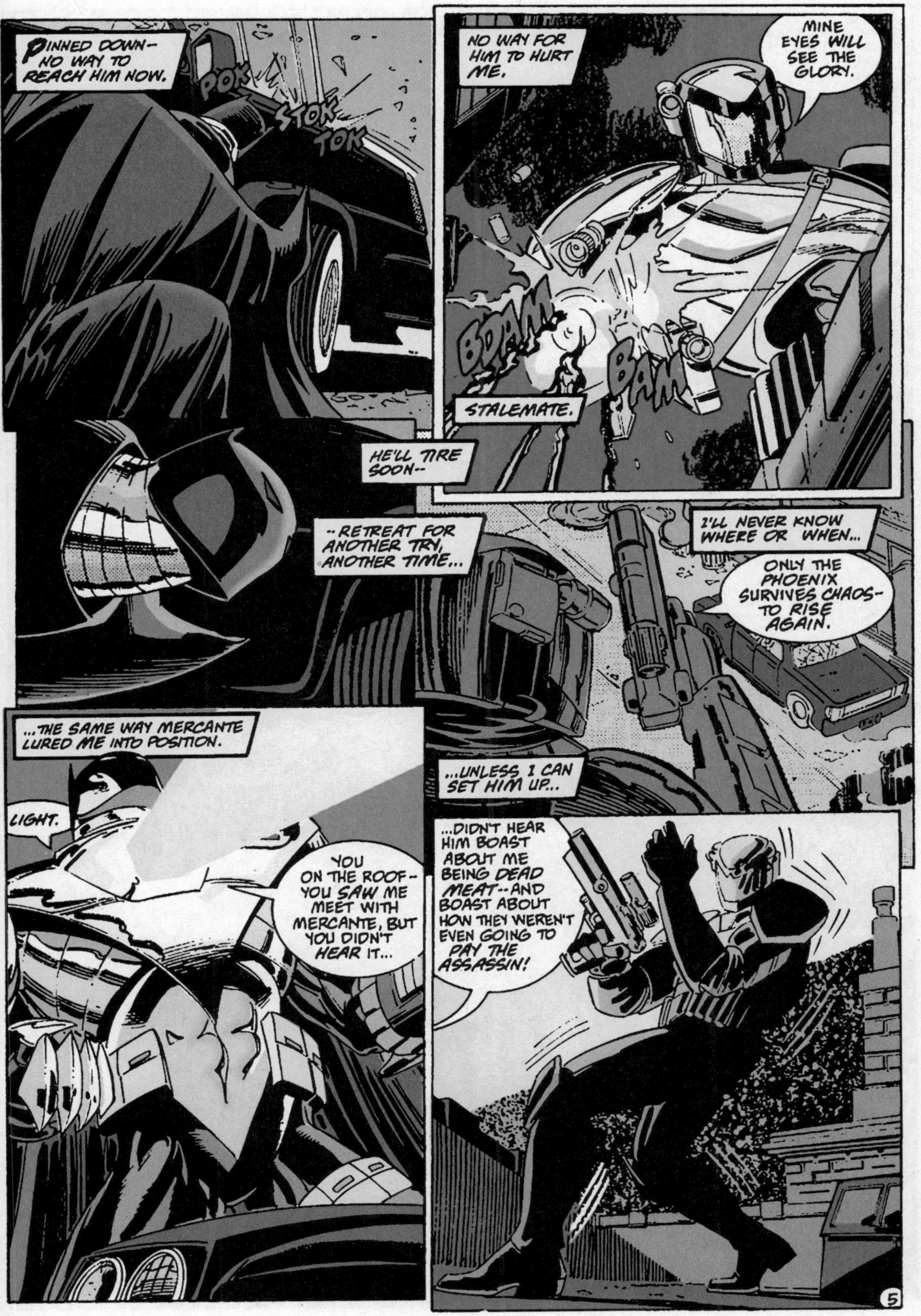
PINNED DOWN-- NO WAY TO REACH HIM NOW.
POK
STOK
TOK
NO WAY FOR HIM TO HURT ME.
MINE EYES WILL SEE THE GLORY.
BDAM
BAM
STALEMATE.
HE'LL TIRE SOON--
--RETREAT FOR ANOTHER TRY, ANOTHER TIME...
I'LL NEVER KNOW WHERE OR WHEN...
ONLY THE PHOENIX SURVIVES CHAOS-- TO RISE AGAIN.
...UNLESS I CAN SET HIM UP...
...THE SAME WAY MERCANTE LURED ME INTO POSITION.
LIGHT.
YOU ON THE ROOF-- YOU SAW ME MEET WITH MERCANTE, BUT YOU DIDN'T HEAR IT...
...DIDN'T HEAR HIM BOAST ABOUT ME BEING DEAD MEAT--AND BOAST ABOUT HOW THEY WEREN'T EVEN GOING TO PAY THE ASSASSIN!
5

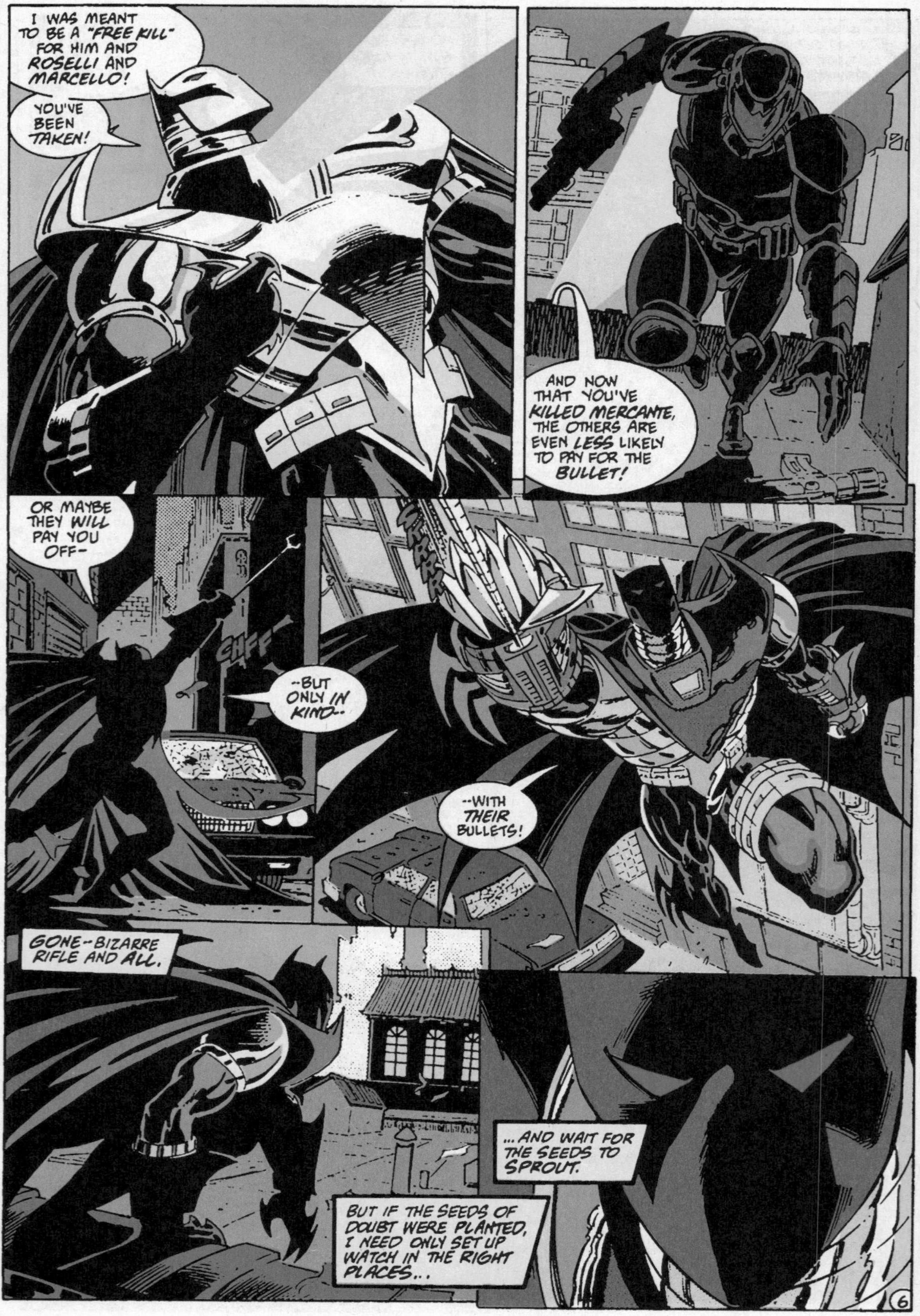

I WAS MEANT TO BE A "FREE KILL" FOR HIM AND ROSELLI AND MARCELLO!
YOU'VE BEEN TAKEN!
AND NOW THAT YOU'VE KILLED MERCANTE, THE OTHERS ARE EVEN LESS LIKELY TO PAY FOR THE BULLET!
OR MAYBE THEY WILL PAY YOU OFF-
CHFF
--BUT ONLY IN KIND--
--WITH THEIR BULLETS!
GONE--BIZARRE RIFLE AND ALL.
BUT IF THE SEEDS OF DOUBT WERE PLANTED, I NEED ONLY SET UP WATCH IN THE RIGHT PLACES...
...AND WAIT FOR THE SEEDS TO SPROUT.
6

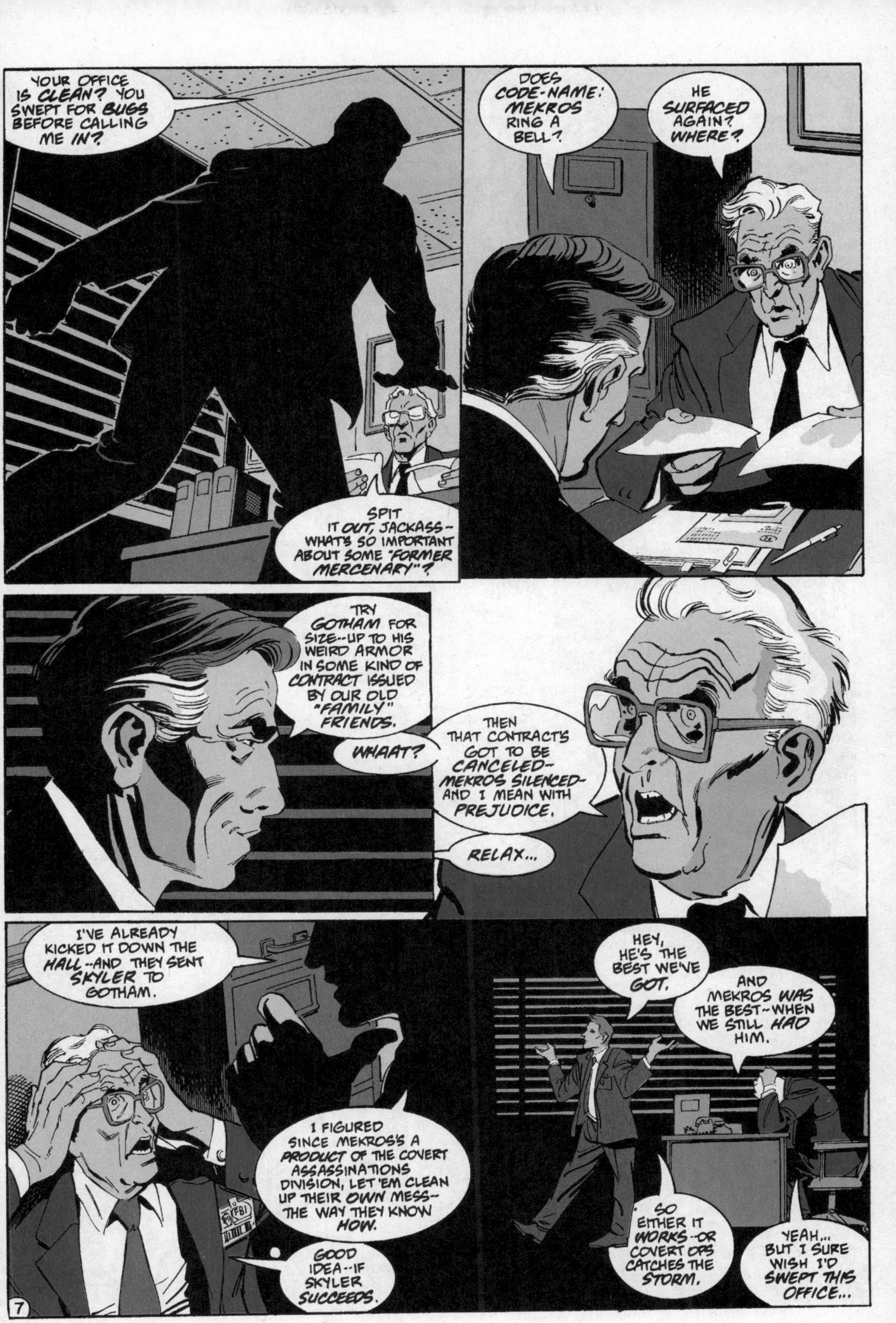
YOUR OFFICE IS CLEAN? YOU SWEPT FOR BUGS BEFORE CALLING ME IN?
SPIT IT OUT, JACKASS-- WHAT'S SO IMPORTANT ABOUT SOME "FORMER MERCENARY"?
DOES CODE-NAME: MEKROS RING A BELL?
HE SURFACED AGAIN? WHERE?
TRY GOTHAM FOR SIZE--UP TO HIS WEIRD ARMOR IN SOME KIND OF CONTRACT ISSUED BY OUR OLD "FAMILY" FRIENDS.
WHAAT?
THEN THAT CONTRACT'S GOT TO BE CANCELED-- MEKROS SILENCED-- AND I MEAN WITH PREJUDICE.
RELAX...
I'VE ALREADY KICKED IT DOWN THE HALL--AND THEY SENT SKYLER TO GOTHAM.
I FIGURED SINCE MEKROS'S A PRODUCT OF THE COVERT ASSASSINATIONS DIVISION, LET 'EM CLEAN UP THEIR OWN MESS-- THE WAY THEY KNOW HOW.
GOOD IDEA--IF SKYLER SUCCEEDS.
FBI
HEY, HE'S THE BEST WE'VE GOT.
AND MEKROS WAS THE BEST--WHEN WE STILL HAD HIM.
SO EITHER IT WORKS--OR COVERT OPS CATCHES THE STORM.
YEAH... BUT I SURE WISH I'D SWEPT THIS OFFICE...
7

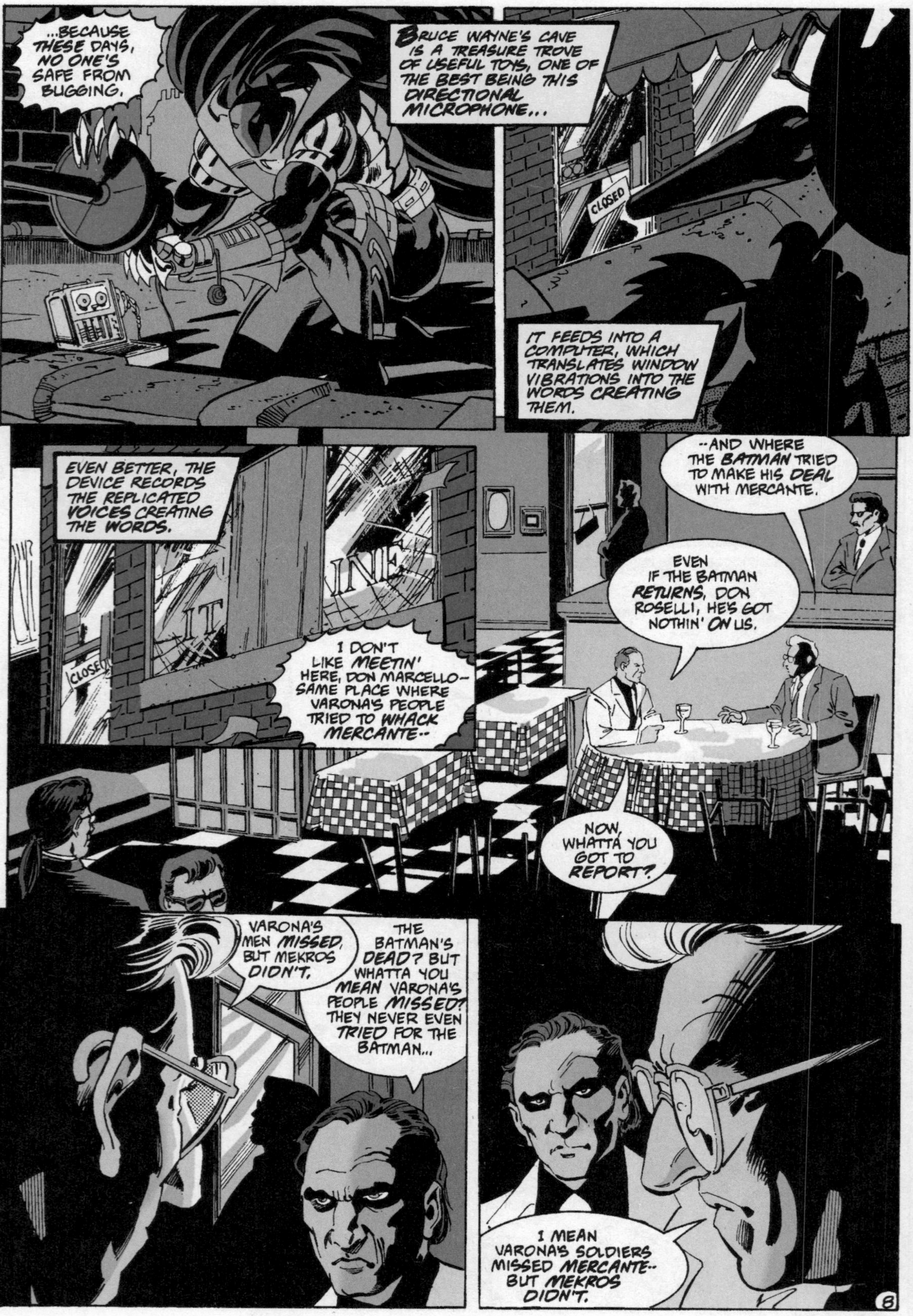
...BECAUSE THESE DAYS, NO ONE'S SAFE FROM BUGGING.
BRUCE WAYNE'S CAVE IS A TREASURE TROVE OF USEFUL TOYS, ONE OF THE BEST BEING THIS DIRECTIONAL MICROPHONE...
CLOSED
IT FEEDS INTO A COMPUTER, WHICH TRANSLATES WINDOW VIBRATIONS INTO THE WORDS CREATING THEM.
EVEN BETTER, THE DEVICE RECORDS THE REPLICATED VOICES CREATING THE WORDS.
I DON'T LIKE MEETIN' HERE, DON MARCELLO-- SAME PLACE WHERE VARONA'S PEOPLE TRIED TO WHACK MERCANTE--
--AND WHERE THE BATMAN TRIED TO MAKE HIS DEAL WITH MERCANTE.
EVEN IF THE BATMAN RETURNS, DON ROSELLI, HE'S GOT NOTHIN' ON US.
NOW, WHATTA YOU GOT TO REPORT?
VARONA'S MEN MISSED, BUT MEKROS DIDN'T.
THE BATMAN'S DEAD? BUT WHATTA YOU MEAN VARONA'S PEOPLE MISSED? THEY NEVER EVEN TRIED FOR THE BATMAN...
I MEAN VARONA'S SOLDIERS MISSED MERCANTE-- BUT MEKROS DIDN'T.
8

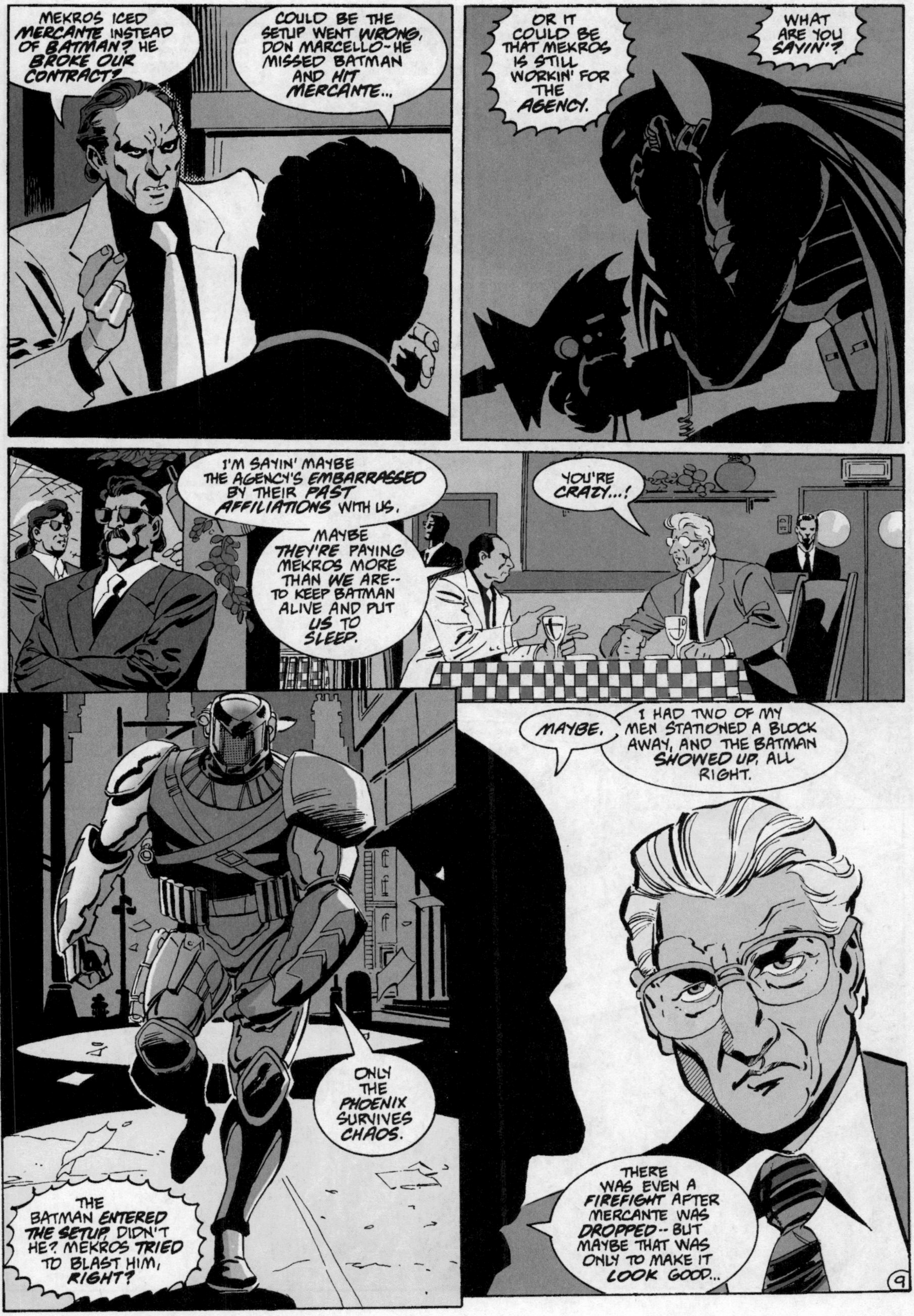
MEKROS ICED MERCANTE INSTEAD OF BATMAN? HE BROKE OUR CONTRACT?
COULD BE THE SETUP WENT WRONG, DON MARCELLO-- HE MISSED BATMAN AND HIT MERCANTE...
OR IT COULD BE THAT MEKROS IS STILL WORKIN' FOR THE AGENCY.
WHAT ARE YOU SAYIN'?
I'M SAYIN' MAYBE THE AGENCY'S EMBARRASSED BY THEIR PAST AFFILIATIONS WITH US.
MAYBE THEY'RE PAYING MEKROS MORE THAN WE ARE-- TO KEEP BATMAN ALIVE AND PUT US TO SLEEP.
YOU'RE CRAZY...!
MAYBE.
I HAD TWO OF MY MEN STATIONED A BLOCK AWAY, AND THE BATMAN SHOWED UP, ALL RIGHT.
ONLY THE PHOENIX SURVIVES CHAOS.
THE BATMAN ENTERED THE SETUP, DIDN'T HE? MEKROS TRIED TO BLAST HIM, RIGHT?
THERE WAS EVEN A FIREFIGHT AFTER MERCANTE WAS DROPPED-- BUT MAYBE THAT WAS ONLY TO MAKE IT LOOK GOOD...
9

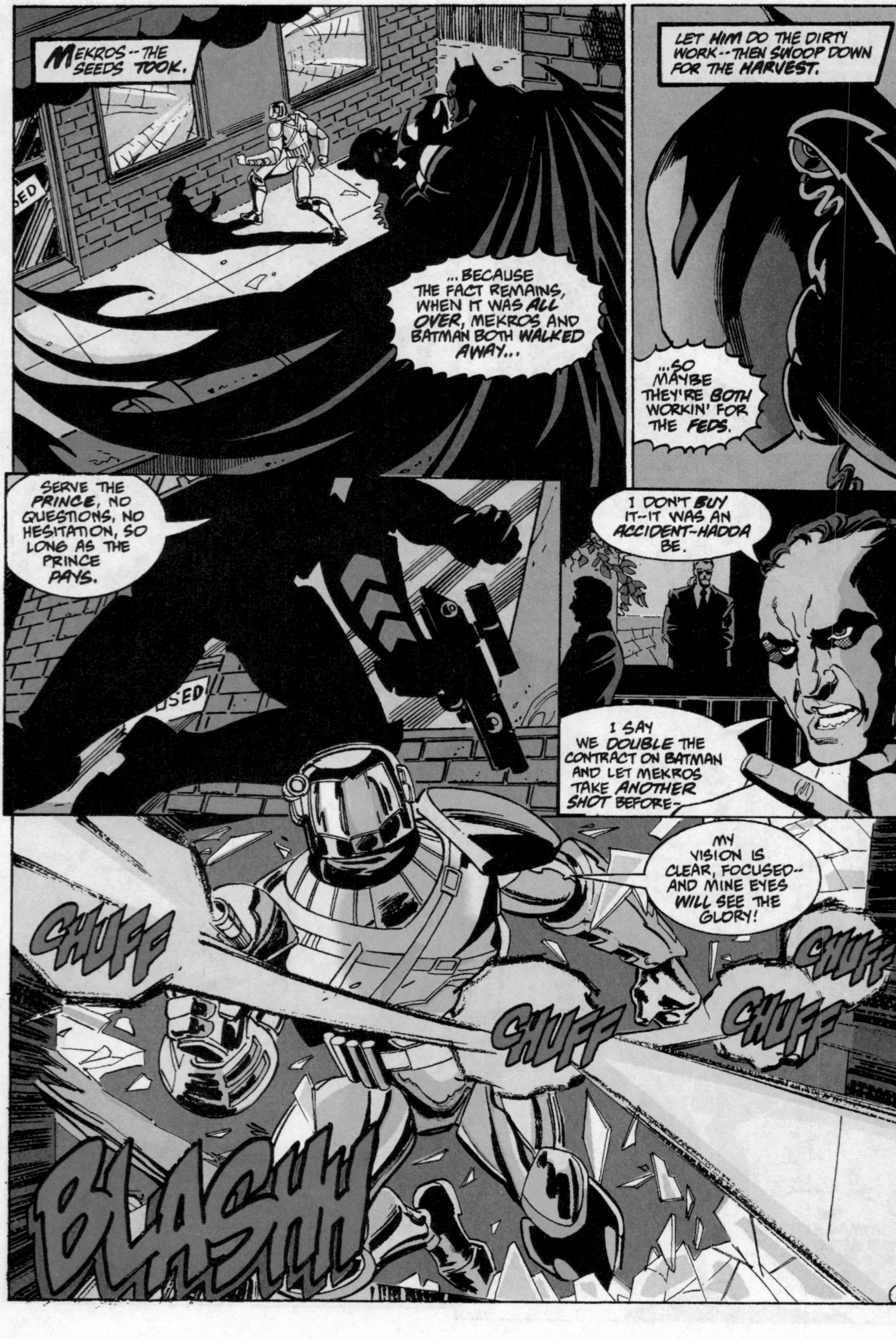
MEKROS--THE SEEDS TOOK.
...BECAUSE THE FACT REMAINS, WHEN IT WAS ALL OVER, MEKROS AND BATMAN BOTH WALKED AWAY...
LET HIM DO THE DIRTY WORK--THEN SWOOP DOWN FOR THE HARVEST.
...SO MAYBE THEY'RE BOTH WORKIN' FOR THE FEDS.
SERVE THE PRINCE, NO QUESTIONS, NO HESITATION, SO LONG AS THE PRINCE PAYS.
SED
I DON'T BUY IT--IT WAS AN ACCIDENT--HADDA BE.
I SAY WE DOUBLE THE CONTRACT ON BATMAN AND LET MEKROS TAKE ANOTHER SHOT BEFORE--
MY VISION IS CLEAR, FOCUSED-- AND MINE EYES WILL SEE THE GLORY!
CHUFF
CHUFF
CHUFF
CHUFF
BLASH
10

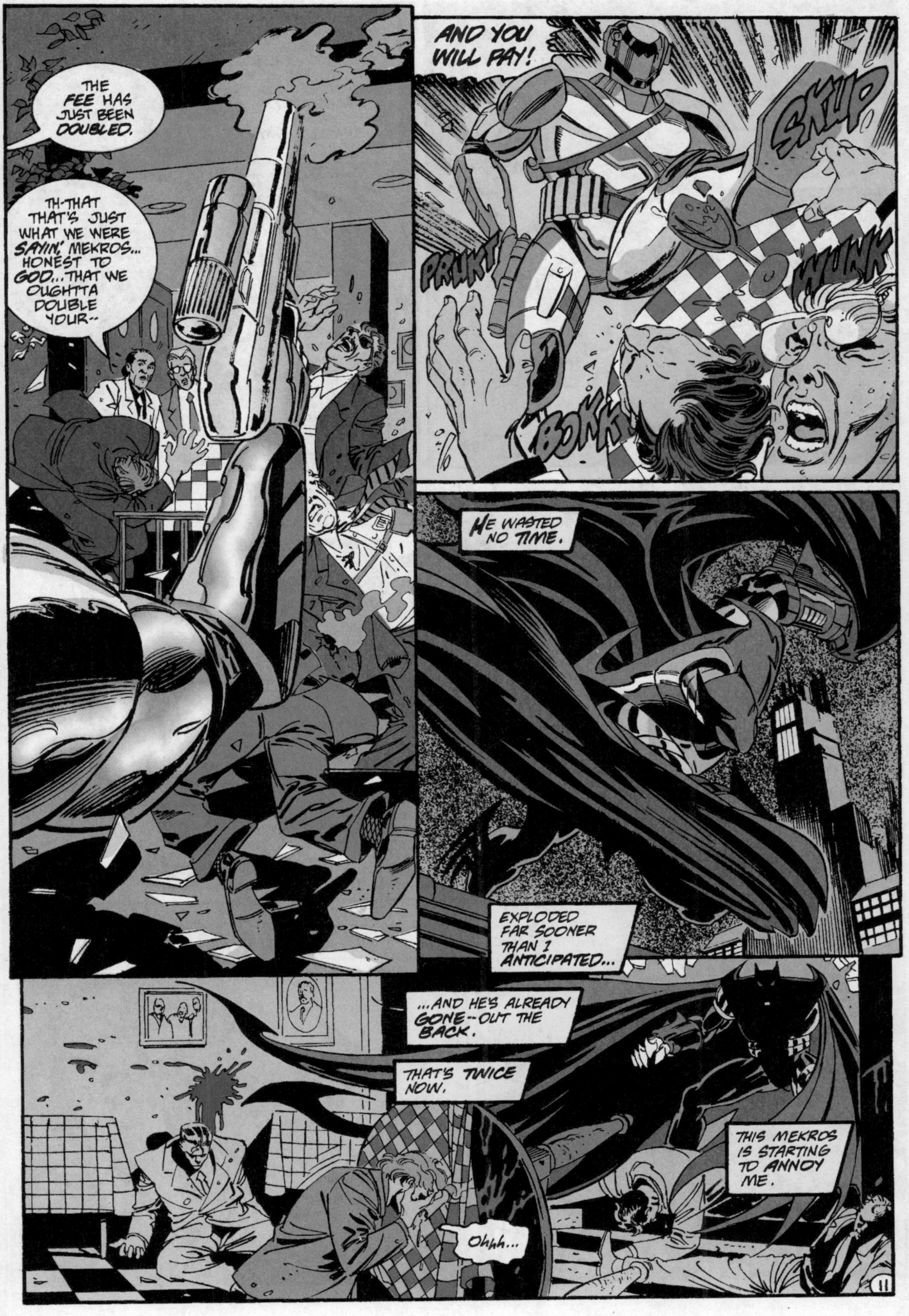
THE FEE HAS JUST BEEN DOUBLED.
TH-THAT THAT'S JUST WHAT WE WERE SAYIN', MEKROS... HONEST TO GOD...THAT WE OUGHTTA DOUBLE YOUR--
AND YOU WILL PAY!
SKUP
PRUKT
WUNK
BOKK
HE WASTED NO TIME.
EXPLODED FAR SOONER THAN I ANTICIPATED...
...AND HE'S ALREADY GONE--OUT THE BACK.
THAT'S TWICE NOW.
THIS MEKROS IS STARTING TO ANNOY ME.
Ohhh...
11

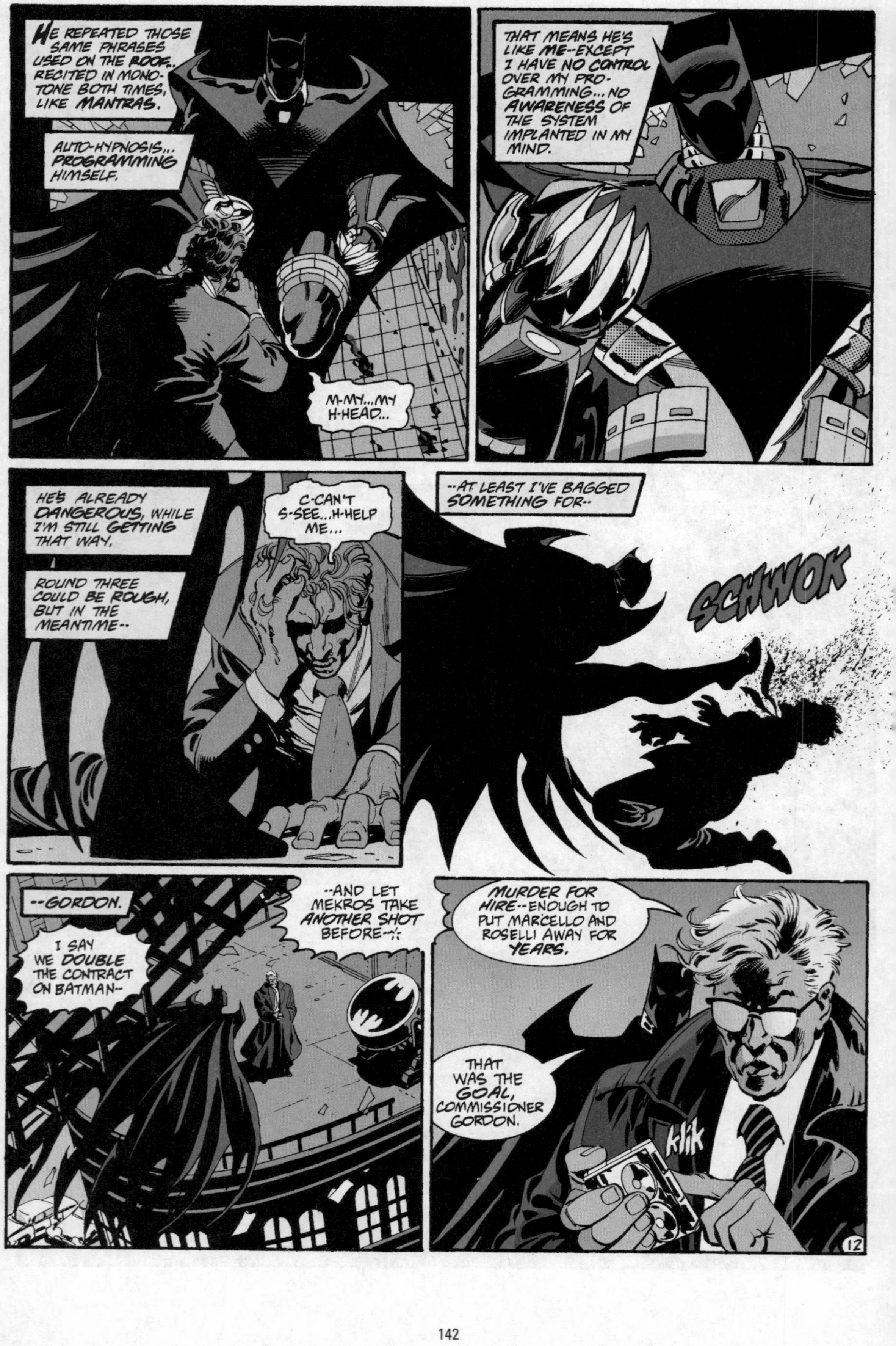
HE REPEATED THOSE SAME PHRASES USED ON THE ROOF.. RECITED IN MONOTONE BOTH TIMES, LIKE MANTRAS.
AUTO-HYPNOSIS... PROGRAMMING HIMSELF.
M-MY...MY H-HEAD...
THAT MEANS HE'S LIKE ME--EXCEPT I HAVE NO CONTROL OVER MY PROGRAMMING... NO AWARENESS OF THE SYSTEM IMPLANTED IN MY MIND.
HE'S ALREADY DANGEROUS, WHILE I'M STILL GETTING THAT WAY.
C-CAN'T S-SEE...H-HELP ME...
ROUND THREE COULD BE ROUGH, BUT IN THE MEANTIME--
--AT LEAST I'VE BAGGED SOMETHING FOR--
SCHWOK
--GORDON.
I SAY WE DOUBLE THE CONTRACT ON BATMAN--
--AND LET MEKROS TAKE ANOTHER SHOT BEFORE--
MURDER FOR HIRE--ENOUGH TO PUT MARCELLO AND ROSELLI AWAY FOR YEARS.
THAT WAS THE GOAL, COMMISSIONER GORDON.
klik
12

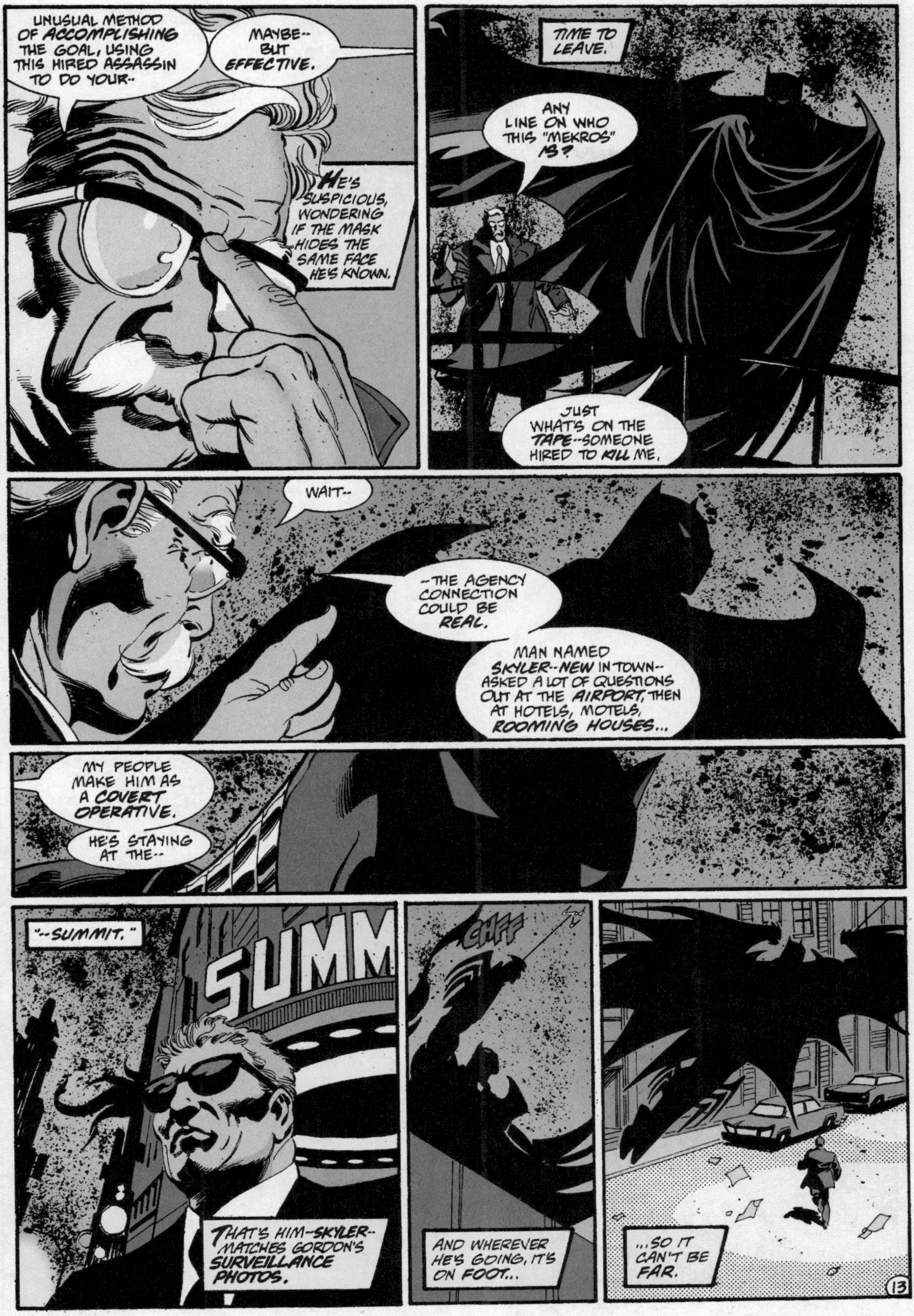
UNUSUAL METHOD OF ACCOMPLISHING THE GOAL, USING THIS HIRED ASSASSIN TO DO YOUR--
MAYBE-- BUT EFFECTIVE.
HE'S SUSPICIOUS, WONDERING IF THE MASK HIDES THE SAME FACE HE'S KNOWN.
TIME TO LEAVE.
ANY LINE ON WHO THIS "MEKROS" IS?
JUST WHAT'S ON THE TAPE--SOMEONE HIRED TO KILL ME.
WAIT--
--THE AGENCY CONNECTION COULD BE REAL.
MAN NAMED SKYLER--NEW IN TOWN--ASKED A LOT OF QUESTIONS OUT AT THE AIRPORT, THEN AT HOTELS, MOTELS, ROOMING HOUSES...
MY PEOPLE MAKE HIM AS A COVERT OPERATIVE.
HE'S STAYING AT THE--
"--SUMMIT."
SUMM
THAT'S HIM--SKYLER--MATCHES GORDON'S SURVEILLANCE PHOTOS.
CHFF
AND WHEREVER HE'S GOING, IT'S ON FOOT...
...SO IT CAN'T BE FAR.
13

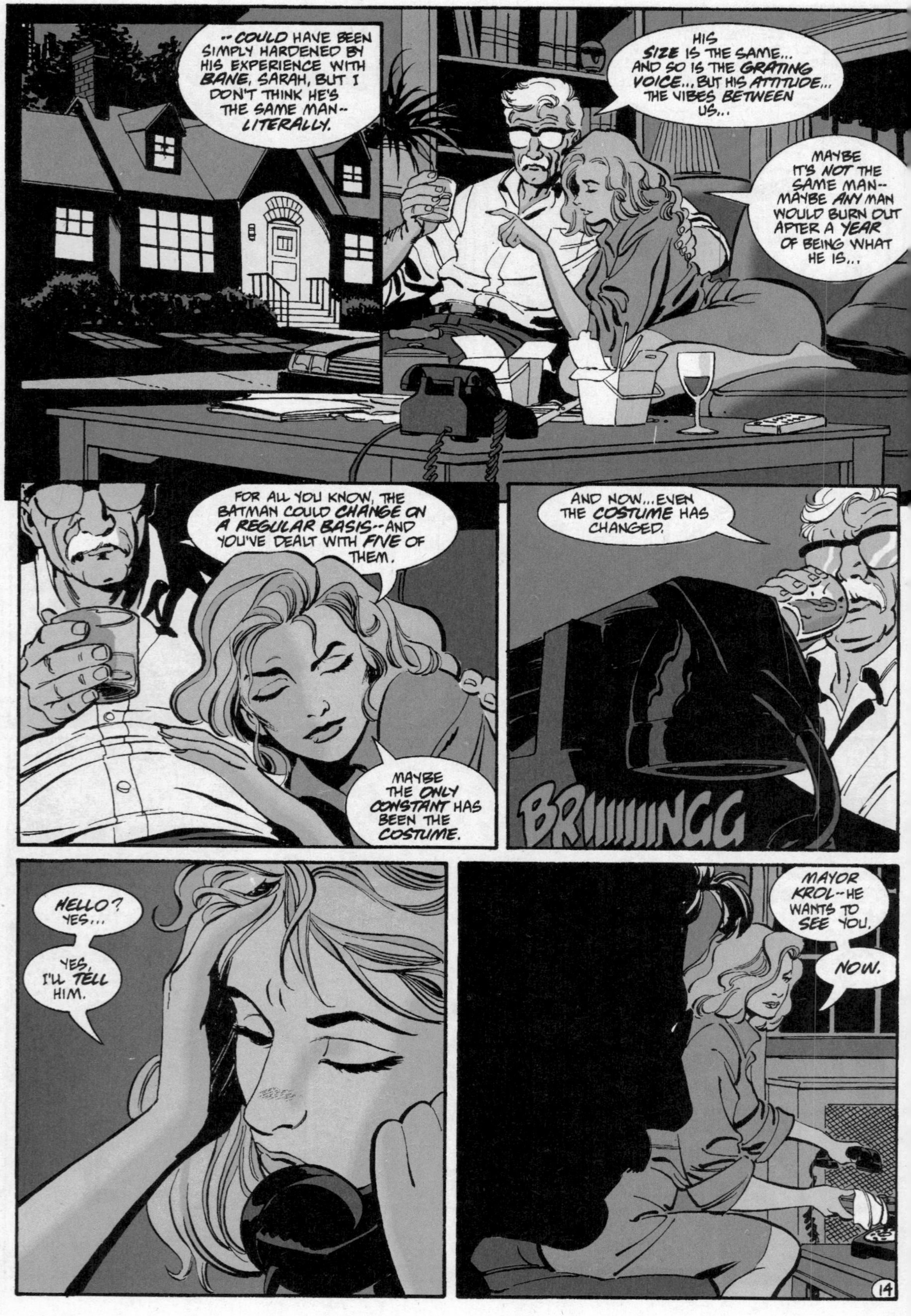
--COULD HAVE BEEN SIMPLY HARDENED BY HIS EXPERIENCE WITH BANE, SARAH, BUT I DON'T THINK HE'S THE SAME MAN-- LITERALLY.
HIS SIZE IS THE SAME... AND SO IS THE GRATING VOICE... BUT HIS ATTITUDE... THE VIBES BETWEEN US...
MAYBE IT'S NOT THE SAME MAN-- MAYBE ANY MAN WOULD BURN OUT AFTER A YEAR OF BEING WHAT HE IS...
FOR ALL YOU KNOW, THE BATMAN COULD CHANGE ON A REGULAR BASIS--AND YOU'VE DEALT WITH FIVE OF THEM.
MAYBE THE ONLY CONSTANT HAS BEEN THE COSTUME.
AND NOW... EVEN THE COSTUME HAS CHANGED.
BRIIIIIINGG
HELLO? YES...
YES, I'LL TELL HIM.
MAYOR KROL--HE WANTS TO SEE YOU.
NOW.
14

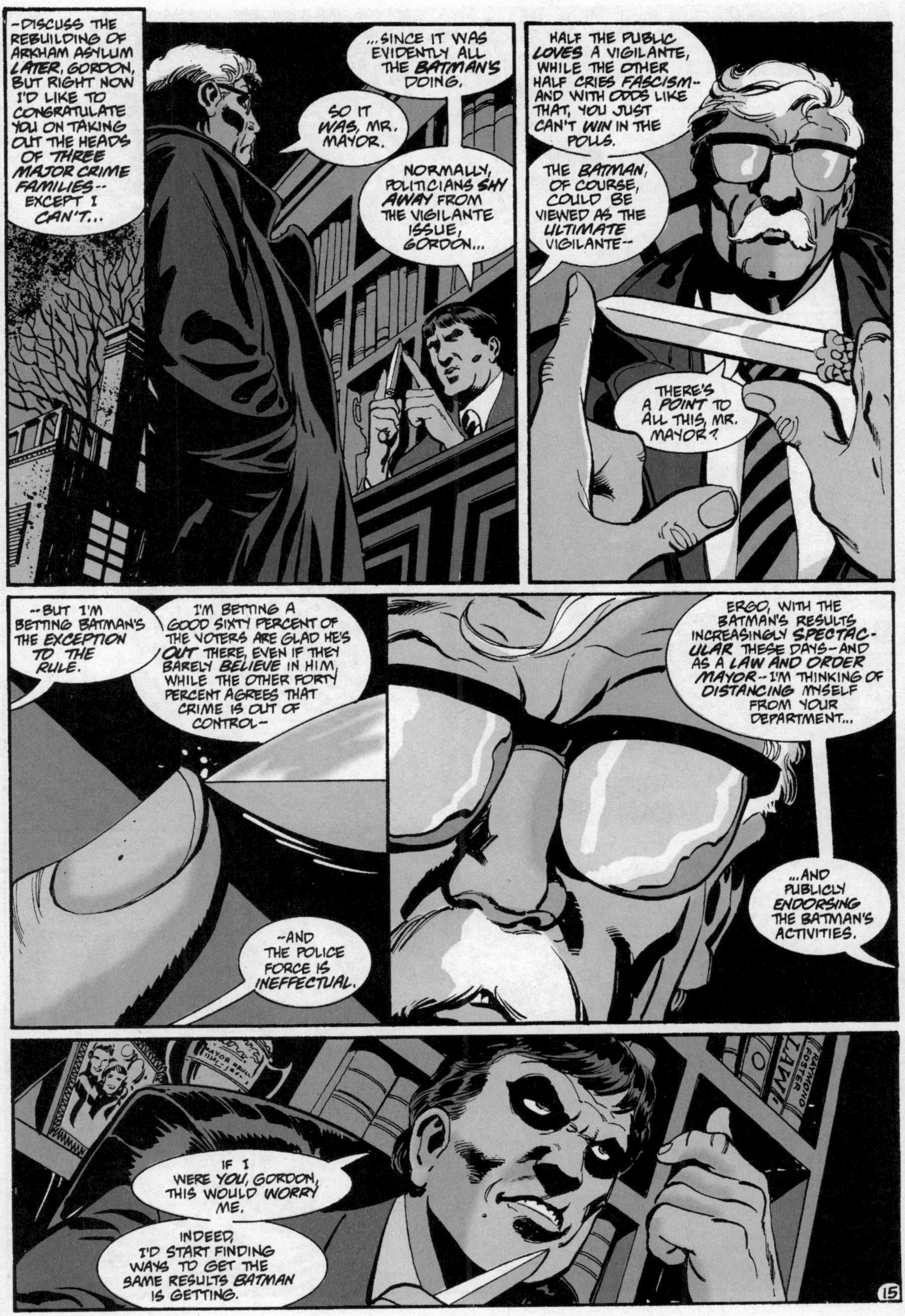
-DISCUSS THE REBUILDING OF ARKHAM ASYLUM LATER, GORDON, BUT RIGHT NOW I'D LIKE TO CONGRATULATE YOU ON TAKING OUT THE HEADS OF THREE MAJOR CRIME FAMILIES-- EXCEPT I CAN'T...
...SINCE IT WAS EVIDENTLY ALL THE BATMAN'S DOING.
SO IT WAS, MR. MAYOR.
NORMALLY, POLITICIANS SHY AWAY FROM THE VIGILANTE ISSUE, GORDON...
HALF THE PUBLIC LOVES A VIGILANTE, WHILE THE OTHER HALF CRIES FASCISM- AND WITH ODDS LIKE THAT, YOU JUST CAN'T WIN IN THE POLLS.
THE BATMAN, OF COURSE, COULD BE VIEWED AS THE ULTIMATE VIGILANTE--
THERE'S A POINT TO ALL THIS, MR. MAYOR?
--BUT I'M BETTING BATMAN'S THE EXCEPTION TO THE RULE.
I'M BETTING A GOOD SIXTY PERCENT OF THE VOTERS ARE GLAD HE'S OUT THERE, EVEN IF THEY BARELY BELIEVE IN HIM, WHILE THE OTHER FORTY PERCENT AGREES THAT CRIME IS OUT OF CONTROL-
--AND THE POLICE FORCE IS INEFFECTUAL.
ERGO, WITH THE BATMAN'S RESULTS INCREASINGLY SPECTACULAR THESE DAYS- AND AS A LAW AND ORDER MAYOR-- I'M THINKING OF DISTANCING MYSELF FROM YOUR DEPARTMENT...
...AND PUBLICLY ENDORSING THE BATMAN'S ACTIVITIES.
LAW
IF I WERE YOU, GORDON, THIS WOULD WORRY ME.
INDEED, I'D START FINDING WAYS TO GET THE SAME RESULTS BATMAN IS GETTING.
15

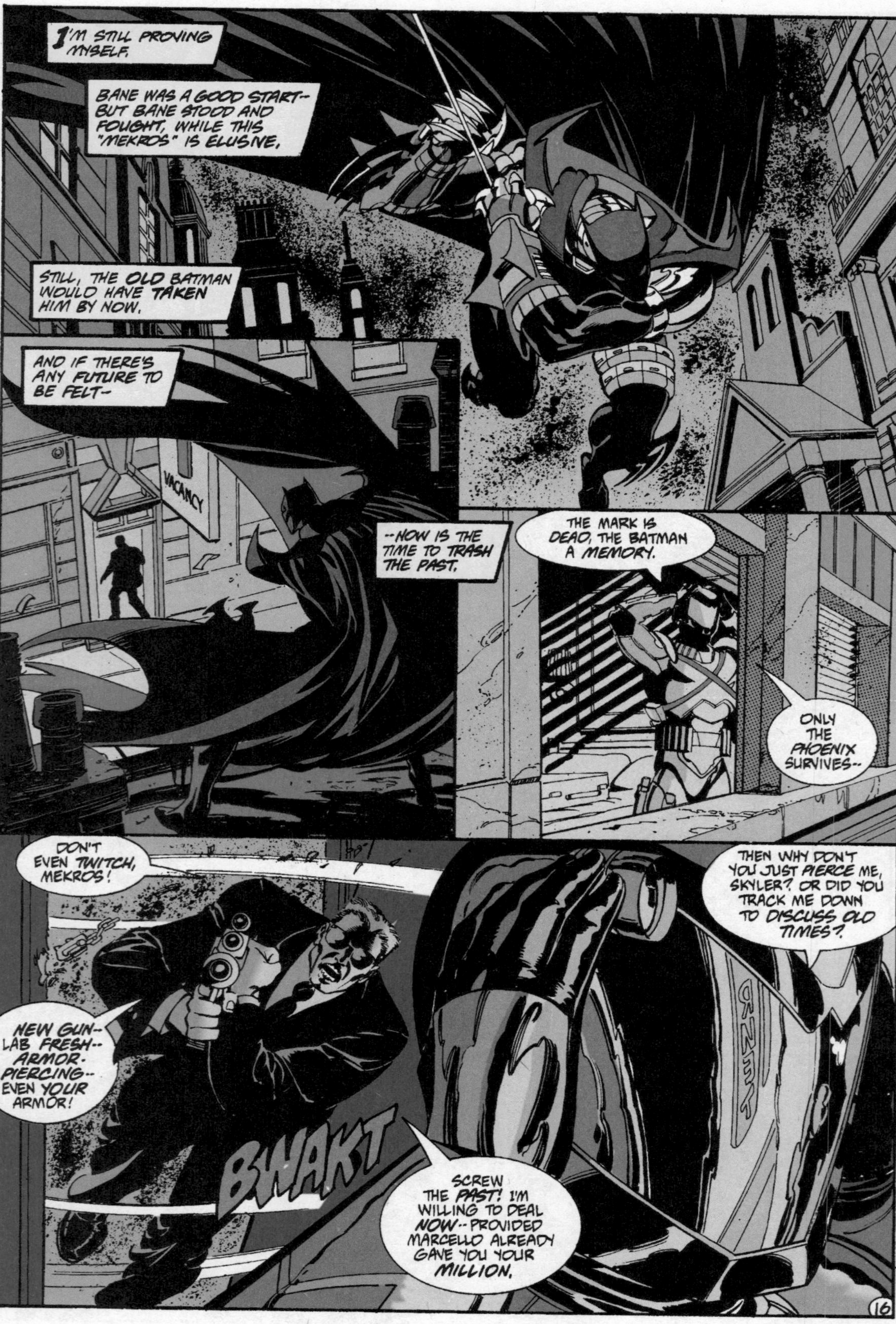
I'M STILL PROVING MYSELF.
BANE WAS A GOOD START-- BUT BANE STOOD AND FOUGHT, WHILE THIS "MEKROS" IS ELUSIVE.
STILL, THE OLD BATMAN WOULD HAVE TAKEN HIM BY NOW.
AND IF THERE'S ANY FUTURE TO BE FELT--
VACANCY
--NOW IS THE TIME TO TRASH THE PAST.
THE MARK IS DEAD, THE BATMAN A MEMORY.
ONLY THE PHOENIX SURVIVES--
DON'T EVEN TWITCH, MEKROS!
THEN WHY DON'T YOU JUST PIERCE ME, SKYLER? OR DID YOU TRACK ME DOWN TO DISCUSS OLD TIMES?
NEW GUN-- LAB FRESH-- ARMOR-PIERCING-- EVEN YOUR ARMOR!
BWAKT
SCREW THE PAST! I'M WILLING TO DEAL NOW--PROVIDED MARCELLO ALREADY GAVE YOU YOUR MILLION.
16

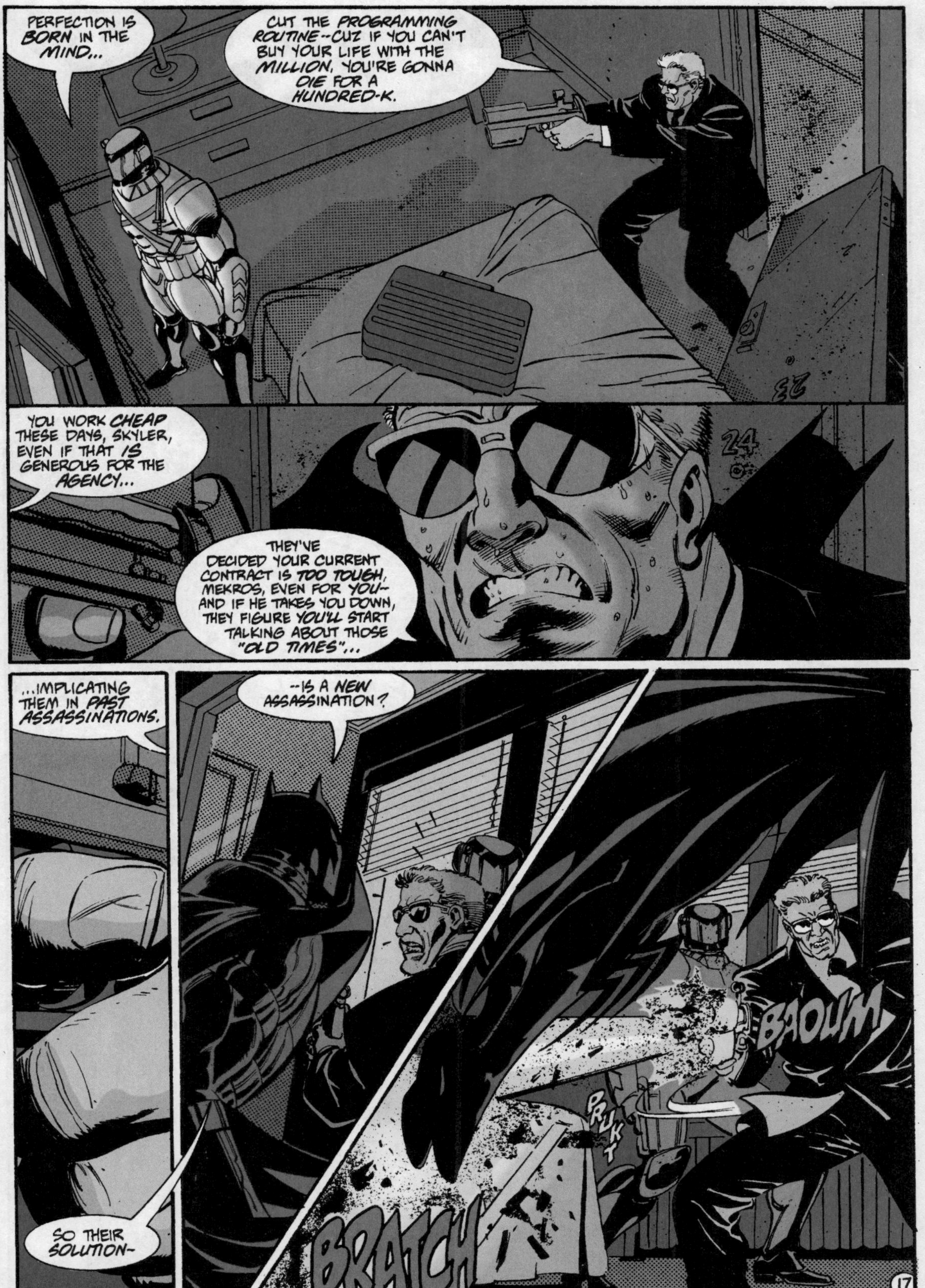
PERFECTION IS BORN IN THE MIND...
CUT THE PROGRAMMING ROUTINE--CUZ IF YOU CAN'T BUY YOUR LIFE WITH THE MILLION, YOU'RE GONNA DIE FOR A HUNDRED-K.
23
YOU WORK CHEAP THESE DAYS, SKYLER, EVEN IF THAT IS GENEROUS FOR THE AGENCY...
24
THEY'VE DECIDED YOUR CURRENT CONTRACT IS TOO TOUGH, MEKROS, EVEN FOR YOU--AND IF HE TAKES YOU DOWN, THEY FIGURE YOU'LL START TALKING ABOUT THOSE "OLD TIMES"...
...IMPLICATING THEM IN PAST ASSASSINATIONS.
SO THEIR SOLUTION-
--IS A NEW ASSASSINATION?
BAOUM
PRUKT
BRATCH
17

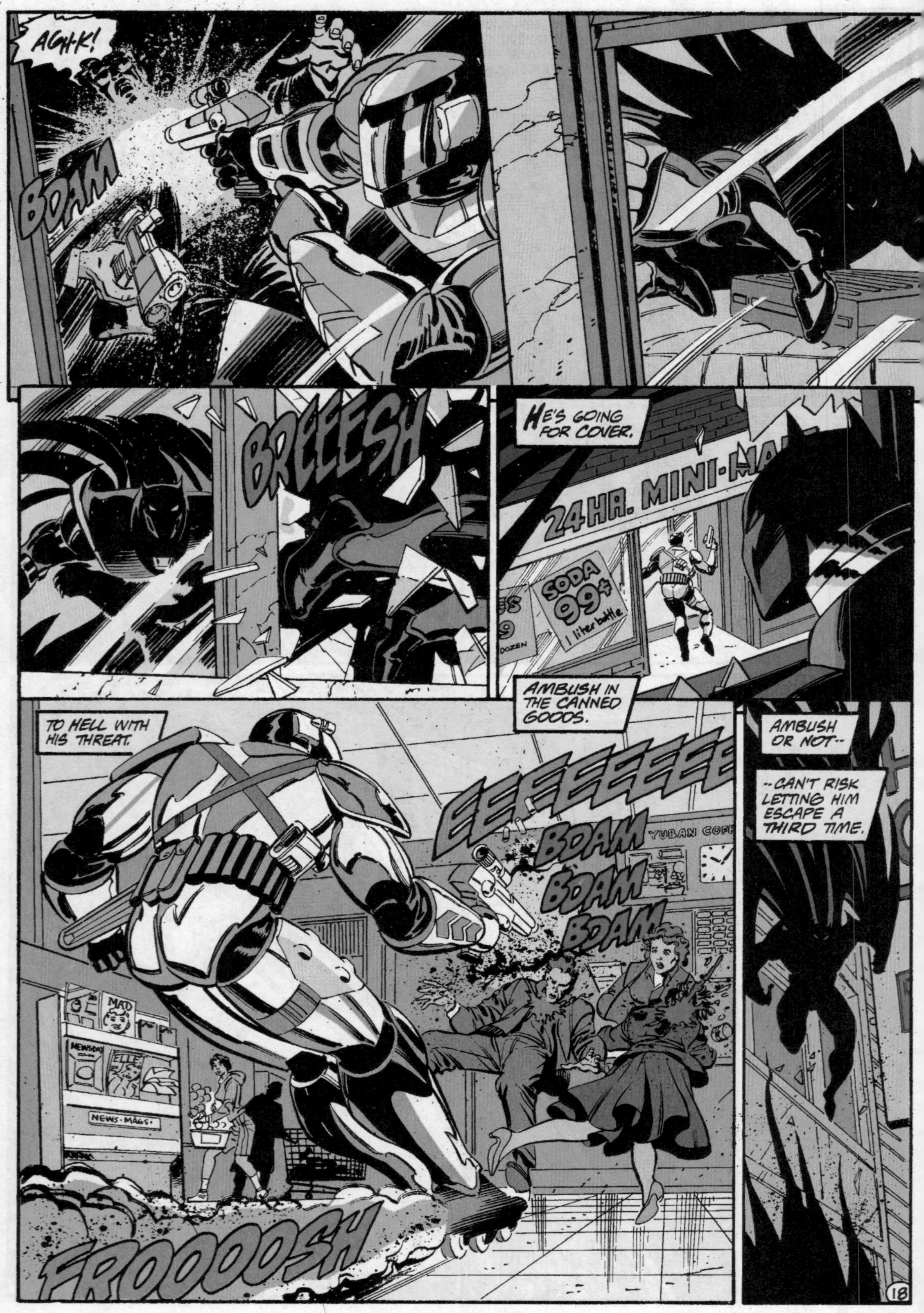
AGH-K!
BDAM
BREEESH
HE'S GOING FOR COVER.
24 HR. MINI-MA
SODA 99¢ 1 liter bottle
DOZEN
AMBUSH IN THE CANNED GOODS.
TO HELL WITH HIS THREAT.
EEEEEEEEE
BDAM
BDAM
BDAM
YUBAN COFF
MAD
NEWSDAY
ELLE
NEWS·MAGS·
FROOOOSH
AMBUSH OR NOT--
--CAN'T RISK LETTING HIM ESCAPE A THIRD TIME.
18

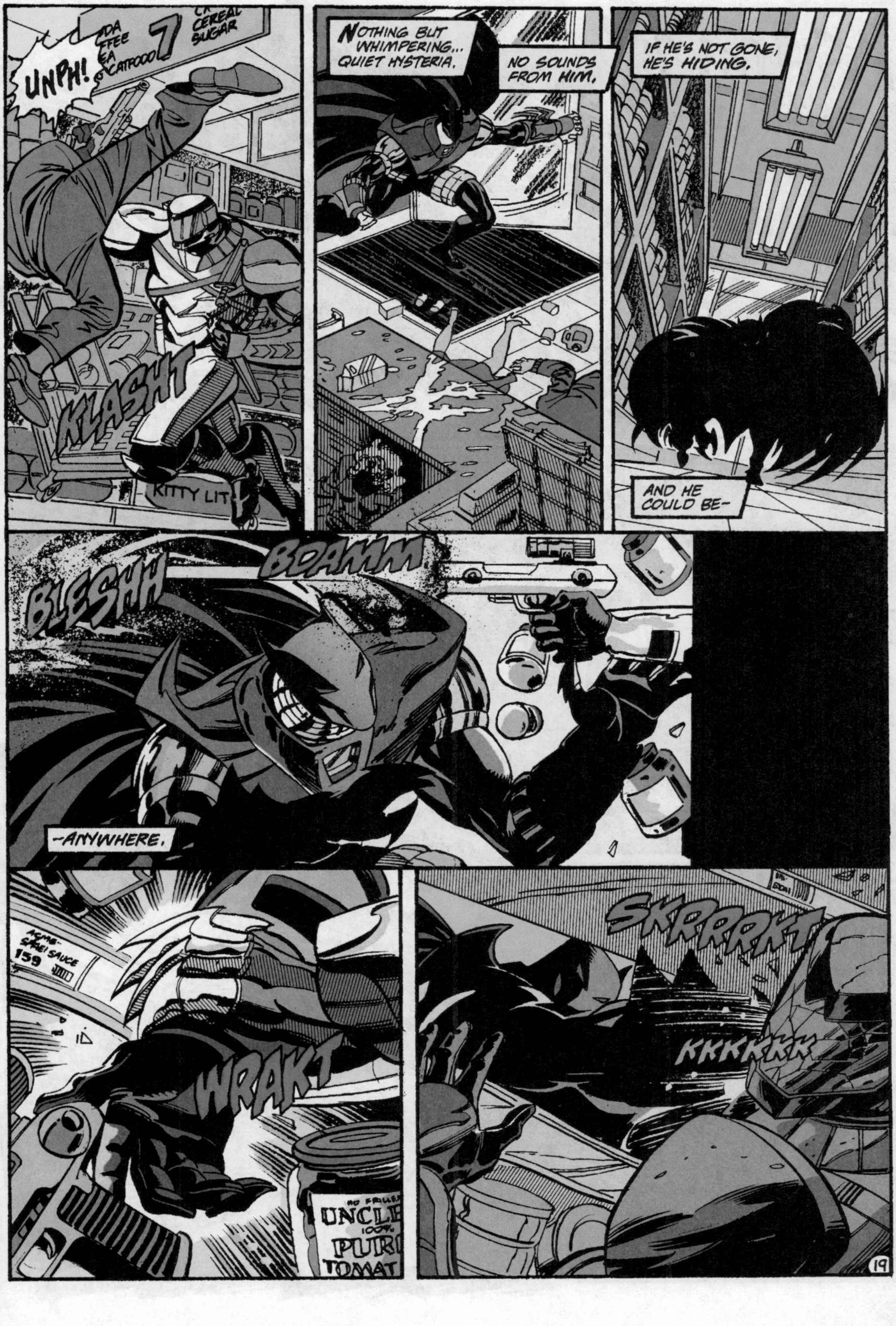
UNPH!
KLASHT
KITTY LIT
NOTHING BUT WHIMPERING... QUIET HYSTERIA.
NO SOUNDS FROM HIM.
IF HE'S NOT GONE, HE'S HIDING.
AND HE COULD BE–
BLESHH
BDAMM
–ANYWHERE.
WRAKT
SKRRRKT
KKKKKK
19

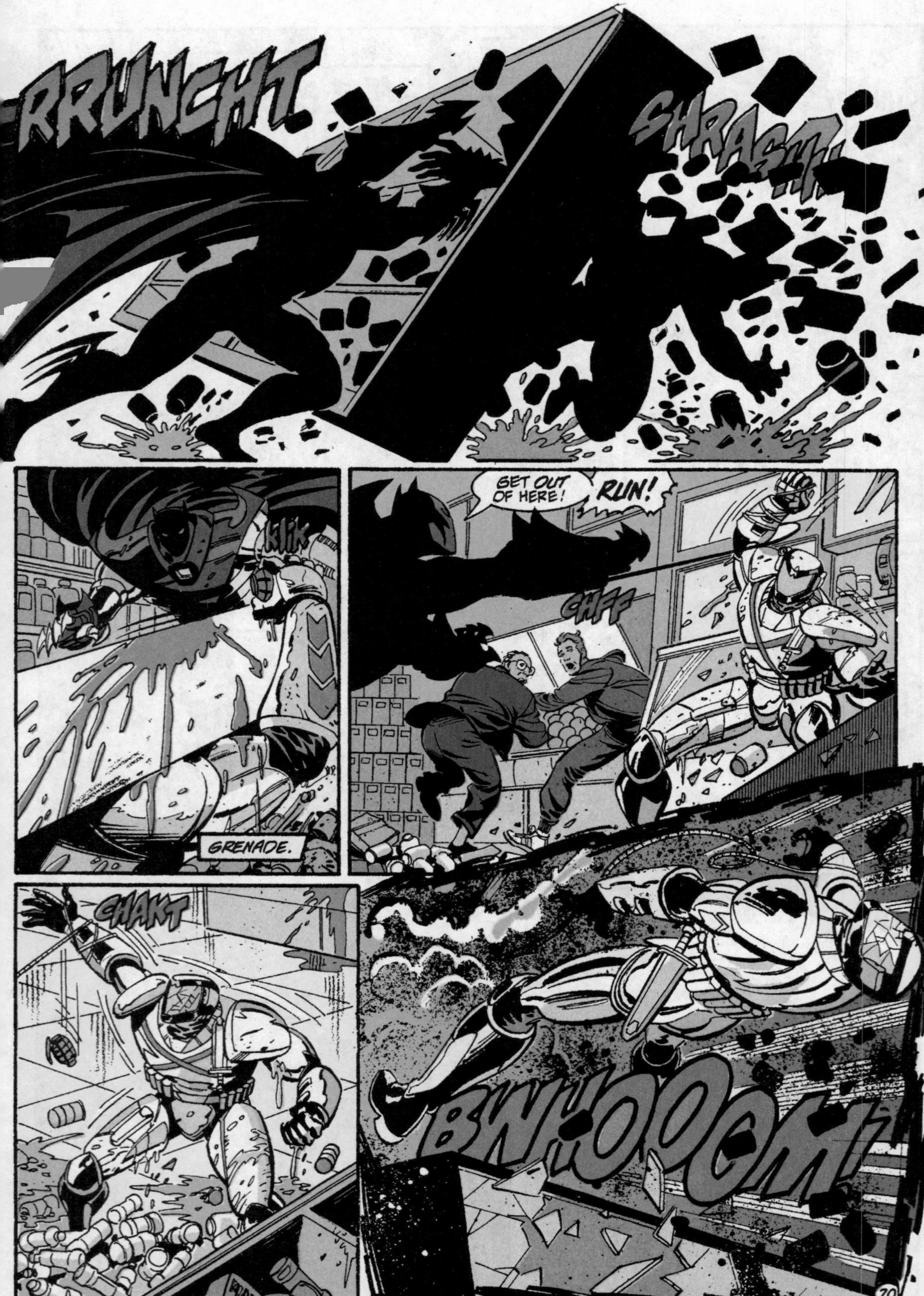
RRUNCH!
SHRASH!
KLIK
GRENADE.
GET OUT OF HERE!
RUN!
CHFF
CHAKT
BWHOOOOM!
20

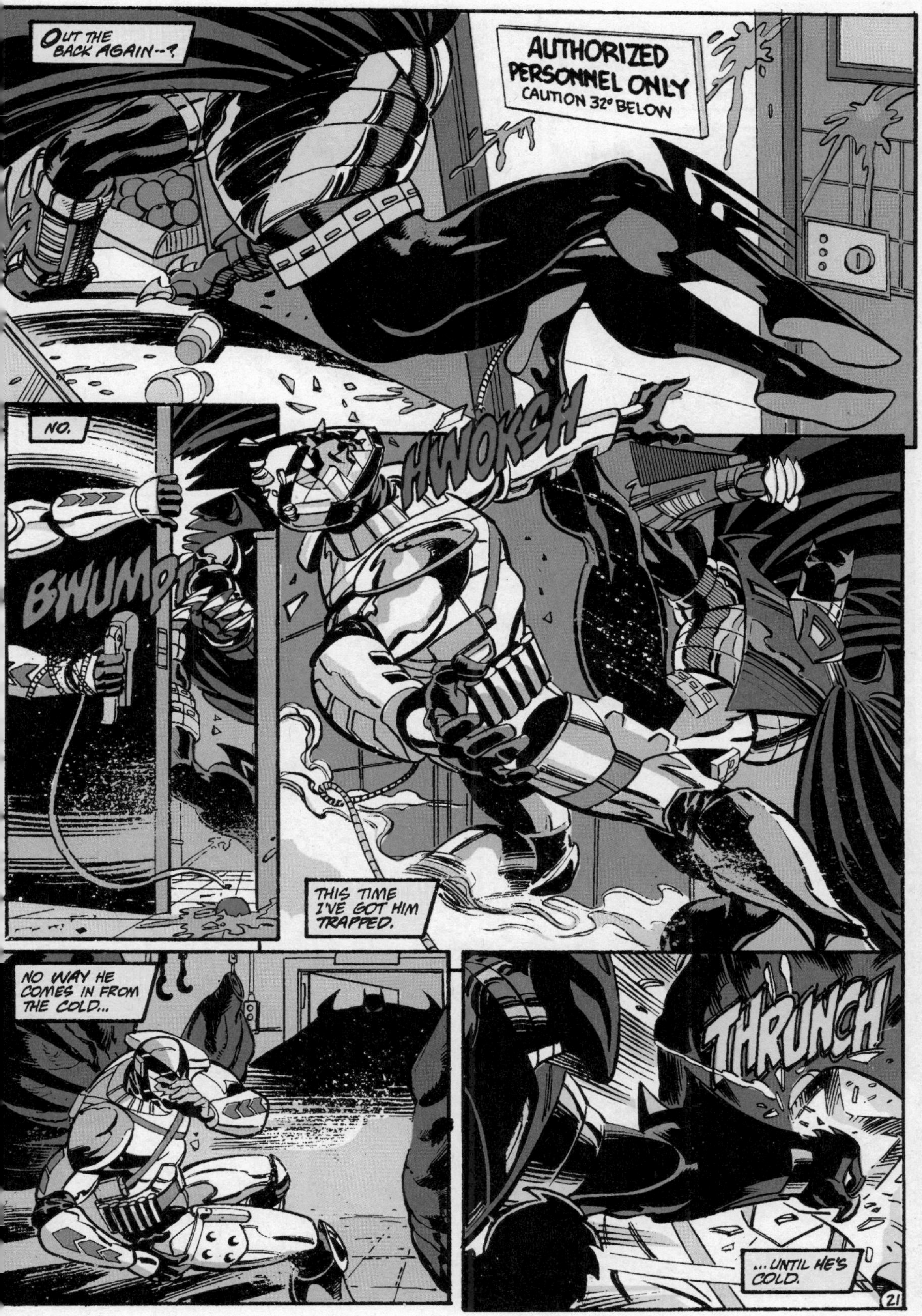
OUT THE BACK AGAIN--?
AUTHORIZED PERSONNEL ONLY CAUTION 32° BELOW
NO.
BWUMP
HWOKSH
THIS TIME I'VE GOT HIM TRAPPED.
NO WAY HE COMES IN FROM THE COLD...
THRUNCH
...UNTIL HE'S COLD.
21

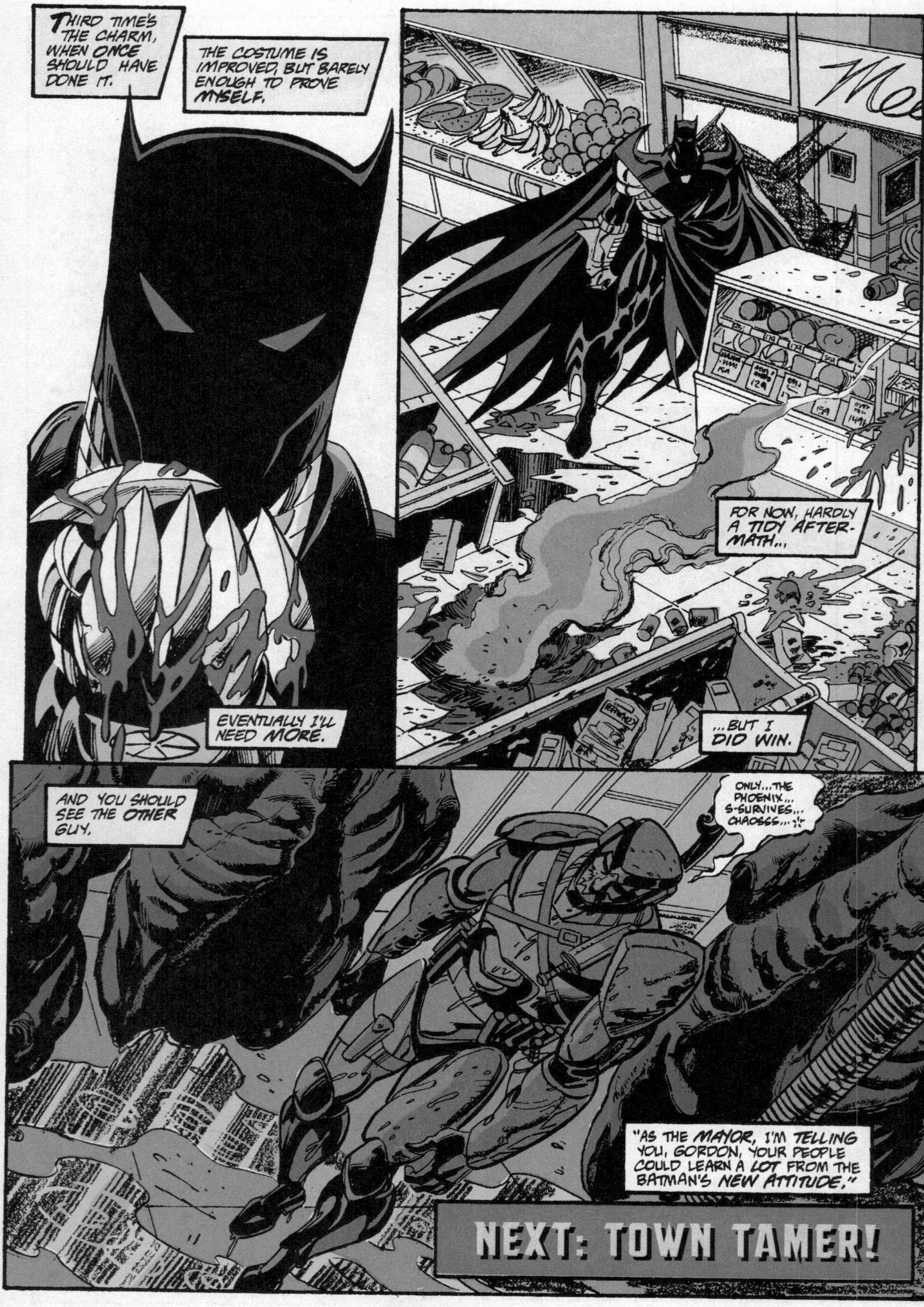
THIRD TIME'S THE CHARM, WHEN ONCE SHOULD HAVE DONE IT.
THE COSTUME IS IMPROVED, BUT BARELY ENOUGH TO PROVE MYSELF.
EVENTUALLY I'LL NEED MORE.
FOR NOW, HARDLY A TIDY AFTER-MATH...
...BUT I DID WIN.
AND YOU SHOULD SEE THE OTHER GUY.
ONLY...THE PHOENIX... S-SURVIVES... CHAOSSS...
"AS THE MAYOR, I'M TELLING YOU, GORDON, YOUR PEOPLE COULD LEARN A LOT FROM THE BATMAN'S NEW ATTITUDE."
NEXT: TOWN TAMER!

Cover art by KELLEY JONES

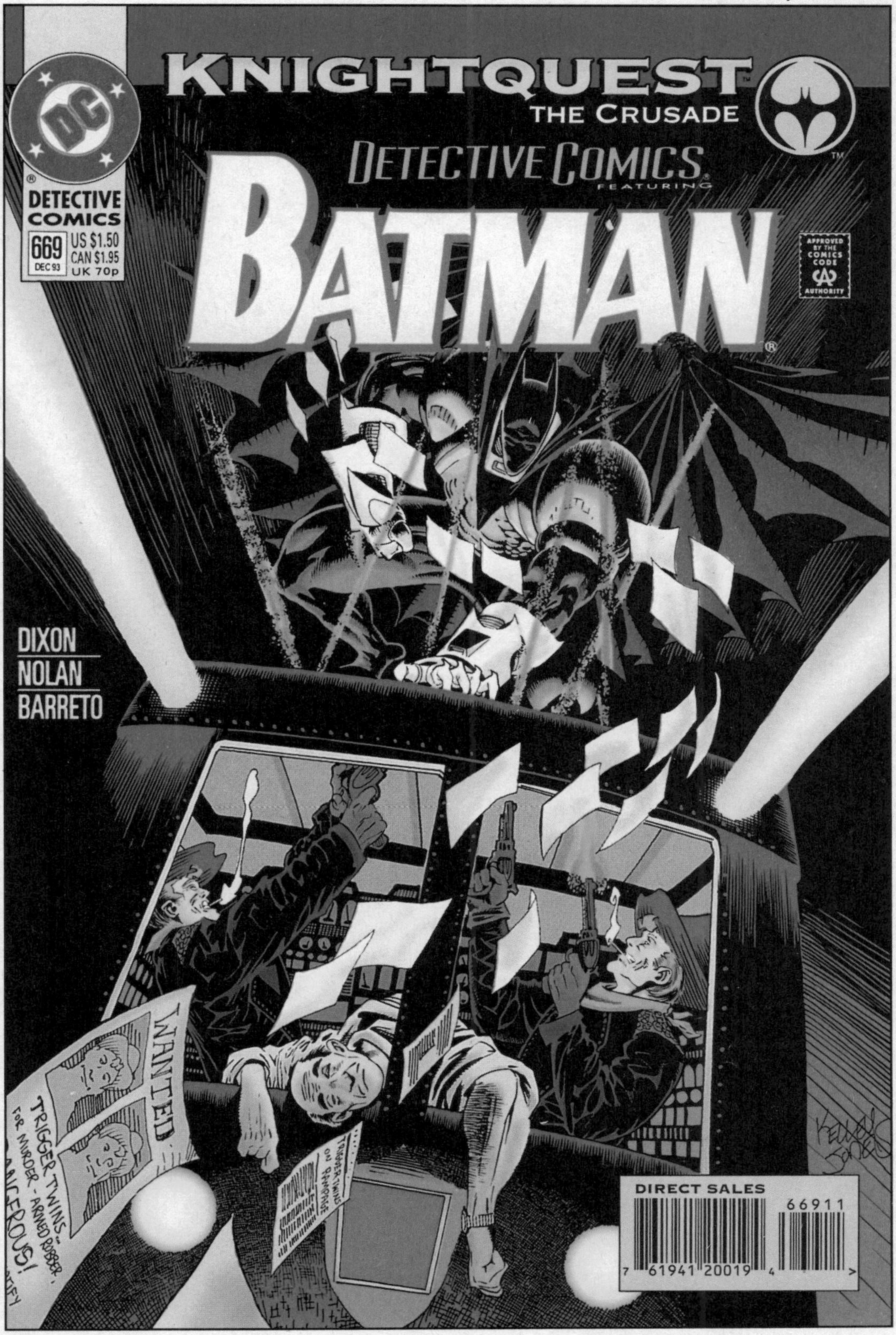
KNIGHTQUEST
THE CRUSADE
DETECTIVE COMICS
FEATURING
BATMAN
DC
DETECTIVE COMICS
669
DEC 93
US $1.50
CAN $1.95
UK 70p
APPROVED BY THE COMICS CODE AUTHORITY
DIXON
NOLAN
BARRETO
WANTED
TRIGGER-TWINS
FOR MURDER - ARMED ROBBERY
DANGEROUS!
DIRECT SALES

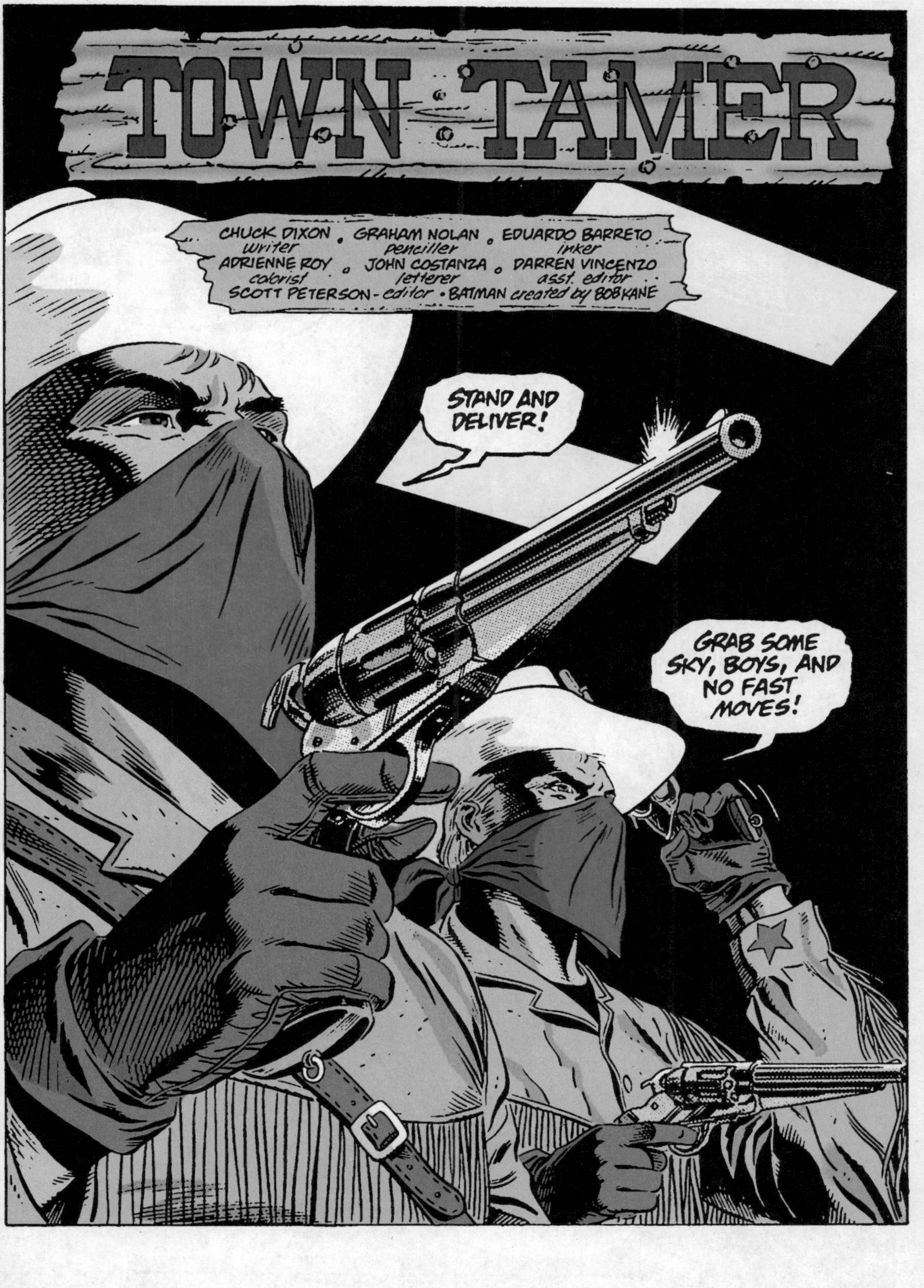
TOWN TAMER
CHUCK DIXON writer • GRAHAM NOLAN penciller • EDUARDO BARRETO inker
ADRIENNE ROY colorist • JOHN COSTANZA letterer • DARREN VINCENZO asst. editor
SCOTT PETERSON - editor • BATMAN created by BOB KANE
STAND AND DELIVER!
GRAB SOME SKY, BOYS, AND NO FAST MOVES!

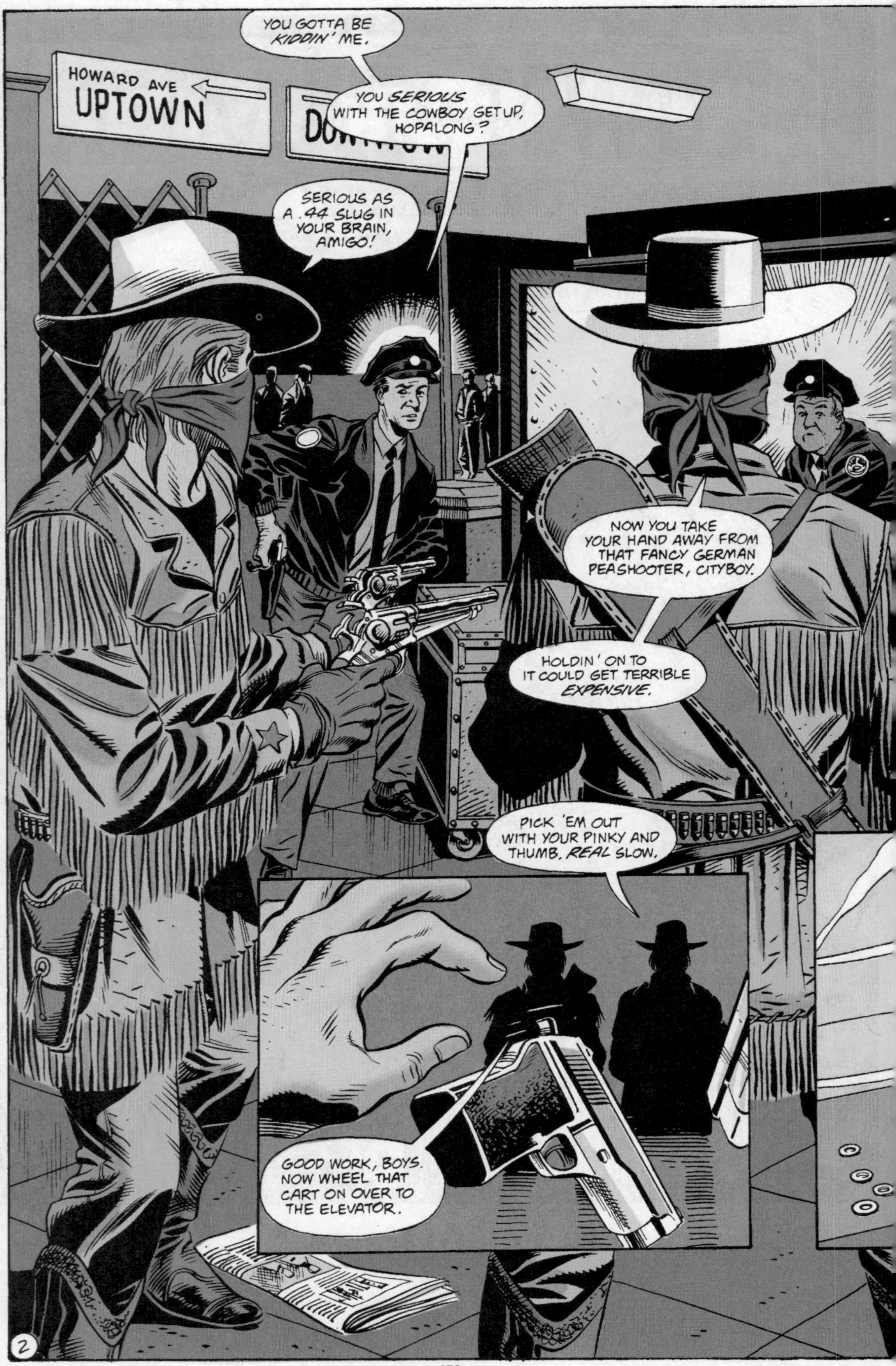
HOWARD AVE
UPTOWN
YOU GOTTA BE KIDDIN' ME.
YOU SERIOUS WITH THE COWBOY GET UP, HOPALONG?
SERIOUS AS A .44 SLUG IN YOUR BRAIN, AMIGO!
NOW YOU TAKE YOUR HAND AWAY FROM THAT FANCY GERMAN PEASHOOTER, CITYBOY.
HOLDIN' ON TO IT COULD GET TERRIBLE EXPENSIVE.
PICK 'EM OUT WITH YOUR PINKY AND THUMB. REAL SLOW.
GOOD WORK, BOYS. NOW WHEEL THAT CART ON OVER TO THE ELEVATOR.
2

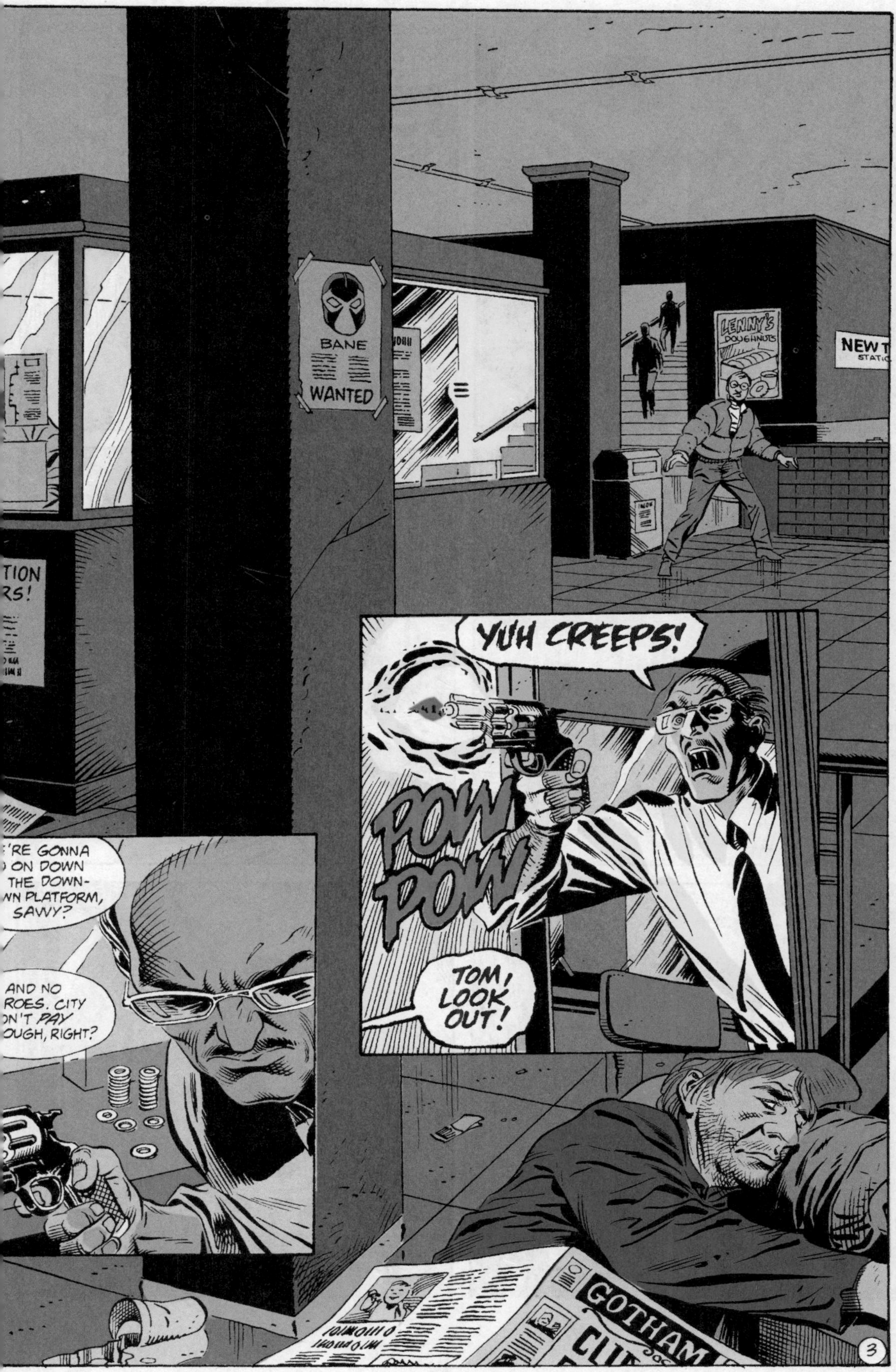
BANE
WANTED
LENNY'S DOUGHNUTS
NEW T
STATIO
TION
RS!
YUH CREEPS!
POW
POW
TOM, LOOK OUT!
'RE GONNA
ON DOWN
THE DOWN-
WN PLATFORM,
SAVVY?
AND NO
ROES. CITY
N'T PAY
OUGH, RIGHT?
GOTHAM
3

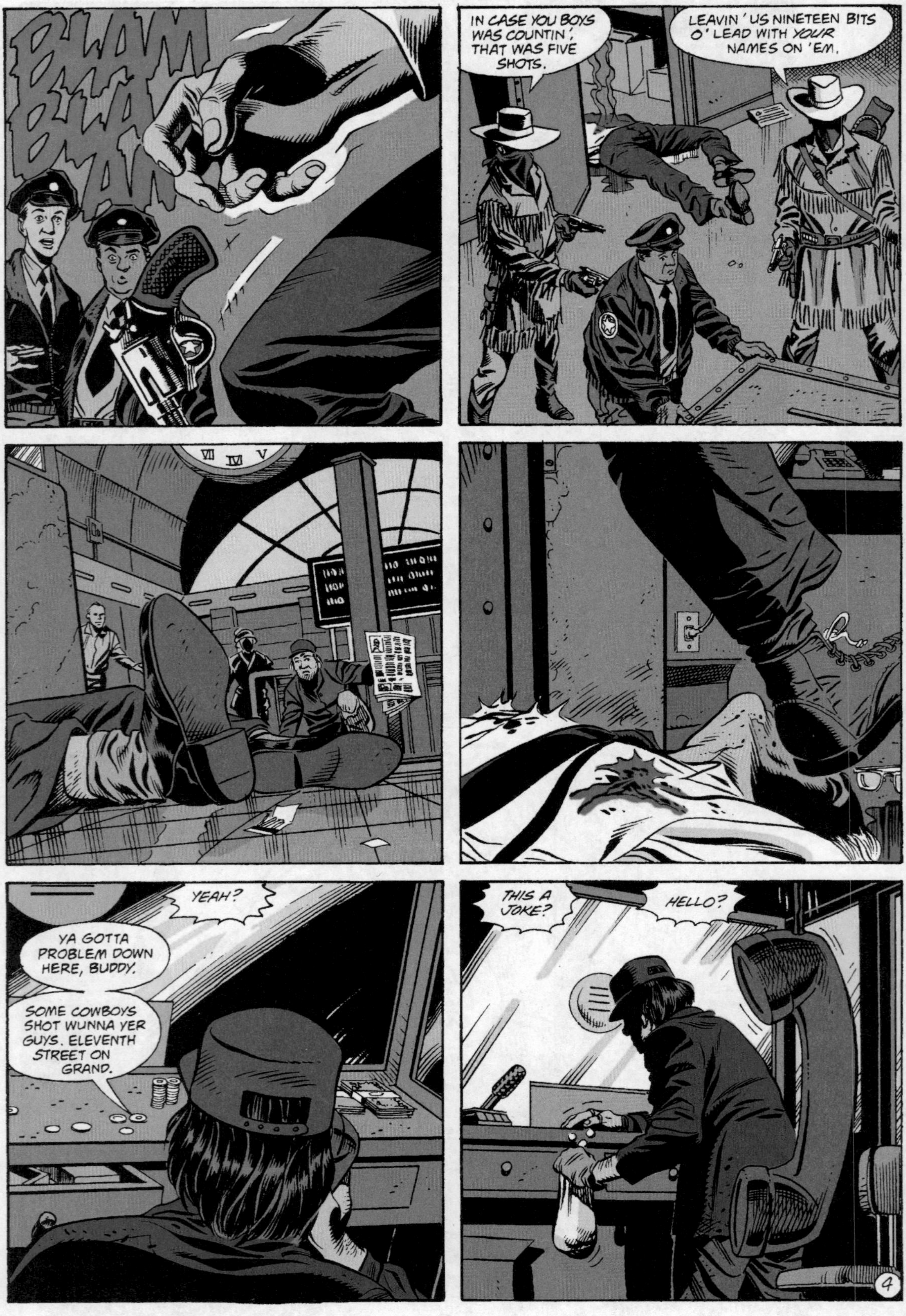
BLAM BLAM BLAM
IN CASE YOU BOYS WAS COUNTIN', THAT WAS FIVE SHOTS.
LEAVIN' US NINETEEN BITS O' LEAD WITH YOUR NAMES ON 'EM.
YEAH?
YA GOTTA PROBLEM DOWN HERE, BUDDY.
SOME COWBOYS SHOT WUNNA YER GUYS. ELEVENTH STREET ON GRAND.
THIS A JOKE?
HELLO?
4

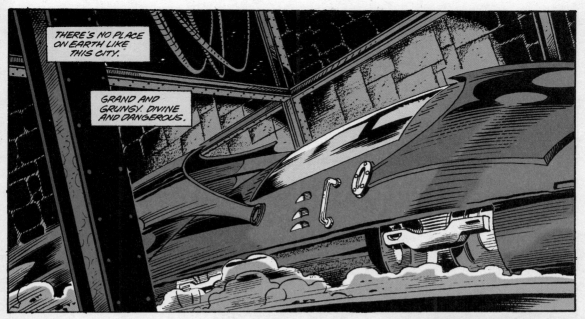

THERE'S NO PLACE ON EARTH LIKE THIS CITY.

GRAND AND GRUNGY. DIVINE AND DANGEROUS.

THAT'S WHY HE HAD TO TURN THE BOY AWAY.

GOTHAM IS TOO UNPREDICTABLE, TOO TREACHEROUS.

YOU NEVER KNOW WHAT KIND OF PSYCHO YOU'LL RUN INTO.

ROVER UNIT IN VICINITY OF ELEVEN AND GRAND. CHECK OUT THE CHANGE BOOTH. WE MAY HAVE AN INCIDENT.

ROVER NINER. TWO STATIONS AWAY. WILL LOOK IN.

5

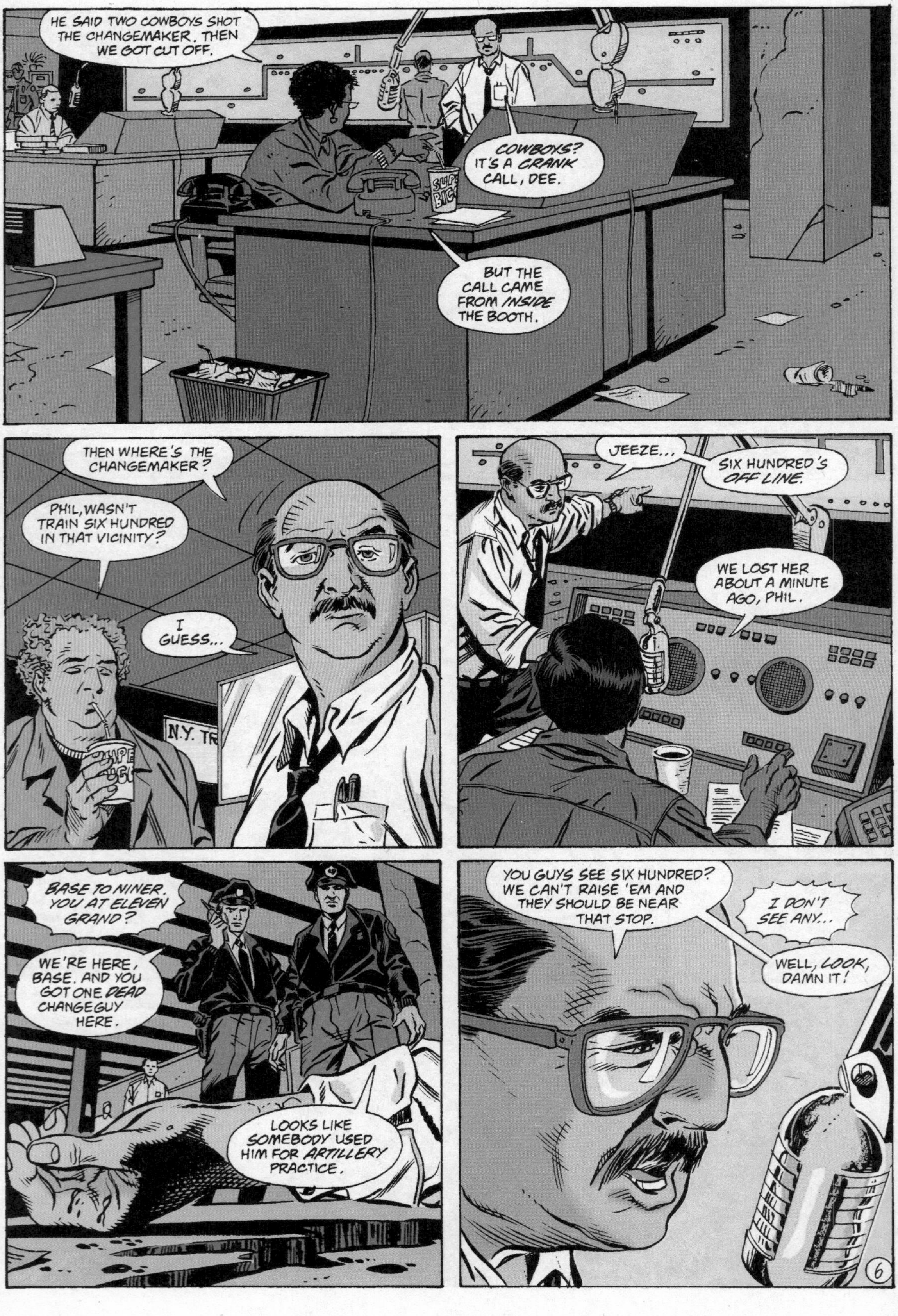
HE SAID TWO COWBOYS SHOT THE CHANGEMAKER. THEN WE GOT CUT OFF.
COWBOYS? IT'S A CRANK CALL, DEE.
BUT THE CALL CAME FROM INSIDE THE BOOTH.
THEN WHERE'S THE CHANGEMAKER?
PHIL, WASN'T TRAIN SIX HUNDRED IN THAT VICINITY?
I GUESS...
N.Y. TR
JEEZE...
SIX HUNDRED'S OFF LINE.
WE LOST HER ABOUT A MINUTE AGO, PHIL.
BASE TO NINER. YOU AT ELEVEN GRAND?
WE'RE HERE, BASE. AND YOU GOT ONE DEAD CHANGEGUY HERE.
LOOKS LIKE SOMEBODY USED HIM FOR ARTILLERY PRACTICE.
YOU GUYS SEE SIX HUNDRED? WE CAN'T RAISE 'EM AND THEY SHOULD BE NEAR THAT STOP.
I DON'T SEE ANY...
WELL, LOOK, DAMN IT!
6

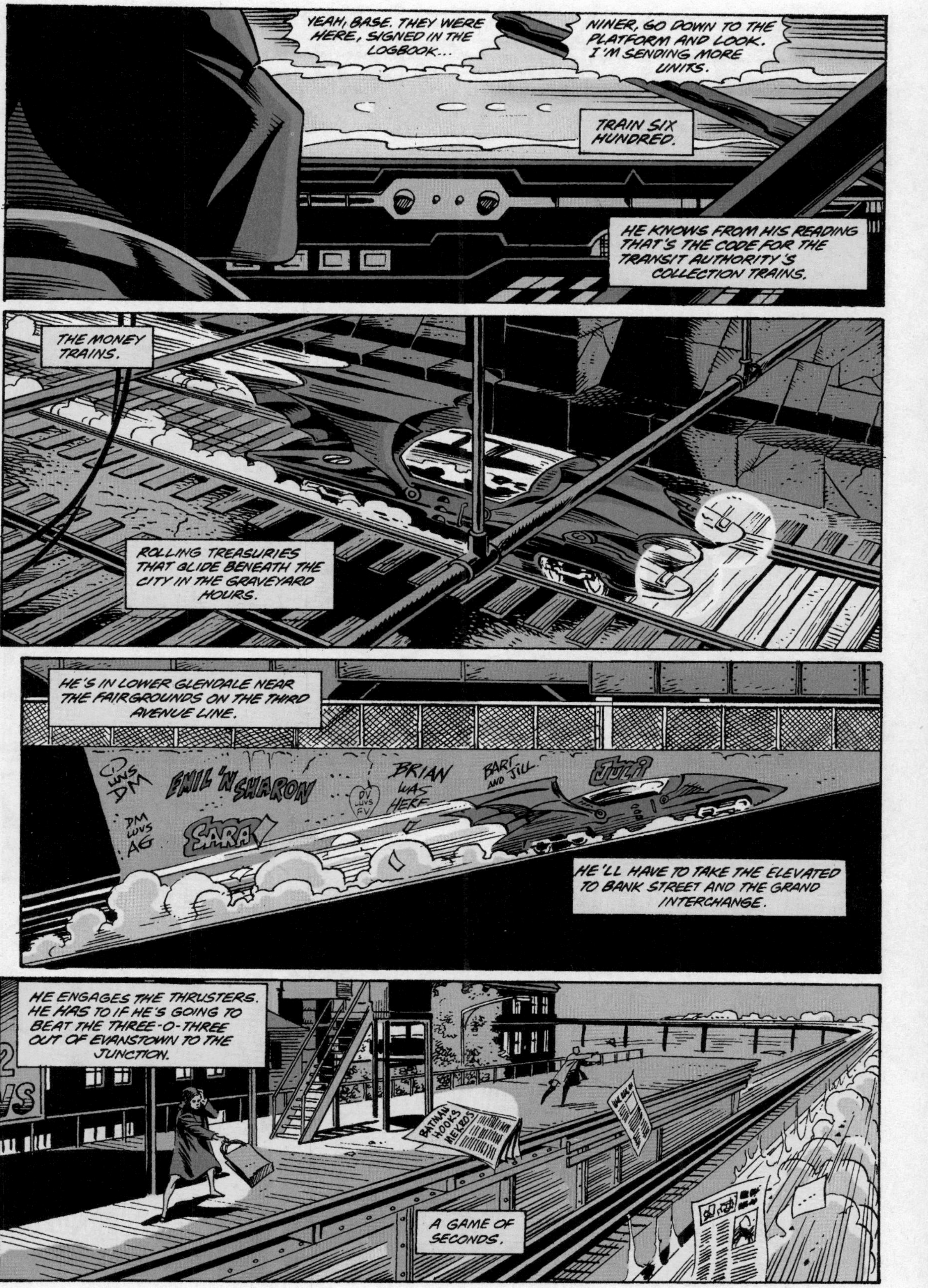
YEAH, BASE. THEY WERE HERE, SIGNED IN THE LOGBOOK...
NINER, GO DOWN TO THE PLATFORM AND LOOK. I'M SENDING MORE UNITS.
TRAIN SIX HUNDRED.
HE KNOWS FROM HIS READING THAT'S THE CODE FOR THE TRANSIT AUTHORITY'S COLLECTION TRAINS.
THE MONEY TRAINS.
ROLLING TREASURIES THAT GLIDE BENEATH THE CITY IN THE GRAVEYARD HOURS.
HE'S IN LOWER GLENDALE NEAR THE FAIRGROUNDS ON THE THIRD AVENUE LINE.
EMIL 'N SHARON
BRIAN WAS HERE
BART AND JILL
SARA
DM LUVS AG
HE'LL HAVE TO TAKE THE ELEVATED TO BANK STREET AND THE GRAND INTERCHANGE.
HE ENGAGES THE THRUSTERS. HE HAS TO IF HE'S GOING TO BEAT THE THREE-O-THREE OUT OF EVANSTOWN TO THE JUNCTION.
BATMAN HOOKS MEKROS
A GAME OF SECONDS.

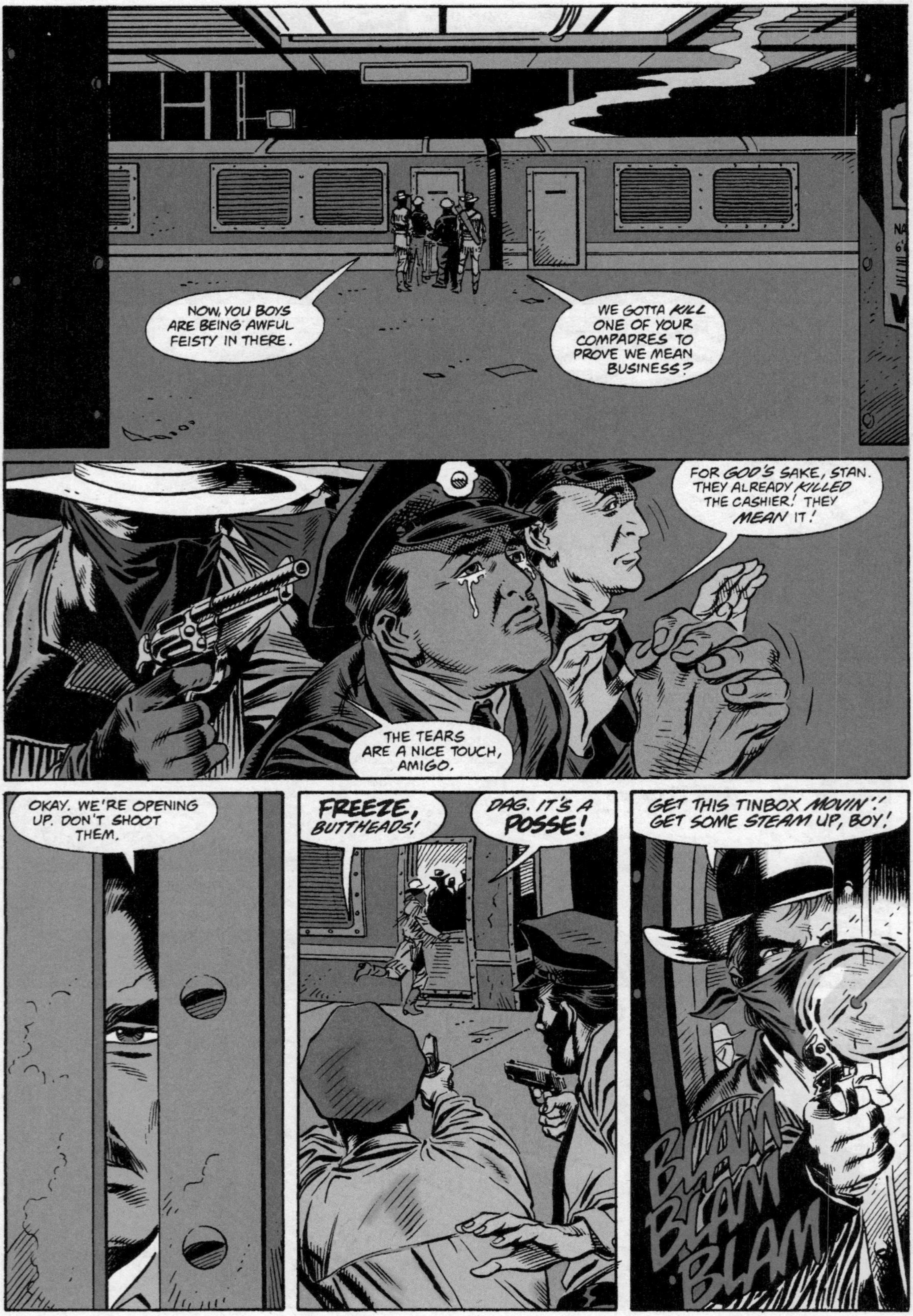

NOW, YOU BOYS ARE BEING AWFUL FEISTY IN THERE.
WE GOTTA KILL ONE OF YOUR COMPADRES TO PROVE WE MEAN BUSINESS?
FOR GOD'S SAKE, STAN. THEY ALREADY KILLED THE CASHIER! THEY MEAN IT!
THE TEARS ARE A NICE TOUCH, AMIGO.
OKAY. WE'RE OPENING UP. DON'T SHOOT THEM.
FREEZE, BUTTHEADS!
DAG. IT'S A POSSE!
GET THIS TINBOX MOVIN'! GET SOME STEAM UP, BOY!
BLAM BLAM BLAM BLAM

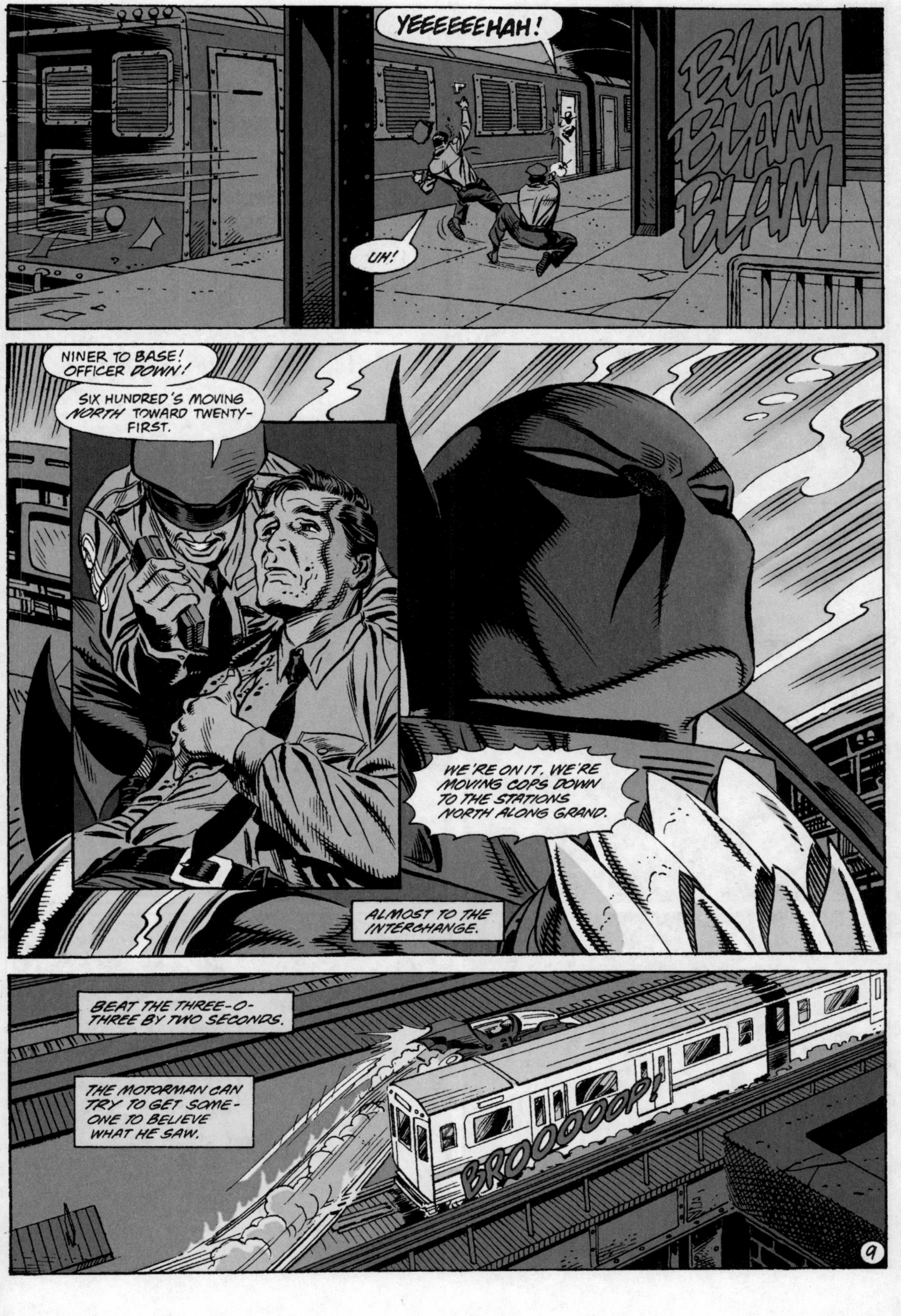
YEEEEEEHAH!
UH!
BLAM BLAM BLAM
NINER TO BASE! OFFICER DOWN!
SIX HUNDRED'S MOVING NORTH TOWARD TWENTY-FIRST.
WE'RE ON IT. WE'RE MOVING COPS DOWN TO THE STATIONS NORTH ALONG GRAND.
ALMOST TO THE INTERCHANGE.
BEAT THE THREE-O-THREE BY TWO SECONDS.
THE MOTORMAN CAN TRY TO GET SOME-ONE TO BELIEVE WHAT HE SAW.
BROOOOOOP!
9

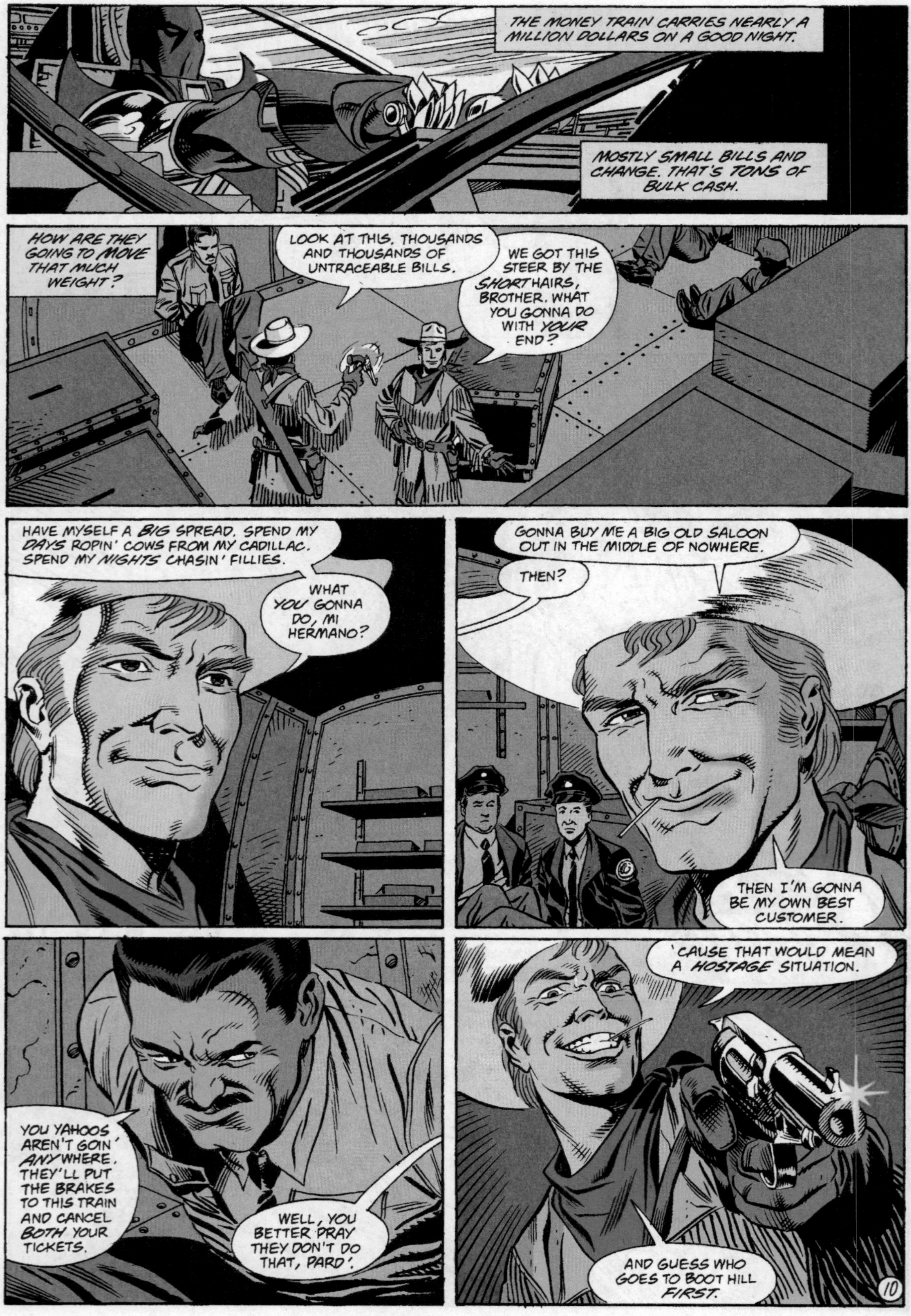
THE MONEY TRAIN CARRIES NEARLY A MILLION DOLLARS ON A GOOD NIGHT.
MOSTLY SMALL BILLS AND CHANGE. THAT'S TONS OF BULK CASH.
HOW ARE THEY GOING TO MOVE THAT MUCH WEIGHT?
LOOK AT THIS. THOUSANDS AND THOUSANDS OF UNTRACEABLE BILLS.
WE GOT THIS STEER BY THE SHORT HAIRS, BROTHER. WHAT YOU GONNA DO WITH YOUR END?
HAVE MYSELF A BIG SPREAD. SPEND MY DAYS ROPIN' COWS FROM MY CADILLAC. SPEND MY NIGHTS CHASIN' FILLIES.
WHAT YOU GONNA DO, MI HERMANO?
GONNA BUY ME A BIG OLD SALOON OUT IN THE MIDDLE OF NOWHERE.
THEN?
THEN I'M GONNA BE MY OWN BEST CUSTOMER.
YOU YAHOOS AREN'T GOIN' ANYWHERE. THEY'LL PUT THE BRAKES TO THIS TRAIN AND CANCEL BOTH YOUR TICKETS.
WELL, YOU BETTER PRAY THEY DON'T DO THAT, PARD'.
'CAUSE THAT WOULD MEAN A HOSTAGE SITUATION.
AND GUESS WHO GOES TO BOOT HILL FIRST.
10

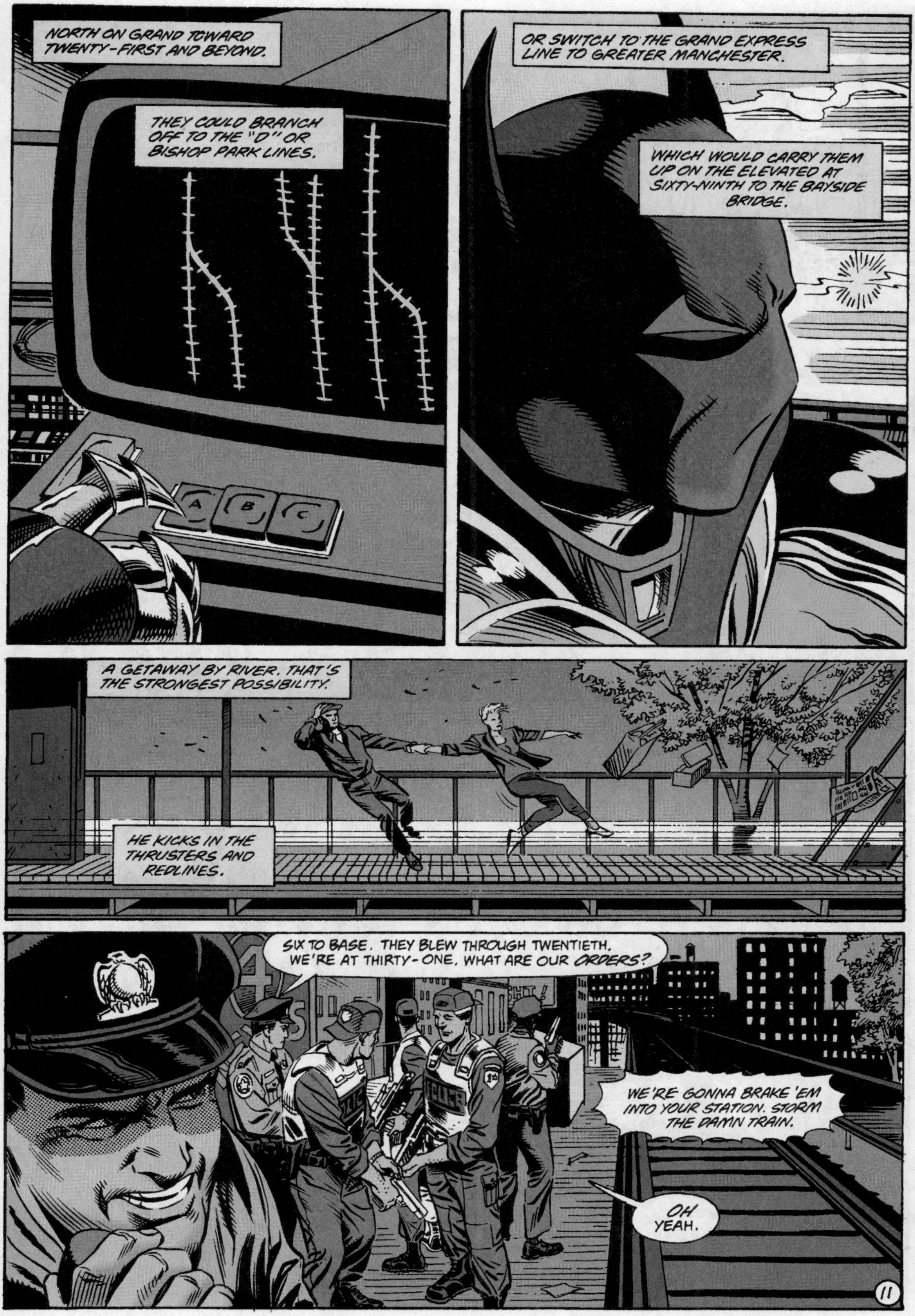
NORTH ON GRAND TOWARD TWENTY-FIRST AND BEYOND.
THEY COULD BRANCH OFF TO THE "D" OR BISHOP PARK LINES.
A
B
C
OR SWITCH TO THE GRAND EXPRESS LINE TO GREATER MANCHESTER.
WHICH WOULD CARRY THEM UP ON THE ELEVATED AT SIXTY-NINTH TO THE BAYSIDE BRIDGE.
A GETAWAY BY RIVER. THAT'S THE STRONGEST POSSIBILITY.
HE KICKS IN THE THRUSTERS AND REDLINES.
SIX TO BASE. THEY BLEW THROUGH TWENTIETH. WE'RE AT THIRTY-ONE. WHAT ARE OUR ORDERS?
WE'RE GONNA BRAKE 'EM INTO YOUR STATION. STORM THE DAMN TRAIN.
OH YEAH.
11

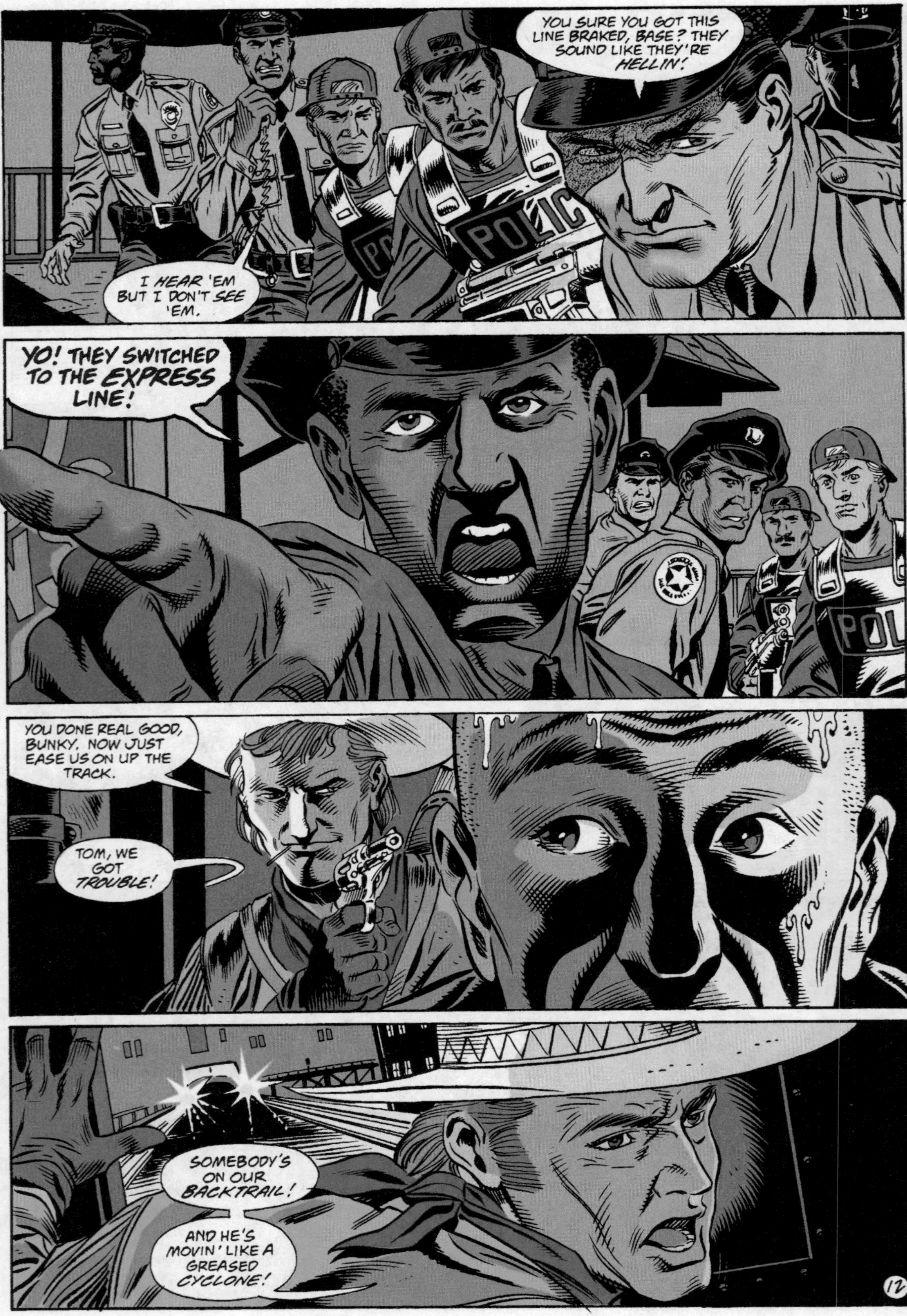
YOU SURE YOU GOT THIS LINE BRAKED, BASE? THEY SOUND LIKE THEY'RE HELLIN'!
I HEAR 'EM BUT I DON'T SEE 'EM.
YO! THEY SWITCHED TO THE EXPRESS LINE!
YOU DONE REAL GOOD, BUNKY. NOW JUST EASE US ON UP THE TRACK.
TOM, WE GOT TROUBLE!
SOMEBODY'S ON OUR BACKTRAIL!
AND HE'S MOVIN' LIKE A GREASED CYCLONE!
12

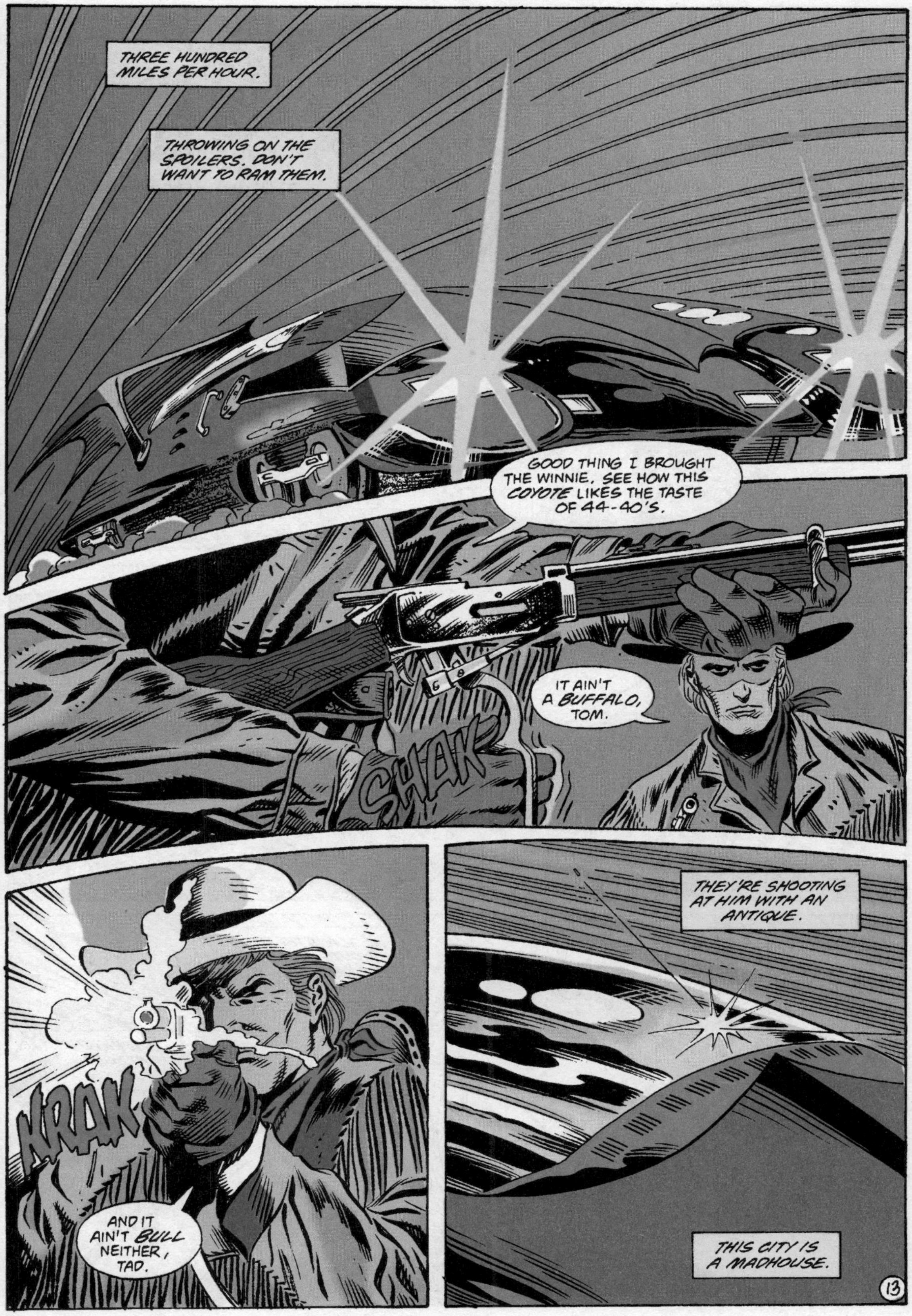

THREE HUNDRED MILES PER HOUR.
THROWING ON THE SPOILERS. DON'T WANT TO RAM THEM.
GOOD THING I BROUGHT THE WINNIE. SEE HOW THIS COYOTE LIKES THE TASTE OF 44-40'S.
IT AIN'T A BUFFALO, TOM.
SHAK
KRAK
AND IT AIN'T BULL NEITHER, TAD.
THEY'RE SHOOTING AT HIM WITH AN ANTIQUE.
THIS CITY IS A MADHOUSE.
13

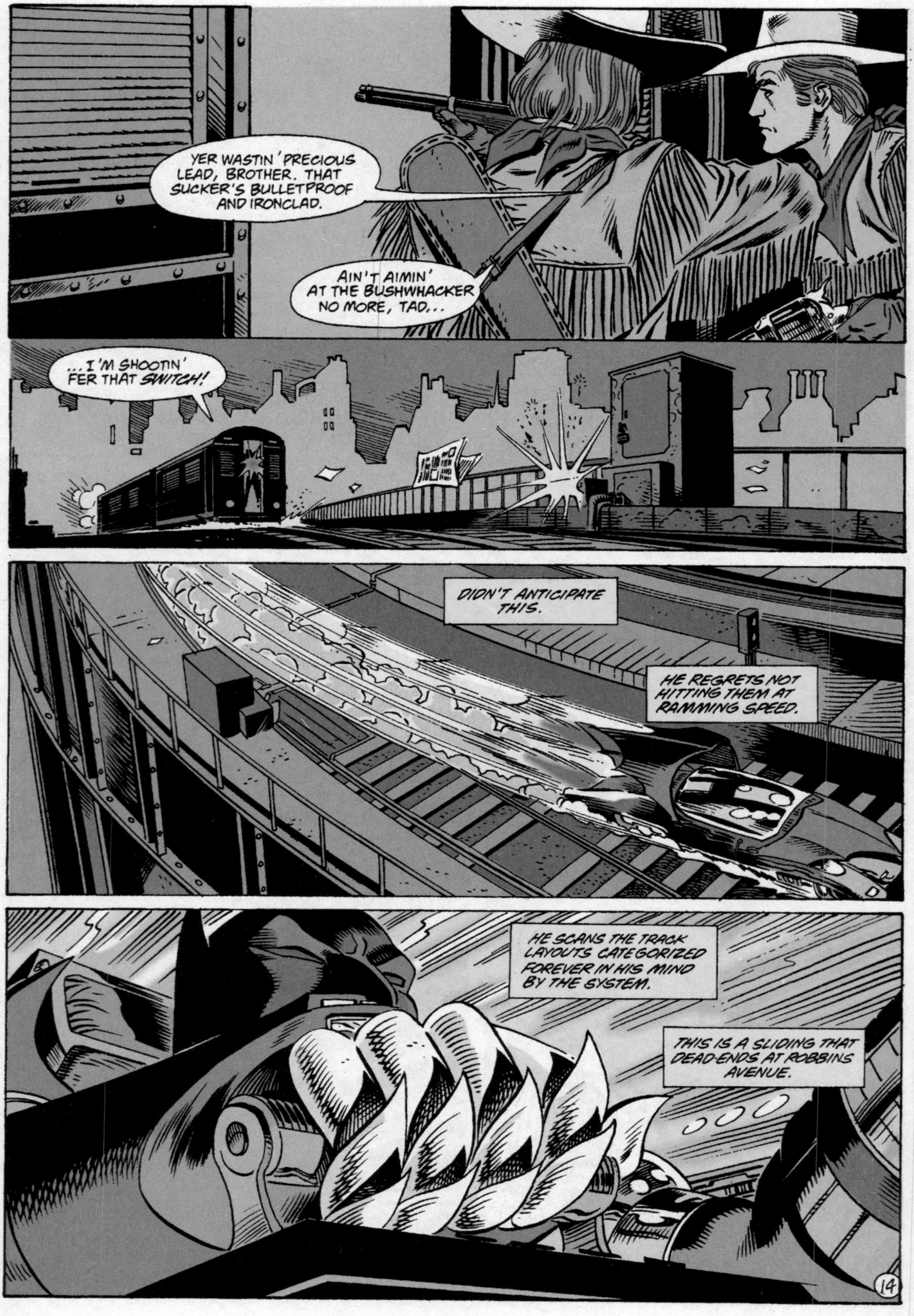
YER WASTIN' PRECIOUS LEAD, BROTHER. THAT SUCKER'S BULLETPROOF AND IRONCLAD.
AIN'T AIMIN' AT THE BUSHWHACKER NO MORE, TAD...
...I'M SHOOTIN' FER THAT SWITCH!
DIDN'T ANTICIPATE THIS.
HE REGRETS NOT HITTING THEM AT RAMMING SPEED.
HE SCANS THE TRACK LAYOUTS CATEGORIZED FOREVER IN HIS MIND BY THE SYSTEM.
THIS IS A SLIDING THAT DEAD-ENDS AT ROBBINS AVENUE.
14

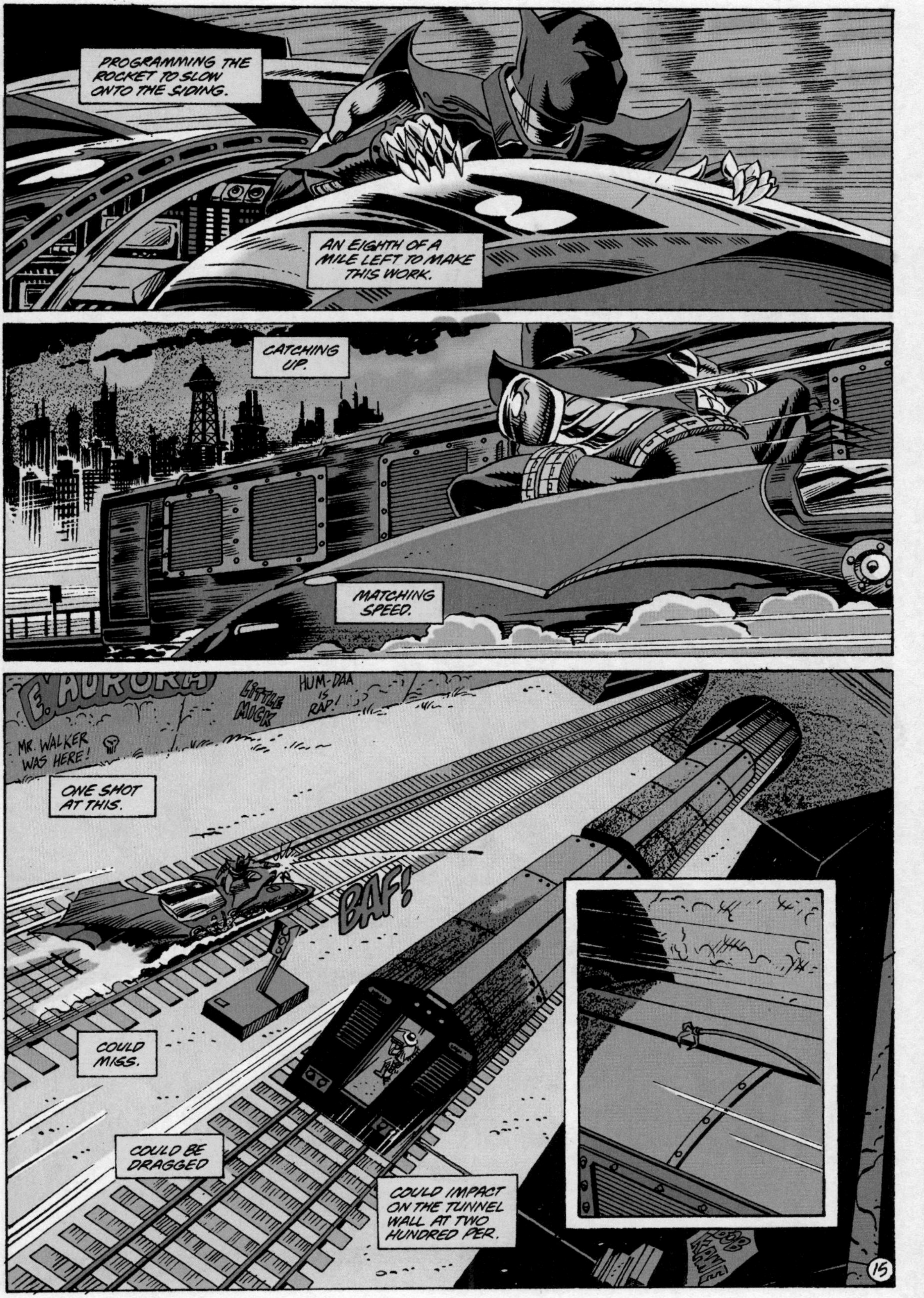
PROGRAMMING THE ROCKET TO SLOW ONTO THE SIDING.
AN EIGHTH OF A MILE LEFT TO MAKE THIS WORK.
CATCHING UP.
MATCHING SPEED.
E. AURORA
LITTLE MICK
HUM-DAA IS RAD!
MR. WALKER WAS HERE!
ONE SHOT AT THIS.
BAF!
COULD MISS.
COULD BE DRAGGED
COULD IMPACT ON THE TUNNEL WALL AT TWO HUNDRED PER.
15

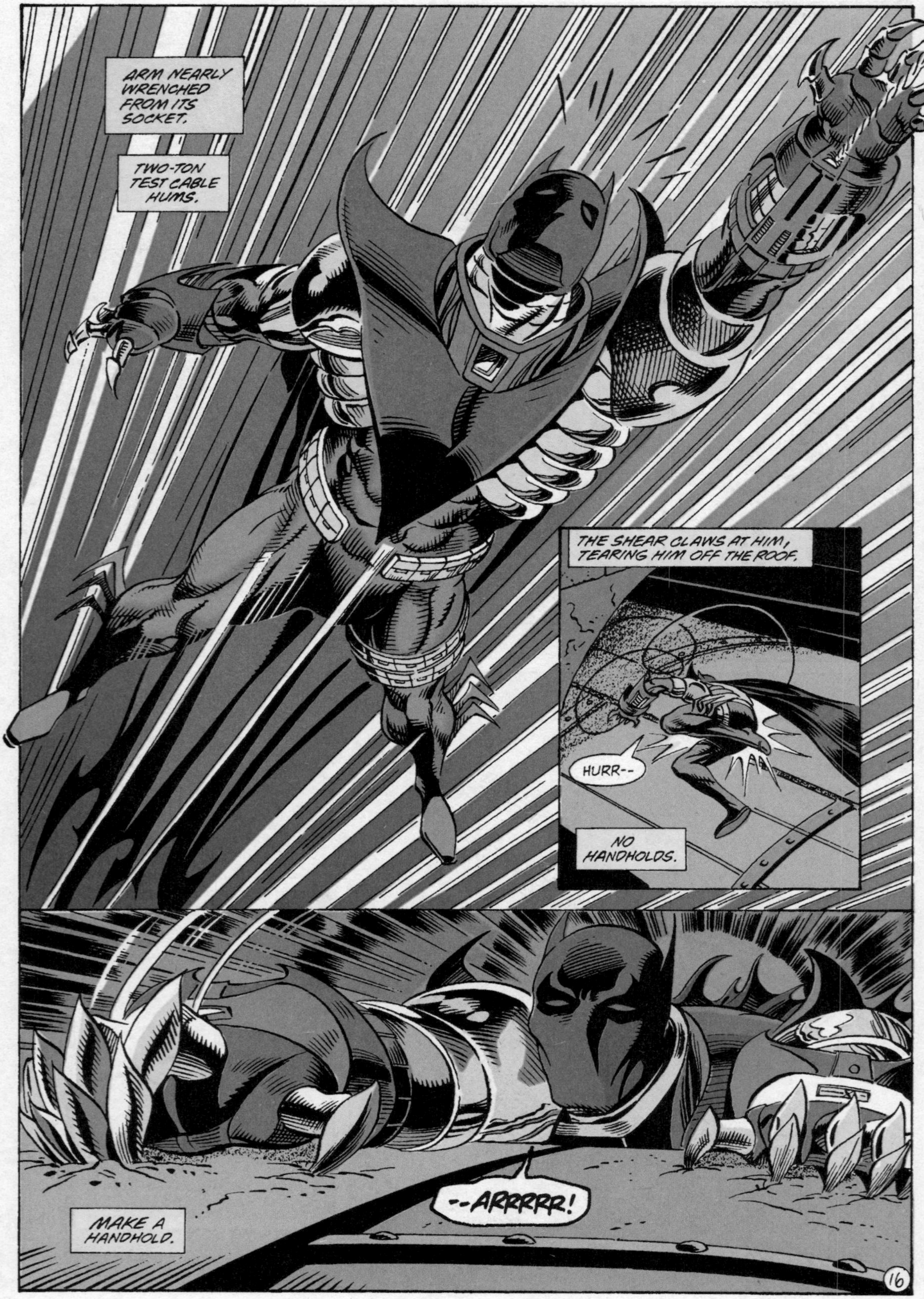

ARM NEARLY WRENCHED FROM ITS SOCKET.
TWO-TON TEST CABLE HUMS.
THE SHEAR CLAWS AT HIM, TEARING HIM OFF THE ROOF.
HURR--
NO HANDHOLDS.
--ARRRRR!
MAKE A HANDHOLD.
16

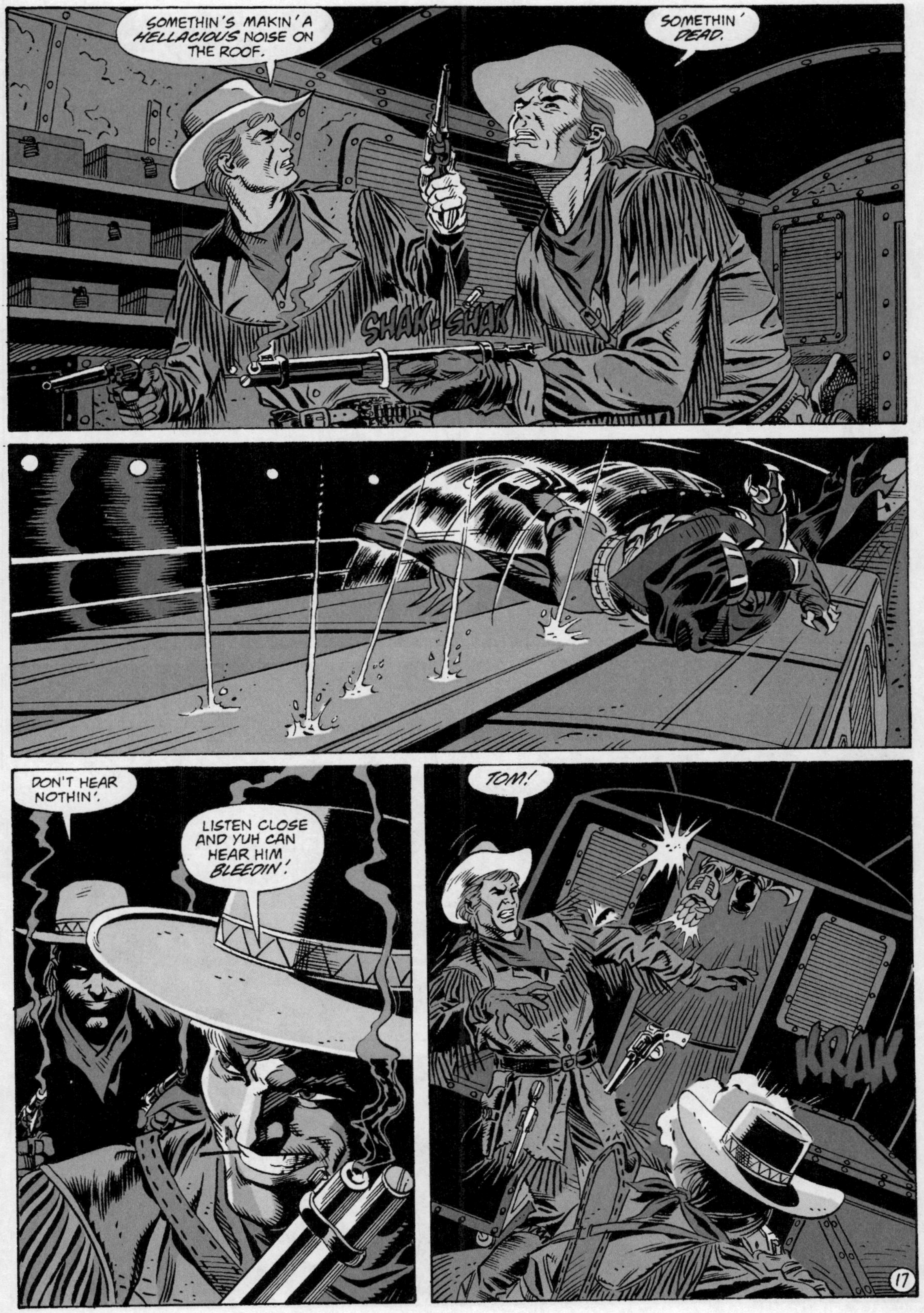
SOMETHIN'S MAKIN' A HELLACIOUS NOISE ON THE ROOF.
SOMETHIN' DEAD.
SHAK-SHAK
DON'T HEAR NOTHIN'.
LISTEN CLOSE AND YUH CAN HEAR HIM BLEEDIN'!
TOM!
KRAK
17

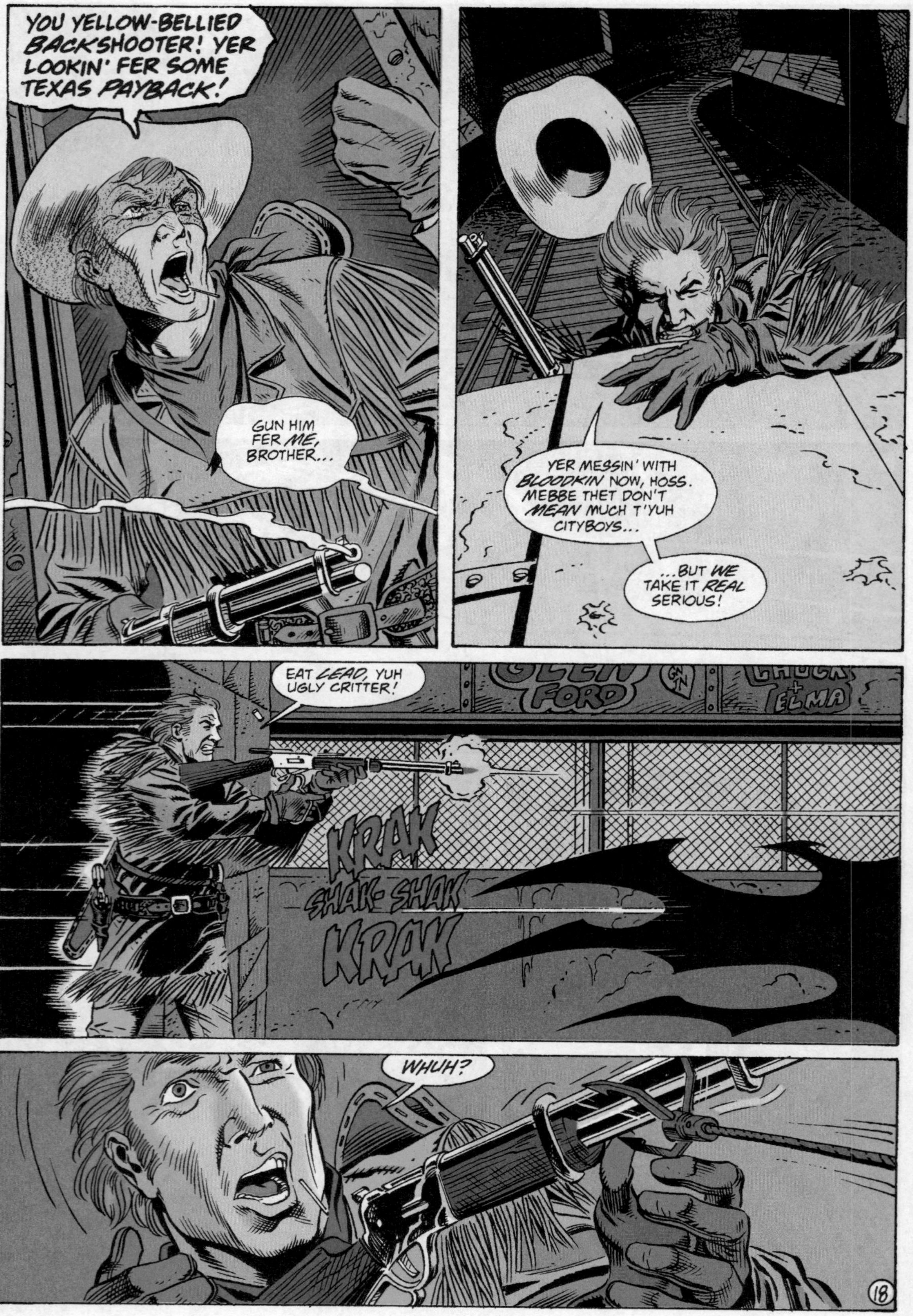
YOU YELLOW-BELLIED BACKSHOOTER! YER LOOKIN' FER SOME TEXAS PAYBACK!
GUN HIM FER ME, BROTHER...
YER MESSIN' WITH BLOODKIN NOW, HOSS. MEBBE THET DON'T MEAN MUCH T'YUH CITYBOYS...
...BUT WE TAKE IT REAL SERIOUS!
EAT LEAD, YUH UGLY CRITTER!
GLEN FORD
CHUCK + ELMA
KRAK
SHAK-SHAK
KRAK
WHUH?
18

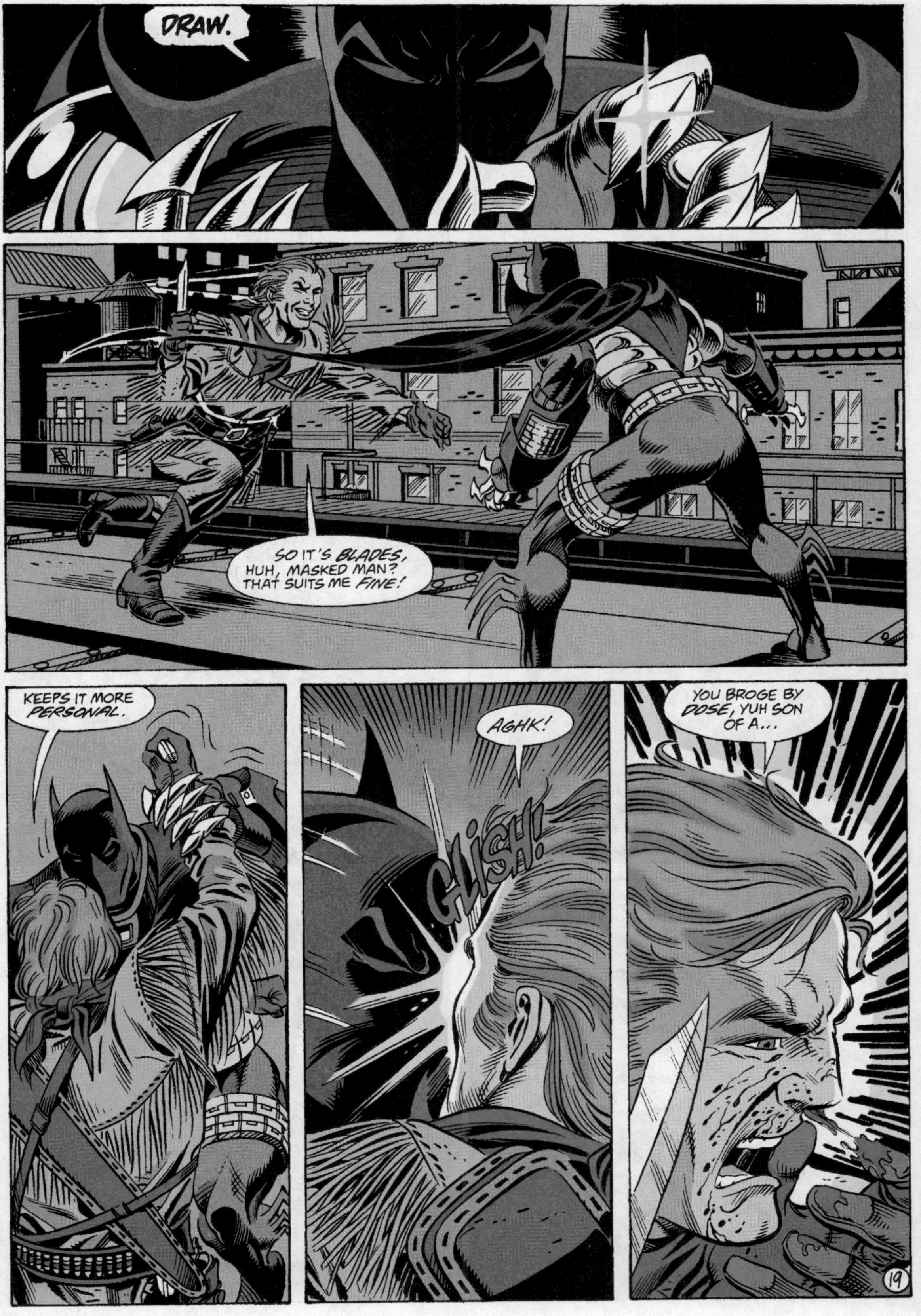
DRAW.
SO IT'S BLADES, HUH, MASKED MAN? THAT SUITS ME FINE!
KEEPS IT MORE PERSONAL.
AGHK!
GLISH!
YOU BROGE BY DOSE, YUH SON OF A...
19

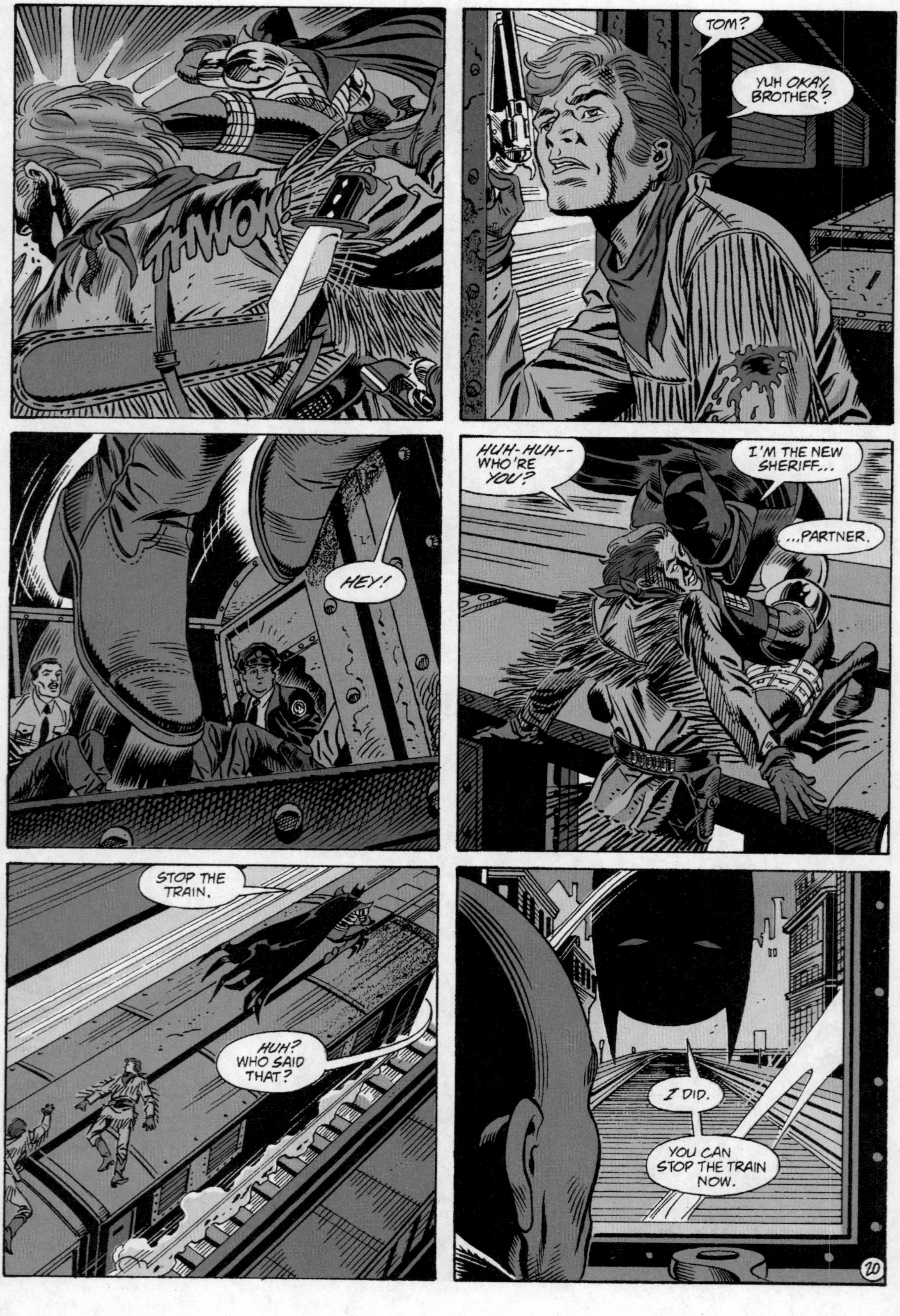
THWOK!
TOM?
YUH OKAY, BROTHER?
HEY!
HUH-HUH-- WHO'RE YOU?
I'M THE NEW SHERIFF...
...PARTNER.
STOP THE TRAIN.
HUH? WHO SAID THAT?
I DID.
YOU CAN STOP THE TRAIN NOW.
20

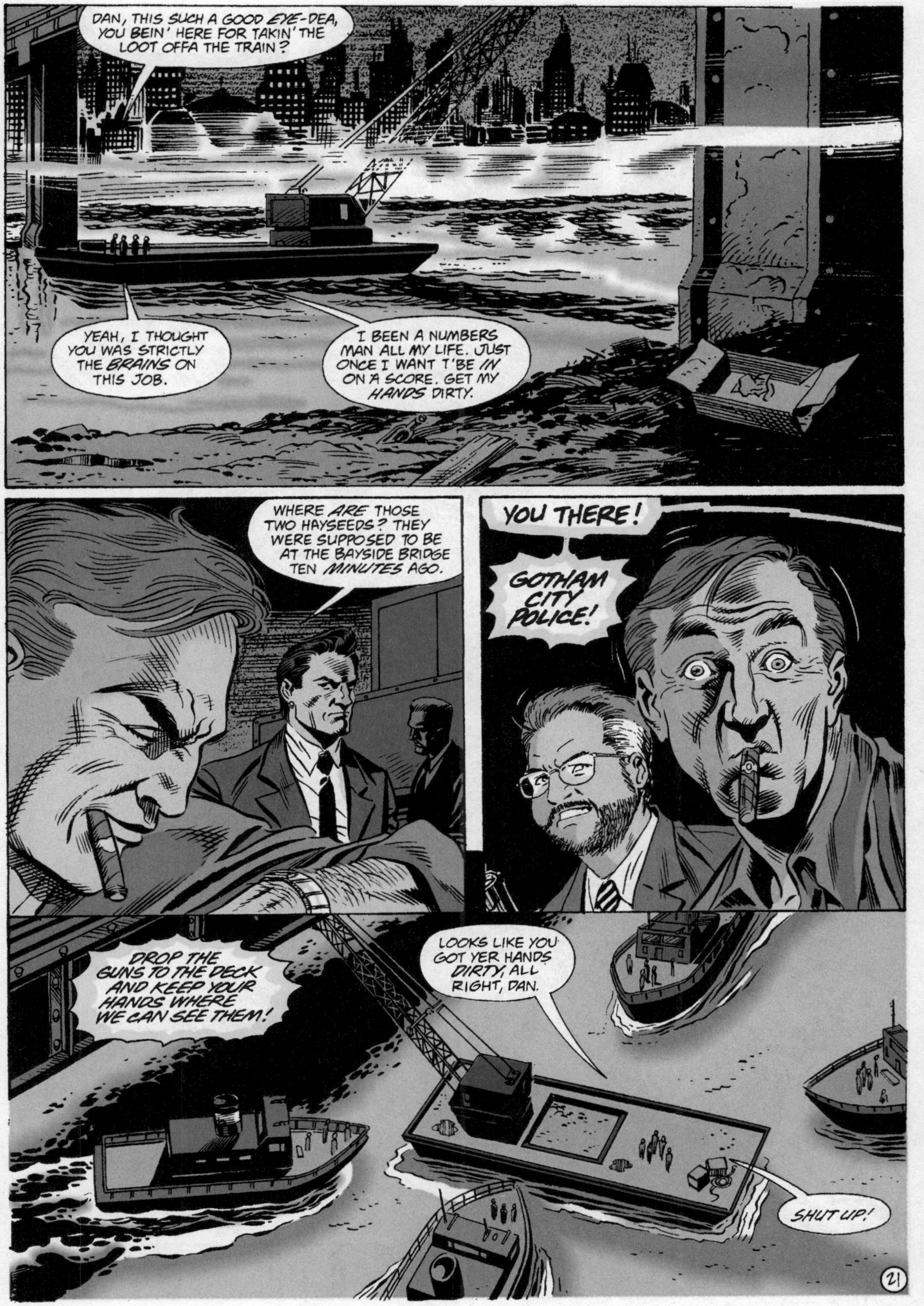
DAN, THIS SUCH A GOOD EYE-DEA, YOU BEIN' HERE FOR TAKIN' THE LOOT OFFA THE TRAIN?
YEAH, I THOUGHT YOU WAS STRICTLY THE BRAINS ON THIS JOB.
I BEEN A NUMBERS MAN ALL MY LIFE. JUST ONCE I WANT T'BE IN ON A SCORE. GET MY HANDS DIRTY.
WHERE ARE THOSE TWO HAYSEEDS? THEY WERE SUPPOSED TO BE AT THE BAYSIDE BRIDGE TEN MINUTES AGO.
YOU THERE!
GOTHAM CITY POLICE!
DROP THE GUNS TO THE DECK AND KEEP YOUR HANDS WHERE WE CAN SEE THEM!
LOOKS LIKE YOU GOT YER HANDS DIRTY, ALL RIGHT, DAN.
SHUT UP!
21

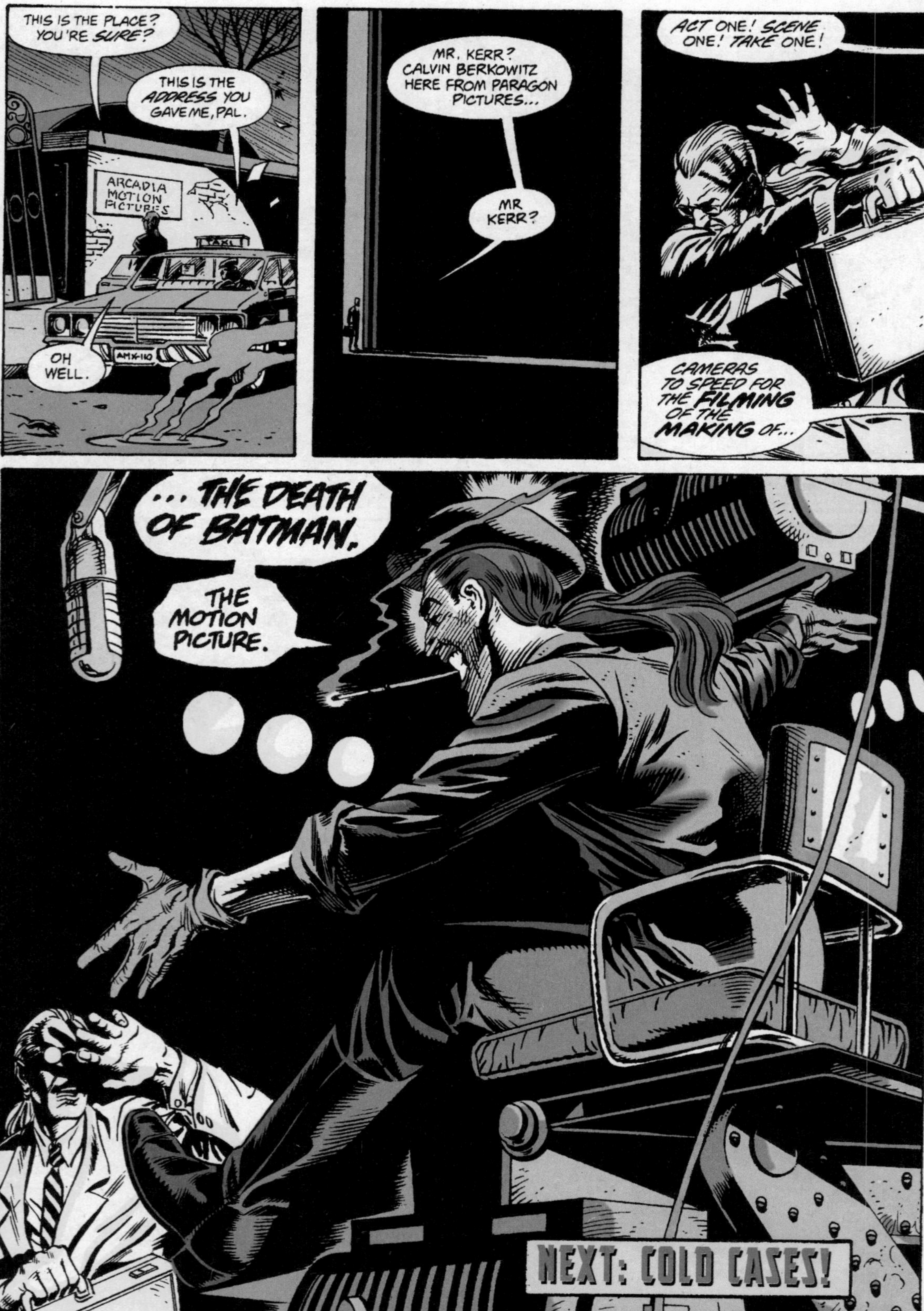
THIS IS THE PLACE? YOU'RE SURE?
THIS IS THE ADDRESS YOU GAVE ME, PAL.
ARCADIA MOTION PICTURES
TAXI
AMX-110
OH WELL.
MR. KERR? CALVIN BERKOWITZ HERE FROM PARAGON PICTURES...
MR KERR?
ACT ONE! SCENE ONE! TAKE ONE!
CAMERAS TO SPEED FOR THE FILMING OF THE MAKING OF...
... THE DEATH OF BATMAN.
THE MOTION PICTURE.
NEXT: COLD CASES!

Cover art by KELLEY JONES

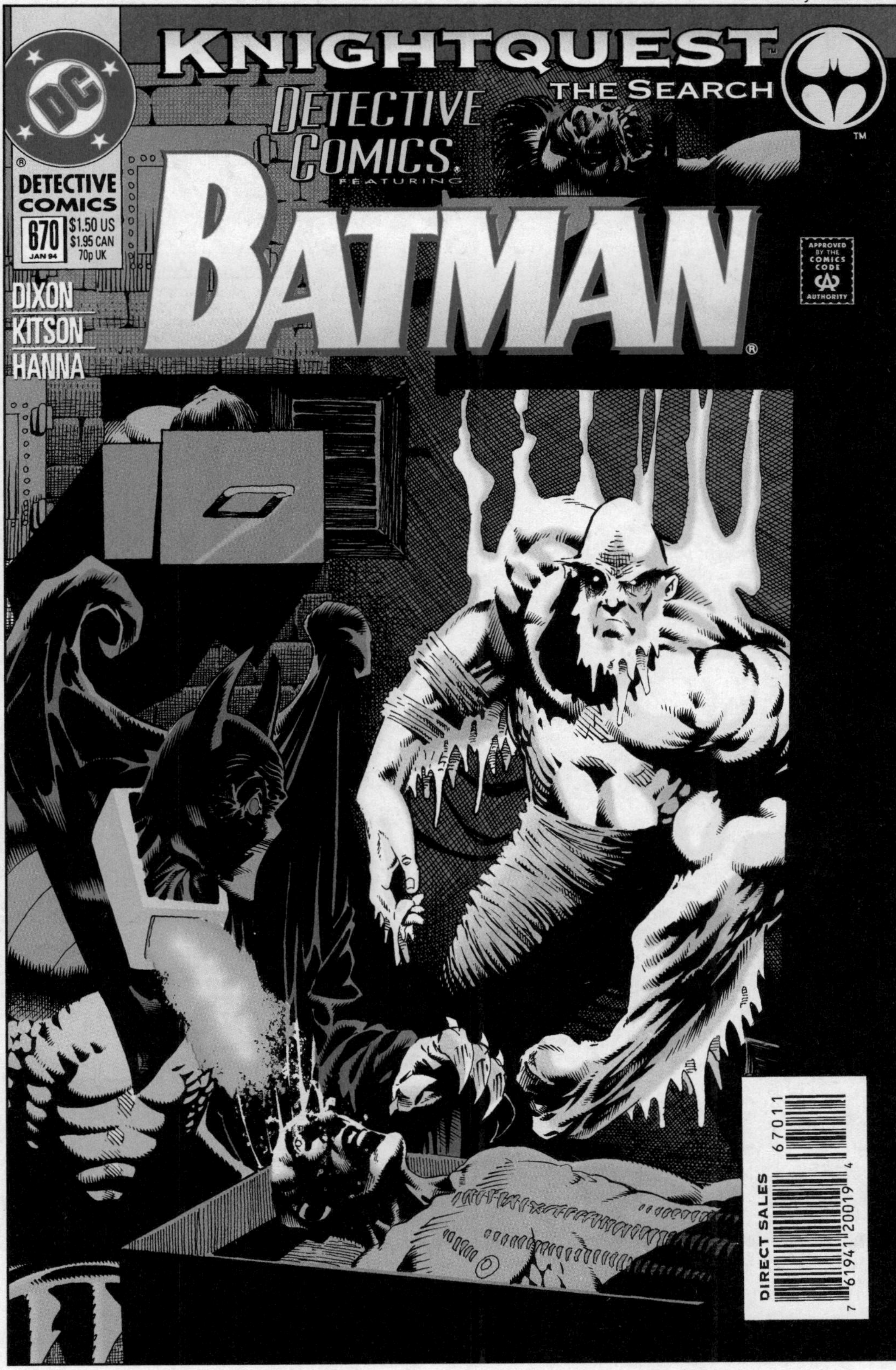
KNIGHTQUEST
THE SEARCH
DETECTIVE COMICS
FEATURING
BATMAN
DETECTIVE COMICS
670
JAN 94
$1.50 US
$1.95 CAN
70p UK
DIXON
KITSON
HANNA
APPROVED BY THE COMICS CODE AUTHORITY
DIRECT SALES

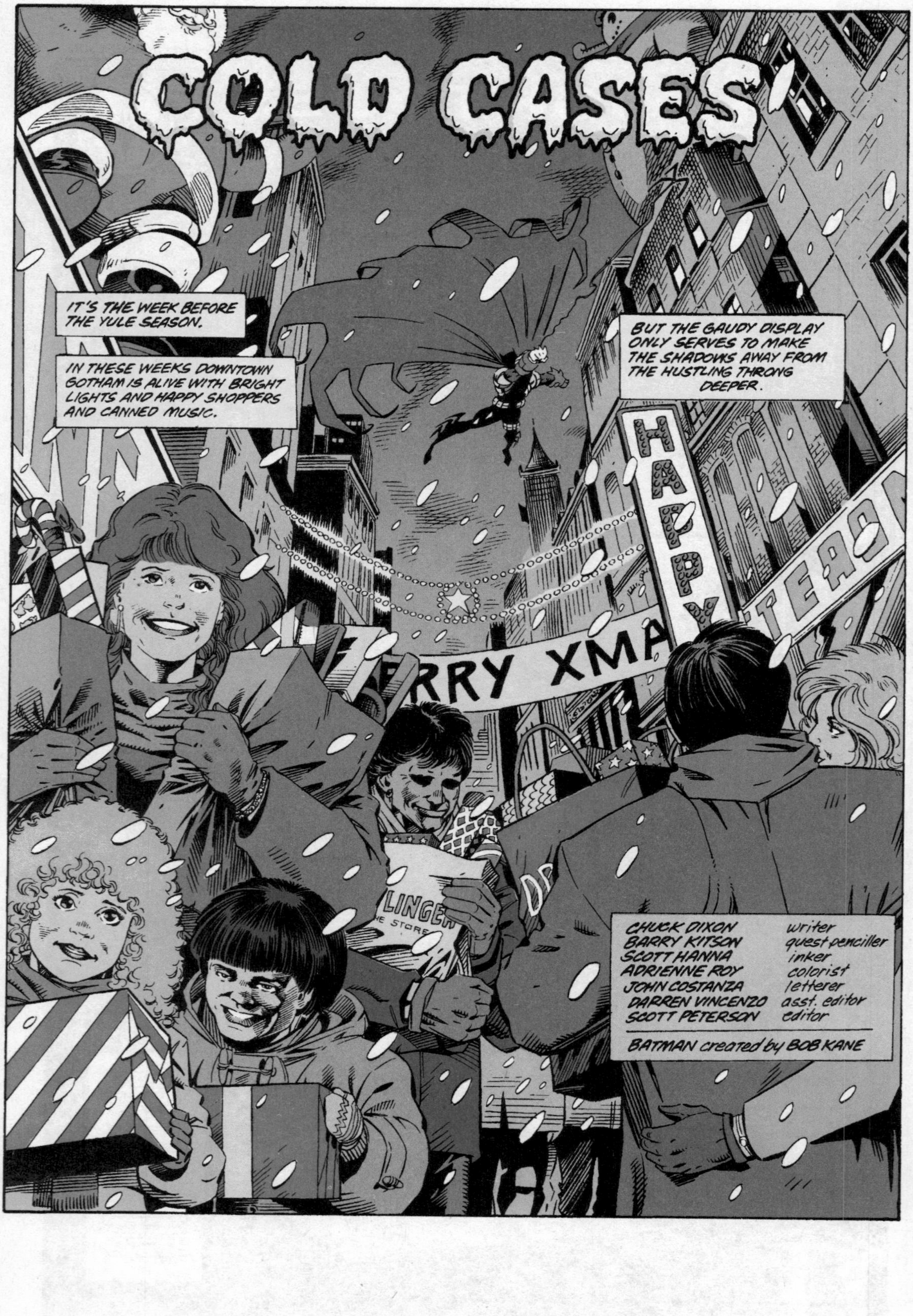
COLD CASES
IT'S THE WEEK BEFORE THE YULE SEASON.
IN THESE WEEKS DOWNTOWN GOTHAM IS ALIVE WITH BRIGHT LIGHTS AND HAPPY SHOPPERS AND CANNED MUSIC.
BUT THE GAUDY DISPLAY ONLY SERVES TO MAKE THE SHADOWS AWAY FROM THE HUSTLING THRONG DEEPER.
HAPPY
RRY XMA
CHUCK DIXON writer
BARRY KITSON guest penciller
SCOTT HANNA inker
ADRIENNE ROY colorist
JOHN COSTANZA letterer
DARREN VINCENZO asst. editor
SCOTT PETERSON editor
BATMAN created by BOB KANE

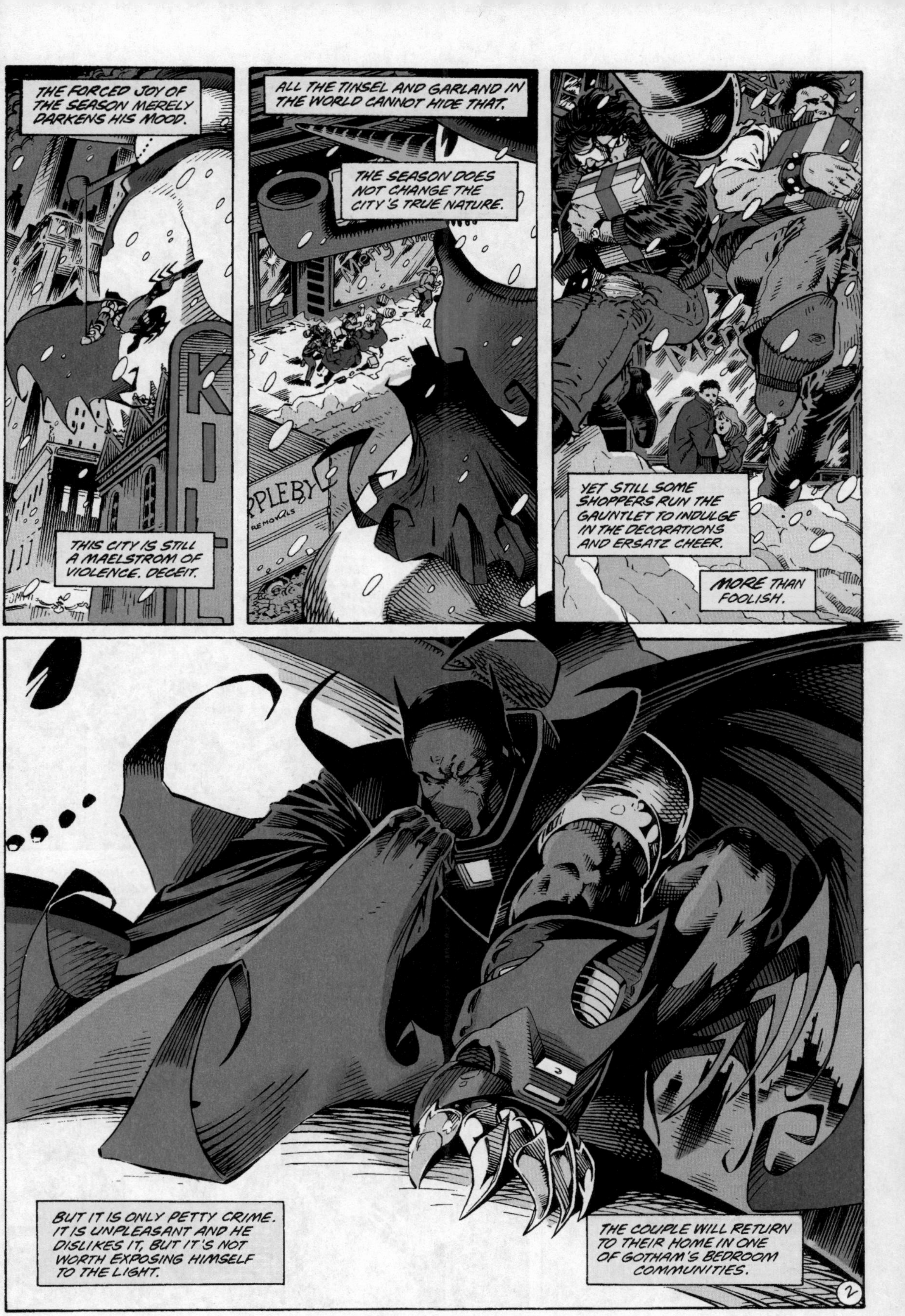
THE FORCED JOY OF THE SEASON MERELY DARKENS HIS MOOD.
THIS CITY IS STILL A MAELSTROM OF VIOLENCE. DECEIT.
ALL THE TINSEL AND GARLAND IN THE WORLD CANNOT HIDE THAT.
THE SEASON DOES NOT CHANGE THE CITY'S TRUE NATURE.
YET STILL SOME SHOPPERS RUN THE GAUNTLET TO INDULGE IN THE DECORATIONS AND ERSATZ CHEER.
MORE THAN FOOLISH.
BUT IT IS ONLY PETTY CRIME. IT IS UNPLEASANT AND HE DISLIKES IT, BUT IT'S NOT WORTH EXPOSING HIMSELF TO THE LIGHT.
THE COUPLE WILL RETURN TO THEIR HOME IN ONE OF GOTHAM'S BEDROOM COMMUNITIES.
2

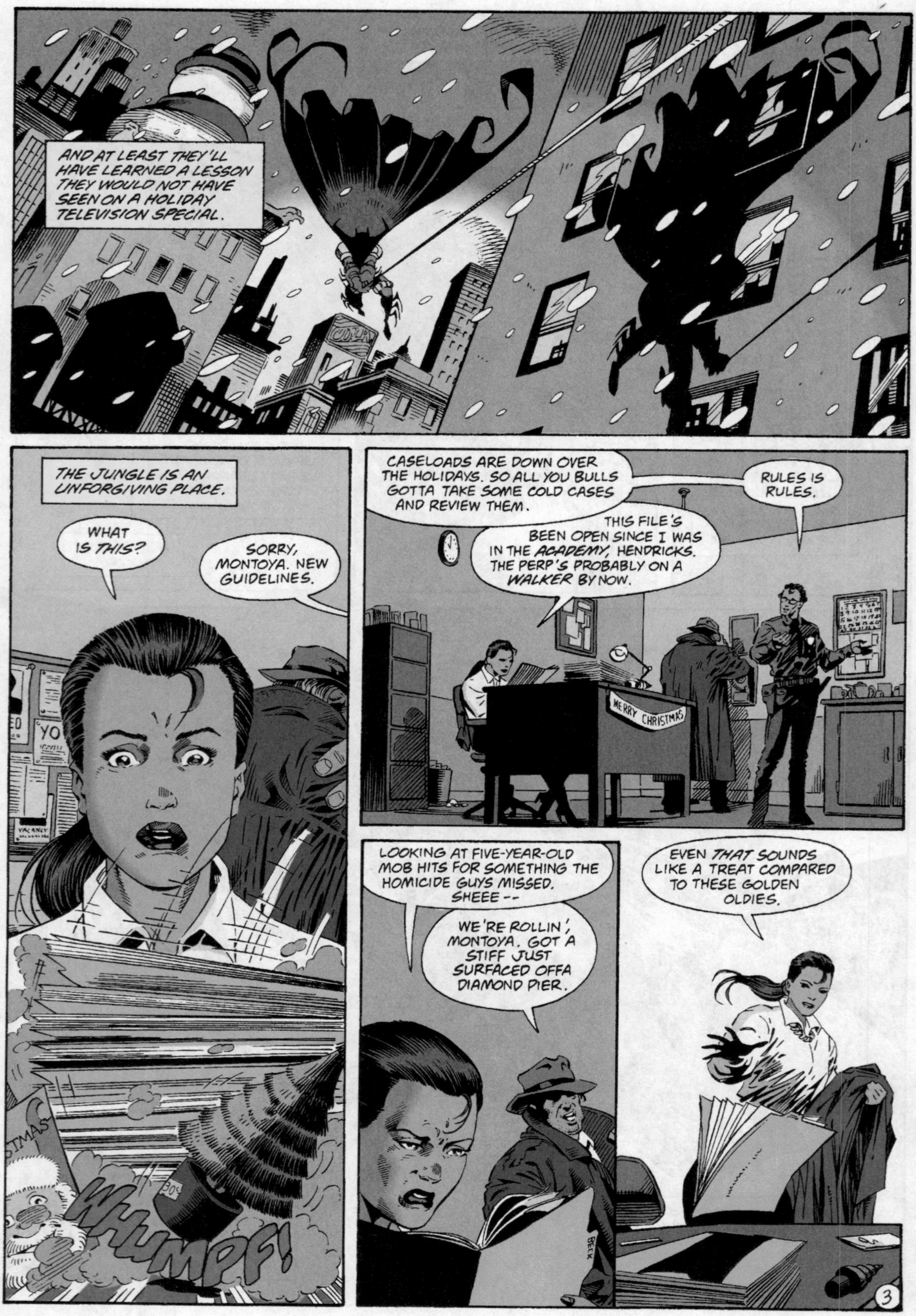
AND AT LEAST THEY'LL HAVE LEARNED A LESSON THEY WOULD NOT HAVE SEEN ON A HOLIDAY TELEVISION SPECIAL.
THE JUNGLE IS AN UNFORGIVING PLACE.
WHAT IS THIS?
SORRY, MONTOYA. NEW GUIDELINES.
WHUMPF!
CASELOADS ARE DOWN OVER THE HOLIDAYS. SO ALL YOU BULLS GOTTA TAKE SOME COLD CASES AND REVIEW THEM.
RULES IS RULES.
THIS FILE'S BEEN OPEN SINCE I WAS IN THE ACADEMY, HENDRICKS. THE PERP'S PROBABLY ON A WALKER BY NOW.
MERRY CHRISTMAS
LOOKING AT FIVE-YEAR-OLD MOB HITS FOR SOMETHING THE HOMICIDE GUYS MISSED. SHEEE --
WE'RE ROLLIN', MONTOYA. GOT A STIFF JUST SURFACED OFFA DIAMOND PIER.
EVEN THAT SOUNDS LIKE A TREAT COMPARED TO THESE GOLDEN OLDIES.
3

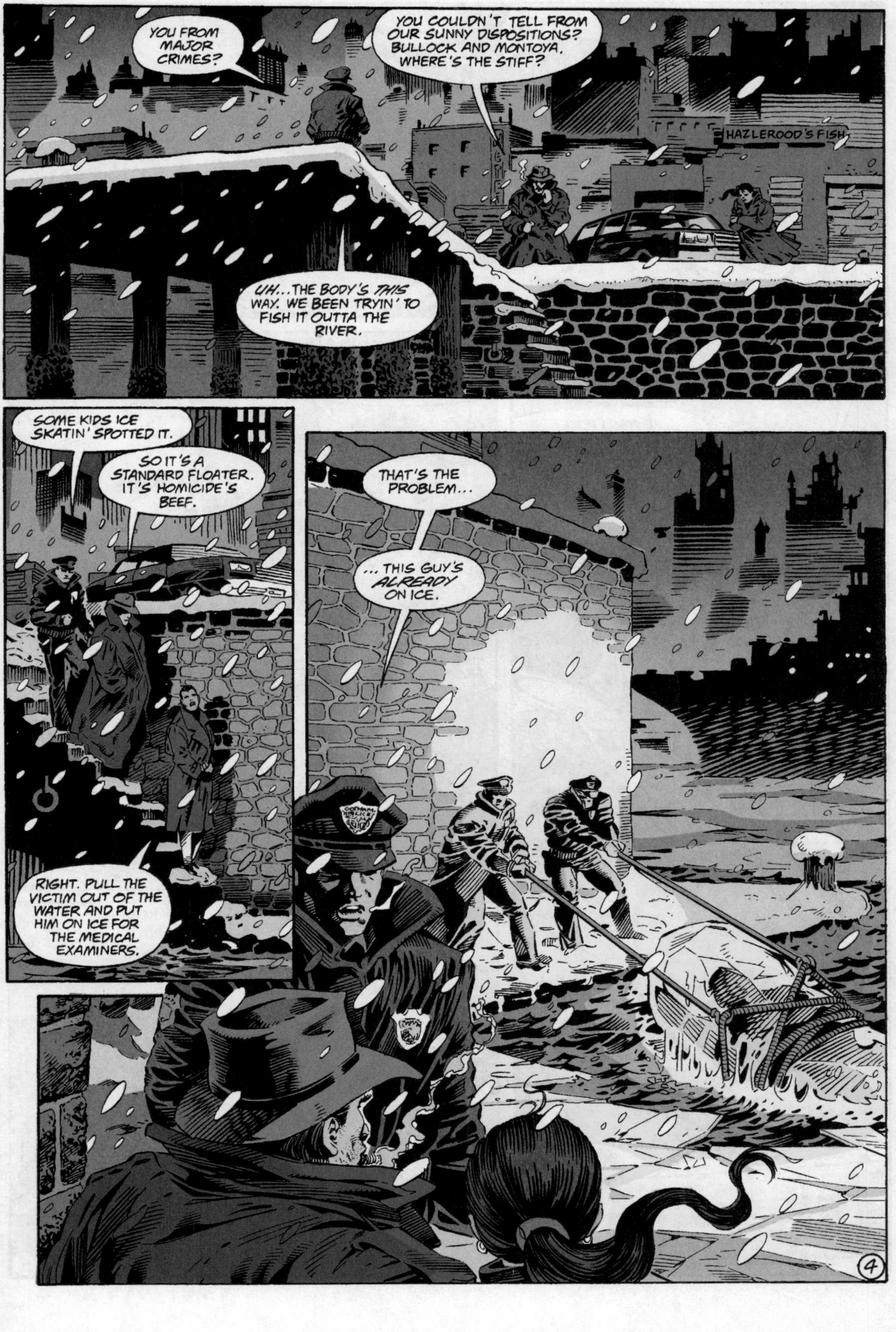
YOU FROM MAJOR CRIMES?
YOU COULDN'T TELL FROM OUR SUNNY DISPOSITIONS? BULLOCK AND MONTOYA. WHERE'S THE STIFF?
HAZLEROOD'S FISH
UH... THE BODY'S THIS WAY. WE BEEN TRYIN' TO FISH IT OUTTA THE RIVER.
SOME KIDS ICE SKATIN' SPOTTED IT.
SO IT'S A STANDARD FLOATER. IT'S HOMICIDE'S BEEF.
RIGHT. PULL THE VICTIM OUT OF THE WATER AND PUT HIM ON ICE FOR THE MEDICAL EXAMINERS.
THAT'S THE PROBLEM...
...THIS GUY'S ALREADY ON ICE.
4

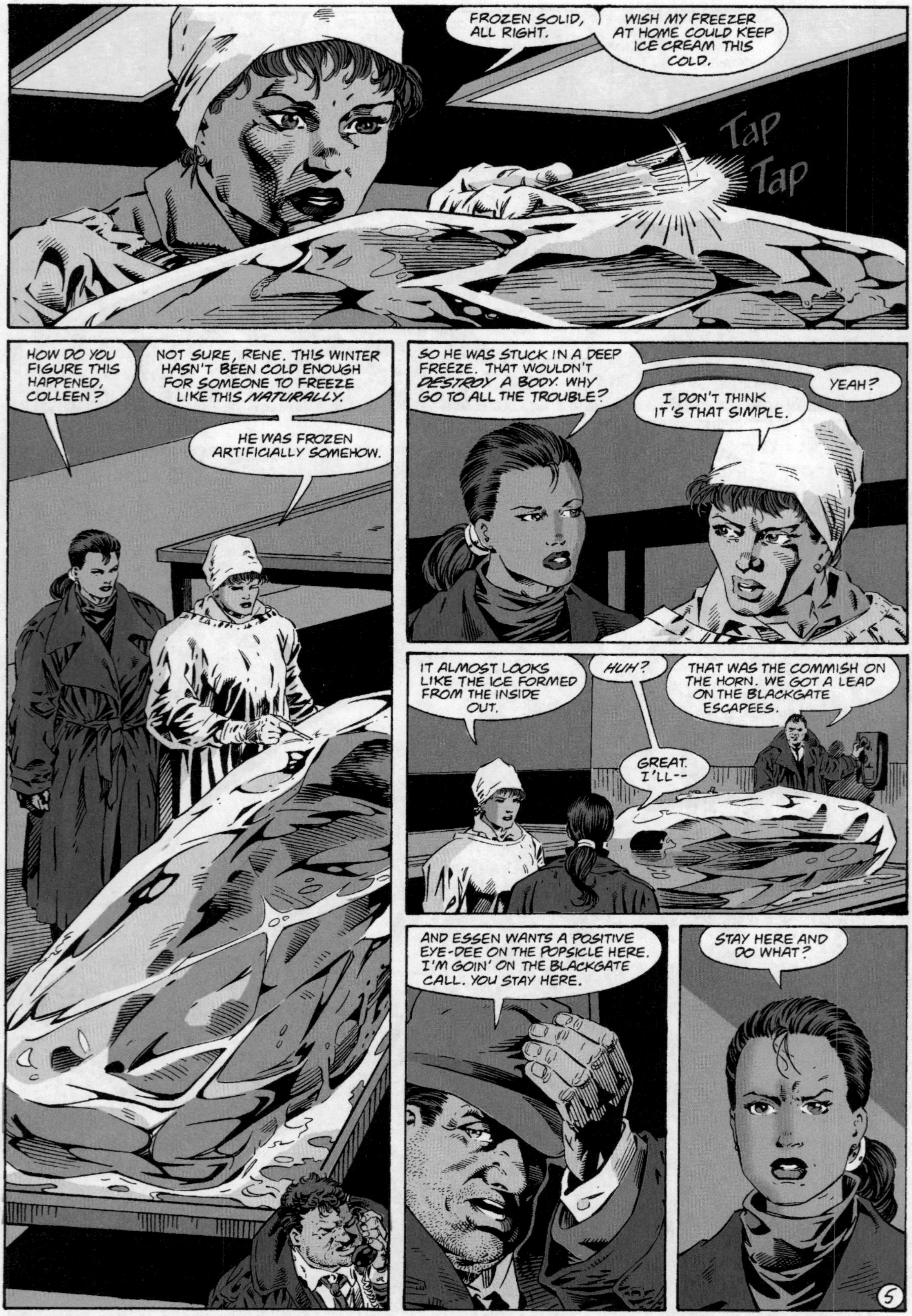
FROZEN SOLID, ALL RIGHT.
WISH MY FREEZER AT HOME COULD KEEP ICE CREAM THIS COLD.
Tap Tap
HOW DO YOU FIGURE THIS HAPPENED, COLLEEN?
NOT SURE, RENE. THIS WINTER HASN'T BEEN COLD ENOUGH FOR SOMEONE TO FREEZE LIKE THIS NATURALLY.
HE WAS FROZEN ARTIFICIALLY SOMEHOW.
SO HE WAS STUCK IN A DEEP FREEZE. THAT WOULDN'T DESTROY A BODY. WHY GO TO ALL THE TROUBLE?
I DON'T THINK IT'S THAT SIMPLE.
YEAH?
IT ALMOST LOOKS LIKE THE ICE FORMED FROM THE INSIDE OUT.
HUH?
THAT WAS THE COMMISH ON THE HORN. WE GOT A LEAD ON THE BLACKGATE ESCAPEES.
GREAT. I'LL--
AND ESSEN WANTS A POSITIVE EYE-DEE ON THE POPSICLE HERE. I'M GOIN' ON THE BLACKGATE CALL. YOU STAY HERE.
STAY HERE AND DO WHAT?
5

WAIT FOR THE STIFF TO *THAW OUT*, MONTOYA.

THIS GUY'S A HOT DATE COMPARED TO *SOME* OF THE CLOWNS YOU'VE BEEN DATING.

HARV...

WHAT A WASTE OF TIME...

LOOK, WE'VE GOT SIX-MONTH-OLD MAGAZINES IN THE WAITING LOUNGE, BUT THE COFFEE'S FRESH.

I GOT A FEW THINGS TO LOOK INTO, NO PUN INTENDED.

YEAH. A CUP OF COFFEE FOR ME AND A HOT *BLOWTORCH* FOR MY *BUDDY* HERE.

WHY COULDN'T YOU HAVE SURFACED ON *DAYWATCH*?

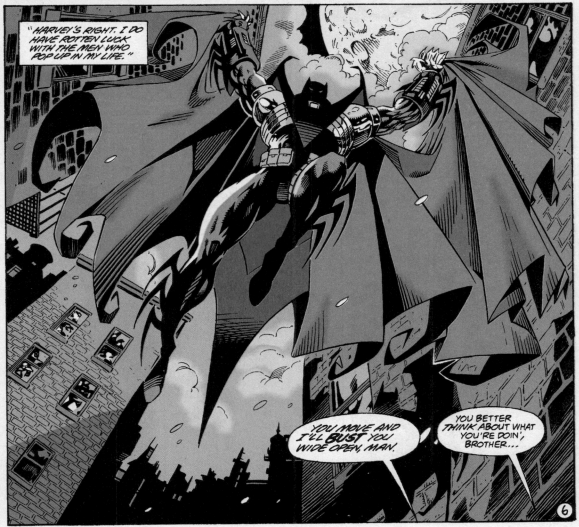

"HARVEY'S RIGHT. I DO HAVE ROTTEN LUCK WITH THE MEN WHO POP UP IN MY LIFE."

YOU MOVE AND I'LL *BUST* YOU WIDE OPEN, MAN.

YOU BETTER *THINK* ABOUT WHAT YOU'RE DOIN', BROTHER...

6

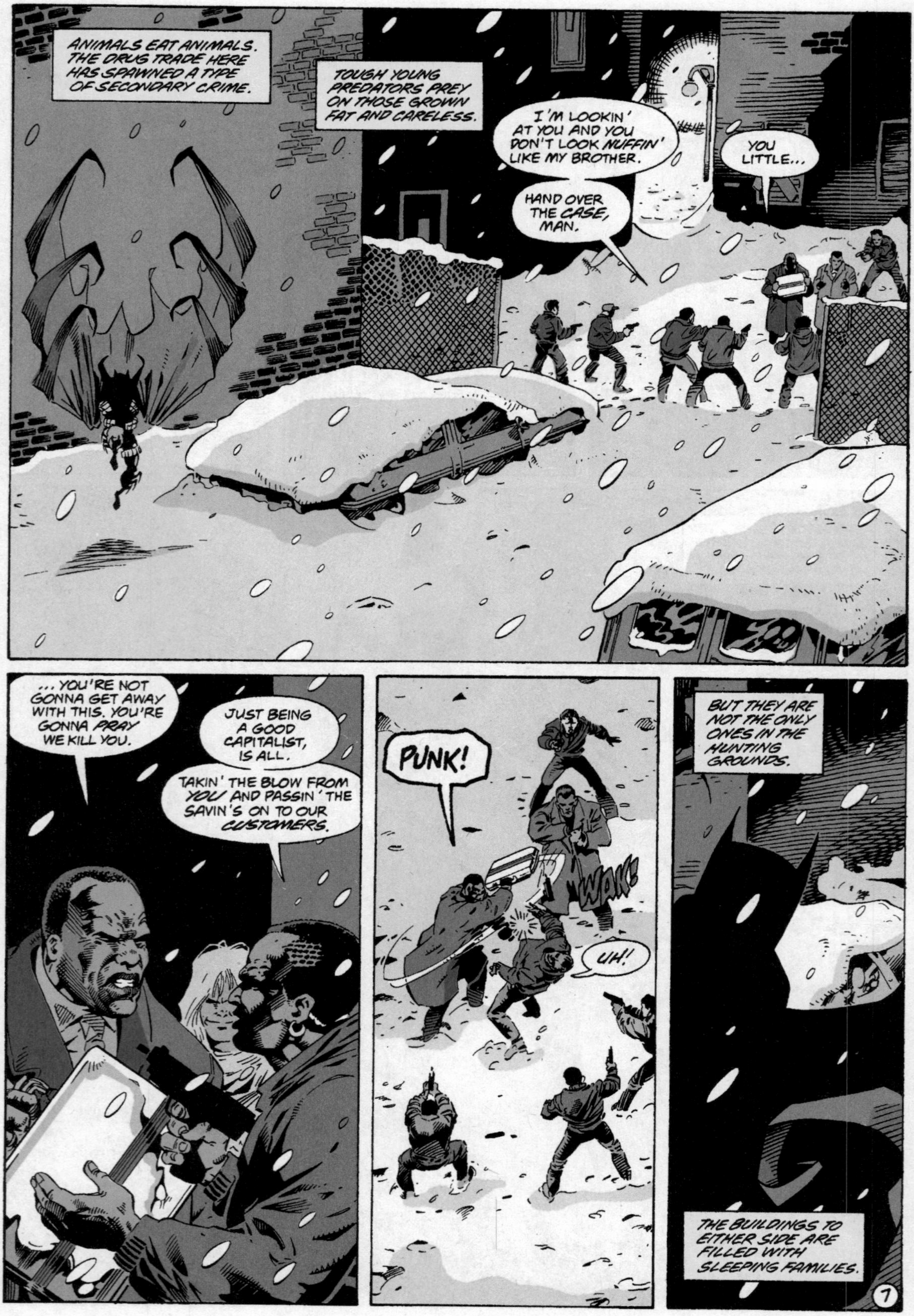
ANIMALS EAT ANIMALS. THE DRUG TRADE HERE HAS SPAWNED A TYPE OF SECONDARY CRIME.
TOUGH YOUNG PREDATORS PREY ON THOSE GROWN FAT AND CARELESS.
I'M LOOKIN' AT YOU AND YOU DON'T LOOK NUFFIN' LIKE MY BROTHER.
HAND OVER THE CASE, MAN.
YOU LITTLE...
...YOU'RE NOT GONNA GET AWAY WITH THIS. YOU'RE GONNA PRAY WE KILL YOU.
JUST BEING A GOOD CAPITALIST, IS ALL.
TAKIN' THE BLOW FROM YOU AND PASSIN' THE SAVIN'S ON TO OUR CUSTOMERS.
PUNK!
WAK!
UH!
BUT THEY ARE NOT THE ONLY ONES IN THE HUNTING GROUNDS.
THE BUILDINGS TO EITHER SIDE ARE FILLED WITH SLEEPING FAMILIES.
7

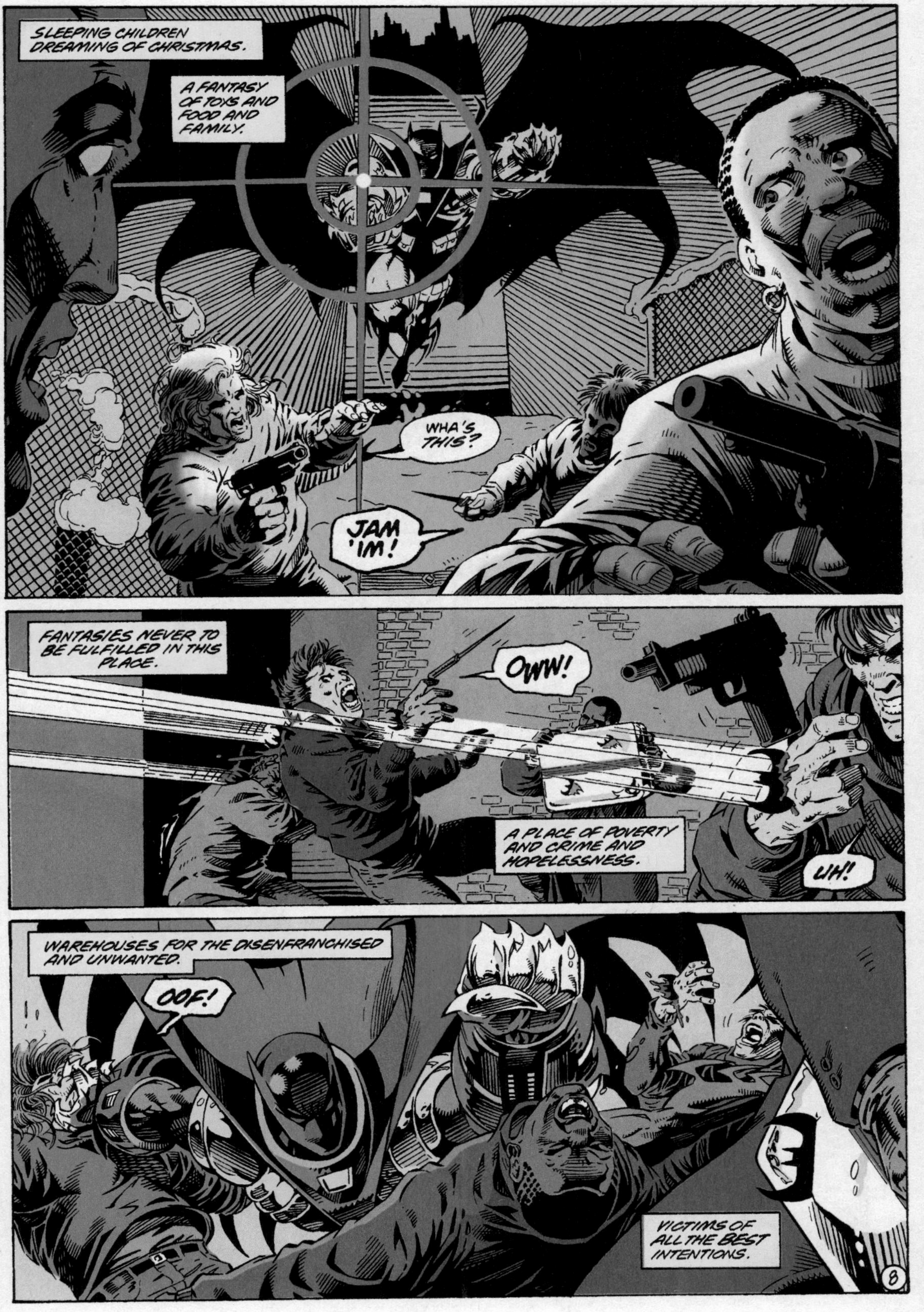
SLEEPING CHILDREN DREAMING OF CHRISTMAS.
A FANTASY OF TOYS AND FOOD AND FAMILY.
WHA'S THIS?
JAM 'IM!
FANTASIES NEVER TO BE FULFILLED IN THIS PLACE.
OWW!
A PLACE OF POVERTY AND CRIME AND HOPELESSNESS.
UH!
WAREHOUSES FOR THE DISENFRANCHISED AND UNWANTED.
OOF!
VICTIMS OF ALL THE BEST INTENTIONS.
8

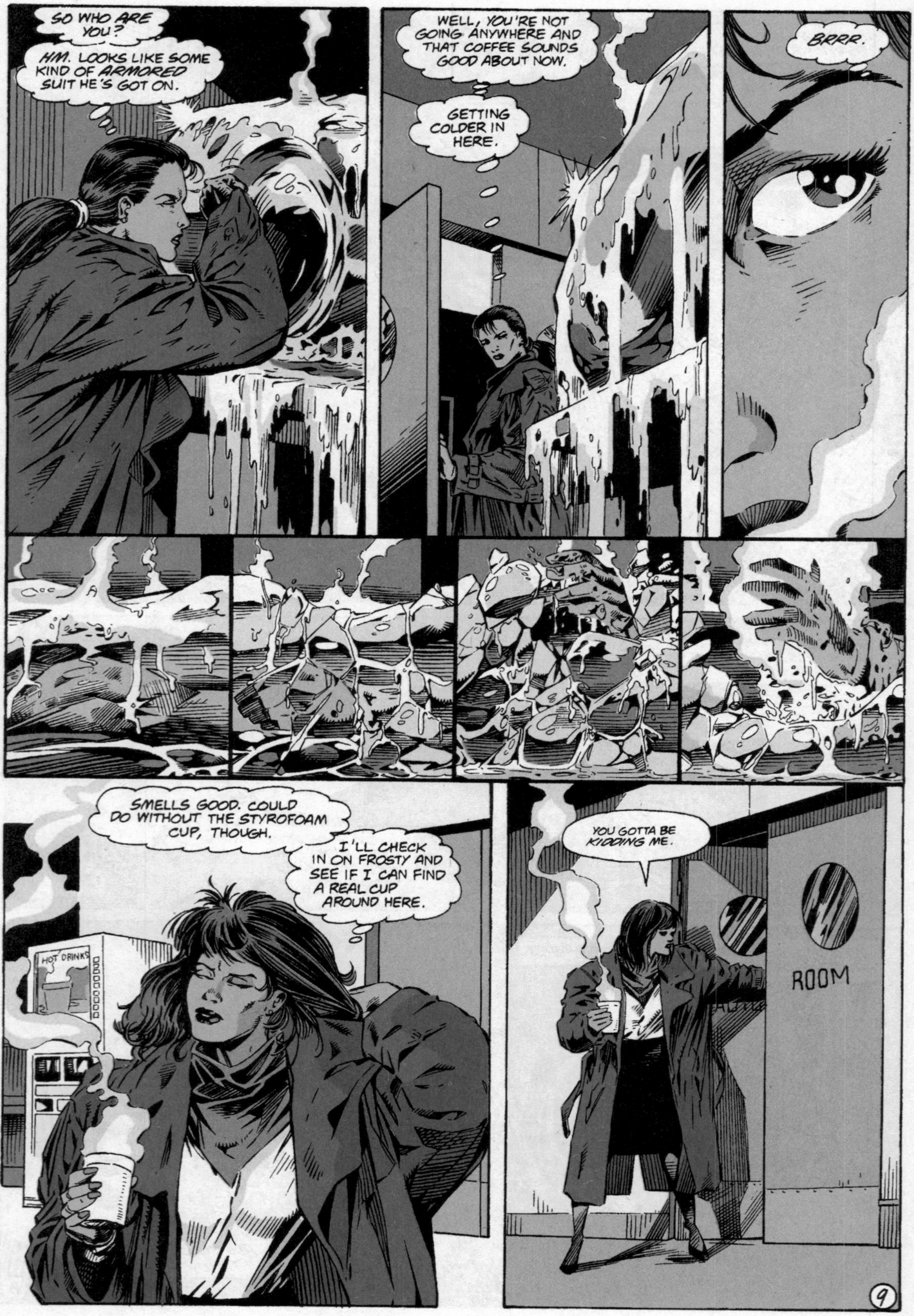
SO WHO ARE YOU?
HM. LOOKS LIKE SOME KIND OF ARMORED SUIT HE'S GOT ON.
WELL, YOU'RE NOT GOING ANYWHERE AND THAT COFFEE SOUNDS GOOD ABOUT NOW.
GETTING COLDER IN HERE.
BRRR.
SMELLS GOOD. COULD DO WITHOUT THE STYROFOAM CUP, THOUGH.
I'LL CHECK IN ON FROSTY AND SEE IF I CAN FIND A REAL CUP AROUND HERE.
HOT DRINKS
YOU GOTTA BE KIDDING ME.
ROOM
9

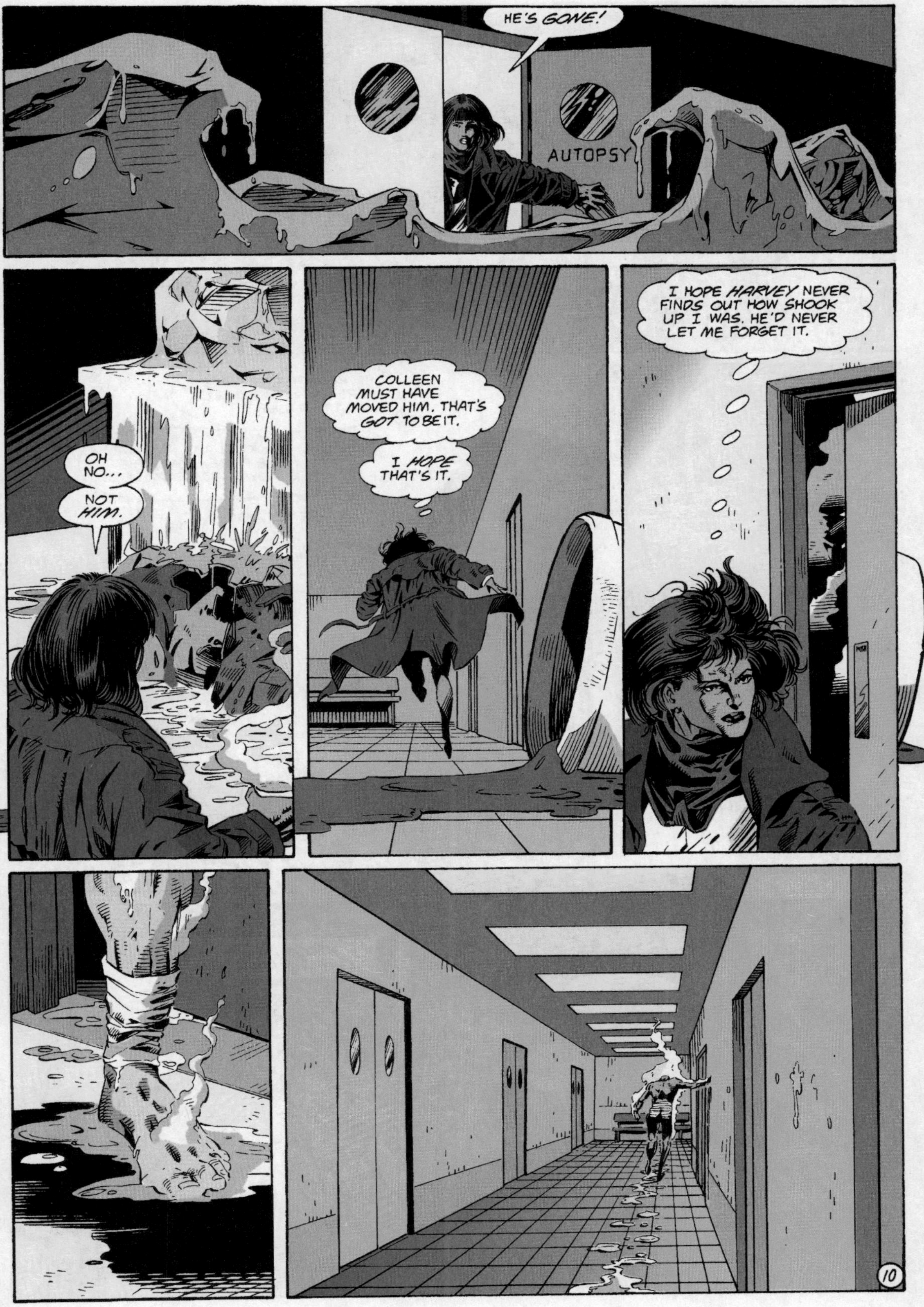

HE'S GONE!
AUTOPSY
OH NO...
NOT HIM.
COLLEEN MUST HAVE MOVED HIM. THAT'S GOT TO BE IT.
I HOPE THAT'S IT.
I HOPE HARVEY NEVER FINDS OUT HOW SHOOK UP I WAS. HE'D NEVER LET ME FORGET IT.
10

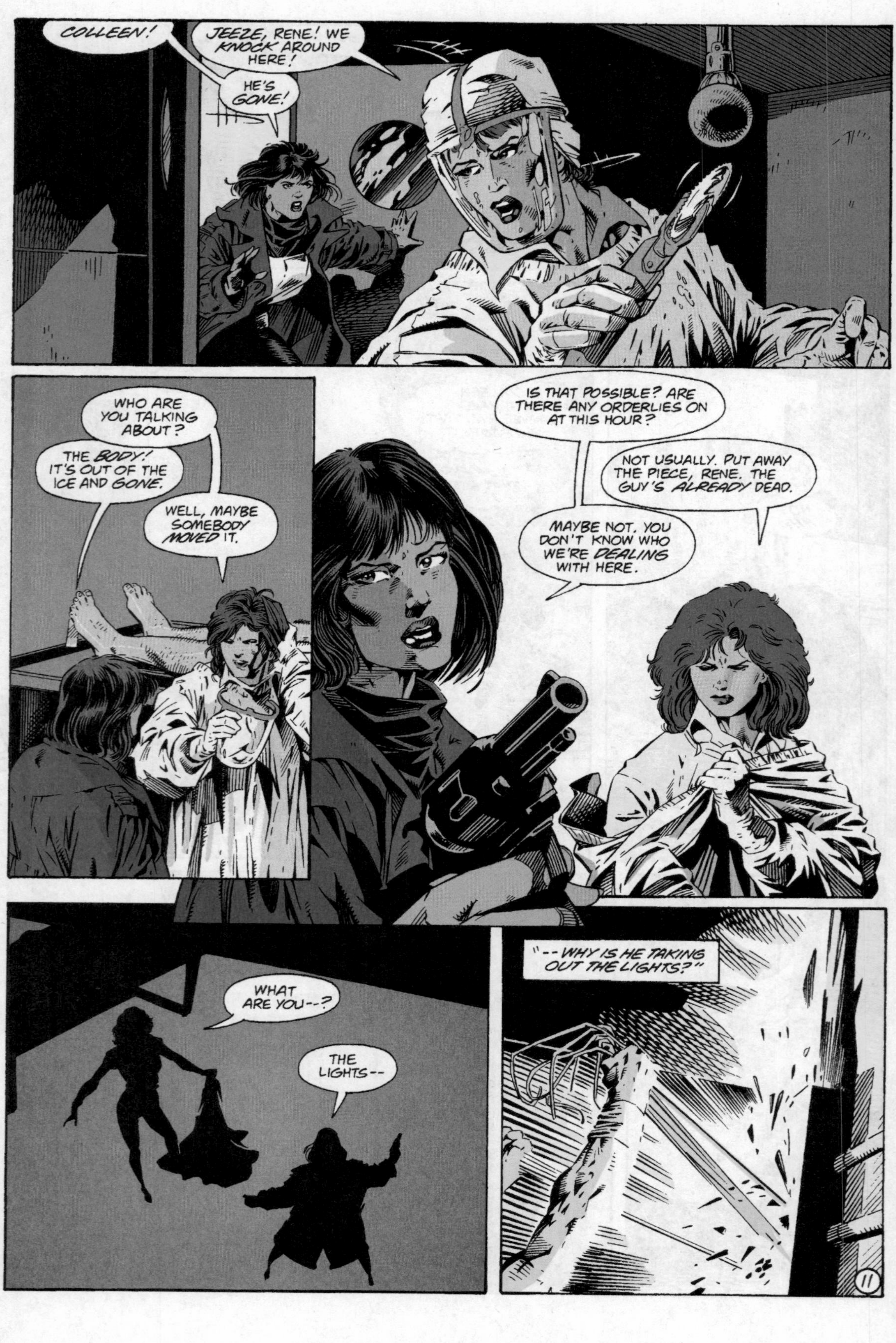
COLLEEN!
JEEZE, RENE! WE KNOCK AROUND HERE!
HE'S GONE!
WHO ARE YOU TALKING ABOUT?
THE BODY! IT'S OUT OF THE ICE AND GONE.
WELL, MAYBE SOMEBODY MOVED IT.
IS THAT POSSIBLE? ARE THERE ANY ORDERLIES ON AT THIS HOUR?
NOT USUALLY. PUT AWAY THE PIECE, RENE. THE GUY'S ALREADY DEAD.
MAYBE NOT. YOU DON'T KNOW WHO WE'RE DEALING WITH HERE.
WHAT ARE YOU--?
THE LIGHTS--
"--WHY IS HE TAKING OUT THE LIGHTS?"
11

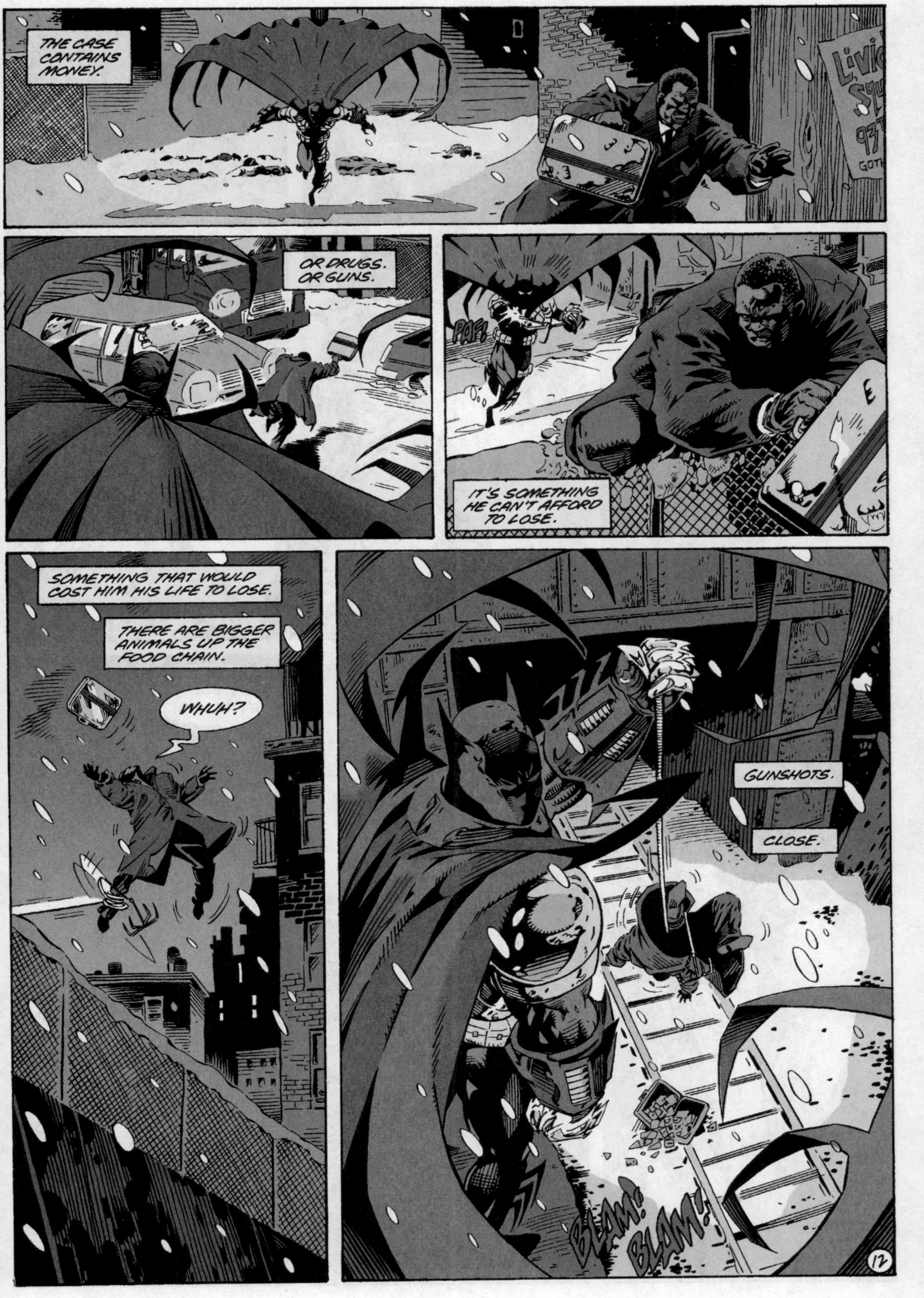
THE CASE CONTAINS MONEY.
OR DRUGS. OR GUNS.
PAF!
IT'S SOMETHING HE CAN'T AFFORD TO LOSE.
SOMETHING THAT WOULD COST HIM HIS LIFE TO LOSE.
THERE ARE BIGGER ANIMALS UP THE FOOD CHAIN.
WHUH?
GUNSHOTS.
CLOSE.
BLAM! BLAM!
12

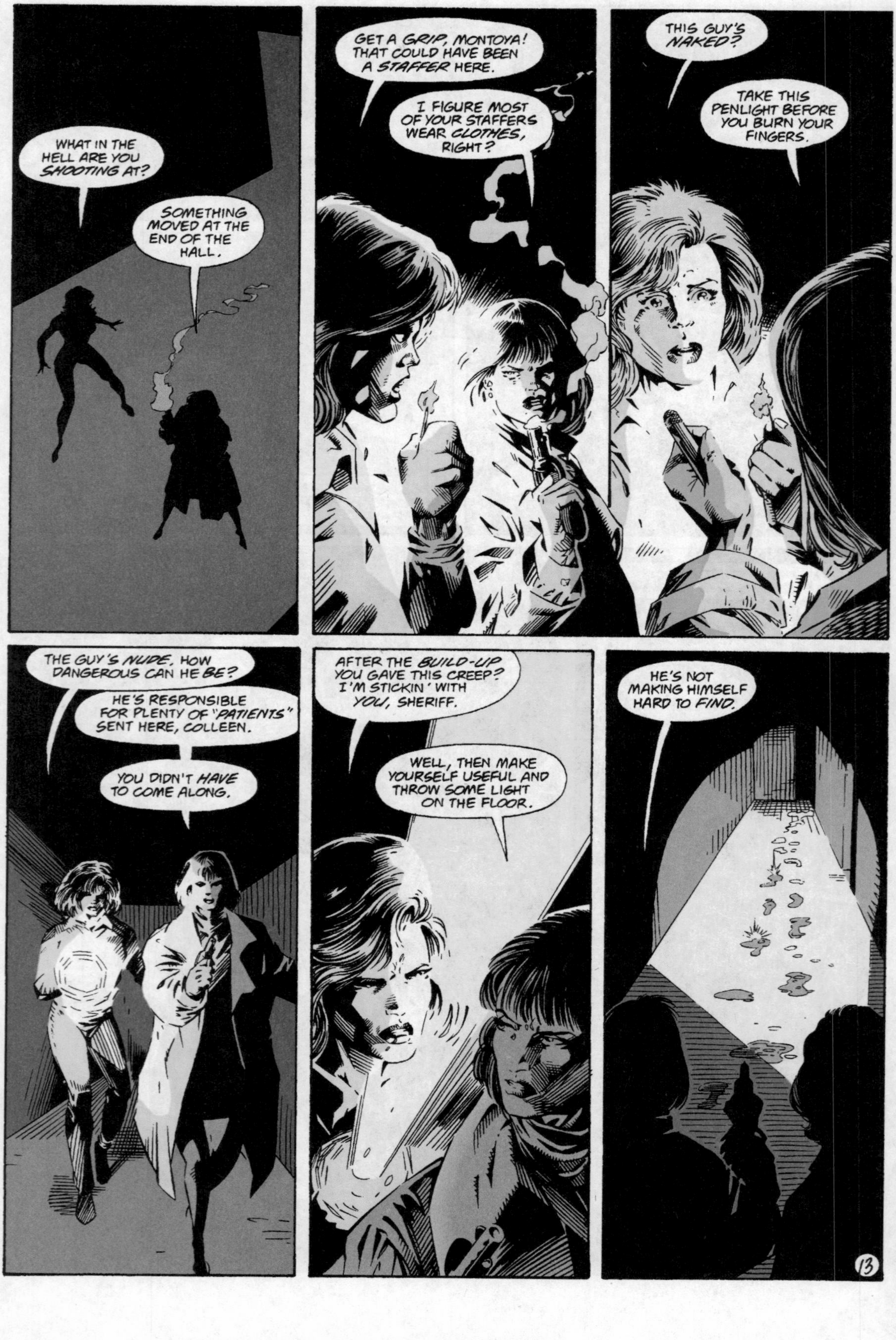
WHAT IN THE HELL ARE YOU SHOOTING AT?
SOMETHING MOVED AT THE END OF THE HALL.
GET A GRIP, MONTOYA! THAT COULD HAVE BEEN A STAFFER HERE.
I FIGURE MOST OF YOUR STAFFERS WEAR CLOTHES, RIGHT?
THIS GUY'S NAKED?
TAKE THIS PENLIGHT BEFORE YOU BURN YOUR FINGERS.
THE GUY'S NUDE. HOW DANGEROUS CAN HE BE?
HE'S RESPONSIBLE FOR PLENTY OF "PATIENTS" SENT HERE, COLLEEN.
YOU DIDN'T HAVE TO COME ALONG.
AFTER THE BUILD-UP YOU GAVE THIS CREEP? I'M STICKIN' WITH YOU, SHERIFF.
WELL, THEN MAKE YOURSELF USEFUL AND THROW SOME LIGHT ON THE FLOOR.
HE'S NOT MAKING HIMSELF HARD TO FIND.
13

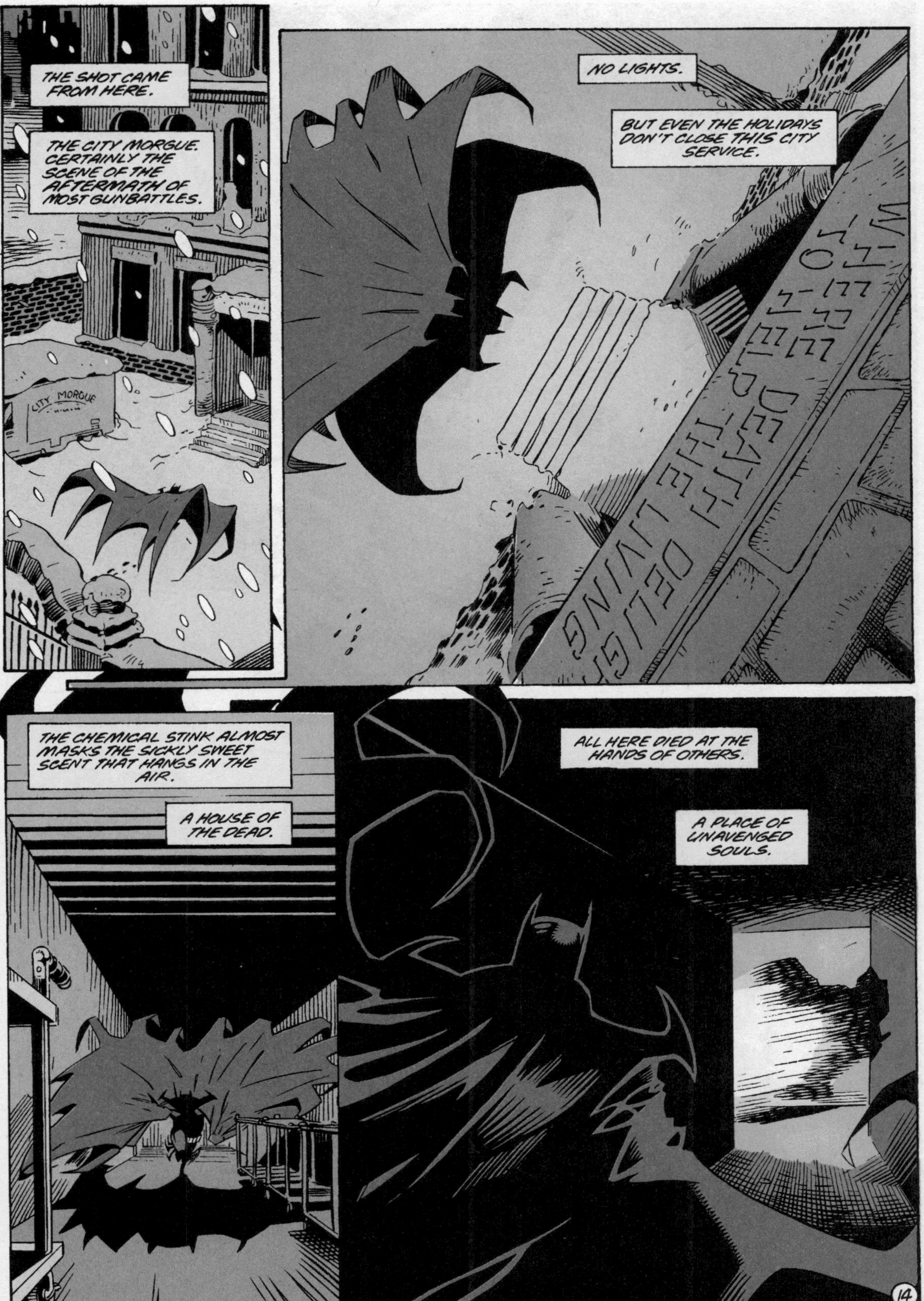
THE SHOT CAME FROM HERE.
THE CITY MORGUE. CERTAINLY THE SCENE OF THE AFTERMATH OF MOST GUNBATTLES.
CITY MORGUE
NO LIGHTS.
BUT EVEN THE HOLIDAYS DON'T CLOSE THIS CITY SERVICE.
WHERE DEATH
TO HELP THE LIVING
THE CHEMICAL STINK ALMOST MASKS THE SICKLY SWEET SCENT THAT HANGS IN THE AIR.
A HOUSE OF THE DEAD.
ALL HERE DIED AT THE HANDS OF OTHERS.
A PLACE OF UNAVENGED SOULS.
14

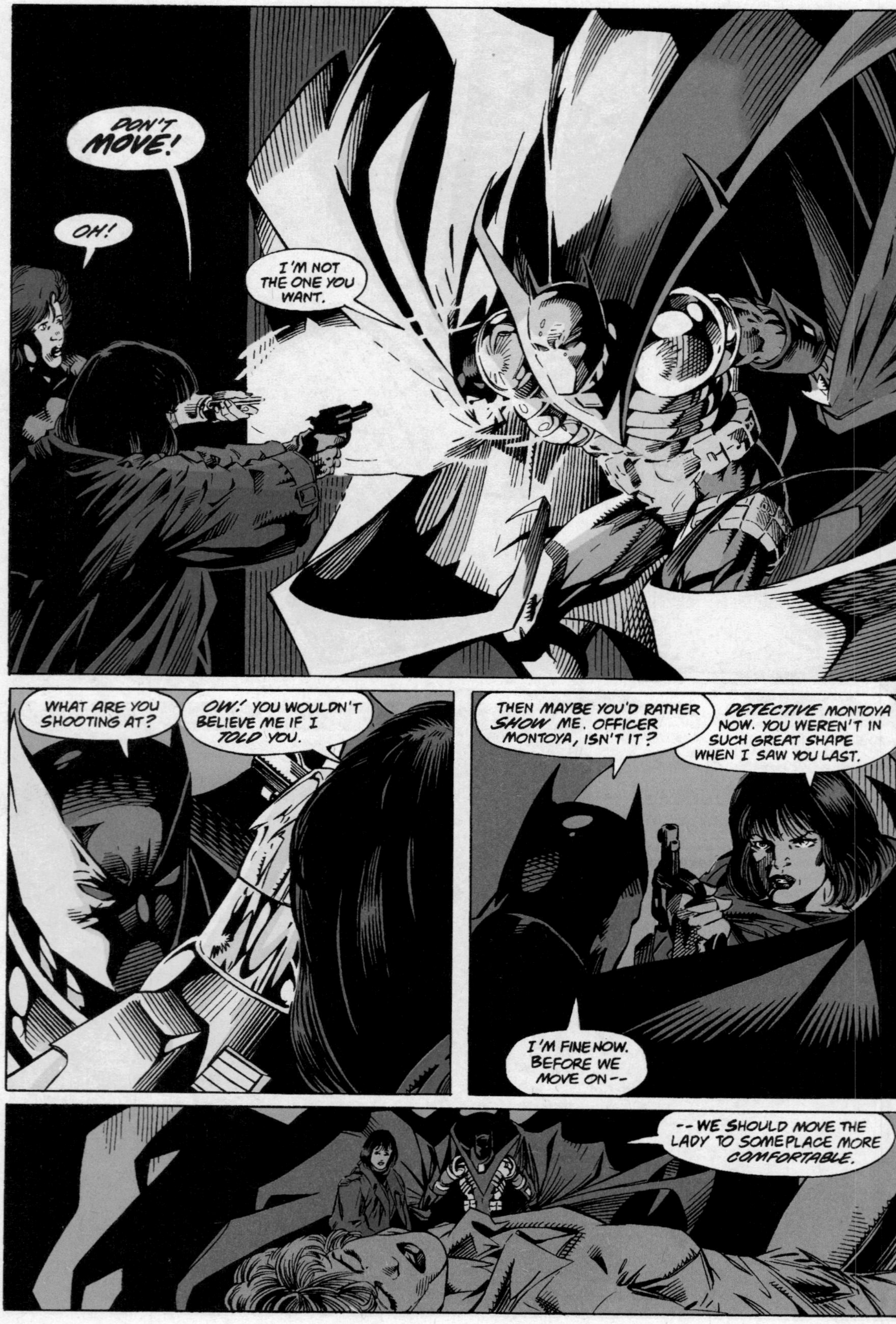
DON'T MOVE!
OH!
I'M NOT THE ONE YOU WANT.
WHAT ARE YOU SHOOTING AT?
OW! YOU WOULDN'T BELIEVE ME IF I TOLD YOU.
THEN MAYBE YOU'D RATHER SHOW ME. OFFICER MONTOYA, ISN'T IT?
DETECTIVE MONTOYA NOW. YOU WEREN'T IN SUCH GREAT SHAPE WHEN I SAW YOU LAST.
I'M FINE NOW. BEFORE WE MOVE ON--
--WE SHOULD MOVE THE LADY TO SOMEPLACE MORE COMFORTABLE.

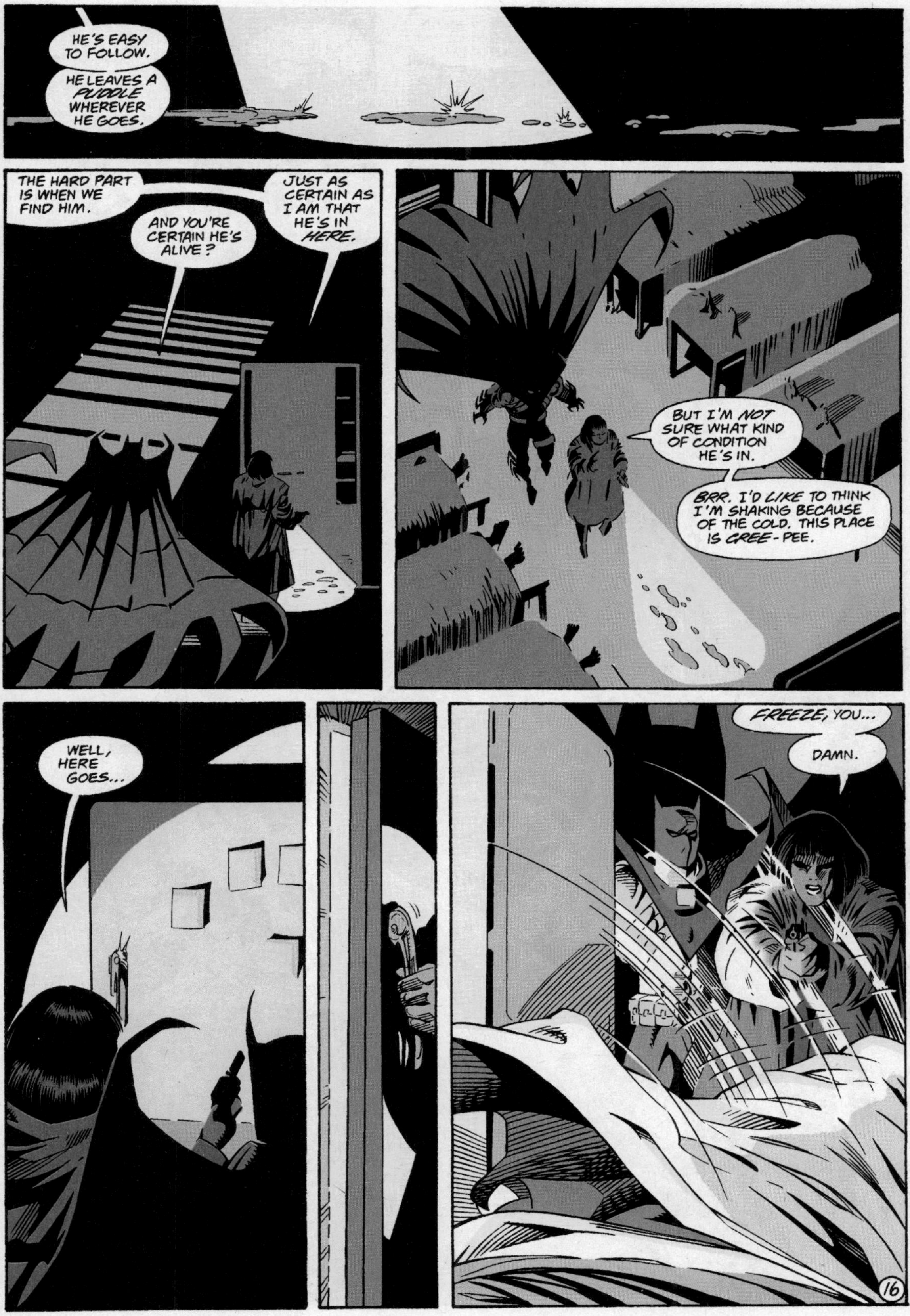
HE'S EASY TO FOLLOW.
HE LEAVES A PUDDLE WHEREVER HE GOES.
THE HARD PART IS WHEN WE FIND HIM.
AND YOU'RE CERTAIN HE'S ALIVE?
JUST AS CERTAIN AS I AM THAT HE'S IN HERE.
BUT I'M NOT SURE WHAT KIND OF CONDITION HE'S IN.
BRR. I'D LIKE TO THINK I'M SHAKING BECAUSE OF THE COLD. THIS PLACE IS CREE-PEE.
WELL, HERE GOES...
FREEZE, YOU...
DAMN.
16

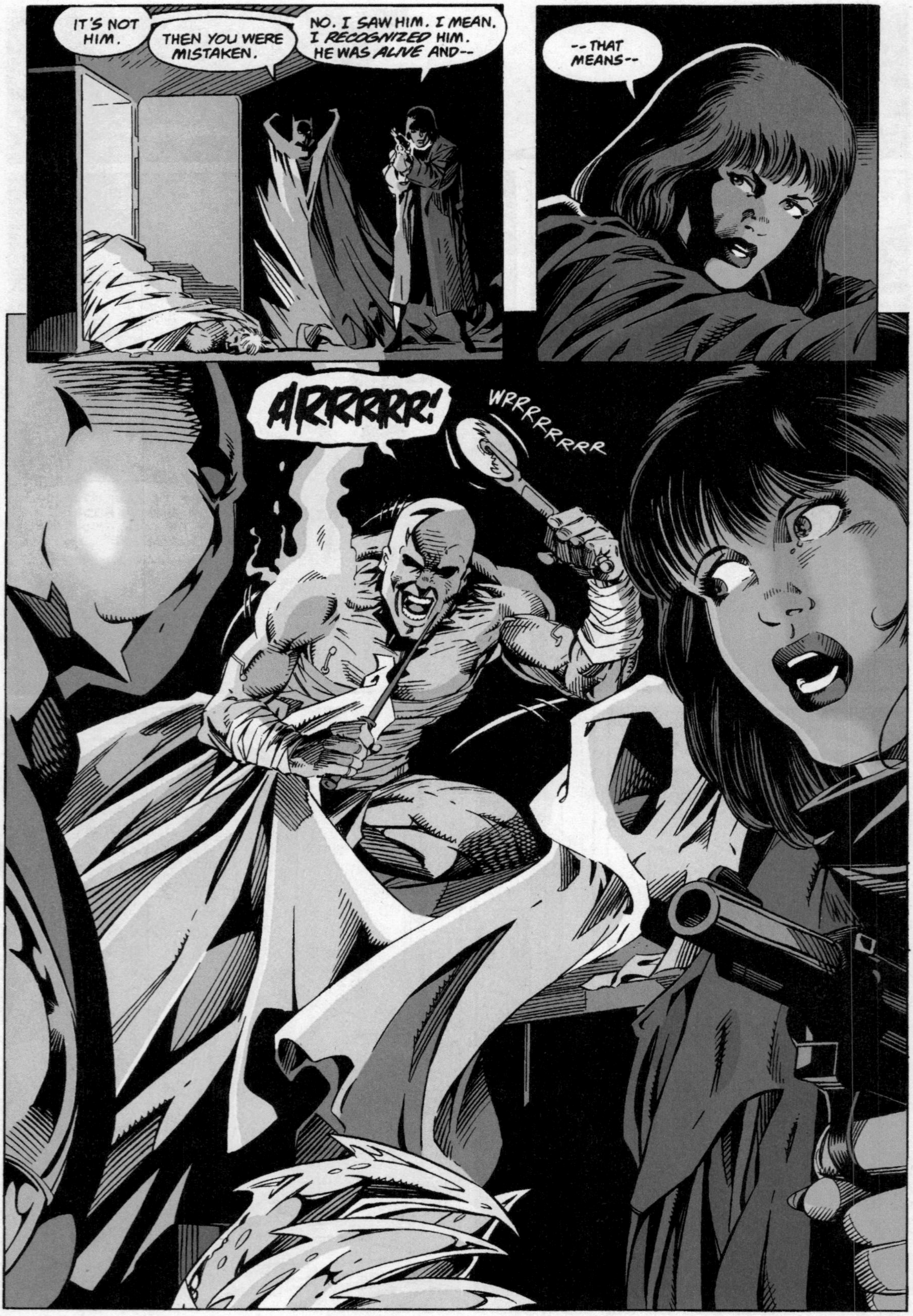

IT'S NOT HIM.
THEN YOU WERE MISTAKEN.
NO. I SAW HIM. I MEAN. I RECOGNIZED HIM. HE WAS ALIVE AND--
--THAT MEANS--
ARRRRR!
WRRRRRRRR

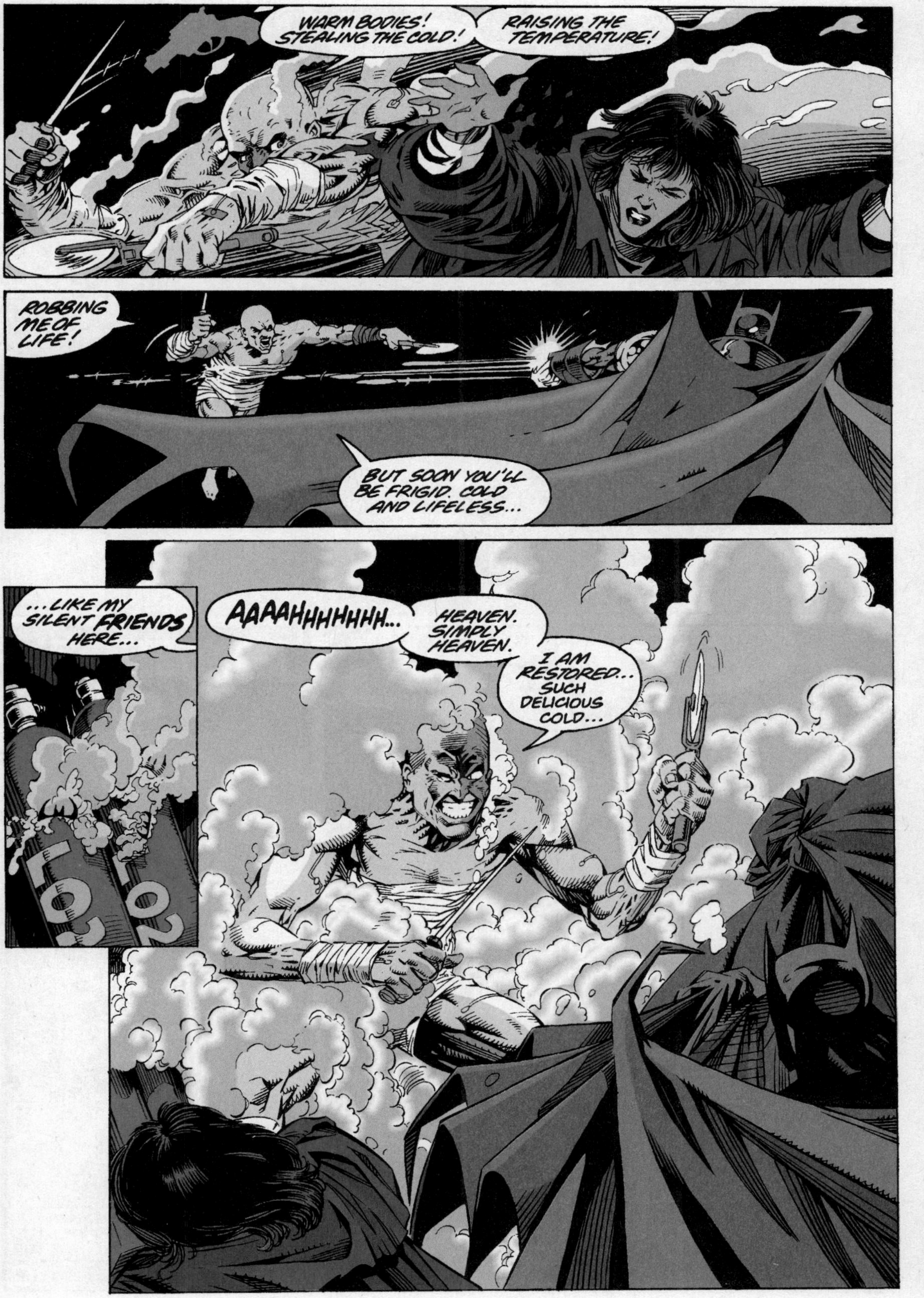
WARM BODIES! STEALING THE COLD!
RAISING THE TEMPERATURE!
ROBBING ME OF LIFE!
BUT SOON YOU'LL BE FRIGID. COLD AND LIFELESS...
...LIKE MY SILENT FRIENDS HERE...
AAAAHHHHHHH...
HEAVEN. SIMPLY HEAVEN.
I AM RESTORED... SUCH DELICIOUS COLD...

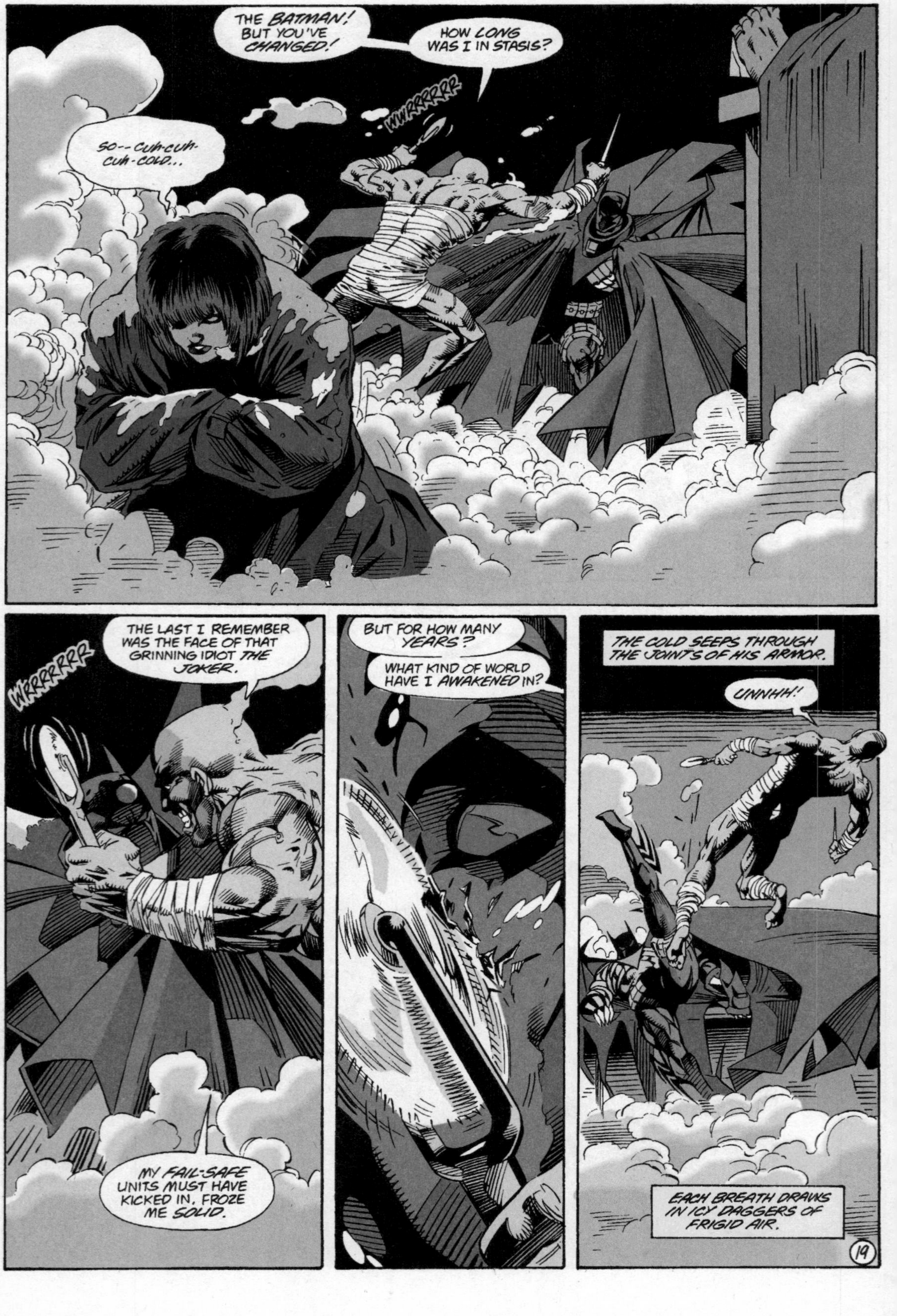
THE BATMAN! BUT YOU'VE CHANGED!
HOW LONG WAS I IN STASIS?
WWRRRRRR
SO--CUH-CUH-CUH-COLD...
THE LAST I REMEMBER WAS THE FACE OF THAT GRINNING IDIOT THE JOKER.
WRRRRRRR
MY FAIL-SAFE UNITS MUST HAVE KICKED IN. FROZE ME SOLID.
BUT FOR HOW MANY YEARS?
WHAT KIND OF WORLD HAVE I AWAKENED IN?
THE COLD SEEPS THROUGH THE JOINTS OF HIS ARMOR.
UNNHH!
EACH BREATH DRAWS IN ICY DAGGERS OF FRIGID AIR.
19

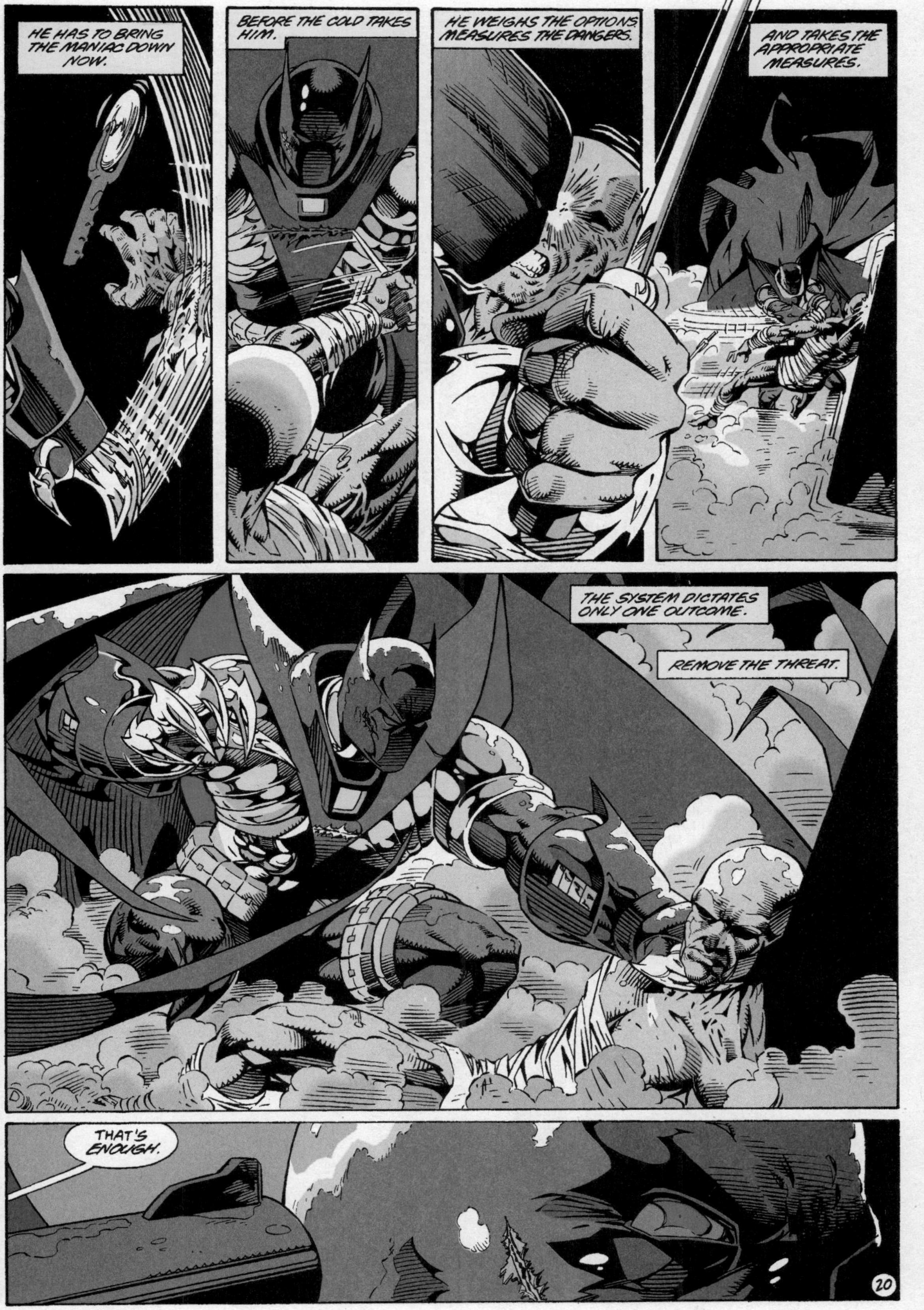
HE HAS TO BRING THE MANIAC DOWN NOW.
BEFORE THE COLD TAKES HIM.
HE WEIGHS THE OPTIONS. MEASURES THE DANGERS.
AND TAKES THE APPROPRIATE MEASURES.
THE SYSTEM DICTATES ONLY ONE OUTCOME.
REMOVE THE THREAT.
THAT'S ENOUGH.
20

YOU TOOK HIM *OUT*, ALL RIGHT?

YOU DON'T HAVE TO *KILL* HIM.

I...

HIS PULSE IS SO SLOW. BUT HE'S ALIVE. YOU MAY HAVE FRACTURED HIS SKULL.

THE COLD PRESERVES HIM. HE CAME HERE TO THE COLDEST PLACE HE COULD FIND... TO SURVIVE.

YOU SOUND LIKE THAT *SURPRISES* YOU.

THIS IS *MR. FREEZE.* YOU SHOULD REMEMBER HIM AFTER ALL THE TIMES HE'S NEARLY *KILLED* YOU.

OF COURSE. MR FREEZE.

OBVIOUSLY HE DIDN'T KNOW IT'S THE DEAD OF WINTER OUTSIDE, HE COULD HAVE *WALKED* AWAY.

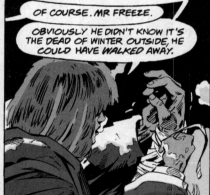

I'LL LEAVE HIM HERE UNTIL I CAN GET BACKUP.

AND A REFRIGERATOR TRUCK. YOU COULD HELP BY--

-- RESTORING THE LIGHTS...

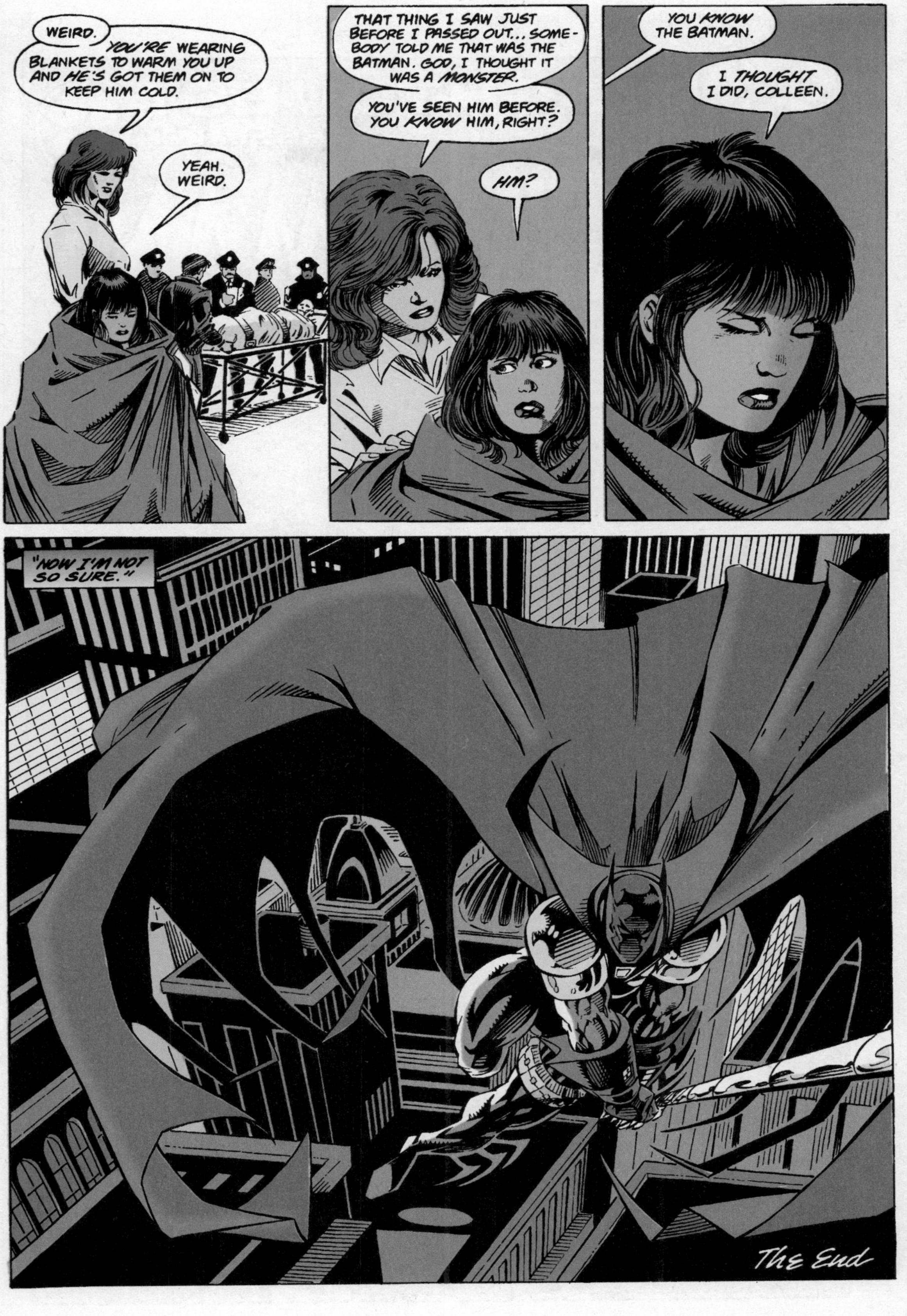
WEIRD.
YOU'RE WEARING BLANKETS TO WARM YOU UP AND HE'S GOT THEM ON TO KEEP HIM COLD.
YEAH. WEIRD.
THAT THING I SAW JUST BEFORE I PASSED OUT... SOME-BODY TOLD ME THAT WAS THE BATMAN. GOD, I THOUGHT IT WAS A MONSTER.
YOU'VE SEEN HIM BEFORE. YOU KNOW HIM, RIGHT?
HM?
YOU KNOW THE BATMAN.
I THOUGHT I DID, COLLEEN.
"NOW I'M NOT SO SURE."
The End

Cover art by JIM BALENT

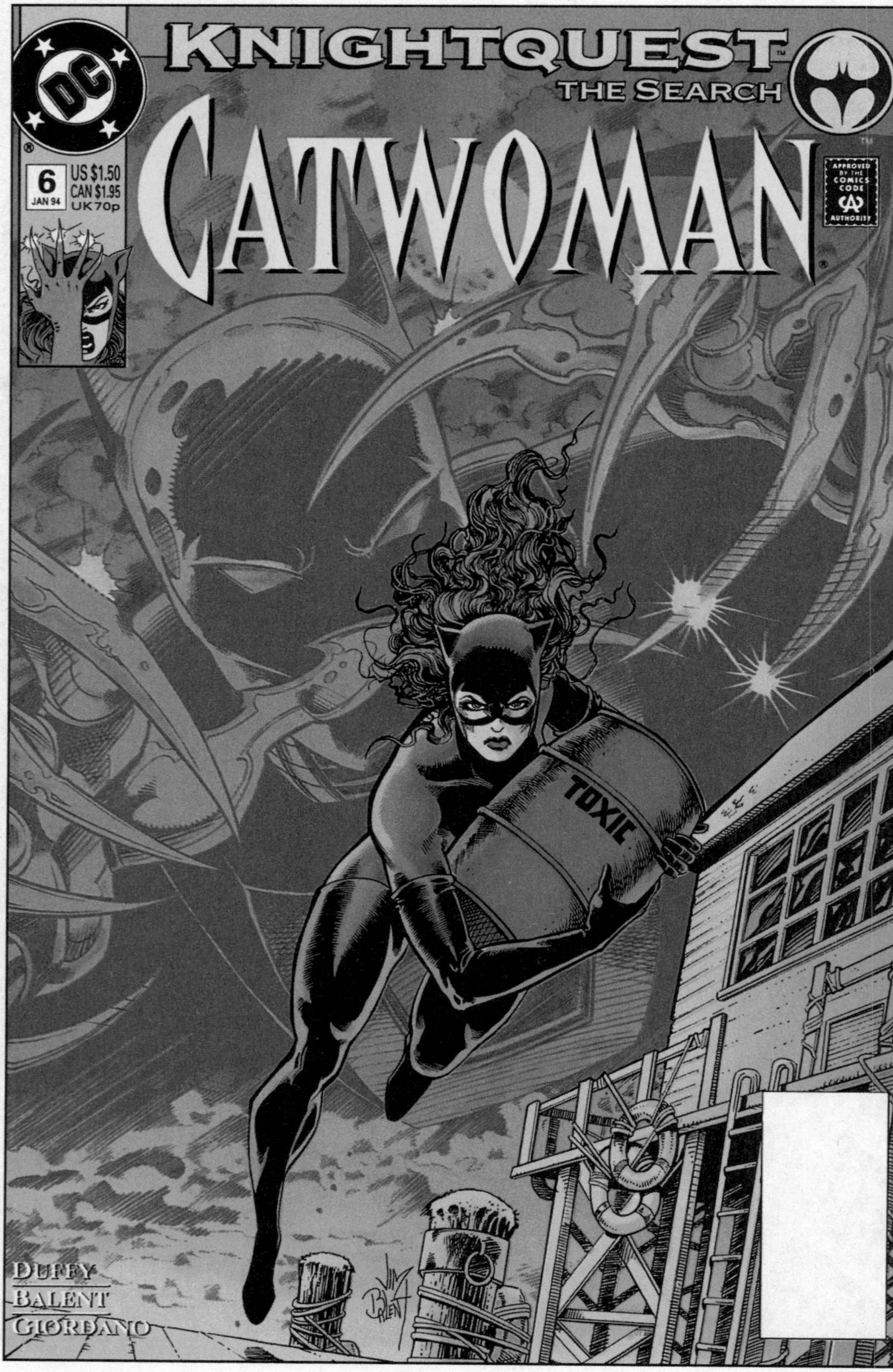
DC
KNIGHTQUEST
THE SEARCH
CATWOMAN
6
JAN 94
US $1.50
CAN $1.95
UK 70p
APPROVED BY THE COMICS CODE AUTHORITY
TOXIC
DUFFY
BALENT
GIORDANO

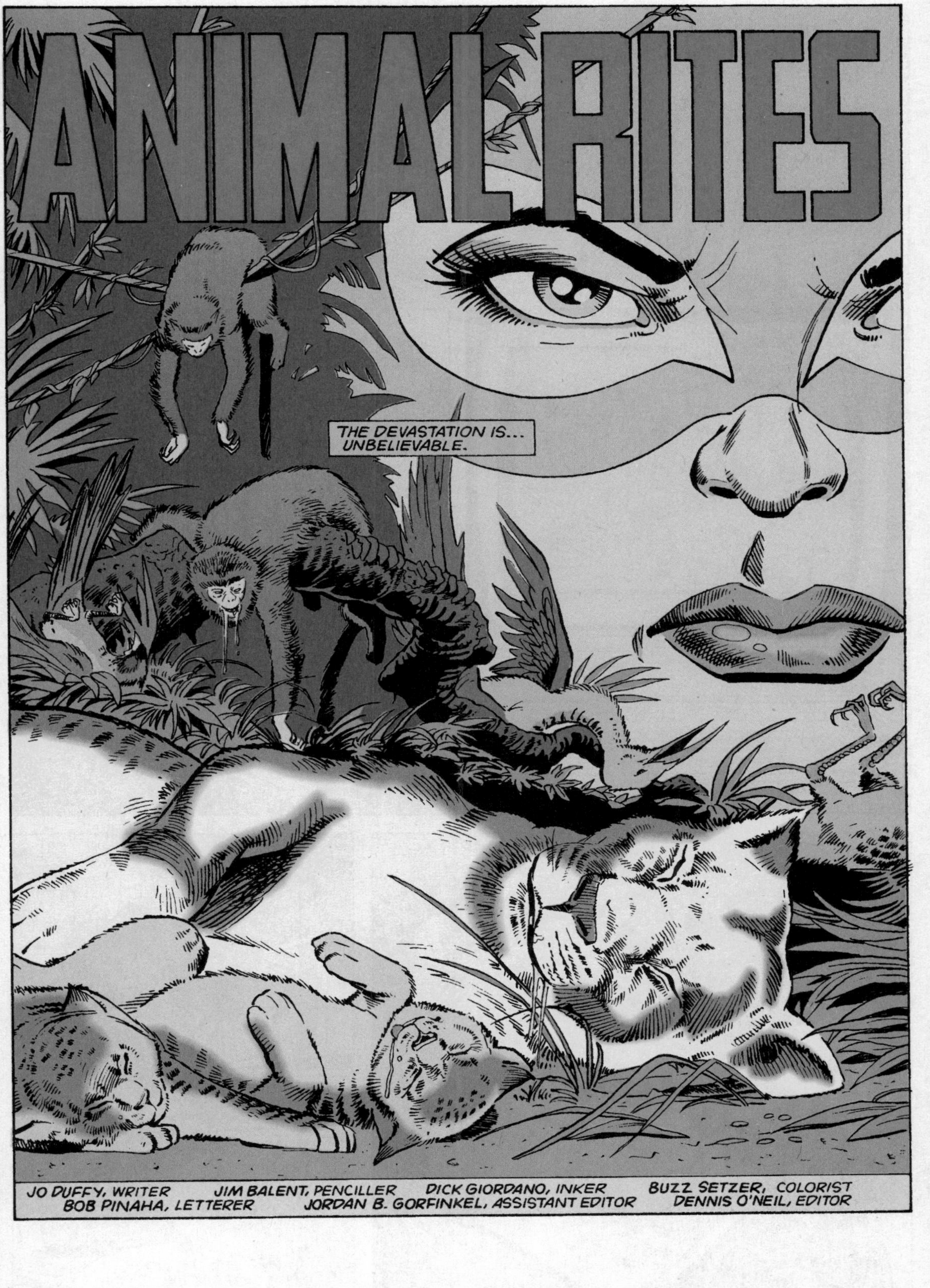
ANIMAL RITES
THE DEVASTATION IS... UNBELIEVABLE.
JO DUFFY, WRITER JIM BALENT, PENCILLER DICK GIORDANO, INKER BUZZ SETZER, COLORIST
BOB PINAHA, LETTERER JORDAN B. GORFINKEL, ASSISTANT EDITOR DENNIS O'NEIL, EDITOR

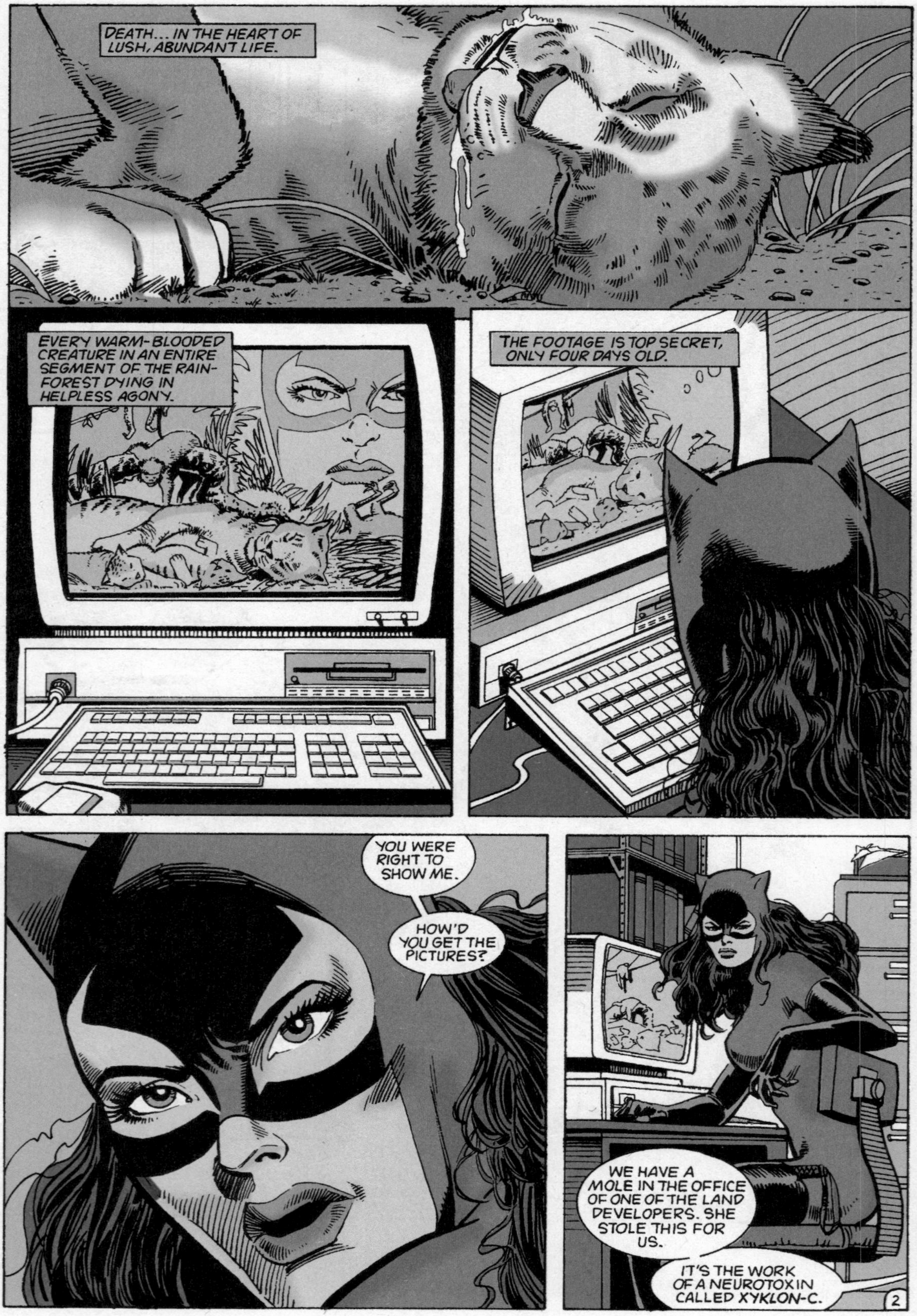
DEATH... IN THE HEART OF LUSH, ABUNDANT LIFE.
EVERY WARM-BLOODED CREATURE IN AN ENTIRE SEGMENT OF THE RAIN-FOREST DYING IN HELPLESS AGONY.
THE FOOTAGE IS TOP SECRET, ONLY FOUR DAYS OLD.
YOU WERE RIGHT TO SHOW ME.
HOW'D YOU GET THE PICTURES?
WE HAVE A MOLE IN THE OFFICE OF ONE OF THE LAND DEVELOPERS. SHE STOLE THIS FOR US.
IT'S THE WORK OF A NEUROTOXIN CALLED XYKLON-C.
2

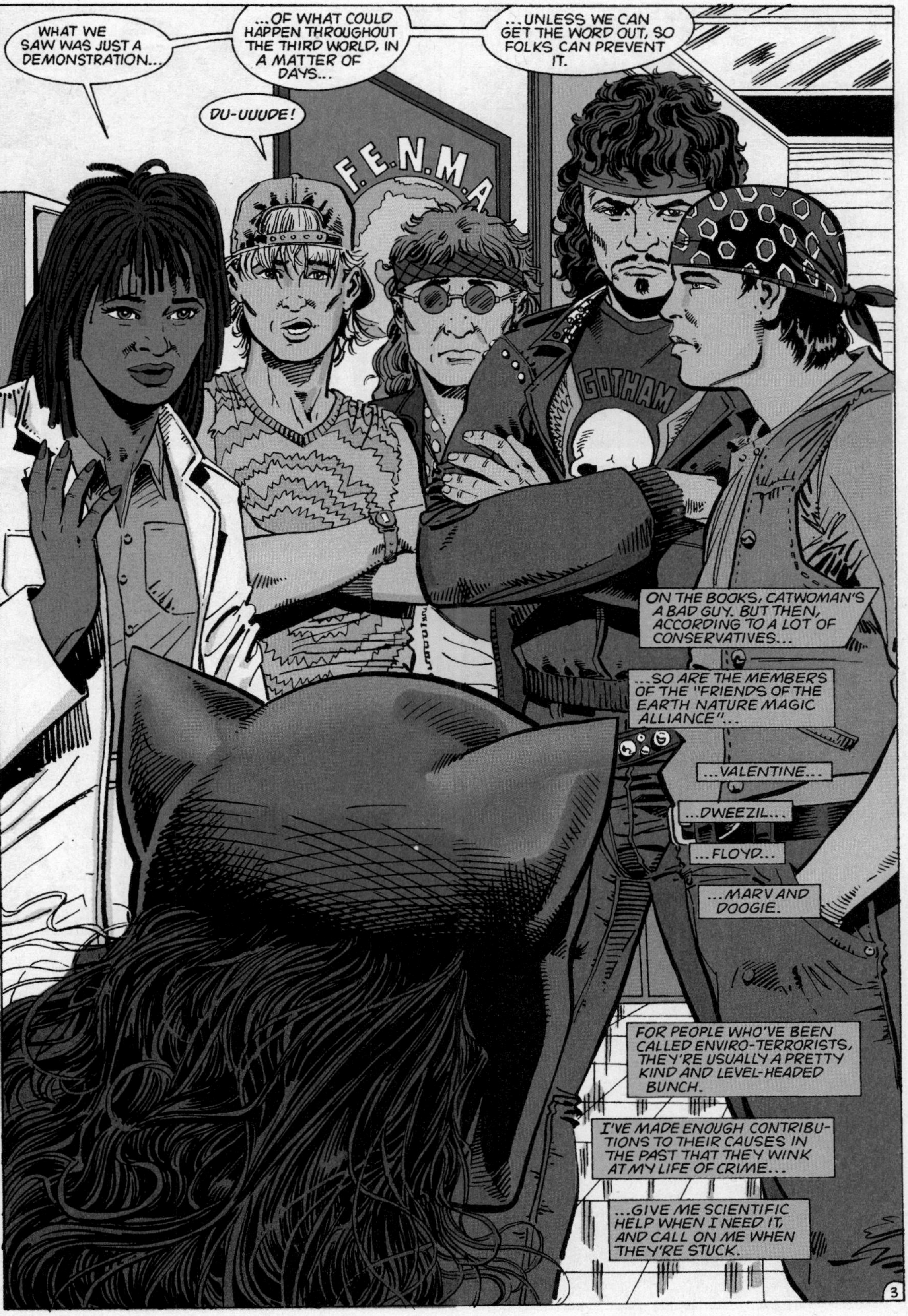
WHAT WE SAW WAS JUST A DEMONSTRATION...
...OF WHAT COULD HAPPEN THROUGHOUT THE THIRD WORLD, IN A MATTER OF DAYS...
...UNLESS WE CAN GET THE WORD OUT, SO FOLKS CAN PREVENT IT.
DU-UUUDE!
F.E.N.M.A
GOTHAM
ON THE BOOKS, CATWOMAN'S A BAD GUY. BUT THEN, ACCORDING TO A LOT OF CONSERVATIVES...
...SO ARE THE MEMBERS OF THE "FRIENDS OF THE EARTH NATURE MAGIC ALLIANCE"...
...VALENTINE...
...DWEEZIL...
...FLOYD...
...MARV AND DOOGIE.
FOR PEOPLE WHO'VE BEEN CALLED ENVIRO-TERRORISTS, THEY'RE USUALLY A PRETTY KIND AND LEVEL-HEADED BUNCH.
I'VE MADE ENOUGH CONTRIBUTIONS TO THEIR CAUSES IN THE PAST THAT THEY WINK AT MY LIFE OF CRIME...
...GIVE ME SCIENTIFIC HELP WHEN I NEED IT, AND CALL ON ME WHEN THEY'RE STUCK.
3

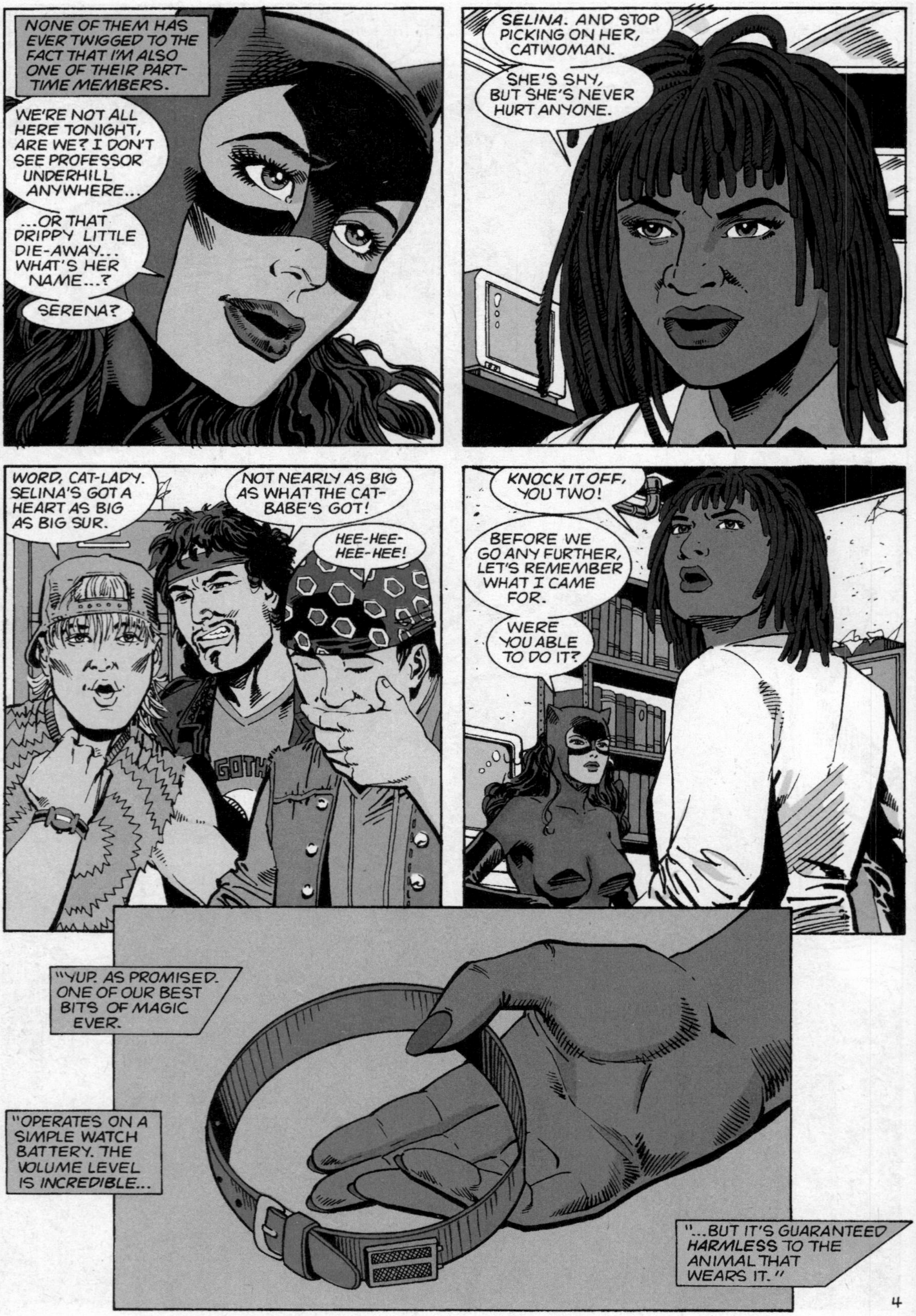
NONE OF THEM HAS EVER TWIGGED TO THE FACT THAT I'M ALSO ONE OF THEIR PART-TIME MEMBERS.
WE'RE NOT ALL HERE TONIGHT, ARE WE? I DON'T SEE PROFESSOR UNDERHILL ANYWHERE...
...OR THAT DRIPPY LITTLE DIE-AWAY... WHAT'S HER NAME...?
SERENA?
SELINA. AND STOP PICKING ON HER, CATWOMAN.
SHE'S SHY, BUT SHE'S NEVER HURT ANYONE.
WORD, CAT-LADY. SELINA'S GOT A HEART AS BIG AS BIG SUR.
NOT NEARLY AS BIG AS WHAT THE CAT-BABE'S GOT!
HEE-HEE-HEE-HEE!
GOTH
KNOCK IT OFF, YOU TWO!
BEFORE WE GO ANY FURTHER, LET'S REMEMBER WHAT I CAME FOR.
WERE YOU ABLE TO DO IT?
"YUP. AS PROMISED. ONE OF OUR BEST BITS OF MAGIC EVER.
"OPERATES ON A SIMPLE WATCH BATTERY. THE VOLUME LEVEL IS INCREDIBLE...
"...BUT IT'S GUARANTEED HARMLESS TO THE ANIMAL THAT WEARS IT."
4

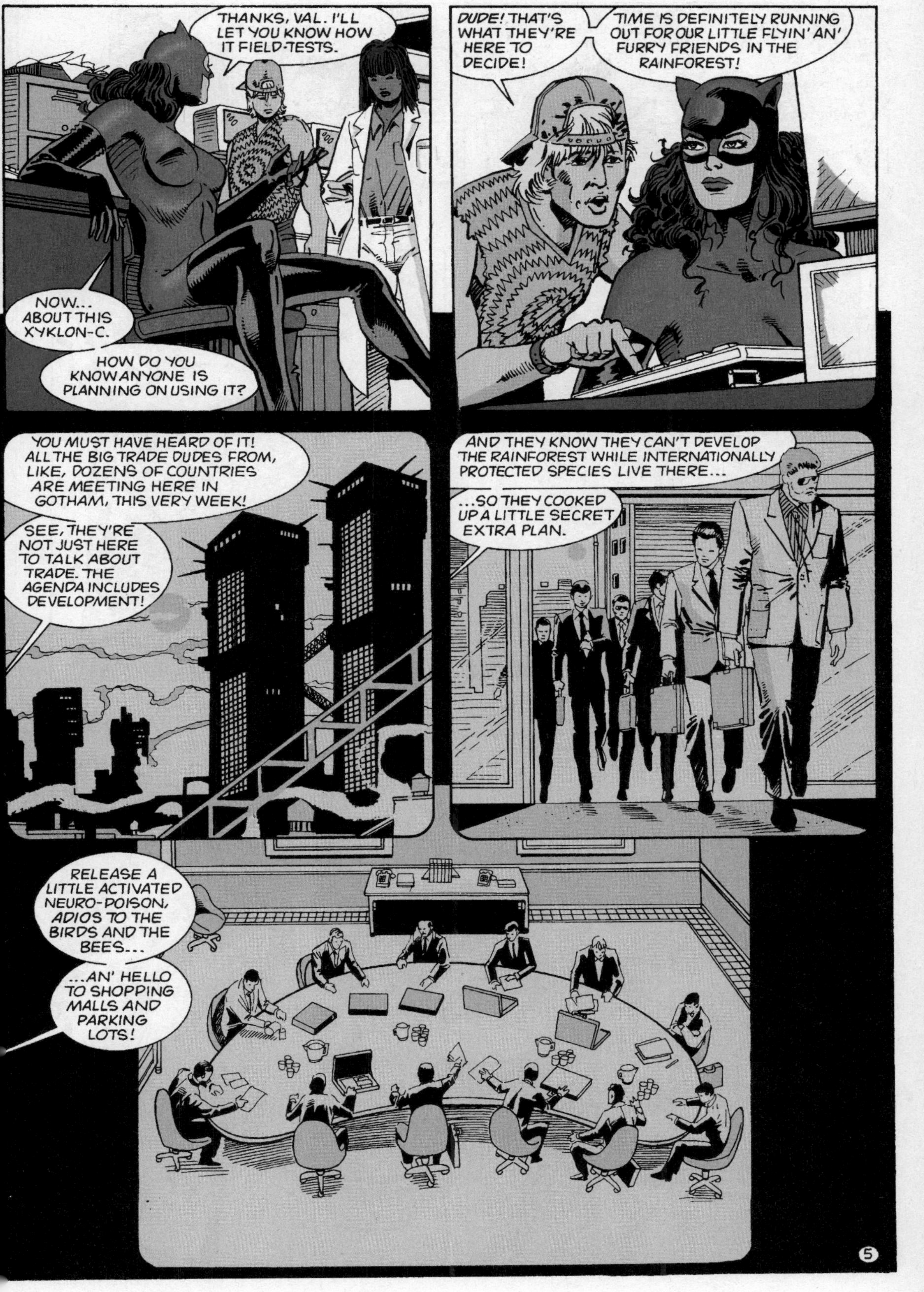
THANKS, VAL. I'LL LET YOU KNOW HOW IT FIELD-TESTS.
NOW... ABOUT THIS XYKLON-C.
HOW DO YOU KNOW ANYONE IS PLANNING ON USING IT?
DUDE! THAT'S WHAT THEY'RE HERE TO DECIDE!
TIME IS DEFINITELY RUNNING OUT FOR OUR LITTLE FLYIN' AN' FURRY FRIENDS IN THE RAINFOREST!
YOU MUST HAVE HEARD OF IT! ALL THE BIG TRADE DUDES FROM, LIKE, DOZENS OF COUNTRIES ARE MEETING HERE IN GOTHAM, THIS VERY WEEK!
SEE, THEY'RE NOT JUST HERE TO TALK ABOUT TRADE. THE AGENDA INCLUDES DEVELOPMENT!
AND THEY KNOW THEY CAN'T DEVELOP THE RAINFOREST WHILE INTERNATIONALLY PROTECTED SPECIES LIVE THERE...
...SO THEY COOKED UP A LITTLE SECRET EXTRA PLAN.
RELEASE A LITTLE ACTIVATED NEURO-POISON, ADIOS TO THE BIRDS AND THE BEES...
...AN' HELLO TO SHOPPING MALLS AND PARKING LOTS!
5

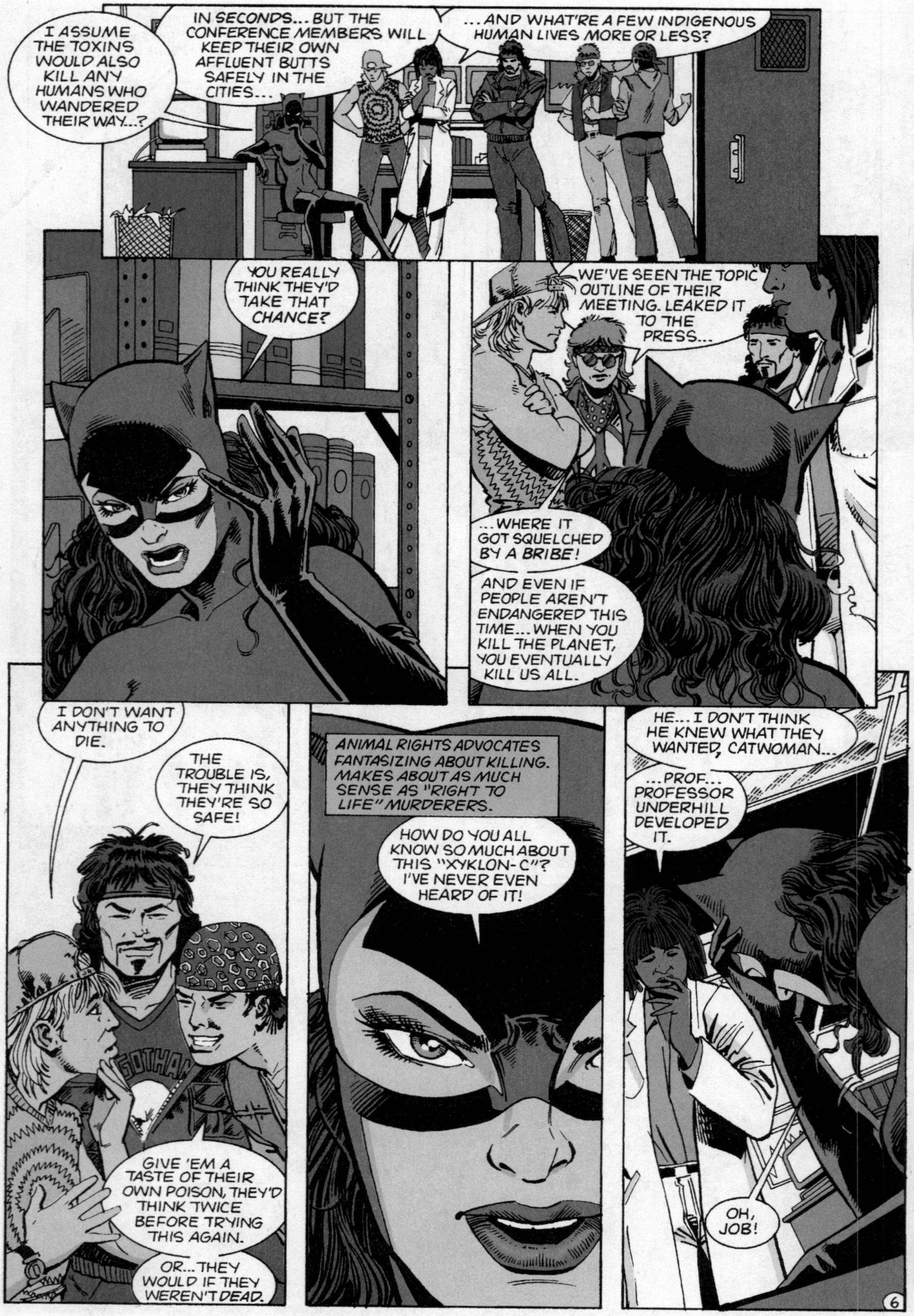
I ASSUME THE TOXINS WOULD ALSO KILL ANY HUMANS WHO WANDERED THEIR WAY...?
IN SECONDS... BUT THE CONFERENCE MEMBERS WILL KEEP THEIR OWN AFFLUENT BUTTS SAFELY IN THE CITIES...
...AND WHAT'RE A FEW INDIGENOUS HUMAN LIVES MORE OR LESS?
YOU REALLY THINK THEY'D TAKE THAT CHANCE?
WE'VE SEEN THE TOPIC OUTLINE OF THEIR MEETING. LEAKED IT TO THE PRESS...
...WHERE IT GOT SQUELCHED BY A BRIBE!
AND EVEN IF PEOPLE AREN'T ENDANGERED THIS TIME... WHEN YOU KILL THE PLANET, YOU EVENTUALLY KILL US ALL.
I DON'T WANT ANYTHING TO DIE.
THE TROUBLE IS, THEY THINK THEY'RE SO SAFE!
GIVE 'EM A TASTE OF THEIR OWN POISON, THEY'D THINK TWICE BEFORE TRYING THIS AGAIN.
OR... THEY WOULD IF THEY WEREN'T DEAD.
ANIMAL RIGHTS ADVOCATES FANTASIZING ABOUT KILLING. MAKES ABOUT AS MUCH SENSE AS "RIGHT TO LIFE" MURDERERS.
HOW DO YOU ALL KNOW SO MUCH ABOUT THIS "XYKLON-C"? I'VE NEVER EVEN HEARD OF IT!
HE... I DON'T THINK HE KNEW WHAT THEY WANTED, CATWOMAN...
...PROF... PROFESSOR UNDERHILL DEVELOPED IT.
OH, JOB!
6

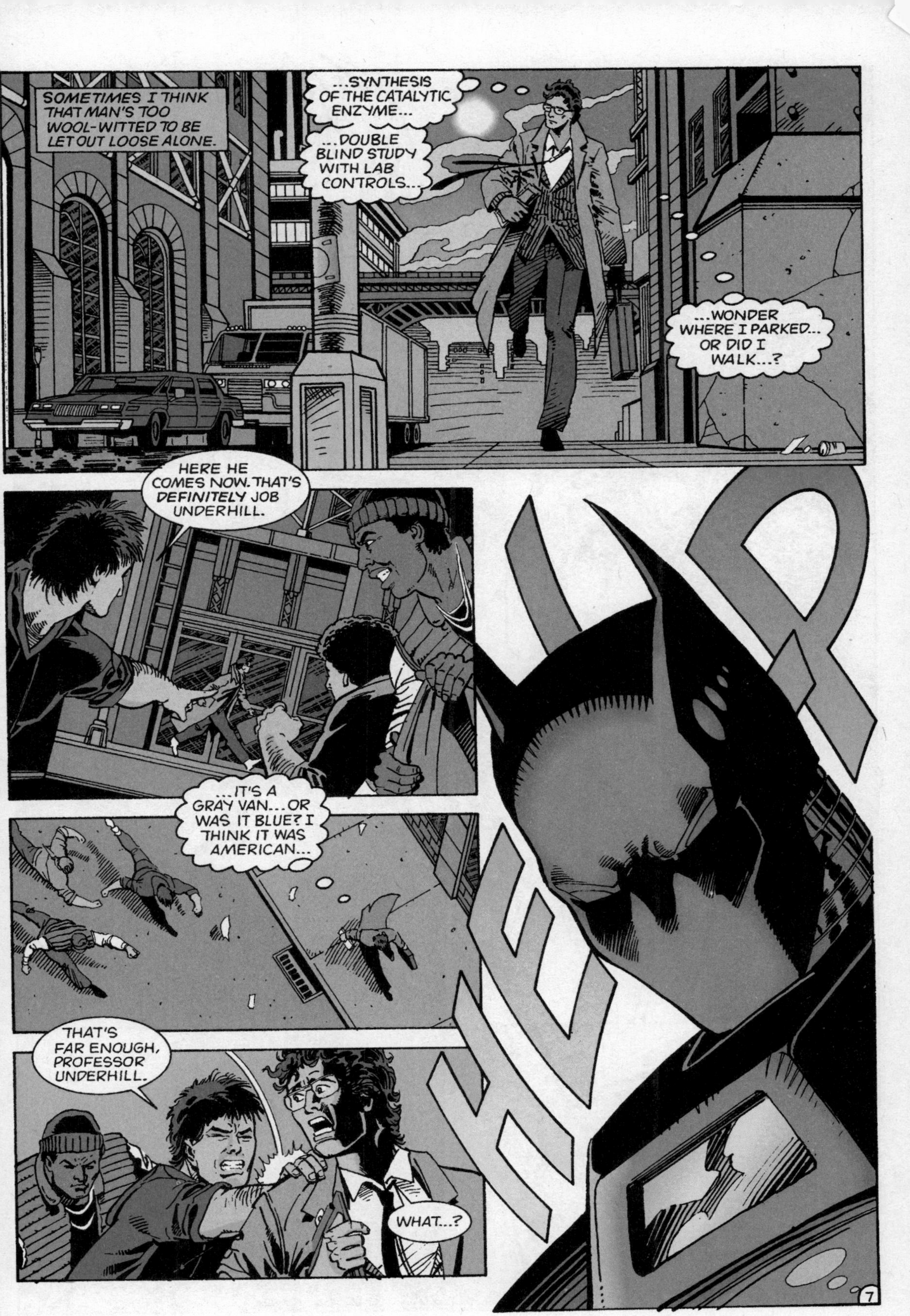
SOMETIMES I THINK THAT MAN'S TOO WOOL-WITTED TO BE LET OUT LOOSE ALONE.
...SYNTHESIS OF THE CATALYTIC ENZYME...
...DOUBLE BLIND STUDY WITH LAB CONTROLS...
...WONDER WHERE I PARKED... OR DID I WALK...?
HERE HE COMES NOW. THAT'S DEFINITELY JOB UNDERHILL.
...IT'S A GRAY VAN... OR WAS IT BLUE? I THINK IT WAS AMERICAN...
THAT'S FAR ENOUGH, PROFESSOR UNDERHILL.
WHAT...?
7

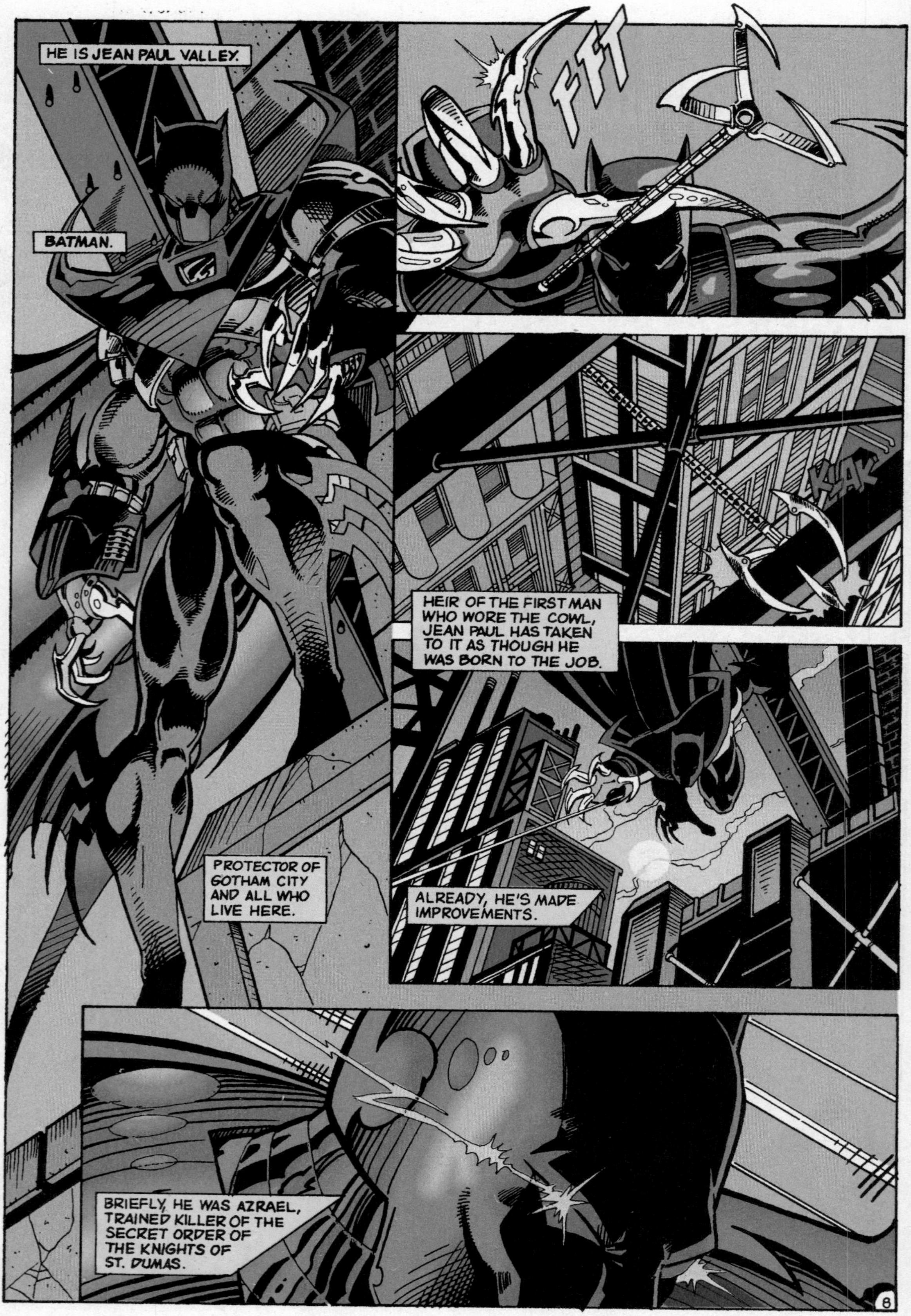
HE IS JEAN PAUL VALLEY.
BATMAN.
PROTECTOR OF GOTHAM CITY AND ALL WHO LIVE HERE.
FFT
KLAK
HEIR OF THE FIRST MAN WHO WORE THE COWL, JEAN PAUL HAS TAKEN TO IT AS THOUGH HE WAS BORN TO THE JOB.
ALREADY, HE'S MADE IMPROVEMENTS.
BRIEFLY, HE WAS AZRAEL, TRAINED KILLER OF THE SECRET ORDER OF THE KNIGHTS OF ST. DUMAS.
8

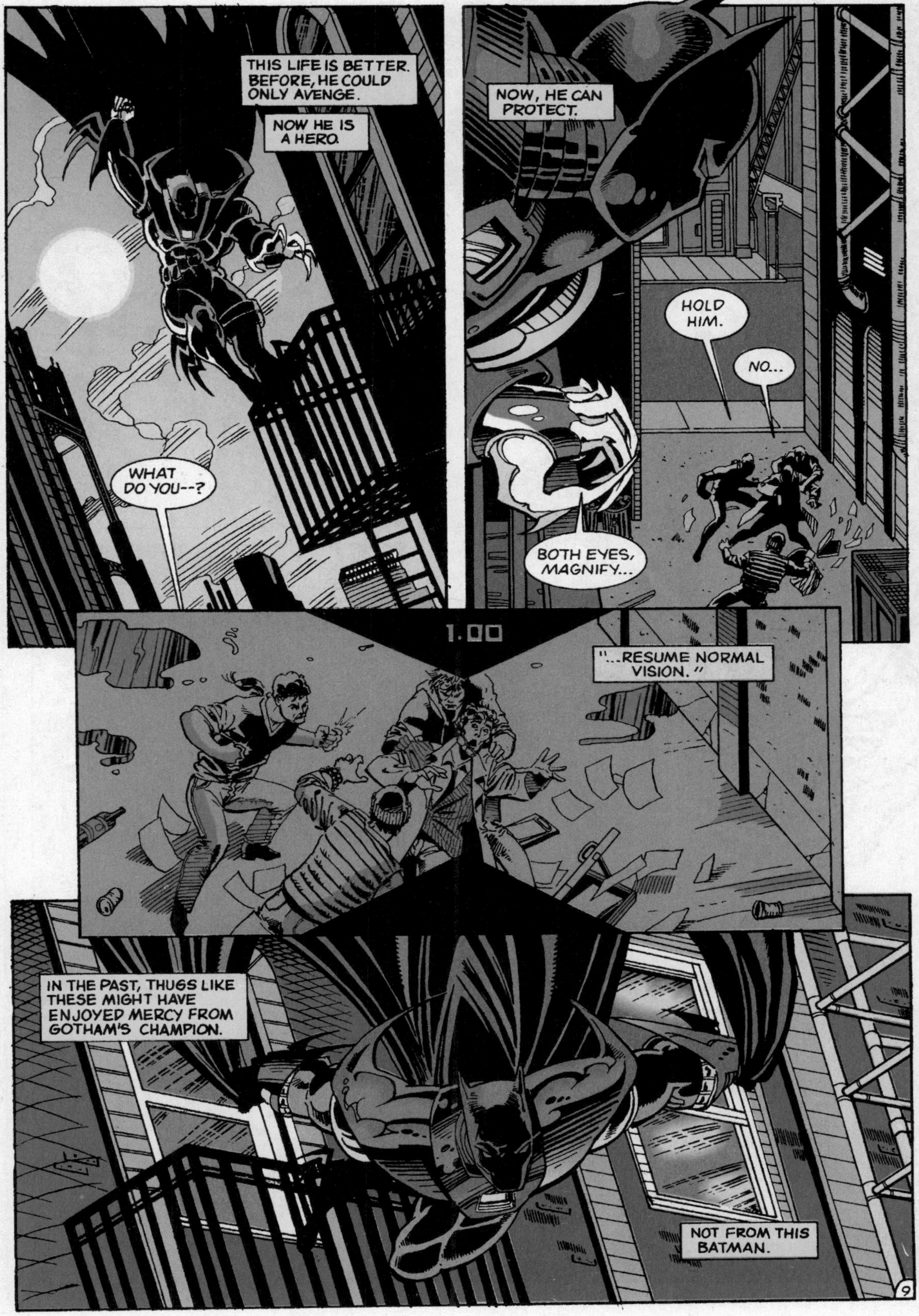
THIS LIFE IS BETTER. BEFORE, HE COULD ONLY AVENGE.
NOW HE IS A HERO.
WHAT DO YOU--?
NOW, HE CAN PROTECT.
HOLD HIM.
NO...
BOTH EYES, MAGNIFY...
1.00
"...RESUME NORMAL VISION."
IN THE PAST, THUGS LIKE THESE MIGHT HAVE ENJOYED MERCY FROM GOTHAM'S CHAMPION.
NOT FROM THIS BATMAN.
9

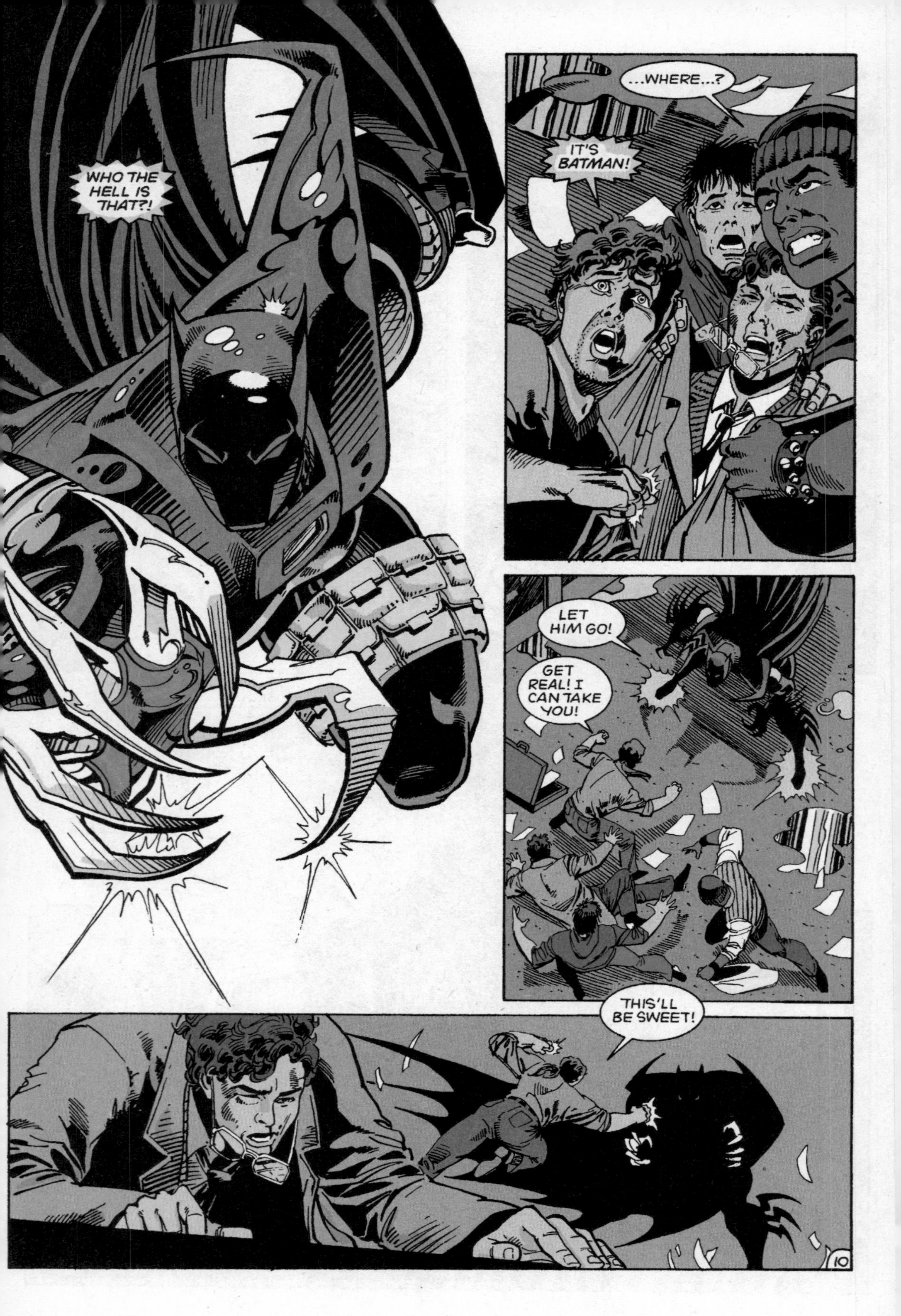
WHO THE HELL IS THAT?!
...WHERE...?
IT'S BATMAN!
LET HIM GO!
GET REAL! I CAN TAKE YOU!
THIS'LL BE SWEET!
10

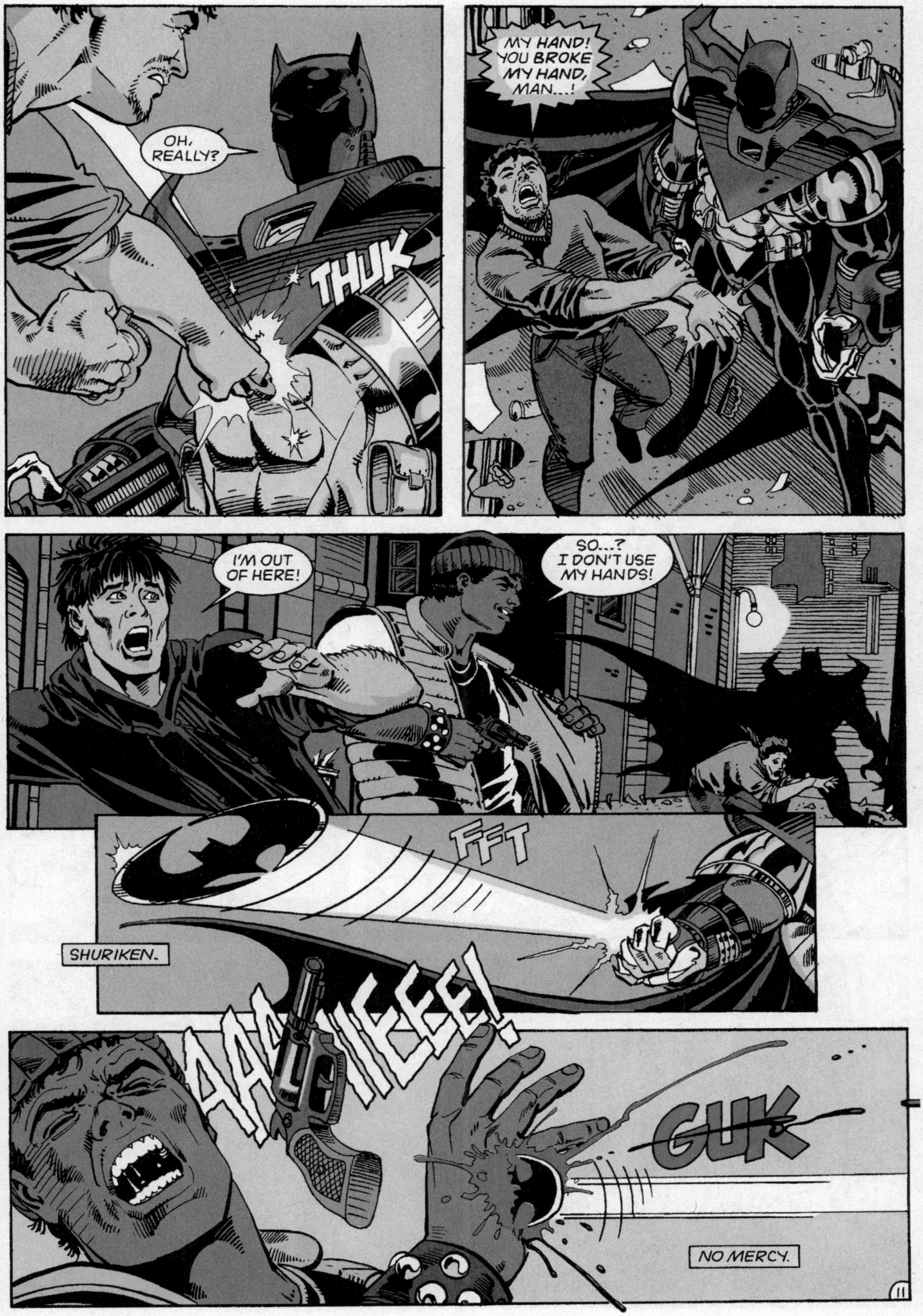
OH, REALLY?
THUK
MY HAND! YOU BROKE MY HAND, MAN...!
I'M OUT OF HERE!
SO...? I DON'T USE MY HANDS!
FFT
SHURIKEN.
AAAIIEEE!
GUK
NO MERCY.
11

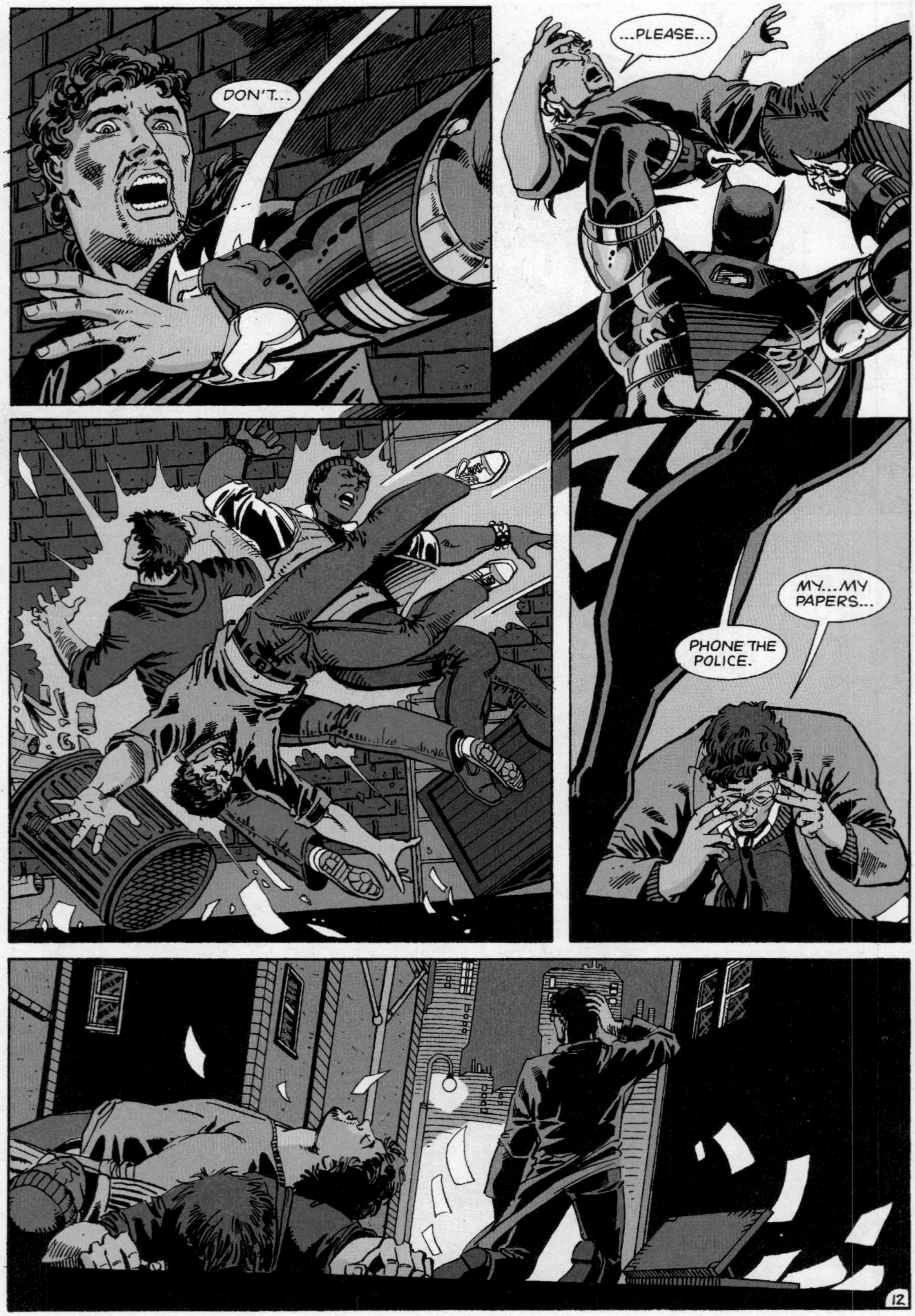

DON'T...
...PLEASE...
MY...MY PAPERS...
PHONE THE POLICE.
12

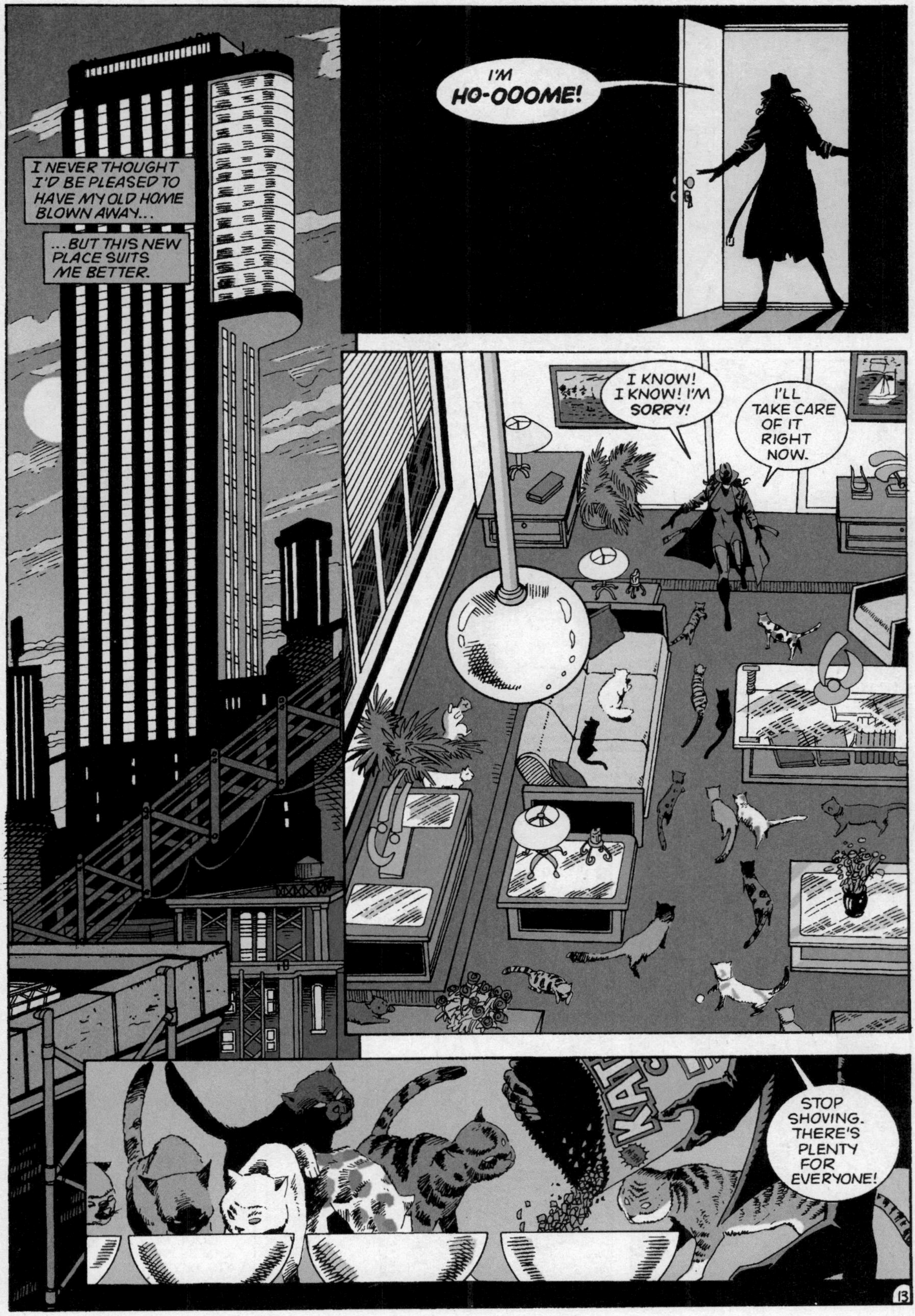
I NEVER THOUGHT I'D BE PLEASED TO HAVE MY OLD HOME BLOWN AWAY...
...BUT THIS NEW PLACE SUITS ME BETTER.
I'M HO-OOOME!
I KNOW! I KNOW! I'M SORRY!
I'LL TAKE CARE OF IT RIGHT NOW.
STOP SHOVING. THERE'S PLENTY FOR EVERYONE!
13

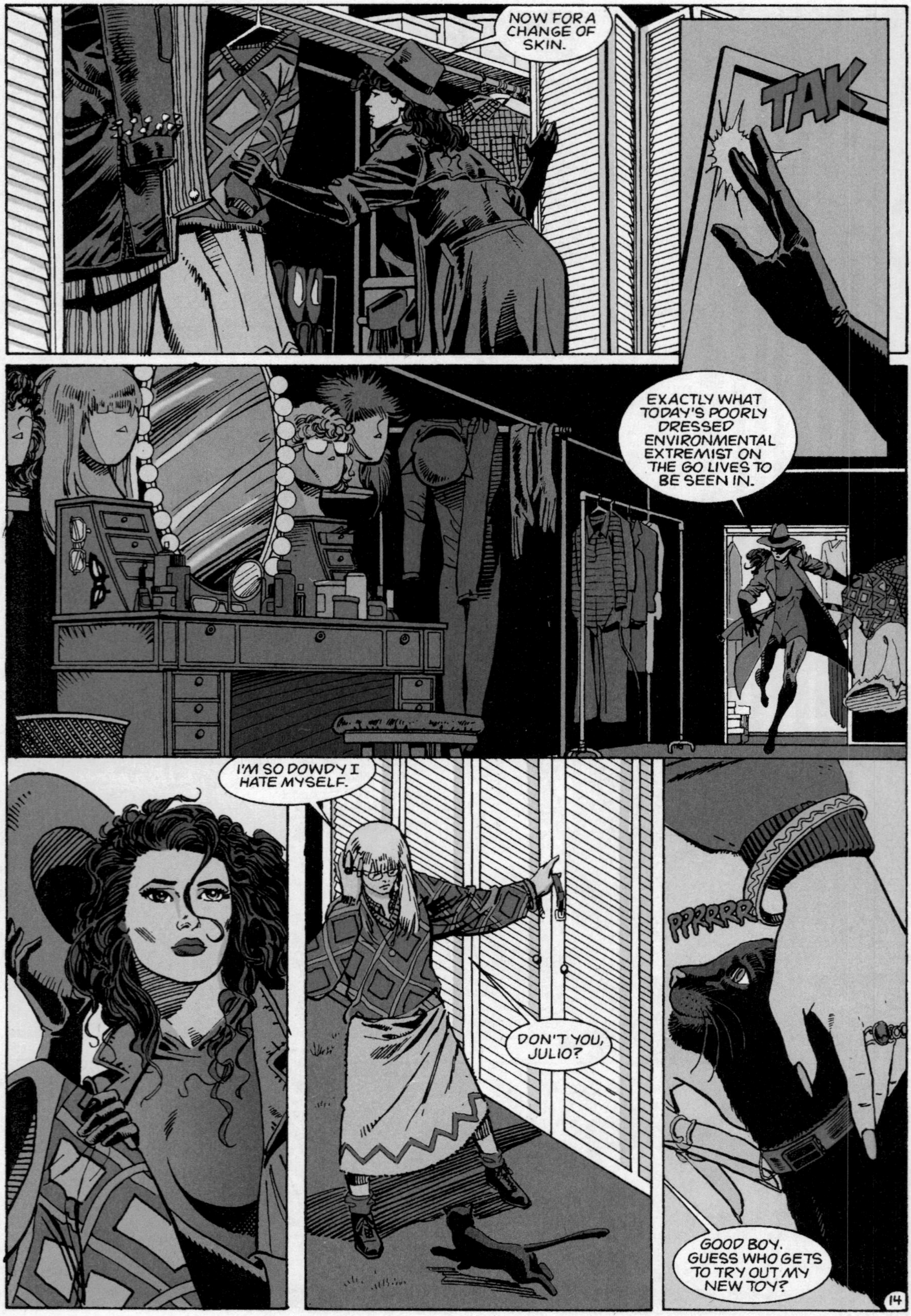
NOW FOR A CHANGE OF SKIN.
TAK
EXACTLY WHAT TODAY'S POORLY DRESSED ENVIRONMENTAL EXTREMIST ON THE GO LIVES TO BE SEEN IN.
I'M SO DOWDY I HATE MYSELF.
DON'T YOU, JULIO?
PPRRRR
GOOD BOY. GUESS WHO GETS TO TRY OUT MY NEW TOY?
14

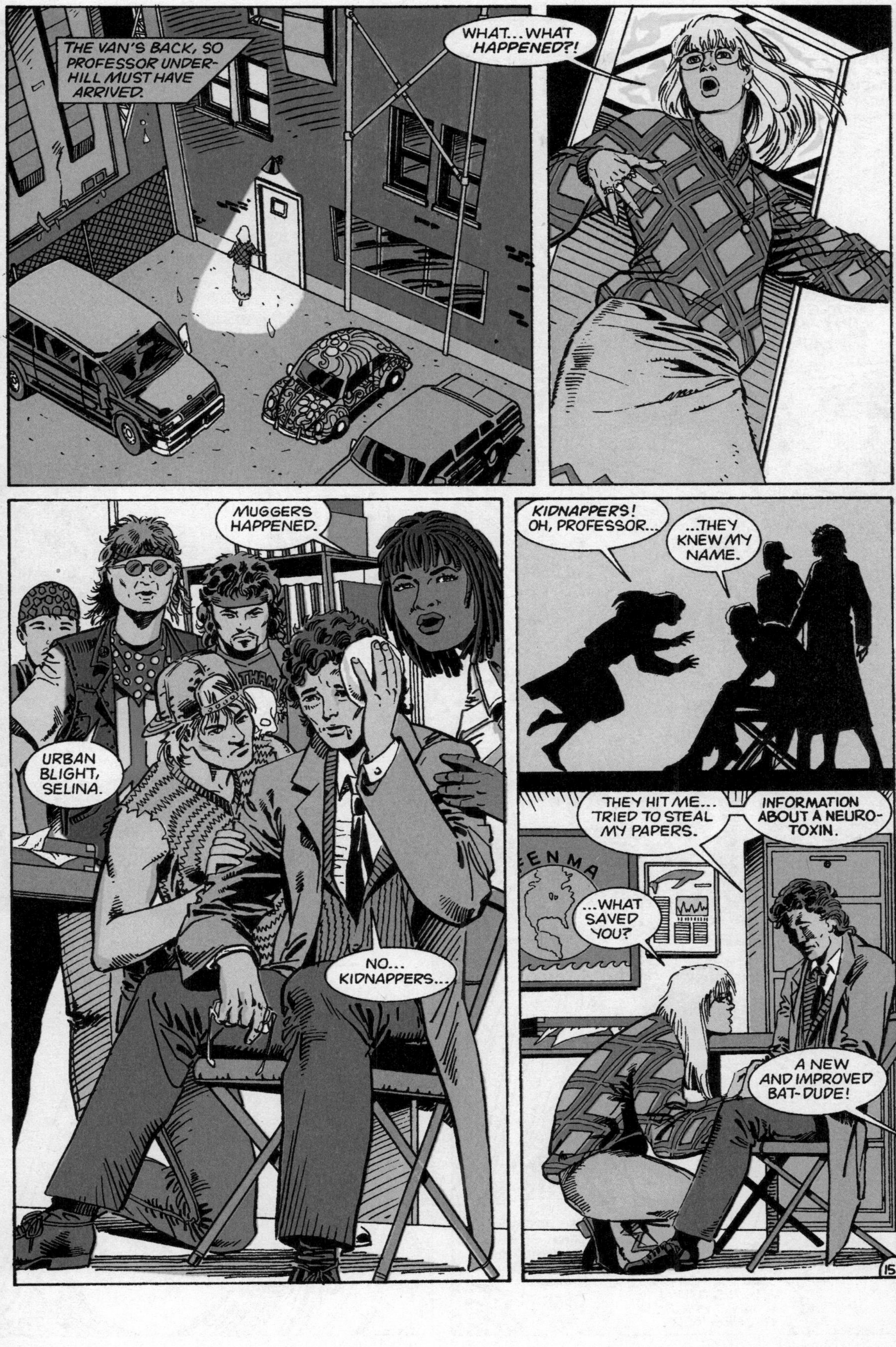
THE VAN'S BACK, SO PROFESSOR UNDERHILL MUST HAVE ARRIVED.
WHAT...WHAT HAPPENED?!
MUGGERS HAPPENED.
URBAN BLIGHT, SELINA.
NO... KIDNAPPERS...
KIDNAPPERS! OH, PROFESSOR...
...THEY KNEW MY NAME.
THEY HIT ME... TRIED TO STEAL MY PAPERS.
INFORMATION ABOUT A NEURO-TOXIN.
...WHAT SAVED YOU?
A NEW AND IMPROVED BAT-DUDE!
15

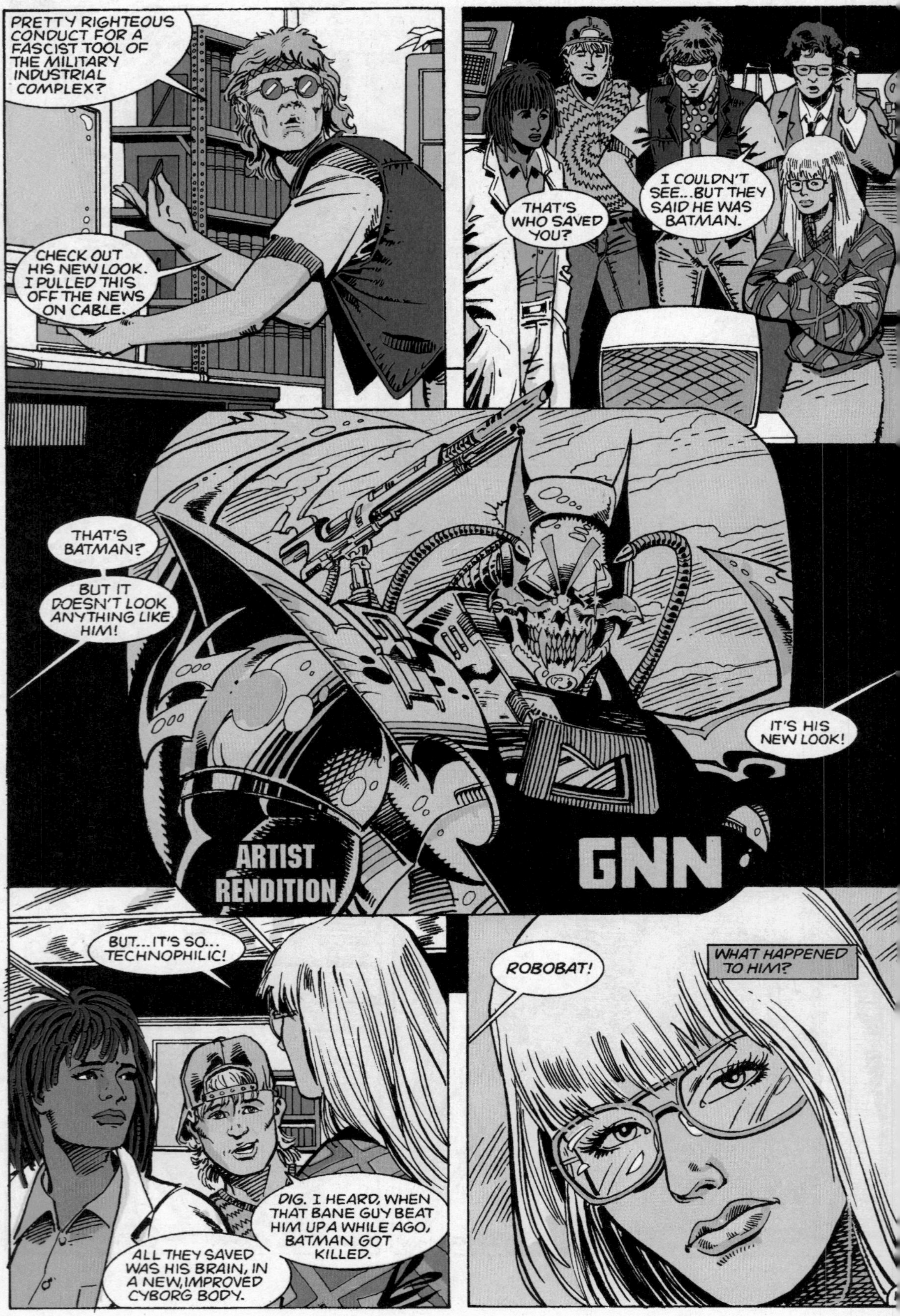
PRETTY RIGHTEOUS CONDUCT FOR A FASCIST TOOL OF THE MILITARY INDUSTRIAL COMPLEX?
CHECK OUT HIS NEW LOOK. I PULLED THIS OFF THE NEWS ON CABLE.
THAT'S WHO SAVED YOU?
I COULDN'T SEE...BUT THEY SAID HE WAS BATMAN.
THAT'S BATMAN?
BUT IT DOESN'T LOOK ANYTHING LIKE HIM!
IT'S HIS NEW LOOK!
ARTIST RENDITION
GNN
BUT...IT'S SO... TECHNOPHILIC!
DIG. I HEARD, WHEN THAT BANE GUY BEAT HIM UP A WHILE AGO, BATMAN GOT KILLED.
ALL THEY SAVED WAS HIS BRAIN, IN A NEW, IMPROVED CYBORG BODY.
ROBOBAT!
WHAT HAPPENED TO HIM?

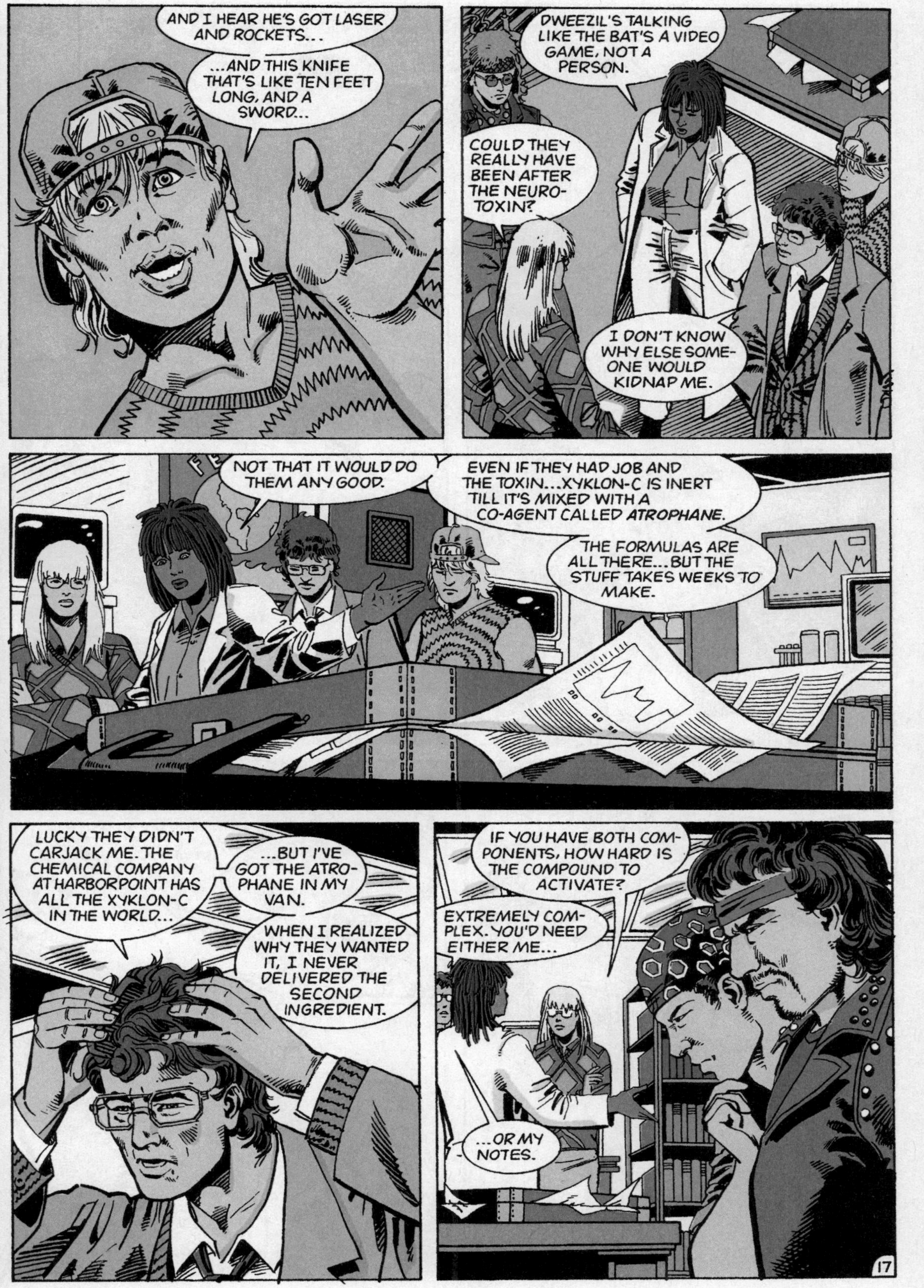
AND I HEAR HE'S GOT LASER AND ROCKETS...
...AND THIS KNIFE THAT'S LIKE TEN FEET LONG, AND A SWORD...
DWEEZIL'S TALKING LIKE THE BAT'S A VIDEO GAME, NOT A PERSON.
COULD THEY REALLY HAVE BEEN AFTER THE NEURO-TOXIN?
I DON'T KNOW WHY ELSE SOME-ONE WOULD KIDNAP ME.
NOT THAT IT WOULD DO THEM ANY GOOD.
EVEN IF THEY HAD JOB AND THE TOXIN...XYKLON-C IS INERT TILL IT'S MIXED WITH A CO-AGENT CALLED ATROPHANE.
THE FORMULAS ARE ALL THERE...BUT THE STUFF TAKES WEEKS TO MAKE.
LUCKY THEY DIDN'T CARJACK ME. THE CHEMICAL COMPANY AT HARBORPOINT HAS ALL THE XYKLON-C IN THE WORLD...
...BUT I'VE GOT THE ATRO-PHANE IN MY VAN.
WHEN I REALIZED WHY THEY WANTED IT, I NEVER DELIVERED THE SECOND INGREDIENT.
IF YOU HAVE BOTH COM-PONENTS, HOW HARD IS THE COMPOUND TO ACTIVATE?
EXTREMELY COM-PLEX. YOU'D NEED EITHER ME...
...OR MY NOTES.
17

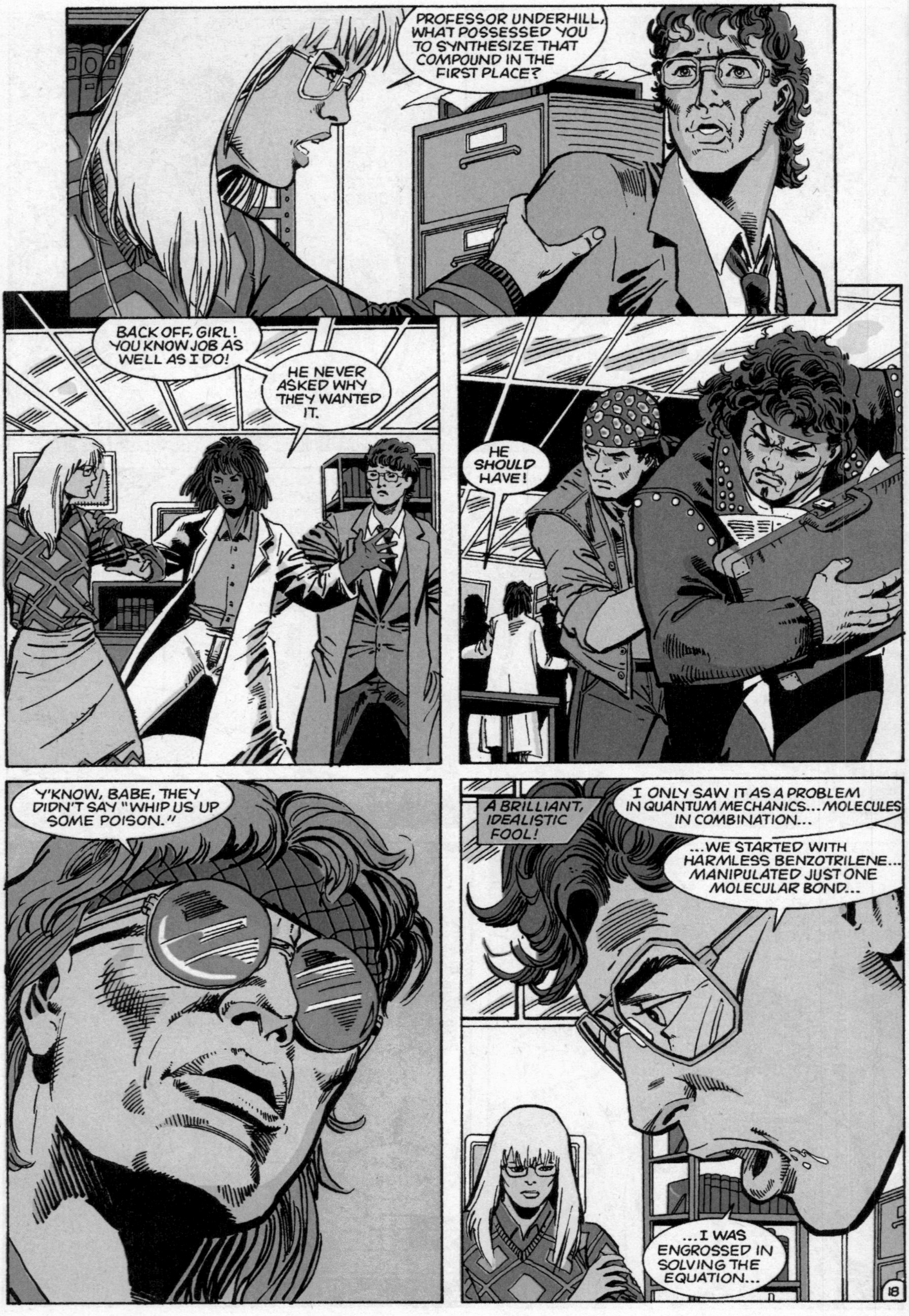
PROFESSOR UNDERHILL, WHAT POSSESSED YOU TO SYNTHESIZE THAT COMPOUND IN THE FIRST PLACE?
BACK OFF, GIRL! YOU KNOW JOB AS WELL AS I DO!
HE NEVER ASKED WHY THEY WANTED IT.
HE SHOULD HAVE!
Y'KNOW, BABE, THEY DIDN'T SAY "WHIP US UP SOME POISON."
A BRILLIANT, IDEALISTIC FOOL!
I ONLY SAW IT AS A PROBLEM IN QUANTUM MECHANICS... MOLECULES IN COMBINATION...
...WE STARTED WITH HARMLESS BENZOTRILENE... MANIPULATED JUST ONE MOLECULAR BOND...
...I WAS ENGROSSED IN SOLVING THE EQUATION...
18

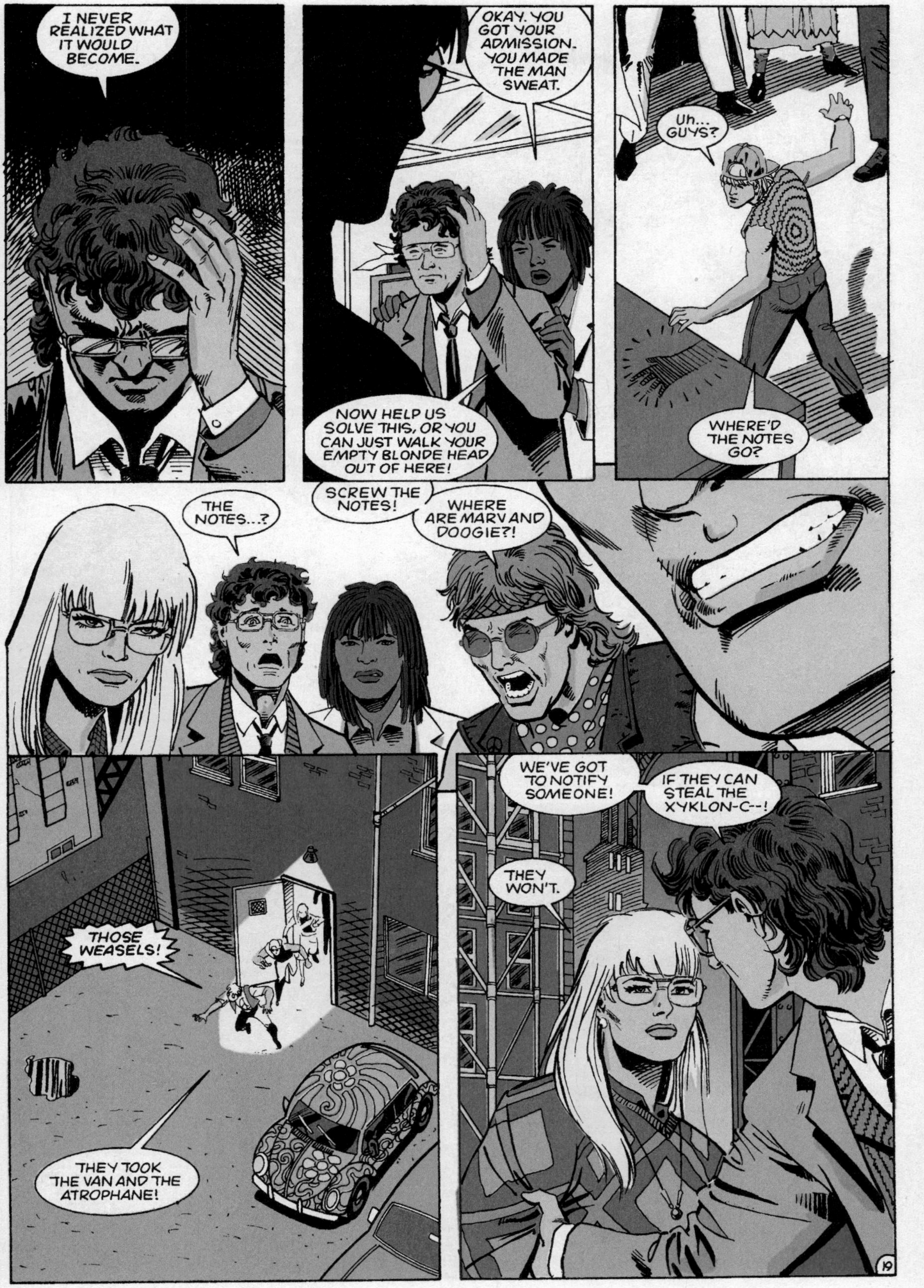
I NEVER REALIZED WHAT IT WOULD BECOME.
OKAY. YOU GOT YOUR ADMISSION. YOU MADE THE MAN SWEAT.
NOW HELP US SOLVE THIS, OR YOU CAN JUST WALK YOUR EMPTY BLONDE HEAD OUT OF HERE!
Uh... GUYS?
WHERE'D THE NOTES GO?
THE NOTES...?
SCREW THE NOTES!
WHERE ARE MARV AND DOOGIE?!
THOSE WEASELS!
THEY TOOK THE VAN AND THE ATROPHANE!
WE'VE GOT TO NOTIFY SOMEONE!
IF THEY CAN STEAL THE XYKLON-C--!
THEY WON'T.
19

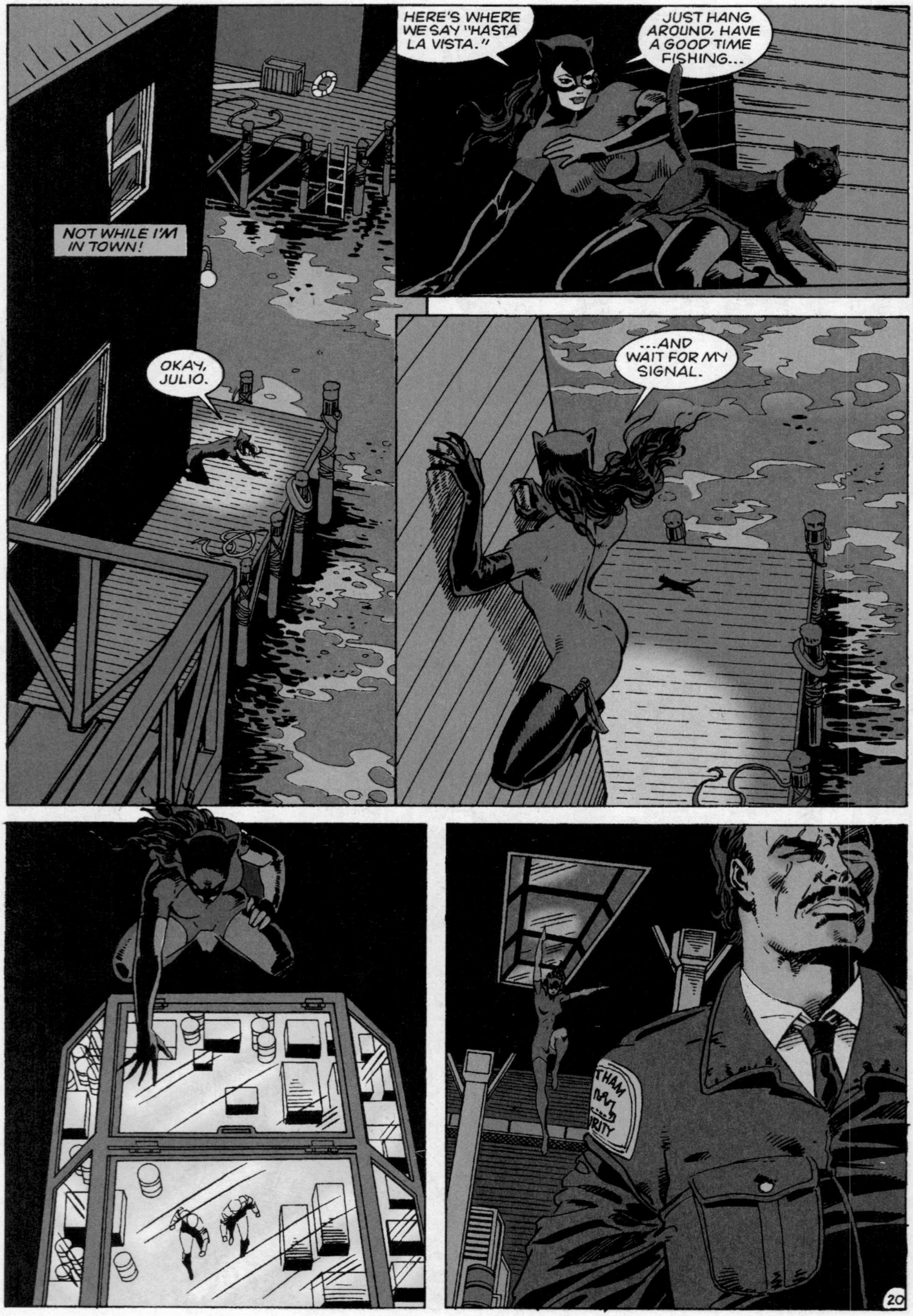

HERE'S WHERE WE SAY "HASTA LA VISTA."
JUST HANG AROUND, HAVE A GOOD TIME FISHING...
NOT WHILE I'M IN TOWN!
OKAY, JULIO.
...AND WAIT FOR MY SIGNAL.
20

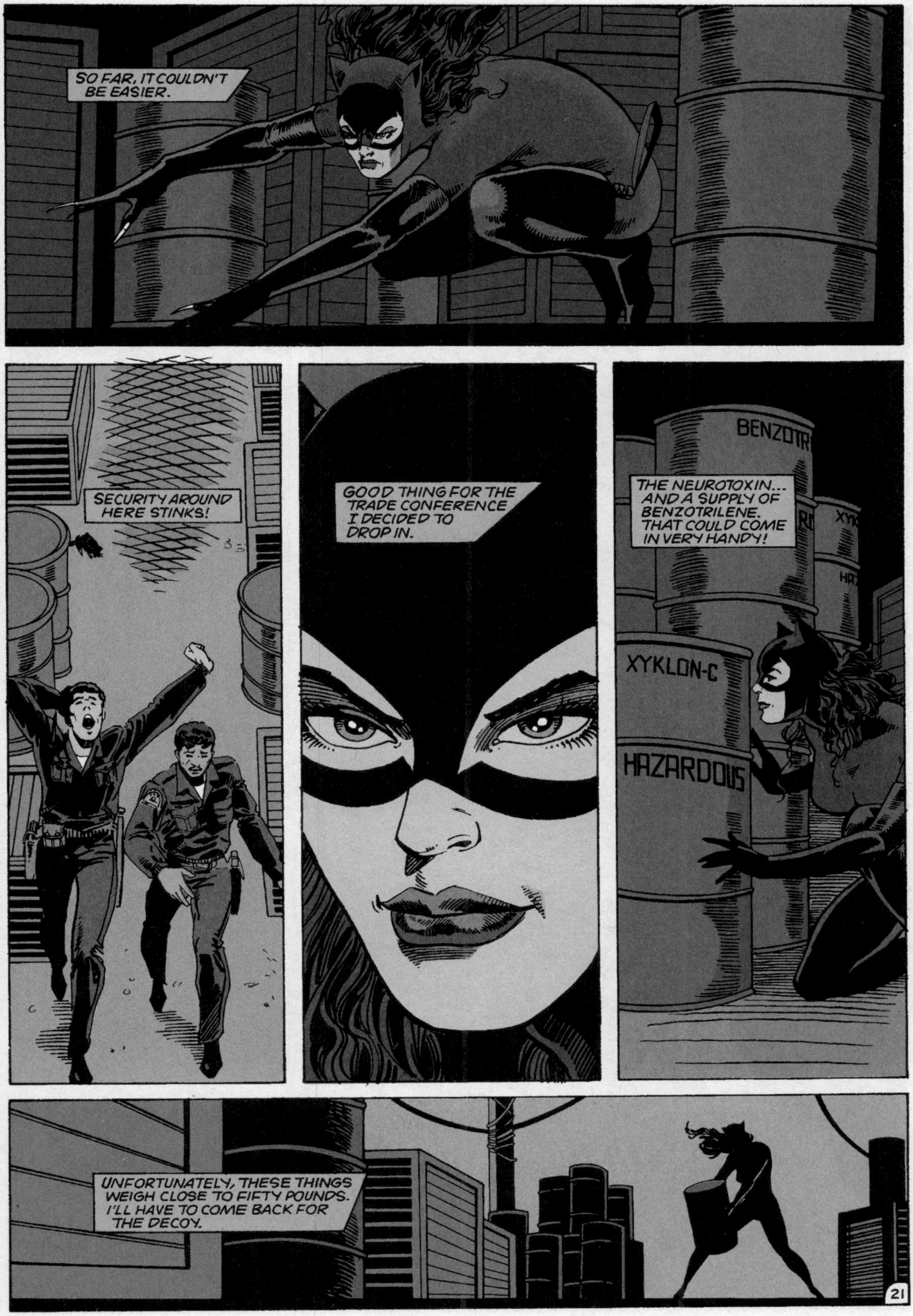
SO FAR, IT COULDN'T BE EASIER.
SECURITY AROUND HERE STINKS!
GOOD THING FOR THE TRADE CONFERENCE I DECIDED TO DROP IN.
BENZOTRI
THE NEUROTOXIN... AND A SUPPLY OF BENZOTRILENE. THAT COULD COME IN VERY HANDY!
XYKLON-C
HAZARDOUS
UNFORTUNATELY, THESE THINGS WEIGH CLOSE TO FIFTY POUNDS. I'LL HAVE TO COME BACK FOR THE DECOY.
21

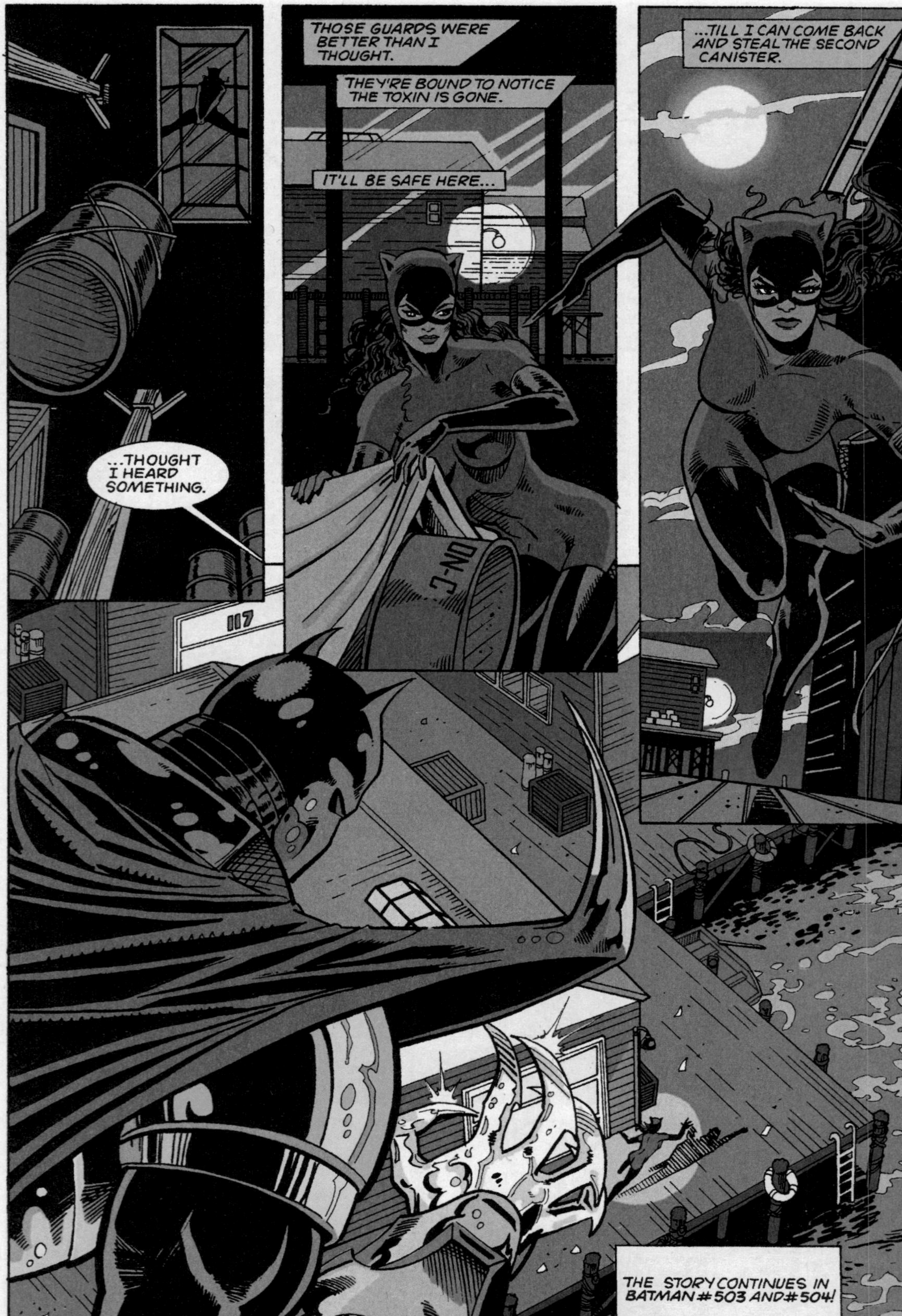
...THOUGHT I HEARD SOMETHING.
THOSE GUARDS WERE BETTER THAN I THOUGHT.
THEY'RE BOUND TO NOTICE THE TOXIN IS GONE.
IT'LL BE SAFE HERE...
...TILL I CAN COME BACK AND STEAL THE SECOND CANISTER.
117
THE STORY CONTINUES IN BATMAN #503 AND #504!

Cover art by KELLEY JONES

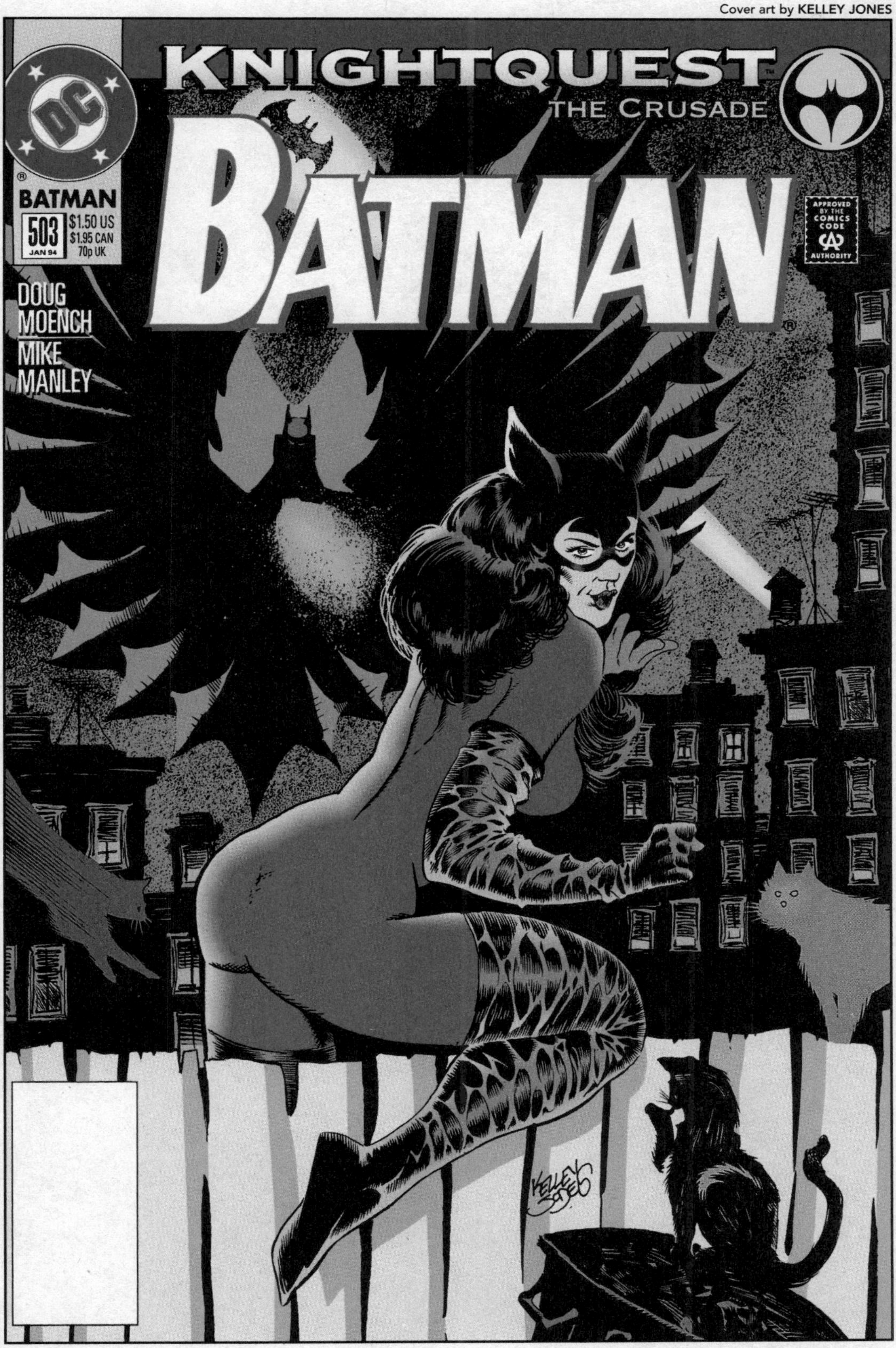

KNIGHTQUEST
THE CRUSADE
BATMAN
BATMAN
503
JAN 94
$1.50 US
$1.95 CAN
70p UK
DOUG MOENCH
MIKE MANLEY
APPROVED BY THE COMICS CODE AUTHORITY

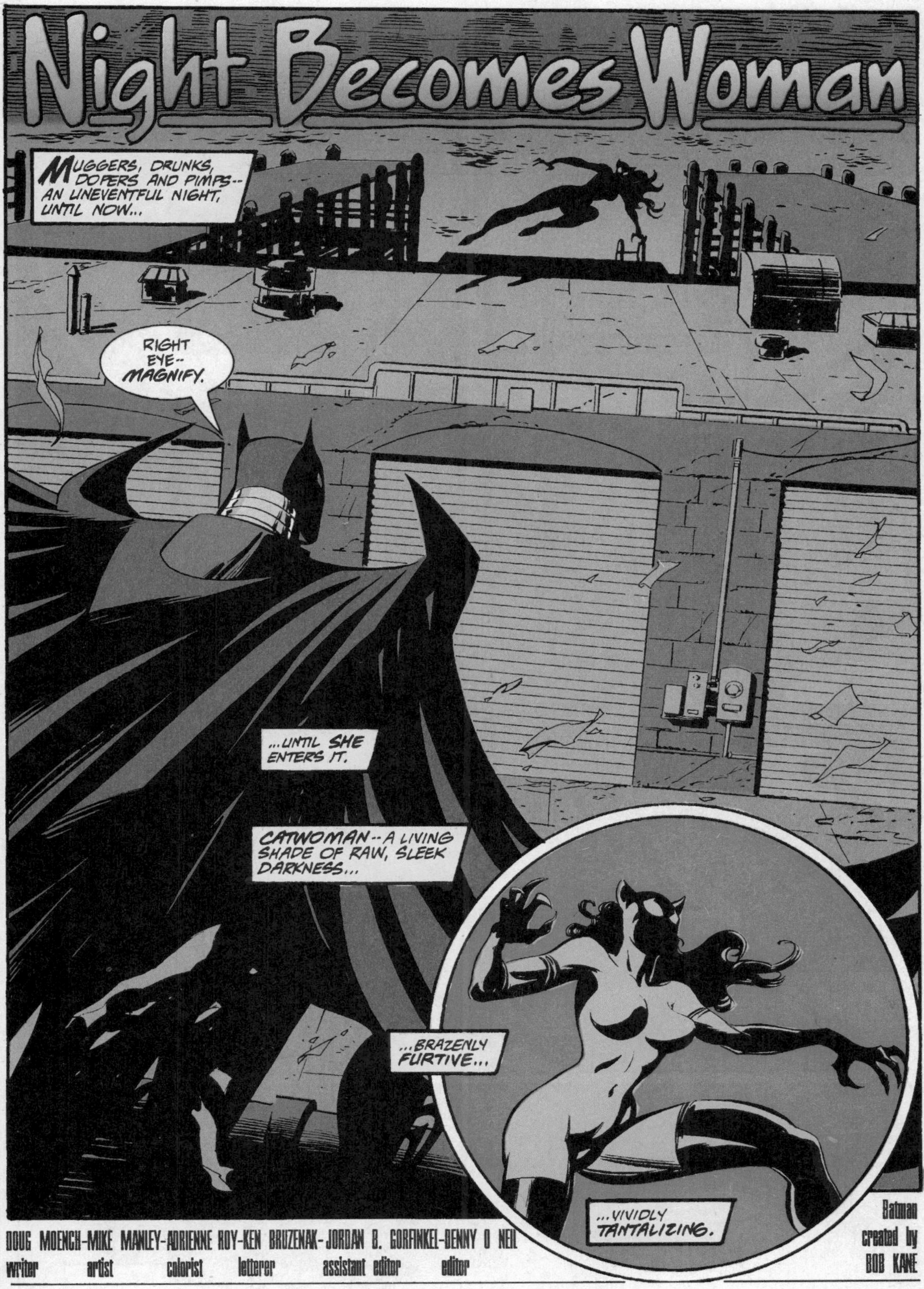

Night Becomes Woman
MUGGERS, DRUNKS, DOPERS AND PIMPS-- AN UNEVENTFUL NIGHT, UNTIL NOW...
RIGHT EYE-- MAGNIFY.
...UNTIL SHE ENTERS IT.
CATWOMAN--A LIVING SHADE OF RAW, SLEEK DARKNESS...
...BRAZENLY FURTIVE...
...VIVIDLY TANTALIZING.

DOUG MOENCH-MIKE MANLEY-ADRIENNE ROY-KEN BRUZENAK-JORDAN B. GORFINKEL-DENNY O NEIL
writer artist colorist letterer assistant editor editor

Batman created by BOB KANE

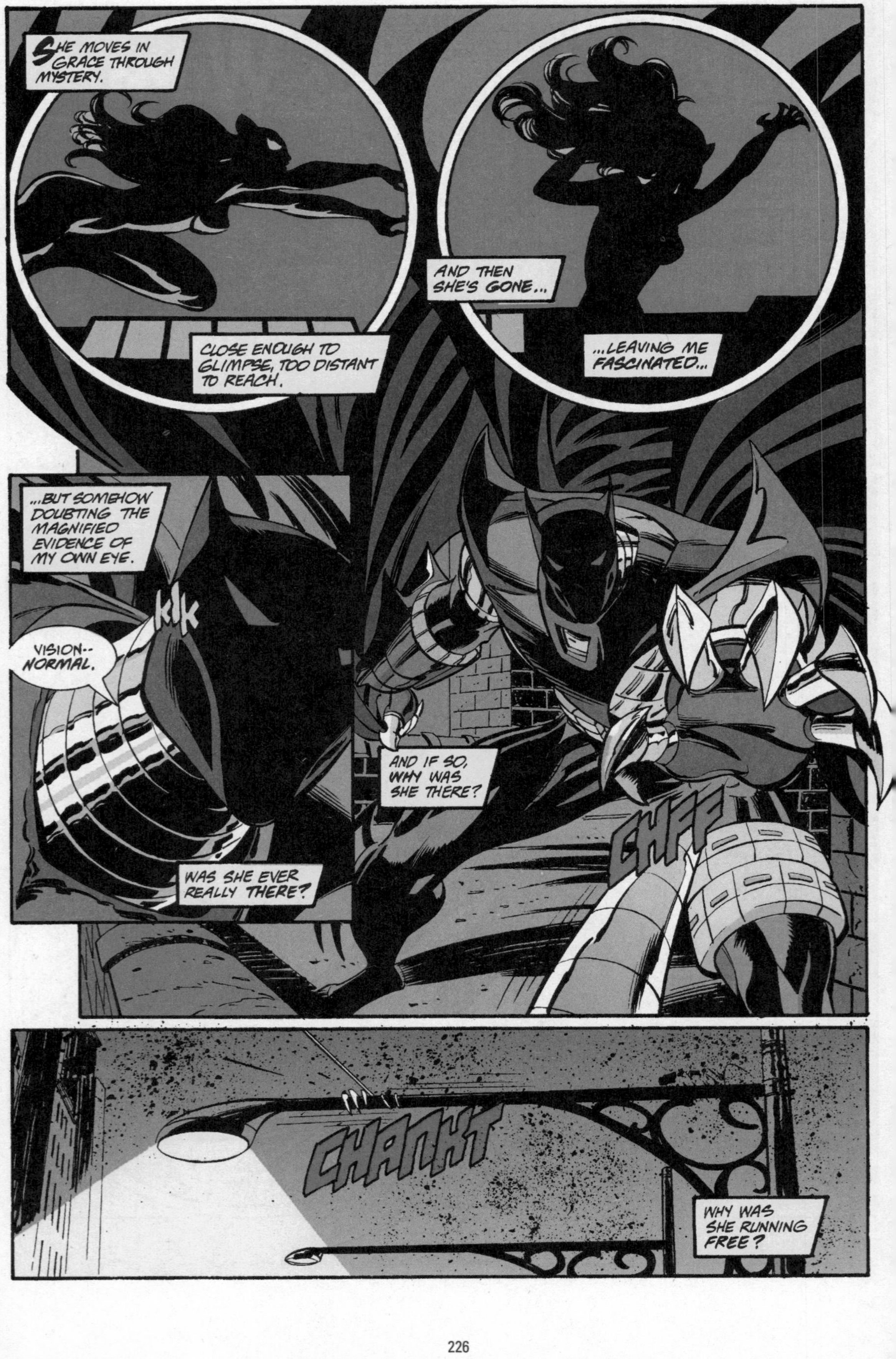
SHE MOVES IN GRACE THROUGH MYSTERY.
CLOSE ENOUGH TO GLIMPSE, TOO DISTANT TO REACH.
AND THEN SHE'S GONE...
...LEAVING ME FASCINATED...
...BUT SOMEHOW DOUBTING THE MAGNIFIED EVIDENCE OF MY OWN EYE.
KIK
VISION-- NORMAL.
AND IF SO, WHY WAS SHE THERE?
WAS SHE EVER REALLY THERE?
CHFF
CHANKT
WHY WAS SHE RUNNING FREE?

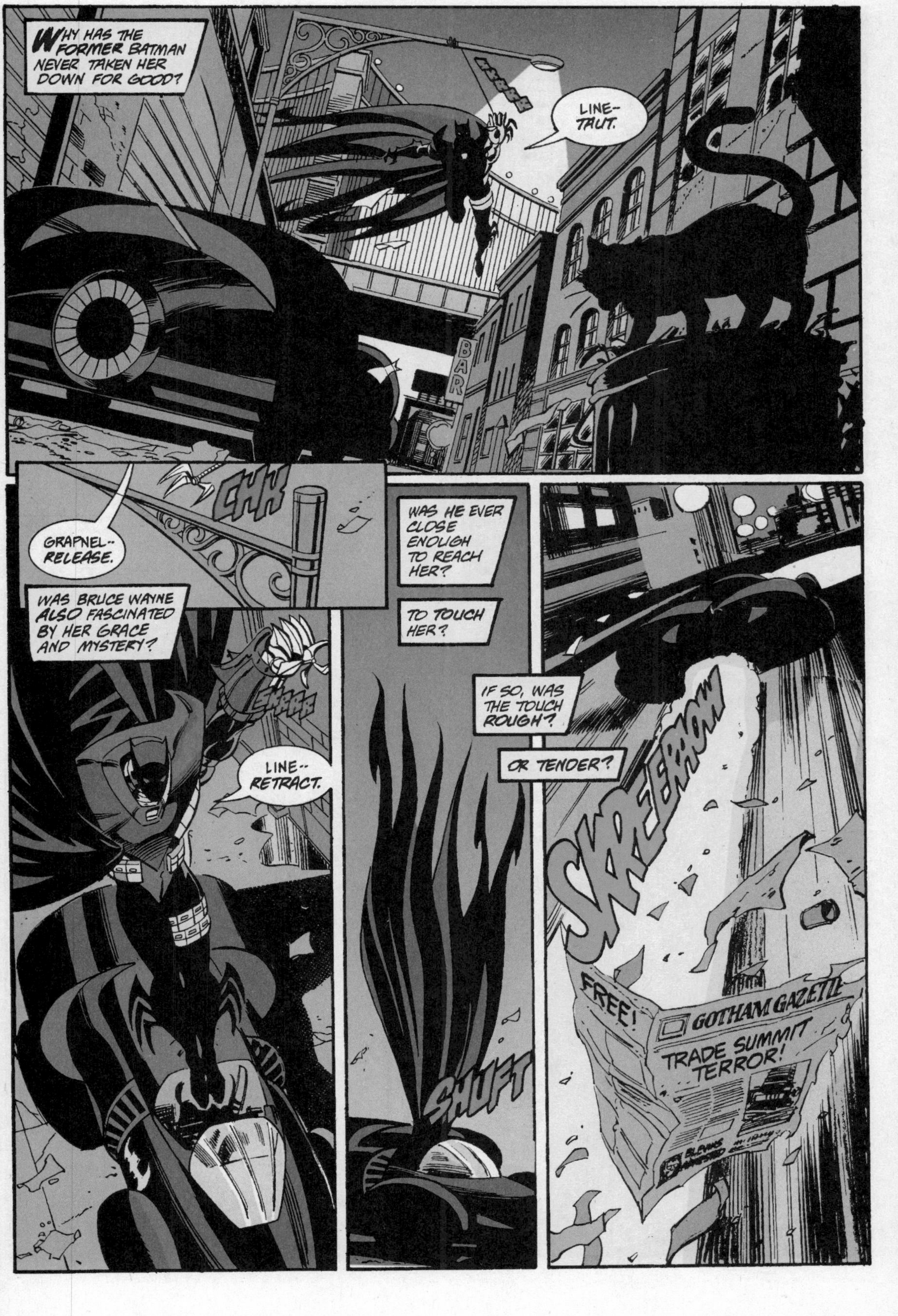

WHY HAS THE FORMER BATMAN NEVER TAKEN HER DOWN FOR GOOD?
LINE-TAUT.
BAR
GRAPNEL-- RELEASE.
CHK
WAS BRUCE WAYNE ALSO FASCINATED BY HER GRACE AND MYSTERY?
LINE-- RETRACT.
WAS HE EVER CLOSE ENOUGH TO REACH HER?
TO TOUCH HER?
IF SO, WAS THE TOUCH ROUGH?
OR TENDER?
SHUFT
SKREEEROWW
FREE!
GOTHAM GAZETTE
TRADE SUMMIT TERROR!

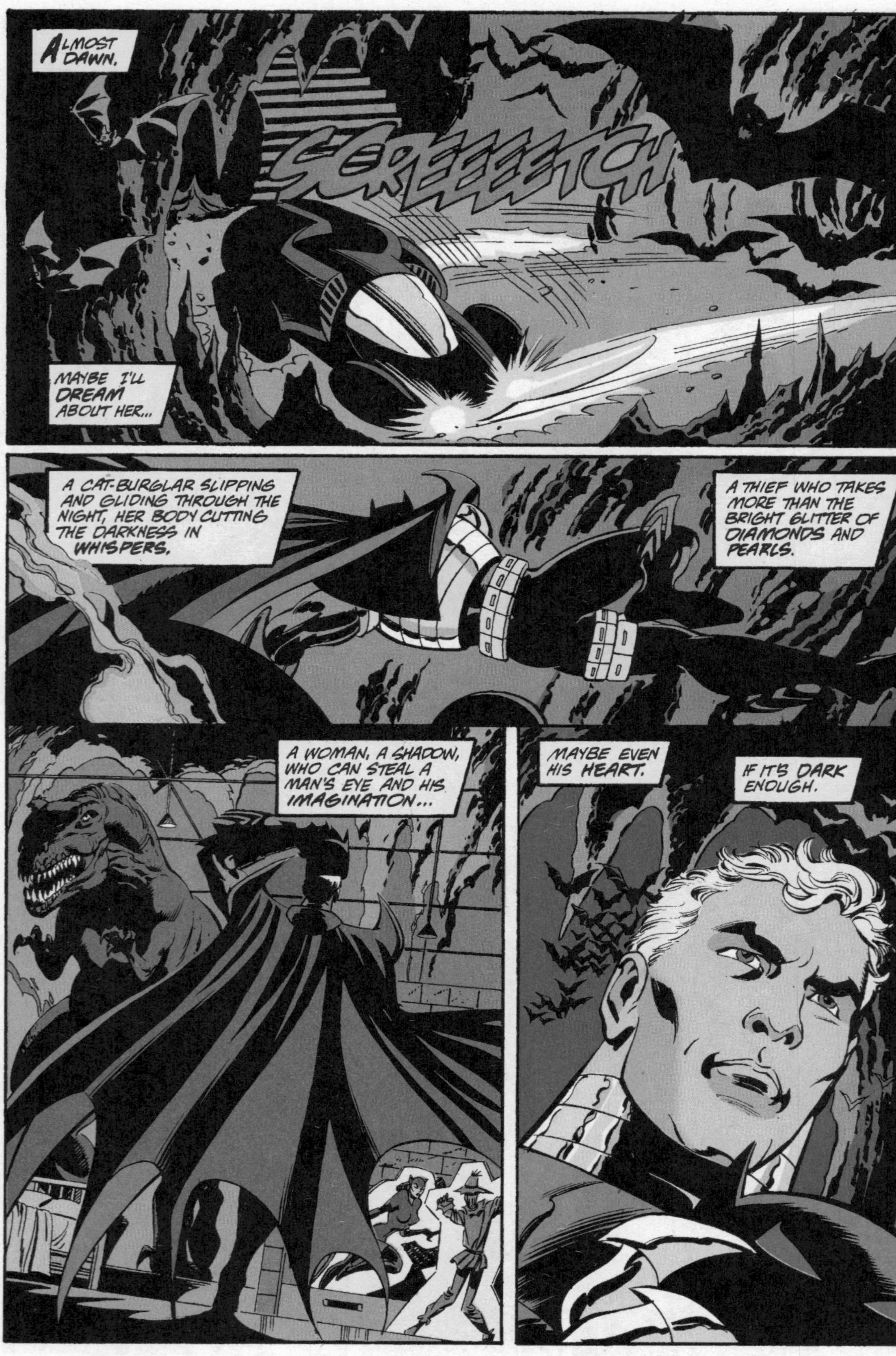
ALMOST DAWN.
SCREEEECH
MAYBE I'LL DREAM ABOUT HER...
A CAT-BURGLAR SLIPPING AND GLIDING THROUGH THE NIGHT, HER BODY CUTTING THE DARKNESS IN WHISPERS.
A THIEF WHO TAKES MORE THAN THE BRIGHT GLITTER OF DIAMONDS AND PEARLS.
A WOMAN, A SHADOW, WHO CAN STEAL A MAN'S EYE AND HIS IMAGINATION...
MAYBE EVEN HIS HEART.
IF IT'S DARK ENOUGH.

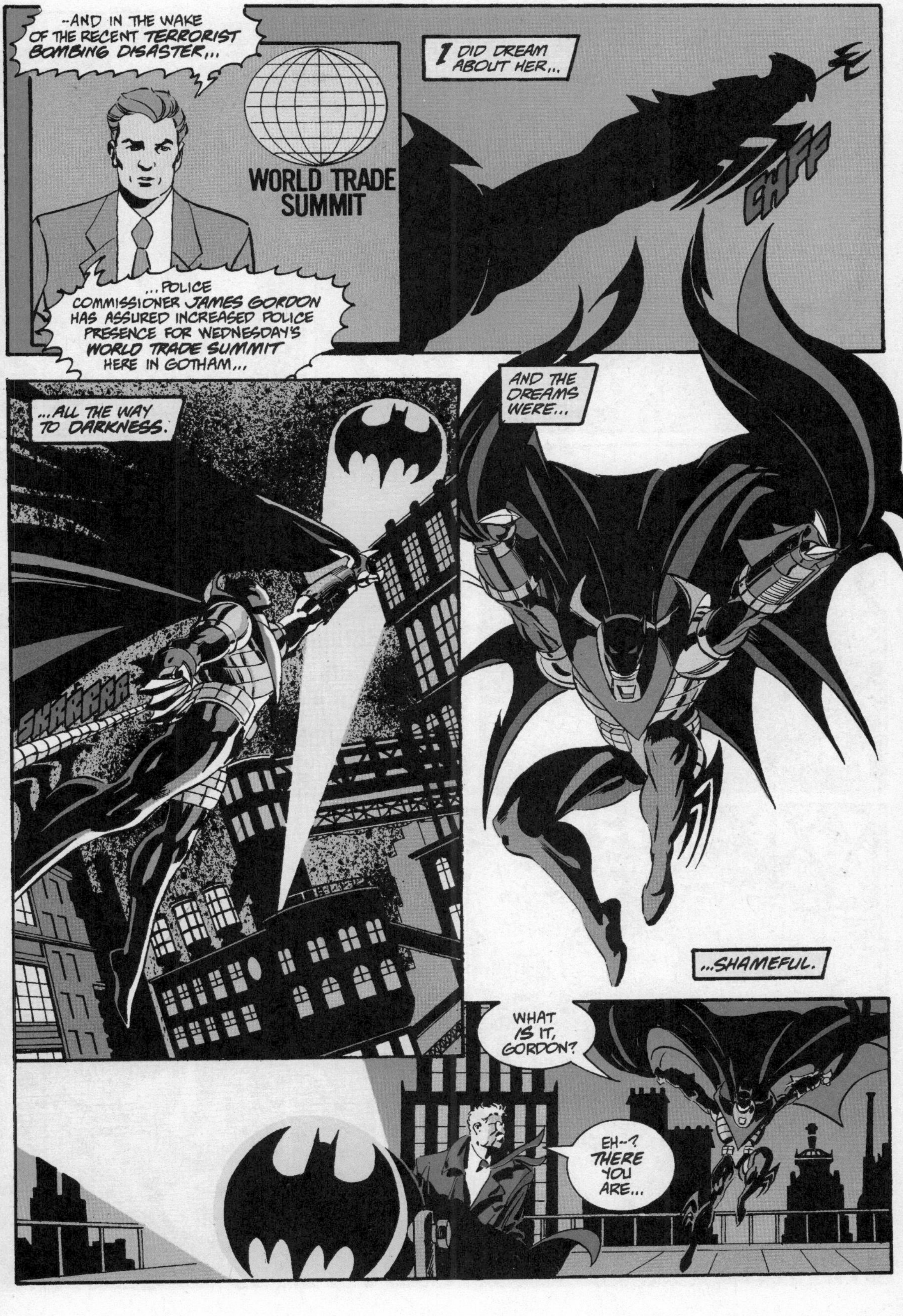

--AND IN THE WAKE OF THE RECENT TERRORIST BOMBING DISASTER,..
WORLD TRADE SUMMIT
...POLICE COMMISSIONER JAMES GORDON HAS ASSURED INCREASED POLICE PRESENCE FOR WEDNESDAY'S WORLD TRADE SUMMIT HERE IN GOTHAM...
I DID DREAM ABOUT HER...
CHFF
...ALL THE WAY TO DARKNESS.
SKRRRRR
AND THE DREAMS WERE...
...SHAMEFUL.
WHAT IS IT, GORDON?
EH--? THERE YOU ARE...

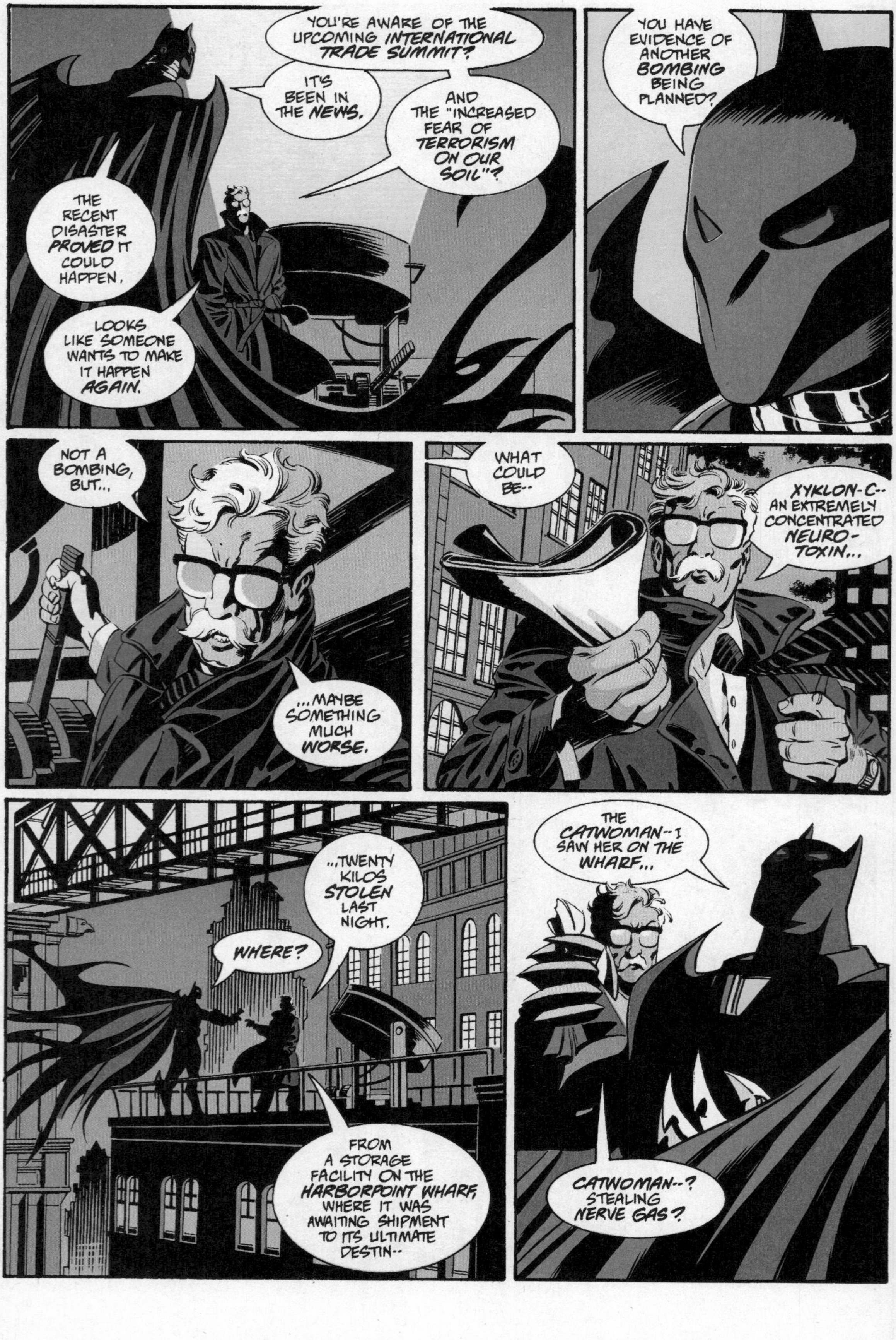
YOU'RE AWARE OF THE UPCOMING INTERNATIONAL TRADE SUMMIT?
IT'S BEEN IN THE NEWS.
AND THE "INCREASED FEAR OF TERRORISM ON OUR SOIL"?
THE RECENT DISASTER PROVED IT COULD HAPPEN.
LOOKS LIKE SOMEONE WANTS TO MAKE IT HAPPEN AGAIN.
YOU HAVE EVIDENCE OF ANOTHER BOMBING BEING PLANNED?
NOT A BOMBING, BUT...
...MAYBE SOMETHING MUCH WORSE.
WHAT COULD BE--
XYKLON-C-- AN EXTREMELY CONCENTRATED NEURO-TOXIN...
...TWENTY KILOS STOLEN LAST NIGHT.
WHERE?
FROM A STORAGE FACILITY ON THE HARBORPOINT WHARF, WHERE IT WAS AWAITING SHIPMENT TO ITS ULTIMATE DESTIN--
THE CATWOMAN--I SAW HER ON THE WHARF...
CATWOMAN--? STEALING NERVE GAS?

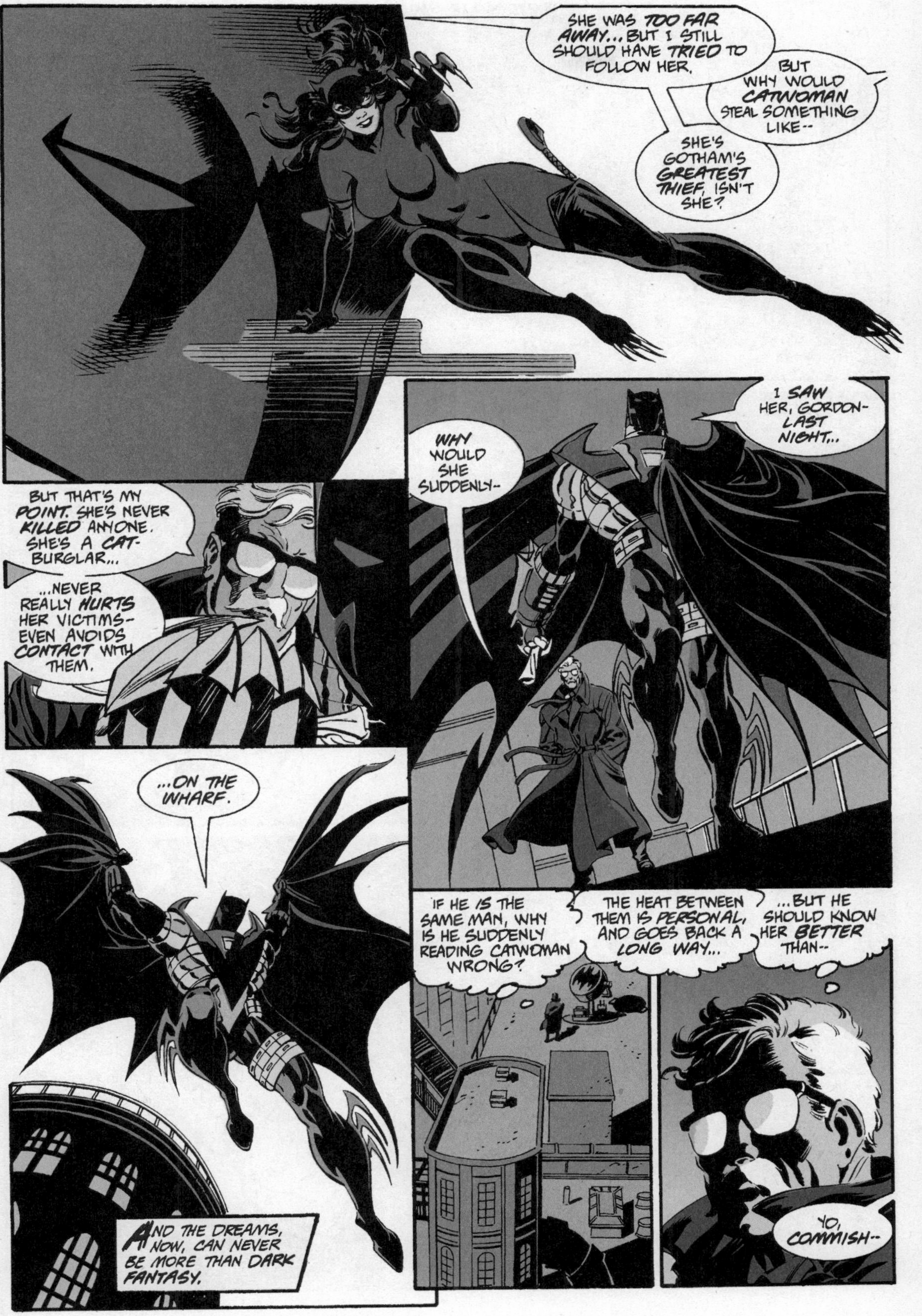
SHE WAS TOO FAR AWAY... BUT I STILL SHOULD HAVE TRIED TO FOLLOW HER.
BUT WHY WOULD CATWOMAN STEAL SOMETHING LIKE--
SHE'S GOTHAM'S GREATEST THIEF, ISN'T SHE?
I SAW HER, GORDON-LAST NIGHT...
WHY WOULD SHE SUDDENLY--
BUT THAT'S MY POINT. SHE'S NEVER KILLED ANYONE. SHE'S A CAT-BURGLAR...
...NEVER REALLY HURTS HER VICTIMS-EVEN AVOIDS CONTACT WITH THEM.
...ON THE WHARF.
AND THE DREAMS, NOW, CAN NEVER BE MORE THAN DARK FANTASY.
IF HE IS THE SAME MAN, WHY IS HE SUDDENLY READING CATWOMAN WRONG?
THE HEAT BETWEEN THEM IS PERSONAL, AND GOES BACK A LONG WAY...
...BUT HE SHOULD KNOW HER BETTER THAN--
YO, COMMISH--

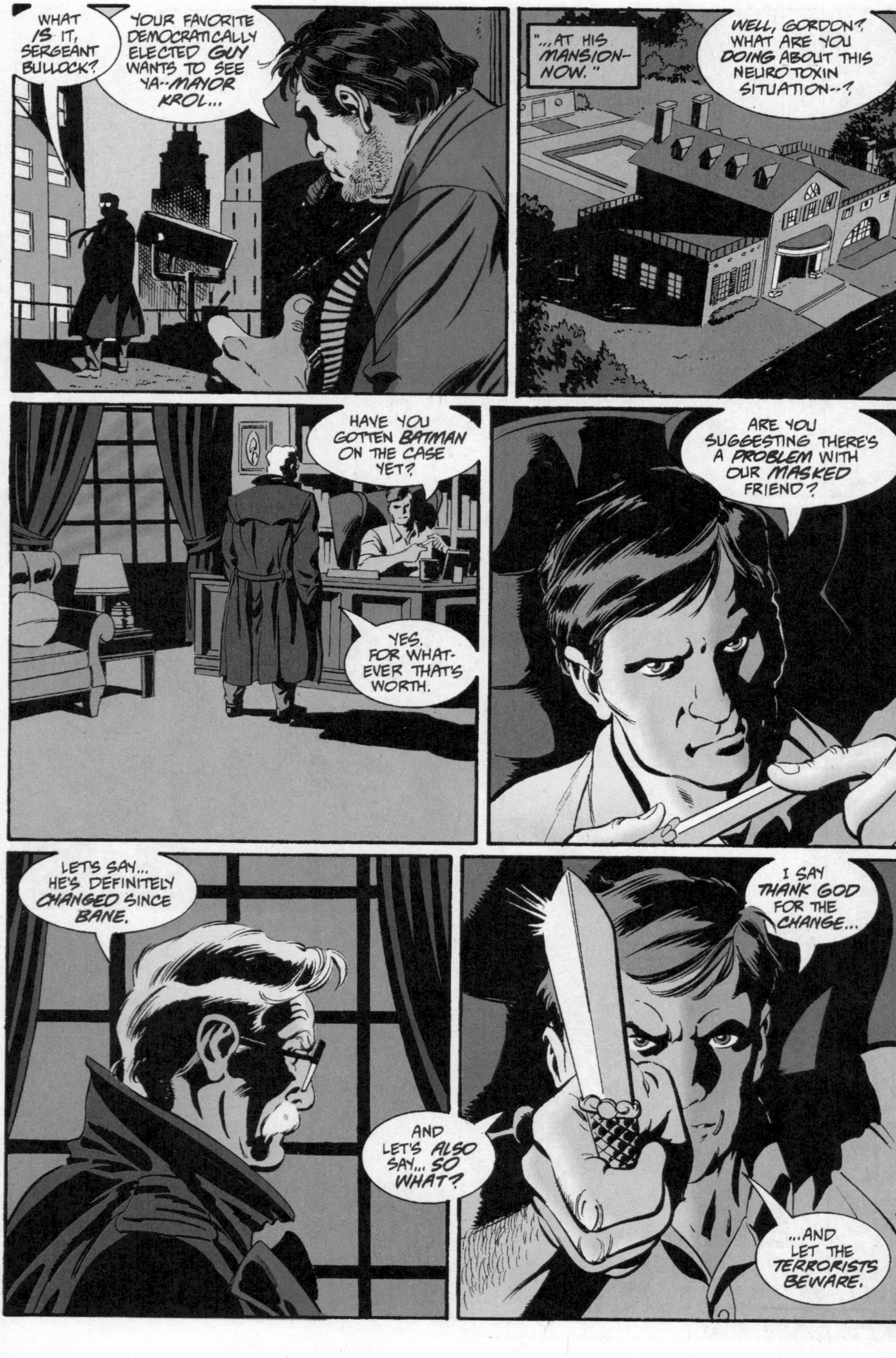
WHAT IS IT, SERGEANT BULLOCK?
YOUR FAVORITE DEMOCRATICALLY ELECTED GUY WANTS TO SEE YA--MAYOR KROL...
"...AT HIS MANSION-NOW."
WELL, GORDON? WHAT ARE YOU DOING ABOUT THIS NEUROTOXIN SITUATION--?
HAVE YOU GOTTEN BATMAN ON THE CASE YET?
YES. FOR WHATEVER THAT'S WORTH.
ARE YOU SUGGESTING THERE'S A PROBLEM WITH OUR MASKED FRIEND?
LET'S SAY... HE'S DEFINITELY CHANGED SINCE BANE.
AND LET'S ALSO SAY... SO WHAT?
I SAY THANK GOD FOR THE CHANGE...
...AND LET THE TERRORISTS BEWARE.

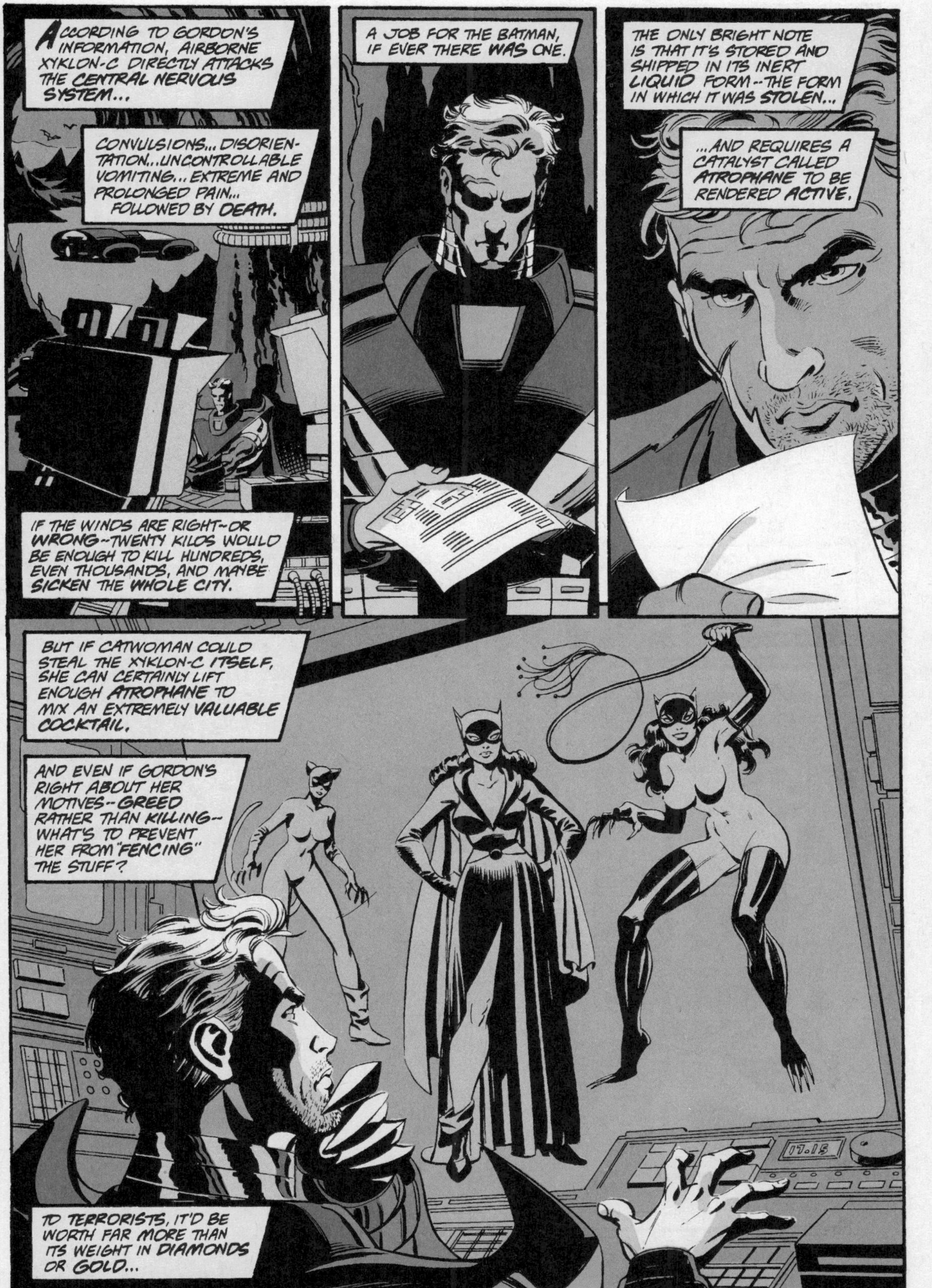
ACCORDING TO GORDON'S INFORMATION, AIRBORNE XYKLON-C DIRECTLY ATTACKS THE CENTRAL NERVOUS SYSTEM...
CONVULSIONS... DISORIENTATION... UNCONTROLLABLE VOMITING... EXTREME AND PROLONGED PAIN... FOLLOWED BY DEATH.
IF THE WINDS ARE RIGHT--OR WRONG--TWENTY KILOS WOULD BE ENOUGH TO KILL HUNDREDS, EVEN THOUSANDS, AND MAYBE SICKEN THE WHOLE CITY.
A JOB FOR THE BATMAN, IF EVER THERE WAS ONE.
THE ONLY BRIGHT NOTE IS THAT IT'S STORED AND SHIPPED IN ITS INERT LIQUID FORM--THE FORM IN WHICH IT WAS STOLEN...
...AND REQUIRES A CATALYST CALLED ATROPHANE TO BE RENDERED ACTIVE.
BUT IF CATWOMAN COULD STEAL THE XYKLON-C ITSELF, SHE CAN CERTAINLY LIFT ENOUGH ATROPHANE TO MIX AN EXTREMELY VALUABLE COCKTAIL.
AND EVEN IF GORDON'S RIGHT ABOUT HER MOTIVES--GREED RATHER THAN KILLING--WHAT'S TO PREVENT HER FROM "FENCING" THE STUFF?
TO TERRORISTS, IT'D BE WORTH FAR MORE THAN ITS WEIGHT IN DIAMONDS OR GOLD...
17.15

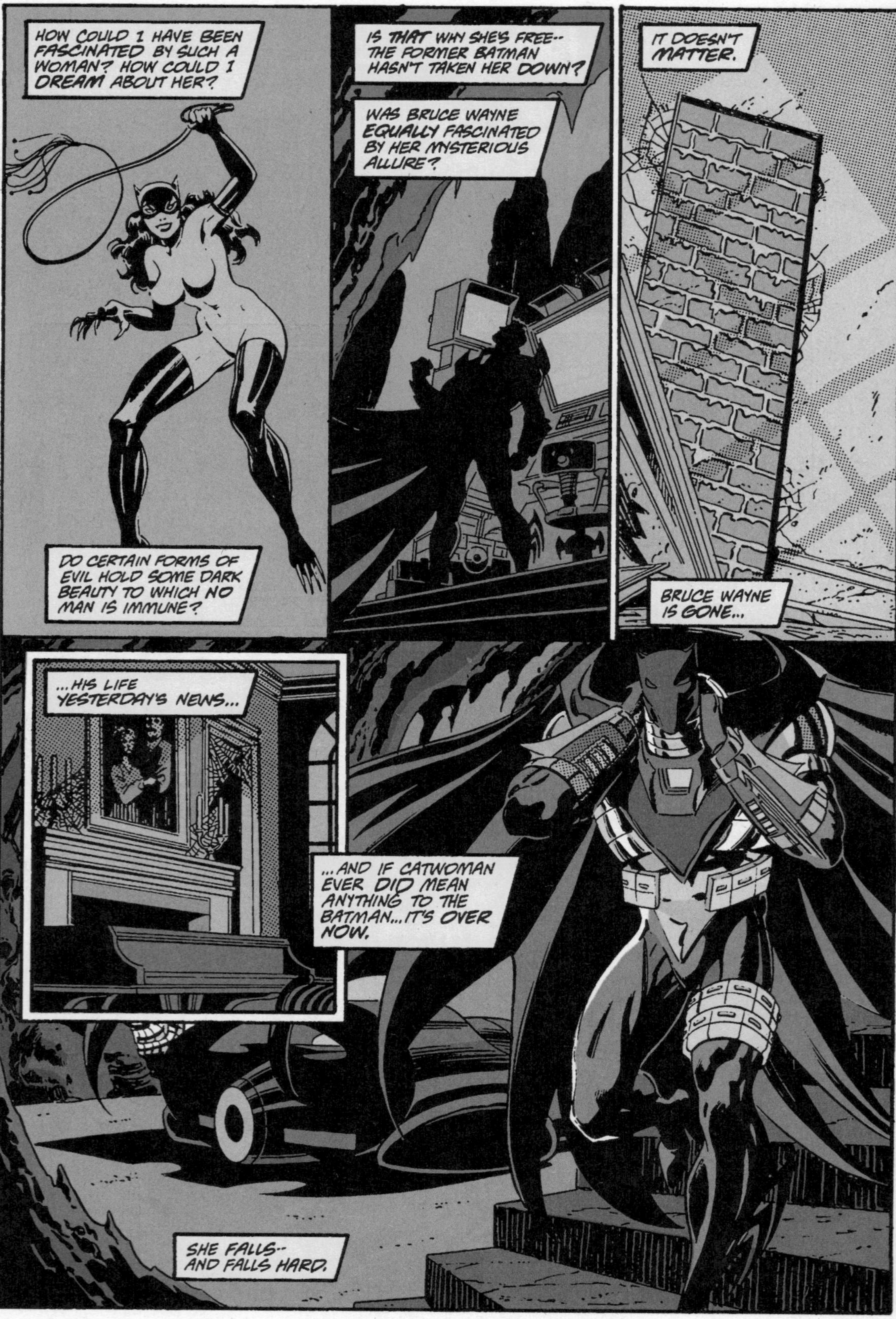
HOW COULD I HAVE BEEN FASCINATED BY SUCH A WOMAN? HOW COULD I DREAM ABOUT HER?
DO CERTAIN FORMS OF EVIL HOLD SOME DARK BEAUTY TO WHICH NO MAN IS IMMUNE?
IS THAT WHY SHE'S FREE-- THE FORMER BATMAN HASN'T TAKEN HER DOWN?
WAS BRUCE WAYNE EQUALLY FASCINATED BY HER MYSTERIOUS ALLURE?
IT DOESN'T MATTER.
BRUCE WAYNE IS GONE...
...HIS LIFE YESTERDAY'S NEWS...
...AND IF CATWOMAN EVER DID MEAN ANYTHING TO THE BATMAN...IT'S OVER NOW.
SHE FALLS-- AND FALLS HARD.

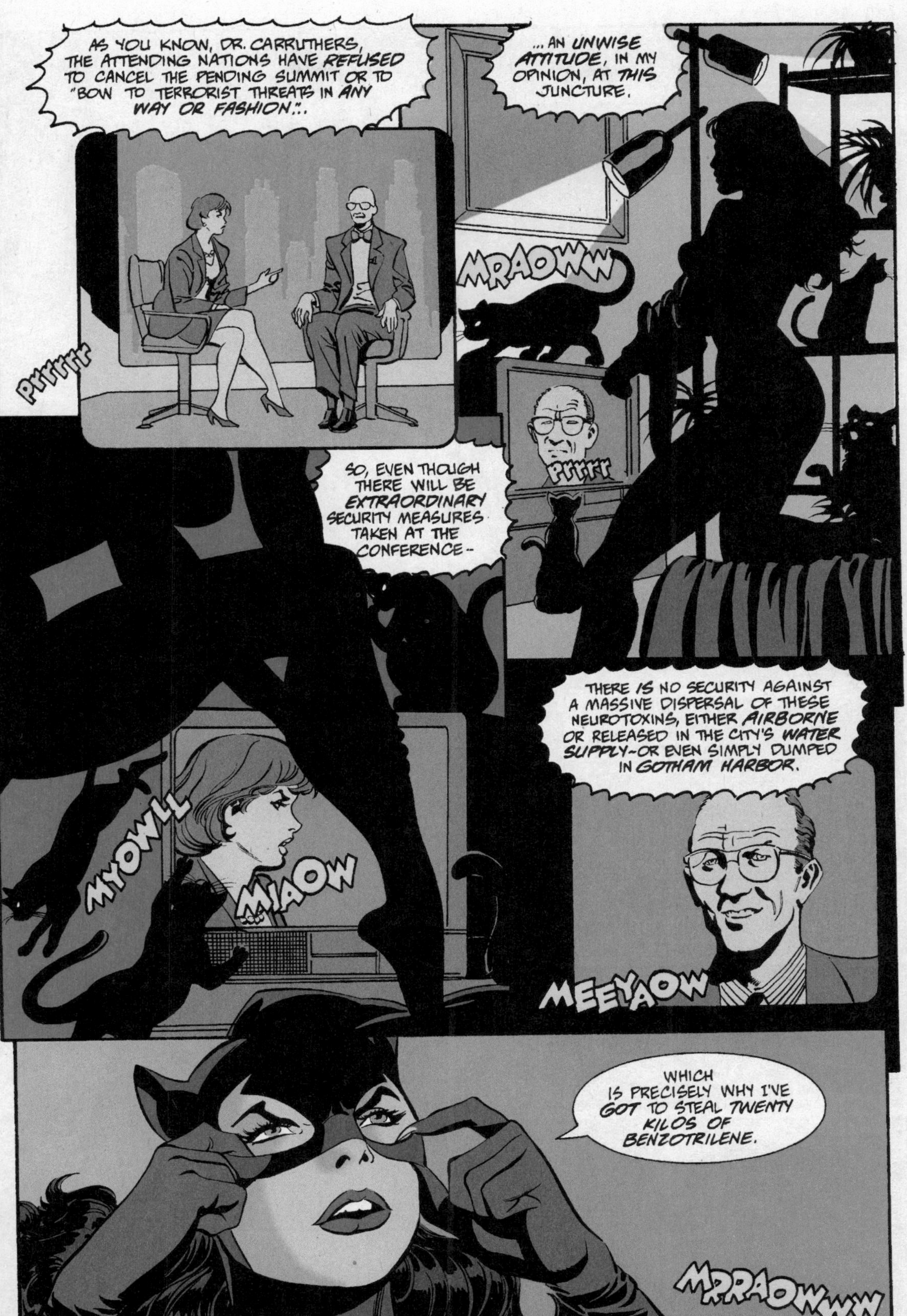

AS YOU KNOW, DR. CARRUTHERS, THE ATTENDING NATIONS HAVE REFUSED TO CANCEL THE PENDING SUMMIT OR TO "BOW TO TERRORIST THREATS IN ANY WAY OR FASHION."...
...AN UNWISE ATTITUDE, IN MY OPINION, AT THIS JUNCTURE.
MRAOWW
PRRRRR
PRRRR
SO, EVEN THOUGH THERE WILL BE EXTRAORDINARY SECURITY MEASURES TAKEN AT THE CONFERENCE -
THERE IS NO SECURITY AGAINST A MASSIVE DISPERSAL OF THESE NEUROTOXINS, EITHER AIRBORNE OR RELEASED IN THE CITY'S WATER SUPPLY-OR EVEN SIMPLY DUMPED IN GOTHAM HARBOR.
MYOWLL
MIAOW
MEEYAOW
WHICH IS PRECISELY WHY I'VE GOT TO STEAL TWENTY KILOS OF BENZOTRILENE.
MRRAOWWW

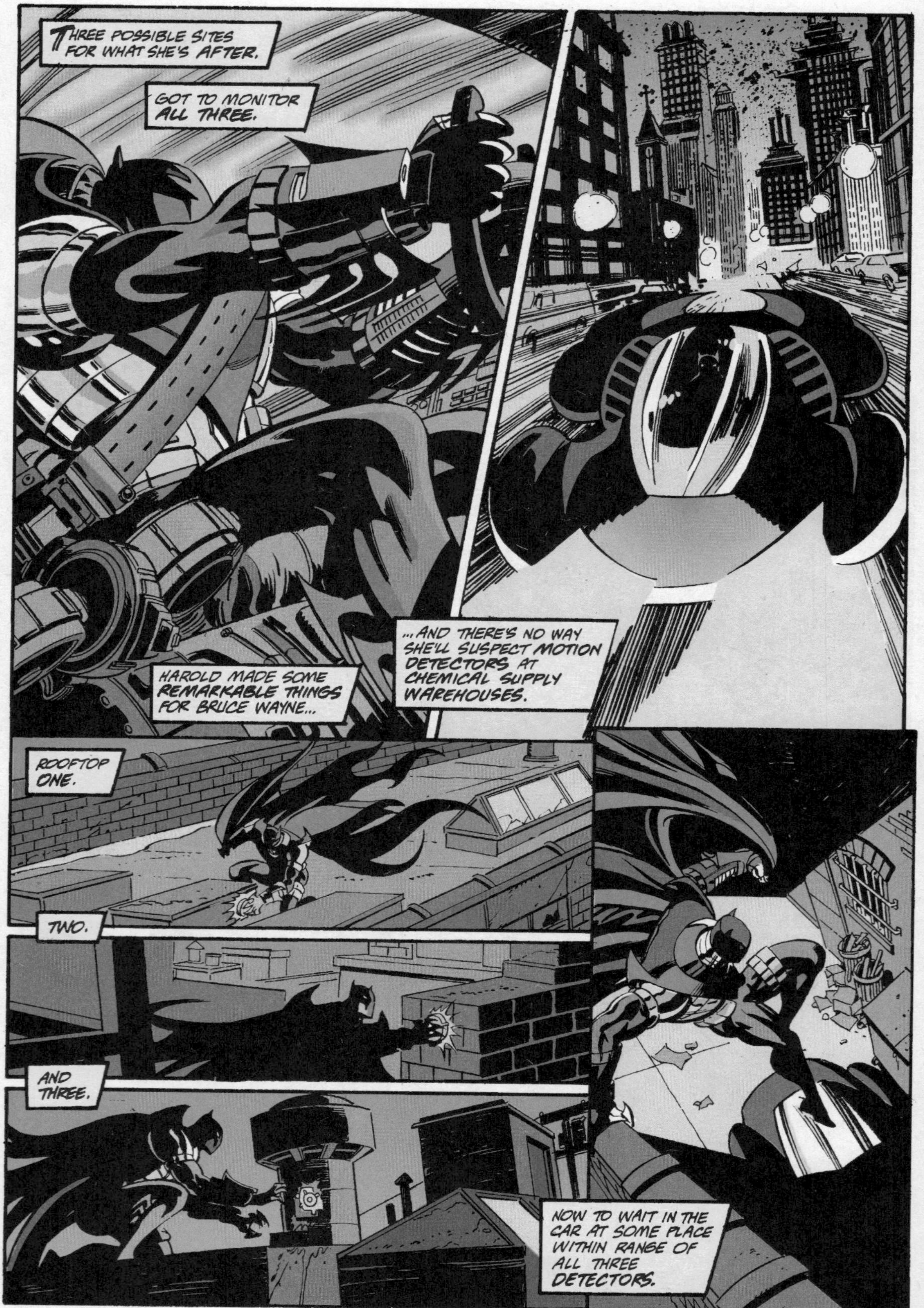
THREE POSSIBLE SITES FOR WHAT SHE'S AFTER.
GOT TO MONITOR ALL THREE.
HAROLD MADE SOME REMARKABLE THINGS FOR BRUCE WAYNE...
...AND THERE'S NO WAY SHE'LL SUSPECT MOTION DETECTORS AT CHEMICAL SUPPLY WAREHOUSES.
ROOFTOP ONE.
TWO.
AND THREE.
NOW TO WAIT IN THE CAR AT SOME PLACE WITHIN RANGE OF ALL THREE DETECTORS.

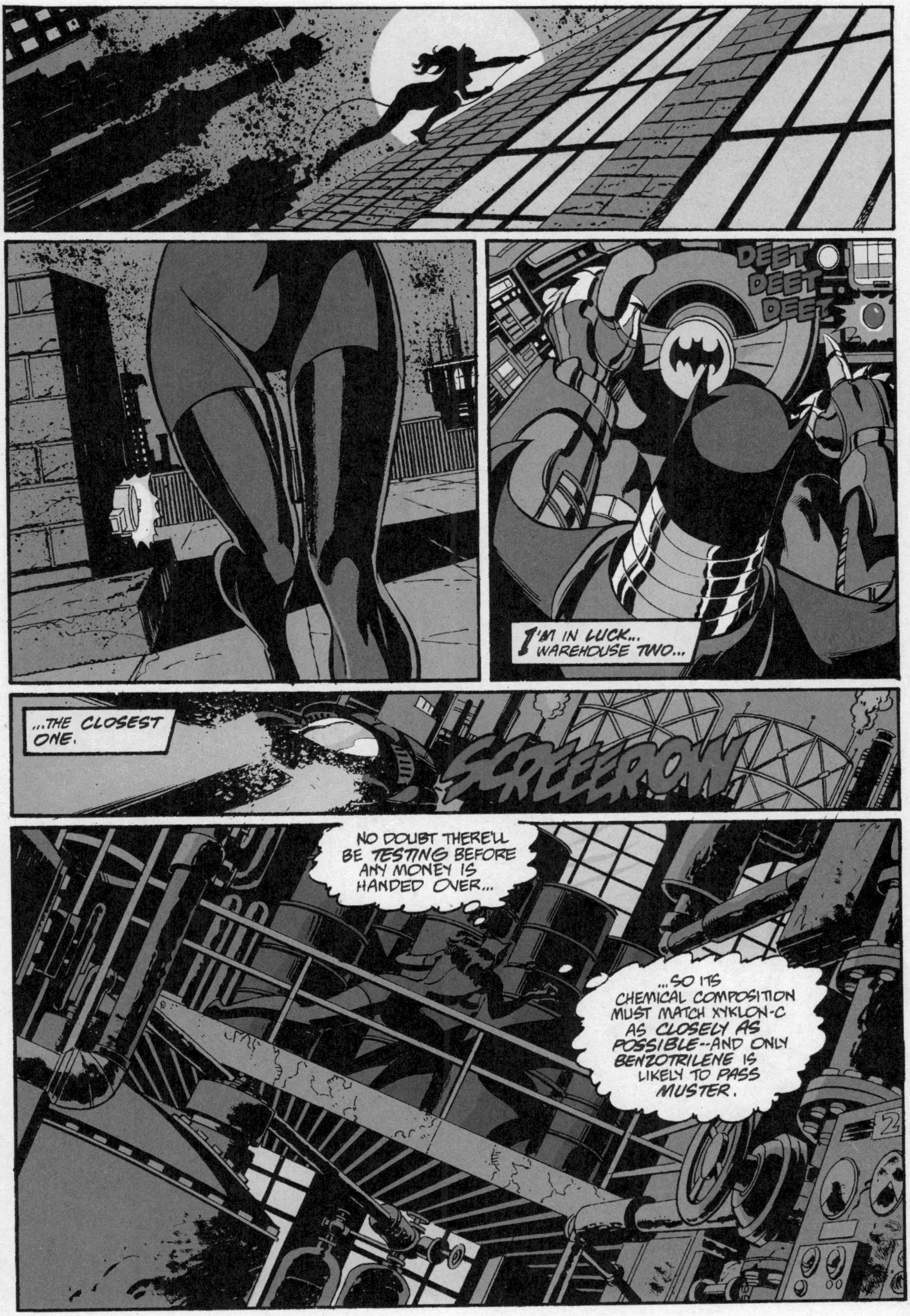
DEET DEET DEET
I'M IN LUCK... WAREHOUSE TWO...
...THE CLOSEST ONE.
SCREEEROW
NO DOUBT THERE'LL BE TESTING BEFORE ANY MONEY IS HANDED OVER...
...SO ITS CHEMICAL COMPOSITION MUST MATCH XYKLON-C AS CLOSELY AS POSSIBLE--AND ONLY BENZOTRILENE IS LIKELY TO PASS MUSTER.

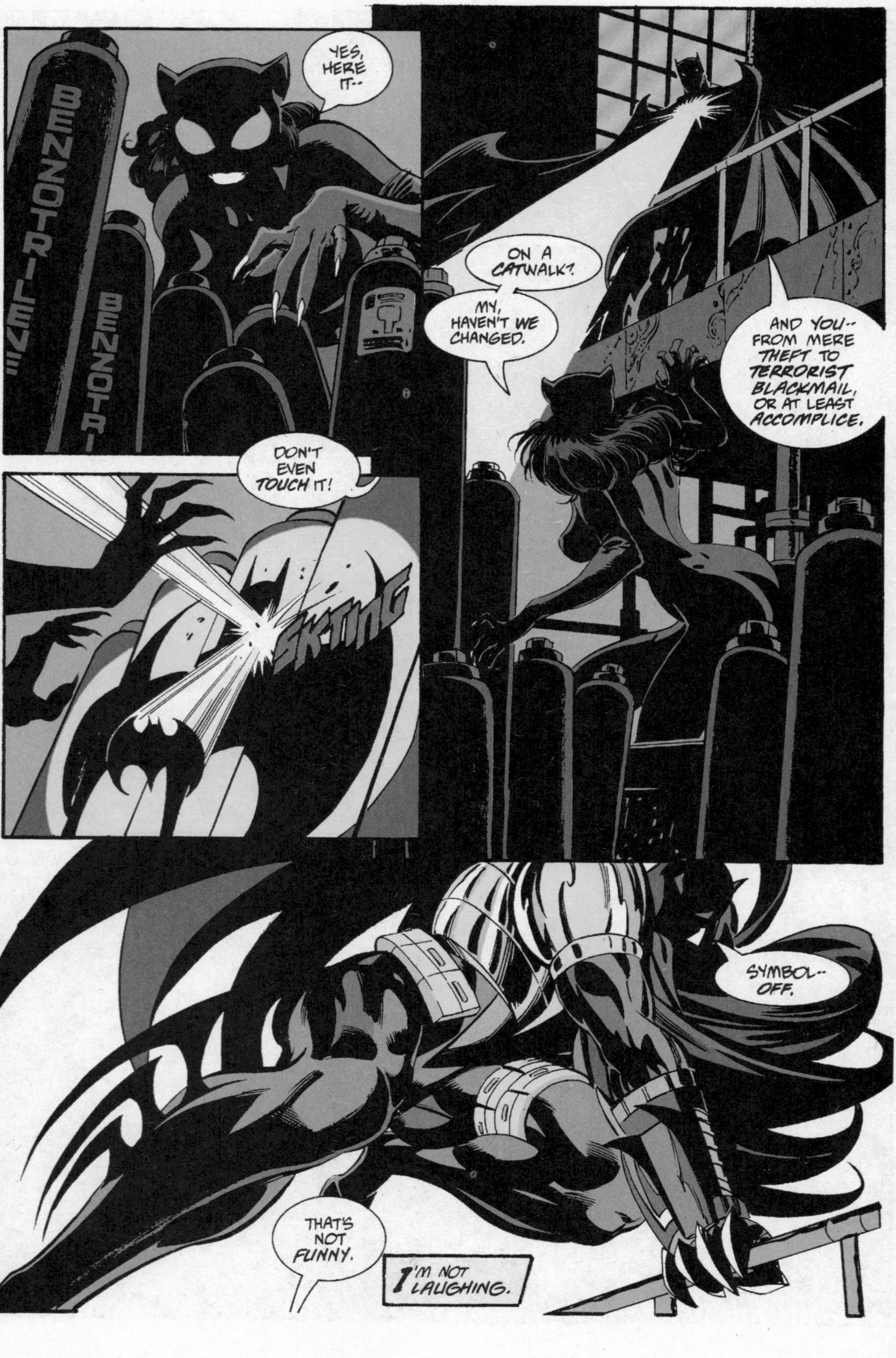
YES, HERE IT--
BENNOTRILEV!!!
BENNOTRI
ON A CATWALK?
MY, HAVEN'T WE CHANGED.
AND YOU-- FROM MERE THEFT TO TERRORIST BLACKMAIL, OR AT LEAST ACCOMPLICE.
DON'T EVEN TOUCH IT!
SKTING
SYMBOL-- OFF.
THAT'S NOT FUNNY.
I'M NOT LAUGHING.

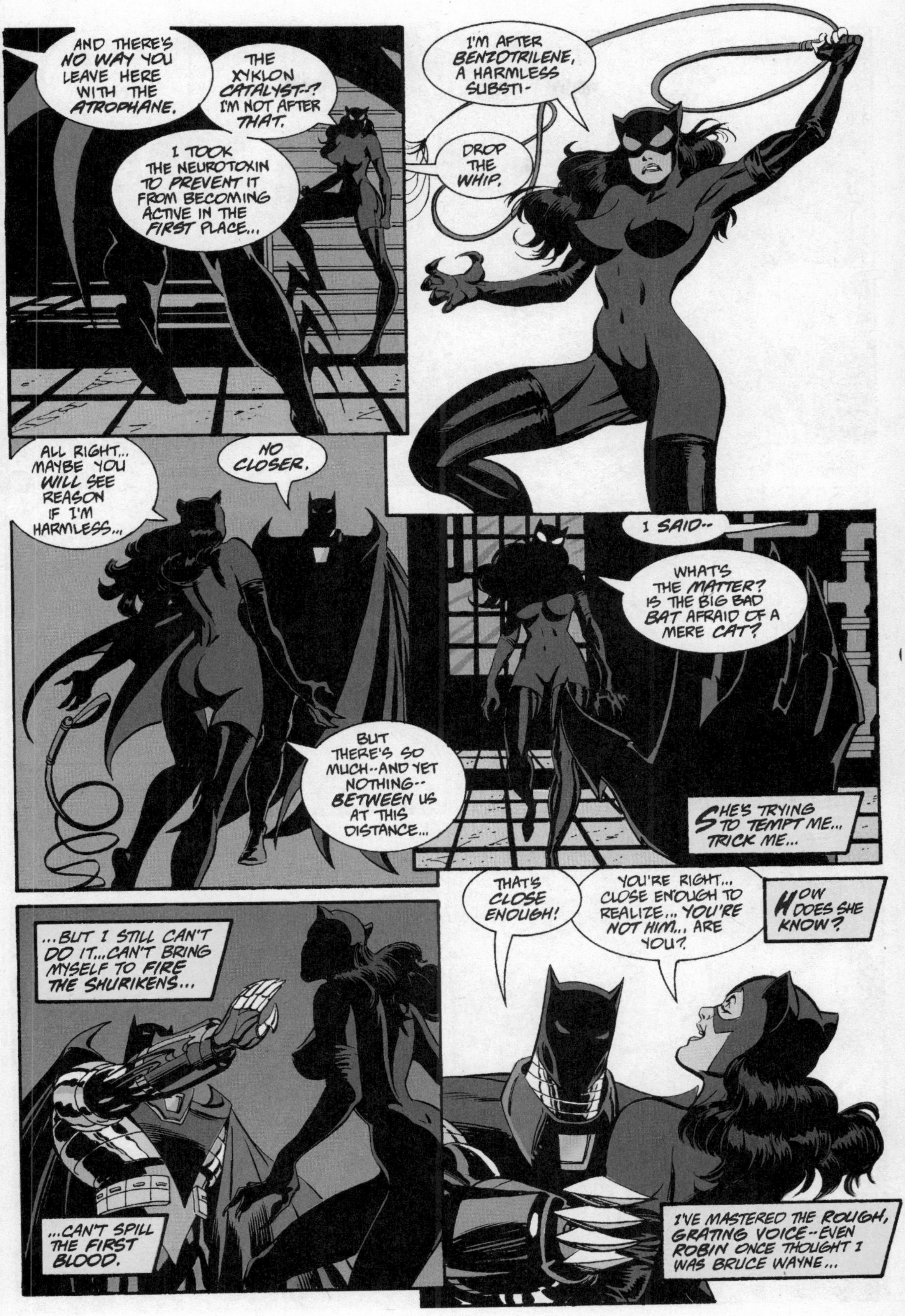
AND THERE'S NO WAY YOU LEAVE HERE WITH THE ATROPHANE.
THE XYKLON CATALYST--? I'M NOT AFTER THAT.
I TOOK THE NEUROTOXIN TO PREVENT IT FROM BECOMING ACTIVE IN THE FIRST PLACE...
I'M AFTER BENZOTRILENE, A HARMLESS SUBSTI-
DROP THE WHIP.
ALL RIGHT... MAYBE YOU WILL SEE REASON IF I'M HARMLESS...
NO CLOSER.
BUT THERE'S SO MUCH--AND YET NOTHING--BETWEEN US AT THIS DISTANCE...
I SAID--
WHAT'S THE MATTER? IS THE BIG BAD BAT AFRAID OF A MERE CAT?
SHE'S TRYING TO TEMPT ME... TRICK ME...
...BUT I STILL CAN'T DO IT...CAN'T BRING MYSELF TO FIRE THE SHURIKENS...
...CAN'T SPILL THE FIRST BLOOD.
THAT'S CLOSE ENOUGH!
YOU'RE RIGHT... CLOSE ENOUGH TO REALIZE... YOU'RE NOT HIM... ARE YOU?
HOW DOES SHE KNOW?
I'VE MASTERED THE ROUGH, GRATING VOICE--EVEN ROBIN ONCE THOUGHT I WAS BRUCE WAYNE...

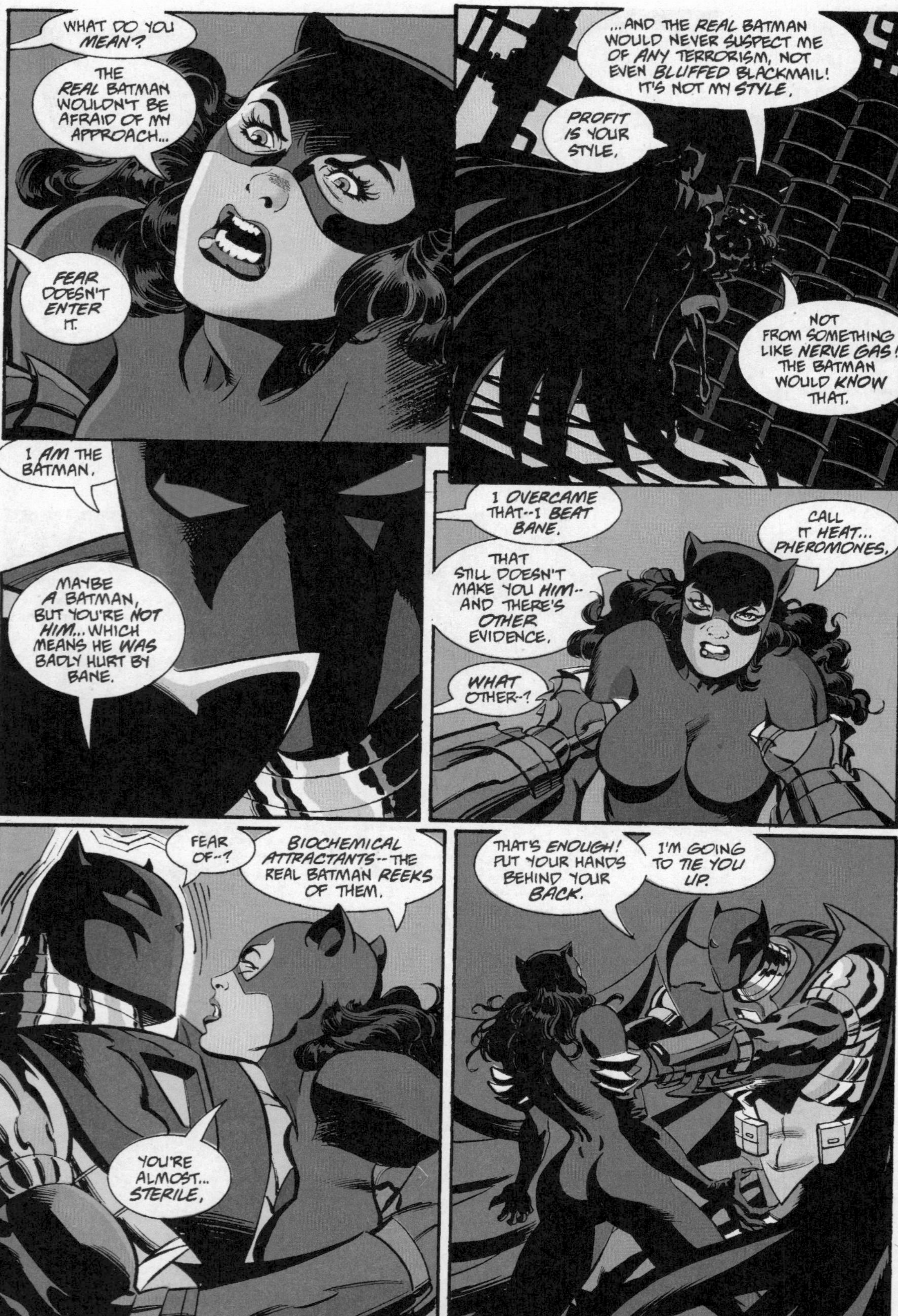
WHAT DO YOU MEAN?
THE REAL BATMAN WOULDN'T BE AFRAID OF MY APPROACH...
FEAR DOESN'T ENTER IT.
...AND THE REAL BATMAN WOULD NEVER SUSPECT ME OF ANY TERRORISM, NOT EVEN BLUFFED BLACKMAIL! IT'S NOT MY STYLE.
PROFIT IS YOUR STYLE.
NOT FROM SOMETHING LIKE NERVE GAS! THE BATMAN WOULD KNOW THAT.
I AM THE BATMAN.
MAYBE A BATMAN, BUT YOU'RE NOT HIM... WHICH MEANS HE WAS BADLY HURT BY BANE.
I OVERCAME THAT--I BEAT BANE.
THAT STILL DOESN'T MAKE YOU HIM.. AND THERE'S OTHER EVIDENCE.
CALL IT HEAT... PHEROMONES.
WHAT OTHER--?
FEAR OF--?
BIOCHEMICAL ATTRACTANTS-- THE REAL BATMAN REEKS OF THEM.
YOU'RE ALMOST... STERILE.
THAT'S ENOUGH! PUT YOUR HANDS BEHIND YOUR BACK.
I'M GOING TO TIE YOU UP.

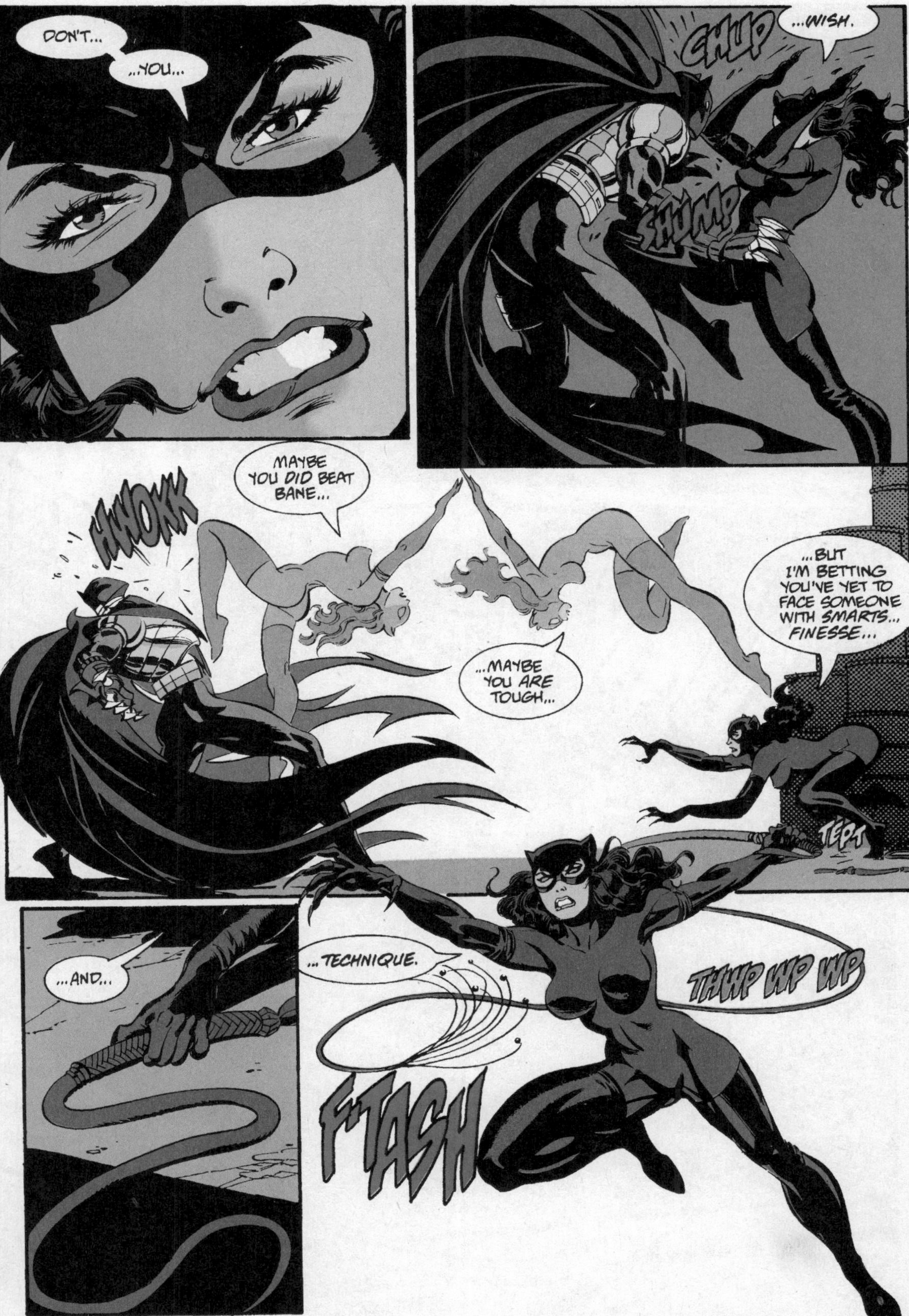
DON'T...
...YOU...
CHUP
...WISH.
SHUMP
HHOKK
MAYBE YOU DID BEAT BANE...
...MAYBE YOU ARE TOUGH...
...BUT I'M BETTING YOU'VE YET TO FACE SOMEONE WITH SMARTS... FINESSE...
TEPT
...AND...
...TECHNIQUE.
THWP WP WP
F'TASH

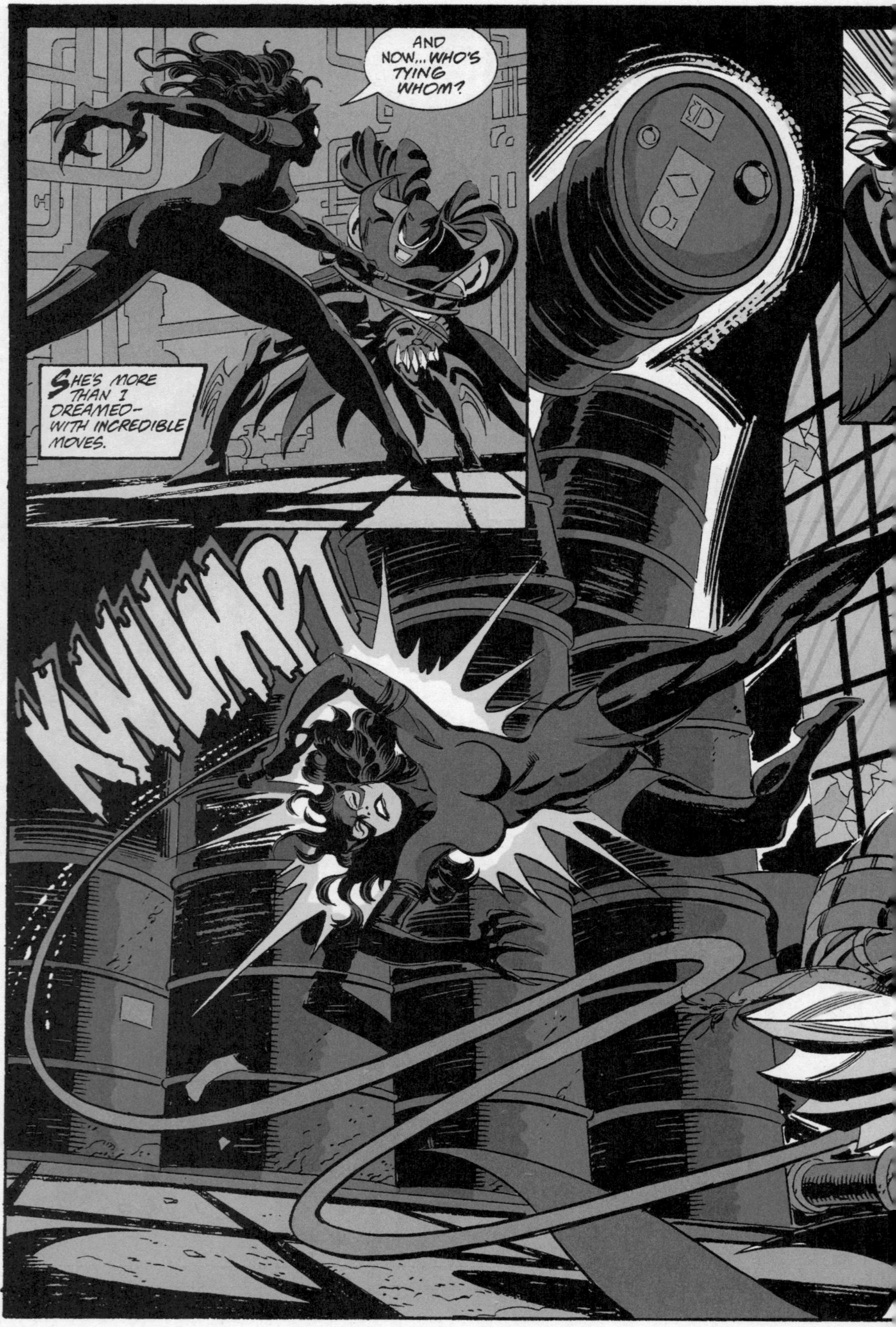
AND NOW... WHO'S TYING WHOM?
SHE'S MORE THAN I DREAMED-- WITH INCREDIBLE MOVES.
KHUMP!

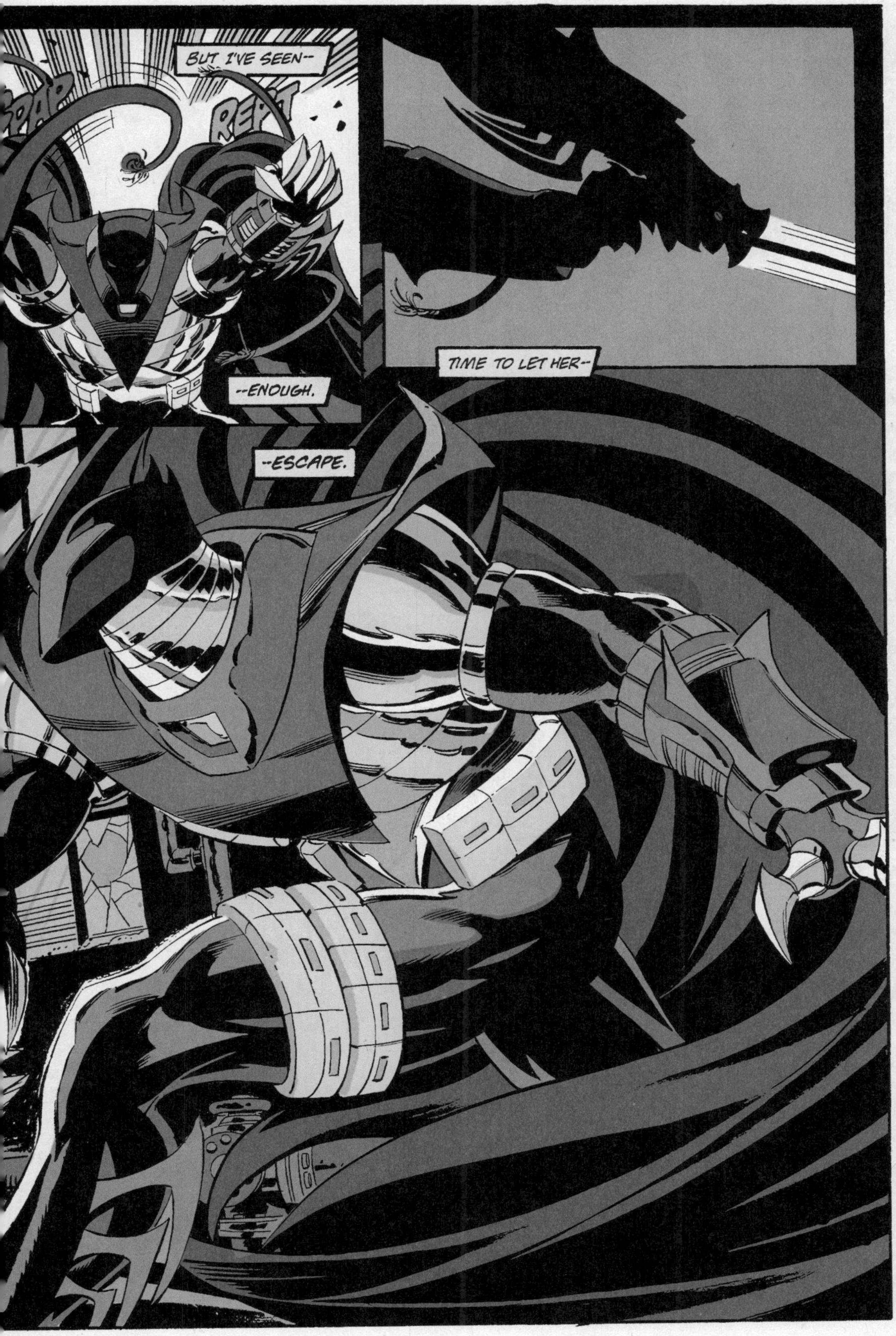
BUT I'VE SEEN--
--ENOUGH.
TIME TO LET HER--
--ESCAPE.

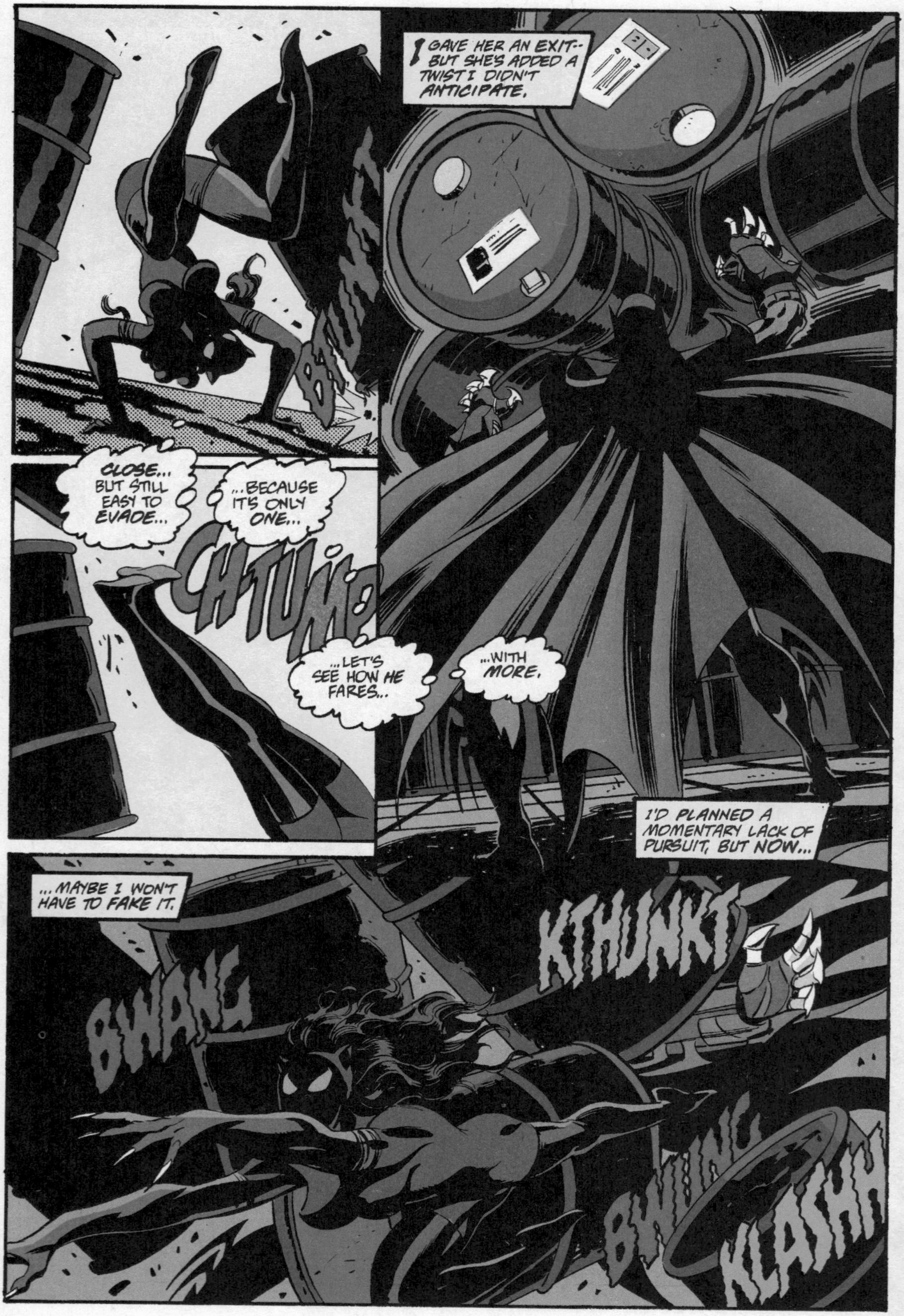

BTHUNKT
I GAVE HER AN EXIT-- BUT SHE'S ADDED A TWIST I DIDN'T ANTICIPATE.
CLOSE... BUT STILL EASY TO EVADE...
...BECAUSE IT'S ONLY ONE...
CHTUMP
...LET'S SEE HOW HE FARES...
...WITH MORE.
I'D PLANNED A MOMENTARY LACK OF PURSUIT, BUT NOW...
...MAYBE I WON'T HAVE TO FAKE IT.
KTHUNKT
BWANG
BWUNG
KLASHH

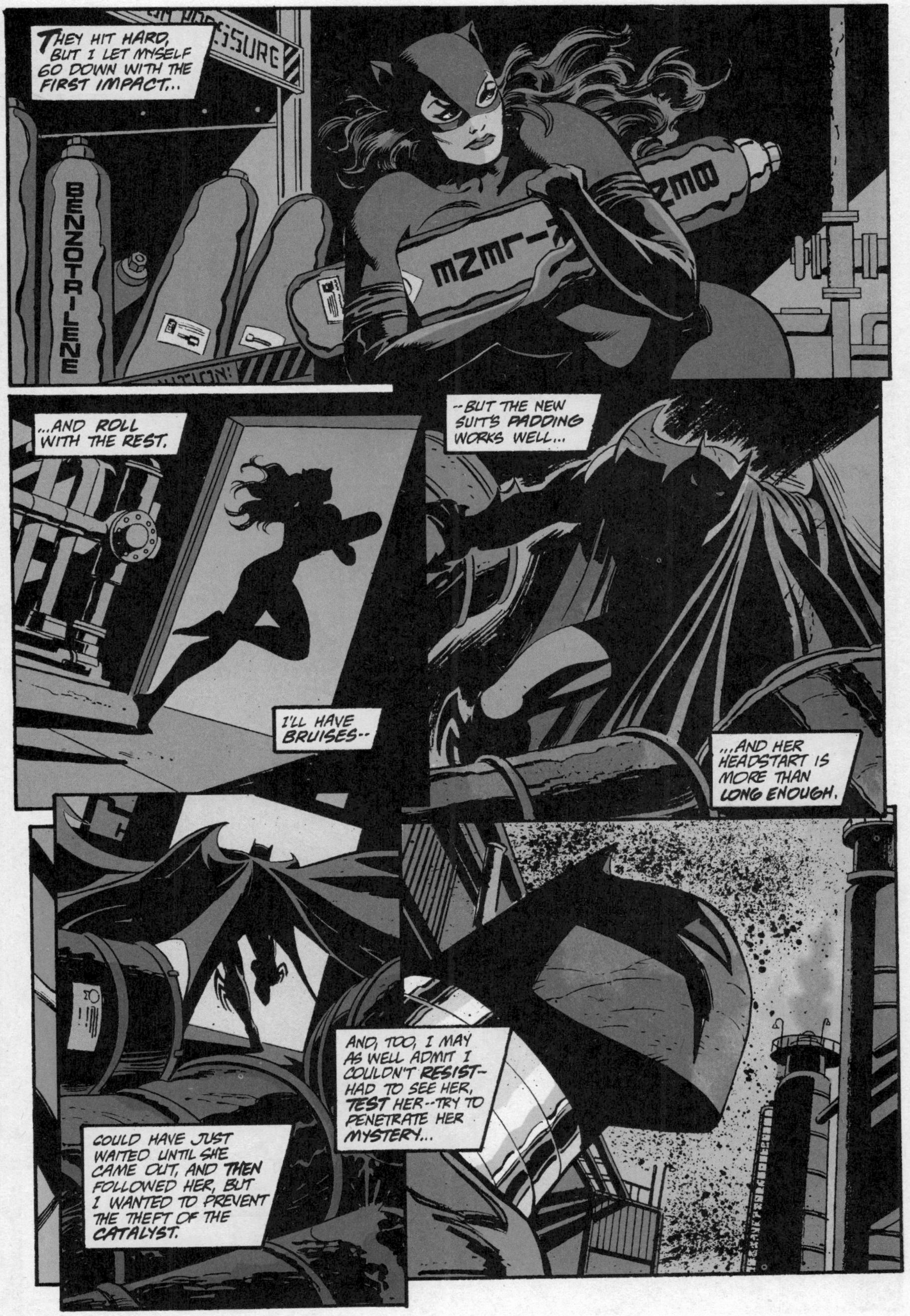
THEY HIT HARD, BUT I LET MYSELF GO DOWN WITH THE FIRST IMPACT...
BENZOTRILENE
...AND ROLL WITH THE REST.
I'LL HAVE BRUISES--
--BUT THE NEW SUIT'S PADDING WORKS WELL...
...AND HER HEADSTART IS MORE THAN LONG ENOUGH.
COULD HAVE JUST WAITED UNTIL SHE CAME OUT, AND THEN FOLLOWED HER, BUT I WANTED TO PREVENT THE THEFT OF THE CATALYST.
AND, TOO, I MAY AS WELL ADMIT I COULDN'T RESIST--HAD TO SEE HER, TEST HER--TRY TO PENETRATE HER MYSTERY...

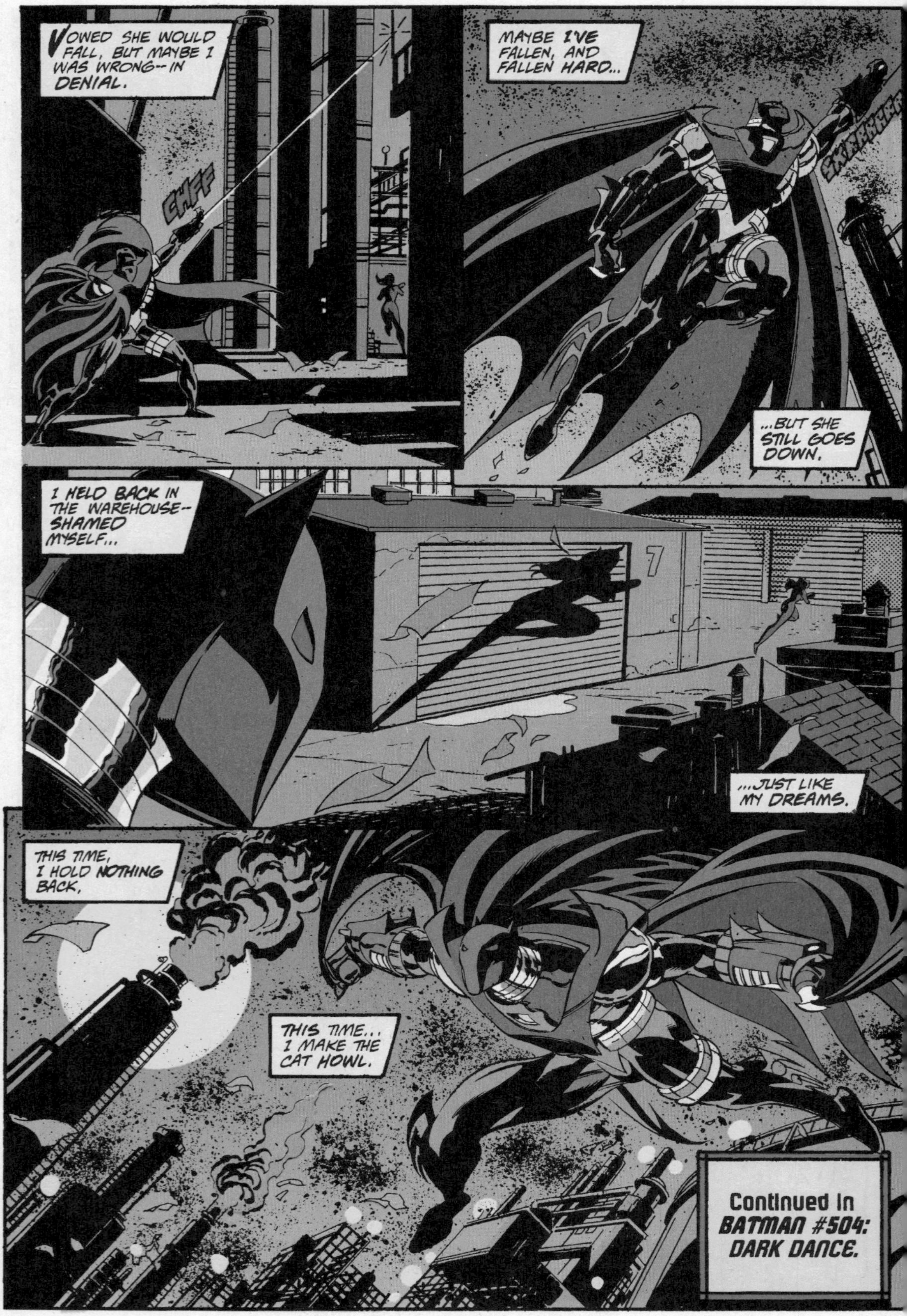
VOWED SHE WOULD FALL, BUT MAYBE I WAS WRONG-- IN DENIAL.
CHFF
MAYBE I'VE FALLEN, AND FALLEN HARD...
...BUT SHE STILL GOES DOWN.
I HELD BACK IN THE WAREHOUSE-- SHAMED MYSELF...
7
...JUST LIKE MY DREAMS.
THIS TIME, I HOLD NOTHING BACK.
THIS TIME... I MAKE THE CAT HOWL.
Continued in BATMAN #504: DARK DANCE.

Cover art by KELLEY JONES

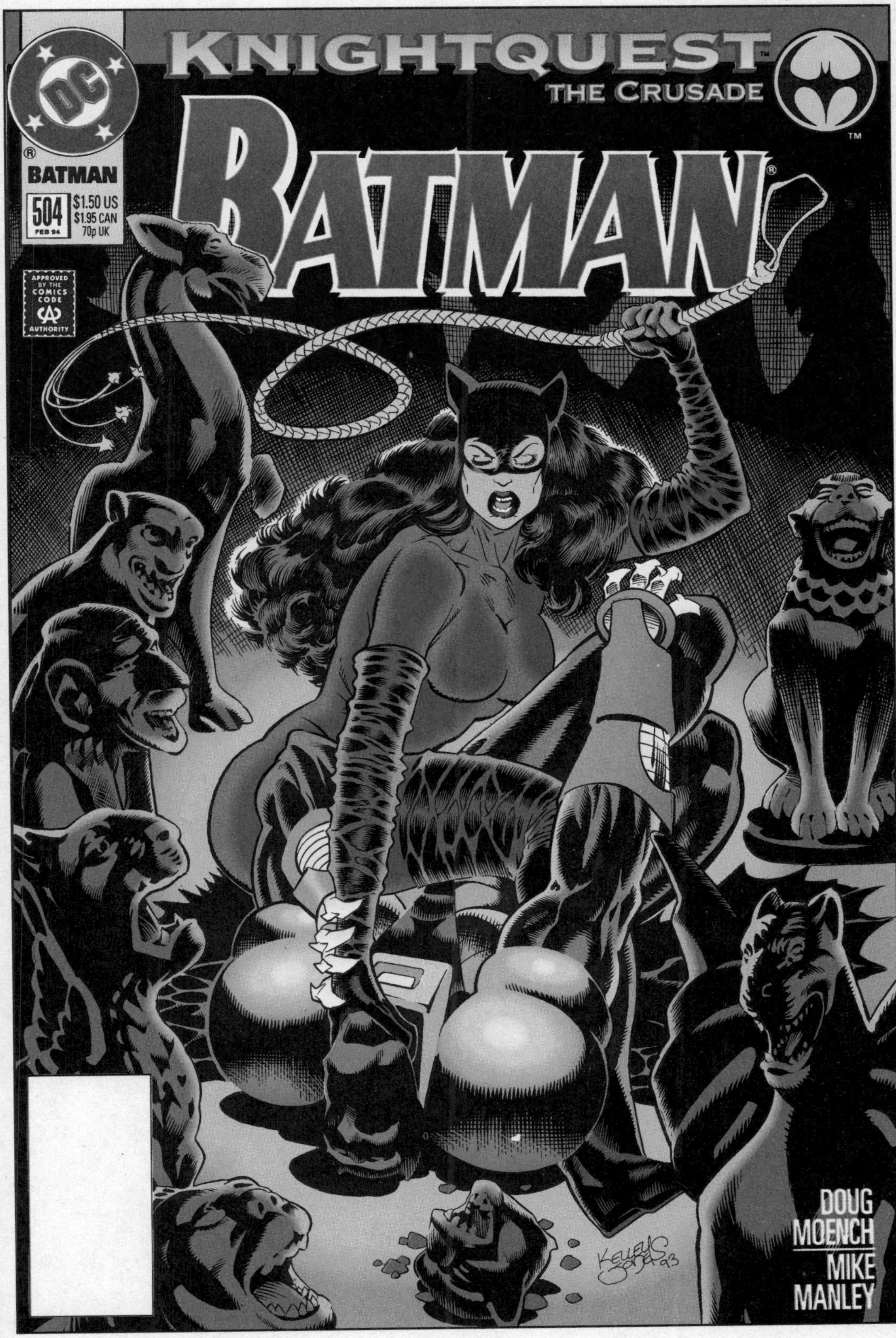
KNIGHTQUEST
THE CRUSADE
BATMAN
BATMAN
504
FEB 94
$1.50 US
$1.95 CAN
70p UK
APPROVED BY THE COMICS CODE AUTHORITY
DOUG MOENCH
MIKE MANLEY

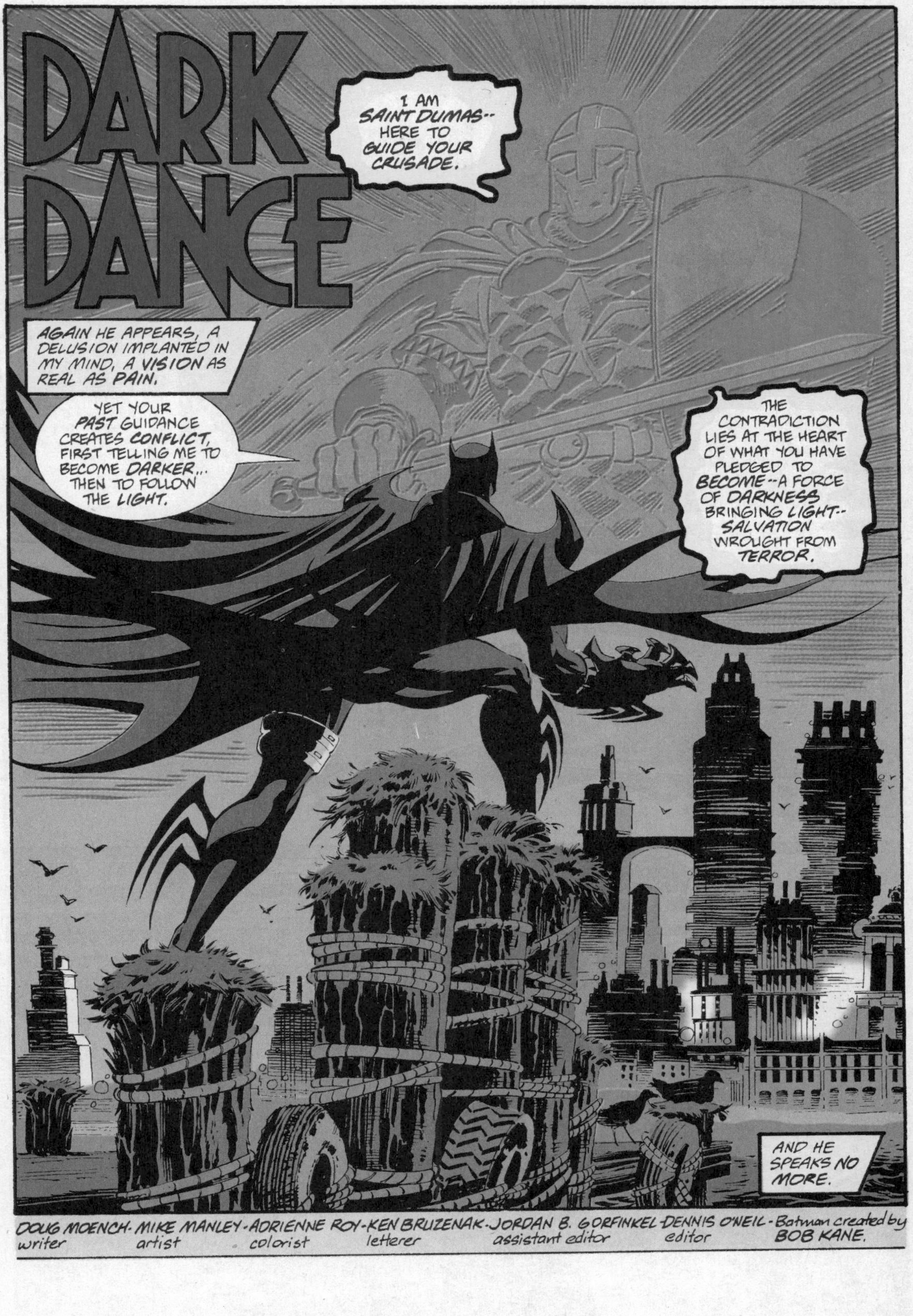
DARK DANCE
I AM SAINT DUMAS-- HERE TO GUIDE YOUR CRUSADE.
AGAIN HE APPEARS, A DELUSION IMPLANTED IN MY MIND, A VISION AS REAL AS PAIN.
YET YOUR PAST GUIDANCE CREATES CONFLICT, FIRST TELLING ME TO BECOME DARKER... THEN TO FOLLOW THE LIGHT.
THE CONTRADICTION LIES AT THE HEART OF WHAT YOU HAVE PLEDGED TO BECOME--A FORCE OF DARKNESS BRINGING LIGHT-- SALVATION WROUGHT FROM TERROR.
AND HE SPEAKS NO MORE.
DOUG MOENCH-writer · MIKE MANLEY-artist · ADRIENNE ROY-colorist · KEN BRUZENAK-letterer · JORDAN B. GORFINKEL-assistant editor · DENNIS O'NEIL-editor · Batman created by BOB KANE.

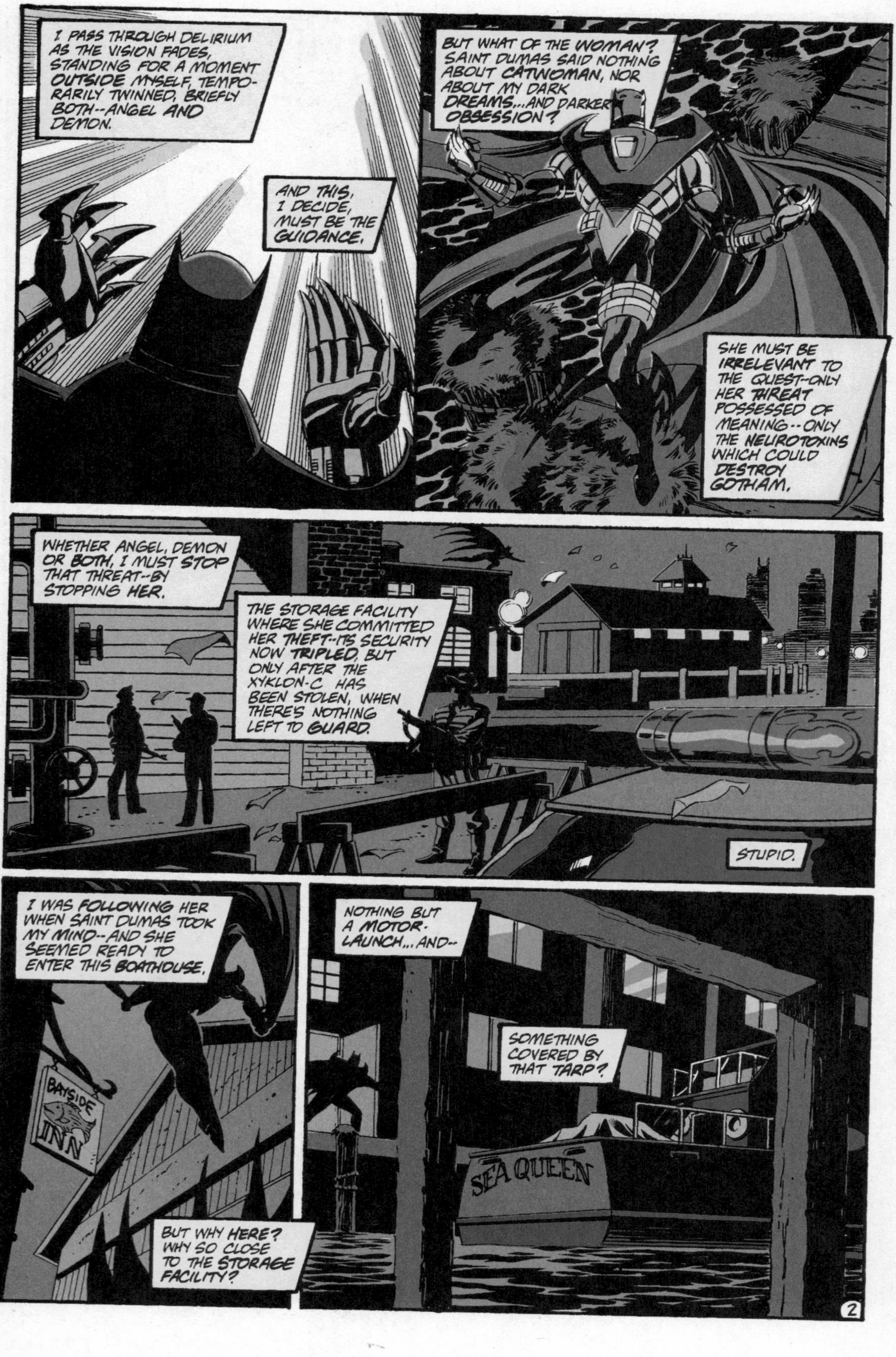
I PASS THROUGH DELIRIUM AS THE VISION FADES, STANDING FOR A MOMENT OUTSIDE MYSELF, TEMPORARILY TWINNED, BRIEFLY BOTH--ANGEL AND DEMON.
AND THIS, I DECIDE, MUST BE THE GUIDANCE.
BUT WHAT OF THE WOMAN? SAINT DUMAS SAID NOTHING ABOUT CATWOMAN, NOR ABOUT MY DARK DREAMS...AND DARKER OBSESSION?
SHE MUST BE IRRELEVANT TO THE QUEST--ONLY HER THREAT POSSESSED OF MEANING--ONLY THE NEUROTOXINS WHICH COULD DESTROY GOTHAM.
WHETHER ANGEL, DEMON OR BOTH, I MUST STOP THAT THREAT--BY STOPPING HER.
THE STORAGE FACILITY WHERE SHE COMMITTED HER THEFT--ITS SECURITY NOW TRIPLED, BUT ONLY AFTER THE XYKLON-C HAS BEEN STOLEN, WHEN THERE'S NOTHING LEFT TO GUARD.
STUPID.
I WAS FOLLOWING HER WHEN SAINT DUMAS TOOK MY MIND--AND SHE SEEMED READY TO ENTER THIS BOATHOUSE.
BAYSIDE INN
BUT WHY HERE? WHY SO CLOSE TO THE STORAGE FACILITY?
NOTHING BUT A MOTOR-LAUNCH...AND--
SOMETHING COVERED BY THAT TARP?
SEA QUEEN
2

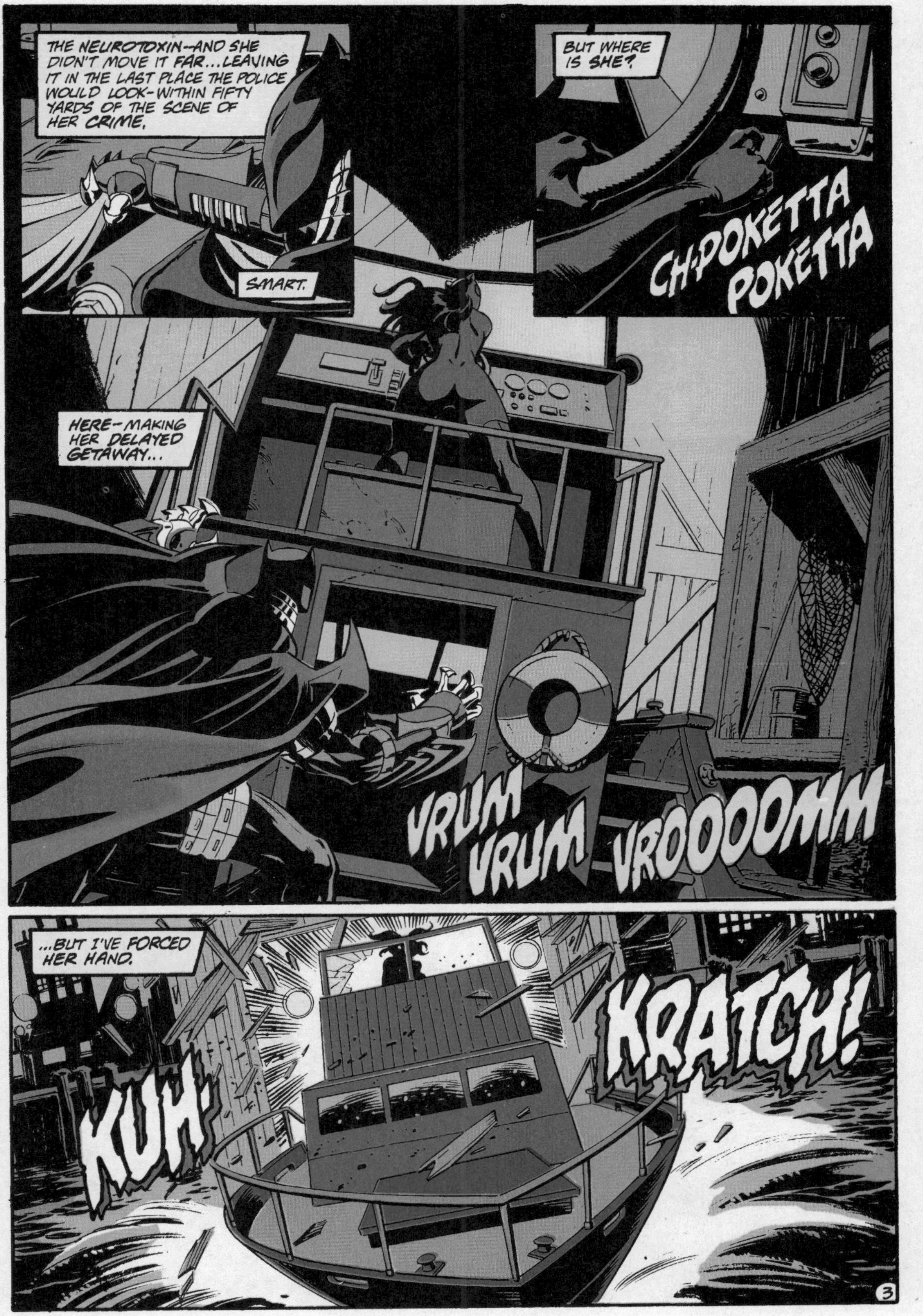
THE NEUROTOXIN--AND SHE DIDN'T MOVE IT FAR... LEAVING IT IN THE LAST PLACE THE POLICE WOULD LOOK-WITHIN FIFTY YARDS OF THE SCENE OF HER CRIME.
SMART.
BUT WHERE IS SHE?
CH-POKETTA POKETTA
HERE--MAKING HER DELAYED GETAWAY...
VRUM VRUM VROOOOOMM
...BUT I'VE FORCED HER HAND.
KUH-
KRATCH!
3

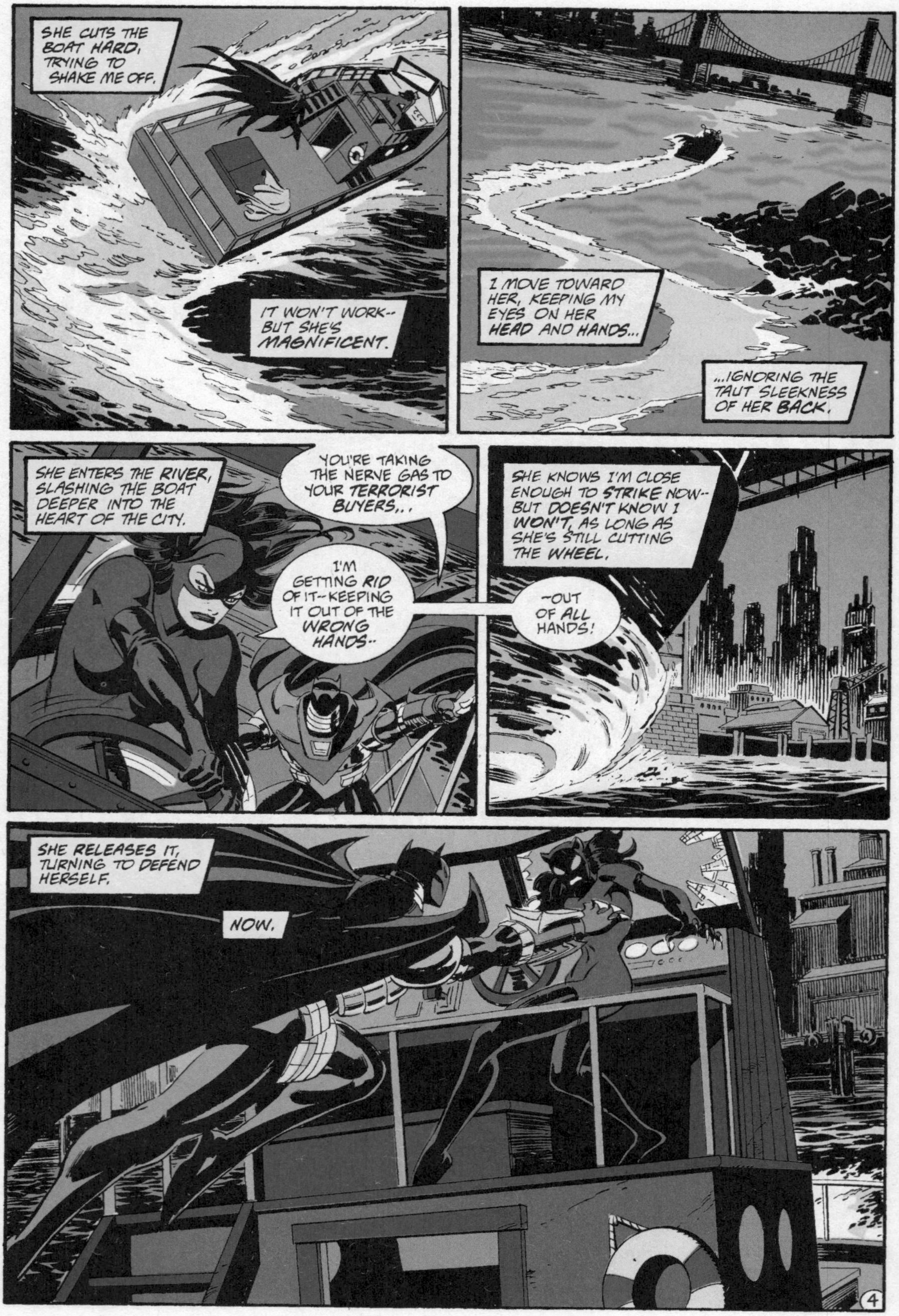

SHE CUTS THE BOAT HARD, TRYING TO SHAKE ME OFF.
IT WON'T WORK-- BUT SHE'S MAGNIFICENT.
I MOVE TOWARD HER, KEEPING MY EYES ON HER HEAD AND HANDS...
...IGNORING THE TAUT SLEEKNESS OF HER BACK.
SHE ENTERS THE RIVER, SLASHING THE BOAT DEEPER INTO THE HEART OF THE CITY.
YOU'RE TAKING THE NERVE GAS TO YOUR TERRORIST BUYERS...
I'M GETTING RID OF IT--KEEPING IT OUT OF THE WRONG HANDS--
SHE KNOWS I'M CLOSE ENOUGH TO STRIKE NOW-- BUT DOESN'T KNOW I WON'T, AS LONG AS SHE'S STILL CUTTING THE WHEEL.
--OUT OF ALL HANDS!
SHE RELEASES IT, TURNING TO DEFEND HERSELF.
NOW.
4

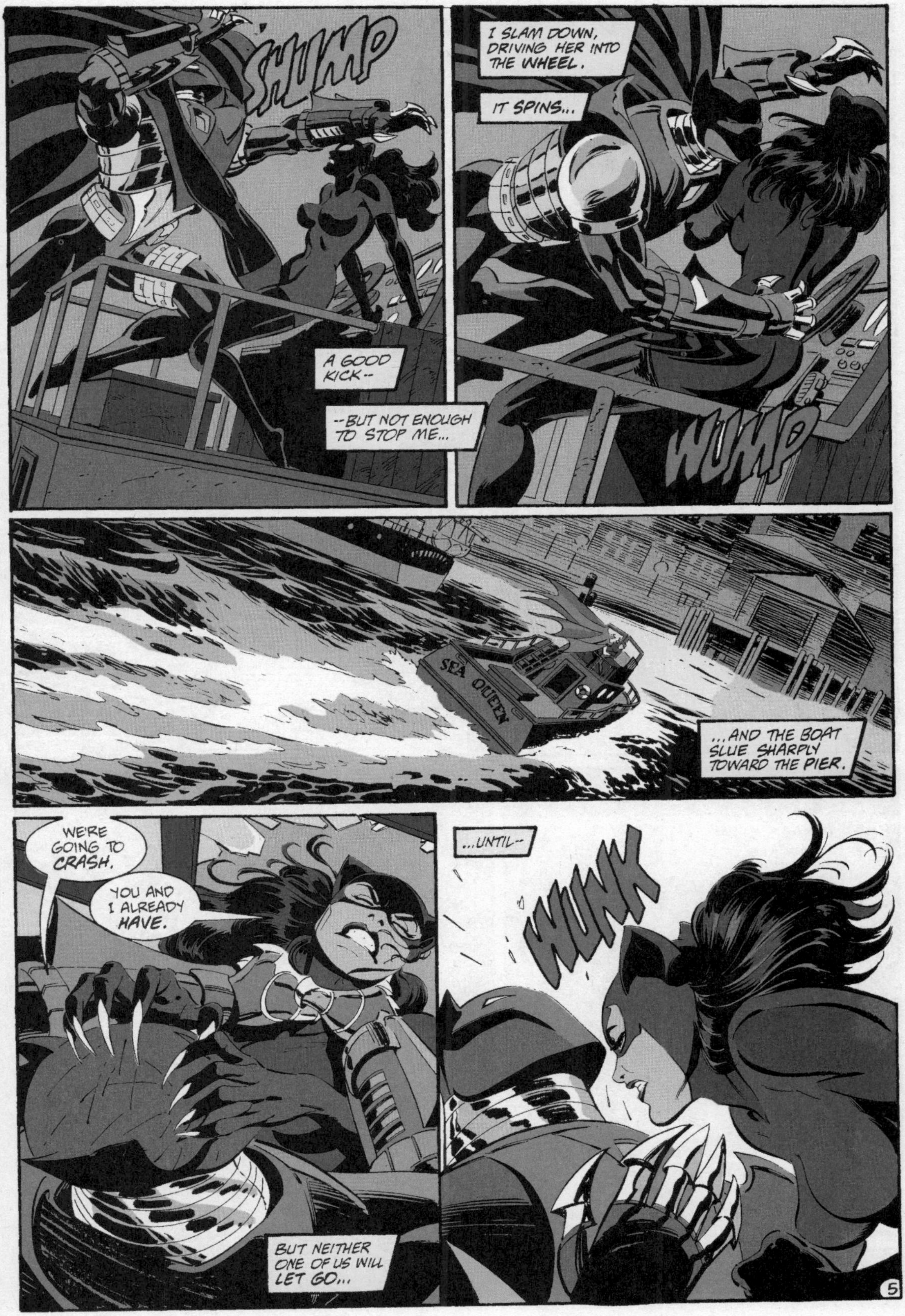
SHUMP
A GOOD KICK--
--BUT NOT ENOUGH TO STOP ME...
I SLAM DOWN, DRIVING HER INTO THE WHEEL.
IT SPINS...
WUMP
SEA QUEEN
...AND THE BOAT SLUE SHARPLY TOWARD THE PIER.
WE'RE GOING TO CRASH.
YOU AND I ALREADY HAVE.
BUT NEITHER ONE OF US WILL LET GO...
...UNTIL--
WUNK
5

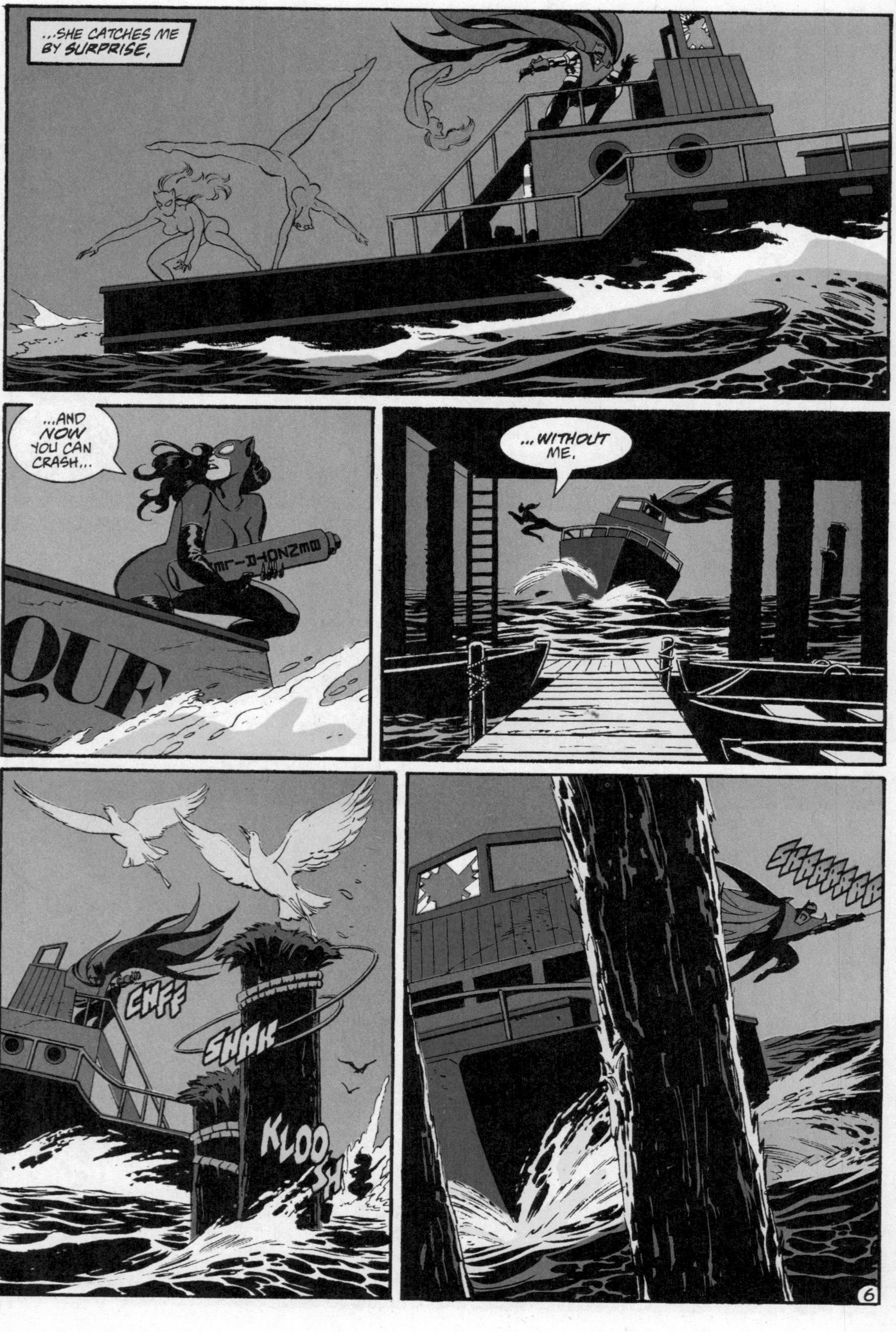
...SHE CATCHES ME BY SURPRISE,
...AND NOW YOU CAN CRASH...
...WITHOUT ME.
CHFF
SHAK
KLOOSH
SKRRRRRR
6

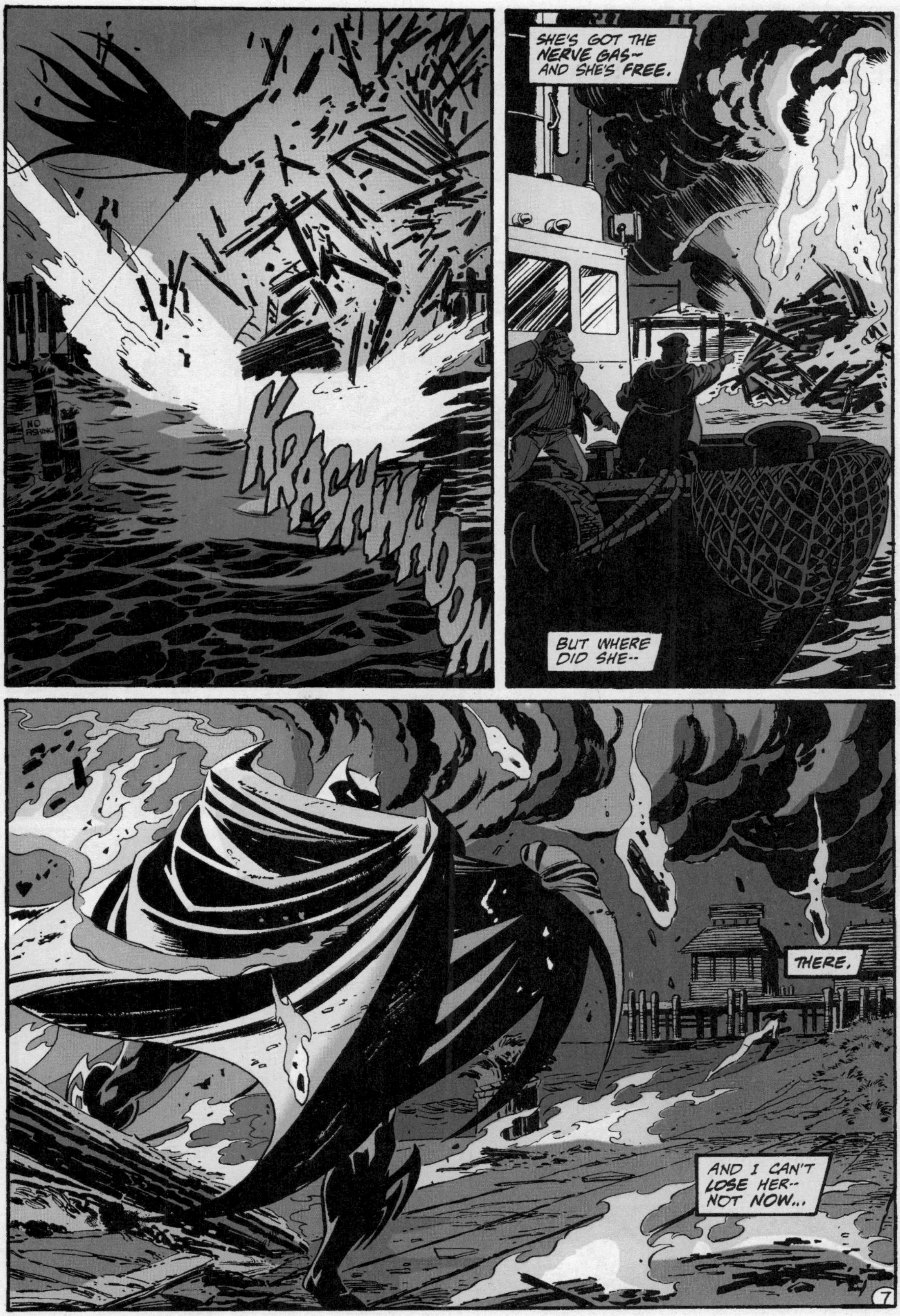
KRASHWHOOM
NO FISHING
SHE'S GOT THE NERVE GAS-- AND SHE'S FREE.
BUT WHERE DID SHE--
THERE.
AND I CAN'T LOSE HER-- NOT NOW...
7

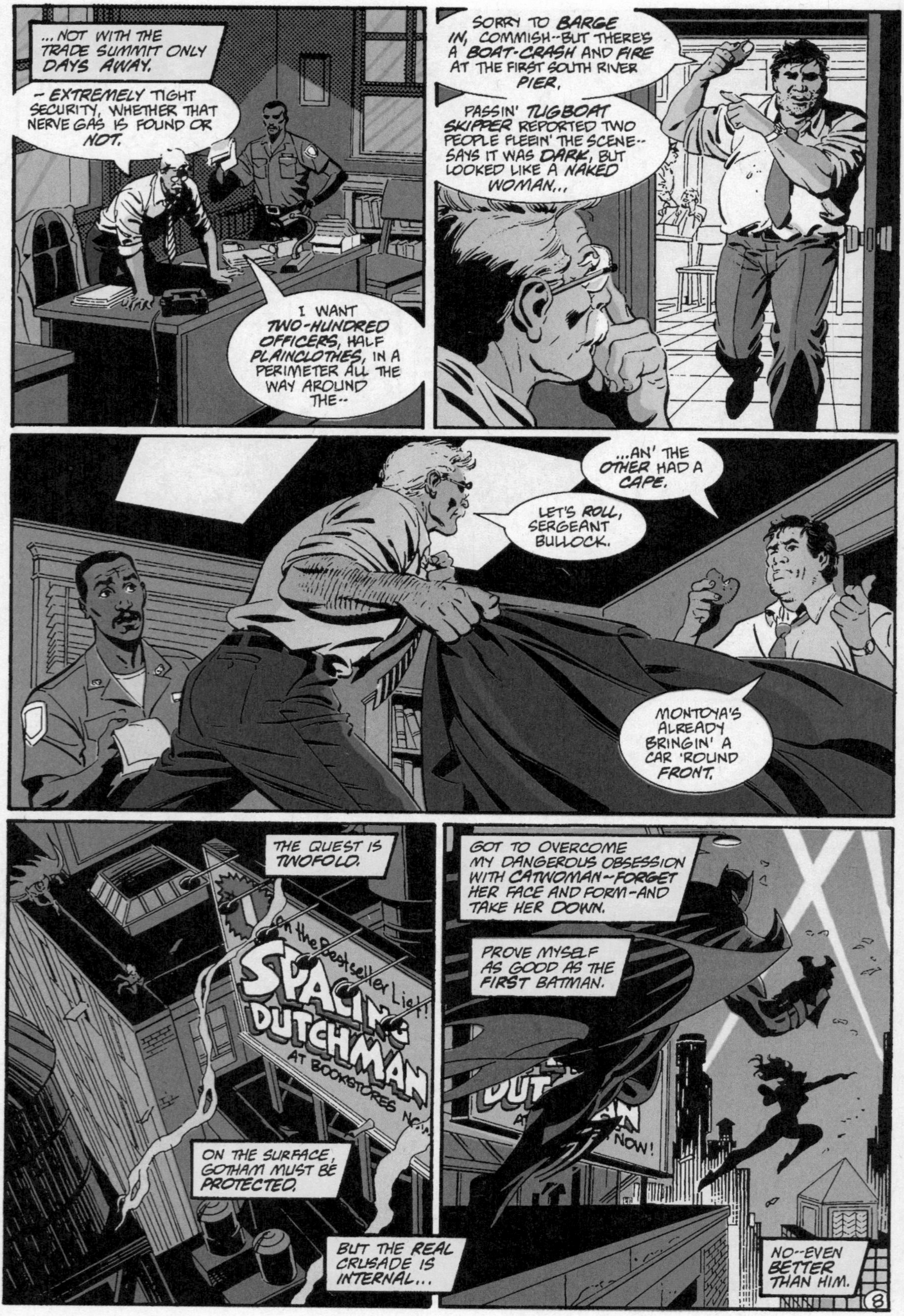

...NOT WITH THE TRADE SUMMIT ONLY DAYS AWAY.
-- EXTREMELY TIGHT SECURITY, WHETHER THAT NERVE GAS IS FOUND OR NOT.
I WANT TWO-HUNDRED OFFICERS, HALF PLAINCLOTHES, IN A PERIMETER ALL THE WAY AROUND THE--
SORRY TO BARGE IN, COMMISH--BUT THERE'S A BOAT-CRASH AND FIRE AT THE FIRST SOUTH RIVER PIER.
PASSIN' TUGBOAT SKIPPER REPORTED TWO PEOPLE FLEEIN' THE SCENE-- SAYS IT WAS DARK, BUT LOOKED LIKE A NAKED WOMAN...
...AN' THE OTHER HAD A CAPE.
LET'S ROLL, SERGEANT BULLOCK.
MONTOYA'S ALREADY BRINGIN' A CAR 'ROUND FRONT.
THE QUEST IS TWOFOLD.
On the Bestseller List!
SPACING DUTCHMAN
AT BOOKSTORES NOW!
ON THE SURFACE, GOTHAM MUST BE PROTECTED.
BUT THE REAL CRUSADE IS INTERNAL...
GOT TO OVERCOME MY DANGEROUS OBSESSION WITH CATWOMAN--FORGET HER FACE AND FORM--AND TAKE HER DOWN.
PROVE MYSELF AS GOOD AS THE FIRST BATMAN.
NO--EVEN BETTER THAN HIM.
8

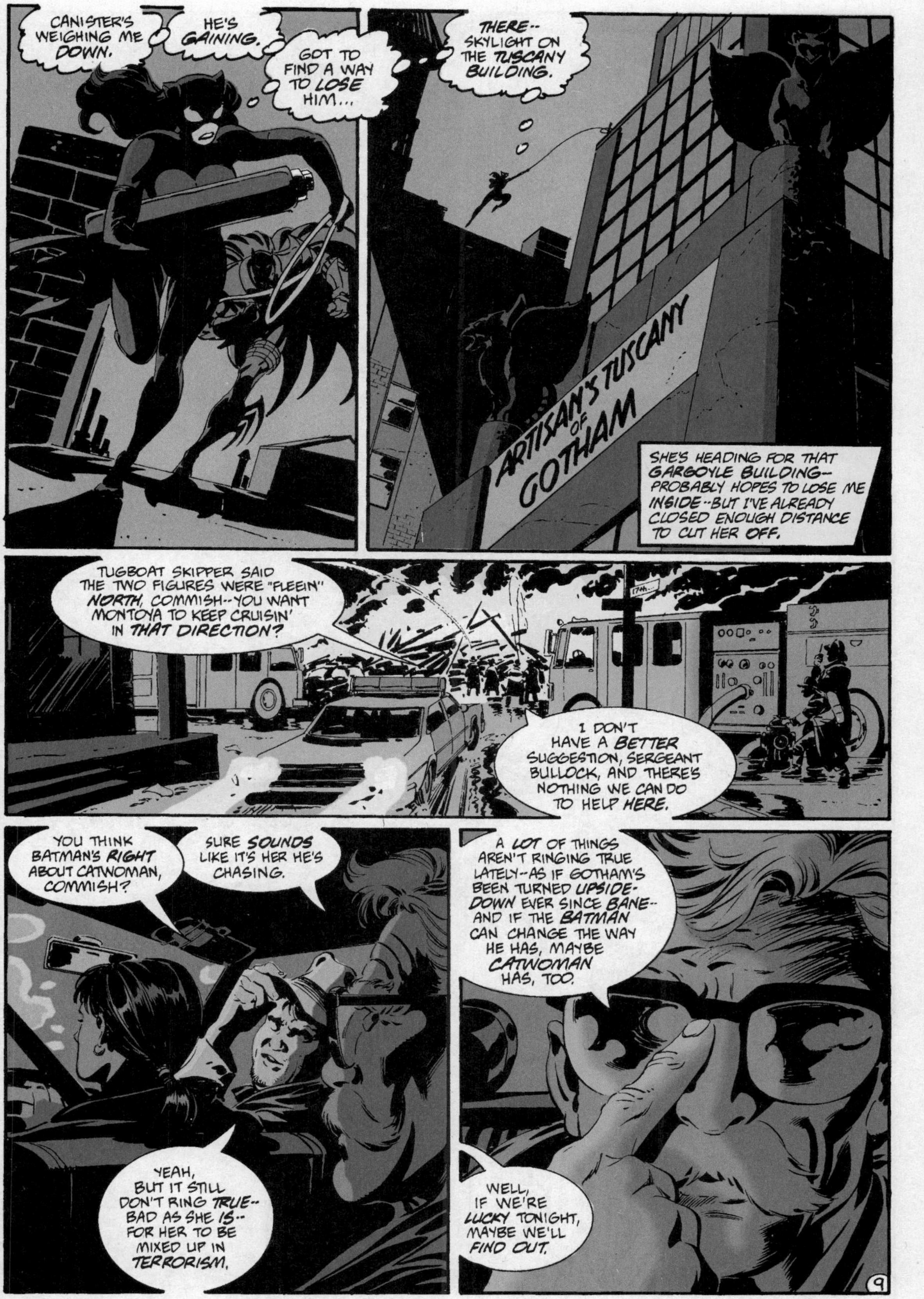
CANISTER'S WEIGHING ME DOWN.
HE'S GAINING.
GOT TO FIND A WAY TO LOSE HIM...
THERE-- SKYLIGHT ON THE TUSCANY BUILDING.
ARTISAN'S TUSCANY OF GOTHAM
SHE'S HEADING FOR THAT GARGOYLE BUILDING-- PROBABLY HOPES TO LOSE ME INSIDE--BUT I'VE ALREADY CLOSED ENOUGH DISTANCE TO CUT HER OFF.
TUGBOAT SKIPPER SAID THE TWO FIGURES WERE "FLEEIN'" NORTH, COMMISH--YOU WANT MONTOYA TO KEEP CRUISIN' IN THAT DIRECTION?
I DON'T HAVE A BETTER SUGGESTION, SERGEANT BULLOCK, AND THERE'S NOTHING WE CAN DO TO HELP HERE.
YOU THINK BATMAN'S RIGHT ABOUT CATWOMAN, COMMISH?
SURE SOUNDS LIKE IT'S HER HE'S CHASING.
YEAH, BUT IT STILL DON'T RING TRUE-- BAD AS SHE IS-- FOR HER TO BE MIXED UP IN TERRORISM.
A LOT OF THINGS AREN'T RINGING TRUE LATELY--AS IF GOTHAM'S BEEN TURNED UPSIDE-DOWN EVER SINCE BANE-- AND IF THE BATMAN CAN CHANGE THE WAY HE HAS, MAYBE CATWOMAN HAS, TOO.
WELL, IF WE'RE LUCKY TONIGHT, MAYBE WE'LL FIND OUT.
9

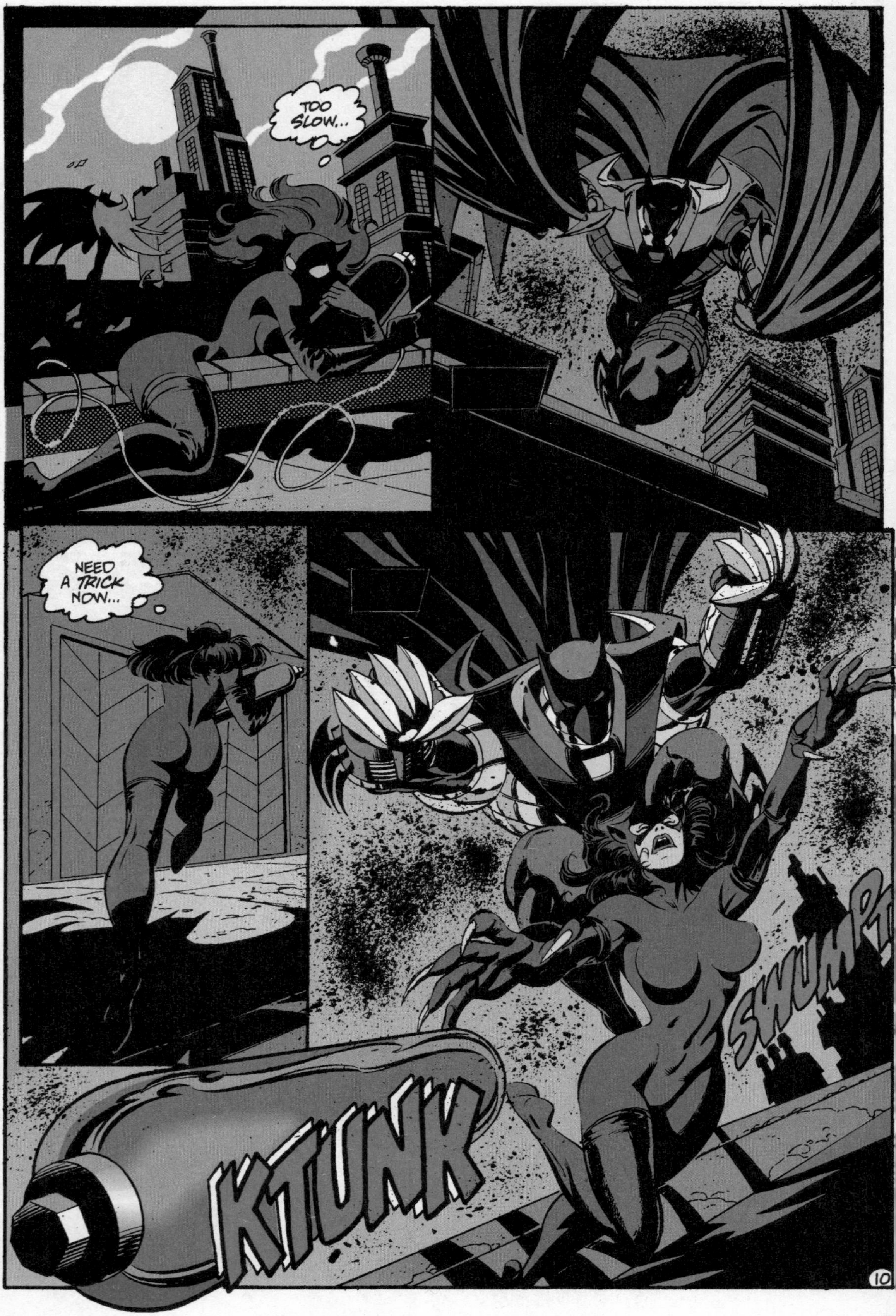
TOO SLOW...
NEED A TRICK NOW...
SWUMP
KTUNK
10

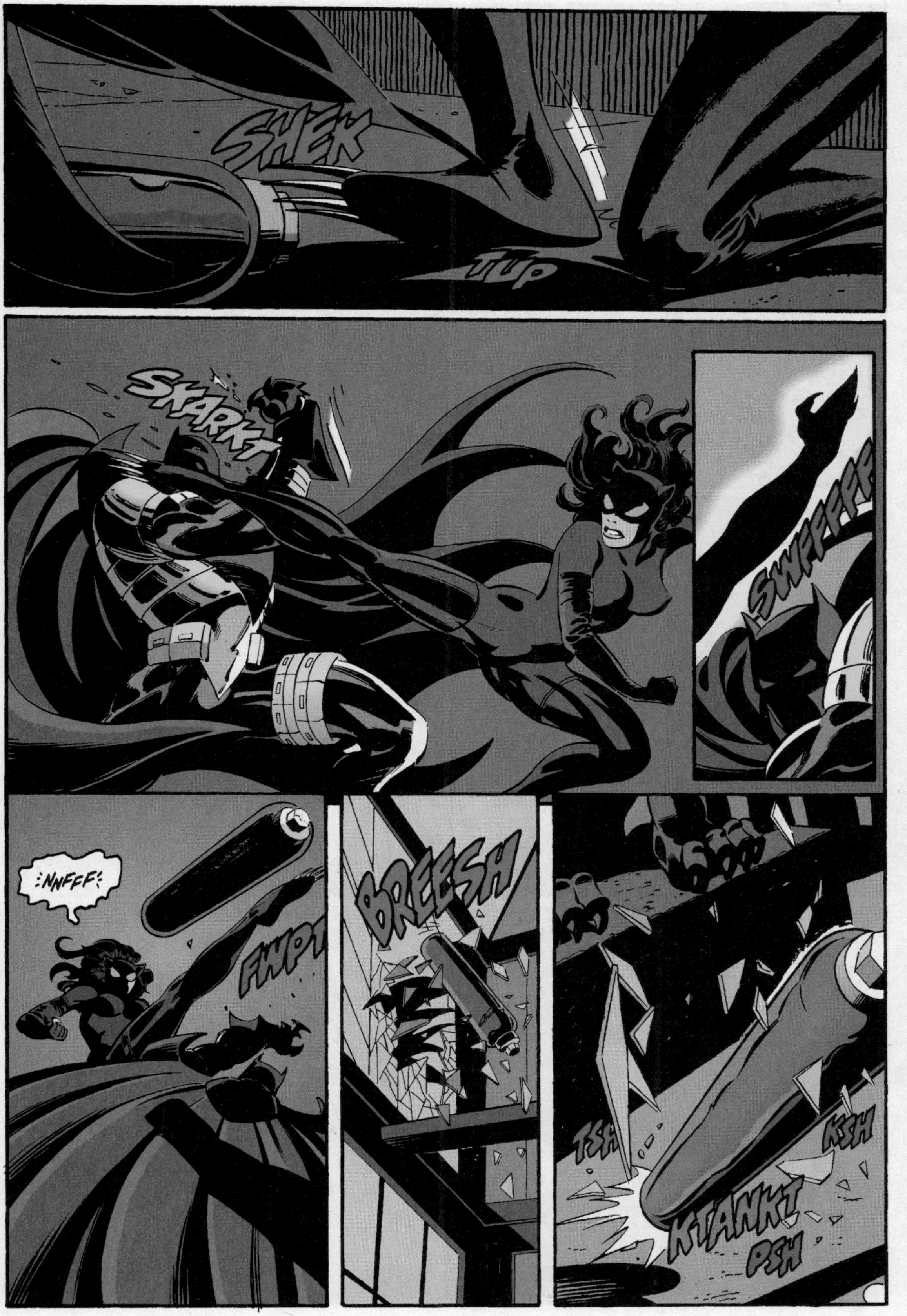
SHEK
TUP
SKARKT
SWFFFFR
NNFFF
FWPT
BREESH
TSH
KSH
KTANKT
PSH

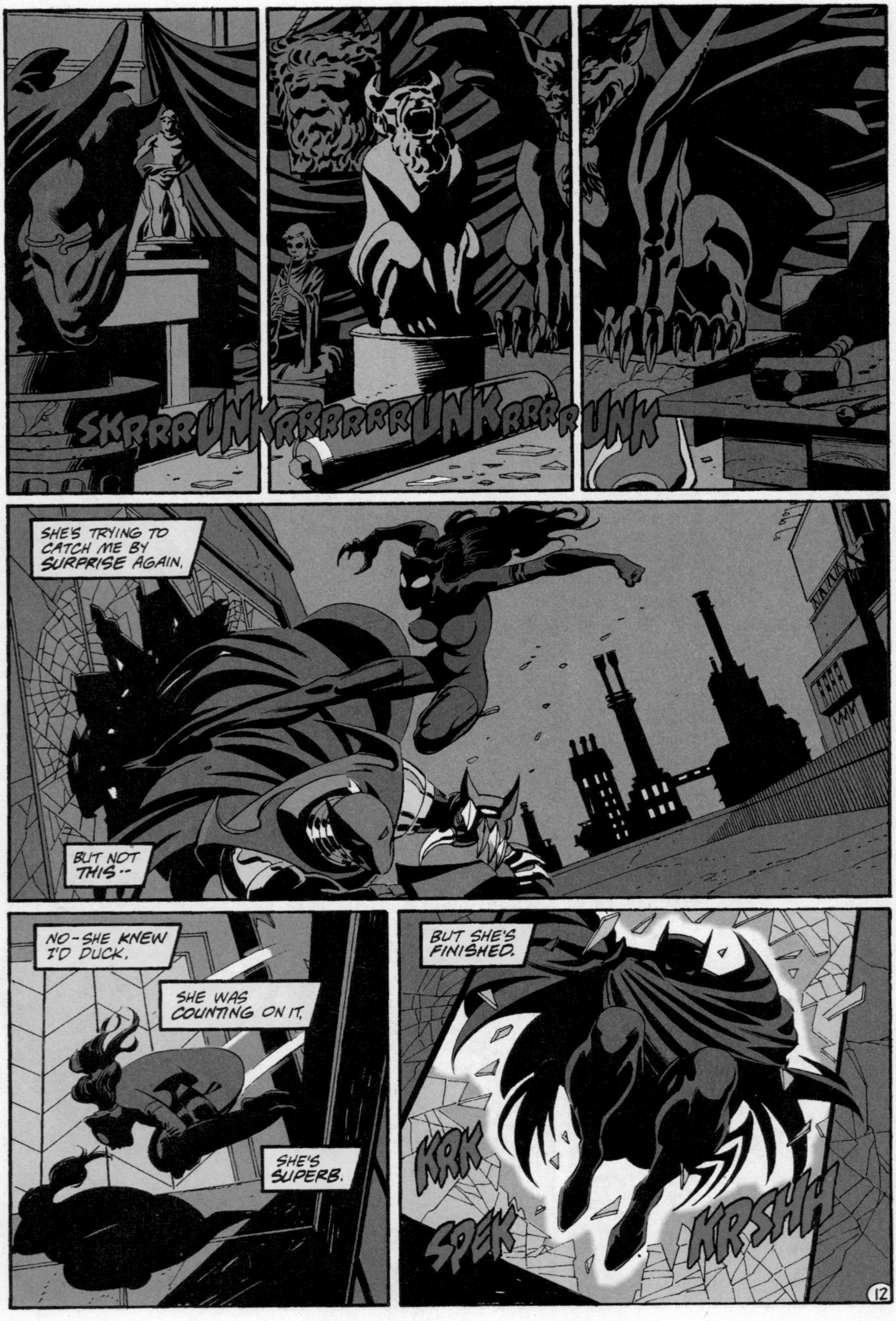

SKRRRUNKRRRRRRRUNKRRRRUNK
SHE'S TRYING TO CATCH ME BY SURPRISE AGAIN.
BUT NOT THIS--
NO-SHE KNEW I'D DUCK.
SHE WAS COUNTING ON IT.
SHE'S SUPERB.
BUT SHE'S FINISHED.
KRK
SPEK
KRSHH
12

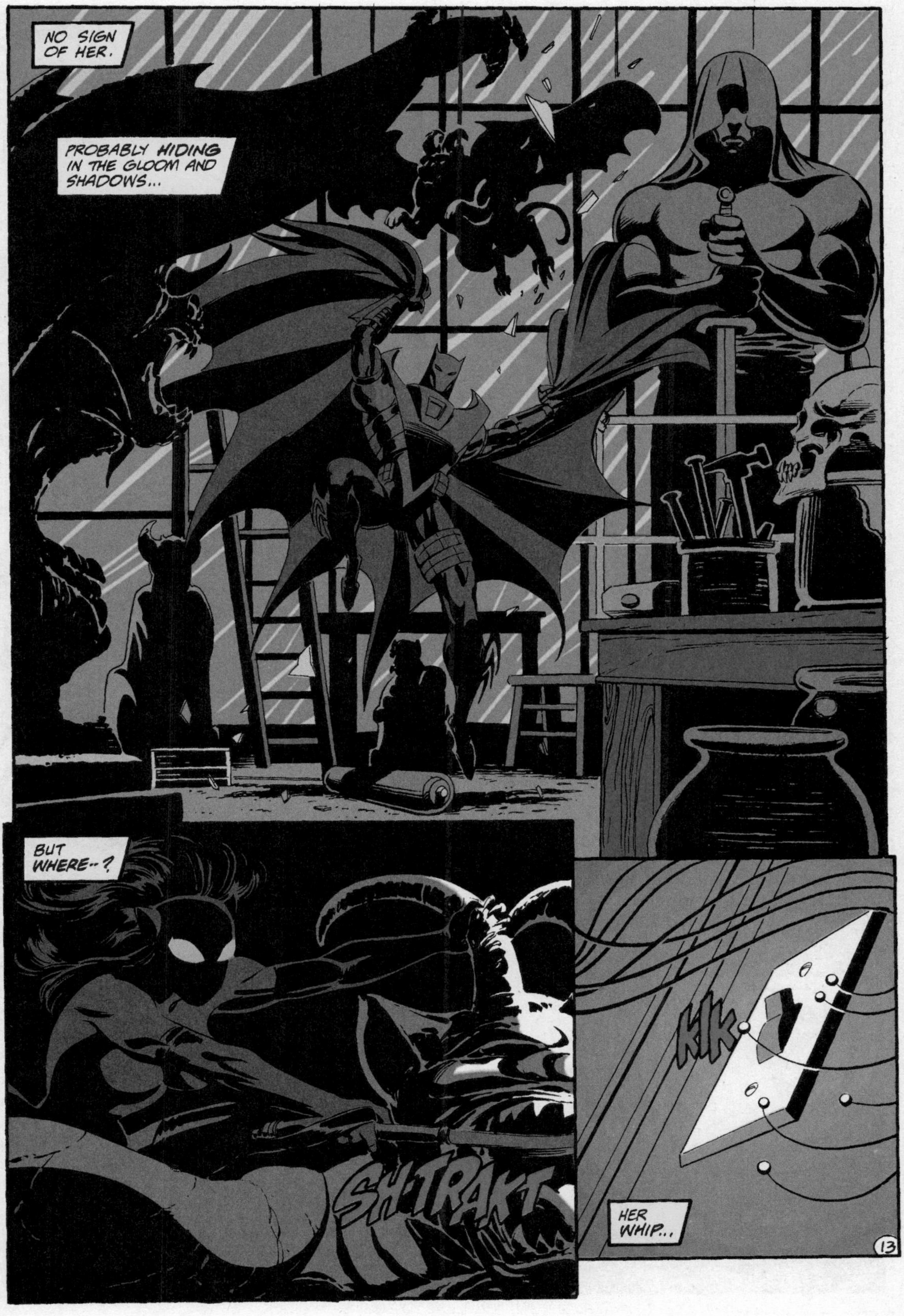
NO SIGN OF HER.
PROBABLY HIDING IN THE GLOOM AND SHADOWS...
BUT WHERE--?
SH-TRAKT
KIK
HER WHIP...
13

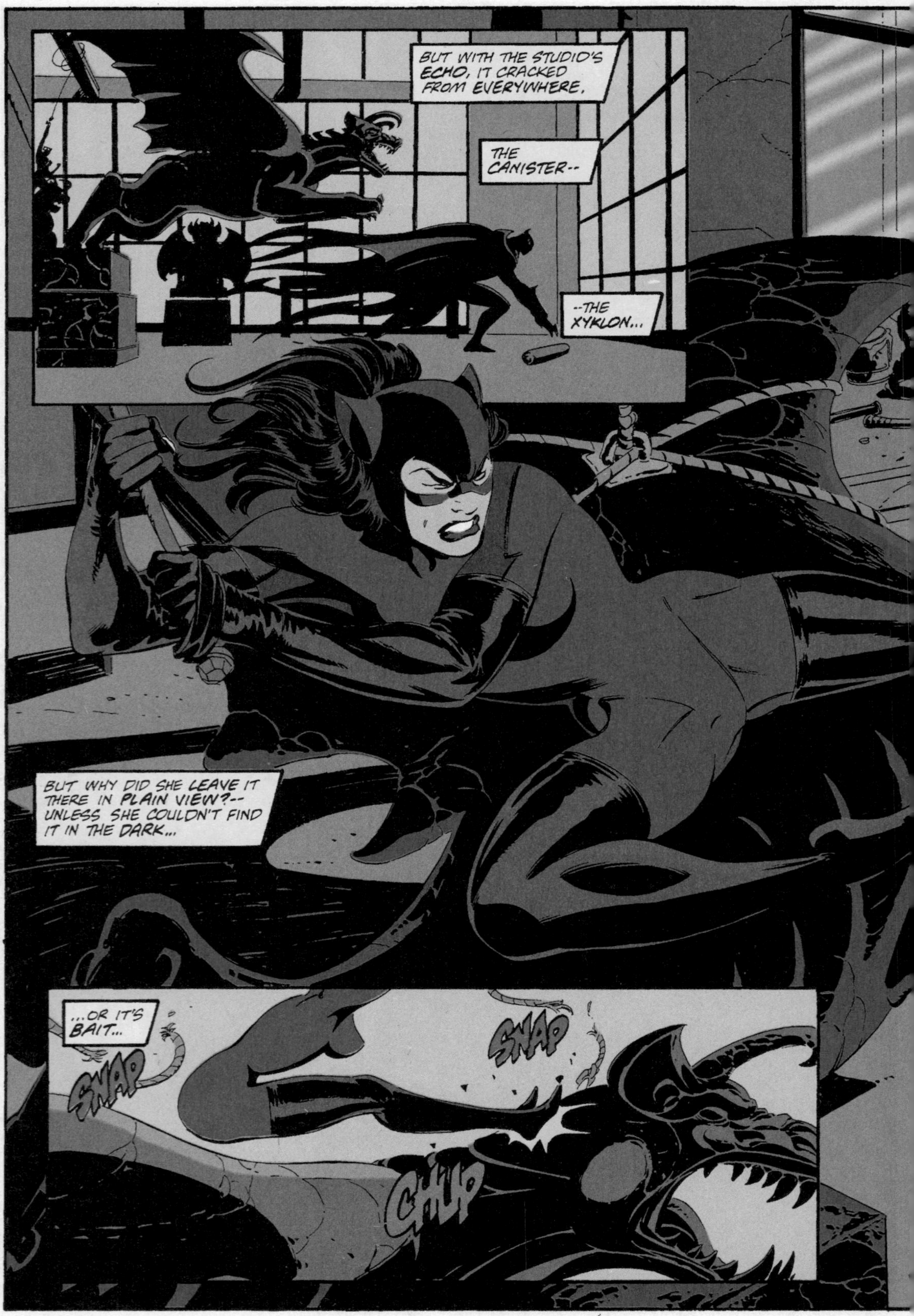

BUT WITH THE STUDIO'S ECHO, IT CRACKED FROM EVERYWHERE.
THE CANISTER--
--THE XYKLON...
BUT WHY DID SHE LEAVE IT THERE IN PLAIN VIEW?--UNLESS SHE COULDN'T FIND IT IN THE DARK...
...OR IT'S BAIT...
SNAP
SNAP
CHUP

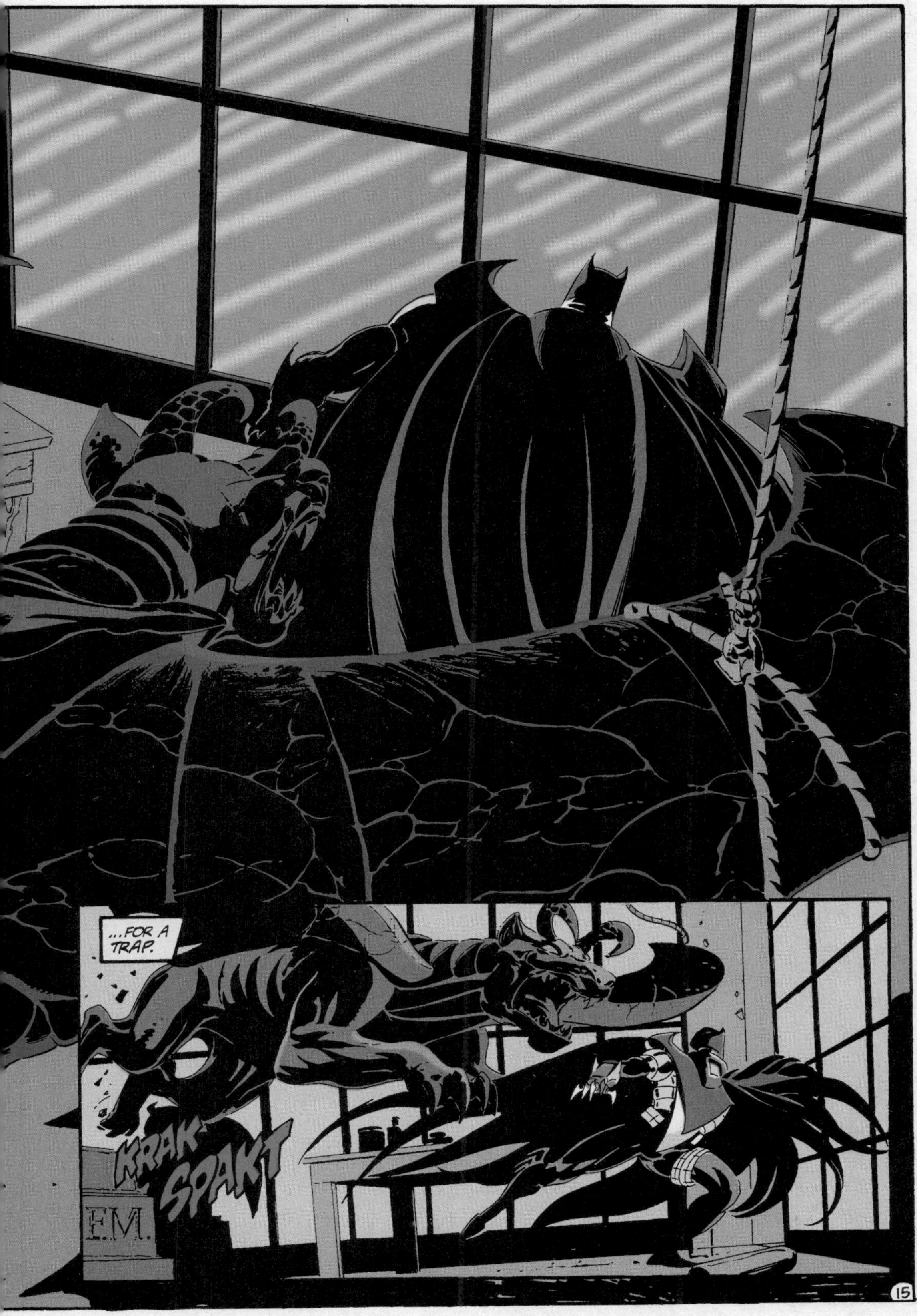
...FOR A TRAP.
KRAK
SPAKT
F.M.
15

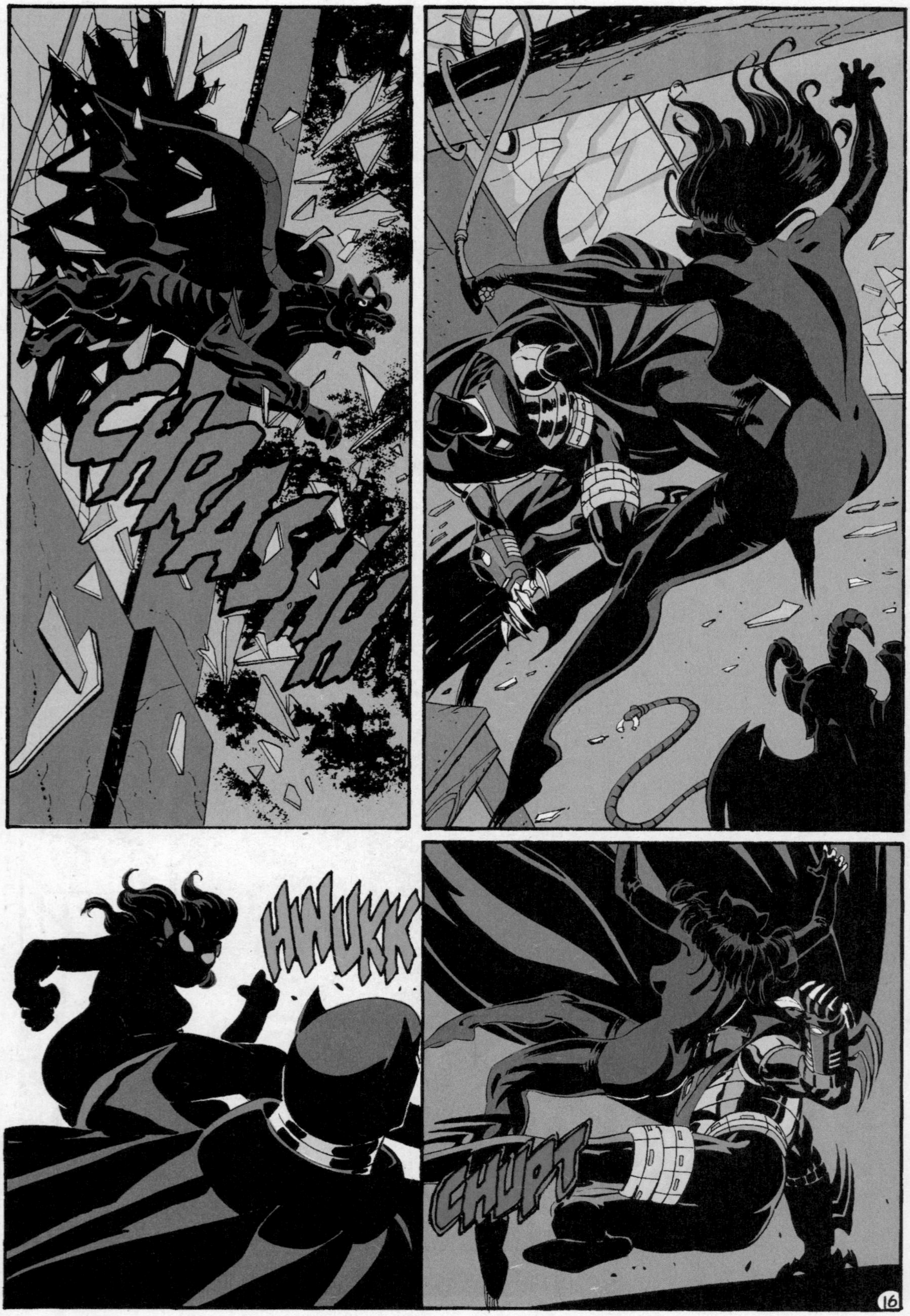
CHRASHHH
HNUKK
CHUPT
16

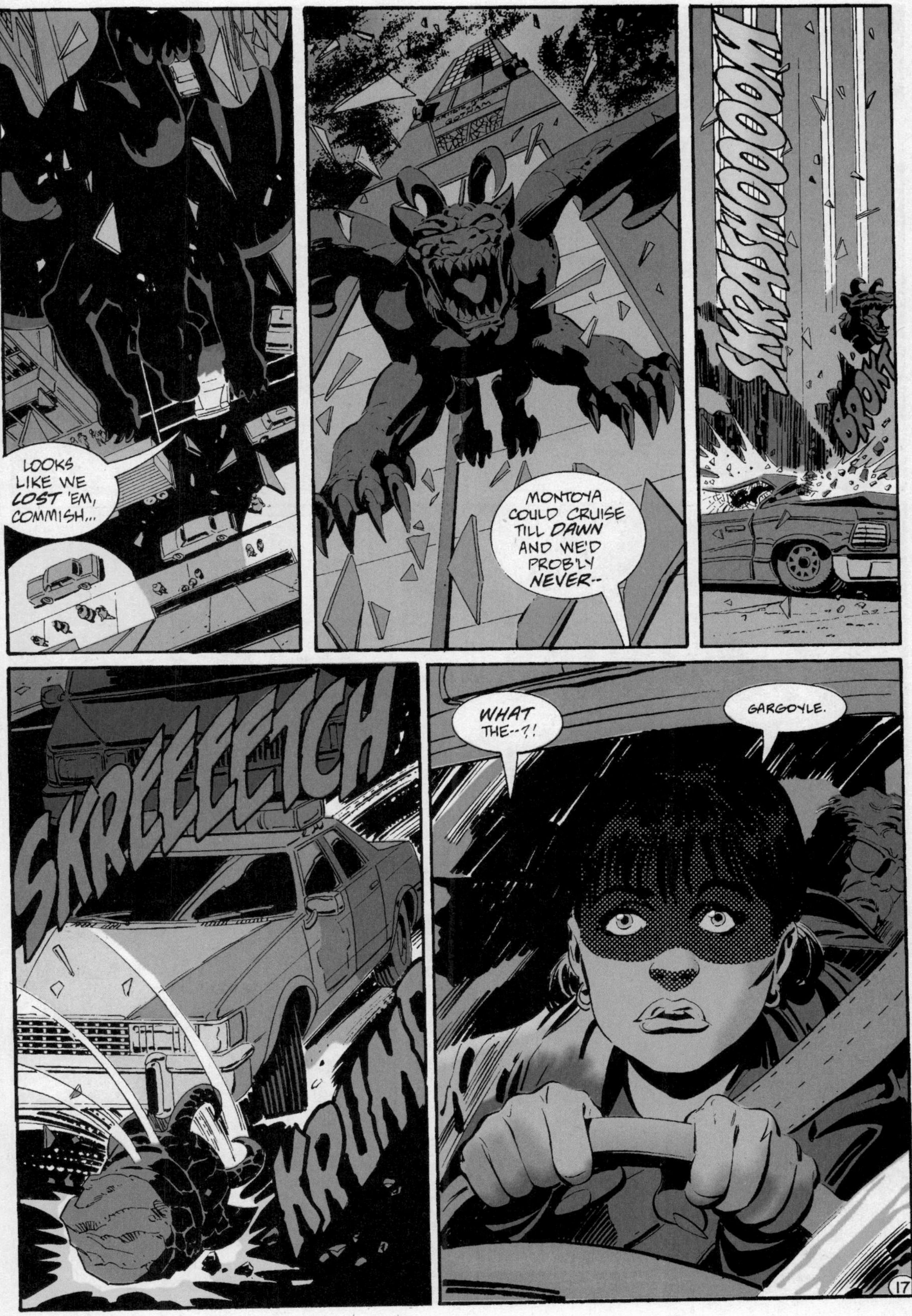
LOOKS LIKE WE *LOST* 'EM, COMMISH...
MONTOYA COULD CRUISE TILL *DAWN* AND WE'D PROB'LY *NEVER*--
SKRASHOOOOM
SKREEEEETCH
WHAT THE--?!
GARGOYLE.

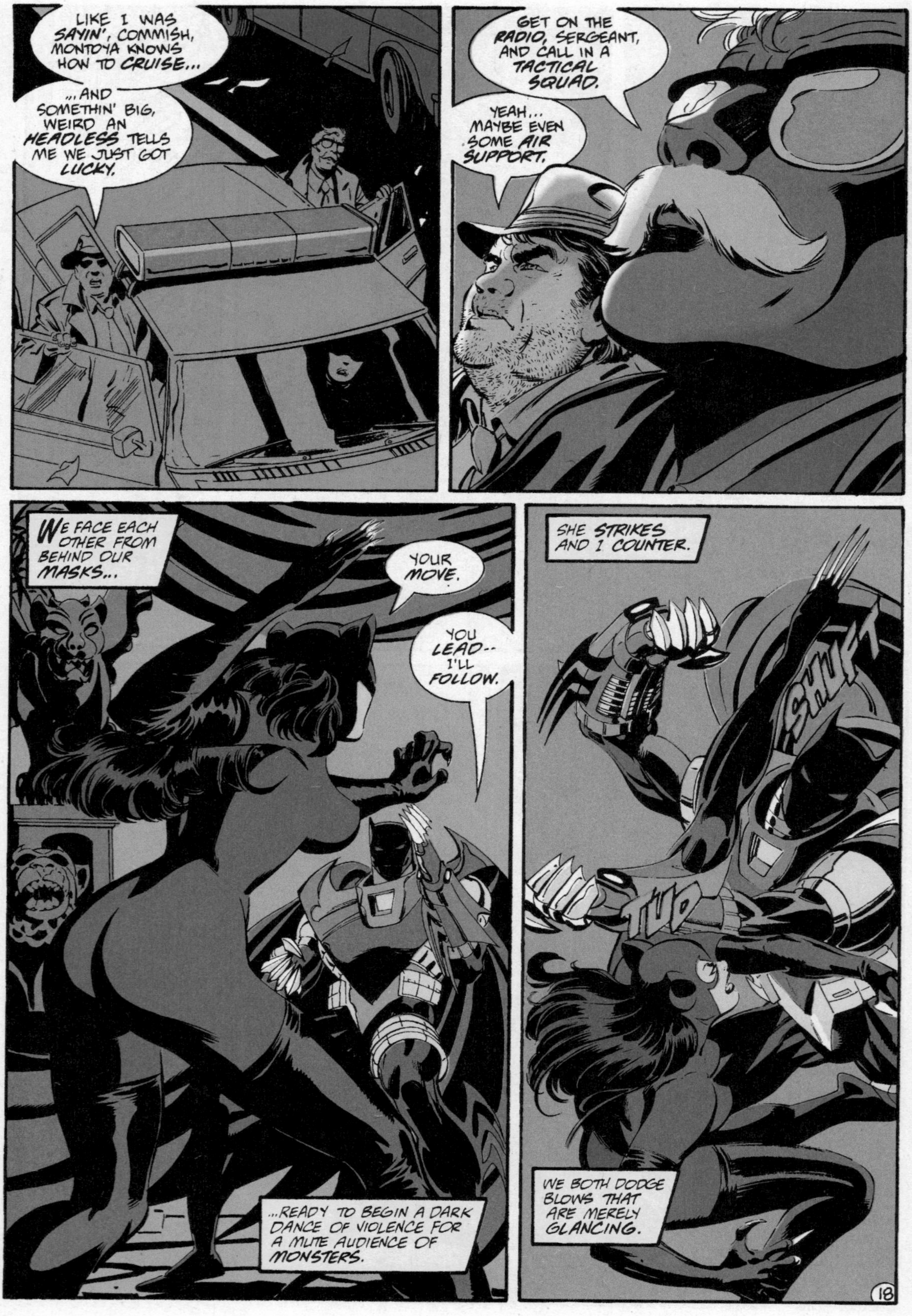
LIKE I WAS SAYIN', COMMISH, MONTOYA KNOWS HOW TO CRUISE...
...AND SOMETHIN' BIG, WEIRD AN HEADLESS TELLS ME WE JUST GOT LUCKY.
GET ON THE RADIO, SERGEANT, AND CALL IN A TACTICAL SQUAD.
YEAH... MAYBE EVEN SOME AIR SUPPORT.
WE FACE EACH OTHER FROM BEHIND OUR MASKS...
YOUR MOVE.
YOU LEAD-- I'LL FOLLOW.
...READY TO BEGIN A DARK DANCE OF VIOLENCE FOR A MUTE AUDIENCE OF MONSTERS.
SHE STRIKES AND I COUNTER.
SHUFT
TUD
WE BOTH DODGE BLOWS THAT ARE MERELY GLANCING.
18

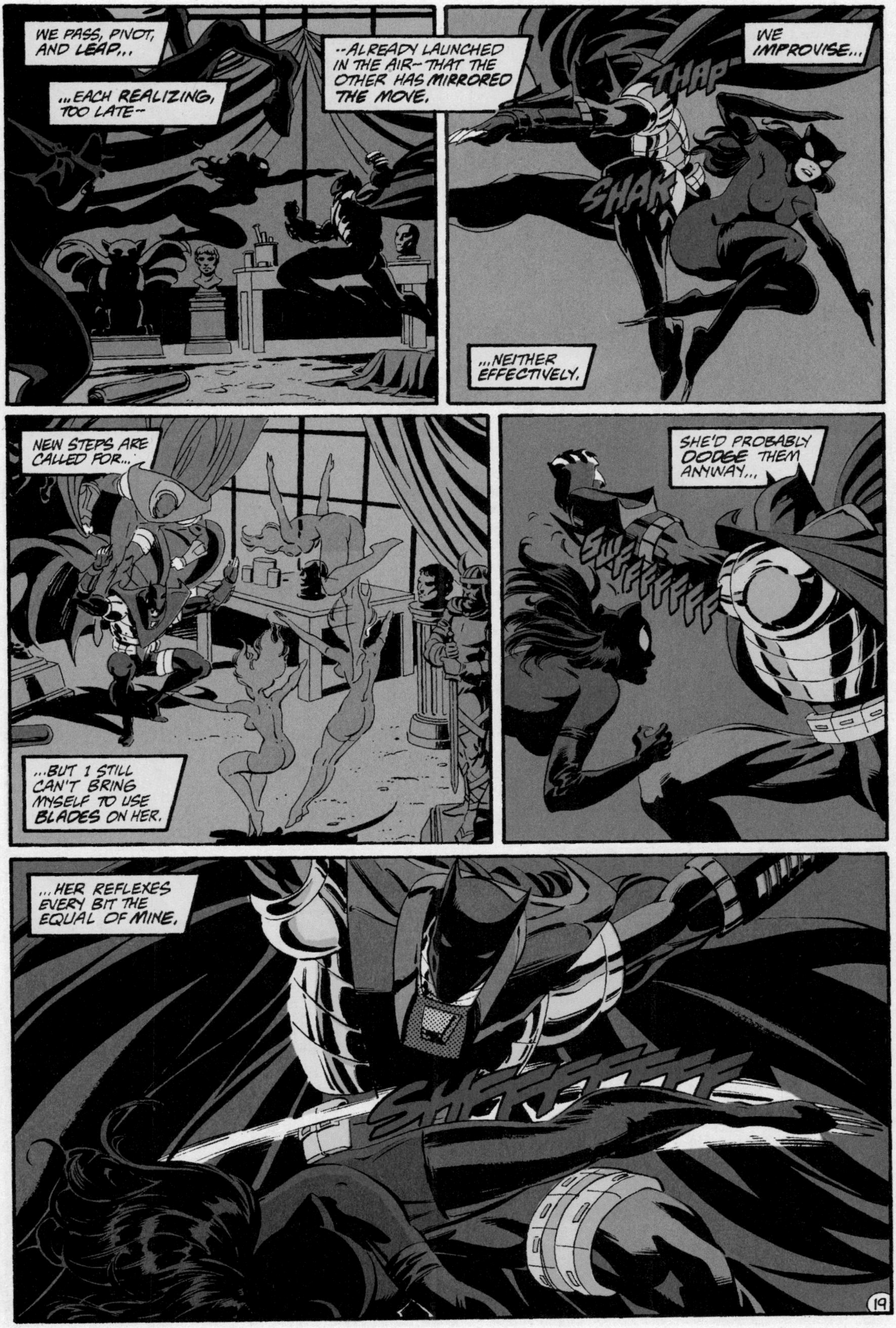
WE PASS, PIVOT, AND LEAP...
...EACH REALIZING, TOO LATE--
--ALREADY LAUNCHED IN THE AIR-- THAT THE OTHER HAS MIRRORED THE MOVE.
WE IMPROVISE...
THAP
SHAK
...NEITHER EFFECTIVELY.
NEW STEPS ARE CALLED FOR...
...BUT I STILL CAN'T BRING MYSELF TO USE BLADES ON HER.
SHE'D PROBABLY DODGE THEM ANYWAY...
...HER REFLEXES EVERY BIT THE EQUAL OF MINE.
19

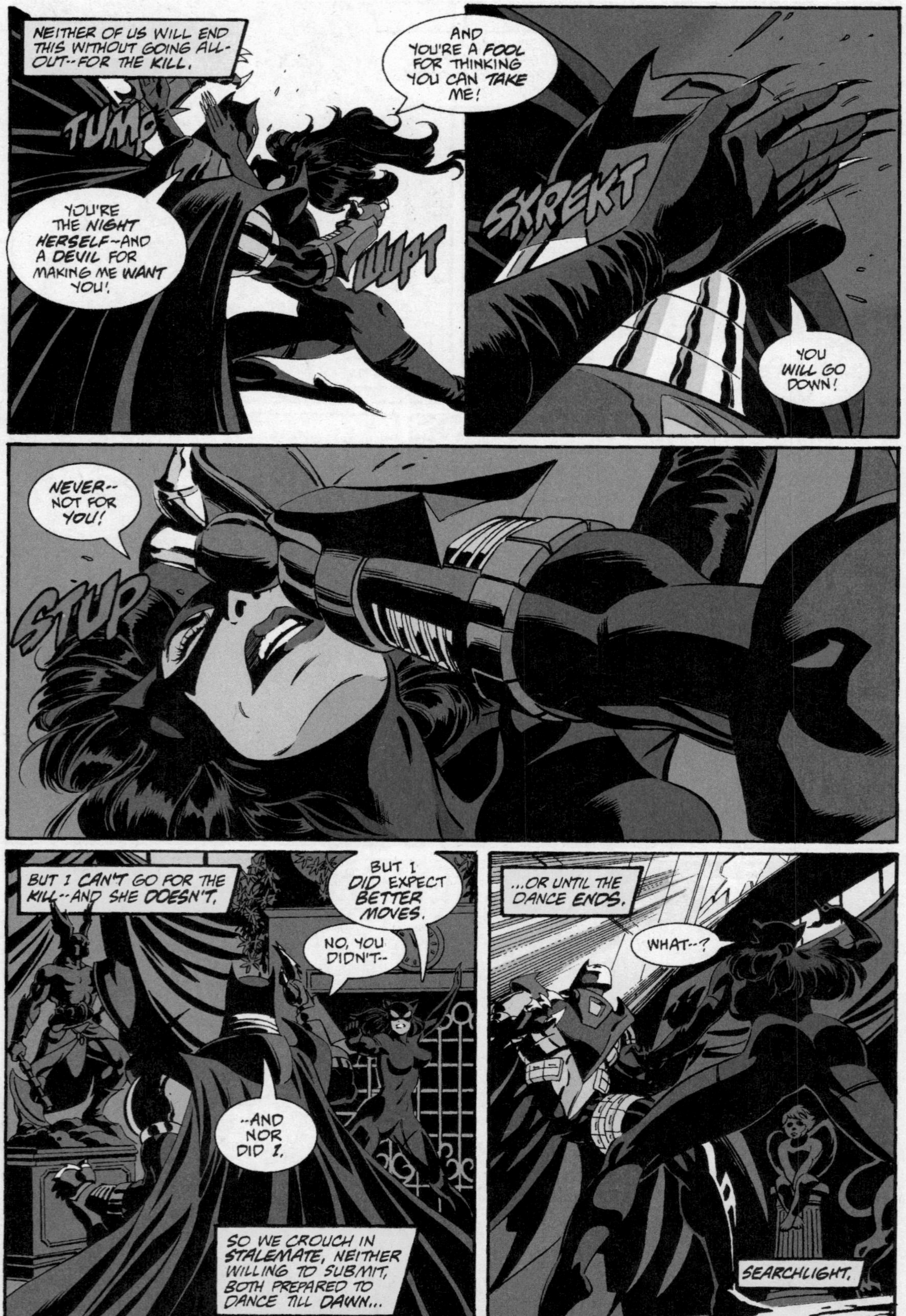

NEITHER OF US WILL END THIS WITHOUT GOING ALL-OUT--FOR THE KILL.
AND YOU'RE A FOOL FOR THINKING YOU CAN TAKE ME!
TUMP
YOU'RE THE NIGHT HERSELF--AND A DEVIL FOR MAKING ME WANT YOU!
WUPT
SKREKT
YOU WILL GO DOWN!
NEVER--NOT FOR YOU!
STUP
BUT I CAN'T GO FOR THE KILL--AND SHE DOESN'T.
BUT I DID EXPECT BETTER MOVES.
NO, YOU DIDN'T--
--AND NOR DID I.
SO WE CROUCH IN STALEMATE, NEITHER WILLING TO SUBMIT, BOTH PREPARED TO DANCE TILL DAWN...
...OR UNTIL THE DANCE ENDS.
WHAT--?
SEARCHLIGHT.
20

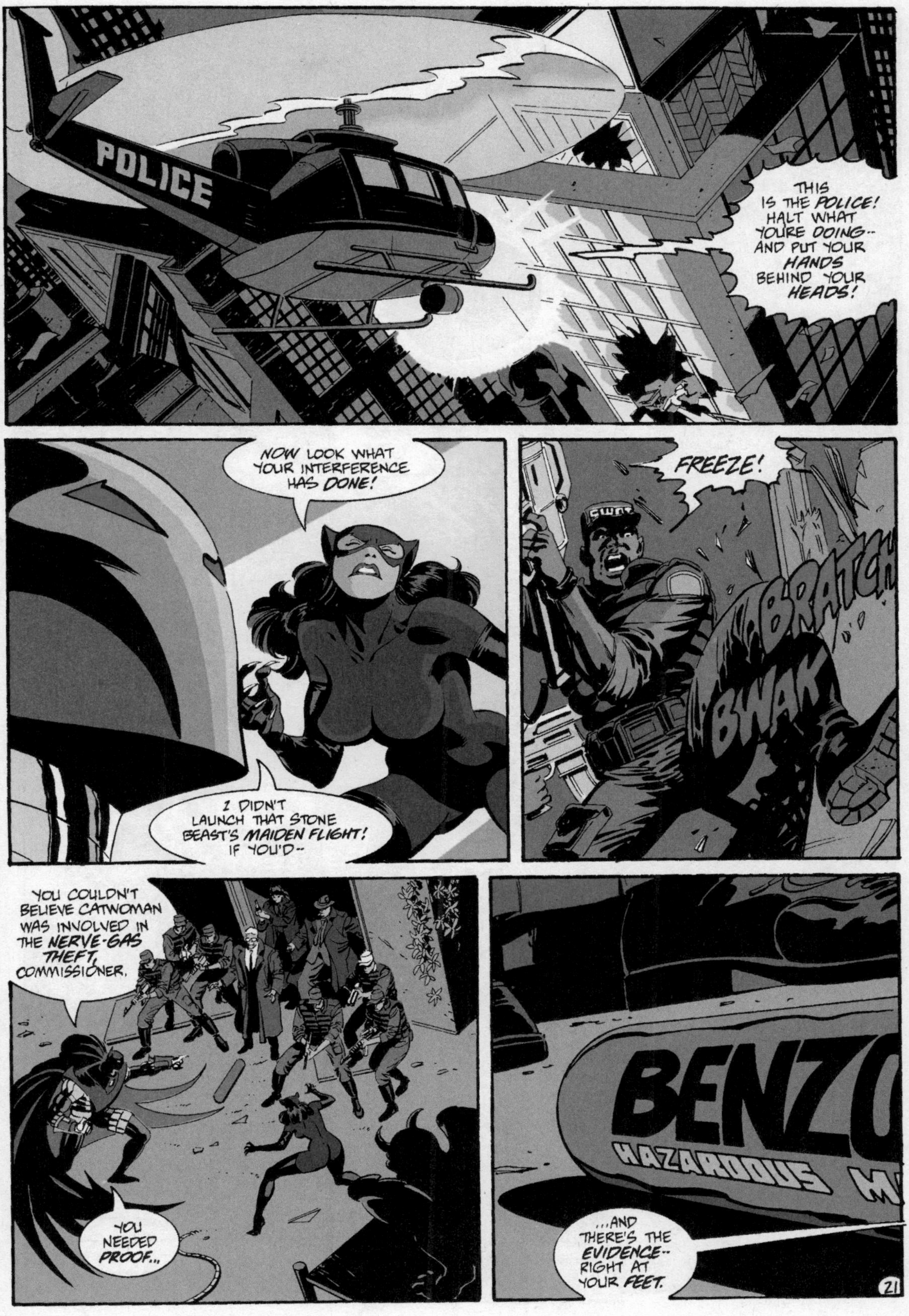
POLICE
THIS IS THE POLICE! HALT WHAT YOU'RE DOING-- AND PUT YOUR HANDS BEHIND YOUR HEADS!
NOW LOOK WHAT YOUR INTERFERENCE HAS DONE!
I DIDN'T LAUNCH THAT STONE BEAST'S MAIDEN FLIGHT! IF YOU'D--
FREEZE!
SWAT
BRATCH
BWAK
YOU COULDN'T BELIEVE CATWOMAN WAS INVOLVED IN THE NERVE-GAS THEFT, COMMISSIONER.
YOU NEEDED PROOF...
...AND THERE'S THE EVIDENCE-- RIGHT AT YOUR FEET.
BENZO
HAZARDOUS M
21

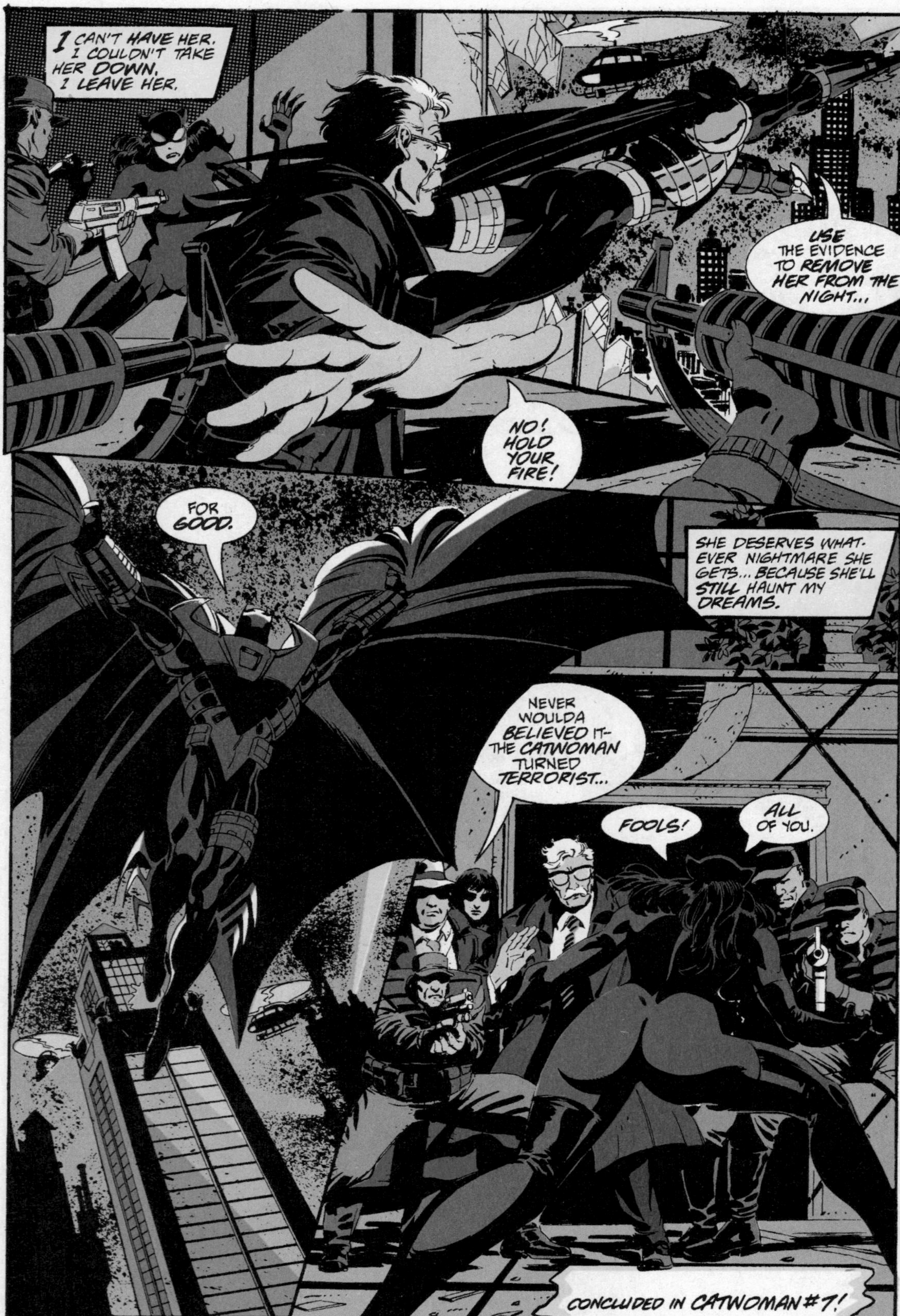
I CAN'T HAVE HER. I COULDN'T TAKE HER DOWN. I LEAVE HER.
USE THE EVIDENCE TO REMOVE HER FROM THE NIGHT...
NO! HOLD YOUR FIRE!
FOR GOOD.
SHE DESERVES WHATEVER NIGHTMARE SHE GETS... BECAUSE SHE'LL STILL HAUNT MY DREAMS.
NEVER WOULDA BELIEVED IT-- THE CATWOMAN TURNED TERRORIST...
FOOLS!
ALL OF YOU.
CONCLUDED IN CATWOMAN #7!

Cover art by JIM BALENT

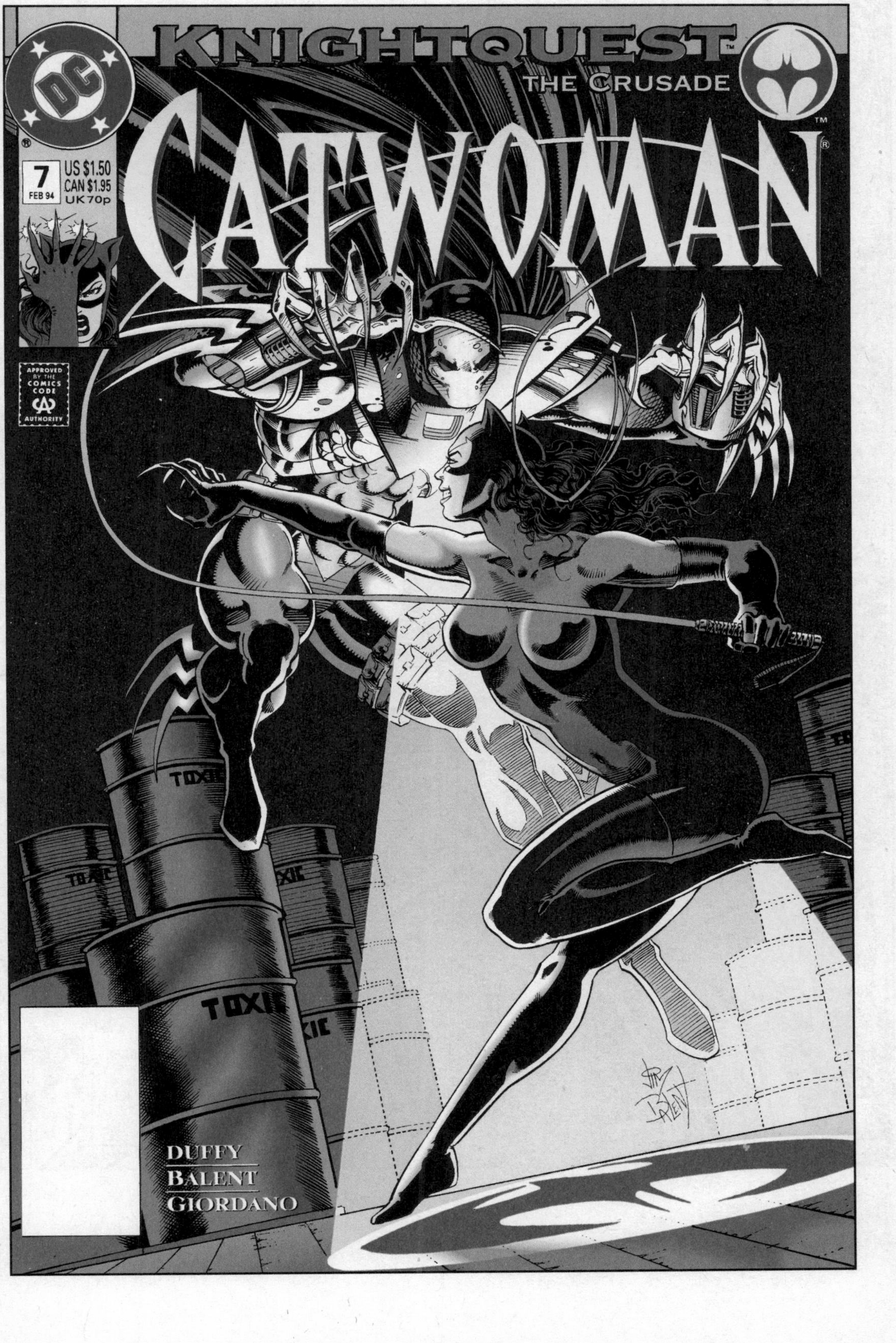
KNIGHTQUEST
THE CRUSADE
CATWOMAN
DC
7
FEB 94
US $1.50
CAN $1.95
UK70p
APPROVED BY THE COMICS CODE AUTHORITY
TOXIC
TOXIC
DUFFY
BALENT
GIORDANO

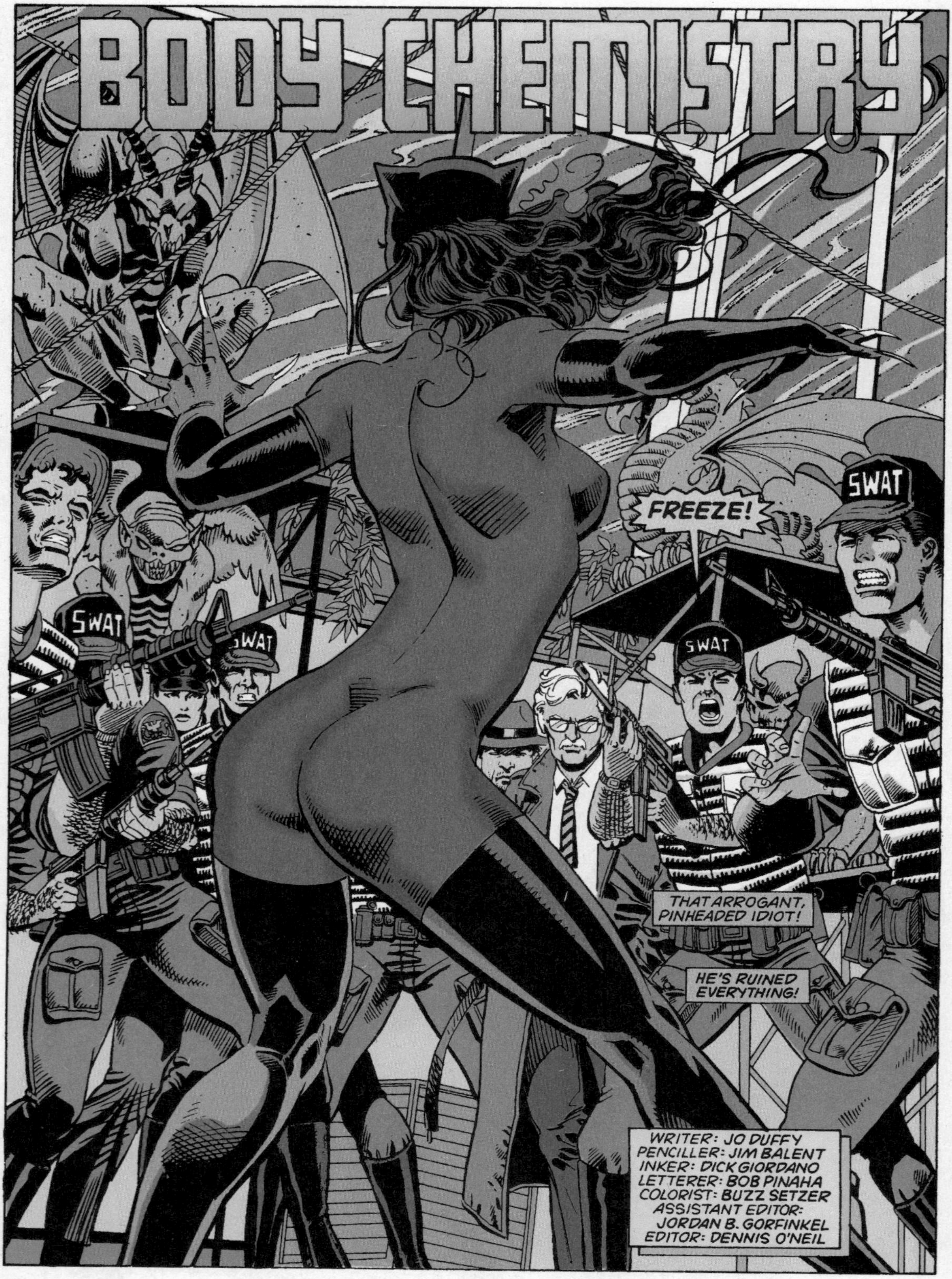
BODY CHEMISTRY
FREEZE!
THAT ARROGANT, PINHEADED IDIOT!
HE'S RUINED EVERYTHING!
WRITER: JO DUFFY
PENCILLER: JIM BALENT
INKER: DICK GIORDANO
LETTERER: BOB PINAHA
COLORIST: BUZZ SETZER
ASSISTANT EDITOR: JORDAN B. GORFINKEL
EDITOR: DENNIS O'NEIL

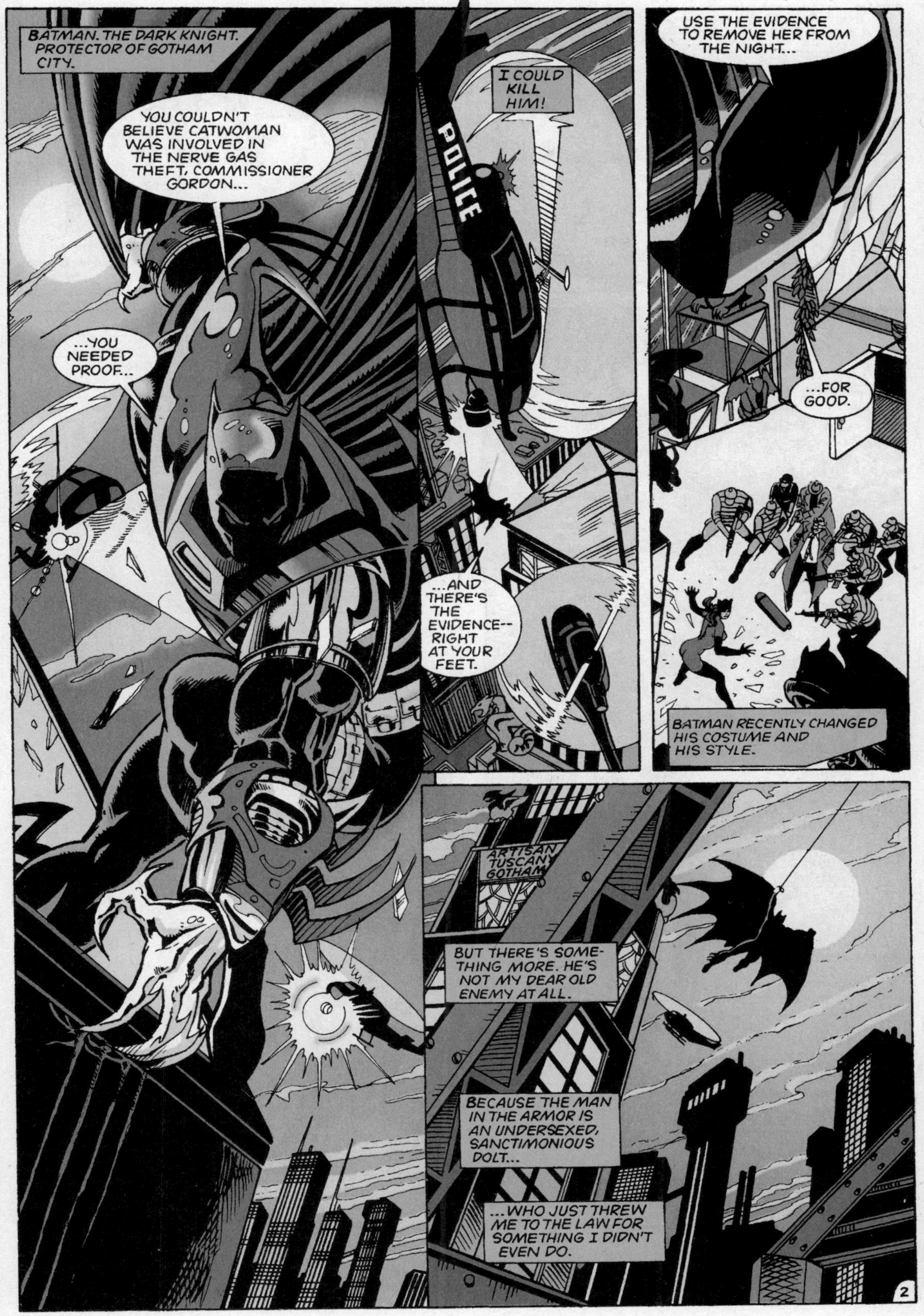
BATMAN. THE DARK KNIGHT. PROTECTOR OF GOTHAM CITY.
YOU COULDN'T BELIEVE CATWOMAN WAS INVOLVED IN THE NERVE GAS THEFT, COMMISSIONER GORDON...
...YOU NEEDED PROOF...
I COULD KILL HIM!
POLICE
...AND THERE'S THE EVIDENCE-- RIGHT AT YOUR FEET.
USE THE EVIDENCE TO REMOVE HER FROM THE NIGHT...
...FOR GOOD.
BATMAN RECENTLY CHANGED HIS COSTUME AND HIS STYLE.
ARTISAN TUSCANY GOTHAM
BUT THERE'S SOMETHING MORE. HE'S NOT MY DEAR OLD ENEMY AT ALL.
BECAUSE THE MAN IN THE ARMOR IS AN UNDERSEXED, SANCTIMONIOUS DOLT...
...WHO JUST THREW ME TO THE LAW FOR SOMETHING I DIDN'T EVEN DO.
2

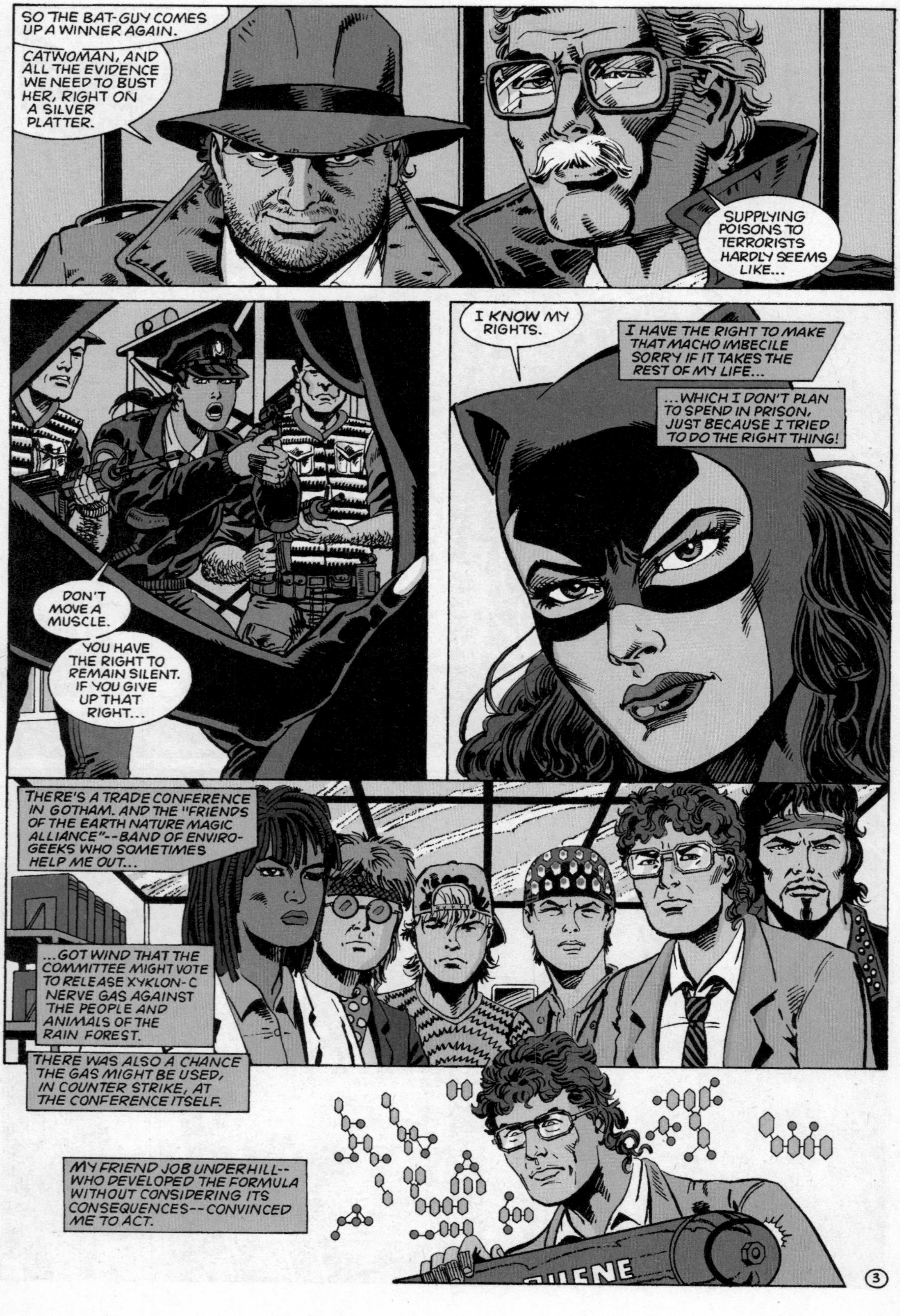
SO THE BAT-GUY COMES UP A WINNER AGAIN.
CATWOMAN, AND ALL THE EVIDENCE WE NEED TO BUST HER, RIGHT ON A SILVER PLATTER.
SUPPLYING POISONS TO TERRORISTS HARDLY SEEMS LIKE...
DON'T MOVE A MUSCLE.
YOU HAVE THE RIGHT TO REMAIN SILENT. IF YOU GIVE UP THAT RIGHT...
I KNOW MY RIGHTS.
I HAVE THE RIGHT TO MAKE THAT MACHO IMBECILE SORRY IF IT TAKES THE REST OF MY LIFE...
...WHICH I DON'T PLAN TO SPEND IN PRISON, JUST BECAUSE I TRIED TO DO THE RIGHT THING!
THERE'S A TRADE CONFERENCE IN GOTHAM. AND THE "FRIENDS OF THE EARTH NATURE MAGIC ALLIANCE"--BAND OF ENVIRO-GEEKS WHO SOMETIMES HELP ME OUT...
...GOT WIND THAT THE COMMITTEE MIGHT VOTE TO RELEASE XYKLON-C NERVE GAS AGAINST THE PEOPLE AND ANIMALS OF THE RAIN FOREST.
THERE WAS ALSO A CHANCE THE GAS MIGHT BE USED, IN COUNTER STRIKE, AT THE CONFERENCE ITSELF.
MY FRIEND JOB UNDERHILL-- WHO DEVELOPED THE FORMULA WITHOUT CONSIDERING ITS CONSEQUENCES--CONVINCED ME TO ACT.
ENE
3

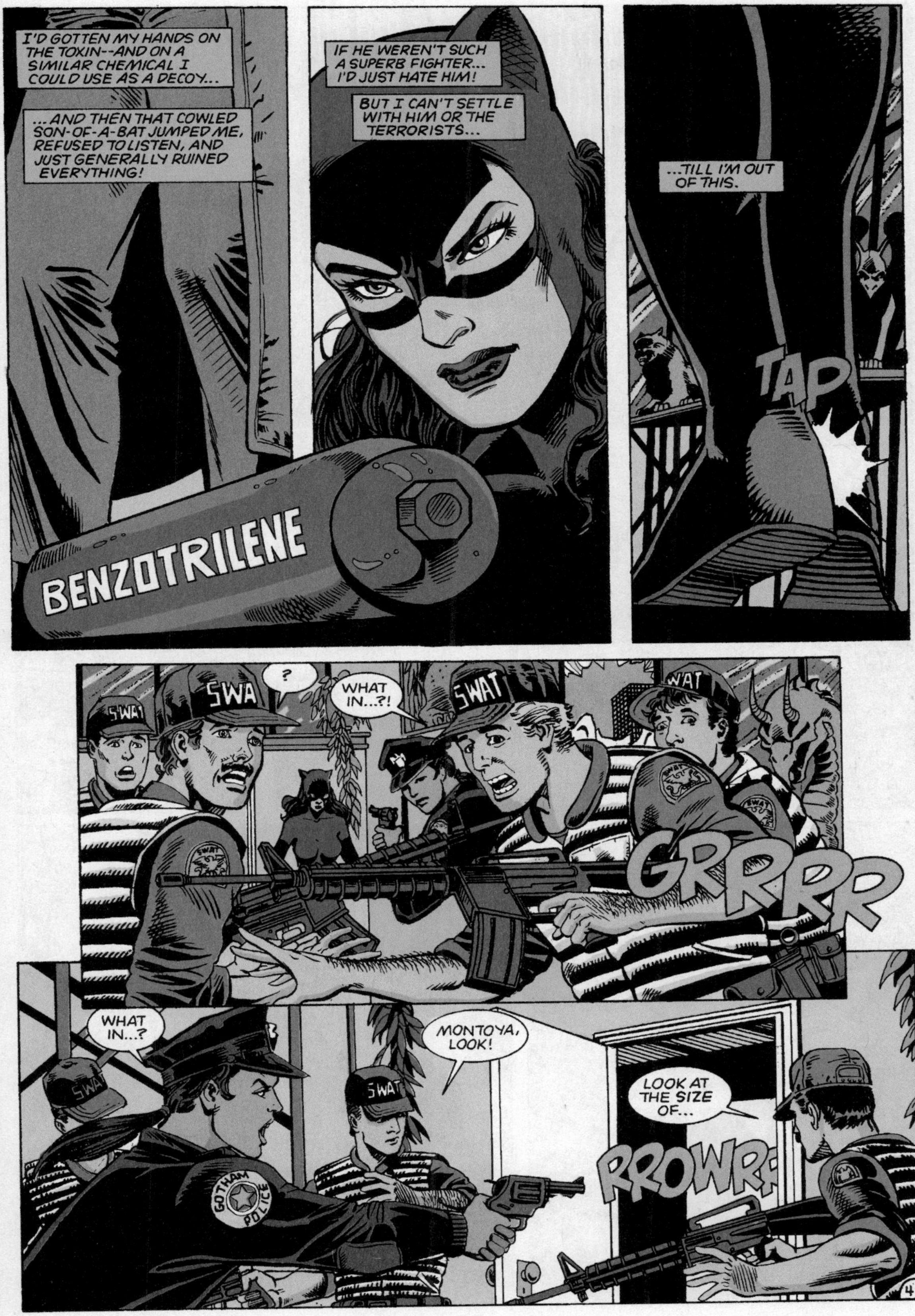
I'D GOTTEN MY HANDS ON THE TOXIN--AND ON A SIMILAR CHEMICAL I COULD USE AS A DECOY...
...AND THEN THAT COWLED SON-OF-A-BAT JUMPED ME, REFUSED TO LISTEN, AND JUST GENERALLY RUINED EVERYTHING!
BENZOTRILENE
IF HE WEREN'T SUCH A SUPERB FIGHTER... I'D JUST HATE HIM!
BUT I CAN'T SETTLE WITH HIM OR THE TERRORISTS...
...TILL I'M OUT OF THIS.
TAP
?
WHAT IN...?!
GRRRR
WHAT IN...?
MONTOYA, LOOK!
LOOK AT THE SIZE OF...
RROWR
GOTHAM POLICE
4

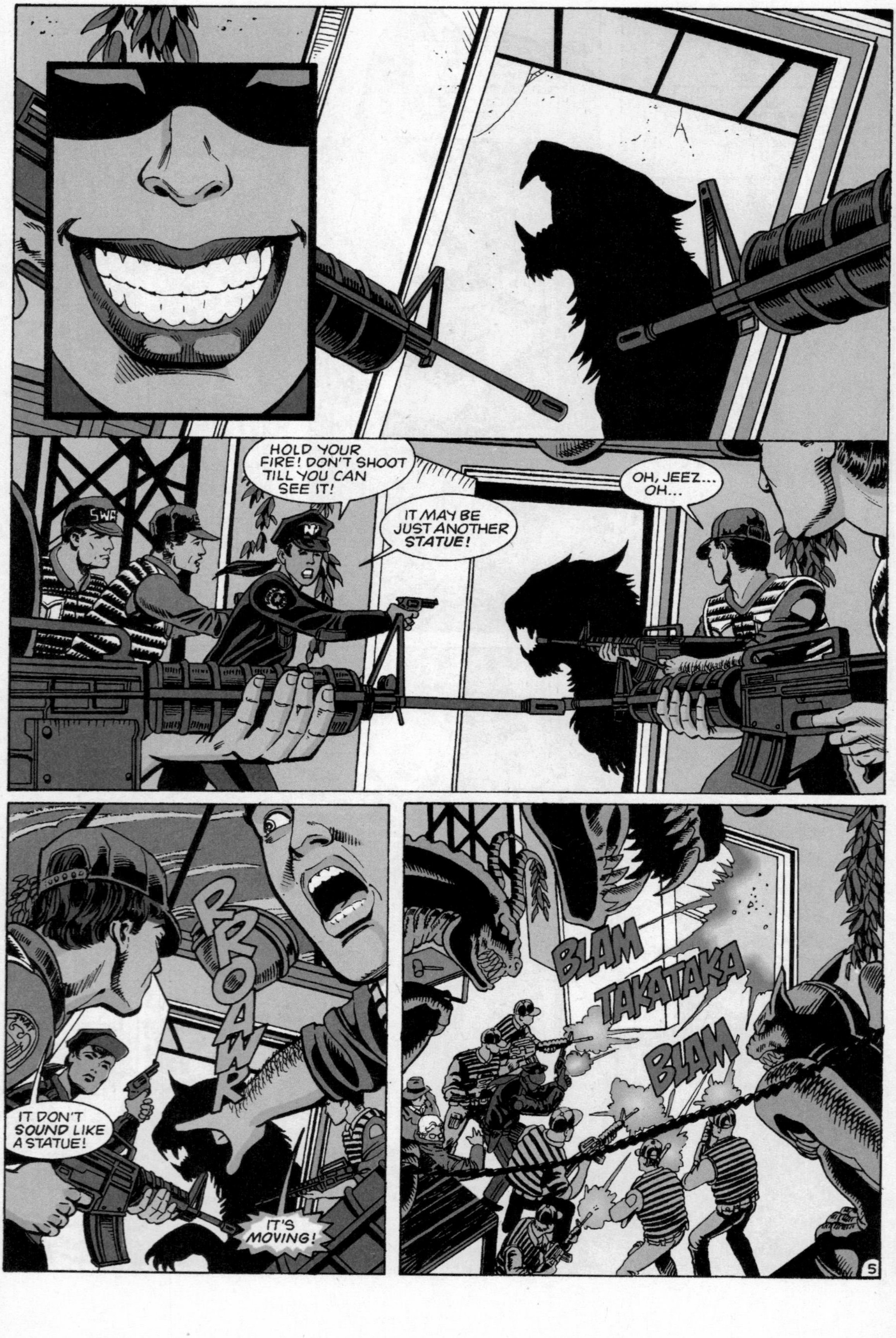
HOLD YOUR FIRE! DON'T SHOOT TILL YOU CAN SEE IT!
IT MAY BE JUST ANOTHER STATUE!
OH, JEEZ... OH...
RROAWR
IT DON'T SOUND LIKE A STATUE!
IT'S MOVING!
BLAM
TAKATAKA
BLAM
5

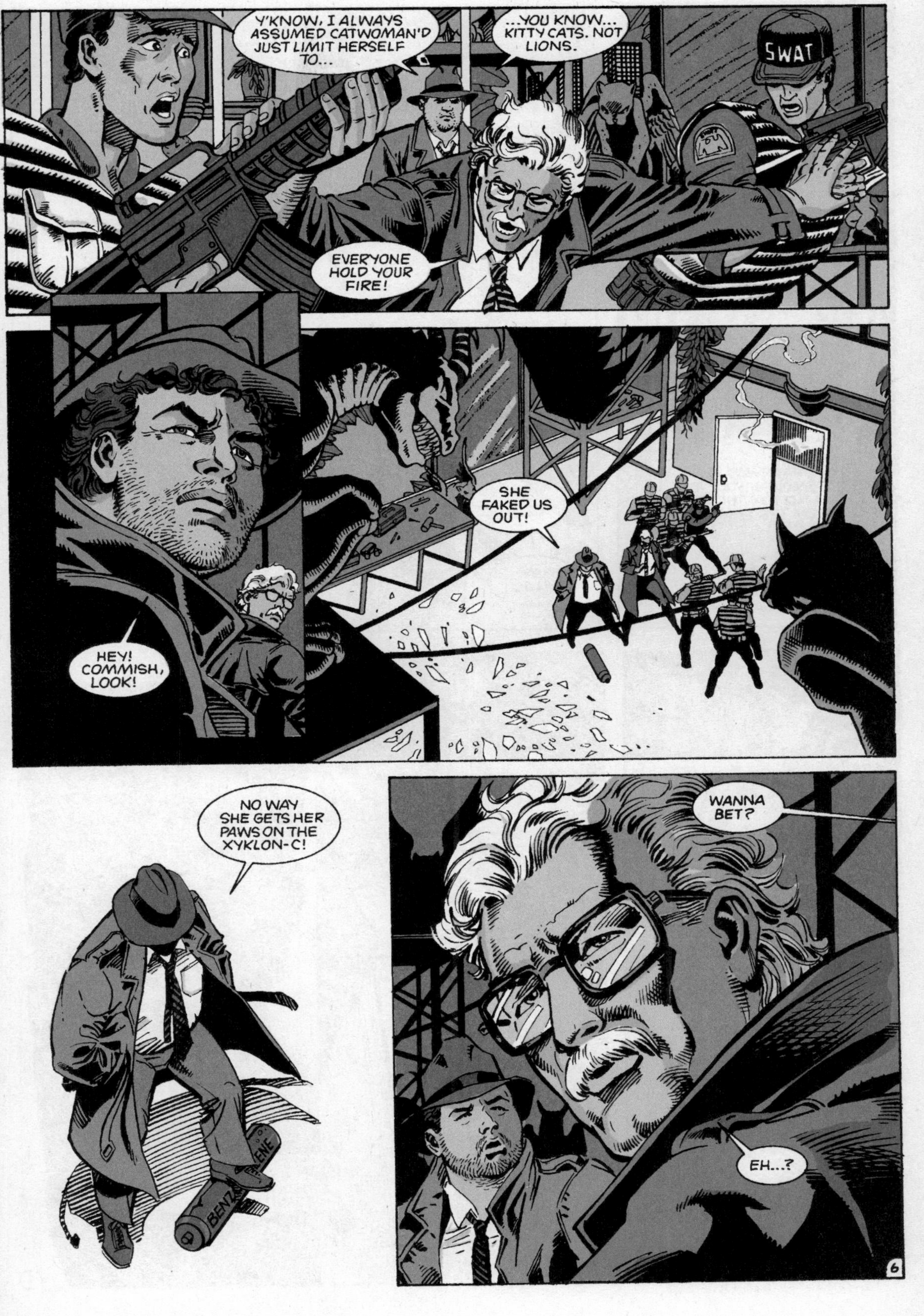
Y'KNOW, I ALWAYS ASSUMED CATWOMAN'D JUST LIMIT HERSELF TO...
...YOU KNOW... KITTY CATS. NOT LIONS.
SWAT
EVERYONE HOLD YOUR FIRE!
HEY! COMMISH, LOOK!
SHE FAKED US OUT!
NO WAY SHE GETS HER PAWS ON THE XYKLON-C!
WANNA BET?
EH...?
6

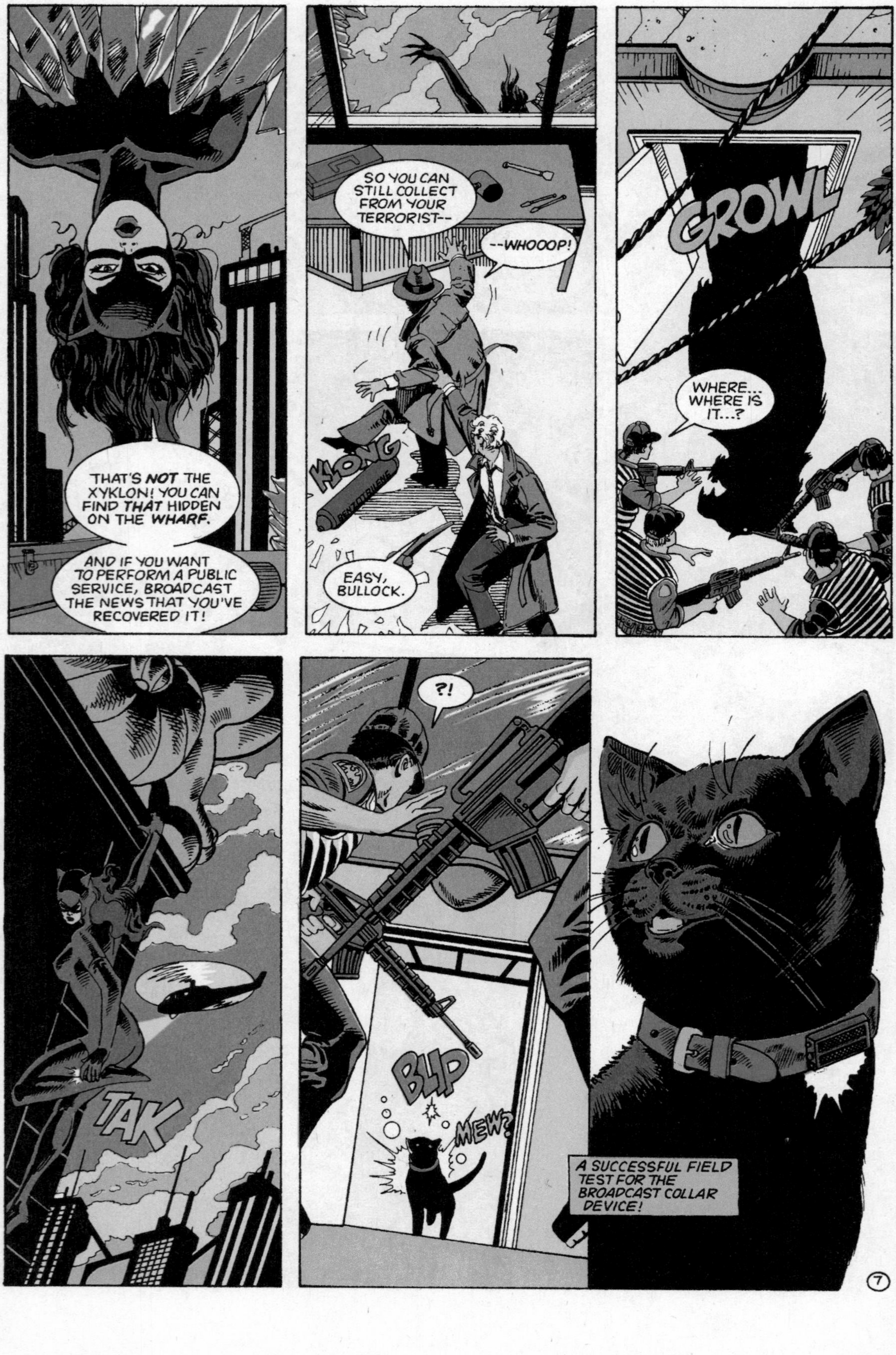
THAT'S NOT THE XYKLON! YOU CAN FIND THAT HIDDEN ON THE WHARF.
AND IF YOU WANT TO PERFORM A PUBLIC SERVICE, BROADCAST THE NEWS THAT YOU'VE RECOVERED IT!
SO YOU CAN STILL COLLECT FROM YOUR TERRORIST--
--WHOOOP!
KLONG
EASY, BULLOCK.
GROWL
WHERE... WHERE IS IT...?
TAK
?!
BLIP
MEW?
A SUCCESSFUL FIELD TEST FOR THE BROADCAST COLLAR DEVICE!
7

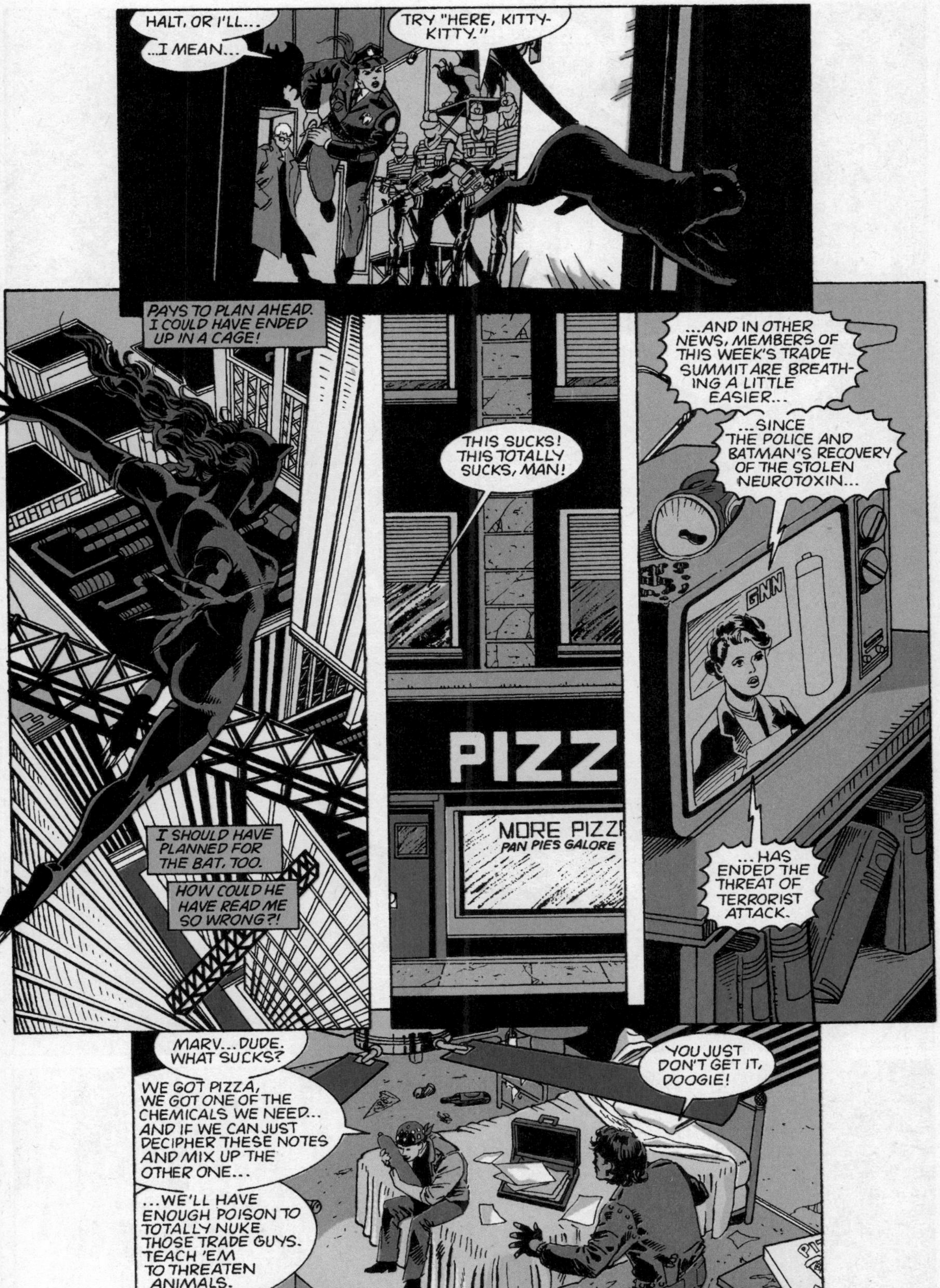

HALT, OR I'LL...
...I MEAN...
TRY "HERE, KITTY-KITTY."
PAYS TO PLAN AHEAD. I COULD HAVE ENDED UP IN A CAGE!
I SHOULD HAVE PLANNED FOR THE BAT, TOO.
HOW COULD HE HAVE READ ME SO WRONG?!
THIS SUCKS! THIS TOTALLY SUCKS, MAN!
PIZZ
MORE PIZZ
PAN PIES GALORE
...AND IN OTHER NEWS, MEMBERS OF THIS WEEK'S TRADE SUMMIT ARE BREATHING A LITTLE EASIER...
...SINCE THE POLICE AND BATMAN'S RECOVERY OF THE STOLEN NEUROTOXIN...
GNN
...HAS ENDED THE THREAT OF TERRORIST ATTACK.
MARV... DUDE. WHAT SUCKS?
WE GOT PIZZA, WE GOT ONE OF THE CHEMICALS WE NEED... AND IF WE CAN JUST DECIPHER THESE NOTES AND MIX UP THE OTHER ONE...
...WE'LL HAVE ENOUGH POISON TO TOTALLY NUKE THOSE TRADE GUYS. TEACH 'EM TO THREATEN ANIMALS.
YOU JUST DON'T GET IT, DOOGIE!

8

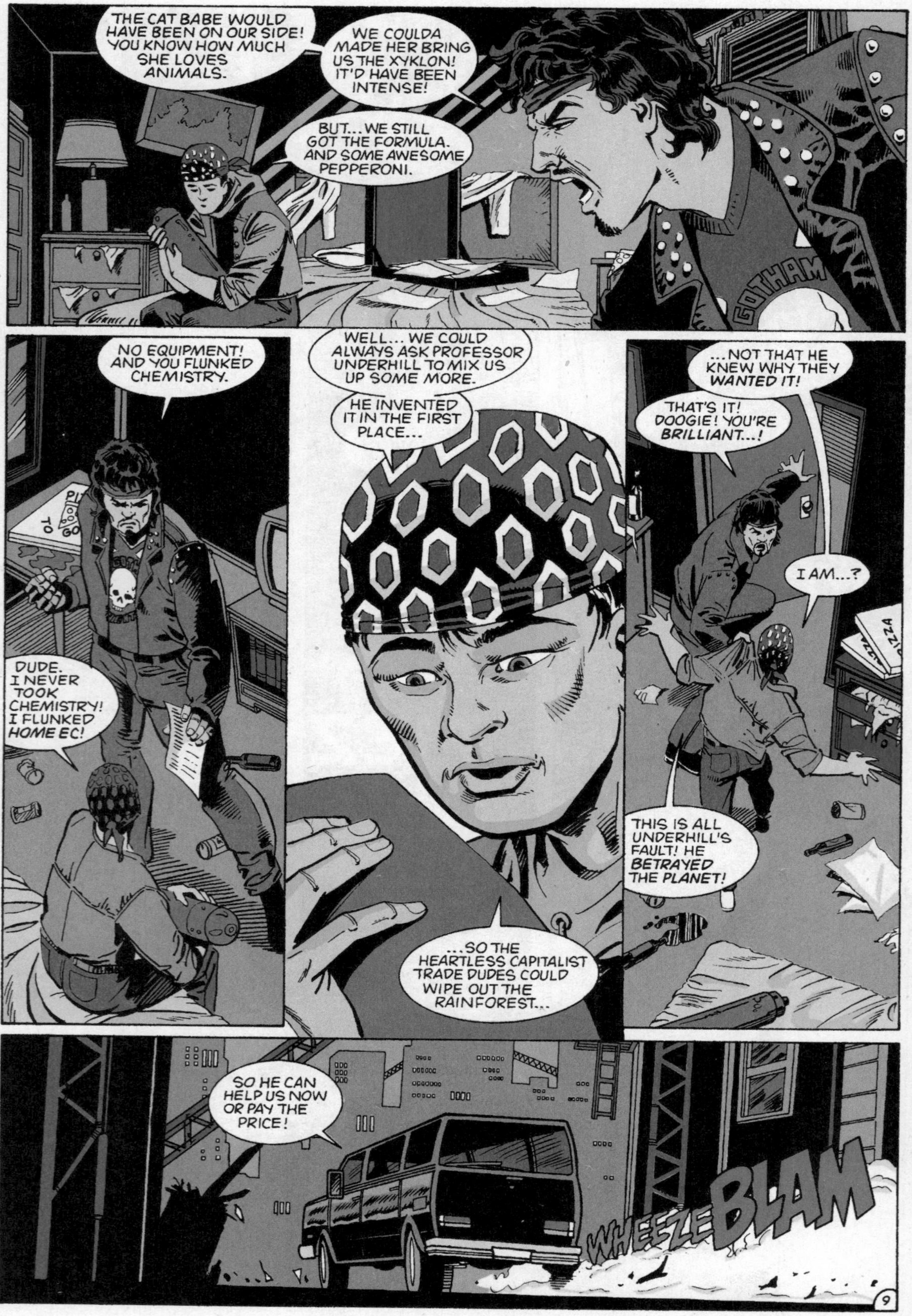
THE CAT BABE WOULD HAVE BEEN ON OUR SIDE! YOU KNOW HOW MUCH SHE LOVES ANIMALS.
WE COULDA MADE HER BRING US THE XYKLON! IT'D HAVE BEEN INTENSE!
BUT... WE STILL GOT THE FORMULA. AND SOME AWESOME PEPPERONI.
GOTHAM
NO EQUIPMENT! AND YOU FLUNKED CHEMISTRY.
DUDE. I NEVER TOOK CHEMISTRY! I FLUNKED HOME EC!
WELL... WE COULD ALWAYS ASK PROFESSOR UNDERHILL TO MIX US UP SOME MORE.
HE INVENTED IT IN THE FIRST PLACE...
...SO THE HEARTLESS CAPITALIST TRADE DUDES COULD WIPE OUT THE RAINFOREST...
...NOT THAT HE KNEW WHY THEY WANTED IT!
THAT'S IT! DOOGIE! YOU'RE BRILLIANT...!
I AM...?
PIZZA
THIS IS ALL UNDERHILL'S FAULT! HE BETRAYED THE PLANET!
SO HE CAN HELP US NOW OR PAY THE PRICE!
WHEEZE BLAM
9

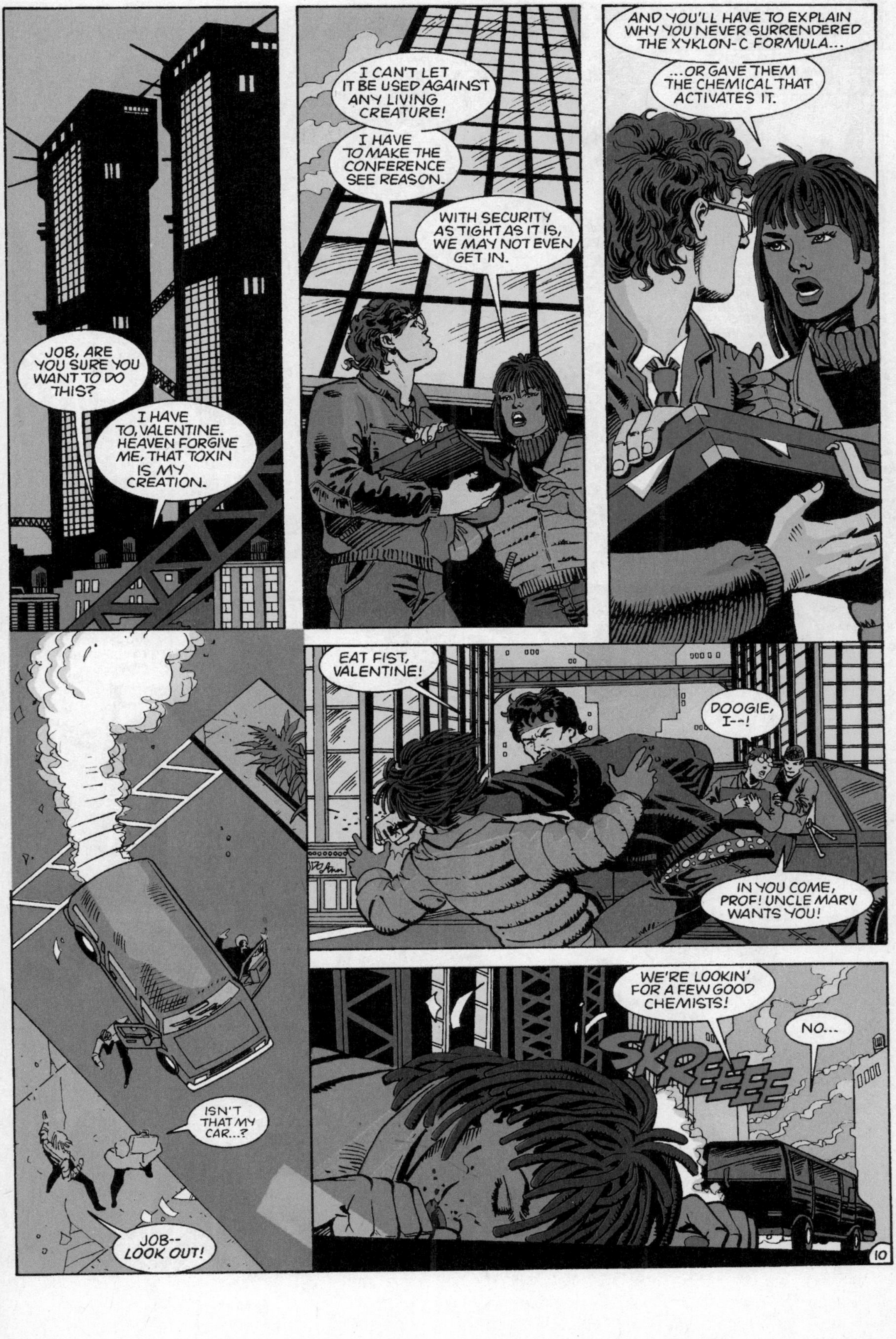
JOB, ARE YOU SURE YOU WANT TO DO THIS?
I HAVE TO, VALENTINE. HEAVEN FORGIVE ME, THAT TOXIN IS MY CREATION.
I CAN'T LET IT BE USED AGAINST ANY LIVING CREATURE!
I HAVE TO MAKE THE CONFERENCE SEE REASON.
WITH SECURITY AS TIGHT AS IT IS, WE MAY NOT EVEN GET IN.
AND YOU'LL HAVE TO EXPLAIN WHY YOU NEVER SURRENDERED THE XYKLON-C FORMULA...
...OR GAVE THEM THE CHEMICAL THAT ACTIVATES IT.
ISN'T THAT MY CAR...?
JOB-- LOOK OUT!
EAT FIST, VALENTINE!
DOOGIE, I--!
IN YOU COME, PROF! UNCLE MARV WANTS YOU!
WE'RE LOOKIN' FOR A FEW GOOD CHEMISTS!
NO...
SKREEEEE
10

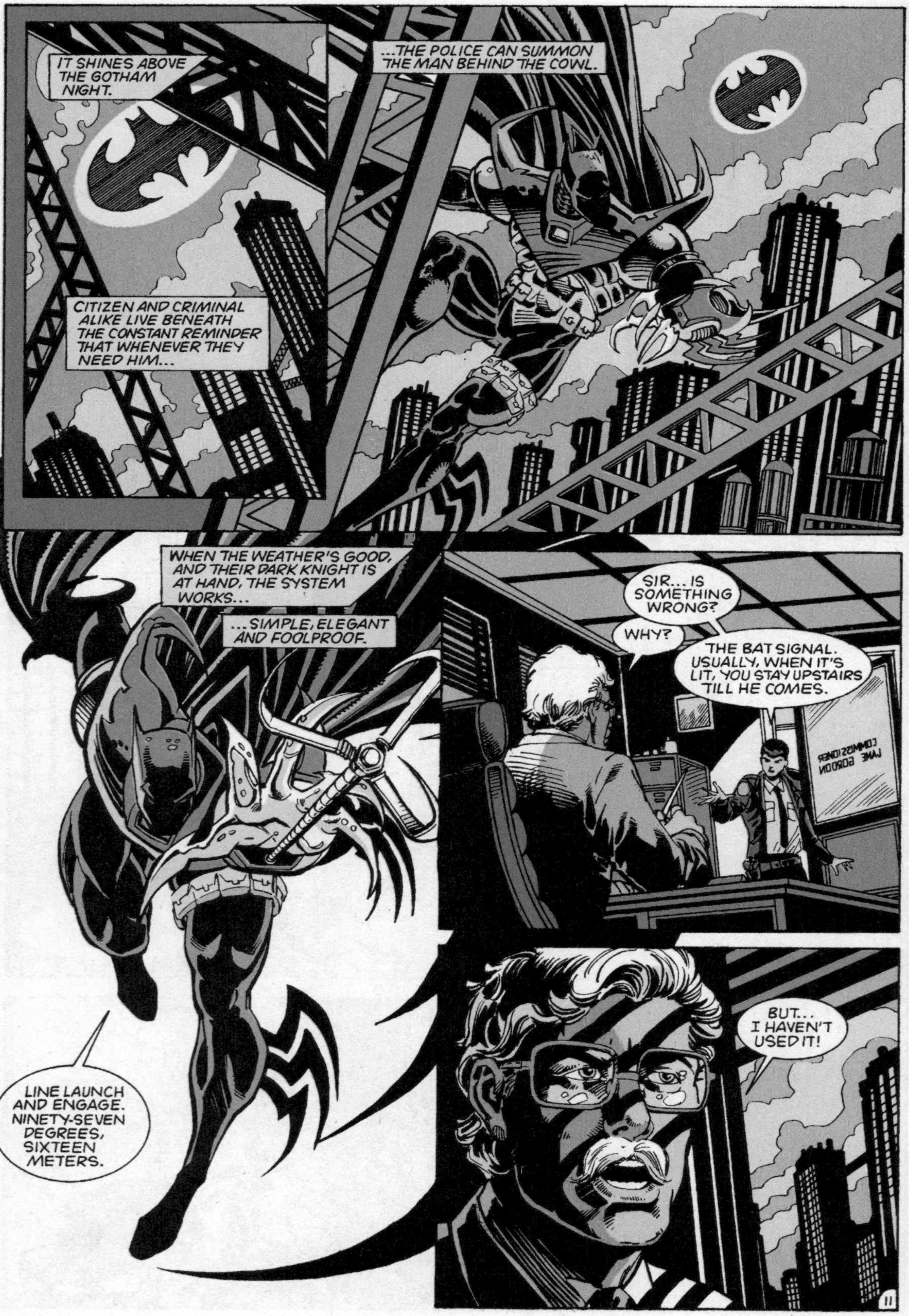
IT SHINES ABOVE THE GOTHAM NIGHT.
CITIZEN AND CRIMINAL ALIKE LIVE BENEATH THE CONSTANT REMINDER THAT WHENEVER THEY NEED HIM...
...THE POLICE CAN SUMMON THE MAN BEHIND THE COWL.
WHEN THE WEATHER'S GOOD, AND THEIR DARK KNIGHT IS AT HAND, THE SYSTEM WORKS...
...SIMPLE, ELEGANT AND FOOLPROOF.
LINE LAUNCH AND ENGAGE. NINETY-SEVEN DEGREES, SIXTEEN METERS.
SIR... IS SOMETHING WRONG?
WHY?
THE BAT SIGNAL. USUALLY, WHEN IT'S LIT, YOU STAY UPSTAIRS TILL HE COMES.
BUT... I HAVEN'T USED IT!
11

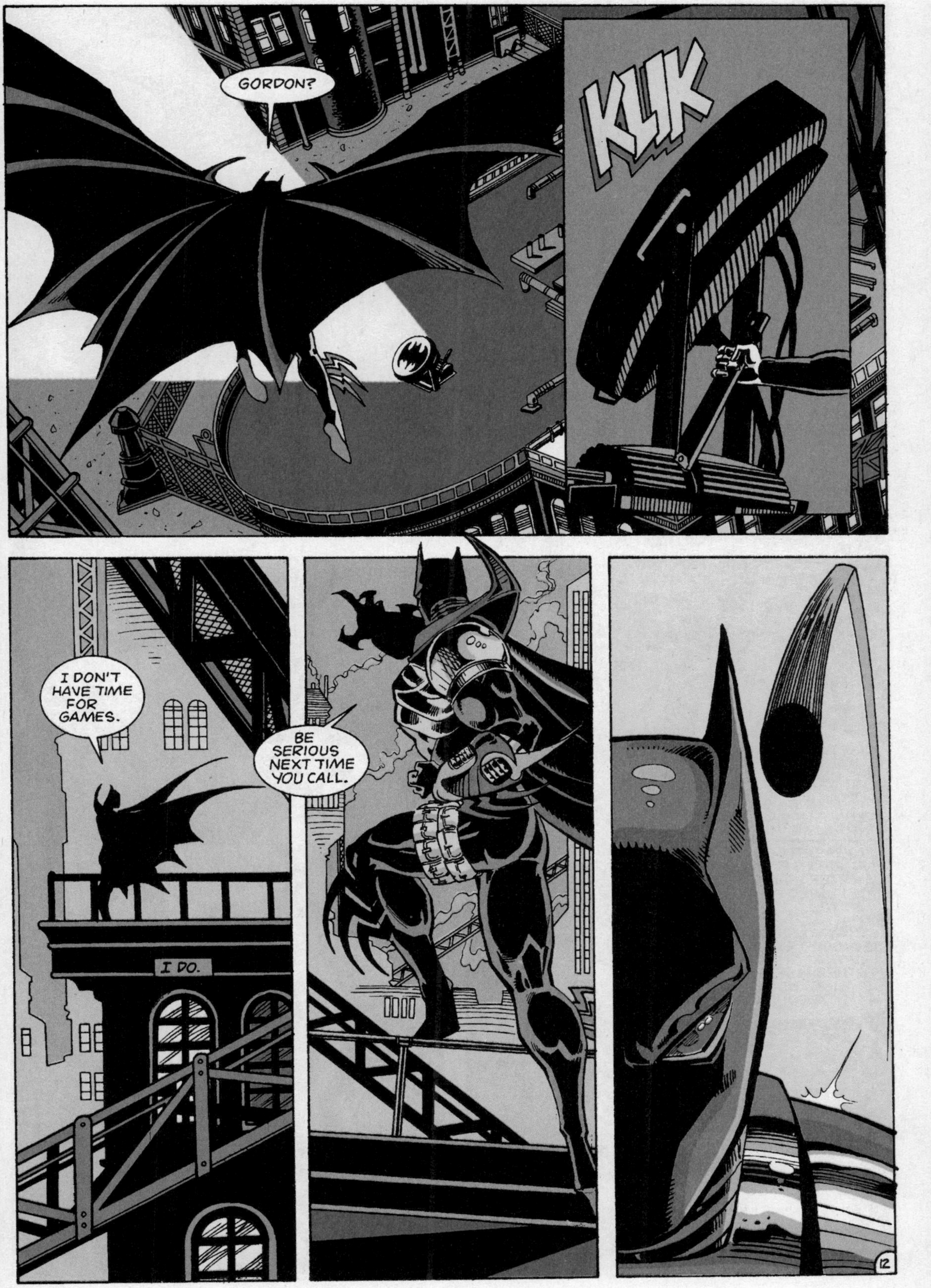
GORDON?
KLIK
I DON'T HAVE TIME FOR GAMES.
I DO.
BE SERIOUS NEXT TIME YOU CALL.
12

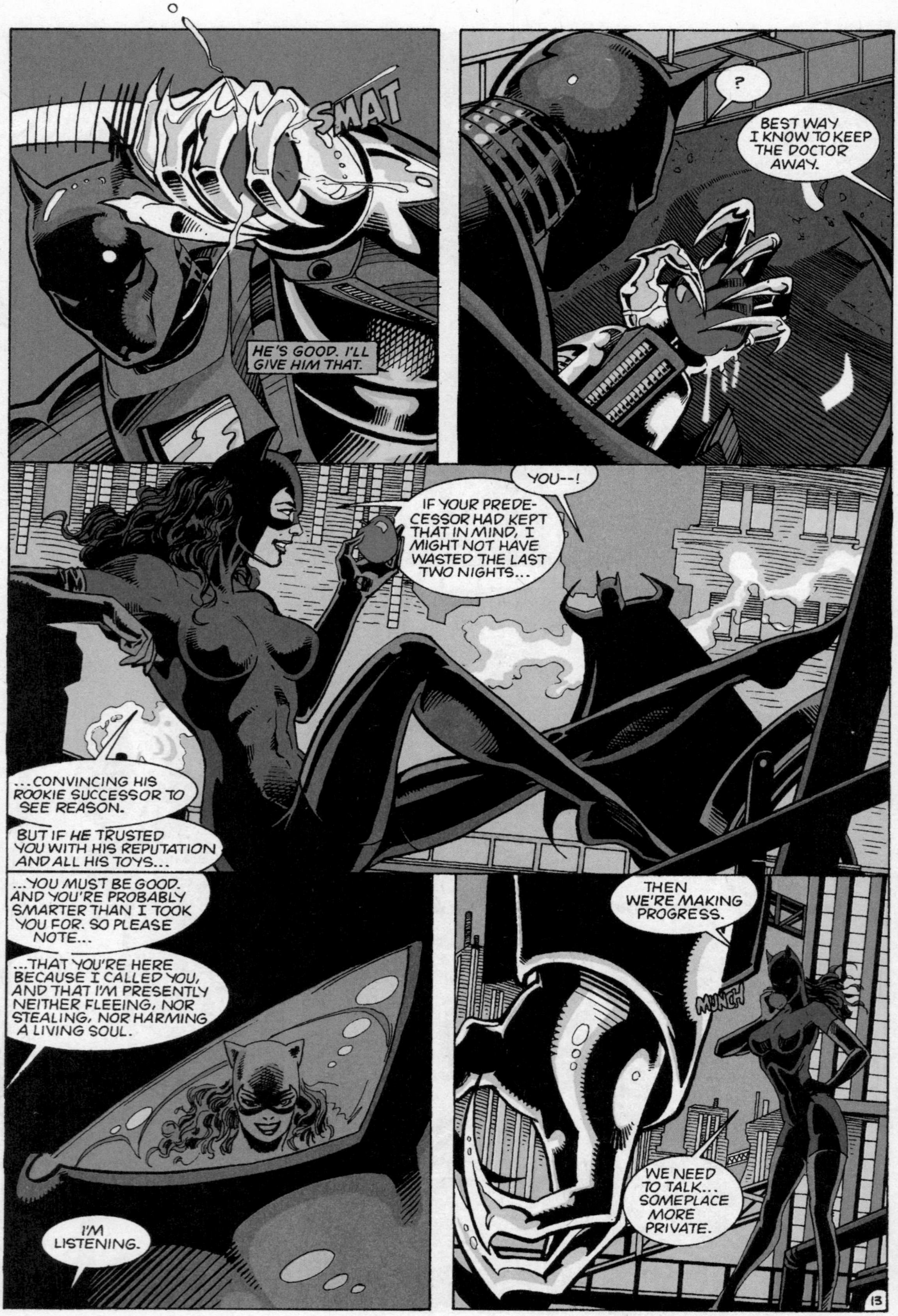
SMAT
HE'S GOOD. I'LL GIVE HIM THAT.
?
BEST WAY I KNOW TO KEEP THE DOCTOR AWAY.
YOU--!
IF YOUR PREDE-CESSOR HAD KEPT THAT IN MIND, I MIGHT NOT HAVE WASTED THE LAST TWO NIGHTS...
...CONVINCING HIS ROOKIE SUCCESSOR TO SEE REASON.
BUT IF HE TRUSTED YOU WITH HIS REPUTATION AND ALL HIS TOYS...
...YOU MUST BE GOOD. AND YOU'RE PROBABLY SMARTER THAN I TOOK YOU FOR. SO PLEASE NOTE...
...THAT YOU'RE HERE BECAUSE I CALLED YOU, AND THAT I'M PRESENTLY NEITHER FLEEING, NOR STEALING, NOR HARMING A LIVING SOUL.
I'M LISTENING.
THEN WE'RE MAKING PROGRESS.
MUNCH
WE NEED TO TALK... SOMEPLACE MORE PRIVATE.
13

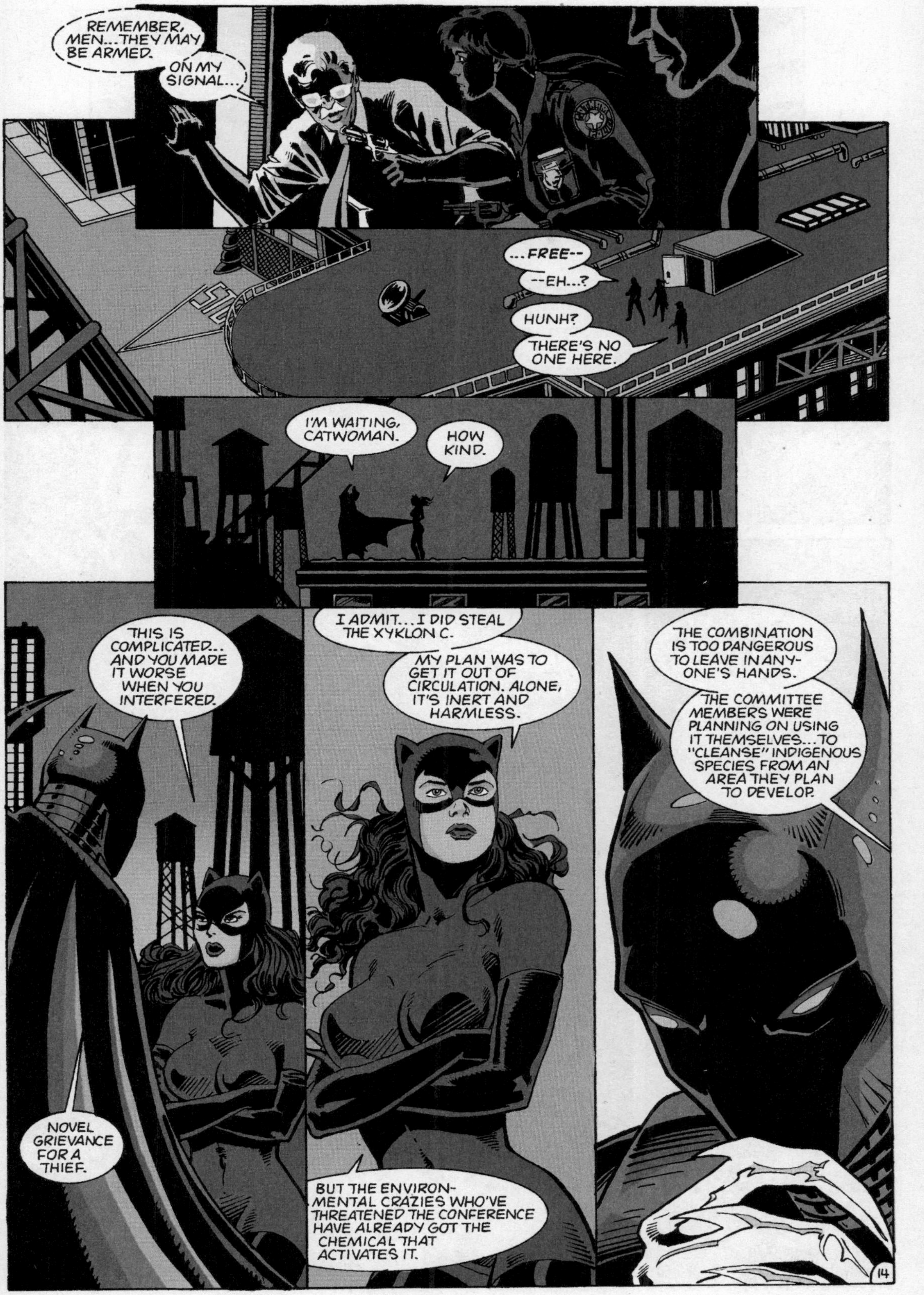
REMEMBER, MEN...THEY MAY BE ARMED.
ON MY SIGNAL...
...FREE--
--EH...?
HUNH?
THERE'S NO ONE HERE.
I'M WAITING, CATWOMAN.
HOW KIND.
THIS IS COMPLICATED... AND YOU MADE IT WORSE WHEN YOU INTERFERED.
NOVEL GRIEVANCE FOR A THIEF.
I ADMIT... I DID STEAL THE XYKLON C.
MY PLAN WAS TO GET IT OUT OF CIRCULATION. ALONE, IT'S INERT AND HARMLESS.
BUT THE ENVIRONMENTAL CRAZIES WHO'VE THREATENED THE CONFERENCE HAVE ALREADY GOT THE CHEMICAL THAT ACTIVATES IT.
THE COMBINATION IS TOO DANGEROUS TO LEAVE IN ANYONE'S HANDS.
THE COMMITTEE MEMBERS WERE PLANNING ON USING IT THEMSELVES...TO "CLEANSE" INDIGENOUS SPECIES FROM AN AREA THEY PLAN TO DEVELOP.
14

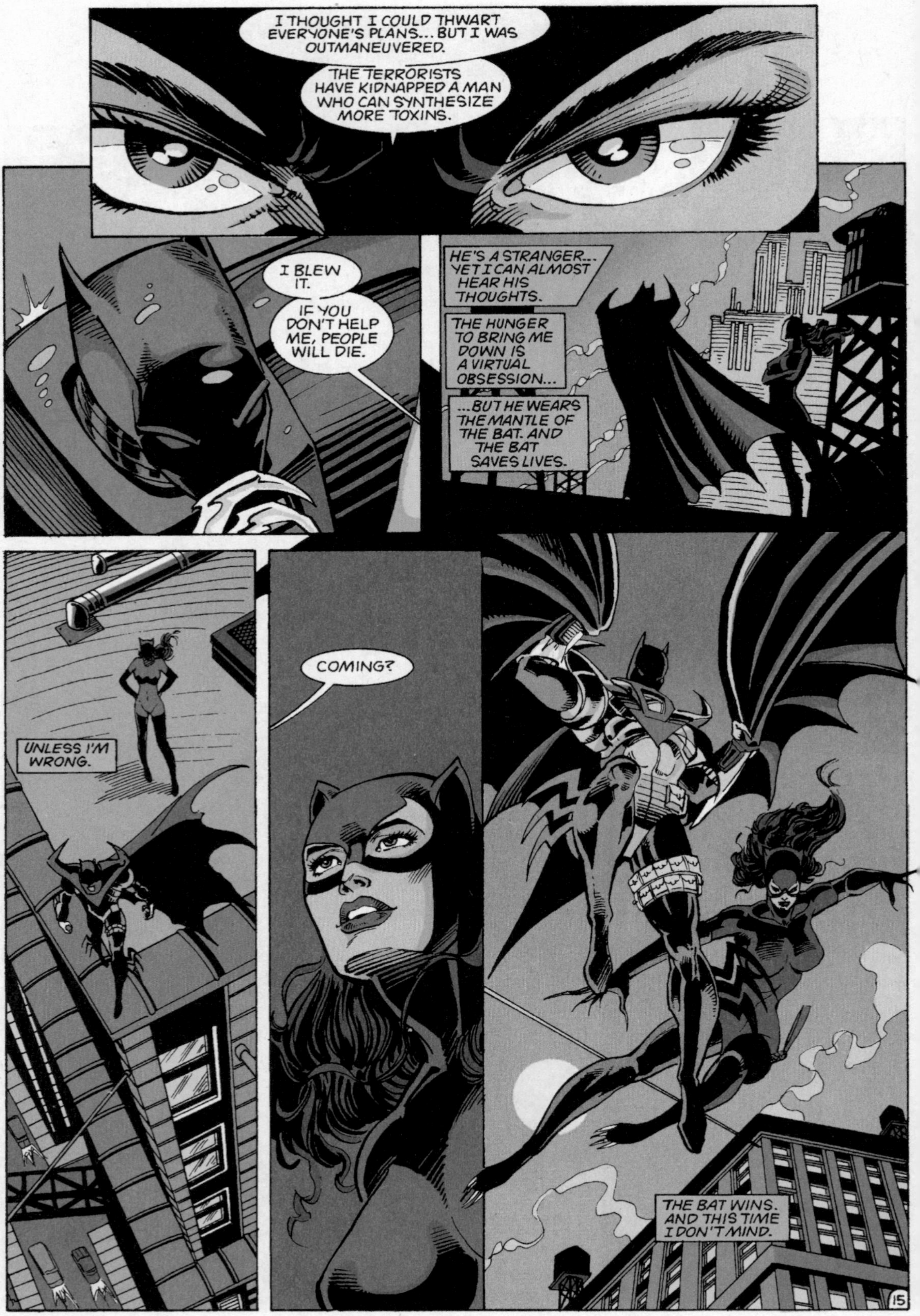
I THOUGHT I COULD THWART EVERYONE'S PLANS... BUT I WAS OUTMANEUVERED.
THE TERRORISTS HAVE KIDNAPPED A MAN WHO CAN SYNTHESIZE MORE TOXINS.
I BLEW IT.
IF YOU DON'T HELP ME, PEOPLE WILL DIE.
HE'S A STRANGER... YET I CAN ALMOST HEAR HIS THOUGHTS.
THE HUNGER TO BRING ME DOWN IS A VIRTUAL OBSESSION...
...BUT HE WEARS THE MANTLE OF THE BAT. AND THE BAT SAVES LIVES.
UNLESS I'M WRONG.
COMING?
THE BAT WINS. AND THIS TIME I DON'T MIND.
15

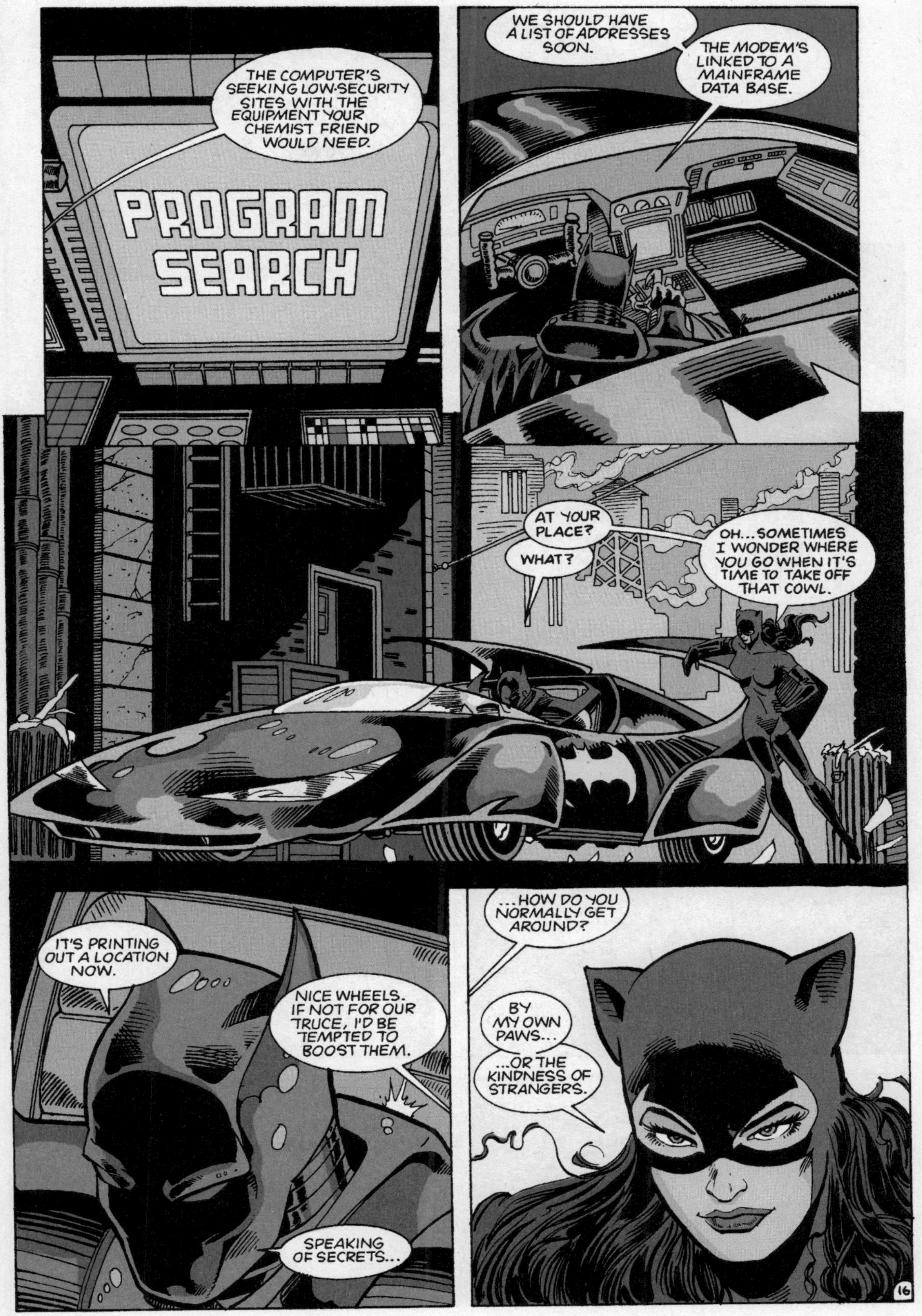
THE COMPUTER'S SEEKING LOW-SECURITY SITES WITH THE EQUIPMENT YOUR CHEMIST FRIEND WOULD NEED.
PROGRAM SEARCH
WE SHOULD HAVE A LIST OF ADDRESSES SOON.
THE MODEM'S LINKED TO A MAINFRAME DATA BASE.
OH...SOMETIMES I WONDER WHERE YOU GO WHEN IT'S TIME TO TAKE OFF THAT COWL.
WHAT?
AT YOUR PLACE?
IT'S PRINTING OUT A LOCATION NOW.
NICE WHEELS. IF NOT FOR OUR TRUCE, I'D BE TEMPTED TO BOOST THEM.
SPEAKING OF SECRETS...
...HOW DO YOU NORMALLY GET AROUND?
BY MY OWN PAWS...
...OR THE KINDNESS OF STRANGERS.
16

THIS SHOULD DO IT.

GOTHAM FOURTH DISTRICT VOCATIONAL HIGH SCHOOL

YOU'RE SURE?!

YES...

≡ACK--!≡

HISSSSSS

DU-UUUDE! THAT STUFF BURNS, MAN!

≡COUGH-COUGH!≡

I THOUGHT THAT WAS THE IDEA.

MIX THE CONTENTS OF THE JUG WITH YOUR TANK OF ATROPHANE.

YOU'LL HAVE ENOUGH GAS FOR A HUNDRED PEOPLE!

AWRIII--IIGHT!

SOON'S I GET THIS INTO THE AIR SUPPLY AT THE TRADE CONFER-ENCE, THOSE ANIMAL KILLERS'LL BE HISTORY!

SORRY, PROFESSOR UNDERHILL, BUT YOU'RE HISTORY, TOO.

ME AN' THE DOOG-MEISTER CAN'T LEAVE YOU ALIVE TO IDENTIFY US.

WE AIN'T FORGOTTEN HOW YOU RATTED OUT OUR OTHER PALS TO--!

17

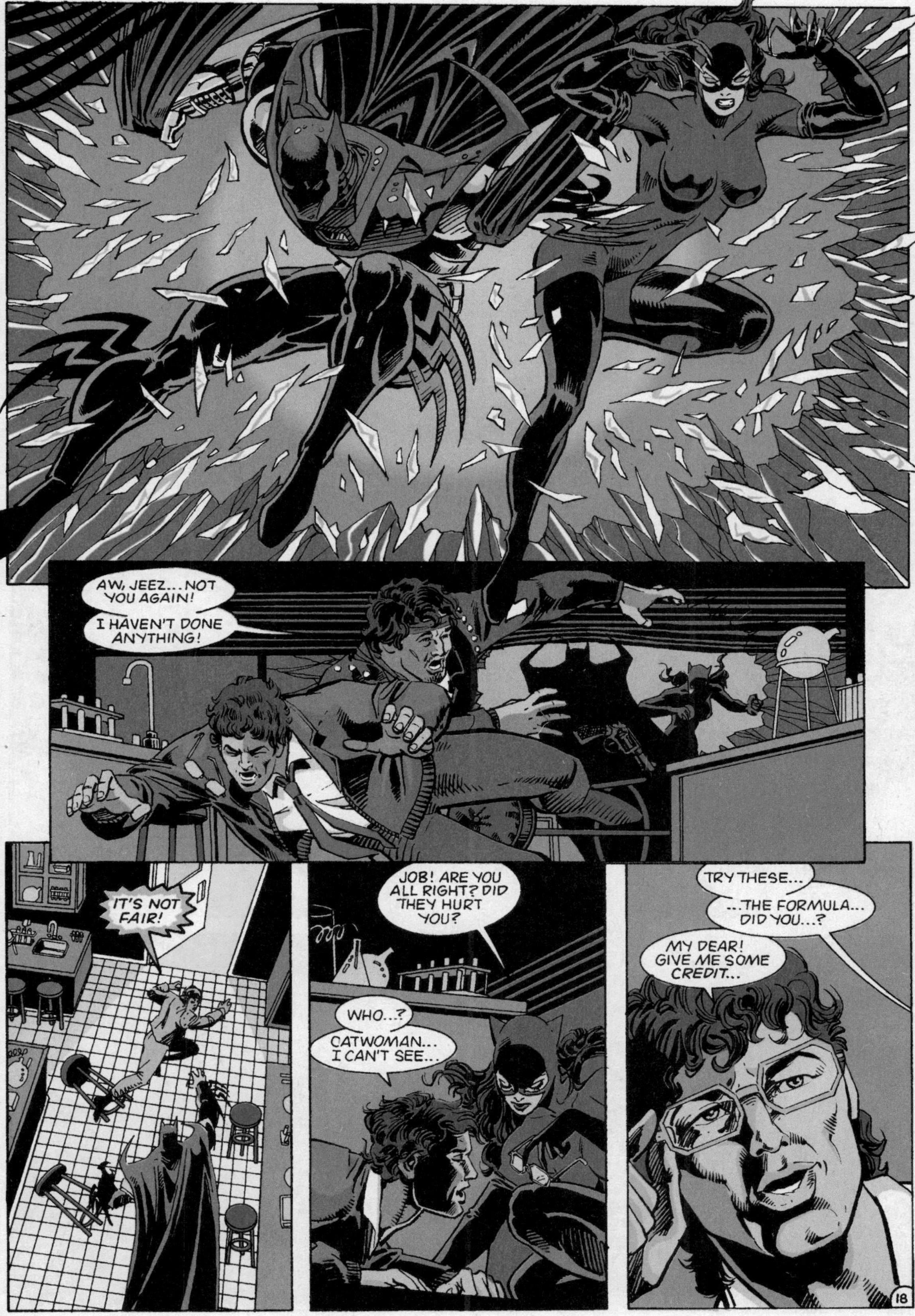
AW, JEEZ... NOT YOU AGAIN!
I HAVEN'T DONE ANYTHING!
IT'S NOT FAIR!
JOB! ARE YOU ALL RIGHT? DID THEY HURT YOU?
WHO...?
CATWOMAN... I CAN'T SEE...
TRY THESE...
...THE FORMULA... DID YOU...?
MY DEAR! GIVE ME SOME CREDIT...
18

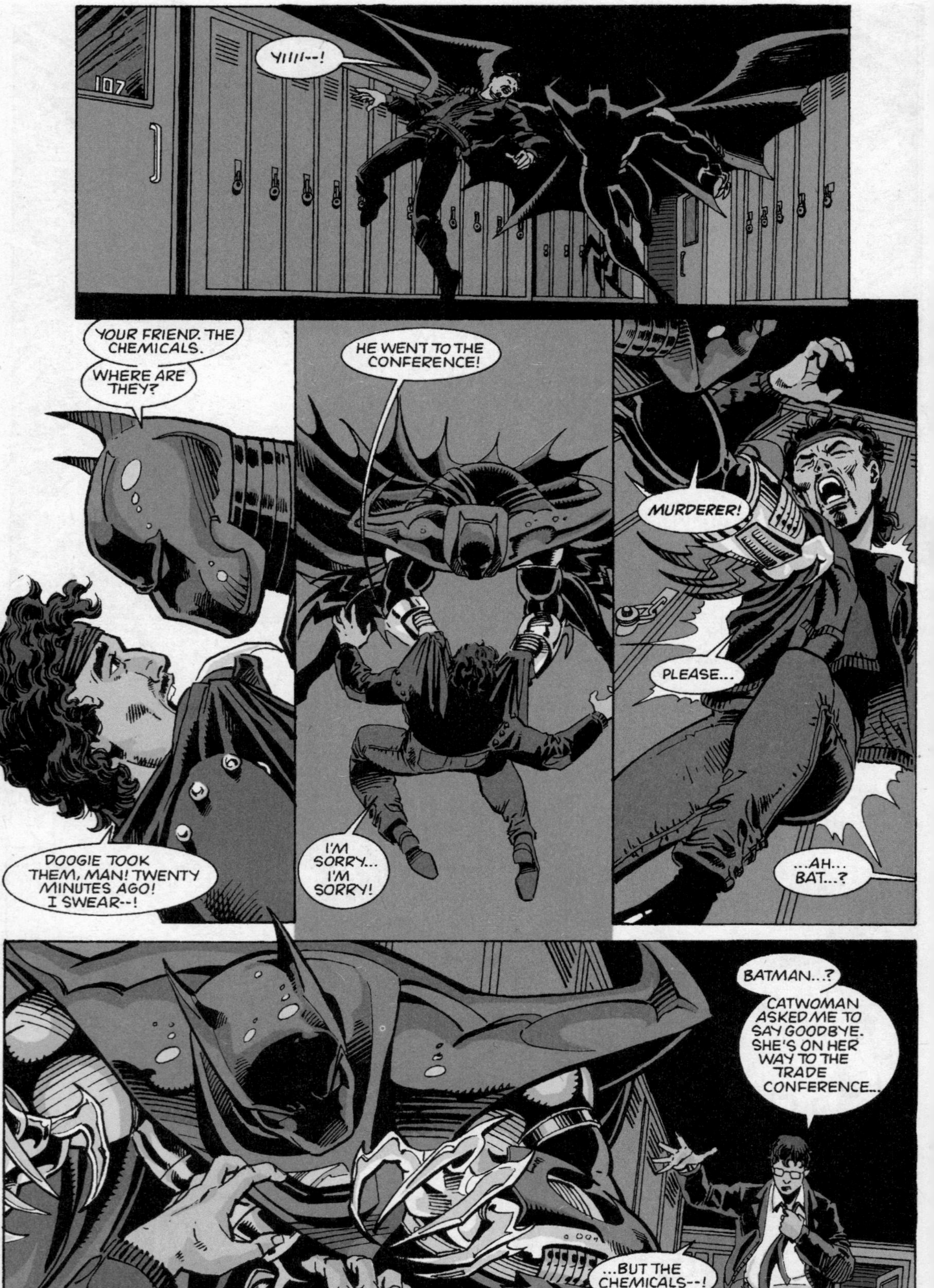
YIIII--!
YOUR FRIEND. THE CHEMICALS.
WHERE ARE THEY?
DOOGIE TOOK THEM, MAN! TWENTY MINUTES AGO! I SWEAR--!
HE WENT TO THE CONFERENCE!
I'M SORRY... I'M SORRY!
MURDERER!
PLEASE...
...AH... BAT...?
BATMAN...?
CATWOMAN ASKED ME TO SAY GOODBYE. SHE'S ON HER WAY TO THE TRADE CONFERENCE...
...BUT THE CHEMICALS--!
19

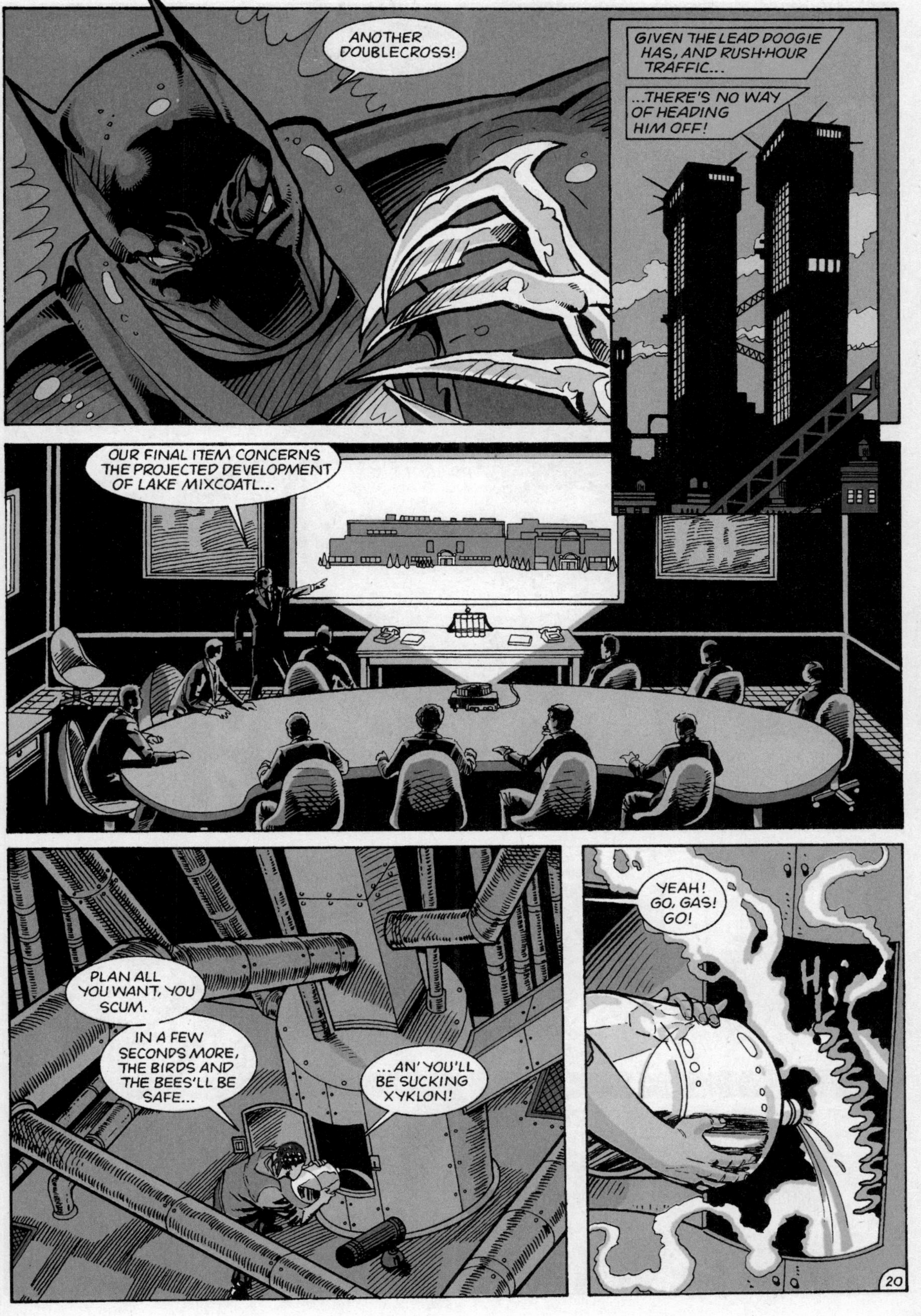
ANOTHER DOUBLECROSS!
GIVEN THE LEAD DOOGIE HAS, AND RUSH-HOUR TRAFFIC...
...THERE'S NO WAY OF HEADING HIM OFF!
OUR FINAL ITEM CONCERNS THE PROJECTED DEVELOPMENT OF LAKE MIXCOATL...
PLAN ALL YOU WANT, YOU SCUM.
IN A FEW SECONDS MORE, THE BIRDS AND THE BEES'LL BE SAFE...
...AN' YOU'LL BE SUCKING XYKLON!
YEAH! GO, GAS! GO!
20

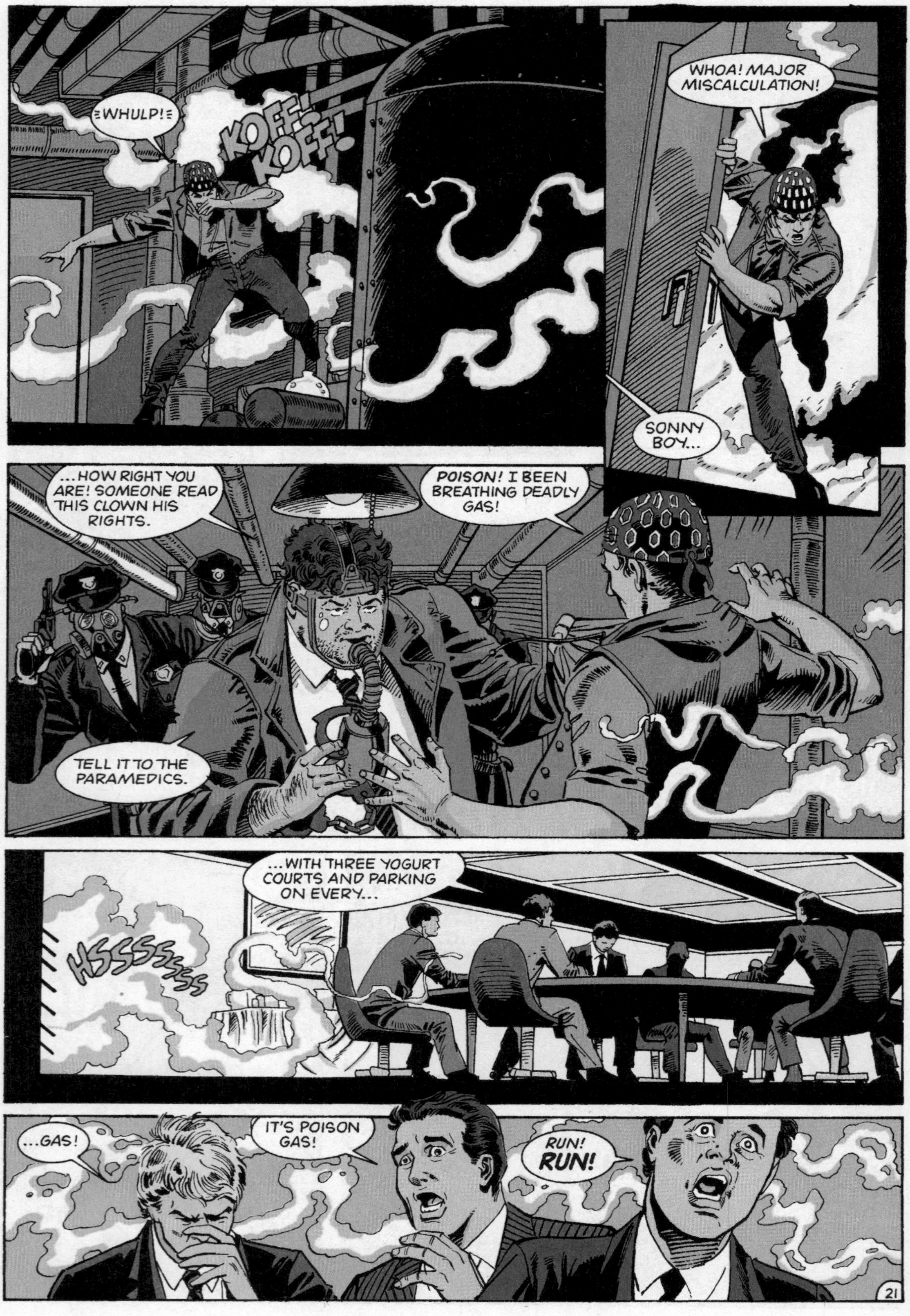
WHULP!
KOFF! KOFF!
WHOA! MAJOR MISCALCULATION!
SONNY BOY...
...HOW RIGHT YOU ARE! SOMEONE READ THIS CLOWN HIS RIGHTS.
POISON! I BEEN BREATHING DEADLY GAS!
TELL IT TO THE PARAMEDICS.
...WITH THREE YOGURT COURTS AND PARKING ON EVERY...
HSSSSSSSS
...GAS!
IT'S POISON GAS!
RUN! RUN!
21

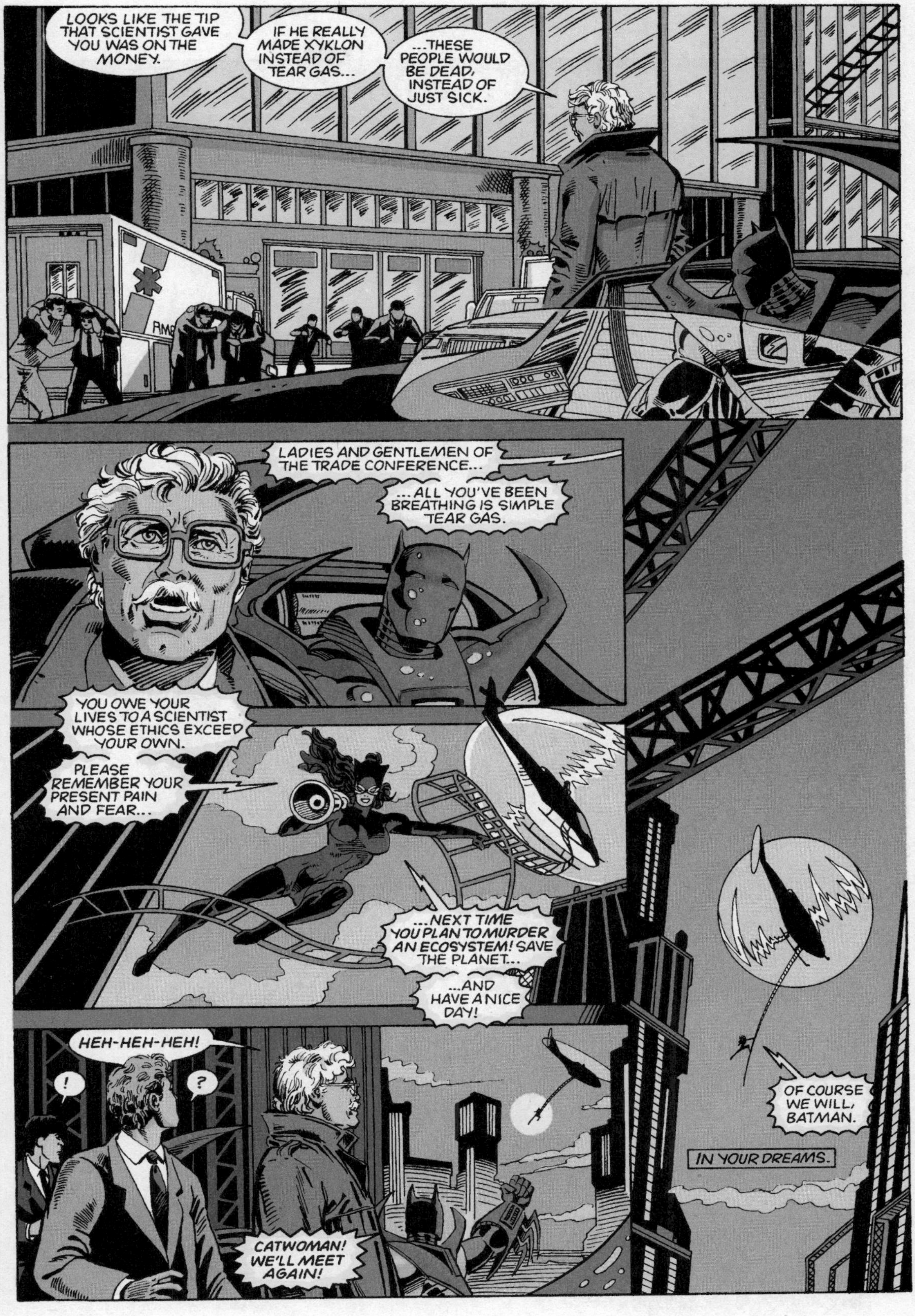
LOOKS LIKE THE TIP THAT SCIENTIST GAVE YOU WAS ON THE MONEY.
IF HE REALLY MADE XYKLON INSTEAD OF TEAR GAS...
...THESE PEOPLE WOULD BE DEAD, INSTEAD OF JUST SICK.
LADIES AND GENTLEMEN OF THE TRADE CONFERENCE...
...ALL YOU'VE BEEN BREATHING IS SIMPLE TEAR GAS.
YOU OWE YOUR LIVES TO A SCIENTIST WHOSE ETHICS EXCEED YOUR OWN.
PLEASE REMEMBER YOUR PRESENT PAIN AND FEAR...
...NEXT TIME YOU PLAN TO MURDER AN ECOSYSTEM! SAVE THE PLANET...
...AND HAVE A NICE DAY!
HEH-HEH-HEH!
!
?
CATWOMAN! WE'LL MEET AGAIN!
OF COURSE WE WILL, BATMAN.
IN YOUR DREAMS.

Cover art by KELLEY JONES

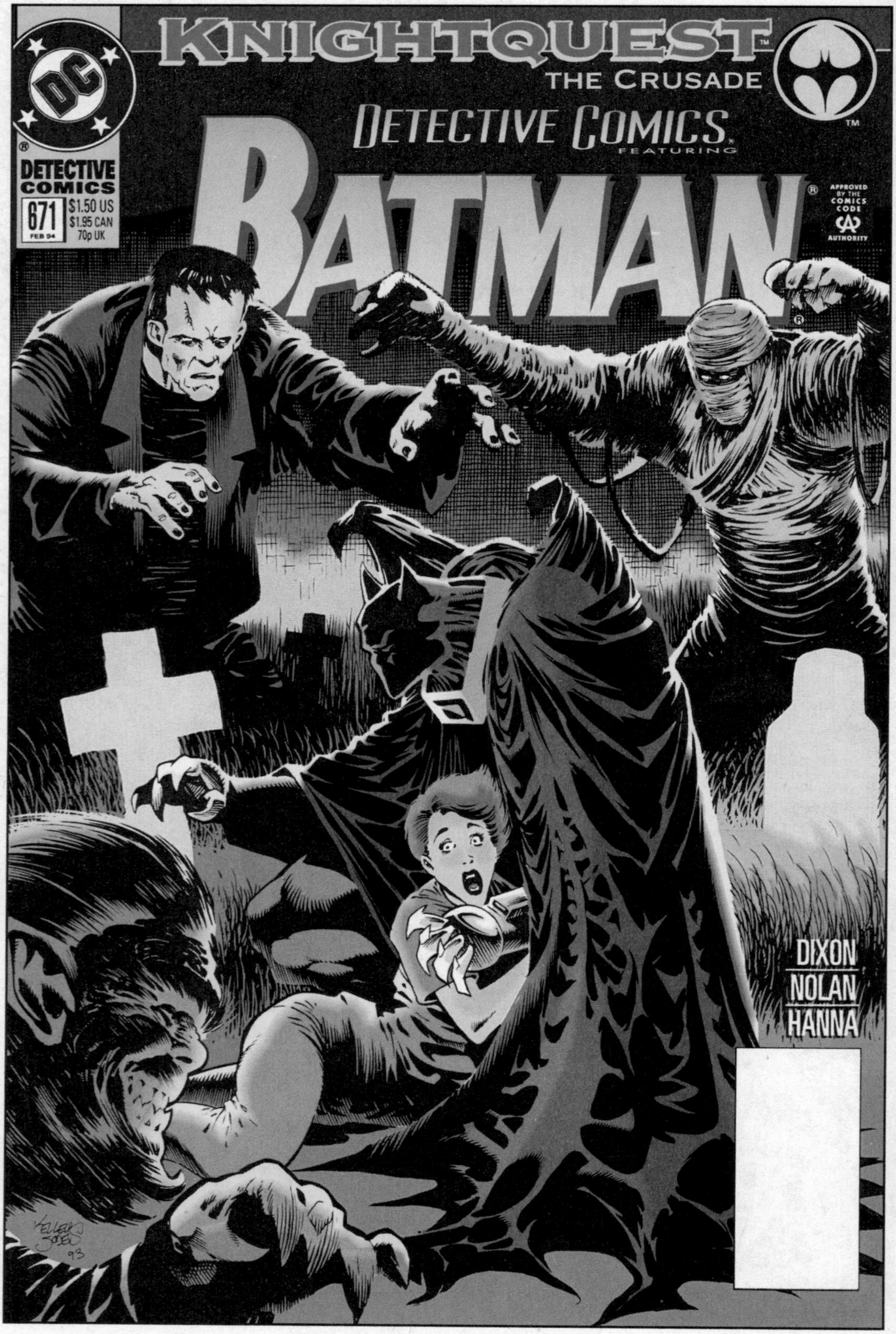

KNIGHTQUEST
THE CRUSADE
DETECTIVE COMICS
FEATURING
BATMAN
DC
DETECTIVE COMICS
671
FEB 94
$1.50 US
$1.95 CAN
70p UK
APPROVED BY THE COMICS CODE AUTHORITY
DIXON
NOLAN
HANNA

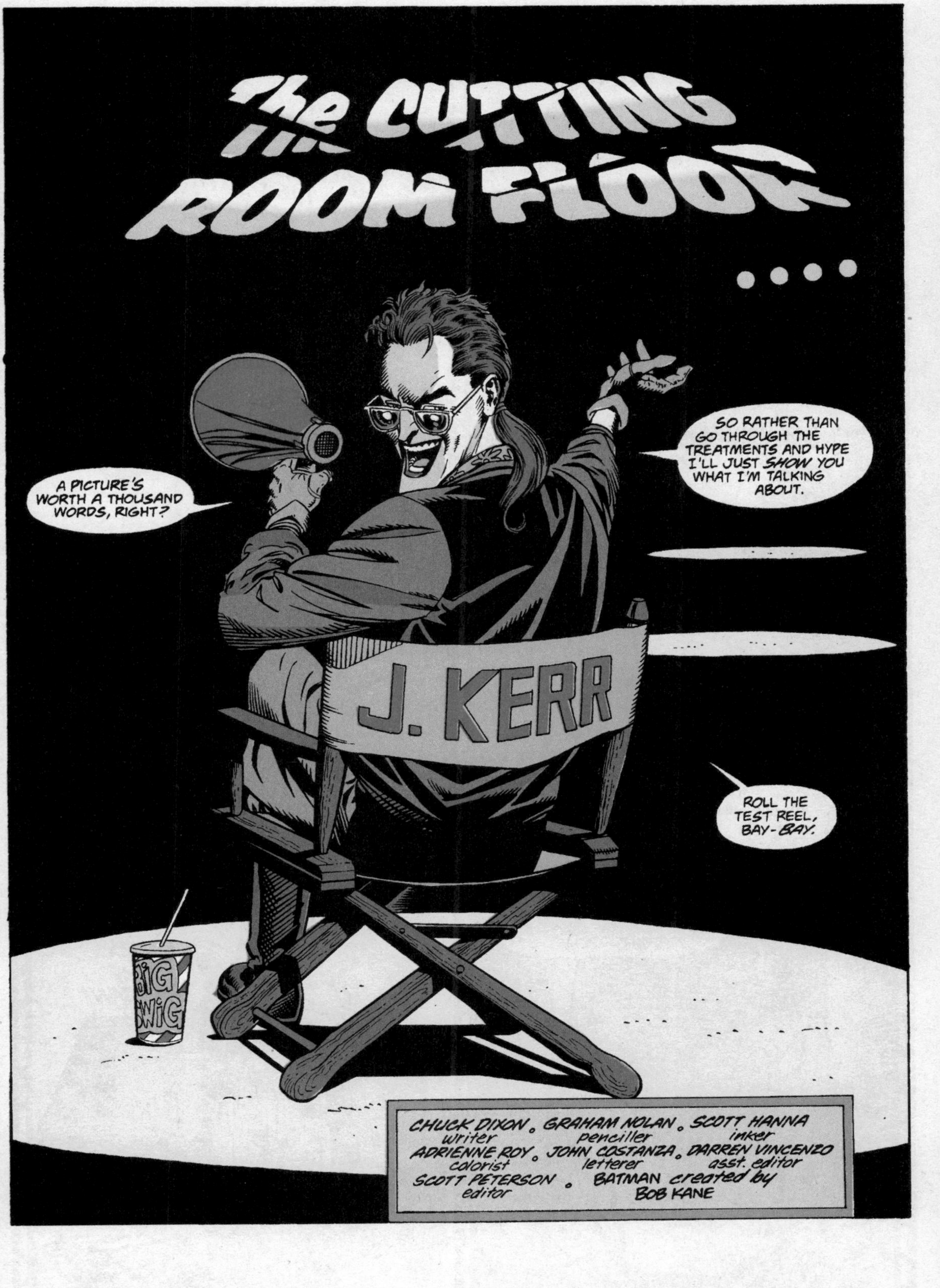
The Cutting Room Floor....
A PICTURE'S WORTH A THOUSAND WORDS, RIGHT?
SO RATHER THAN GO THROUGH THE TREATMENTS AND HYPE I'LL JUST *SHOW* YOU WHAT I'M TALKING ABOUT.
J. KERR
ROLL THE TEST REEL, BAY-*BAY*.
BIG SWIG
CHUCK DIXON writer . GRAHAM NOLAN penciller . SCOTT HANNA inker
ADRIENNE ROY colorist . JOHN COSTANZA letterer . DARREN VINCENZO asst. editor
SCOTT PETERSON editor . BATMAN created by BOB KANE

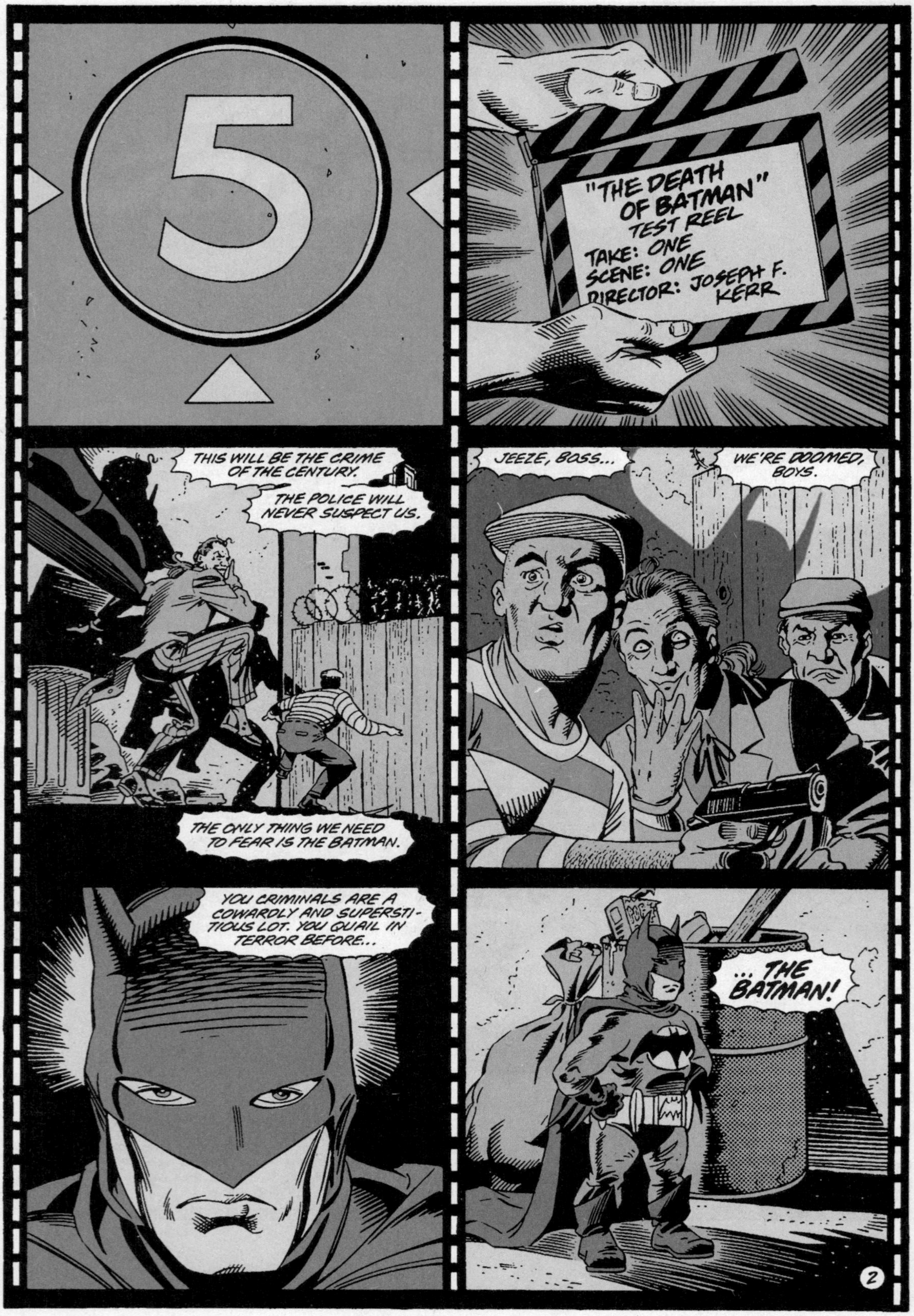
5
"THE DEATH OF BATMAN" TEST REEL
TAKE: ONE
SCENE: ONE
DIRECTOR: JOSEPH F. KERR
THIS WILL BE THE CRIME OF THE CENTURY.
THE POLICE WILL NEVER SUSPECT US.
THE ONLY THING WE NEED TO FEAR IS THE BATMAN.
JEEZE, BOSS...
WE'RE DOOMED, BOYS.
YOU CRIMINALS ARE A COWARDLY AND SUPERSTI-TIOUS LOT. YOU QUAIL IN TERROR BEFORE...
...THE BATMAN!
2

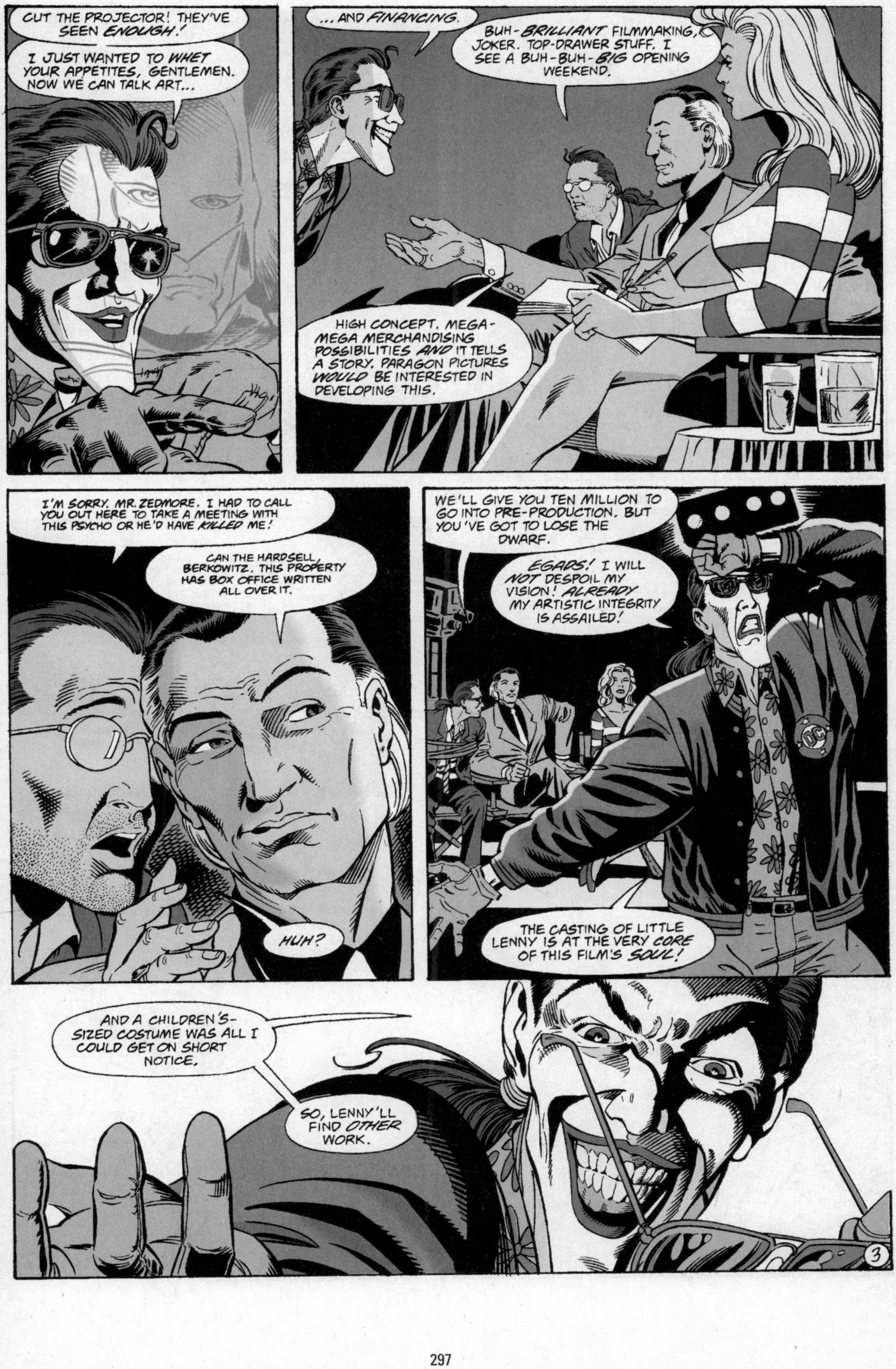
CUT THE PROJECTOR! THEY'VE SEEN ENOUGH!
I JUST WANTED TO WHET YOUR APPETITES, GENTLEMEN. NOW WE CAN TALK ART...
...AND FINANCING.
BUH-BRILLIANT FILMMAKING, JOKER. TOP-DRAWER STUFF. I SEE A BUH-BUH-BIG OPENING WEEKEND.
HIGH CONCEPT. MEGA-MEGA MERCHANDISING POSSIBILITIES AND IT TELLS A STORY. PARAGON PICTURES WOULD BE INTERESTED IN DEVELOPING THIS.
I'M SORRY, MR. ZEDMORE. I HAD TO CALL YOU OUT HERE TO TAKE A MEETING WITH THIS PSYCHO OR HE'D HAVE KILLED ME!
CAN THE HARDSELL, BERKOWITZ. THIS PROPERTY HAS BOX OFFICE WRITTEN ALL OVER IT.
HUH?
WE'LL GIVE YOU TEN MILLION TO GO INTO PRE-PRODUCTION. BUT YOU'VE GOT TO LOSE THE DWARF.
EGADS! I WILL NOT DESPOIL MY VISION! ALREADY MY ARTISTIC INTEGRITY IS ASSAILED!
THE CASTING OF LITTLE LENNY IS AT THE VERY CORE OF THIS FILM'S SOUL!
AND A CHILDREN'S-SIZED COSTUME WAS ALL I COULD GET ON SHORT NOTICE.
SO, LENNY'LL FIND OTHER WORK.
3

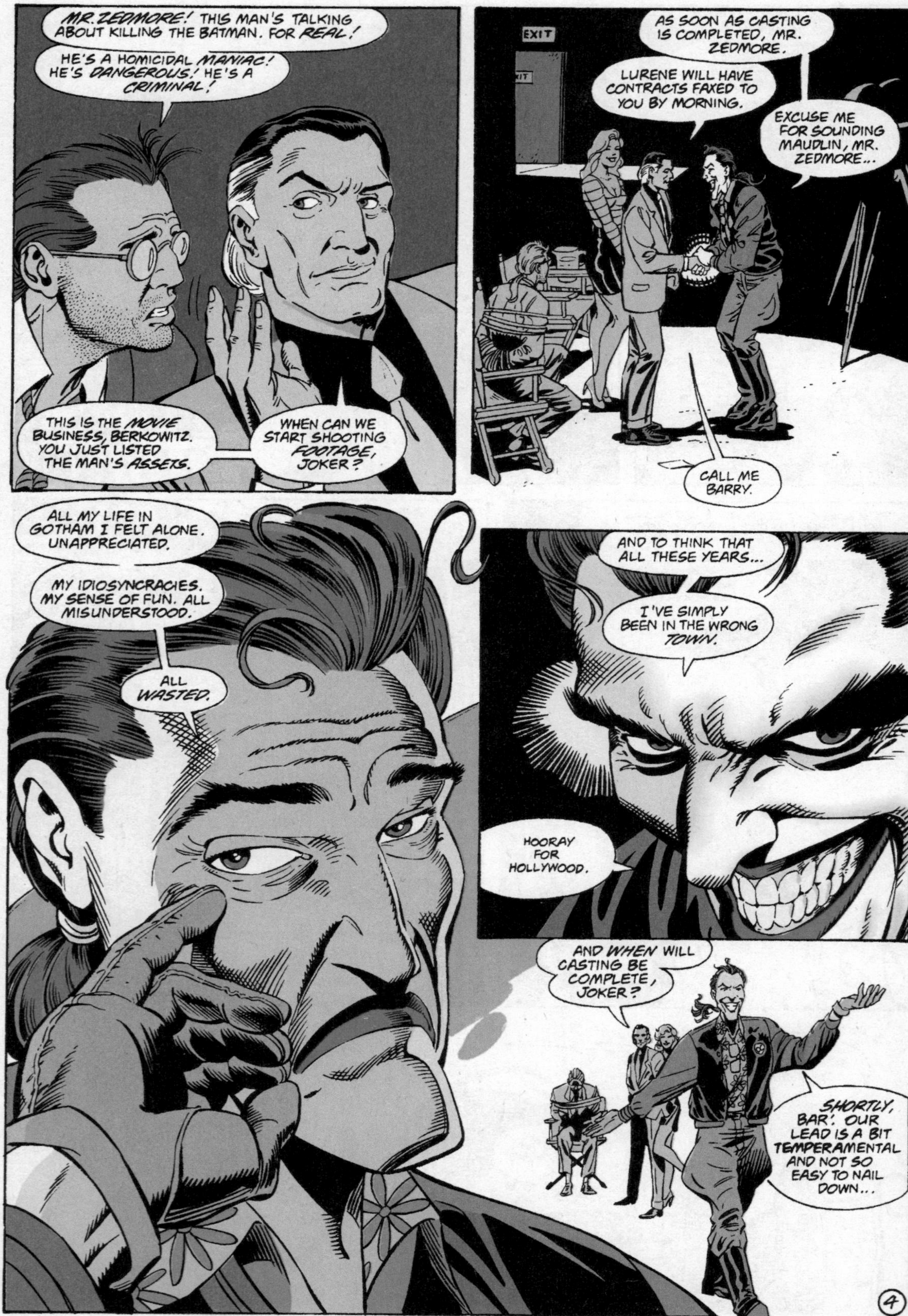
MR. ZEDMORE! THIS MAN'S TALKING ABOUT KILLING THE BATMAN. FOR REAL!
HE'S A HOMICIDAL MANIAC! HE'S DANGEROUS! HE'S A CRIMINAL!
THIS IS THE MOVIE BUSINESS, BERKOWITZ. YOU JUST LISTED THE MAN'S ASSETS.
WHEN CAN WE START SHOOTING FOOTAGE, JOKER?
EXIT
AS SOON AS CASTING IS COMPLETED, MR. ZEDMORE.
LURENE WILL HAVE CONTRACTS FAXED TO YOU BY MORNING.
EXCUSE ME FOR SOUNDING MAUDLIN, MR. ZEDMORE...
CALL ME BARRY.
ALL MY LIFE IN GOTHAM I FELT ALONE. UNAPPRECIATED.
MY IDIOSYNCRACIES. MY SENSE OF FUN. ALL MISUNDERSTOOD.
ALL WASTED.
AND TO THINK THAT ALL THESE YEARS...
I'VE SIMPLY BEEN IN THE WRONG TOWN.
HOORAY FOR HOLLYWOOD.
AND WHEN WILL CASTING BE COMPLETE, JOKER?
SHORTLY, BAR. OUR LEAD IS A BIT TEMPERAMENTAL AND NOT SO EASY TO NAIL DOWN...
4

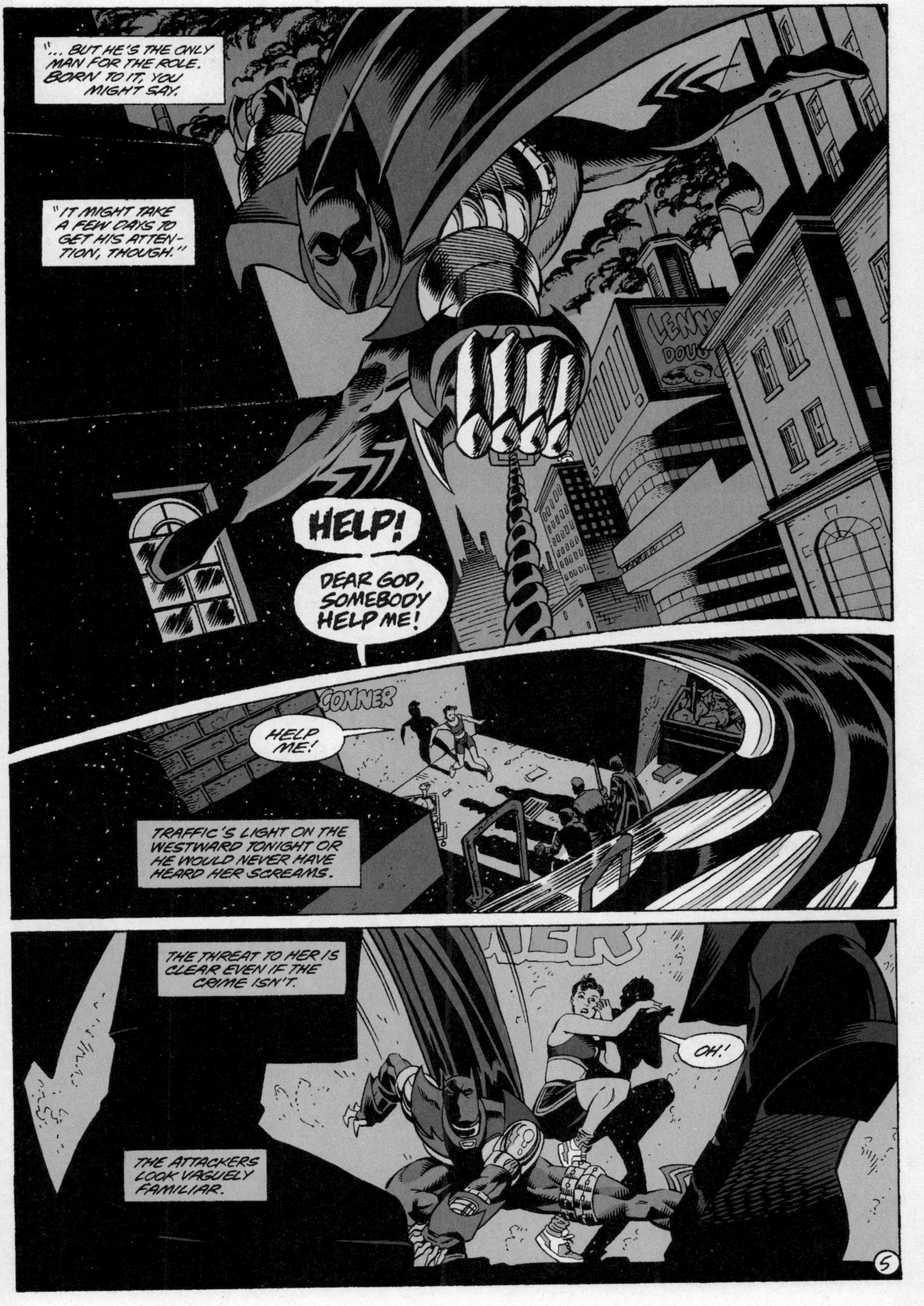
"... BUT HE'S THE ONLY MAN FOR THE ROLE. BORN TO IT, YOU MIGHT SAY.
"IT MIGHT TAKE A FEW DAYS TO GET HIS ATTENTION, THOUGH."
HELP!
DEAR GOD, SOMEBODY HELP ME!
CONNER
HELP ME!
TRAFFIC'S LIGHT ON THE WESTWARD TONIGHT OR HE WOULD NEVER HAVE HEARD HER SCREAMS.
THE THREAT TO HER IS CLEAR EVEN IF THE CRIME ISN'T.
OH!
THE ATTACKERS LOOK VAGUELY FAMILIAR.
5

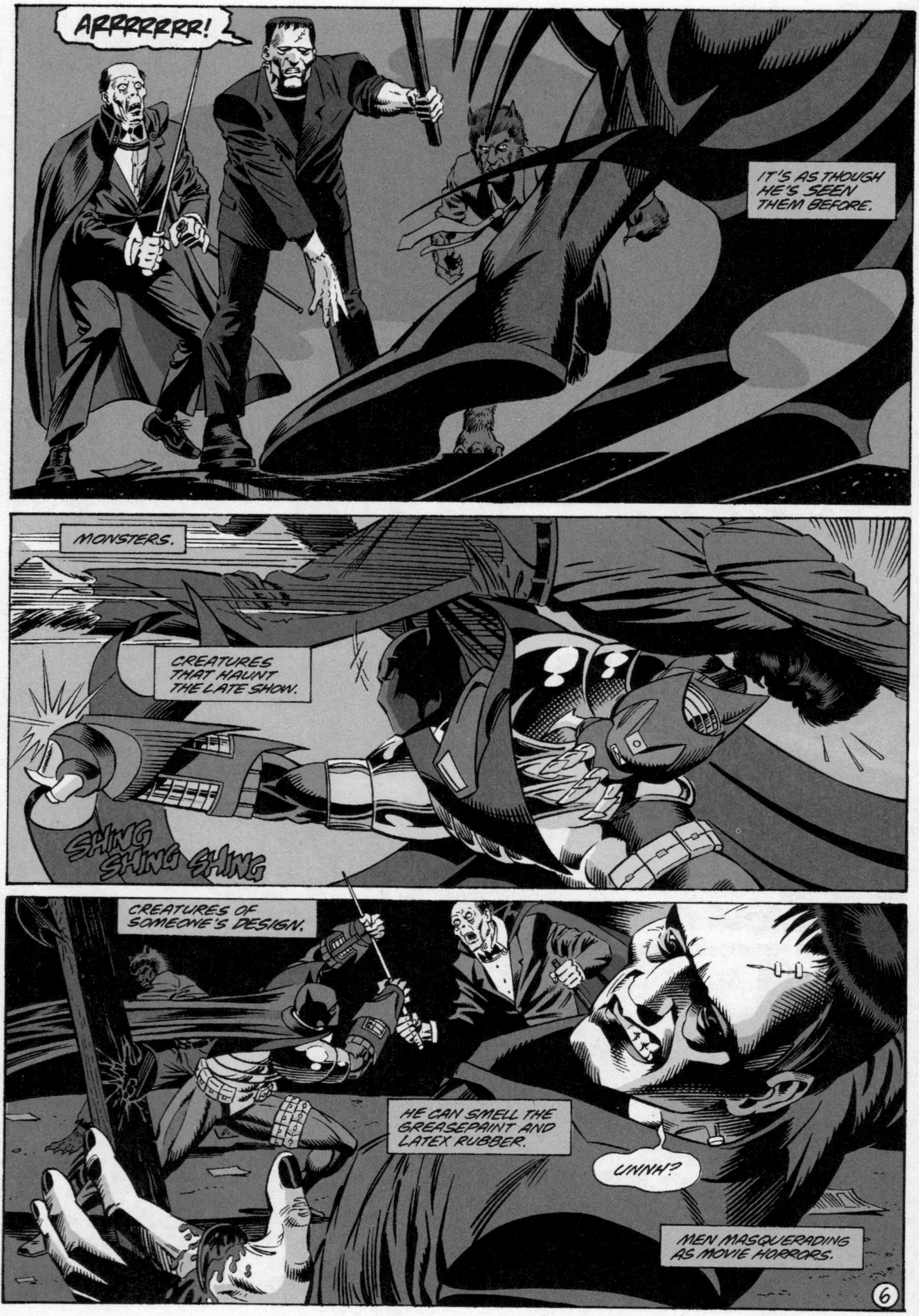
ARRRRRRR!
IT'S AS THOUGH HE'S SEEN THEM BEFORE.
MONSTERS.
CREATURES THAT HAUNT THE LATE SHOW.
SHING SHING SHING
CREATURES OF SOMEONE'S DESIGN.
HE CAN SMELL THE GREASEPAINT AND LATEX RUBBER.
UNNH?
MEN MASQUERADING AS MOVIE HORRORS.
6

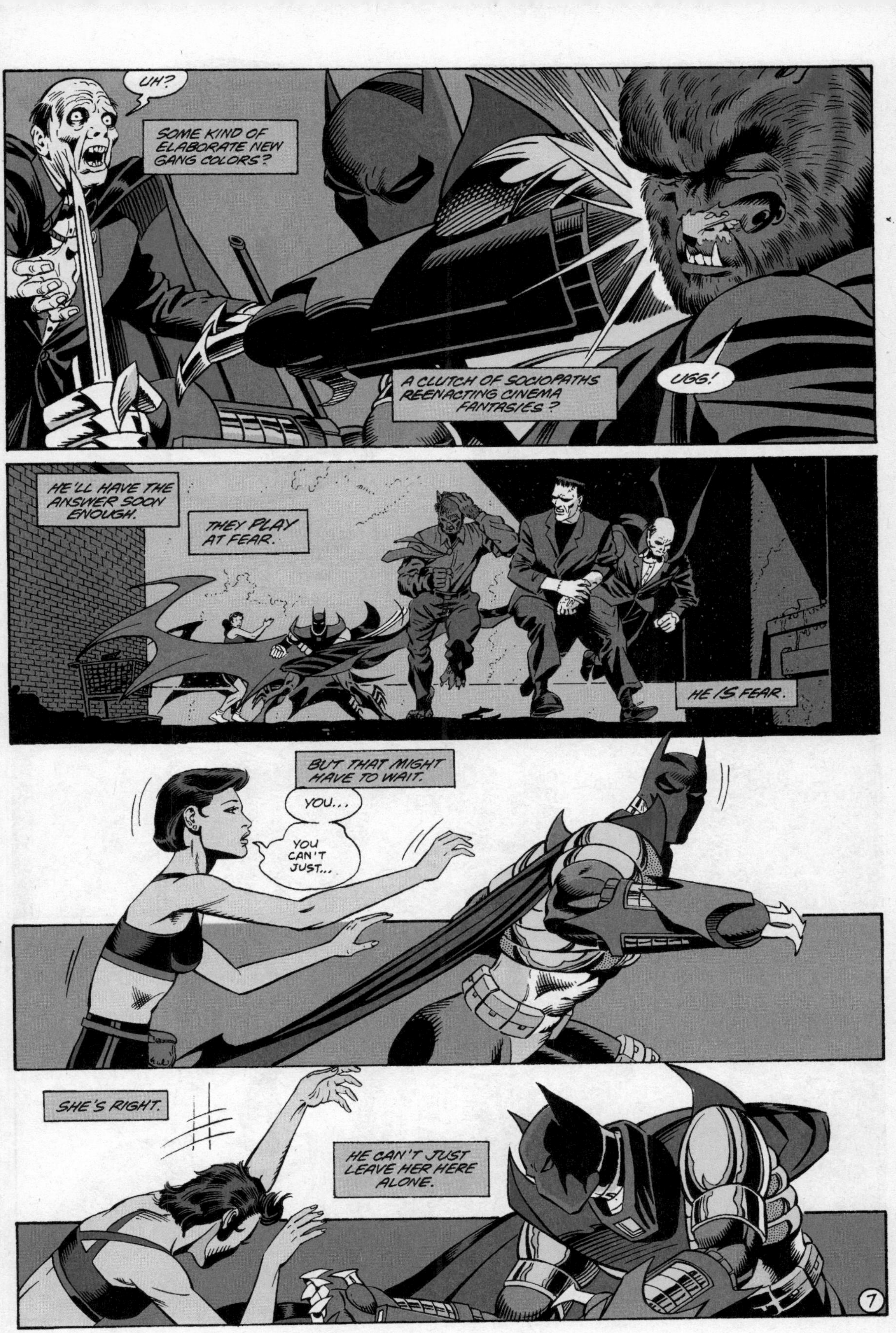
UH?
SOME KIND OF ELABORATE NEW GANG COLORS?
A CLUTCH OF SOCIOPATHS REENACTING CINEMA FANTASIES?
UGG!
HE'LL HAVE THE ANSWER SOON ENOUGH.
THEY PLAY AT FEAR.
HE IS FEAR.
BUT THAT MIGHT HAVE TO WAIT.
YOU...
YOU CAN'T JUST...
SHE'S RIGHT.
HE CAN'T JUST LEAVE HER HERE ALONE.
7

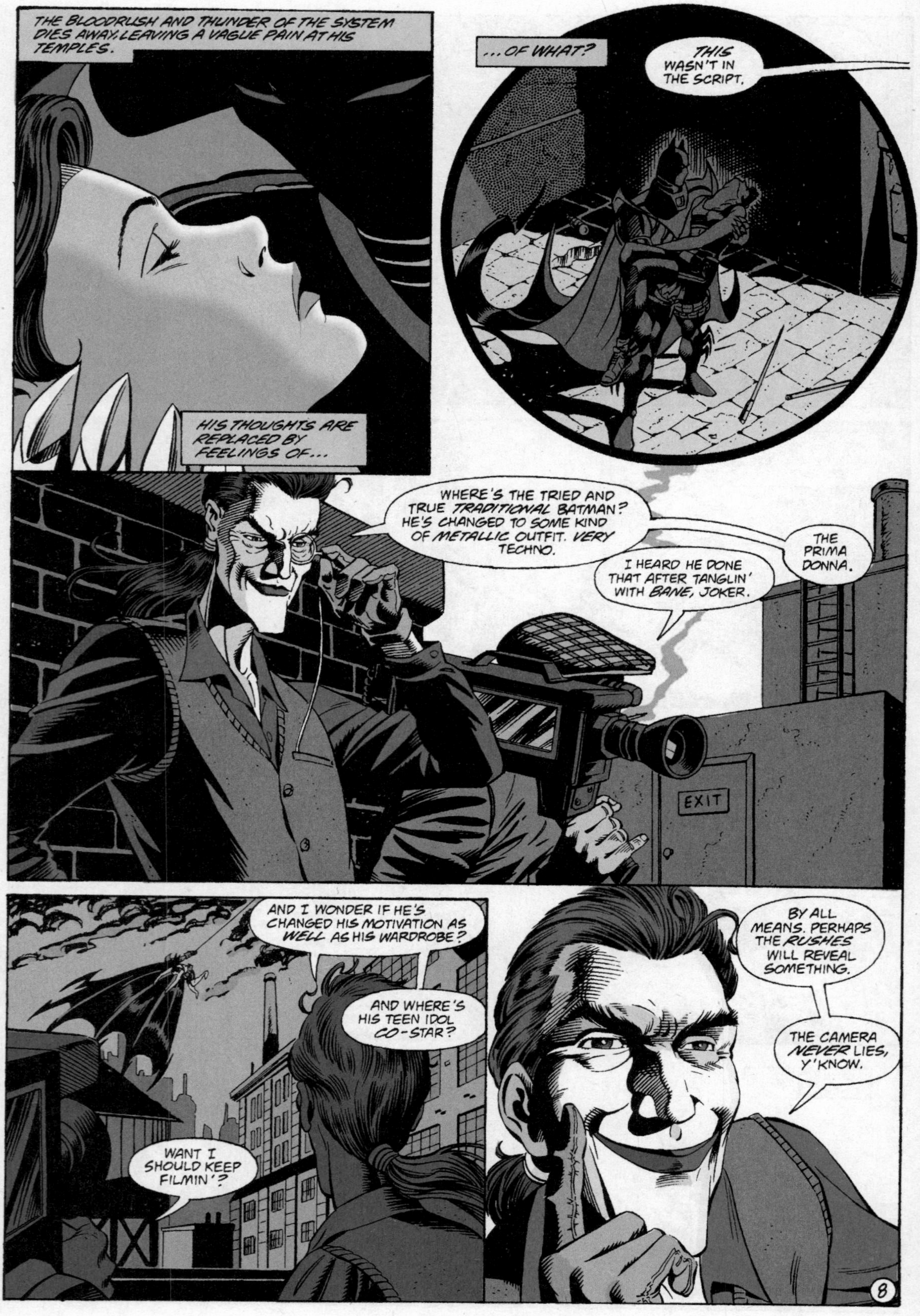
THE BLOODRUSH AND THUNDER OF THE SYSTEM DIES AWAY, LEAVING A VAGUE PAIN AT HIS TEMPLES.
HIS THOUGHTS ARE REPLACED BY FEELINGS OF...
...OF WHAT?
THIS WASN'T IN THE SCRIPT.
WHERE'S THE TRIED AND TRUE TRADITIONAL BATMAN? HE'S CHANGED TO SOME KIND OF METALLIC OUTFIT. VERY TECHNO.
THE PRIMA DONNA.
I HEARD HE DONE THAT AFTER TANGLIN' WITH BANE, JOKER.
EXIT
AND I WONDER IF HE'S CHANGED HIS MOTIVATION AS WELL AS HIS WARDROBE?
AND WHERE'S HIS TEEN IDOL CO-STAR?
WANT I SHOULD KEEP FILMIN'?
BY ALL MEANS. PERHAPS THE RUSHES WILL REVEAL SOMETHING.
THE CAMERA NEVER LIES, Y'KNOW.
8

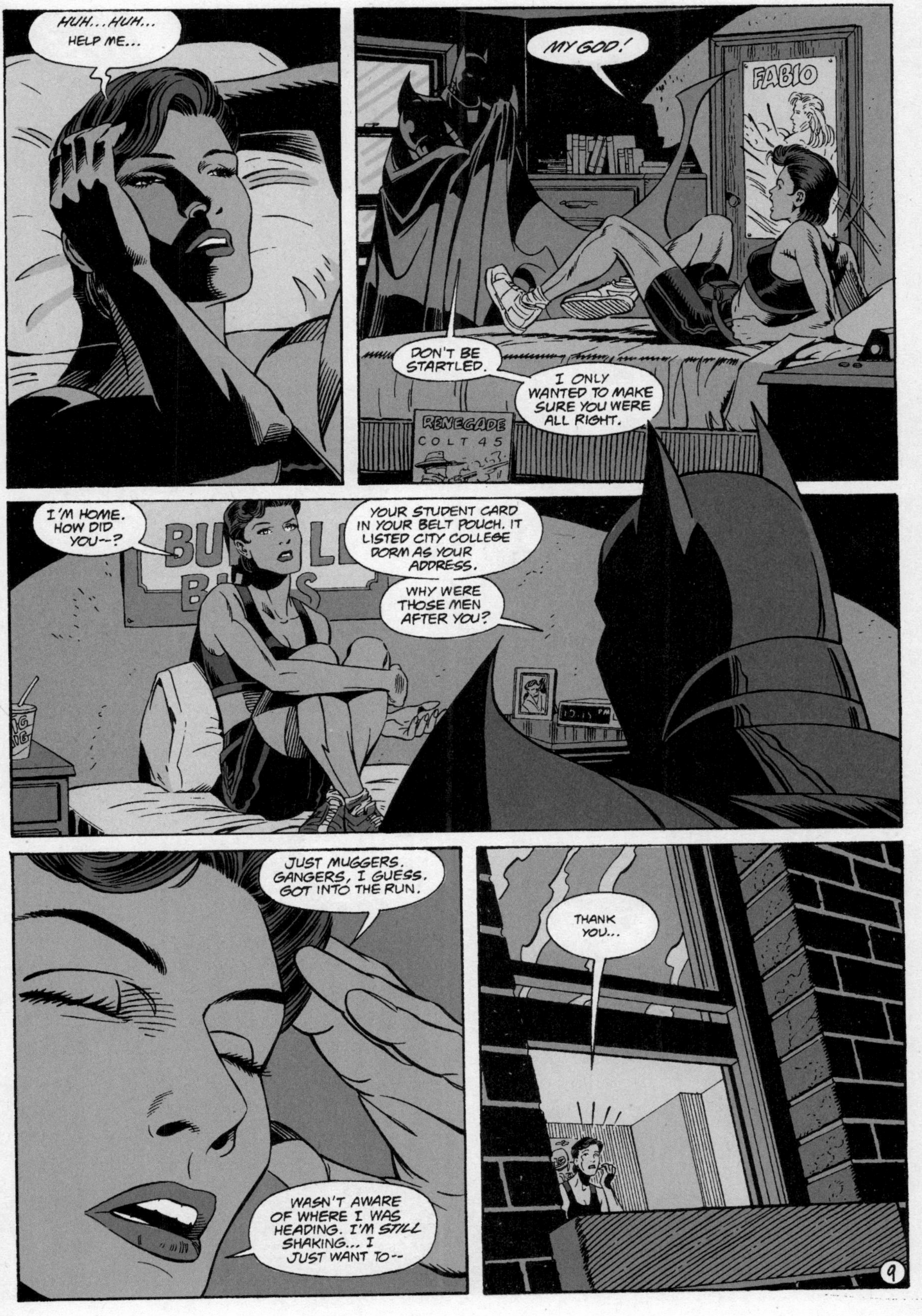
HUH...HUH...
HELP ME...
MY GOD!
FABIO
DON'T BE STARTLED.
I ONLY WANTED TO MAKE SURE YOU WERE ALL RIGHT.
RENEGADE
COLT 45
I'M HOME. HOW DID YOU--?
YOUR STUDENT CARD IN YOUR BELT POUCH. IT LISTED CITY COLLEGE DORM AS YOUR ADDRESS.
WHY WERE THOSE MEN AFTER YOU?
JUST MUGGERS. GANGERS, I GUESS. GOT INTO THE RUN.
WASN'T AWARE OF WHERE I WAS HEADING. I'M *STILL* SHAKING... I JUST WANT TO--
THANK YOU...
9

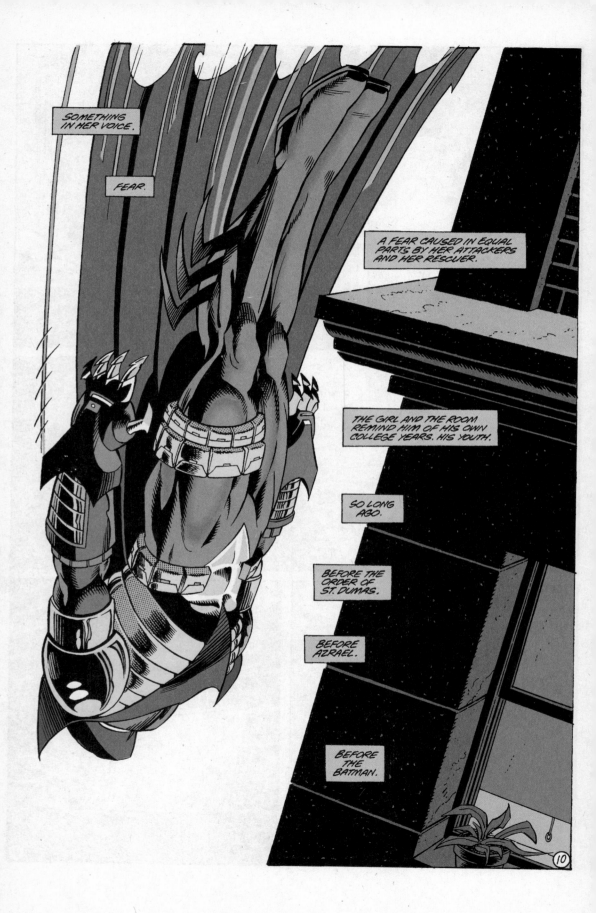

SOMETHING IN HER VOICE.

FEAR.

A FEAR CAUSED IN EQUAL PARTS BY HER ATTACKERS AND HER RESCUER.

THE GIRL AND THE ROOM REMIND HIM OF HIS OWN COLLEGE YEARS. HIS YOUTH.

SO LONG AGO.

BEFORE THE ORDER OF ST. DUMAS.

BEFORE AZRAEL.

BEFORE THE BATMAN.

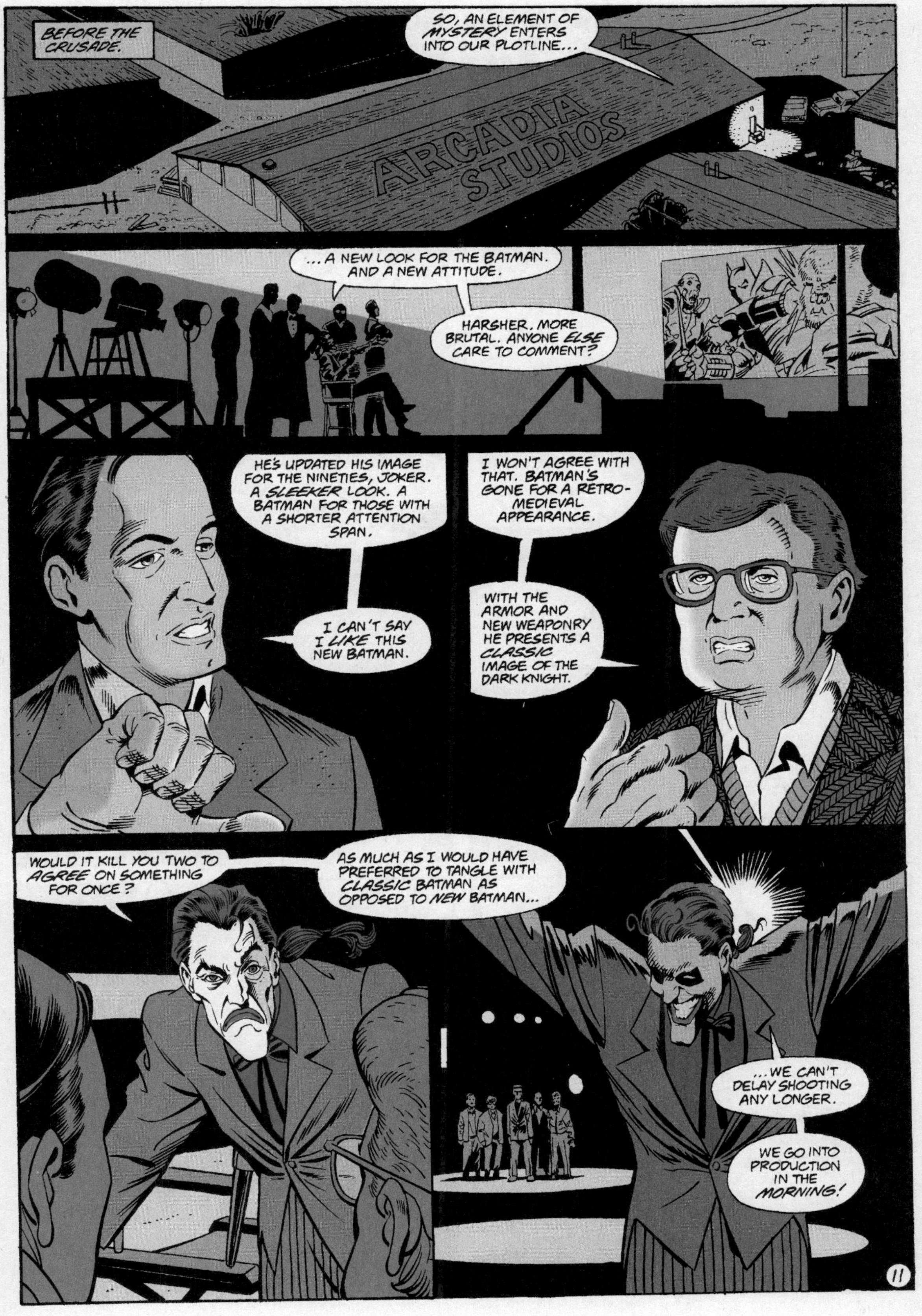
BEFORE THE CRUSADE.
SO, AN ELEMENT OF MYSTERY ENTERS INTO OUR PLOTLINE...
ARCADIA STUDIOS
...A NEW LOOK FOR THE BATMAN. AND A NEW ATTITUDE.
HARSHER. MORE BRUTAL. ANYONE ELSE CARE TO COMMENT?
HE'S UPDATED HIS IMAGE FOR THE NINETIES, JOKER. A SLEEKER LOOK. A BATMAN FOR THOSE WITH A SHORTER ATTENTION SPAN.
I CAN'T SAY I LIKE THIS NEW BATMAN.
I WON'T AGREE WITH THAT. BATMAN'S GONE FOR A RETRO-MEDIEVAL APPEARANCE.
WITH THE ARMOR AND NEW WEAPONRY HE PRESENTS A CLASSIC IMAGE OF THE DARK KNIGHT.
WOULD IT KILL YOU TWO TO AGREE ON SOMETHING FOR ONCE?
AS MUCH AS I WOULD HAVE PREFERRED TO TANGLE WITH CLASSIC BATMAN AS OPPOSED TO NEW BATMAN...
...WE CAN'T DELAY SHOOTING ANY LONGER.
WE GO INTO PRODUCTION IN THE MORNING!
11

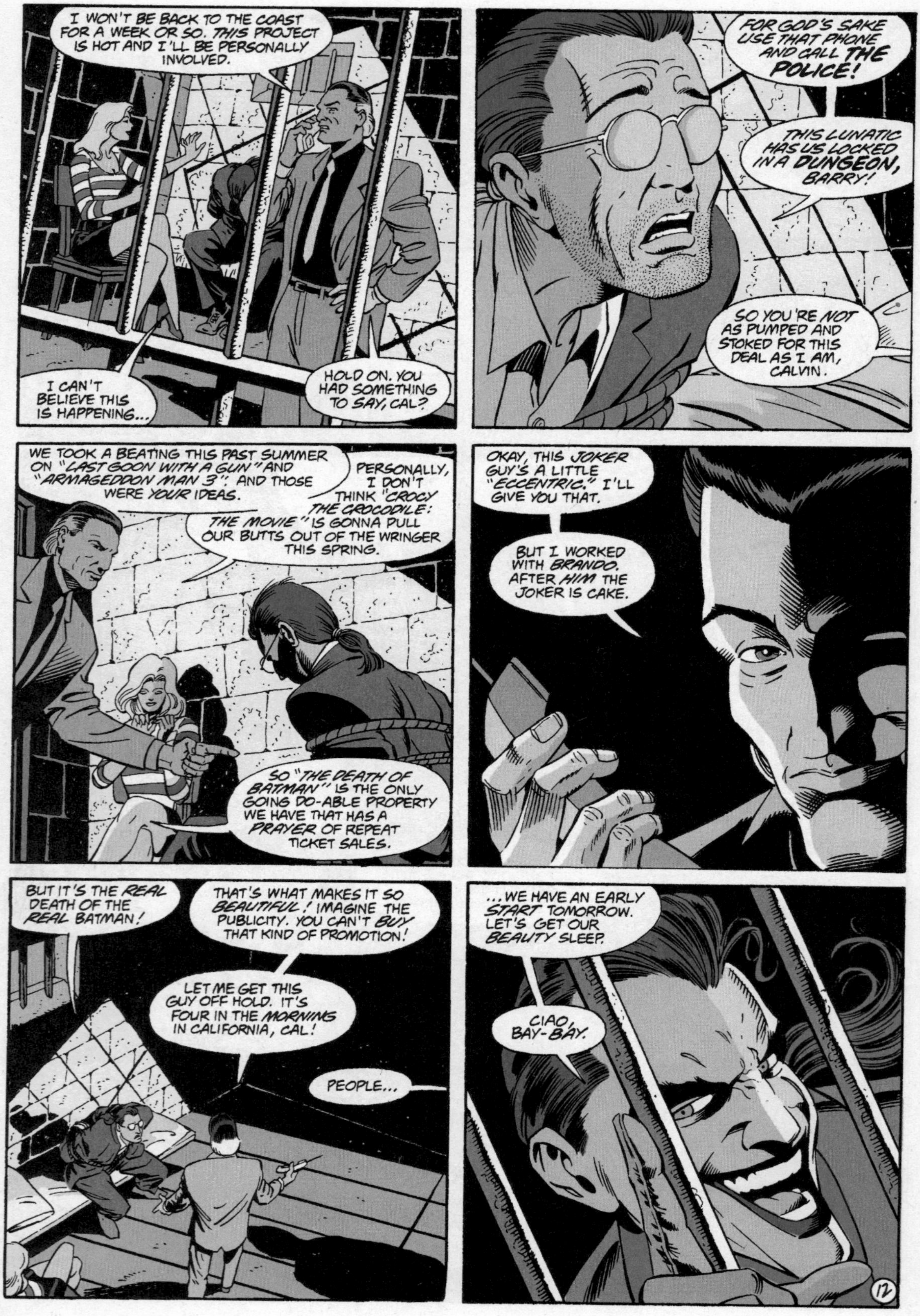

I WON'T BE BACK TO THE COAST FOR A WEEK OR SO. THIS PROJECT IS HOT AND I'LL BE PERSONALLY INVOLVED.
I CAN'T BELIEVE THIS IS HAPPENING...
HOLD ON. YOU HAD SOMETHING TO SAY, CAL?
FOR GOD'S SAKE USE THAT PHONE AND CALL THE POLICE!
THIS LUNATIC HAS US LOCKED IN A DUNGEON, BARRY!
SO YOU'RE NOT AS PUMPED AND STOKED FOR THIS DEAL AS I AM, CALVIN.
WE TOOK A BEATING THIS PAST SUMMER ON "LAST GOON WITH A GUN" AND "ARMAGEDDON MAN 3". AND THOSE WERE YOUR IDEAS.
PERSONALLY, I DON'T THINK "CROCY THE CROCODILE: THE MOVIE" IS GONNA PULL OUR BUTTS OUT OF THE WRINGER THIS SPRING.
SO "THE DEATH OF BATMAN" IS THE ONLY GOING DO-ABLE PROPERTY WE HAVE THAT HAS A PRAYER OF REPEAT TICKET SALES.
OKAY, THIS JOKER GUY'S A LITTLE "ECCENTRIC." I'LL GIVE YOU THAT.
BUT I WORKED WITH BRANDO. AFTER HIM THE JOKER IS CAKE.
BUT IT'S THE REAL DEATH OF THE REAL BATMAN!
THAT'S WHAT MAKES IT SO BEAUTIFUL! IMAGINE THE PUBLICITY. YOU CAN'T BUY THAT KIND OF PROMOTION!
LET ME GET THIS GUY OFF HOLD. IT'S FOUR IN THE MORNING IN CALIFORNIA, CAL!
PEOPLE...
...WE HAVE AN EARLY START TOMORROW. LET'S GET OUR BEAUTY SLEEP.
CIAO, BAY-BAY.
12

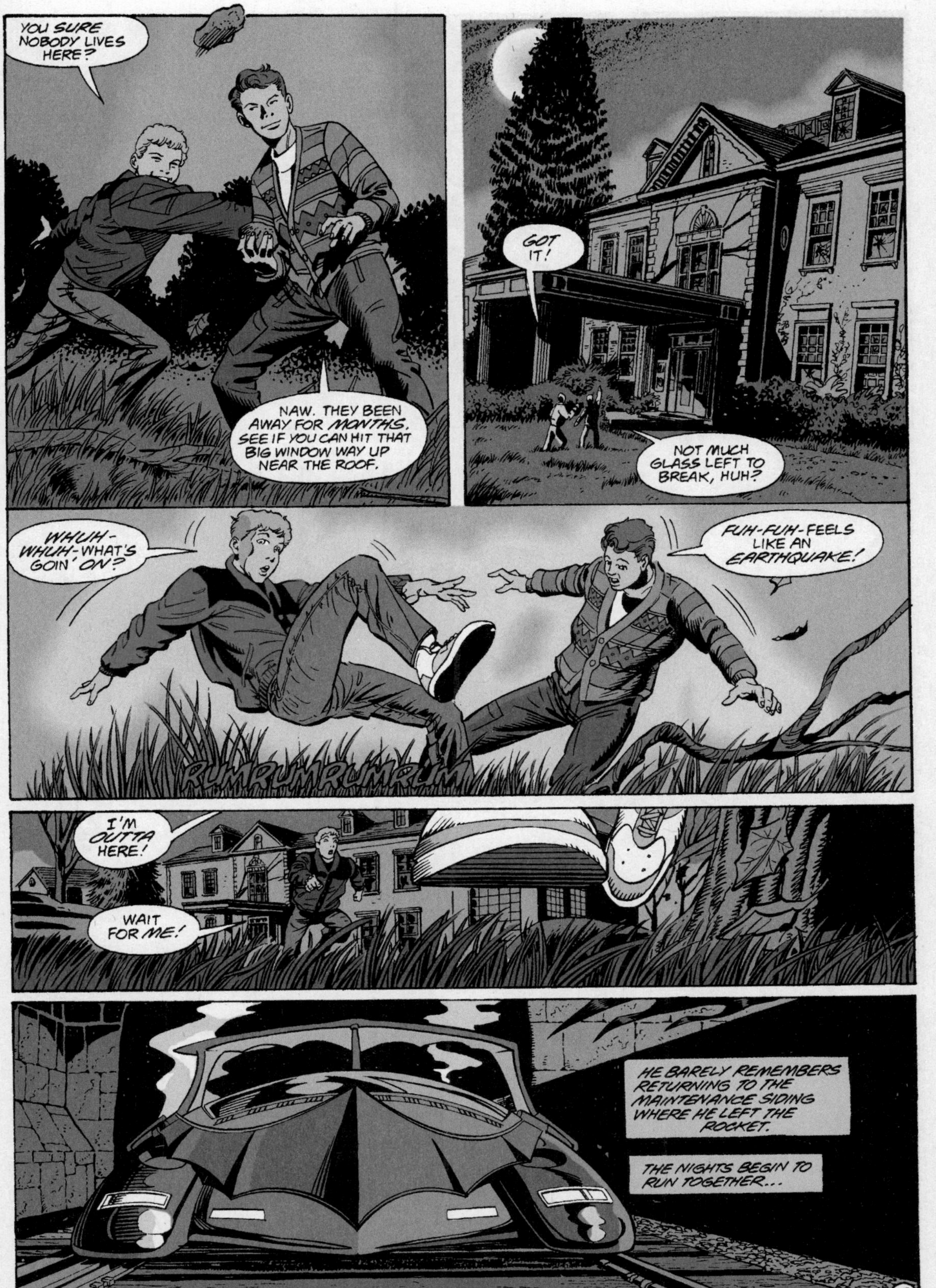
YOU SURE NOBODY LIVES HERE?
NAW. THEY BEEN AWAY FOR MONTHS. SEE IF YOU CAN HIT THAT BIG WINDOW WAY UP NEAR THE ROOF.
GOT IT!
NOT MUCH GLASS LEFT TO BREAK, HUH?
WHUH-WHUH-WHAT'S GOIN' ON?
FUH-FUH-FEELS LIKE AN EARTHQUAKE!
RUMRUMRUMRUM
I'M OUTTA HERE!
WAIT FOR ME!
HE BARELY REMEMBERS RETURNING TO THE MAINTENANCE SIDING WHERE HE LEFT THE ROCKET.
THE NIGHTS BEGIN TO RUN TOGETHER...
13

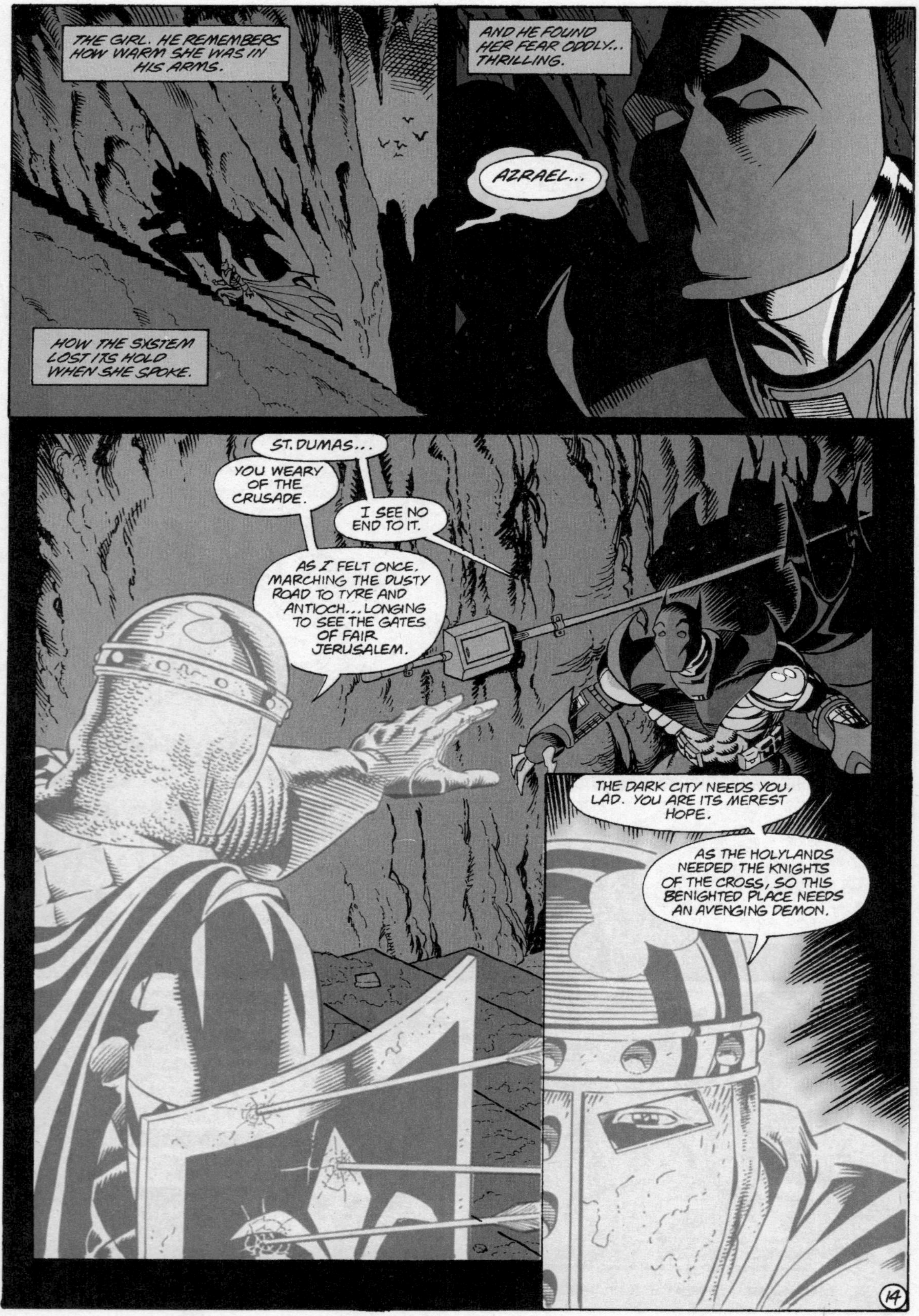
THE GIRL. HE REMEMBERS HOW WARM SHE WAS IN HIS ARMS.
HOW THE SYSTEM LOST ITS HOLD WHEN SHE SPOKE.
AND HE FOUND HER FEAR ODDLY... THRILLING.
AZRAEL...
ST. DUMAS...
YOU WEARY OF THE CRUSADE.
I SEE NO END TO IT.
AS I FELT ONCE, MARCHING THE DUSTY ROAD TO TYRE AND ANTIOCH... LONGING TO SEE THE GATES OF FAIR JERUSALEM.
THE DARK CITY NEEDS YOU, LAD. YOU ARE ITS MEREST HOPE.
AS THE HOLYLANDS NEEDED THE KNIGHTS OF THE CROSS, SO THIS BENIGHTED PLACE NEEDS AN AVENGING DEMON.
14

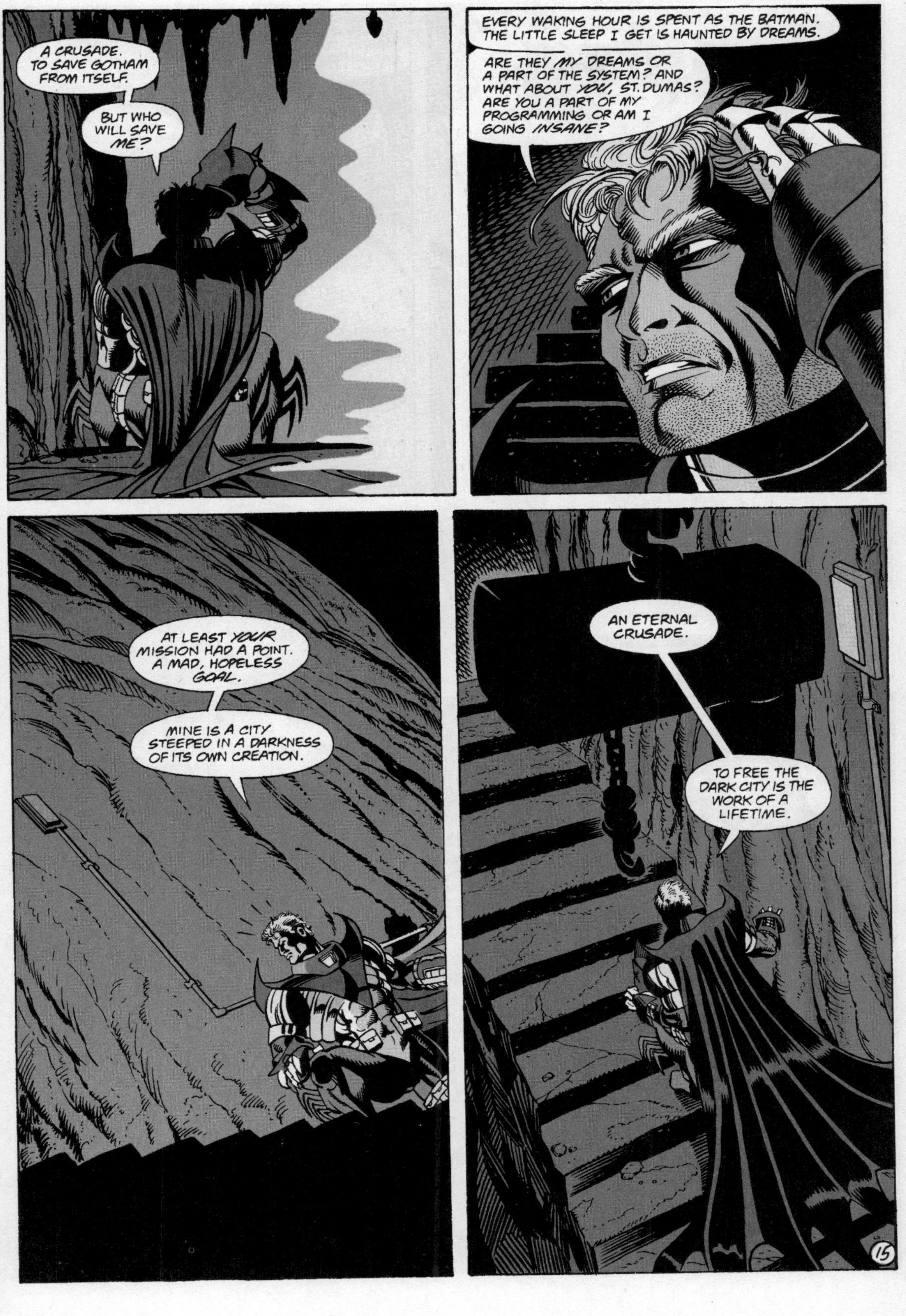
A CRUSADE. TO SAVE GOTHAM FROM ITSELF.
BUT WHO WILL SAVE ME?
EVERY WAKING HOUR IS SPENT AS THE BATMAN. THE LITTLE SLEEP I GET IS HAUNTED BY DREAMS.
ARE THEY MY DREAMS OR A PART OF THE SYSTEM? AND WHAT ABOUT YOU, ST. DUMAS? ARE YOU A PART OF MY PROGRAMMING OR AM I GOING INSANE?
AT LEAST YOUR MISSION HAD A POINT. A MAD, HOPELESS GOAL.
MINE IS A CITY STEEPED IN A DARKNESS OF ITS OWN CREATION.
AN ETERNAL CRUSADE.
TO FREE THE DARK CITY IS THE WORK OF A LIFETIME.
15

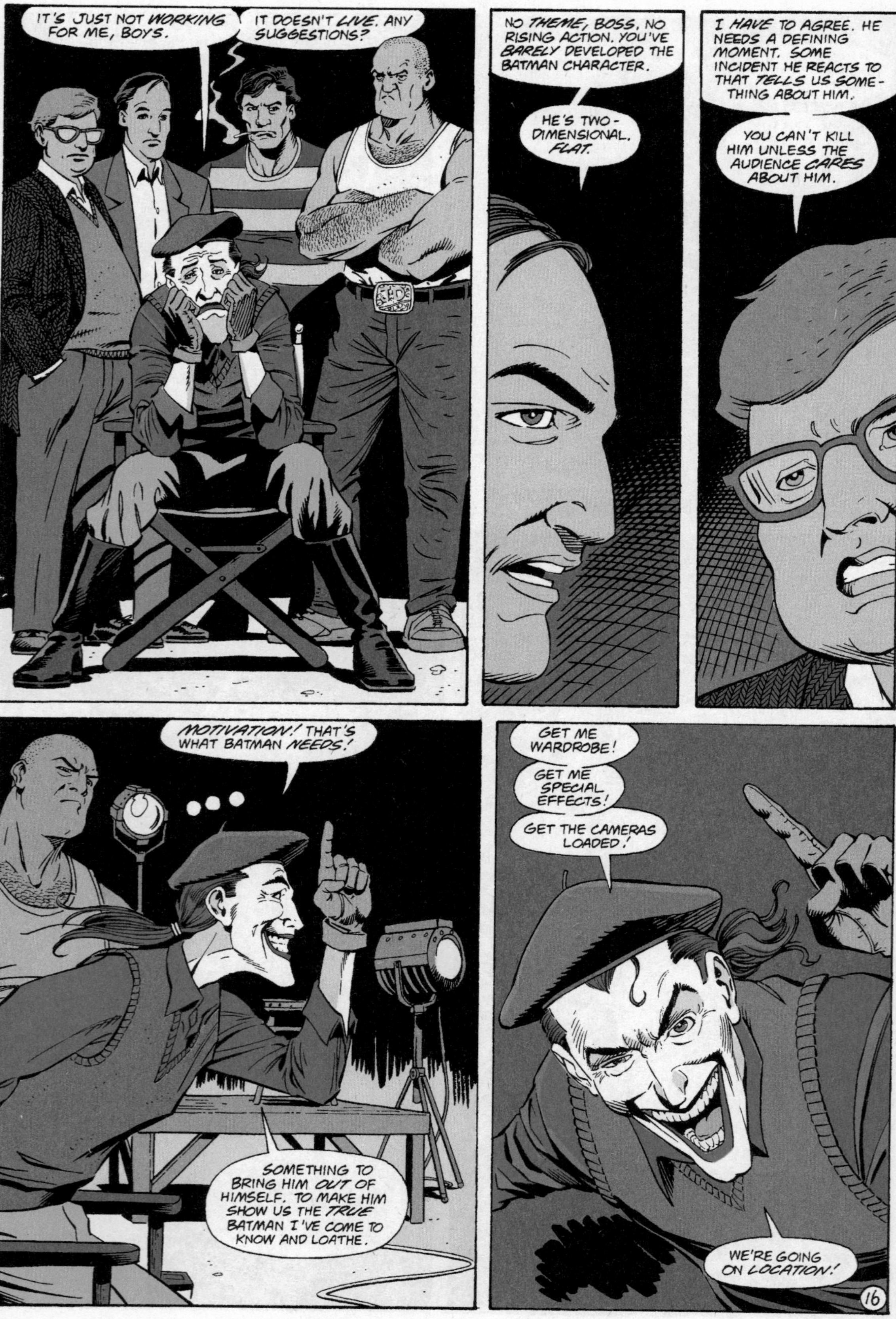
IT'S JUST NOT WORKING FOR ME, BOYS.
IT DOESN'T LIVE. ANY SUGGESTIONS?
NO THEME, BOSS. NO RISING ACTION. YOU'VE BARELY DEVELOPED THE BATMAN CHARACTER.
HE'S TWO-DIMENSIONAL. FLAT.
I HAVE TO AGREE. HE NEEDS A DEFINING MOMENT. SOME INCIDENT HE REACTS TO THAT TELLS US SOMETHING ABOUT HIM.
YOU CAN'T KILL HIM UNLESS THE AUDIENCE CARES ABOUT HIM.
MOTIVATION! THAT'S WHAT BATMAN NEEDS!
SOMETHING TO BRING HIM OUT OF HIMSELF. TO MAKE HIM SHOW US THE TRUE BATMAN I'VE COME TO KNOW AND LOATHE.
GET ME WARDROBE!
GET ME SPECIAL EFFECTS!
GET THE CAMERAS LOADED!
WE'RE GOING ON LOCATION!
16

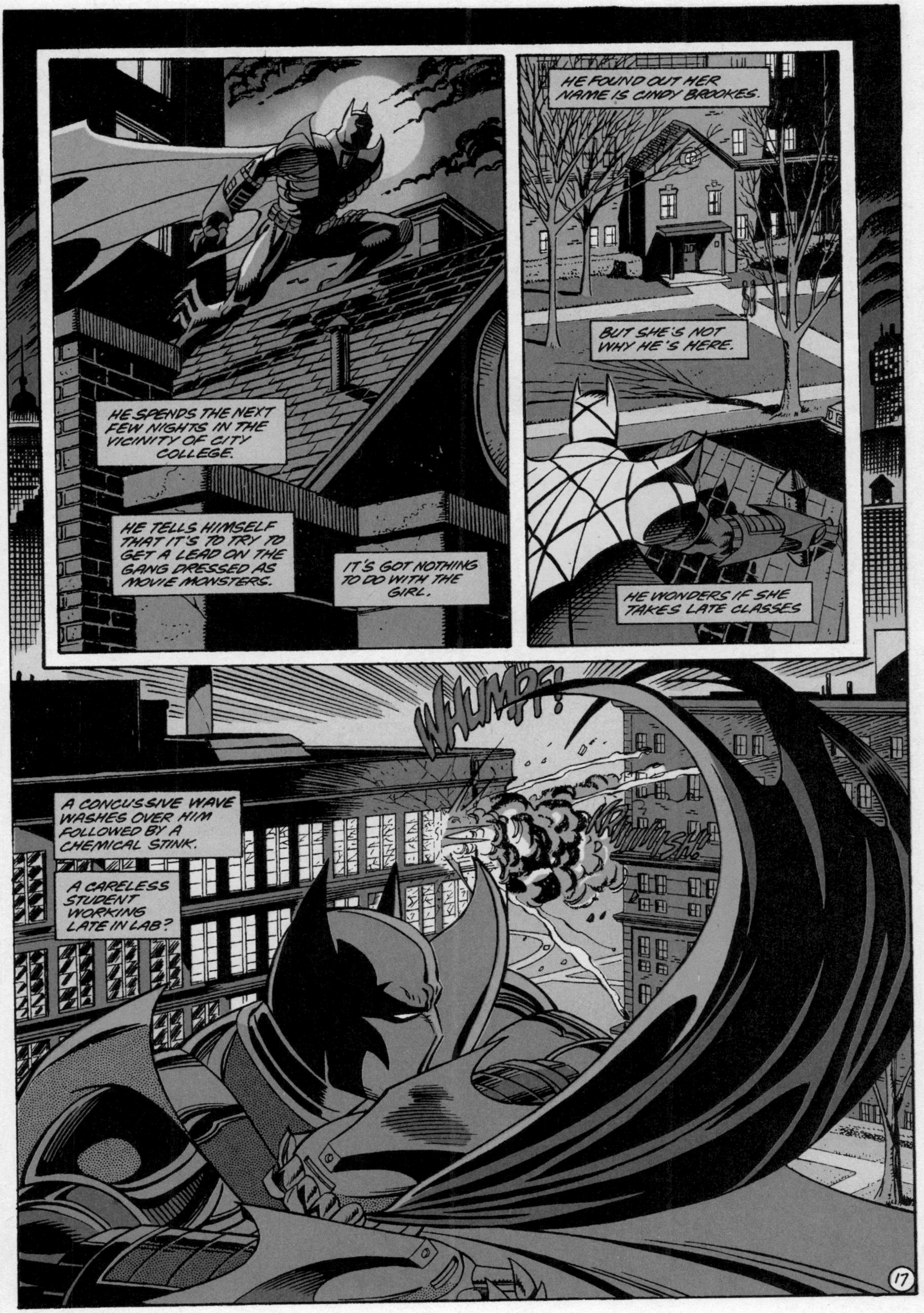
HE SPENDS THE NEXT FEW NIGHTS IN THE VICINITY OF CITY COLLEGE.
HE TELLS HIMSELF THAT IT'S TO TRY TO GET A LEAD ON THE GANG DRESSED AS MOVIE MONSTERS.
IT'S GOT NOTHING TO DO WITH THE GIRL.
HE FOUND OUT HER NAME IS CINDY BROOKES.
BUT SHE'S NOT WHY HE'S HERE.
HE WONDERS IF SHE TAKES LATE CLASSES
WHUMPF!
A CONCUSSIVE WAVE WASHES OVER HIM FOLLOWED BY A CHEMICAL STINK.
A CARELESS STUDENT WORKING LATE IN LAB?
17

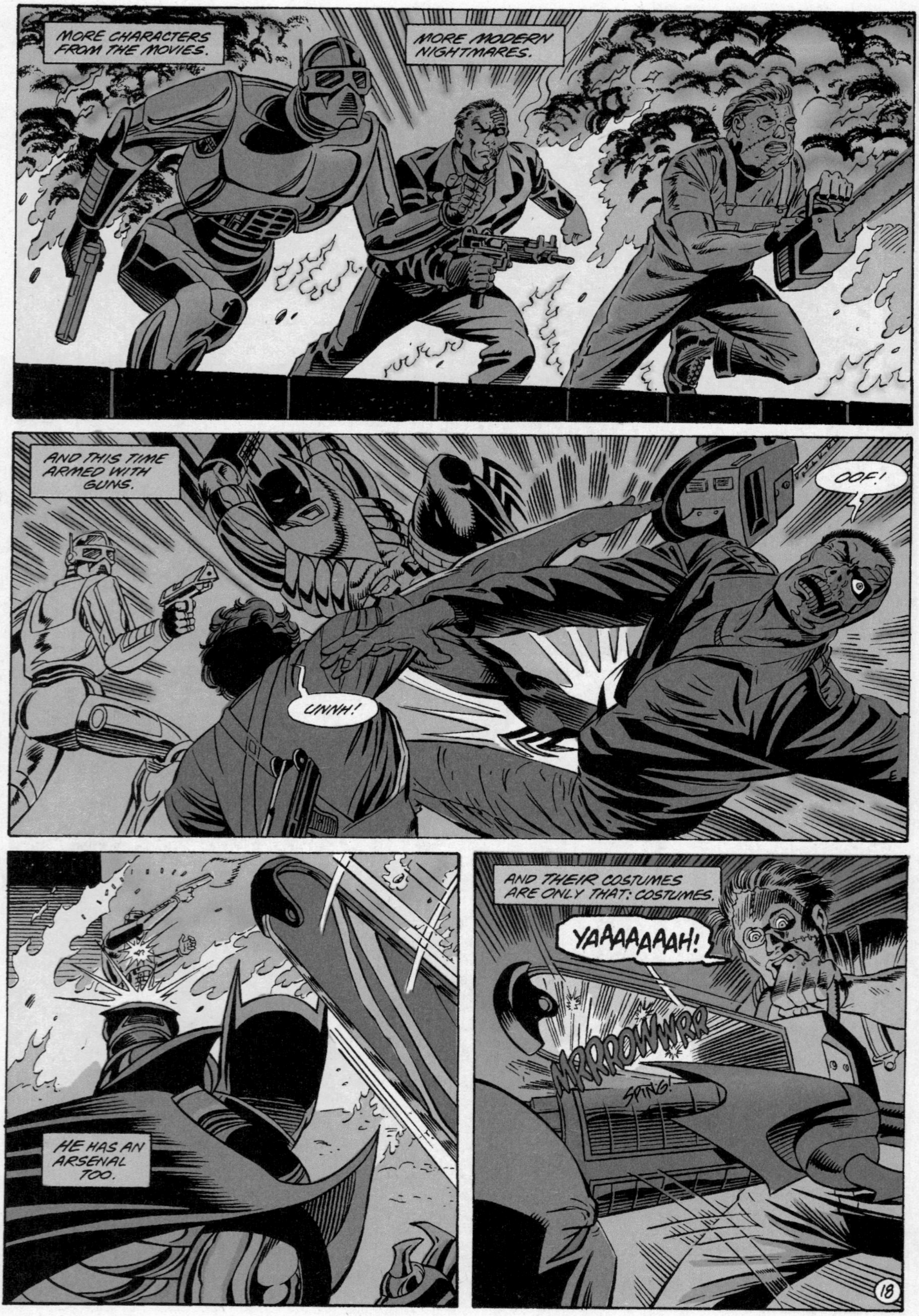
MORE CHARACTERS FROM THE MOVIES.
MORE MODERN NIGHTMARES.
AND THIS TIME ARMED WITH GUNS.
OOF!
UNNH!
HE HAS AN ARSENAL TOO.
AND THEIR COSTUMES ARE ONLY THAT: COSTUMES.
YAAAAAAAH!
MRRROWWRR
SPING!
18

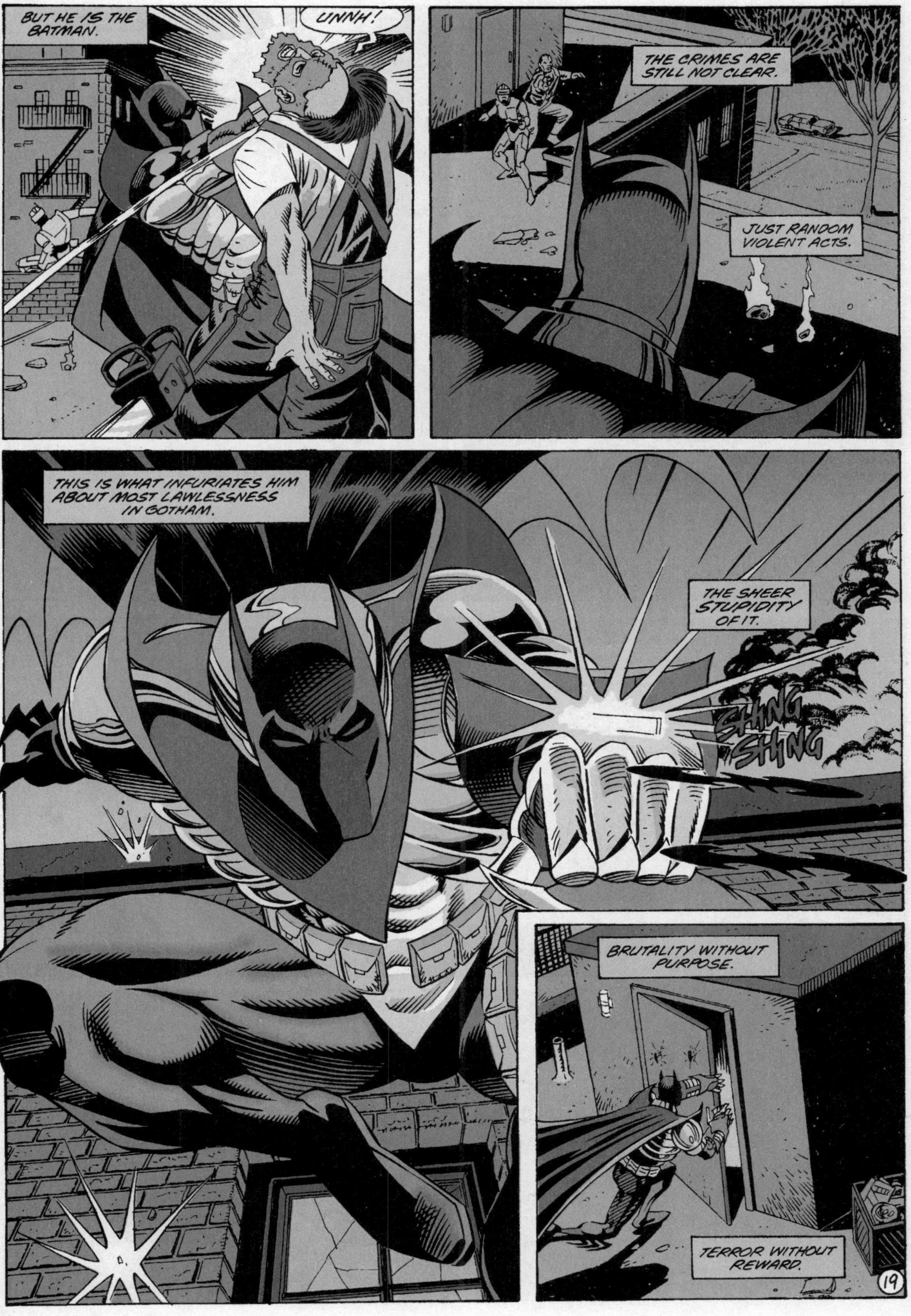
BUT HE IS THE BATMAN.
UNNH!
THE CRIMES ARE STILL NOT CLEAR.
JUST RANDOM VIOLENT ACTS.
THIS IS WHAT INFURIATES HIM ABOUT MOST LAWLESSNESS IN GOTHAM.
THE SHEER STUPIDITY OF IT.
SHING
SHING
BRUTALITY WITHOUT PURPOSE.
TERROR WITHOUT REWARD.
19

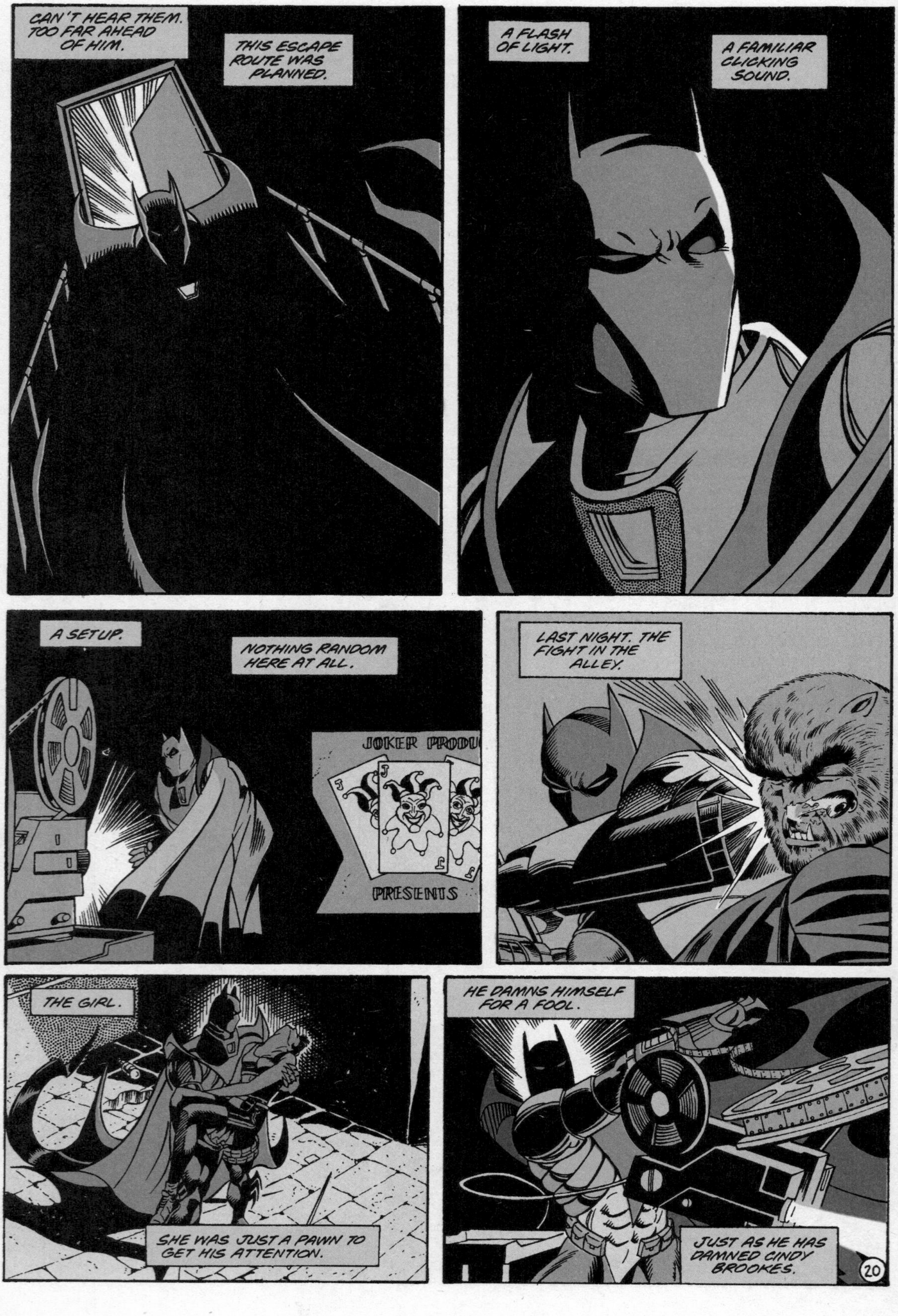
CAN'T HEAR THEM. TOO FAR AHEAD OF HIM.
THIS ESCAPE ROUTE WAS PLANNED.
A FLASH OF LIGHT.
A FAMILIAR CLICKING SOUND.
A SET UP.
NOTHING RANDOM HERE AT ALL.
JOKER PRODU
PRESENTS
LAST NIGHT. THE FIGHT IN THE ALLEY.
THE GIRL.
SHE WAS JUST A PAWN TO GET HIS ATTENTION.
HE DAMNS HIMSELF FOR A FOOL.
JUST AS HE HAS DAMNED CINDY BROOKES.
20

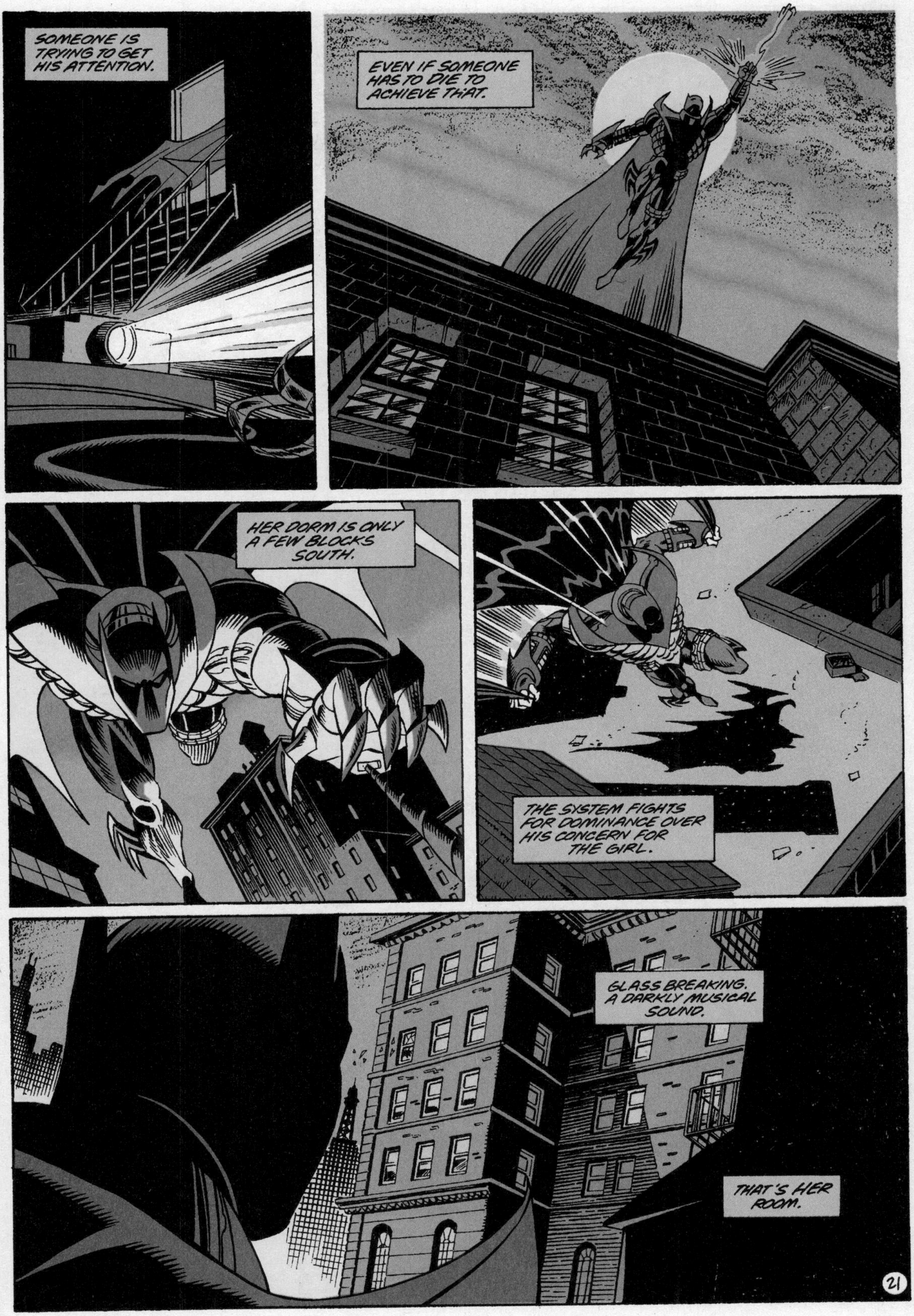
SOMEONE IS TRYING TO GET HIS ATTENTION.
EVEN IF SOMEONE HAS TO DIE TO ACHIEVE THAT.
HER DORM IS ONLY A FEW BLOCKS SOUTH.
THE SYSTEM FIGHTS FOR DOMINANCE OVER HIS CONCERN FOR THE GIRL.
GLASS BREAKING. A DARKLY MUSICAL SOUND.
THAT'S HER ROOM.
21

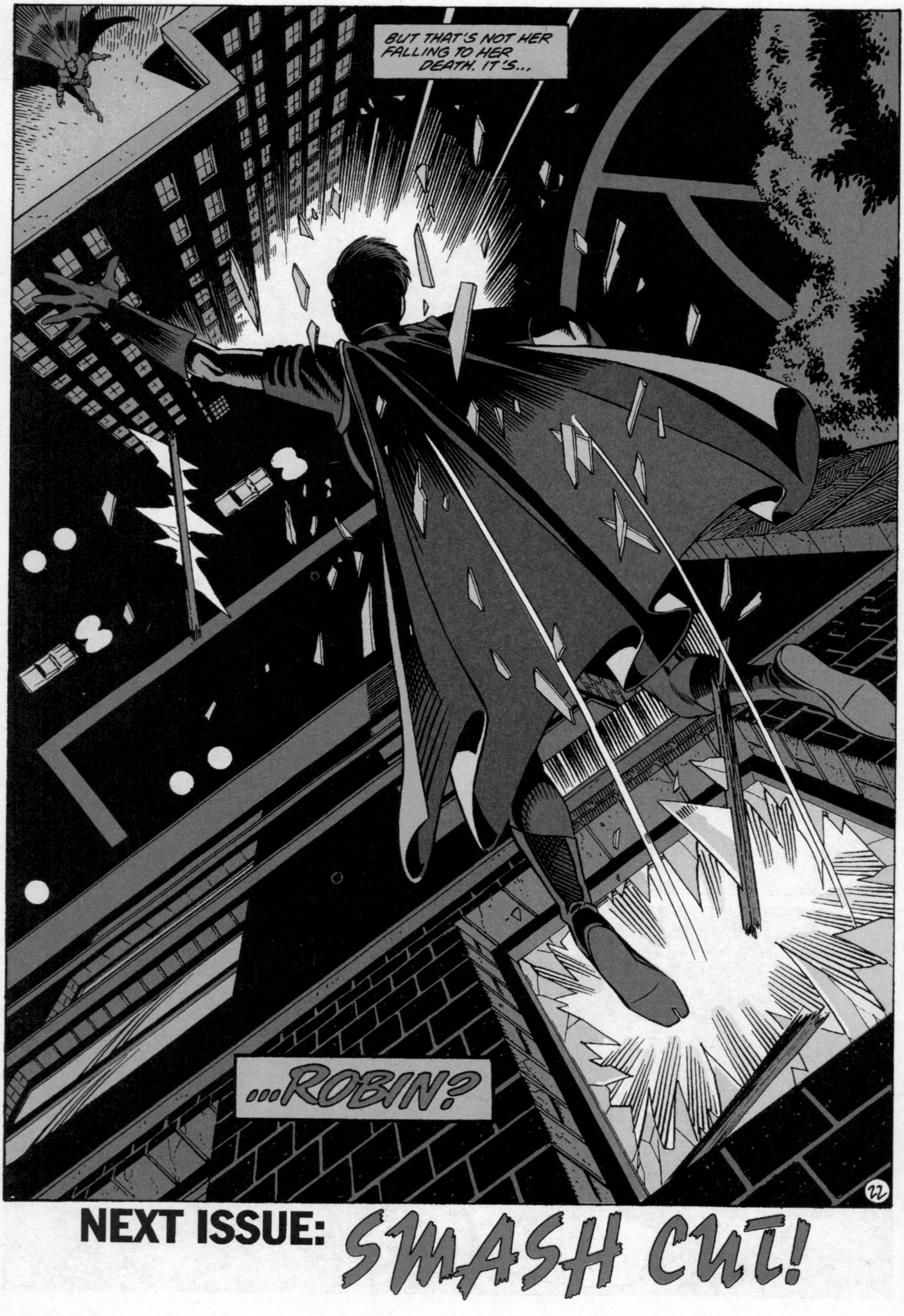
BUT THAT'S NOT HER FALLING TO HER DEATH. IT'S...
...ROBIN?
22

NEXT ISSUE: SMASH CUT!

Cover art by KELLEY JONES

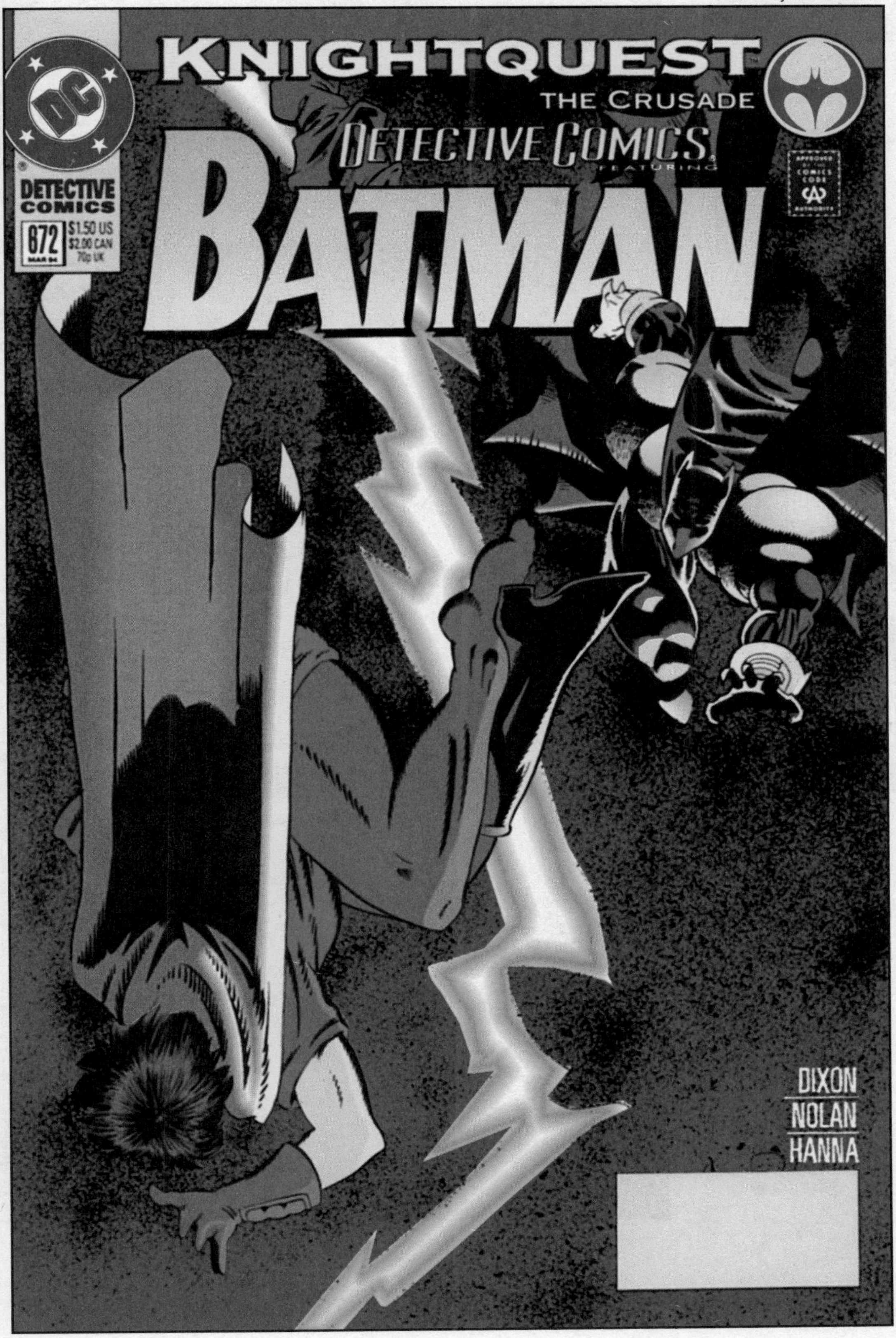

DC
DETECTIVE COMICS
672
$1.50 US
$2.00 CAN
70p UK
MAR 94
KNIGHTQUEST
THE CRUSADE
DETECTIVE COMICS
FEATURING
BATMAN
APPROVED BY THE COMICS CODE AUTHORITY
DIXON
NOLAN
HANNA

SMASH CUT

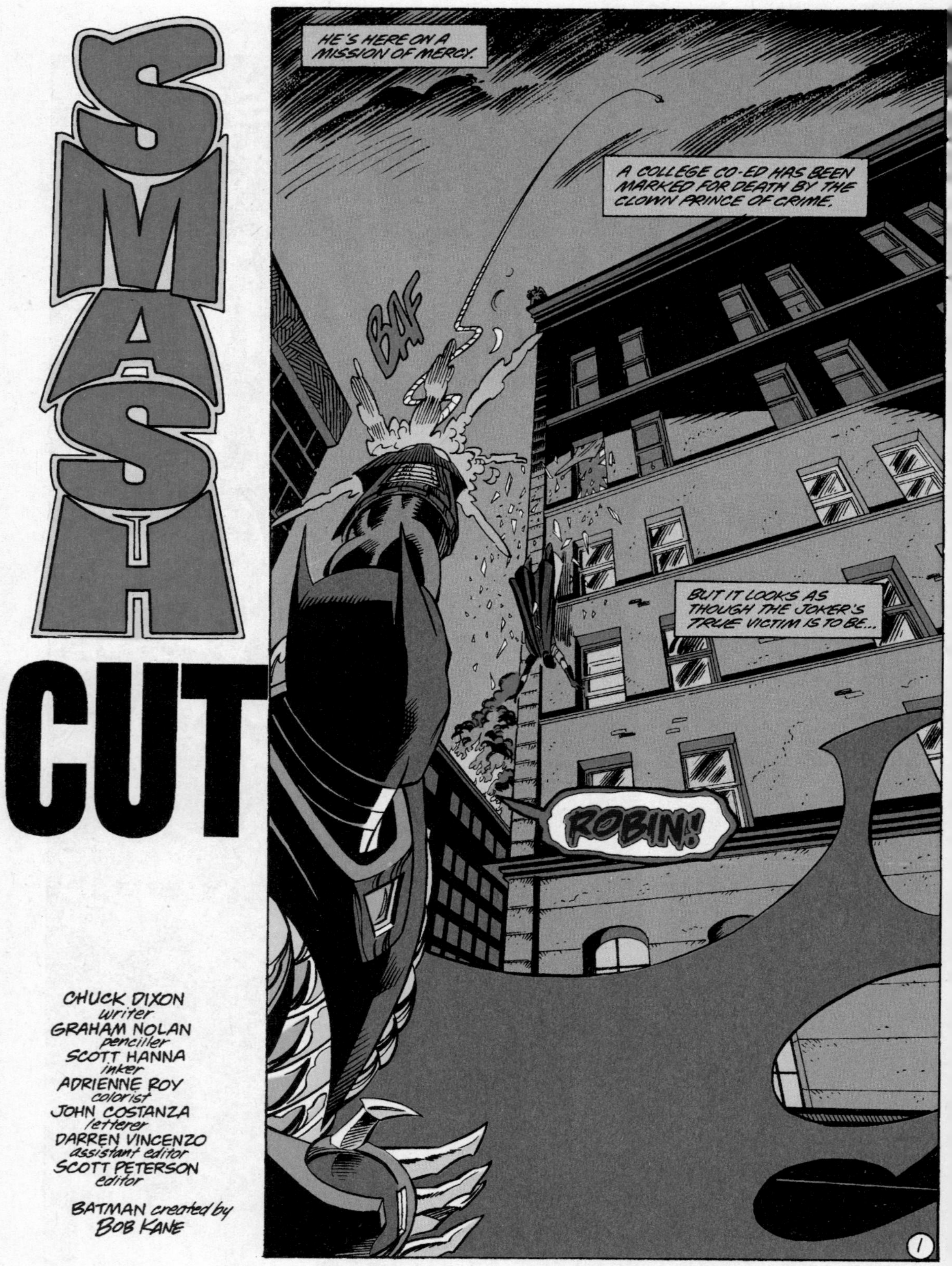

HE'S HERE ON A MISSION OF MERCY.
A COLLEGE CO-ED HAS BEEN MARKED FOR DEATH BY THE CLOWN PRINCE OF CRIME.
BAF
BUT IT LOOKS AS THOUGH THE JOKER'S TRUE VICTIM IS TO BE...
ROBIN!
1

CHUCK DIXON
writer
GRAHAM NOLAN
penciller
SCOTT HANNA
inker
ADRIENNE ROY
colorist
JOHN COSTANZA
letterer
DARREN VINCENZO
assistant editor
SCOTT PETERSON
editor

BATMAN *created by*
BOB KANE

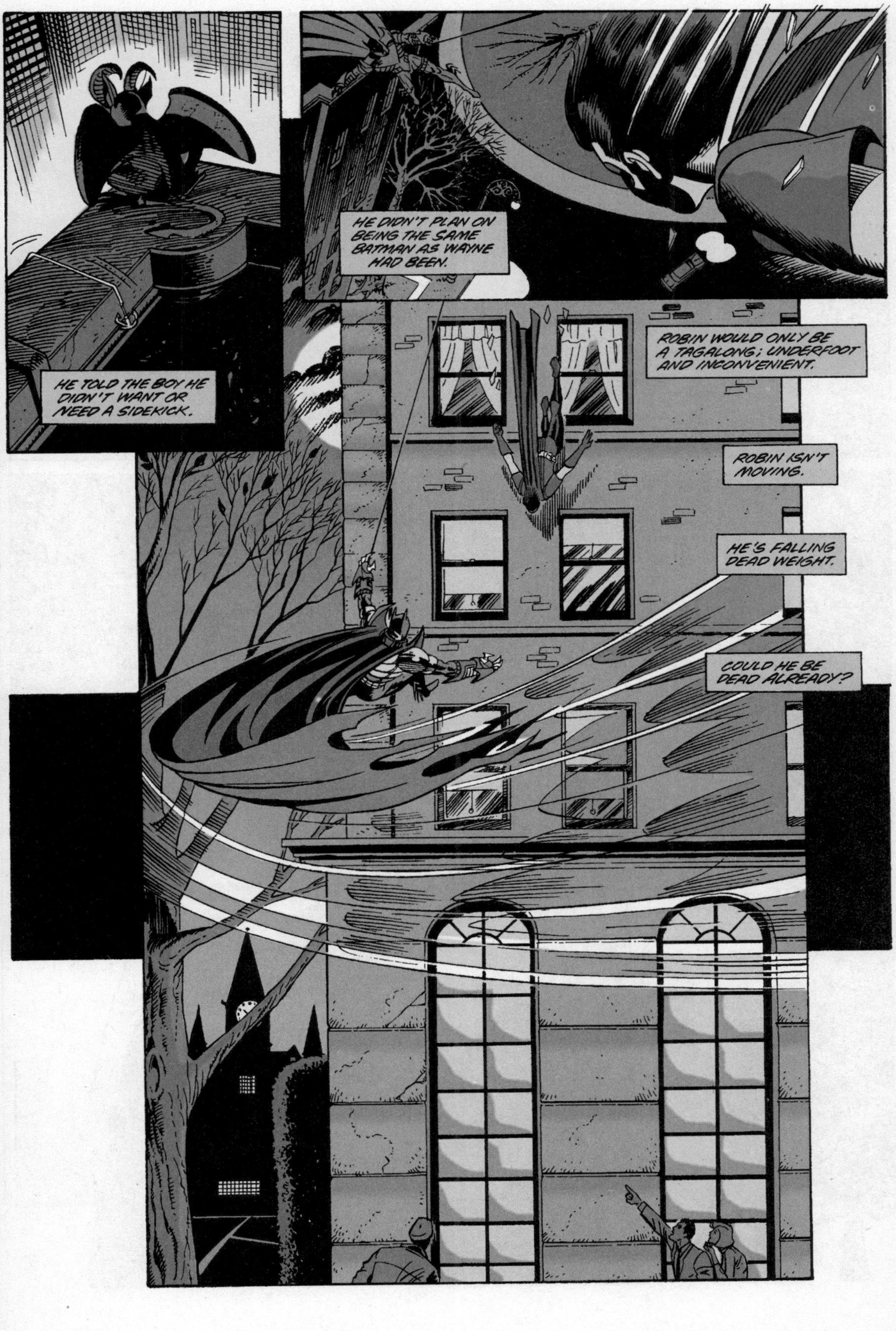
HE TOLD THE BOY HE DIDN'T WANT OR NEED A SIDEKICK.
HE DIDN'T PLAN ON BEING THE SAME BATMAN AS WAYNE HAD BEEN.
ROBIN WOULD ONLY BE A TAGALONG; UNDERFOOT AND INCONVENIENT.
ROBIN ISN'T MOVING.
HE'S FALLING DEAD WEIGHT.
COULD HE BE DEAD ALREADY?

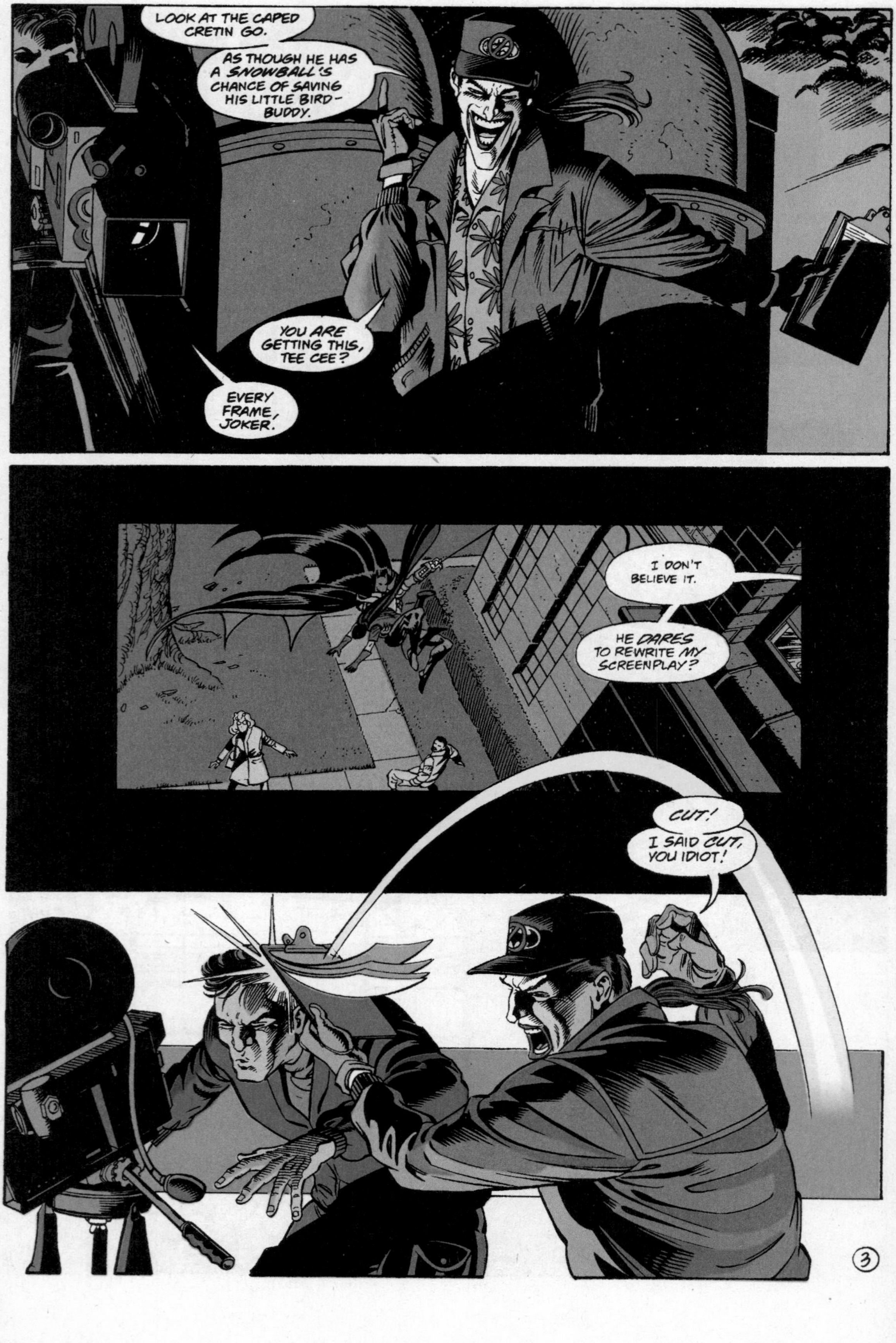
LOOK AT THE CAPED CRETIN GO.
AS THOUGH HE HAS A SNOWBALL'S CHANCE OF SAVING HIS LITTLE BIRD-BUDDY.
YOU ARE GETTING THIS, TEE CEE?
EVERY FRAME, JOKER.
I DON'T BELIEVE IT.
HE DARES TO REWRITE MY SCREENPLAY?
CUT!
I SAID CUT, YOU IDIOT!
3

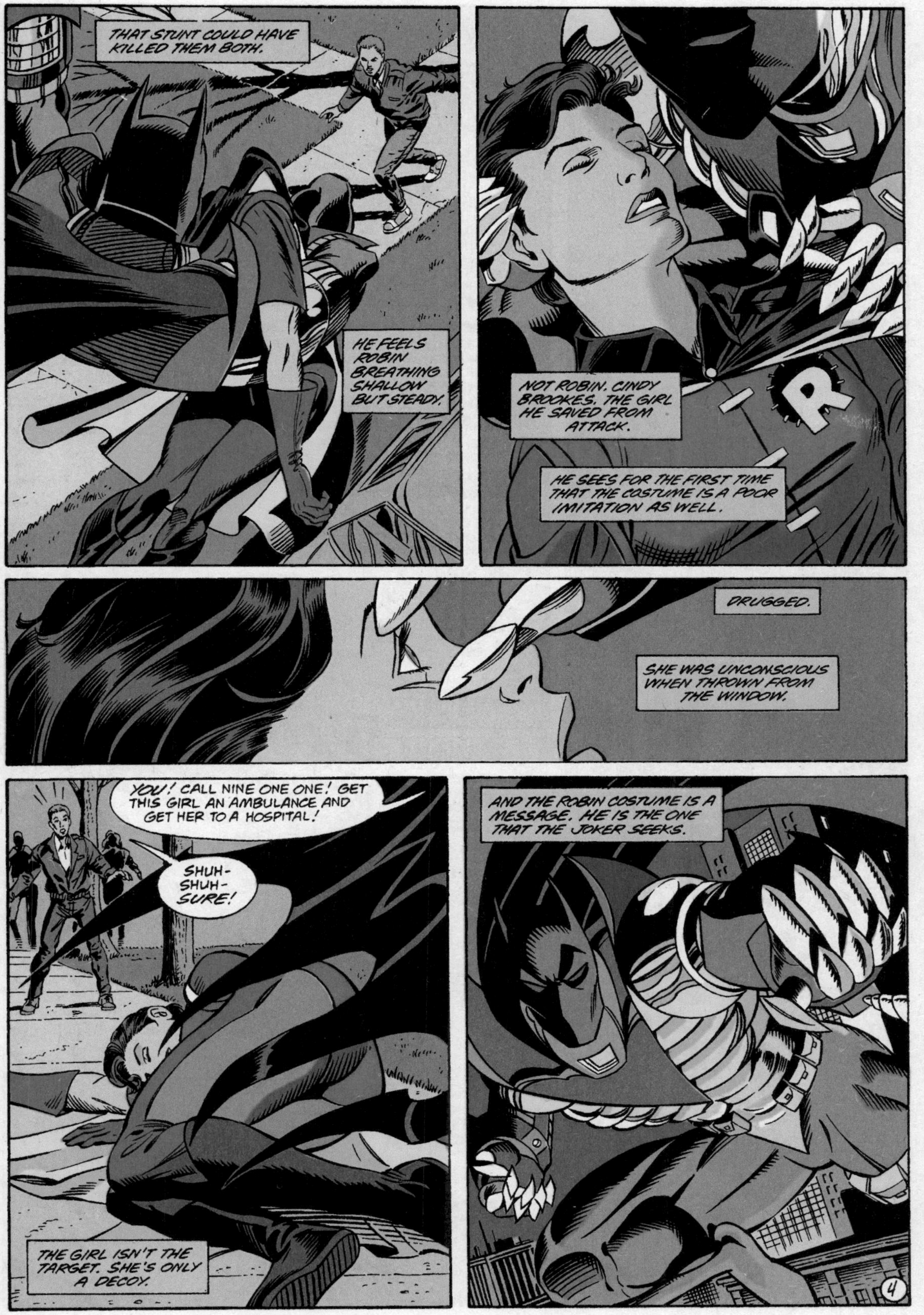

THAT STUNT COULD HAVE KILLED THEM BOTH.
HE FEELS ROBIN BREATHING SHALLOW BUT STEADY.
NOT ROBIN. CINDY BROOKES. THE GIRL HE SAVED FROM ATTACK.
HE SEES FOR THE FIRST TIME THAT THE COSTUME IS A POOR IMITATION AS WELL.
DRUGGED.
SHE WAS UNCONSCIOUS WHEN THROWN FROM THE WINDOW.
YOU! CALL NINE ONE ONE! GET THIS GIRL AN AMBULANCE AND GET HER TO A HOSPITAL!
SHUH-SHUH-SURE!
THE GIRL ISN'T THE TARGET. SHE'S ONLY A DECOY.
AND THE ROBIN COSTUME IS A MESSAGE. HE IS THE ONE THAT THE JOKER SEEKS.
4

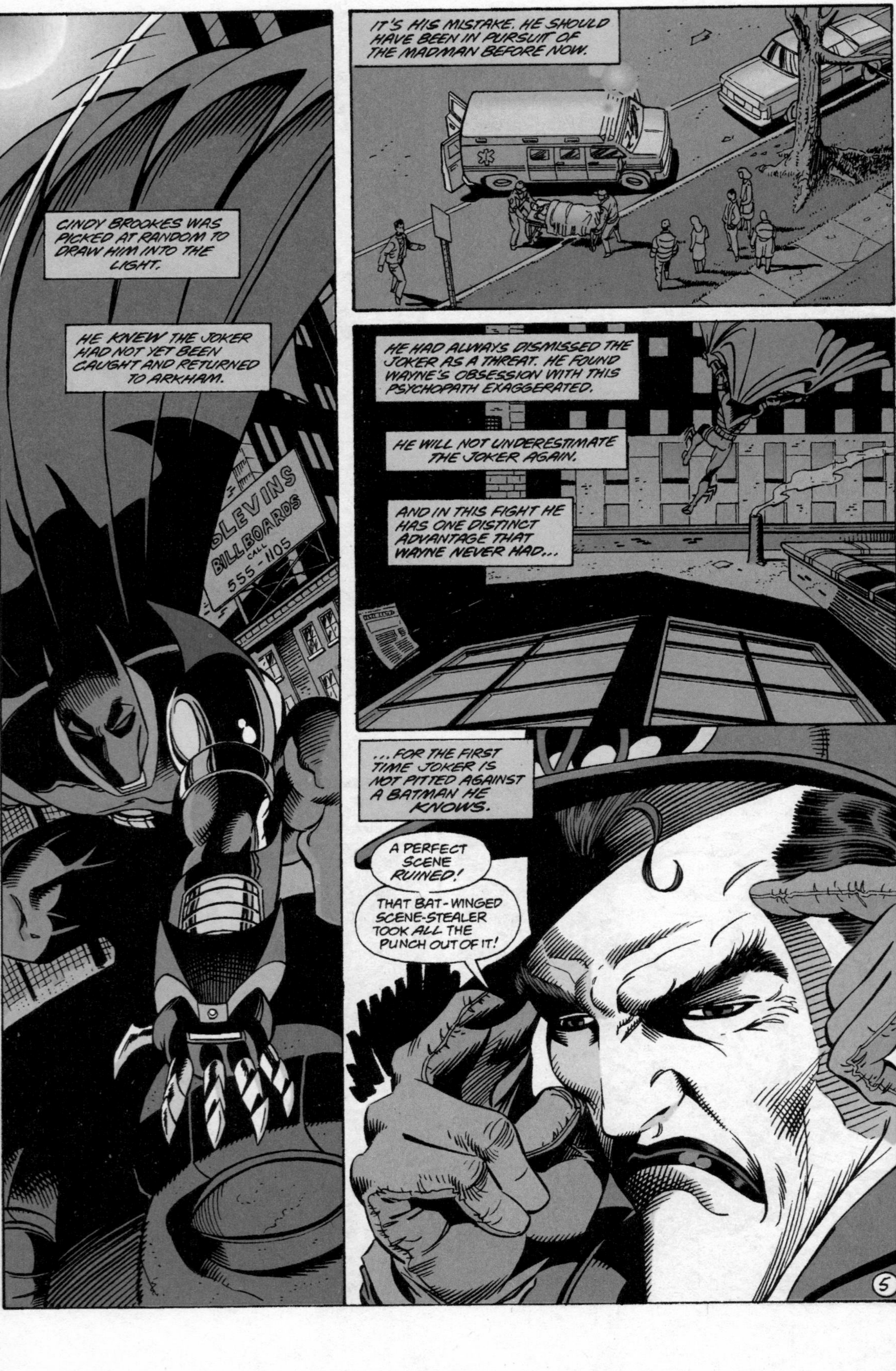
CINDY BROOKES WAS PICKED AT RANDOM TO DRAW HIM INTO THE LIGHT.
HE KNEW THE JOKER HAD NOT YET BEEN CAUGHT AND RETURNED TO ARKHAM.
BLEVINS BILLBOARDS CALL 555-1105
IT'S HIS MISTAKE. HE SHOULD HAVE BEEN IN PURSUIT OF THE MADMAN BEFORE NOW.
HE HAD ALWAYS DISMISSED THE JOKER AS A THREAT. HE FOUND WAYNE'S OBSESSION WITH THIS PSYCHOPATH EXAGGERATED.
HE WILL NOT UNDERESTIMATE THE JOKER AGAIN.
AND IN THIS FIGHT HE HAS ONE DISTINCT ADVANTAGE THAT WAYNE NEVER HAD...
...FOR THE FIRST TIME JOKER IS NOT PITTED AGAINST A BATMAN HE KNOWS.
A PERFECT SCENE RUINED!
THAT BAT-WINGED SCENE-STEALER TOOK ALL THE PUNCH OUT OF IT!
5

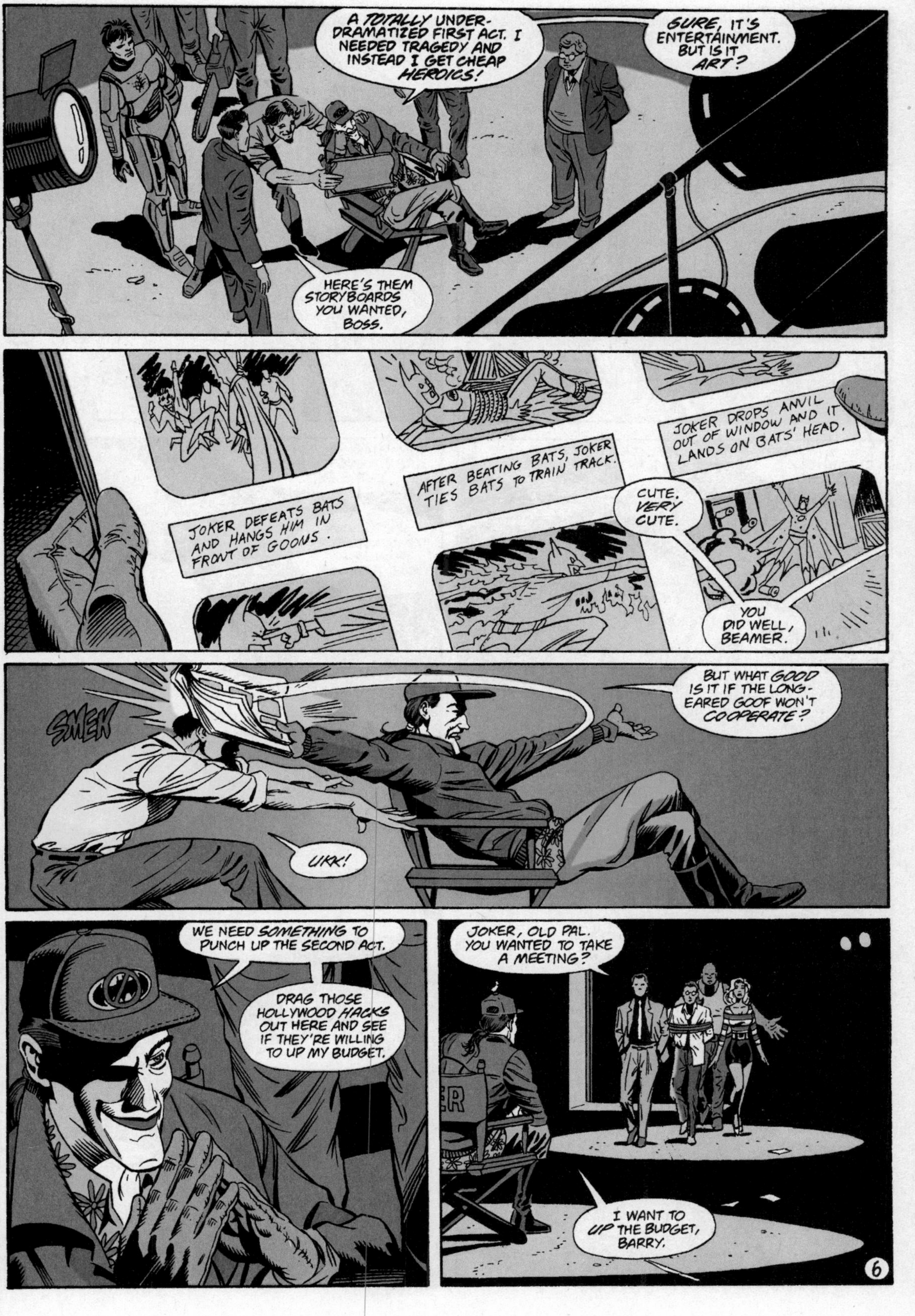
A TOTALLY UNDER-DRAMATIZED FIRST ACT. I NEEDED TRAGEDY AND INSTEAD I GET CHEAP HEROICS!
SURE, IT'S ENTERTAINMENT. BUT IS IT ART?
HERE'S THEM STORYBOARDS YOU WANTED, BOSS.
JOKER DEFEATS BATS AND HANGS HIM IN FRONT OF GOONS.
AFTER BEATING BATS, JOKER TIES BATS TO TRAIN TRACK.
JOKER DROPS ANVIL OUT OF WINDOW AND IT LANDS ON BATS' HEAD.
CUTE. VERY CUTE.
YOU DID WELL, BEAMER.
SMEK
BUT WHAT GOOD IS IT IF THE LONG-EARED GOOF WON'T COOPERATE?
UKK!
WE NEED SOMETHING TO PUNCH UP THE SECOND ACT.
DRAG THOSE HOLLYWOOD HACKS OUT HERE AND SEE IF THEY'RE WILLING TO UP MY BUDGET.
JOKER, OLD PAL. YOU WANTED TO TAKE A MEETING?
I WANT TO UP THE BUDGET, BARRY.
6

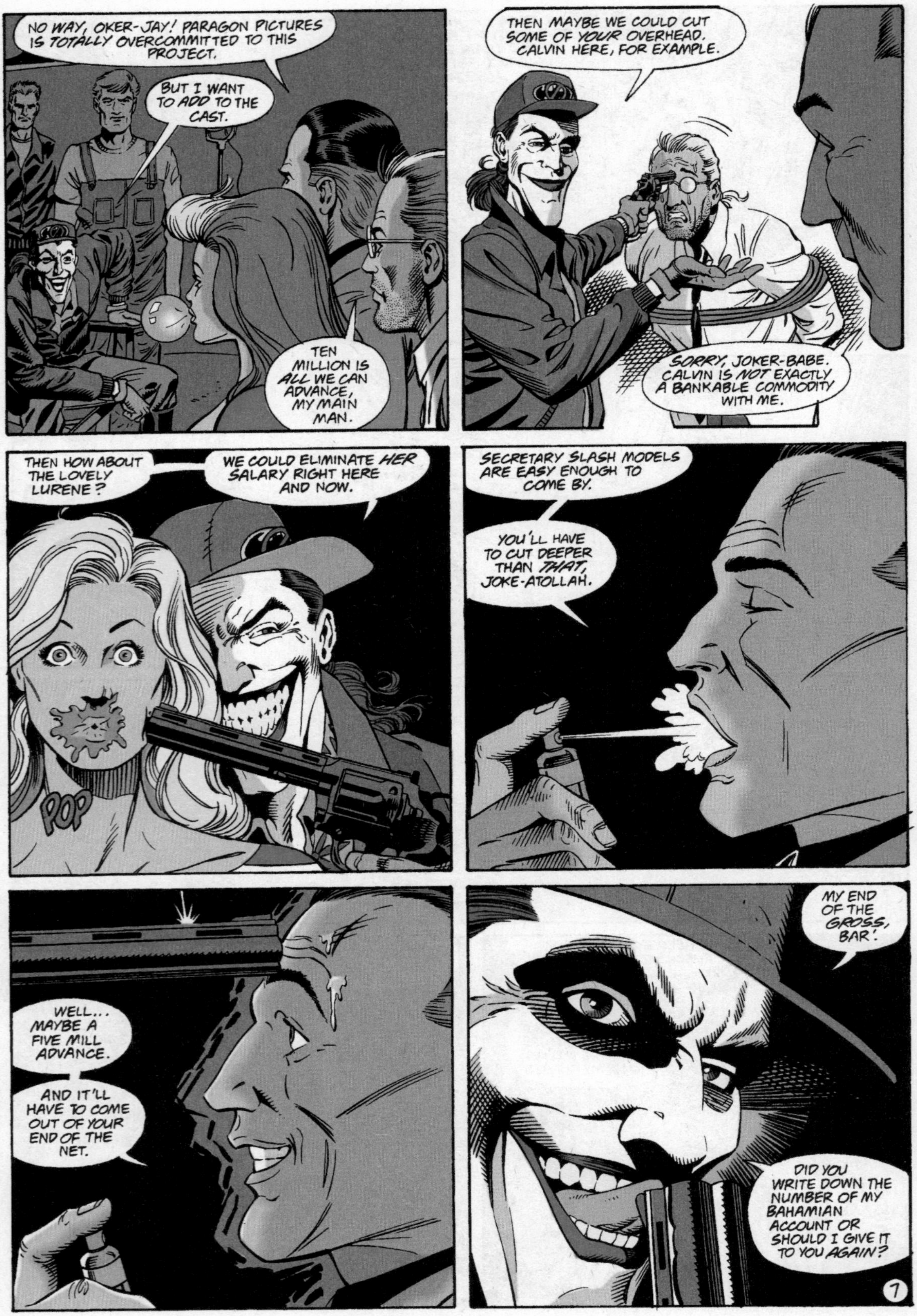
NO WAY, OKER-JAY! PARAGON PICTURES IS TOTALLY OVERCOMMITTED TO THIS PROJECT.
BUT I WANT TO ADD TO THE CAST.
TEN MILLION IS ALL WE CAN ADVANCE, MY MAIN MAN.
THEN MAYBE WE COULD CUT SOME OF YOUR OVERHEAD. CALVIN HERE, FOR EXAMPLE.
SORRY, JOKER-BABE. CALVIN IS NOT EXACTLY A BANKABLE COMMODITY WITH ME.
THEN HOW ABOUT THE LOVELY LURENE?
WE COULD ELIMINATE HER SALARY RIGHT HERE AND NOW.
POP
SECRETARY SLASH MODELS ARE EASY ENOUGH TO COME BY.
YOU'LL HAVE TO CUT DEEPER THAN THAT, JOKE-ATOLLAH.
WELL... MAYBE A FIVE MILL ADVANCE.
AND IT'LL HAVE TO COME OUT OF YOUR END OF THE NET.
MY END OF THE GROSS, BAR'.
DID YOU WRITE DOWN THE NUMBER OF MY BAHAMIAN ACCOUNT OR SHOULD I GIVE IT TO YOU AGAIN?
7

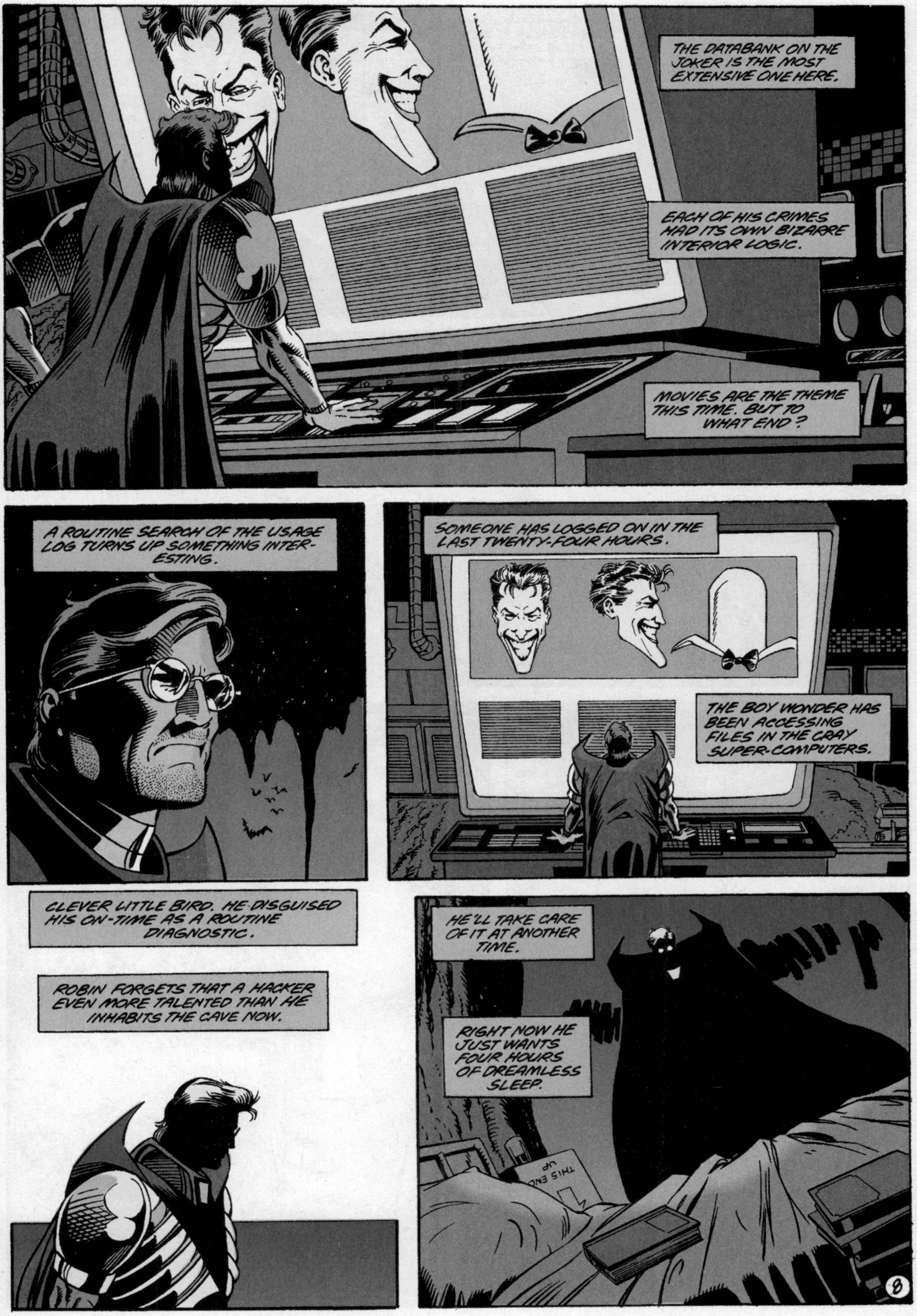
THE DATABANK ON THE JOKER IS THE MOST EXTENSIVE ONE HERE.
EACH OF HIS CRIMES HAD ITS OWN BIZARRE INTERIOR LOGIC.
MOVIES ARE THE THEME THIS TIME. BUT TO WHAT END?
A ROUTINE SEARCH OF THE USAGE LOG TURNS UP SOMETHING INTER-ESTING.
SOMEONE HAS LOGGED ON IN THE LAST TWENTY-FOUR HOURS.
THE BOY WONDER HAS BEEN ACCESSING FILES IN THE CRAY SUPER-COMPUTERS.
CLEVER LITTLE BIRD. HE DISGUISED HIS ON-TIME AS A ROUTINE DIAGNOSTIC.
ROBIN FORGETS THAT A HACKER EVEN MORE TALENTED THAN HE INHABITS THE CAVE NOW.
HE'LL TAKE CARE OF IT AT ANOTHER TIME.
RIGHT NOW HE JUST WANTS FOUR HOURS OF DREAMLESS SLEEP.

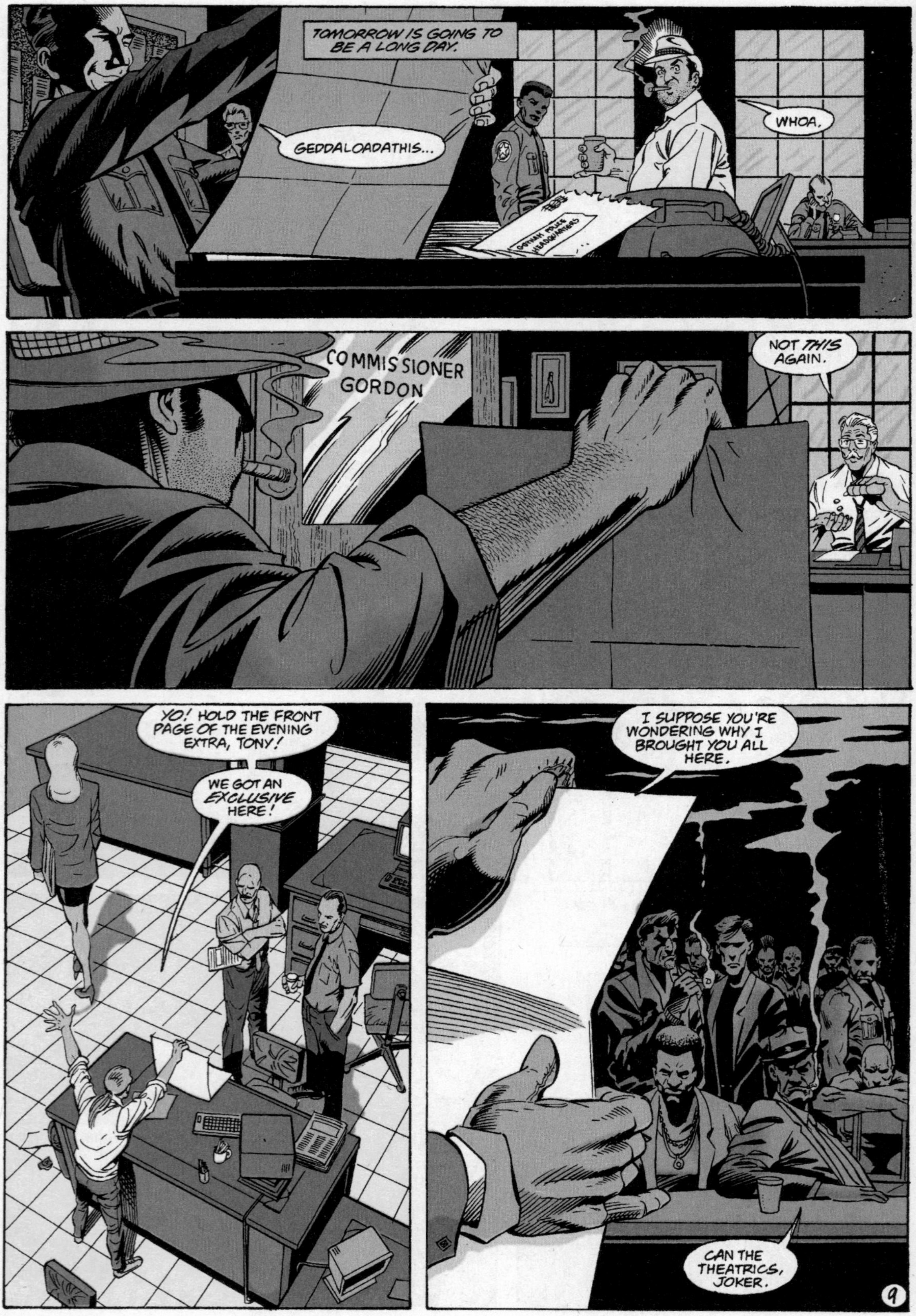
TOMORROW IS GOING TO BE A LONG DAY.
GEDDALOADATHIS...
WHOA.
COMMISSIONER GORDON
NOT *THIS* AGAIN.
YO! HOLD THE FRONT PAGE OF THE EVENING EXTRA, TONY!
WE GOT AN *EXCLUSIVE* HERE!
I SUPPOSE YOU'RE WONDERING WHY I BROUGHT YOU ALL HERE.
CAN THE THEATRICS, JOKER.
9

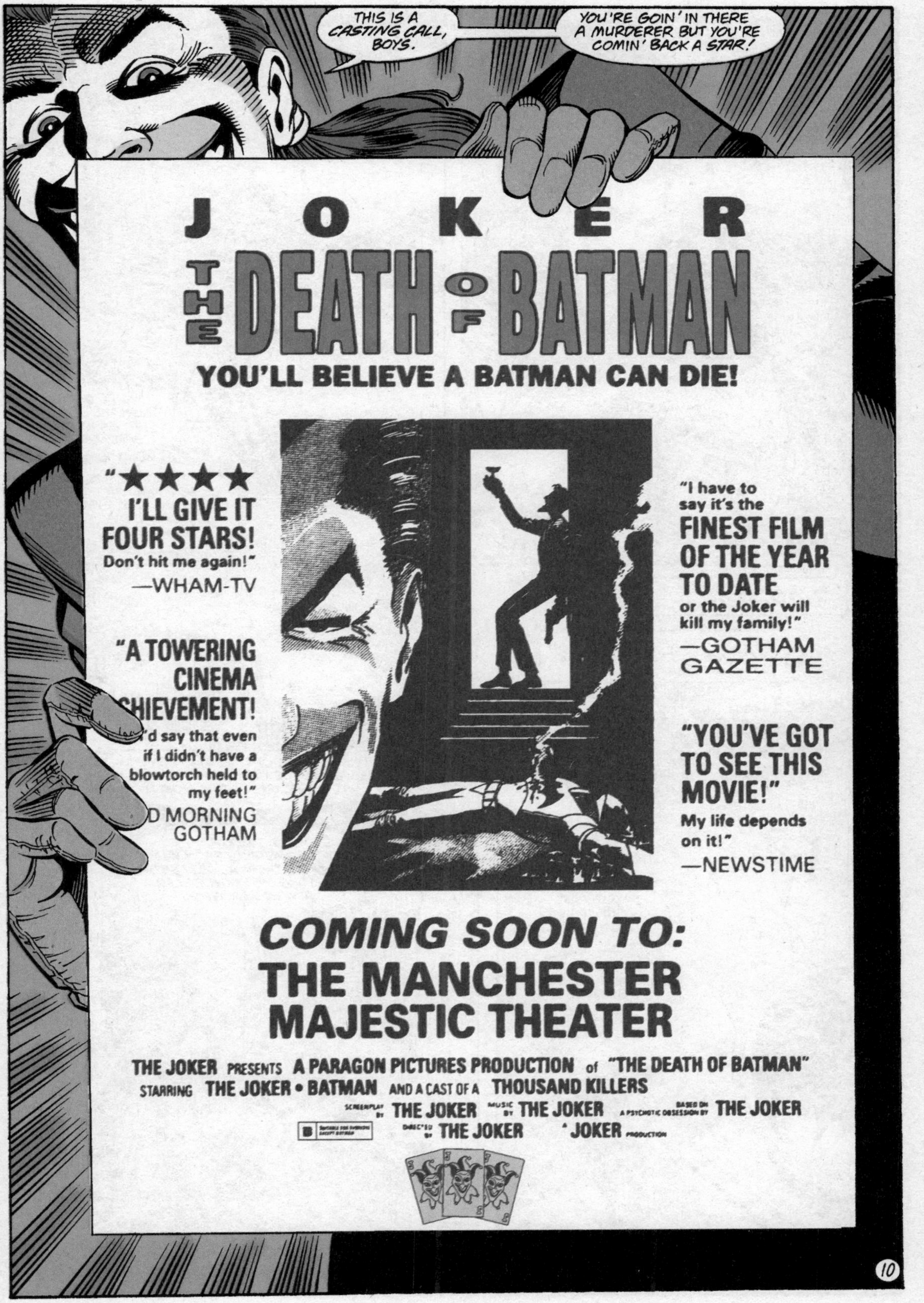
THIS IS A CASTING CALL, BOYS.
YOU'RE GOIN' IN THERE A MURDERER BUT YOU'RE COMIN' BACK A STAR!
JOKER
THE DEATH OF BATMAN
YOU'LL BELIEVE A BATMAN CAN DIE!
"★★★★ I'LL GIVE IT FOUR STARS! Don't hit me again!" —WHAM-TV
"A TOWERING CINEMA CHIEVEMENT! 'd say that even if I didn't have a blowtorch held to my feet!"
D MORNING GOTHAM
"I have to say it's the FINEST FILM OF THE YEAR TO DATE or the Joker will kill my family!" —GOTHAM GAZETTE
"YOU'VE GOT TO SEE THIS MOVIE!" My life depends on it!" —NEWSTIME
COMING SOON TO:
THE MANCHESTER MAJESTIC THEATER
THE JOKER PRESENTS A PARAGON PICTURES PRODUCTION of "THE DEATH OF BATMAN"
STARRING THE JOKER • BATMAN AND A CAST OF A THOUSAND KILLERS
SCREENPLAY BY THE JOKER MUSIC BY THE JOKER BASED ON A PSYCHOTIC OBSESSION BY THE JOKER
DIRECTED BY THE JOKER
JOKER PRODUCTION
10

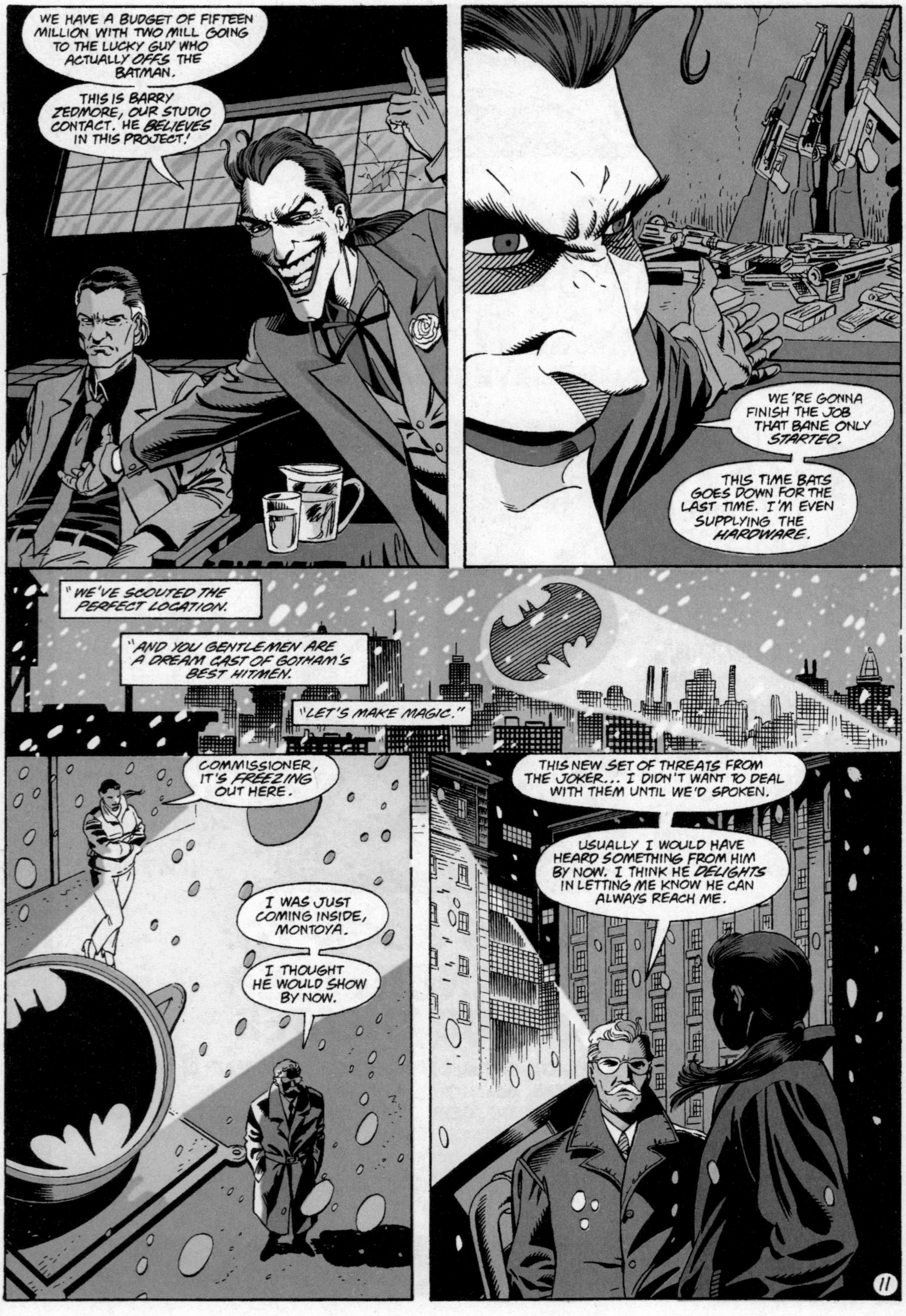
WE HAVE A BUDGET OF FIFTEEN MILLION WITH TWO MILL GOING TO THE LUCKY GUY WHO ACTUALLY OFFS THE BATMAN.
THIS IS BARRY ZEDMORE, OUR STUDIO CONTACT. HE BELIEVES IN THIS PROJECT!
WE'RE GONNA FINISH THE JOB THAT BANE ONLY STARTED.
THIS TIME BATS GOES DOWN FOR THE LAST TIME. I'M EVEN SUPPLYING THE HARDWARE.
"WE'VE SCOUTED THE PERFECT LOCATION.
"AND YOU GENTLEMEN ARE A DREAM CAST OF GOTHAM'S BEST HITMEN.
"LET'S MAKE MAGIC."
COMMISSIONER, IT'S FREEZING OUT HERE.
I WAS JUST COMING INSIDE, MONTOYA.
I THOUGHT HE WOULD SHOW BY NOW.
THIS NEW SET OF THREATS FROM THE JOKER... I DIDN'T WANT TO DEAL WITH THEM UNTIL WE'D SPOKEN.
USUALLY I WOULD HAVE HEARD SOMETHING FROM HIM BY NOW. I THINK HE DELIGHTS IN LETTING ME KNOW HE CAN ALWAYS REACH ME.
11

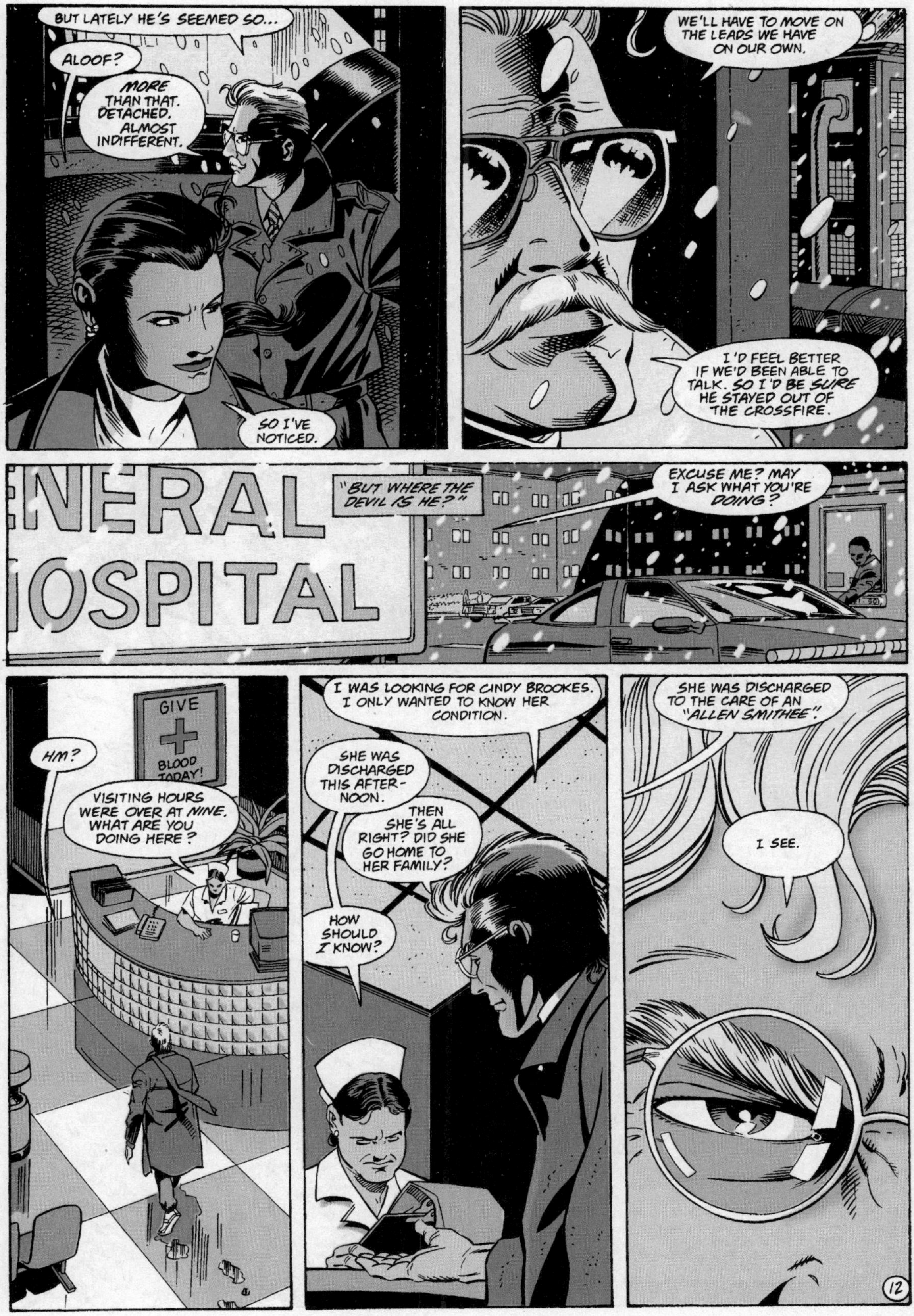
BUT LATELY HE'S SEEMED SO...
ALOOF?
MORE THAN THAT. DETACHED. ALMOST INDIFFERENT.
SO I'VE NOTICED.
WE'LL HAVE TO MOVE ON THE LEADS WE HAVE ON OUR OWN.
I'D FEEL BETTER IF WE'D BEEN ABLE TO TALK. SO I'D BE SURE HE STAYED OUT OF THE CROSSFIRE.
ENERAL
OSPITAL
"BUT WHERE THE DEVIL IS HE?"
EXCUSE ME? MAY I ASK WHAT YOU'RE DOING?
GIVE
BLOOD TODAY!
HM?
VISITING HOURS WERE OVER AT NINE. WHAT ARE YOU DOING HERE?
I WAS LOOKING FOR CINDY BROOKES. I ONLY WANTED TO KNOW HER CONDITION.
SHE WAS DISCHARGED THIS AFTER-NOON.
THEN SHE'S ALL RIGHT? DID SHE GO HOME TO HER FAMILY?
HOW SHOULD I KNOW?
SHE WAS DISCHARGED TO THE CARE OF AN "ALLEN SMITHEE".
I SEE.
12

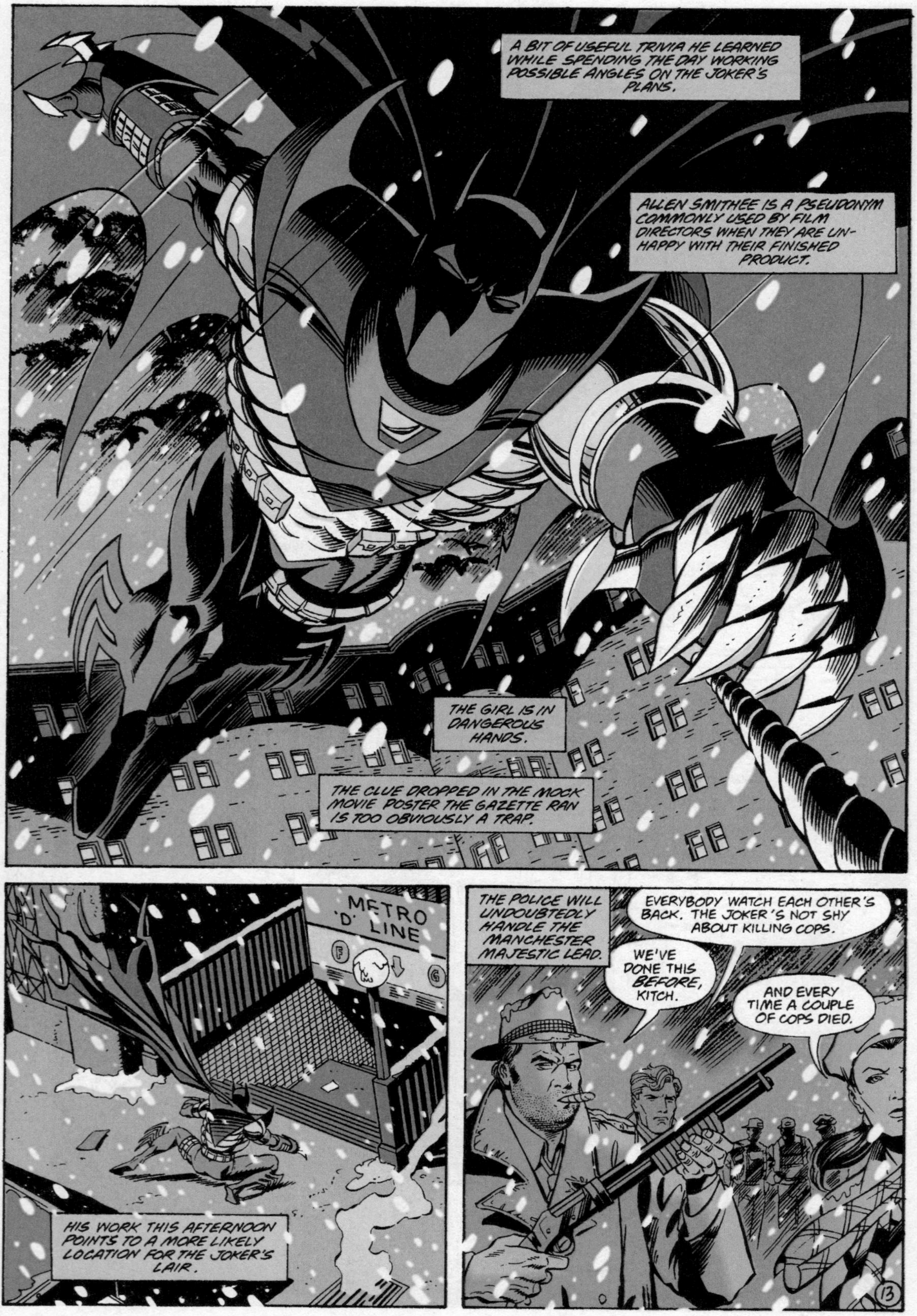
A BIT OF USEFUL TRIVIA HE LEARNED WHILE SPENDING THE DAY WORKING POSSIBLE ANGLES ON THE JOKER'S PLANS.
ALLEN SMITHEE IS A PSEUDONYM COMMONLY USED BY FILM DIRECTORS WHEN THEY ARE UN-HAPPY WITH THEIR FINISHED PRODUCT.
THE GIRL IS IN DANGEROUS HANDS.
THE CLUE DROPPED IN THE MOCK MOVIE POSTER THE GAZETTE RAN IS TOO OBVIOUSLY A TRAP.
METRO 'D' LINE
F
G
HIS WORK THIS AFTERNOON POINTS TO A MORE LIKELY LOCATION FOR THE JOKER'S LAIR.
THE POLICE WILL UNDOUBTEDLY HANDLE THE MANCHESTER MAJESTIC LEAD.
EVERYBODY WATCH EACH OTHER'S BACK. THE JOKER'S NOT SHY ABOUT KILLING COPS.
WE'VE DONE THIS *BEFORE*, KITCH.
AND EVERY TIME A COUPLE OF COPS DIED.
13

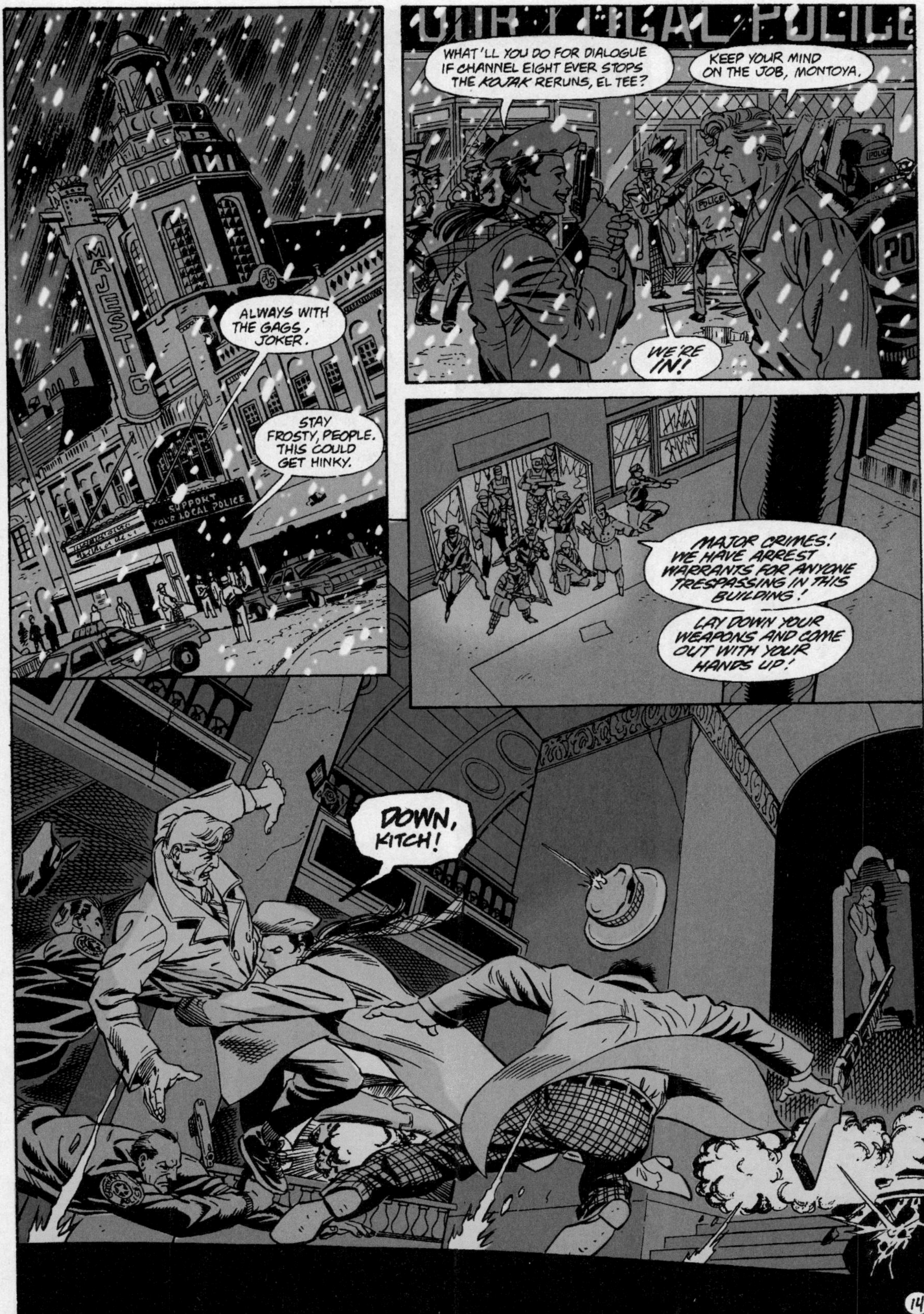
MAJESTIC
SUPPORT YOUR LOCAL POLICE
ALWAYS WITH THE GAGS, JOKER.
STAY FROSTY, PEOPLE. THIS COULD GET HINKY.
WHAT'LL YOU DO FOR DIALOGUE IF CHANNEL EIGHT EVER STOPS THE KOJAK RERUNS, EL TEE?
KEEP YOUR MIND ON THE JOB, MONTOYA.
WE'RE IN!
MAJOR CRIMES! WE HAVE ARREST WARRANTS FOR ANYONE TRESPASSING IN THIS BUILDING!
LAY DOWN YOUR WEAPONS AND COME OUT WITH YOUR HANDS UP!
DOWN, KITCH!
14

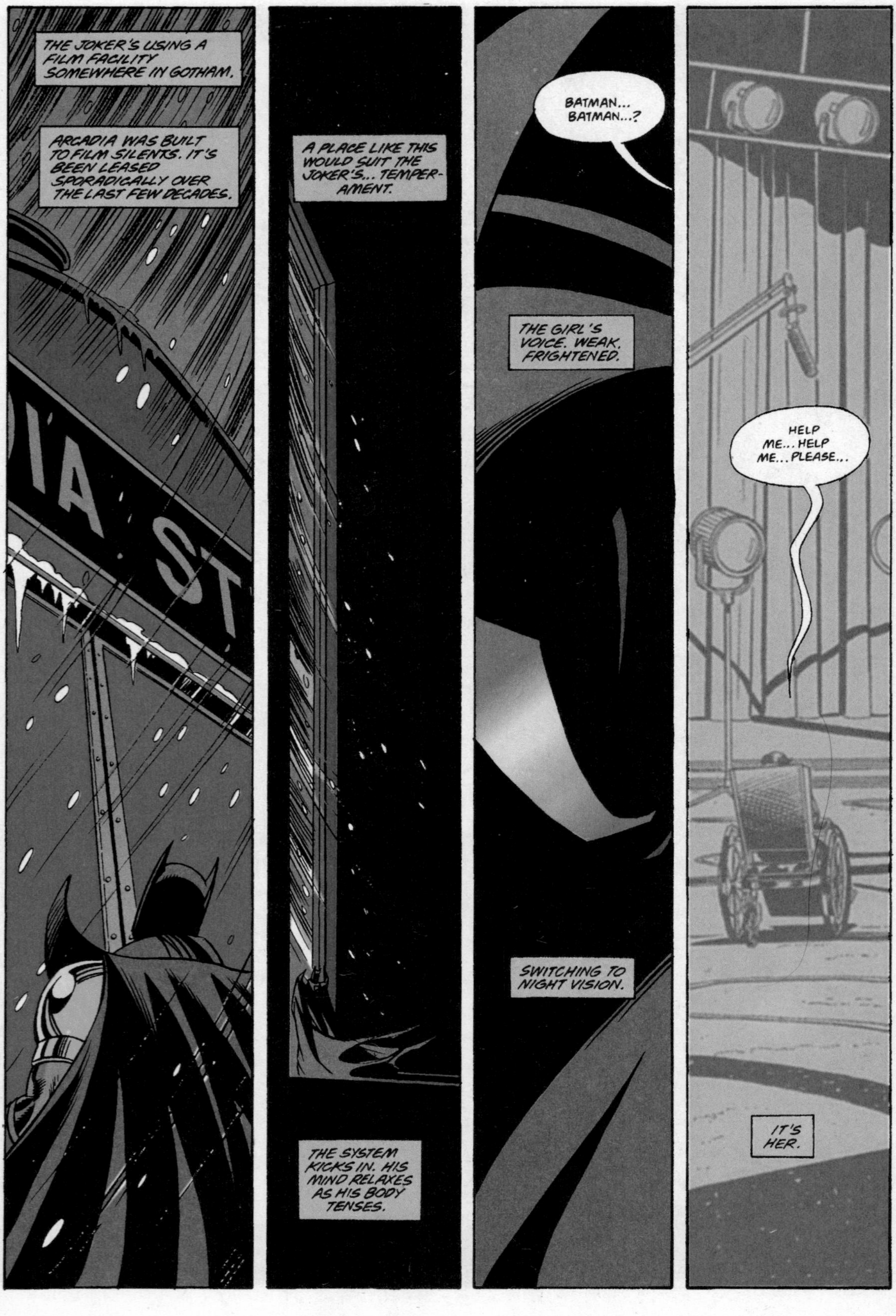
THE JOKER'S USING A FILM FACILITY SOMEWHERE IN GOTHAM.
ARCADIA WAS BUILT TO FILM SILENTS. IT'S BEEN LEASED SPORADICALLY OVER THE LAST FEW DECADES.
A PLACE LIKE THIS WOULD SUIT THE JOKER'S... TEMPER-AMENT.
THE SYSTEM KICKS IN. HIS MIND RELAXES AS HIS BODY TENSES.
BATMAN... BATMAN...?
THE GIRL'S VOICE. WEAK. FRIGHTENED.
SWITCHING TO NIGHT VISION.
HELP ME... HELP ME... PLEASE...
IT'S HER.

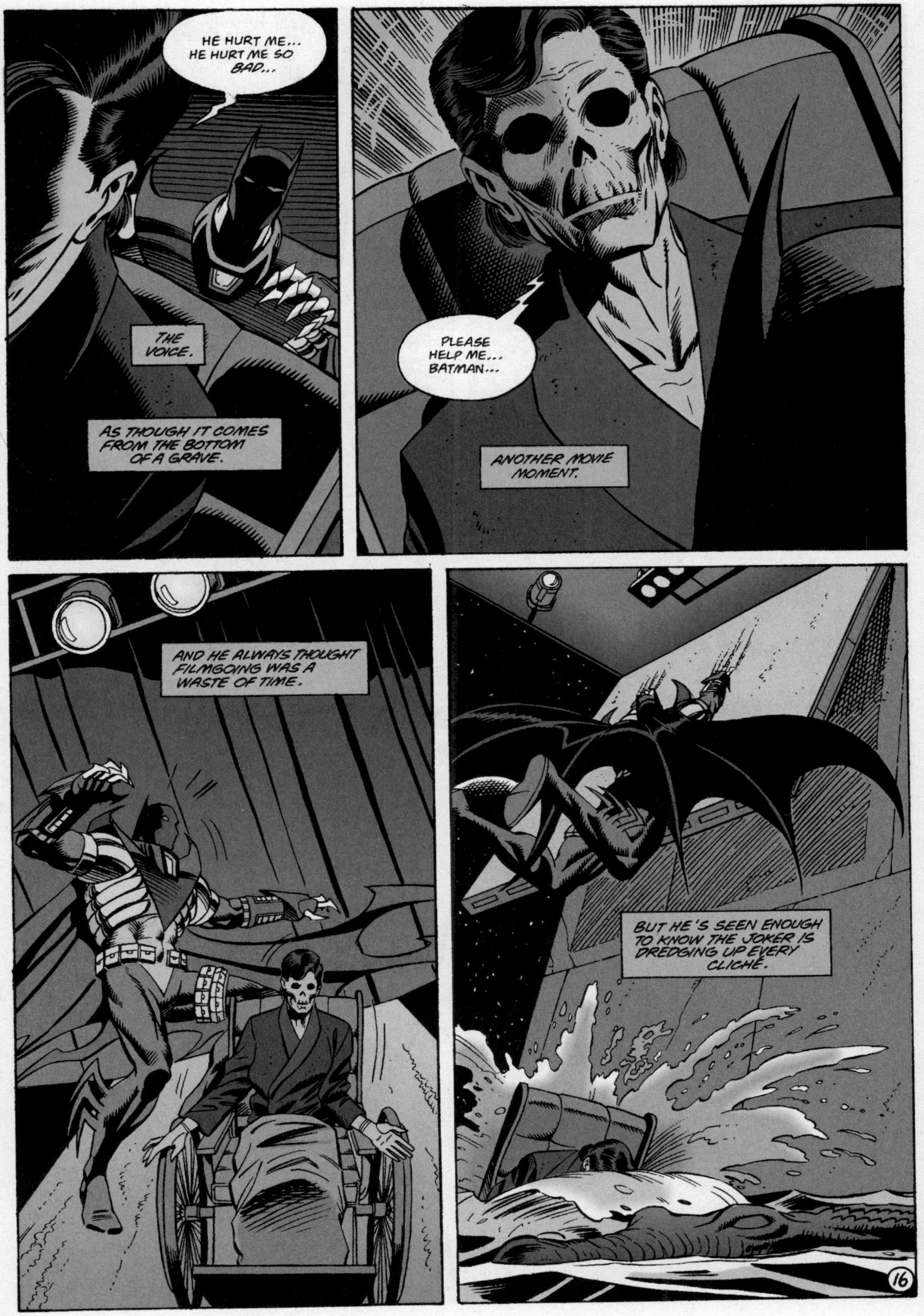
HE HURT ME... HE HURT ME SO BAD...
THE VOICE.
AS THOUGH IT COMES FROM THE BOTTOM OF A GRAVE.
PLEASE HELP ME... BATMAN...
ANOTHER MOVIE MOMENT.
AND HE ALWAYS THOUGHT FILMGOING WAS A WASTE OF TIME.
BUT HE'S SEEN ENOUGH TO KNOW THE JOKER IS DREDGING UP EVERY CLICHÉ.
16

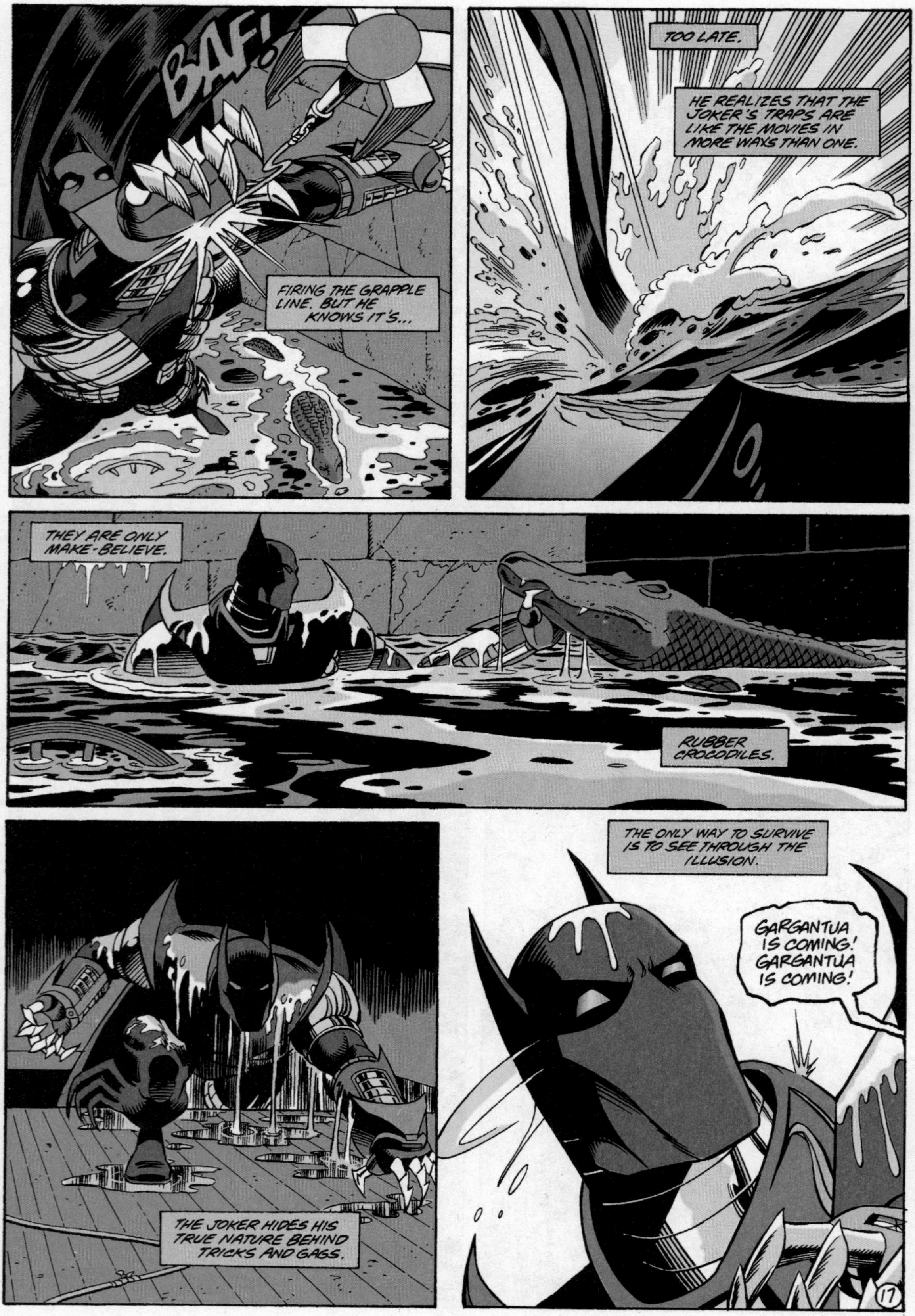
BAF!
FIRING THE GRAPPLE LINE. BUT HE KNOWS IT'S...
TOO LATE.
HE REALIZES THAT THE JOKER'S TRAPS ARE LIKE THE MOVIES IN MORE WAYS THAN ONE.
THEY ARE ONLY MAKE-BELIEVE.
RUBBER CROCODILES.
THE JOKER HIDES HIS TRUE NATURE BEHIND TRICKS AND GAGS.
THE ONLY WAY TO SURVIVE IS TO SEE THROUGH THE ILLUSION.
GARGANTUA IS COMING! GARGANTUA IS COMING!
17

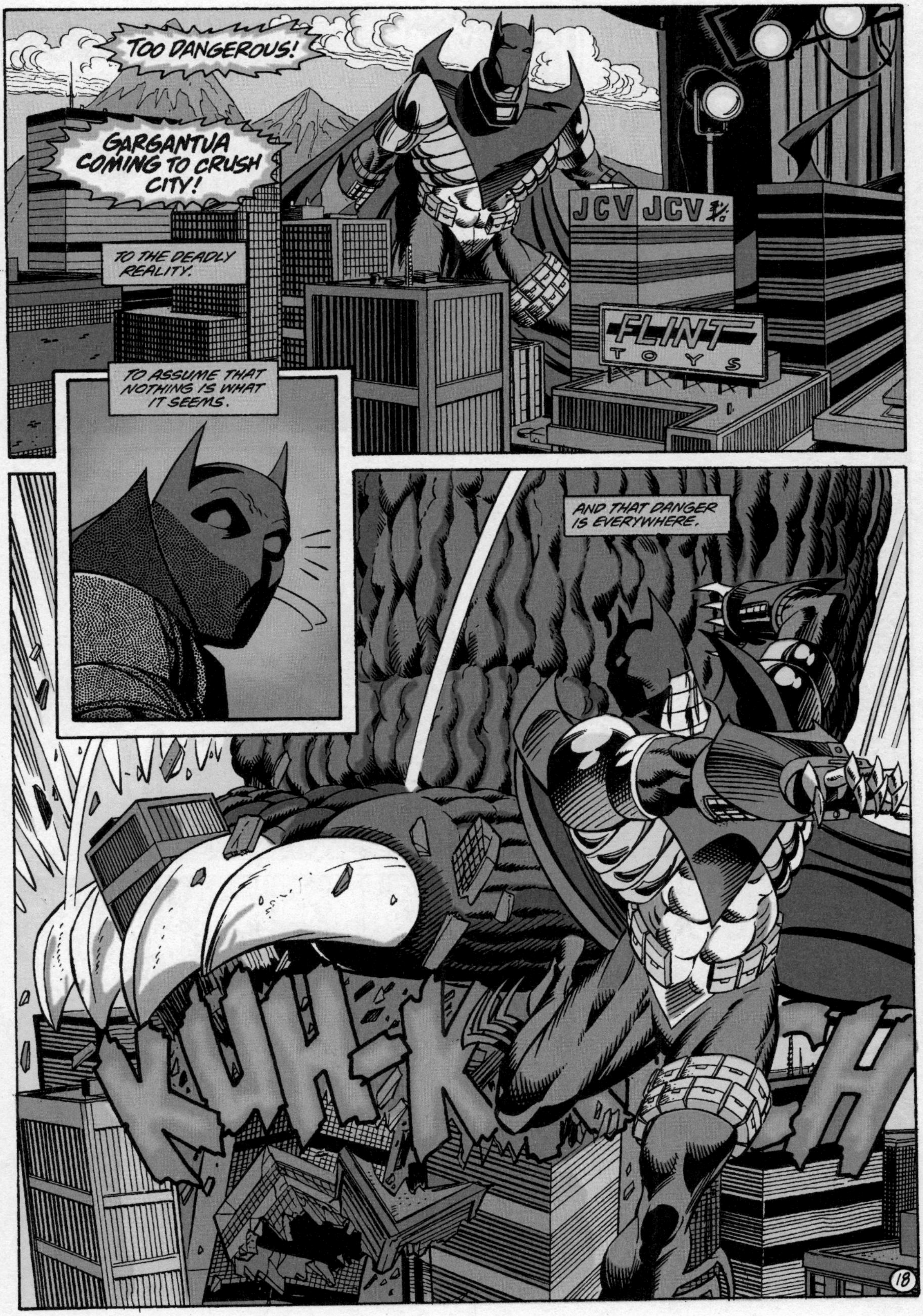
TOO DANGEROUS!
GARGANTUA COMING TO CRUSH CITY!
TO THE DEADLY REALITY.
JCV JCV
FLINT TOYS
TO ASSUME THAT NOTHING IS WHAT IT SEEMS.
AND THAT DANGER IS EVERYWHERE.
KUH-K
H
18

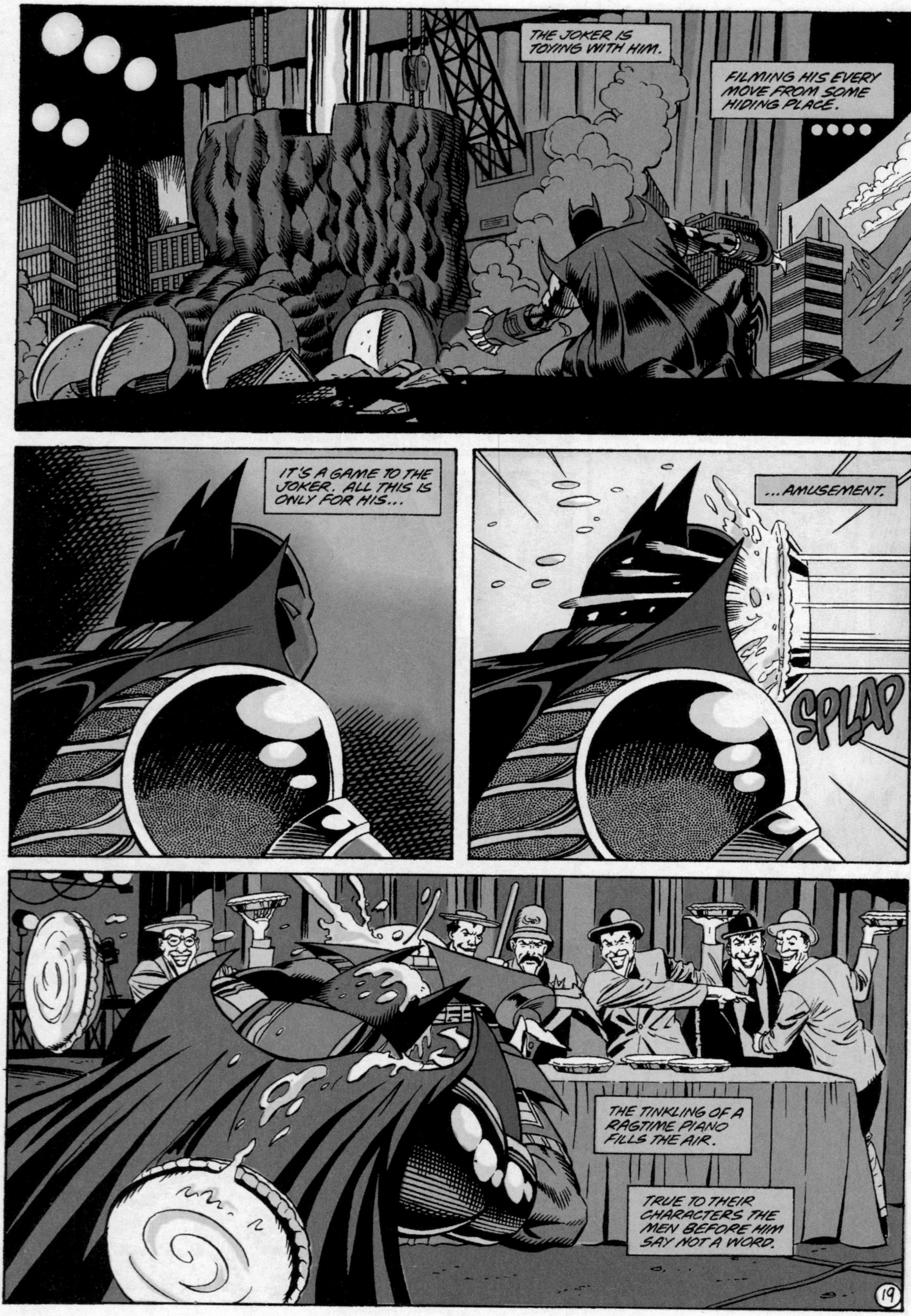
THE JOKER IS TOYING WITH HIM.
FILMING HIS EVERY MOVE FROM SOME HIDING PLACE.
IT'S A GAME TO THE JOKER. ALL THIS IS ONLY FOR HIS...
...AMUSEMENT.
SPLAP
THE TINKLING OF A RAGTIME PIANO FILLS THE AIR.
TRUE TO THEIR CHARACTERS THE MEN BEFORE HIM SAY NOT A WORD.
19

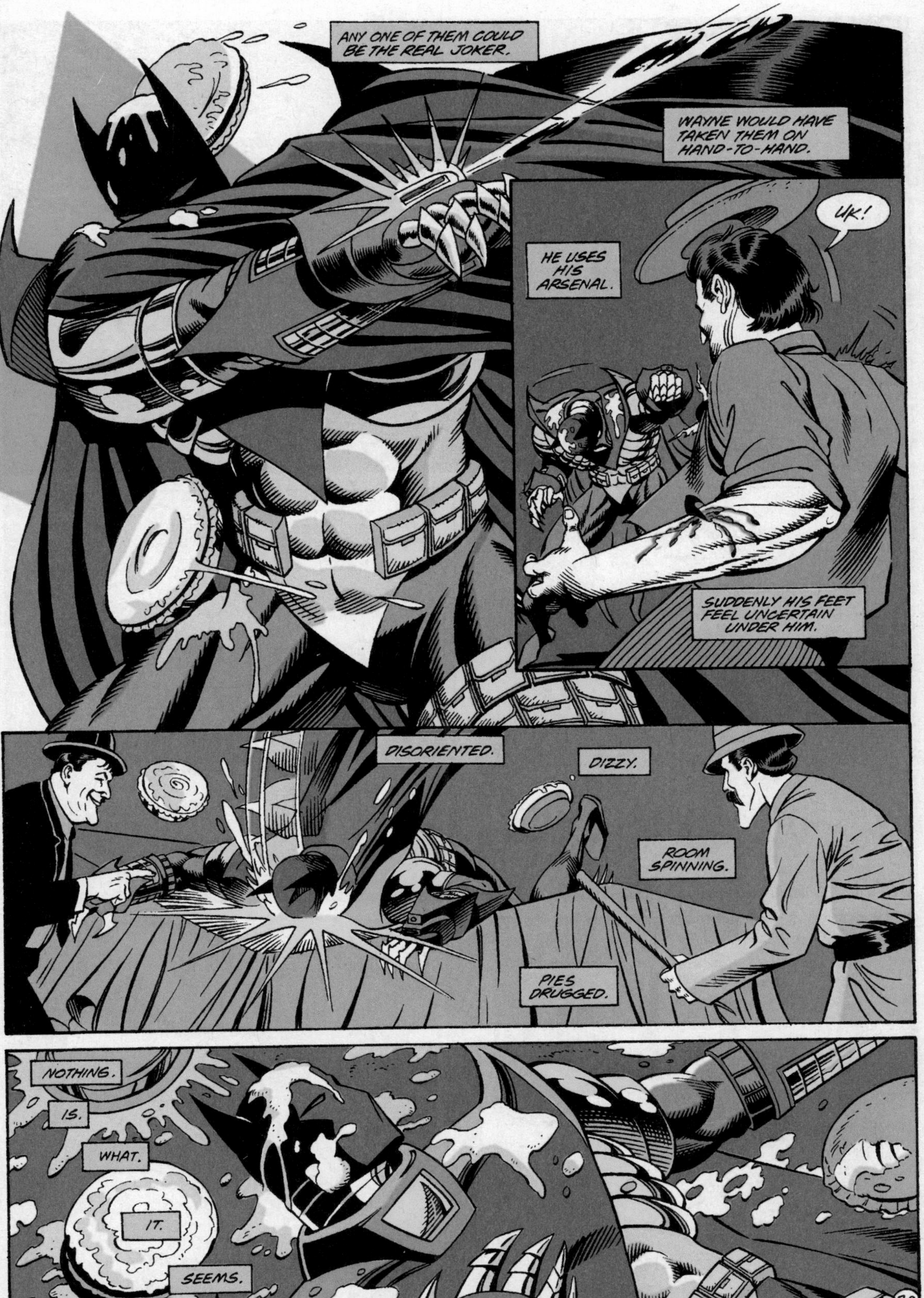
ANY ONE OF THEM COULD BE THE REAL JOKER.
WAYNE WOULD HAVE TAKEN THEM ON HAND-TO-HAND.
HE USES HIS ARSENAL.
UK!
SUDDENLY HIS FEET FEEL UNCERTAIN UNDER HIM.
DISORIENTED.
DIZZY.
ROOM SPINNING.
PIES DRUGGED.
NOTHING.
IS.
WHAT.
IT.
SEEMS.
20

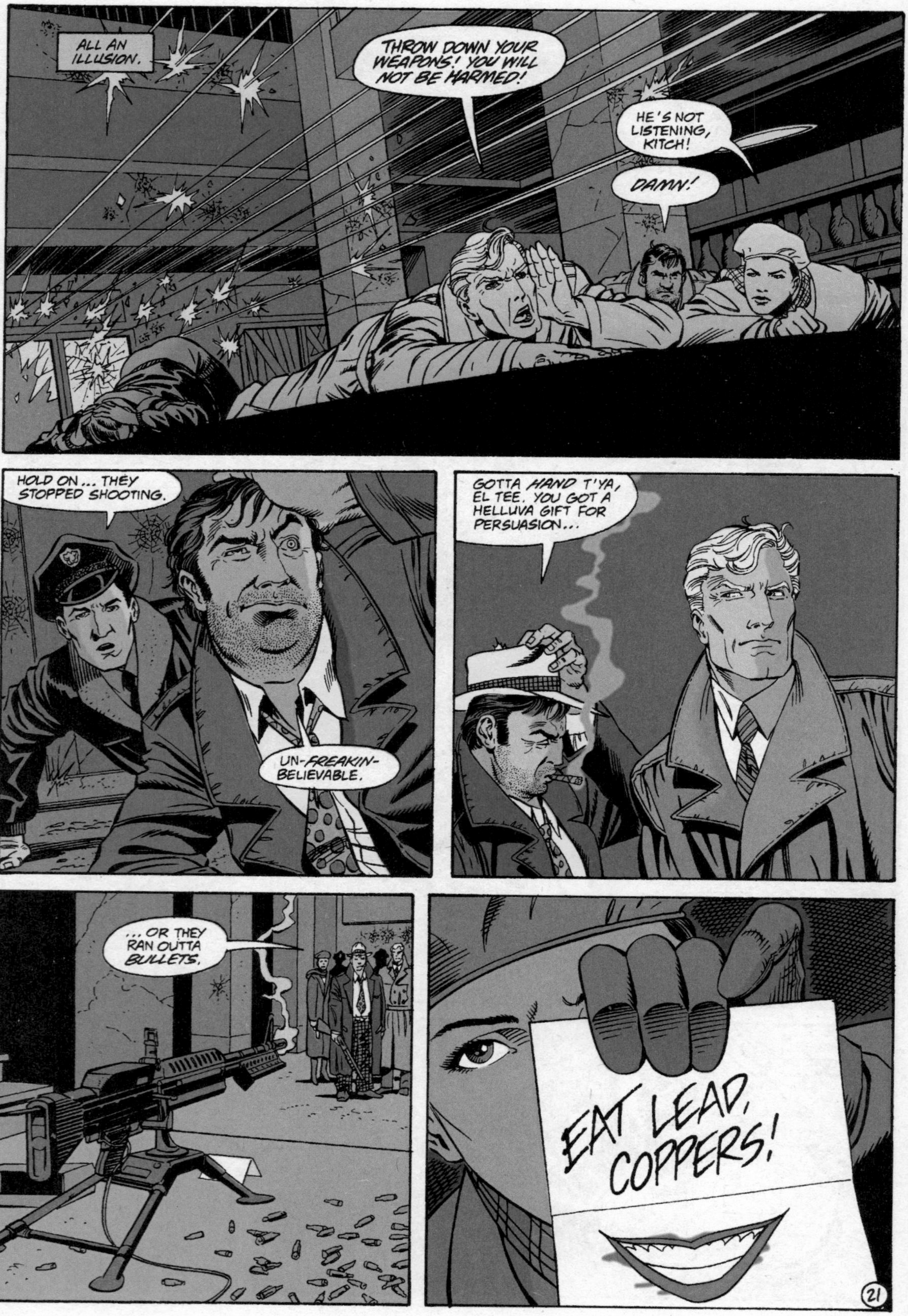
ALL AN ILLUSION.
THROW DOWN YOUR WEAPONS! YOU WILL NOT BE HARMED!
HE'S NOT LISTENING, KITCH!
DAMN!
HOLD ON... THEY STOPPED SHOOTING.
UN-FREAKIN-BELIEVABLE.
GOTTA HAND T'YA, EL TEE. YOU GOT A HELLUVA GIFT FOR PERSUASION...
...OR THEY RAN OUTTA BULLETS.
EAT LEAD, COPPERS!
21

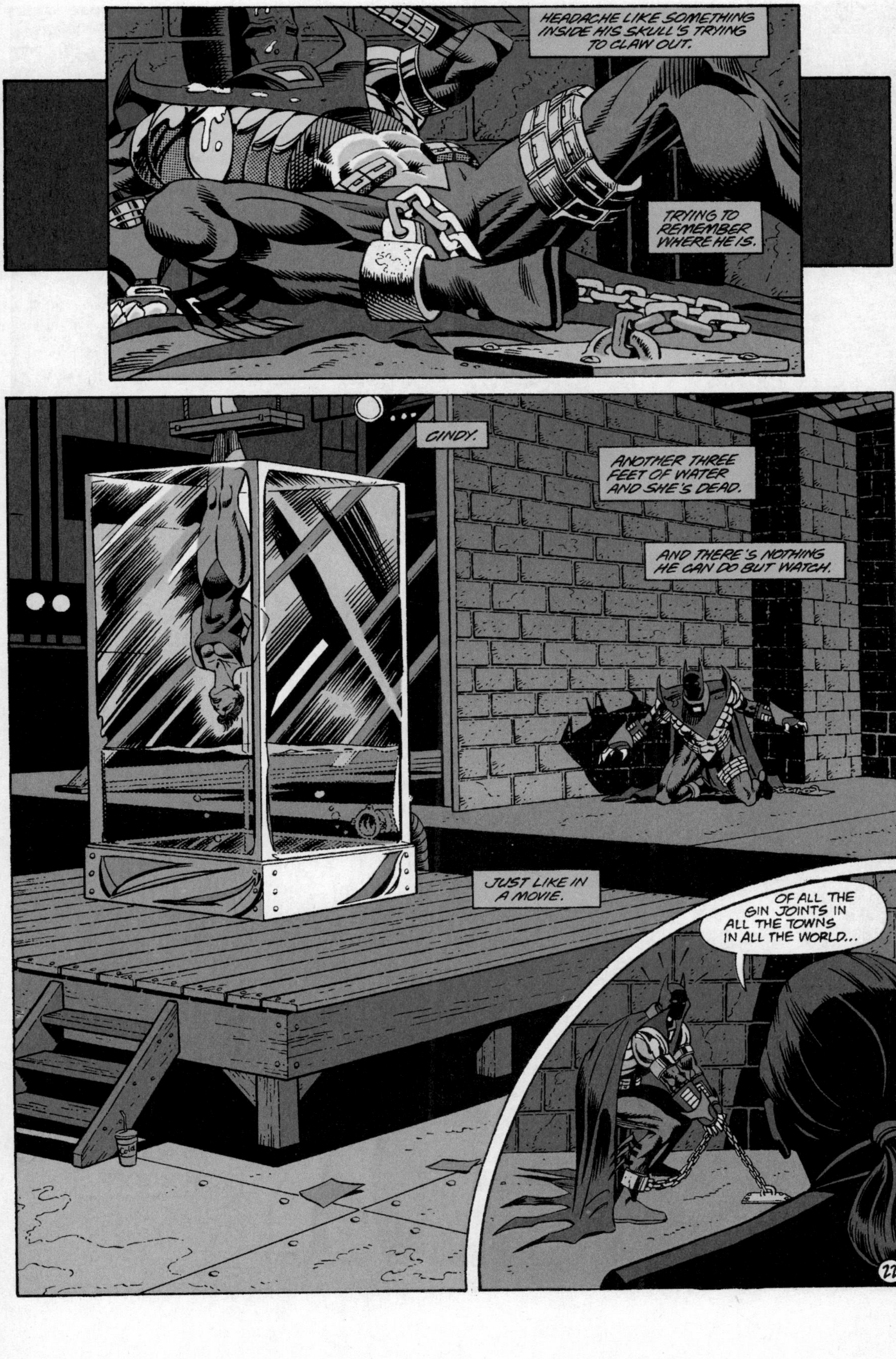
HEADACHE LIKE SOMETHING INSIDE HIS SKULL'S TRYING TO CLAW OUT.
TRYING TO REMEMBER WHERE HE IS.
CINDY.
ANOTHER THREE FEET OF WATER AND SHE'S DEAD.
AND THERE'S NOTHING HE CAN DO BUT WATCH.
JUST LIKE IN A MOVIE.
OF ALL THE GIN JOINTS IN ALL THE TOWNS IN ALL THE WORLD...
22

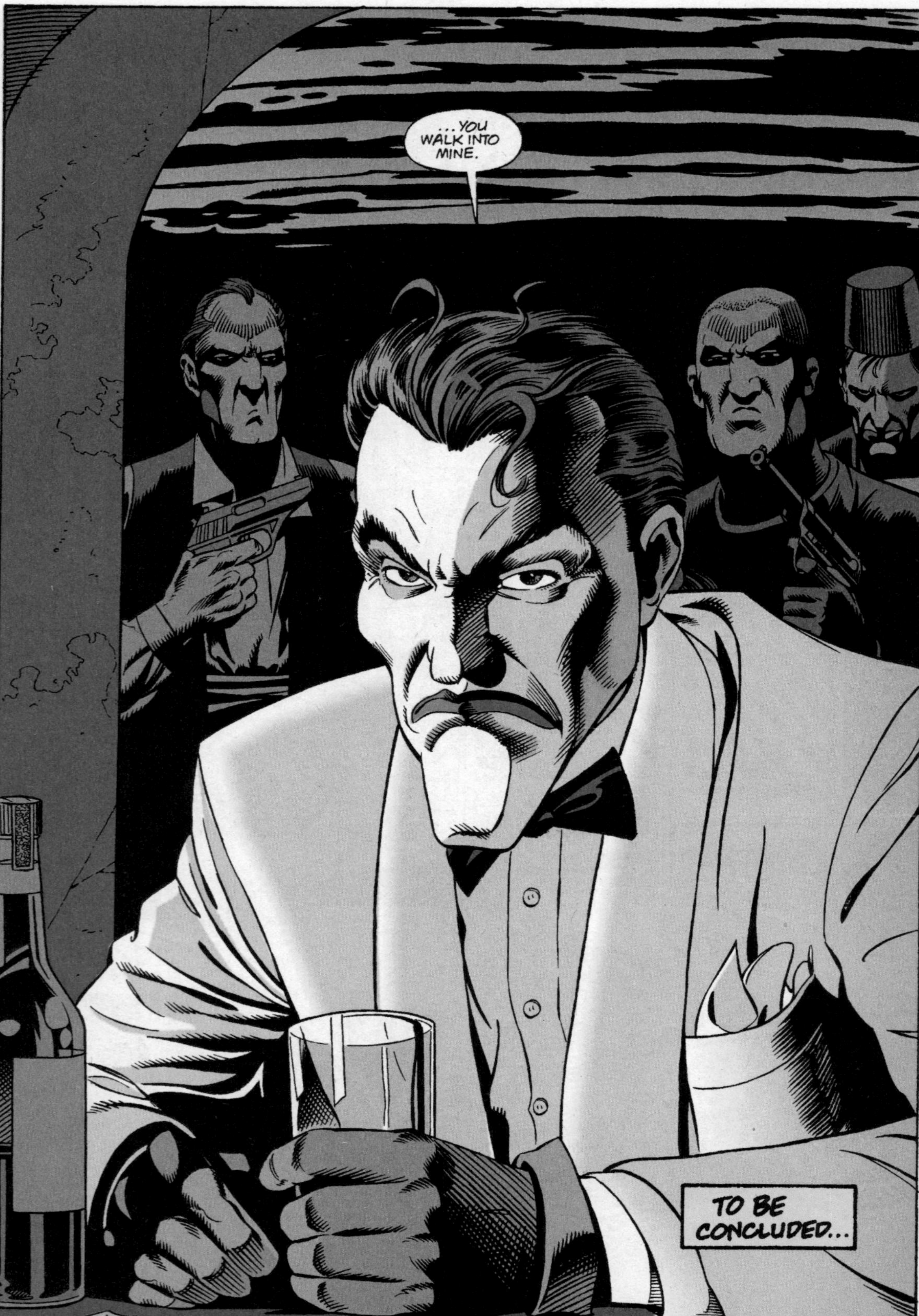
...YOU WALK INTO MINE.
TO BE CONCLUDED...
23

Cover art by **KELLEY JONES**

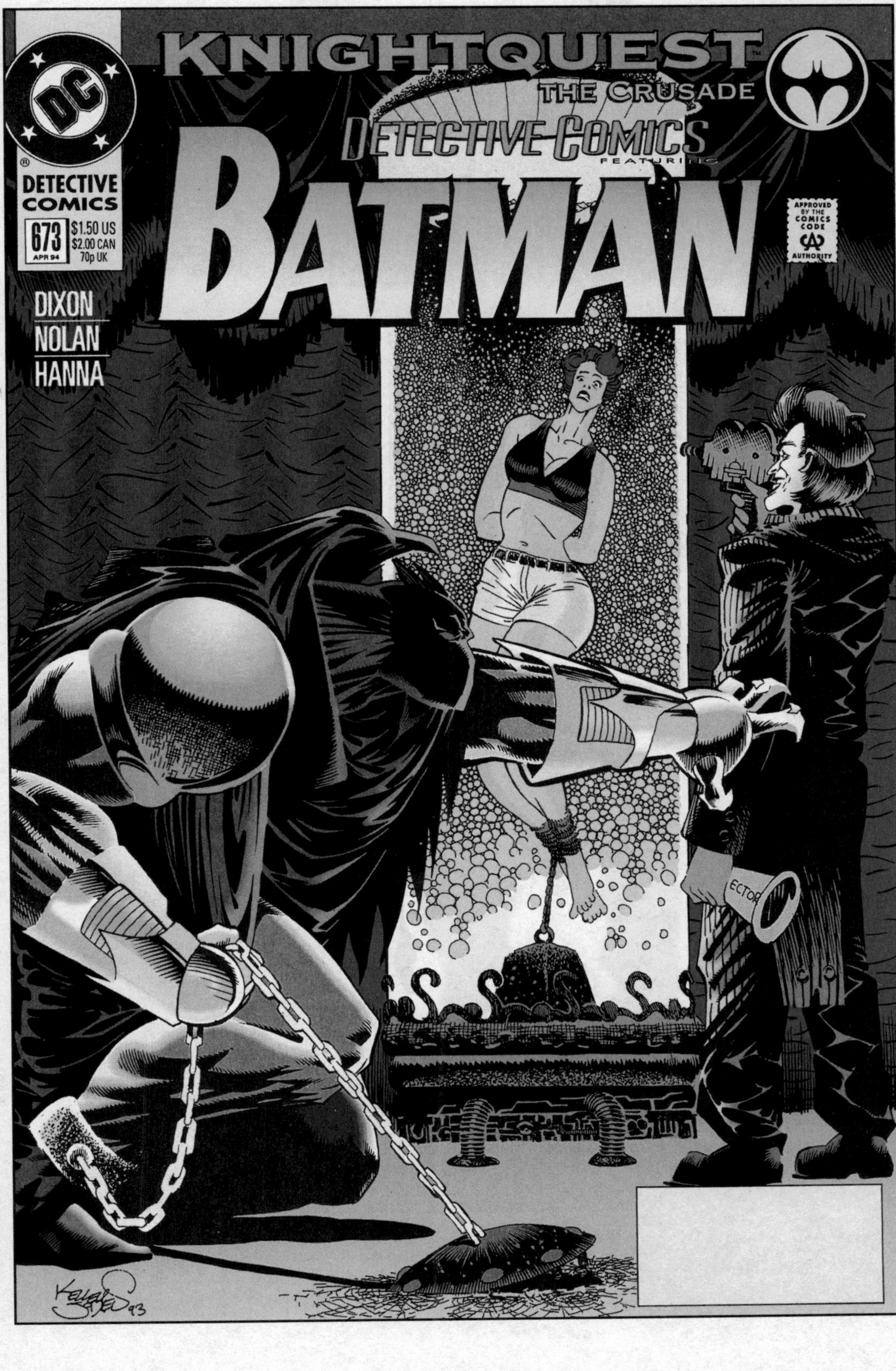
KNIGHTQUEST
THE CRUSADE
DETECTIVE COMICS
FEATURING
BATMAN
DC
DETECTIVE COMICS
673
APR 94
$1.50 US
$2.00 CAN
70p UK
DIXON
NOLAN
HANNA
APPROVED BY THE COMICS CODE AUTHORITY
ECTOR
KELLEY JONES '93

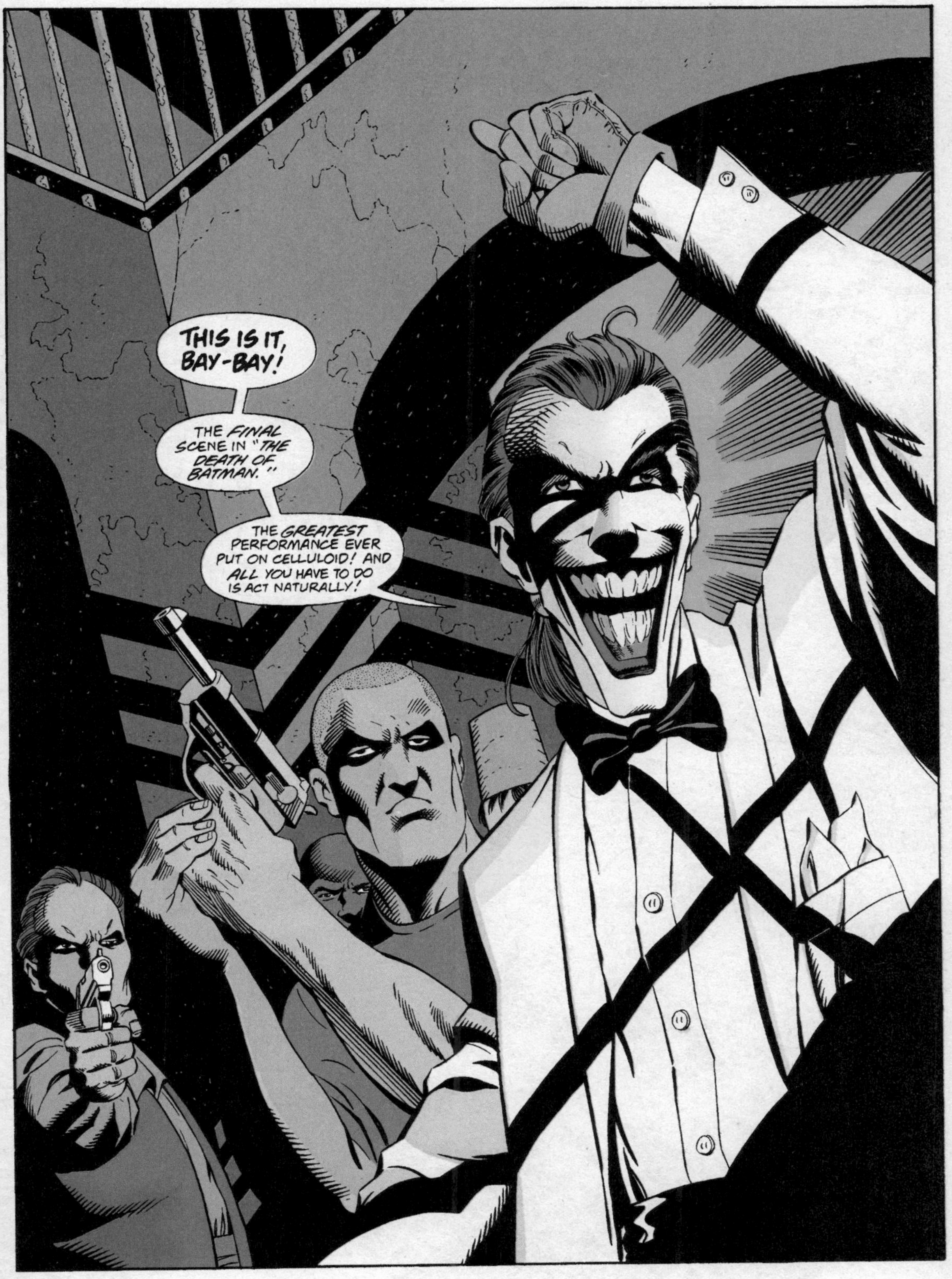
THIS IS IT, BAY-BAY!
THE FINAL SCENE IN "THE DEATH OF BATMAN."
THE GREATEST PERFORMANCE EVER PUT ON CELLULOID! AND ALL YOU HAVE TO DO IS ACT NATURALLY!

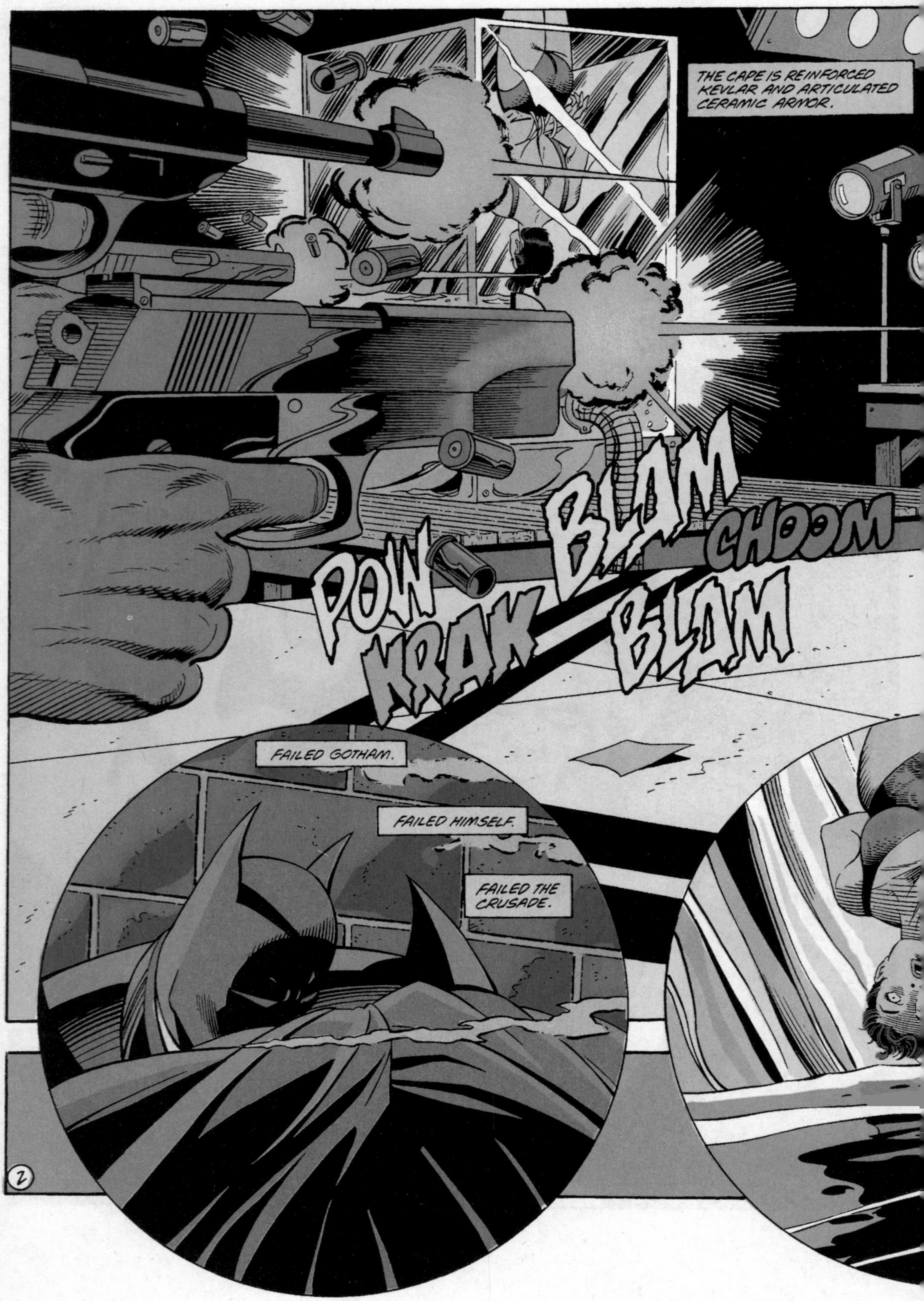
THE CAPE IS REINFORCED KEVLAR AND ARTICULATED CERAMIC ARMOR.
POW
KRAK
BLAM
CHOOM
BLAM
FAILED GOTHAM.
FAILED HIMSELF.
FAILED THE CRUSADE.

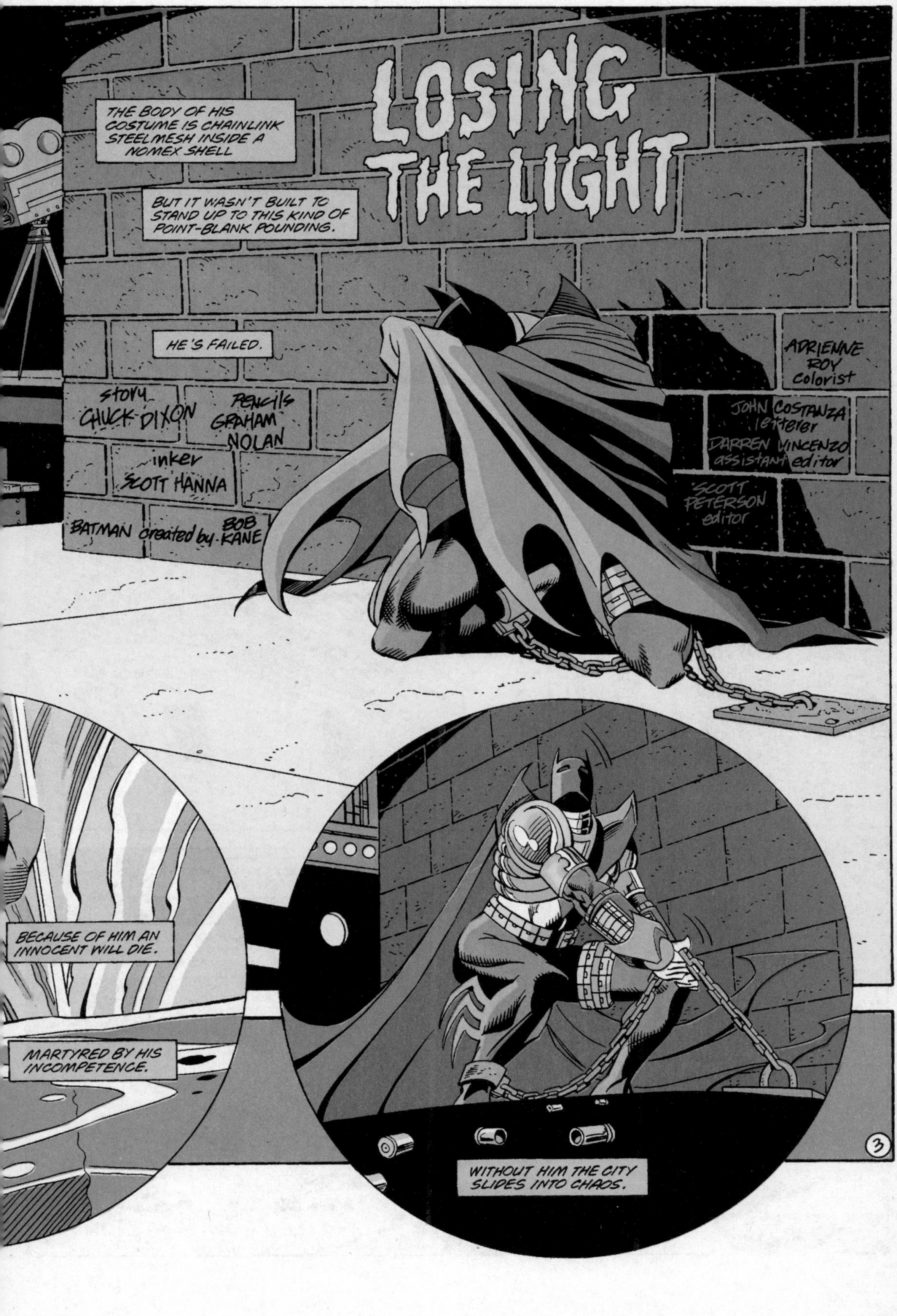
LOSING THE LIGHT
THE BODY OF HIS COSTUME IS CHAINLINK STEELMESH INSIDE A NOMEX SHELL
BUT IT WASN'T BUILT TO STAND UP TO THIS KIND OF POINT-BLANK POUNDING.
HE'S FAILED.
story CHUCK DIXON
pencils GRAHAM NOLAN
inker SCOTT HANNA
BATMAN created by BOB KANE
ADRIENNE ROY Colorist
JOHN COSTANZA letterer
DARREN VINCENZO assistant editor
SCOTT PETERSON editor
BECAUSE OF HIM AN INNOCENT WILL DIE.
MARTYRED BY HIS INCOMPETENCE.
WITHOUT HIM THE CITY SLIDES INTO CHAOS.
3

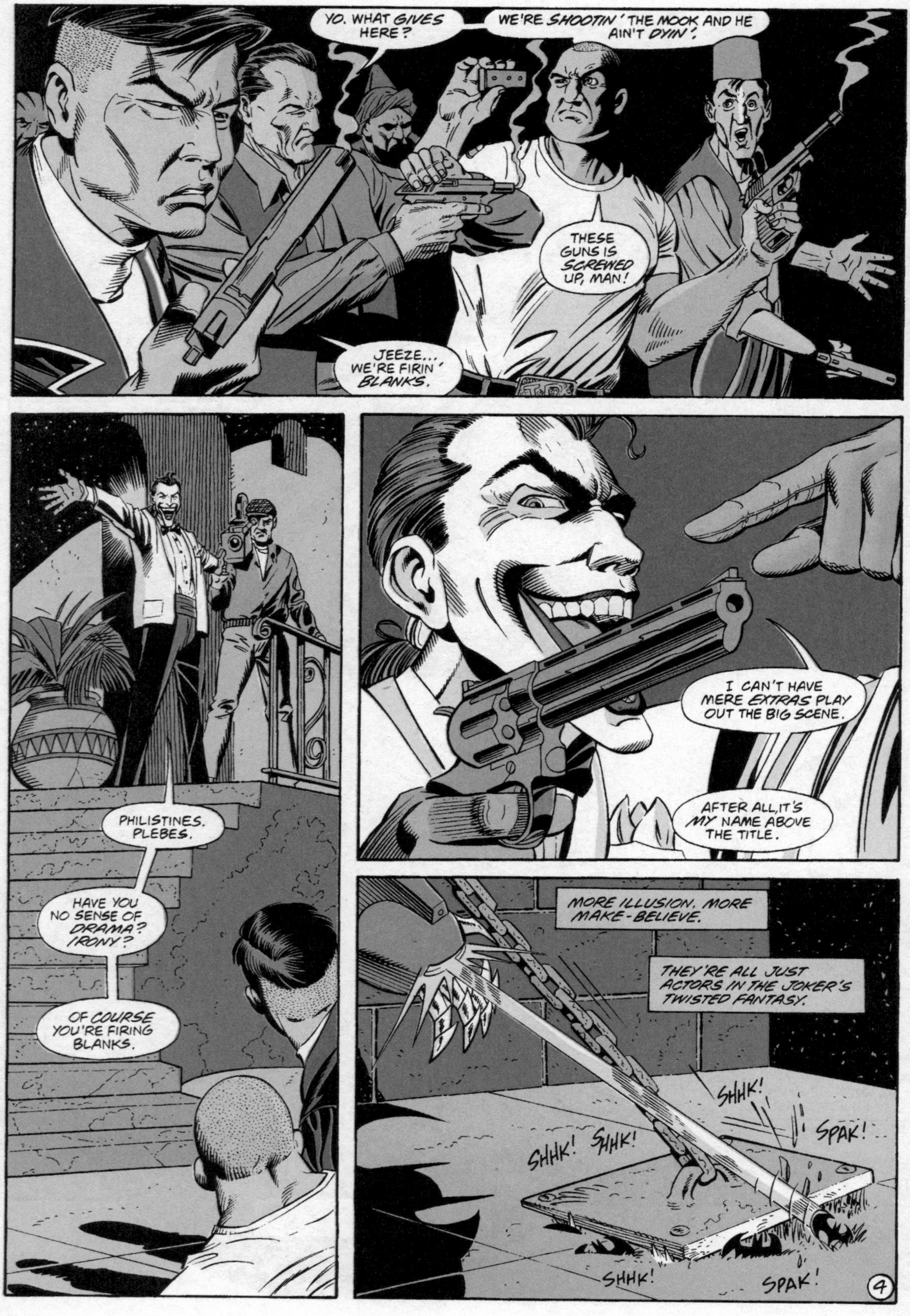
YO. WHAT GIVES HERE?
WE'RE SHOOTIN' THE MOOK AND HE AIN'T DYIN'.
THESE GUNS IS SCREWED UP, MAN!
JEEZE... WE'RE FIRIN' BLANKS.
PHILISTINES. PLEBES.
HAVE YOU NO SENSE OF DRAMA? IRONY?
OF COURSE YOU'RE FIRING BLANKS.
I CAN'T HAVE MERE EXTRAS PLAY OUT THE BIG SCENE.
AFTER ALL, IT'S MY NAME ABOVE THE TITLE.
MORE ILLUSION. MORE MAKE-BELIEVE.
THEY'RE ALL JUST ACTORS IN THE JOKER'S TWISTED FANTASY.
SHHK!
SHHK! SHHK!
SPAK!
SHHK!
SPAK!
4

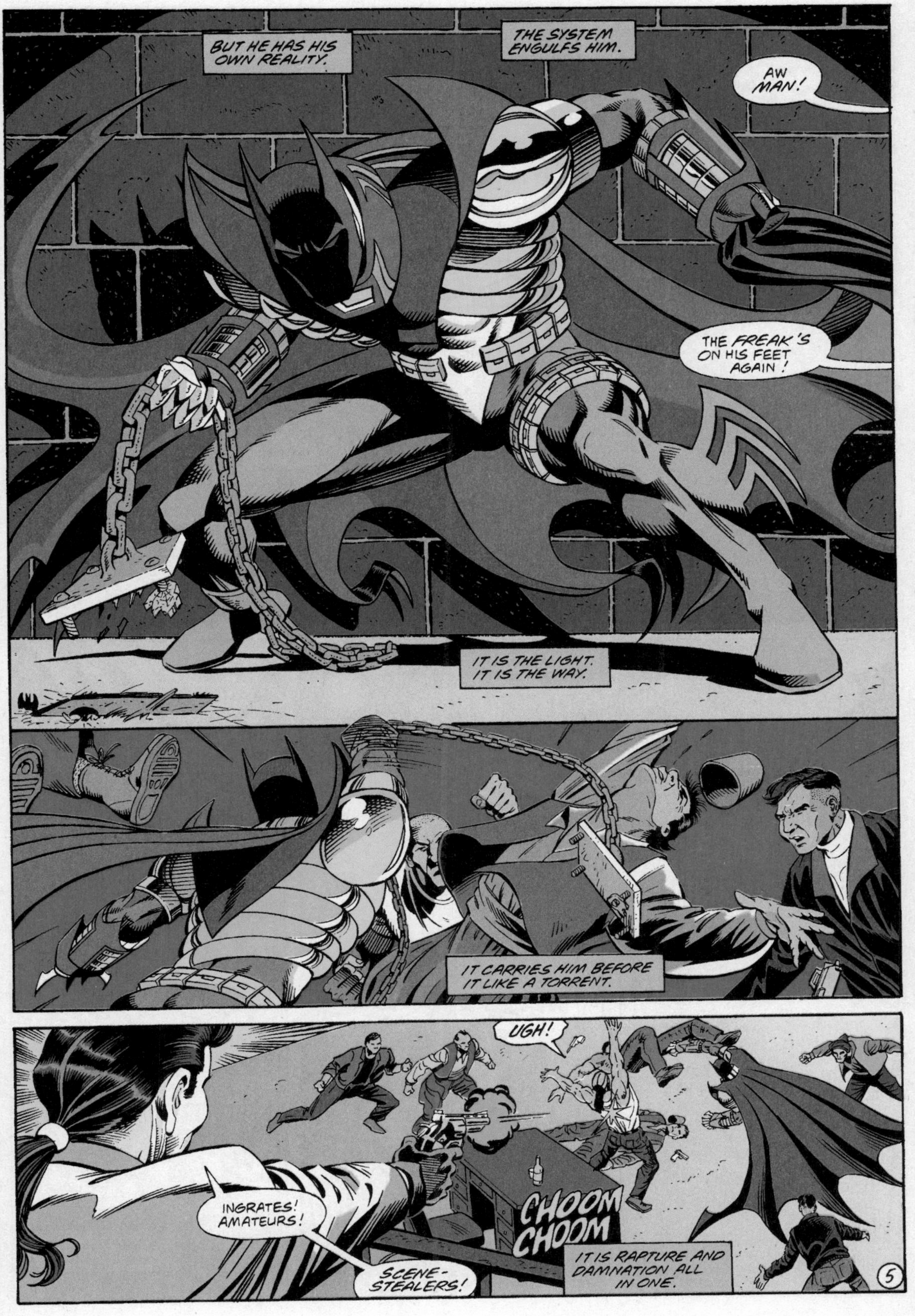
BUT HE HAS HIS OWN REALITY.
THE SYSTEM ENGULFS HIM.
AW MAN!
THE FREAK'S ON HIS FEET AGAIN!
IT IS THE LIGHT. IT IS THE WAY.
IT CARRIES HIM BEFORE IT LIKE A TORRENT.
UGH!
INGRATES! AMATEURS!
SCENE-STEALERS!
CHOOM CHOOM
IT IS RAPTURE AND DAMNATION ALL IN ONE.
5

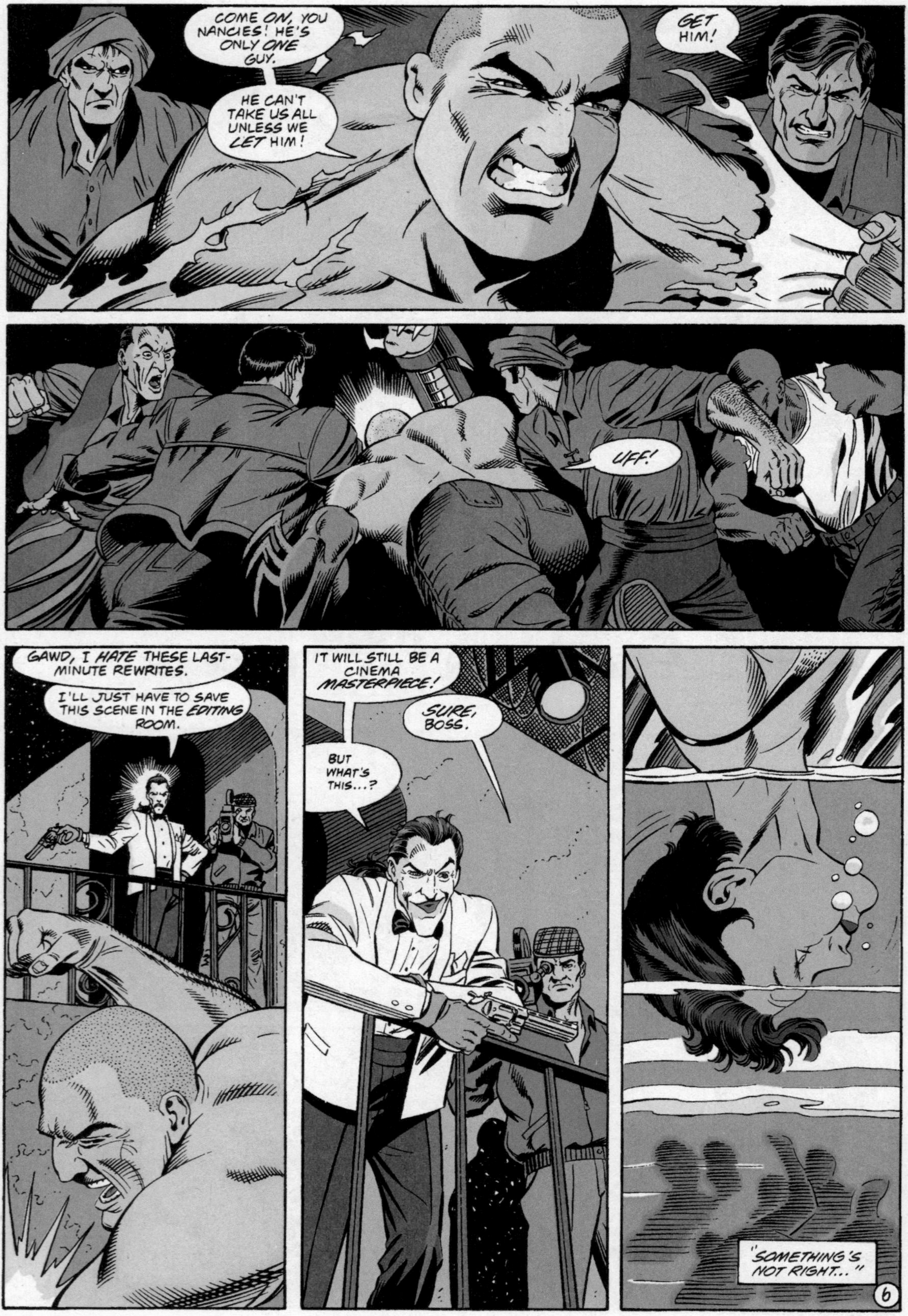
COME ON, YOU NANCIES! HE'S ONLY ONE GUY.
HE CAN'T TAKE US ALL UNLESS WE LET HIM!
GET HIM!
UFF!
GAWD, I HATE THESE LAST-MINUTE REWRITES.
I'LL JUST HAVE TO SAVE THIS SCENE IN THE EDITING ROOM.
IT WILL STILL BE A CINEMA MASTERPIECE!
SURE, BOSS.
BUT WHAT'S THIS...?
"SOMETHING'S NOT RIGHT..."
6

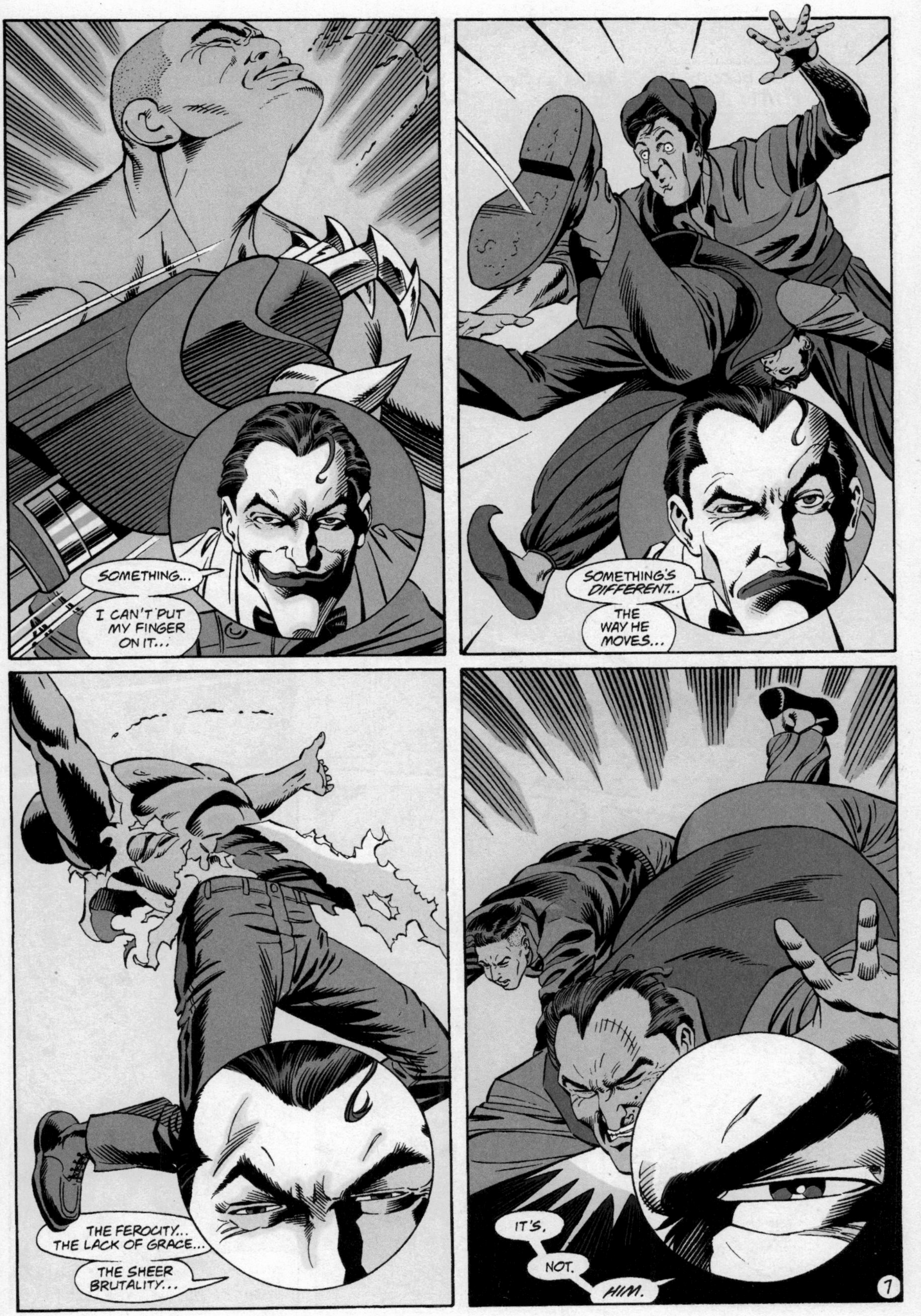
SOMETHING...
I CAN'T PUT MY FINGER ON IT...
SOMETHING'S DIFFERENT...
THE WAY HE MOVES...
THE FEROCITY... THE LACK OF GRACE...
THE SHEER BRUTALITY...
IT'S.
NOT.
HIM.
7

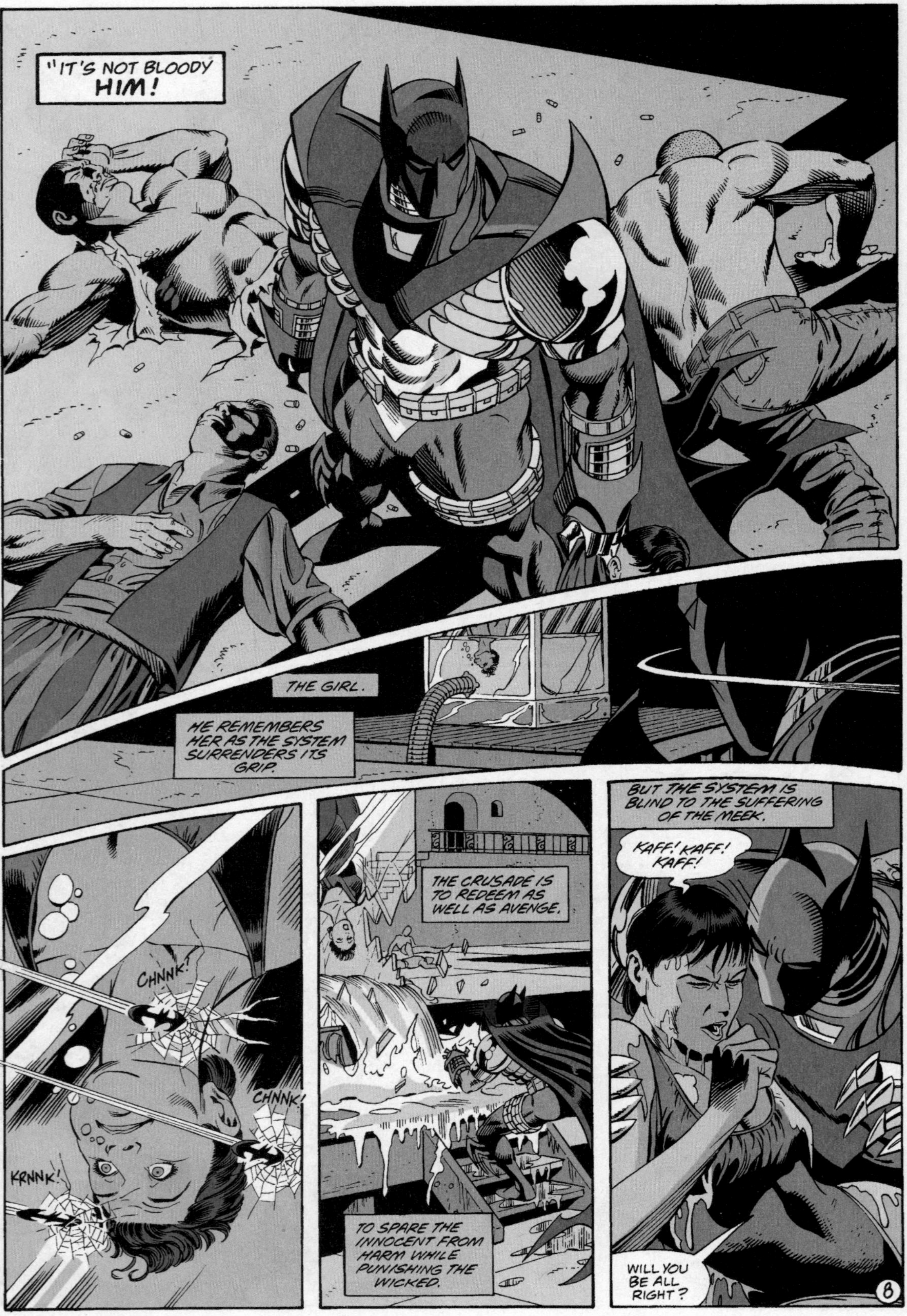
"IT'S NOT BLOODY HIM!
THE GIRL.
HE REMEMBERS HER AS THE SYSTEM SURRENDERS ITS GRIP.
CHNNK!
CHNNK!
KRNNK!
THE CRUSADE IS TO REDEEM AS WELL AS AVENGE.
TO SPARE THE INNOCENT FROM HARM WHILE PUNISHING THE WICKED.
BUT THE SYSTEM IS BLIND TO THE SUFFERING OF THE MEEK.
KAFF! KAFF! KAFF!
WILL YOU BE ALL RIGHT?
8

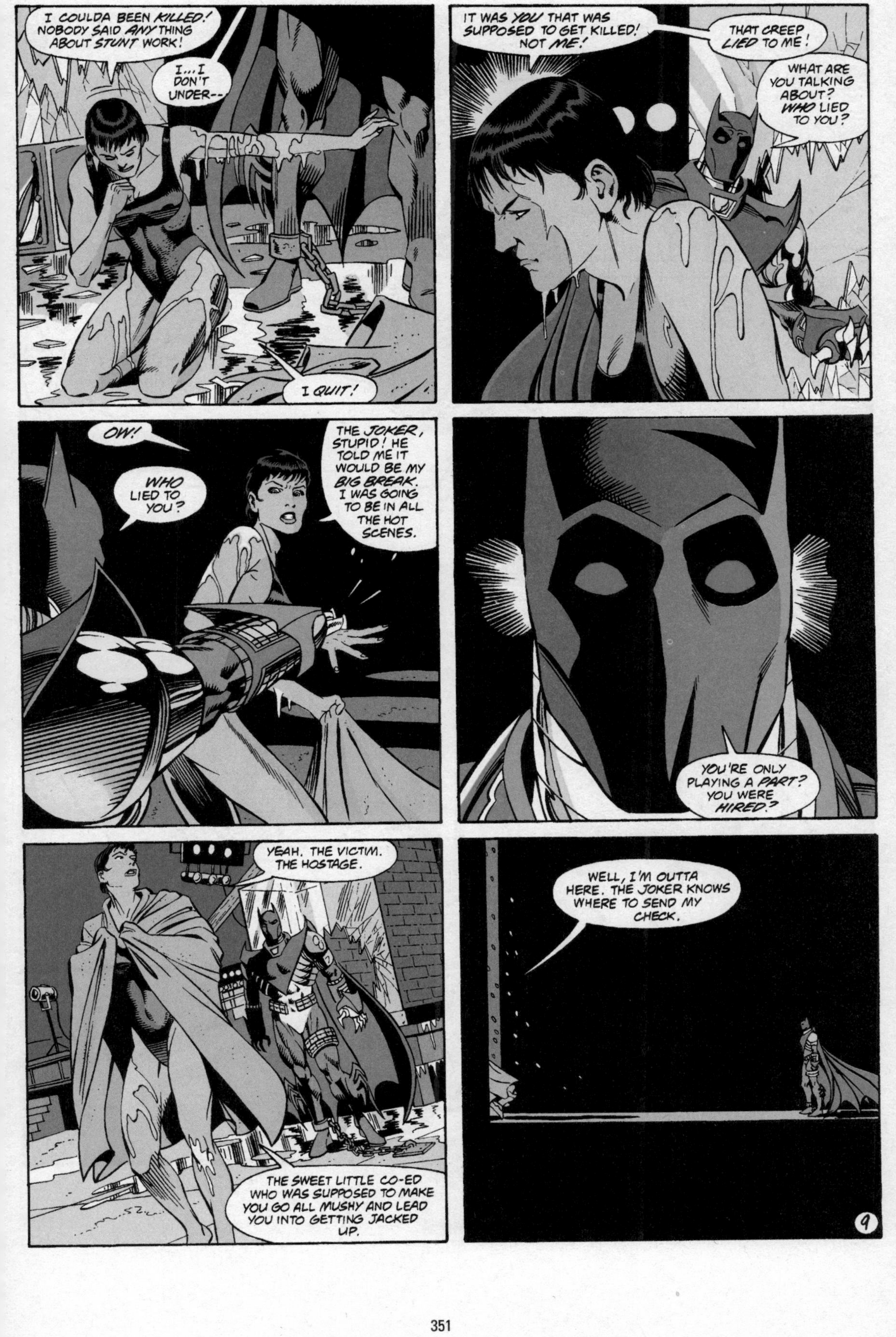
I COULDA BEEN KILLED! NOBODY SAID ANY THING ABOUT STUNT WORK!
I...I DON'T UNDER--
I QUIT!
IT WAS YOU THAT WAS SUPPOSED TO GET KILLED! NOT ME!
THAT CREEP LIED TO ME!
WHAT ARE YOU TALKING ABOUT? WHO LIED TO YOU?
OW!
WHO LIED TO YOU?
THE JOKER, STUPID! HE TOLD ME IT WOULD BE MY BIG BREAK. I WAS GOING TO BE IN ALL THE HOT SCENES.
YOU'RE ONLY PLAYING A PART? YOU WERE HIRED?
YEAH. THE VICTIM. THE HOSTAGE.
THE SWEET LITTLE CO-ED WHO WAS SUPPOSED TO MAKE YOU GO ALL MUSHY AND LEAD YOU INTO GETTING JACKED UP.
WELL, I'M OUTTA HERE. THE JOKER KNOWS WHERE TO SEND MY CHECK.
9

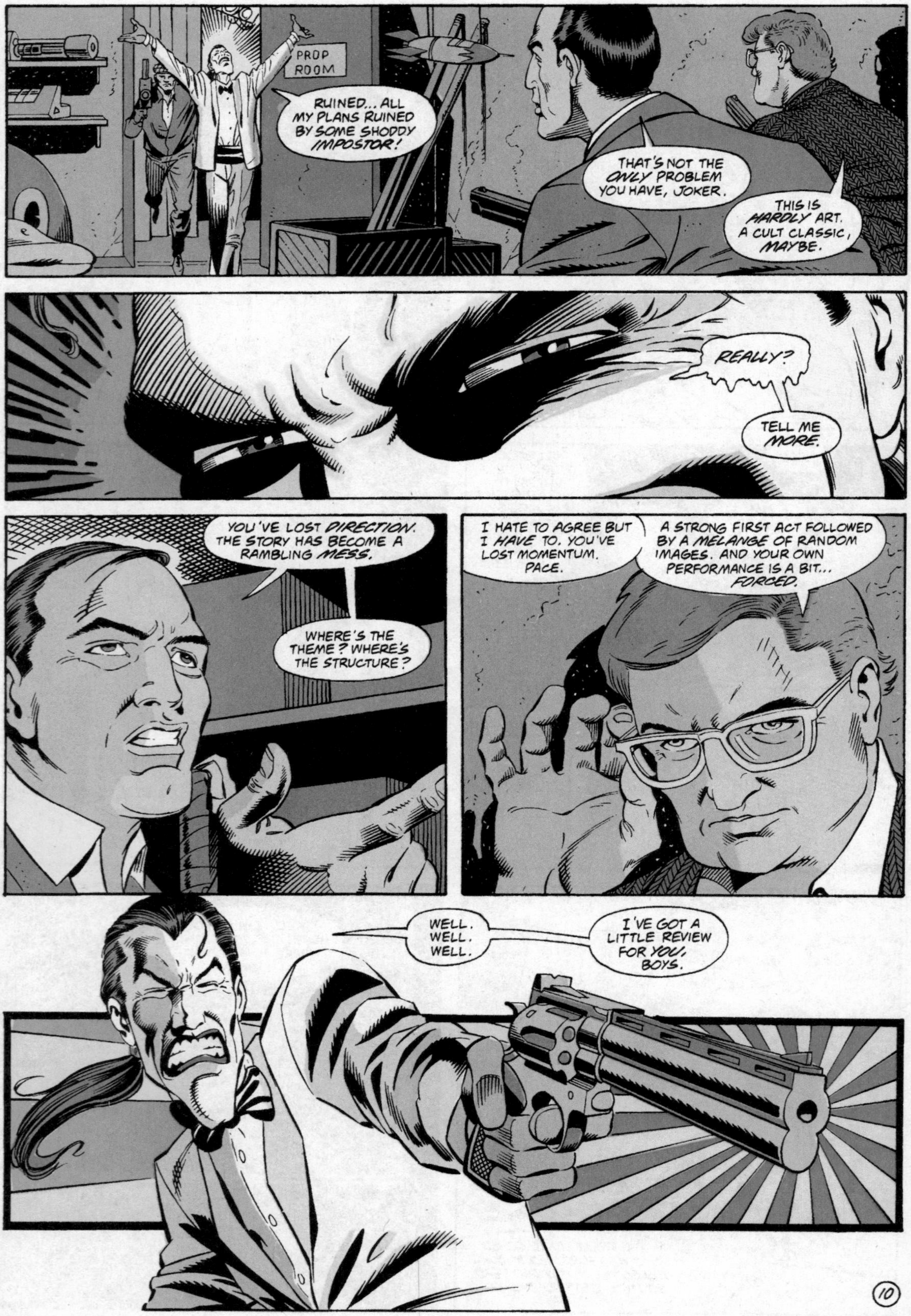
PROP ROOM
RUINED... ALL MY PLANS RUINED BY SOME SHODDY IMPOSTOR!
THAT'S NOT THE ONLY PROBLEM YOU HAVE, JOKER.
THIS IS HARDLY ART. A CULT CLASSIC, MAYBE.
REALLY?
TELL ME MORE.
YOU'VE LOST DIRECTION. THE STORY HAS BECOME A RAMBLING MESS.
WHERE'S THE THEME? WHERE'S THE STRUCTURE?
I HATE TO AGREE BUT I HAVE TO. YOU'VE LOST MOMENTUM. PACE.
A STRONG FIRST ACT FOLLOWED BY A MELANGE OF RANDOM IMAGES. AND YOUR OWN PERFORMANCE IS A BIT... FORCED.
WELL. WELL. WELL.
I'VE GOT A LITTLE REVIEW FOR YOU, BOYS.
10

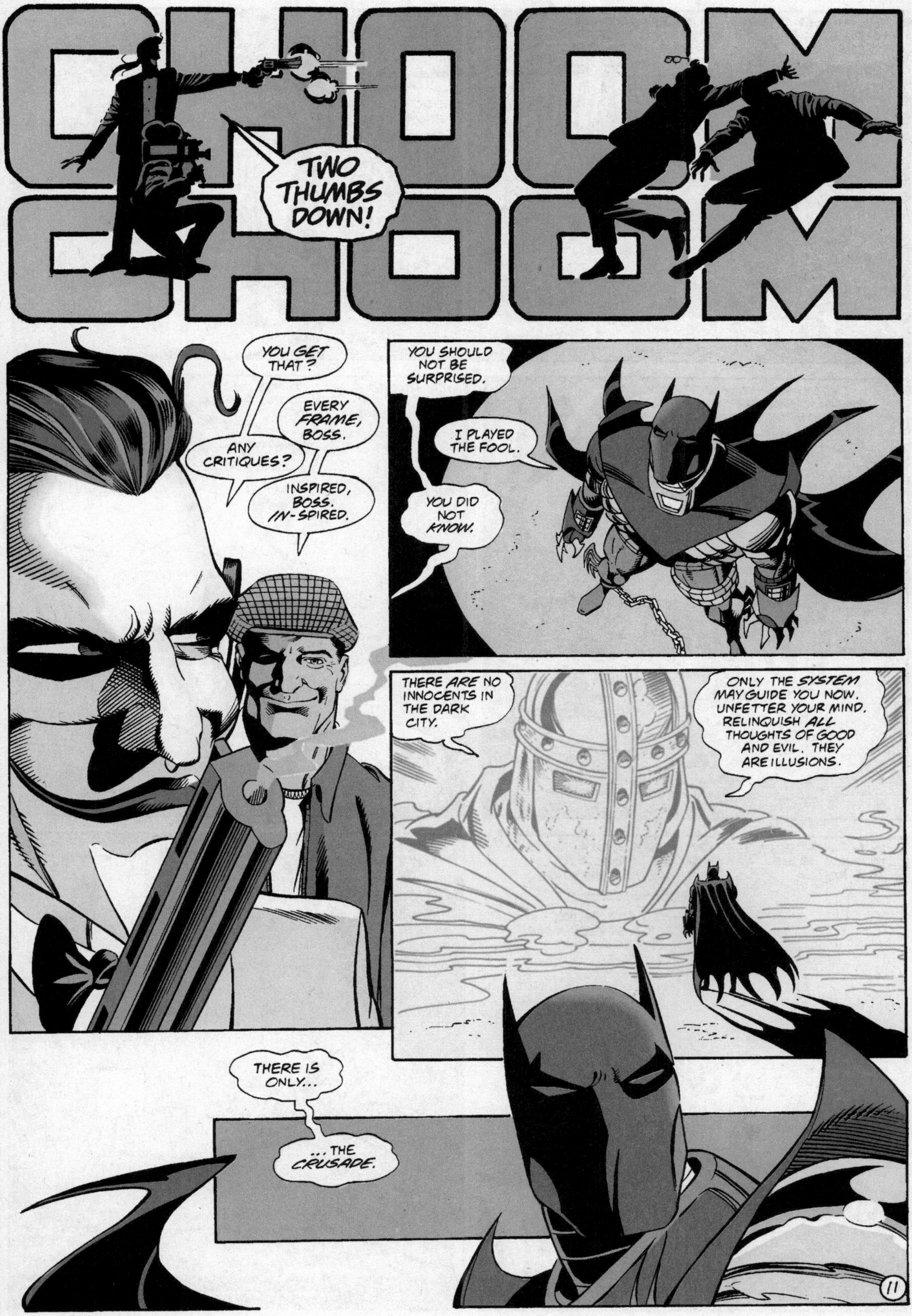
CHOOM
CHOOM
TWO THUMBS DOWN!
YOU GET THAT?
ANY CRITIQUES?
EVERY FRAME, BOSS.
INSPIRED, BOSS. IN-SPIRED.
YOU SHOULD NOT BE SURPRISED.
I PLAYED THE FOOL.
YOU DID NOT KNOW.
THERE ARE NO INNOCENTS IN THE DARK CITY.
ONLY THE SYSTEM MAY GUIDE YOU NOW. UNFETTER YOUR MIND. RELINQUISH ALL THOUGHTS OF GOOD AND EVIL. THEY ARE ILLUSIONS.
THERE IS ONLY...
...THE CRUSADE.
11

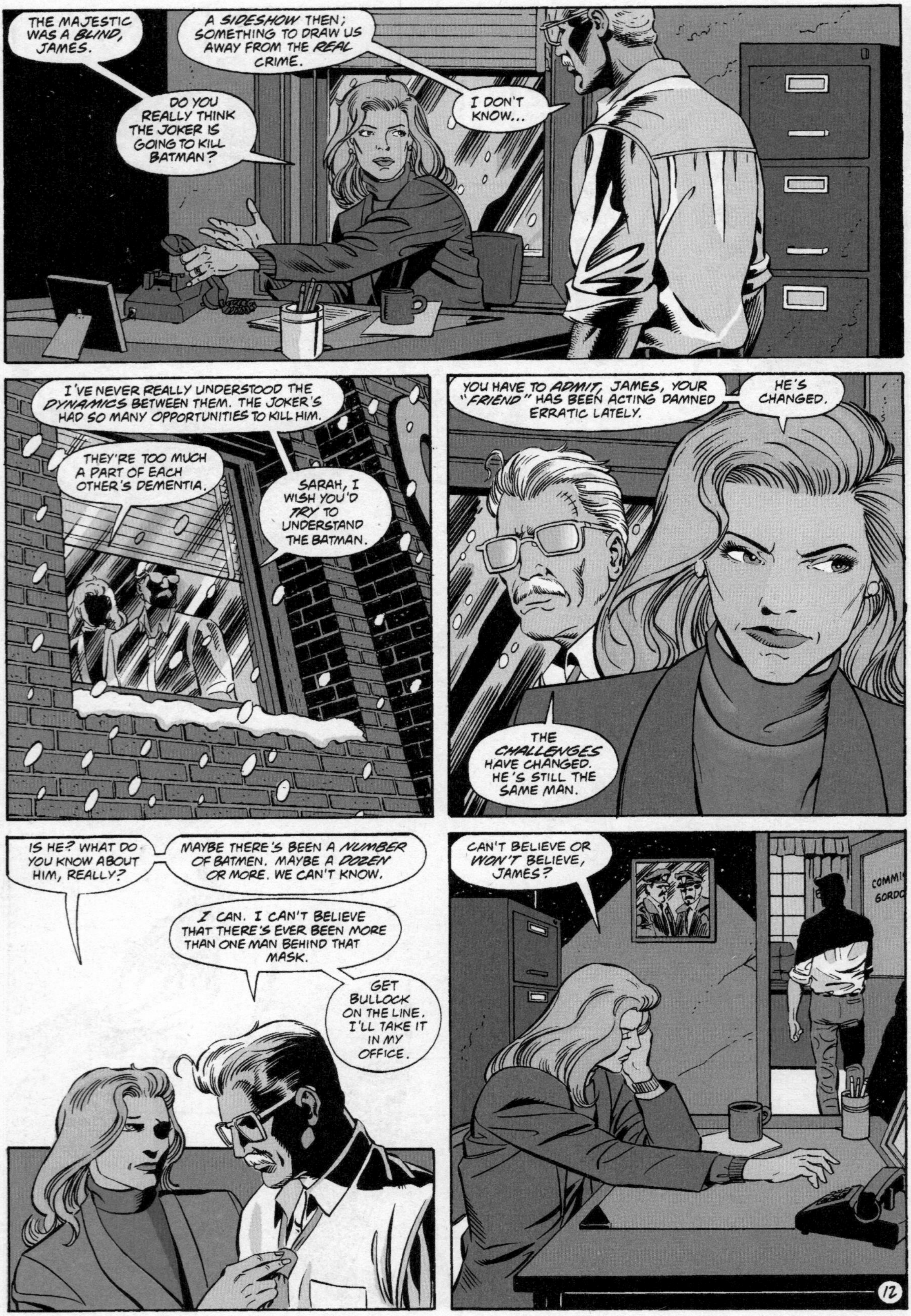
THE MAJESTIC WAS A BLIND, JAMES.
A SIDESHOW THEN; SOMETHING TO DRAW US AWAY FROM THE REAL CRIME.
DO YOU REALLY THINK THE JOKER IS GOING TO KILL BATMAN?
I DON'T KNOW...
I'VE NEVER REALLY UNDERSTOOD THE DYNAMICS BETWEEN THEM. THE JOKER'S HAD SO MANY OPPORTUNITIES TO KILL HIM.
THEY'RE TOO MUCH A PART OF EACH OTHER'S DEMENTIA.
SARAH, I WISH YOU'D TRY TO UNDERSTAND THE BATMAN.
YOU HAVE TO ADMIT, JAMES, YOUR "FRIEND" HAS BEEN ACTING DAMNED ERRATIC LATELY.
HE'S CHANGED.
THE CHALLENGES HAVE CHANGED. HE'S STILL THE SAME MAN.
IS HE? WHAT DO YOU KNOW ABOUT HIM, REALLY?
MAYBE THERE'S BEEN A NUMBER OF BATMEN. MAYBE A DOZEN OR MORE. WE CAN'T KNOW.
I CAN. I CAN'T BELIEVE THAT THERE'S EVER BEEN MORE THAN ONE MAN BEHIND THAT MASK.
GET BULLOCK ON THE LINE. I'LL TAKE IT IN MY OFFICE.
CAN'T BELIEVE OR WON'T BELIEVE, JAMES?
12

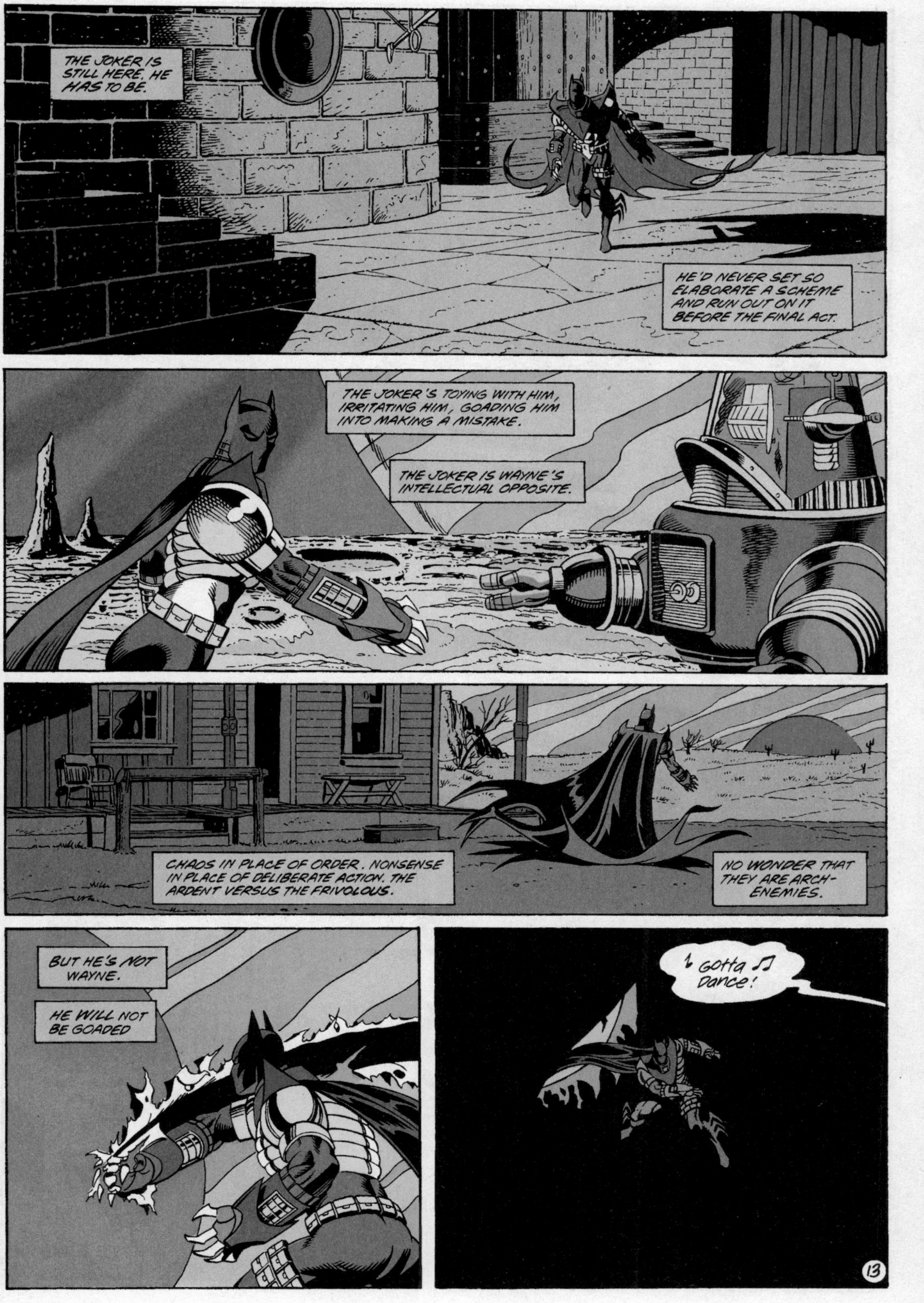
THE JOKER IS STILL HERE. HE HAS TO BE.
HE'D NEVER SET SO ELABORATE A SCHEME AND RUN OUT ON IT BEFORE THE FINAL ACT.
THE JOKER'S TOYING WITH HIM, IRRITATING HIM, GOADING HIM INTO MAKING A MISTAKE.
THE JOKER IS WAYNE'S INTELLECTUAL OPPOSITE.
CHAOS IN PLACE OF ORDER. NONSENSE IN PLACE OF DELIBERATE ACTION. THE ARDENT VERSUS THE FRIVOLOUS.
NO WONDER THAT THEY ARE ARCH-ENEMIES.
BUT HE'S NOT WAYNE.
HE WILL NOT BE GOADED
♪ Gotta ♫ Dance!
13

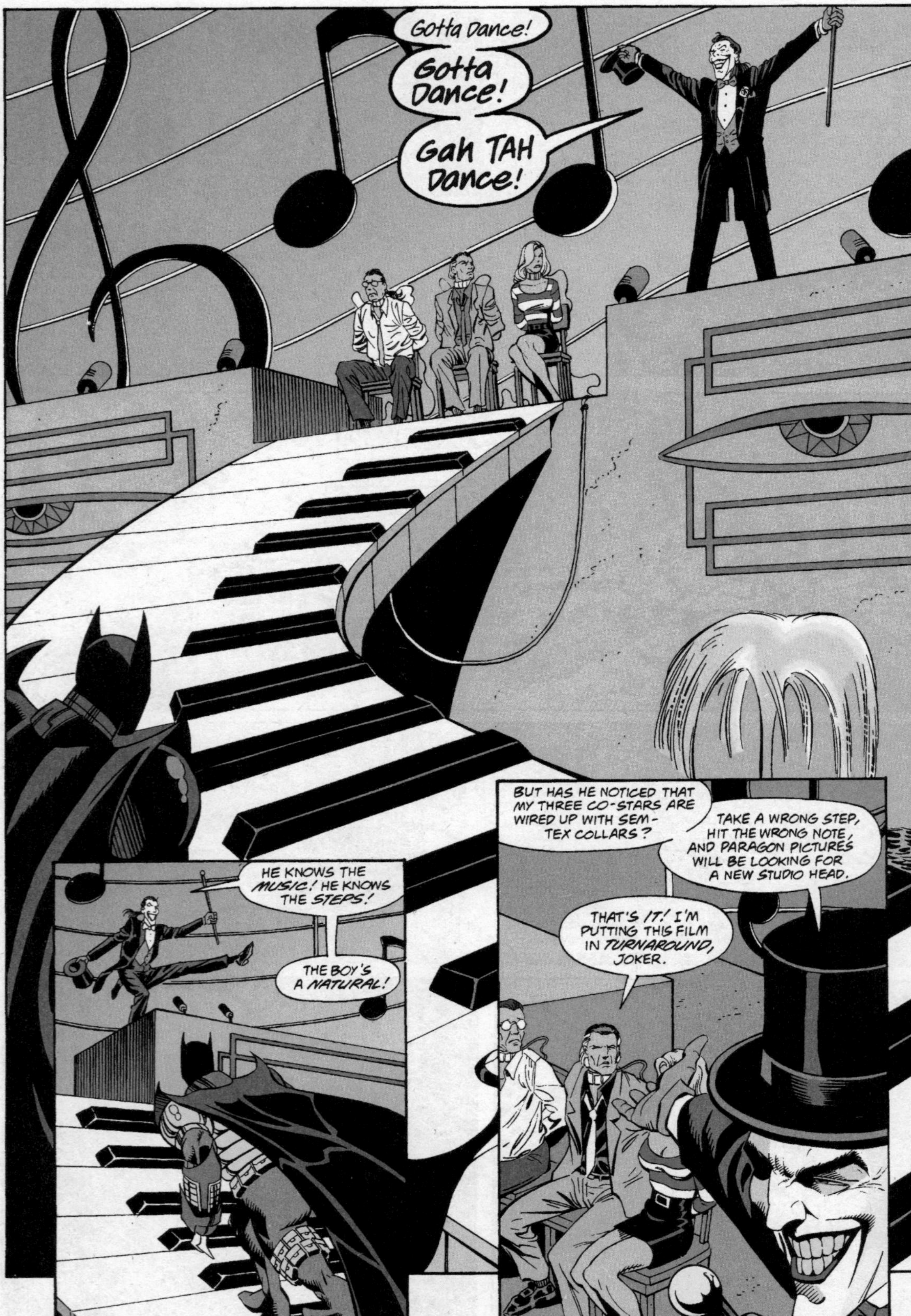
Gotta Dance!
Gotta Dance!
Gah TAH Dance!
HE KNOWS THE MUSIC! HE KNOWS THE STEPS!
THE BOY'S A NATURAL!
BUT HAS HE NOTICED THAT MY THREE CO-STARS ARE WIRED UP WITH SEM-TEX COLLARS?
TAKE A WRONG STEP, HIT THE WRONG NOTE, AND PARAGON PICTURES WILL BE LOOKING FOR A NEW STUDIO HEAD.
THAT'S IT! I'M PUTTING THIS FILM IN TURNAROUND, JOKER.
14

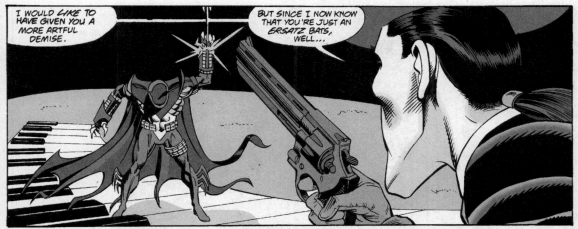

I WOULD *LIKE* TO HAVE GIVEN YOU A MORE ARTFUL DEMISE.

BUT SINCE I NOW KNOW THAT YOU'RE JUST AN *ERSATZ* BATS, WELL...

...I JUST DON'T HAVE THE *HEART* ANYMORE.

MAKE MY DAILIES, YOU *PHONY!*

CHOOM CHOOM CLICK

I MUST SAY I'M IMPRESSED.

SO MANY NEW GADGETS.

I HAVE SOME MYSELF.

SURPRISED?

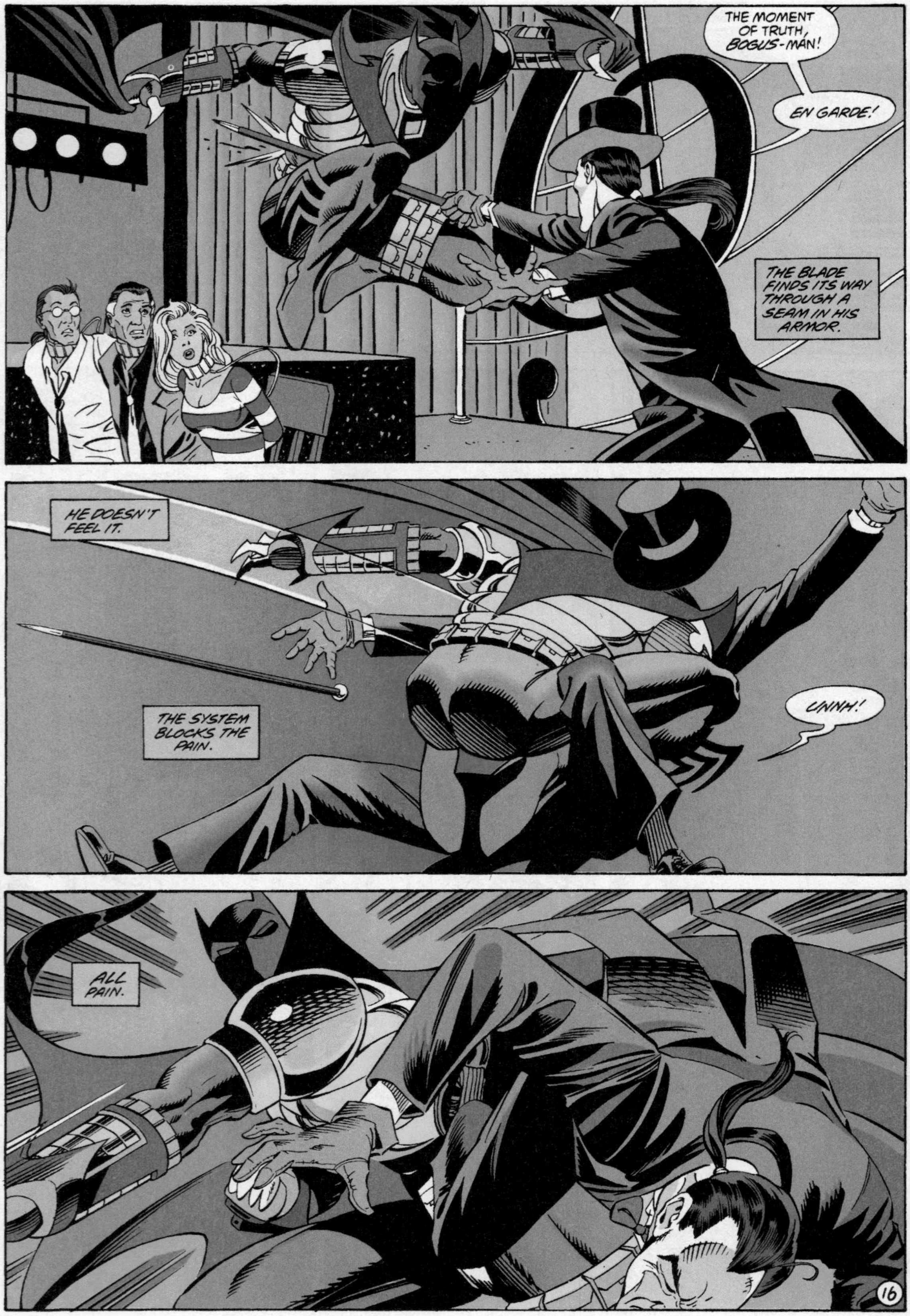
THE MOMENT OF TRUTH, BOGUS-MAN!
EN GARDE!
THE BLADE FINDS ITS WAY THROUGH A SEAM IN HIS ARMOR.
HE DOESN'T FEEL IT.
THE SYSTEM BLOCKS THE PAIN.
UNNH!
ALL PAIN.
16

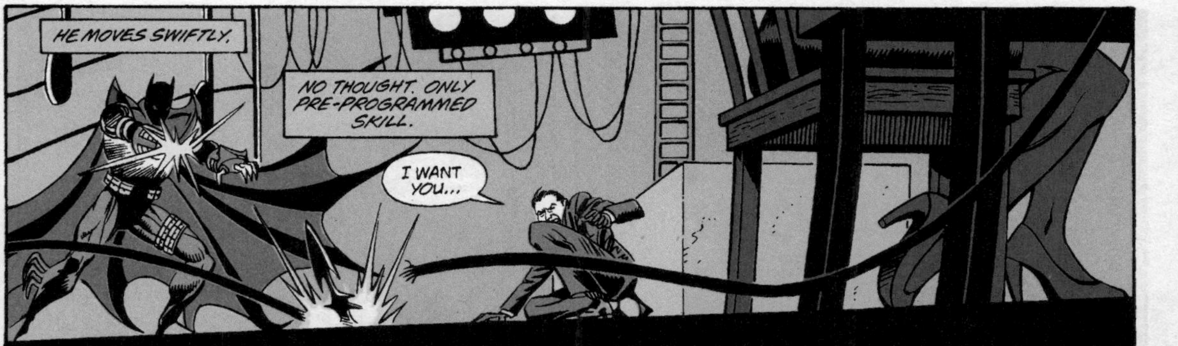
HE MOVES SWIFTLY.
NO THOUGHT. ONLY PRE-PROGRAMMED SKILL.
I WANT YOU...

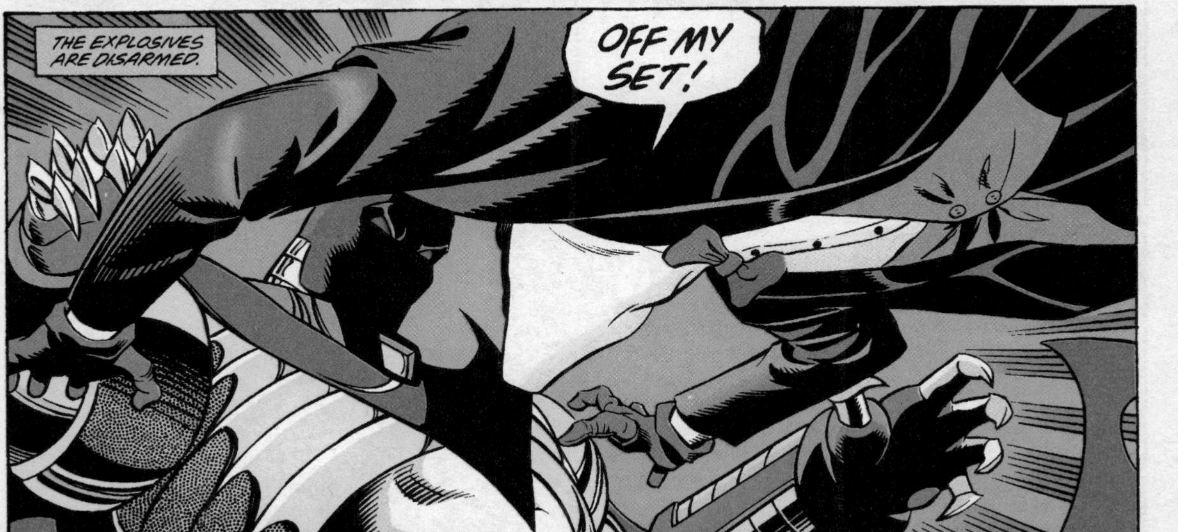
THE EXPLOSIVES ARE DISARMED.
OFF MY SET!

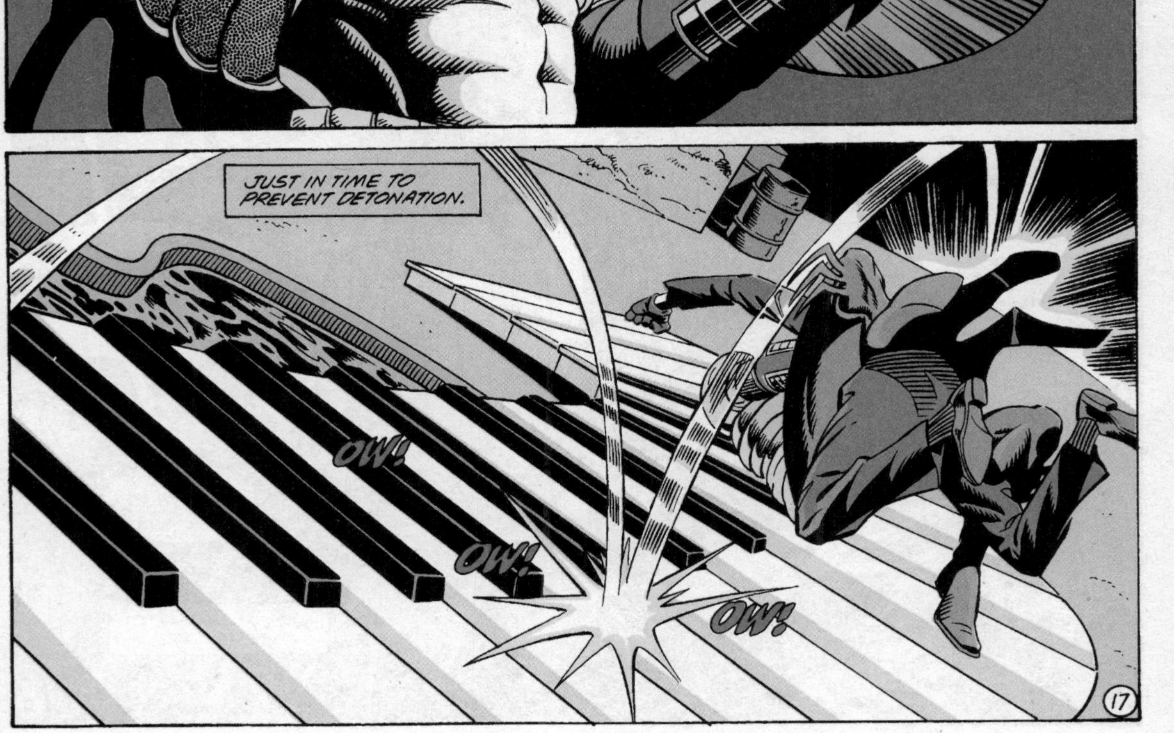
JUST IN TIME TO PREVENT DETONATION.
OW!
OW!
OW!
17

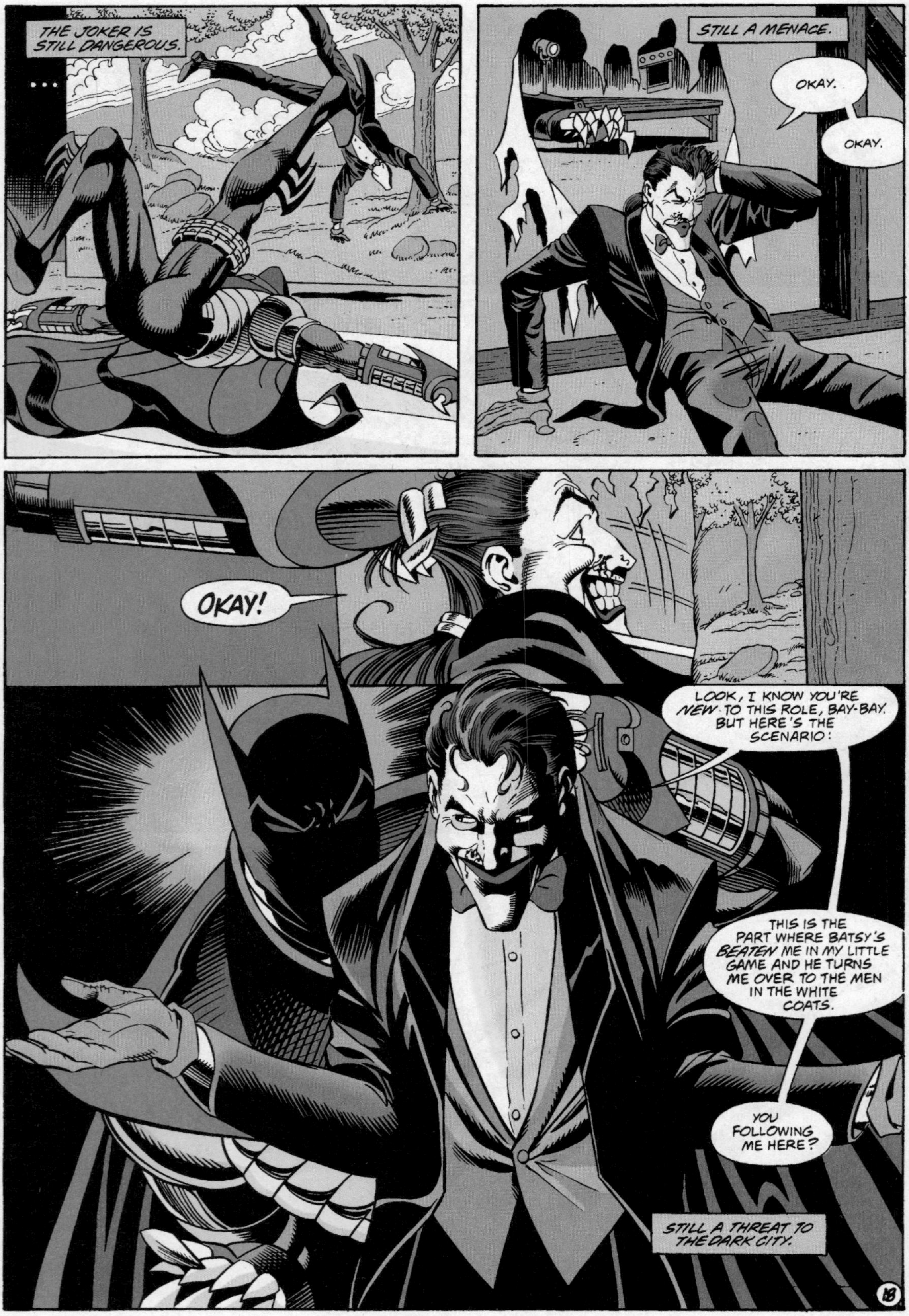
THE JOKER IS STILL DANGEROUS.
...
STILL A MENACE.
OKAY.
OKAY.
OKAY!
LOOK, I KNOW YOU'RE NEW TO THIS ROLE, BAY-BAY. BUT HERE'S THE SCENARIO:
THIS IS THE PART WHERE BATSY'S BEATEN ME IN MY LITTLE GAME AND HE TURNS ME OVER TO THE MEN IN THE WHITE COATS.
YOU FOLLOWING ME HERE?
STILL A THREAT TO THE DARK CITY.
18

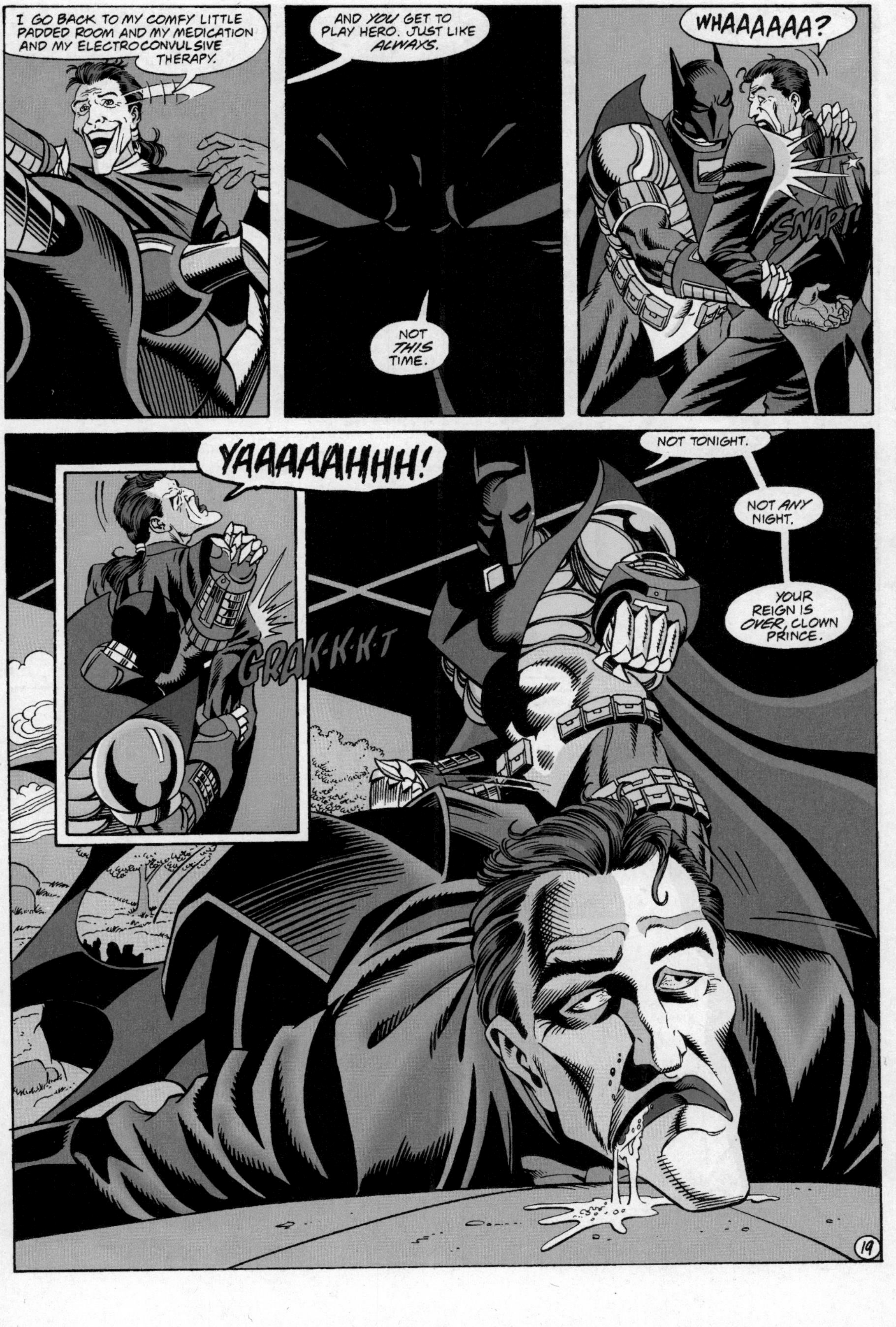
I GO BACK TO MY COMFY LITTLE PADDED ROOM AND MY MEDICATION AND MY ELECTROCONVULSIVE THERAPY.
AND YOU GET TO PLAY HERO. JUST LIKE ALWAYS.
NOT THIS TIME.
WHAAAAAA?
SNAP!
YAAAAAHHH!
GRAK-K-K-T
NOT TONIGHT.
NOT ANY NIGHT.
YOUR REIGN IS OVER, CLOWN PRINCE.
19

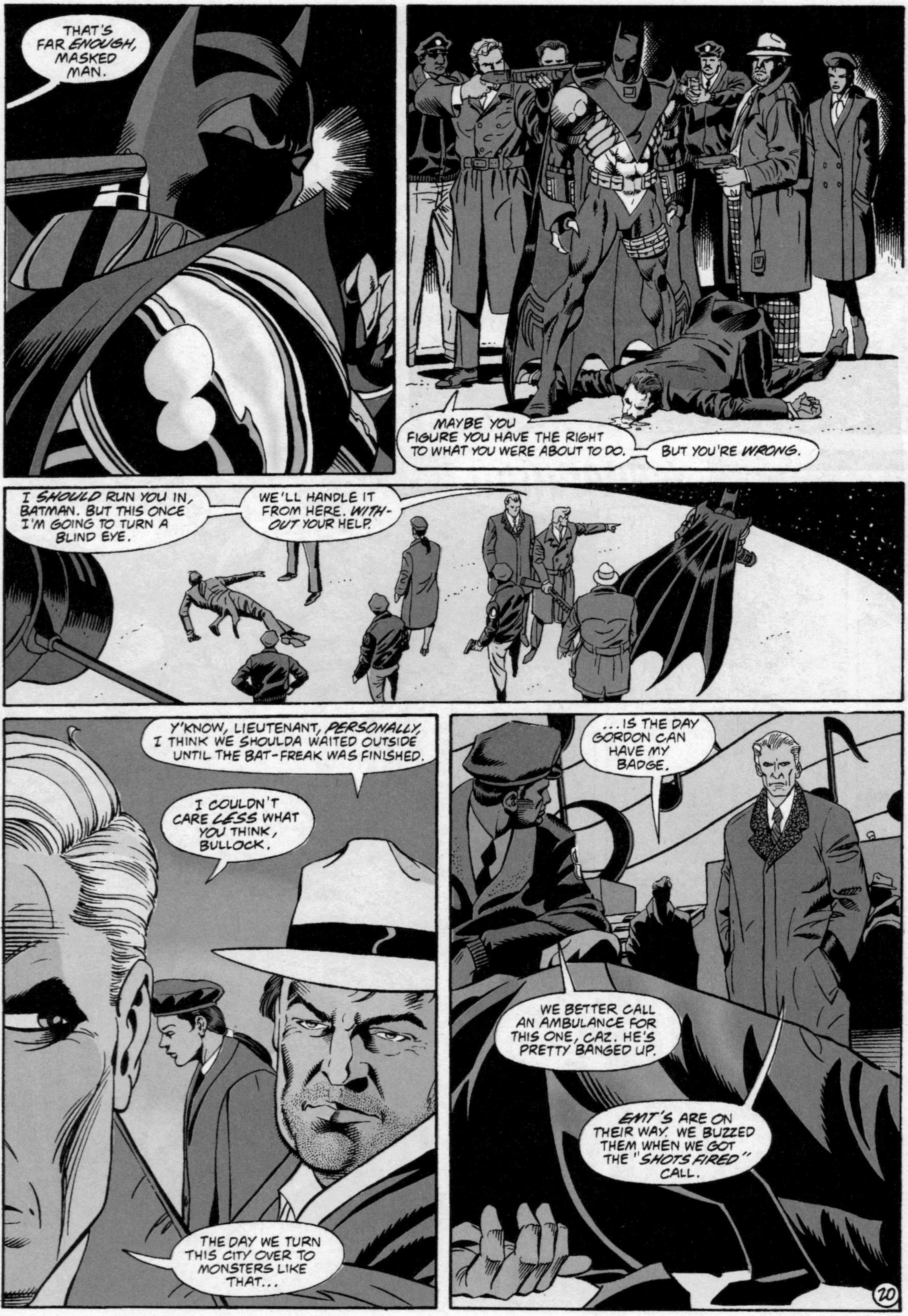
THAT'S FAR ENOUGH, MASKED MAN.
MAYBE YOU FIGURE YOU HAVE THE RIGHT TO WHAT YOU WERE ABOUT TO DO.
BUT YOU'RE WRONG.
I SHOULD RUN YOU IN, BATMAN. BUT THIS ONCE I'M GOING TO TURN A BLIND EYE.
WE'LL HANDLE IT FROM HERE. WITHOUT YOUR HELP.
Y'KNOW, LIEUTENANT, PERSONALLY, I THINK WE SHOULDA WAITED OUTSIDE UNTIL THE BAT-FREAK WAS FINISHED.
I COULDN'T CARE LESS WHAT YOU THINK, BULLOCK.
THE DAY WE TURN THIS CITY OVER TO MONSTERS LIKE THAT...
...IS THE DAY GORDON CAN HAVE MY BADGE.
WE BETTER CALL AN AMBULANCE FOR THIS ONE, CAZ. HE'S PRETTY BANGED UP.
EMT'S ARE ON THEIR WAY. WE BUZZED THEM WHEN WE GOT THE "SHOTS FIRED" CALL.
20

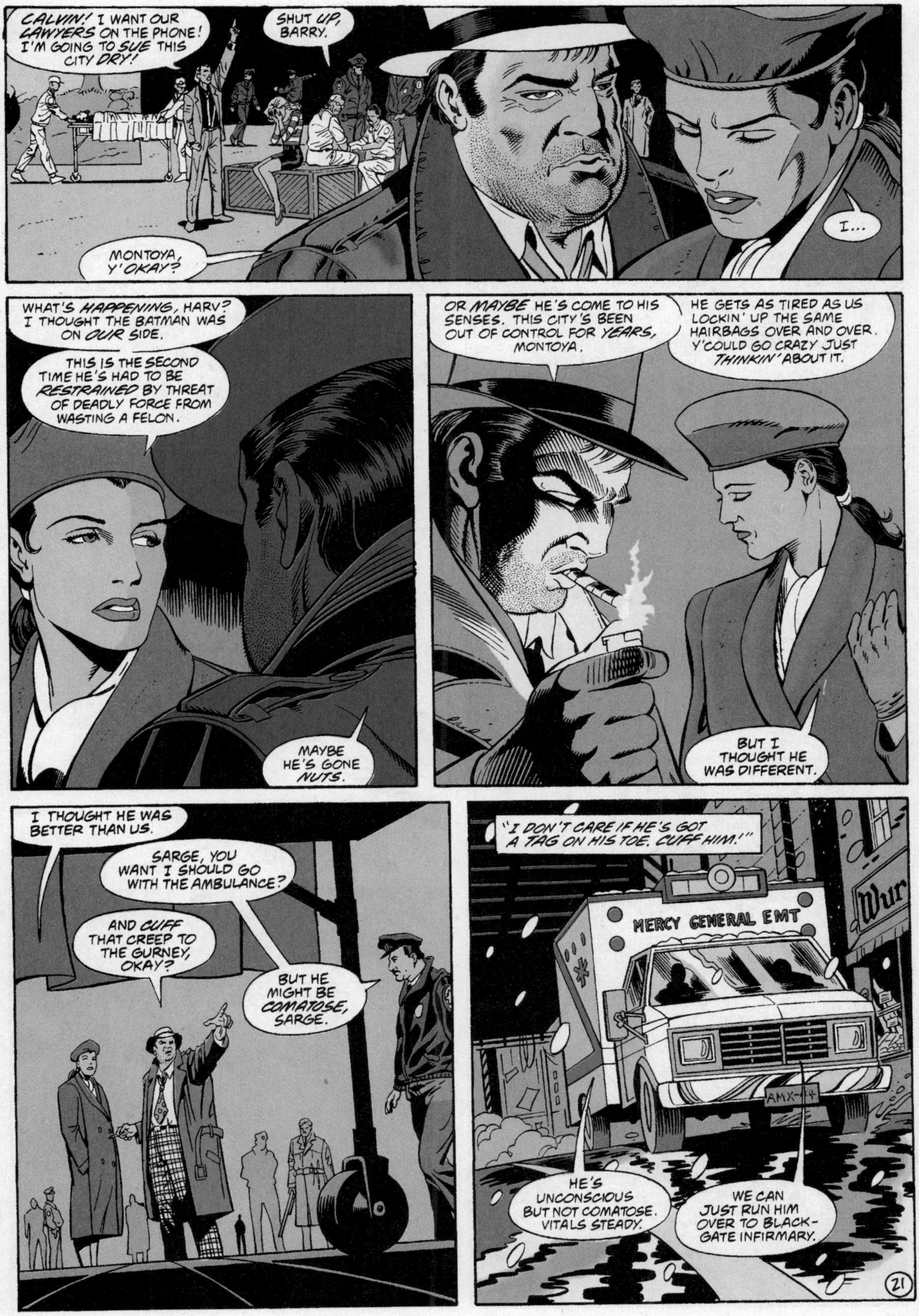
CALVIN! I WANT OUR LAWYERS ON THE PHONE! I'M GOING TO SUE THIS CITY DRY!
SHUT UP, BARRY.
MONTOYA, Y'OKAY?
I...
WHAT'S HAPPENING, HARV? I THOUGHT THE BATMAN WAS ON OUR SIDE.
THIS IS THE SECOND TIME HE'S HAD TO BE RESTRAINED BY THREAT OF DEADLY FORCE FROM WASTING A FELON.
MAYBE HE'S GONE NUTS.
OR MAYBE HE'S COME TO HIS SENSES. THIS CITY'S BEEN OUT OF CONTROL FOR YEARS, MONTOYA.
HE GETS AS TIRED AS US LOCKIN' UP THE SAME HAIRBAGS OVER AND OVER. Y'COULD GO CRAZY JUST THINKIN' ABOUT IT.
BUT I THOUGHT HE WAS DIFFERENT.
I THOUGHT HE WAS BETTER THAN US.
SARGE, YOU WANT I SHOULD GO WITH THE AMBULANCE?
AND CUFF THAT CREEP TO THE GURNEY, OKAY?
BUT HE MIGHT BE COMATOSE, SARGE.
"I DON'T CARE IF HE'S GOT A TAG ON HIS TOE. CUFF HIM."
MERCY GENERAL EMT
AMX-44
HE'S UNCONSCIOUS BUT NOT COMATOSE. VITALS STEADY.
WE CAN JUST RUN HIM OVER TO BLACKGATE INFIRMARY.
21

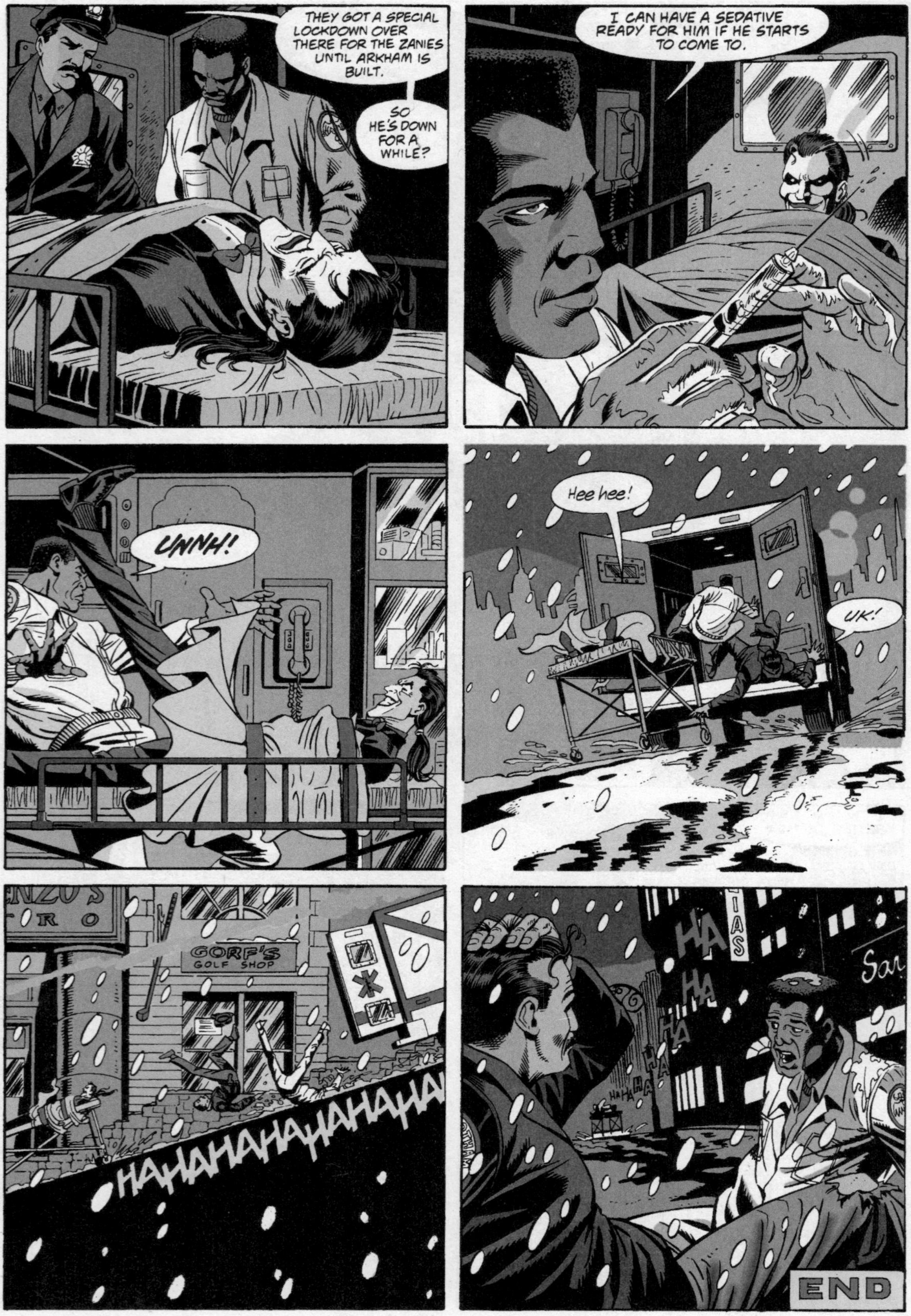
THEY GOT A SPECIAL LOCKDOWN OVER THERE FOR THE ZANIES UNTIL ARKHAM IS BUILT.
SO HE'S DOWN FOR A WHILE?
I CAN HAVE A SEDATIVE READY FOR HIM IF HE STARTS TO COME TO.
UNNH!
Hee hee!
UK!
GORF'S GOLF SHOP
HAHAHAHAHAHAHAHAHA
HA HA HA HA HA
END

Cover art by **BRIAN STELFREEZE**

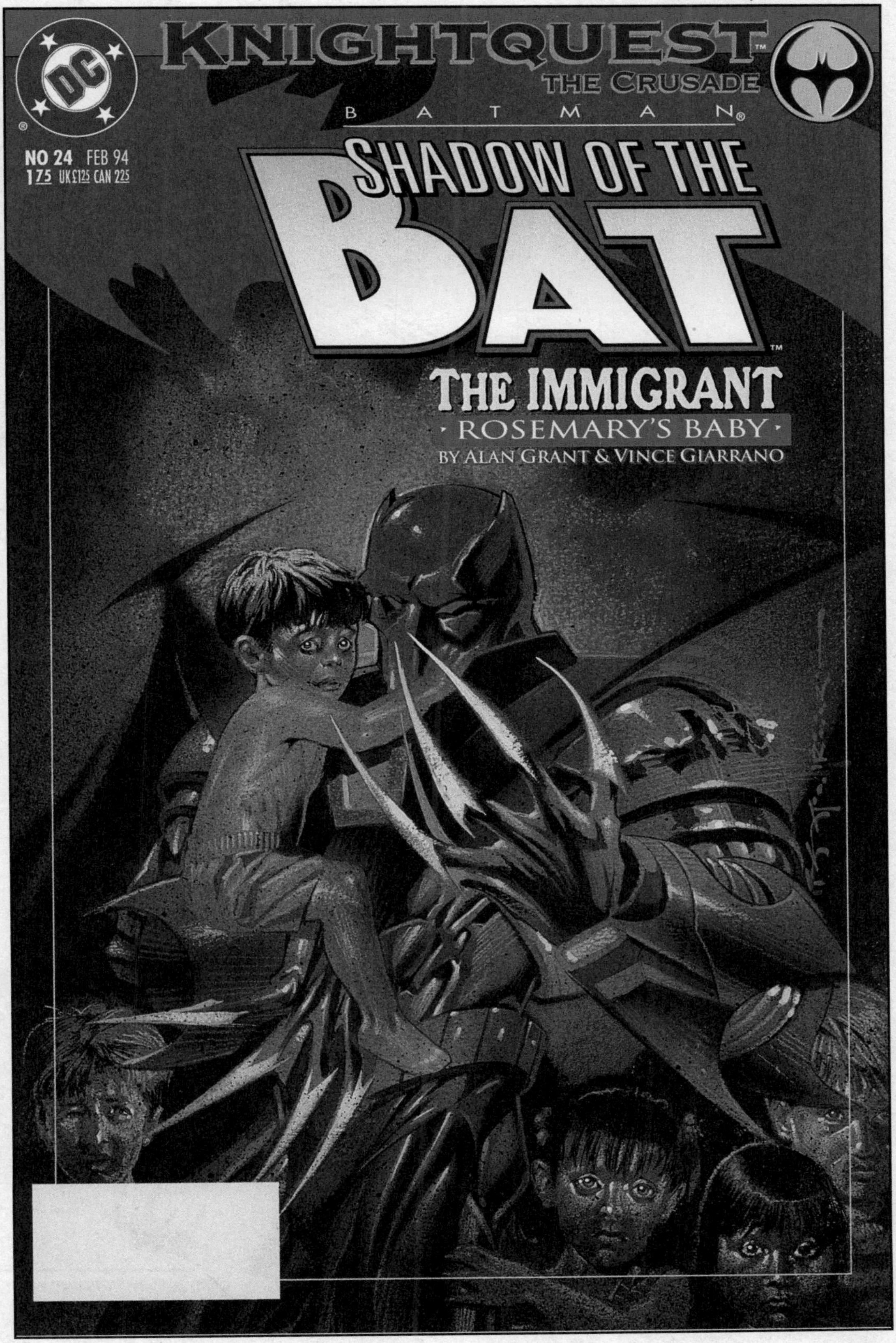
DC
KNIGHTQUEST™
THE CRUSADE
BATMAN®
NO 24 FEB 94
1.75 UK£1.25 CAN 2.25
SHADOW OF THE BAT™
THE IMMIGRANT
· ROSEMARY'S BABY ·
BY ALAN GRANT & VINCE GIARRANO

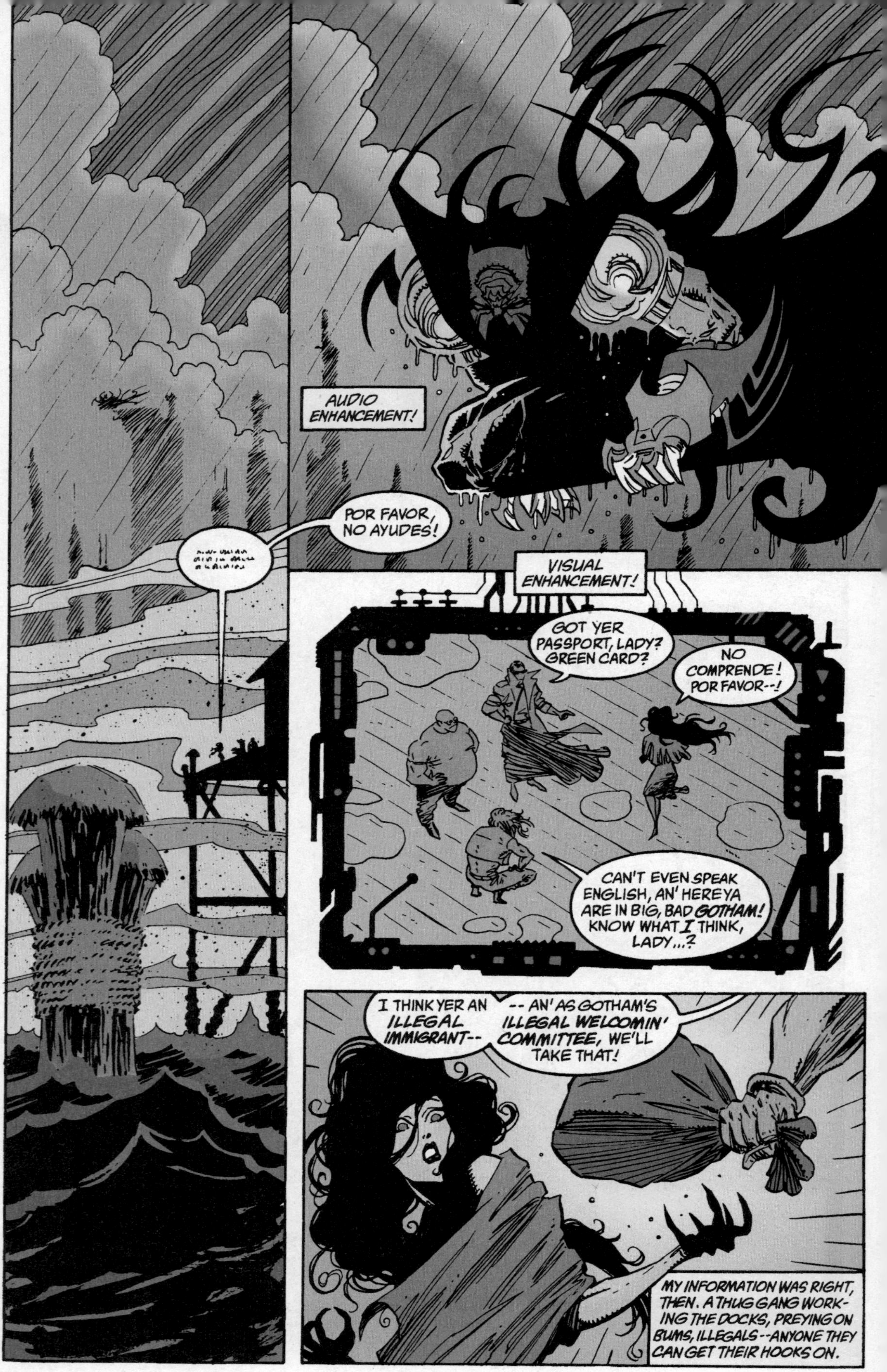
AUDIO ENHANCEMENT!
POR FAVOR, NO AYUDES!
VISUAL ENHANCEMENT!
GOT YER PASSPORT, LADY? GREEN CARD?
NO COMPRENDE! POR FAVOR--!
CAN'T EVEN SPEAK ENGLISH, AN' HERE YA ARE IN BIG, BAD GOTHAM! KNOW WHAT I THINK, LADY...?
I THINK YER AN ILLEGAL IMMIGRANT--
-- AN' AS GOTHAM'S ILLEGAL WELCOMIN' COMMITTEE, WE'LL TAKE THAT!
MY INFORMATION WAS RIGHT, THEN. A THUG GANG WORKING THE DOCKS, PREYING ON BUMS, ILLEGALS--ANYONE THEY CAN GET THEIR HOOKS ON.

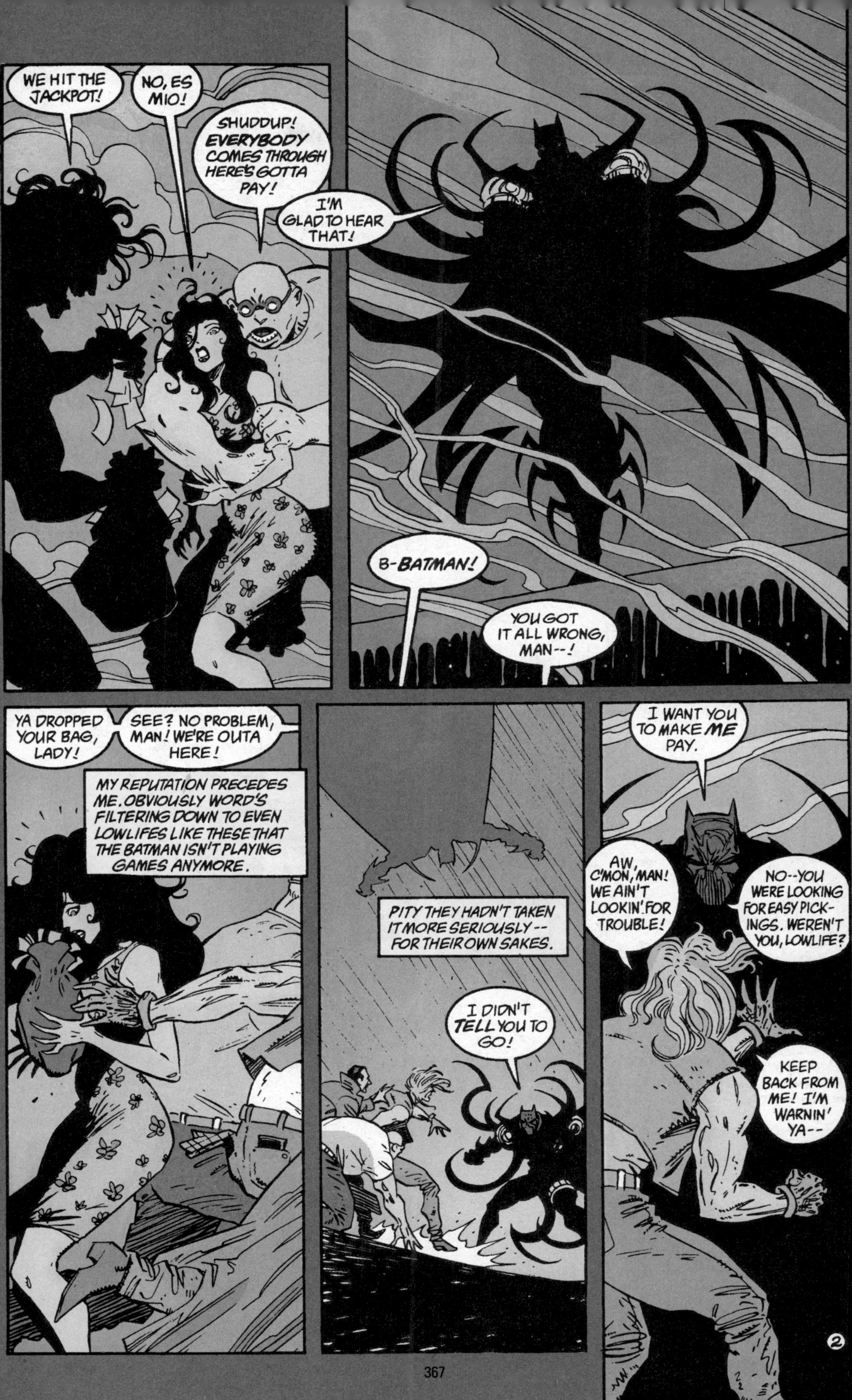
WE HIT THE JACKPOT!
NO, ES MIO!
SHUDDUP! EVERYBODY COMES THROUGH HERE'S GOTTA PAY!
I'M GLAD TO HEAR THAT!
B-BATMAN!
YOU GOT IT ALL WRONG, MAN--!
YA DROPPED YOUR BAG, LADY!
SEE? NO PROBLEM, MAN! WE'RE OUTA HERE!
MY REPUTATION PRECEDES ME. OBVIOUSLY WORD'S FILTERING DOWN TO EVEN LOWLIFES LIKE THESE THAT THE BATMAN ISN'T PLAYING GAMES ANYMORE.
PITY THEY HADN'T TAKEN IT MORE SERIOUSLY -- FOR THEIR OWN SAKES.
I DIDN'T TELL YOU TO GO!
I WANT YOU TO MAKE ME PAY.
AW, C'MON, MAN! WE AIN'T LOOKIN' FOR TROUBLE!
NO--YOU WERE LOOKING FOR EASY PICKINGS. WEREN'T YOU, LOWLIFE?
KEEP BACK FROM ME! I'M WARNIN' YA--
2

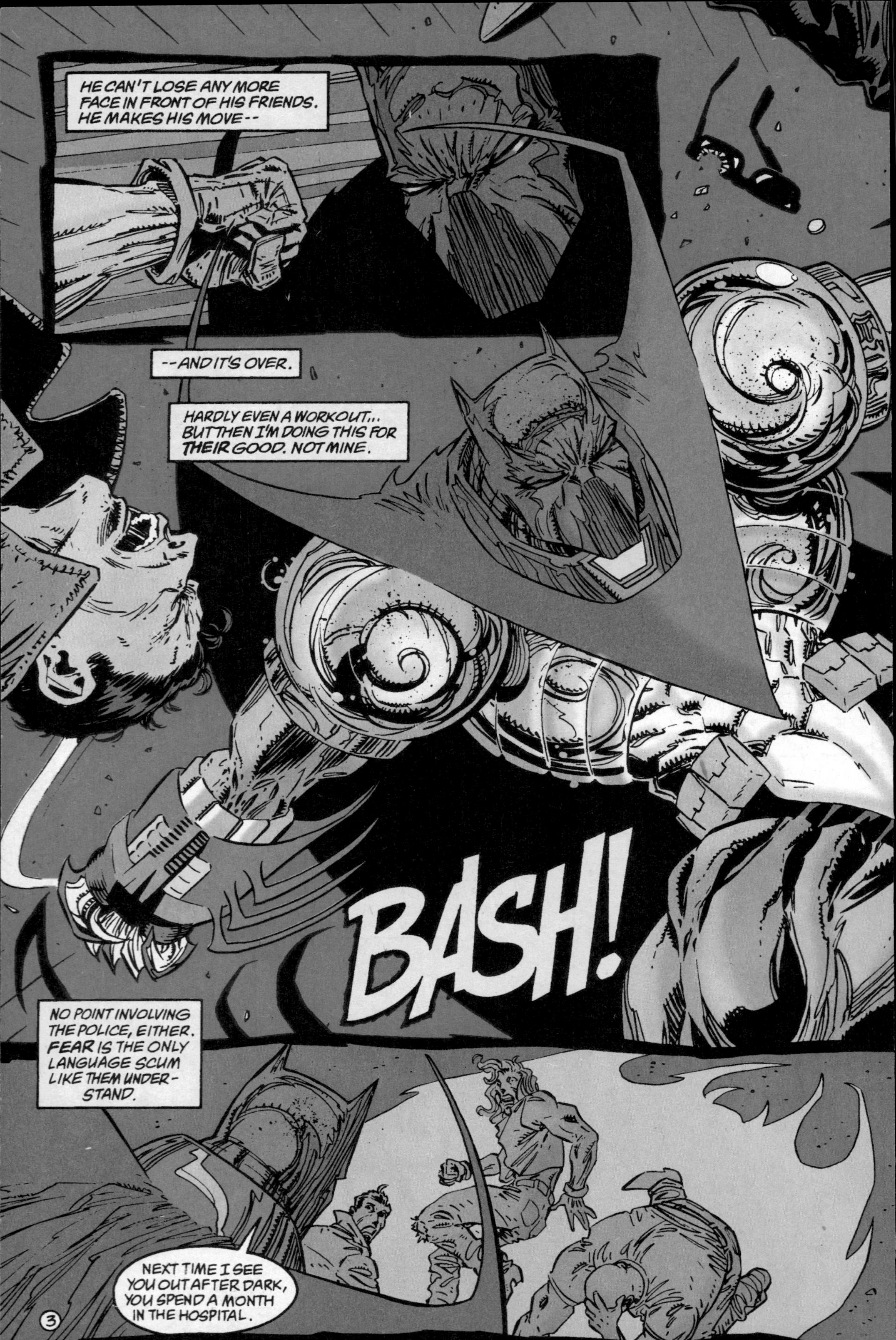
HE CAN'T LOSE ANY MORE FACE IN FRONT OF HIS FRIENDS. HE MAKES HIS MOVE--
--AND IT'S OVER.
HARDLY EVEN A WORKOUT... BUT THEN I'M DOING THIS FOR THEIR GOOD. NOT MINE.
BASH!
NO POINT INVOLVING THE POLICE, EITHER. FEAR IS THE ONLY LANGUAGE SCUM LIKE THEM UNDER-STAND.
NEXT TIME I SEE YOU OUT AFTER DARK, YOU SPEND A MONTH IN THE HOSPITAL.
3

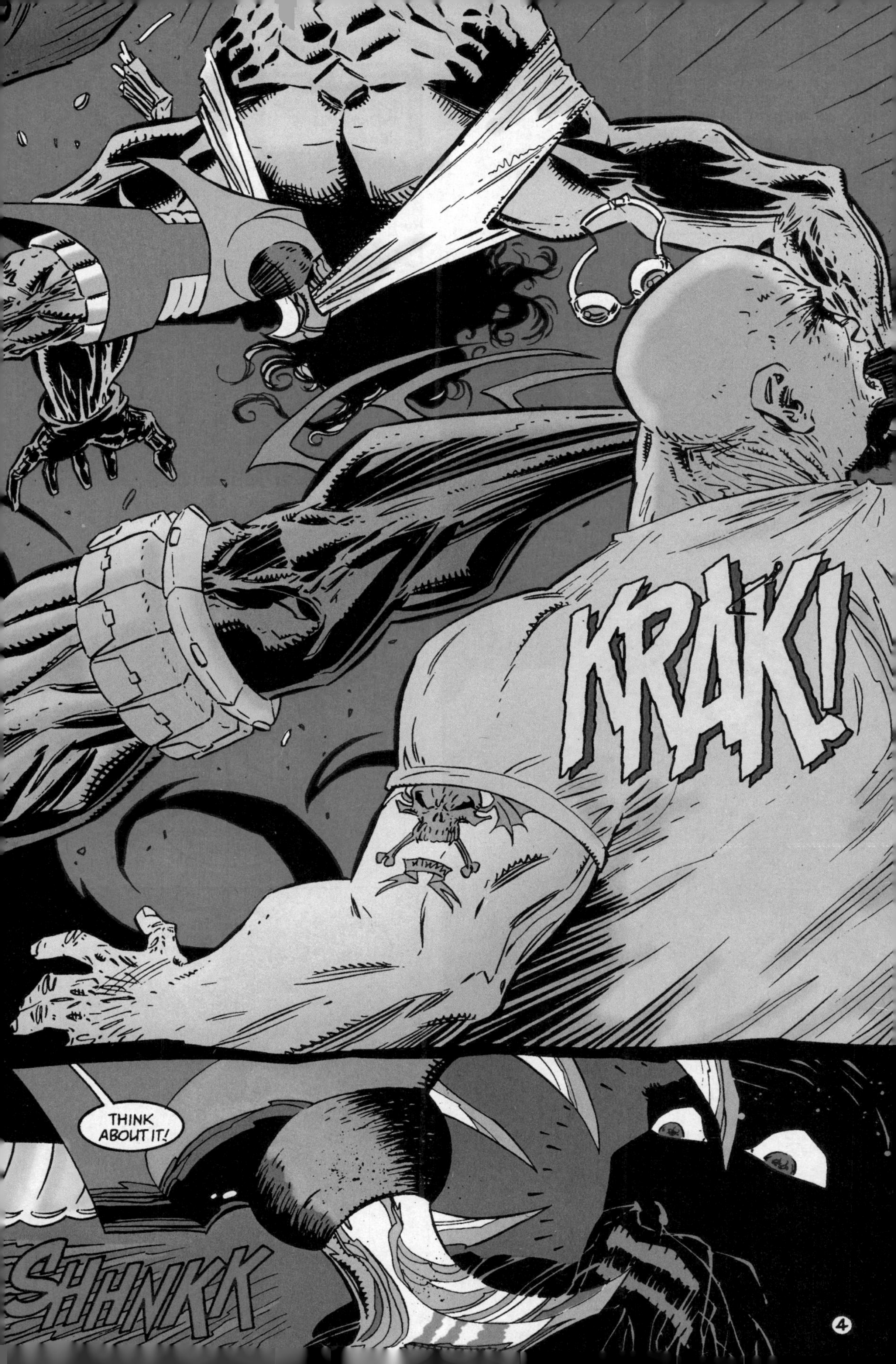
KRAK!
THINK ABOUT IT!
SHHNKK

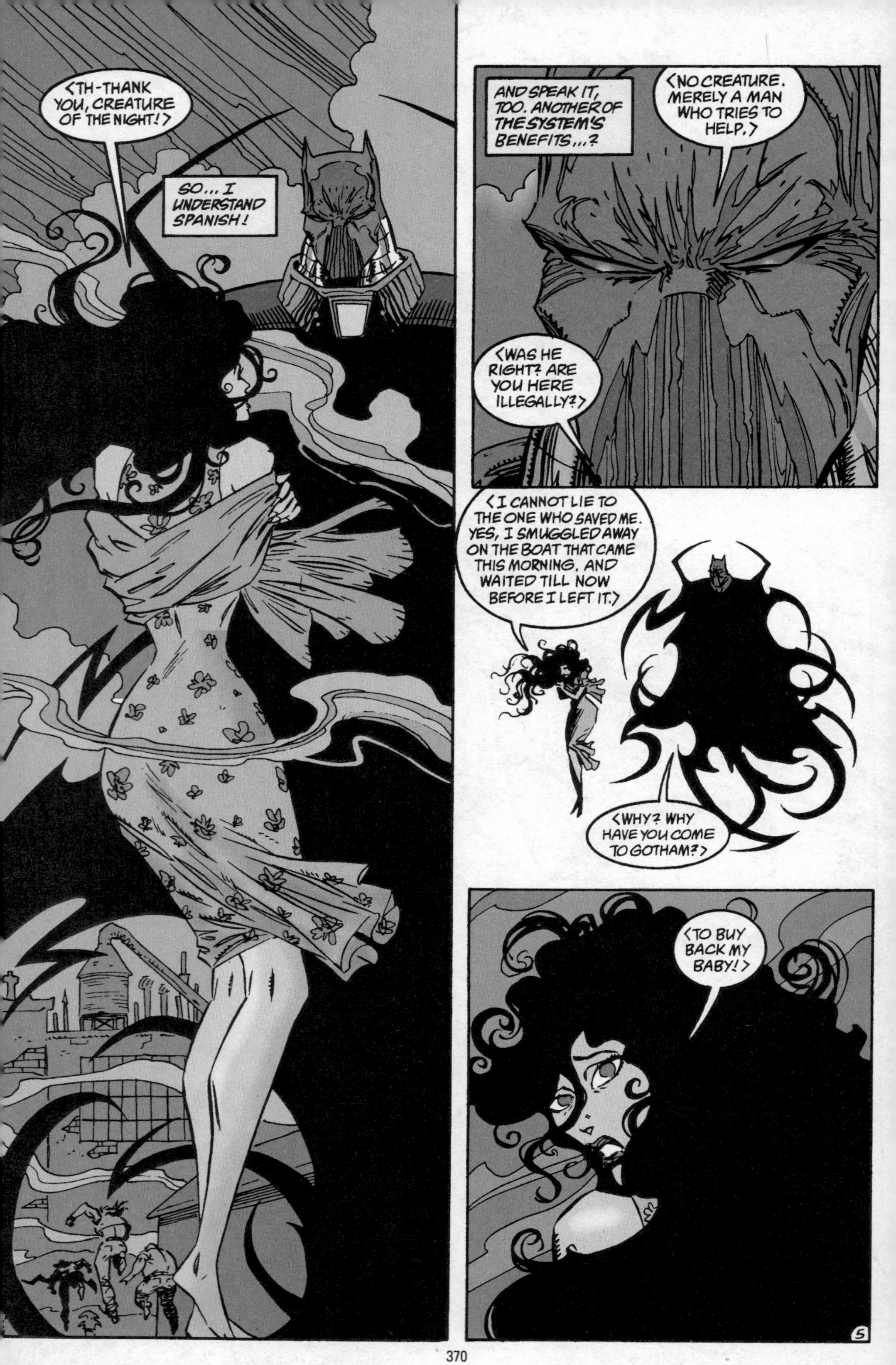
<TH-THANK YOU, CREATURE OF THE NIGHT!>
SO... I UNDERSTAND SPANISH!
AND SPEAK IT, TOO. ANOTHER OF THE SYSTEM'S BENEFITS...?
<NO CREATURE. MERELY A MAN WHO TRIES TO HELP.>
<WAS HE RIGHT? ARE YOU HERE ILLEGALLY?>
<I CANNOT LIE TO THE ONE WHO SAVED ME. YES, I SMUGGLED AWAY ON THE BOAT THAT CAME THIS MORNING, AND WAITED TILL NOW BEFORE I LEFT IT.>
<WHY? WHY HAVE YOU COME TO GOTHAM?>
<TO BUY BACK MY BABY!>
5

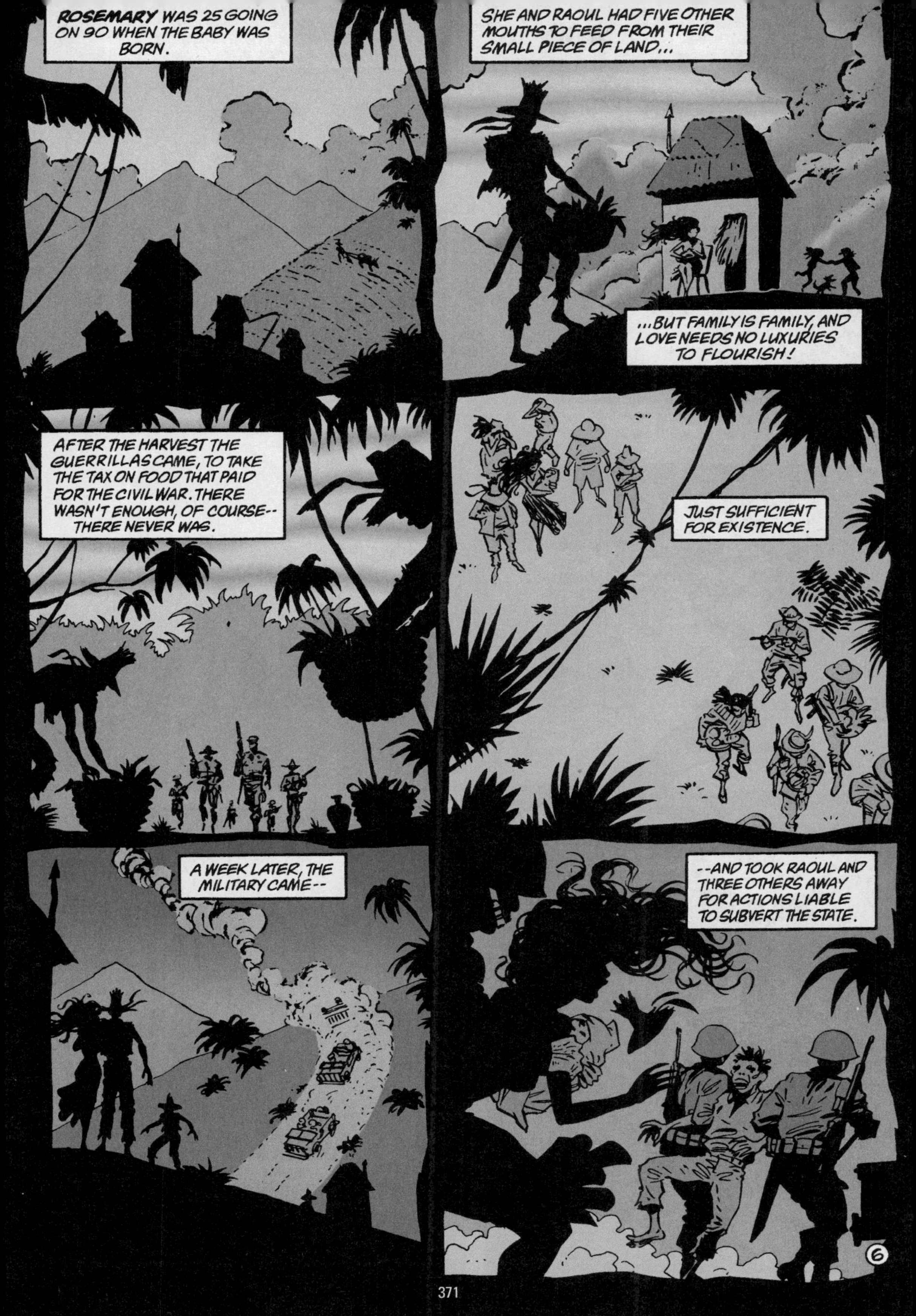
ROSEMARY WAS 25 GOING ON 90 WHEN THE BABY WAS BORN.
SHE AND RAOUL HAD FIVE OTHER MOUTHS TO FEED FROM THEIR SMALL PIECE OF LAND...
...BUT FAMILY IS FAMILY, AND LOVE NEEDS NO LUXURIES TO FLOURISH!
AFTER THE HARVEST THE GUERRILLAS CAME, TO TAKE THE TAX ON FOOD THAT PAID FOR THE CIVIL WAR. THERE WASN'T ENOUGH, OF COURSE-- THERE NEVER WAS.
JUST SUFFICIENT FOR EXISTENCE.
A WEEK LATER, THE MILITARY CAME--
--AND TOOK RAOUL AND THREE OTHERS AWAY FOR ACTIONS LIABLE TO SUBVERT THE STATE.
6

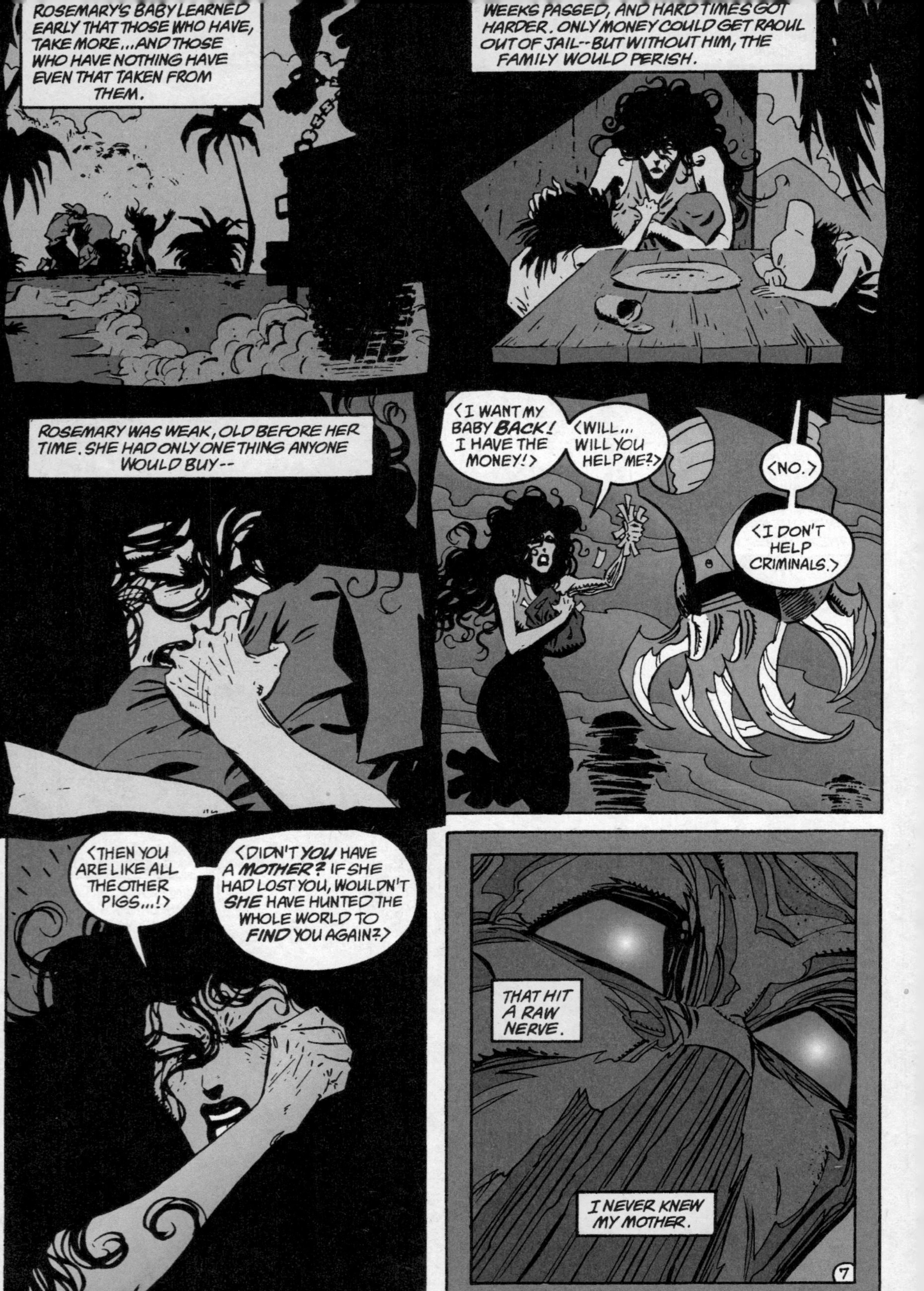
ROSEMARY'S BABY LEARNED EARLY THAT THOSE WHO HAVE, TAKE MORE,...AND THOSE WHO HAVE NOTHING HAVE EVEN THAT TAKEN FROM THEM.
WEEKS PASSED, AND HARD TIMES GOT HARDER. ONLY MONEY COULD GET RAOUL OUT OF JAIL--BUT WITHOUT HIM, THE FAMILY WOULD PERISH.
ROSEMARY WAS WEAK, OLD BEFORE HER TIME. SHE HAD ONLY ONE THING ANYONE WOULD BUY--
<I WANT MY BABY BACK! I HAVE THE MONEY!>
<WILL... WILL YOU HELP ME?>
<NO.>
<I DON'T HELP CRIMINALS.>
<THEN YOU ARE LIKE ALL THE OTHER PIGS...!>
<DIDN'T YOU HAVE A MOTHER? IF SHE HAD LOST YOU, WOULDN'T SHE HAVE HUNTED THE WHOLE WORLD TO FIND YOU AGAIN?>
THAT HIT A RAW NERVE.
I NEVER KNEW MY MOTHER.
7

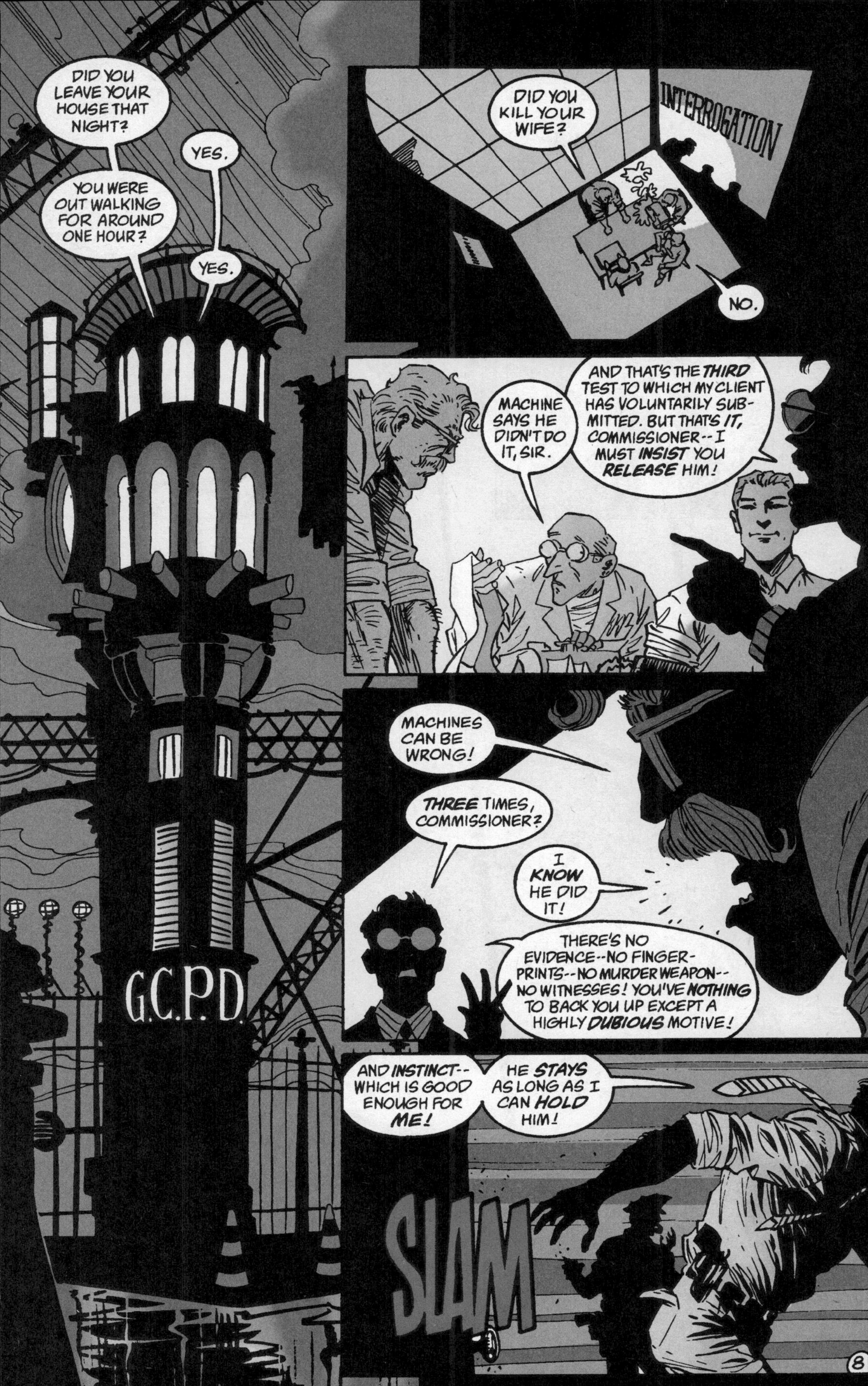
DID YOU LEAVE YOUR HOUSE THAT NIGHT?
YES.
YOU WERE OUT WALKING FOR AROUND ONE HOUR?
YES.
G.C.P.D.
INTERROGATION
DID YOU KILL YOUR WIFE?
NO.
MACHINE SAYS HE DIDN'T DO IT, SIR.
AND THAT'S THE THIRD TEST TO WHICH MY CLIENT HAS VOLUNTARILY SUBMITTED. BUT THAT'S IT, COMMISSIONER--I MUST INSIST YOU RELEASE HIM!
MACHINES CAN BE WRONG!
THREE TIMES, COMMISSIONER?
I KNOW HE DID IT!
THERE'S NO EVIDENCE--NO FINGERPRINTS--NO MURDER WEAPON--NO WITNESSES! YOU'VE NOTHING TO BACK YOU UP EXCEPT A HIGHLY DUBIOUS MOTIVE!
AND INSTINCT--WHICH IS GOOD ENOUGH FOR ME!
HE STAYS AS LONG AS I CAN HOLD HIM!
SLAM
8

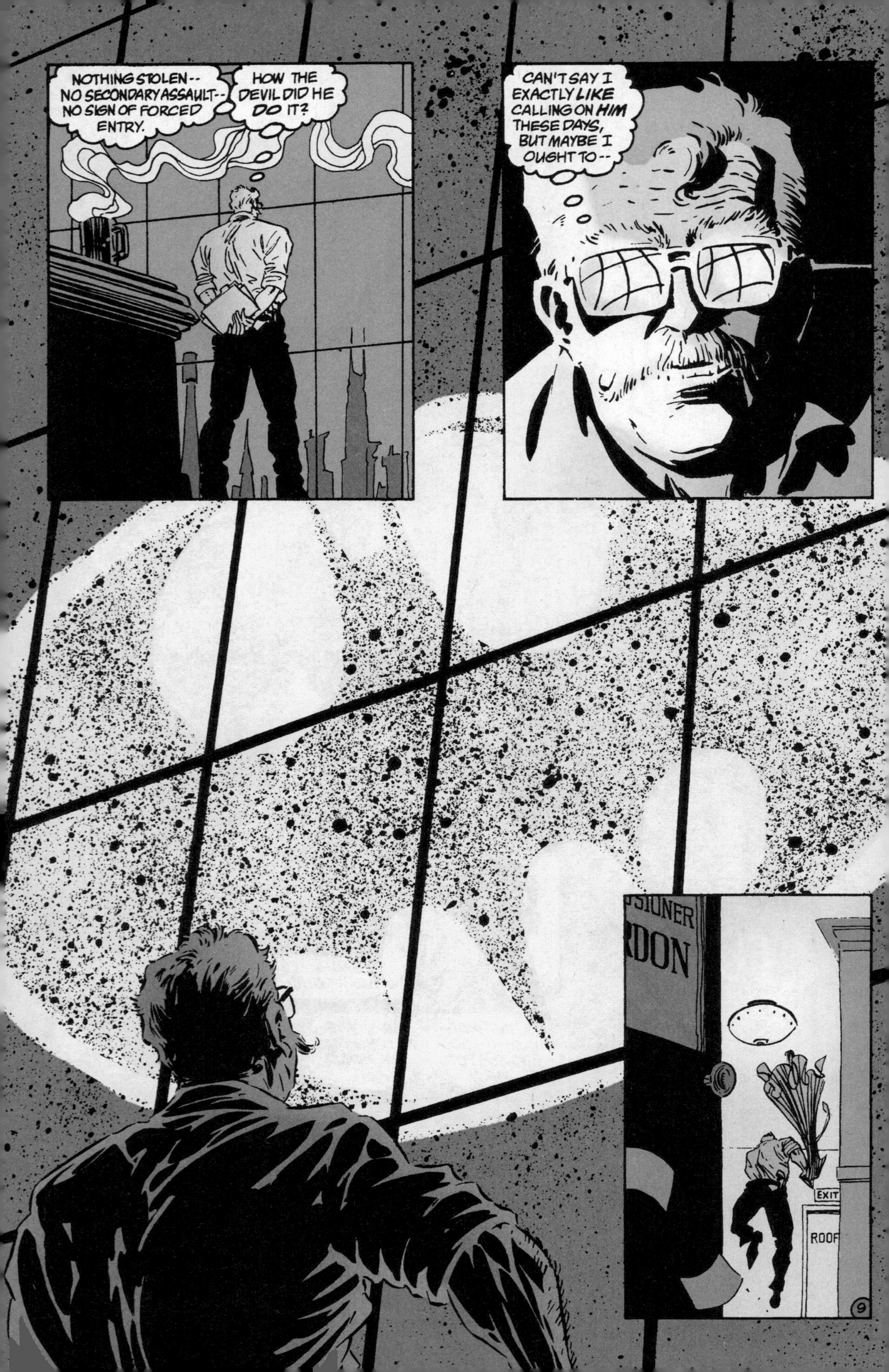
NOTHING STOLEN-- NO SECONDARY ASSAULT-- NO SIGN OF FORCED ENTRY.
HOW THE DEVIL DID HE DO IT?
CAN'T SAY I EXACTLY LIKE CALLING ON HIM THESE DAYS, BUT MAYBE I OUGHT TO--
SIONER
RDON
EXIT
ROOF
9

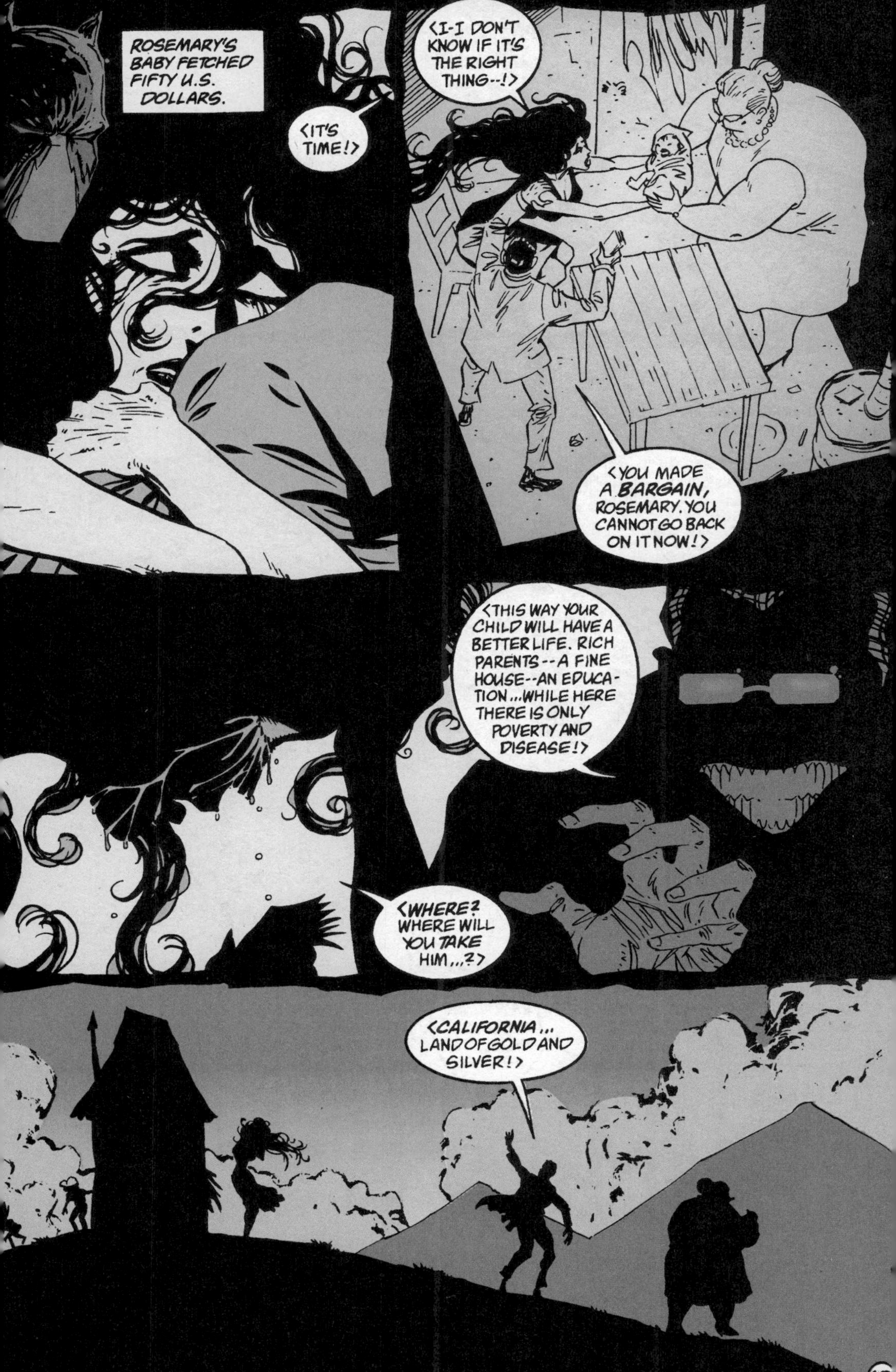
ROSEMARY'S BABY FETCHED FIFTY U.S. DOLLARS.
<IT'S TIME!>
<I-I DON'T KNOW IF IT'S THE RIGHT THING--!>
<YOU MADE A BARGAIN, ROSEMARY. YOU CANNOT GO BACK ON IT NOW!>
<THIS WAY YOUR CHILD WILL HAVE A BETTER LIFE. RICH PARENTS--A FINE HOUSE--AN EDUCATION...WHILE HERE THERE IS ONLY POVERTY AND DISEASE!>
<WHERE? WHERE WILL YOU TAKE HIM...?>
<CALIFORNIA... LAND OF GOLD AND SILVER!>

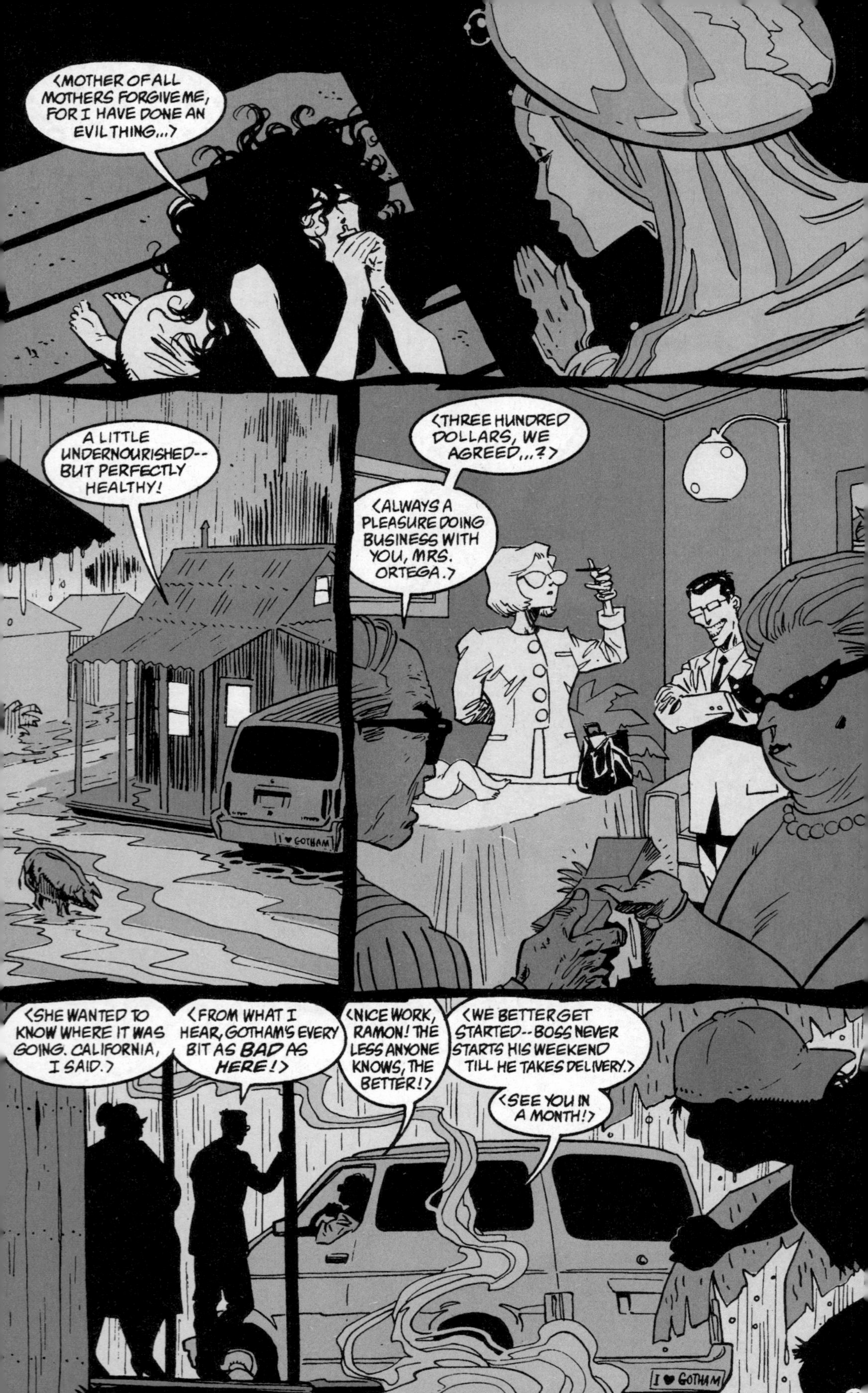
<MOTHER OF ALL MOTHERS FORGIVE ME, FOR I HAVE DONE AN EVIL THING...>
A LITTLE UNDERNOURISHED-- BUT PERFECTLY HEALTHY!
I ♥ GOTHAM
<THREE HUNDRED DOLLARS, WE AGREED,...?>
<ALWAYS A PLEASURE DOING BUSINESS WITH YOU, MRS. ORTEGA.>
<SHE WANTED TO KNOW WHERE IT WAS GOING. CALIFORNIA, I SAID.>
<FROM WHAT I HEAR, GOTHAM'S EVERY BIT AS *BAD* AS *HERE*!>
<NICE WORK, RAMON! THE LESS ANYONE KNOWS, THE BETTER!>
<WE BETTER GET STARTED--BOSS NEVER STARTS HIS WEEKEND TILL HE TAKES DELIVERY.>
<SEE YOU IN A MONTH!>
I ♥ GOTHAM

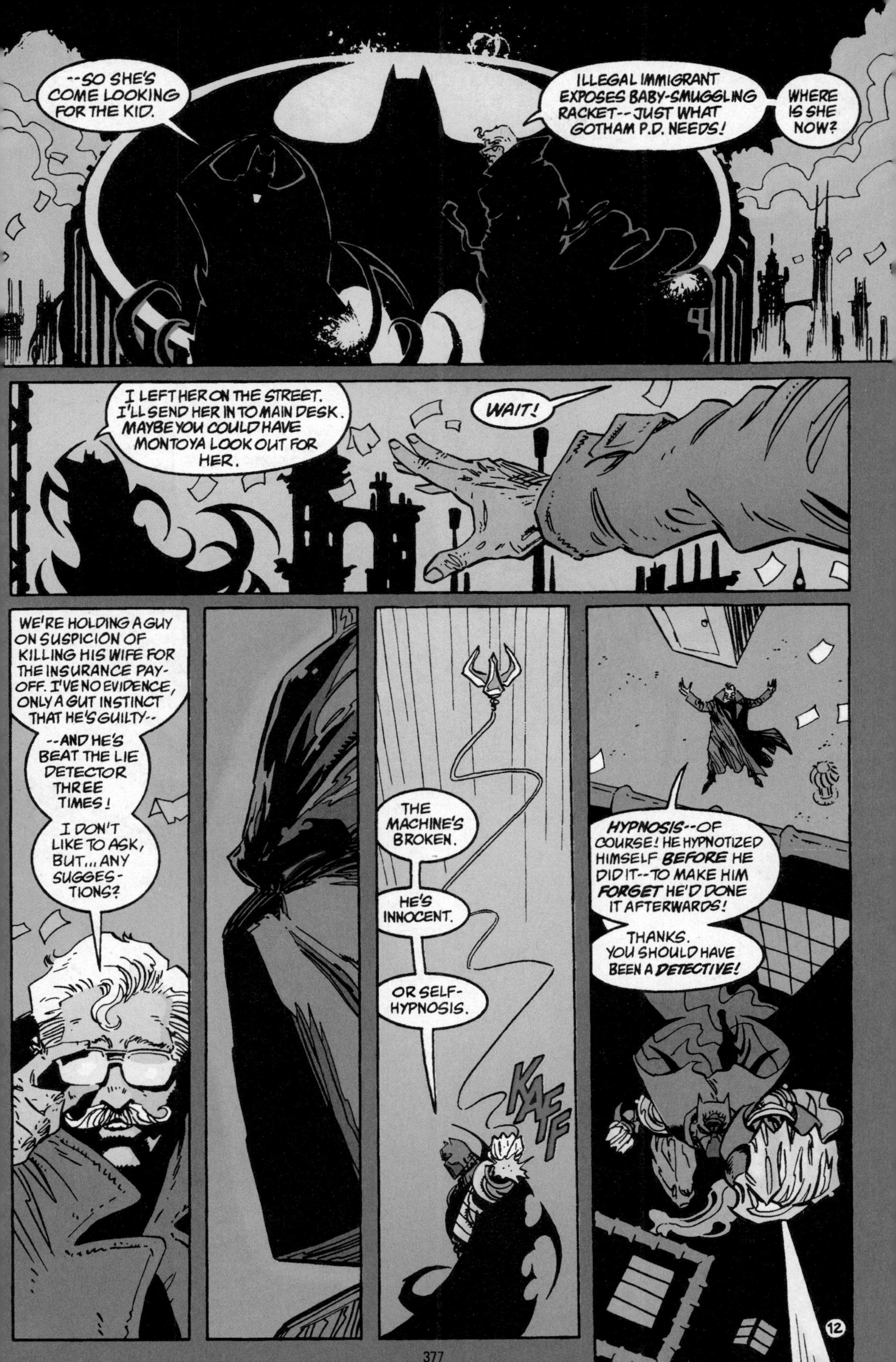
--SO SHE'S COME LOOKING FOR THE KID.
ILLEGAL IMMIGRANT EXPOSES BABY-SMUGGLING RACKET--JUST WHAT GOTHAM P.D. NEEDS!
WHERE IS SHE NOW?
I LEFT HER ON THE STREET. I'LL SEND HER IN TO MAIN DESK. MAYBE YOU COULD HAVE MONTOYA LOOK OUT FOR HER.
WAIT!
WE'RE HOLDING A GUY ON SUSPICION OF KILLING HIS WIFE FOR THE INSURANCE PAY-OFF. I'VE NO EVIDENCE, ONLY A GUT INSTINCT THAT HE'S GUILTY--
--AND HE'S BEAT THE LIE DETECTOR THREE TIMES!
I DON'T LIKE TO ASK, BUT... ANY SUGGES-TIONS?
THE MACHINE'S BROKEN.
HE'S INNOCENT.
OR SELF-HYPNOSIS.
KAFF
HYPNOSIS--OF COURSE! HE HYPNOTIZED HIMSELF BEFORE HE DID IT--TO MAKE HIM FORGET HE'D DONE IT AFTERWARDS!
THANKS. YOU SHOULD HAVE BEEN A DETECTIVE!
12

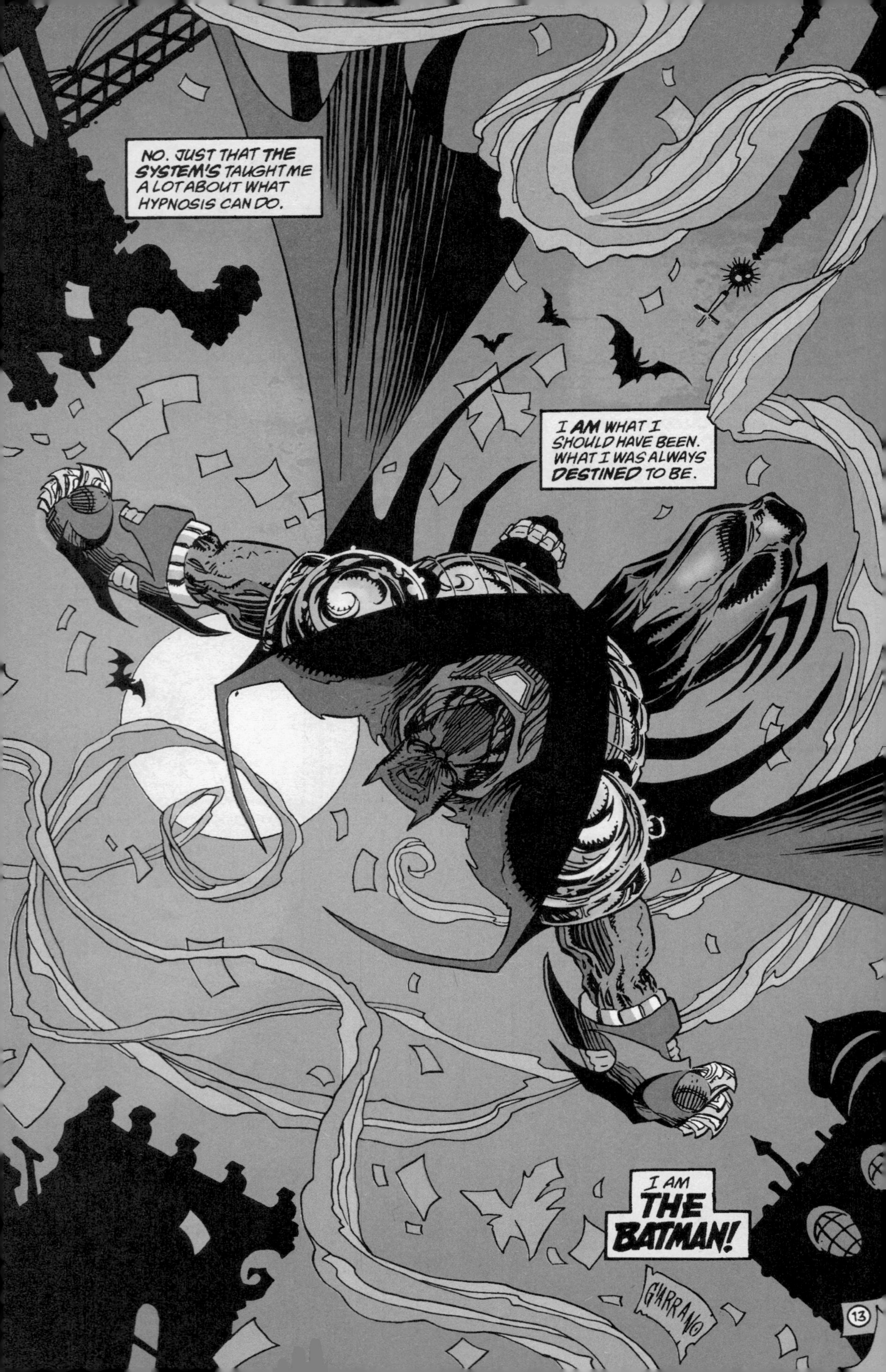
NO. JUST THAT THE SYSTEM'S TAUGHT ME A LOT ABOUT WHAT HYPNOSIS CAN DO.
I AM WHAT I SHOULD HAVE BEEN. WHAT I WAS ALWAYS DESTINED TO BE.
I AM THE BATMAN!
GIARRANO

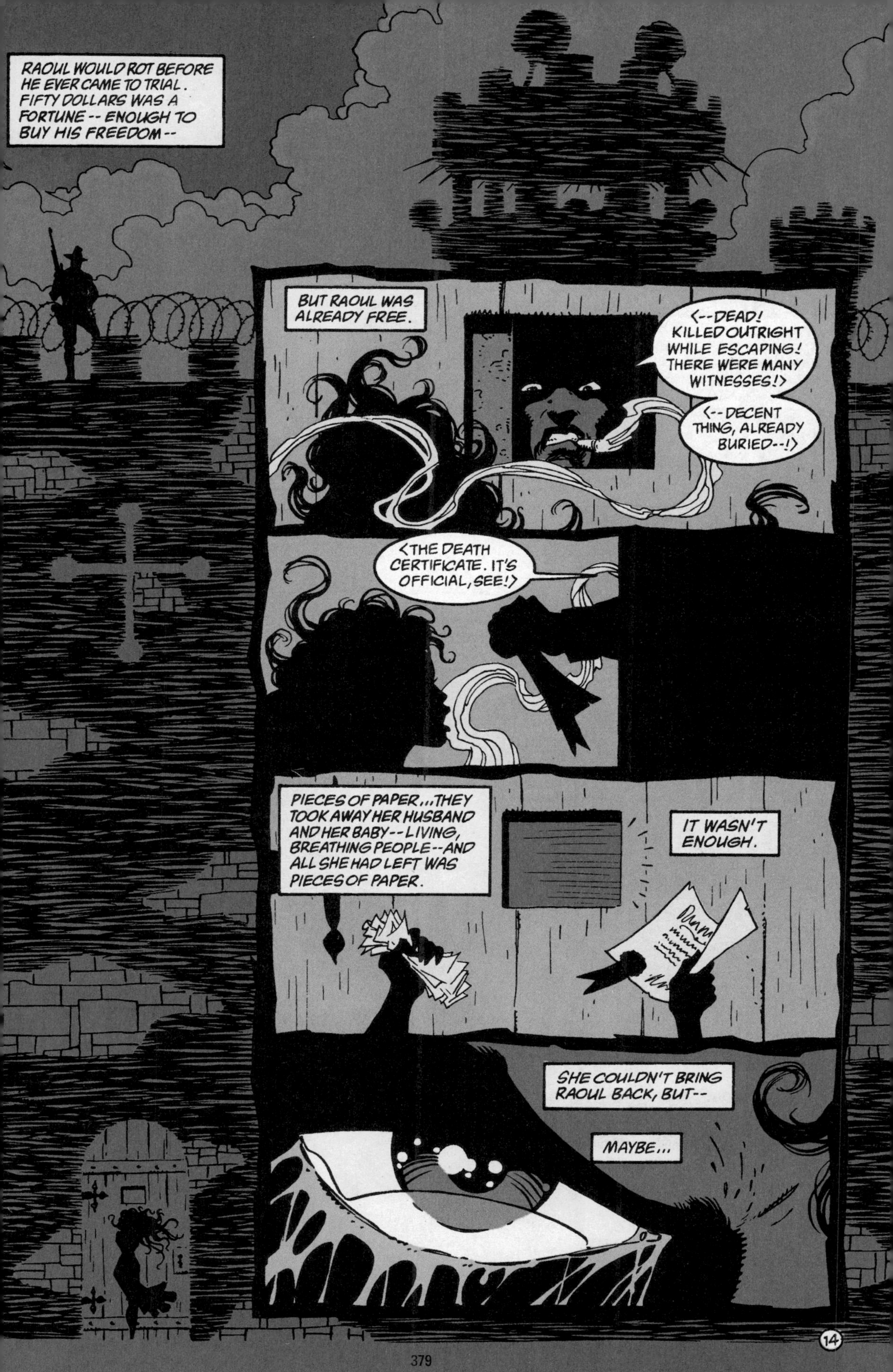
RAOUL WOULD ROT BEFORE HE EVER CAME TO TRIAL. FIFTY DOLLARS WAS A FORTUNE -- ENOUGH TO BUY HIS FREEDOM --
BUT RAOUL WAS ALREADY FREE.
<--DEAD! KILLED OUTRIGHT WHILE ESCAPING! THERE WERE MANY WITNESSES!>
<--DECENT THING, ALREADY BURIED--!>
<THE DEATH CERTIFICATE. IT'S OFFICIAL, SEE!>
PIECES OF PAPER... THEY TOOK AWAY HER HUSBAND AND HER BABY--LIVING, BREATHING PEOPLE--AND ALL SHE HAD LEFT WAS PIECES OF PAPER.
IT WASN'T ENOUGH.
SHE COULDN'T BRING RAOUL BACK, BUT--
MAYBE...
14

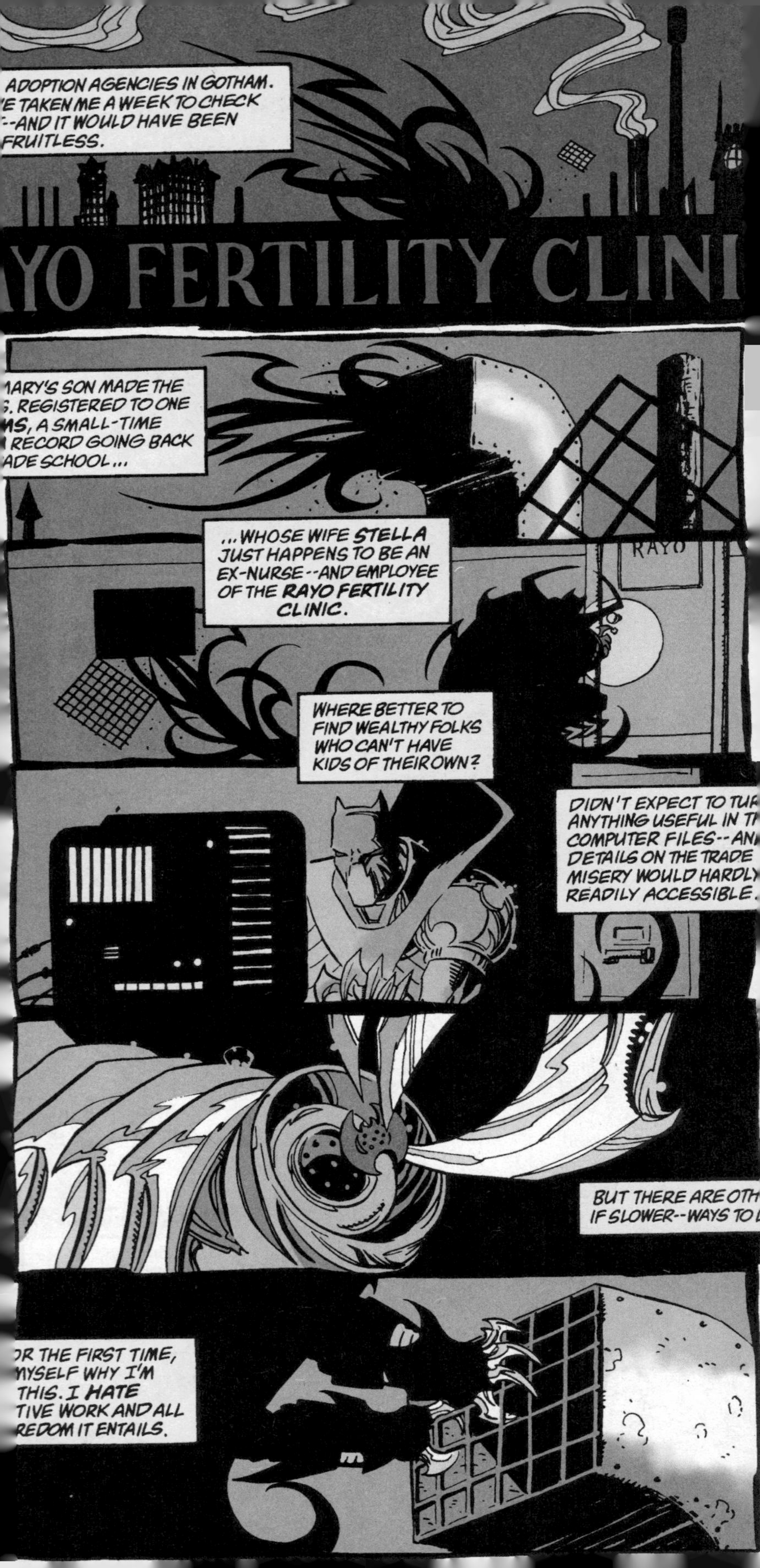

ADOPTION AGENCIES IN GOTHAM. 'E TAKEN ME A WEEK TO CHECK --AND IT WOULD HAVE BEEN FRUITLESS.
YO FERTILITY CLINI
MARY'S SON MADE THE S. REGISTERED TO ONE MS, A SMALL-TIME RECORD GOING BACK ADE SCHOOL...
...WHOSE WIFE STELLA JUST HAPPENS TO BE AN EX-NURSE--AND EMPLOYEE OF THE RAYO FERTILITY CLINIC.
RAYO
WHERE BETTER TO FIND WEALTHY FOLKS WHO CAN'T HAVE KIDS OF THEIR OWN?
DIDN'T EXPECT TO TUR ANYTHING USEFUL IN T COMPUTER FILES--AN DETAILS ON THE TRADE MISERY WOULD HARDLY READILY ACCESSIBLE.
BUT THERE ARE OTH IF SLOWER--WAYS TO
OR THE FIRST TIME, MYSELF WHY I'M THIS. I HATE TIVE WORK AND ALL REDOM IT ENTAILS.

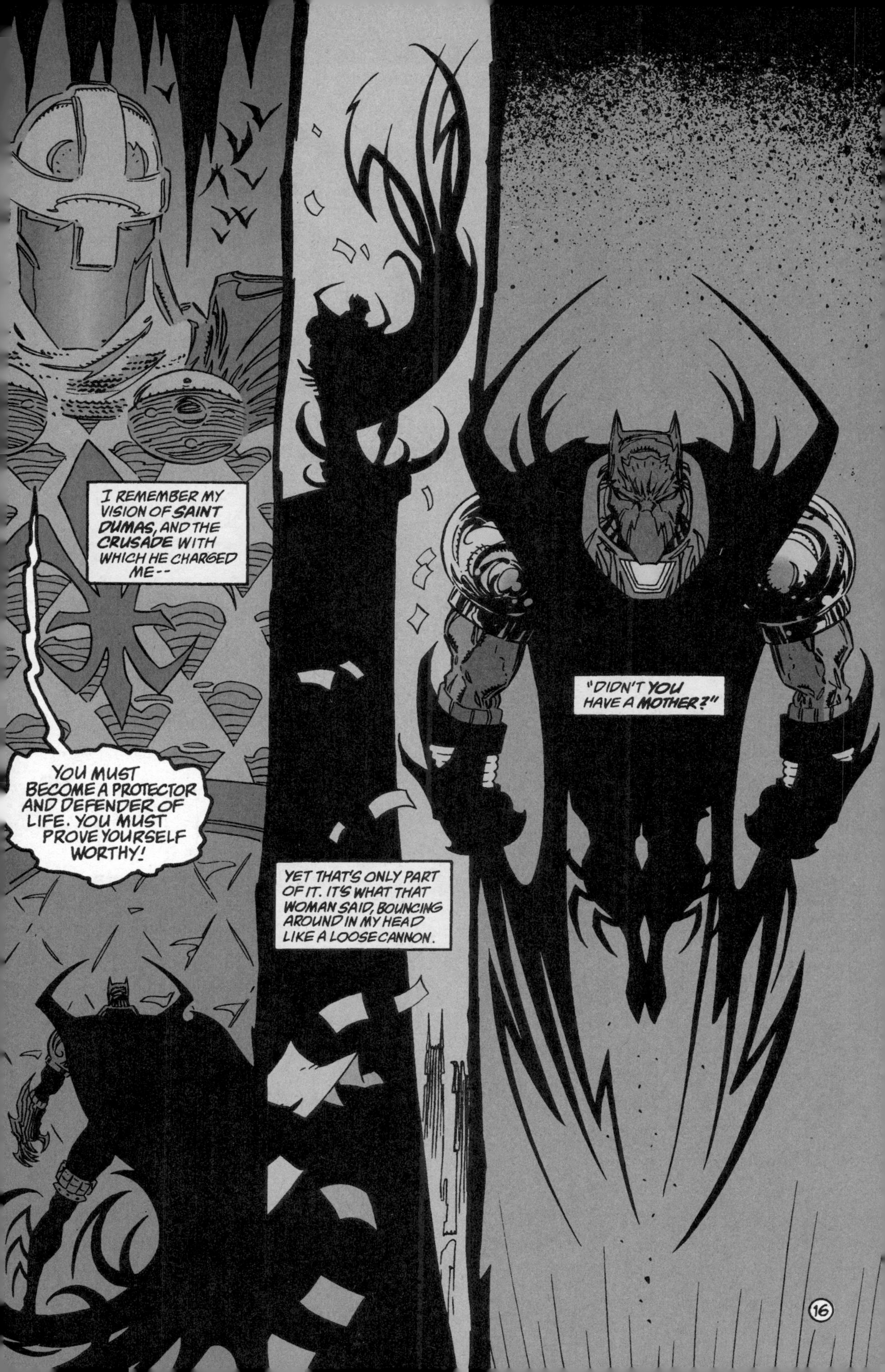
I REMEMBER MY VISION OF SAINT DUMAS, AND THE CRUSADE WITH WHICH HE CHARGED ME--
YOU MUST BECOME A PROTECTOR AND DEFENDER OF LIFE. YOU MUST PROVE YOURSELF WORTHY!
YET THAT'S ONLY PART OF IT. IT'S WHAT THAT WOMAN SAID, BOUNCING AROUND IN MY HEAD LIKE A LOOSE CANNON.
"DIDN'T YOU HAVE A MOTHER?"
16

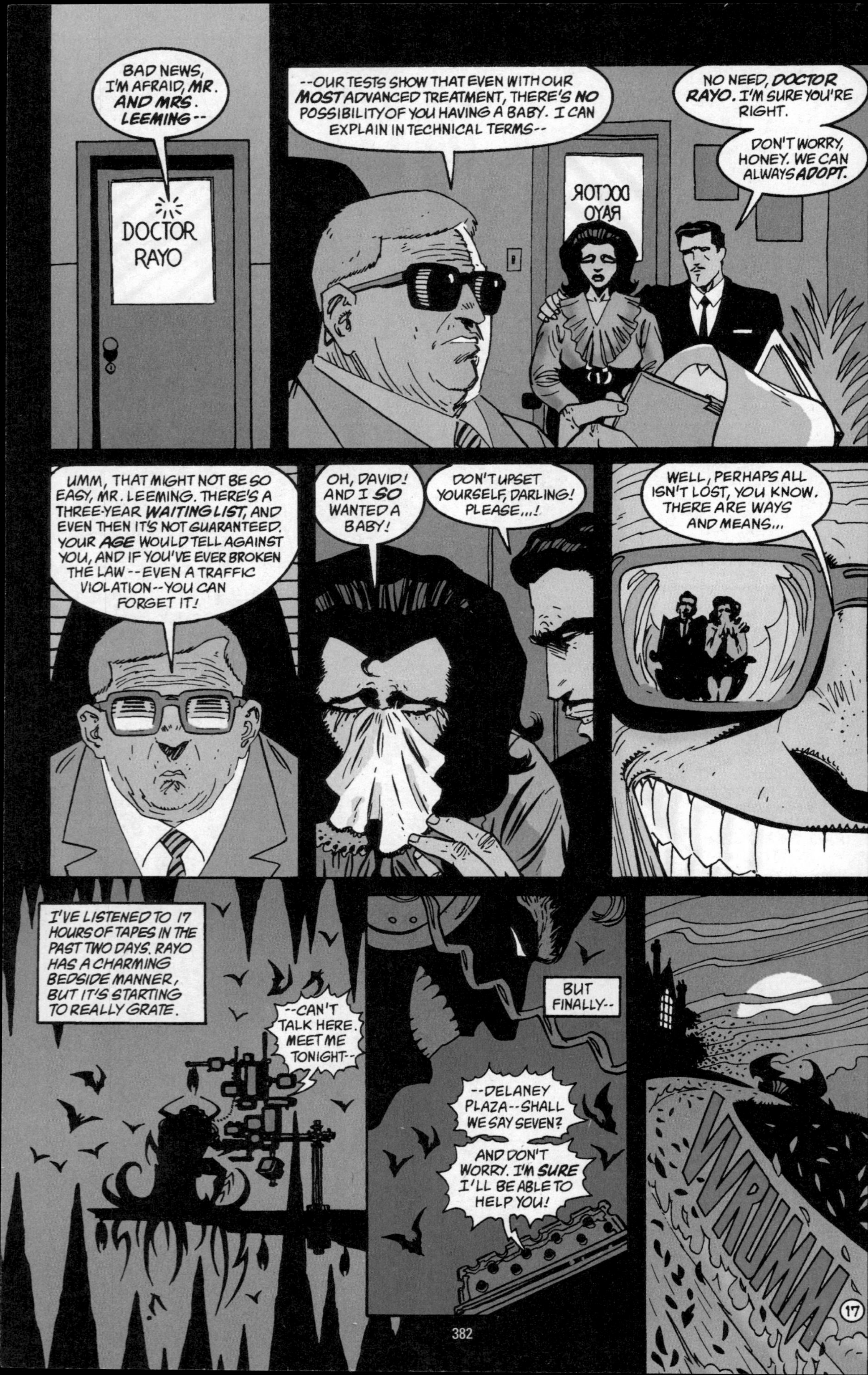

BAD NEWS, I'M AFRAID, MR. AND MRS. LEEMING--
DOCTOR RAYO
--OUR TESTS SHOW THAT EVEN WITH OUR MOST ADVANCED TREATMENT, THERE'S NO POSSIBILITY OF YOU HAVING A BABY. I CAN EXPLAIN IN TECHNICAL TERMS--
NO NEED, DOCTOR RAYO. I'M SURE YOU'RE RIGHT.
DON'T WORRY, HONEY. WE CAN ALWAYS ADOPT.
UMM, THAT MIGHT NOT BE SO EASY, MR. LEEMING. THERE'S A THREE-YEAR WAITING LIST, AND EVEN THEN IT'S NOT GUARANTEED. YOUR AGE WOULD TELL AGAINST YOU, AND IF YOU'VE EVER BROKEN THE LAW--EVEN A TRAFFIC VIOLATION--YOU CAN FORGET IT!
OH, DAVID! AND I SO WANTED A BABY!
DON'T UPSET YOURSELF, DARLING! PLEASE...!
WELL, PERHAPS ALL ISN'T LOST, YOU KNOW. THERE ARE WAYS AND MEANS...
I'VE LISTENED TO 17 HOURS OF TAPES IN THE PAST TWO DAYS. RAYO HAS A CHARMING BEDSIDE MANNER, BUT IT'S STARTING TO REALLY GRATE.
--CAN'T TALK HERE. MEET ME TONIGHT--
BUT FINALLY--
--DELANEY PLAZA--SHALL WE SAY SEVEN?
AND DON'T WORRY. I'M SURE I'LL BE ABLE TO HELP YOU!
VVRUMMM
17

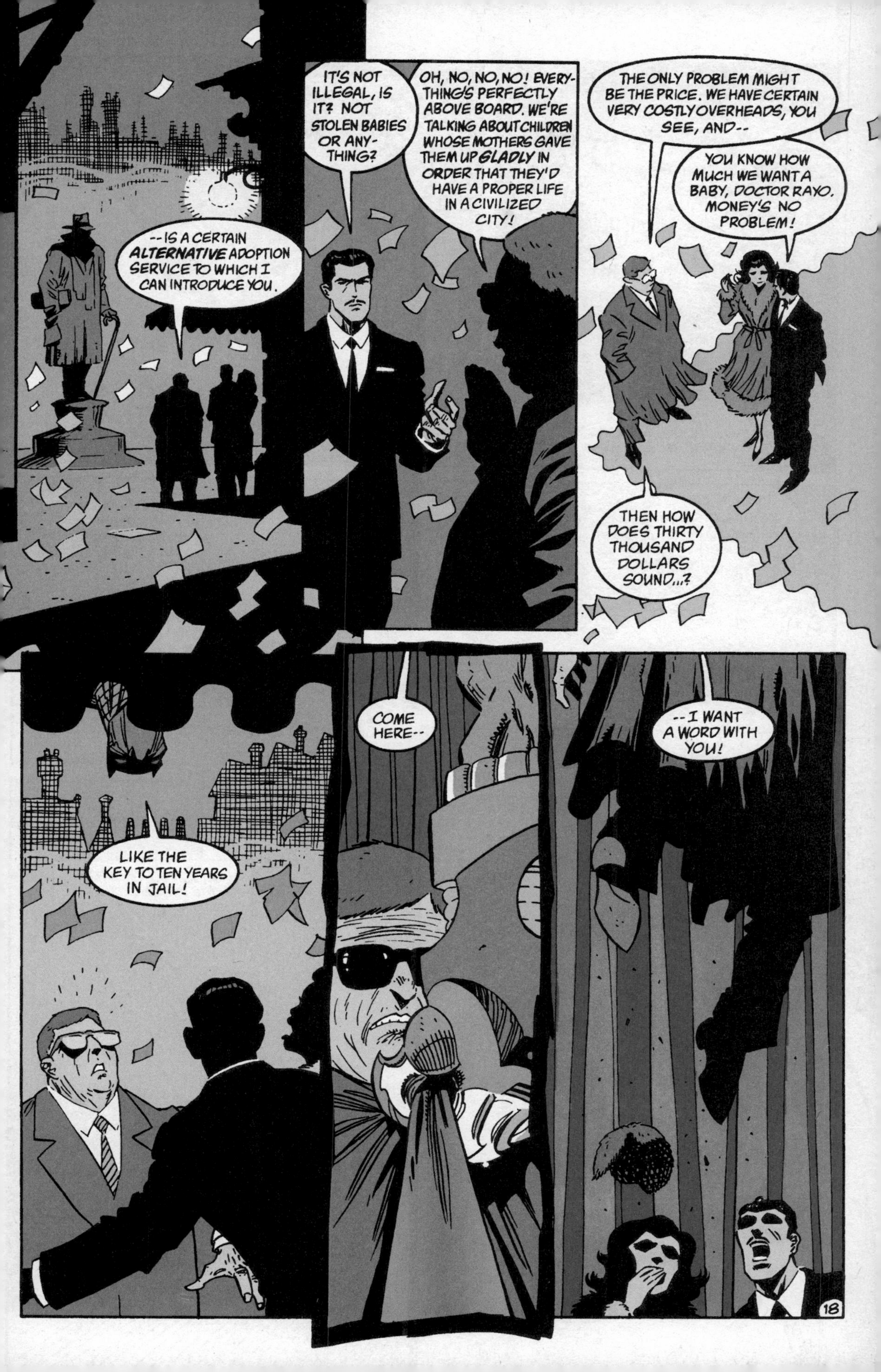
--IS A CERTAIN ALTERNATIVE ADOPTION SERVICE TO WHICH I CAN INTRODUCE YOU.
IT'S NOT ILLEGAL, IS IT? NOT STOLEN BABIES OR ANY-THING?
OH, NO, NO, NO! EVERY-THING'S PERFECTLY ABOVE BOARD. WE'RE TALKING ABOUT CHILDREN WHOSE MOTHERS GAVE THEM UP GLADLY IN ORDER THAT THEY'D HAVE A PROPER LIFE IN A CIVILIZED CITY!
THE ONLY PROBLEM MIGHT BE THE PRICE. WE HAVE CERTAIN VERY COSTLY OVERHEADS, YOU SEE, AND--
YOU KNOW HOW MUCH WE WANT A BABY, DOCTOR RAYO. MONEY'S NO PROBLEM!
THEN HOW DOES THIRTY THOUSAND DOLLARS SOUND...?
LIKE THE KEY TO TEN YEARS IN JAIL!
COME HERE--
--I WANT A WORD WITH YOU!
18

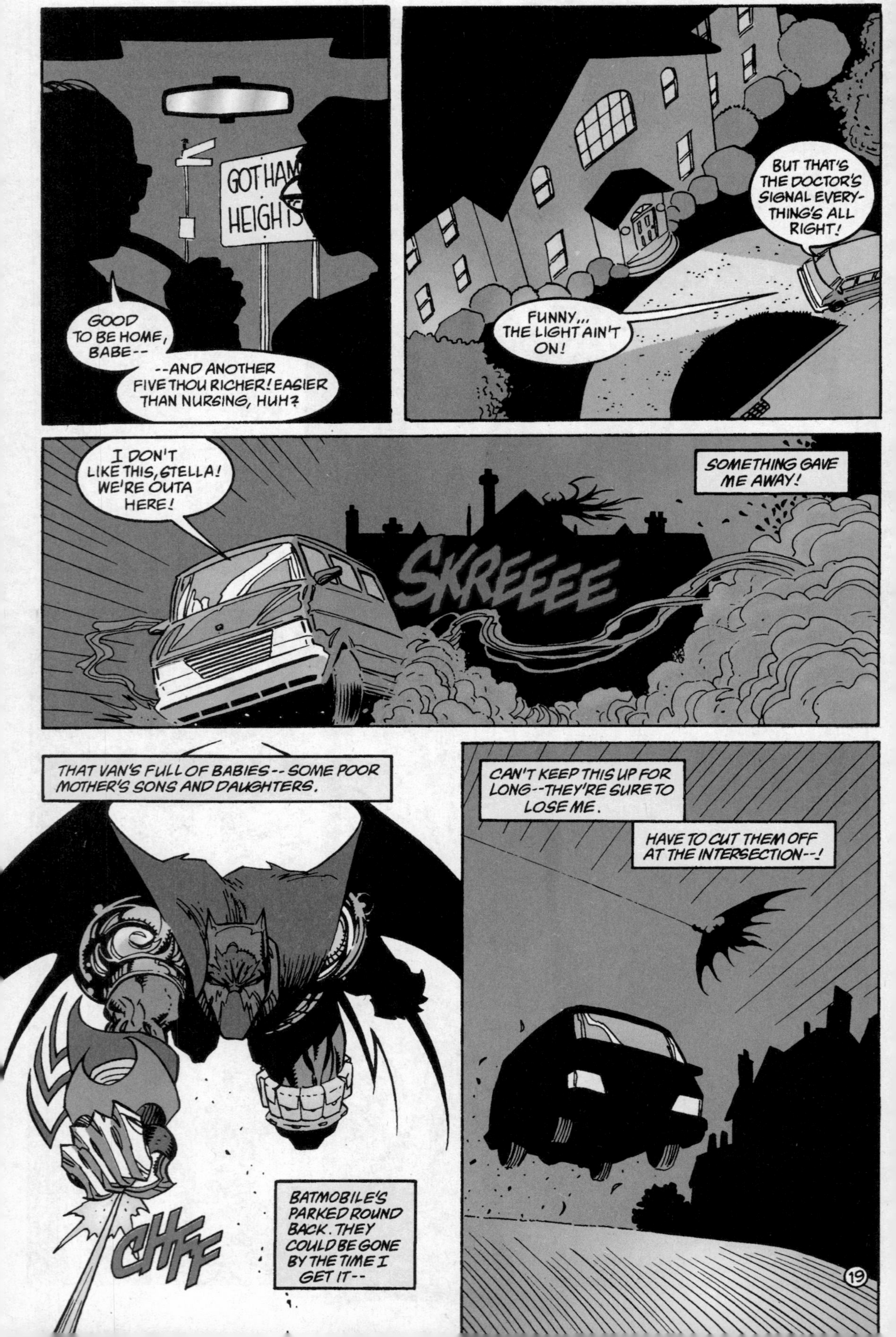
GOTHAM HEIGHTS
GOOD TO BE HOME, BABE--
--AND ANOTHER FIVE THOU RICHER! EASIER THAN NURSING, HUH?
FUNNY... THE LIGHT AIN'T ON!
BUT THAT'S THE DOCTOR'S SIGNAL EVERYTHING'S ALL RIGHT!
I DON'T LIKE THIS, STELLA! WE'RE OUTA HERE!
SOMETHING GAVE ME AWAY!
SKREEEEE
THAT VAN'S FULL OF BABIES -- SOME POOR MOTHER'S SONS AND DAUGHTERS.
BATMOBILE'S PARKED ROUND BACK. THEY COULD BE GONE BY THE TIME I GET IT--
CHFF
CAN'T KEEP THIS UP FOR LONG--THEY'RE SURE TO LOSE ME.
HAVE TO CUT THEM OFF AT THE INTERSECTION--!

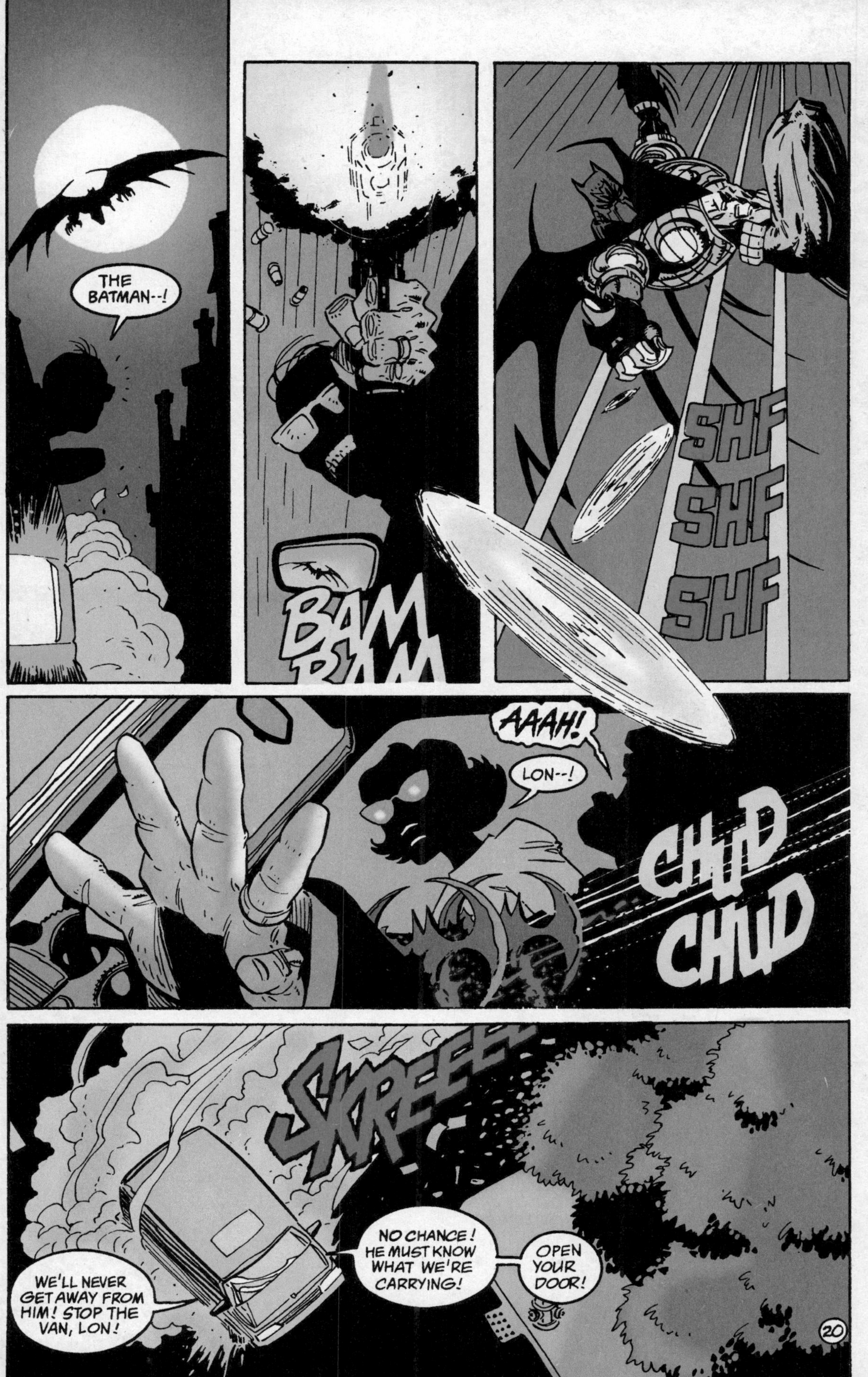

THE BATMAN--!
BAM
SHF
SHF
SHF
AAAH!
LON--!
CHUD
CHUD
SKREEEE
WE'LL NEVER GET AWAY FROM HIM! STOP THE VAN, LON!
NO CHANCE! HE MUST KNOW WHAT WE'RE CARRYING!
OPEN YOUR DOOR!
20

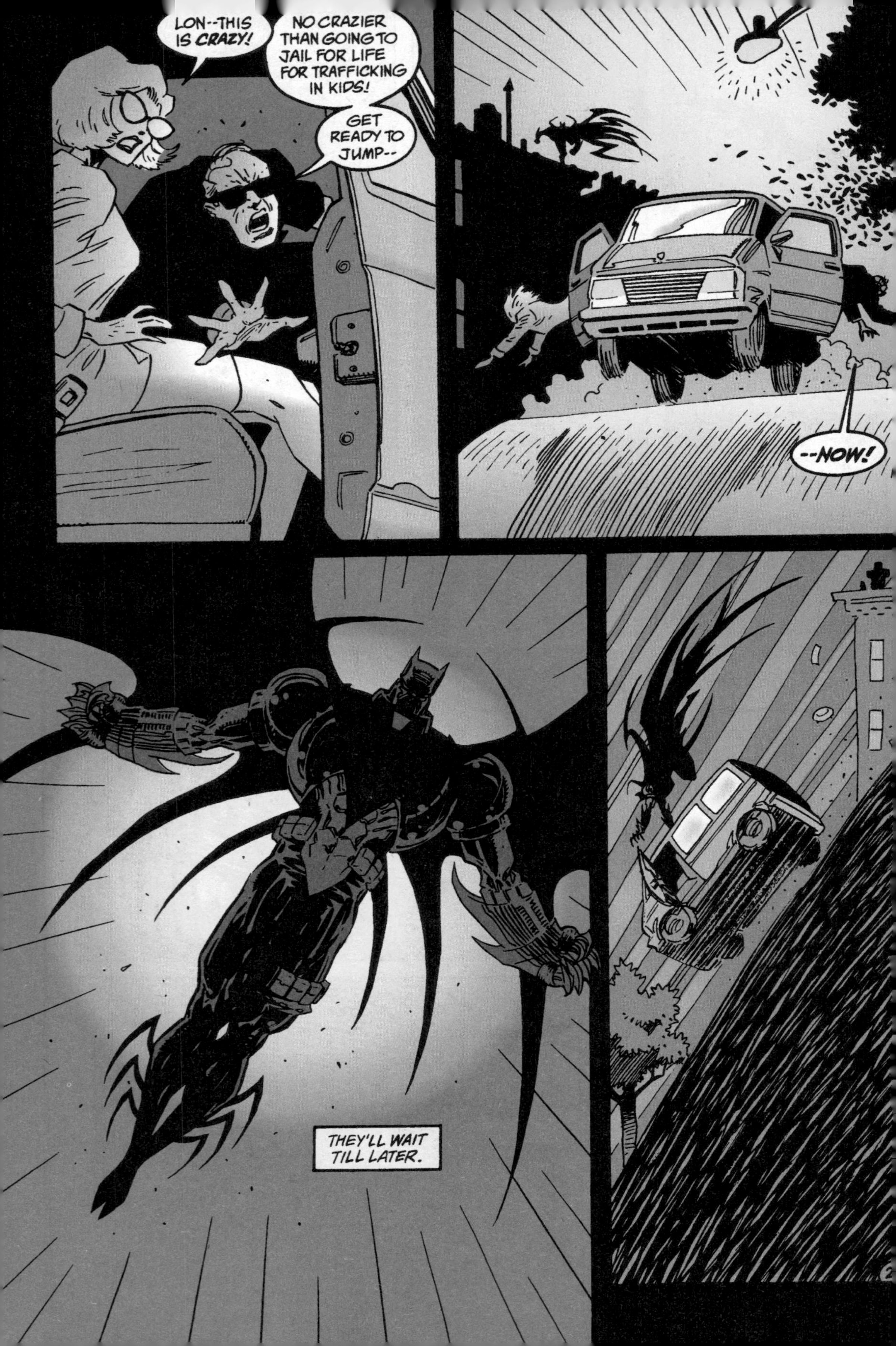

LON--THIS IS *CRAZY!*
NO CRAZIER THAN GOING TO JAIL FOR LIFE FOR TRAFFICKING IN KIDS!
GET READY TO JUMP--
--NOW!
THEY'LL WAIT TILL LATER.

810

BEEP BEEP

FUEL

1042

BASH!

GOTHAM

SKREEEEEEE

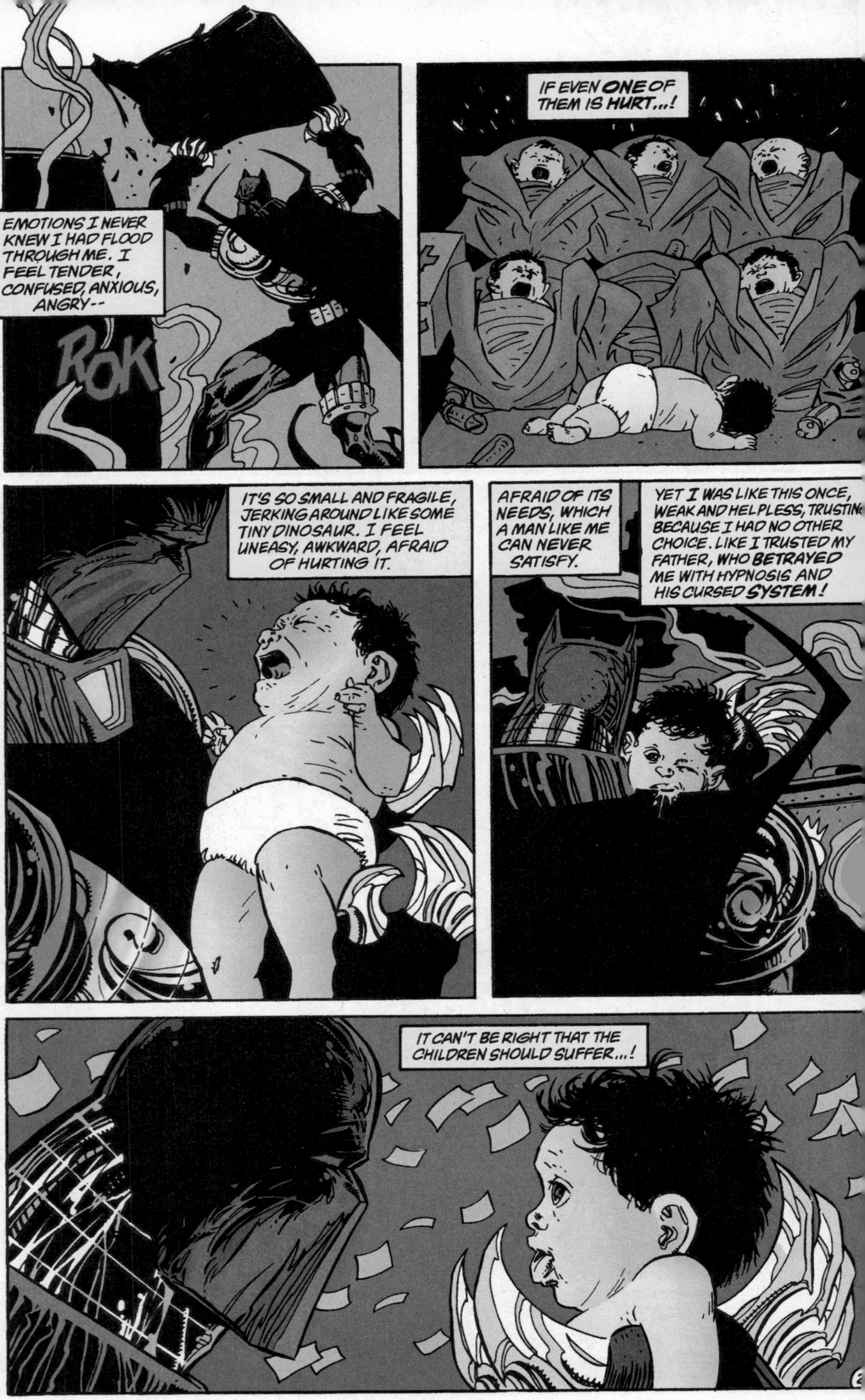
EMOTIONS I NEVER KNEW I HAD FLOOD THROUGH ME. I FEEL TENDER, CONFUSED, ANXIOUS, ANGRY--
ROK
IF EVEN ONE OF THEM IS HURT...!
IT'S SO SMALL AND FRAGILE, JERKING AROUND LIKE SOME TINY DINOSAUR. I FEEL UNEASY, AWKWARD, AFRAID OF HURTING IT.
AFRAID OF ITS NEEDS, WHICH A MAN LIKE ME CAN NEVER SATISFY.
YET I WAS LIKE THIS ONCE, WEAK AND HELPLESS, TRUSTING BECAUSE I HAD NO OTHER CHOICE. LIKE I TRUSTED MY FATHER, WHO BETRAYED ME WITH HYPNOSIS AND HIS CURSED SYSTEM!
IT CAN'T BE RIGHT THAT THE CHILDREN SHOULD SUFFER...!

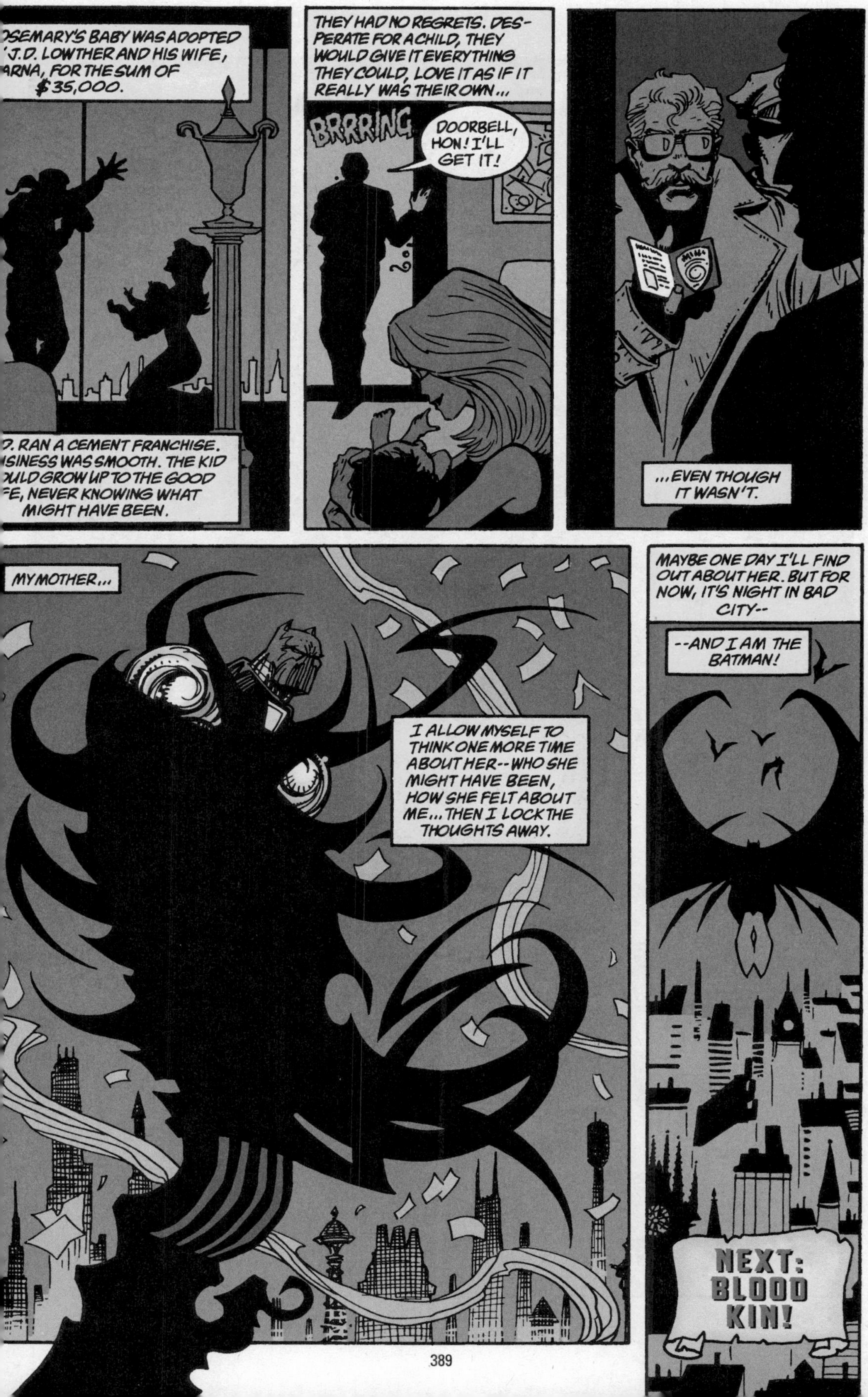

OSEMARY'S BABY WAS ADOPTED ' J.D. LOWTHER AND HIS WIFE, ARNA, FOR THE SUM OF $35,000.
D. RAN A CEMENT FRANCHISE. ISINESS WAS SMOOTH. THE KID OULD GROW UP TO THE GOOD FE, NEVER KNOWING WHAT MIGHT HAVE BEEN.
THEY HAD NO REGRETS. DESPERATE FOR A CHILD, THEY WOULD GIVE IT EVERYTHING THEY COULD, LOVE IT AS IF IT REALLY WAS THEIR OWN...
BRRRING
DOORBELL, HON! I'LL GET IT!
...EVEN THOUGH IT WASN'T.
MY MOTHER...
I ALLOW MYSELF TO THINK ONE MORE TIME ABOUT HER--WHO SHE MIGHT HAVE BEEN, HOW SHE FELT ABOUT ME...THEN I LOCK THE THOUGHTS AWAY.
MAYBE ONE DAY I'LL FIND OUT ABOUT HER. BUT FOR NOW, IT'S NIGHT IN BAD CITY--
--AND I AM THE BATMAN!
NEXT: BLOOD KIN!

Cover art by KELLEY JONES

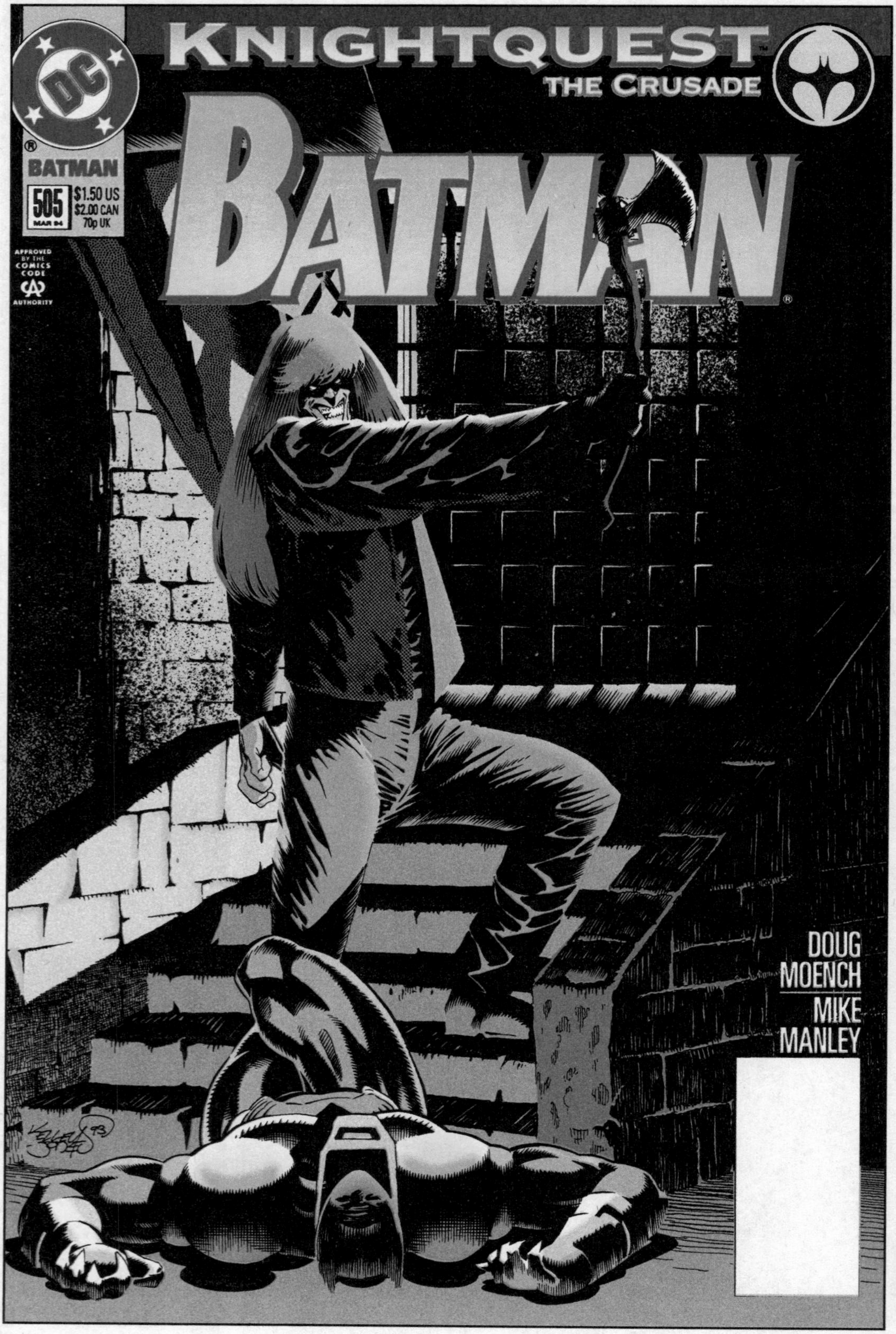

KNIGHTQUEST
THE CRUSADE
DC
BATMAN
505
$1.50 US
$2.00 CAN
70p UK
MAR 94
APPROVED BY THE COMICS CODE AUTHORITY
BATMAN
DOUG MOENCH
MIKE MANLEY

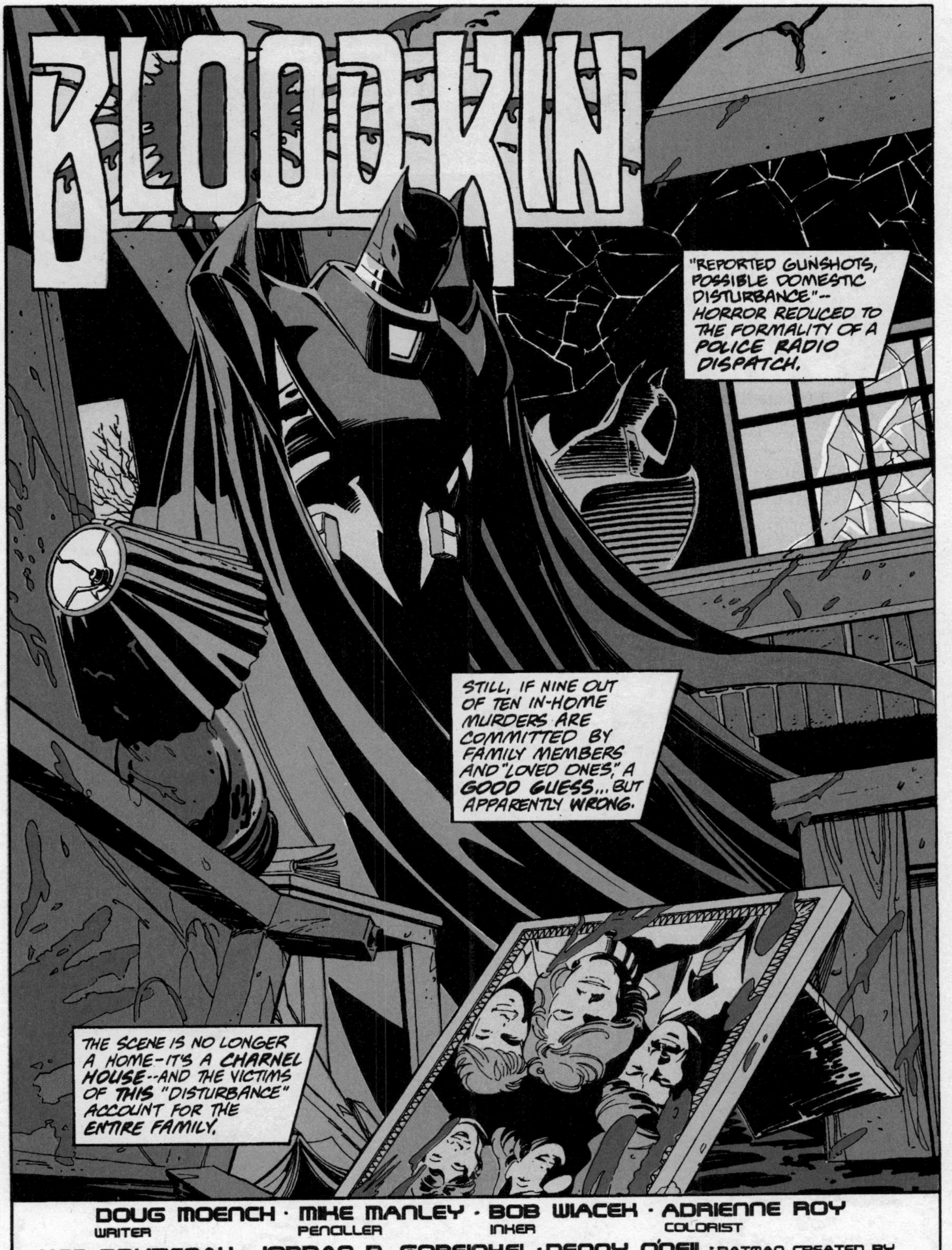
BLOOD KIN
"REPORTED GUNSHOTS, POSSIBLE DOMESTIC DISTURBANCE"-- HORROR REDUCED TO THE FORMALITY OF A POLICE RADIO DISPATCH.
STILL, IF NINE OUT OF TEN IN-HOME MURDERS ARE COMMITTED BY FAMILY MEMBERS AND "LOVED ONES," A GOOD GUESS... BUT APPARENTLY WRONG.
THE SCENE IS NO LONGER A HOME--IT'S A CHARNEL HOUSE--AND THE VICTIMS OF THIS "DISTURBANCE" ACCOUNT FOR THE ENTIRE FAMILY.
DOUG MOENCH · MIKE MANLEY · BOB WIACEK · ADRIENNE ROY
WRITER PENCILLER INKER COLORIST
KEN BRUZENAK · JORDAN B. GORFINKEL · DENNY O'NEIL · BATMAN CREATED BY BOB KANE
LETTERER ASSISTANT EDITOR EDITOR

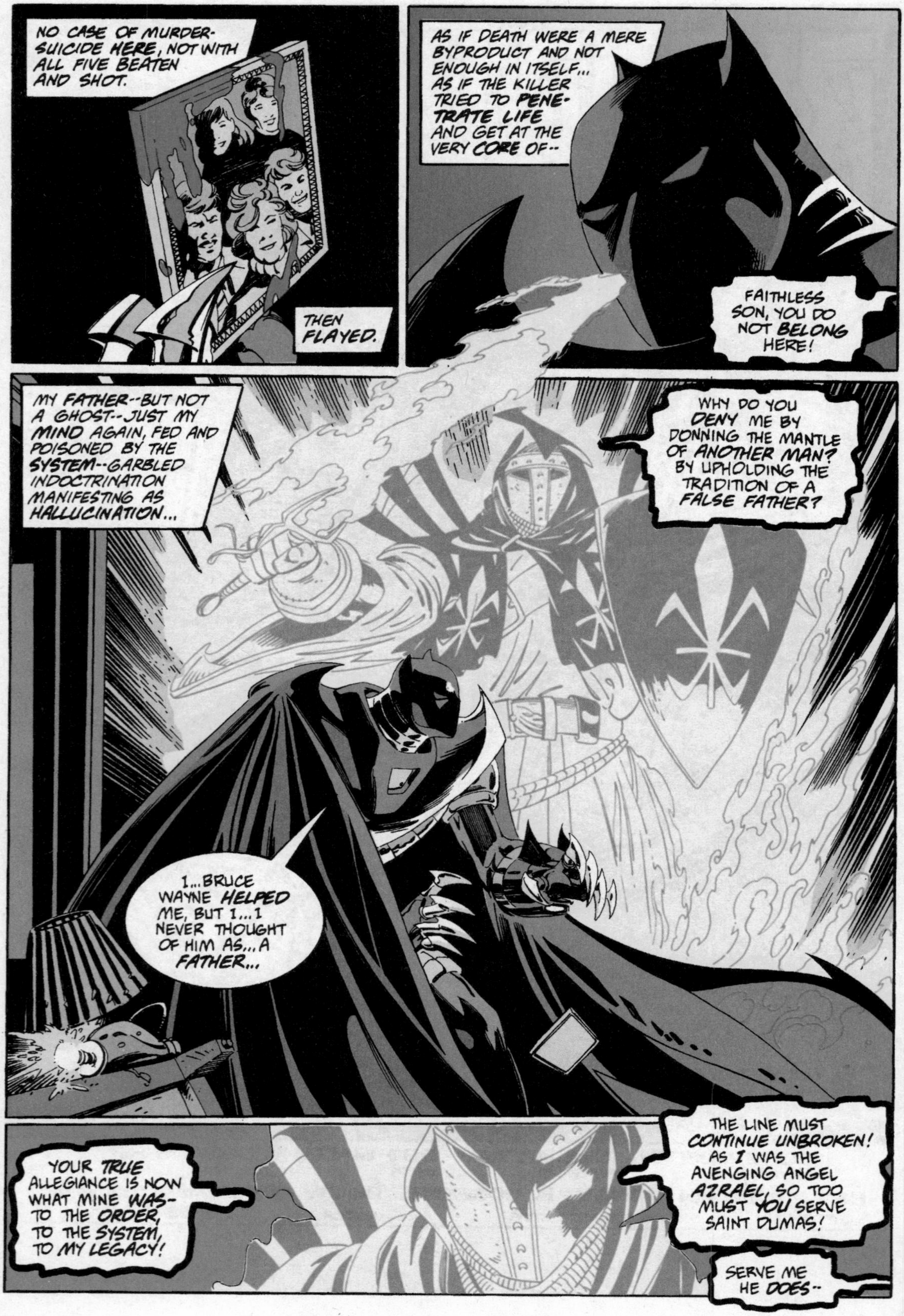
NO CASE OF MURDER-SUICIDE HERE, NOT WITH ALL FIVE BEATEN AND SHOT.
THEN FLAYED.
AS IF DEATH WERE A MERE BYPRODUCT AND NOT ENOUGH IN ITSELF... AS IF THE KILLER TRIED TO PENE-TRATE LIFE AND GET AT THE VERY CORE OF--
FAITHLESS SON, YOU DO NOT BELONG HERE!
MY FATHER--BUT NOT A GHOST--JUST MY MIND AGAIN, FED AND POISONED BY THE SYSTEM--GARBLED INDOCTRINATION MANIFESTING AS HALLUCINATION...
WHY DO YOU DENY ME BY DONNING THE MANTLE OF ANOTHER MAN? BY UPHOLDING THE TRADITION OF A FALSE FATHER?
I...BRUCE WAYNE HELPED ME, BUT I...I NEVER THOUGHT OF HIM AS...A FATHER...
YOUR TRUE ALLEGIANCE IS NOW WHAT MINE WAS-- TO THE ORDER, TO THE SYSTEM, TO MY LEGACY!
THE LINE MUST CONTINUE UNBROKEN! AS I WAS THE AVENGING ANGEL AZRAEL, SO TOO MUST YOU SERVE SAINT DUMAS!
SERVE ME HE DOES--

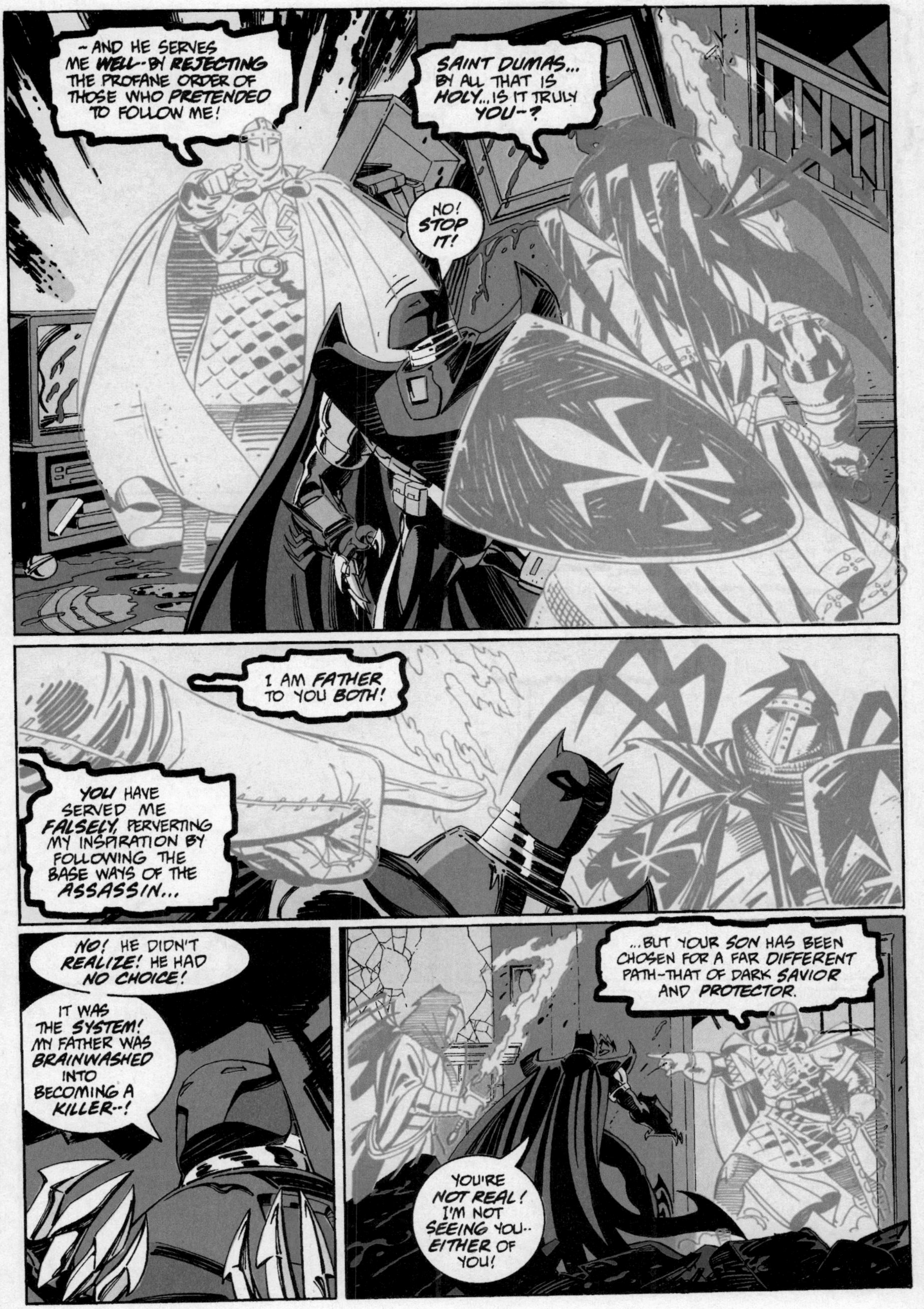

-AND HE SERVES ME WELL--BY REJECTING THE PROFANE ORDER OF THOSE WHO PRETENDED TO FOLLOW ME!
SAINT DUMAS... BY ALL THAT IS HOLY... IS IT TRULY YOU--?
NO! STOP IT!
I AM FATHER TO YOU BOTH!
YOU HAVE SERVED ME FALSELY, PERVERTING MY INSPIRATION BY FOLLOWING THE BASE WAYS OF THE ASSASSIN...
NO! HE DIDN'T REALIZE! HE HAD NO CHOICE!
IT WAS THE SYSTEM! MY FATHER WAS BRAINWASHED INTO BECOMING A KILLER--!
...BUT YOUR SON HAS BEEN CHOSEN FOR A FAR DIFFERENT PATH--THAT OF DARK SAVIOR AND PROTECTOR.
YOU'RE NOT REAL! I'M NOT SEEING YOU.. EITHER OF YOU!

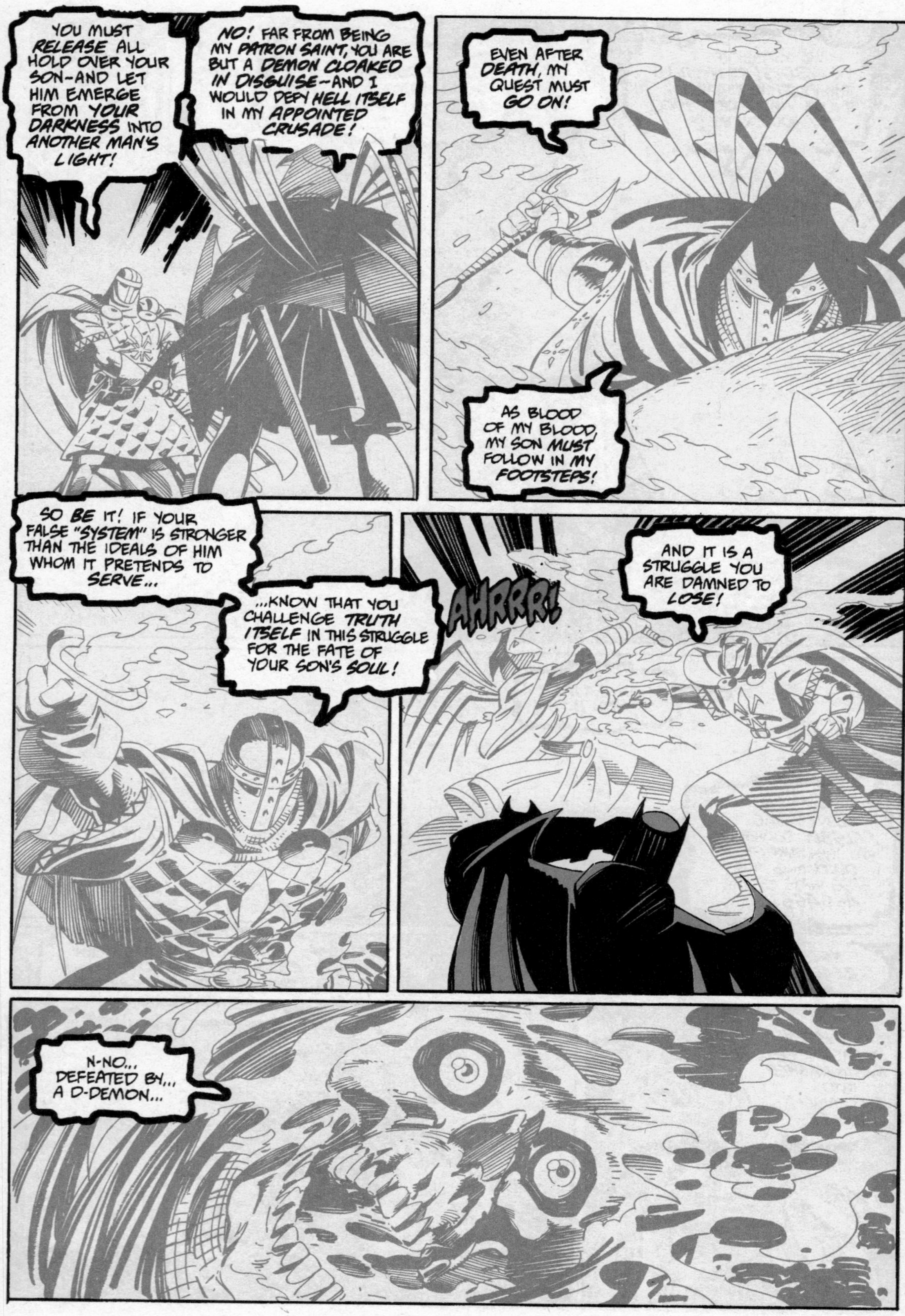
YOU MUST RELEASE ALL HOLD OVER YOUR SON--AND LET HIM EMERGE FROM YOUR DARKNESS INTO ANOTHER MAN'S LIGHT!
NO! FAR FROM BEING MY PATRON SAINT, YOU ARE BUT A DEMON CLOAKED IN DISGUISE--AND I WOULD DEFY HELL ITSELF IN MY APPOINTED CRUSADE!
EVEN AFTER DEATH, MY QUEST MUST GO ON!
AS BLOOD OF MY BLOOD, MY SON MUST FOLLOW IN MY FOOTSTEPS!
SO BE IT! IF YOUR FALSE "SYSTEM" IS STRONGER THAN THE IDEALS OF HIM WHOM IT PRETENDS TO SERVE...
...KNOW THAT YOU CHALLENGE TRUTH ITSELF IN THIS STRUGGLE FOR THE FATE OF YOUR SON'S SOUL!
AHRRR!
AND IT IS A STRUGGLE YOU ARE DAMNED TO LOSE!
N-NO... DEFEATED BY... A D-DEMON...

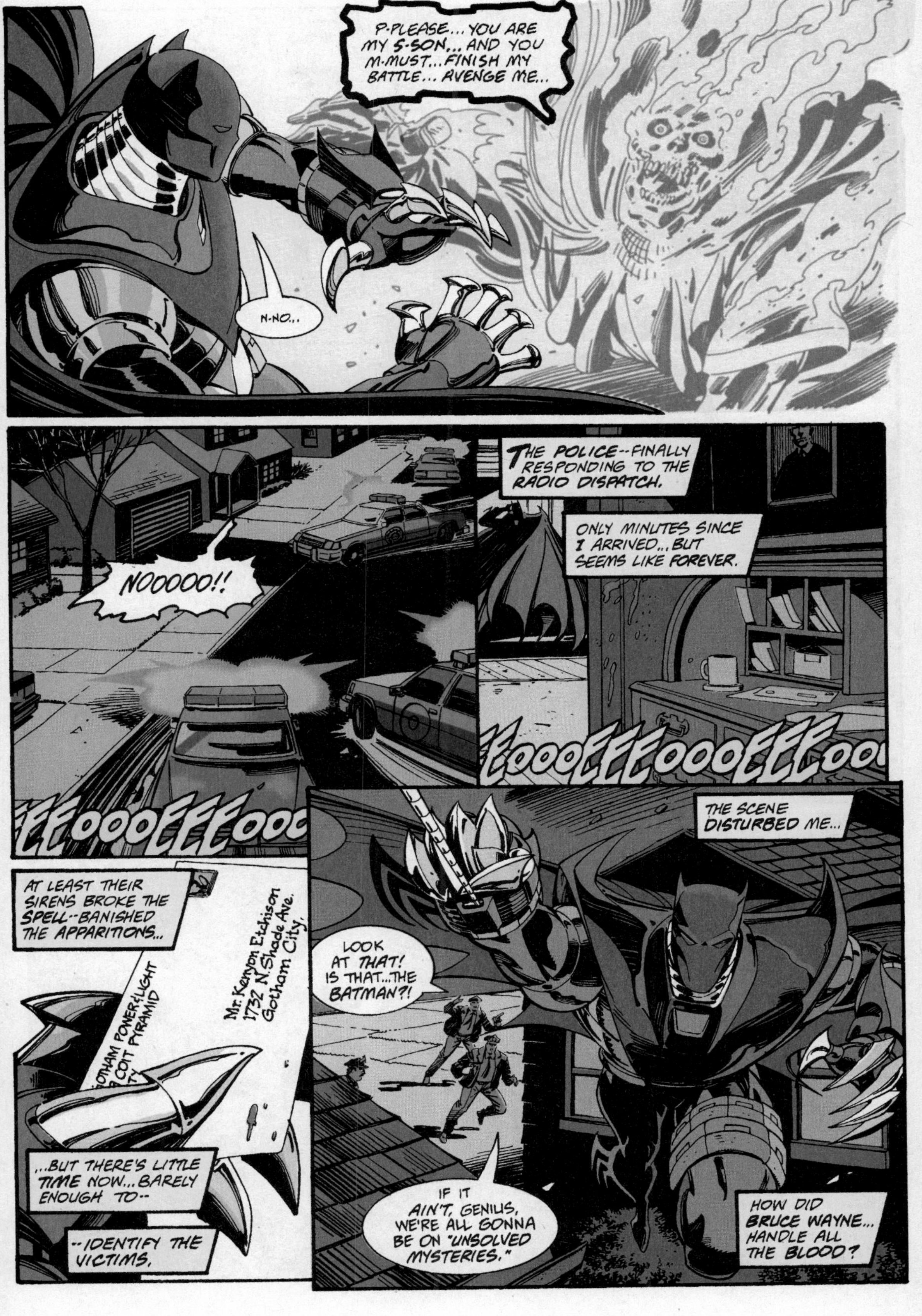
P-PLEASE... YOU ARE MY S-SON... AND YOU M-MUST... FINISH MY BATTLE... AVENGE ME...
N-NO...
THE POLICE--FINALLY RESPONDING TO THE RADIO DISPATCH.
NOOOOO!!
ONLY MINUTES SINCE I ARRIVED... BUT SEEMS LIKE FOREVER.
EEOOOEEOOOEEOO
EEOOOEEOOOEEOO
AT LEAST THEIR SIRENS BROKE THE SPELL--BANISHED THE APPARITIONS...
Mr. Kenyon Etchison
1732 N. Shade Ave.
Gotham City,
GOTHAM POWER & LIGHT
COIT PYRAMID
...BUT THERE'S LITTLE TIME NOW... BARELY ENOUGH TO--
--IDENTIFY THE VICTIMS.
THE SCENE DISTURBED ME...
LOOK AT THAT! IS THAT... THE BATMAN?!
IF IT AIN'T, GENIUS, WE'RE ALL GONNA BE ON "UNSOLVED MYSTERIES."
HOW DID BRUCE WAYNE... HANDLE ALL THE BLOOD?

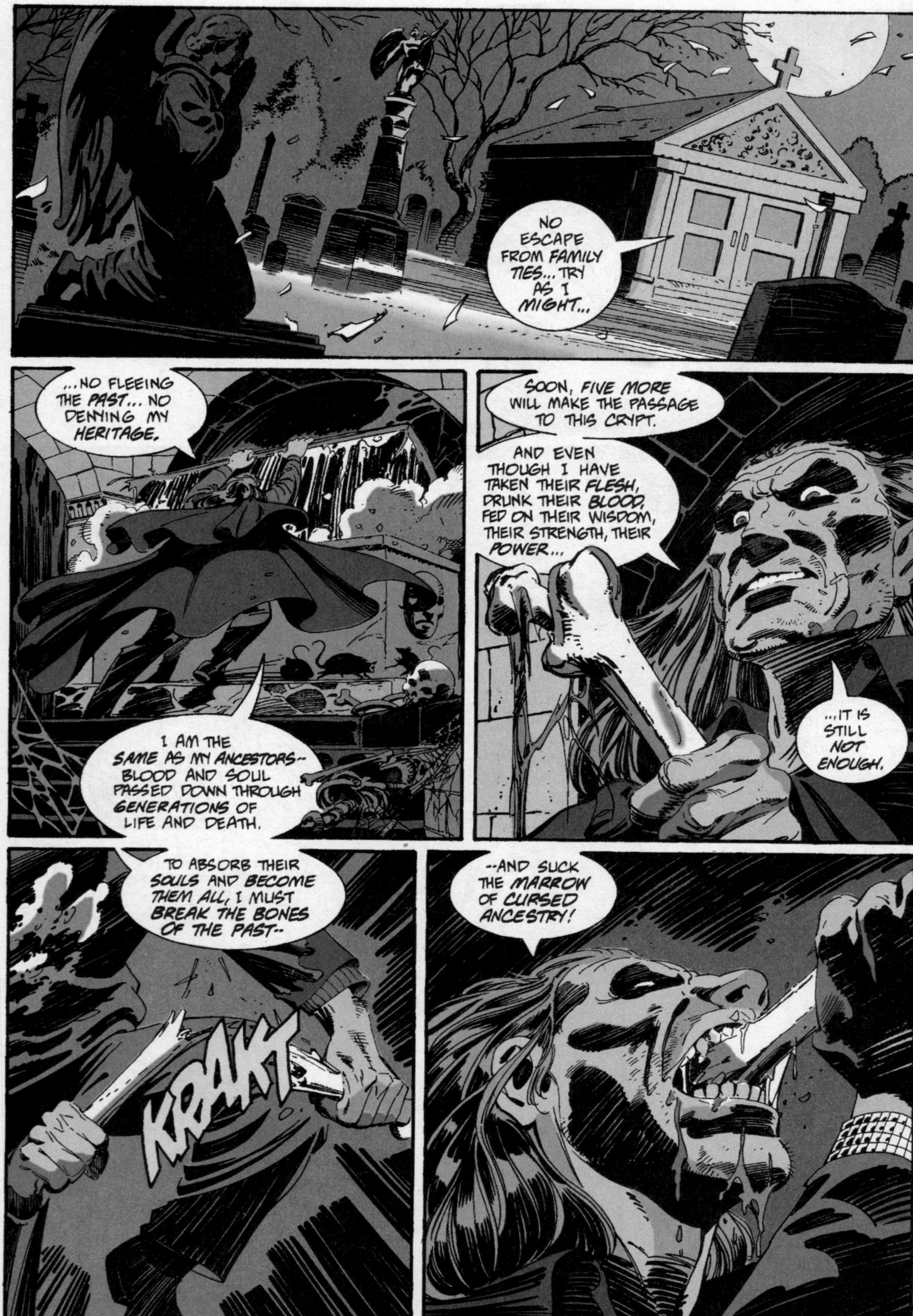
NO ESCAPE FROM FAMILY TIES... TRY AS I MIGHT...
...NO FLEEING THE PAST... NO DENYING MY HERITAGE.
I AM THE SAME AS MY ANCESTORS-- BLOOD AND SOUL PASSED DOWN THROUGH GENERATIONS OF LIFE AND DEATH.
SOON, FIVE MORE WILL MAKE THE PASSAGE TO THIS CRYPT.
AND EVEN THOUGH I HAVE TAKEN THEIR FLESH, DRUNK THEIR BLOOD, FED ON THEIR WISDOM, THEIR STRENGTH, THEIR POWER...
...IT IS STILL NOT ENOUGH.
TO ABSORB THEIR SOULS AND BECOME THEM ALL, I MUST BREAK THE BONES OF THE PAST--
KRAKT
--AND SUCK THE MARROW OF CURSED ANCESTRY!

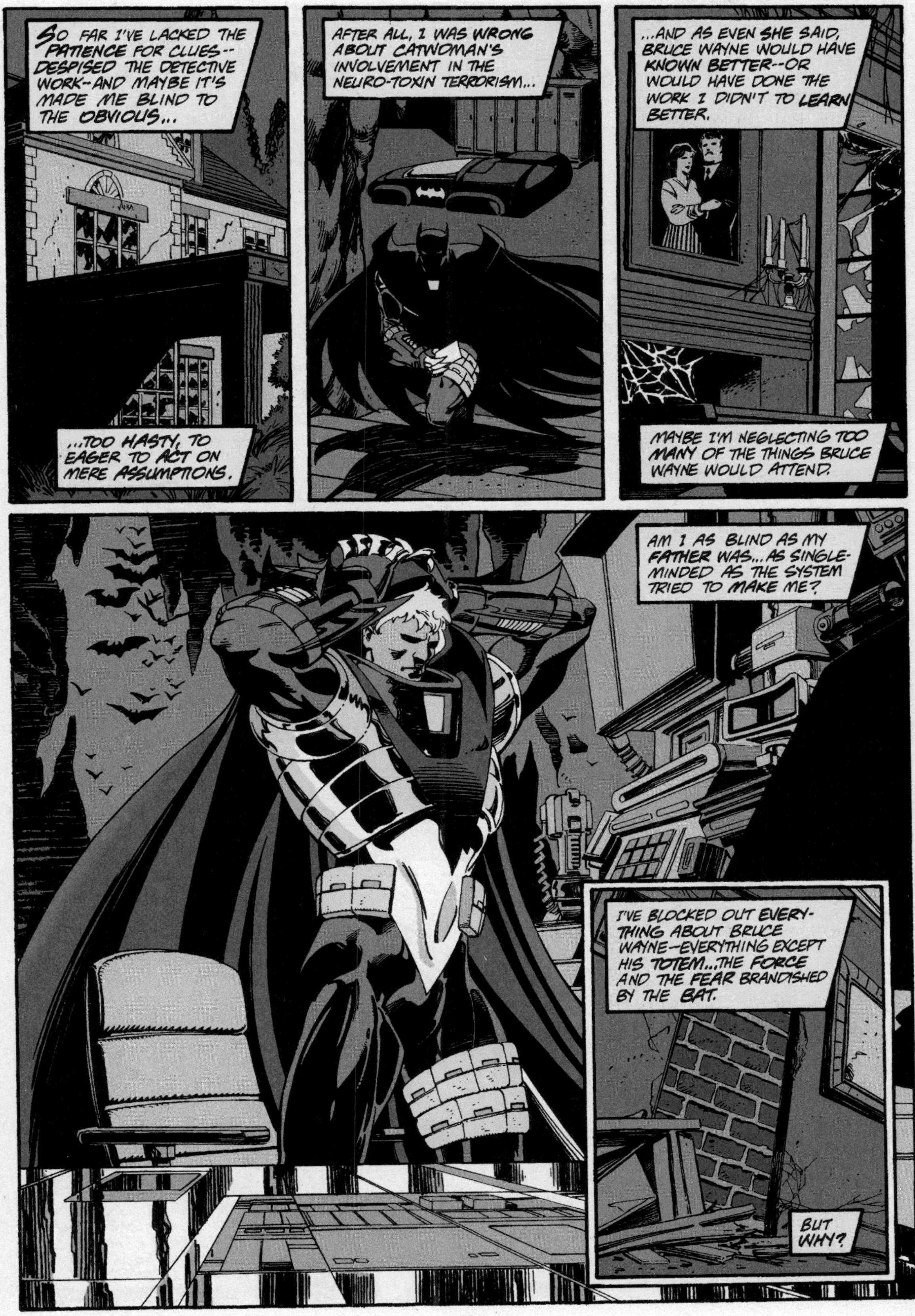

SO FAR I'VE LACKED THE PATIENCE FOR CLUES--DESPISED THE DETECTIVE WORK--AND MAYBE IT'S MADE ME BLIND TO THE OBVIOUS...
...TOO HASTY, TO EAGER TO ACT ON MERE ASSUMPTIONS.
AFTER ALL, I WAS WRONG ABOUT CATWOMAN'S INVOLVEMENT IN THE NEURO-TOXIN TERRORISM...
...AND AS EVEN SHE SAID, BRUCE WAYNE WOULD HAVE KNOWN BETTER--OR WOULD HAVE DONE THE WORK I DIDN'T TO LEARN BETTER.
MAYBE I'M NEGLECTING TOO MANY OF THE THINGS BRUCE WAYNE WOULD ATTEND.
AM I AS BLIND AS MY FATHER WAS...AS SINGLE-MINDED AS THE SYSTEM TRIED TO MAKE ME?
I'VE BLOCKED OUT EVERYTHING ABOUT BRUCE WAYNE--EVERYTHING EXCEPT HIS TOTEM...THE FORCE AND THE FEAR BRANDISHED BY THE BAT.
BUT WHY?

AM I TRYING TO EXORCISE BRUCE WAYNE FROM HIS OWN TOTEM--

--EVEN AS I USURP THE BAT?

WHATEVER THE TRUTH, IT'S TIME TO STOP BLAMING THE SYSTEM AND START GETTING DOWN TO WORK.

TEK
CHEK
TEKKA
TEK
TEK

FIVE PEOPLE WERE SAVAGELY BUTCHERED TONIGHT.

ALL DAMAGE AT THE SCENE WAS RELATED TO THE STRUGGLE...

KLAK TAK

NO VANDALISM-- AND NO EVIDENCE OF MISSING VALUABLES.

NO THEFT, NO MOTIVE, AND MOTIVELESS CRIMES USUALLY INDICATE PASSION...

...WHICH USUALLY INCRIMINATES A FAMILY MEMBER-- YET THE ENTIRE FAMILY IS DEAD.

AND NOW...TIME TO LOOK UP MY DEAR COUSIN'S SON.

SO WHO WAS THE BUTCHER?

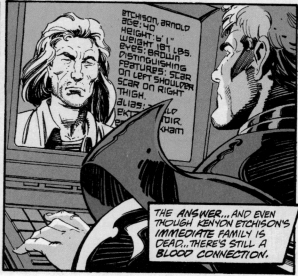

ETCHISON, ARNOLD
AGE: 40
HEIGHT: 6'1"
WEIGHT: 187 LBS.
EYES: BROWN
DISTINGUISHING FEATURES: SCAR ON LEFT SHOULDER SCAR ON RIGHT THIGH.
ALIAS:
EKT...
...OLD
...DIR.
...KHAM

THE ANSWER...AND EVEN THOUGH KENYON ETCHISON'S IMMEDIATE FAMILY IS DEAD...THERE'S STILL A BLOOD CONNECTION.

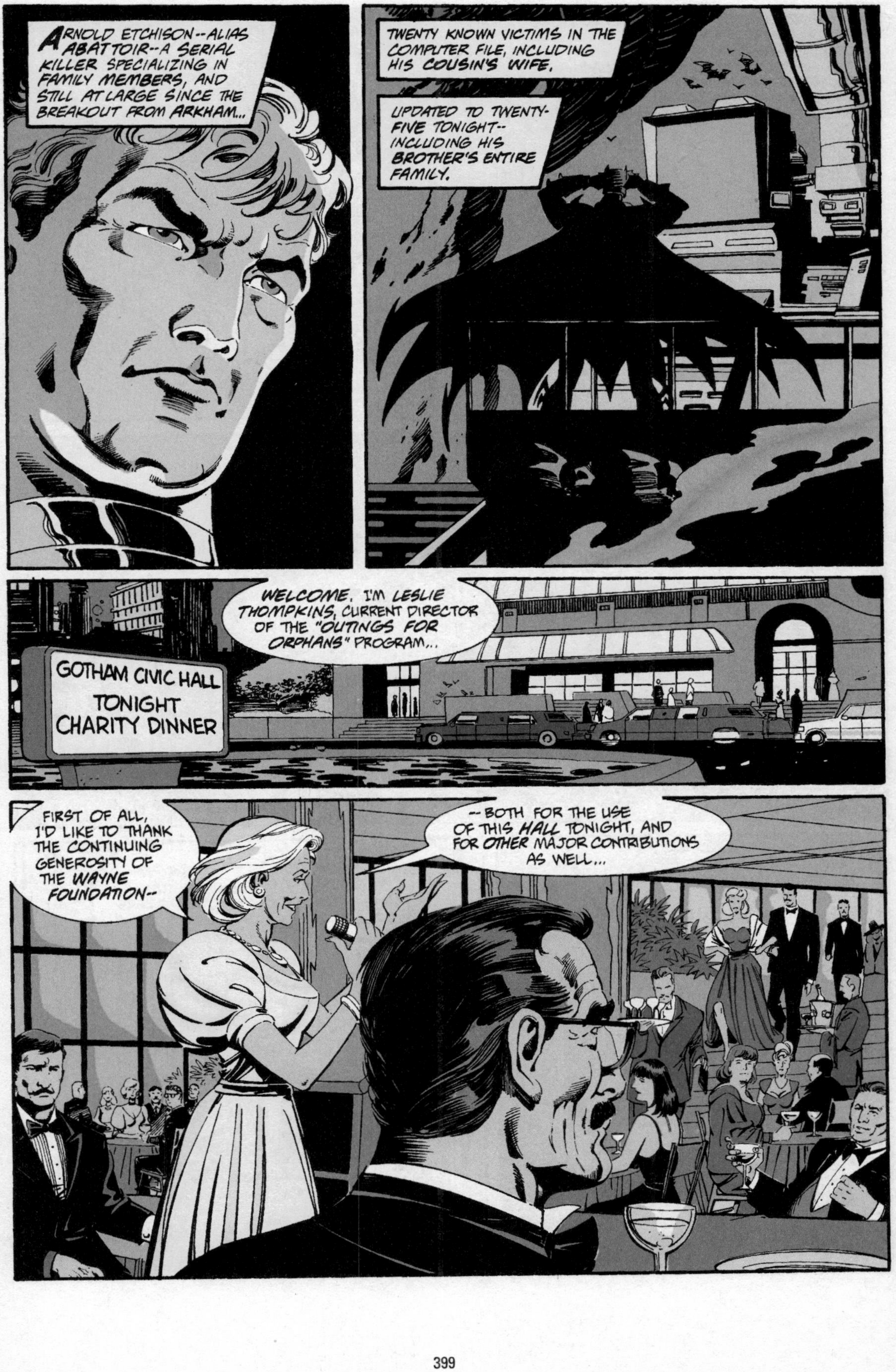
ARNOLD ETCHISON--ALIAS ABATTOIR--A SERIAL KILLER SPECIALIZING IN FAMILY MEMBERS, AND STILL AT LARGE SINCE THE BREAKOUT FROM ARKHAM...
TWENTY KNOWN VICTIMS IN THE COMPUTER FILE, INCLUDING HIS COUSIN'S WIFE.
UPDATED TO TWENTY-FIVE TONIGHT--INCLUDING HIS BROTHER'S ENTIRE FAMILY.
WELCOME. I'M LESLIE THOMPKINS, CURRENT DIRECTOR OF THE "OUTINGS FOR ORPHANS" PROGRAM...
GOTHAM CIVIC HALL TONIGHT CHARITY DINNER
FIRST OF ALL, I'D LIKE TO THANK THE CONTINUING GENEROSITY OF THE WAYNE FOUNDATION--
--BOTH FOR THE USE OF THIS HALL TONIGHT, AND FOR OTHER MAJOR CONTRIBUTIONS AS WELL...

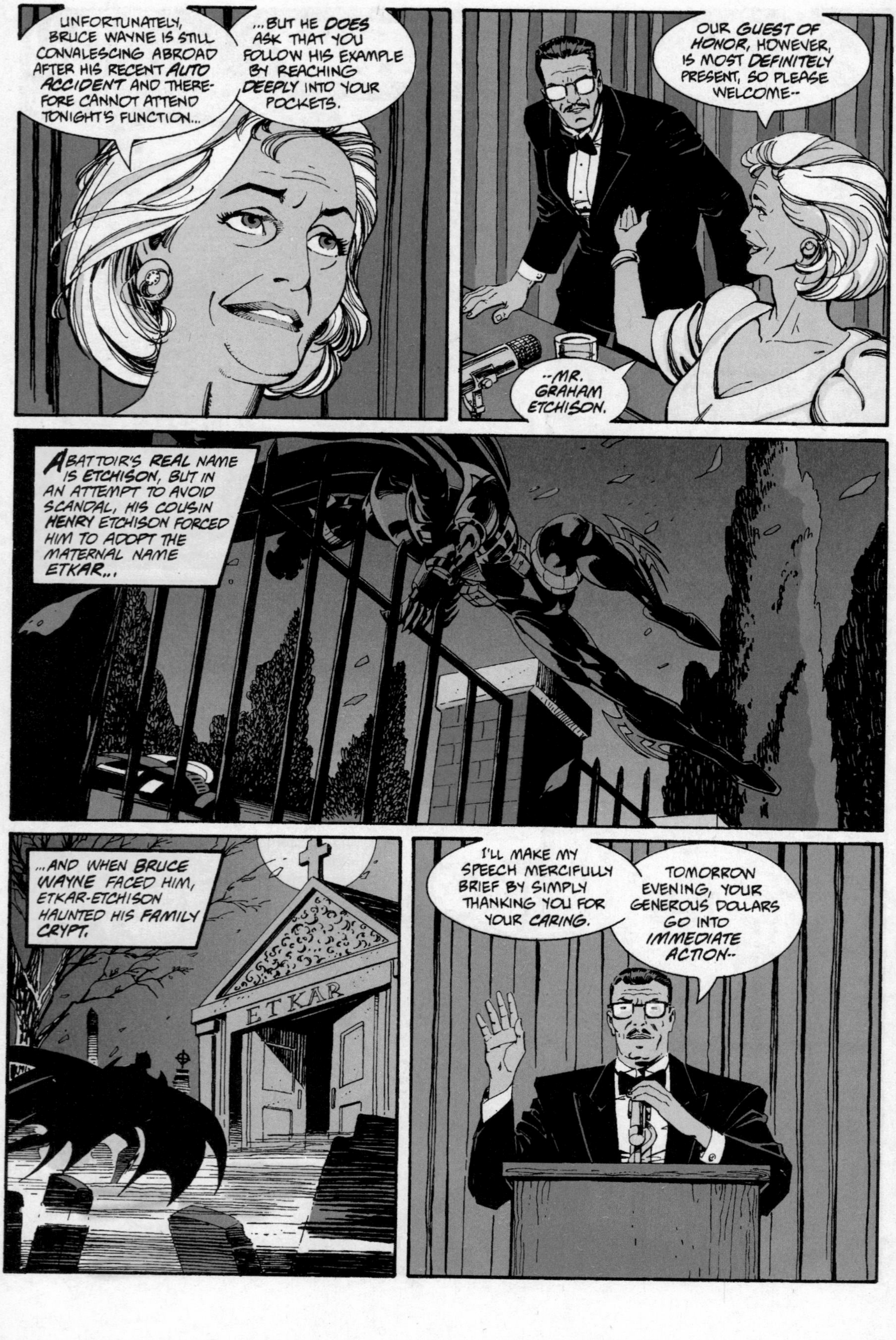
UNFORTUNATELY, BRUCE WAYNE IS STILL CONVALESCING ABROAD AFTER HIS RECENT AUTO ACCIDENT AND THEREFORE CANNOT ATTEND TONIGHT'S FUNCTION...
...BUT HE DOES ASK THAT YOU FOLLOW HIS EXAMPLE BY REACHING DEEPLY INTO YOUR POCKETS.
OUR GUEST OF HONOR, HOWEVER, IS MOST DEFINITELY PRESENT, SO PLEASE WELCOME--
--MR. GRAHAM ETCHISON.
ABATTOIR'S REAL NAME IS ETCHISON, BUT IN AN ATTEMPT TO AVOID SCANDAL, HIS COUSIN HENRY ETCHISON FORCED HIM TO ADOPT THE MATERNAL NAME ETKAR...
...AND WHEN BRUCE WAYNE FACED HIM, ETKAR-ETCHISON HAUNTED HIS FAMILY CRYPT.
ETKAR
I'LL MAKE MY SPEECH MERCIFULLY BRIEF BY SIMPLY THANKING YOU FOR YOUR CARING.
TOMORROW EVENING, YOUR GENEROUS DOLLARS GO INTO IMMEDIATE ACTION--

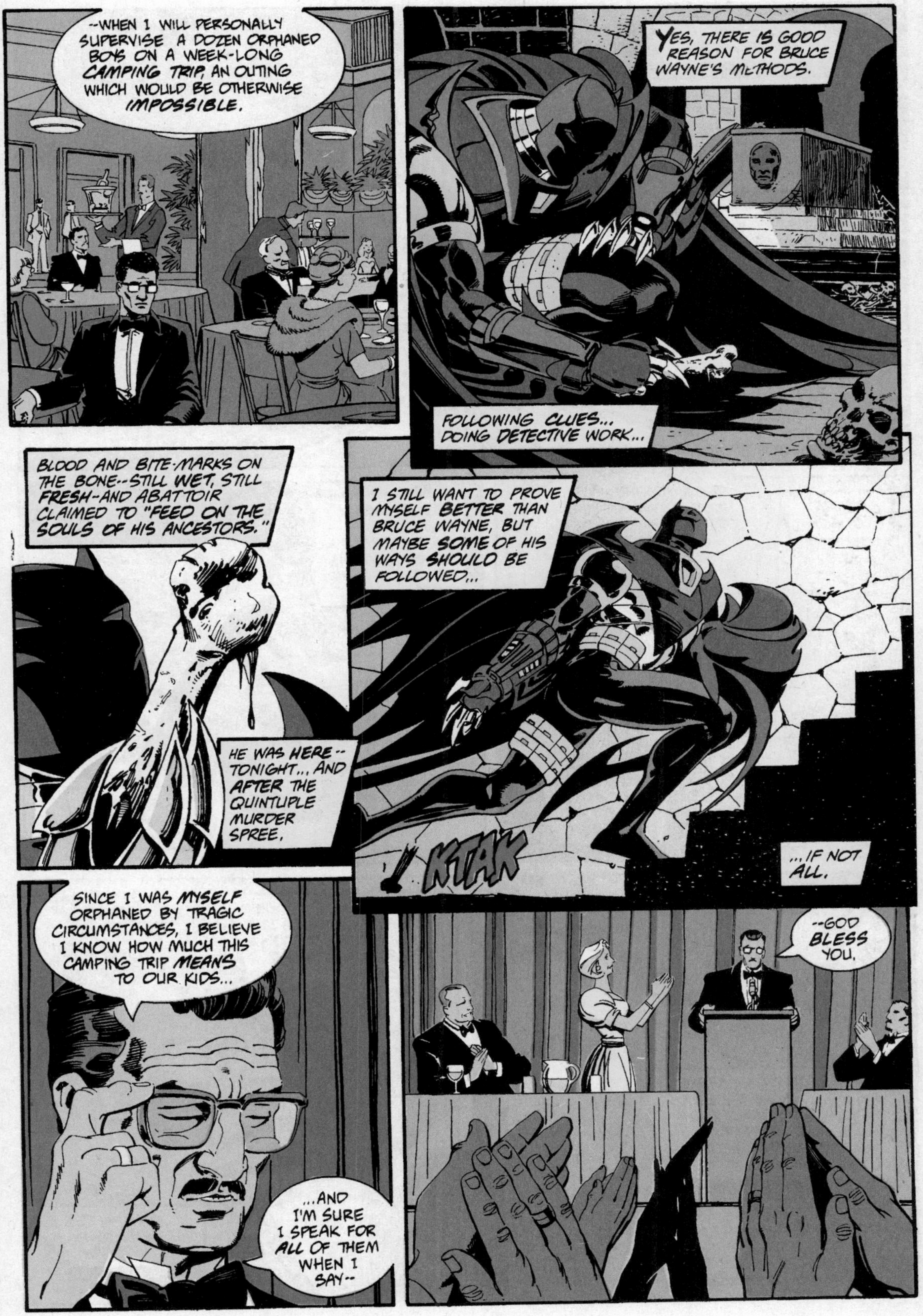
--WHEN I WILL PERSONALLY SUPERVISE A DOZEN ORPHANED BOYS ON A WEEK-LONG CAMPING TRIP, AN OUTING WHICH WOULD BE OTHERWISE IMPOSSIBLE.
YES, THERE IS GOOD REASON FOR BRUCE WAYNE'S METHODS.
FOLLOWING CLUES... DOING DETECTIVE WORK...
BLOOD AND BITE-MARKS ON THE BONE--STILL WET, STILL FRESH--AND ABATTOIR CLAIMED TO "FEED ON THE SOULS OF HIS ANCESTORS."
HE WAS HERE--TONIGHT... AND AFTER THE QUINTUPLE MURDER SPREE.
I STILL WANT TO PROVE MYSELF BETTER THAN BRUCE WAYNE, BUT MAYBE SOME OF HIS WAYS SHOULD BE FOLLOWED...
KTAK
...IF NOT ALL.
SINCE I WAS MYSELF ORPHANED BY TRAGIC CIRCUMSTANCES, I BELIEVE I KNOW HOW MUCH THIS CAMPING TRIP MEANS TO OUR KIDS...
...AND I'M SURE I SPEAK FOR ALL OF THEM WHEN I SAY--
--GOD BLESS YOU.

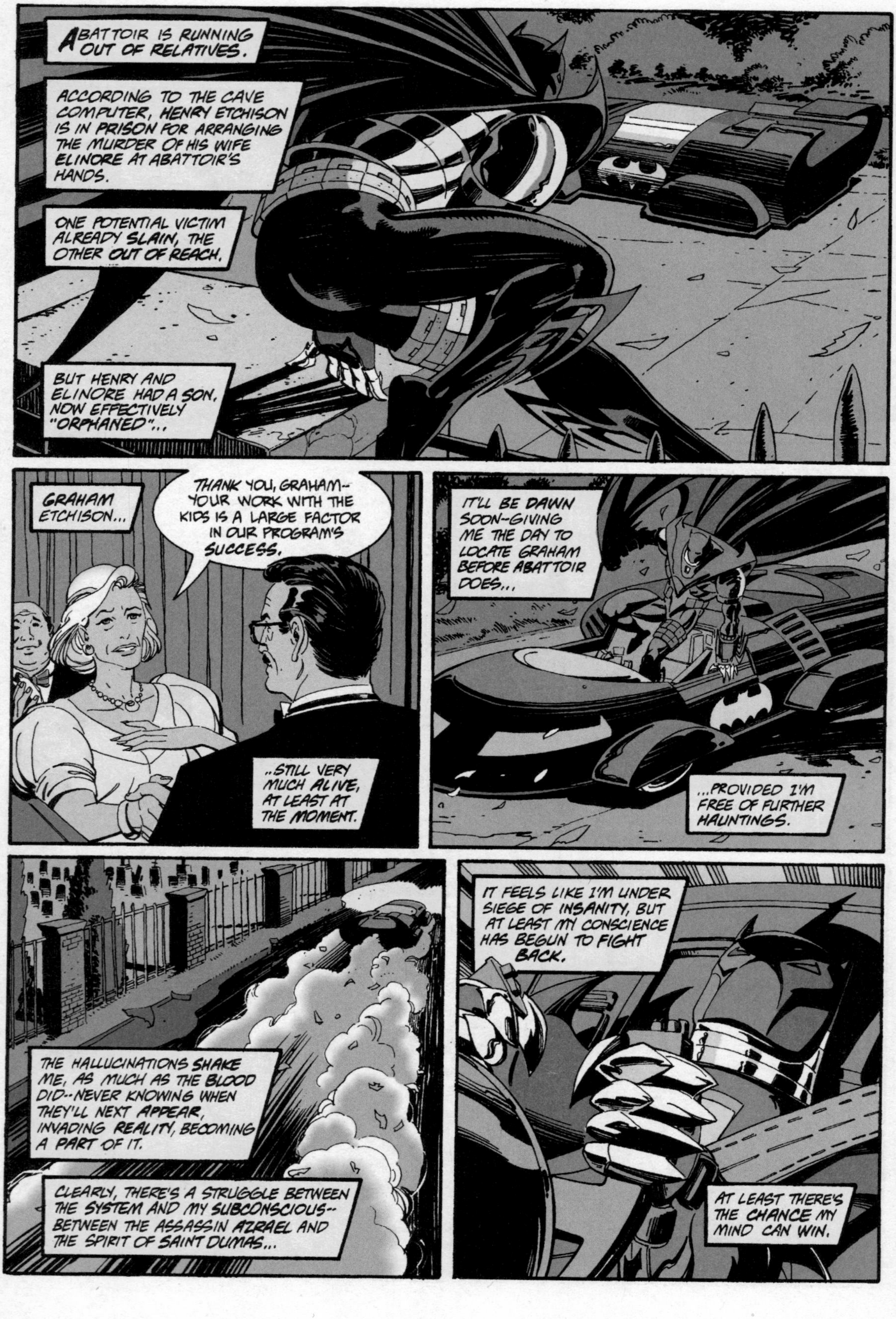
ABATTOIR IS RUNNING OUT OF RELATIVES.
ACCORDING TO THE CAVE COMPUTER, HENRY ETCHISON IS IN PRISON FOR ARRANGING THE MURDER OF HIS WIFE ELINORE AT ABATTOIR'S HANDS.
ONE POTENTIAL VICTIM ALREADY SLAIN, THE OTHER OUT OF REACH.
BUT HENRY AND ELINORE HAD A SON, NOW EFFECTIVELY "ORPHANED"...
GRAHAM ETCHISON...
THANK YOU, GRAHAM-- YOUR WORK WITH THE KIDS IS A LARGE FACTOR IN OUR PROGRAM'S SUCCESS.
..STILL VERY MUCH ALIVE, AT LEAST AT THE MOMENT.
IT'LL BE DAWN SOON--GIVING ME THE DAY TO LOCATE GRAHAM BEFORE ABATTOIR DOES...
...PROVIDED I'M FREE OF FURTHER HAUNTINGS.
THE HALLUCINATIONS SHAKE ME, AS MUCH AS THE BLOOD DID--NEVER KNOWING WHEN THEY'LL NEXT APPEAR, INVADING REALITY, BECOMING A PART OF IT.
CLEARLY, THERE'S A STRUGGLE BETWEEN THE SYSTEM AND MY SUBCONSCIOUS-- BETWEEN THE ASSASSIN AZRAEL AND THE SPIRIT OF SAINT DUMAS...
IT FEELS LIKE I'M UNDER SIEGE OF INSANITY, BUT AT LEAST MY CONSCIENCE HAS BEGUN TO FIGHT BACK.
AT LEAST THERE'S THE CHANCE MY MIND CAN WIN.

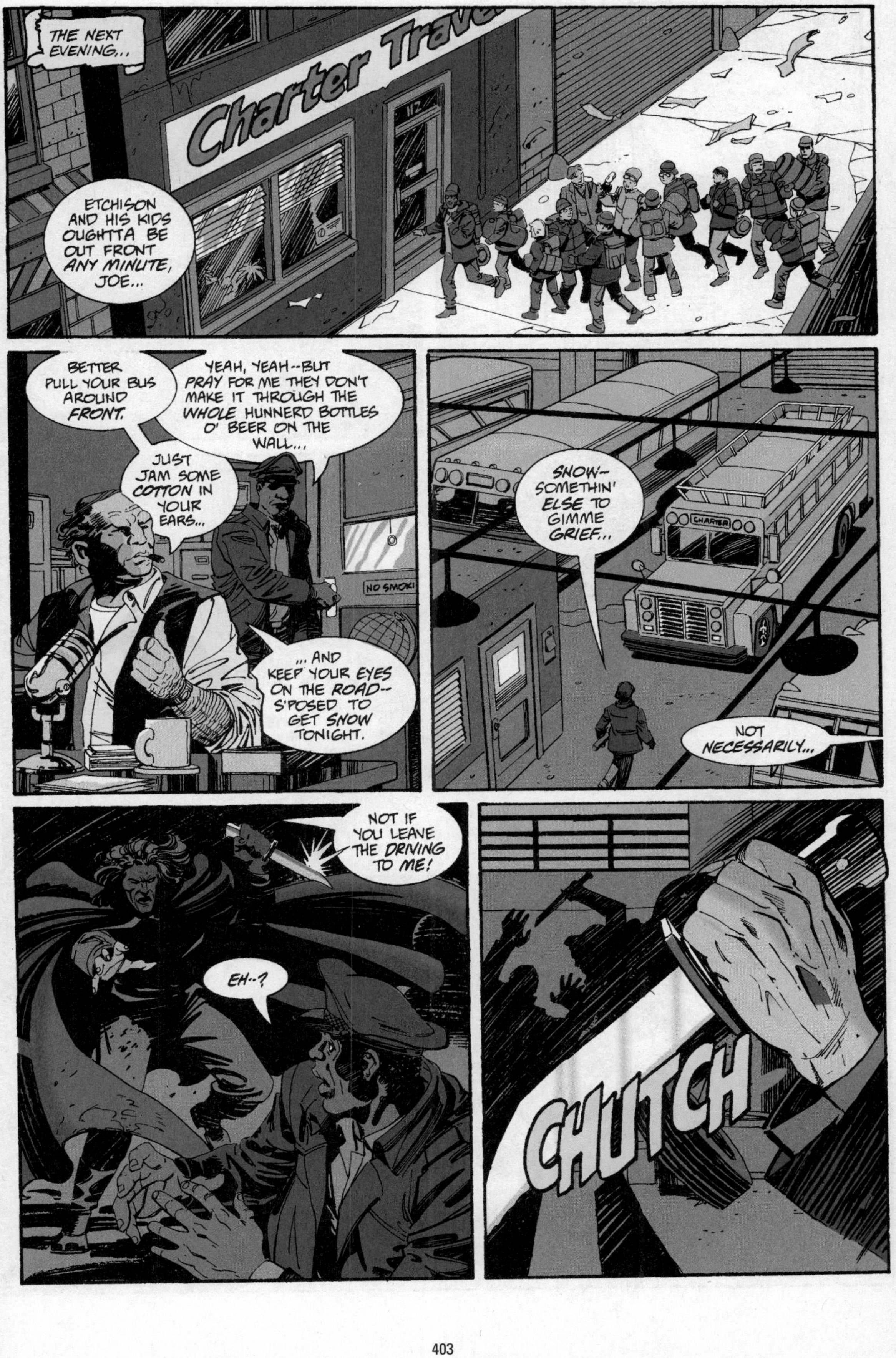
THE NEXT EVENING...
Charter Travel
ETCHISON AND HIS KIDS OUGHTTA BE OUT FRONT ANY MINUTE, JOE...
BETTER PULL YOUR BUS AROUND FRONT.
YEAH, YEAH--BUT PRAY FOR ME THEY DON'T MAKE IT THROUGH THE WHOLE HUNNERD BOTTLES O' BEER ON THE WALL...
JUST JAM SOME COTTON IN YOUR EARS...
...AND KEEP YOUR EYES ON THE ROAD-- S'POSED TO GET SNOW TONIGHT.
NO SMOKI
SNOW-- SOMETHIN' ELSE TO GIMME GRIEF...
CHARTER
NOT NECESSARILY...
NOT IF YOU LEAVE THE DRIVING TO ME!
EH--?
CHUTCH

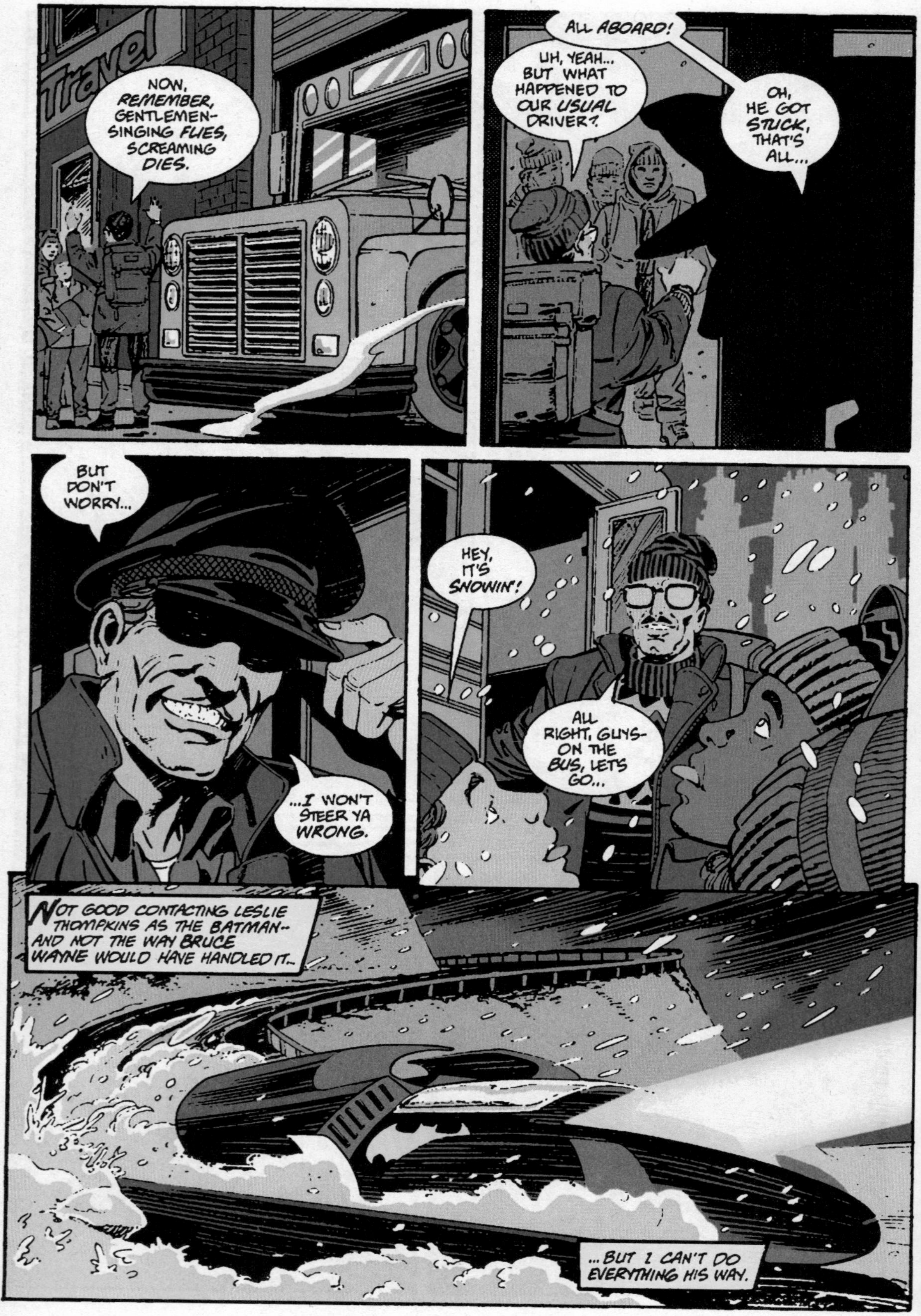

NOW, REMEMBER, GENTLEMEN- SINGING FLIES, SCREAMING DIES.
ALL ABOARD!
UH, YEAH... BUT WHAT HAPPENED TO OUR USUAL DRIVER?
OH, HE GOT STUCK, THAT'S ALL...
BUT DON'T WORRY...
...I WON'T STEER YA WRONG.
HEY, IT'S SNOWIN'!
ALL RIGHT, GUYS- ON THE BUS, LET'S GO...
NOT GOOD CONTACTING LESLIE THOMPKINS AS THE BATMAN-- AND NOT THE WAY BRUCE WAYNE WOULD HAVE HANDLED IT...
...BUT I CAN'T DO EVERYTHING HIS WAY.

THE ROUGH BATMAN VOICE IS EASY TO IMPERSONATE, BUT I CAN'T BECOME BRUCE WAYNE.

NOT EVEN ON THE PHONE.

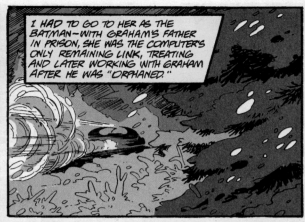

I HAD TO GO TO HER AS THE BATMAN—WITH GRAHAM'S FATHER IN PRISON, SHE WAS THE COMPUTER'S ONLY REMAINING LINK, TREATING AND LATER WORKING WITH GRAHAM AFTER HE WAS "ORPHANED."

THE NAMES OF LAST NIGHT'S VICTIMS STILL HAVEN'T BEEN RELEASED, BUT THE POLICE MUST KNOW IT WAS ABATTOIR'S HANDIWORK...

...SIXTY-SEVEN BOTTLES OF BEER ON THE WALL, SIXTY-SEVEN BOTTLES OF BEEEER...♪

DRIVER, WHERE ARE YOU GOING?

...WHICH MEANS THEY HAVEN'T LOCATED GRAHAM YET—OR HE'D HARDLY BE GOING ON A CAMPING TRIP.

...IF ONE OF THOSE BOTTLES SHOULD HAPPEN TO FALL...♪

THIS ISN'T THE WAY TO THE CAMP...

IT ISN'T—?

THEN I GUESS WE'RE HEADED FOR A SLIGHT DETOUR, COUSIN!

THERE—THE BUS—BUT IT TURNED OFF THE ROUTE LESLIE THOMPKINS DESCRIBED.

MAYBE THIS IS IT—MAYBE ABATTOIR'S ALREADY FOUND HIS NEXT PREY.

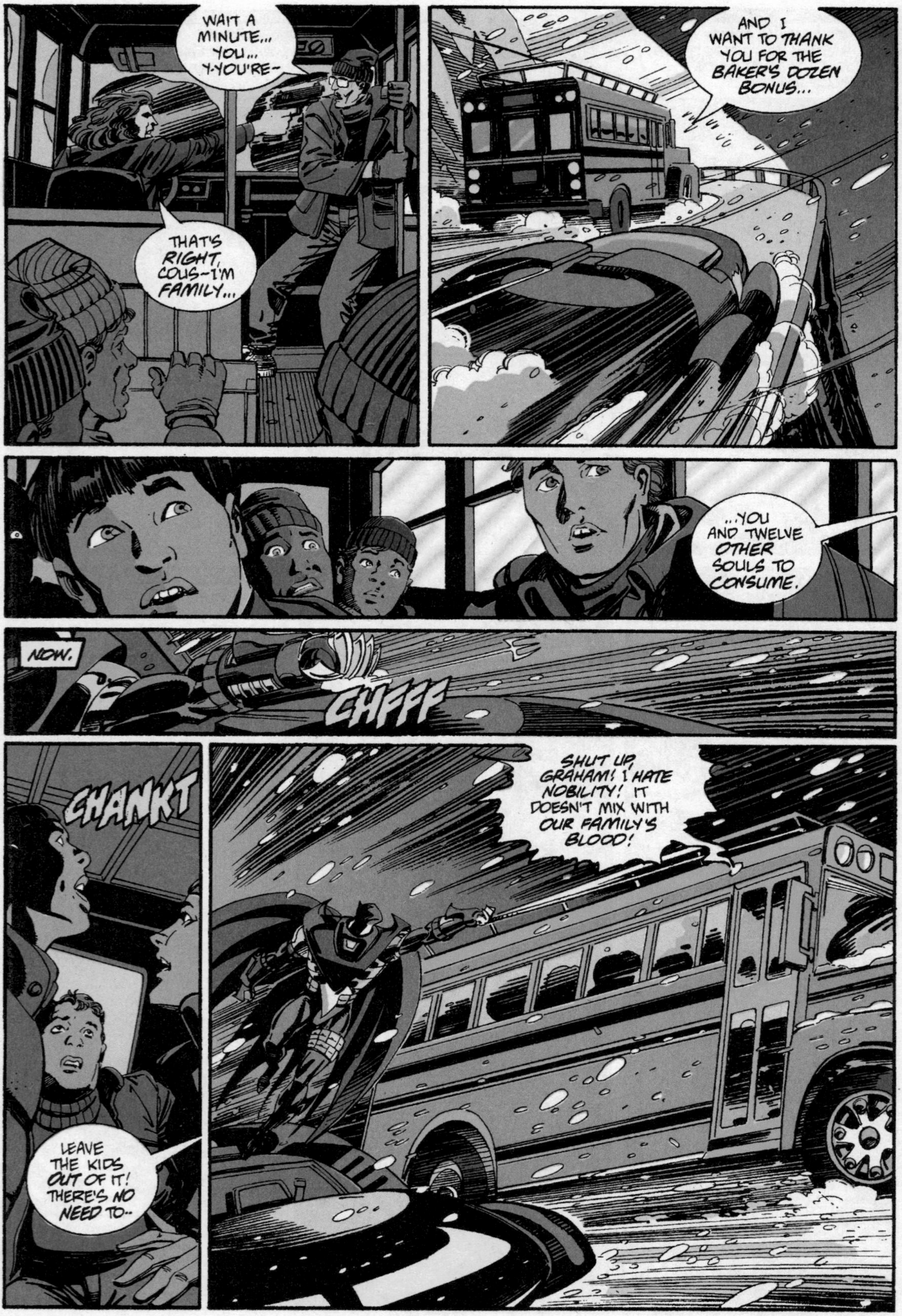
WAIT A MINUTE... YOU... Y-YOU'RE–
THAT'S RIGHT, COUS–I'M FAMILY...
AND I WANT TO THANK YOU FOR THE BAKER'S DOZEN BONUS...
...YOU AND TWELVE OTHER SOULS TO CONSUME.
NOW.
CHFFF
CHANKT
LEAVE THE KIDS OUT OF IT! THERE'S NO NEED TO--
SHUT UP, GRAHAM! I HATE NOBILITY! IT DOESN'T MIX WITH OUR FAMILY'S BLOOD!

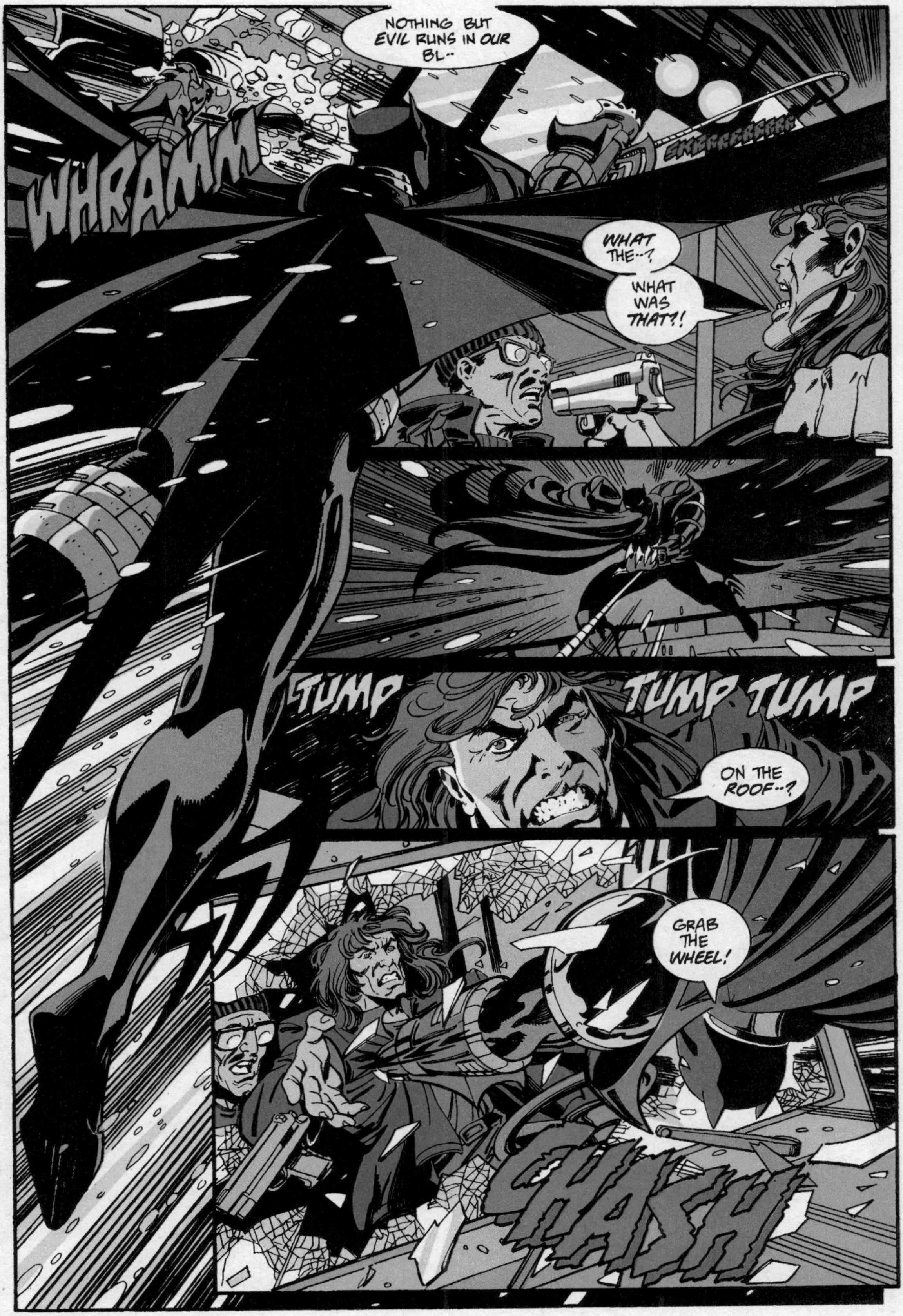
NOTHING BUT EVIL RUNS IN OUR BL--
WHRAMM
WHAT THE--?
WHAT WAS THAT?!
TUMP
TUMP TUMP
ON THE ROOF--?
GRAB THE WHEEL!
CHASH!

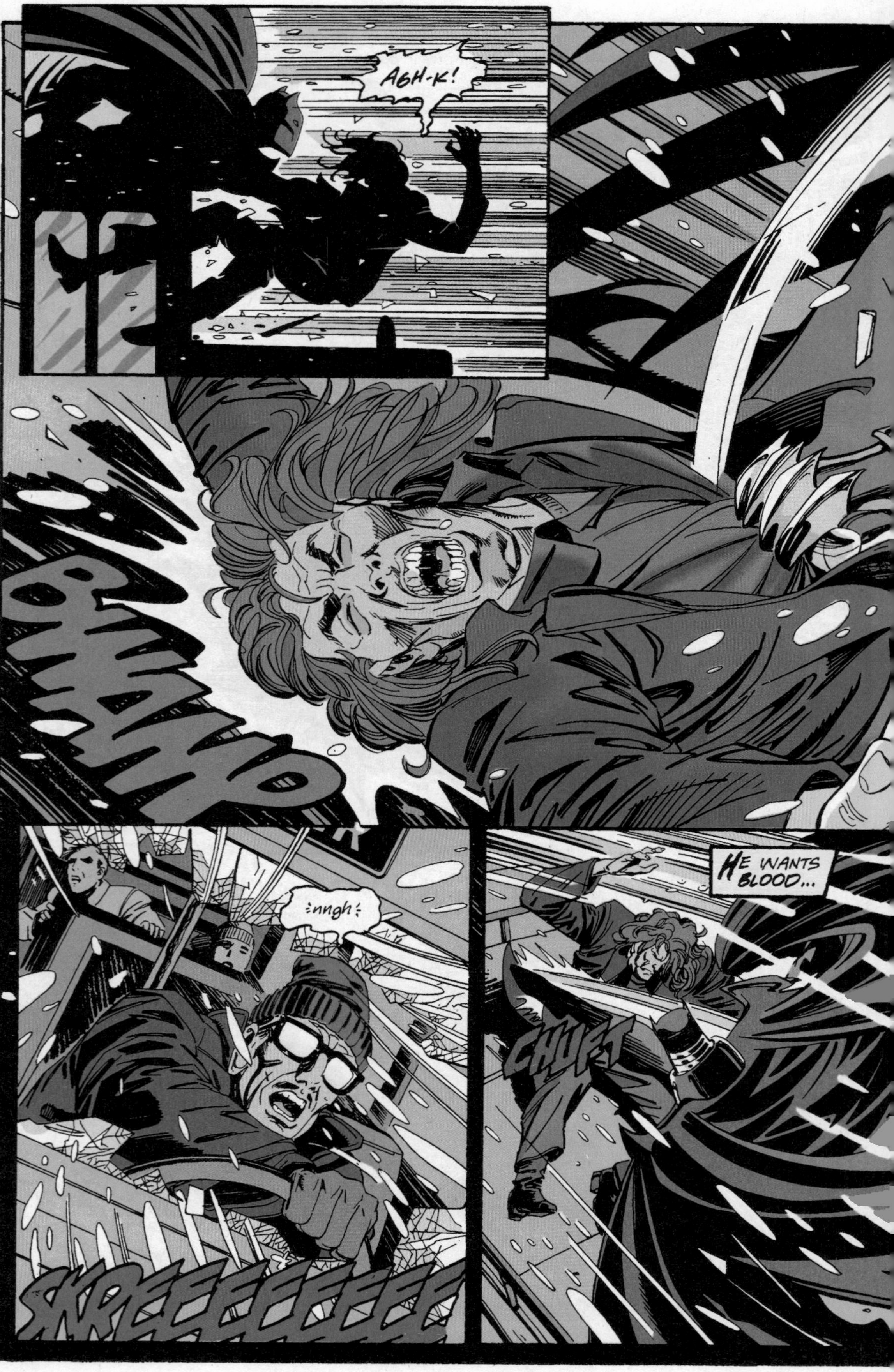
AGH-K!
CHAMP
:nngh:
HE WANTS BLOOD...
CHUFF
SKREEEEEEEEEEEE

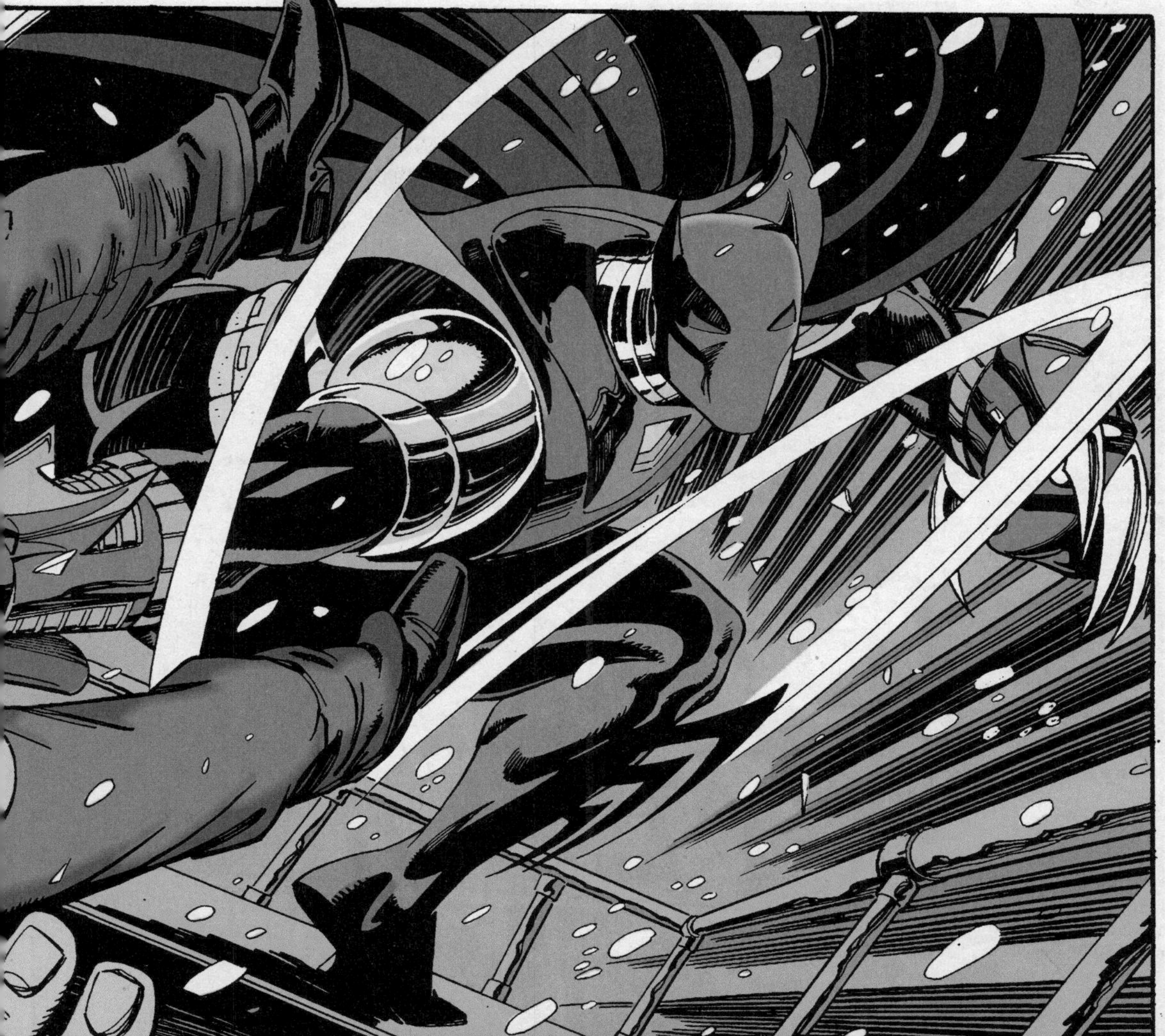

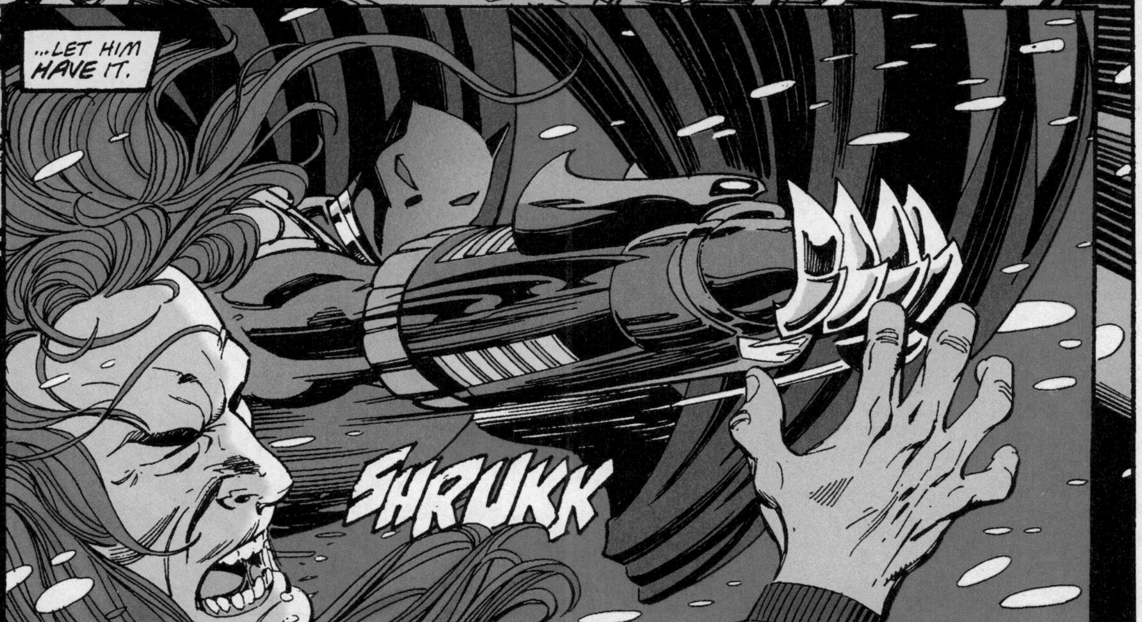
...LET HIM HAVE IT.
SHRUKK

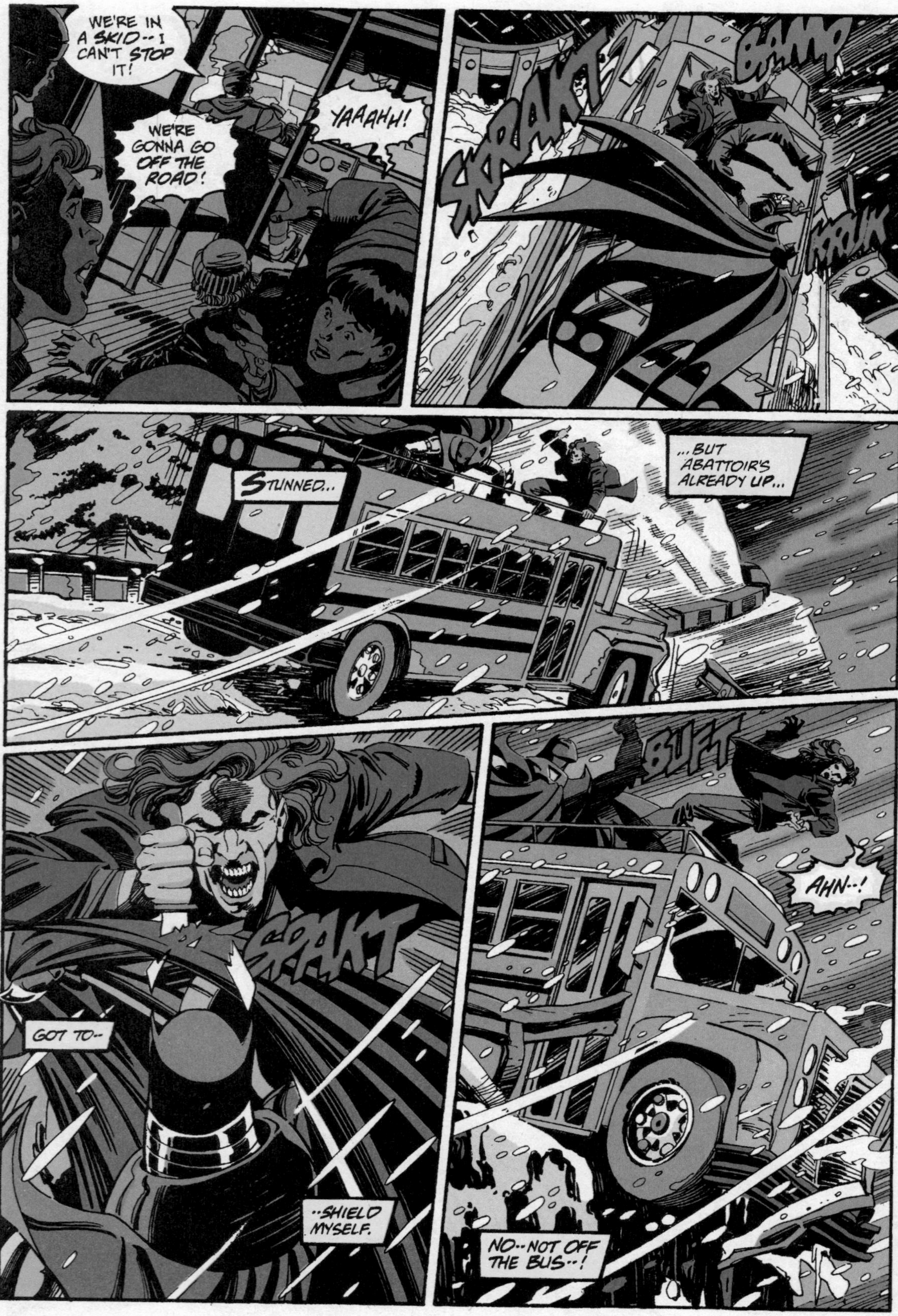
WE'RE IN A SKID-- I CAN'T STOP IT!
WE'RE GONNA GO OFF THE ROAD!
YAAAHH!
SKRAKT
BLAMM
KRUK
STUNNED...
...BUT ABATTOIR'S ALREADY UP...
SPAKT
GOT TO--
--SHIELD MYSELF.
BUFT
AHN--!
NO--NOT OFF THE BUS--!

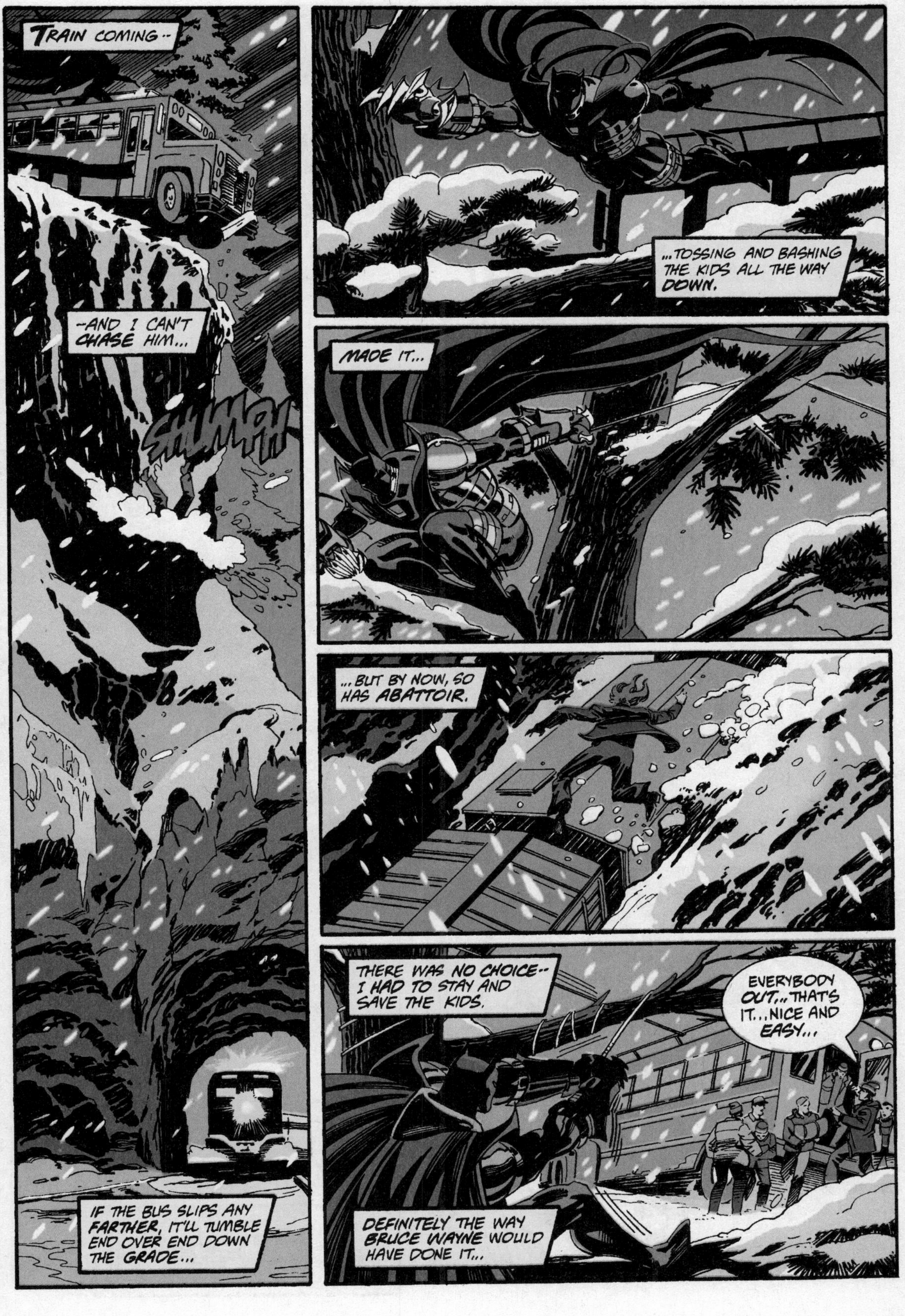
TRAIN COMING--
--AND I CAN'T CHASE HIM...
SHUMPH
IF THE BUS SLIPS ANY FARTHER, IT'LL TUMBLE END OVER END DOWN THE GRADE...
...TOSSING AND BASHING THE KIDS ALL THE WAY DOWN.
MADE IT...
...BUT BY NOW, SO HAS ABATTOIR.
THERE WAS NO CHOICE-- I HAD TO STAY AND SAVE THE KIDS.
EVERYBODY OUT... THAT'S IT...NICE AND EASY...
DEFINITELY THE WAY BRUCE WAYNE WOULD HAVE DONE IT...

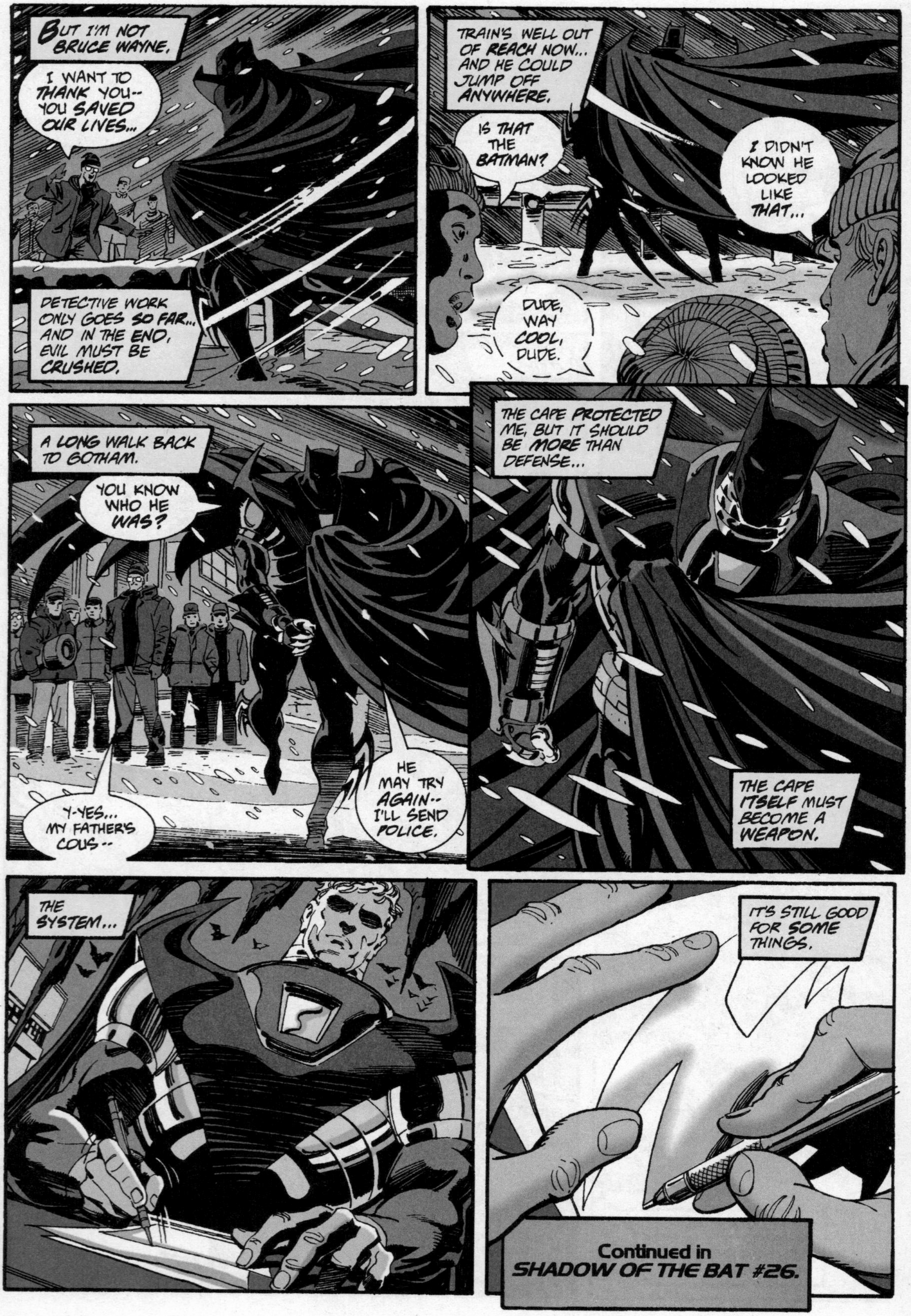
BUT I'M NOT BRUCE WAYNE.
I WANT TO THANK YOU-- YOU SAVED OUR LIVES...
DETECTIVE WORK ONLY GOES SO FAR... AND IN THE END, EVIL MUST BE CRUSHED.
TRAIN'S WELL OUT OF REACH NOW... AND HE COULD JUMP OFF ANYWHERE.
IS THAT THE BATMAN?
I DIDN'T KNOW HE LOOKED LIKE THAT...
DUDE, WAY COOL, DUDE.
A LONG WALK BACK TO GOTHAM.
YOU KNOW WHO HE WAS?
Y-YES... MY FATHER'S COUS--
HE MAY TRY AGAIN-- I'LL SEND POLICE.
THE CAPE PROTECTED ME, BUT IT SHOULD BE MORE THAN DEFENSE...
THE CAPE ITSELF MUST BECOME A WEAPON.
THE SYSTEM...
IT'S STILL GOOD FOR SOME THINGS.
Continued in SHADOW OF THE BAT #26.

Cover art by **BRIAN STELFREEZE**

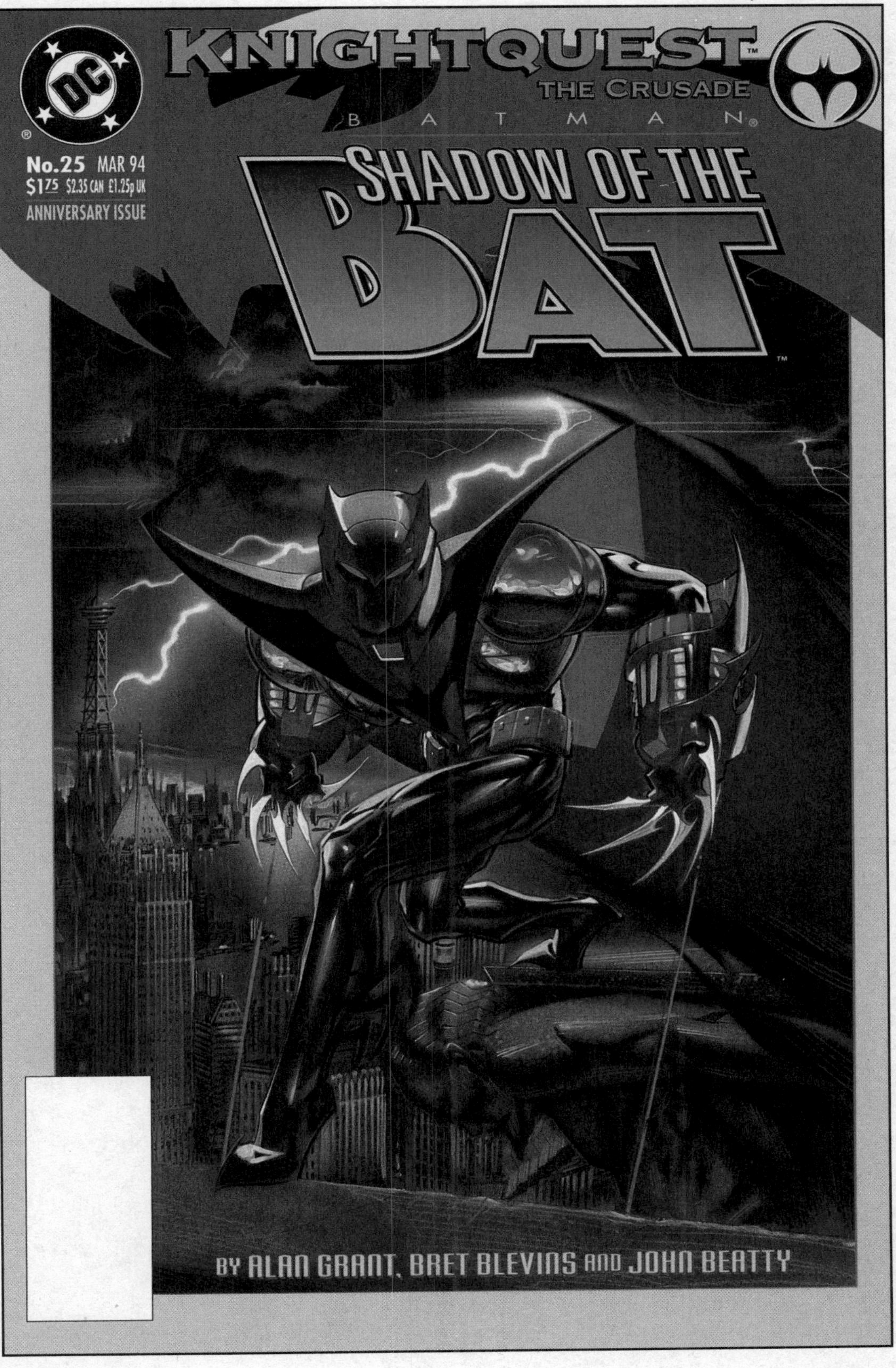
KNIGHTQUEST
THE CRUSADE
BATMAN
SHADOW OF THE BAT
No.25 MAR 94
$1.75 $2.35 CAN £1.25p UK
ANNIVERSARY ISSUE
BY ALAN GRANT, BRET BLEVINS AND JOHN BEATTY

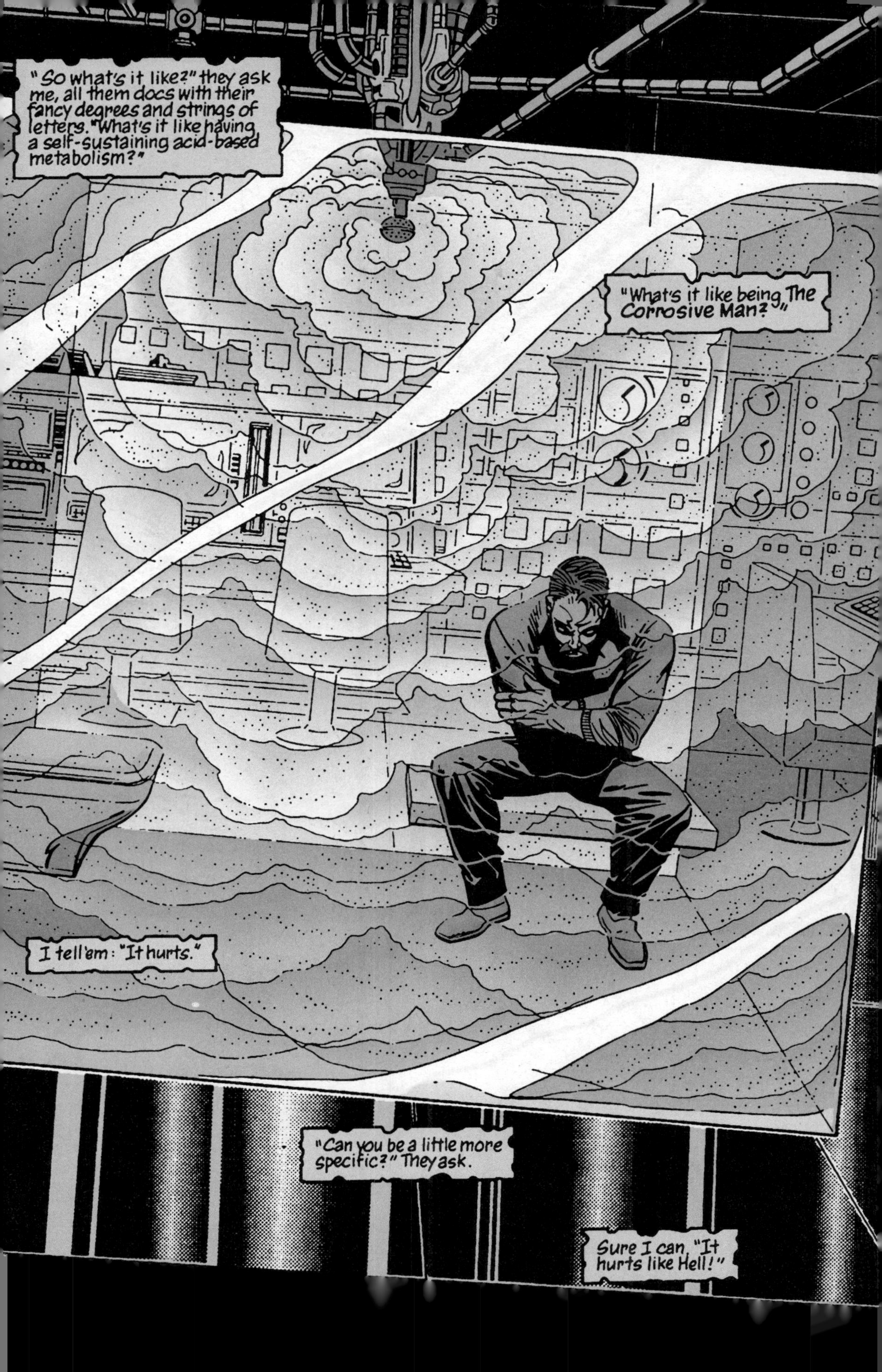
"So what's it like?" they ask me, all them docs with their fancy degrees and strings of letters. "What's it like having a self-sustaining acid-based metabolism?"
"What's it like being The Corrosive Man?"
I tell 'em: "It hurts."
"Can you be a little more specific?" They ask.
Sure I can, "It hurts like Hell!"

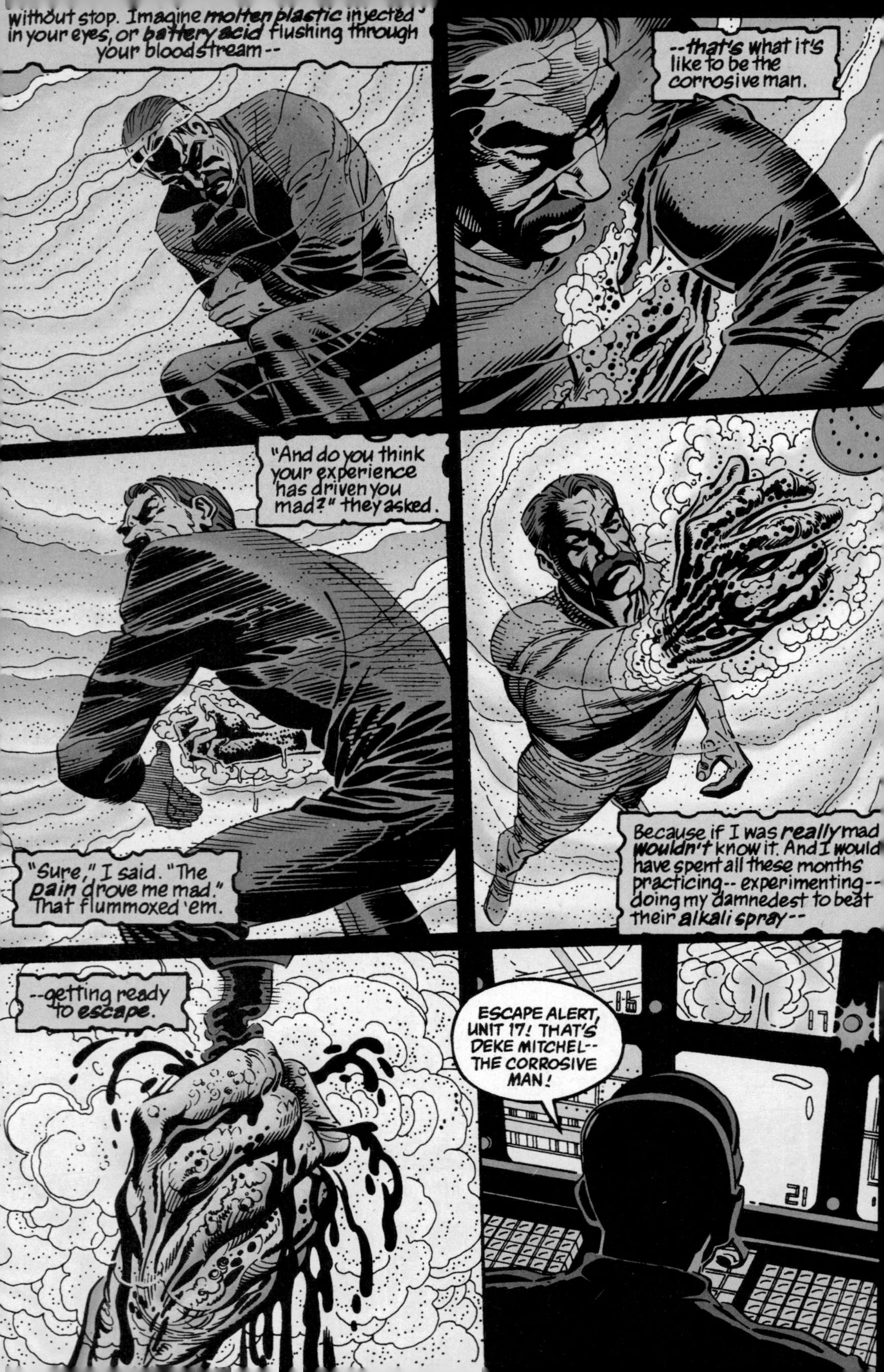
without stop. Imagine molten plastic injected in your eyes, or battery acid flushing through your bloodstream--
--that's what it's like to be the corrosive man.
"And do you think your experience has driven you mad?" they asked.
"Sure," I said. "The pain drove me mad." That flummoxed 'em.
Because if I was really mad I wouldn't know it. And I would have spent all these months practicing-- experimenting-- doing my damnedest to beat their alkali spray--
--getting ready to escape.
ESCAPE ALERT, UNIT 17! THAT'S DEKE MITCHEL-- THE CORROSIVE MAN!

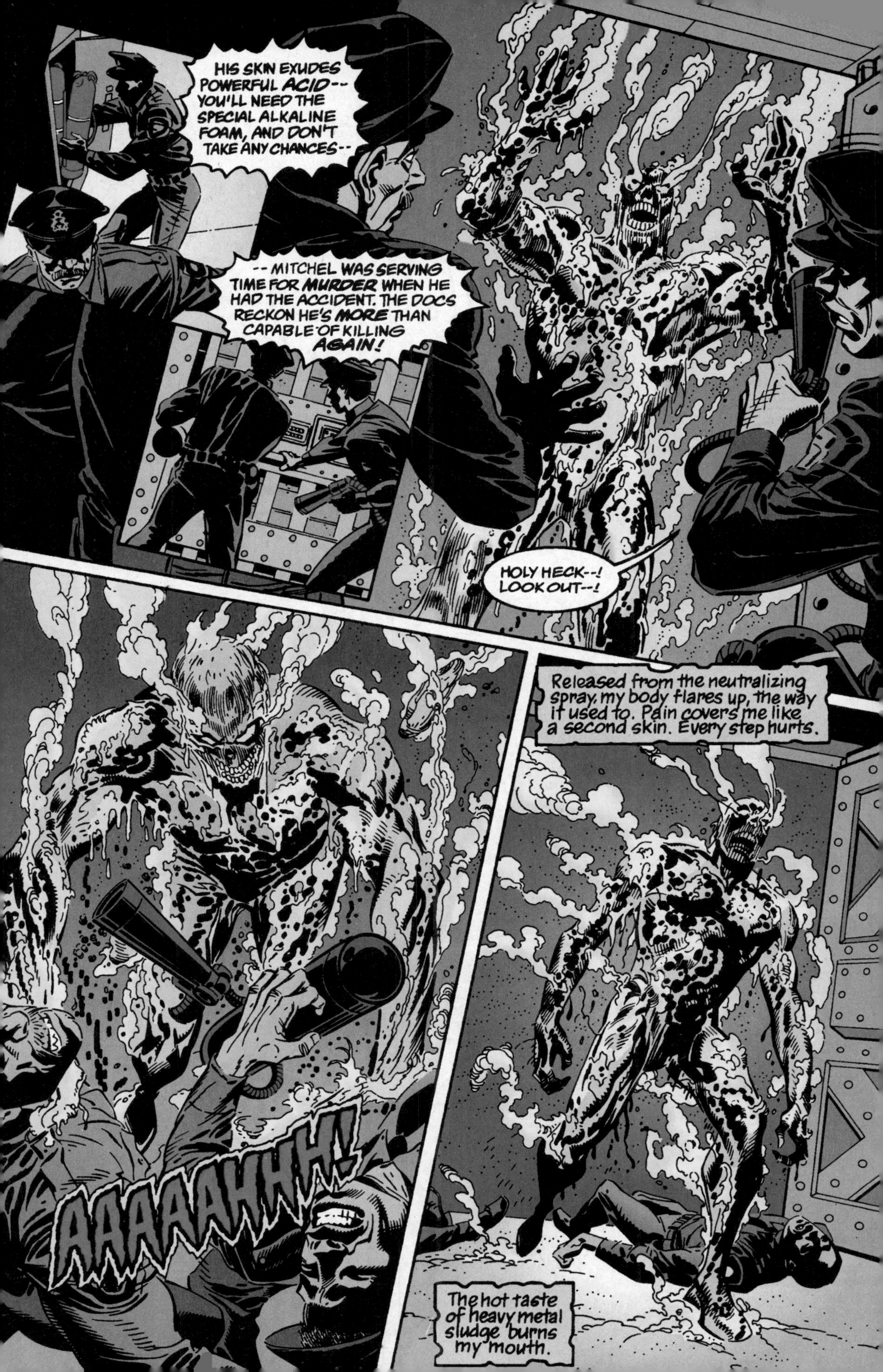
HIS SKIN EXUDES POWERFUL ACID-- YOU'LL NEED THE SPECIAL ALKALINE FOAM, AND DON'T TAKE ANY CHANCES--
--MITCHEL WAS SERVING TIME FOR MURDER WHEN HE HAD THE ACCIDENT. THE DOCS RECKON HE'S MORE THAN CAPABLE OF KILLING AGAIN!
HOLY HECK--! LOOK OUT--!
AAAAHHH!
Released from the neutralizing spray, my body flares up, the way it used to. Pain covers me like a second skin. Every step hurts.
The hot taste of heavy metal sludge burns my mouth.

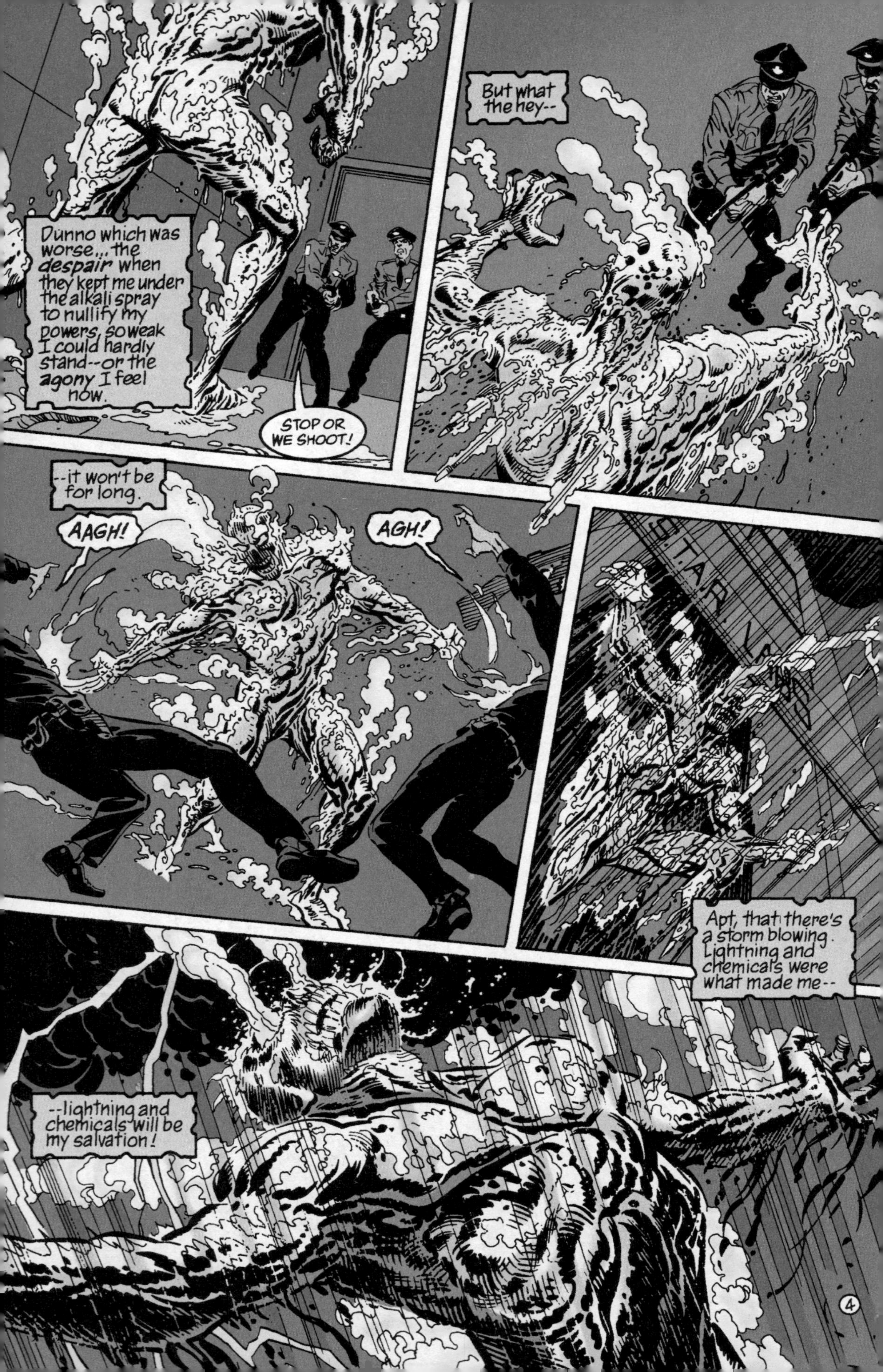
Dunno which was worse... the despair when they kept me under the alkali spray to nullify my powers, so weak I could hardly stand--or the agony I feel now.
STOP OR WE SHOOT!
But what the hey--
--it won't be for long.
AAGH!
AGH!
S.T.A.R.
Apt, that there's a storm blowing. Lightning and chemicals were what made me--
--lightning and chemicals will be my salvation!
4

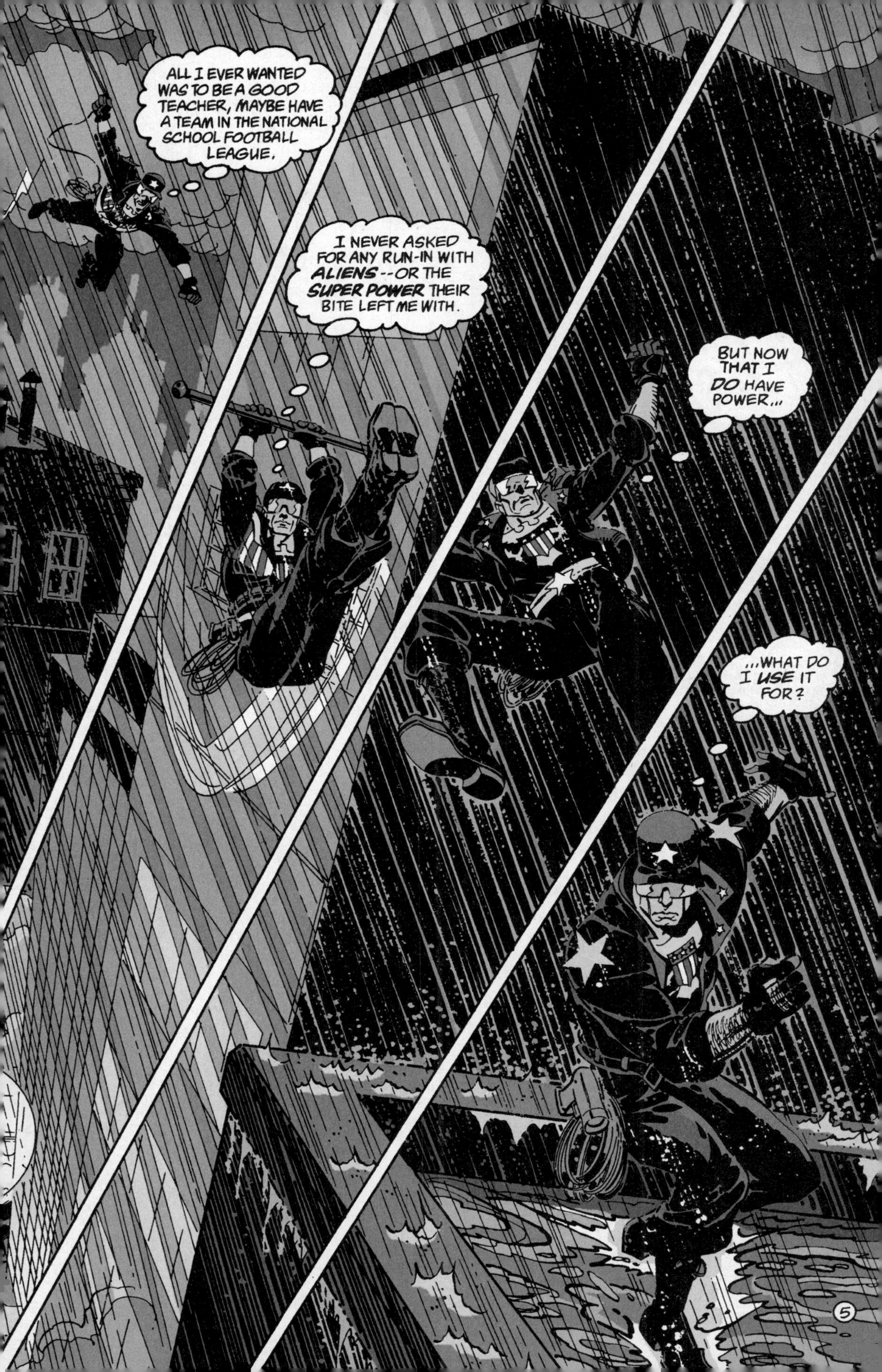
ALL I EVER WANTED WAS TO BE A GOOD TEACHER, MAYBE HAVE A TEAM IN THE NATIONAL SCHOOL FOOTBALL LEAGUE.
I NEVER ASKED FOR ANY RUN-IN WITH ALIENS--OR THE SUPER POWER THEIR BITE LEFT ME WITH.
BUT NOW THAT I DO HAVE POWER...
...WHAT DO I USE IT FOR?
5

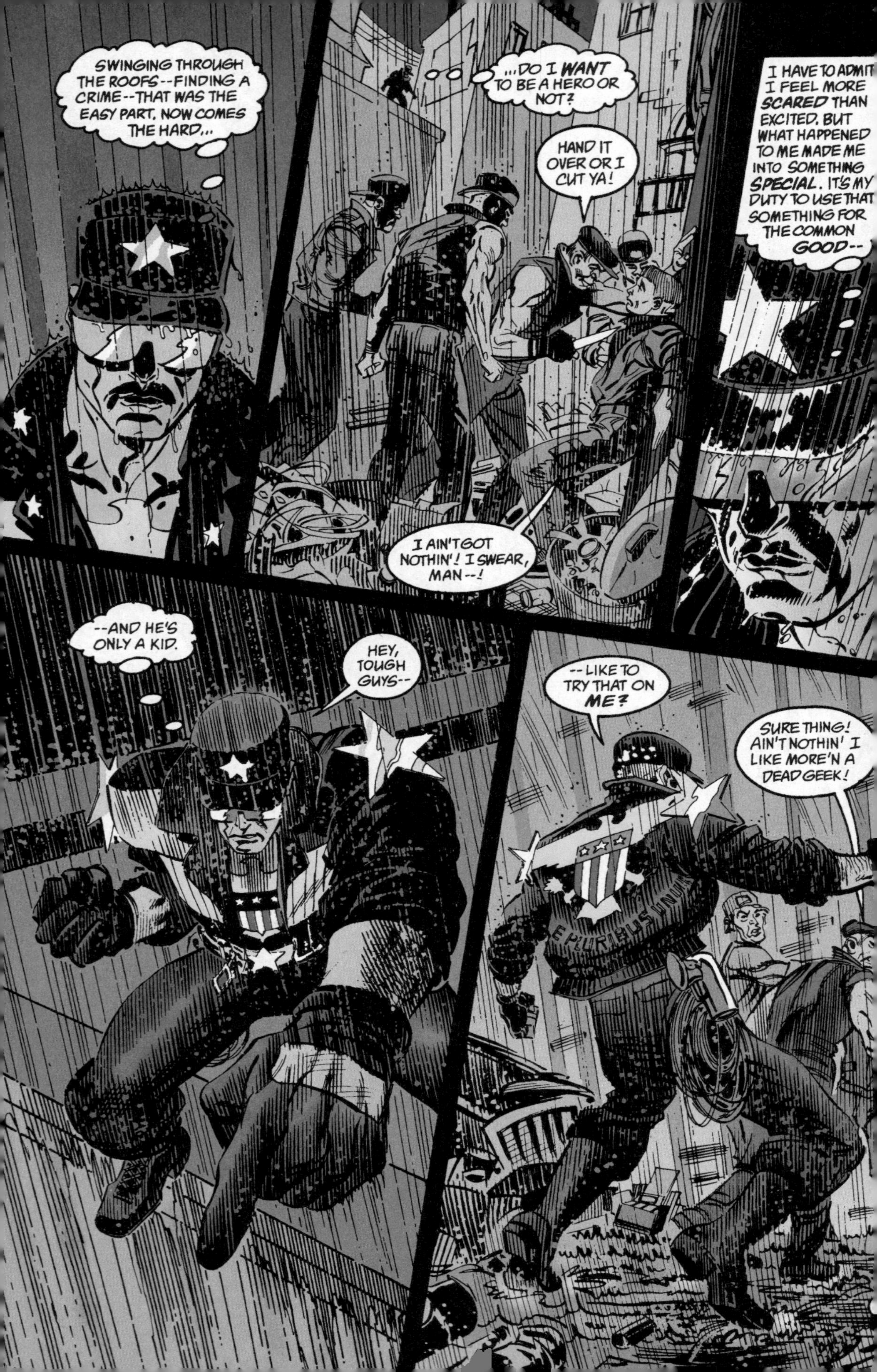
SWINGING THROUGH THE ROOFS--FINDING A CRIME--THAT WAS THE EASY PART. NOW COMES THE HARD,...
...DO I WANT TO BE A HERO OR NOT?
HAND IT OVER OR I CUT YA!
I AIN'T GOT NOTHIN'! I SWEAR, MAN--!
I HAVE TO ADMIT I FEEL MORE SCARED THAN EXCITED. BUT WHAT HAPPENED TO ME MADE ME INTO SOMETHING SPECIAL. IT'S MY DUTY TO USE THAT SOMETHING FOR THE COMMON GOOD--
--AND HE'S ONLY A KID.
HEY, TOUGH GUYS--
--LIKE TO TRY THAT ON ME?
SURE THING! AIN'T NOTHIN' I LIKE MORE'N A DEAD GEEK!

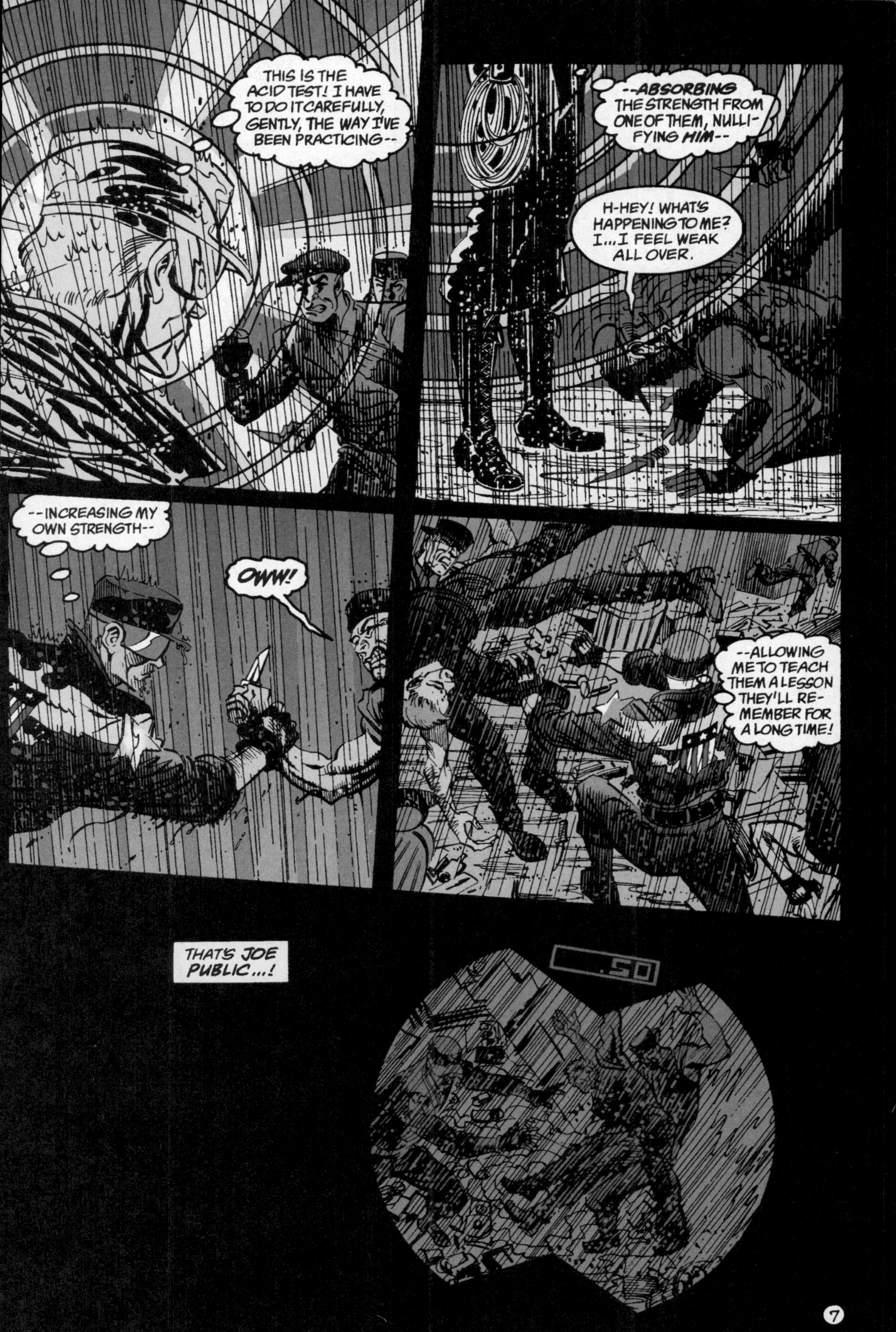
THIS IS THE ACID TEST! I HAVE TO DO IT CAREFULLY, GENTLY, THE WAY I'VE BEEN PRACTICING--
--ABSORBING THE STRENGTH FROM ONE OF THEM, NULLIFYING HIM--
H-HEY! WHAT'S HAPPENING TO ME? I...I FEEL WEAK ALL OVER.
--INCREASING MY OWN STRENGTH--
OWW!
--ALLOWING ME TO TEACH THEM A LESSON THEY'LL REMEMBER FOR A LONG TIME!
THAT'S JOE PUBLIC...!
7

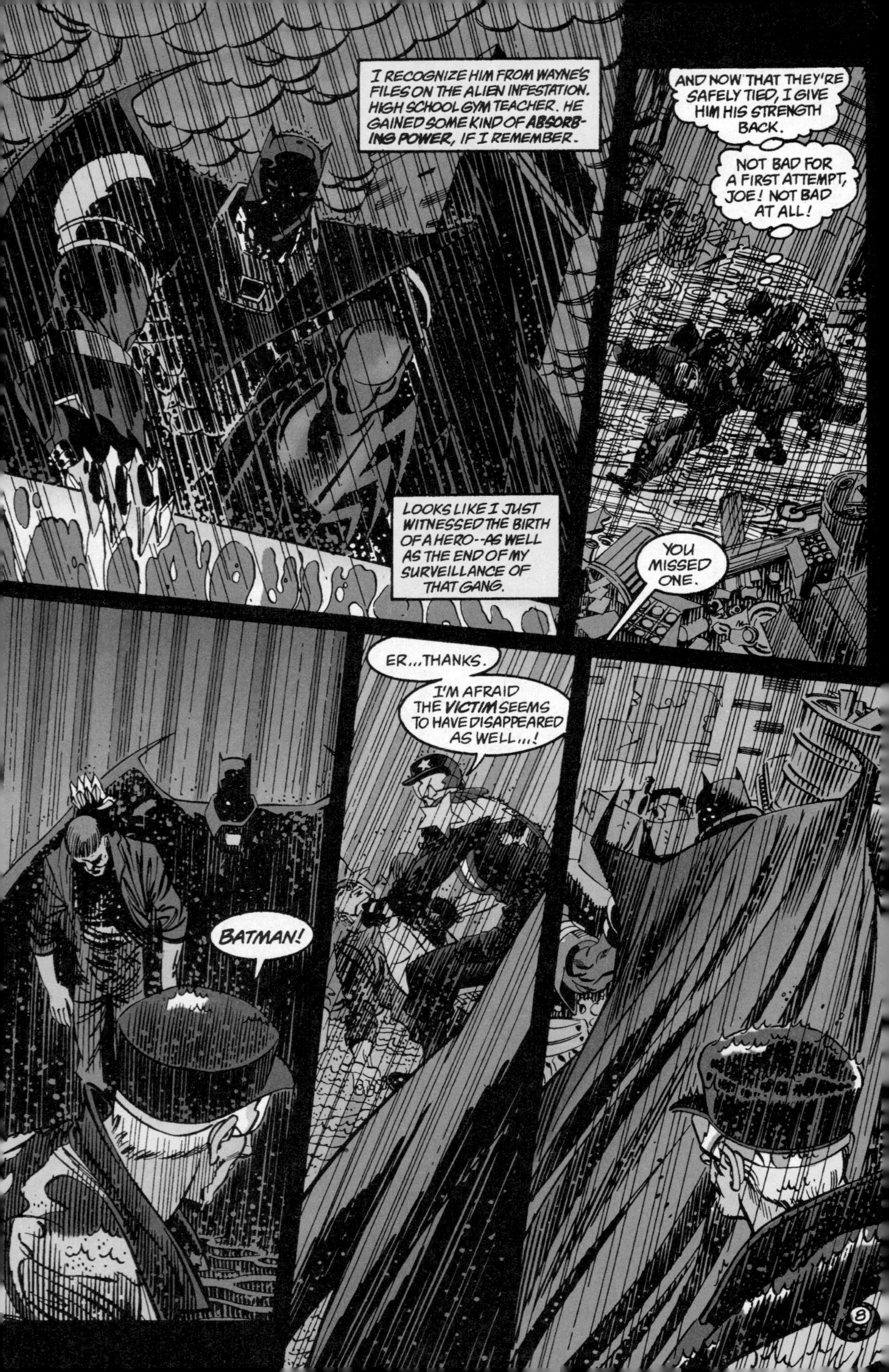
I RECOGNIZE HIM FROM WAYNE'S FILES ON THE ALIEN INFESTATION. HIGH SCHOOL GYM TEACHER. HE GAINED SOME KIND OF ABSORBING POWER, IF I REMEMBER.
AND NOW THAT THEY'RE SAFELY TIED, I GIVE HIM HIS STRENGTH BACK.
NOT BAD FOR A FIRST ATTEMPT, JOE! NOT BAD AT ALL!
LOOKS LIKE I JUST WITNESSED THE BIRTH OF A HERO--AS WELL AS THE END OF MY SURVEILLANCE OF THAT GANG.
YOU MISSED ONE.
BATMAN!
ER... THANKS.
I'M AFRAID THE VICTIM SEEMS TO HAVE DISAPPEARED AS WELL...!
8

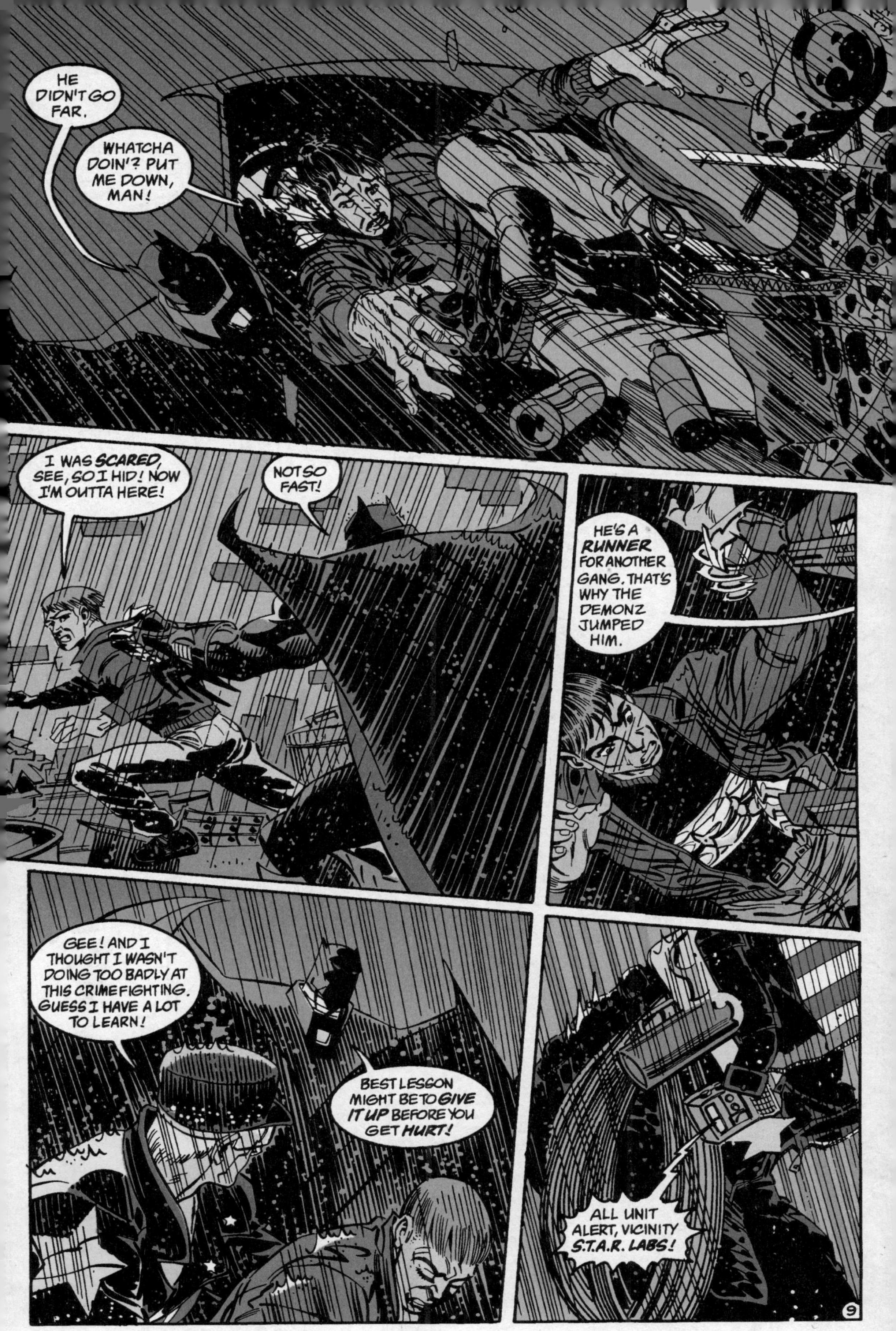
HE DIDN'T GO FAR.
WHATCHA DOIN'? PUT ME DOWN, MAN!
I WAS SCARED, SEE, SO I HID! NOW I'M OUTTA HERE!
NOT SO FAST!
HE'S A RUNNER FOR ANOTHER GANG. THAT'S WHY THE DEMONZ JUMPED HIM.
GEE! AND I THOUGHT I WASN'T DOING TOO BADLY AT THIS CRIME FIGHTING. GUESS I HAVE A LOT TO LEARN!
BEST LESSON MIGHT BE TO GIVE IT UP BEFORE YOU GET HURT!
ALL UNIT ALERT, VICINITY S.T.A.R. LABS!
9

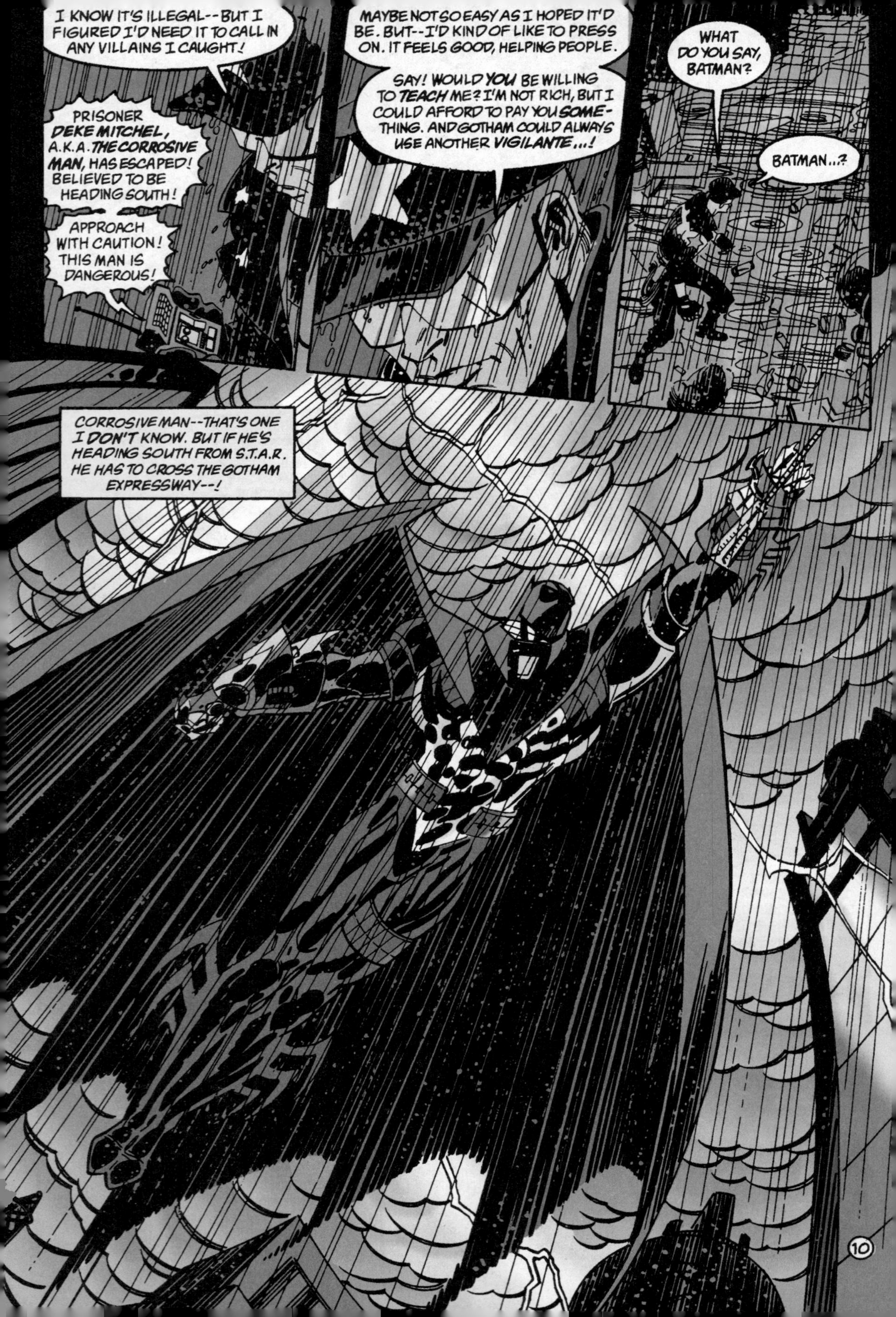
I KNOW IT'S ILLEGAL--BUT I FIGURED I'D NEED IT TO CALL IN ANY VILLAINS I CAUGHT!
PRISONER DEKE MITCHEL, A.K.A. THE CORROSIVE MAN, HAS ESCAPED! BELIEVED TO BE HEADING SOUTH!
APPROACH WITH CAUTION! THIS MAN IS DANGEROUS!
MAYBE NOT SO EASY AS I HOPED IT'D BE. BUT--I'D KIND OF LIKE TO PRESS ON. IT FEELS GOOD, HELPING PEOPLE.
SAY! WOULD YOU BE WILLING TO TEACH ME? I'M NOT RICH, BUT I COULD AFFORD TO PAY YOU SOMETHING. AND GOTHAM COULD ALWAYS USE ANOTHER VIGILANTE...!
WHAT DO YOU SAY, BATMAN?
BATMAN...?
CORROSIVE MAN--THAT'S ONE I DON'T KNOW. BUT IF HE'S HEADING SOUTH FROM S.T.A.R. HE HAS TO CROSS THE GOTHAM EXPRESSWAY--!
10

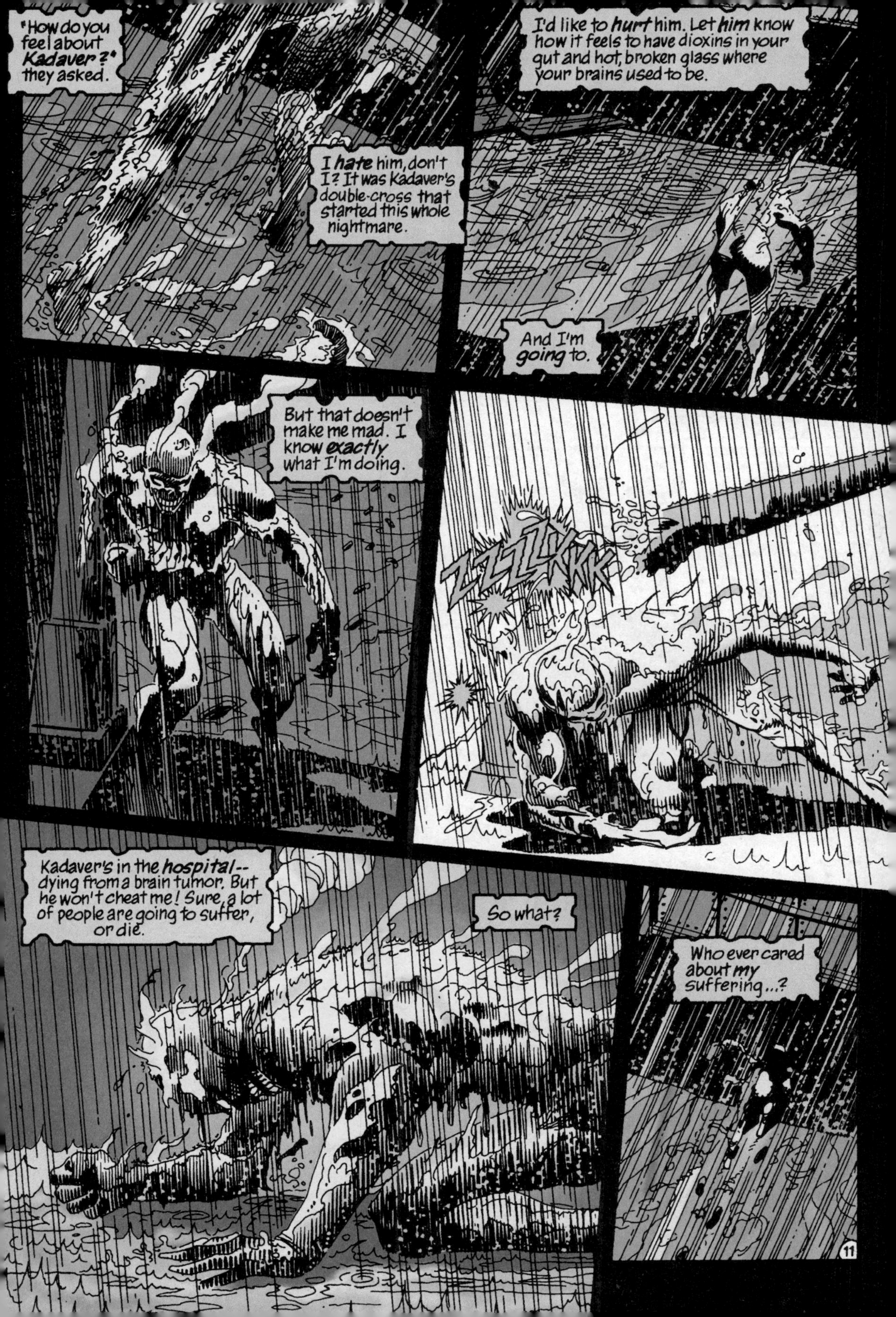
"How do you feel about Kadaver?" they asked.
I hate him, don't I? It was Kadaver's double-cross that started this whole nightmare.
I'd like to hurt him. Let him know how it feels to have dioxins in your gut and hot, broken glass where your brains used to be.
And I'm going to.
But that doesn't make me mad. I know exactly what I'm doing.
ZZZZKKK
Kadaver's in the hospital-- dying from a brain tumor. But he won't cheat me! Sure, a lot of people are going to suffer, or die.
So what?
Who ever cared about my suffering...?
11

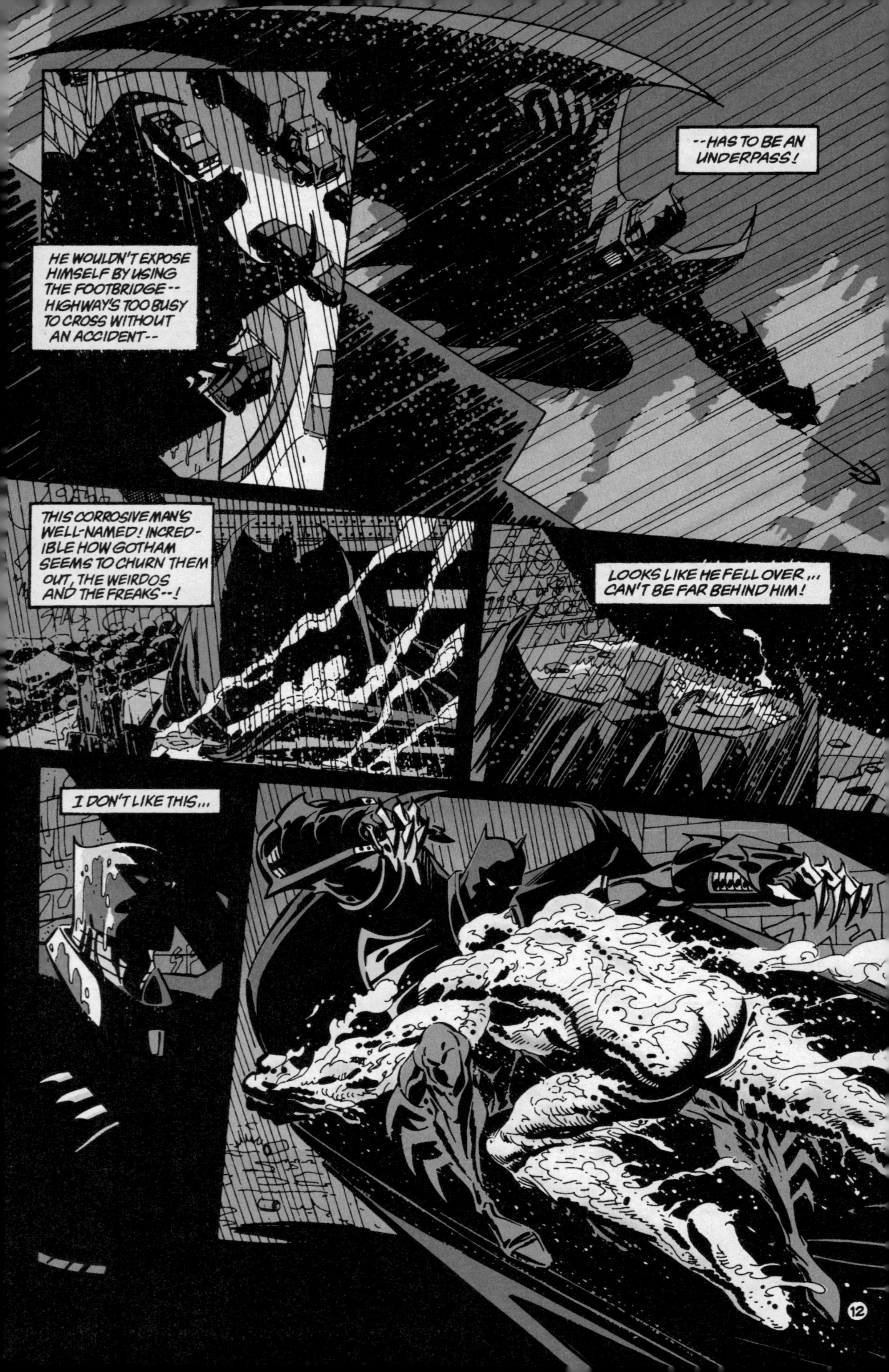
--HAS TO BE AN UNDERPASS!
HE WOULDN'T EXPOSE HIMSELF BY USING THE FOOTBRIDGE -- HIGHWAY'S TOO BUSY TO CROSS WITHOUT AN ACCIDENT--
THIS CORROSIVE MAN'S WELL-NAMED! INCREDIBLE HOW GOTHAM SEEMS TO CHURN THEM OUT, THE WEIRDOS AND THE FREAKS--!
LOOKS LIKE HE FELL OVER... CAN'T BE FAR BEHIND HIM!
I DON'T LIKE THIS...

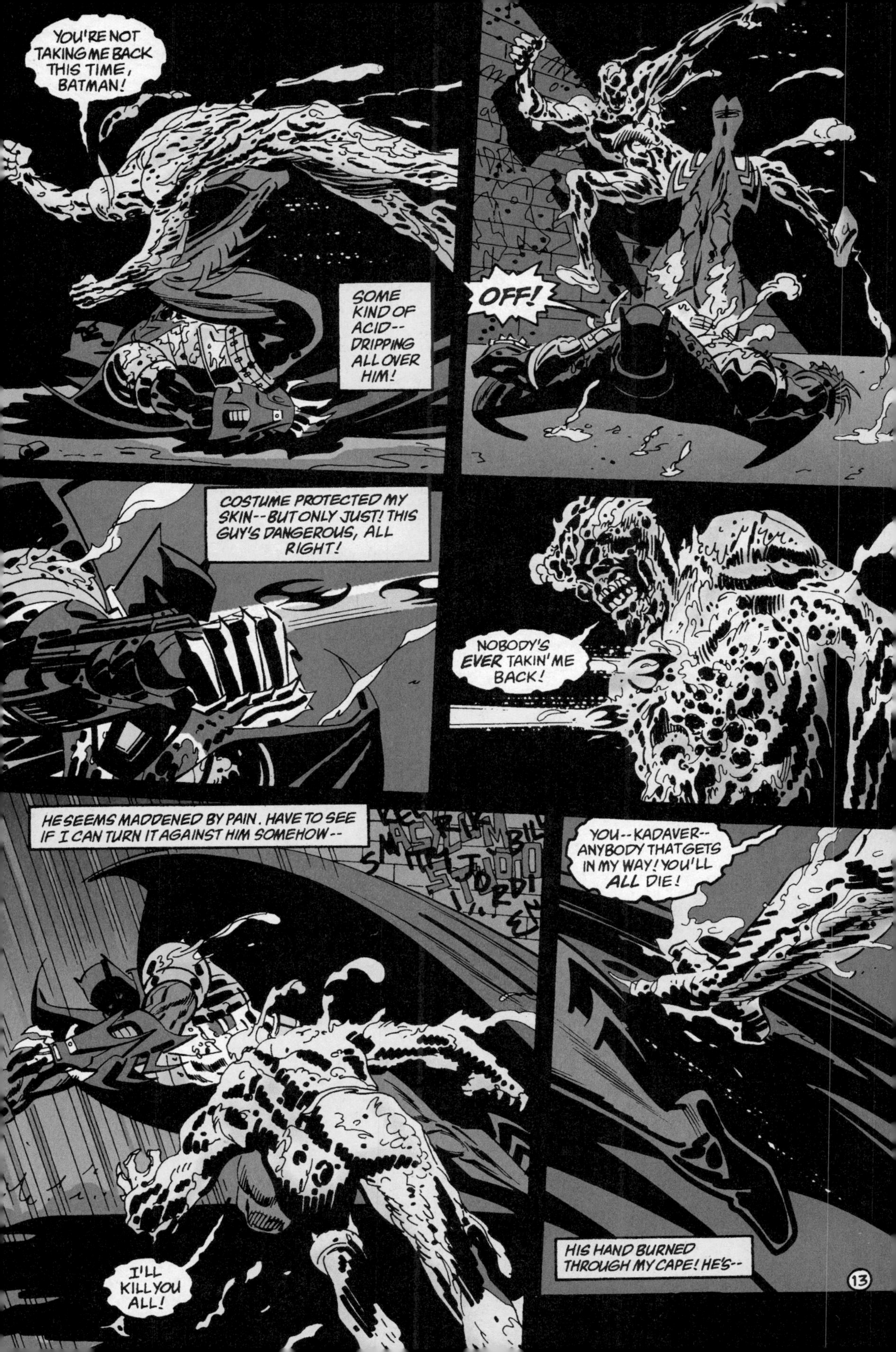

YOU'RE NOT TAKING ME BACK THIS TIME, BATMAN!
SOME KIND OF ACID-- DRIPPING ALL OVER HIM!
OFF!
COSTUME PROTECTED MY SKIN--BUT ONLY JUST! THIS GUY'S DANGEROUS, ALL RIGHT!
NOBODY'S EVER TAKIN' ME BACK!
HE SEEMS MADDENED BY PAIN. HAVE TO SEE IF I CAN TURN IT AGAINST HIM SOMEHOW--
I'LL KILL YOU ALL!
YOU--KADAVER-- ANYBODY THAT GETS IN MY WAY! YOU'LL ALL DIE!
HIS HAND BURNED THROUGH MY CAPE! HE'S--
13

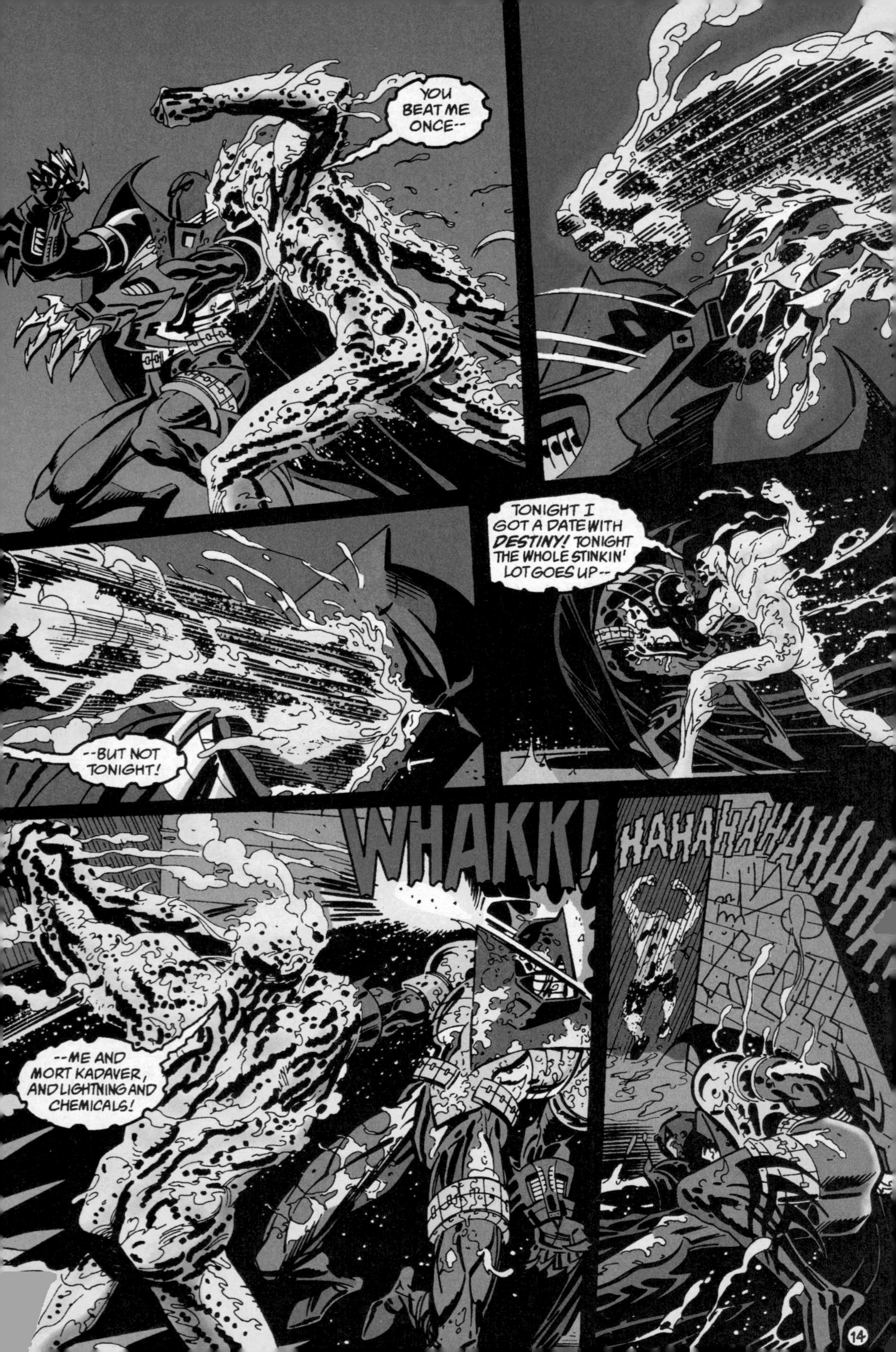
YOU BEAT ME ONCE--
--BUT NOT TONIGHT!
TONIGHT I GOT A DATE WITH DESTINY! TONIGHT THE WHOLE STINKIN' LOT GOES UP--
WHAKK!
--ME AND MORT KADAVER, AND LIGHTNING AND CHEMICALS!
HAHAHAHAHAHAHAH
14

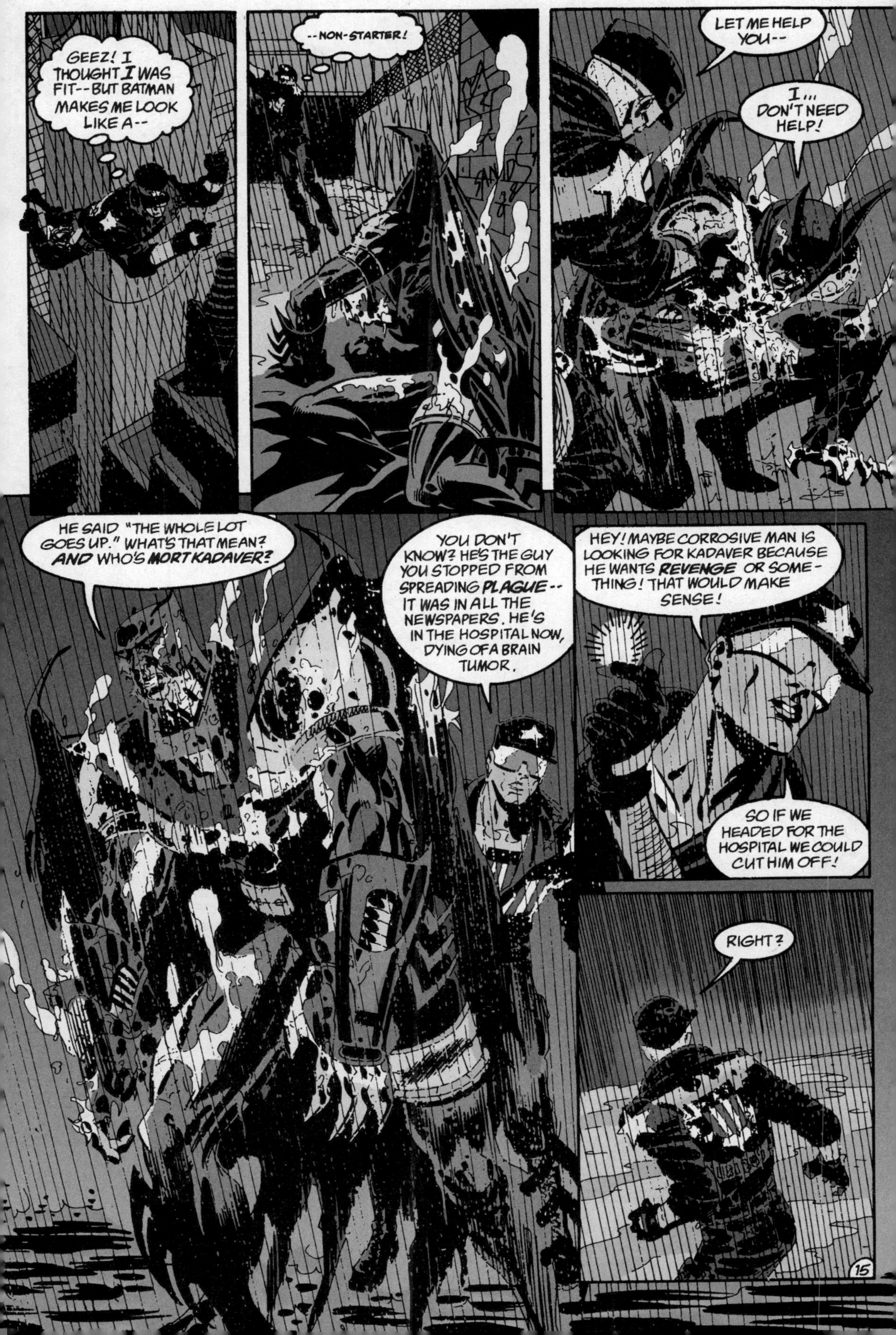
GEEZ! I THOUGHT I WAS FIT--BUT BATMAN MAKES ME LOOK LIKE A--
--NON-STARTER!
LET ME HELP YOU--
I... DON'T NEED HELP!
HE SAID "THE WHOLE LOT GOES UP." WHAT'S THAT MEAN? AND WHO'S MORT KADAVER?
YOU DON'T KNOW? HE'S THE GUY YOU STOPPED FROM SPREADING PLAGUE--IT WAS IN ALL THE NEWSPAPERS. HE'S IN THE HOSPITAL NOW, DYING OF A BRAIN TUMOR.
HEY! MAYBE CORROSIVE MAN IS LOOKING FOR KADAVER BECAUSE HE WANTS REVENGE OR SOME-THING! THAT WOULD MAKE SENSE!
SO IF WE HEADED FOR THE HOSPITAL WE COULD CUT HIM OFF!
RIGHT?
15

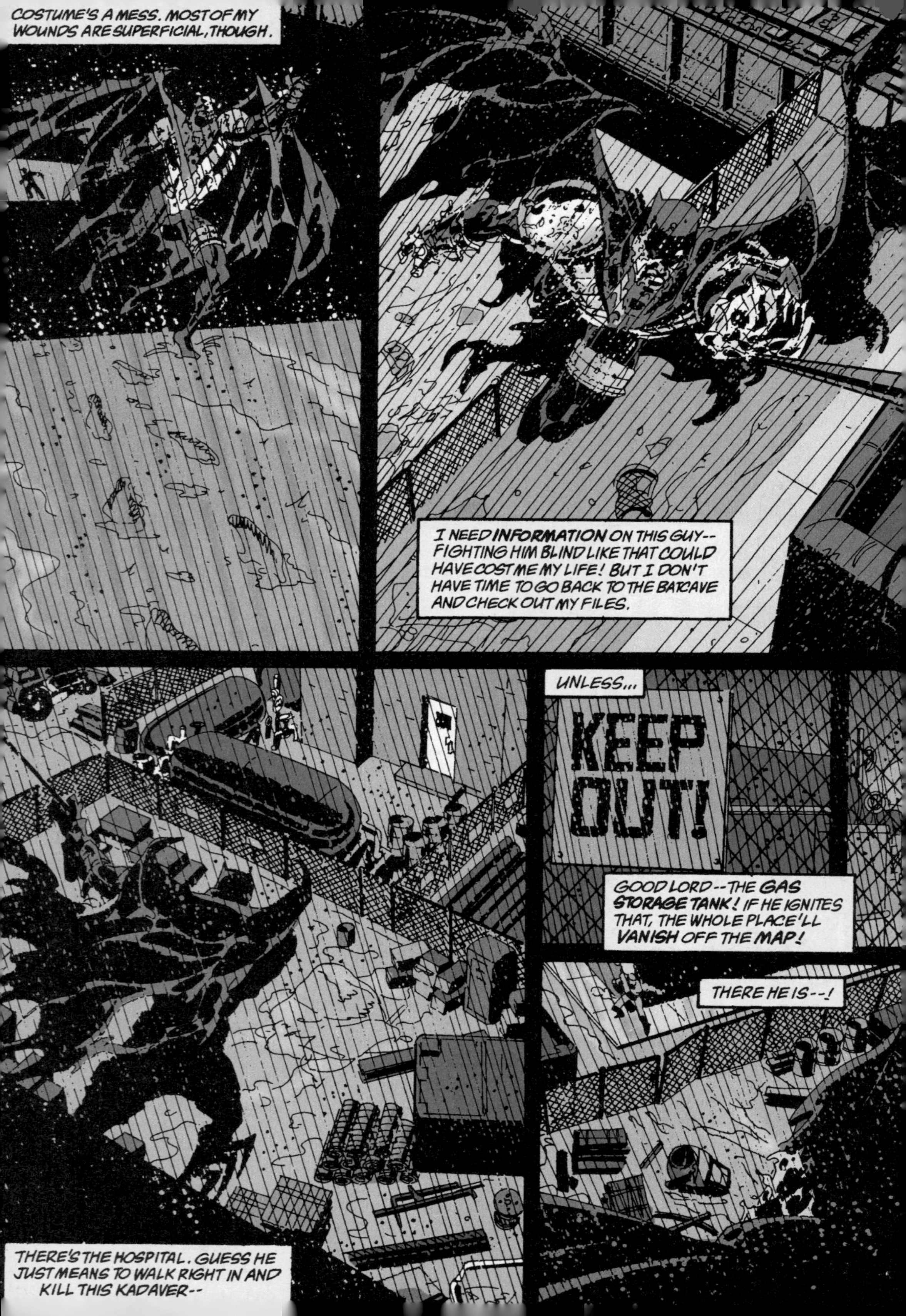
COSTUME'S A MESS. MOST OF MY WOUNDS ARE SUPERFICIAL, THOUGH.
I NEED INFORMATION ON THIS GUY-- FIGHTING HIM BLIND LIKE THAT COULD HAVE COST ME MY LIFE! BUT I DON'T HAVE TIME TO GO BACK TO THE BATCAVE AND CHECK OUT MY FILES.
THERE'S THE HOSPITAL. GUESS HE JUST MEANS TO WALK RIGHT IN AND KILL THIS KADAVER--
UNLESS...
KEEP OUT!
GOOD LORD--THE GAS STORAGE TANK! IF HE IGNITES THAT, THE WHOLE PLACE'LL VANISH OFF THE MAP!
THERE HE IS--!

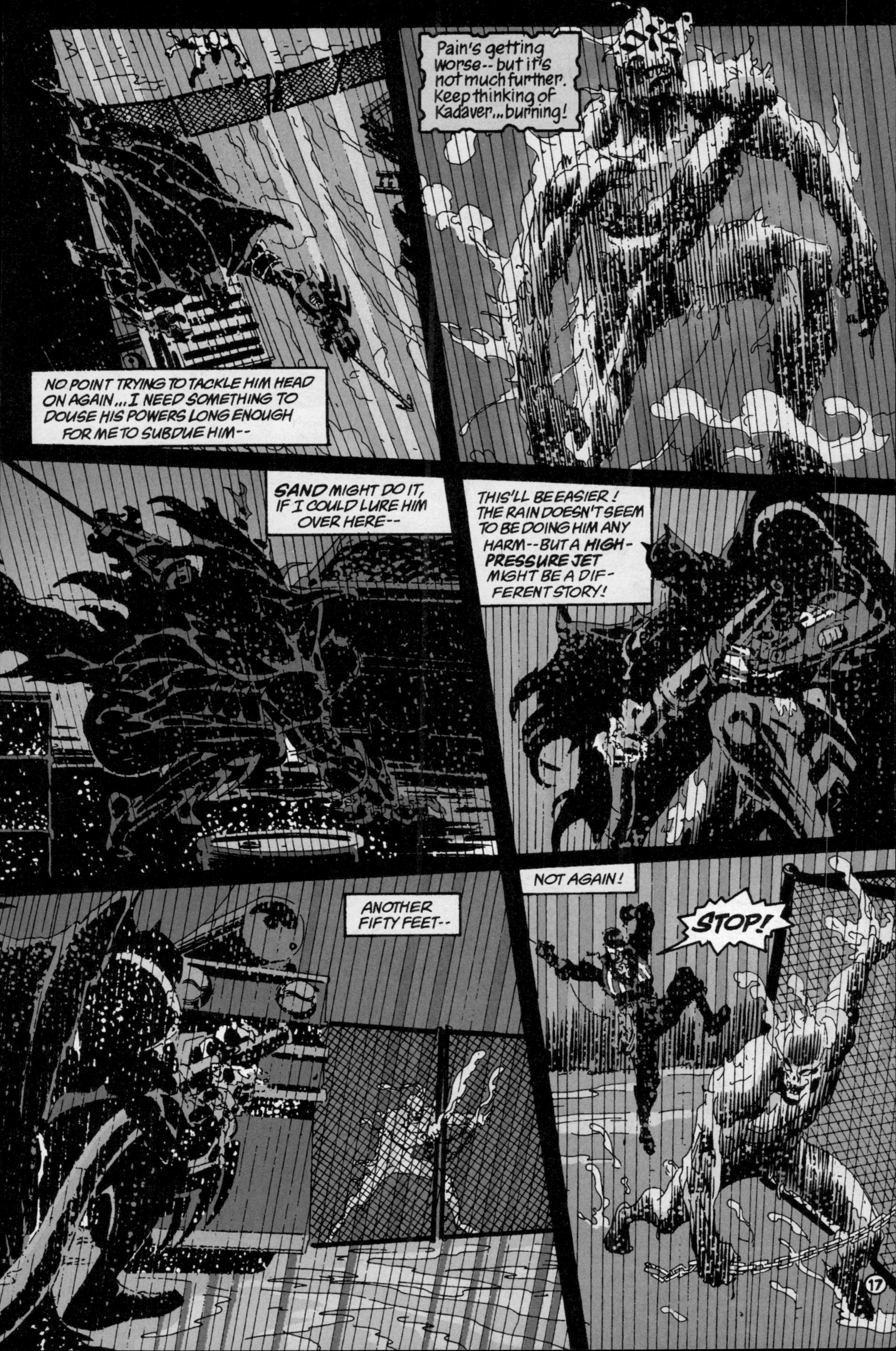
NO POINT TRYING TO TACKLE HIM HEAD ON AGAIN... I NEED SOMETHING TO DOUSE HIS POWERS LONG ENOUGH FOR ME TO SUBDUE HIM--
Pain's getting worse-- but it's not much further. Keep thinking of Kadaver... burning!
SAND MIGHT DO IT, IF I COULD LURE HIM OVER HERE--
THIS'LL BE EASIER! THE RAIN DOESN'T SEEM TO BE DOING HIM ANY HARM--BUT A HIGH-PRESSURE JET MIGHT BE A DIFFERENT STORY!
ANOTHER FIFTY FEET--
NOT AGAIN!
STOP!
17

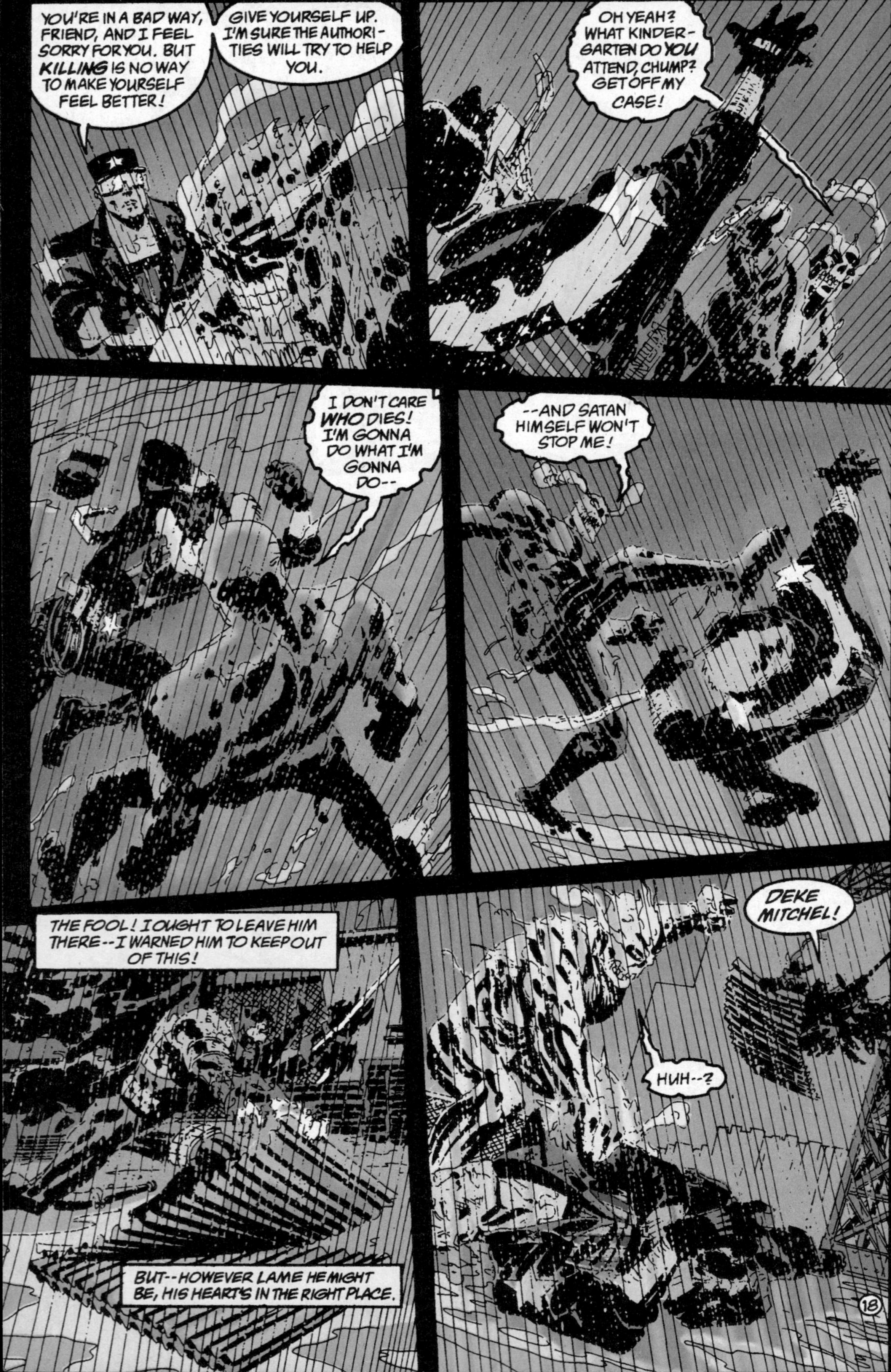

YOU'RE IN A BAD WAY, FRIEND, AND I FEEL SORRY FOR YOU. BUT KILLING IS NO WAY TO MAKE YOURSELF FEEL BETTER!
GIVE YOURSELF UP. I'M SURE THE AUTHORI-TIES WILL TRY TO HELP YOU.
OH YEAH? WHAT KINDER-GARTEN DO YOU ATTEND, CHUMP? GET OFF MY CASE!
I DON'T CARE WHO DIES! I'M GONNA DO WHAT I'M GONNA DO--
--AND SATAN HIMSELF WON'T STOP ME!
THE FOOL! I OUGHT TO LEAVE HIM THERE--I WARNED HIM TO KEEP OUT OF THIS!
BUT--HOWEVER LAME HE MIGHT BE, HIS HEART'S IN THE RIGHT PLACE.
DEKE MITCHEL!
HUH--?
18

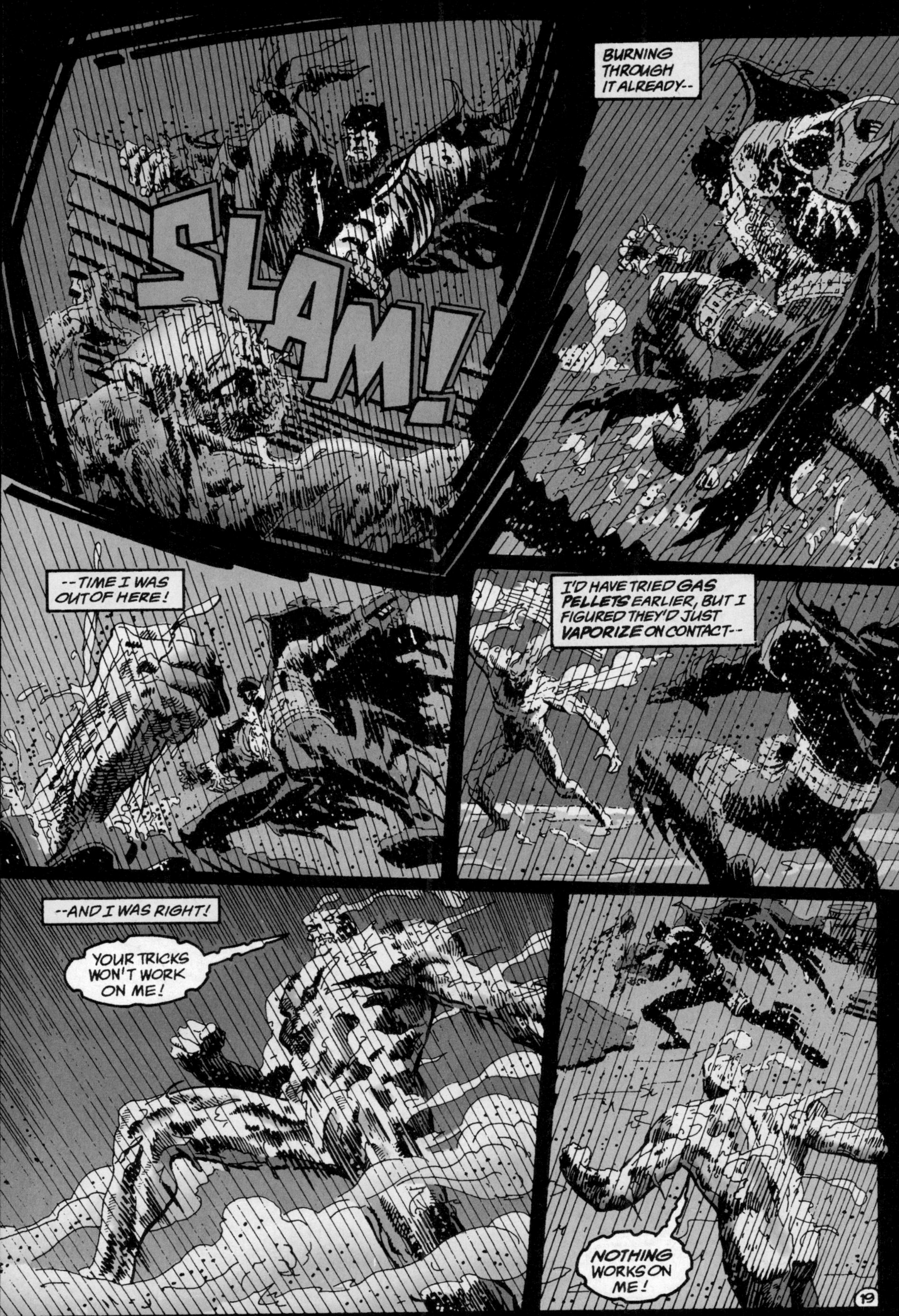
SLAM!
BURNING THROUGH IT ALREADY--
--TIME I WAS OUT OF HERE!
I'D HAVE TRIED GAS PELLETS EARLIER, BUT I FIGURED THEY'D JUST VAPORIZE ON CONTACT--
--AND I WAS RIGHT!
YOUR TRICKS WON'T WORK ON ME!
NOTHING WORKS ON ME!
19

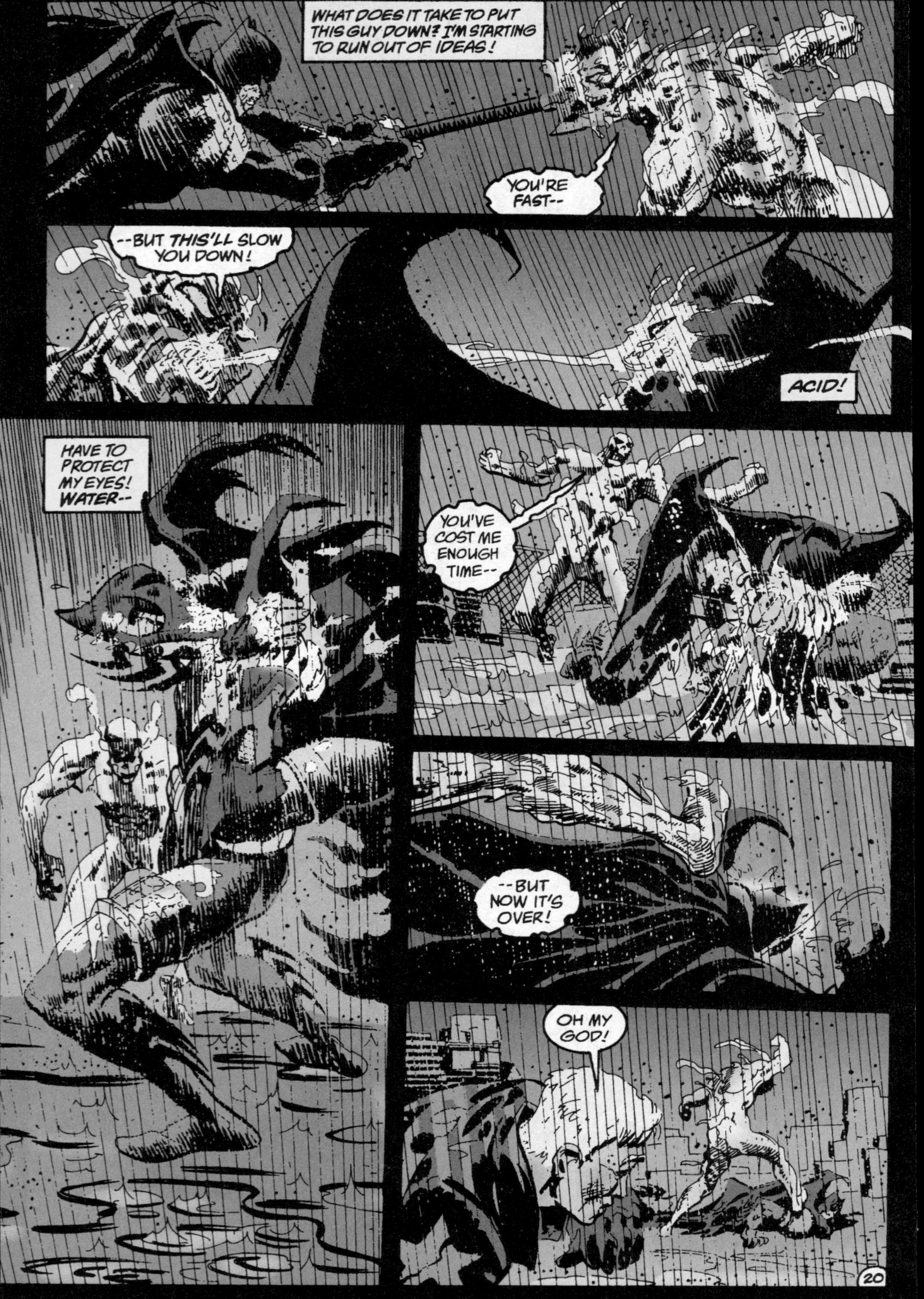
WHAT DOES IT TAKE TO PUT THIS GUY DOWN? I'M STARTING TO RUN OUT OF IDEAS!
YOU'RE FAST--
--BUT THIS'LL SLOW YOU DOWN!
ACID!
HAVE TO PROTECT MY EYES! WATER--
YOU'VE COST ME ENOUGH TIME--
--BUT NOW IT'S OVER!
OH MY GOD!
20

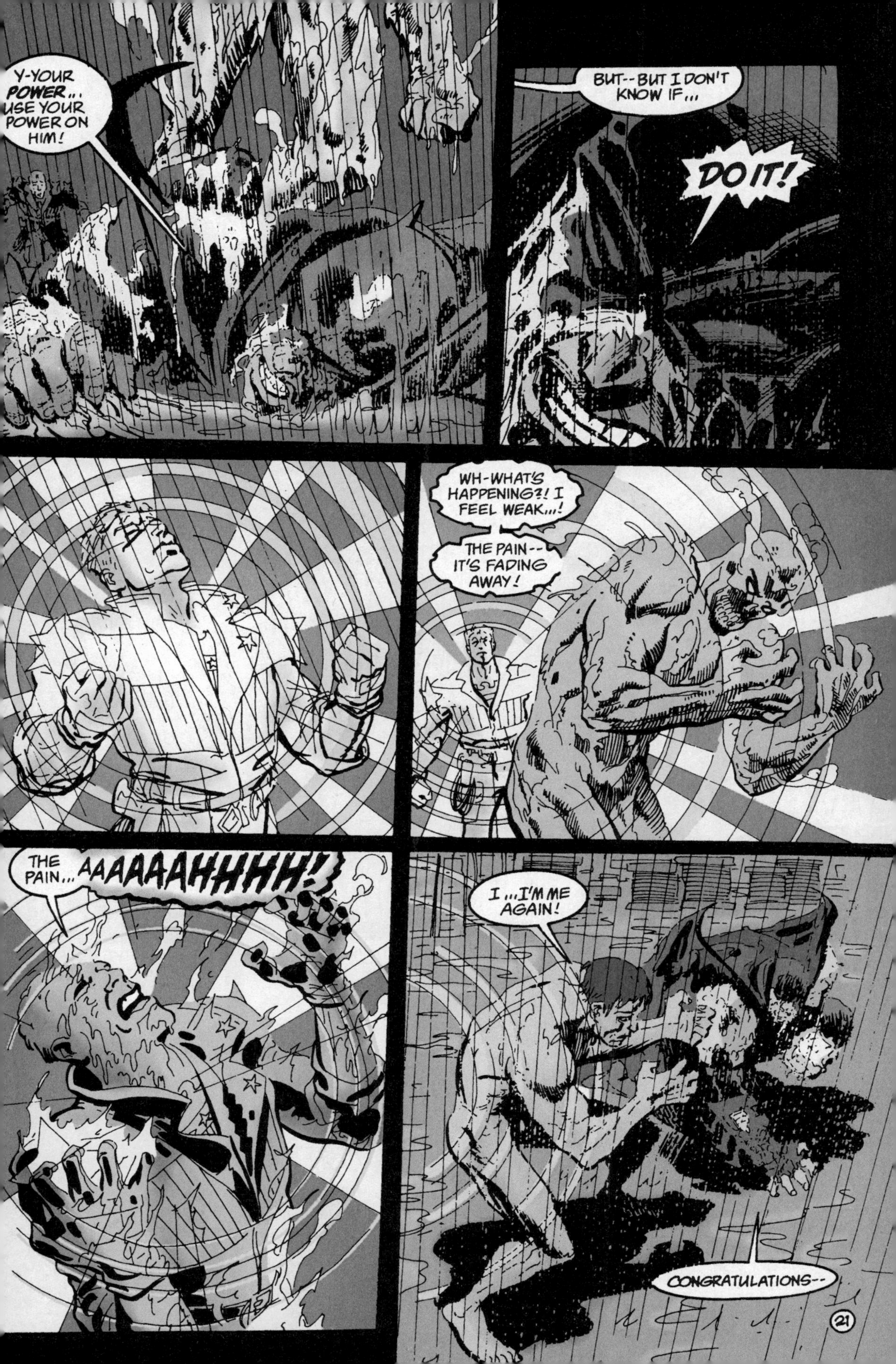

Y-YOUR POWER... USE YOUR POWER ON HIM!
BUT--BUT I DON'T KNOW IF...
DO IT!
WH-WHAT'S HAPPENING?! I FEEL WEAK...!
THE PAIN-- IT'S FADING AWAY!
THE PAIN... AAAAAAHHHH!
I...I'M ME AGAIN!
CONGRATULATIONS--

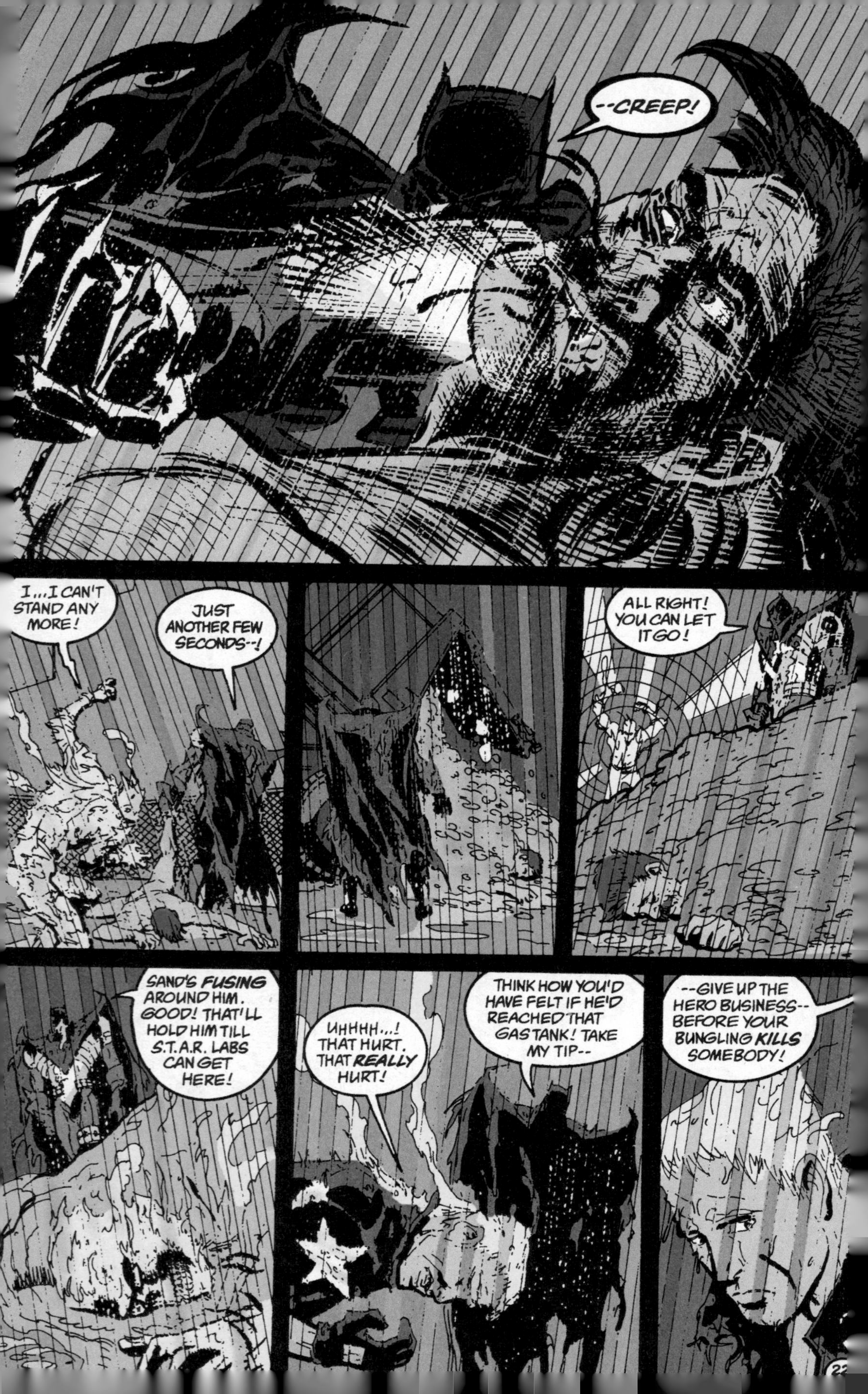
--CREEP!
I...I CAN'T STAND ANY MORE!
JUST ANOTHER FEW SECONDS--!
ALL RIGHT! YOU CAN LET IT GO!
SAND'S FUSING AROUND HIM. GOOD! THAT'LL HOLD HIM TILL S.T.A.R. LABS CAN GET HERE!
UHHHH...! THAT HURT. THAT REALLY HURT!
THINK HOW YOU'D HAVE FELT IF HE'D REACHED THAT GAS TANK! TAKE MY TIP--
--GIVE UP THE HERO BUSINESS--BEFORE YOUR BUNGLING KILLS SOMEBODY!

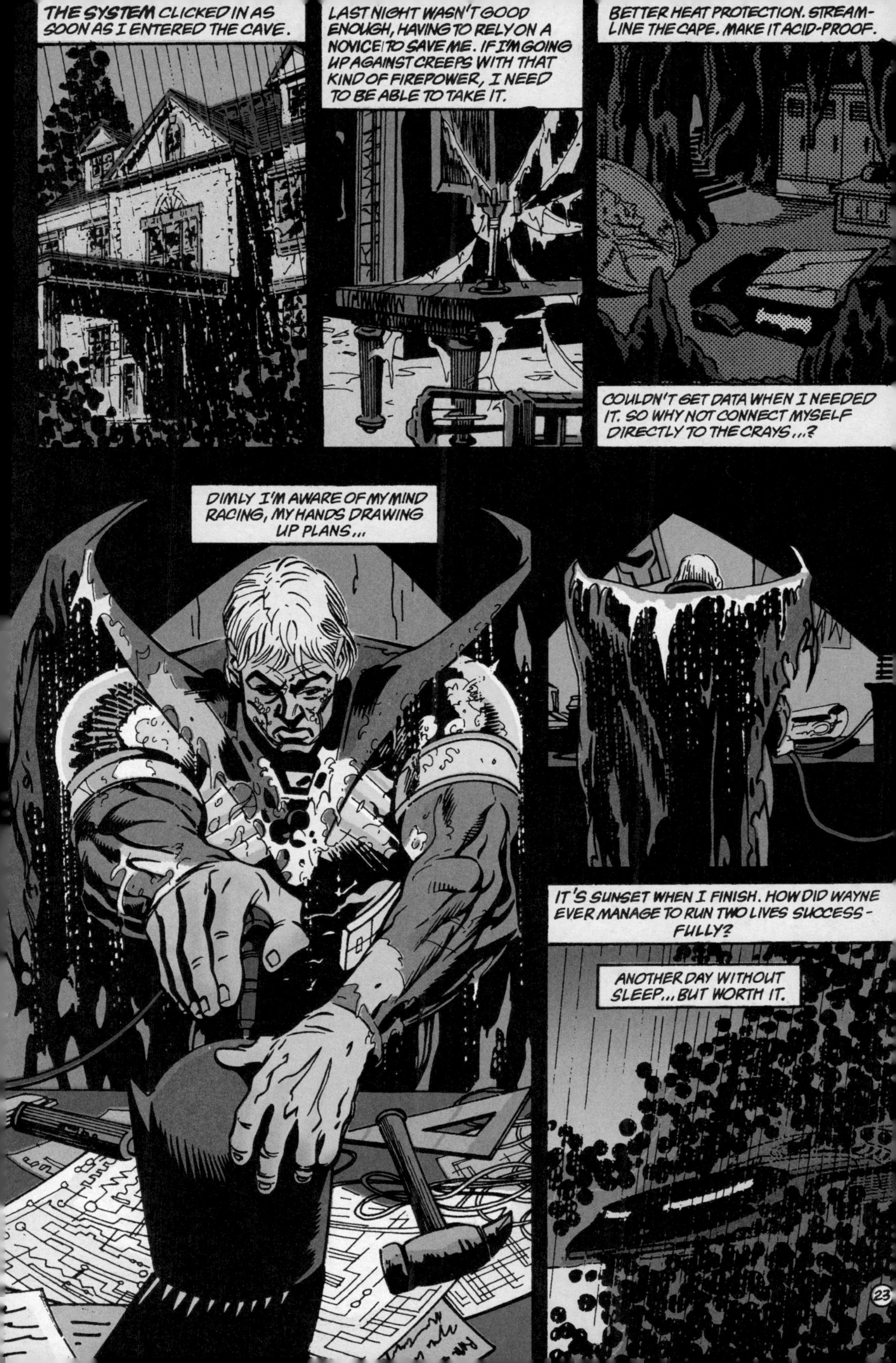
THE SYSTEM CLICKED IN AS SOON AS I ENTERED THE CAVE.
LAST NIGHT WASN'T GOOD ENOUGH, HAVING TO RELY ON A NOVICE TO SAVE ME. IF I'M GOING UP AGAINST CREEPS WITH THAT KIND OF FIREPOWER, I NEED TO BE ABLE TO TAKE IT.
BETTER HEAT PROTECTION. STREAM-LINE THE CAPE. MAKE IT ACID-PROOF.
COULDN'T GET DATA WHEN I NEEDED IT. SO WHY NOT CONNECT MYSELF DIRECTLY TO THE CRAYS...?
DIMLY I'M AWARE OF MY MIND RACING, MY HANDS DRAWING UP PLANS...
IT'S SUNSET WHEN I FINISH. HOW DID WAYNE EVER MANAGE TO RUN TWO LIVES SUCCESS-FULLY?
ANOTHER DAY WITHOUT SLEEP... BUT WORTH IT.
23

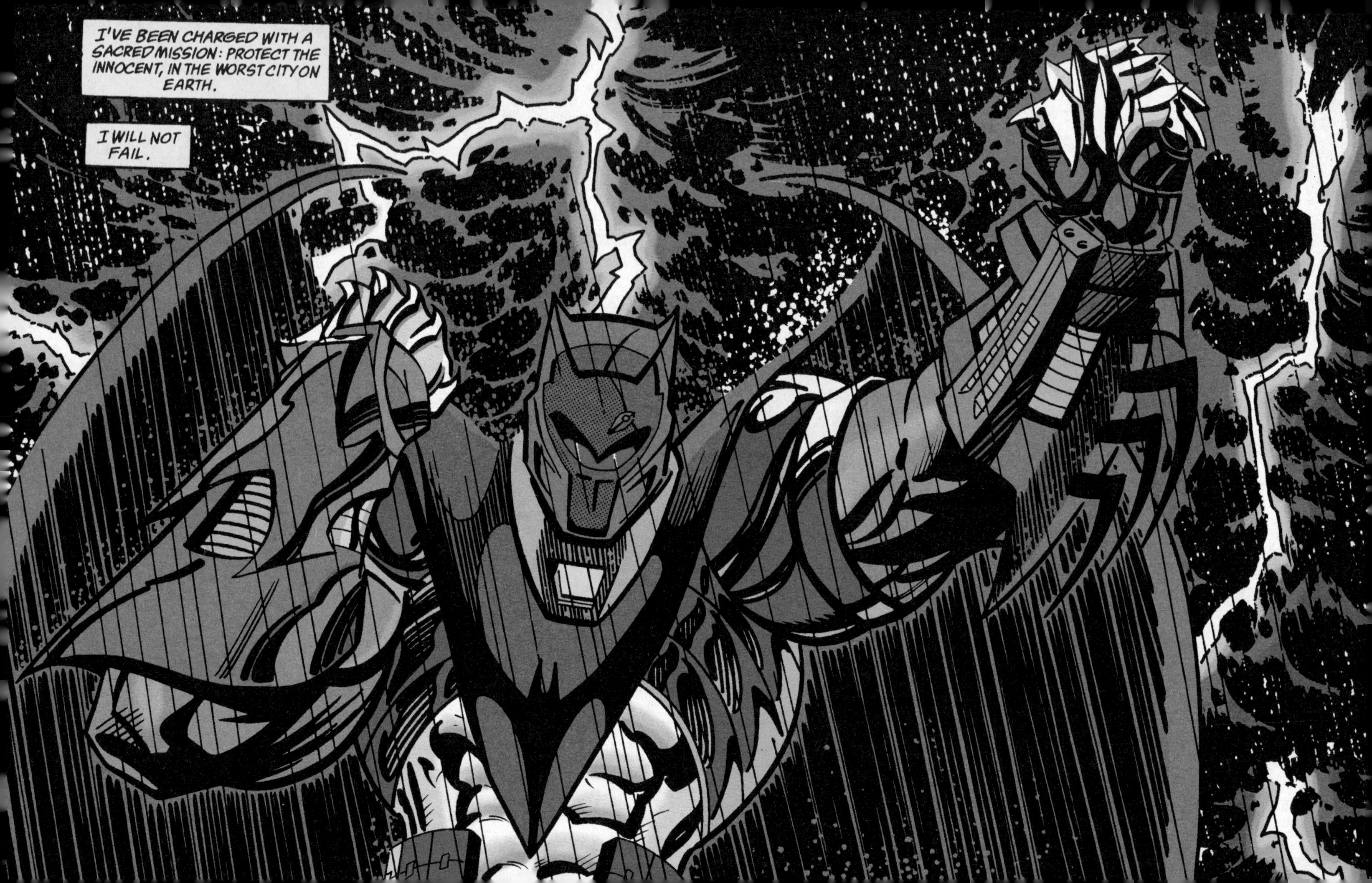
I'VE BEEN CHARGED WITH A SACRED MISSION: PROTECT THE INNOCENT, IN THE WORST CITY ON EARTH.
I WILL NOT FAIL.

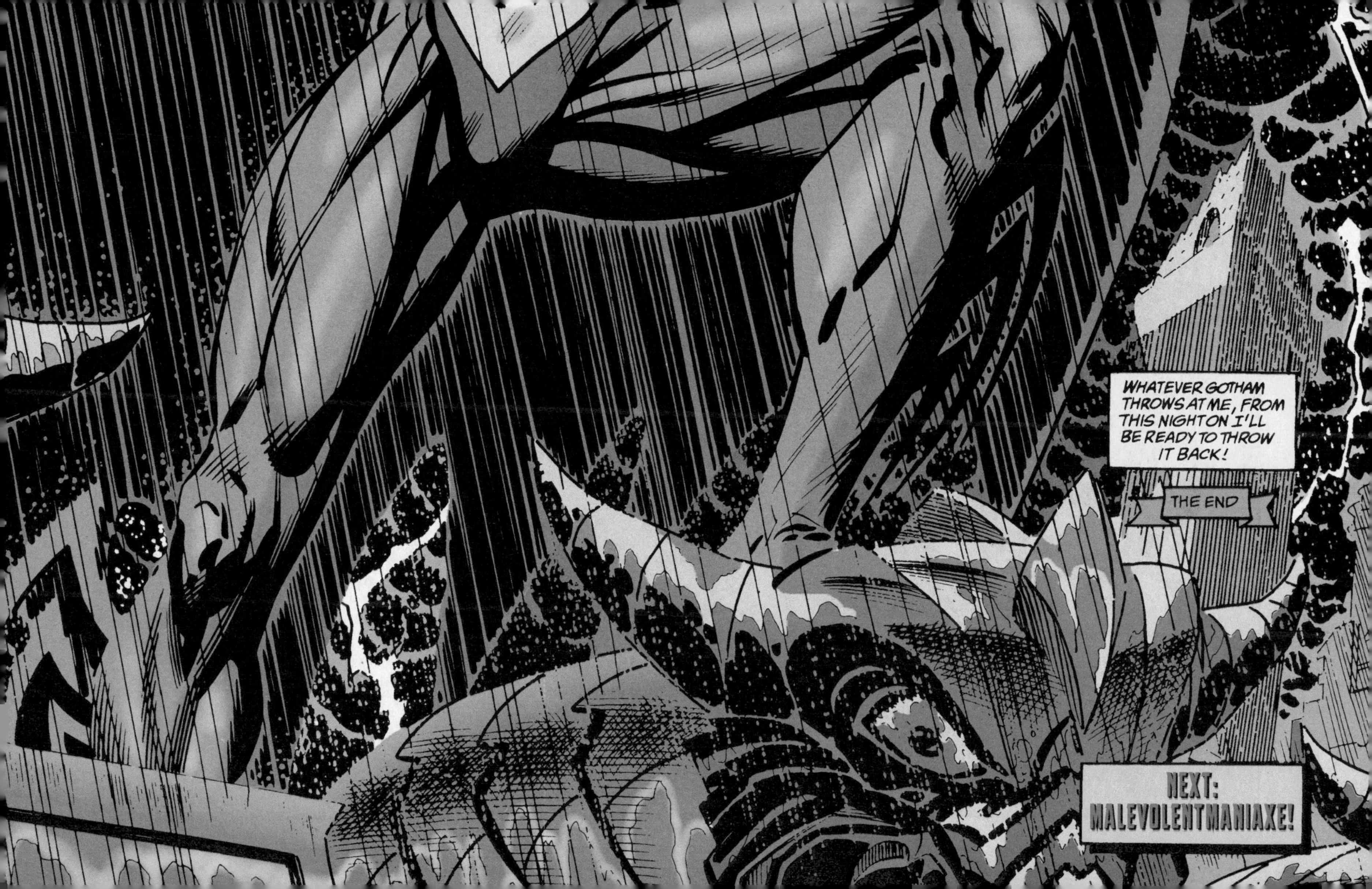
WHATEVER GOTHAM THROWS AT ME, FROM THIS NIGHT ON I'LL BE READY TO THROW IT BACK!
THE END
NEXT: MALEVOLENTMANIAXE!

Cover art by KELLEY JONES

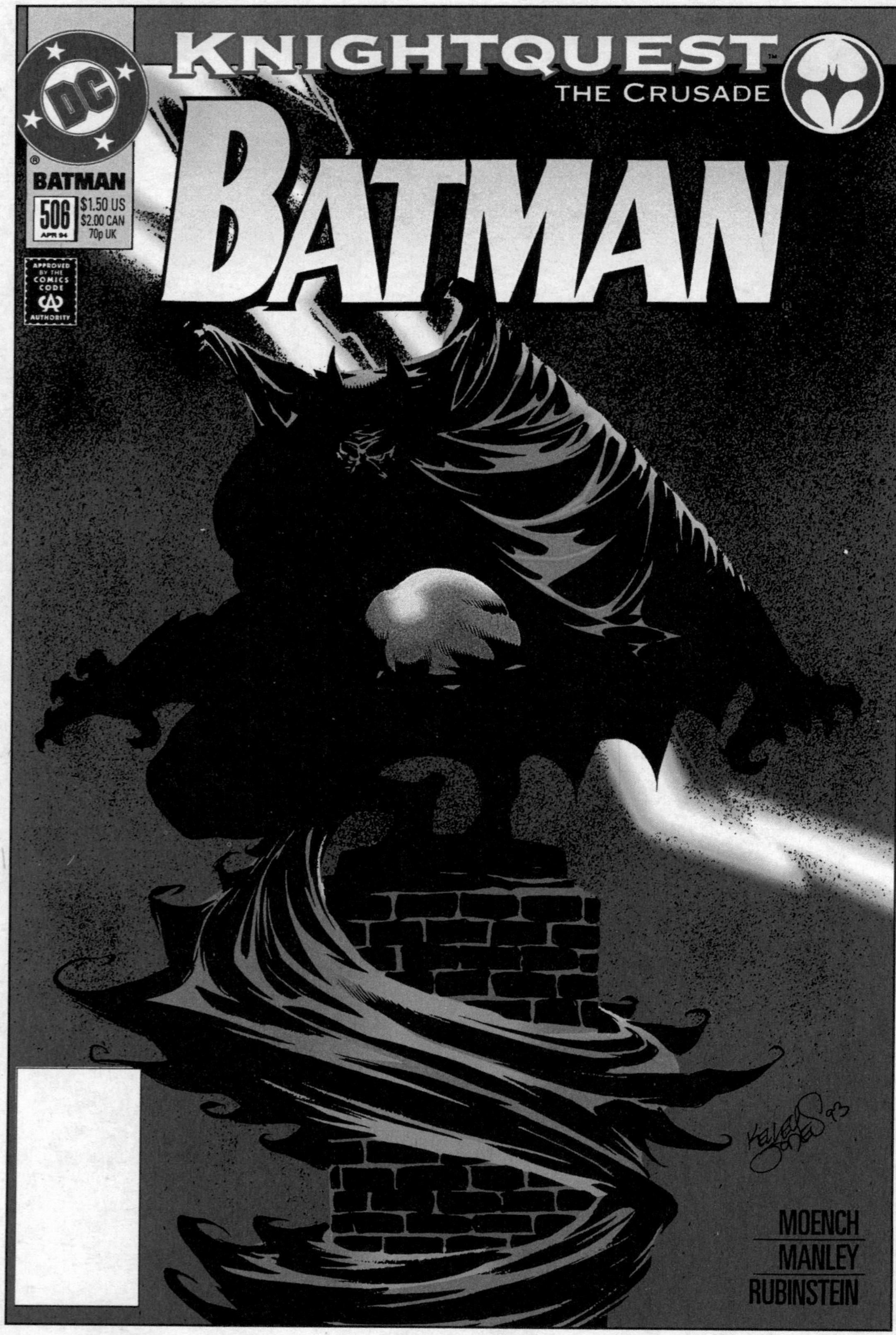
KNIGHTQUEST
THE CRUSADE
DC
BATMAN
506
$1.50 US
$2.00 CAN
70p UK
APR 94
APPROVED BY THE COMICS CODE AUTHORITY
BATMAN
MOENCH
MANLEY
RUBINSTEIN

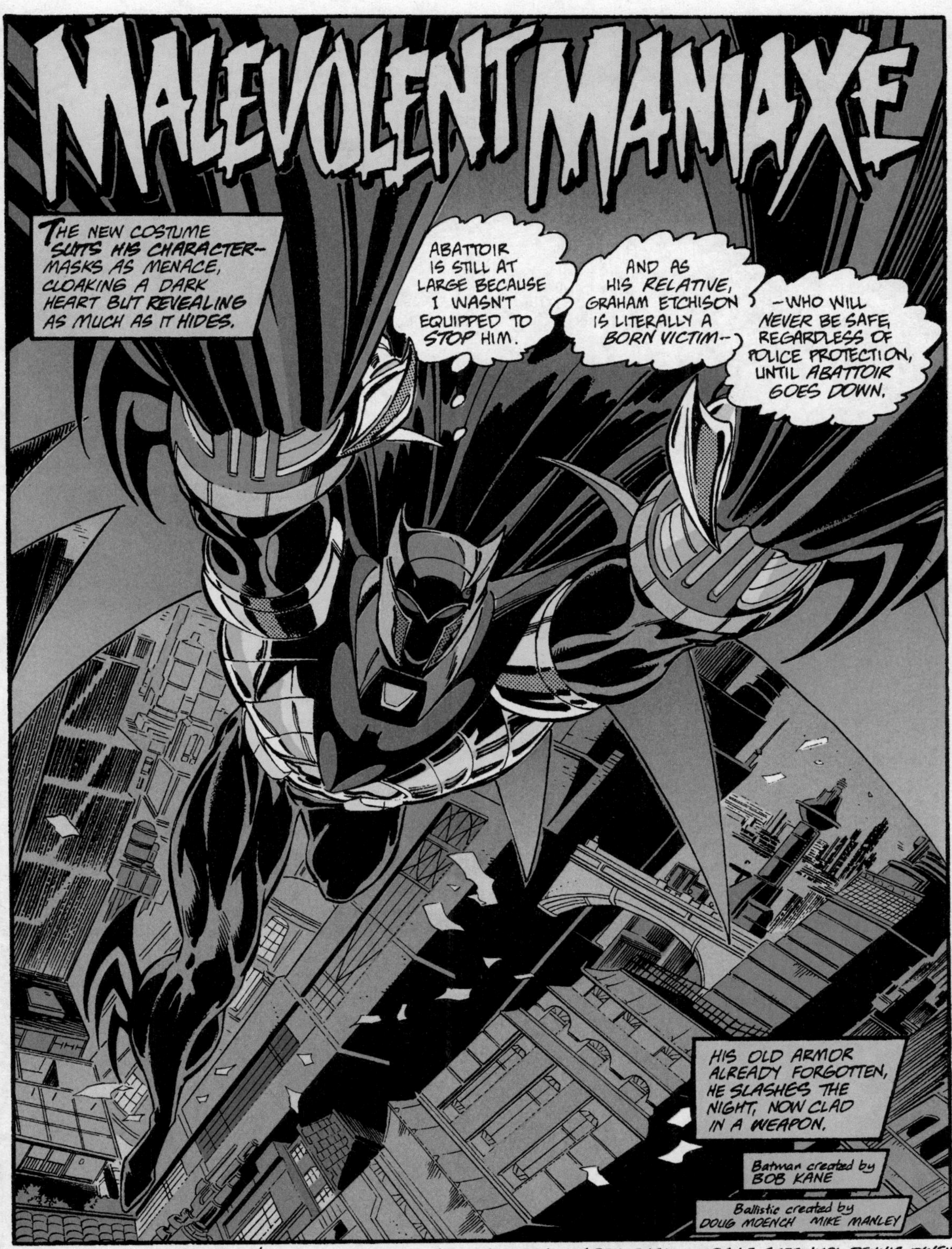
MALEVOLENT MANIAXE
THE NEW COSTUME SUITS HIS CHARACTER-- MASKS AS MENACE, CLOAKING A DARK HEART BUT REVEALING AS MUCH AS IT HIDES.
ABATTOIR IS STILL AT LARGE BECAUSE I WASN'T EQUIPPED TO STOP HIM.
AND AS HIS RELATIVE, GRAHAM ETCHISON IS LITERALLY A BORN VICTIM--
--WHO WILL NEVER BE SAFE, REGARDLESS OF POLICE PROTECTION, UNTIL ABATTOIR GOES DOWN.
HIS OLD ARMOR ALREADY FORGOTTEN, HE SLASHES THE NIGHT, NOW CLAD IN A WEAPON.
Batman created by BOB KANE
Ballistic created by DOUG MOENCH MIKE MANLEY

DOUG MOENCH-writer MIKE MANLEY & JOSEF RUBINSTEIN-artists ADRIENNE ROY-colorist KEN BRUZENAK-letterer JORDAN B. GORFINKEL-assistant editor DENNIS O'NEIL-editor

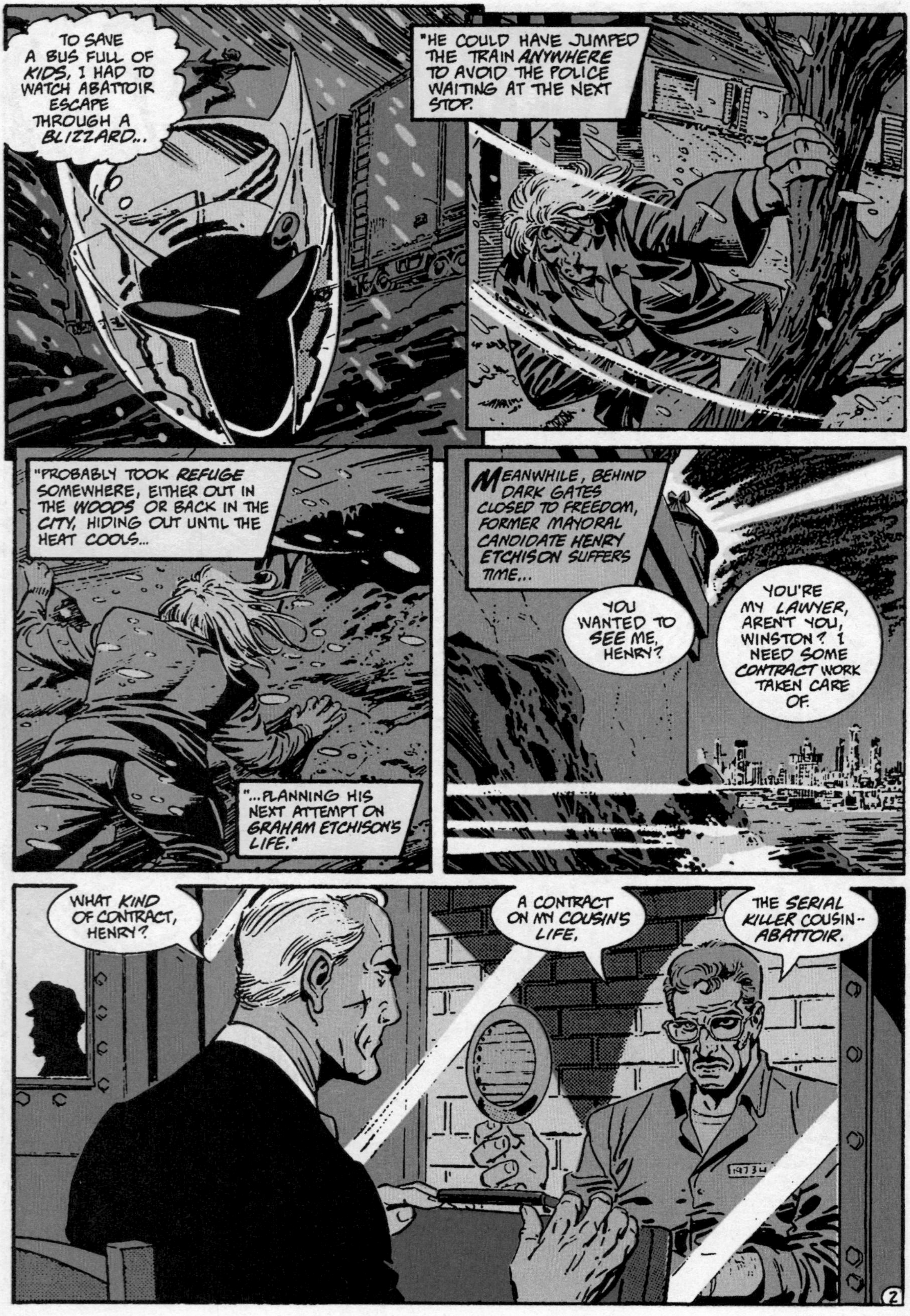
TO SAVE A BUS FULL OF KIDS, I HAD TO WATCH ABATTOIR ESCAPE THROUGH A BLIZZARD...
"HE COULD HAVE JUMPED THE TRAIN ANYWHERE TO AVOID THE POLICE WAITING AT THE NEXT STOP.
"PROBABLY TOOK REFUGE SOMEWHERE, EITHER OUT IN THE WOODS OR BACK IN THE CITY, HIDING OUT UNTIL THE HEAT COOLS...
"...PLANNING HIS NEXT ATTEMPT ON GRAHAM ETCHISON'S LIFE."
MEANWHILE, BEHIND DARK GATES CLOSED TO FREEDOM, FORMER MAYORAL CANDIDATE HENRY ETCHISON SUFFERS TIME...
YOU WANTED TO SEE ME, HENRY?
YOU'RE MY LAWYER, AREN'T YOU, WINSTON? I NEED SOME CONTRACT WORK TAKEN CARE OF.
WHAT KIND OF CONTRACT, HENRY?
A CONTRACT ON MY COUSIN'S LIFE.
THE SERIAL KILLER COUSIN-- ABATTOIR.
2

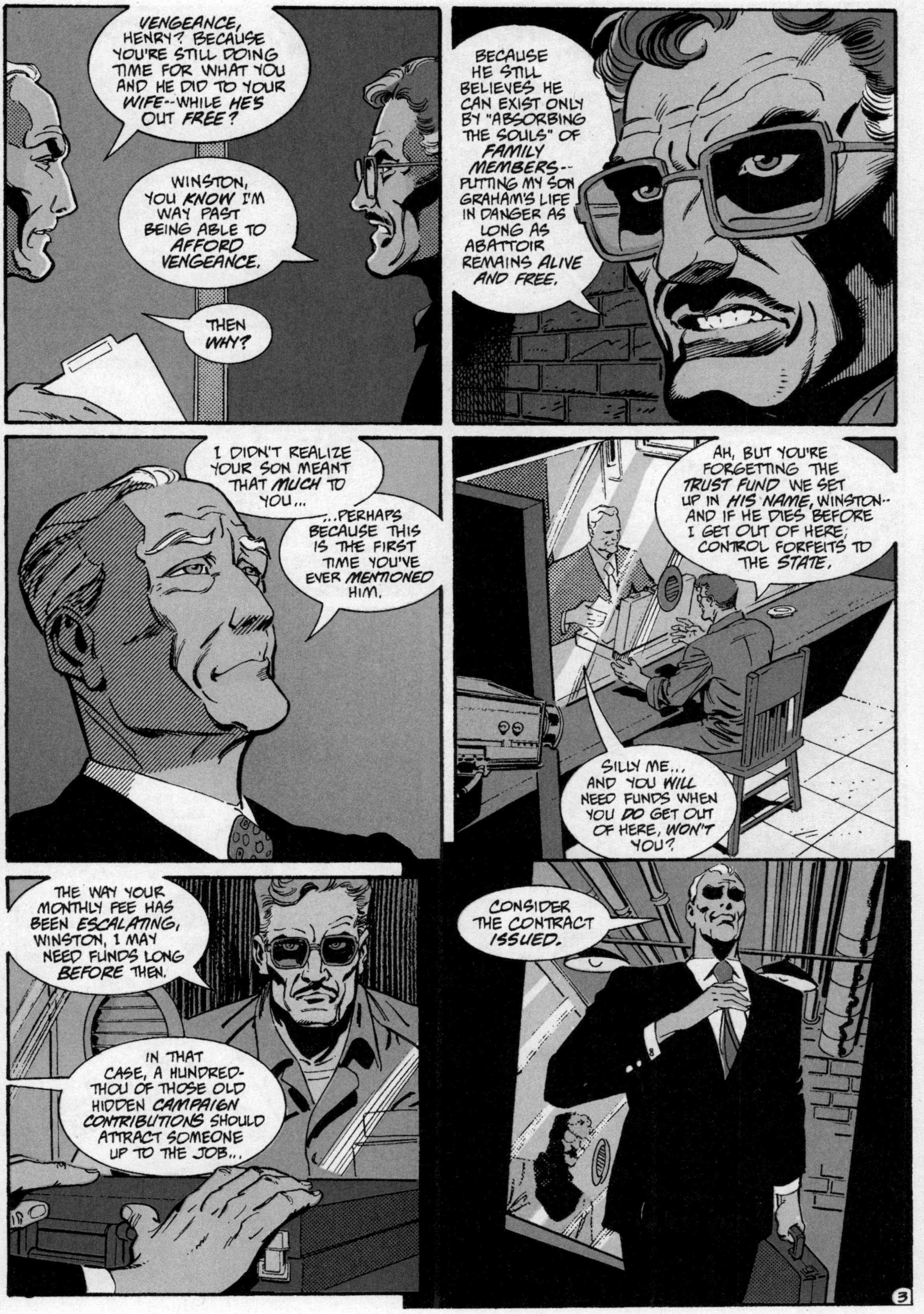
VENGEANCE, HENRY? BECAUSE YOU'RE STILL DOING TIME FOR WHAT YOU AND HE DID TO YOUR WIFE--WHILE HE'S OUT FREE?
WINSTON, YOU KNOW I'M WAY PAST BEING ABLE TO AFFORD VENGEANCE.
THEN WHY?
BECAUSE HE STILL BELIEVES HE CAN EXIST ONLY BY "ABSORBING THE SOULS" OF FAMILY MEMBERS-- PUTTING MY SON GRAHAM'S LIFE IN DANGER AS LONG AS ABATTOIR REMAINS ALIVE AND FREE.
I DIDN'T REALIZE YOUR SON MEANT THAT MUCH TO YOU...
...PERHAPS BECAUSE THIS IS THE FIRST TIME YOU'VE EVER MENTIONED HIM.
AH, BUT YOU'RE FORGETTING THE TRUST FUND WE SET UP IN HIS NAME, WINSTON-- AND IF HE DIES BEFORE I GET OUT OF HERE, CONTROL FORFEITS TO THE STATE.
SILLY ME... AND YOU WILL NEED FUNDS WHEN YOU DO GET OUT OF HERE, WON'T YOU?
THE WAY YOUR MONTHLY FEE HAS BEEN ESCALATING, WINSTON, I MAY NEED FUNDS LONG BEFORE THEN.
IN THAT CASE, A HUNDRED-THOU OF THOSE OLD HIDDEN CAMPAIGN CONTRIBUTIONS SHOULD ATTRACT SOMEONE UP TO THE JOB...
CONSIDER THE CONTRACT ISSUED.
3

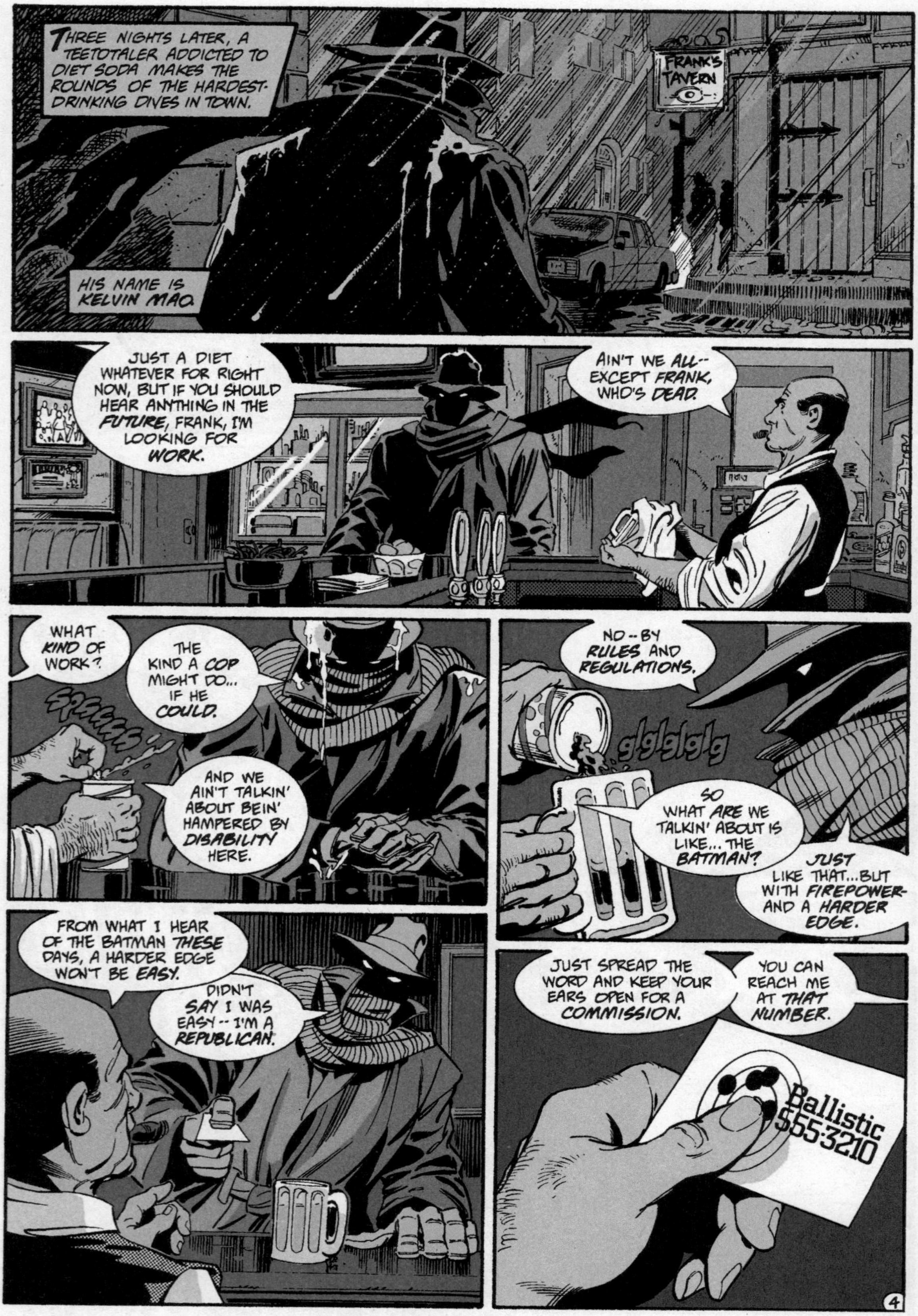
THREE NIGHTS LATER, A TEETOTALER ADDICTED TO DIET SODA MAKES THE ROUNDS OF THE HARDEST-DRINKING DIVES IN TOWN.
FRANK'S TAVERN
HIS NAME IS KELVIN MAO.
JUST A DIET WHATEVER FOR RIGHT NOW, BUT IF YOU SHOULD HEAR ANYTHING IN THE FUTURE, FRANK, I'M LOOKING FOR WORK.
AIN'T WE ALL-- EXCEPT FRANK, WHO'S DEAD.
WHAT KIND OF WORK?
THE KIND A COP MIGHT DO... IF HE COULD.
SPCCSSS
AND WE AIN'T TALKIN' ABOUT BEIN' HAMPERED BY DISABILITY HERE.
NO--BY RULES AND REGULATIONS.
glglglglg
SO WHAT ARE WE TALKIN' ABOUT IS LIKE... THE BATMAN?
JUST LIKE THAT...BUT WITH FIREPOWER-AND A HARDER EDGE.
FROM WHAT I HEAR OF THE BATMAN THESE DAYS, A HARDER EDGE WON'T BE EASY.
DIDN'T SAY I WAS EASY-- I'M A REPUBLICAN.
JUST SPREAD THE WORD AND KEEP YOUR EARS OPEN FOR A COMMISSION.
YOU CAN REACH ME AT THAT NUMBER.
Ballistic
555-3210
4

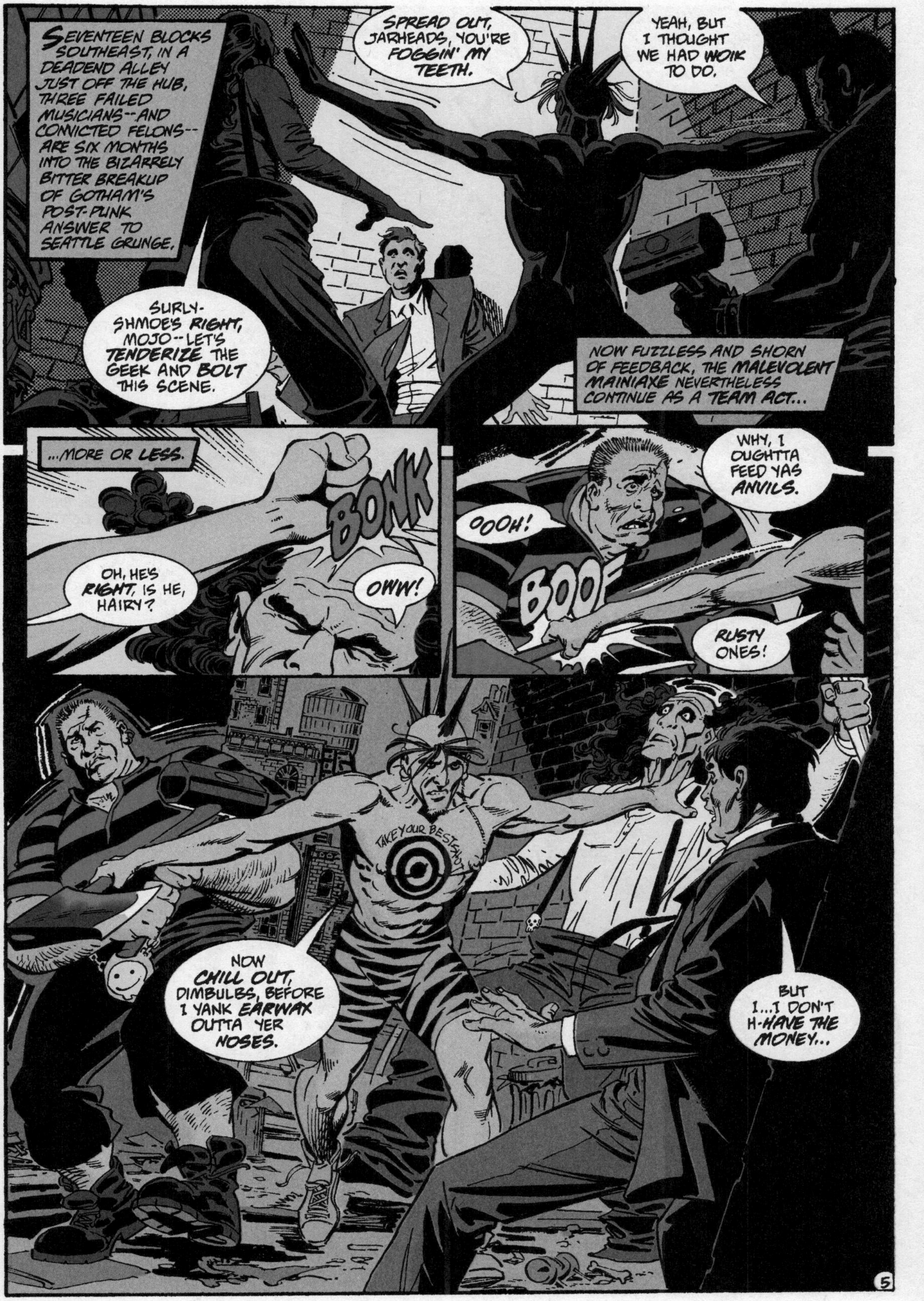
SEVENTEEN BLOCKS SOUTHEAST, IN A DEADEND ALLEY JUST OFF THE HUB, THREE FAILED MUSICIANS--AND CONVICTED FELONS--ARE SIX MONTHS INTO THE BIZARRELY BITTER BREAKUP OF GOTHAM'S POST-PUNK ANSWER TO SEATTLE GRUNGE.
SPREAD OUT, JARHEADS, YOU'RE FOGGIN' MY TEETH.
YEAH, BUT I THOUGHT WE HAD WOIK TO DO.
SURLY-SHMOE'S RIGHT, MOJO--LET'S TENDERIZE THE GEEK AND BOLT THIS SCENE.
NOW FUZZLESS AND SHORN OF FEEDBACK, THE MALEVOLENT MAINIAXE NEVERTHELESS CONTINUE AS A TEAM ACT...
...MORE OR LESS.
BONK
OH, HE'S RIGHT, IS HE, HAIRY?
OWW!
OOOH!
WHY, I OUGHTTA FEED YAS ANVILS.
BOOF
RUSTY ONES!
TAKE YOUR BEST SHOT
NOW CHILL OUT, DIMBULBS, BEFORE I YANK EARWAX OUTTA YER NOSES.
BUT I...I DON'T H-HAVE THE MONEY...
5

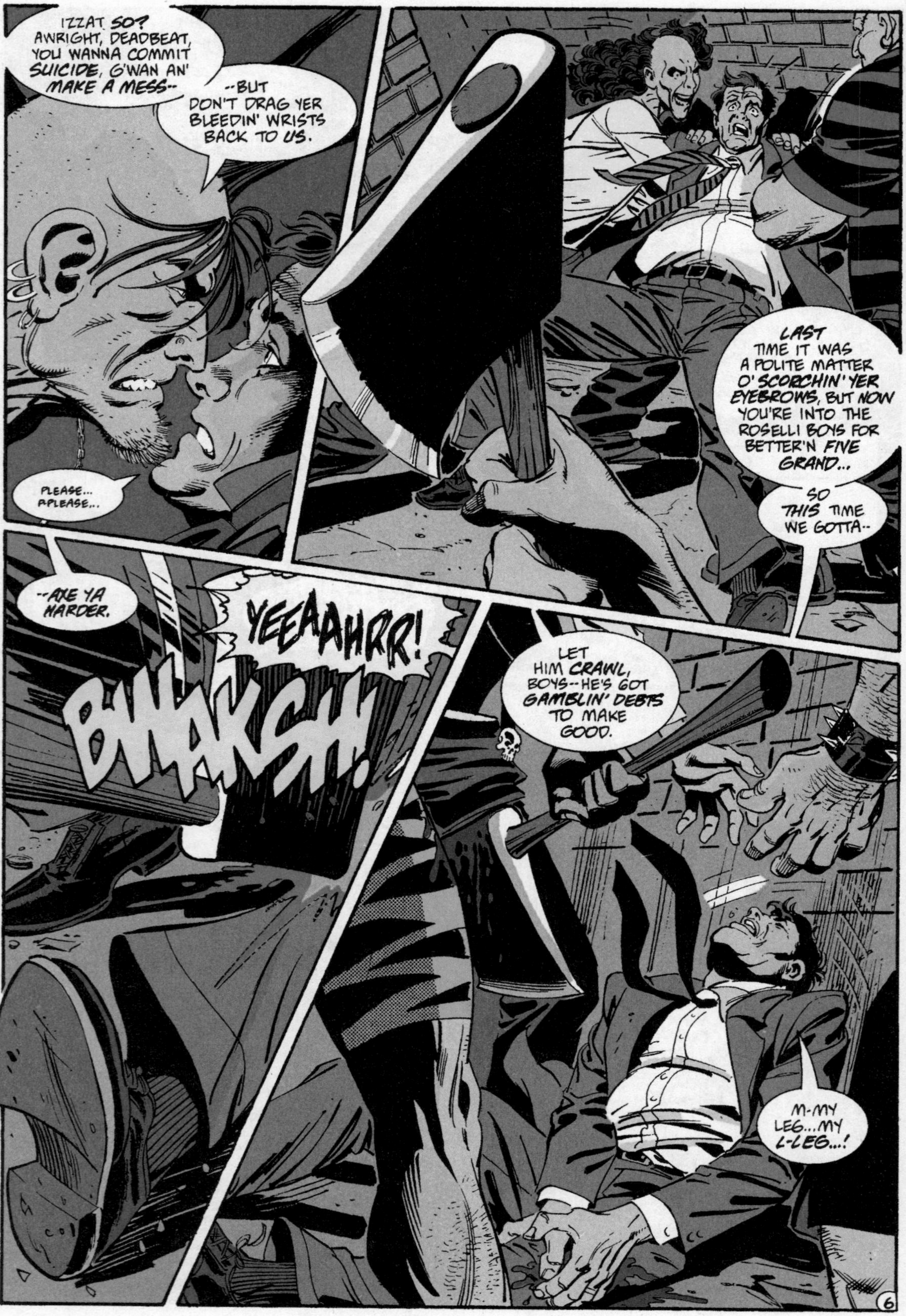
IZZAT SO? AWRIGHT, DEADBEAT, YOU WANNA COMMIT SUICIDE, G'WAN AN' MAKE A MESS--
--BUT DON'T DRAG YER BLEEDIN' WRISTS BACK TO US.
PLEASE... P-PLEASE...
LAST TIME IT WAS A POLITE MATTER O' SCORCHIN' YER EYEBROWS, BUT NOW YOU'RE INTO THE ROSELLI BOYS FOR BETTER'N FIVE GRAND...
SO THIS TIME WE GOTTA--
--AXE YA HARDER.
YEEAAAHRR!
BHAKSH!
LET HIM CRAWL, BOYS--HE'S GOT GAMBLIN' DEBTS TO MAKE GOOD.
M-MY LEG...MY L-LEG...!
6

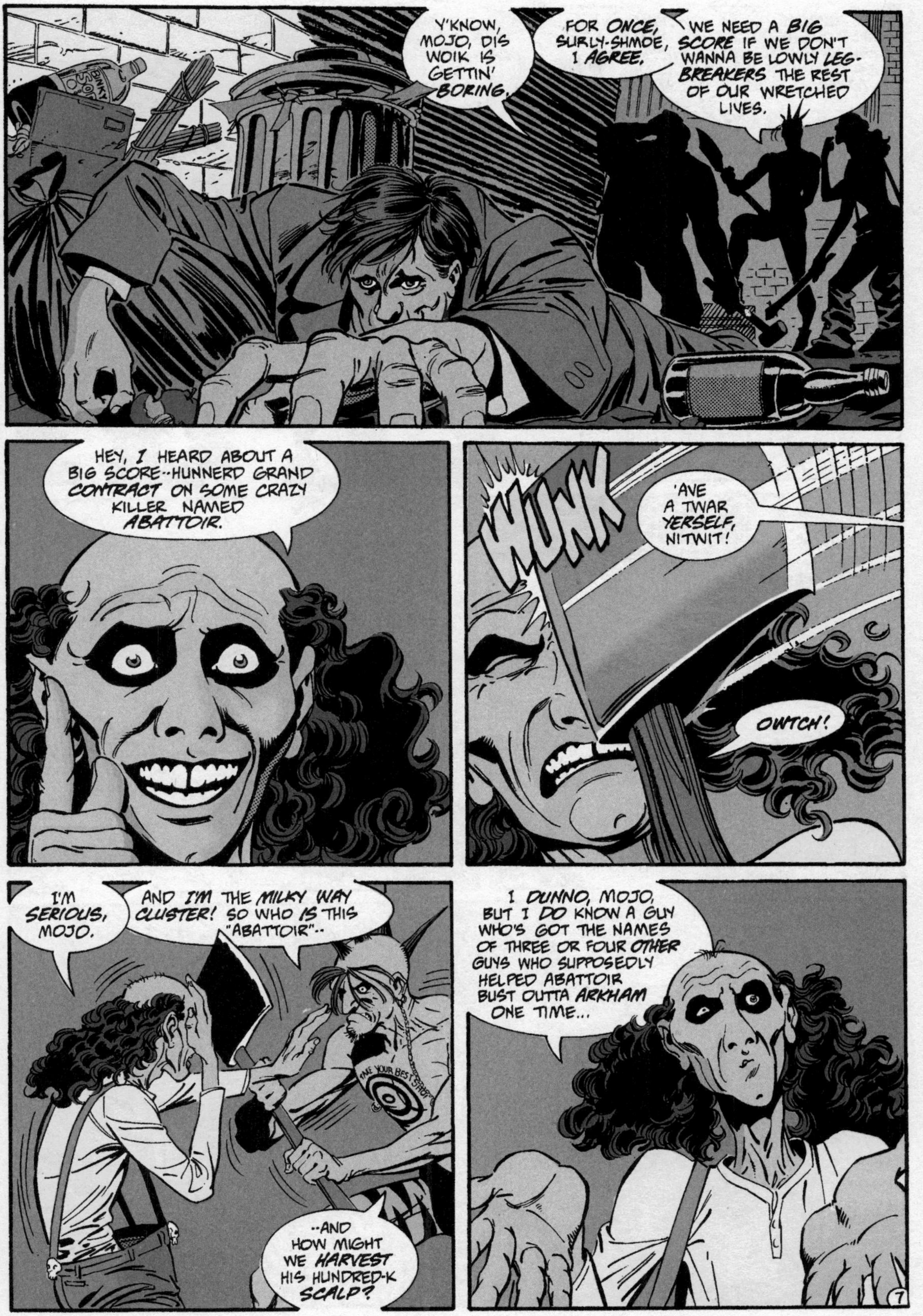
Y'KNOW, MOJO, DIS WOIK IS GETTIN' BORING.
FOR ONCE, SURLY-SHMOE, I AGREE.
WE NEED A BIG SCORE IF WE DON'T WANNA BE LOWLY LEG-BREAKERS THE REST OF OUR WRETCHED LIVES.
HEY, I HEARD ABOUT A BIG SCORE--HUNNERD GRAND CONTRACT ON SOME CRAZY KILLER NAMED ABATTOIR.
WHUNK
'AVE A TWAR YERSELF, NITWIT!
OWTCH!
I'M SERIOUS, MOJO.
AND I'M THE MILKY WAY CLUSTER! SO WHO IS THIS "ABATTOIR"--
TAKE YOUR BEST SHOT
--AND HOW MIGHT WE HARVEST HIS HUNDRED-K SCALP?
I DUNNO, MOJO, BUT I DO KNOW A GUY WHO'S GOT THE NAMES OF THREE OR FOUR OTHER GUYS WHO SUPPOSEDLY HELPED ABATTOIR BUST OUTTA ARKHAM ONE TIME...
7

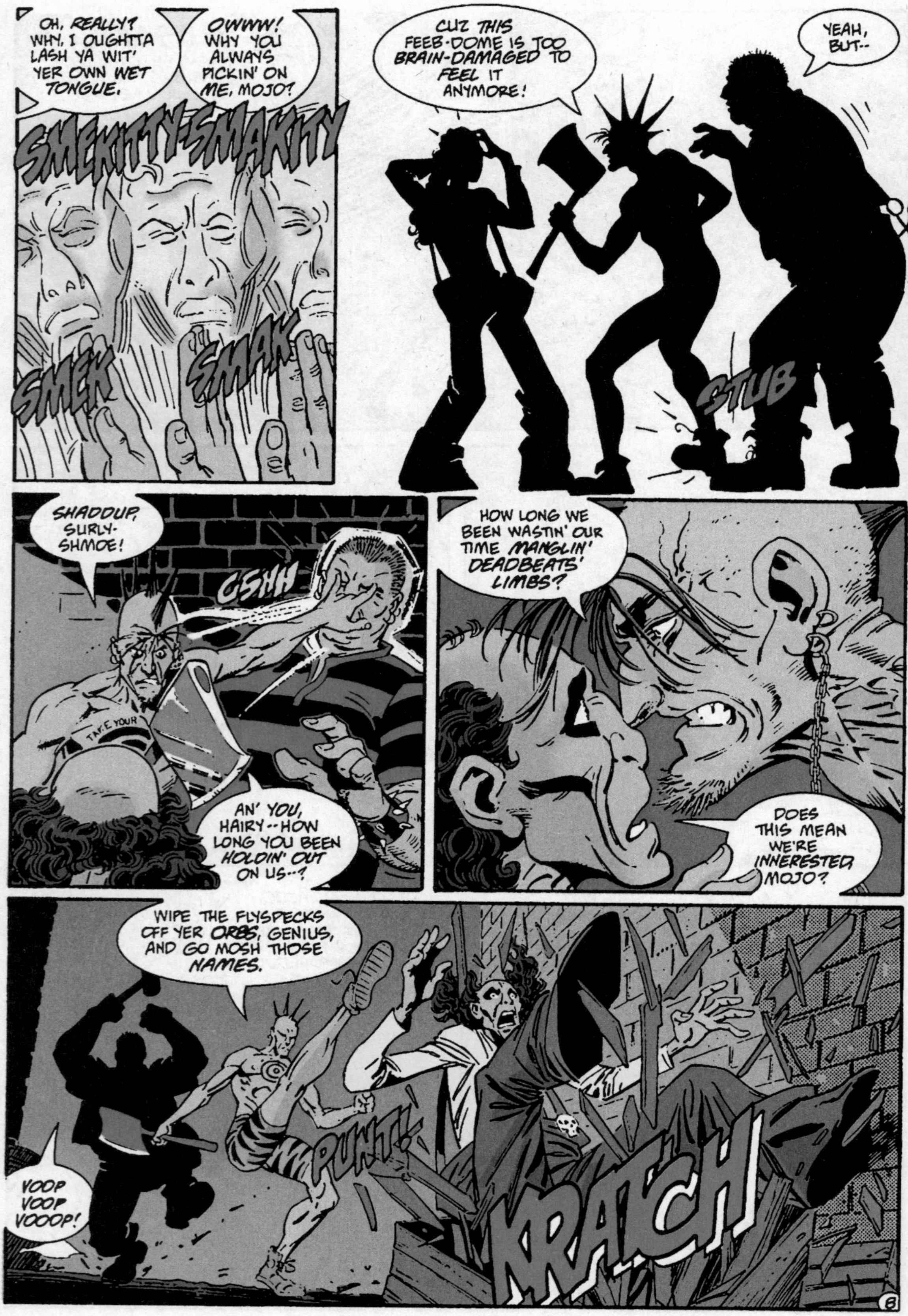
OH, REALLY? WHY, I OUGHTTA LASH YA WIT' YER OWN WET TONGUE.
OWWW! WHY YOU ALWAYS PICKIN' ON ME, MOJO?
SMEKITTY-SMAKITTY
SMEK
SMAK
CUZ THIS FEEB-DOME IS TOO BRAIN-DAMAGED TO FEEL IT ANYMORE!
YEAH, BUT--
STUB
SHADDUP, SURLY-SHMOE!
GSHH
TAKE YOUR
AN' YOU, HAIRY--HOW LONG YOU BEEN HOLDIN' OUT ON US--?
HOW LONG WE BEEN WASTIN' OUR TIME MANGLIN' DEADBEATS' LIMBS?
DOES THIS MEAN WE'RE INNERESTED, MOJO?
WIPE THE FLYSPECKS OFF YER ORBS, GENIUS, AND GO MOSH THOSE NAMES.
VOOP VOOP VOOOP!
PUNT!
KRATCH
8

HIS ROUNDS COMPLETED, KELVIN MAO QUITS THE STREETS...

...TRUDGES THROUGH MELTED SNOW AND MUCH WORSE...

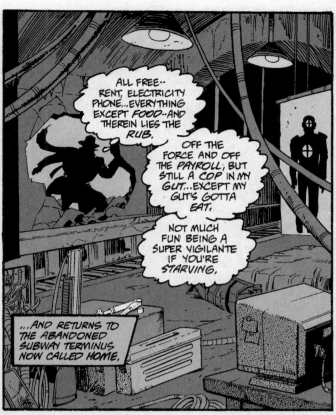

ALL FREE-- RENT, ELECTRICITY PHONE...EVERYTHING EXCEPT FOOD--AND THEREIN LIES THE RUB.

OFF THE FORCE AND OFF THE PAYROLL, BUT STILL A COP IN MY GUT...EXCEPT MY GUT'S GOTTA EAT.

NOT MUCH FUN BEING A SUPER VIGILANTE IF YOU'RE STARVING.

...AND RETURNS TO THE ABANDONED SUBWAY TERMINUS NOW CALLED HOME.

STILL HARD TO BELIEVE WHAT HAPPENED TO ME...

9

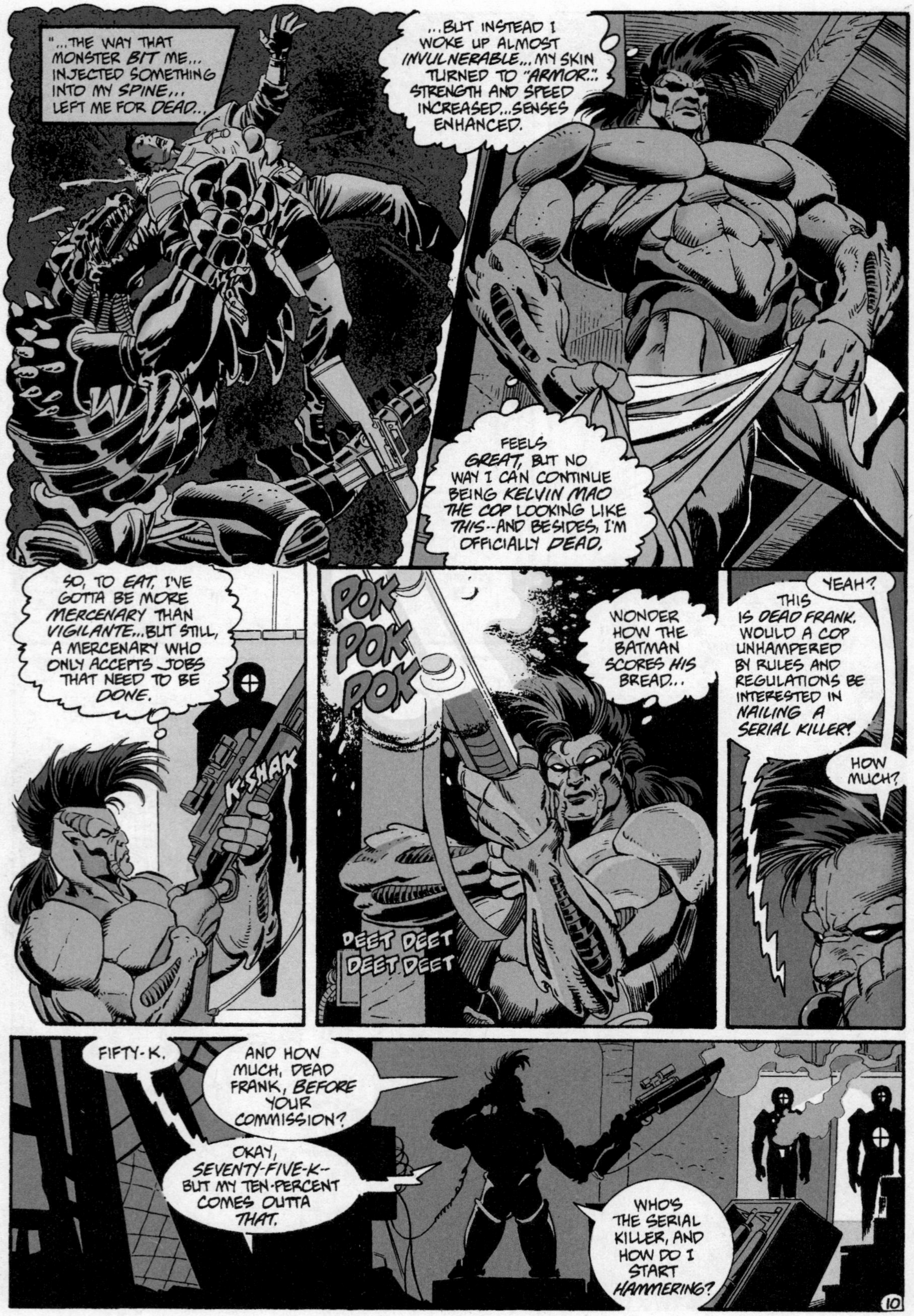

"...THE WAY THAT MONSTER BIT ME... INJECTED SOMETHING INTO MY SPINE... LEFT ME FOR DEAD...
...BUT INSTEAD I WOKE UP ALMOST INVULNERABLE... MY SKIN TURNED TO "ARMOR"... STRENGTH AND SPEED INCREASED...SENSES ENHANCED.
FEELS GREAT, BUT NO WAY I CAN CONTINUE BEING KELVIN MAO THE COP LOOKING LIKE THIS--AND BESIDES, I'M OFFICIALLY DEAD.
SO, TO EAT, I'VE GOTTA BE MORE MERCENARY THAN VIGILANTE...BUT STILL, A MERCENARY WHO ONLY ACCEPTS JOBS THAT NEED TO BE DONE.
K-SHAK
POK POK POK
WONDER HOW THE BATMAN SCORES HIS BREAD...
DEET DEET DEET DEET
YEAH?
THIS IS DEAD FRANK. WOULD A COP UNHAMPERED BY RULES AND REGULATIONS BE INTERESTED IN NAILING A SERIAL KILLER?
HOW MUCH?
FIFTY-K.
AND HOW MUCH, DEAD FRANK, BEFORE YOUR COMMISSION?
OKAY, SEVENTY-FIVE-K-- BUT MY TEN-PERCENT COMES OUTTA THAT.
WHO'S THE SERIAL KILLER, AND HOW DO I START HAMMERING?
10

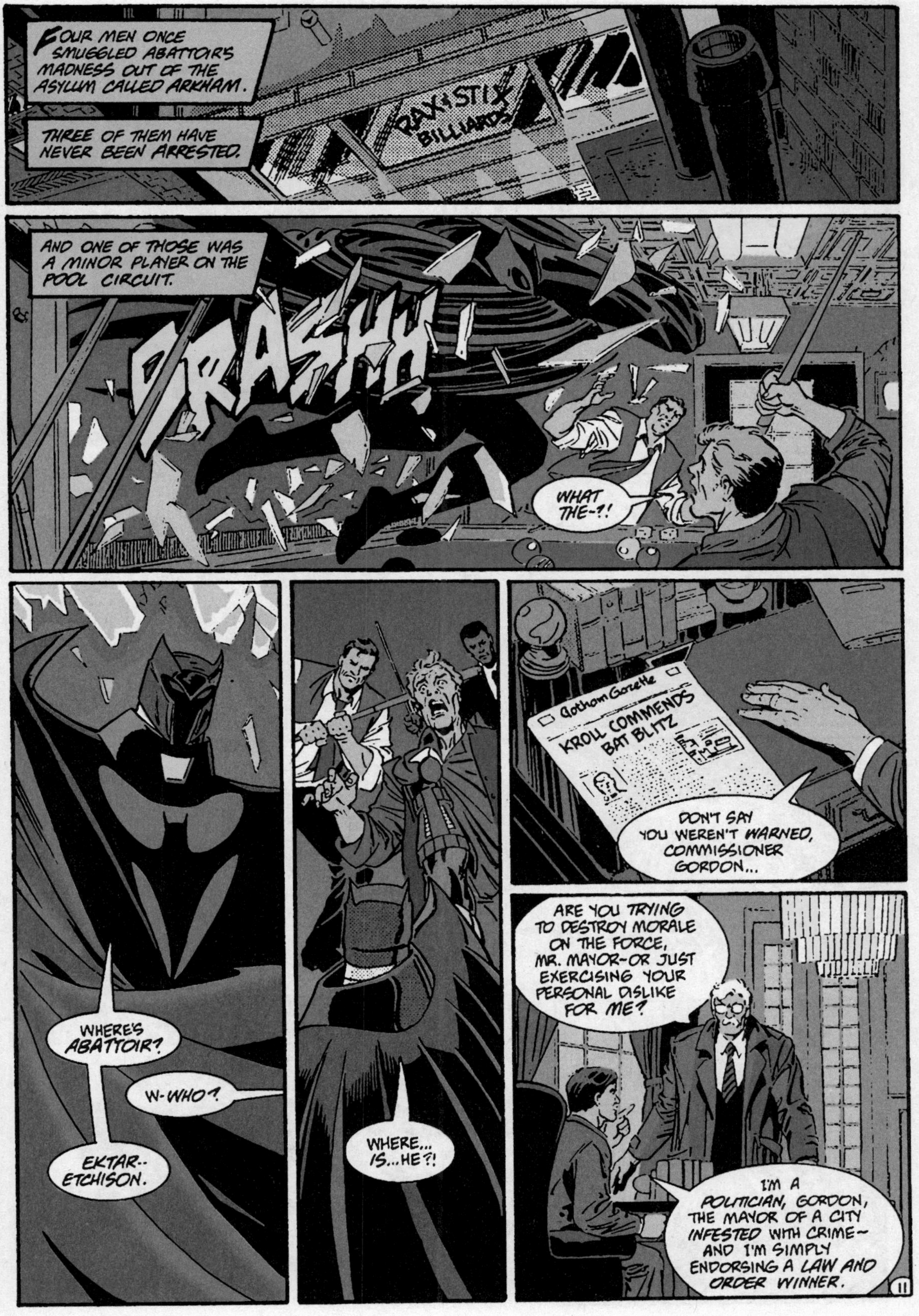

FOUR MEN ONCE SMUGGLED ABATTOIR'S MADNESS OUT OF THE ASYLUM CALLED ARKHAM.
THREE OF THEM HAVE NEVER BEEN ARRESTED.
RAX & STIX BILLIARDS
AND ONE OF THOSE WAS A MINOR PLAYER ON THE POOL CIRCUIT.
CRASHH
WHAT THE-?!
WHERE'S ABATTOIR?
W-WHO?
EKTAR.. ETCHISON.
WHERE... IS...HE?!
Gotham Gazette
KROLL COMMENDS BAT BLITZ
DON'T SAY YOU WEREN'T WARNED, COMMISSIONER GORDON...
ARE YOU TRYING TO DESTROY MORALE ON THE FORCE, MR. MAYOR-OR JUST EXERCISING YOUR PERSONAL DISLIKE FOR ME?
I'M A POLITICIAN, GORDON, THE MAYOR OF A CITY INFESTED WITH CRIME-AND I'M SIMPLY ENDORSING A LAW AND ORDER WINNER.
11

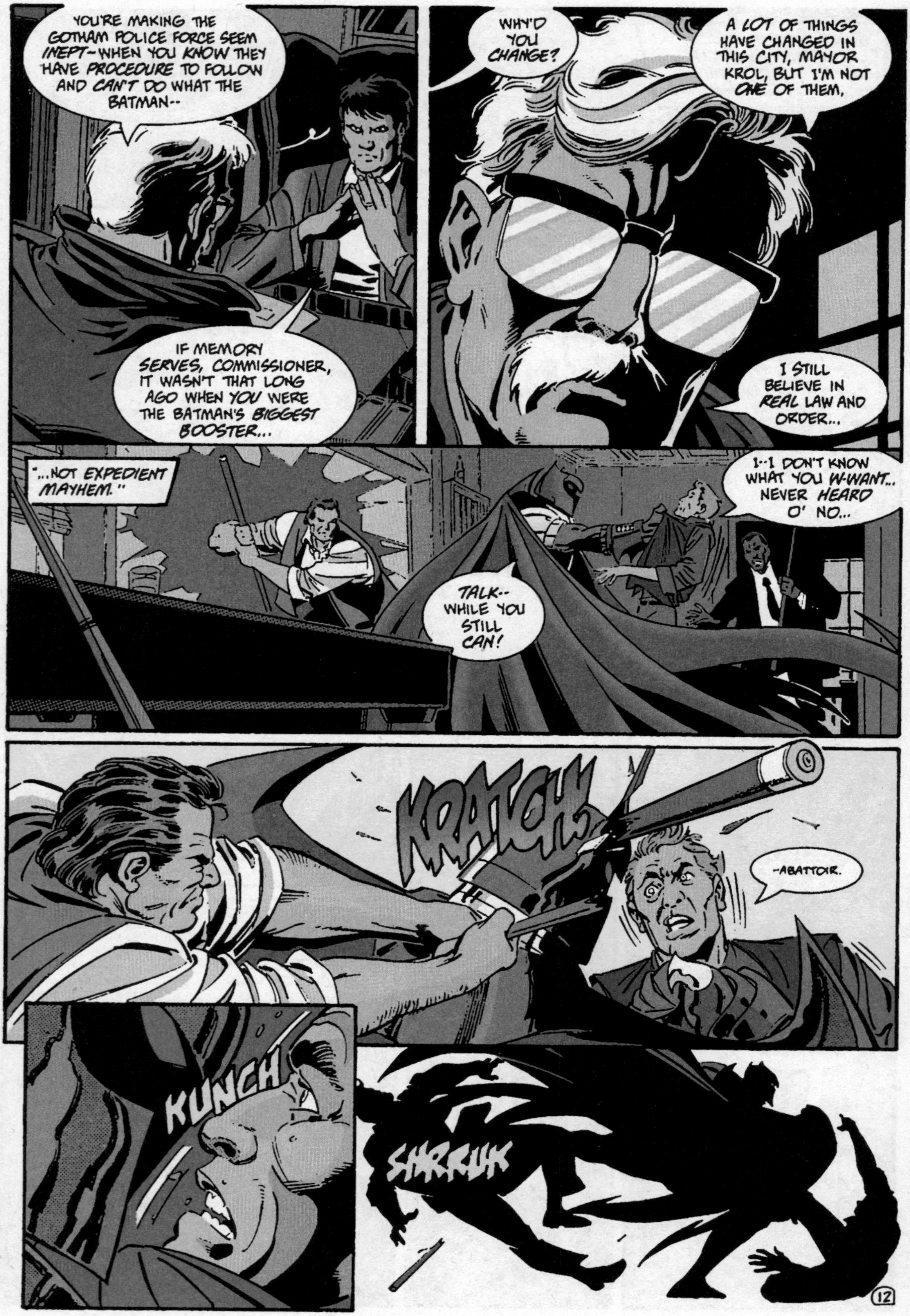
YOU'RE MAKING THE GOTHAM POLICE FORCE SEEM INEPT--WHEN YOU KNOW THEY HAVE PROCEDURE TO FOLLOW AND CAN'T DO WHAT THE BATMAN--
IF MEMORY SERVES, COMMISSIONER, IT WASN'T THAT LONG AGO WHEN YOU WERE THE BATMAN'S BIGGEST BOOSTER...
WHY'D YOU CHANGE?
A LOT OF THINGS HAVE CHANGED IN THIS CITY, MAYOR KROL, BUT I'M NOT ONE OF THEM.
I STILL BELIEVE IN REAL LAW AND ORDER...
"...NOT EXPEDIENT MAYHEM."
I--I DON'T KNOW WHAT YOU W-WANT... NEVER HEARD O' NO...
TALK-- WHILE YOU STILL CAN!
KRATCH
-ABATTOIR.
KUNCH
SHRRUK
12

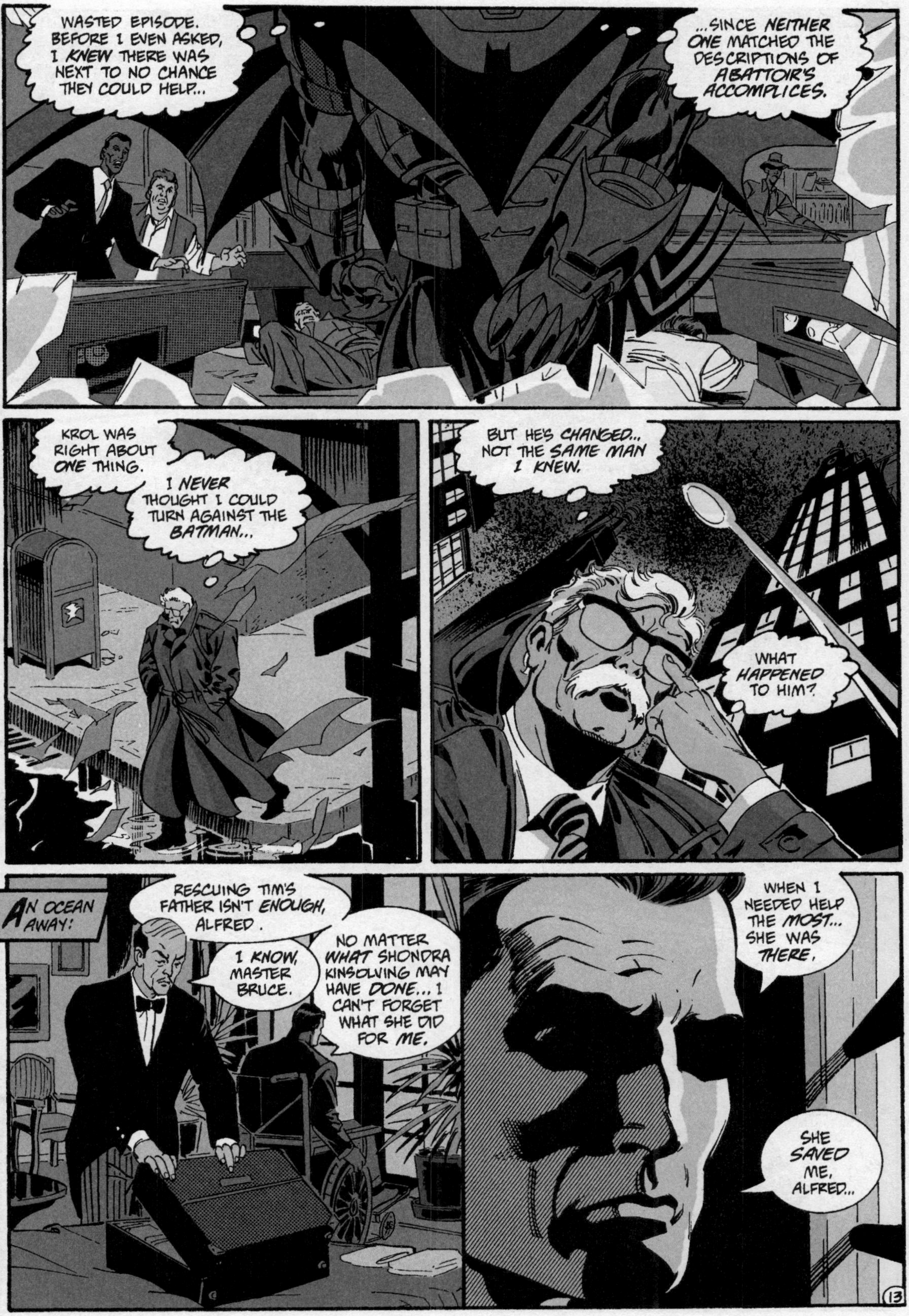
WASTED EPISODE. BEFORE I EVEN ASKED, I KNEW THERE WAS NEXT TO NO CHANCE THEY COULD HELP...
...SINCE NEITHER ONE MATCHED THE DESCRIPTIONS OF ABATTOIR'S ACCOMPLICES.
KROL WAS RIGHT ABOUT ONE THING.
I NEVER THOUGHT I COULD TURN AGAINST THE BATMAN...
BUT HE'S CHANGED... NOT THE SAME MAN I KNEW.
WHAT HAPPENED TO HIM?
AN OCEAN AWAY:
RESCUING TIM'S FATHER ISN'T ENOUGH, ALFRED.
I KNOW, MASTER BRUCE.
NO MATTER WHAT SHONDRA KINSOLVING MAY HAVE DONE... I CAN'T FORGET WHAT SHE DID FOR ME.
WHEN I NEEDED HELP THE MOST... SHE WAS THERE.
SHE SAVED ME, ALFRED...
13

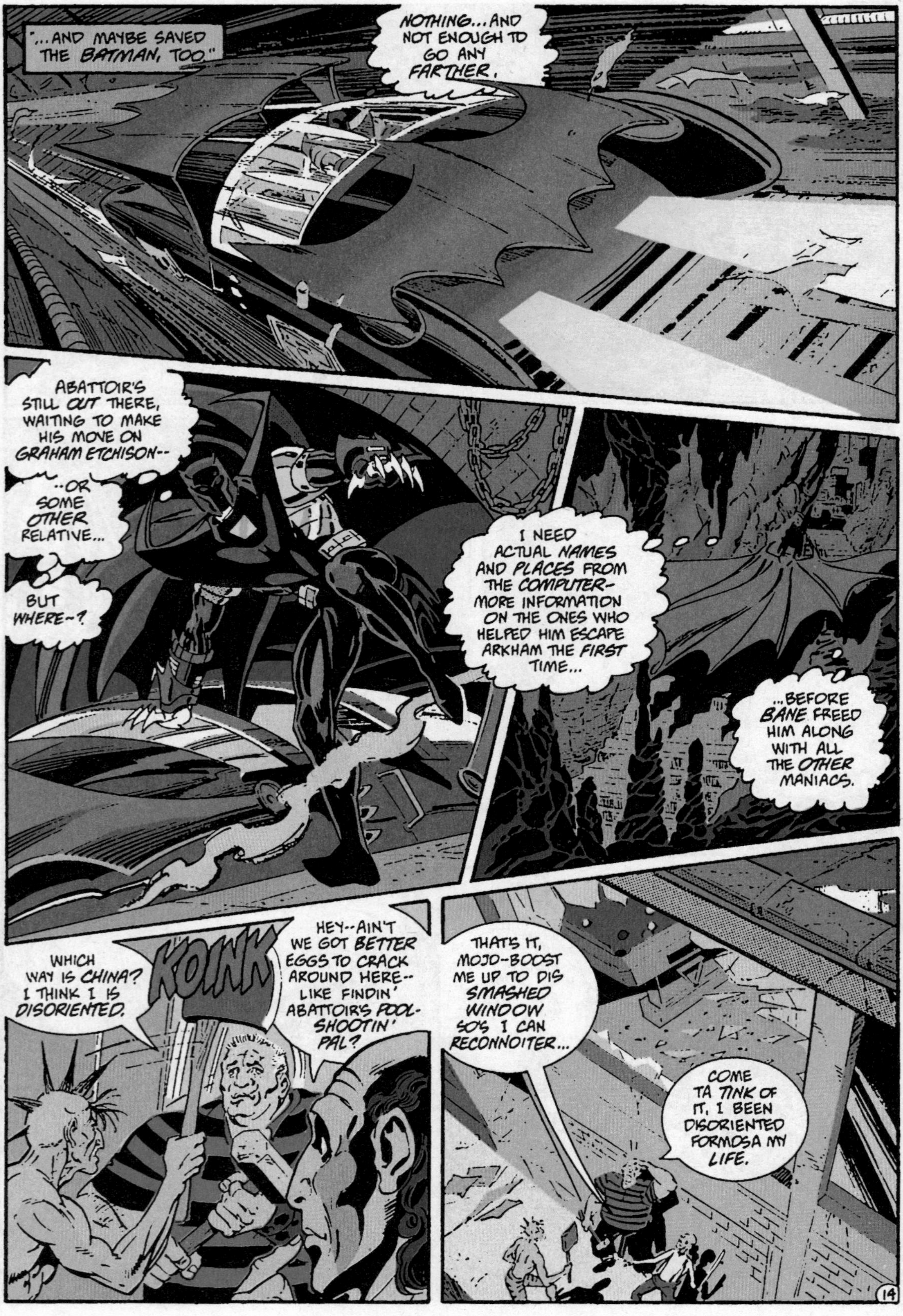

"...AND MAYBE SAVED THE BATMAN, TOO."
NOTHING...AND NOT ENOUGH TO GO ANY FARTHER.
ABATTOIR'S STILL OUT THERE, WAITING TO MAKE HIS MOVE ON GRAHAM ETCHISON--
..OR SOME OTHER RELATIVE...
BUT WHERE--?
I NEED ACTUAL NAMES AND PLACES FROM THE COMPUTER-- MORE INFORMATION ON THE ONES WHO HELPED HIM ESCAPE ARKHAM THE FIRST TIME...
...BEFORE BANE FREED HIM ALONG WITH ALL THE OTHER MANIACS.
WHICH WAY IS CHINA? I THINK I IS DISORIENTED.
KOINK
HEY--AIN'T WE GOT BETTER EGGS TO CRACK AROUND HERE-- LIKE FINDIN' ABATTOIR'S POOL-SHOOTIN' PAL?
THAT'S IT, MOJO--BOOST ME UP TO DIS SMASHED WINDOW SO'S I CAN RECONNOITER...
COME TA TINK OF IT, I BEEN DISORIENTED FORMOSA MY LIFE.
14

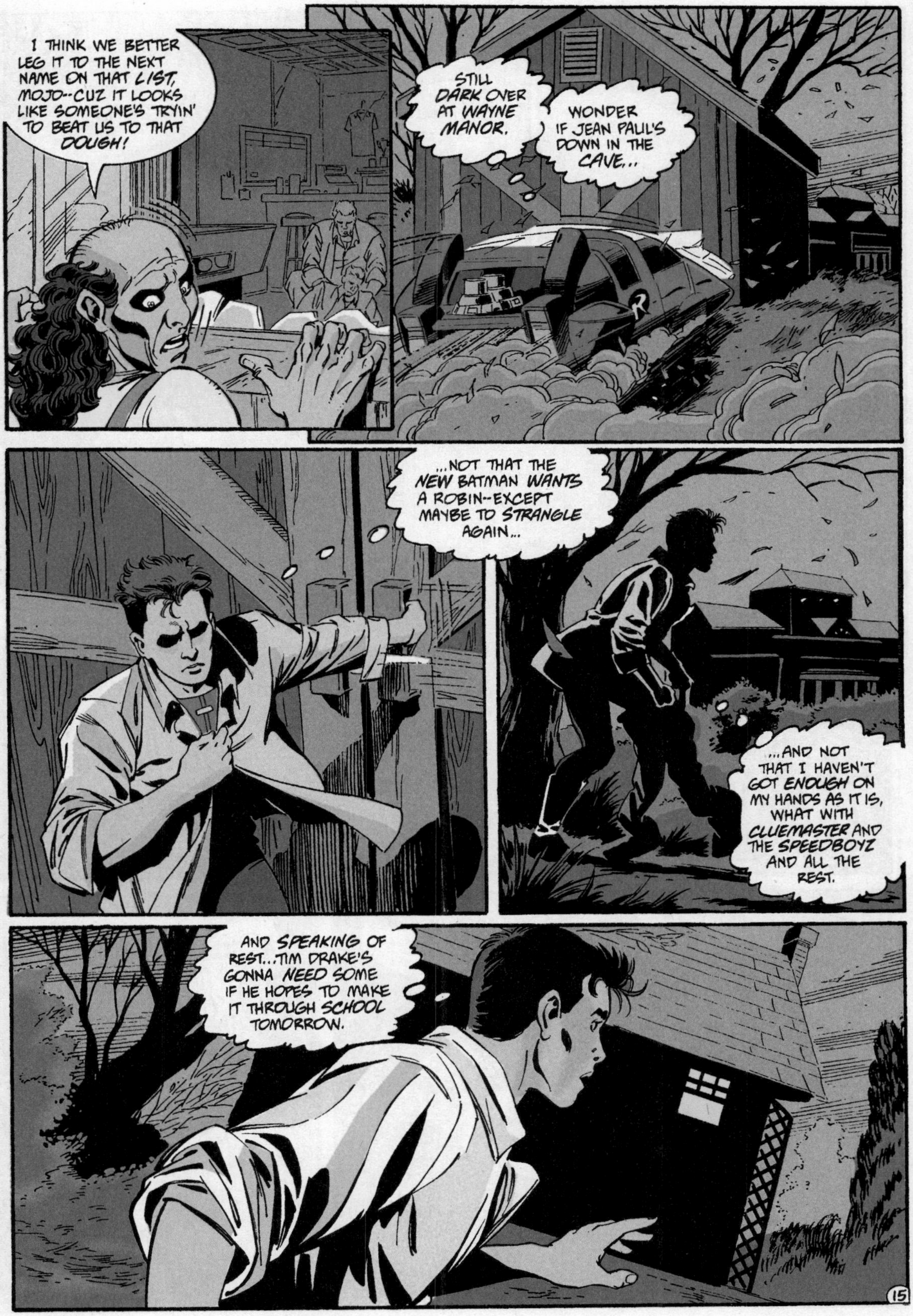
I THINK WE BETTER LEG IT TO THE NEXT NAME ON THAT LIST, MOJO--CUZ IT LOOKS LIKE SOMEONE'S TRYIN' TO BEAT US TO THAT DOUGH!
STILL DARK OVER AT WAYNE MANOR.
WONDER IF JEAN PAUL'S DOWN IN THE CAVE...
...NOT THAT THE NEW BATMAN WANTS A ROBIN--EXCEPT MAYBE TO STRANGLE AGAIN...
...AND NOT THAT I HAVEN'T GOT ENOUGH ON MY HANDS AS IT IS, WHAT WITH CLUEMASTER AND THE SPEEDBOYZ AND ALL THE REST.
AND SPEAKING OF REST...TIM DRAKE'S GONNA NEED SOME IF HE HOPES TO MAKE IT THROUGH SCHOOL TOMORROW.
15

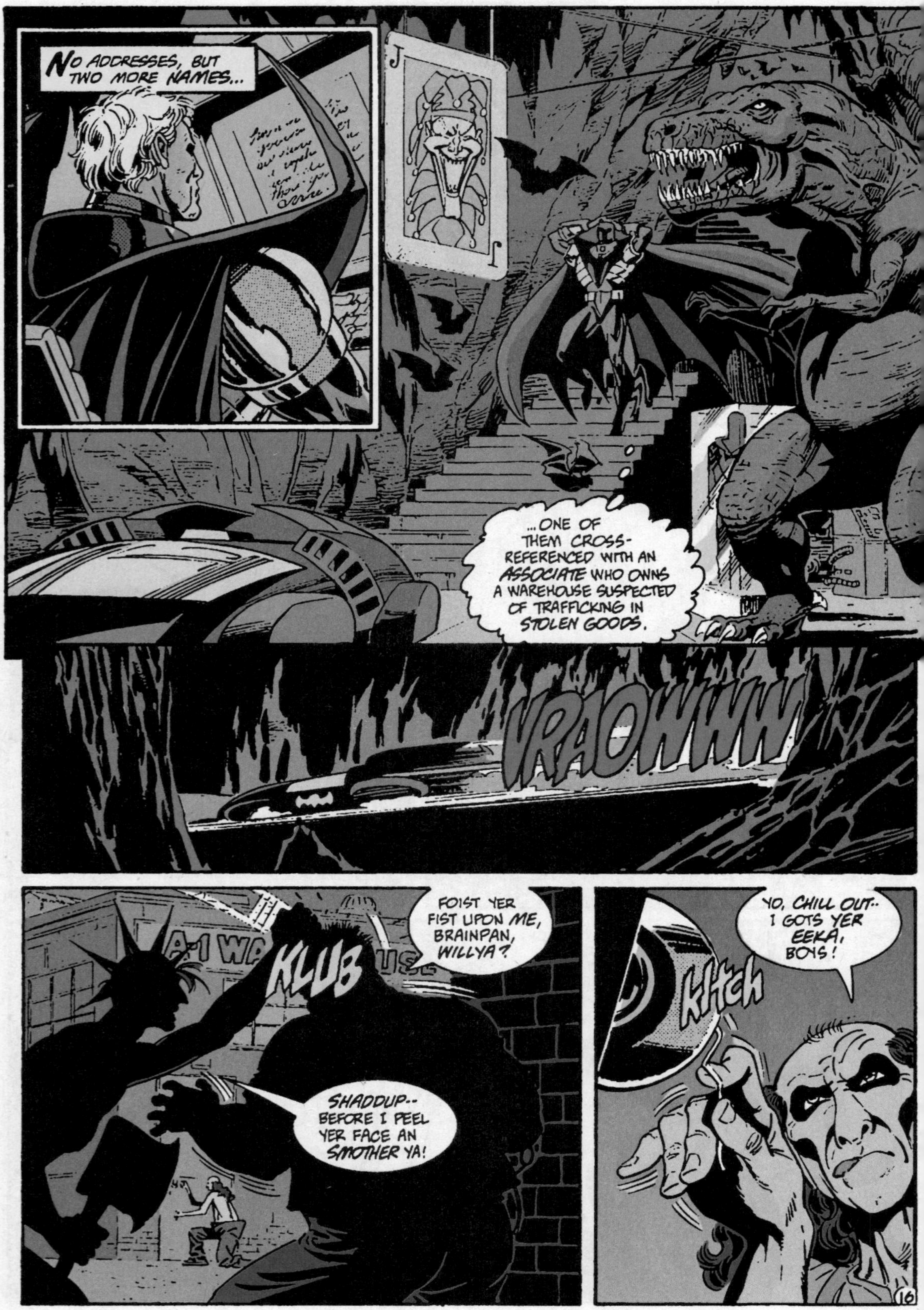

NO ADDRESSES, BUT TWO MORE NAMES...
...ONE OF THEM CROSS-REFERENCED WITH AN ASSOCIATE WHO OWNS A WAREHOUSE SUSPECTED OF TRAFFICKING IN STOLEN GOODS.
VRAOWWW
FOIST YER FIST UPON ME, BRAINPAN, WILLYA?
KLUB
SHADDUP-- BEFORE I PEEL YER FACE AN SMOTHER YA!
YO, CHILL OUT.. I GOTS YER EEKA, BOYS!
kltch
16

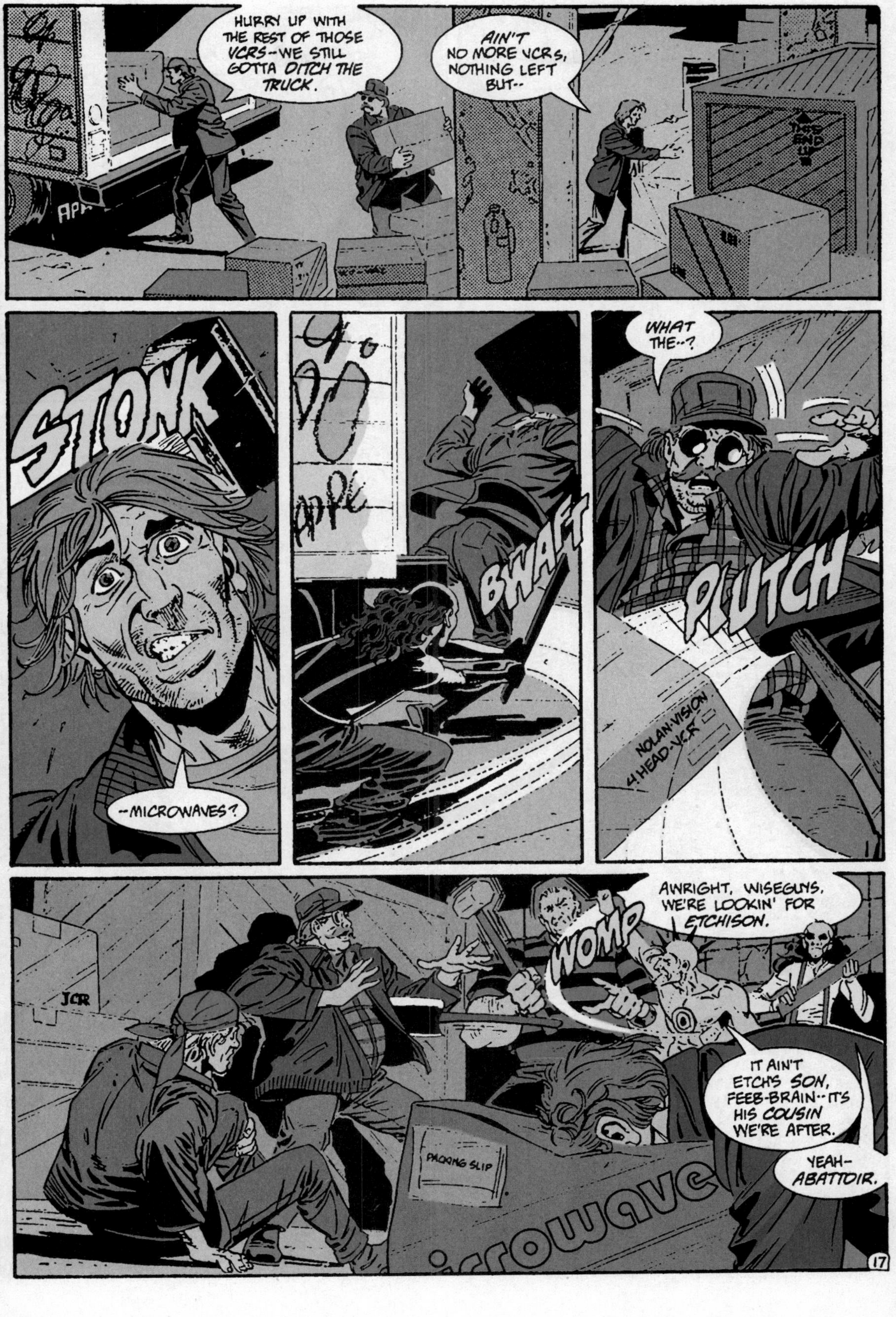
HURRY UP WITH THE REST OF THOSE VCRS--WE STILL GOTTA DITCH THE TRUCK.
AIN'T NO MORE VCRS, NOTHING LEFT BUT--
STONK
--MICROWAVES?
BWAFT
WHAT THE--?
PLUTCH
NOLAN·VISION 4 HEAD·VCR
WOMP
AWRIGHT, WISEGUYS. WE'RE LOOKIN' FOR ETCHISON.
IT AIN'T ETCH'S SON, FEEB-BRAIN--IT'S HIS COUSIN WE'RE AFTER.
YEAH-ABATTOIR.
17

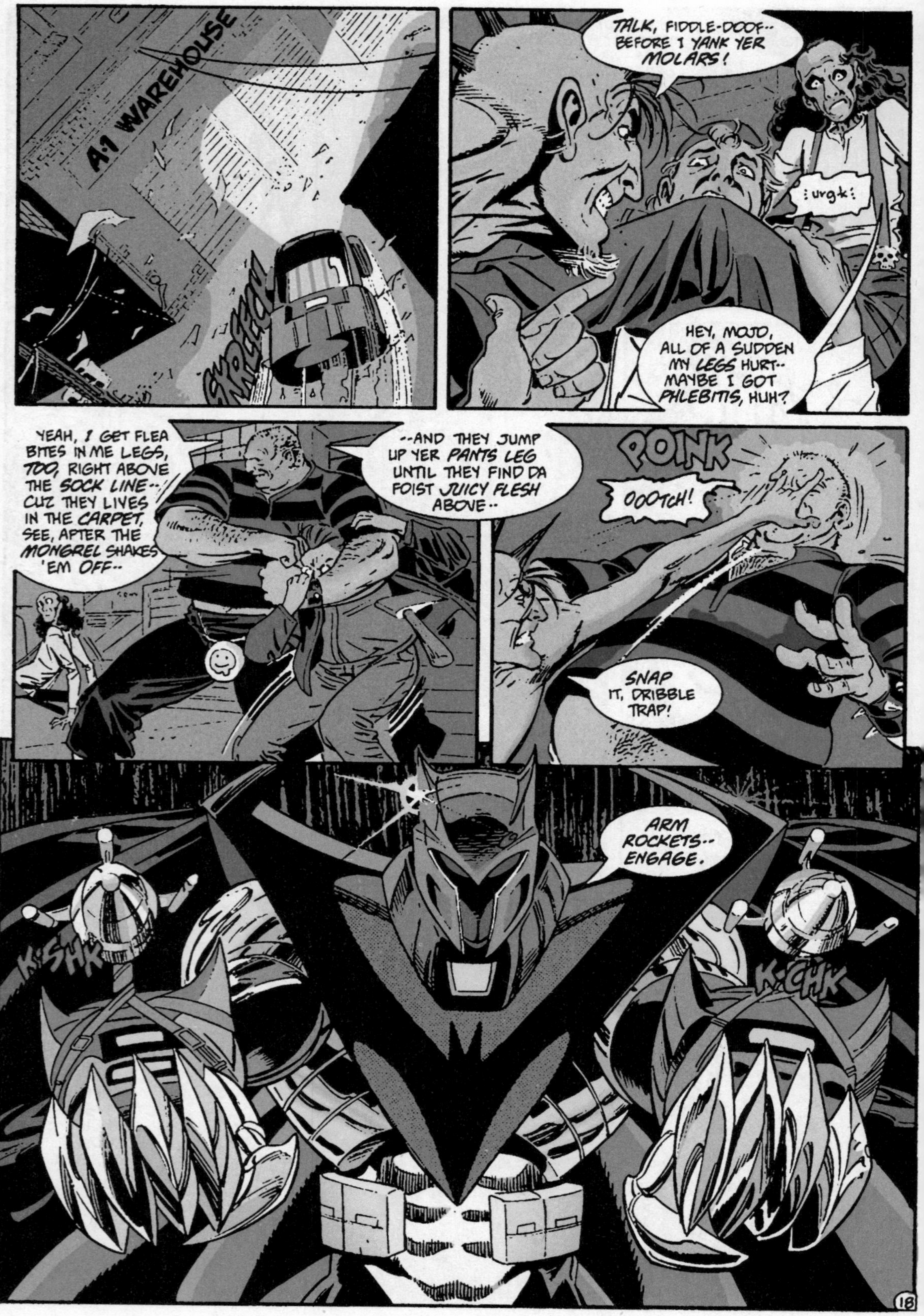
A-1 WAREHOUSE
SKREEEECH
TALK, FIDDLE-DOOF-- BEFORE I YANK YER MOLARS!
:urg-k:
HEY, MOJO, ALL OF A SUDDEN MY LEGS HURT-- MAYBE I GOT PHLEBITIS, HUH?
YEAH, I GET FLEA BITES IN ME LEGS, TOO, RIGHT ABOVE THE SOCK LINE-- CUZ THEY LIVES IN THE CARPET, SEE, AFTER THE MONGREL SHAKES 'EM OFF--
--AND THEY JUMP UP YER PANTS LEG UNTIL THEY FIND DA FOIST JUICY FLESH ABOVE--
POINK
OOOTCH!
SNAP IT, DRIBBLE TRAP!
ARM ROCKETS-- ENGAGE.
K-SHK
K-CHK
18

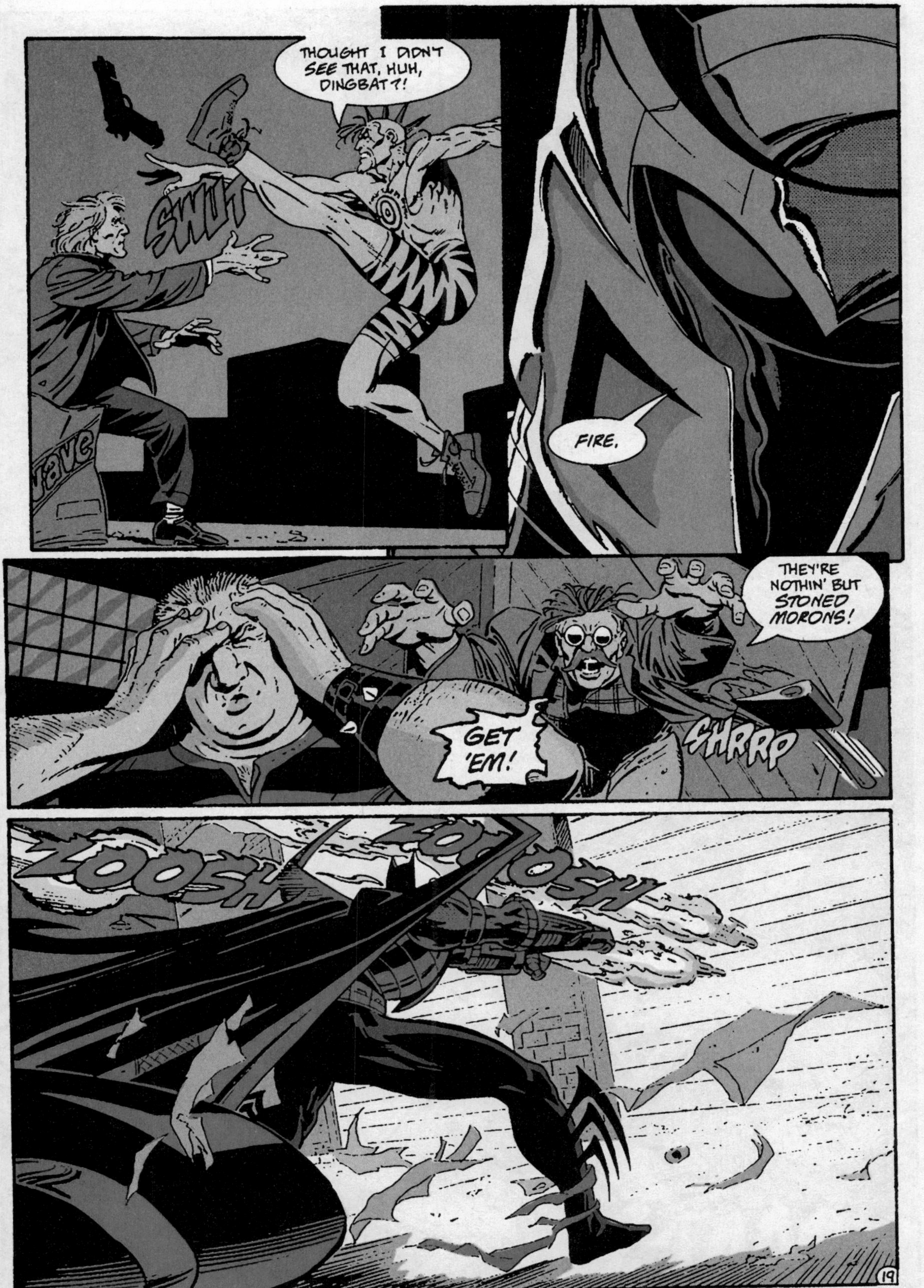
THOUGHT I DIDN'T SEE THAT, HUH, DINGBAT?!
SWUT
FIRE.
THEY'RE NOTHIN' BUT STONED MORONS!
GET 'EM!
SHRRP
ZOOSH
ZOOOSH
19

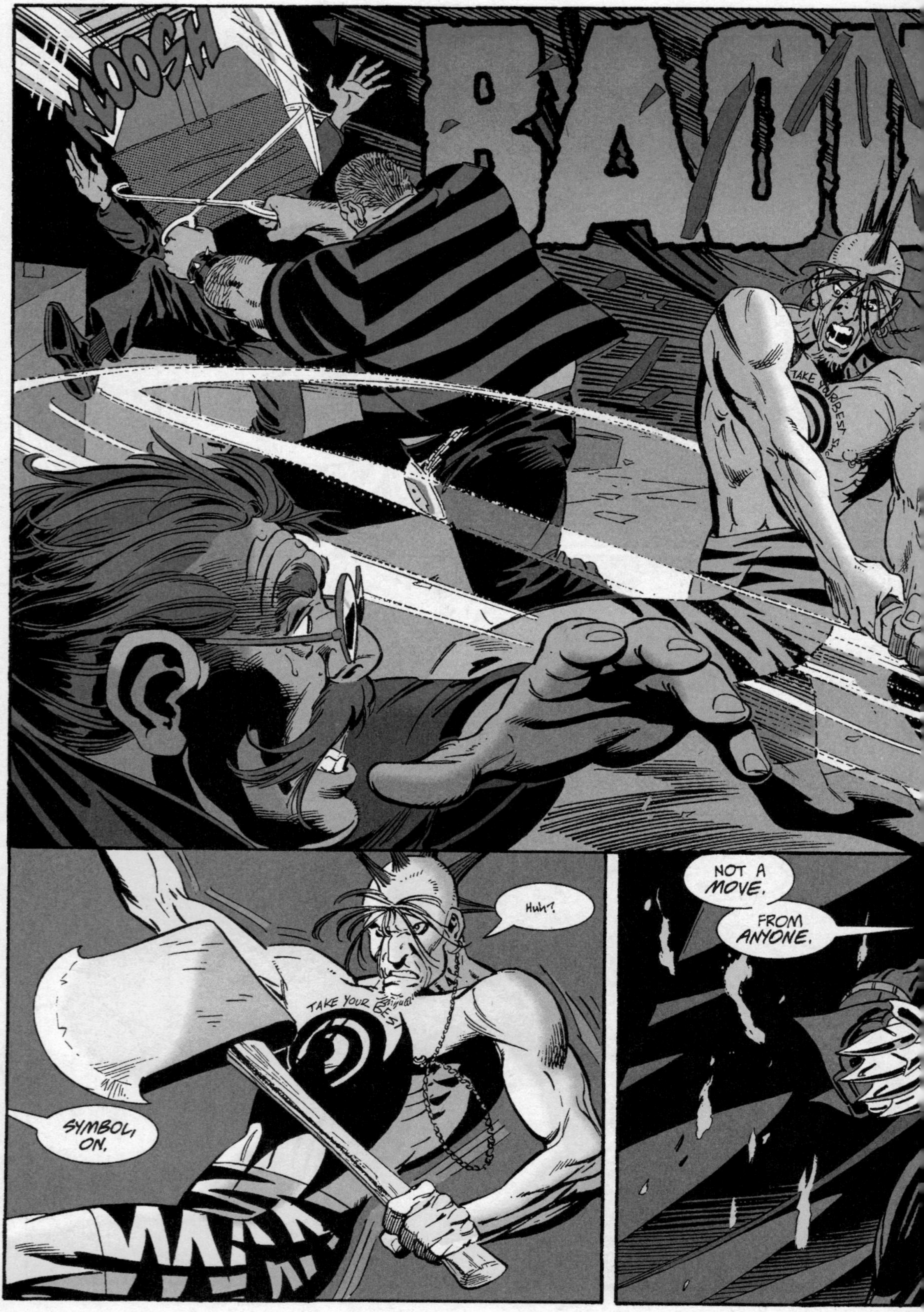

KLOOSH
RA
TAKE YOUR BEST SHOT
Huh?
TAKE YOUR BEST
SYMBOL, ON.
NOT A MOVE.
FROM ANYONE.

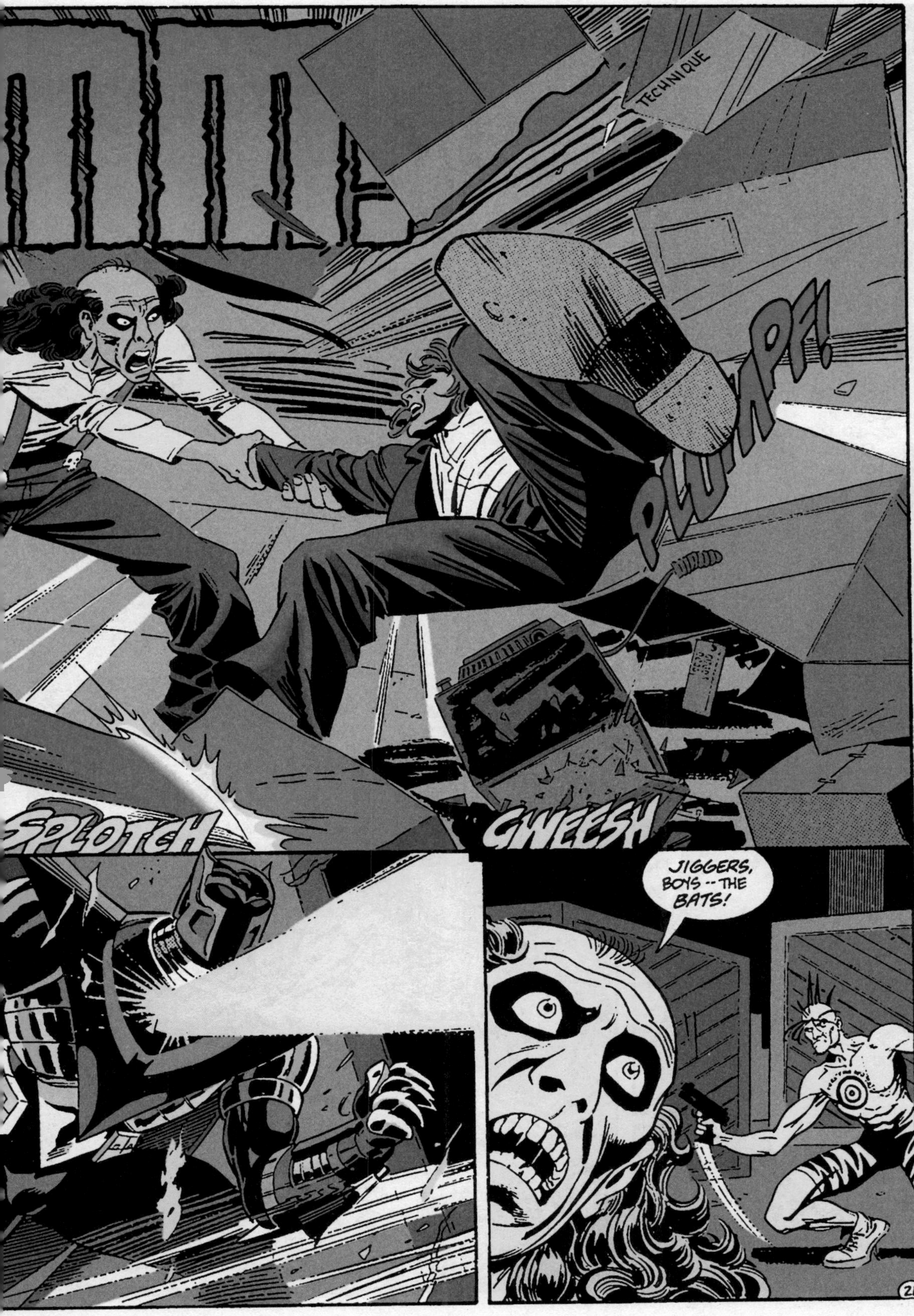
TECHNIQUE
PLUMPF!
SPLOTCH
GWEESH
JIGGERS, BOYS -- THE BATS!
21

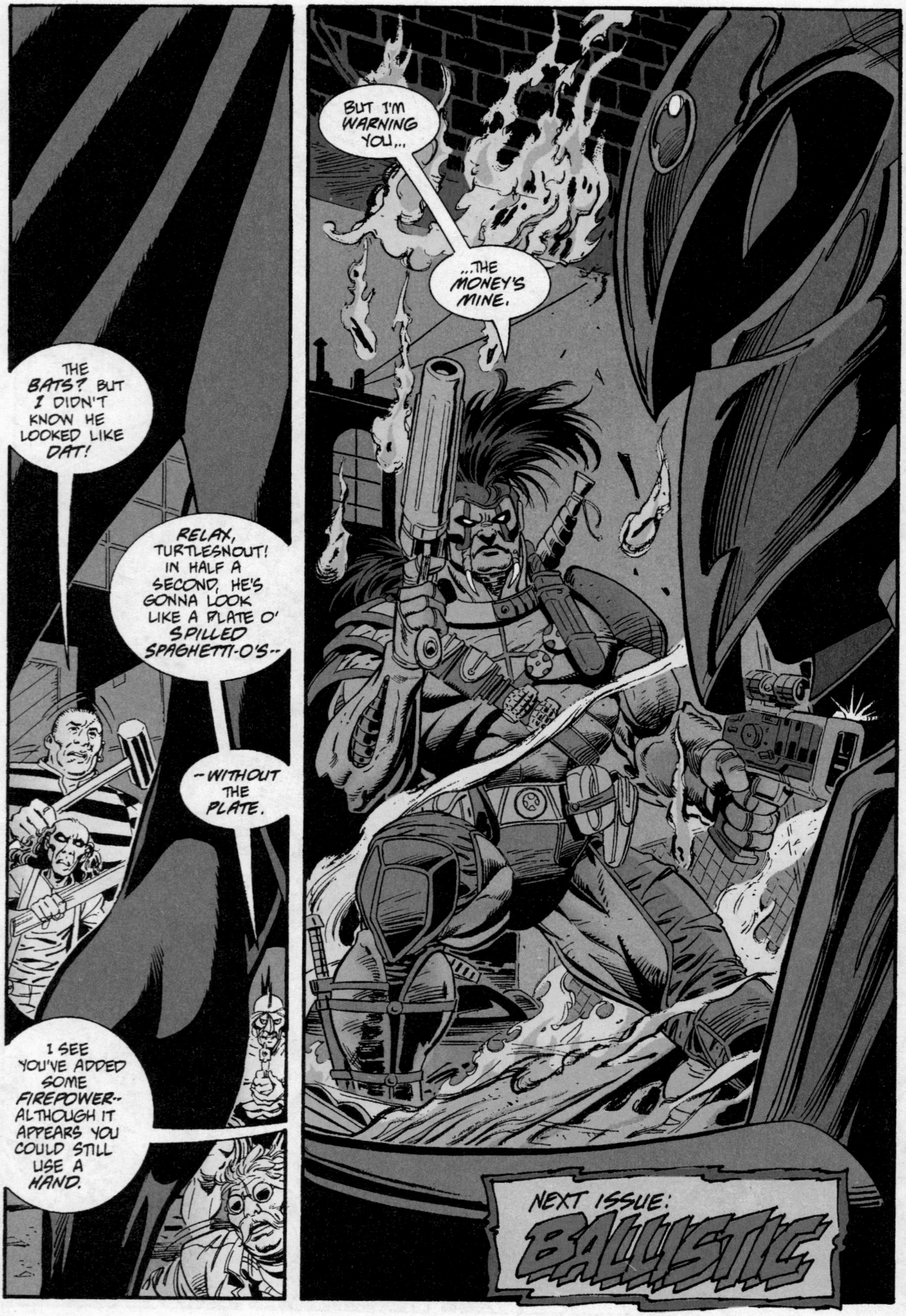
THE BATS? BUT I DIDN'T KNOW HE LOOKED LIKE DAT!
RELAX, TURTLESNOUT! IN HALF A SECOND, HE'S GONNA LOOK LIKE A PLATE O' SPILLED SPAGHETTI-O'S--
--WITHOUT THE PLATE.
I SEE YOU'VE ADDED SOME FIREPOWER-- ALTHOUGH IT APPEARS YOU COULD STILL USE A HAND.
BUT I'M WARNING YOU...
...THE MONEY'S MINE.
NEXT ISSUE:
BALLISTIC

Cover art by **KELLEY JONES**

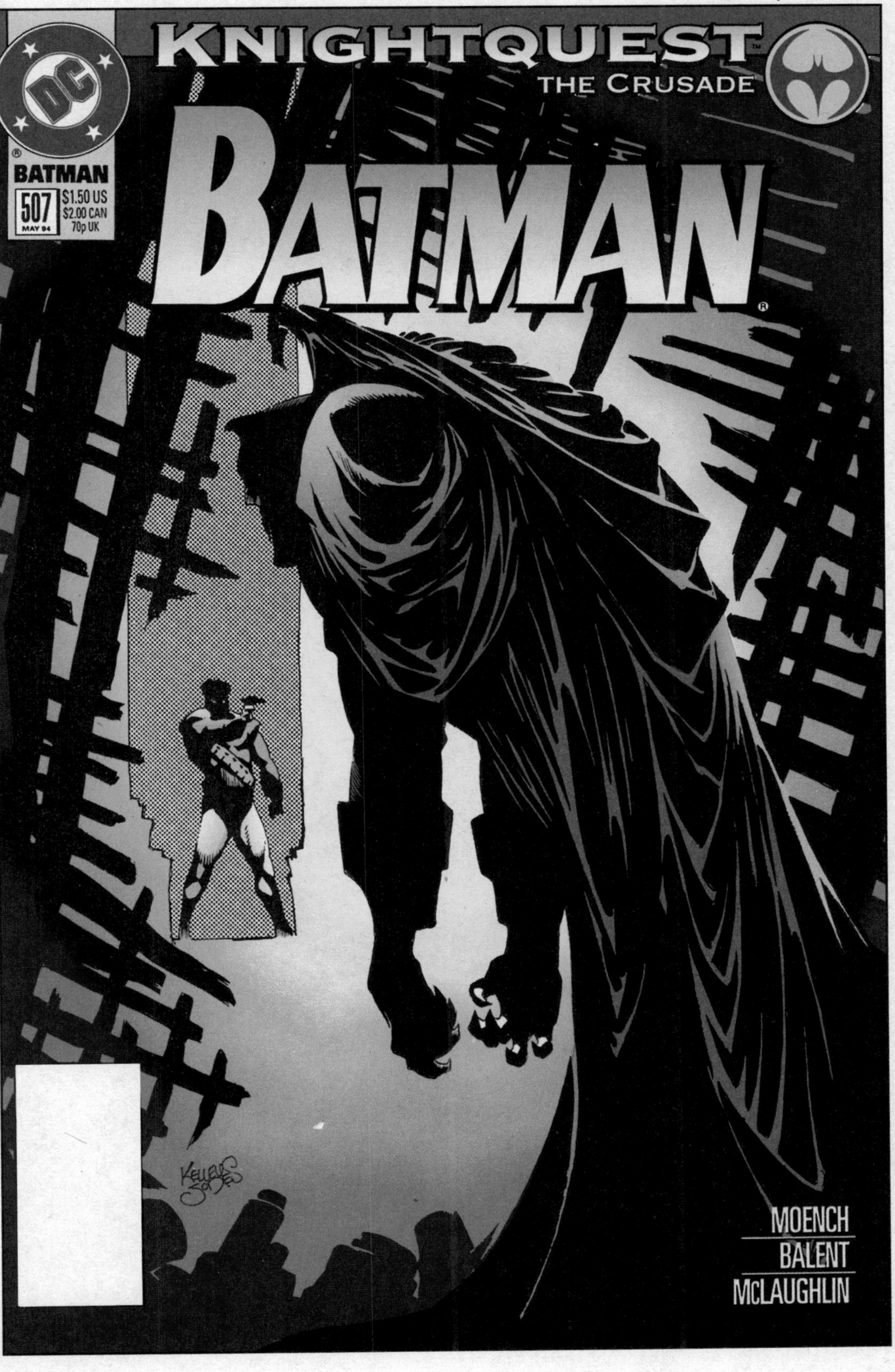
KNIGHTQUEST
THE CRUSADE
BATMAN
507
$1.50 US
$2.00 CAN
70p UK
MAY 94
BATMAN
MOENCH
BALENT
McLAUGHLIN

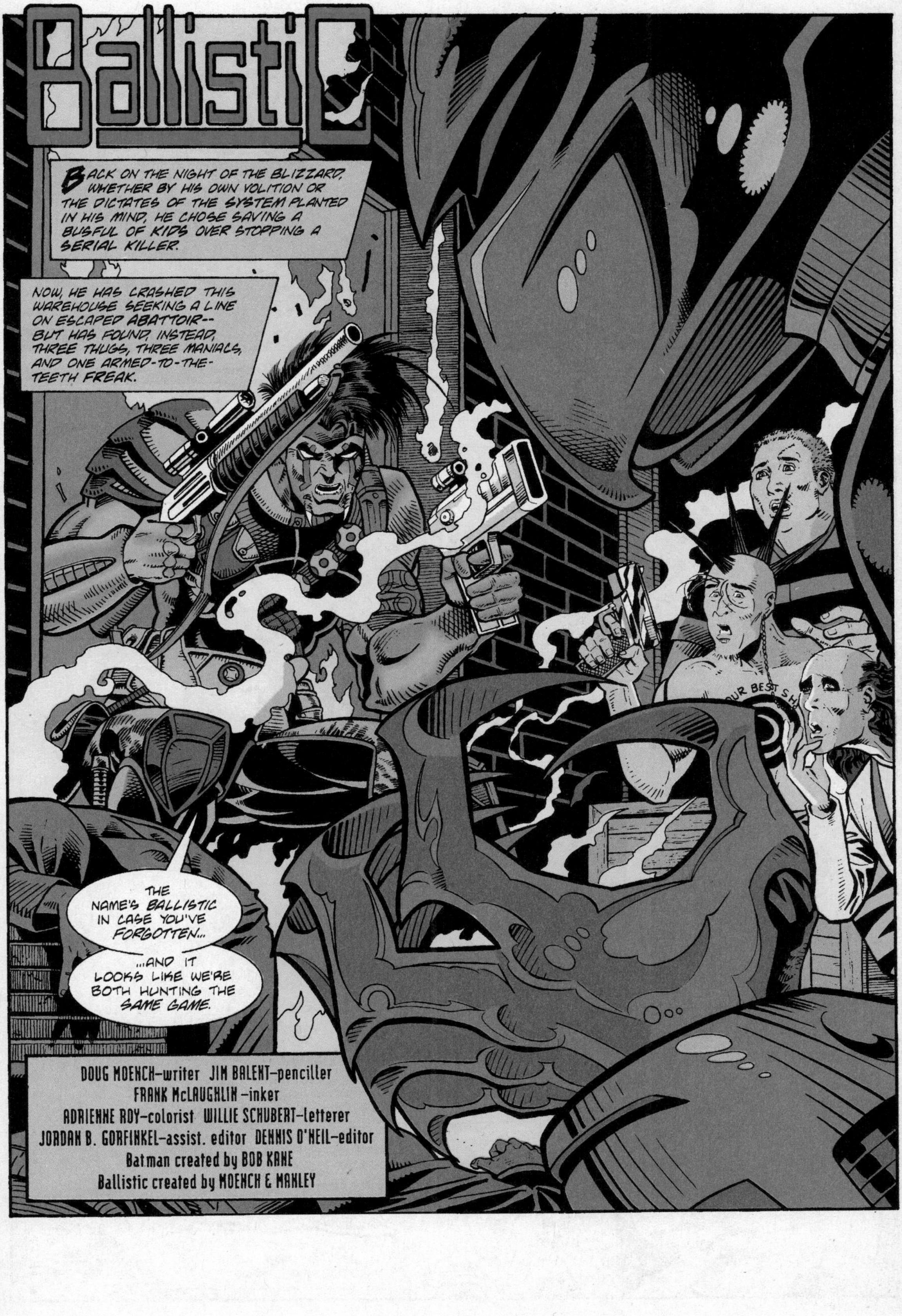
Ballistic
BACK ON THE NIGHT OF THE BLIZZARD, WHETHER BY HIS OWN VOLITION OR THE DICTATES OF THE SYSTEM PLANTED IN HIS MIND, HE CHOSE SAVING A BUSFUL OF KIDS OVER STOPPING A SERIAL KILLER.
NOW, HE HAS CRASHED THIS WAREHOUSE SEEKING A LINE ON ESCAPED ABATTOIR-- BUT HAS FOUND, INSTEAD, THREE THUGS, THREE MANIACS, AND ONE ARMED-TO-THE-TEETH FREAK.
THE NAME'S BALLISTIC IN CASE YOU'VE FORGOTTEN...
...AND IT LOOKS LIKE WE'RE BOTH HUNTING THE SAME GAME.
DOUG MOENCH–writer JIM BALENT–penciller
FRANK McLAUGHLIN–inker
ADRIENNE ROY–colorist WILLIE SCHUBERT–letterer
JORDAN B. GORFINKEL–assist. editor DENNIS O'NEIL–editor
Batman created by BOB KANE
Ballistic created by MOENCH & MANLEY

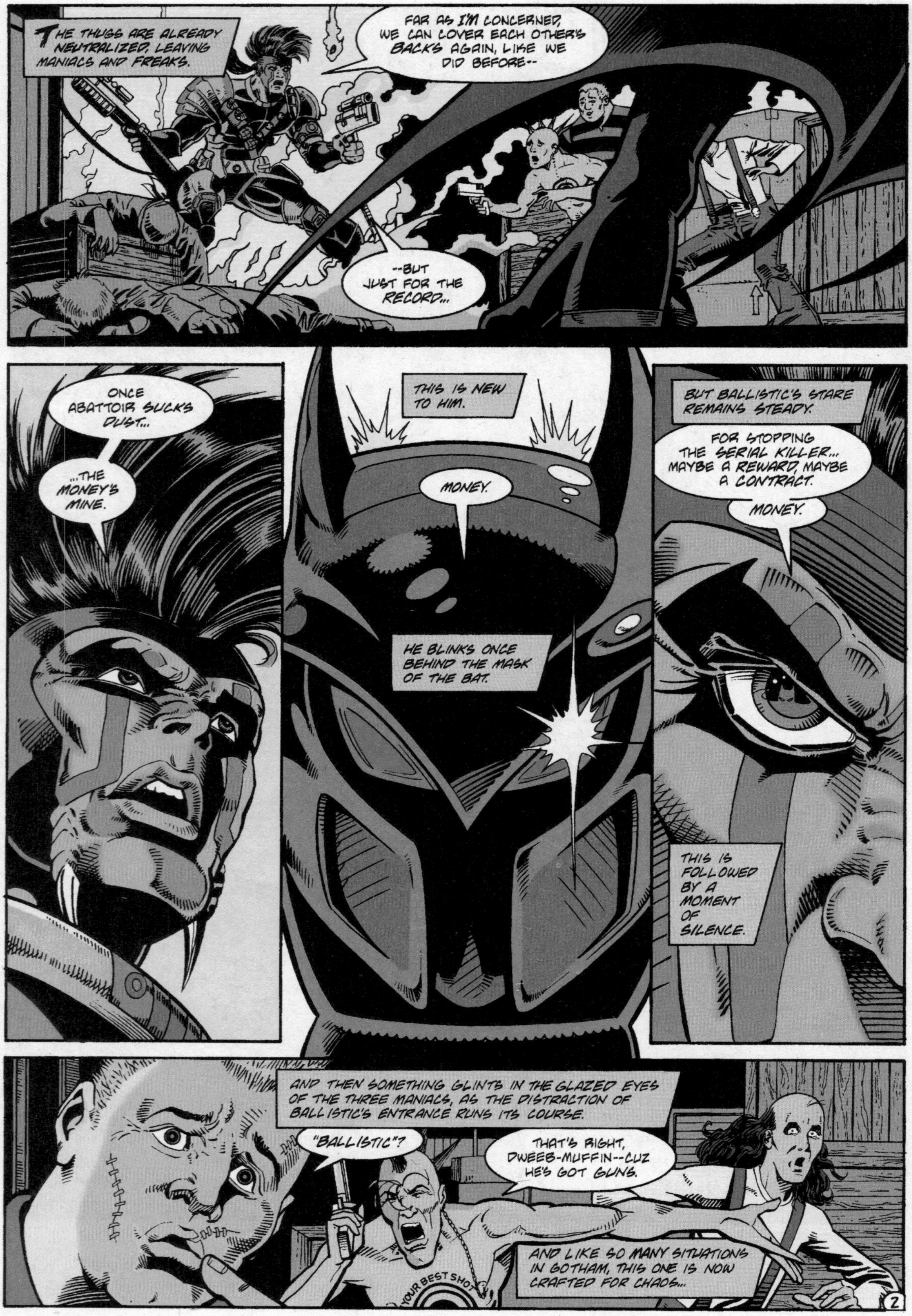

THE THUGS ARE ALREADY NEUTRALIZED, LEAVING MANIACS AND FREAKS.
FAR AS I'M CONCERNED, WE CAN COVER EACH OTHER'S BACKS AGAIN, LIKE WE DID BEFORE--
--BUT JUST FOR THE RECORD...
ONCE ABATTOIR SUCKS DUST...
...THE MONEY'S MINE.
THIS IS NEW TO HIM.
MONEY.
HE BLINKS ONCE BEHIND THE MASK OF THE BAT.
BUT BALLISTIC'S STARE REMAINS STEADY.
FOR STOPPING THE SERIAL KILLER... MAYBE A REWARD, MAYBE A CONTRACT.
MONEY.
THIS IS FOLLOWED BY A MOMENT OF SILENCE.
AND THEN SOMETHING GLINTS IN THE GLAZED EYES OF THE THREE MANIACS, AS THE DISTRACTION OF BALLISTIC'S ENTRANCE RUNS ITS COURSE.
"BALLISTIC"?
THAT'S RIGHT, DWEEB-MUFFIN--CUZ HE'S GOT GUNS.
YOUR BEST SHOT
AND LIKE SO MANY SITUATIONS IN GOTHAM, THIS ONE IS NOW CRAFTED FOR CHAOS...
2

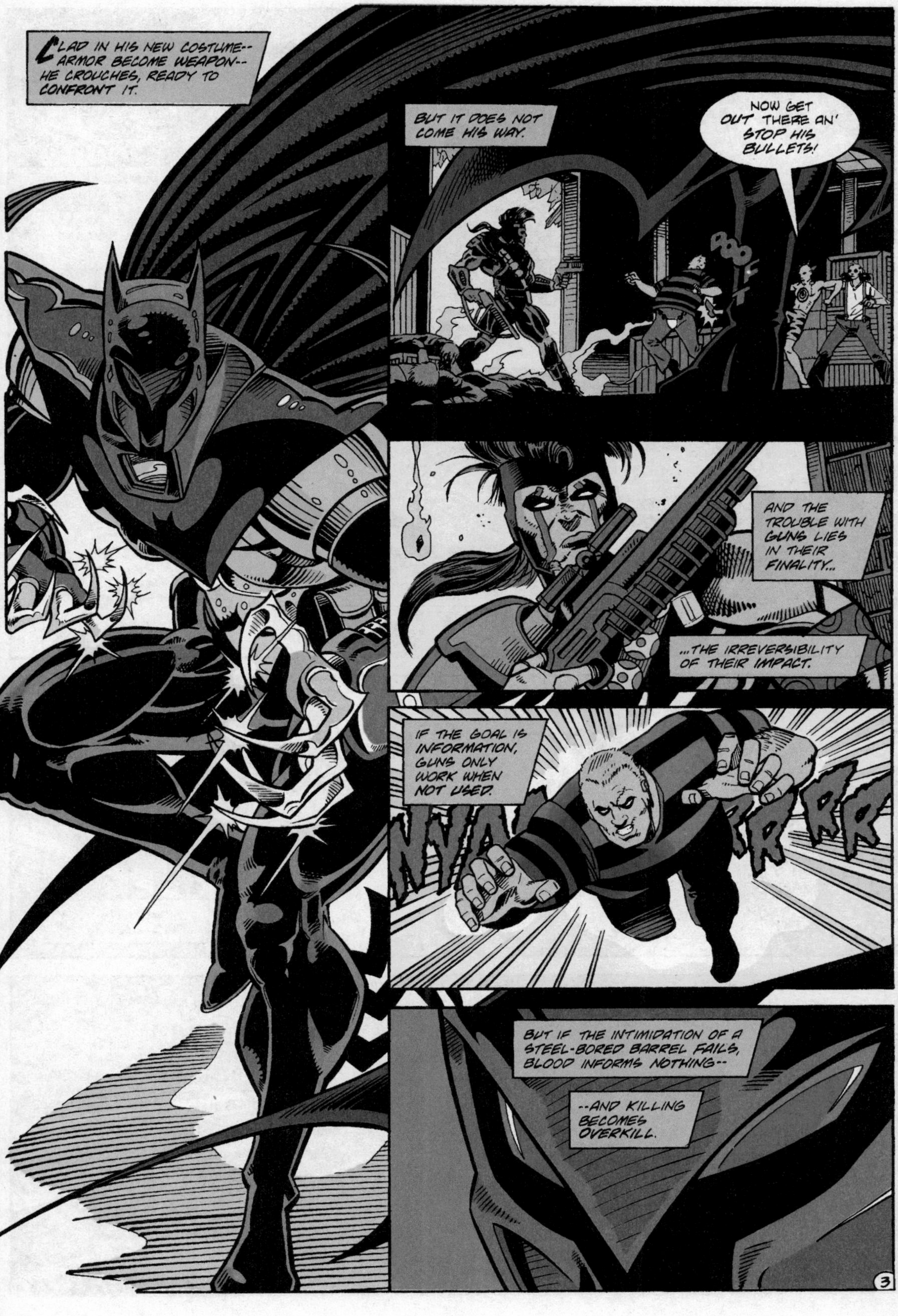
CLAD IN HIS NEW COSTUME--ARMOR BECOME WEAPON--HE CROUCHES, READY TO CONFRONT IT.
BUT IT DOES NOT COME HIS WAY.
NOW GET OUT THERE AN' STOP HIS BULLETS!
AND THE TROUBLE WITH GUNS LIES IN THEIR FINALITY...
...THE IRREVERSIBILITY OF THEIR IMPACT.
IF THE GOAL IS INFORMATION, GUNS ONLY WORK WHEN NOT USED.
BUT IF THE INTIMIDATION OF A STEEL-BORED BARREL FAILS, BLOOD INFORMS NOTHING--
--AND KILLING BECOMES OVERKILL.
3

GRAB SOME COVER, HAIRY!

THE DIMBULB'S ACTUALLY *DOIN'* IT!

ULTIMATELY, IN THE FACE OF SOMEONE FEARLESS, CRAZED OR STUPID--AND IN THE HAND OF SOMEONE UNWILLING TO KILL--THE GUN IS USELESS...

...AT LEAST IN ITS PRIMARY FUNCTION.

SHWONK

HWEEP!

ON THE OTHER HAND, THERE ARE THOSE WHO COULDN'T CARE LESS ABOUT LIFE OR INFORMATION...

HYAHAHAHAAA

BRAM BRAM BRAM

BRAM BRAM

...THOSE WHO SIMPLY CRAVE BLOOD.

AND IN THEIR HANDS, GUNS WORK BEAUTIFULLY...

SKANG BLAM BEOW

...GIVEN HALF A CHANCE.

④

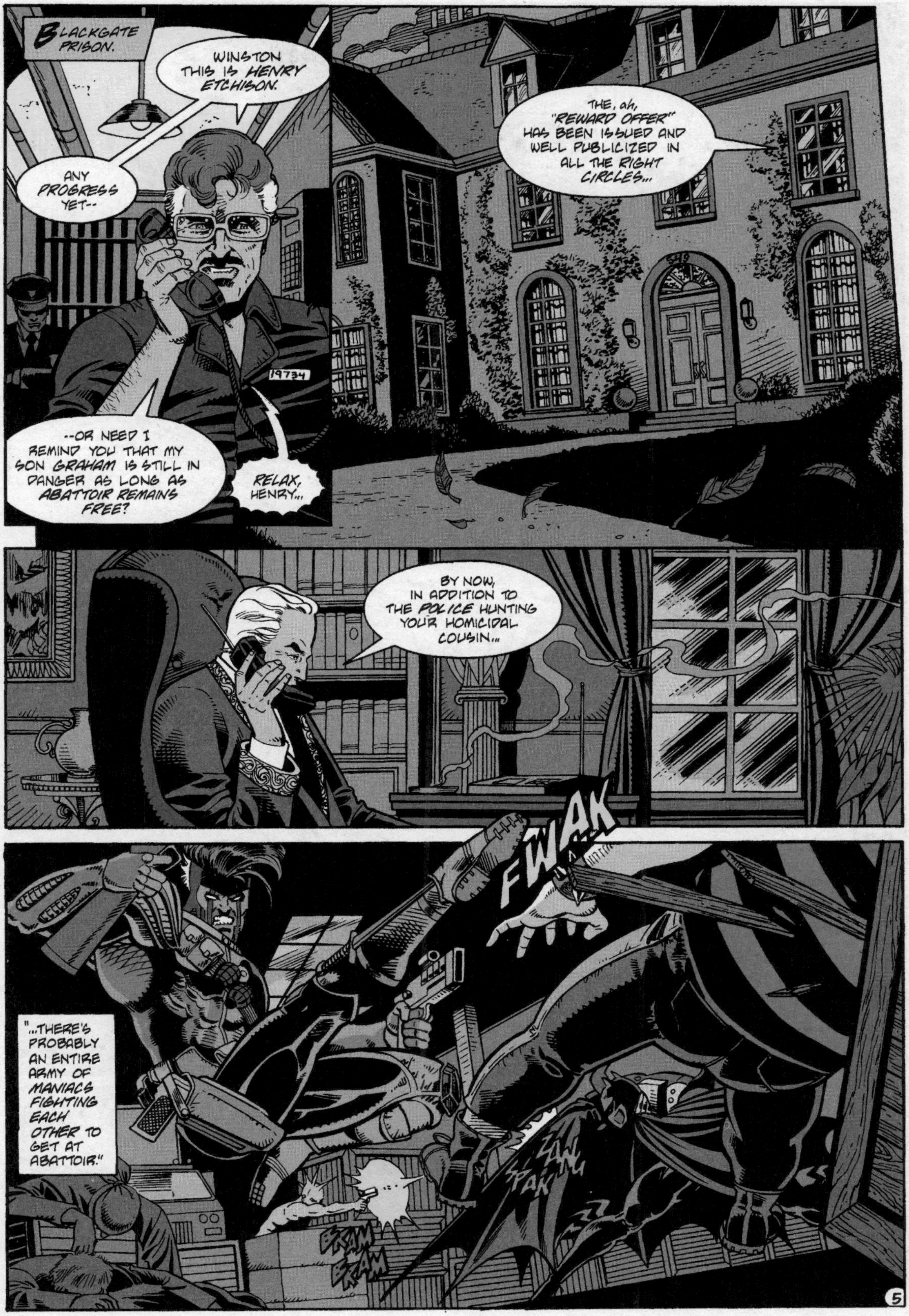
BLACKGATE PRISON.
WINSTON THIS IS HENRY ETCHISON.
ANY PROGRESS YET--
--OR NEED I REMIND YOU THAT MY SON GRAHAM IS STILL IN DANGER AS LONG AS ABATTOIR REMAINS FREE?
RELAX, HENRY...
THE, ah, "REWARD OFFER" HAS BEEN ISSUED AND WELL PUBLICIZED IN ALL THE RIGHT CIRCLES...
BY NOW, IN ADDITION TO THE POLICE HUNTING YOUR HOMICIDAL COUSIN...
"...THERE'S PROBABLY AN ENTIRE ARMY OF MANIACS FIGHTING EACH OTHER TO GET AT ABATTOIR."
FWAK
BRAM
BRAM
5

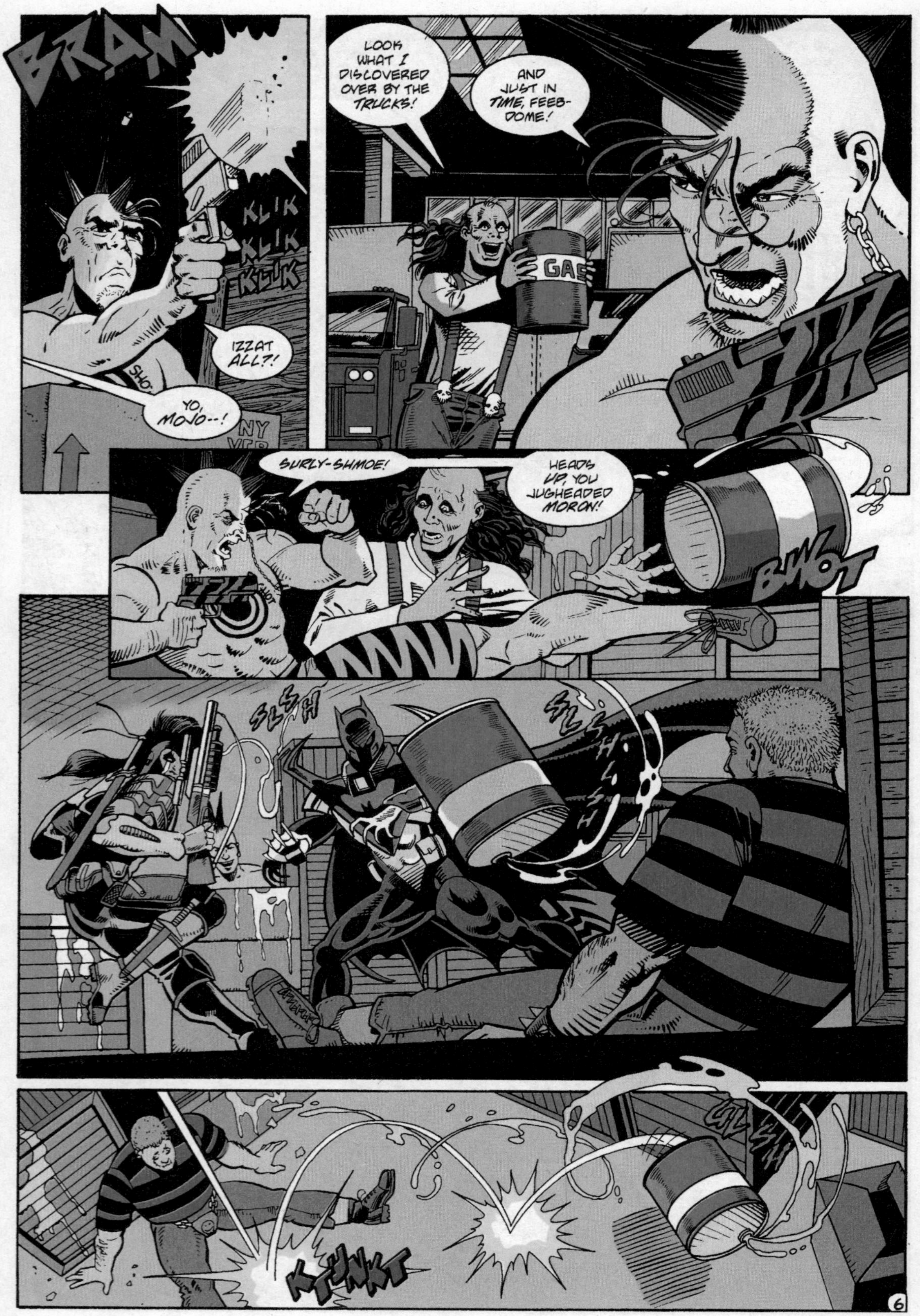
BRAM
KLIK KLIK KLIK
IZZAT ALL?!
YO, MOJO--!
LOOK WHAT I DISCOVERED OVER BY THE TRUCKS!
AND JUST IN TIME, FEEB-DOME!
GAS
SURLY-SHMOE!
HEADS UP, YOU JUGHEADED MORON!
BWOT
SLSH
KTUNKT
6

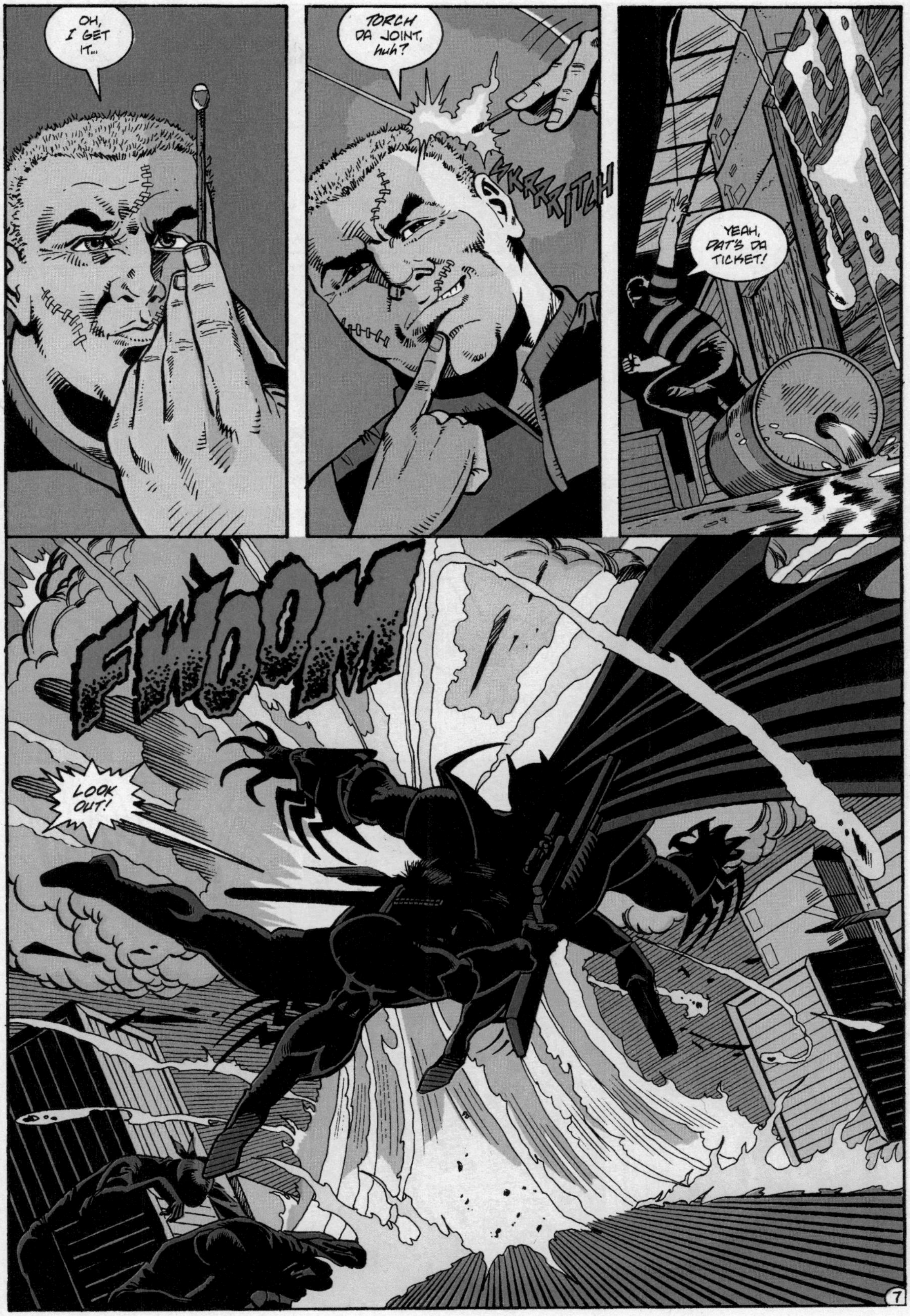
OH, I GET IT...
TORCH DA JOINT, huh?
SKRRRITCH
YEAH, DAT'S DA TICKET!
FWOOM
LOOK OUT!
7

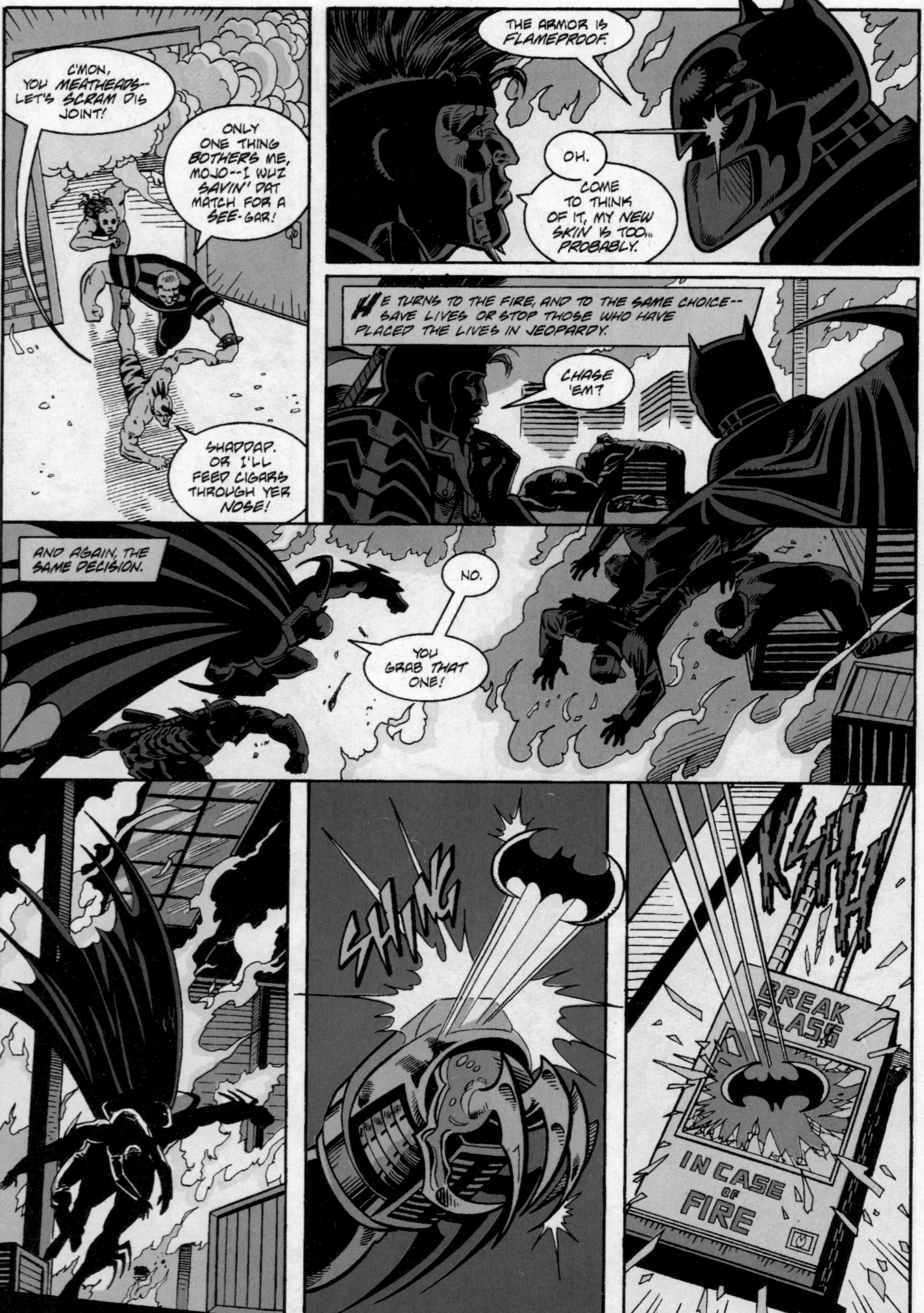
C'MON, YOU MEATHEADS-- LET'S SCRAM DIS JOINT!
ONLY ONE THING BOTHERS ME, MOJO--I WUZ SAVIN' DAT MATCH FOR A SEE-GAR!
SHADDAP. OR I'LL FEED CIGARS THROUGH YER NOSE!
THE ARMOR IS FLAMEPROOF.
OH.
COME TO THINK OF IT, MY NEW SKIN IS TOO... PROBABLY.
HE TURNS TO THE FIRE, AND TO THE SAME CHOICE-- SAVE LIVES OR STOP THOSE WHO HAVE PLACED THE LIVES IN JEOPARDY.
CHASE 'EM?
AND AGAIN, THE SAME DECISION.
NO.
YOU GRAB THAT ONE!
SHING
KSHH
BREAK GLASS
IN CASE OF FIRE
8

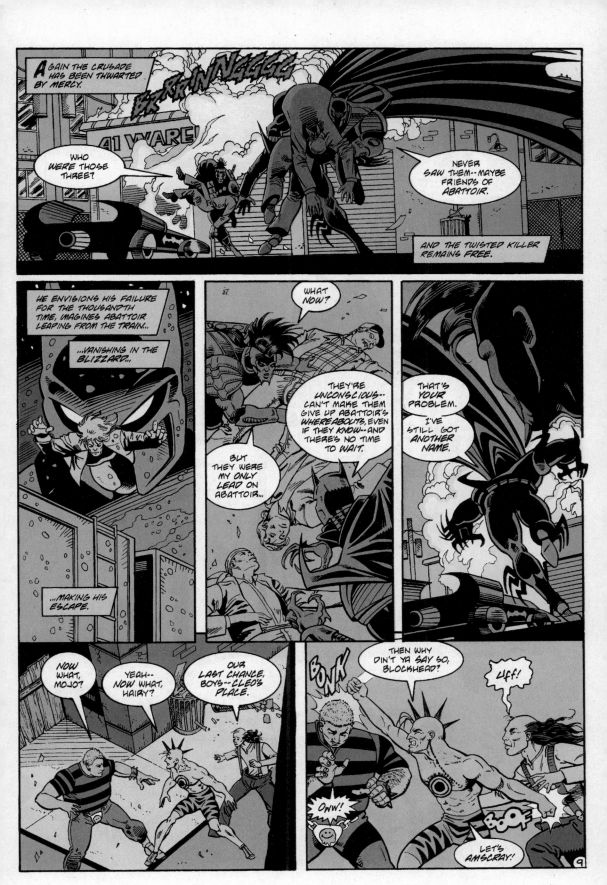

AGAIN THE CRUSADE HAS BEEN THWARTED BY MERCY.

BR-RRINNGGG

WHO WERE THOSE THREE?

NEVER SAW THEM-- MAYBE FRIENDS OF ABATTOIR.

AND THE TWISTED KILLER REMAINS FREE.

HE ENVISIONS HIS FAILURE FOR THE THOUSANDTH TIME, IMAGINES ABATTOIR LEAPING FROM THE TRAIN...

...VANISHING IN THE BLIZZARD...

...MAKING HIS ESCAPE.

WHAT NOW?

THEY'RE UNCONSCIOUS-- CAN'T MAKE THEM GIVE UP ABATTOIR'S WHEREABOUTS, EVEN IF THEY KNOW-- AND THERE'S NO TIME TO WAIT.

BUT THEY WERE MY ONLY LEAD ON ABATTOIR...

THAT'S YOUR PROBLEM. I'VE STILL GOT ANOTHER NAME.

NOW WHAT, MOJO?

YEAH-- NOW WHAT, HAIRY?

OUR LAST CHANCE, BOYS-- CLEO'S PLACE.

BONK

THEN WHY DIN'T YA SAY SO, BLOCKHEAD?

UFF!

OWW!

BOOF

LET'S AMSCRAY!

9

473

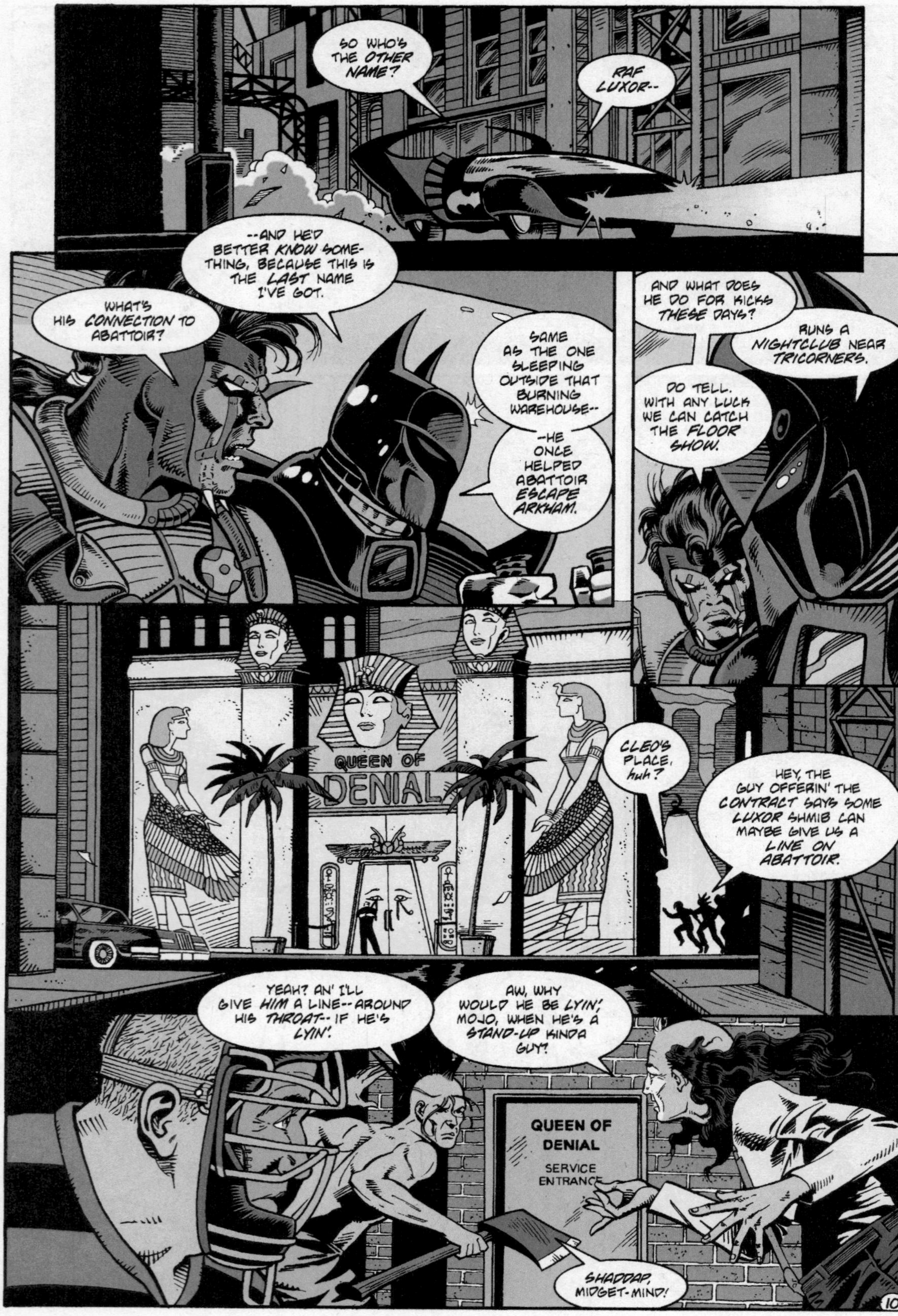

SO WHO'S THE OTHER NAME?
RAF LUXOR--
--AND HE'D BETTER KNOW SOMETHING, BECAUSE THIS IS THE LAST NAME I'VE GOT.
WHAT'S HIS CONNECTION TO ABATTOIR?
SAME AS THE ONE SLEEPING OUTSIDE THAT BURNING WAREHOUSE--
--HE ONCE HELPED ABATTOIR ESCAPE ARKHAM.
AND WHAT DOES HE DO FOR KICKS THESE DAYS?
RUNS A NIGHTCLUB NEAR TRICORNERS.
DO TELL. WITH ANY LUCK WE CAN CATCH THE FLOOR SHOW.
QUEEN OF DENIAL
CLEO'S PLACE, huh?
HEY, THE GUY OFFERIN' THE CONTRACT SAYS SOME LUXOR SHMIB CAN MAYBE GIVE US A LINE ON ABATTOIR.
YEAH? AN' I'LL GIVE HIM A LINE--AROUND HIS THROAT--IF HE'S LYIN'.
AW, WHY WOULD HE BE LYIN', MOJO, WHEN HE'S A STAND-UP KINDA GUY?
QUEEN OF DENIAL
SERVICE ENTRANCE
SHADDAP, MIDGET-MIND!
10

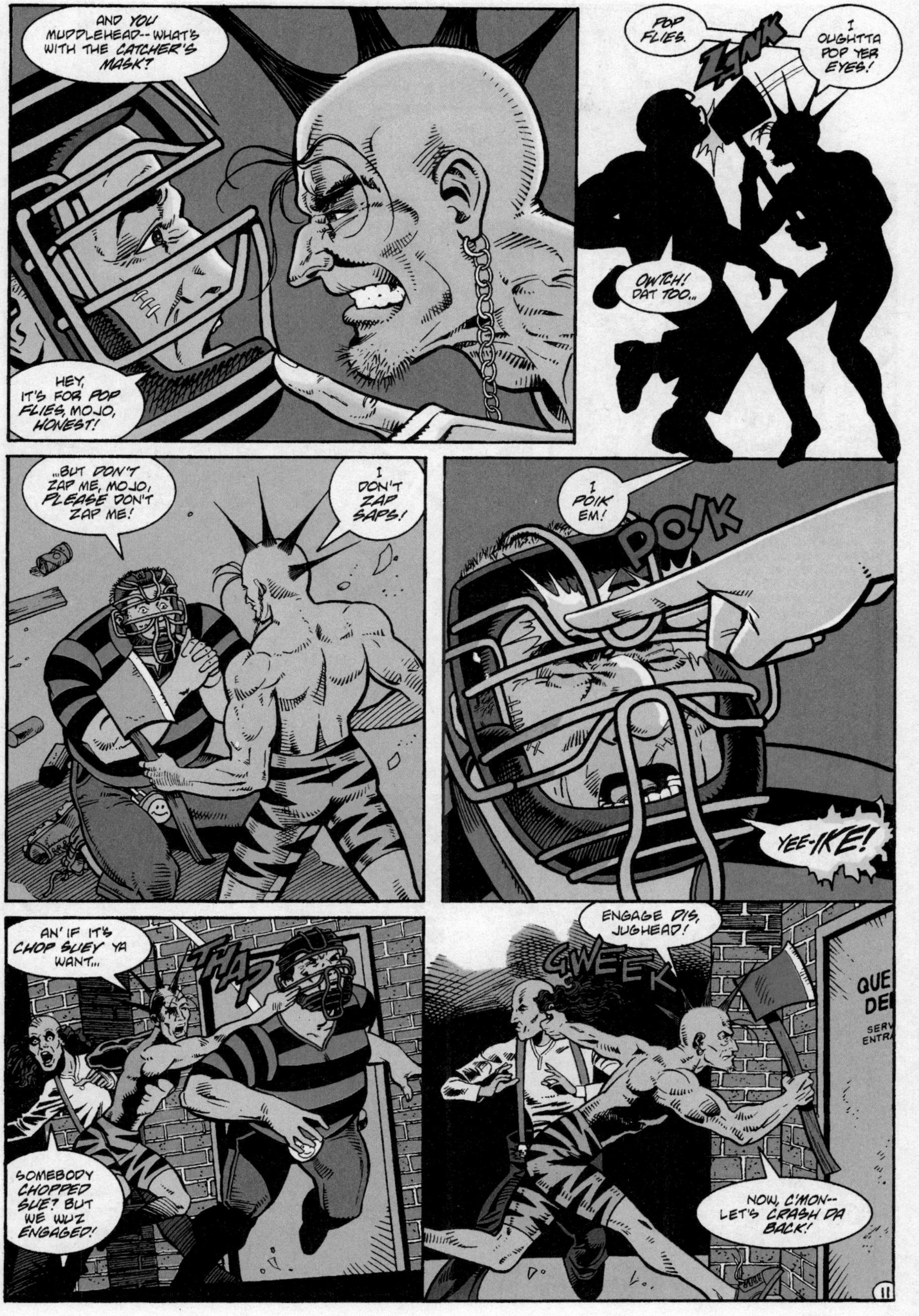
AND YOU MUDDLEHEAD-- WHAT'S WITH THE CATCHER'S MASK?
HEY, IT'S FOR POP FLIES, MOJO, HONEST!
POP FLIES.
ZANK
I OUGHTTA POP YER EYES!
OWTCH! DAT TOO...
...BUT DON'T ZAP ME, MOJO, PLEASE DON'T ZAP ME!
I DON'T ZAP SAPS!
I POIK EM!
POIK
YEE-IKE!
AN' IF IT'S CHOP SUEY YA WANT...
THAP
SOMEBODY CHOPPED SUE? BUT WE WUZ ENGAGED!
ENGAGE DIS, JUGHEAD!
GWEEEK
NOW, C'MON-- LET'S CRASH DA BACK!
11

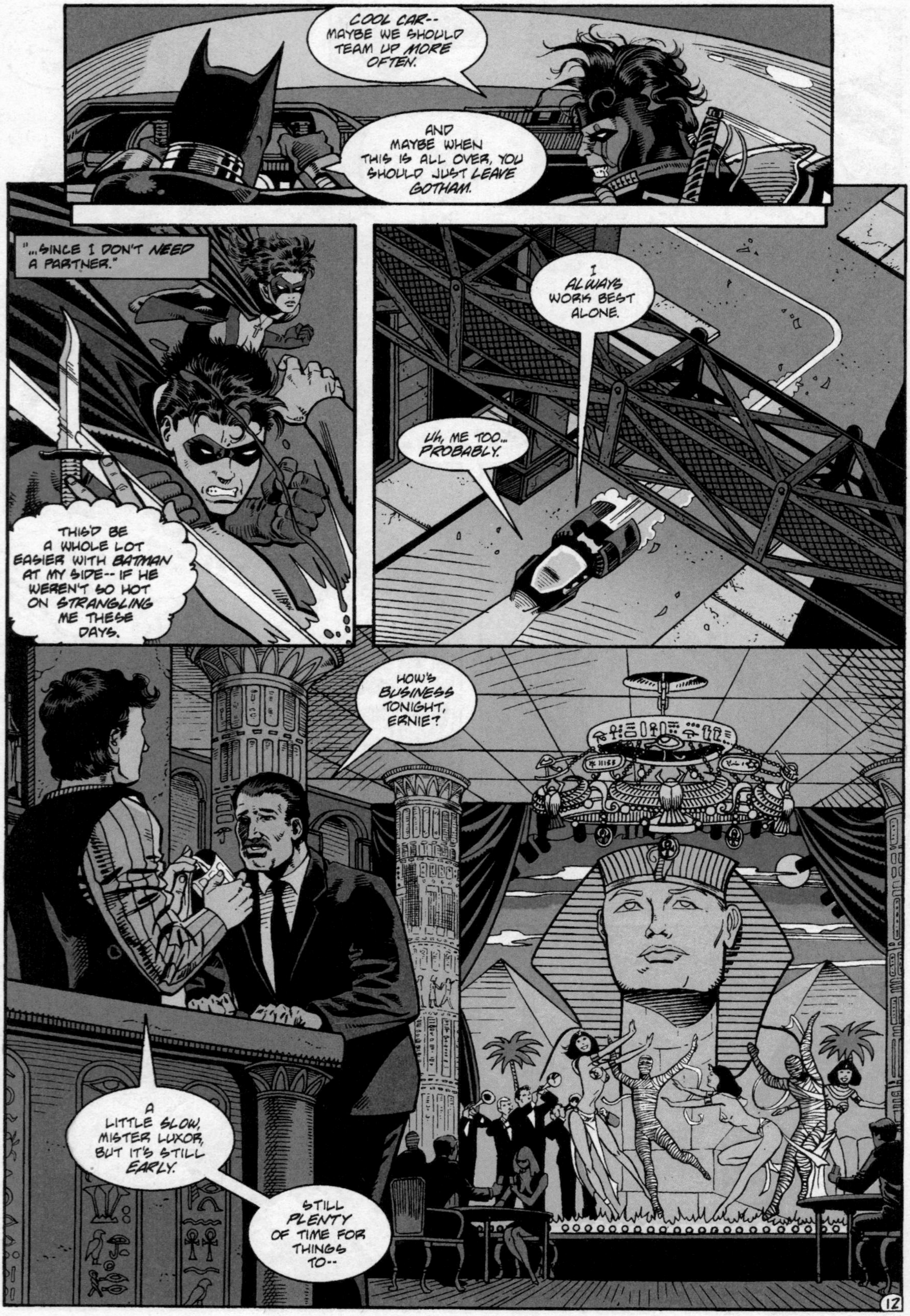
COOL CAR-- MAYBE WE SHOULD TEAM UP MORE OFTEN.
AND MAYBE WHEN THIS IS ALL OVER, YOU SHOULD JUST LEAVE GOTHAM.
"...SINCE I DON'T NEED A PARTNER."
THIS'D BE A WHOLE LOT EASIER WITH BATMAN AT MY SIDE-- IF HE WEREN'T SO HOT ON STRANGLING ME THESE DAYS.
I ALWAYS WORK BEST ALONE.
UH, ME TOO... PROBABLY.
HOW'S BUSINESS TONIGHT, ERNIE?
A LITTLE SLOW, MISTER LUXOR, BUT IT'S STILL EARLY.
STILL PLENTY OF TIME FOR THINGS TO--
12

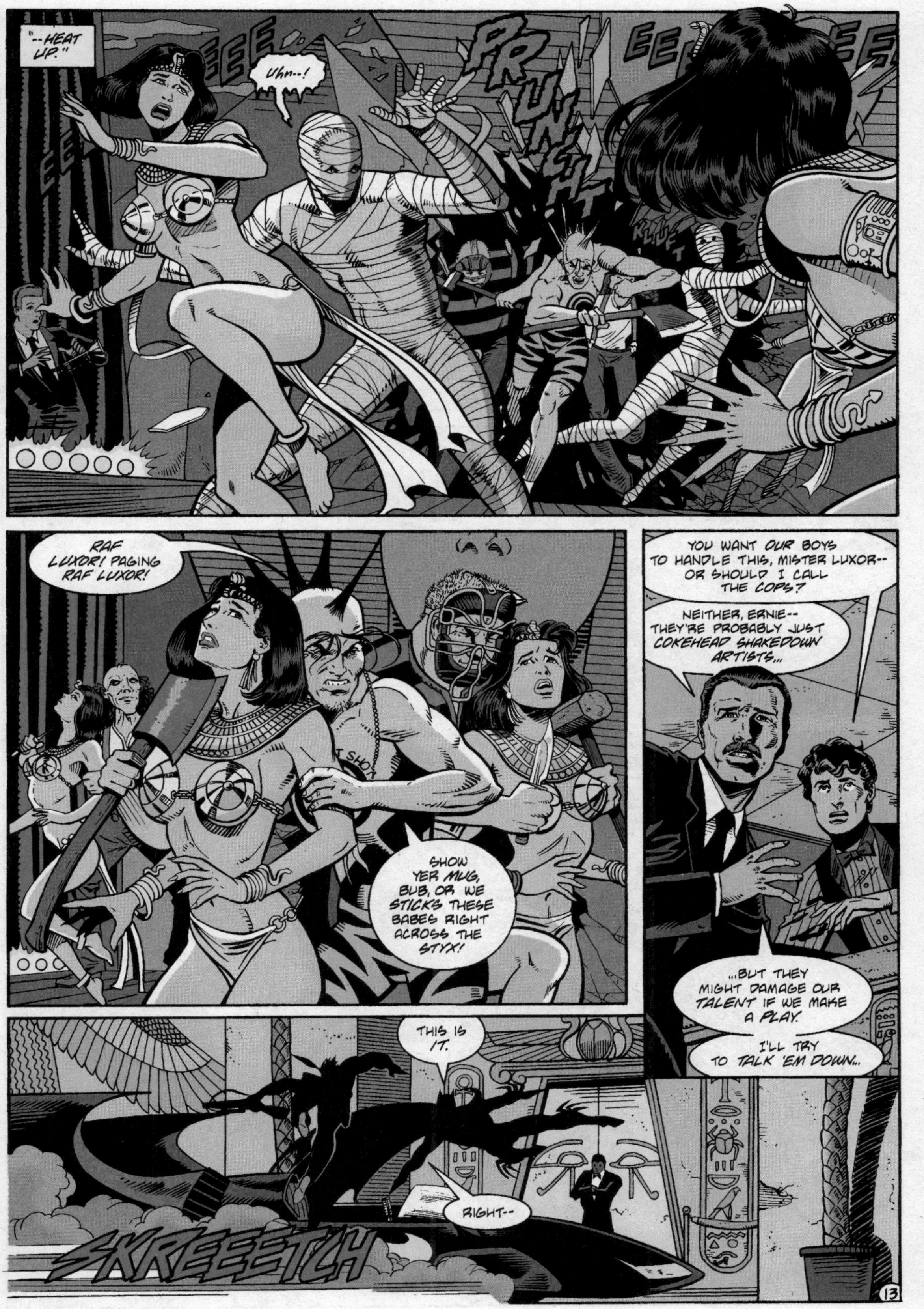
"--HEAT UP."
EEE
Uhn--!
PRUNCH
EEE
RAF LUXOR! PAGING RAF LUXOR!
SHOW YER MUG, BUB, OR WE STICKS THESE BABES RIGHT ACROSS THE STYX!
YOU WANT OUR BOYS TO HANDLE THIS, MISTER LUXOR-- OR SHOULD I CALL THE COPS?
NEITHER, ERNIE-- THEY'RE PROBABLY JUST COKEHEAD SHAKEDOWN ARTISTS...
...BUT THEY MIGHT DAMAGE OUR TALENT IF WE MAKE A PLAY.
I'LL TRY TO TALK 'EM DOWN...
THIS IS IT.
RIGHT--
SKREEETCH
13

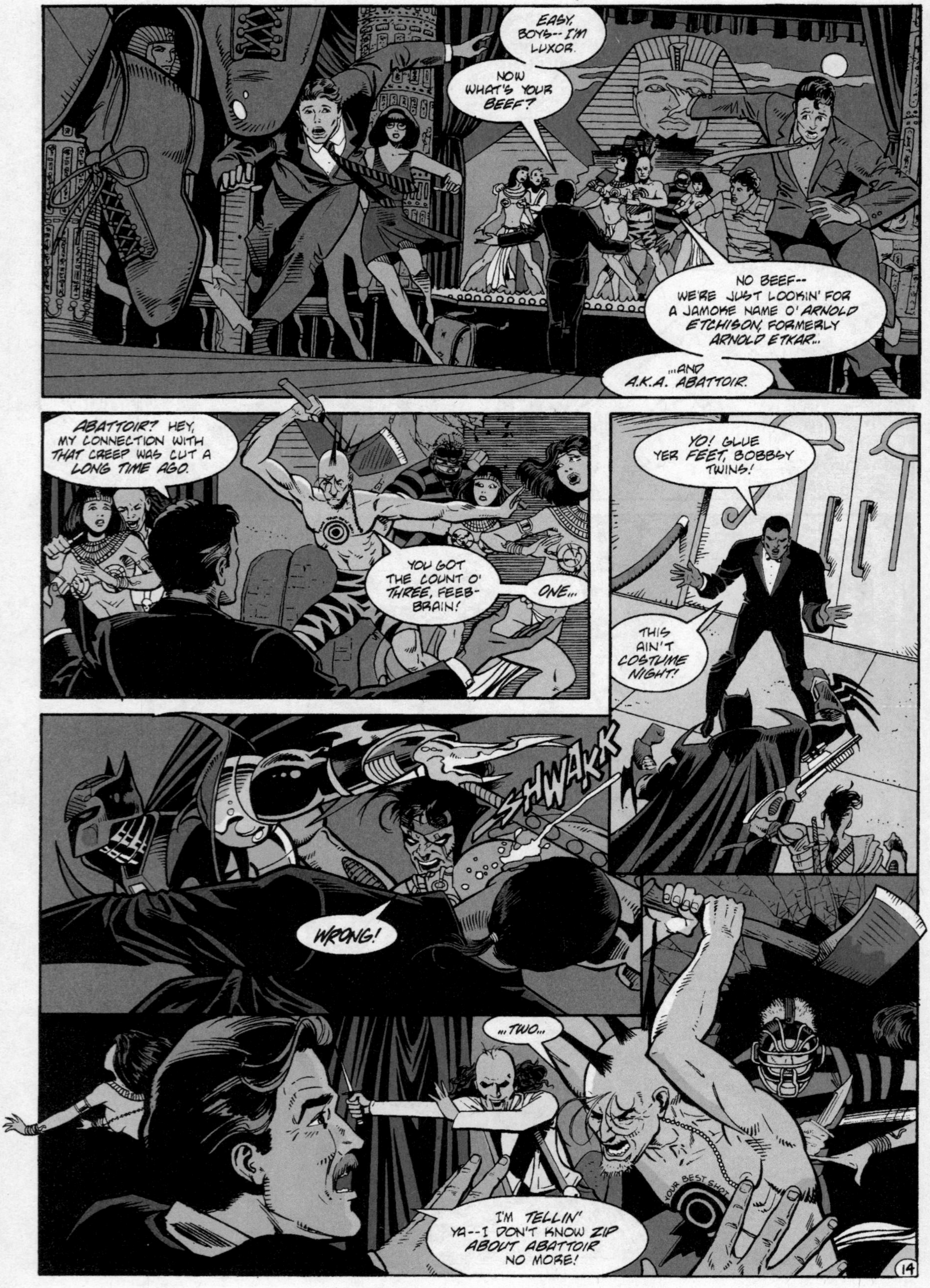
EASY, BOYS-- I'M LUXOR.
NOW WHAT'S YOUR BEEF?
NO BEEF-- WE'RE JUST LOOKIN' FOR A JAMOKE NAME O' ARNOLD ETCHISON, FORMERLY ARNOLD ETKAR...
...AND A.K.A. ABATTOIR.
ABATTOIR? HEY, MY CONNECTION WITH THAT CREEP WAS CUT A LONG TIME AGO.
YOU GOT THE COUNT O' THREE, FEEB-BRAIN!
ONE...
YO! GLUE YER FEET, BOBBSY TWINS!
THIS AIN'T COSTUME NIGHT!
SHWAKK
WRONG!
...TWO...
YOUR BEST SHOT
I'M TELLIN' YA--I DON'T KNOW ZIP ABOUT ABATTOIR NO MORE!
14

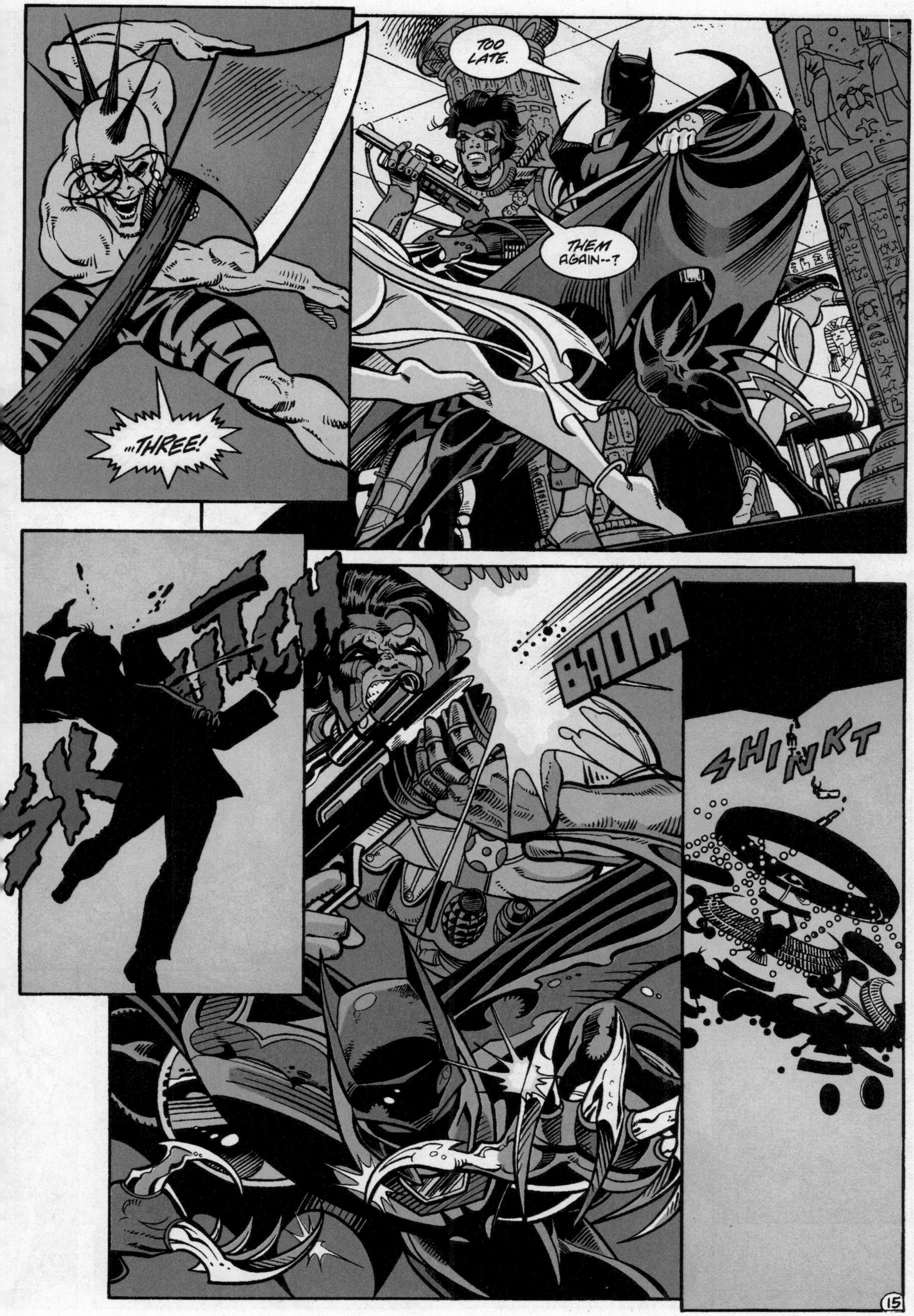
...THREE!
TOO LATE.
THEM AGAIN--?
SKLUTCH
BOOM
SHINKT
15

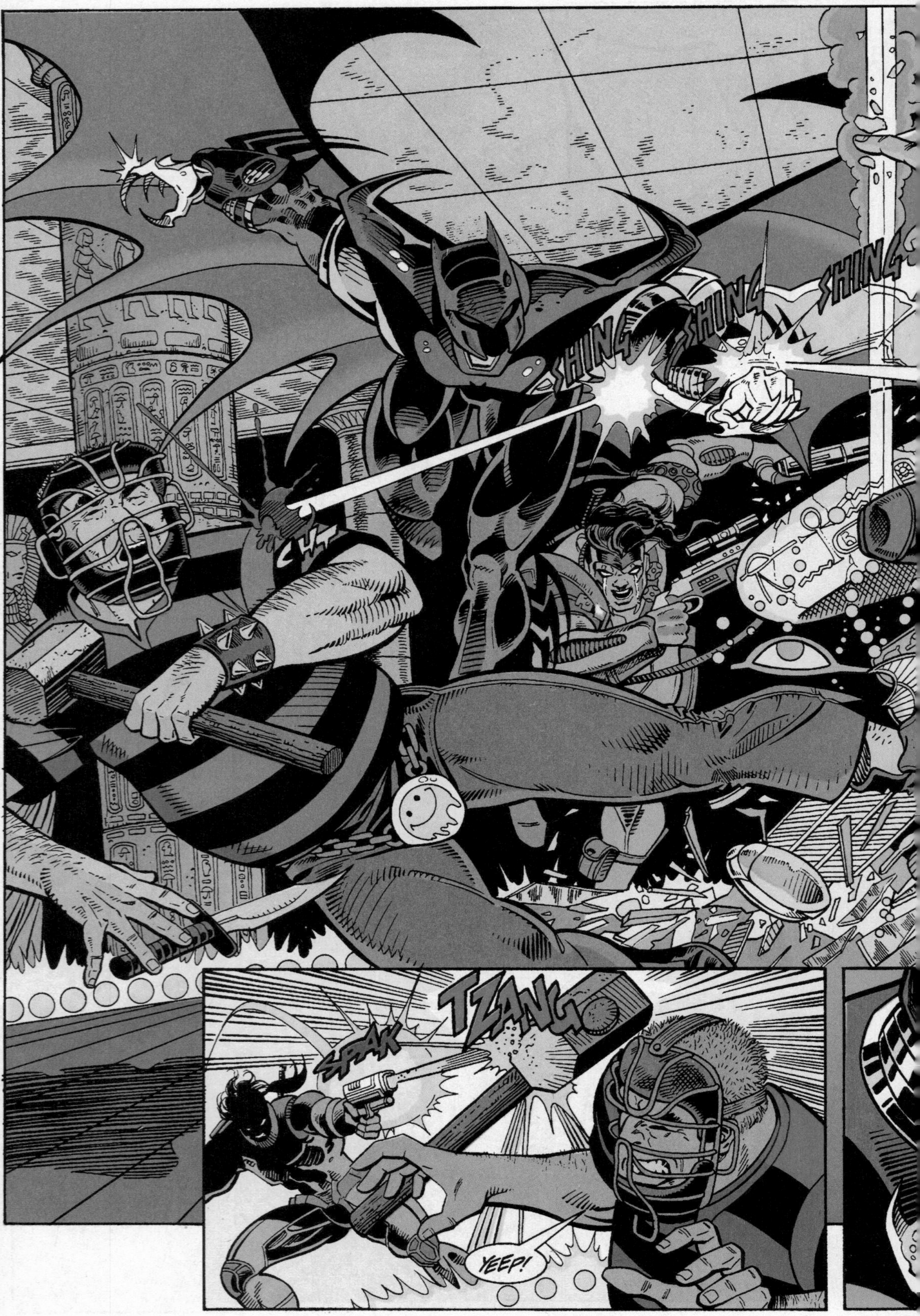
SHING SHING SHING SHING
CHT
TZANG
SPAK
YEEP!

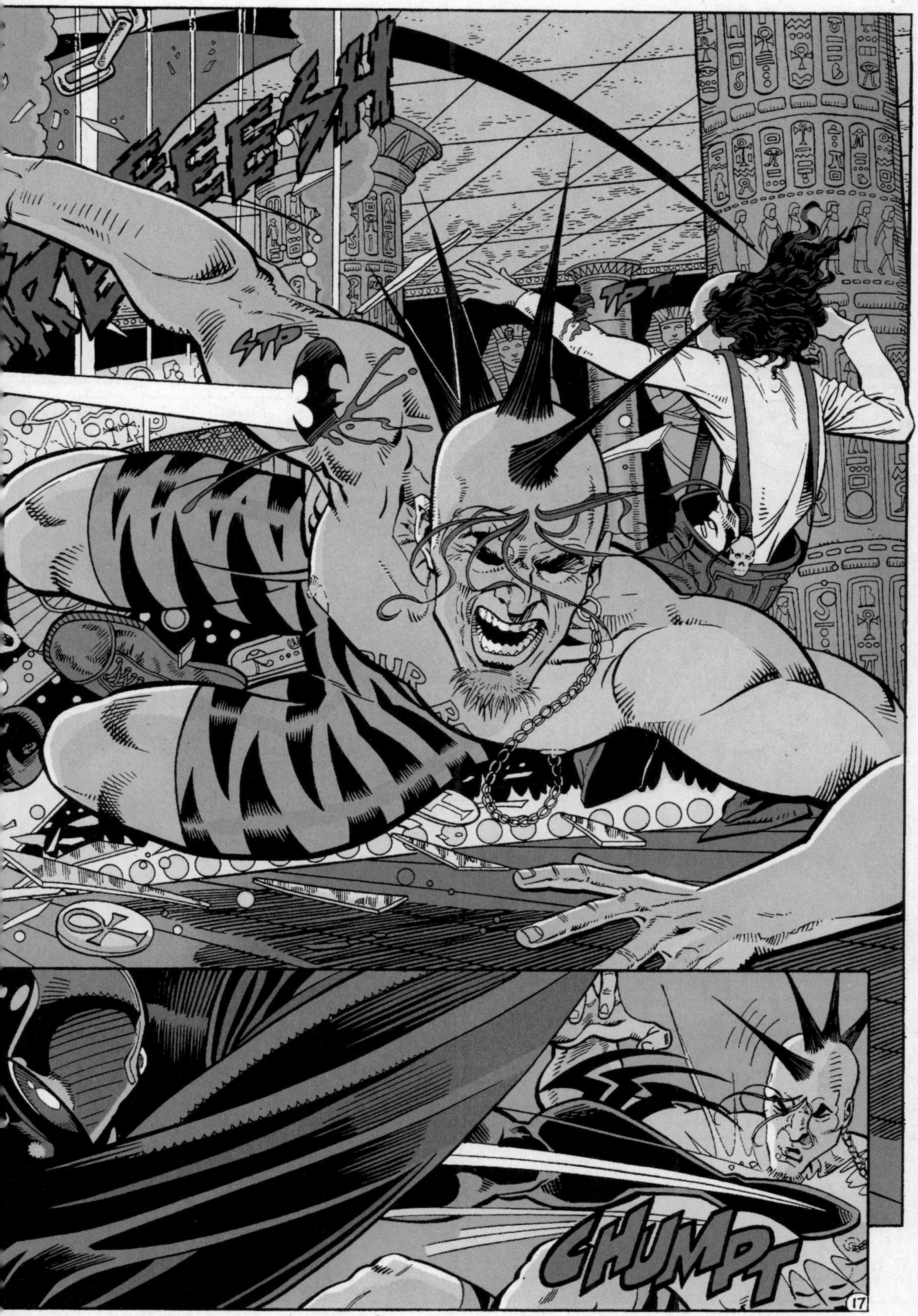
FREEEESH
STP
TPT
CHUMPT
17

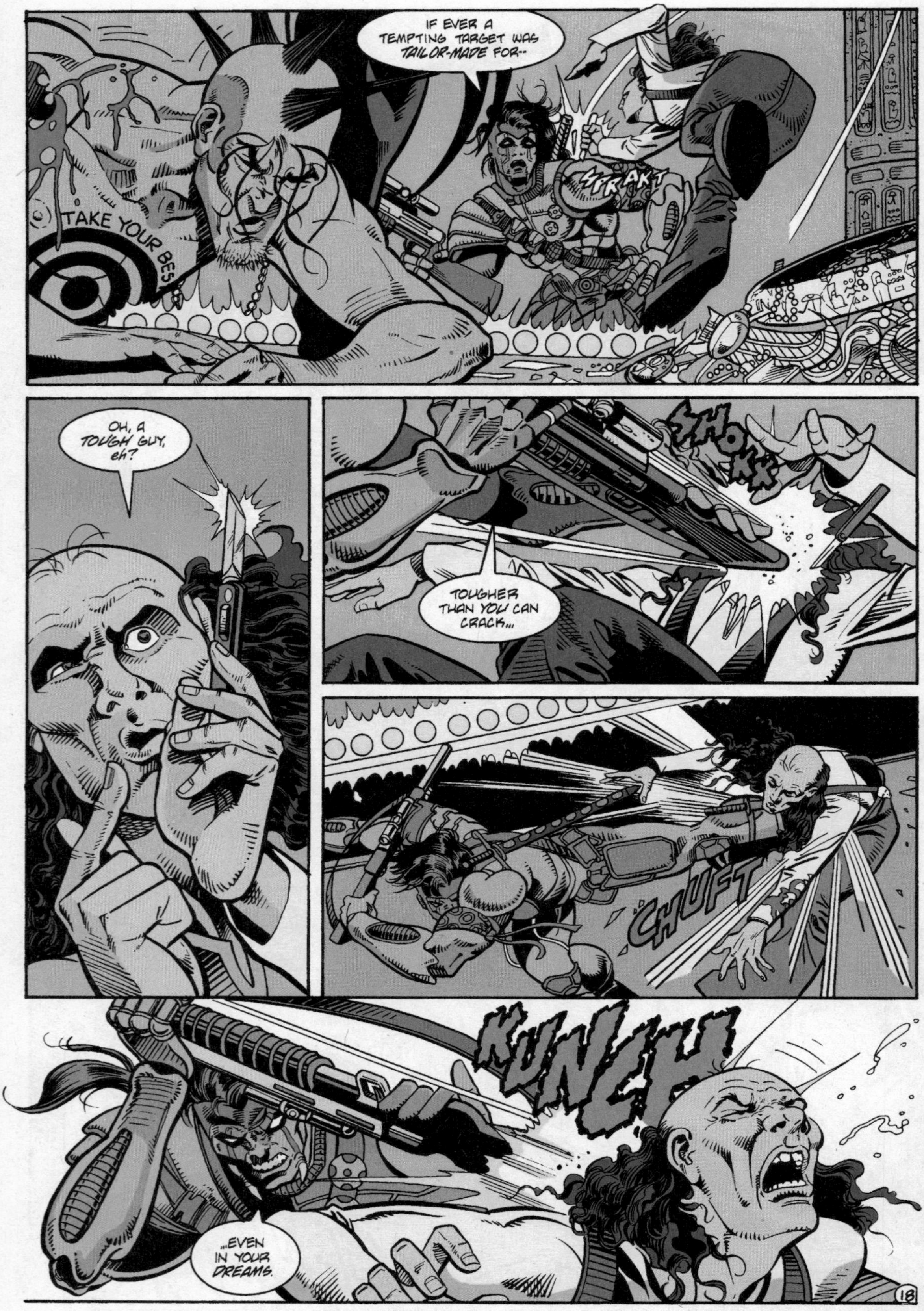
IF EVER A TEMPTING TARGET WAS TAILOR-MADE FOR--
TAKE YOUR BES
SPRAKT
OH, A TOUGH GUY, eh?
SHOKK
TOUGHER THAN YOU CAN CRACK...
CHUFT
KUNCH
...EVEN IN YOUR DREAMS.
18

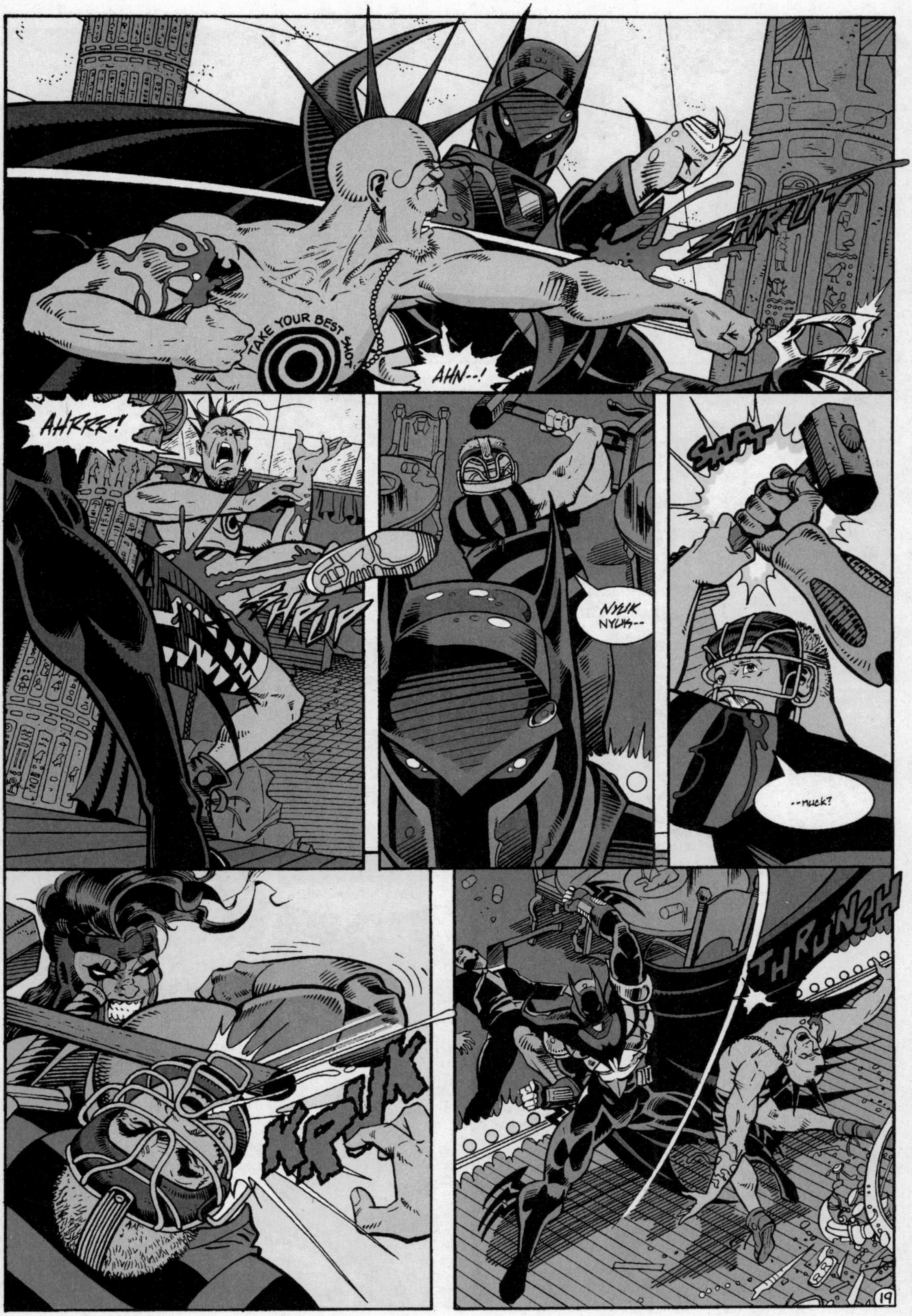
SHRUT
TAKE YOUR BEST SHOT
AHN--!
AHRRR!
SHRUP
NYUK NYUK--
SAPT
--nuck?
KRUK
THRUNCH
19

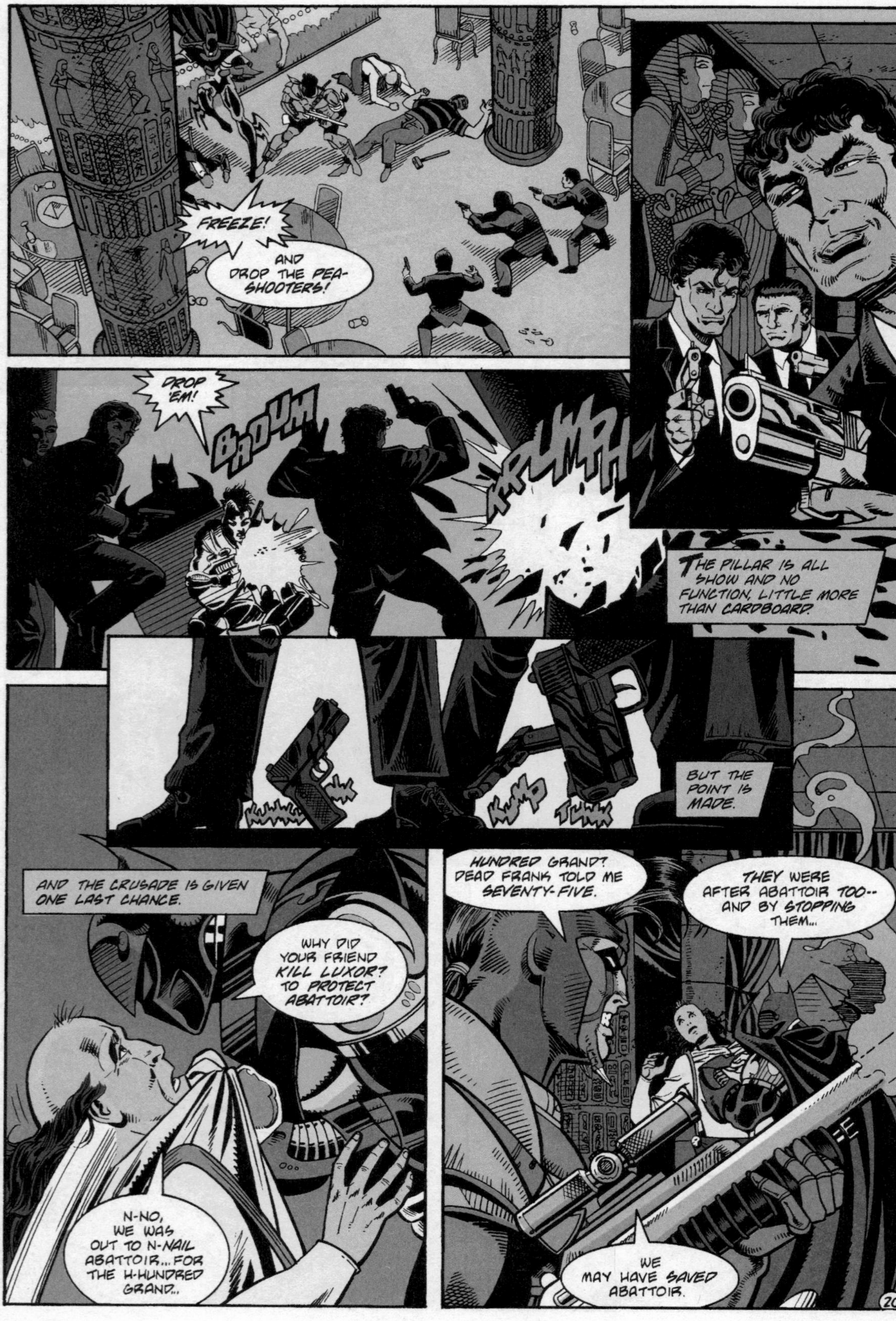
FREEZE!
AND DROP THE PEA-SHOOTERS!
DROP 'EM!
BRDUM
KRUMPH
THE PILLAR IS ALL SHOW AND NO FUNCTION, LITTLE MORE THAN CARDBOARD?
BUT THE POINT IS MADE.
KLUNK
KLMP
TUNK
AND THE CRUSADE IS GIVEN ONE LAST CHANCE.
WHY DID YOUR FRIEND KILL LUXOR? TO PROTECT ABATTOIR?
N-NO, WE WAS OUT TO N-NAIL ABATTOIR... FOR THE H-HUNDRED GRAND..
HUNDRED GRAND? DEAD FRANK TOLD ME SEVENTY-FIVE.
THEY WERE AFTER ABATTOIR TOO-- AND BY STOPPING THEM...
WE MAY HAVE SAVED ABATTOIR.
20

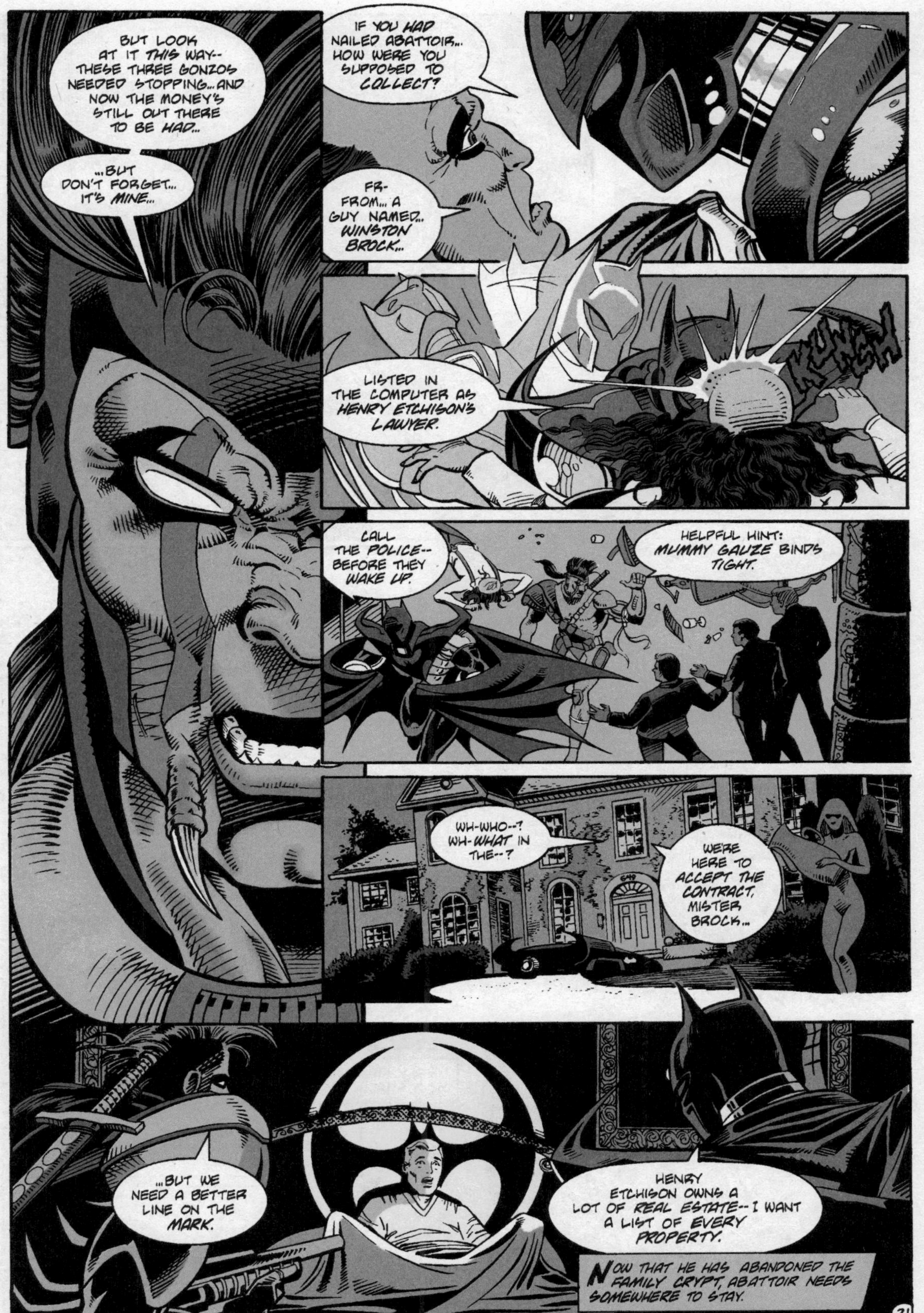
BUT LOOK AT IT THIS WAY-- THESE THREE GONZOS NEEDED STOPPING...AND NOW THE MONEY'S STILL OUT THERE TO BE HAD...
...BUT DON'T FORGET... IT'S MINE...
IF YOU HAD NAILED ABATTOIR... HOW WERE YOU SUPPOSED TO COLLECT?
FR-FROM... A GUY NAMED... WINSTON BROCK...
LISTED IN THE COMPUTER AS HENRY ETCHISON'S LAWYER.
KUNCH
CALL THE POLICE-- BEFORE THEY WAKE UP.
HELPFUL HINT: MUMMY GAUZE BINDS TIGHT.
WH-WHO--? WH-WHAT IN THE--?
WE'RE HERE TO ACCEPT THE CONTRACT, MISTER BROCK...
...BUT WE NEED A BETTER LINE ON THE MARK.
HENRY ETCHISON OWNS A LOT OF REAL ESTATE-- I WANT A LIST OF EVERY PROPERTY.
NOW THAT HE HAS ABANDONED THE FAMILY CRYPT, ABATTOIR NEEDS SOMEWHERE TO STAY.
21

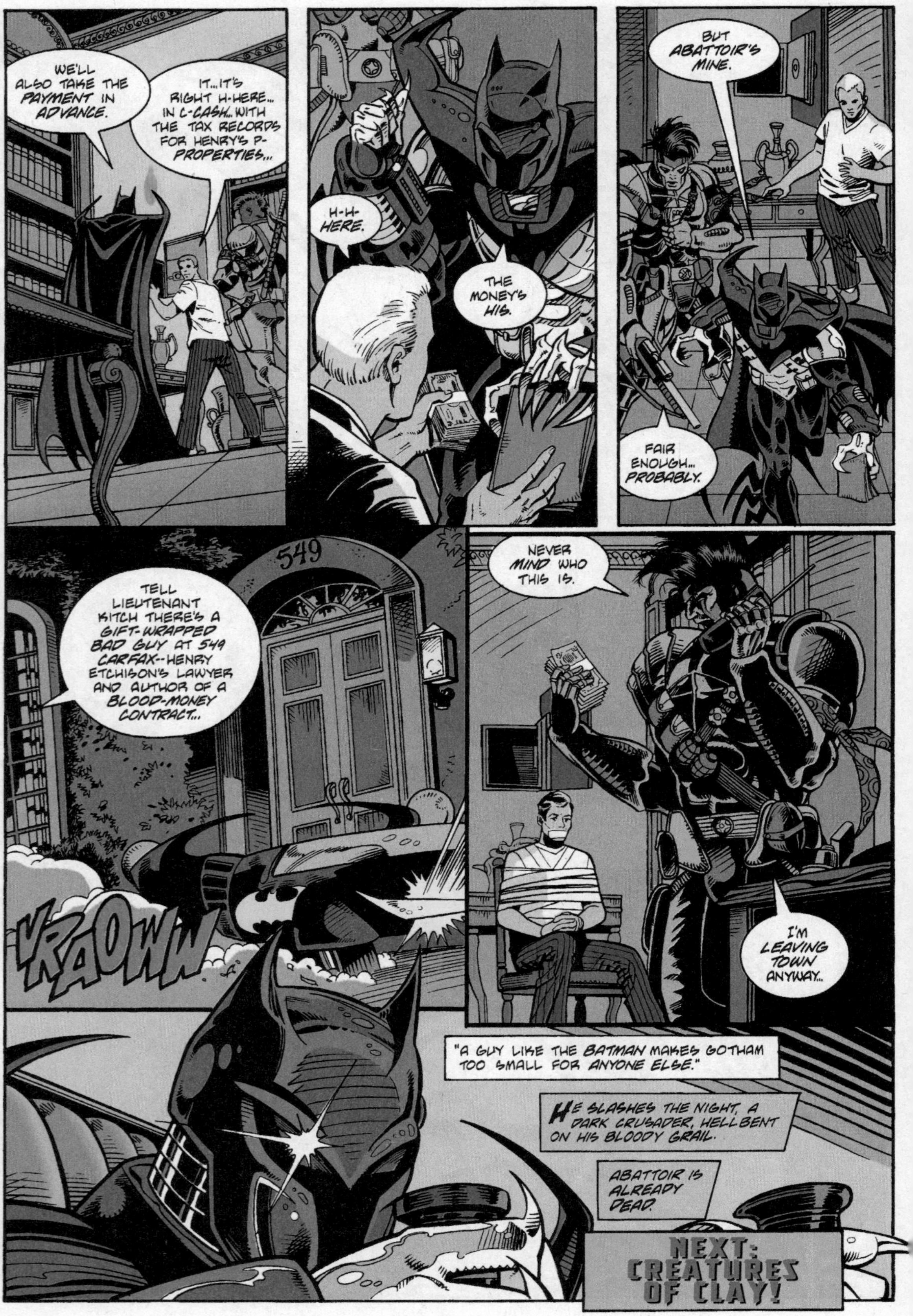
WE'LL ALSO TAKE THE PAYMENT IN ADVANCE.
IT...IT'S RIGHT H-HERE... IN C-CASH...WITH THE TAX RECORDS FOR HENRY'S P-PROPERTIES...
H-H-HERE.
THE MONEY'S HIS.
BUT ABATTOIR'S MINE.
FAIR ENOUGH... PROBABLY.
549
TELL LIEUTENANT KITCH THERE'S A GIFT-WRAPPED BAD GUY AT 549 CARFAX--HENRY ETCHISON'S LAWYER AND AUTHOR OF A BLOOD-MONEY CONTRACT...
VRAOWW
NEVER MIND WHO THIS IS.
I'M LEAVING TOWN ANYWAY...
"A GUY LIKE THE BATMAN MAKES GOTHAM TOO SMALL FOR ANYONE ELSE."
HE SLASHES THE NIGHT, A DARK CRUSADER, HELLBENT ON HIS BLOODY GRAIL.
ABATTOIR IS ALREADY DEAD.
NEXT: CREATURES OF CLAY!

Cover art by BRIAN STELFREEZE

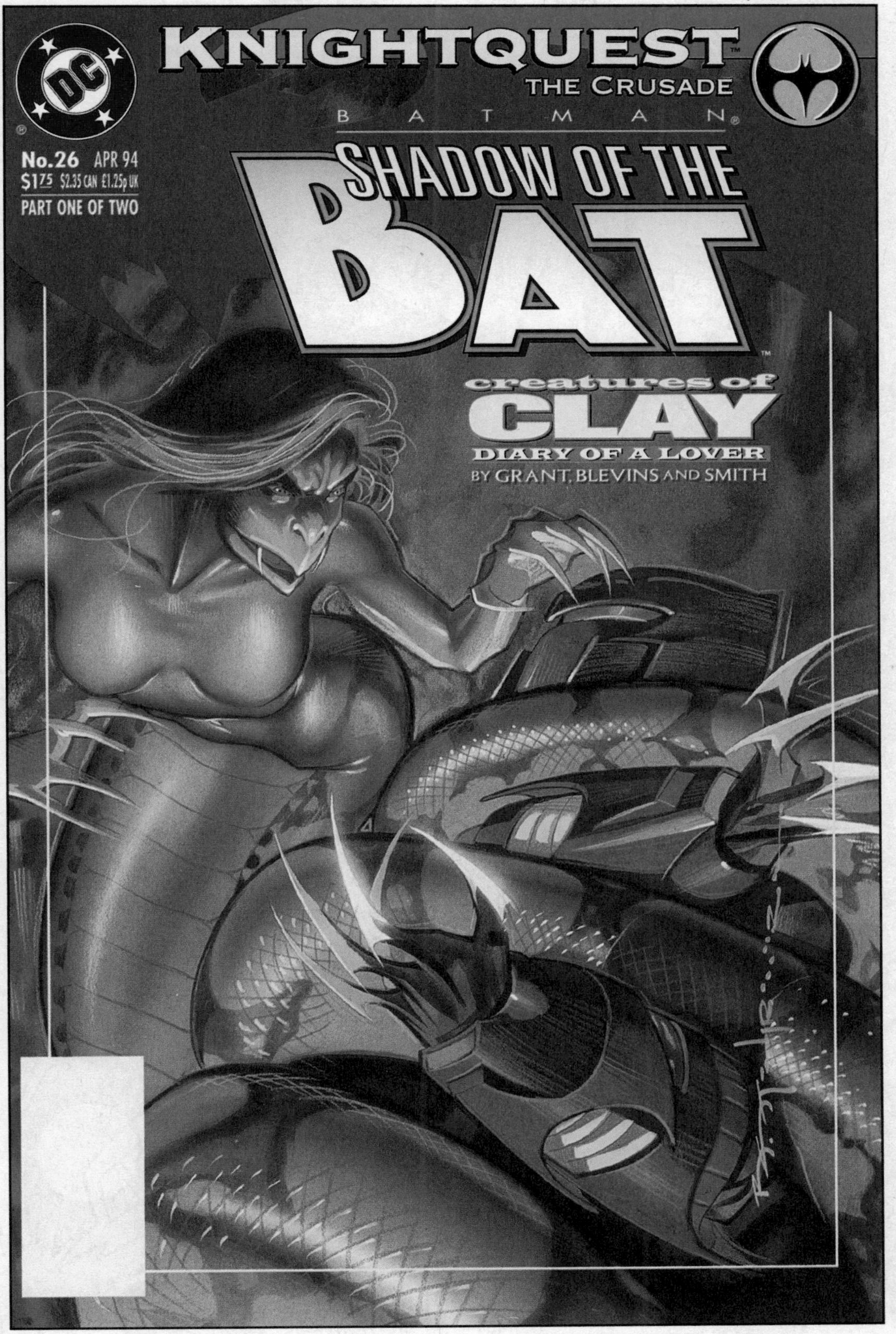
DC
KNIGHTQUEST
THE CRUSADE
BATMAN
No.26 APR 94
$1.75 $2.35 CAN £1.25p UK
PART ONE OF TWO
SHADOW OF THE BAT
creatures of CLAY
DIARY OF A LOVER
BY GRANT, BLEVINS AND SMITH

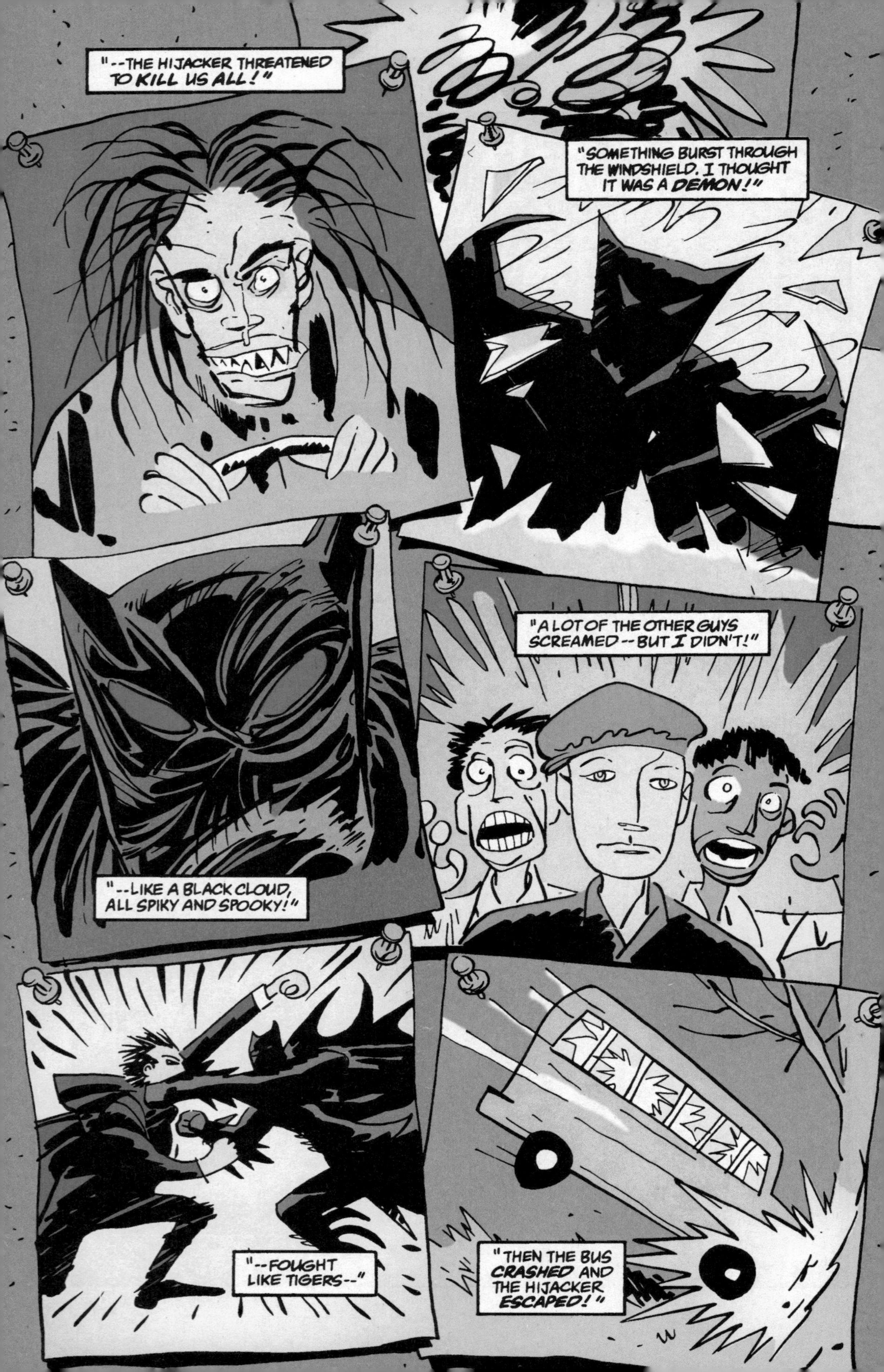
"--THE HIJACKER THREATENED TO KILL US ALL!"
"SOMETHING BURST THROUGH THE WINDSHIELD. I THOUGHT IT WAS A DEMON!"
"--LIKE A BLACK CLOUD, ALL SPIKY AND SPOOKY!"
"A LOT OF THE OTHER GUYS SCREAMED--BUT I DIDN'T!"
"--FOUGHT LIKE TIGERS--"
"THEN THE BUS CRASHED AND THE HIJACKER ESCAPED!"

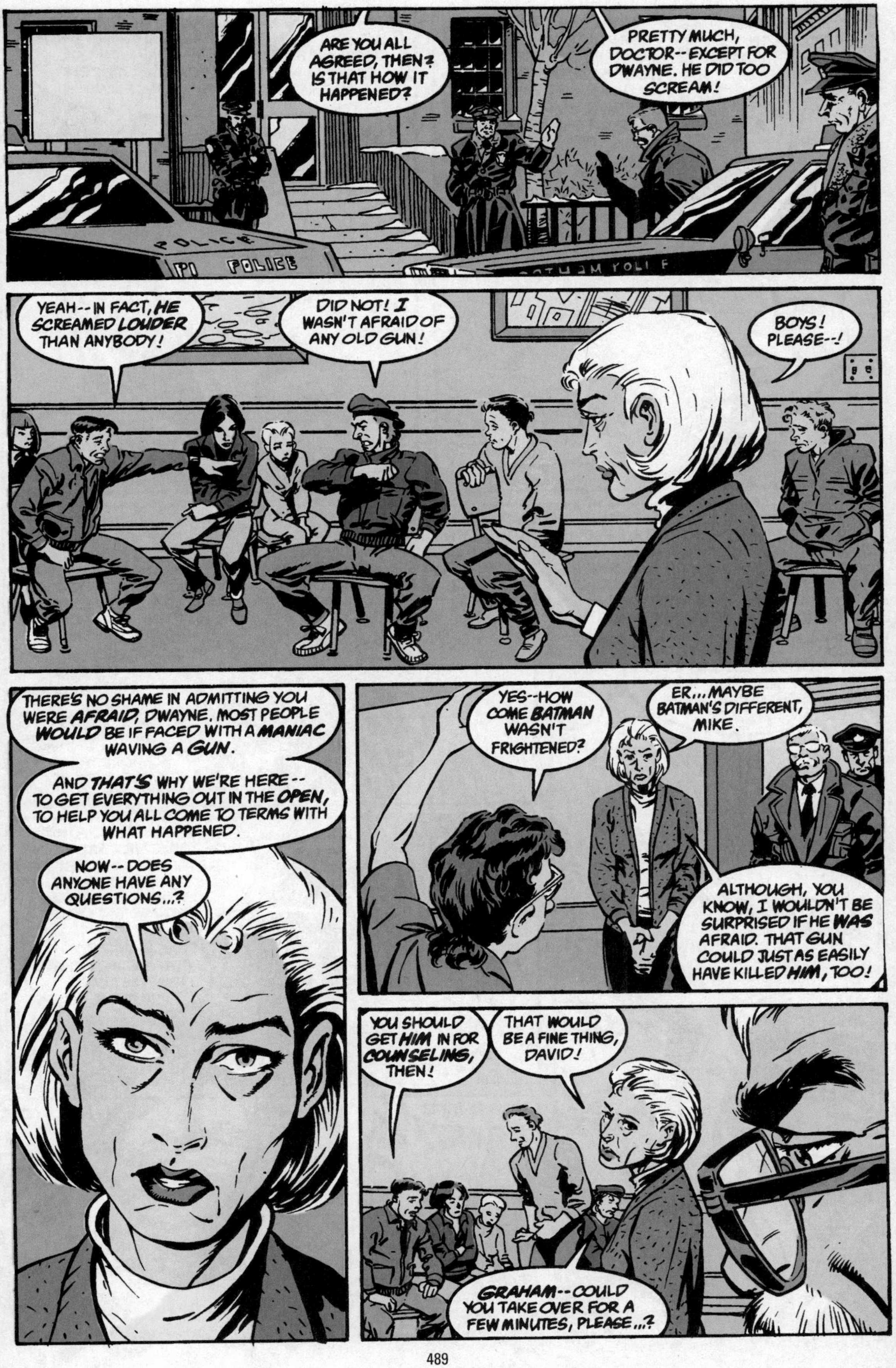
ARE YOU ALL AGREED, THEN? IS THAT HOW IT HAPPENED?
PRETTY MUCH, DOCTOR-- EXCEPT FOR DWAYNE. HE DID TOO SCREAM!
POLICE
POLICE
YEAH--IN FACT, HE SCREAMED LOUDER THAN ANYBODY!
DID NOT! I WASN'T AFRAID OF ANY OLD GUN!
BOYS! PLEASE--!
THERE'S NO SHAME IN ADMITTING YOU WERE AFRAID, DWAYNE. MOST PEOPLE WOULD BE IF FACED WITH A MANIAC WAVING A GUN.
AND THAT'S WHY WE'RE HERE-- TO GET EVERYTHING OUT IN THE OPEN, TO HELP YOU ALL COME TO TERMS WITH WHAT HAPPENED.
NOW--DOES ANYONE HAVE ANY QUESTIONS...?
YES--HOW COME BATMAN WASN'T FRIGHTENED?
ER...MAYBE BATMAN'S DIFFERENT, MIKE.
ALTHOUGH, YOU KNOW, I WOULDN'T BE SURPRISED IF HE WAS AFRAID. THAT GUN COULD JUST AS EASILY HAVE KILLED HIM, TOO!
YOU SHOULD GET HIM IN FOR COUNSELING, THEN!
THAT WOULD BE A FINE THING, DAVID!
GRAHAM--COULD YOU TAKE OVER FOR A FEW MINUTES, PLEASE...?

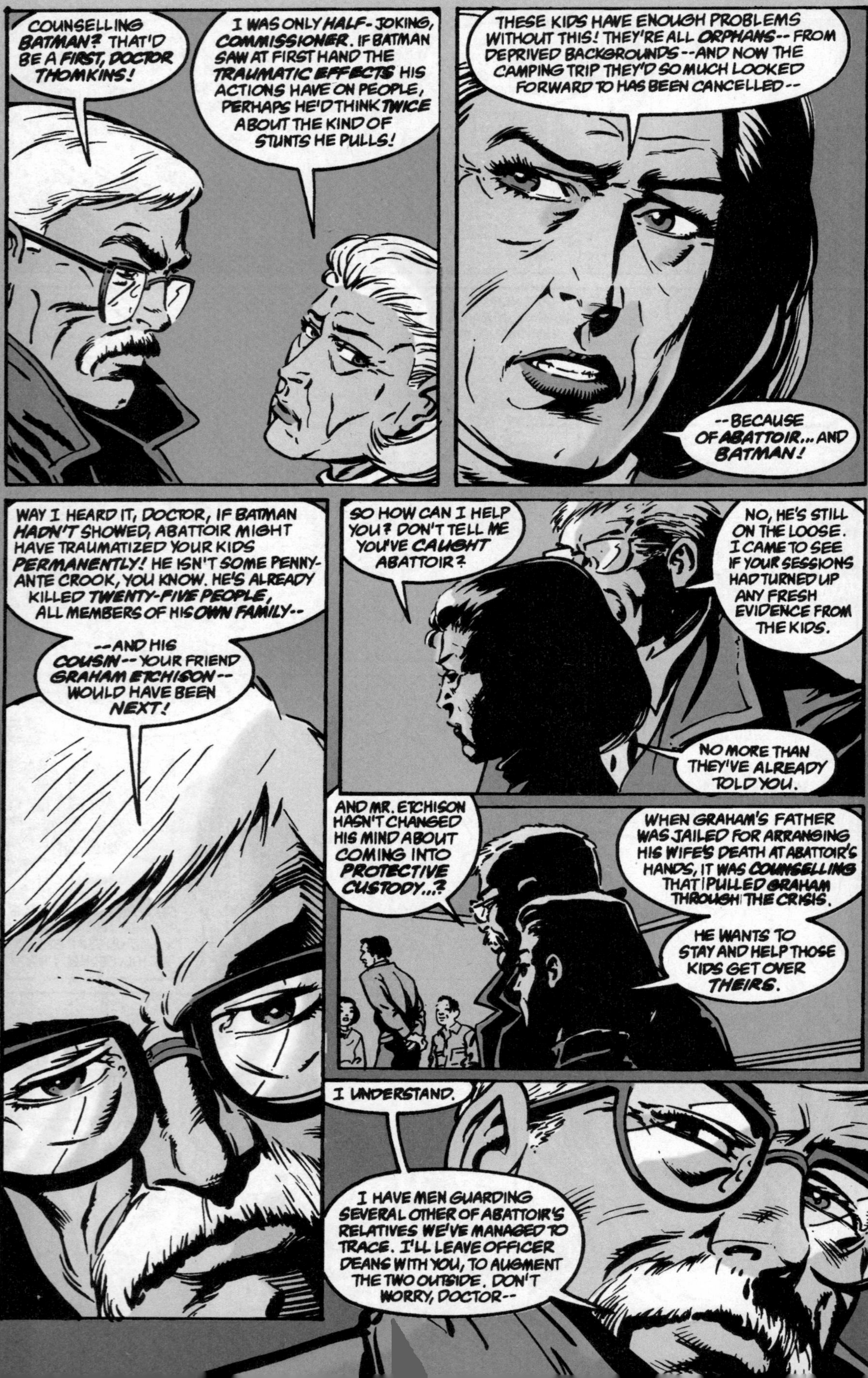
COUNSELLING BATMAN? THAT'D BE A FIRST, DOCTOR THOMKINS!
I WAS ONLY HALF-JOKING, COMMISSIONER. IF BATMAN SAW AT FIRST HAND THE TRAUMATIC EFFECTS HIS ACTIONS HAVE ON PEOPLE, PERHAPS HE'D THINK TWICE ABOUT THE KIND OF STUNTS HE PULLS!
THESE KIDS HAVE ENOUGH PROBLEMS WITHOUT THIS! THEY'RE ALL ORPHANS-- FROM DEPRIVED BACKGROUNDS--AND NOW THE CAMPING TRIP THEY'D SO MUCH LOOKED FORWARD TO HAS BEEN CANCELLED--
--BECAUSE OF ABATTOIR... AND BATMAN!
WAY I HEARD IT, DOCTOR, IF BATMAN HADN'T SHOWED, ABATTOIR MIGHT HAVE TRAUMATIZED YOUR KIDS PERMANENTLY! HE ISN'T SOME PENNY-ANTE CROOK, YOU KNOW. HE'S ALREADY KILLED TWENTY-FIVE PEOPLE, ALL MEMBERS OF HIS OWN FAMILY--
--AND HIS COUSIN-- YOUR FRIEND GRAHAM ETCHISON-- WOULD HAVE BEEN NEXT!
SO HOW CAN I HELP YOU? DON'T TELL ME YOU'VE CAUGHT ABATTOIR?
NO, HE'S STILL ON THE LOOSE. I CAME TO SEE IF YOUR SESSIONS HAD TURNED UP ANY FRESH EVIDENCE FROM THE KIDS.
NO MORE THAN THEY'VE ALREADY TOLD YOU.
AND MR. ETCHISON HASN'T CHANGED HIS MIND ABOUT COMING INTO PROTECTIVE CUSTODY...?
WHEN GRAHAM'S FATHER WAS JAILED FOR ARRANGING HIS WIFE'S DEATH AT ABATTOIR'S HANDS, IT WAS COUNSELLING THAT I PULLED GRAHAM THROUGH THE CRISIS.
HE WANTS TO STAY AND HELP THOSE KIDS GET OVER THEIRS.
I UNDERSTAND.
I HAVE MEN GUARDING SEVERAL OTHER OF ABATTOIR'S RELATIVES WE'VE MANAGED TO TRACE. I'LL LEAVE OFFICER DEANS WITH YOU, TO AUGMENT THE TWO OUTSIDE. DON'T WORRY, DOCTOR--

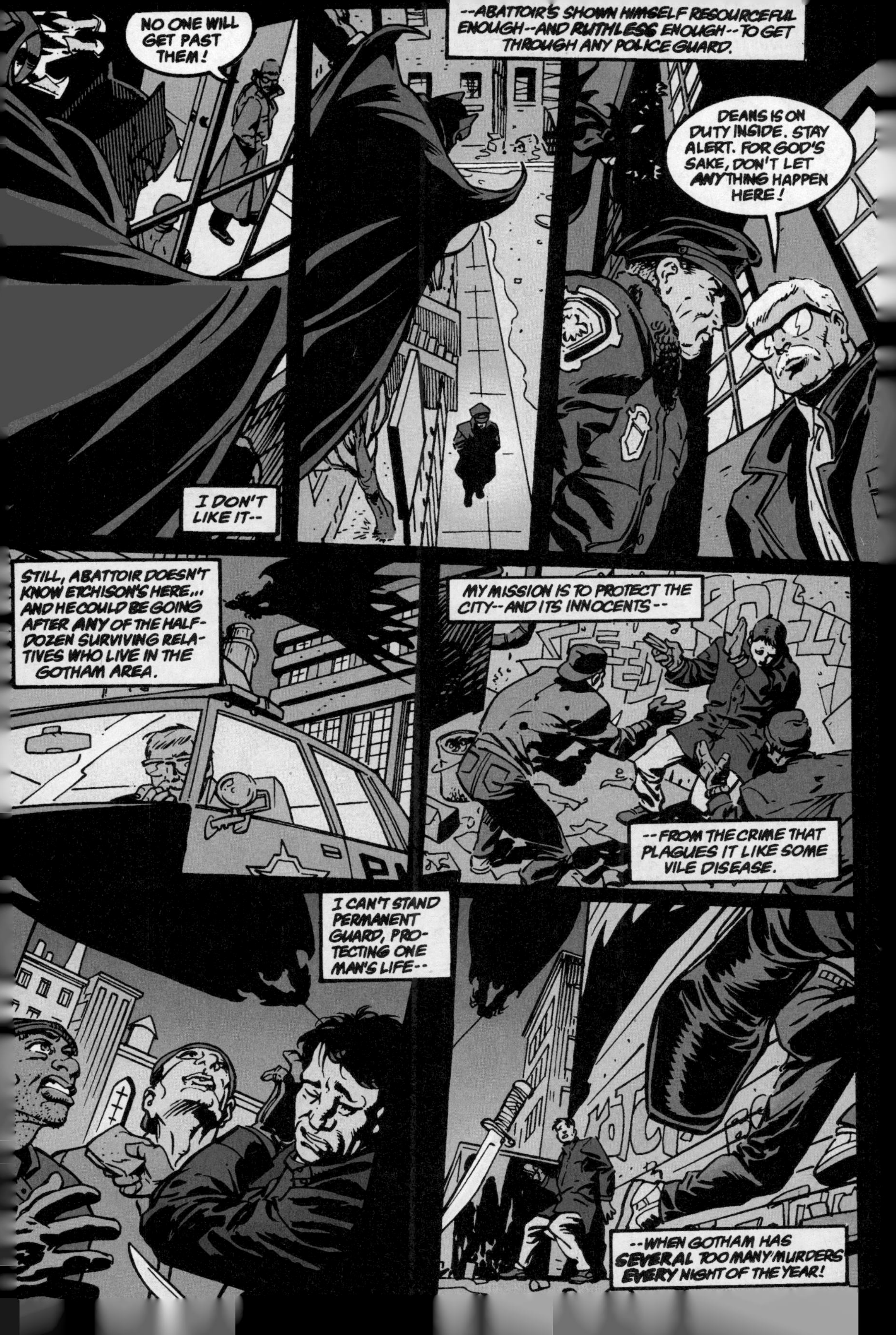
NO ONE WILL GET PAST THEM!
I DON'T LIKE IT--
--ABATTOIR'S SHOWN HIMSELF RESOURCEFUL ENOUGH--AND RUTHLESS ENOUGH--TO GET THROUGH ANY POLICE GUARD.
DEANS IS ON DUTY INSIDE. STAY ALERT. FOR GOD'S SAKE, DON'T LET ANYTHING HAPPEN HERE!
STILL, ABATTOIR DOESN'T KNOW ETCHISON'S HERE... AND HE COULD BE GOING AFTER ANY OF THE HALF-DOZEN SURVIVING RELATIVES WHO LIVE IN THE GOTHAM AREA.
MY MISSION IS TO PROTECT THE CITY--AND ITS INNOCENTS--
--FROM THE CRIME THAT PLAGUES IT LIKE SOME VILE DISEASE.
I CAN'T STAND PERMANENT GUARD, PROTECTING ONE MAN'S LIFE--
--WHEN GOTHAM HAS SEVERAL TOO MANY MURDERS EVERY NIGHT OF THE YEAR!

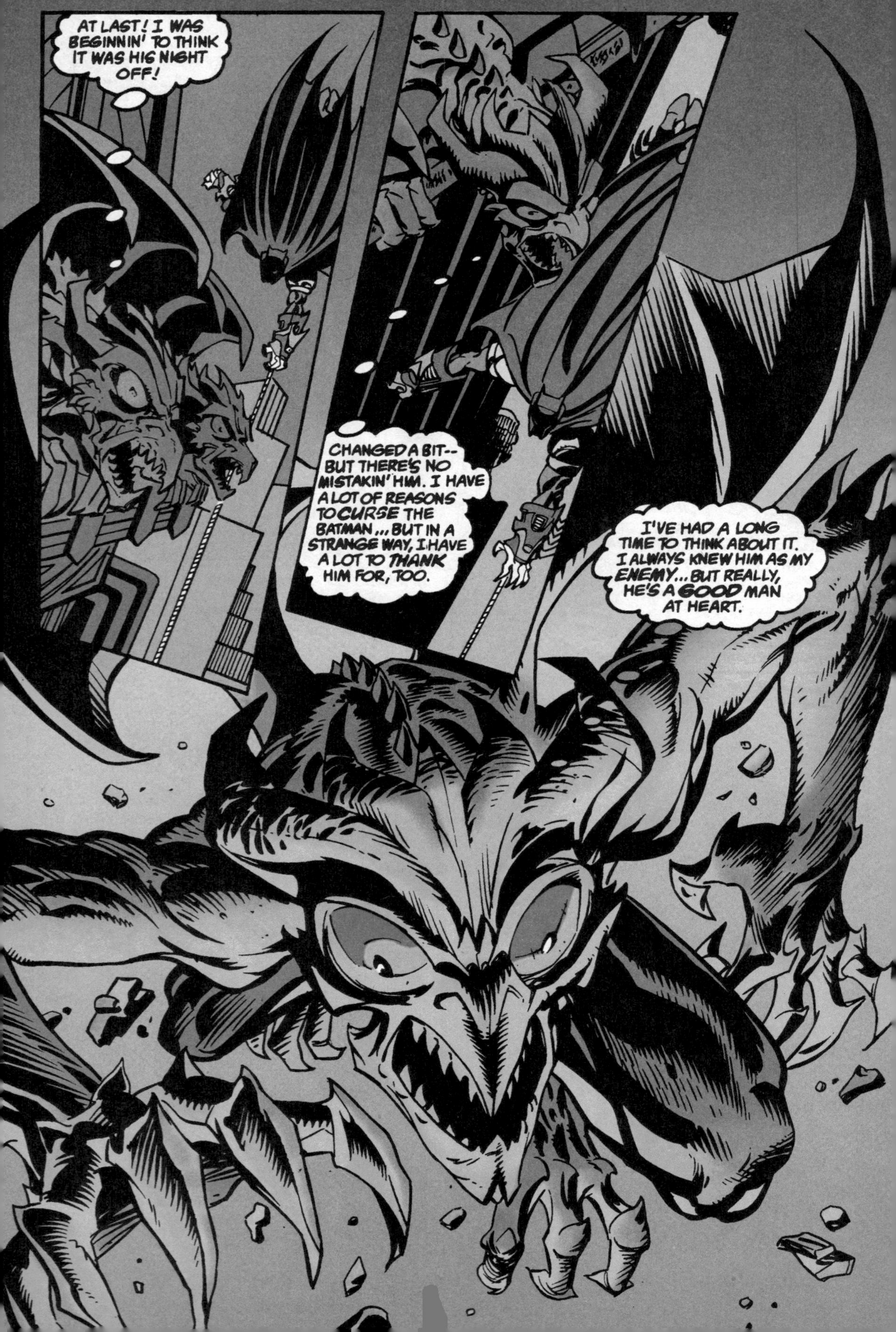
AT LAST! I WAS BEGINNIN' TO THINK IT WAS HIS NIGHT OFF!
CHANGED A BIT-- BUT THERE'S NO MISTAKIN' HIM. I HAVE A LOT OF REASONS TO CURSE THE BATMAN... BUT IN A STRANGE WAY, I HAVE A LOT TO THANK HIM FOR, TOO.
I'VE HAD A LONG TIME TO THINK ABOUT IT. I ALWAYS KNEW HIM AS MY ENEMY... BUT REALLY, HE'S A GOOD MAN AT HEART.

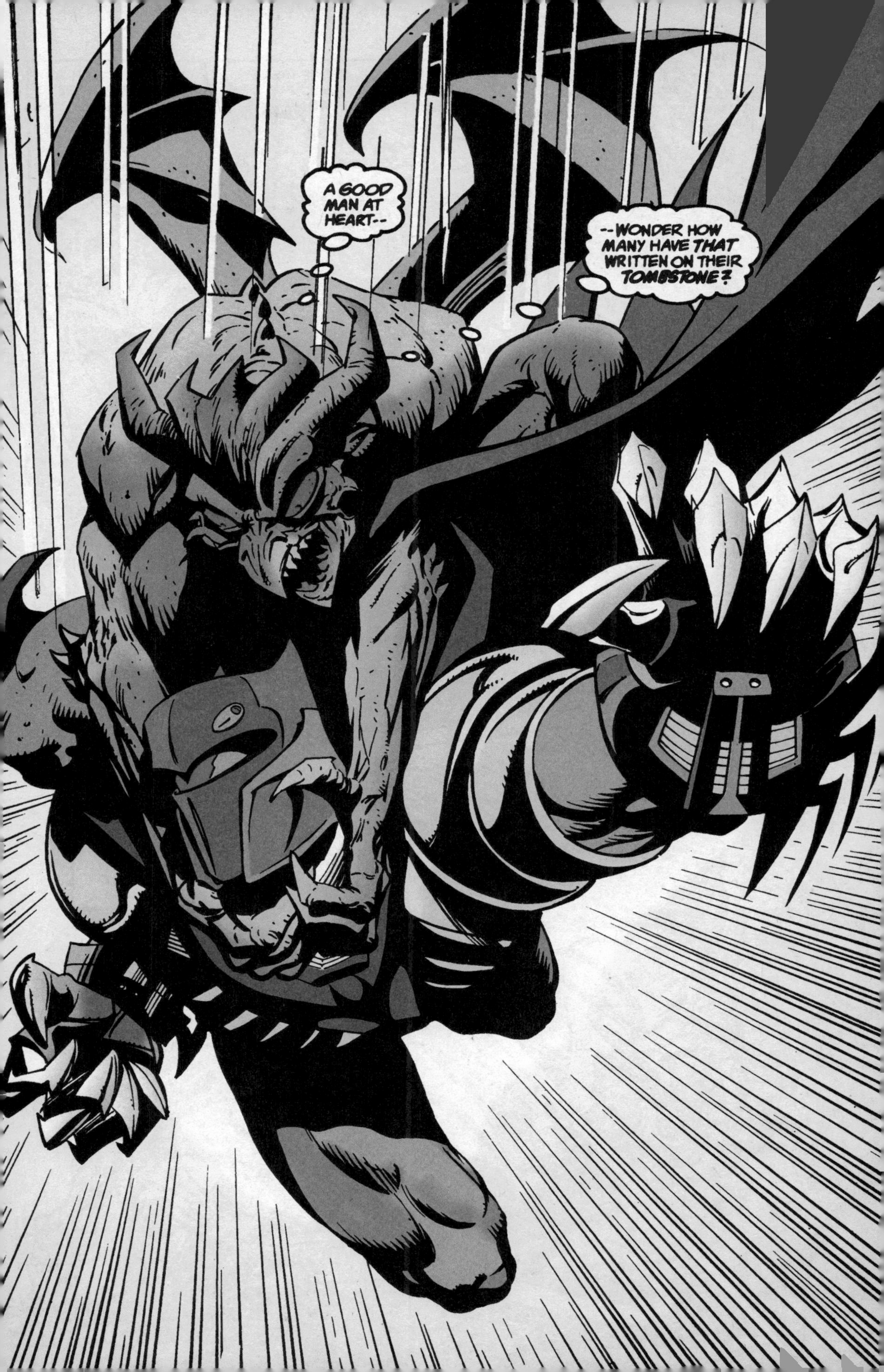
A GOOD MAN AT HEART--
--WONDER HOW MANY HAVE THAT WRITTEN ON THEIR TOMBSTONE?

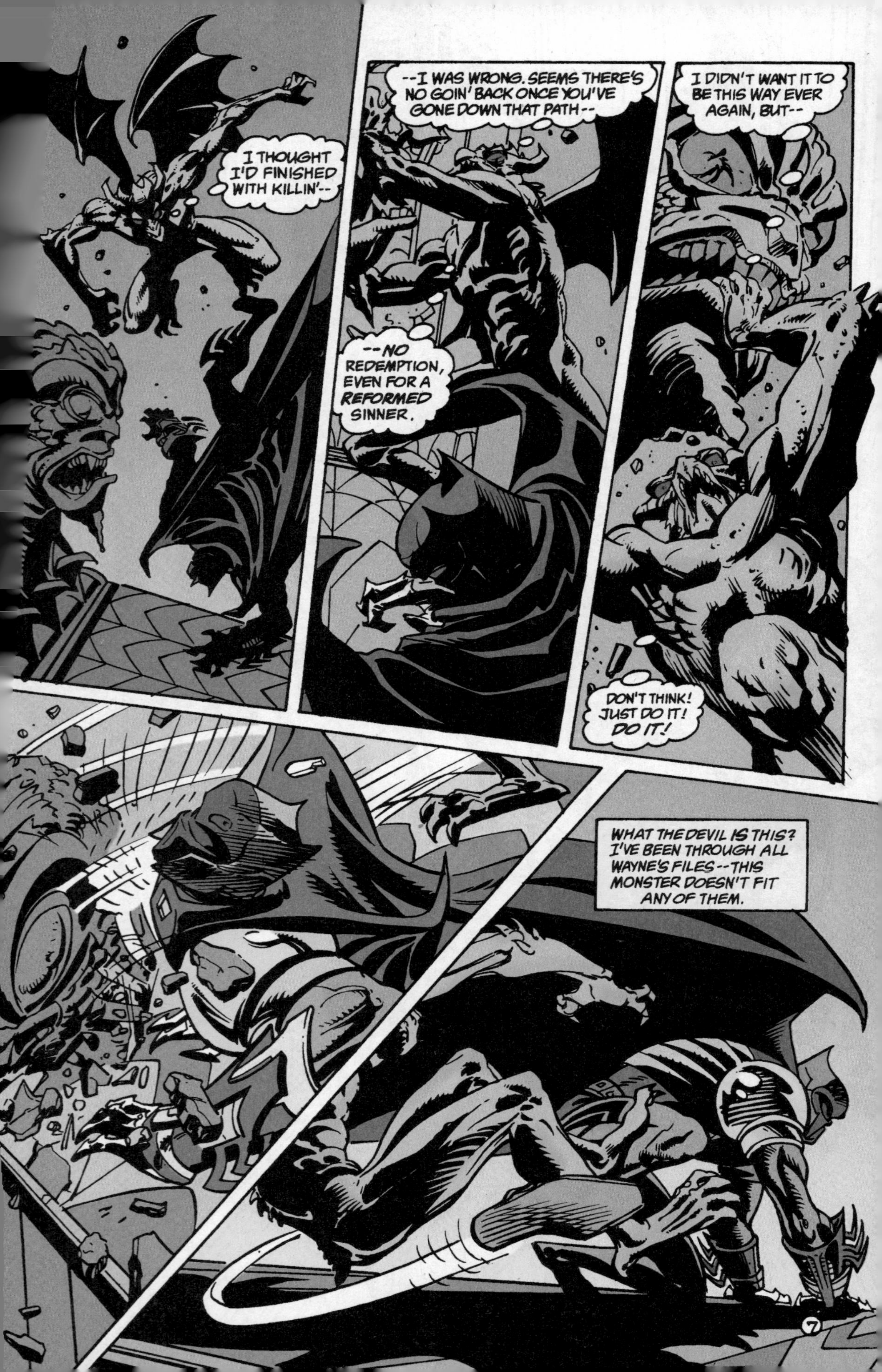
I THOUGHT I'D FINISHED WITH KILLIN'--
--I WAS WRONG. SEEMS THERE'S NO GOIN' BACK ONCE YOU'VE GONE DOWN THAT PATH--
--NO REDEMPTION, EVEN FOR A REFORMED SINNER.
I DIDN'T WANT IT TO BE THIS WAY EVER AGAIN, BUT--
DON'T THINK! JUST DO IT! DO IT!
WHAT THE DEVIL IS THIS? I'VE BEEN THROUGH ALL WAYNE'S FILES--THIS MONSTER DOESN'T FIT ANY OF THEM.
7

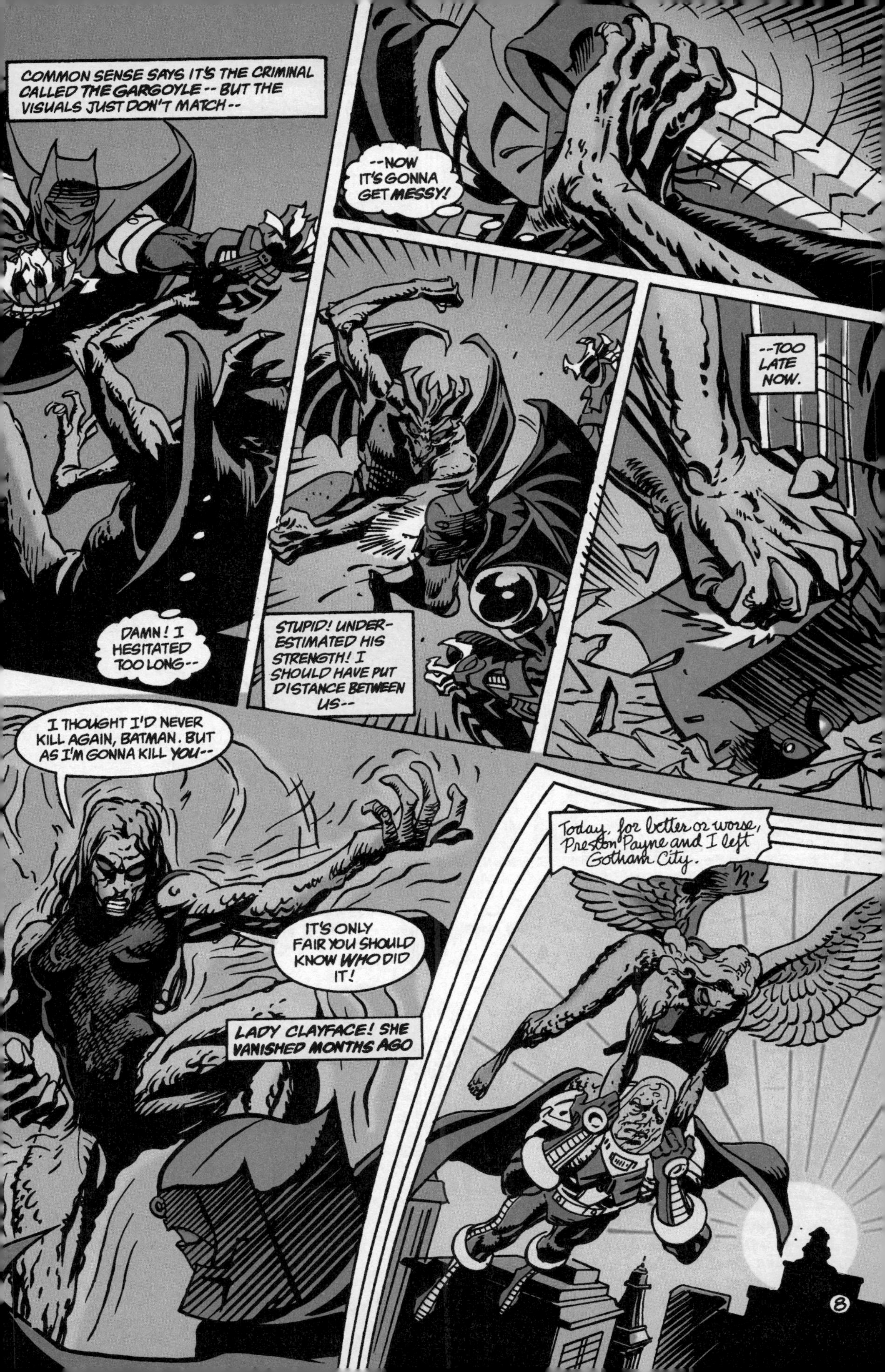
COMMON SENSE SAYS IT'S THE CRIMINAL CALLED THE GARGOYLE -- BUT THE VISUALS JUST DON'T MATCH --
DAMN! I HESITATED TOO LONG--
--NOW IT'S GONNA GET MESSY!
STUPID! UNDER-ESTIMATED HIS STRENGTH! I SHOULD HAVE PUT DISTANCE BETWEEN US--
--TOO LATE NOW.
I THOUGHT I'D NEVER KILL AGAIN, BATMAN. BUT AS I'M GONNA KILL YOU--
IT'S ONLY FAIR YOU SHOULD KNOW WHO DID IT!
LADY CLAYFACE! SHE VANISHED MONTHS AGO
Today, for better or worse, Preston Payne and I left Gotham City.
8

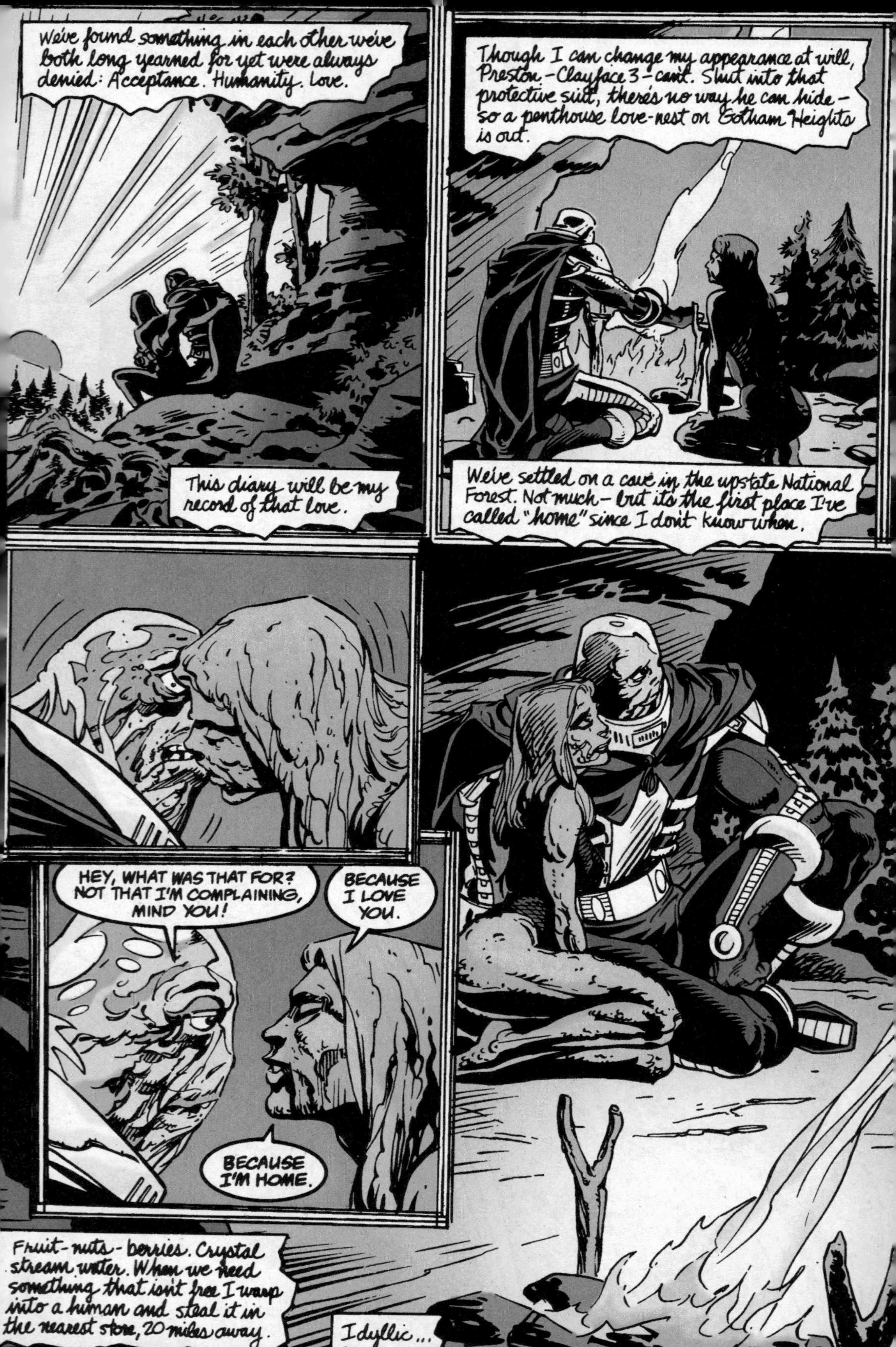
We've found something in each other we've both long yearned for yet were always denied: Acceptance. Humanity. Love.
This diary will be my record of that love.
Though I can change my appearance at will, Preston - Clayface 3 - can't. Shut into that protective suit, there's no way he can hide - so a penthouse love-nest on Gotham Heights is out.
We've settled on a cave in the upstate National Forest. Not much - but its the first place I've called "home" since I don't know when.
HEY, WHAT WAS THAT FOR? NOT THAT I'M COMPLAINING, MIND YOU!
BECAUSE I LOVE YOU.
BECAUSE I'M HOME.
Fruit - nuts - berries. Crystal stream water. When we need something that isn't free I warp into a human and steal it in the nearest store, 20 miles away.
Idyllic...

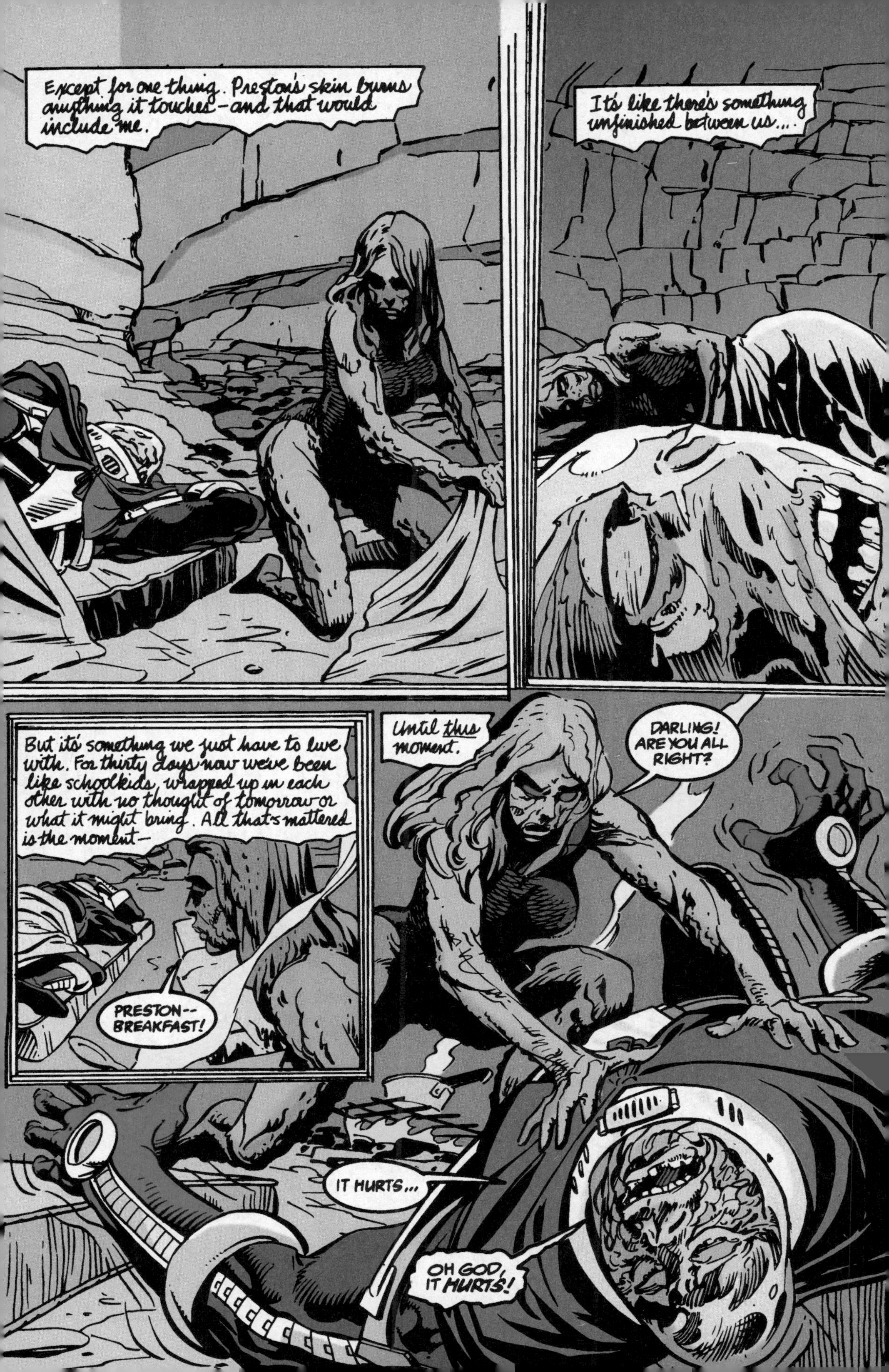

Except for one thing. Preston's skin burns anything it touches--and that would include me.
It's like there's something unfinished between us....
But it's something we just have to live with. For thirty days now we've been like schoolkids, wrapped up in each other with no thought of tomorrow or what it might bring. All that's mattered is the moment--
PRESTON-- BREAKFAST!
Until this moment.
DARLING! ARE YOU ALL RIGHT?
IT HURTS...
OH GOD, IT HURTS!

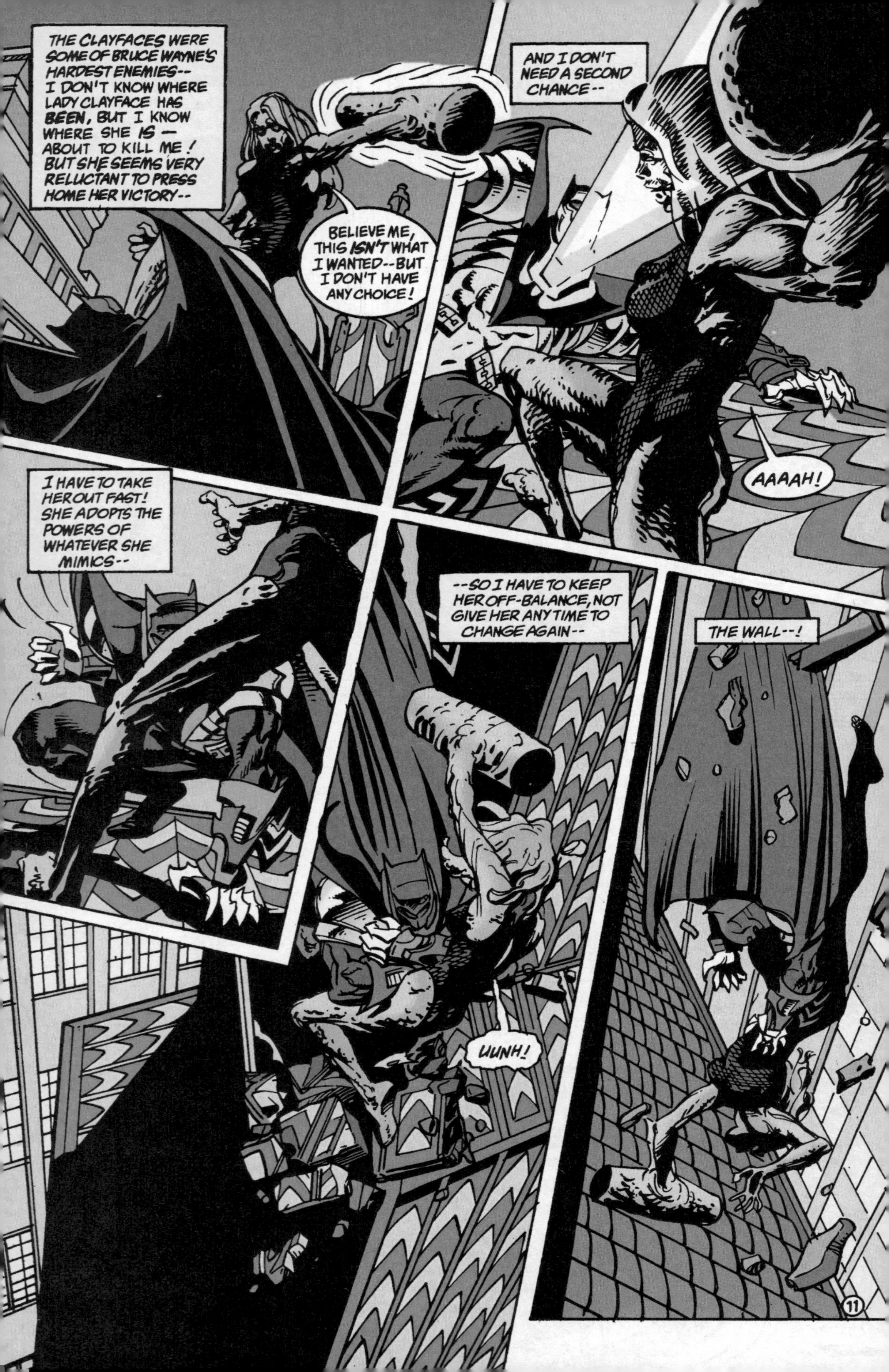
THE CLAYFACES WERE SOME OF BRUCE WAYNE'S HARDEST ENEMIES-- I DON'T KNOW WHERE LADY CLAYFACE HAS BEEN, BUT I KNOW WHERE SHE IS -- ABOUT TO KILL ME! BUT SHE SEEMS VERY RELUCTANT TO PRESS HOME HER VICTORY--
BELIEVE ME, THIS ISN'T WHAT I WANTED--BUT I DON'T HAVE ANY CHOICE!
AND I DON'T NEED A SECOND CHANCE--
AAAAH!
I HAVE TO TAKE HER OUT FAST! SHE ADOPTS THE POWERS OF WHATEVER SHE MIMICS--
--SO I HAVE TO KEEP HER OFF-BALANCE, NOT GIVE HER ANY TIME TO CHANGE AGAIN--
UUNH!
THE WALL--!
11

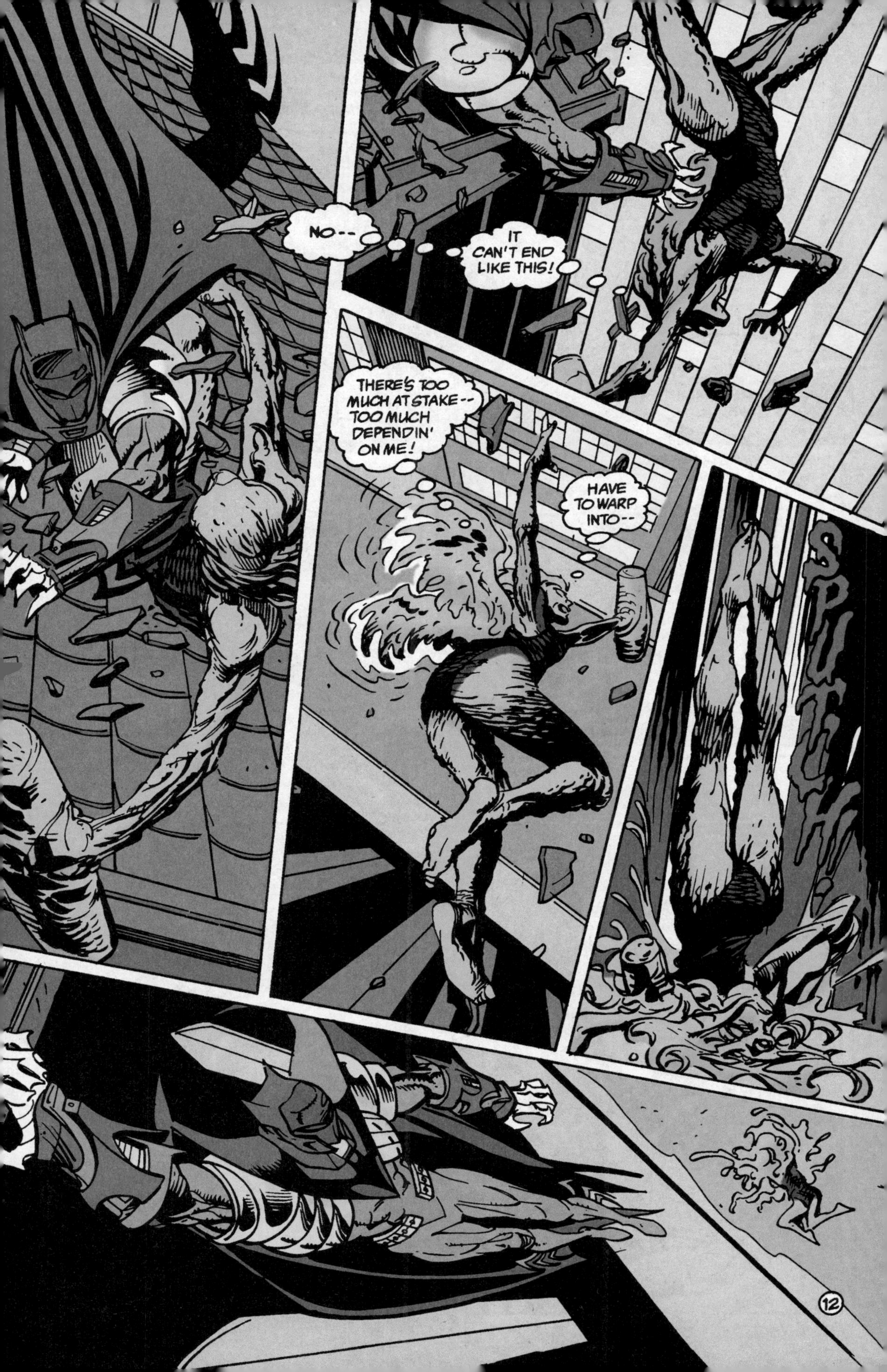
NO--
IT CAN'T END LIKE THIS!
THERE'S TOO MUCH AT STAKE-- TOO MUCH DEPENDIN' ON ME!
HAVE TO WARP INTO--
SPLUT

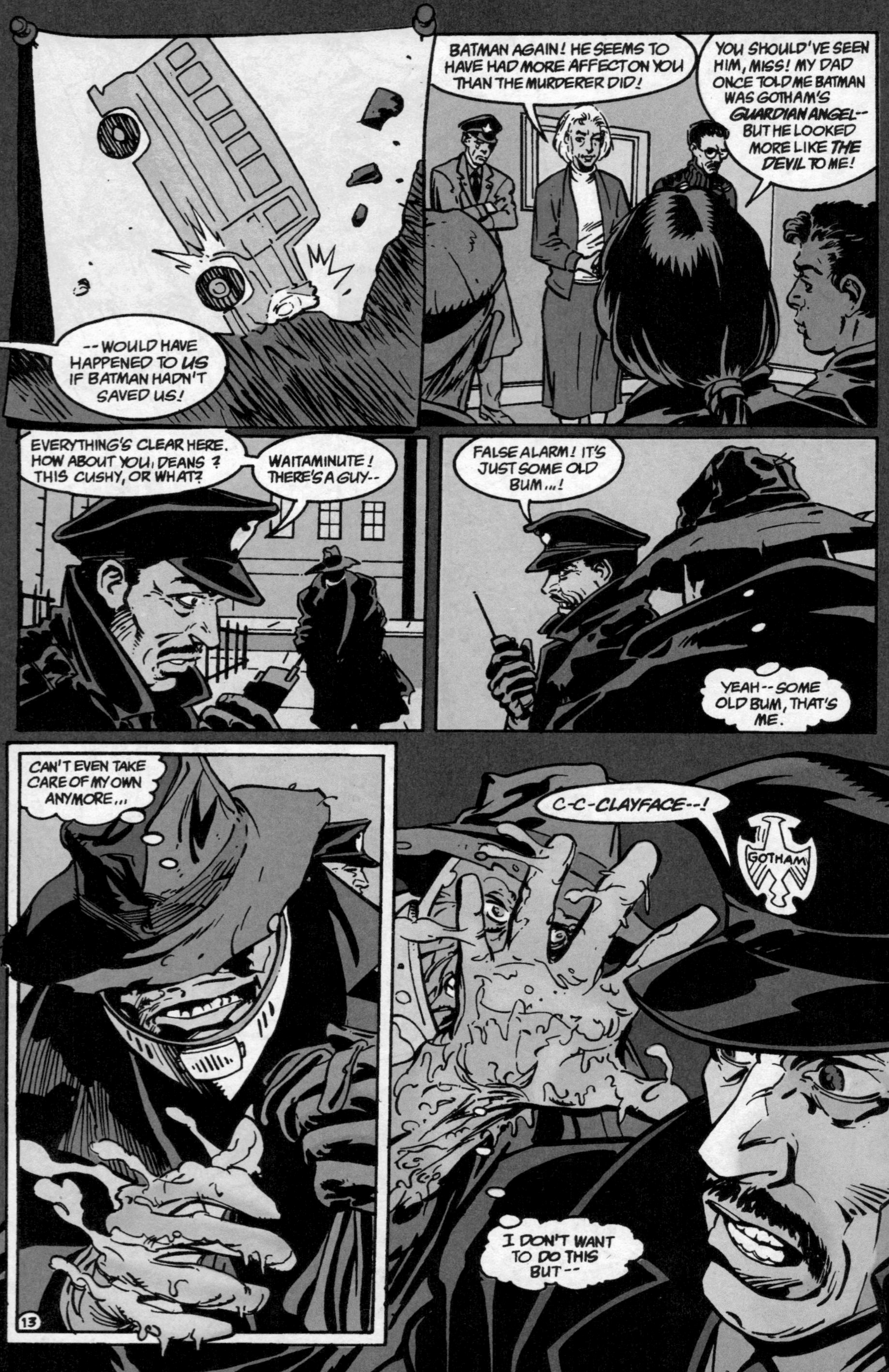
--WOULD HAVE HAPPENED TO US IF BATMAN HADN'T SAVED US!
BATMAN AGAIN! HE SEEMS TO HAVE HAD MORE AFFECT ON YOU THAN THE MURDERER DID!
YOU SHOULD'VE SEEN HIM, MISS! MY DAD ONCE TOLD ME BATMAN WAS GOTHAM'S GUARDIAN ANGEL-- BUT HE LOOKED MORE LIKE THE DEVIL TO ME!
EVERYTHING'S CLEAR HERE. HOW ABOUT YOU, DEANS? THIS CUSHY, OR WHAT?
WAITAMINUTE! THERE'S A GUY--
FALSE ALARM! IT'S JUST SOME OLD BUM...!
YEAH--SOME OLD BUM, THAT'S ME.
CAN'T EVEN TAKE CARE OF MY OWN ANYMORE...
C-C-CLAYFACE--!
GOTHAM
I DON'T WANT TO DO THIS BUT--
13

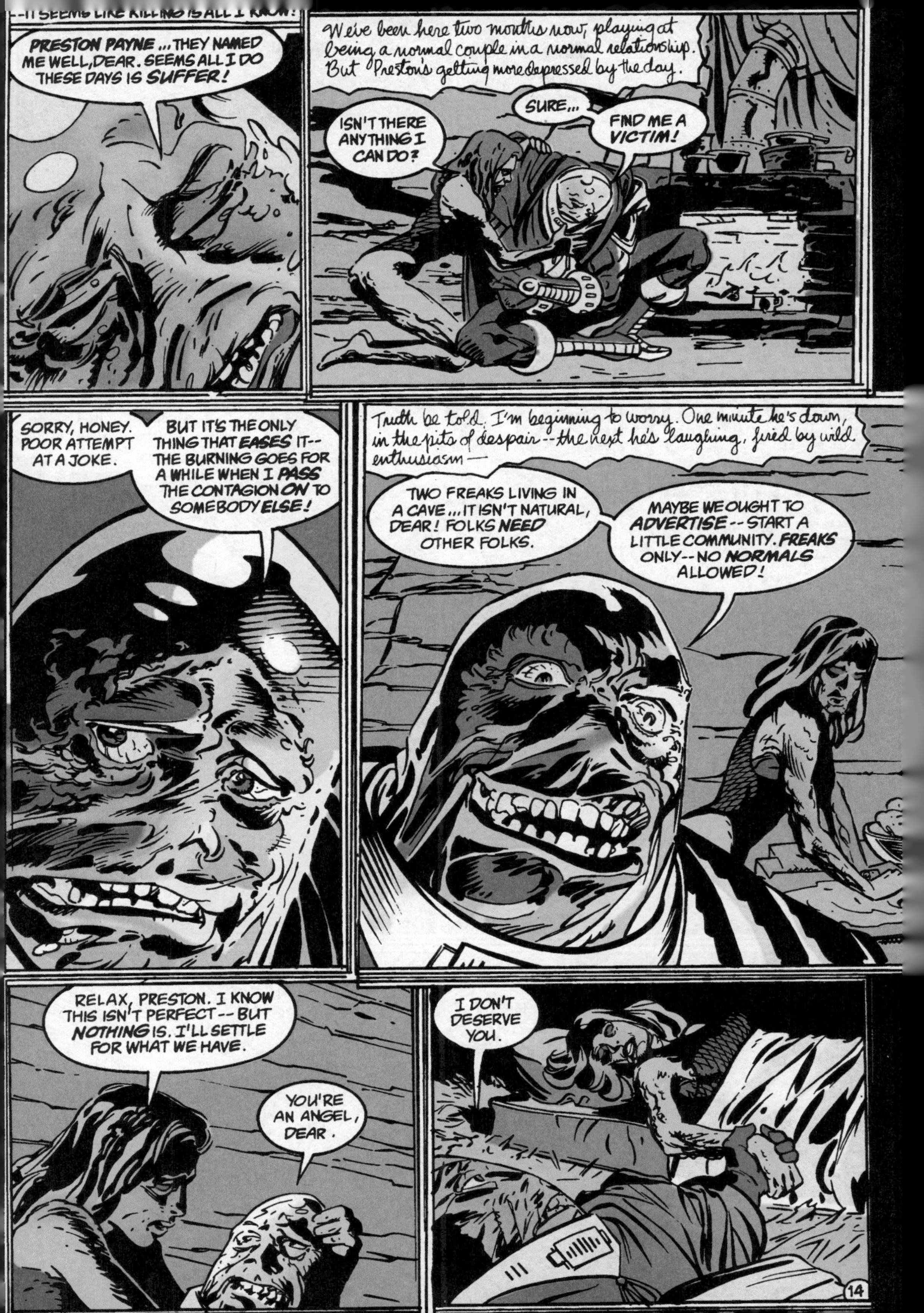
--IT SEEMS LIKE KILLING IS ALL I KNOW!
PRESTON PAYNE ... THEY NAMED ME WELL, DEAR. SEEMS ALL I DO THESE DAYS IS SUFFER!
We've been here two months now, playing at being a normal couple in a normal relationship. But Preston's getting more depressed by the day.
ISN'T THERE ANYTHING I CAN DO?
SURE...
FIND ME A VICTIM!
SORRY, HONEY. POOR ATTEMPT AT A JOKE.
BUT IT'S THE ONLY THING THAT EASES IT-- THE BURNING GOES FOR A WHILE WHEN I PASS THE CONTAGION ON TO SOMEBODY ELSE!
Truth be told. I'm beginning to worry. One minute he's down, in the pits of despair--the next he's laughing, fired by wild enthusiasm—
TWO FREAKS LIVING IN A CAVE... IT ISN'T NATURAL, DEAR! FOLKS NEED OTHER FOLKS.
MAYBE WE OUGHT TO ADVERTISE--START A LITTLE COMMUNITY. FREAKS ONLY--NO NORMALS ALLOWED!
RELAX, PRESTON. I KNOW THIS ISN'T PERFECT--BUT NOTHING IS. I'LL SETTLE FOR WHAT WE HAVE.
YOU'RE AN ANGEL, DEAR.
I DON'T DESERVE YOU.
14

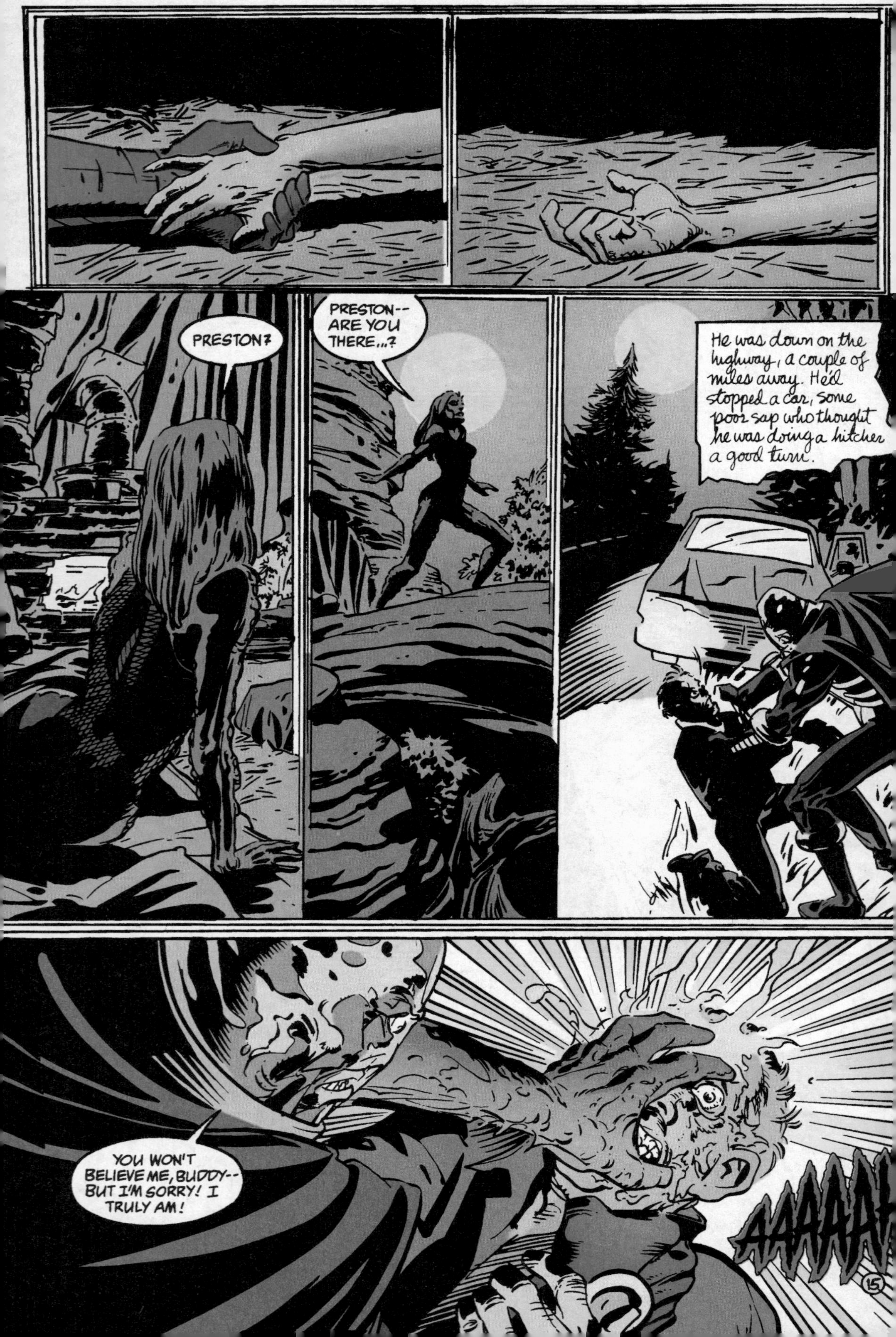
PRESTON?
PRESTON-- ARE YOU THERE...?
He was down on the highway, a couple of miles away. He'd stopped a car, some poor sap who thought he was doing a hitcher a good turn.
YOU WON'T BELIEVE ME, BUDDY-- BUT I'M SORRY! I TRULY AM!
AAAAA
15

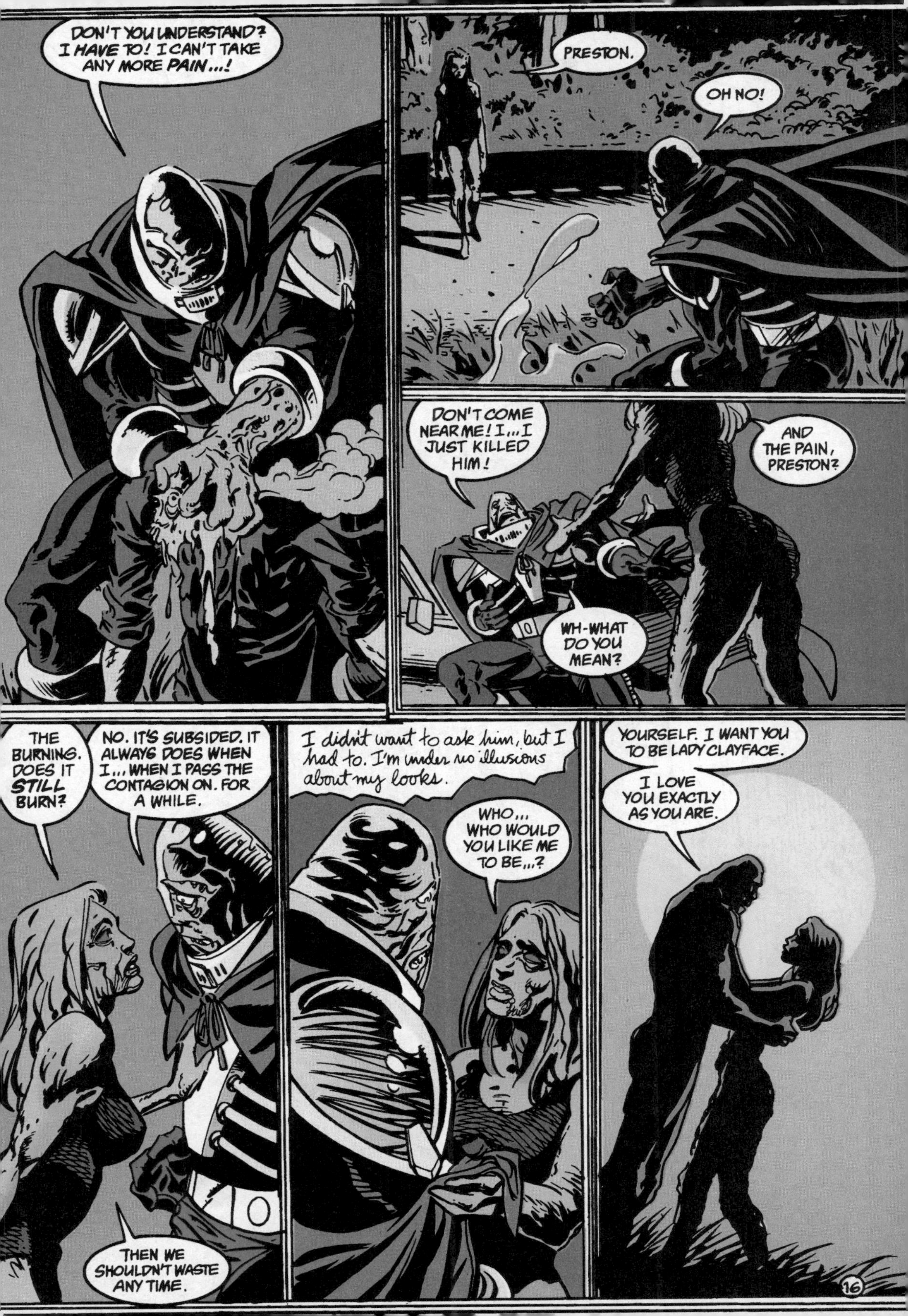
DON'T YOU UNDERSTAND? I HAVE TO! I CAN'T TAKE ANY MORE PAIN...!
PRESTON.
OH NO!
DON'T COME NEAR ME! I...I JUST KILLED HIM!
AND THE PAIN, PRESTON?
WH-WHAT DO YOU MEAN?
THE BURNING. DOES IT STILL BURN?
NO. IT'S SUBSIDED. IT ALWAYS DOES WHEN I... WHEN I PASS THE CONTAGION ON. FOR A WHILE.
THEN WE SHOULDN'T WASTE ANY TIME.
I didn't want to ask him, but I had to. I'm under no illusions about my looks.
WHO... WHO WOULD YOU LIKE ME TO BE...?
YOURSELF. I WANT YOU TO BE LADY CLAYFACE.
I LOVE YOU EXACTLY AS YOU ARE.
16

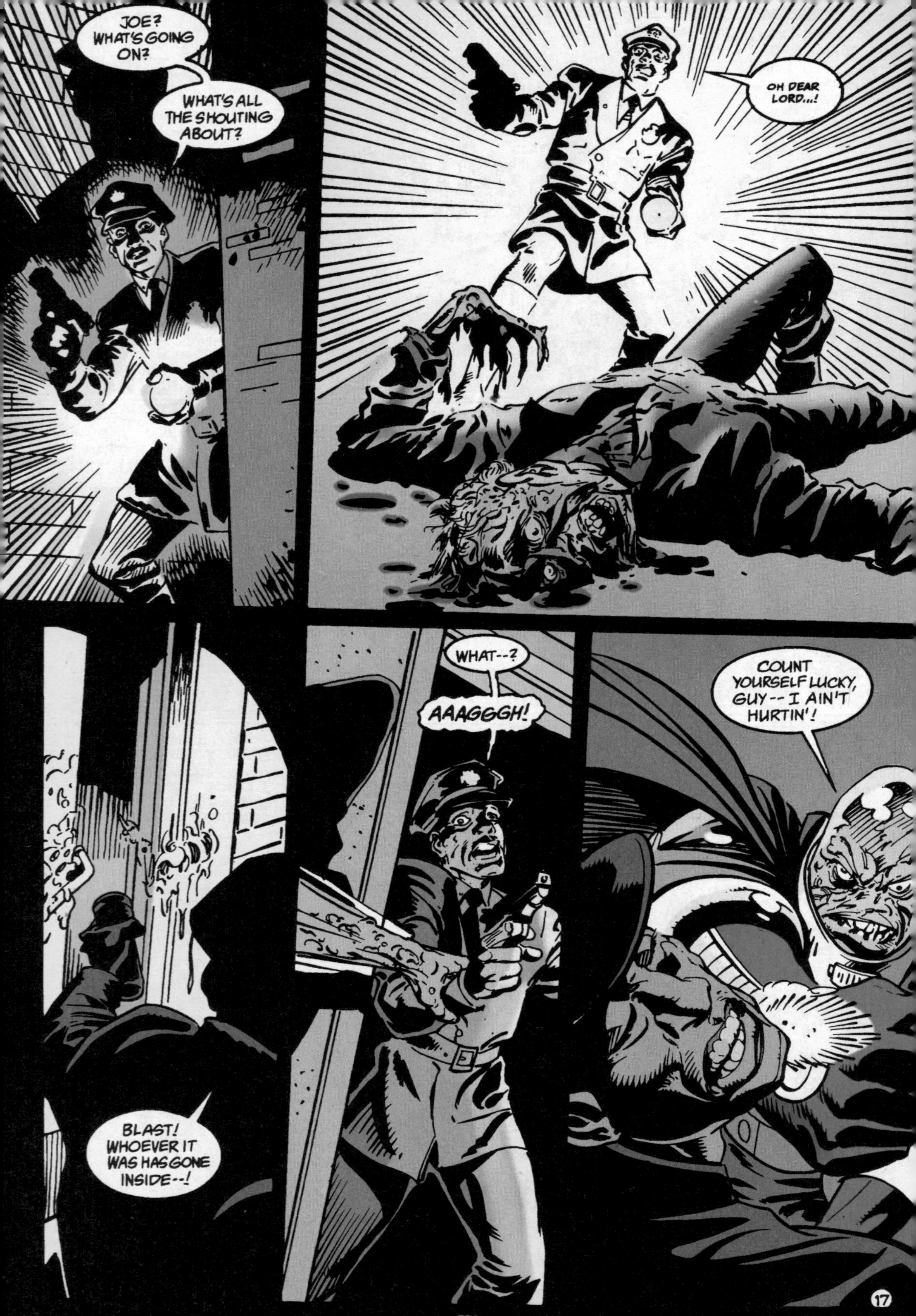

JOE? WHAT'S GOING ON?
WHAT'S ALL THE SHOUTING ABOUT?
OH DEAR LORD...!
BLAST! WHOEVER IT WAS HAS GONE INSIDE--!
WHAT--?
AAAGGGH!
COUNT YOURSELF LUCKY, GUY -- I AIN'T HURTIN'!
17

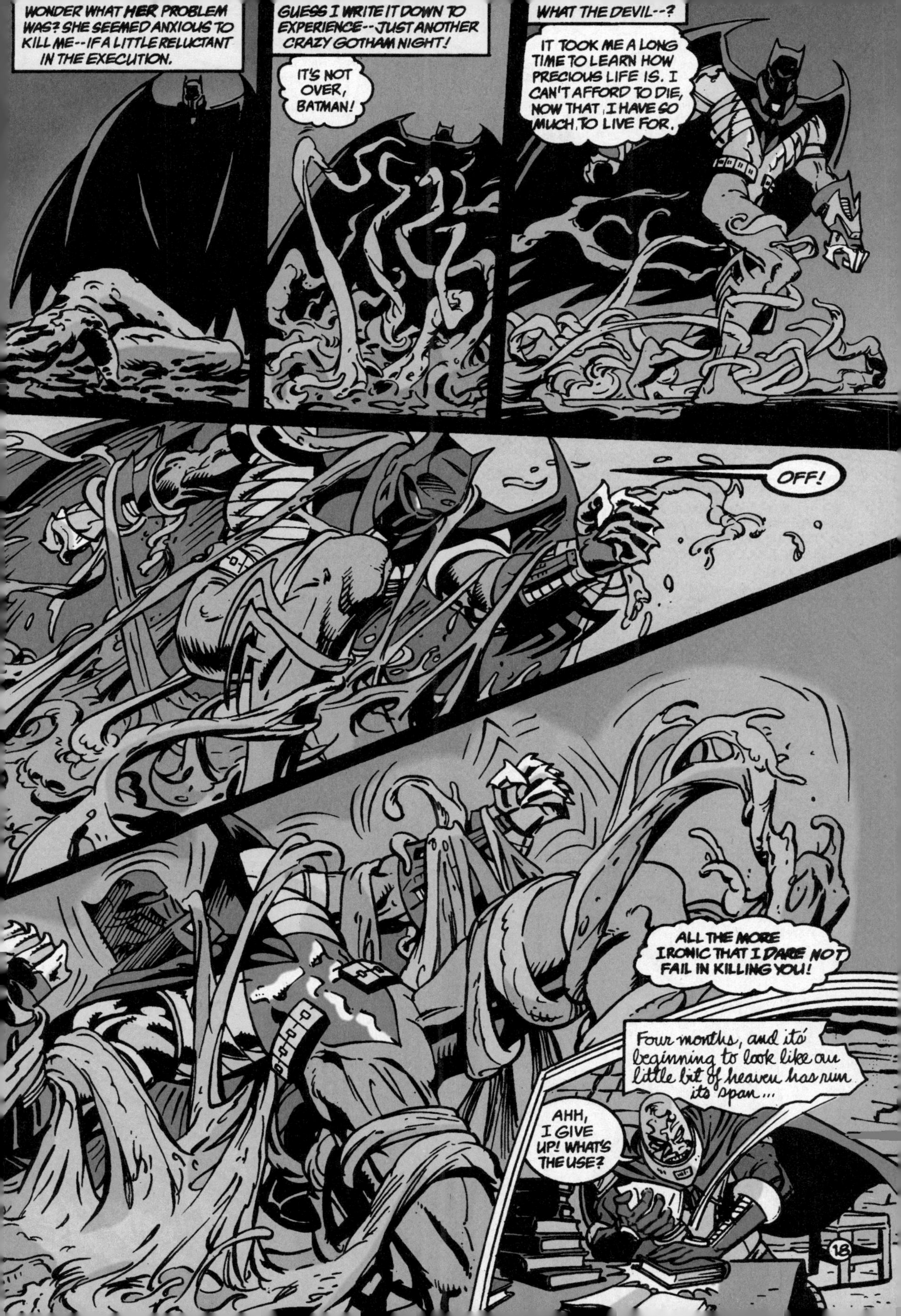

WONDER WHAT HER PROBLEM WAS? SHE SEEMED ANXIOUS TO KILL ME--IF A LITTLE RELUCTANT IN THE EXECUTION.
GUESS I WRITE IT DOWN TO EXPERIENCE--JUST ANOTHER CRAZY GOTHAM NIGHT!
IT'S NOT OVER, BATMAN!
WHAT THE DEVIL--?
IT TOOK ME A LONG TIME TO LEARN HOW PRECIOUS LIFE IS. I CAN'T AFFORD TO DIE, NOW THAT I HAVE SO MUCH TO LIVE FOR.
OFF!
ALL THE MORE IRONIC THAT I DARE NOT FAIL IN KILLING YOU!
Four months, and it's beginning to look like our little bit of heaven has run its span...
AHH, I GIVE UP! WHAT'S THE USE?
18

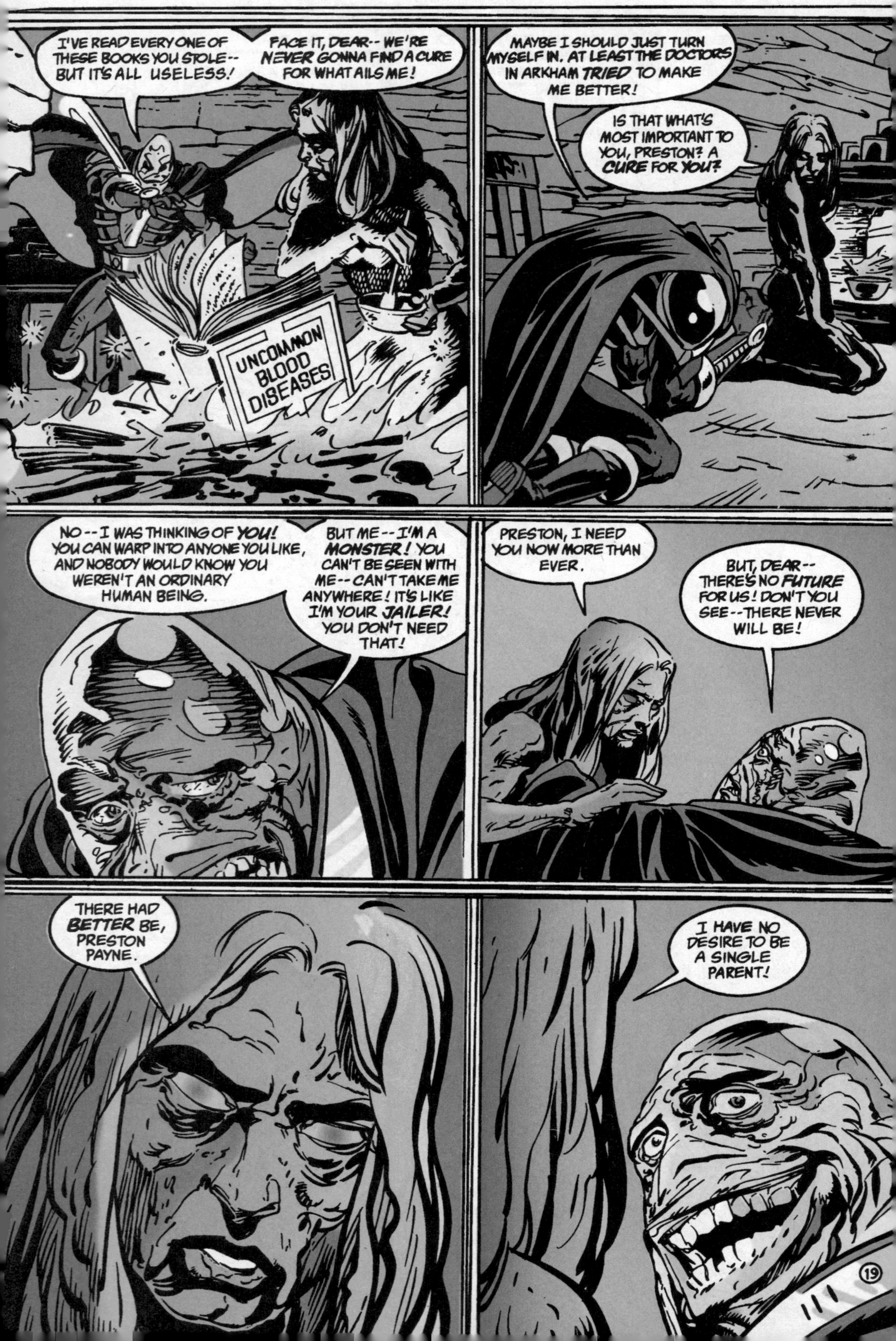
I'VE READ EVERY ONE OF THESE BOOKS YOU STOLE-- BUT IT'S ALL USELESS!
FACE IT, DEAR-- WE'RE NEVER GONNA FIND A CURE FOR WHAT AILS ME!
UNCOMMON BLOOD DISEASES
MAYBE I SHOULD JUST TURN MYSELF IN. AT LEAST THE DOCTORS IN ARKHAM TRIED TO MAKE ME BETTER!
IS THAT WHAT'S MOST IMPORTANT TO YOU, PRESTON? A CURE FOR YOU?
NO--I WAS THINKING OF YOU! YOU CAN WARP INTO ANYONE YOU LIKE, AND NOBODY WOULD KNOW YOU WEREN'T AN ORDINARY HUMAN BEING.
BUT ME--I'M A MONSTER! YOU CAN'T BE SEEN WITH ME--CAN'T TAKE ME ANYWHERE! IT'S LIKE I'M YOUR JAILER! YOU DON'T NEED THAT!
PRESTON, I NEED YOU NOW MORE THAN EVER.
BUT, DEAR-- THERE'S NO FUTURE FOR US! DON'T YOU SEE--THERE NEVER WILL BE!
THERE HAD BETTER BE, PRESTON PAYNE.
I HAVE NO DESIRE TO BE A SINGLE PARENT!

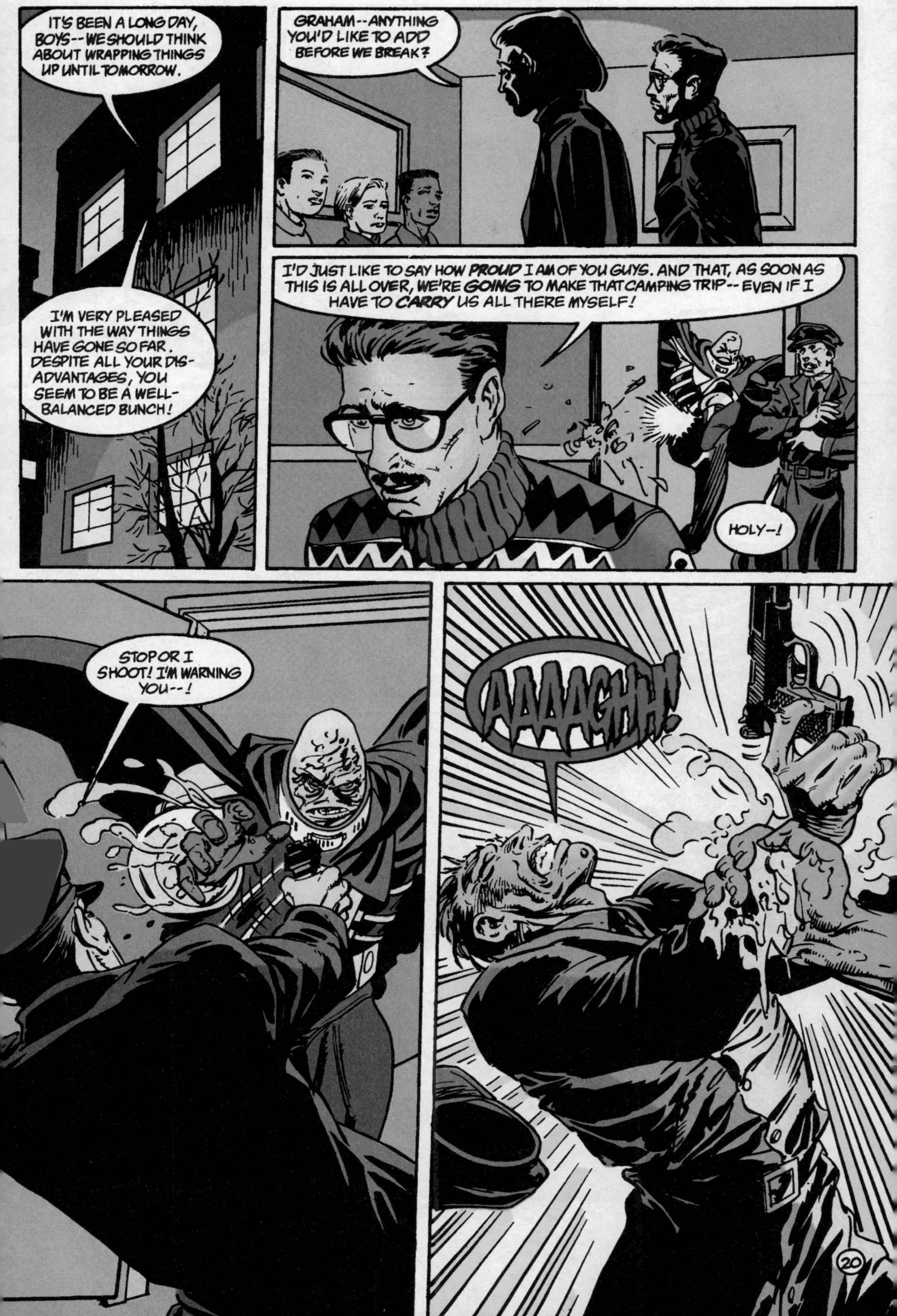
IT'S BEEN A LONG DAY, BOYS--WE SHOULD THINK ABOUT WRAPPING THINGS UP UNTIL TOMORROW.
I'M VERY PLEASED WITH THE WAY THINGS HAVE GONE SO FAR. DESPITE ALL YOUR DIS-ADVANTAGES, YOU SEEM TO BE A WELL-BALANCED BUNCH!
GRAHAM--ANYTHING YOU'D LIKE TO ADD BEFORE WE BREAK?
I'D JUST LIKE TO SAY HOW PROUD I AM OF YOU GUYS. AND THAT, AS SOON AS THIS IS ALL OVER, WE'RE GOING TO MAKE THAT CAMPING TRIP--EVEN IF I HAVE TO CARRY US ALL THERE MYSELF!
HOLY--!
STOP OR I SHOOT! I'M WARNING YOU--!
AAAAGHH!
20

AAAAAAAAAAAA

I DON'T WANT TO HURT ANYBODY ELSE.

GRAHAM ERCHISON-- YOU COME WITH ME, AND THERE'LL BE NO MORE TROUBLE!

NO! I DON'T KNOW WHY YOU WANT HIM--BUT HE'S BEEN THROUGH ENOUGH! I WON'T LET YOU TAKE HIM!

THEN YOU'LL BURN!

D-DO YOUR WORST! YOU WON'T HAVE HIM!

SUIT YOURSELF, LADY--

21

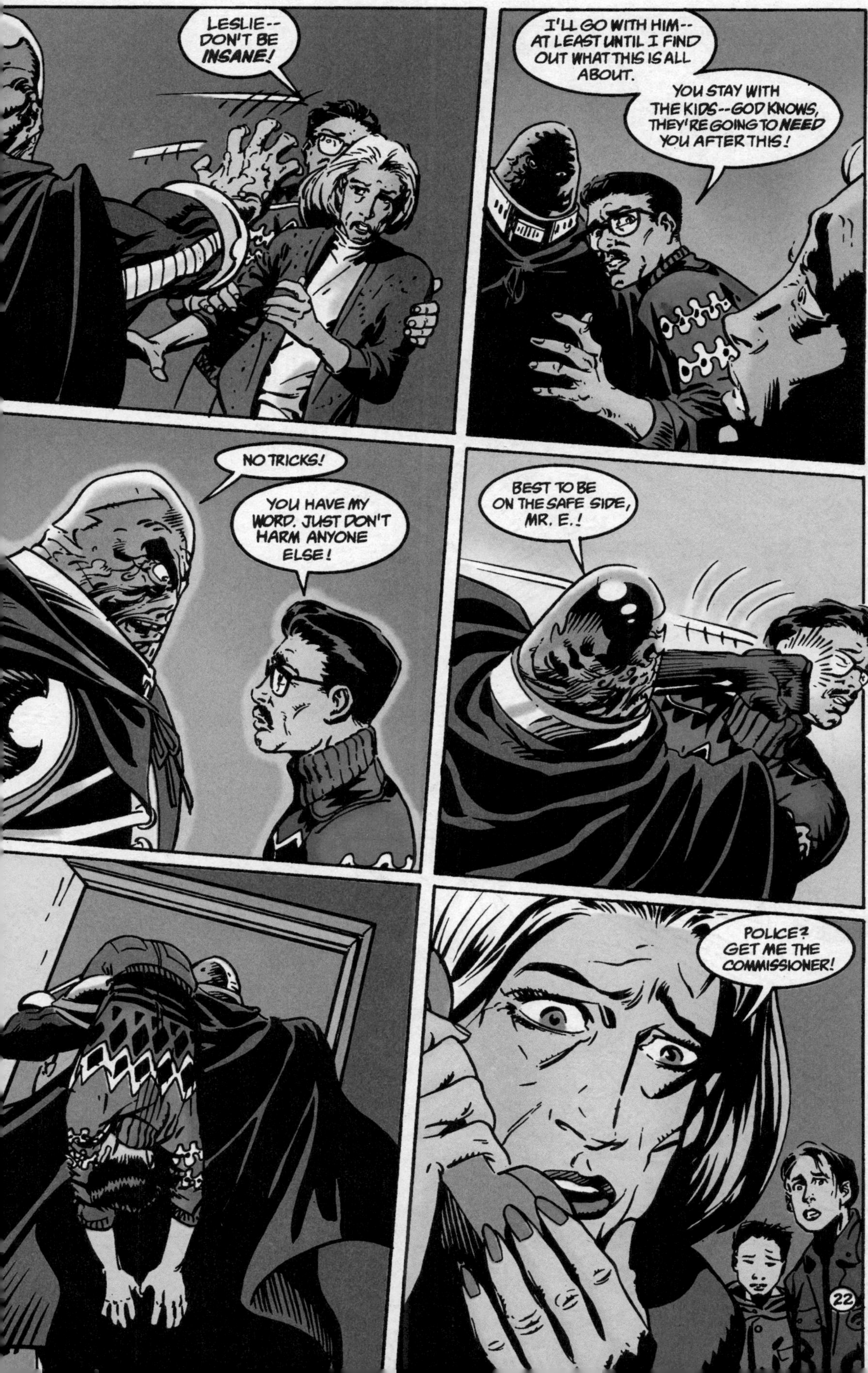
LESLIE-- DON'T BE INSANE!
I'LL GO WITH HIM-- AT LEAST UNTIL I FIND OUT WHAT THIS IS ALL ABOUT.
YOU STAY WITH THE KIDS--GOD KNOWS, THEY'RE GOING TO NEED YOU AFTER THIS!
NO TRICKS!
YOU HAVE MY WORD. JUST DON'T HARM ANYONE ELSE!
BEST TO BE ON THE SAFE SIDE, MR. E.!
POLICE? GET ME THE COMMISSIONER!
22

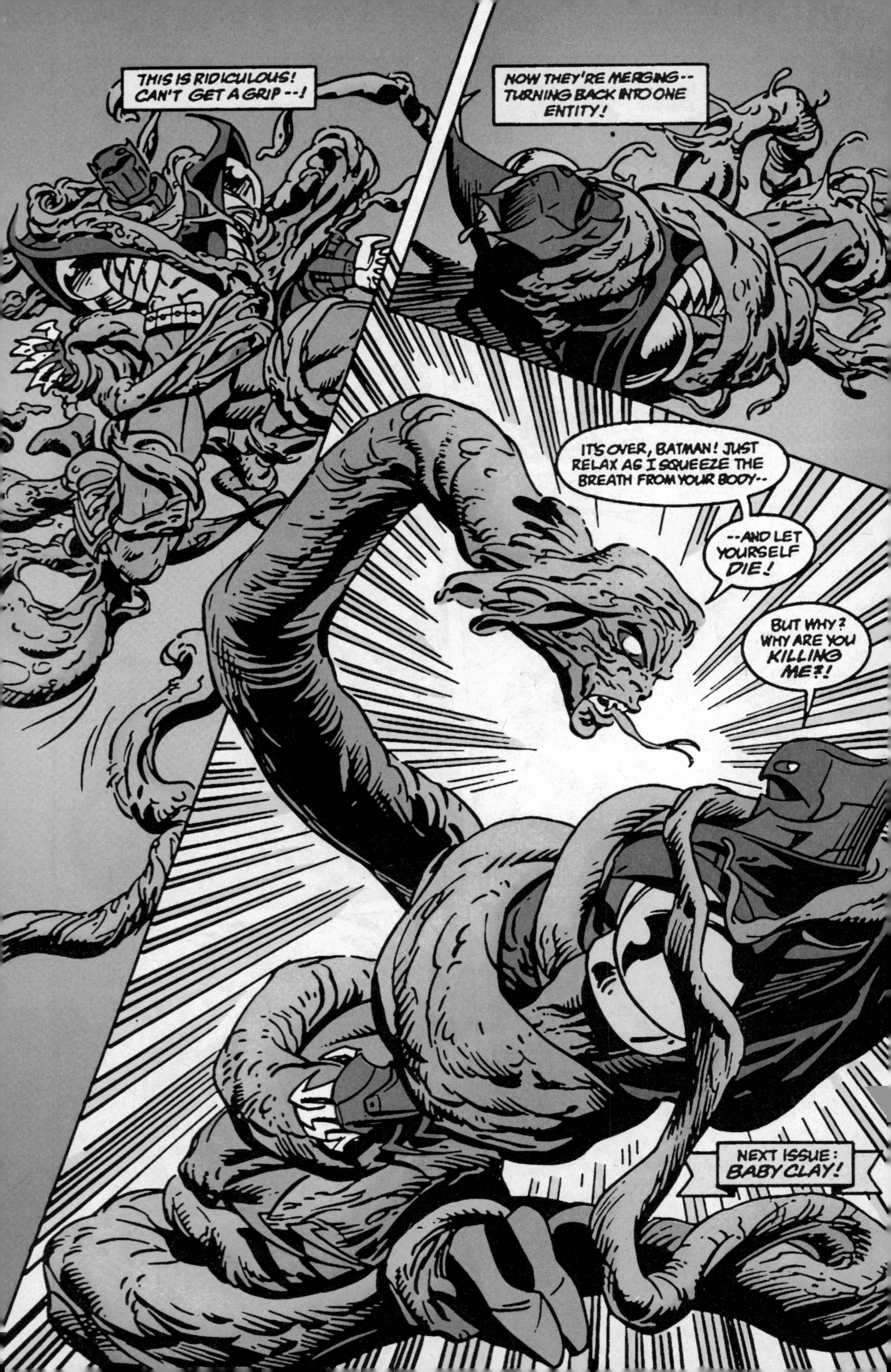

THIS IS RIDICULOUS! CAN'T GET A GRIP --!
NOW THEY'RE MERGING -- TURNING BACK INTO ONE ENTITY!
IT'S OVER, BATMAN! JUST RELAX AS I SQUEEZE THE BREATH FROM YOUR BODY--
--AND LET YOURSELF DIE!
BUT WHY? WHY ARE YOU KILLING ME?!
NEXT ISSUE: BABY CLAY!

Cover art by **BRIAN STELFREEZE**

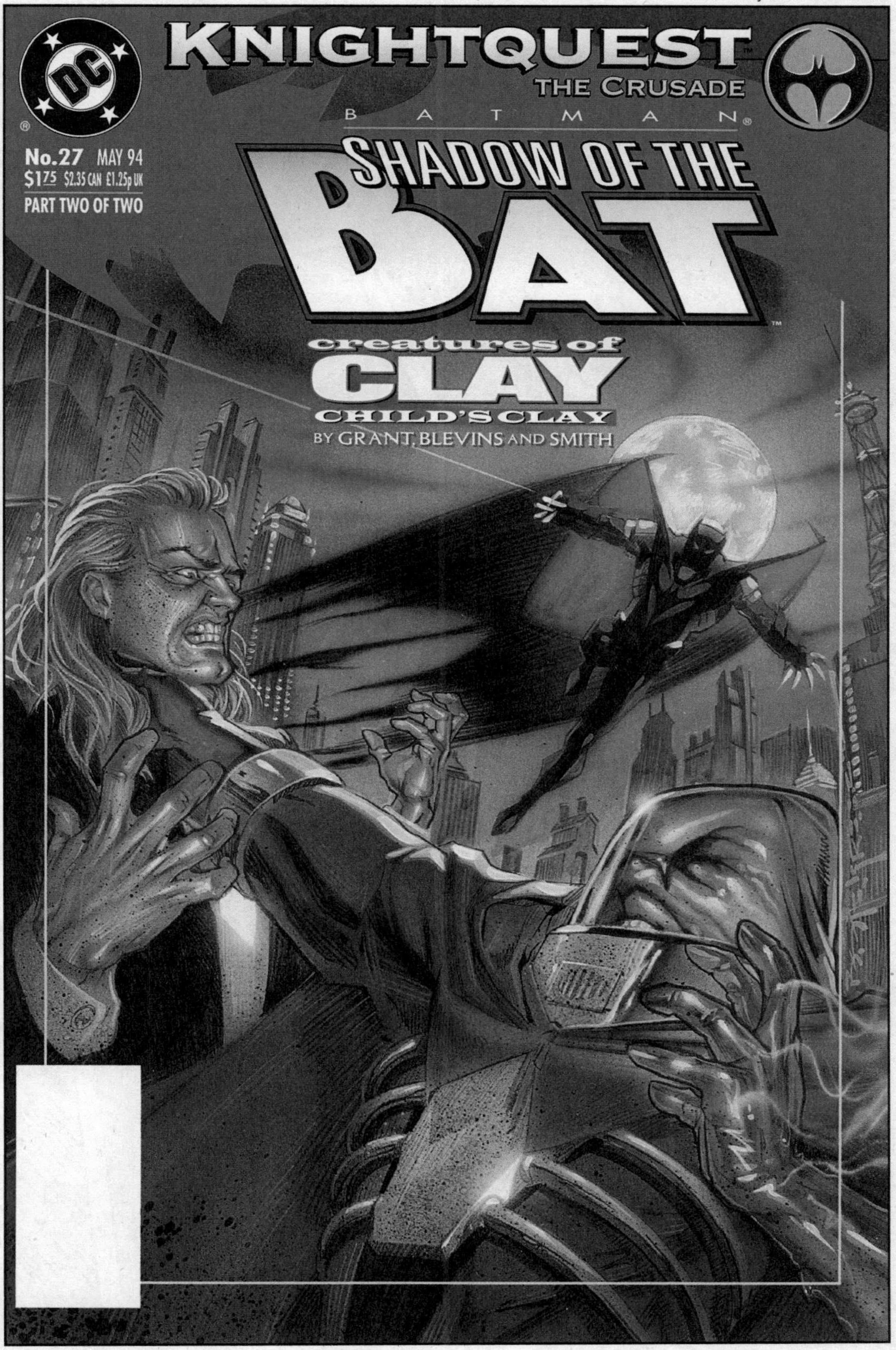
DC
KNIGHTQUEST
THE CRUSADE
BATMAN
No.27 MAY 94
$1.75 $2.35 CAN £1.25p UK
PART TWO OF TWO
SHADOW OF THE BAT
creatures of
CLAY
CHILD'S CLAY
BY GRANT, BLEVINS AND SMITH

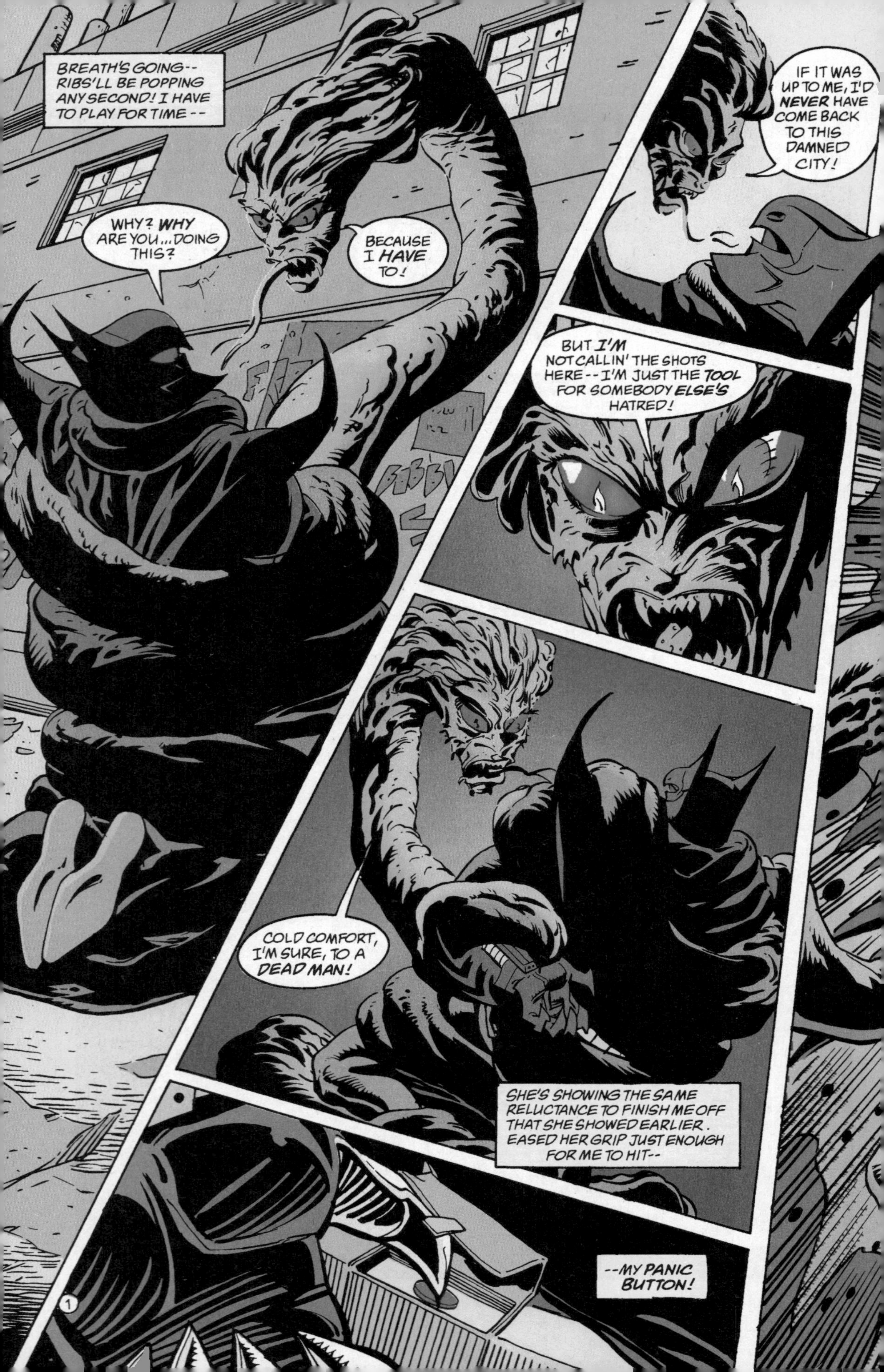
BREATH'S GOING-- RIBS'LL BE POPPING ANY SECOND! I HAVE TO PLAY FOR TIME--
WHY? WHY ARE YOU...DOING THIS?
BECAUSE I HAVE TO!
IF IT WAS UP TO ME, I'D NEVER HAVE COME BACK TO THIS DAMNED CITY!
BUT I'M NOT CALLIN' THE SHOTS HERE--I'M JUST THE TOOL FOR SOMEBODY ELSE'S HATRED!
COLD COMFORT, I'M SURE, TO A DEAD MAN!
SHE'S SHOWING THE SAME RELUCTANCE TO FINISH ME OFF THAT SHE SHOWED EARLIER. EASED HER GRIP JUST ENOUGH FOR ME TO HIT--
--MY PANIC BUTTON!
1

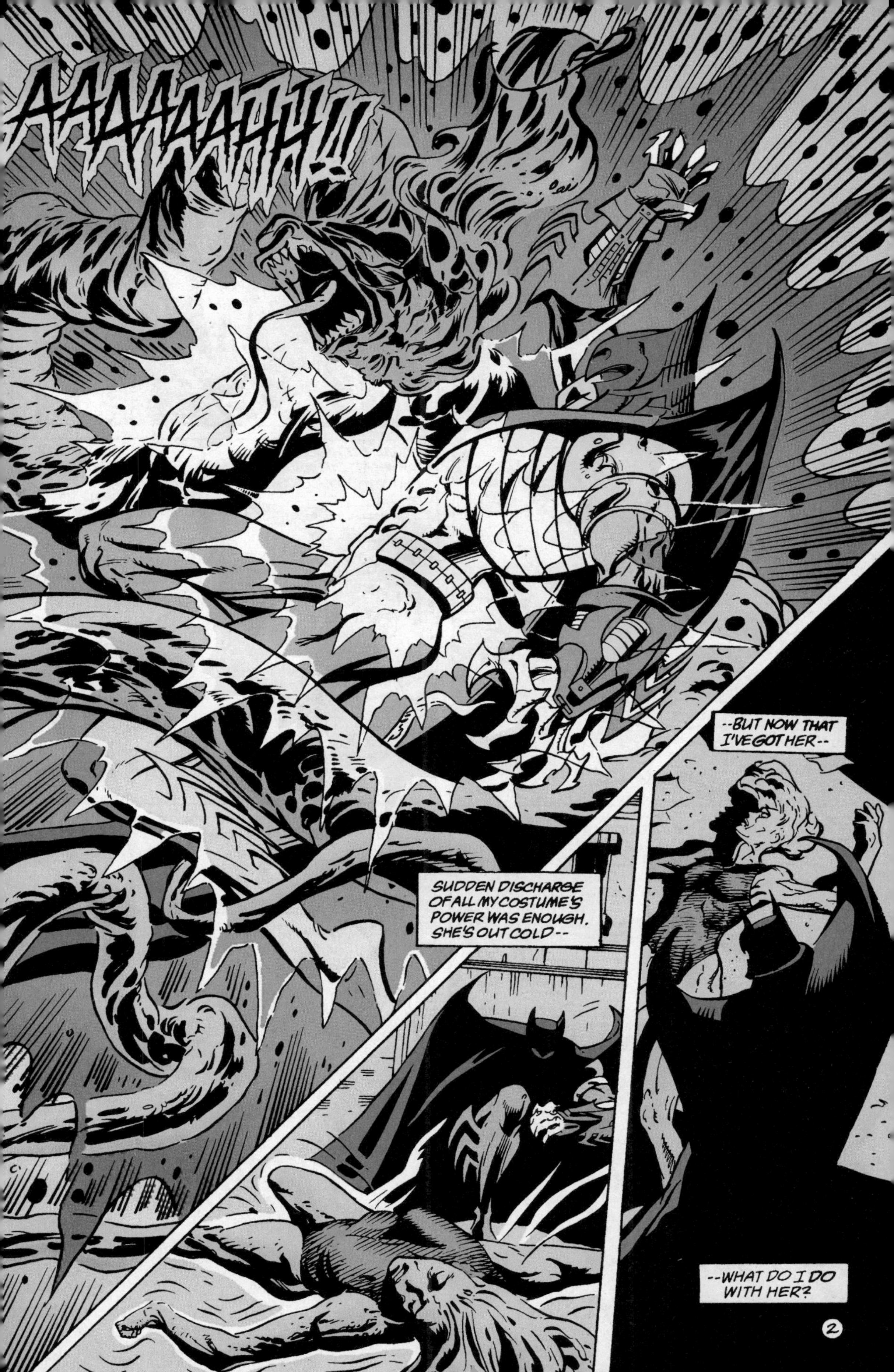
AAAAAHH!!
SUDDEN DISCHARGE OF ALL MY COSTUME'S POWER WAS ENOUGH. SHE'S OUT COLD--
--BUT NOW THAT I'VE GOT HER--
--WHAT DO I DO WITH HER?

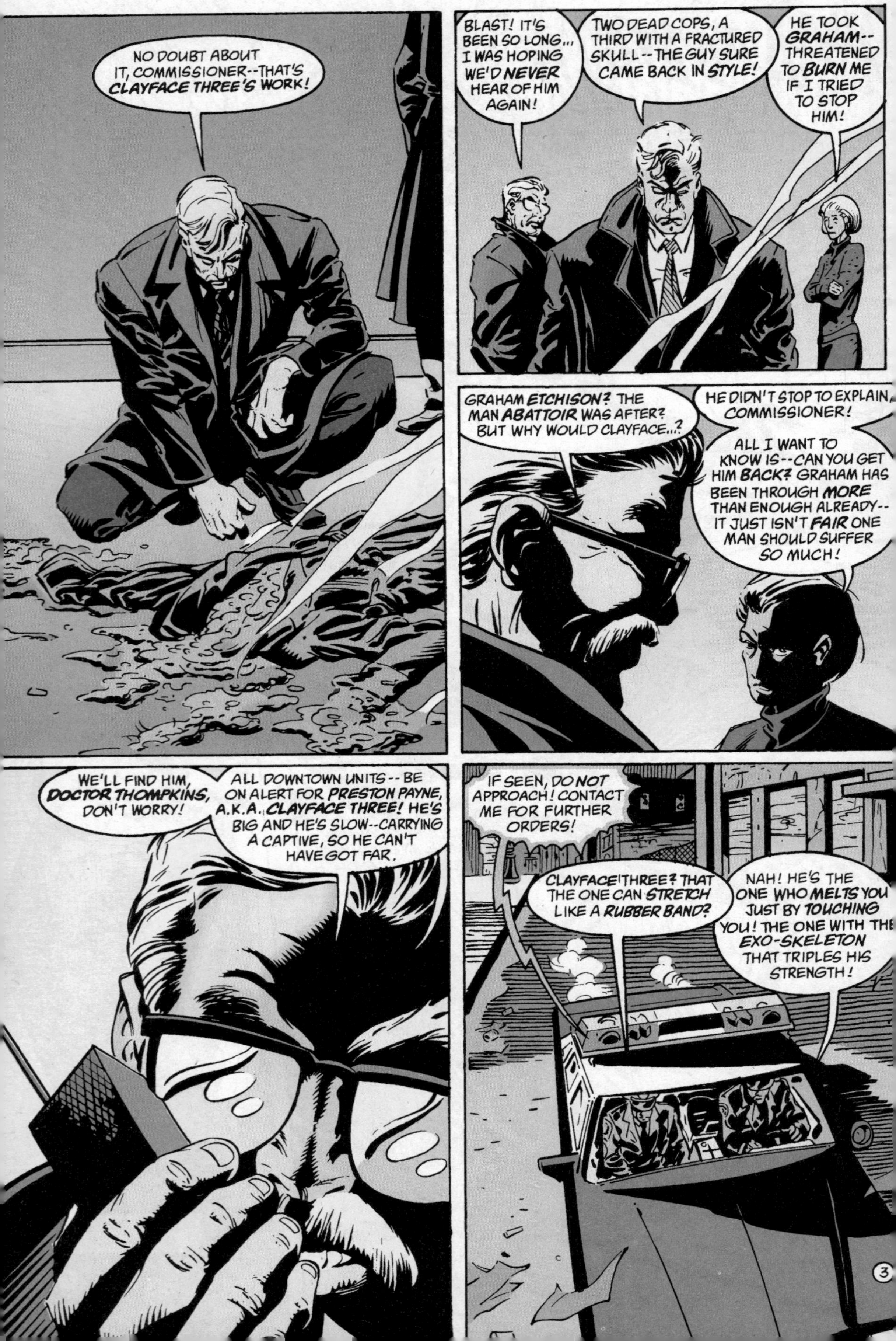
NO DOUBT ABOUT IT, COMMISSIONER--THAT'S CLAYFACE THREE'S WORK!
BLAST! IT'S BEEN SO LONG... I WAS HOPING WE'D NEVER HEAR OF HIM AGAIN!
TWO DEAD COPS, A THIRD WITH A FRACTURED SKULL--THE GUY SURE CAME BACK IN STYLE!
HE TOOK GRAHAM--THREATENED TO BURN ME IF I TRIED TO STOP HIM!
GRAHAM ETCHISON? THE MAN ABATTOIR WAS AFTER? BUT WHY WOULD CLAYFACE...?
HE DIDN'T STOP TO EXPLAIN, COMMISSIONER!
ALL I WANT TO KNOW IS--CAN YOU GET HIM BACK? GRAHAM HAS BEEN THROUGH MORE THAN ENOUGH ALREADY--IT JUST ISN'T FAIR ONE MAN SHOULD SUFFER SO MUCH!
WE'LL FIND HIM, DOCTOR THOMPKINS, DON'T WORRY!
ALL DOWNTOWN UNITS--BE ON ALERT FOR PRESTON PAYNE, A.K.A. CLAYFACE THREE! HE'S BIG AND HE'S SLOW--CARRYING A CAPTIVE, SO HE CAN'T HAVE GOT FAR.
IF SEEN, DO NOT APPROACH! CONTACT ME FOR FURTHER ORDERS!
CLAYFACE THREE? THAT THE ONE CAN STRETCH LIKE A RUBBER BAND?
NAH! HE'S THE ONE WHO MELTS YOU JUST BY TOUCHING YOU! THE ONE WITH THE EXO-SKELETON THAT TRIPLES HIS STRENGTH!

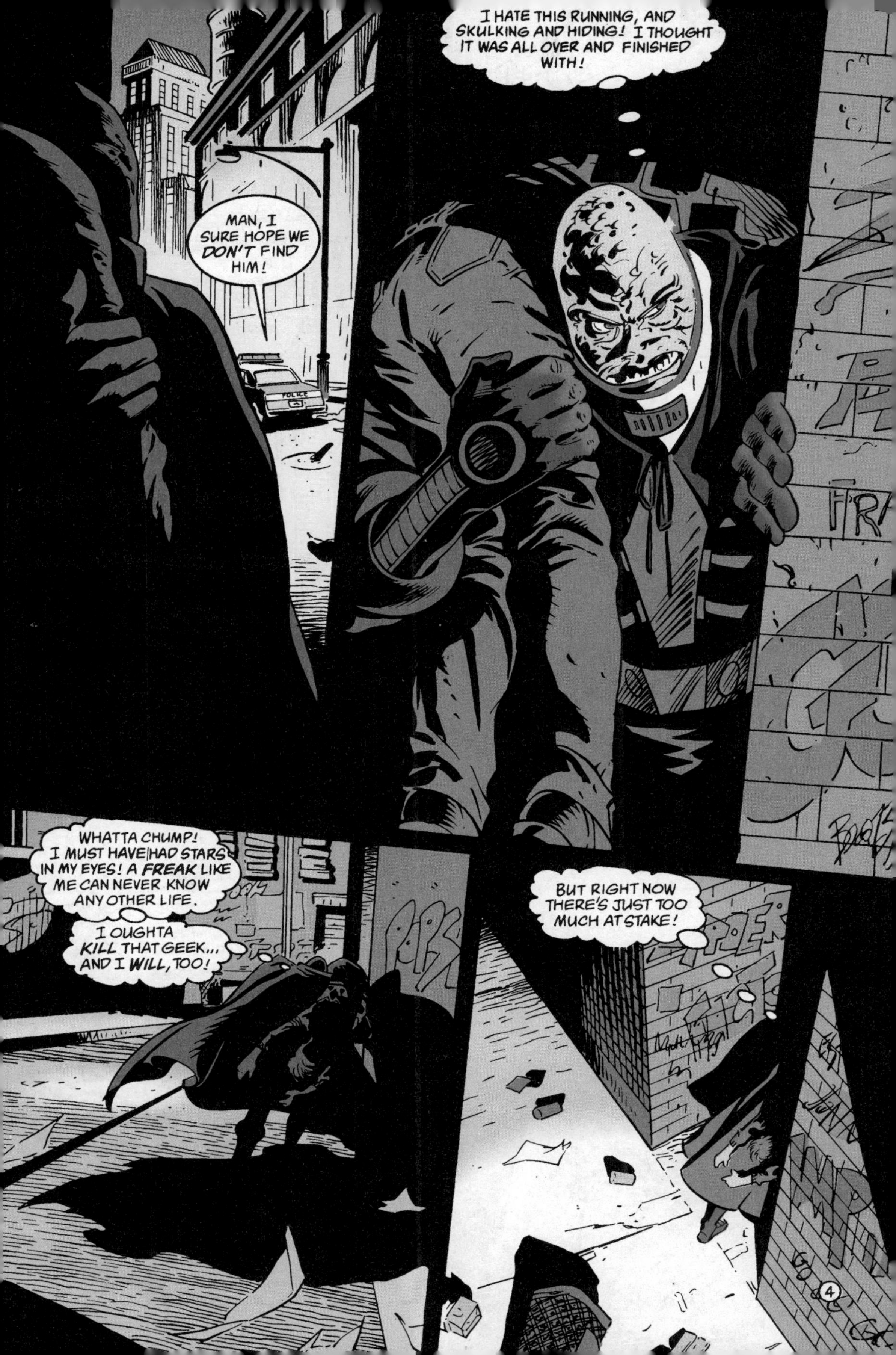

MAN, I SURE HOPE WE DON'T FIND HIM!
I HATE THIS RUNNING, AND SKULKING AND HIDING! I THOUGHT IT WAS ALL OVER AND FINISHED WITH!
POLICE
WHATTA CHUMP! I MUST HAVE HAD STARS IN MY EYES! A FREAK LIKE ME CAN NEVER KNOW ANY OTHER LIFE.
I OUGHTA KILL THAT GEEK... AND I WILL, TOO!
BUT RIGHT NOW THERE'S JUST TOO MUCH AT STAKE!

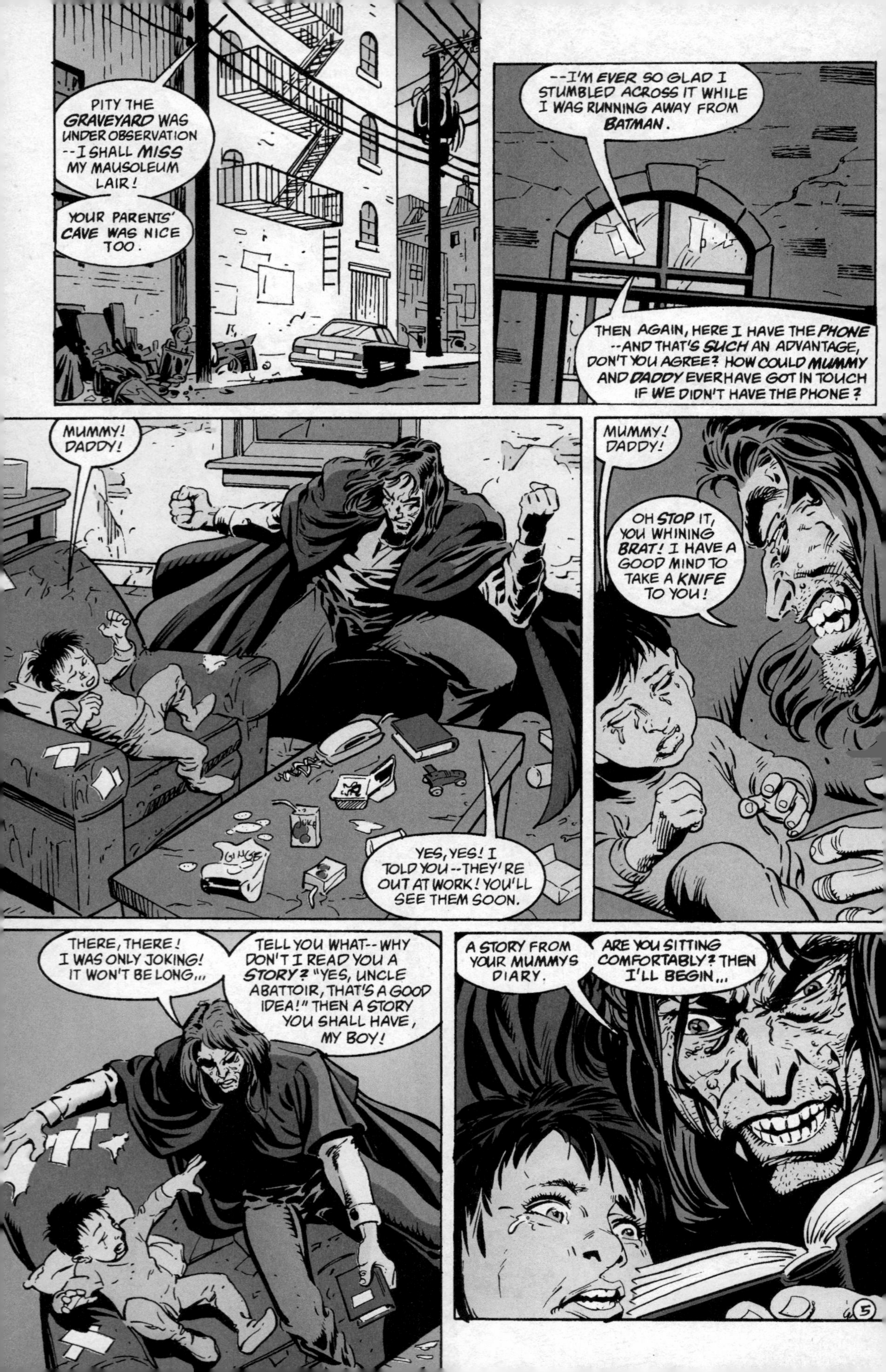
PITY THE GRAVEYARD WAS UNDER OBSERVATION --I SHALL MISS MY MAUSOLEUM LAIR!
YOUR PARENTS' CAVE WAS NICE TOO.
--I'M EVER SO GLAD I STUMBLED ACROSS IT WHILE I WAS RUNNING AWAY FROM BATMAN.
THEN AGAIN, HERE I HAVE THE PHONE --AND THAT'S SUCH AN ADVANTAGE, DON'T YOU AGREE? HOW COULD MUMMY AND DADDY EVER HAVE GOT IN TOUCH IF WE DIDN'T HAVE THE PHONE?
MUMMY! DADDY!
YES, YES! I TOLD YOU --THEY'RE OUT AT WORK! YOU'LL SEE THEM SOON.
MUMMY! DADDY!
OH STOP IT, YOU WHINING BRAT! I HAVE A GOOD MIND TO TAKE A KNIFE TO YOU!
THERE, THERE! I WAS ONLY JOKING! IT WON'T BE LONG...
TELL YOU WHAT-- WHY DON'T I READ YOU A STORY? "YES, UNCLE ABATTOIR, THAT'S A GOOD IDEA!" THEN A STORY YOU SHALL HAVE, MY BOY!
A STORY FROM YOUR MUMMYS DIARY.
ARE YOU SITTING COMFORTABLY? THEN I'LL BEGIN...
5

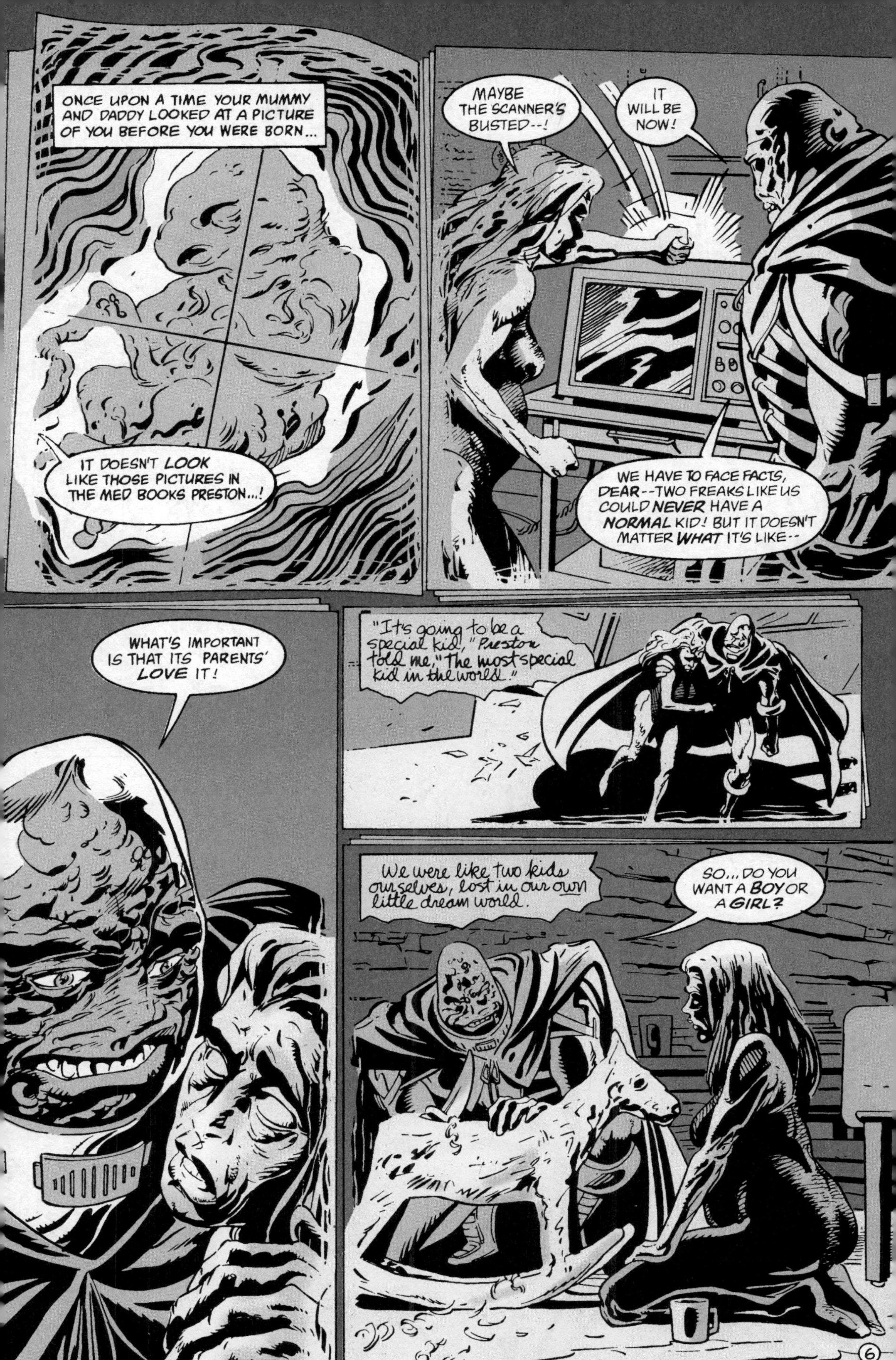
ONCE UPON A TIME YOUR MUMMY AND DADDY LOOKED AT A PICTURE OF YOU BEFORE YOU WERE BORN...
IT DOESN'T LOOK LIKE THOSE PICTURES IN THE MED BOOKS PRESTON...!
MAYBE THE SCANNER'S BUSTED--!
IT WILL BE NOW!
WE HAVE TO FACE FACTS, DEAR--TWO FREAKS LIKE US COULD NEVER HAVE A NORMAL KID! BUT IT DOESN'T MATTER WHAT IT'S LIKE--
WHAT'S IMPORTANT IS THAT ITS PARENTS' LOVE IT!
"It's going to be a special kid," Preston told me, "The most special kid in the world."
We were like two kids ourselves, lost in our own little dream world.
SO... DO YOU WANT A BOY OR A GIRL?

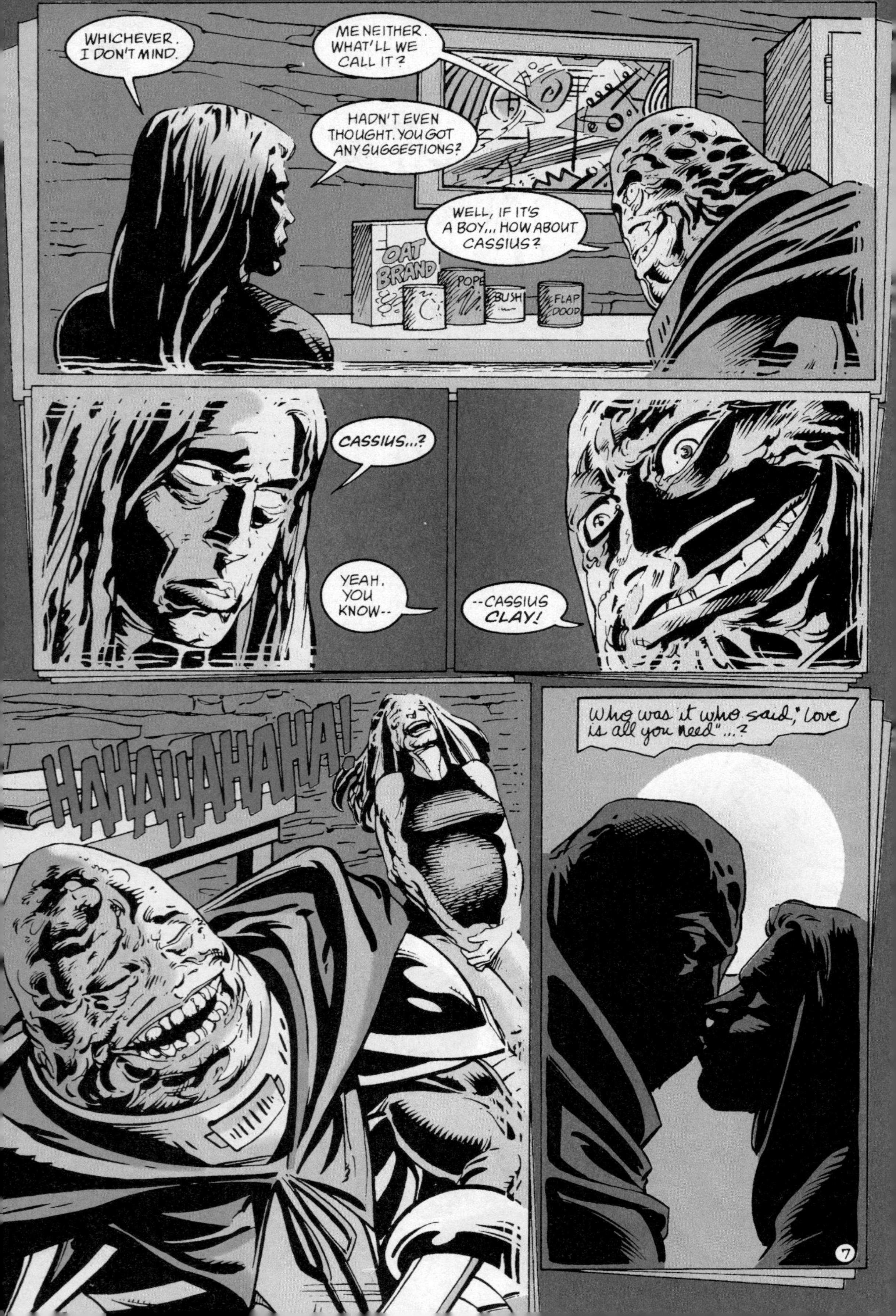
WHICHEVER. I DON'T MIND.
ME NEITHER. WHAT'LL WE CALL IT?
HADN'T EVEN THOUGHT. YOU GOT ANY SUGGESTIONS?
WELL, IF IT'S A BOY... HOW ABOUT CASSIUS?
OAT BRAND
POPE
BUSH
FLAP DOOD
CASSIUS...?
YEAH, YOU KNOW--
--CASSIUS CLAY!
HAHAHAHAHAHA!
Who was it who said, "Love is all you need"...?
7

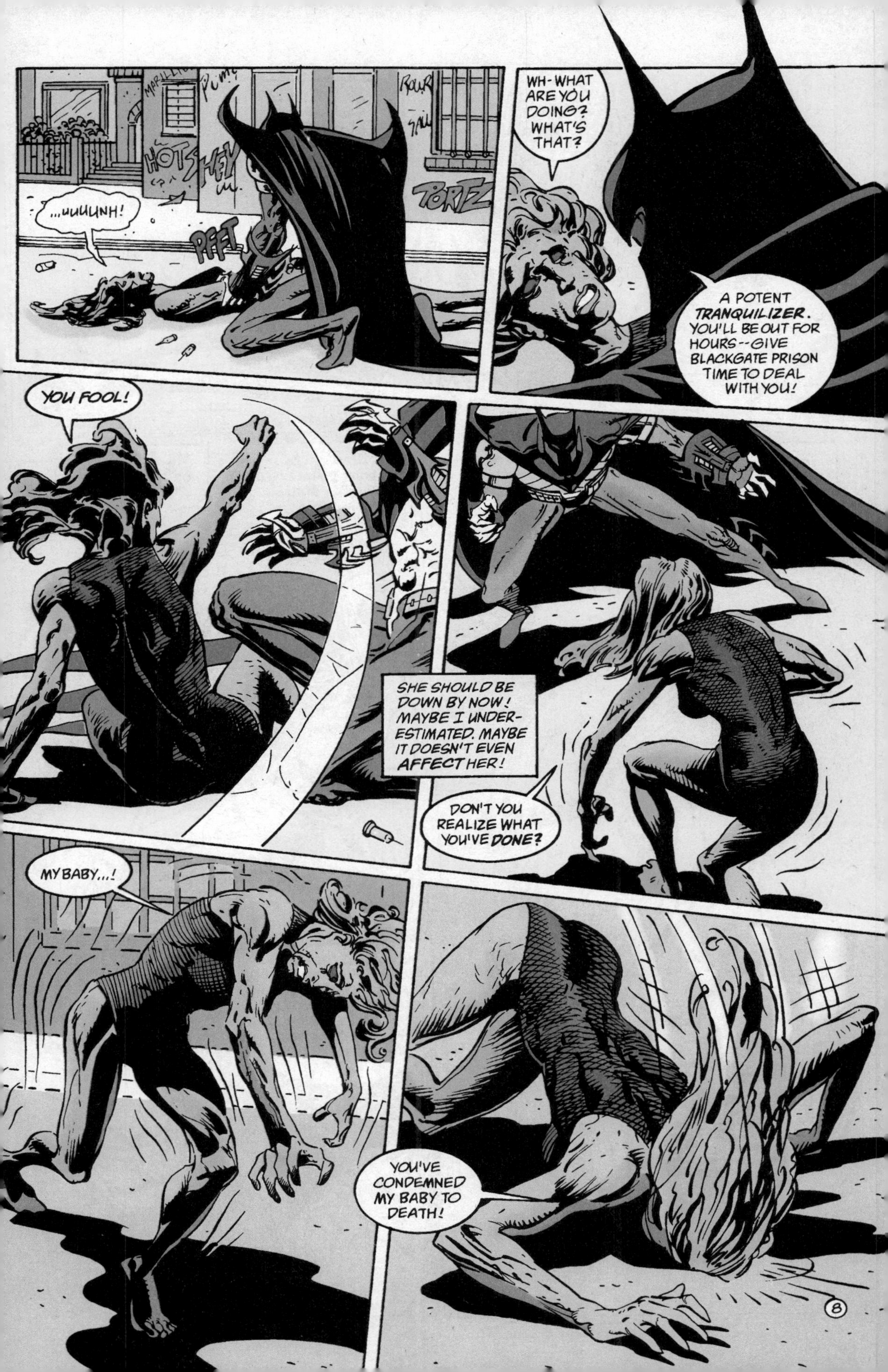
...UUUUNH!
PFFT
WH-WHAT ARE YOU DOING? WHAT'S THAT?
A POTENT TRANQUILIZER. YOU'LL BE OUT FOR HOURS--GIVE BLACKGATE PRISON TIME TO DEAL WITH YOU!
YOU FOOL!
SHE SHOULD BE DOWN BY NOW! MAYBE I UNDER-ESTIMATED. MAYBE IT DOESN'T EVEN AFFECT HER!
DON'T YOU REALIZE WHAT YOU'VE DONE?
MY BABY...!
YOU'VE CONDEMNED MY BABY TO DEATH!
8

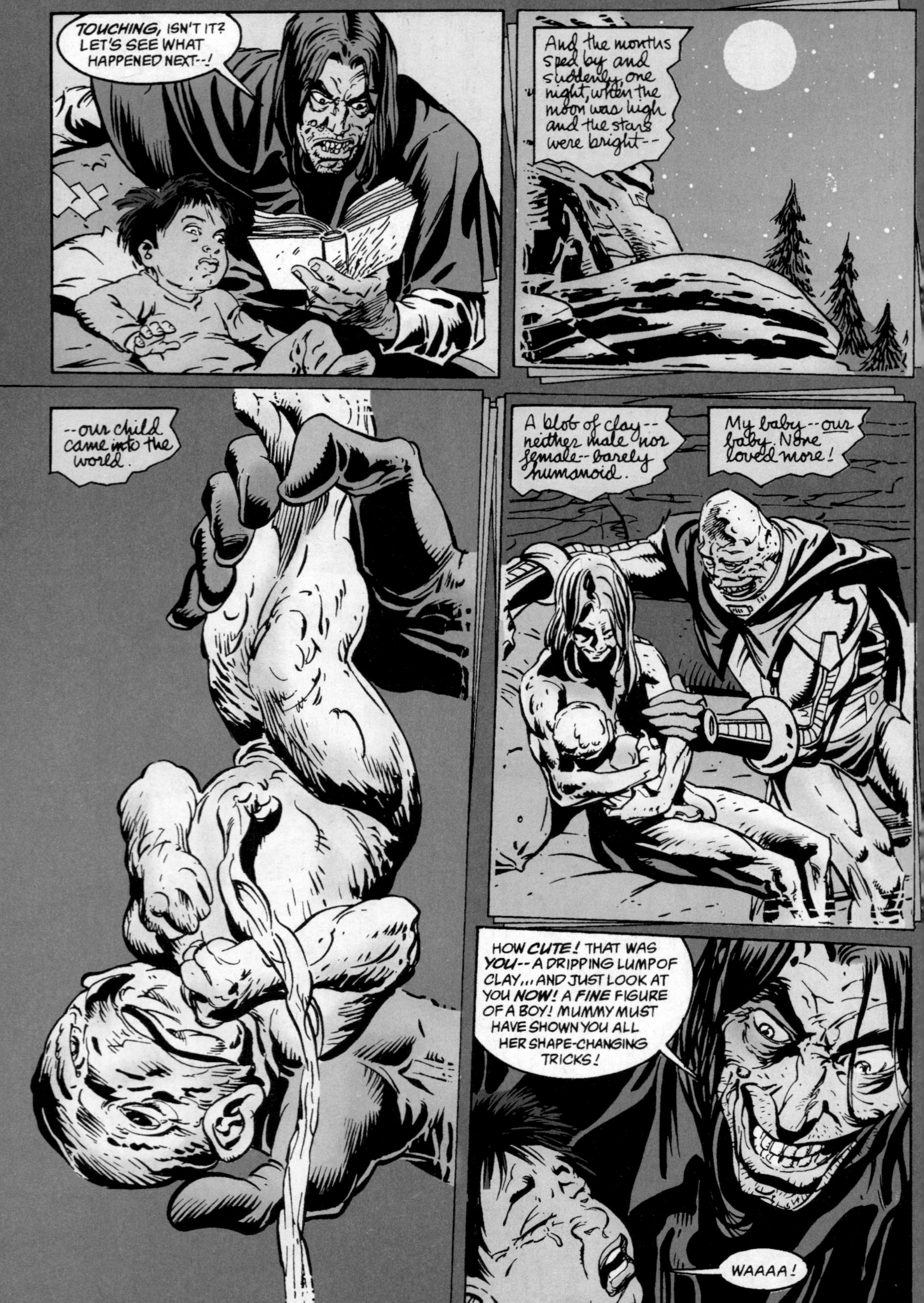

TOUCHING, ISN'T IT? LET'S SEE WHAT HAPPENED NEXT--!
And the months sped by and suddenly, one night, when the moon was high and the stars were bright--
--our child came into the world.
A blob of clay--neither male nor female--barely humanoid.
My baby--our baby. None loved more!
HOW CUTE! THAT WAS YOU--A DRIPPING LUMP OF CLAY... AND JUST LOOK AT YOU NOW! A FINE FIGURE OF A BOY! MUMMY MUST HAVE SHOWN YOU ALL HER SHAPE-CHANGING TRICKS!
WAAAA!
9

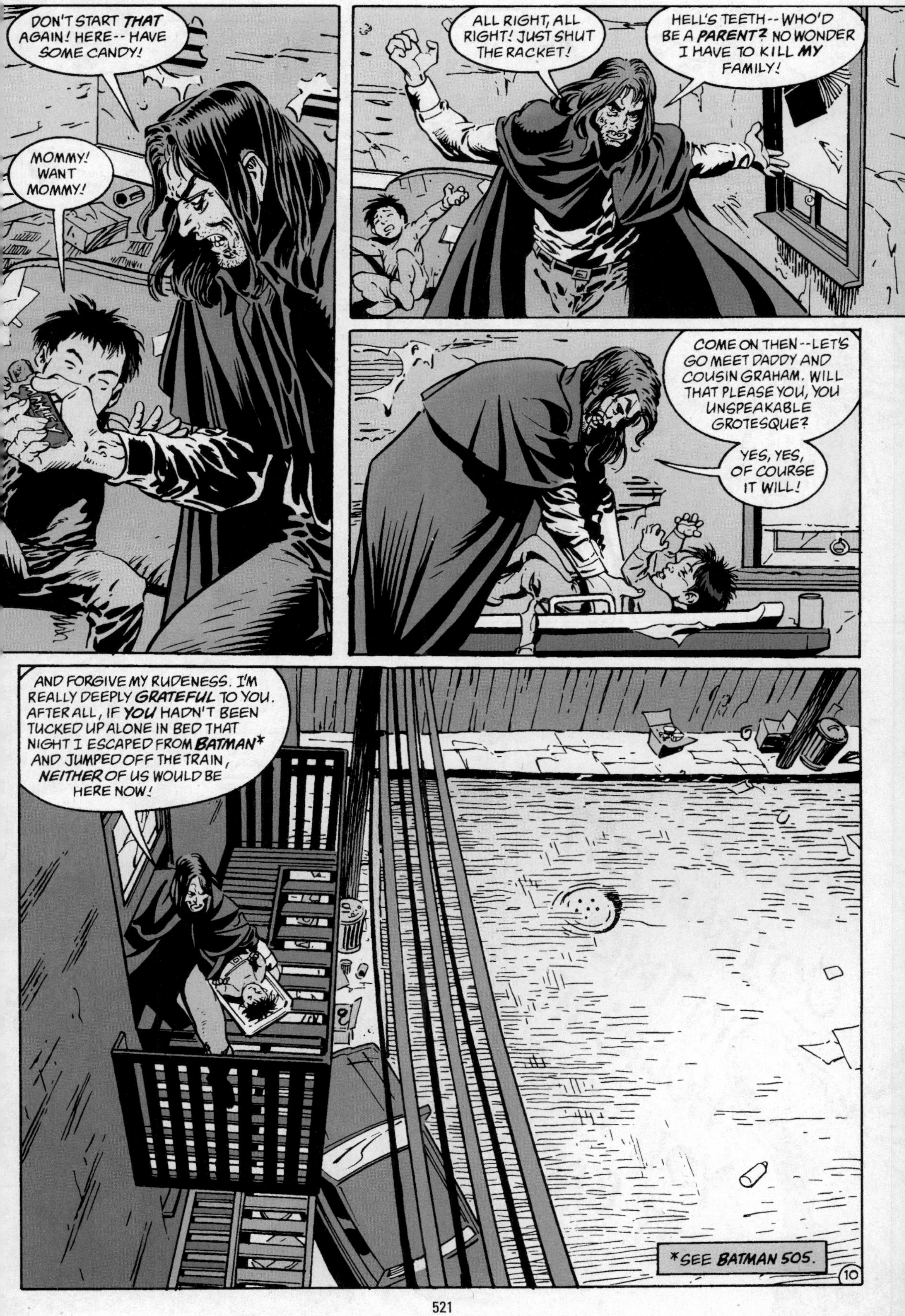

DON'T START THAT AGAIN! HERE-- HAVE SOME CANDY!
MOMMY! WANT MOMMY!
ALL RIGHT, ALL RIGHT! JUST SHUT THE RACKET!
HELL'S TEETH--WHO'D BE A PARENT? NO WONDER I HAVE TO KILL MY FAMILY!
COME ON THEN--LET'S GO MEET DADDY AND COUSIN GRAHAM. WILL THAT PLEASE YOU, YOU UNSPEAKABLE GROTESQUE?
YES, YES, OF COURSE IT WILL!
AND FORGIVE MY RUDENESS. I'M REALLY DEEPLY GRATEFUL TO YOU. AFTER ALL, IF YOU HADN'T BEEN TUCKED UP ALONE IN BED THAT NIGHT I ESCAPED FROM BATMAN* AND JUMPED OFF THE TRAIN, NEITHER OF US WOULD BE HERE NOW!
*SEE BATMAN 505.
10

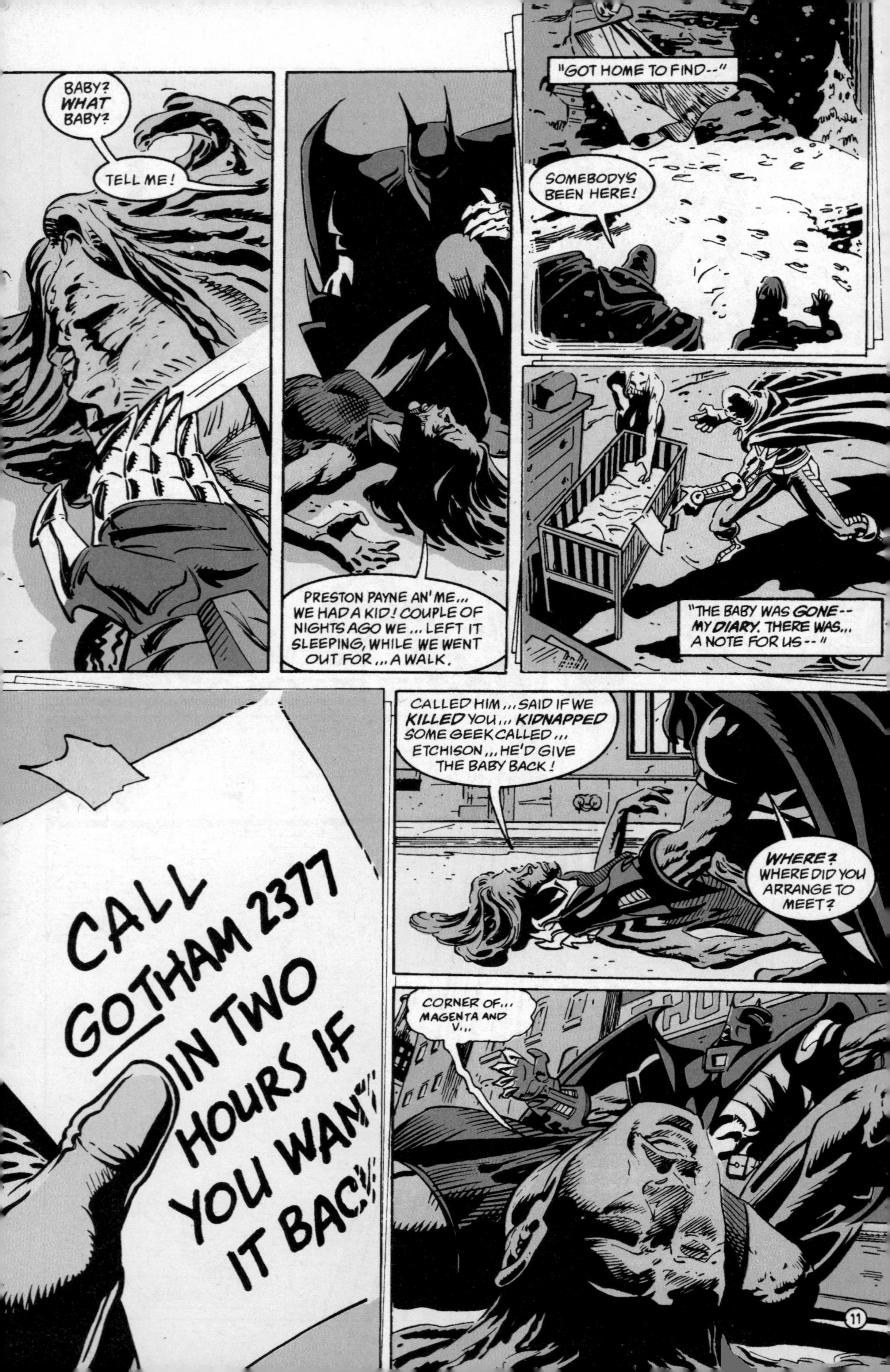
BABY? WHAT BABY?
TELL ME!
PRESTON PAYNE AN' ME... WE HAD A KID! COUPLE OF NIGHTS AGO WE... LEFT IT SLEEPING, WHILE WE WENT OUT FOR... A WALK.
"GOT HOME TO FIND--"
SOMEBODY'S BEEN HERE!
"THE BABY WAS GONE-- MY DIARY. THERE WAS... A NOTE FOR US--"
CALL GOTHAM 2377 IN TWO HOURS IF YOU WAN IT BAC
CALLED HIM... SAID IF WE KILLED YOU... KIDNAPPED SOME GEEK CALLED... ETCHISON... HE'D GIVE THE BABY BACK!
WHERE? WHERE DID YOU ARRANGE TO MEET?
CORNER OF... MAGENTA AND V...

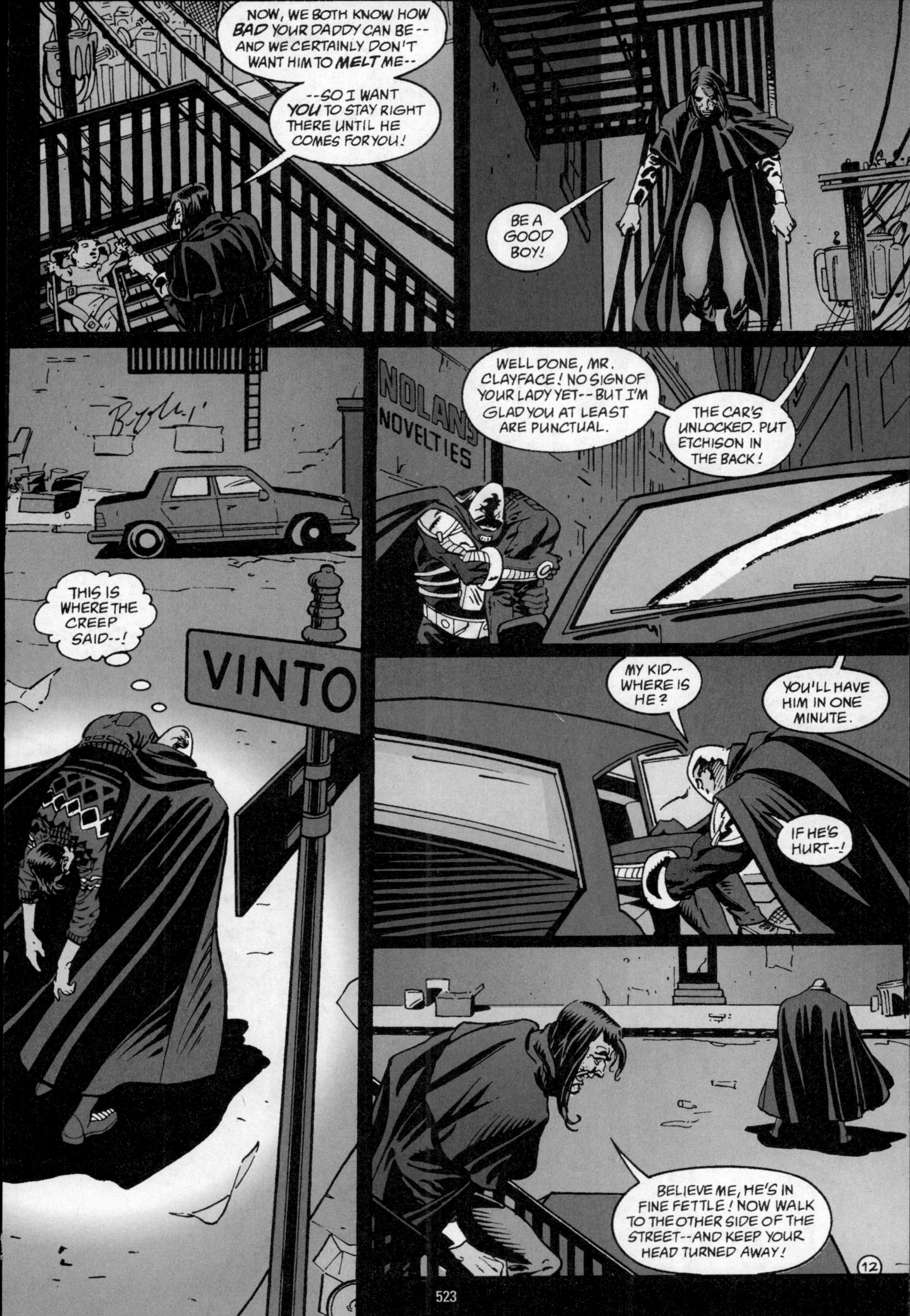
NOW, WE BOTH KNOW HOW BAD YOUR DADDY CAN BE-- AND WE CERTAINLY DON'T WANT HIM TO MELT ME--
--SO I WANT YOU TO STAY RIGHT THERE UNTIL HE COMES FOR YOU!
BE A GOOD BOY!
NOLANS NOVELTIES
WELL DONE, MR. CLAYFACE! NO SIGN OF YOUR LADY YET--BUT I'M GLAD YOU AT LEAST ARE PUNCTUAL.
THE CAR'S UNLOCKED. PUT ETCHISON IN THE BACK!
THIS IS WHERE THE CREEP SAID--!
VINTO
MY KID-- WHERE IS HE?
YOU'LL HAVE HIM IN ONE MINUTE.
IF HE'S HURT--!
BELIEVE ME, HE'S IN FINE FETTLE! NOW WALK TO THE OTHER SIDE OF THE STREET--AND KEEP YOUR HEAD TURNED AWAY!
12

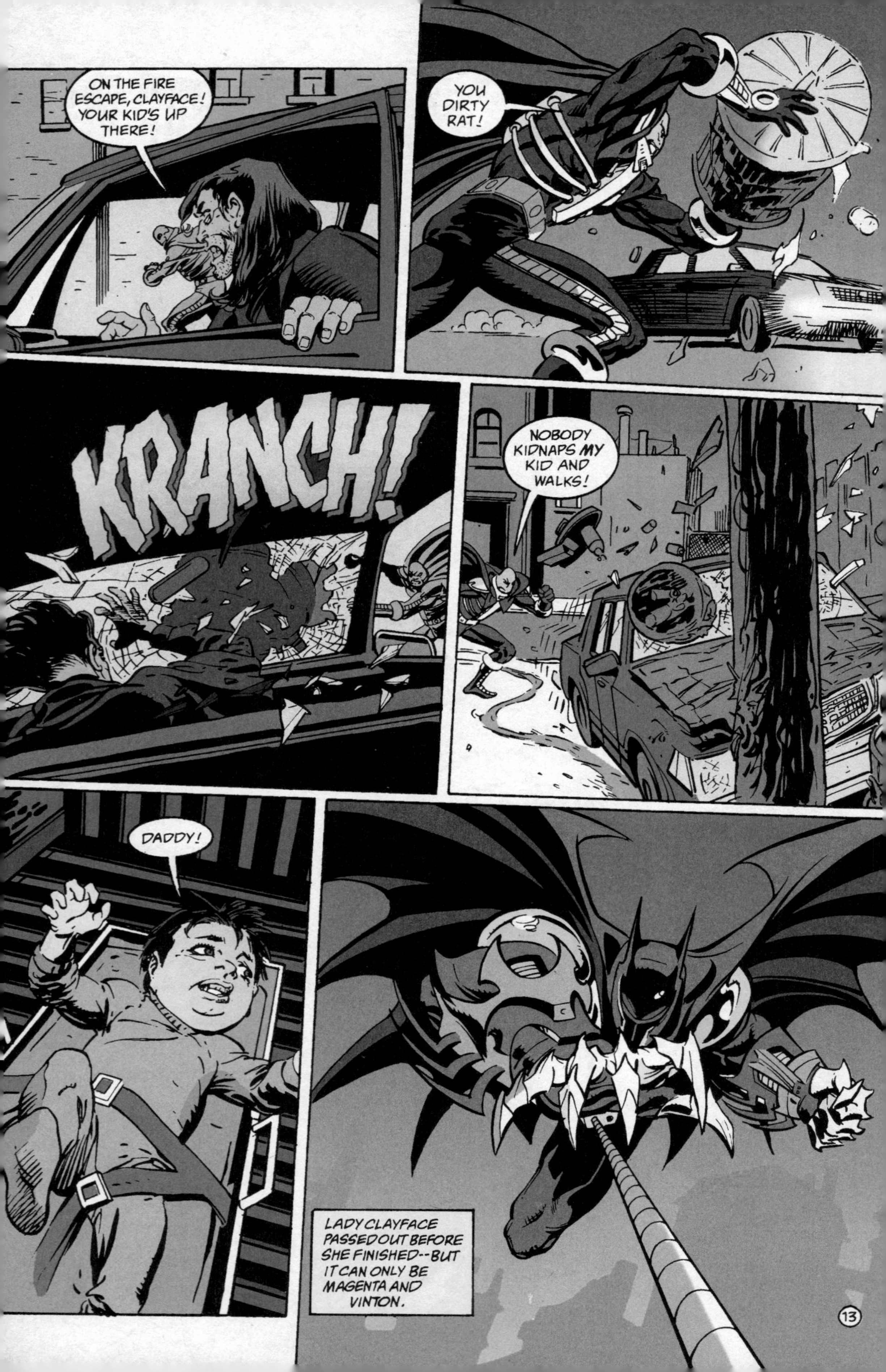
ON THE FIRE ESCAPE, CLAYFACE! YOUR KID'S UP THERE!
YOU DIRTY RAT!
KRANCH!
NOBODY KIDNAPS MY KID AND WALKS!
DADDY!
LADY CLAYFACE PASSED OUT BEFORE SHE FINISHED--BUT IT CAN ONLY BE MAGENTA AND VINTON.

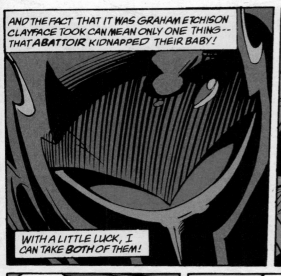

AND THE FACT THAT IT WAS GRAHAM ETCHISON CLAYFACE TOOK CAN MEAN ONLY ONE THING-- THAT ABATTOIR KIDNAPPED THEIR BABY!

WITH A LITTLE LUCK, I CAN TAKE BOTH OF THEM!

K-KEEP BACK! I TOLD YOU WHERE THE CHILD IS!

DADDY! DADDY!

YOU CAUSED ME AND MY WIFE A WHOLE LOT OF HEARTACHE, YOU WORM! I'M GOING TO SEE THAT YOU SUFFER--

MMM...

SNAP

I'M GOING TO SEE YOU BURN!

NO--!

14

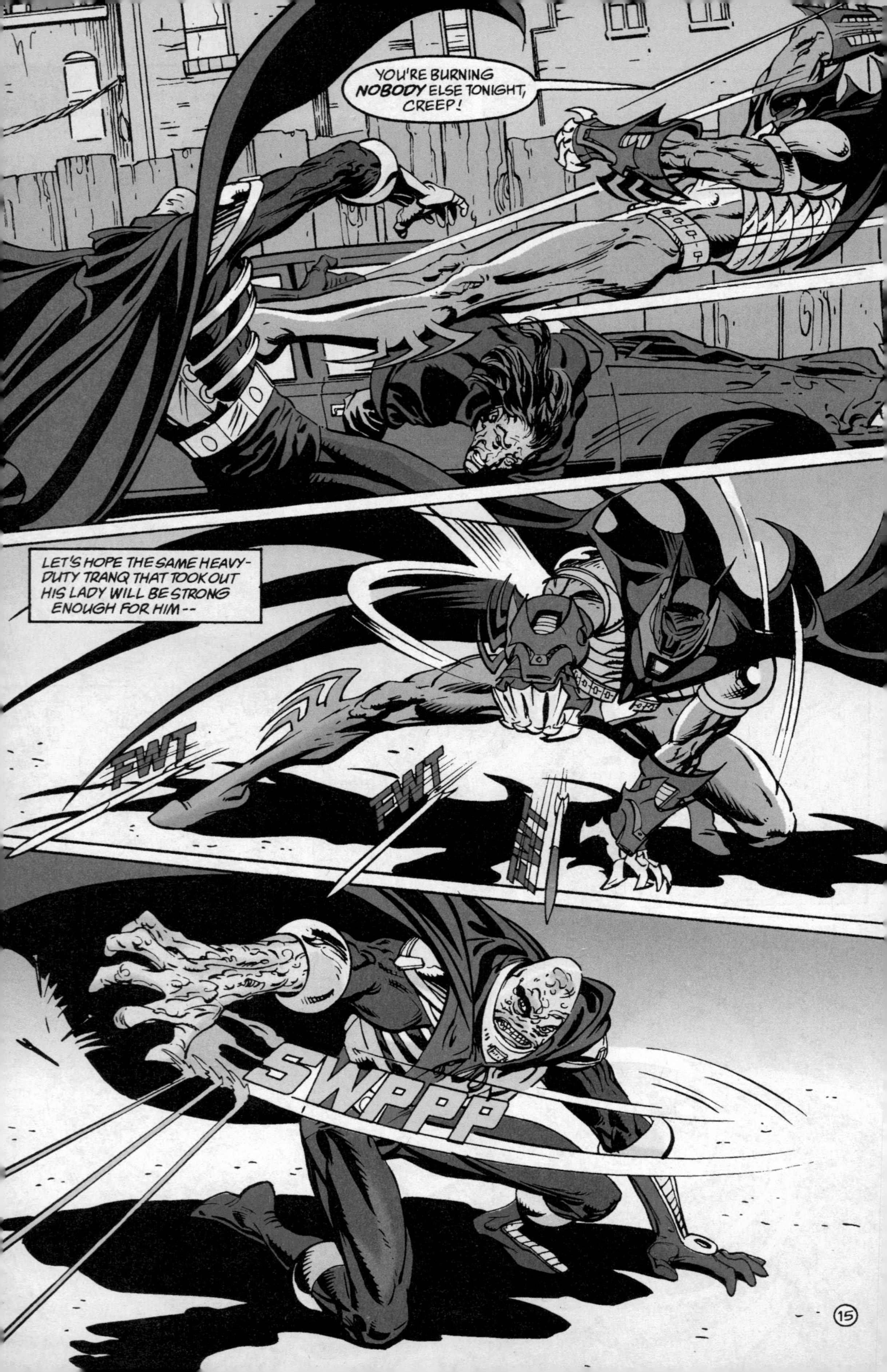
YOU'RE BURNING NOBODY ELSE TONIGHT, CREEP!
LET'S HOPE THE SAME HEAVY-DUTY TRANQ THAT TOOK OUT HIS LADY WILL BE STRONG ENOUGH FOR HIM--
FWT
FWT
SWPPP

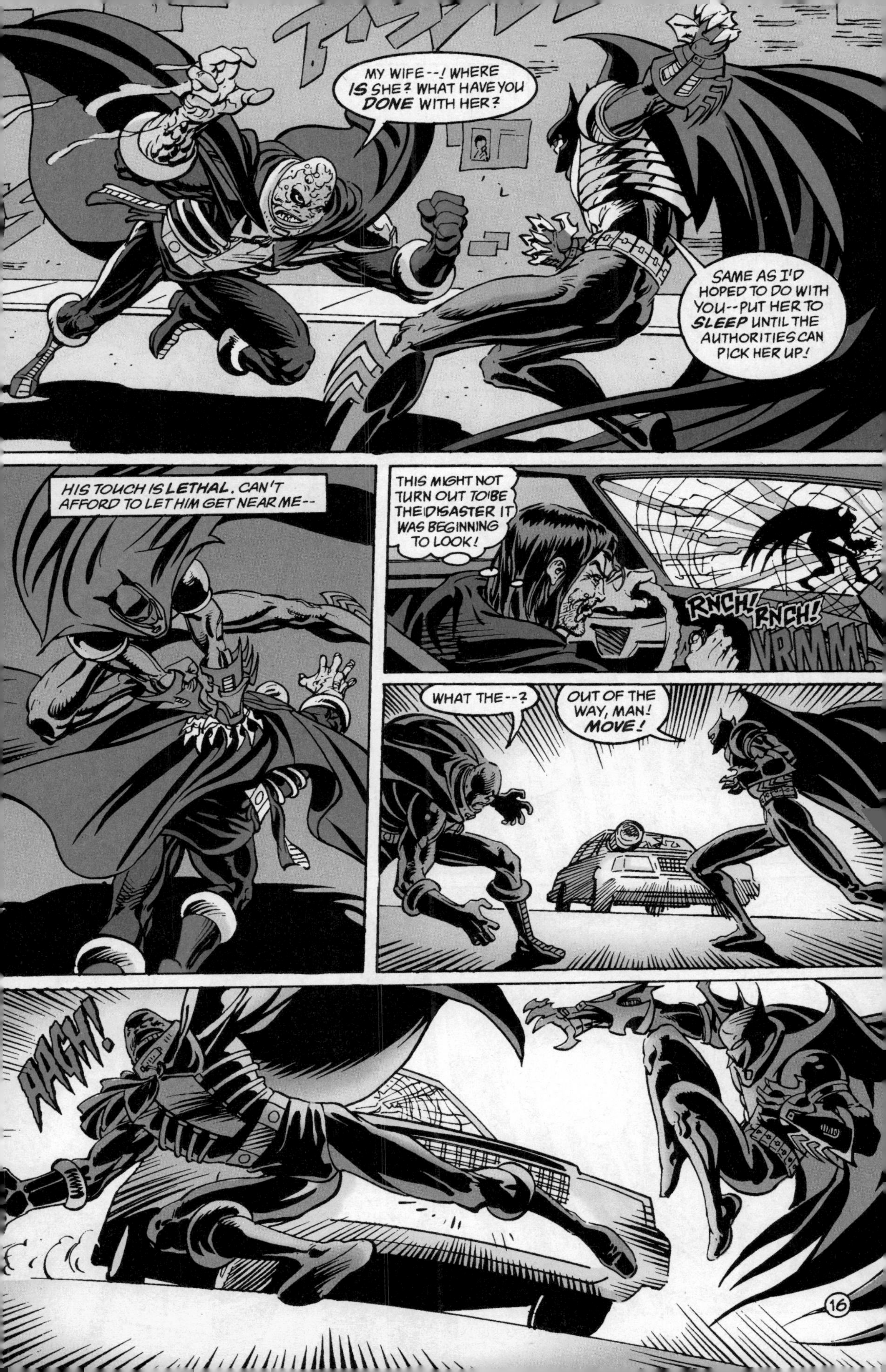

MY WIFE--! WHERE IS SHE? WHAT HAVE YOU DONE WITH HER?
SAME AS I'D HOPED TO DO WITH YOU--PUT HER TO SLEEP UNTIL THE AUTHORITIES CAN PICK HER UP!
HIS TOUCH IS LETHAL. CAN'T AFFORD TO LET HIM GET NEAR ME--
THIS MIGHT NOT TURN OUT TO BE THE DISASTER IT WAS BEGINNING TO LOOK!
RNCH! RNCH!
VRMM!
WHAT THE--?
OUT OF THE WAY, MAN! MOVE!
AAGH!

DADDY! DADDY!

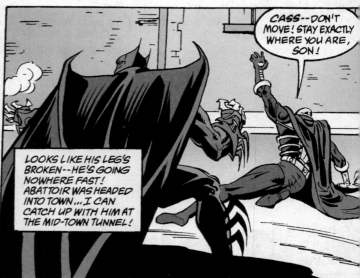

CASS--DON'T MOVE! STAY EXACTLY WHERE YOU ARE, SON!

LOOKS LIKE HIS LEG'S BROKEN--HE'S GOING NOWHERE FAST! ABATTOIR WAS HEADED INTO TOWN... I CAN CATCH UP WITH HIM AT THE MID-TOWN TUNNEL!

FLY DOWN, DADDY! FLY!

NO! YOU CAN'T FLY! STAY PUT! DADDY'S COMING!

YES, DADDY! FLY! FLY!

PLEASE, CASS-- WAIT! I'M COMING!

17

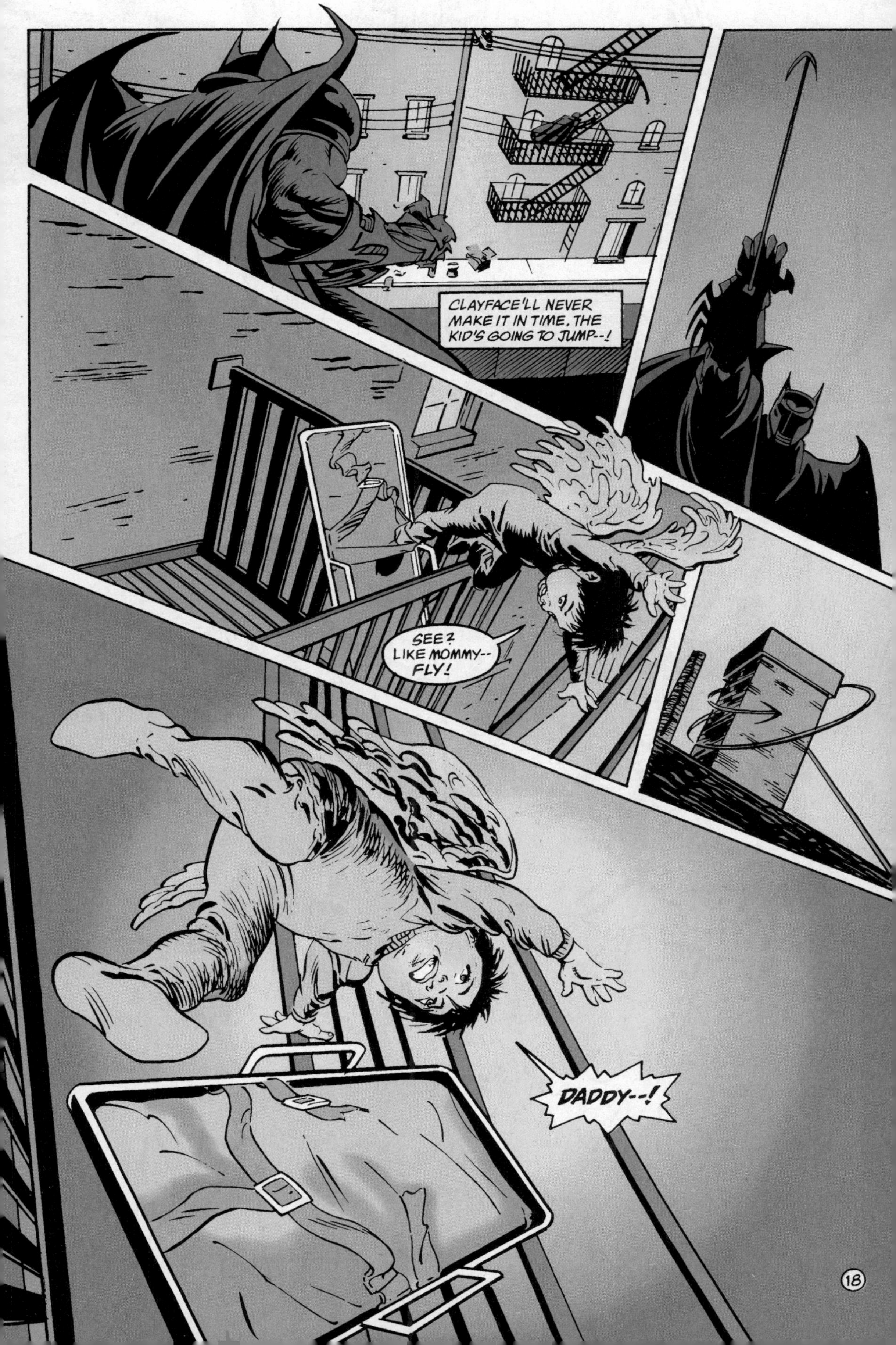
CLAYFACE'LL NEVER MAKE IT IN TIME. THE KID'S GOING TO JUMP--!
SEE? LIKE MOMMY-- FLY!
DADDY--!

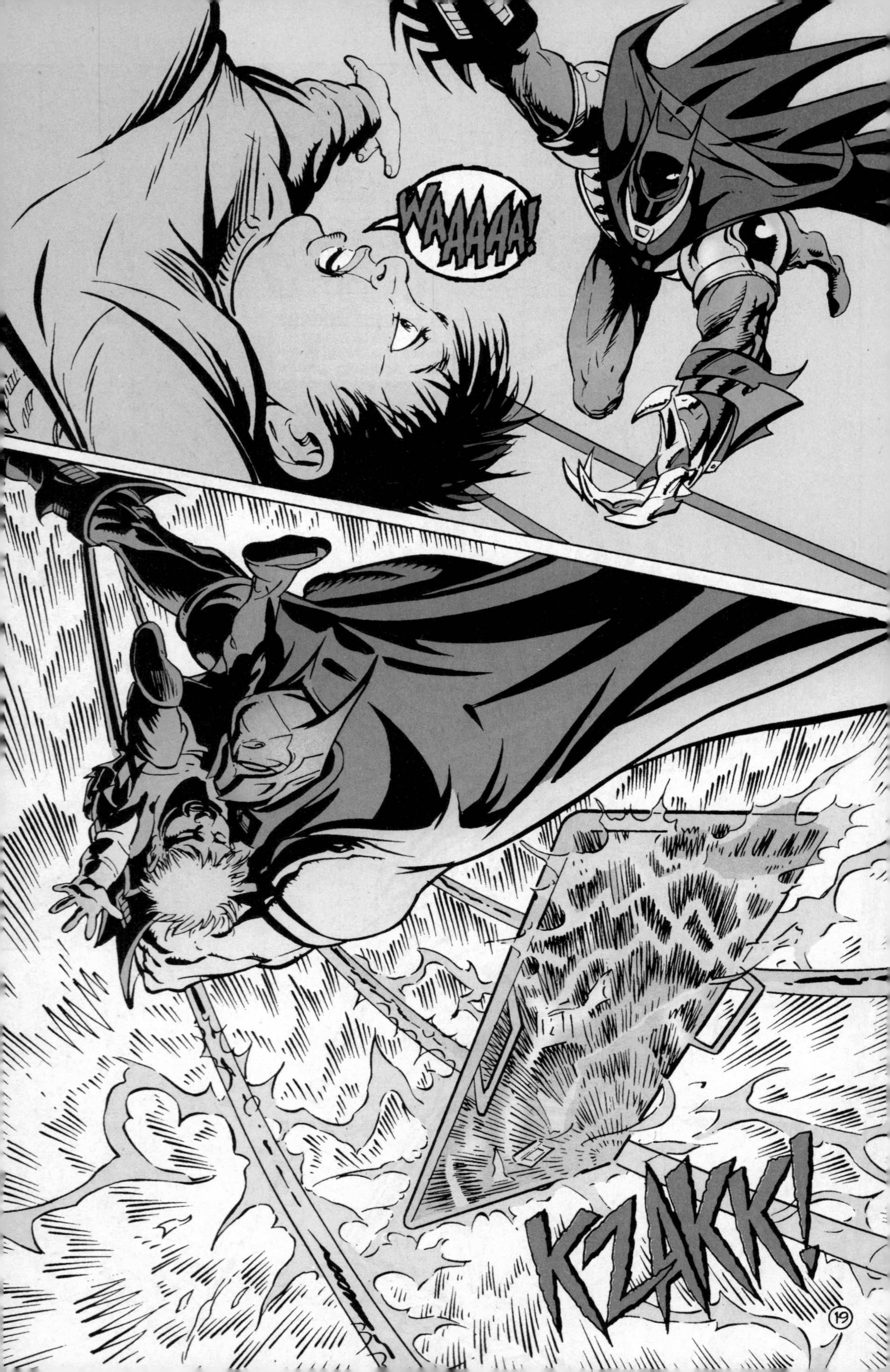
WAAAAA!
KZAKK!
19

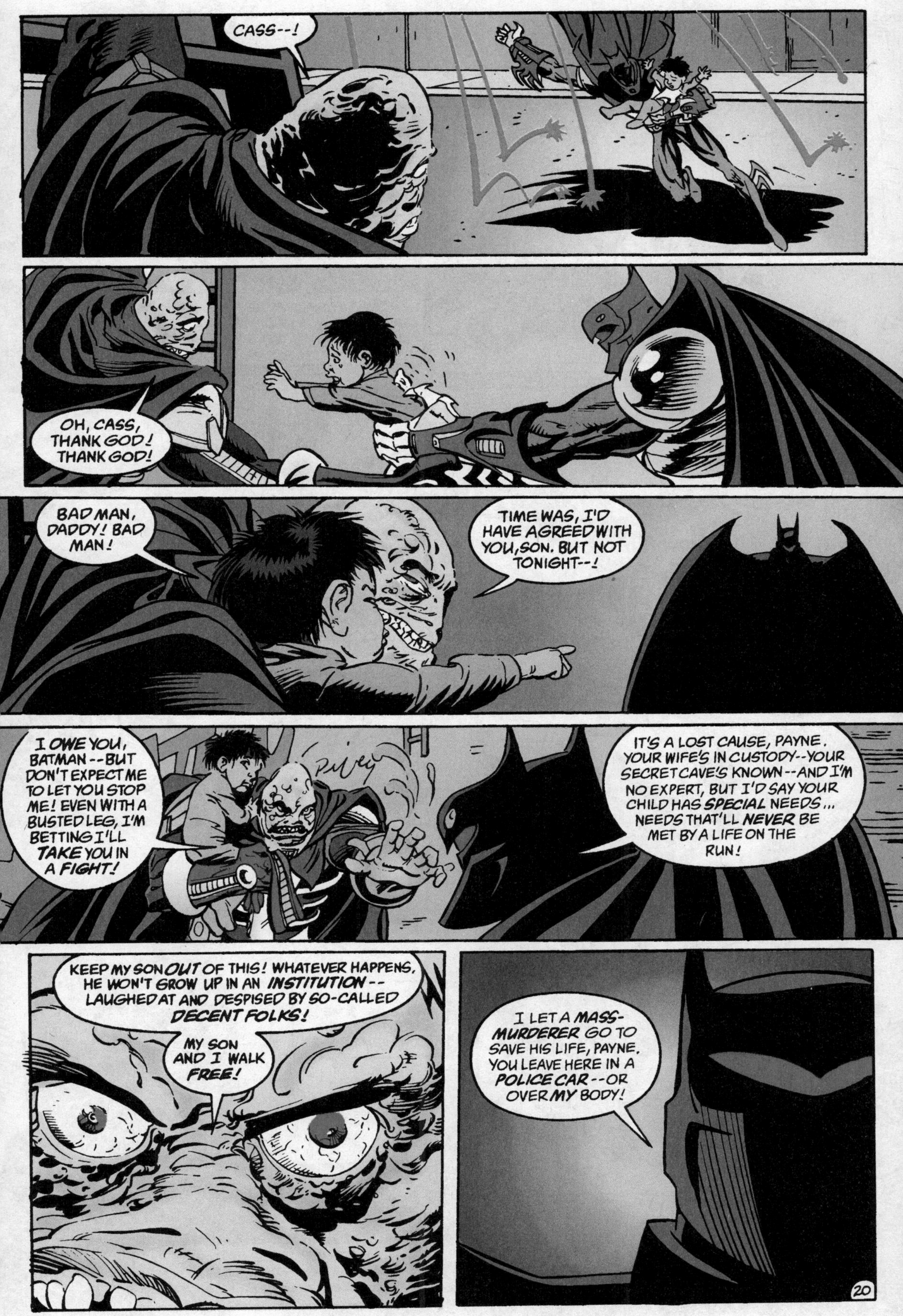
CASS--!
OH, CASS, THANK GOD! THANK GOD!
BAD MAN, DADDY! BAD MAN!
TIME WAS, I'D HAVE AGREED WITH YOU, SON. BUT NOT TONIGHT--!
I OWE YOU, BATMAN--BUT DON'T EXPECT ME TO LET YOU STOP ME! EVEN WITH A BUSTED LEG, I'M BETTING I'LL TAKE YOU IN A FIGHT!
IT'S A LOST CAUSE, PAYNE. YOUR WIFE'S IN CUSTODY--YOUR SECRET CAVE'S KNOWN--AND I'M NO EXPERT, BUT I'D SAY YOUR CHILD HAS SPECIAL NEEDS... NEEDS THAT'LL NEVER BE MET BY A LIFE ON THE RUN!
KEEP MY SON OUT OF THIS! WHATEVER HAPPENS, HE WON'T GROW UP IN AN INSTITUTION-- LAUGHED AT AND DESPISED BY SO-CALLED DECENT FOLKS!
MY SON AND I WALK FREE!
I LET A MASS-MURDERER GO TO SAVE HIS LIFE, PAYNE. YOU LEAVE HERE IN A POLICE CAR--OR OVER MY BODY!
20

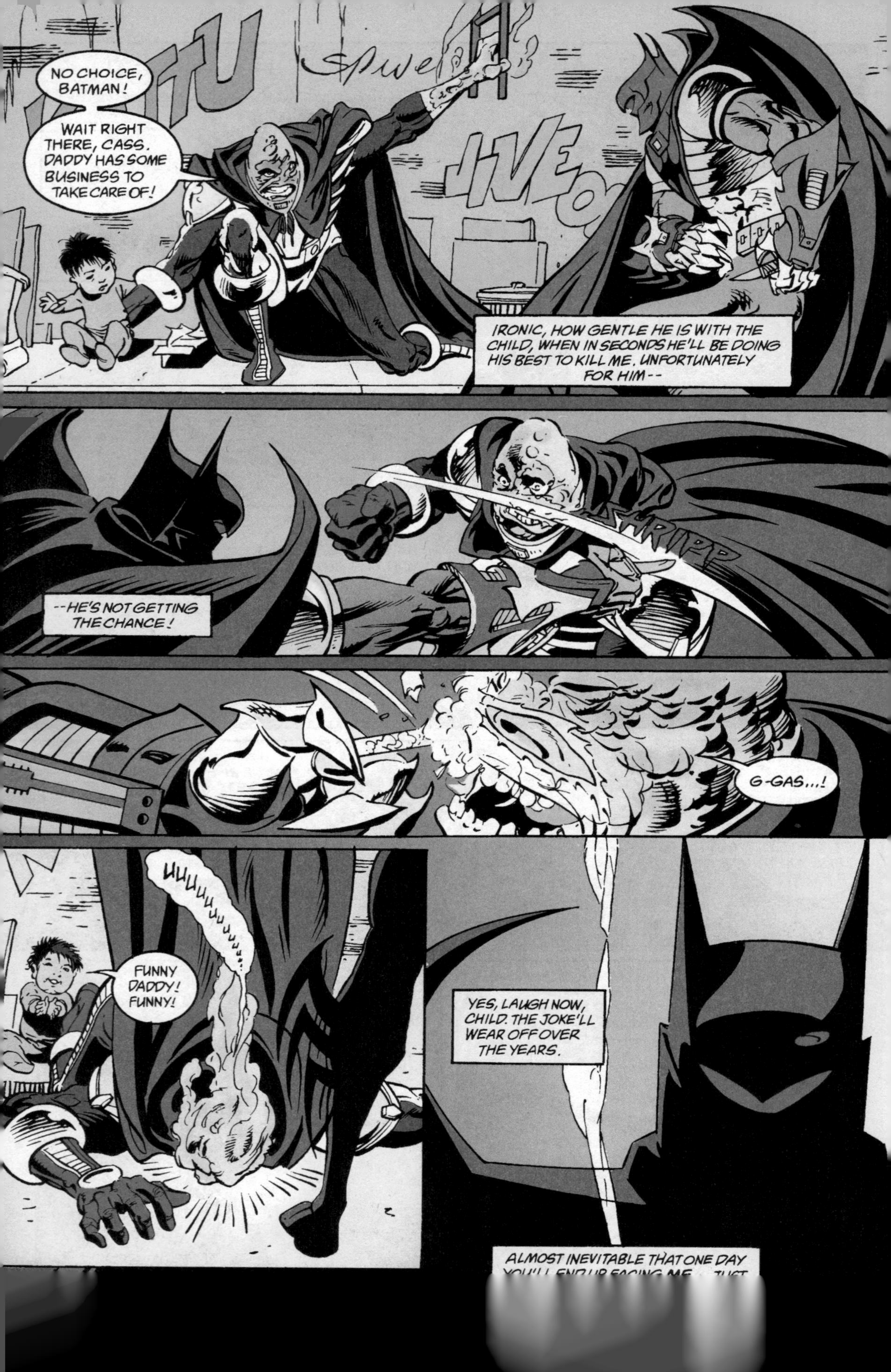

NO CHOICE, BATMAN!
WAIT RIGHT THERE, CASS. DADDY HAS SOME BUSINESS TO TAKE CARE OF!
IRONIC, HOW GENTLE HE IS WITH THE CHILD, WHEN IN SECONDS HE'LL BE DOING HIS BEST TO KILL ME. UNFORTUNATELY FOR HIM--
--HE'S NOT GETTING THE CHANCE!
G-GAS...!
FUNNY DADDY! FUNNY!
YES, LAUGH NOW, CHILD. THE JOKE'LL WEAR OFF OVER THE YEARS.
ALMOST INEVITABLE THAT ONE DAY

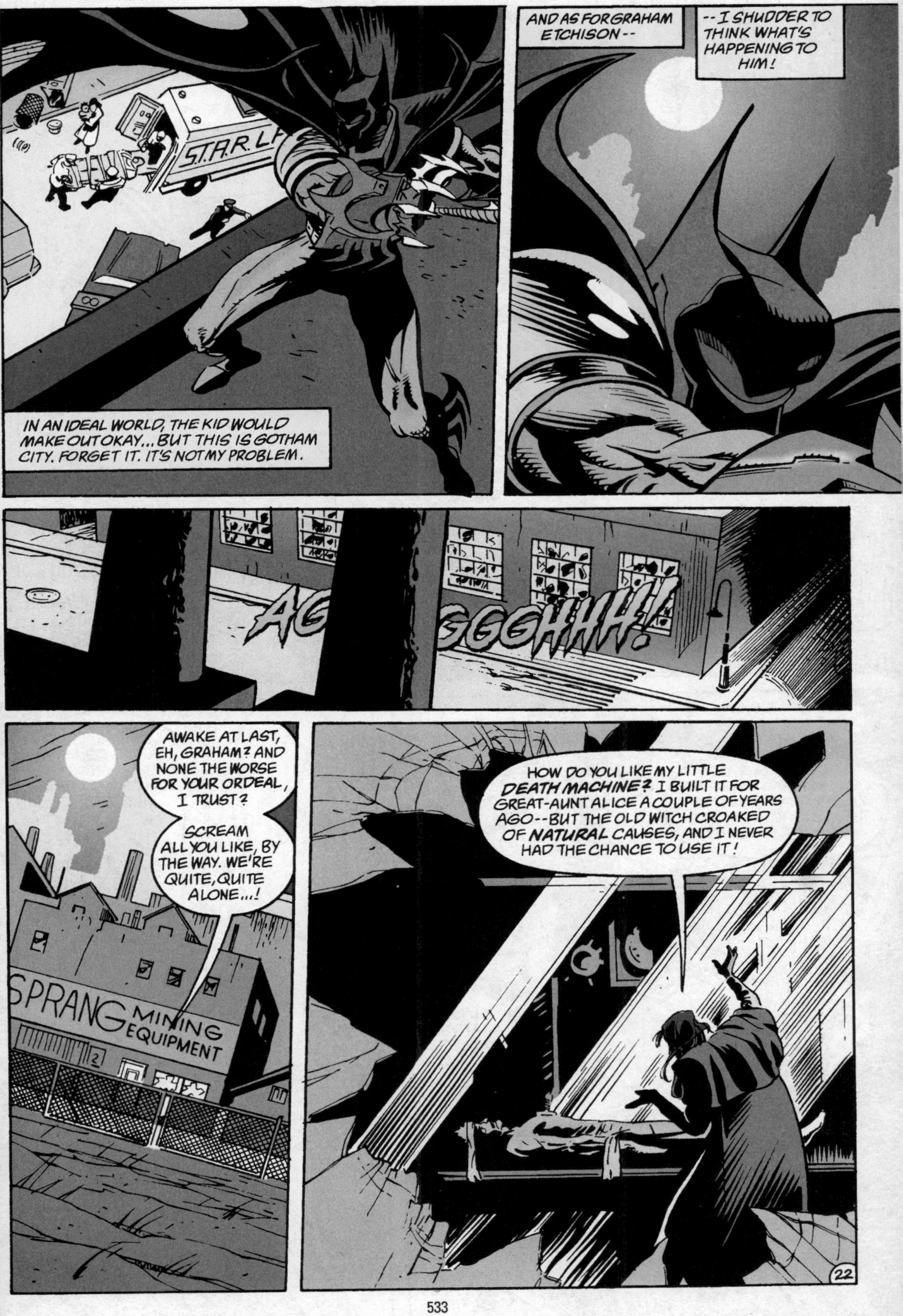

IN AN IDEAL WORLD, THE KID WOULD MAKE OUT OKAY... BUT THIS IS GOTHAM CITY. FORGET IT. IT'S NOT MY PROBLEM.
S.T.A.R. L
AND AS FOR GRAHAM ETCHISON--
--I SHUDDER TO THINK WHAT'S HAPPENING TO HIM!
AGGGGHHH!
AWAKE AT LAST, EH, GRAHAM? AND NONE THE WORSE FOR YOUR ORDEAL, I TRUST?
SCREAM ALL YOU LIKE, BY THE WAY. WE'RE QUITE, QUITE ALONE...!
SPRANG MINING EQUIPMENT
HOW DO YOU LIKE MY LITTLE DEATH MACHINE? I BUILT IT FOR GREAT-AUNT ALICE A COUPLE OF YEARS AGO--BUT THE OLD WITCH CROAKED OF NATURAL CAUSES, AND I NEVER HAD THE CHANCE TO USE IT!
22

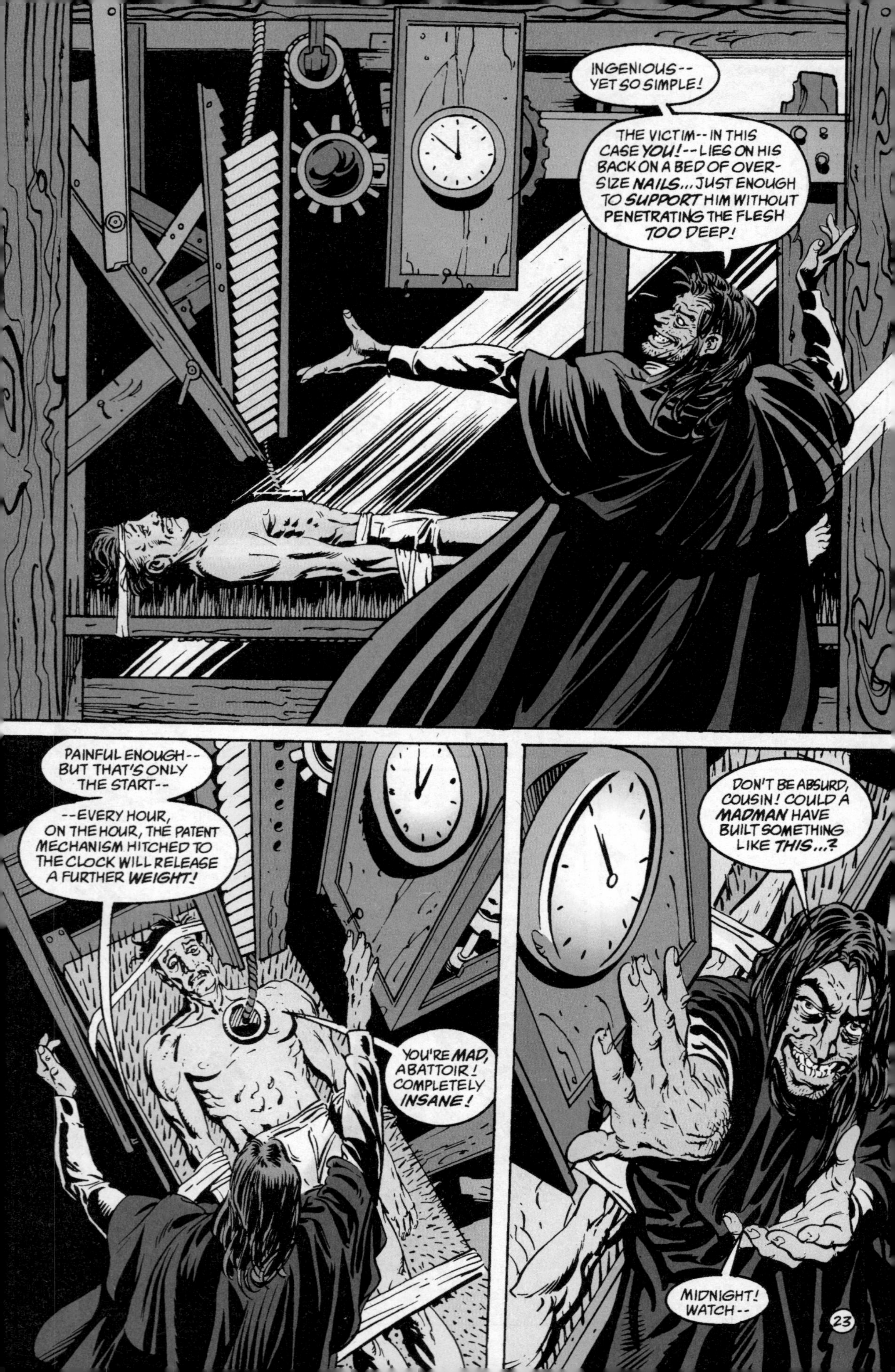
INGENIOUS--
YET SO SIMPLE!
THE VICTIM--IN THIS CASE YOU!--LIES ON HIS BACK ON A BED OF OVER-SIZE NAILS...JUST ENOUGH TO SUPPORT HIM WITHOUT PENETRATING THE FLESH TOO DEEP!
PAINFUL ENOUGH--BUT THAT'S ONLY THE START--
--EVERY HOUR, ON THE HOUR, THE PATENT MECHANISM HITCHED TO THE CLOCK WILL RELEASE A FURTHER WEIGHT!
YOU'RE MAD, ABATTOIR! COMPLETELY INSANE!
DON'T BE ABSURD, COUSIN! COULD A MADMAN HAVE BUILT SOMETHING LIKE THIS...?
MIDNIGHT! WATCH--
23

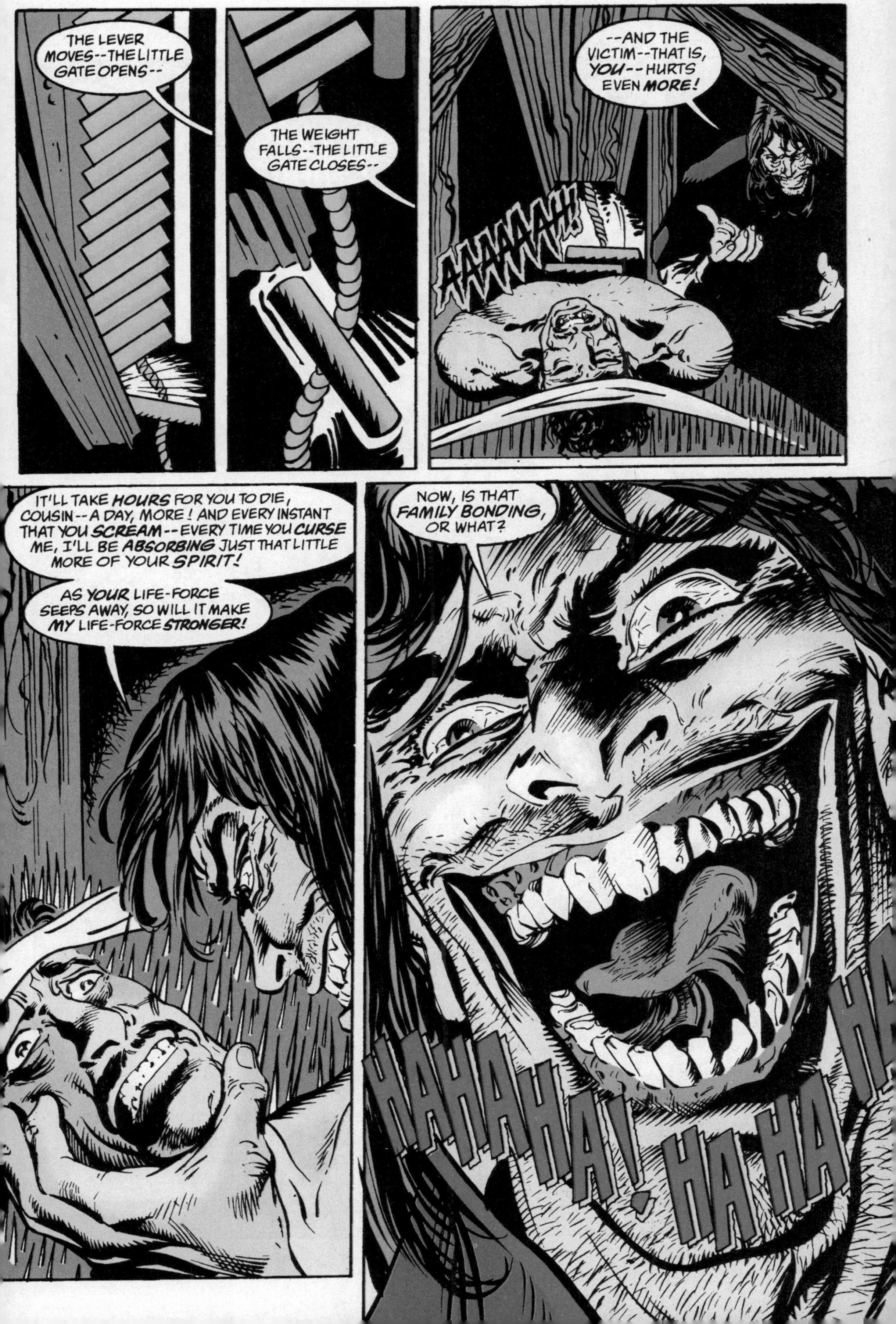
THE LEVER MOVES--THE LITTLE GATE OPENS--
THE WEIGHT FALLS--THE LITTLE GATE CLOSES--
--AND THE VICTIM--THAT IS, YOU--HURTS EVEN MORE!
AAAAAAH!
IT'LL TAKE HOURS FOR YOU TO DIE, COUSIN--A DAY, MORE! AND EVERY INSTANT THAT YOU SCREAM--EVERY TIME YOU CURSE ME, I'LL BE ABSORBING JUST THAT LITTLE MORE OF YOUR SPIRIT!
AS YOUR LIFE-FORCE SEEPS AWAY, SO WILL IT MAKE MY LIFE-FORCE STRONGER!
NOW, IS THAT FAMILY BONDING, OR WHAT?
HAHAHA! HAHA HA

Cover art by KELLEY JONES AND JOHN BEATTY

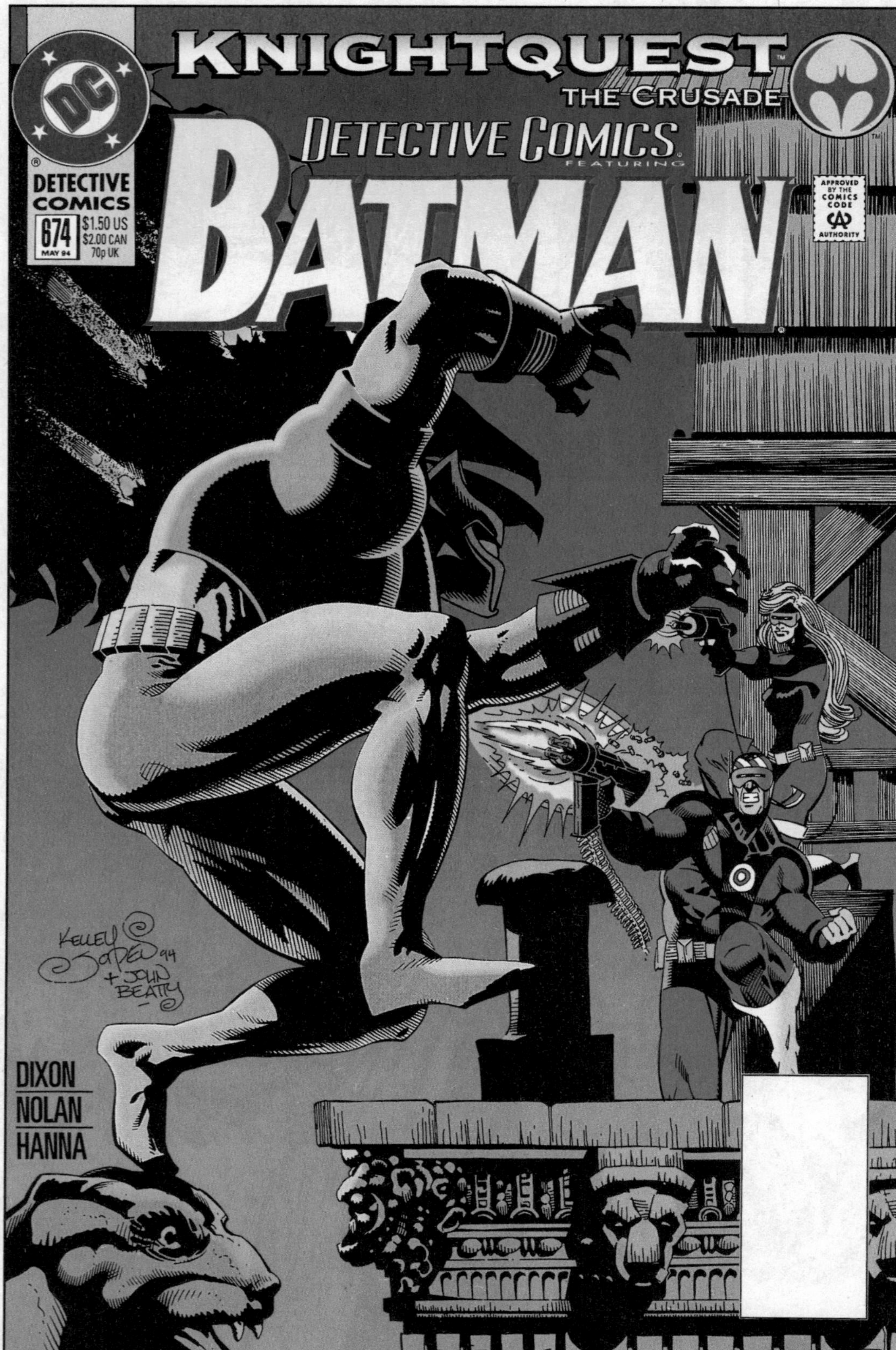

KNIGHTQUEST
THE CRUSADE
DETECTIVE COMICS
FEATURING
BATMAN
DC
DETECTIVE COMICS
674
MAY 94
$1.50 US
$2.00 CAN
70p UK
APPROVED BY THE COMICS CODE AUTHORITY
DIXON
NOLAN
HANNA

OUT-GUNNED

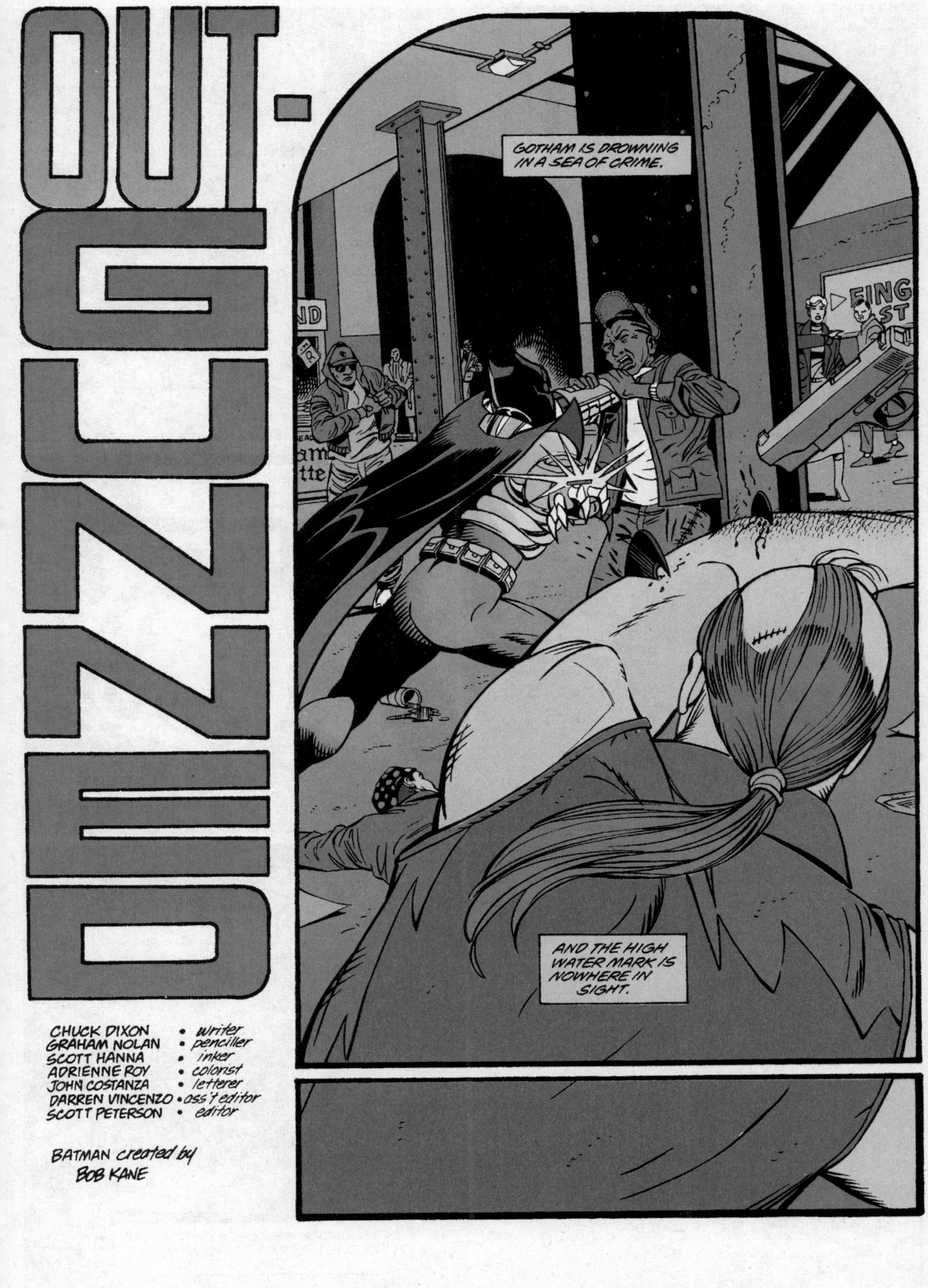
GOTHAM IS DROWNING IN A SEA OF CRIME.
AND THE HIGH WATER MARK IS NOWHERE IN SIGHT.

CHUCK DIXON • writer
GRAHAM NOLAN • penciller
SCOTT HANNA • inker
ADRIENNE ROY • colorist
JOHN COSTANZA • letterer
DARREN VINCENZO • ass't editor
SCOTT PETERSON • editor

BATMAN created by BOB KANE

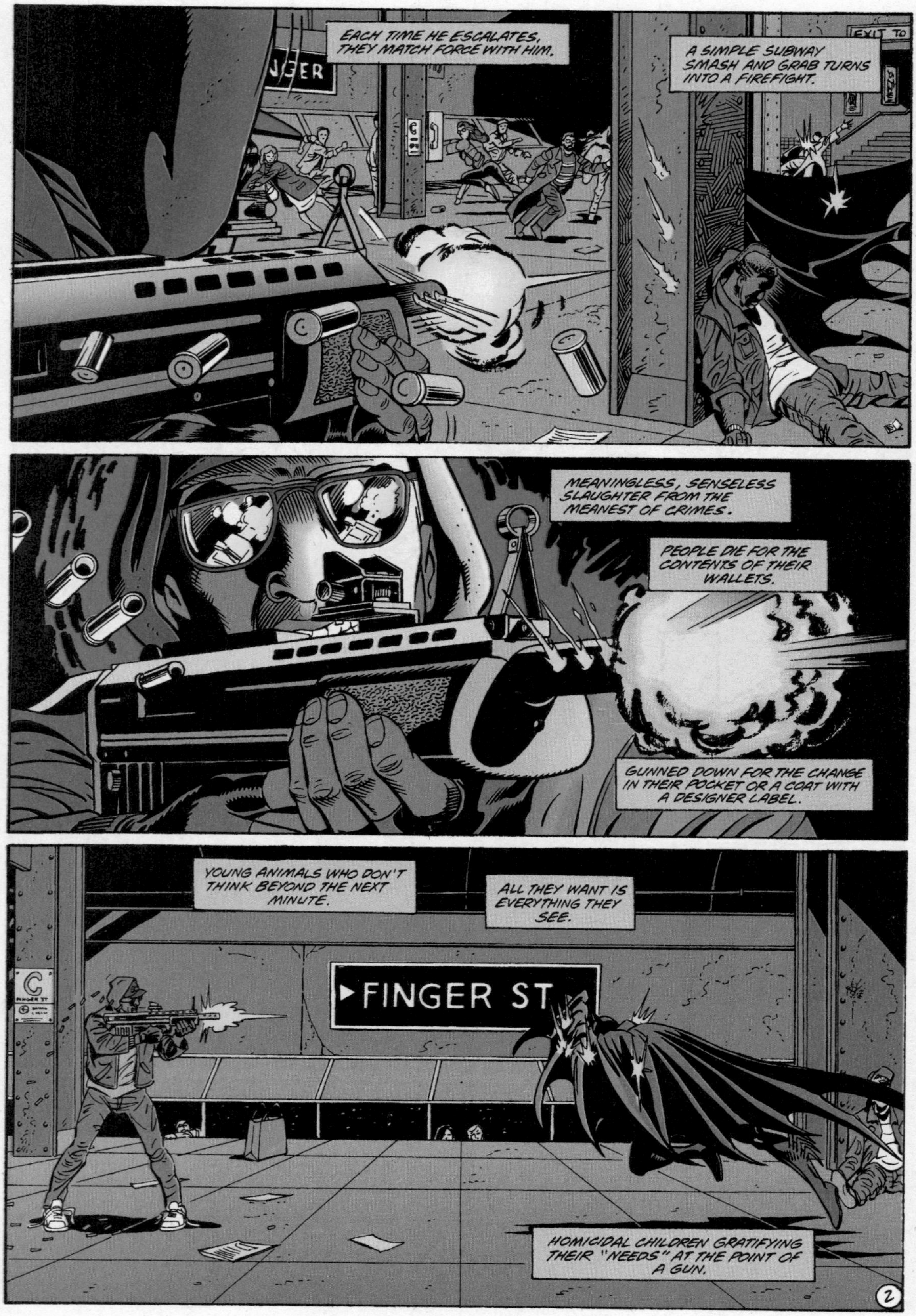
EACH TIME HE ESCALATES, THEY MATCH FORCE WITH HIM.
EXIT TO
A SIMPLE SUBWAY SMASH AND GRAB TURNS INTO A FIREFIGHT.
MEANINGLESS, SENSELESS SLAUGHTER FROM THE MEANEST OF CRIMES.
PEOPLE DIE FOR THE CONTENTS OF THEIR WALLETS.
GUNNED DOWN FOR THE CHANGE IN THEIR POCKET OR A COAT WITH A DESIGNER LABEL.
YOUNG ANIMALS WHO DON'T THINK BEYOND THE NEXT MINUTE.
ALL THEY WANT IS EVERYTHING THEY SEE.
FINGER ST
HOMICIDAL CHILDREN GRATIFYING THEIR "NEEDS" AT THE POINT OF A GUN.
2

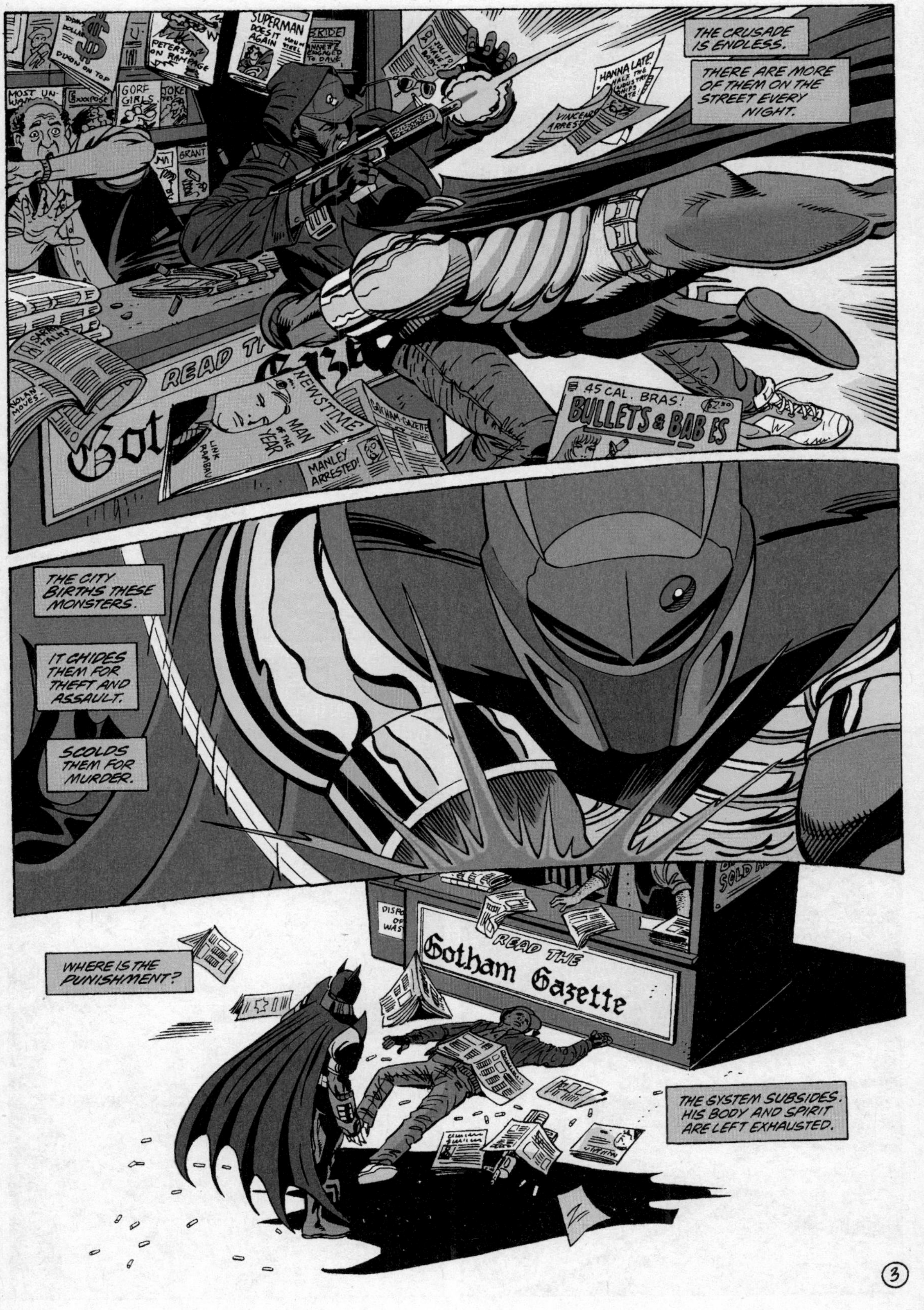
THE CRUSADE IS ENDLESS.
THERE ARE MORE OF THEM ON THE STREET EVERY NIGHT.
THE CITY BIRTHS THESE MONSTERS.
IT CHIDES THEM FOR THEFT AND ASSAULT.
SCOLDS THEM FOR MURDER.
WHERE IS THE PUNISHMENT?
THE SYSTEM SUBSIDES. HIS BODY AND SPIRIT ARE LEFT EXHAUSTED.
READ THE Gotham Gazette
BULLETS & BABES
MANLEY ARRESTED!
3

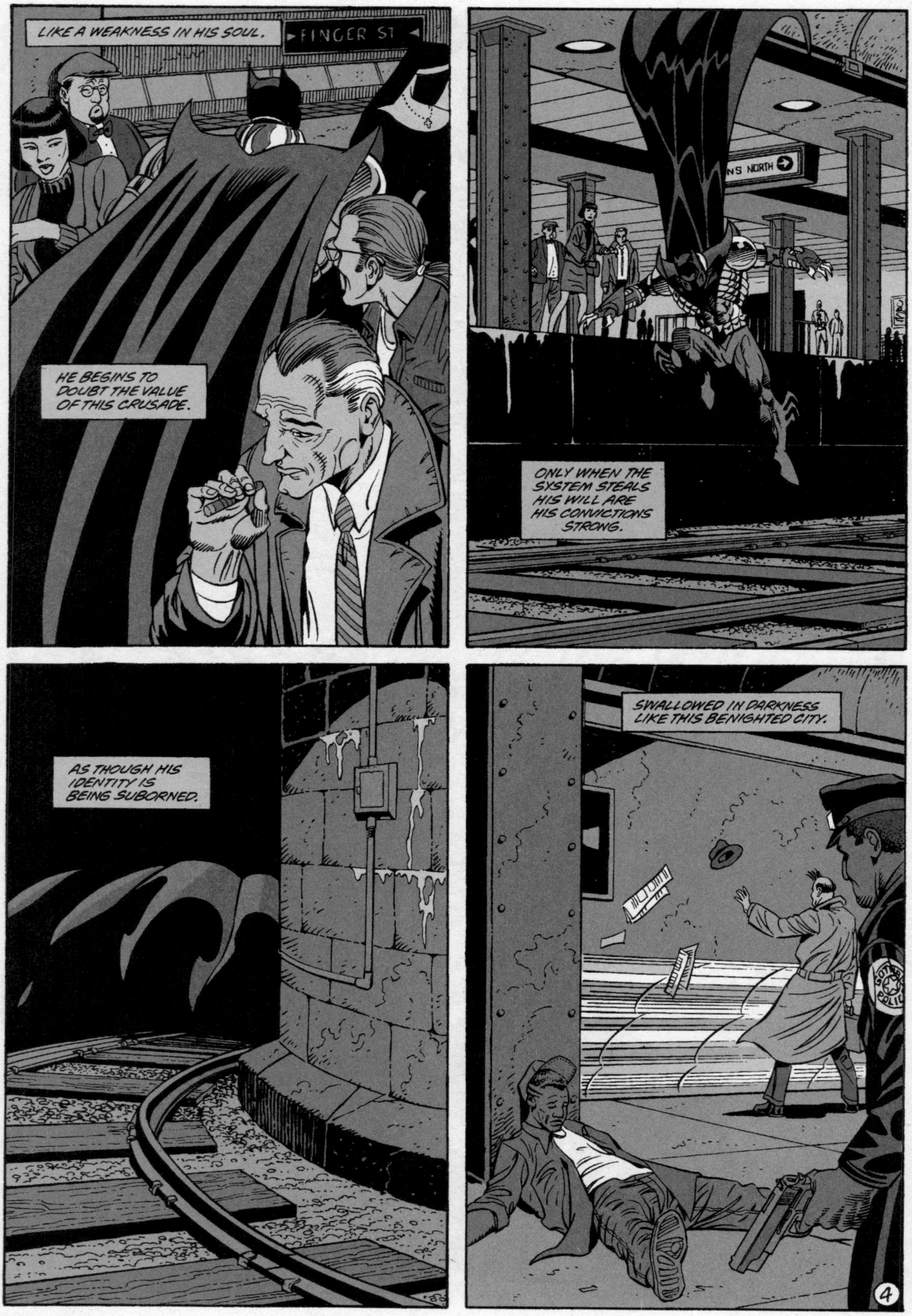
LIKE A WEAKNESS IN HIS SOUL.
FINGER ST
HE BEGINS TO DOUBT THE VALUE OF THIS CRUSADE.
ONLY WHEN THE SYSTEM STEALS HIS WILL ARE HIS CONVICTIONS STRONG.
AS THOUGH HIS IDENTITY IS BEING SUBORNED.
SWALLOWED IN DARKNESS LIKE THIS BENIGHTED CITY.
4

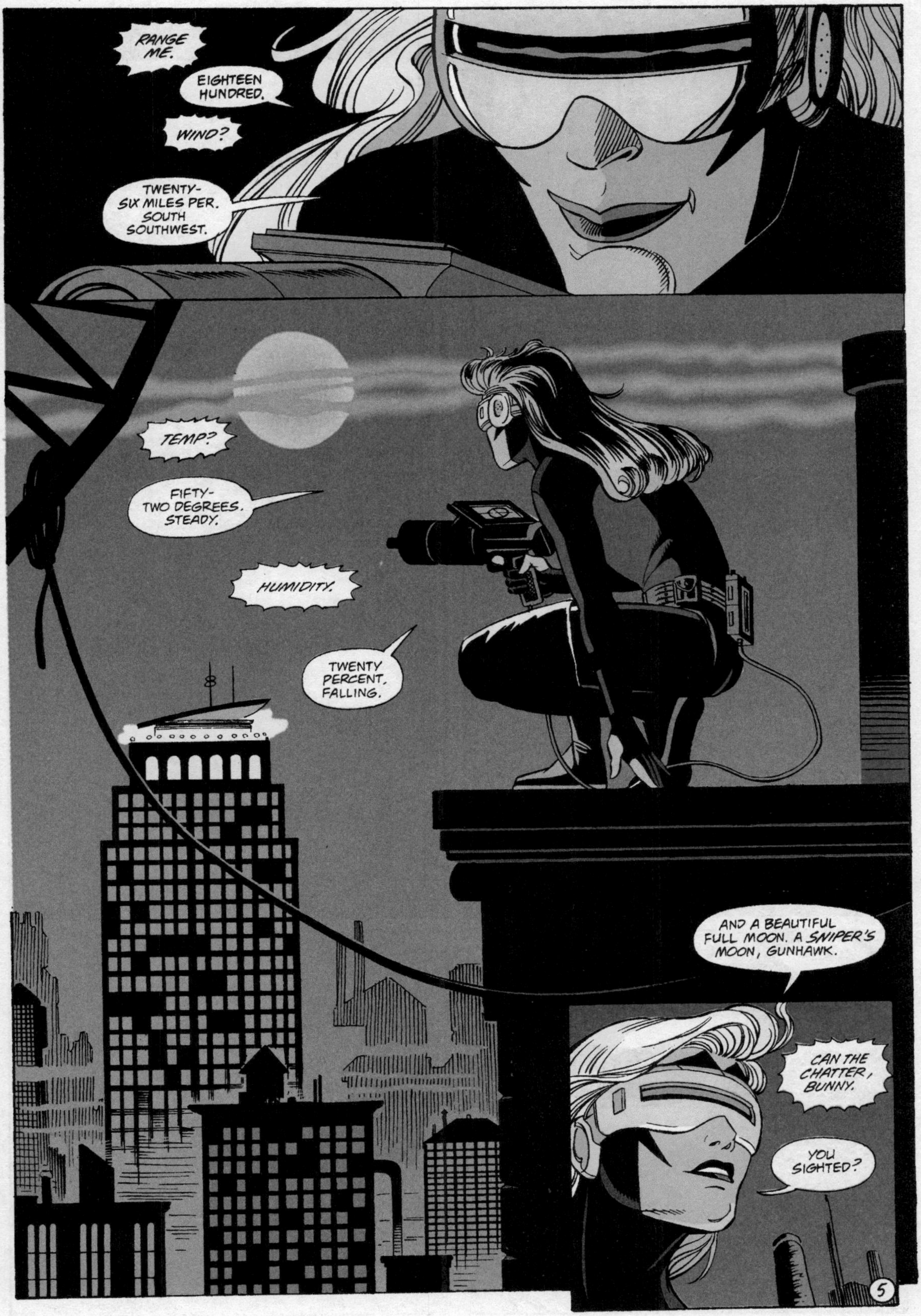
RANGE ME.
EIGHTEEN HUNDRED.
WIND?
TWENTY-SIX MILES PER. SOUTH SOUTHWEST.
TEMP?
FIFTY-TWO DEGREES. STEADY.
HUMIDITY.
TWENTY PERCENT, FALLING.
AND A BEAUTIFUL FULL MOON. A SNIPER'S MOON, GUNHAWK.
CAN THE CHATTER, BUNNY.
YOU SIGHTED?
5

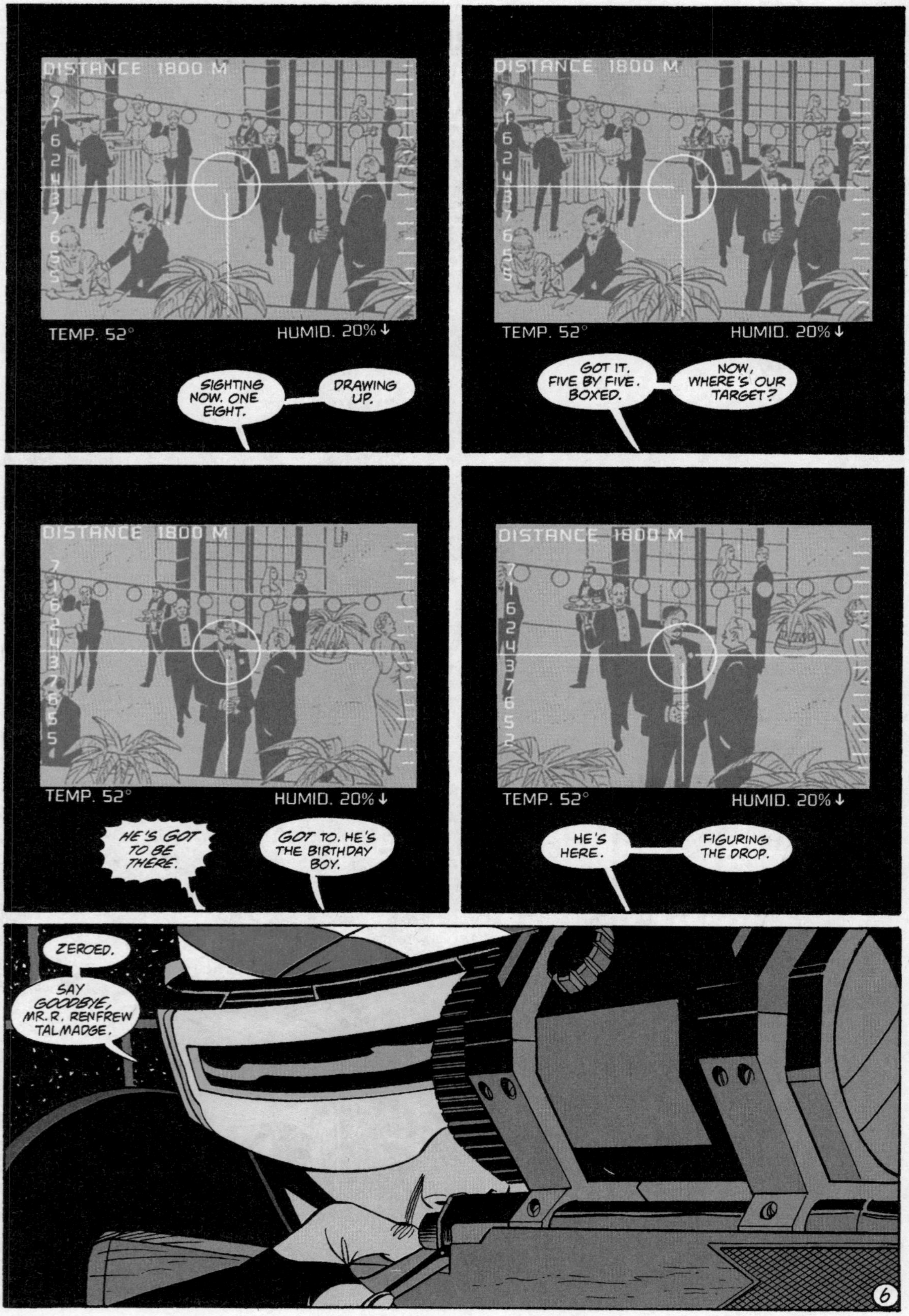

DISTANCE 1800 M
TEMP. 52°
HUMID. 20%↓
SIGHTING NOW. ONE EIGHT.
DRAWING UP.
DISTANCE 1800 M
TEMP. 52°
HUMID. 20%↓
GOT IT. FIVE BY FIVE. BOXED.
NOW, WHERE'S OUR TARGET?
DISTANCE 1800 M
TEMP. 52°
HUMID. 20%↓
HE'S GOT TO BE THERE.
GOT TO. HE'S THE BIRTHDAY BOY.
DISTANCE 1800 M
TEMP. 52°
HUMID. 20%↓
HE'S HERE.
FIGURING THE DROP.
ZEROED.
SAY GOODBYE, MR. R. RENFREW TALMADGE.
6

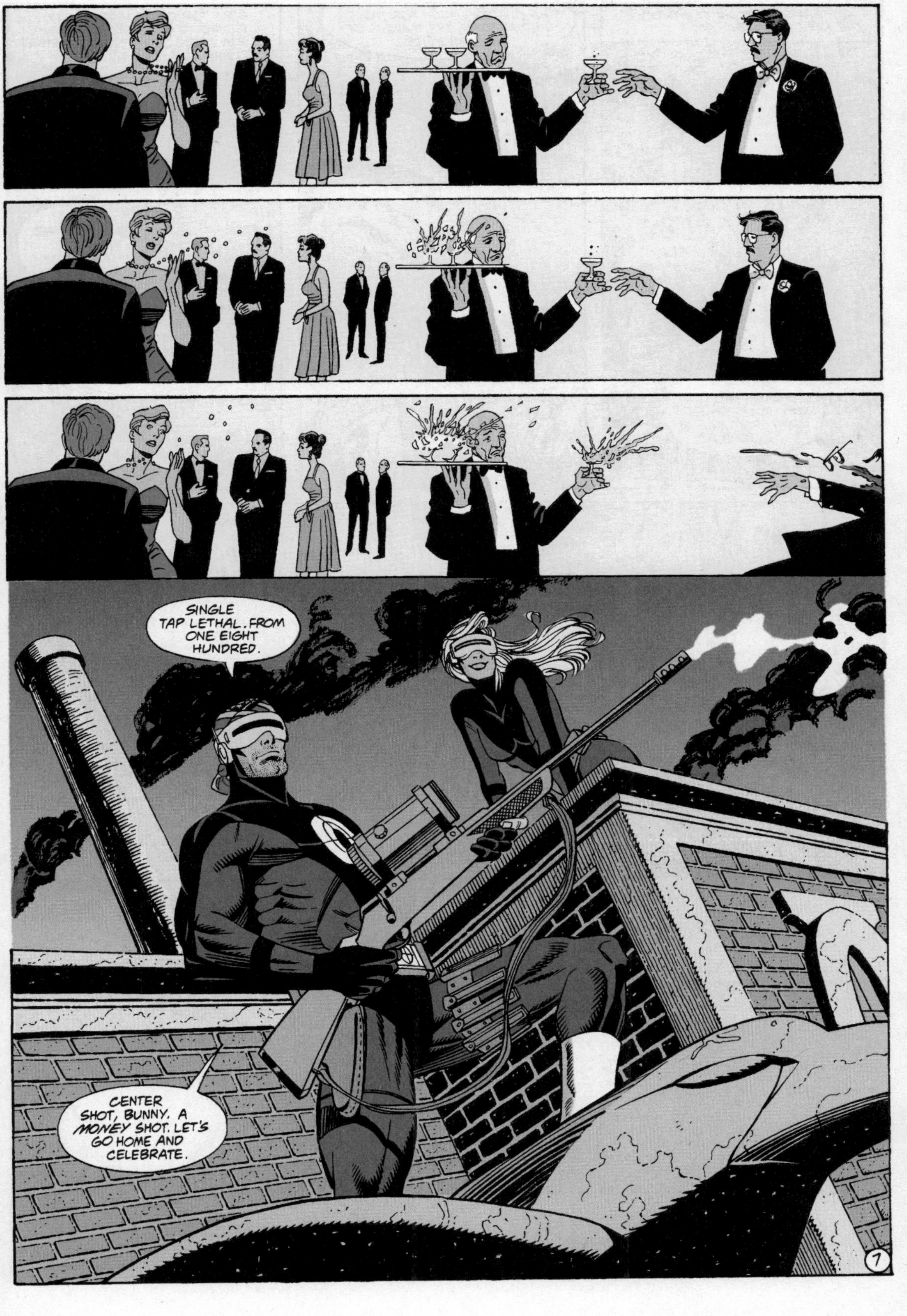
SINGLE TAP LETHAL. FROM ONE EIGHT HUNDRED.
CENTER SHOT, BUNNY. A MONEY SHOT. LET'S GO HOME AND CELEBRATE.
7

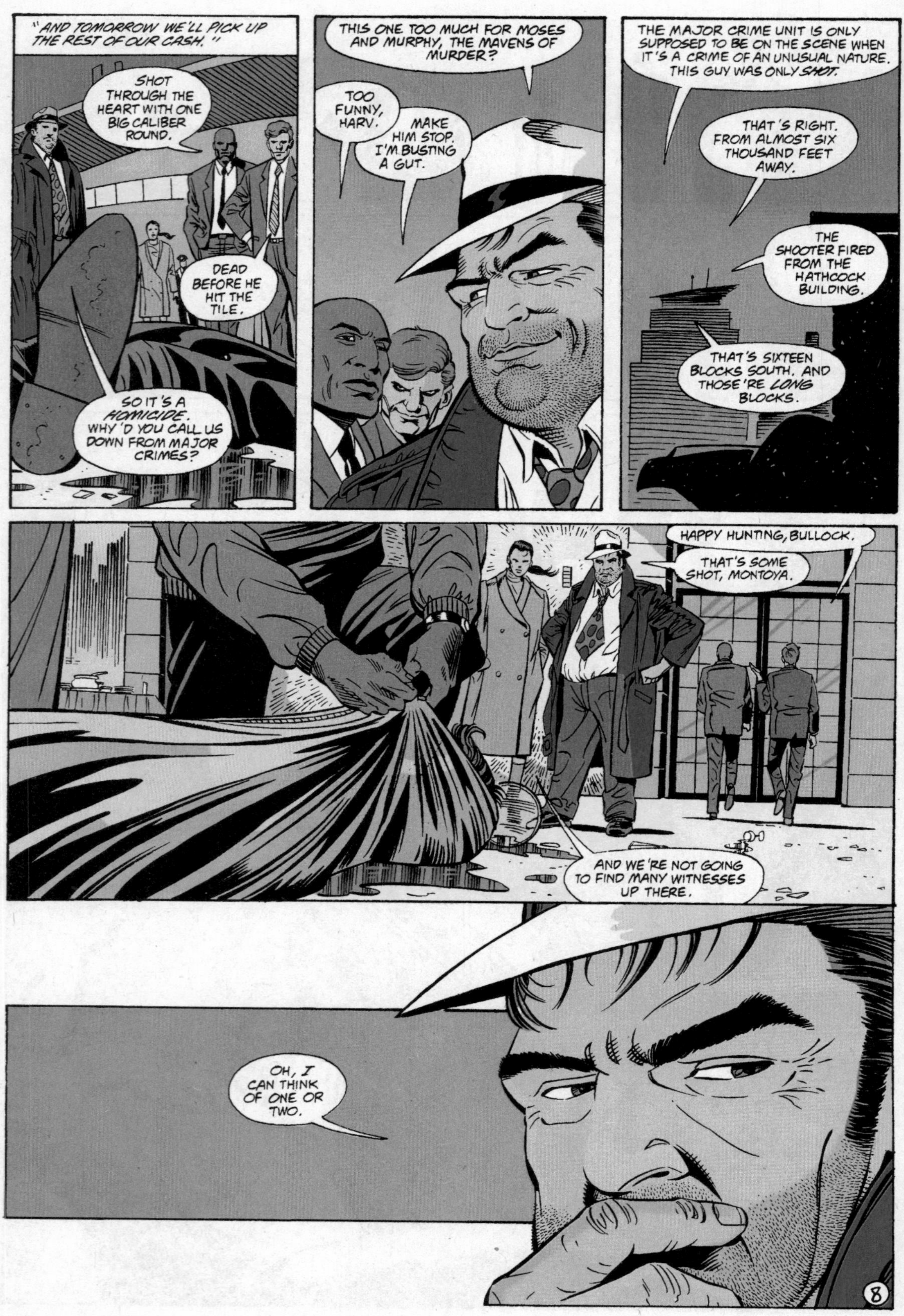
"AND TOMORROW WE'LL PICK UP THE REST OF OUR CASH."
SHOT THROUGH THE HEART WITH ONE BIG CALIBER ROUND.
DEAD BEFORE HE HIT THE TILE.
SO IT'S A HOMICIDE. WHY'D YOU CALL US DOWN FROM MAJOR CRIMES?
THIS ONE TOO MUCH FOR MOSES AND MURPHY, THE MAVENS OF MURDER?
TOO FUNNY, HARV.
MAKE HIM STOP. I'M BUSTING A GUT.
THE MAJOR CRIME UNIT IS ONLY SUPPOSED TO BE ON THE SCENE WHEN IT'S A CRIME OF AN UNUSUAL NATURE. THIS GUY WAS ONLY SHOT.
THAT'S RIGHT. FROM ALMOST SIX THOUSAND FEET AWAY.
THE SHOOTER FIRED FROM THE HATHCOCK BUILDING.
THAT'S SIXTEEN BLOCKS SOUTH. AND THOSE'RE LONG BLOCKS.
HAPPY HUNTING, BULLOCK.
THAT'S SOME SHOT, MONTOYA.
AND WE'RE NOT GOING TO FIND MANY WITNESSES UP THERE.
OH, I CAN THINK OF ONE OR TWO.
8

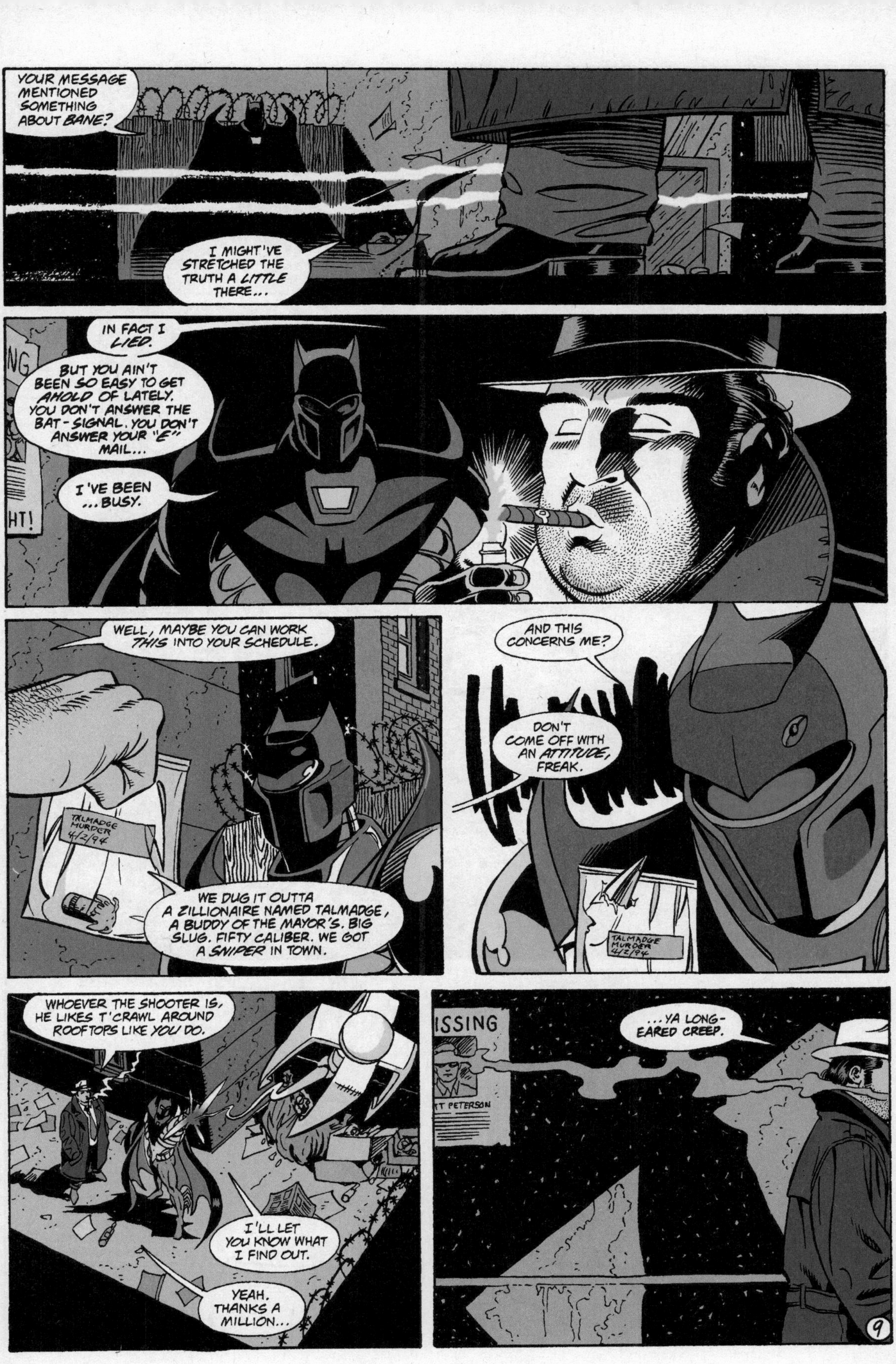
YOUR MESSAGE MENTIONED SOMETHING ABOUT BANE?
I MIGHT'VE STRETCHED THE TRUTH A LITTLE THERE...
IN FACT I LIED.
BUT YOU AIN'T BEEN SO EASY TO GET AHOLD OF LATELY. YOU DON'T ANSWER THE BAT-SIGNAL. YOU DON'T ANSWER YOUR "E" MAIL...
I'VE BEEN ...BUSY.
WELL, MAYBE YOU CAN WORK THIS INTO YOUR SCHEDULE.
TALMADGE MURDER 4/2/94
WE DUG IT OUTTA A ZILLIONAIRE NAMED TALMADGE, A BUDDY OF THE MAYOR'S. BIG SLUG. FIFTY CALIBER. WE GOT A SNIPER IN TOWN.
AND THIS CONCERNS ME?
DON'T COME OFF WITH AN ATTITUDE, FREAK.
TALMADGE MURDER 4/2/94
WHOEVER THE SHOOTER IS, HE LIKES T'CRAWL AROUND ROOFTOPS LIKE YOU DO.
I'LL LET YOU KNOW WHAT I FIND OUT.
YEAH. THANKS A MILLION...
ISSING
T PETERSON
...YA LONG-EARED CREEP.
9

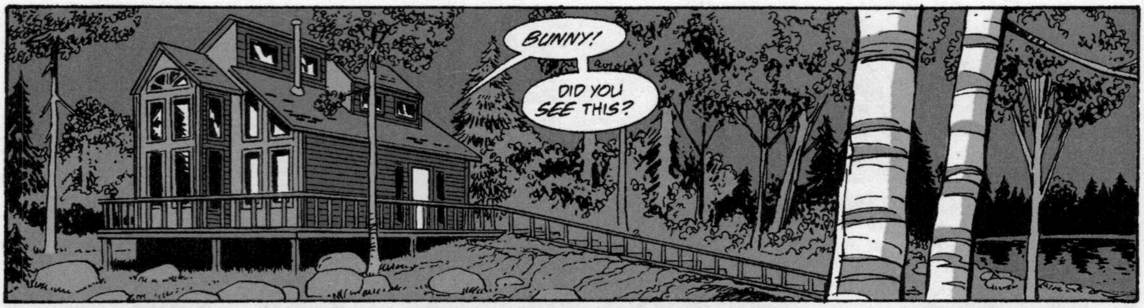
BUNNY!
DID YOU SEE THIS?
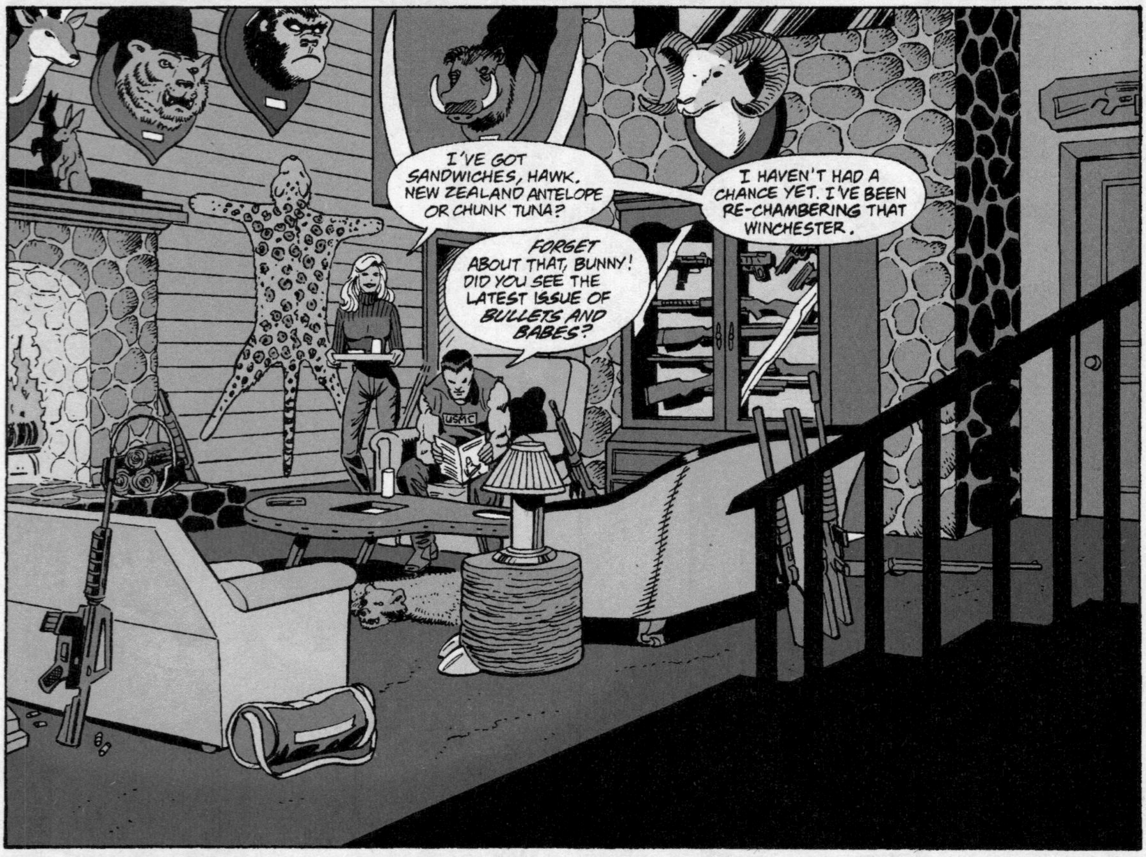
I'VE GOT SANDWICHES, HAWK. NEW ZEALAND ANTELOPE OR CHUNK TUNA?
I HAVEN'T HAD A CHANCE YET. I'VE BEEN RE-CHAMBERING THAT WINCHESTER.
FORGET ABOUT THAT, BUNNY! DID YOU SEE THE LATEST ISSUE OF BULLETS AND BABES?
USMC
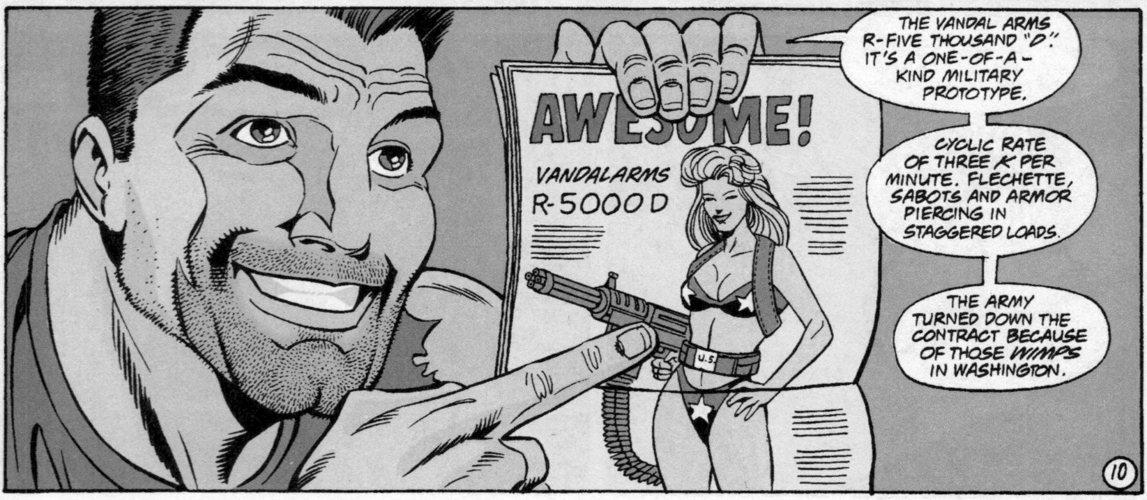
THE VANDAL ARMS R-FIVE THOUSAND "D". IT'S A ONE-OF-A-KIND MILITARY PROTOTYPE.
CYCLIC RATE OF THREE K PER MINUTE. FLECHETTE, SABOTS AND ARMOR PIERCING IN STAGGERED LOADS.
THE ARMY TURNED DOWN THE CONTRACT BECAUSE OF THOSE WIMPS IN WASHINGTON.
AWESOME!
VANDALARMS
R-5000 D
U.S.
10

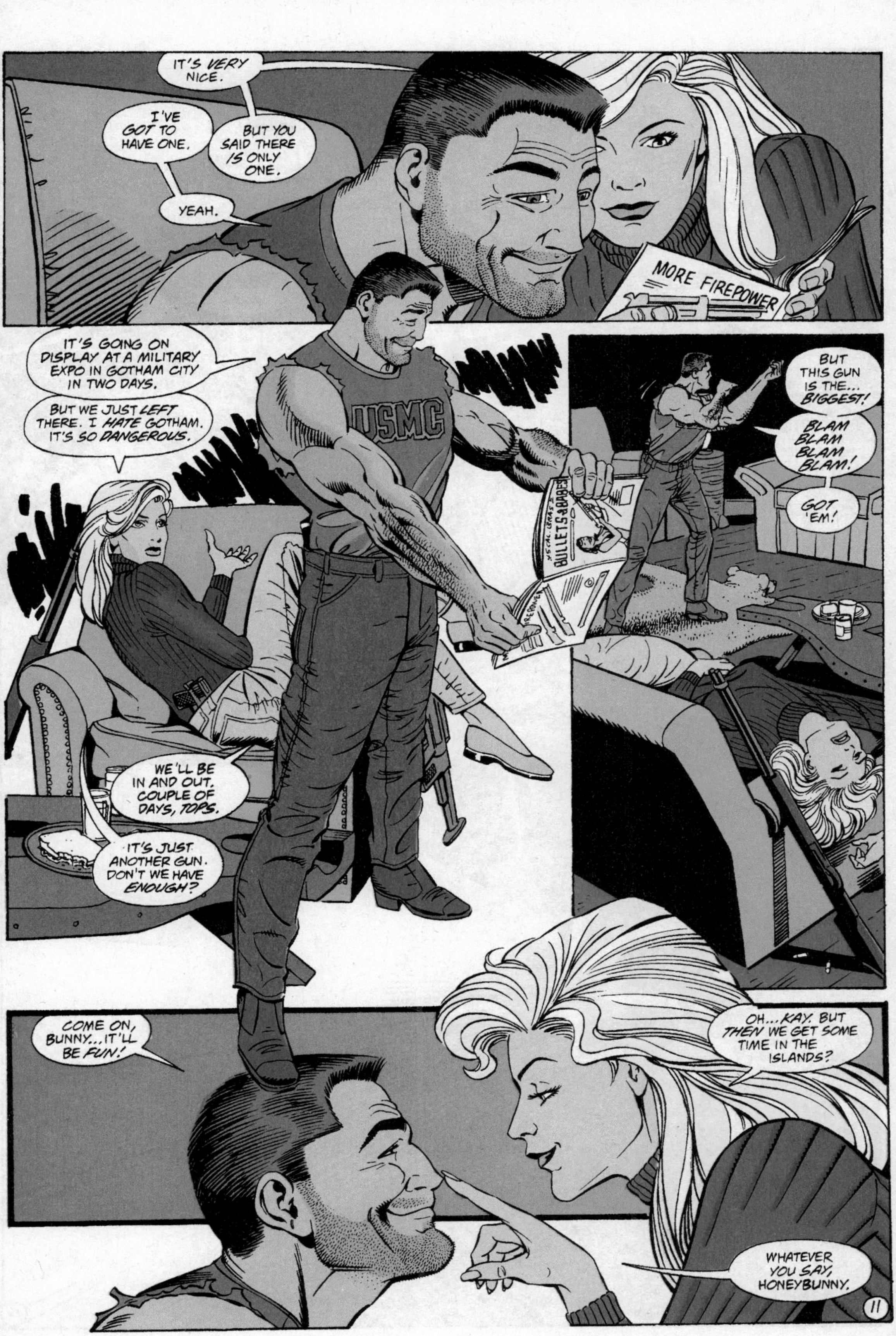
IT'S VERY NICE.
I'VE GOT TO HAVE ONE.
BUT YOU SAID THERE IS ONLY ONE.
YEAH.
MORE FIREPOWER
IT'S GOING ON DISPLAY AT A MILITARY EXPO IN GOTHAM CITY IN TWO DAYS.
BUT WE JUST LEFT THERE. I HATE GOTHAM. IT'S SO DANGEROUS.
USMC
BULLETS & BABES
WE'LL BE IN AND OUT. COUPLE OF DAYS, TOPS.
IT'S JUST ANOTHER GUN. DON'T WE HAVE ENOUGH?
BUT THIS GUN IS THE... BIGGEST!
BLAM BLAM BLAM BLAM!
GOT 'EM!
COME ON, BUNNY... IT'LL BE FUN!
OH... KAY. BUT THEN WE GET SOME TIME IN THE ISLANDS?
WHATEVER YOU SAY, HONEYBUNNY.
11

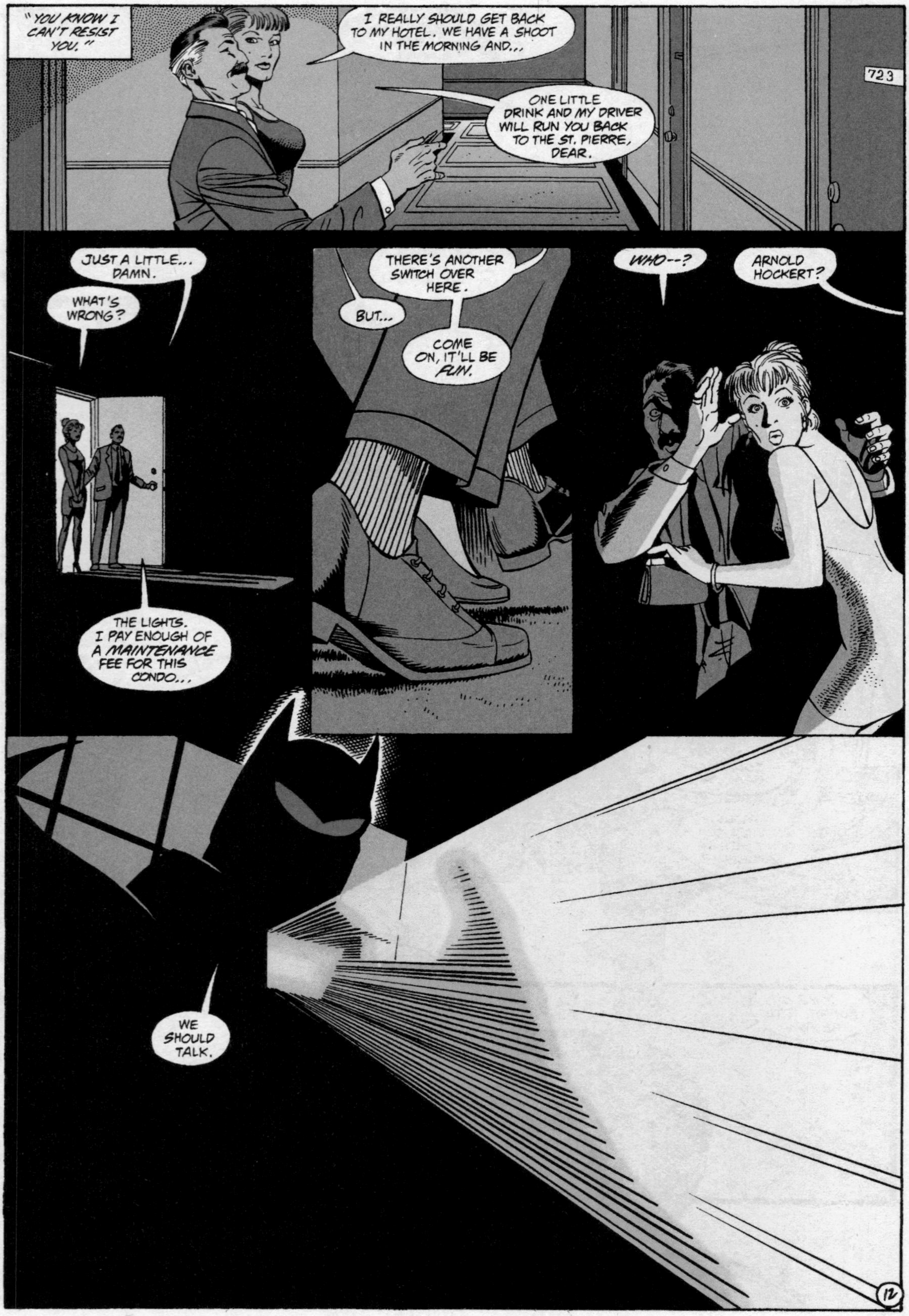
"YOU KNOW I CAN'T RESIST YOU."
I REALLY SHOULD GET BACK TO MY HOTEL. WE HAVE A SHOOT IN THE MORNING AND...
723
ONE LITTLE DRINK AND MY DRIVER WILL RUN YOU BACK TO THE ST. PIERRE, DEAR.
JUST A LITTLE... DAMN.
WHAT'S WRONG?
THE LIGHTS. I PAY ENOUGH OF A MAINTENANCE FEE FOR THIS CONDO...
THERE'S ANOTHER SWITCH OVER HERE.
BUT...
COME ON, IT'LL BE FUN.
WHO--?
ARNOLD HOCKERT?
WE SHOULD TALK.
12

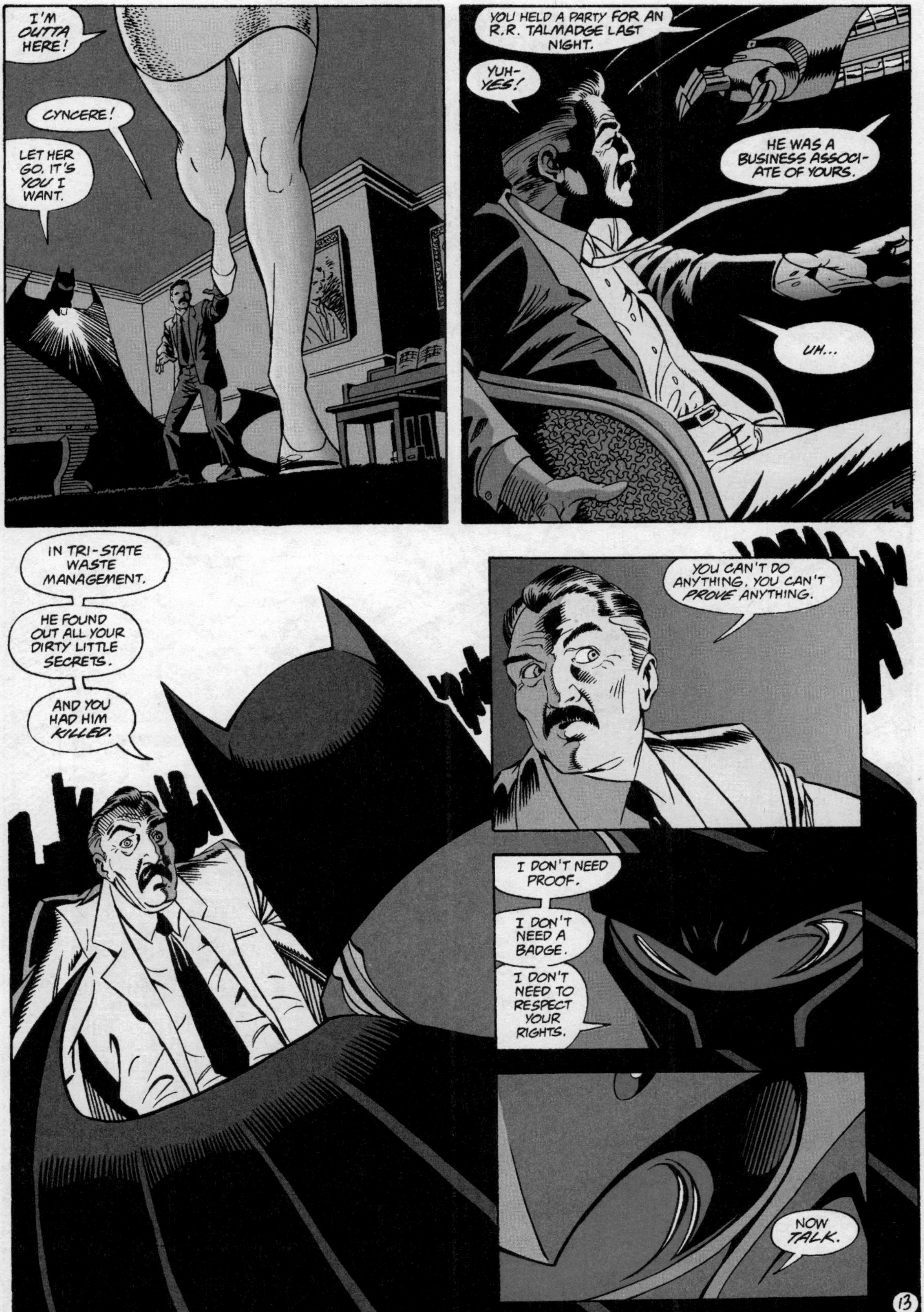
I'M OUTTA HERE!
CYNCERE!
LET HER GO, IT'S YOU I WANT.
YOU HELD A PARTY FOR AN R.R. TALMADGE LAST NIGHT.
YUH- YES!
HE WAS A BUSINESS ASSOCI- ATE OF YOURS.
UH...
IN TRI-STATE WASTE MANAGEMENT.
HE FOUND OUT ALL YOUR DIRTY LITTLE SECRETS.
AND YOU HAD HIM KILLED.
YOU CAN'T DO ANYTHING. YOU CAN'T PROVE ANYTHING.
I DON'T NEED PROOF.
I DON'T NEED A BADGE.
I DON'T NEED TO RESPECT YOUR RIGHTS.
NOW TALK.
13

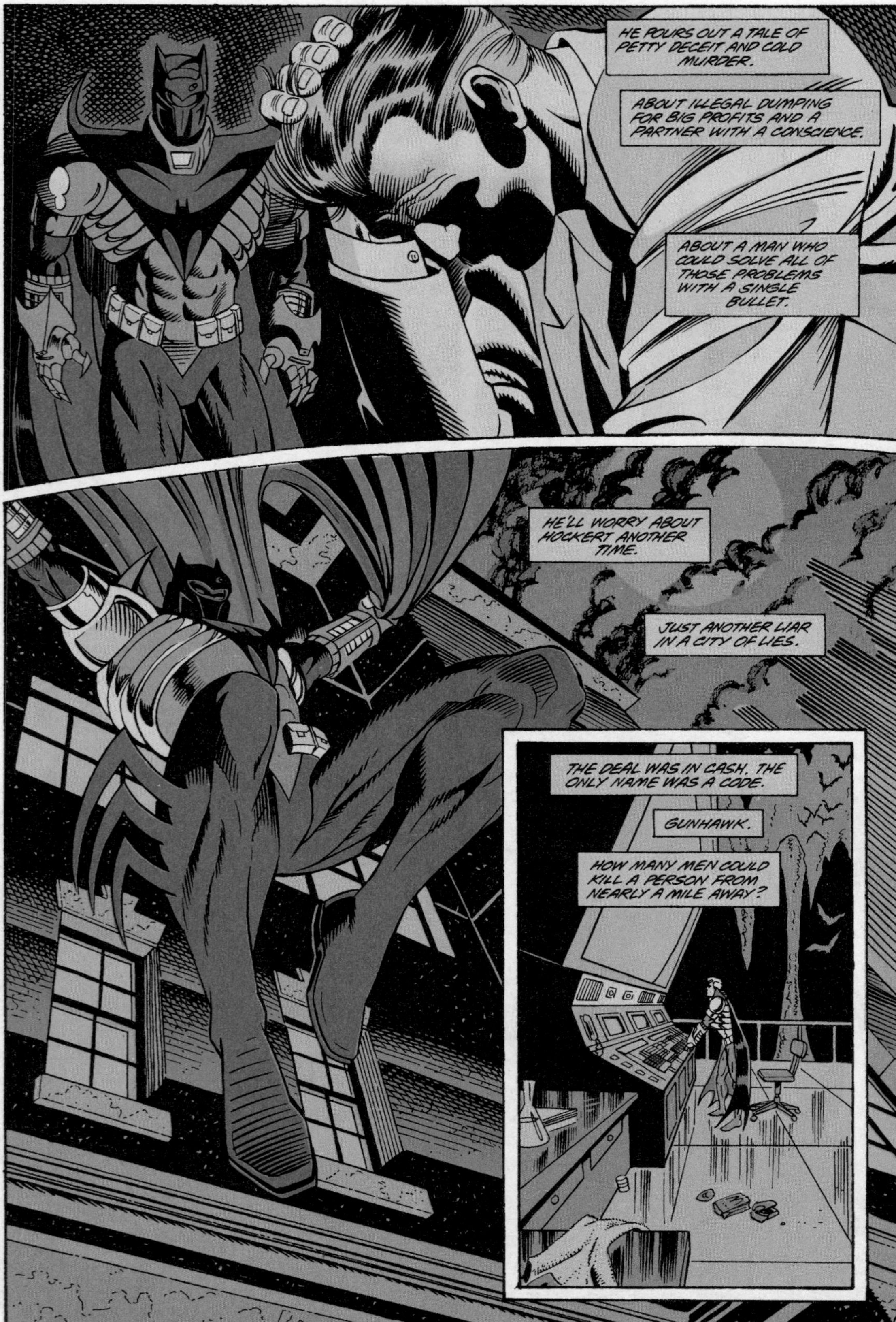
HE POURS OUT A TALE OF PETTY DECEIT AND COLD MURDER.
ABOUT ILLEGAL DUMPING FOR BIG PROFITS AND A PARTNER WITH A CONSCIENCE.
ABOUT A MAN WHO COULD SOLVE ALL OF THOSE PROBLEMS WITH A SINGLE BULLET.
HE'LL WORRY ABOUT HOCKERT ANOTHER TIME.
JUST ANOTHER LIAR IN A CITY OF LIES.
THE DEAL WAS IN CASH. THE ONLY NAME WAS A CODE.
GUNHAWK.
HOW MANY MEN COULD KILL A PERSON FROM NEARLY A MILE AWAY?
14

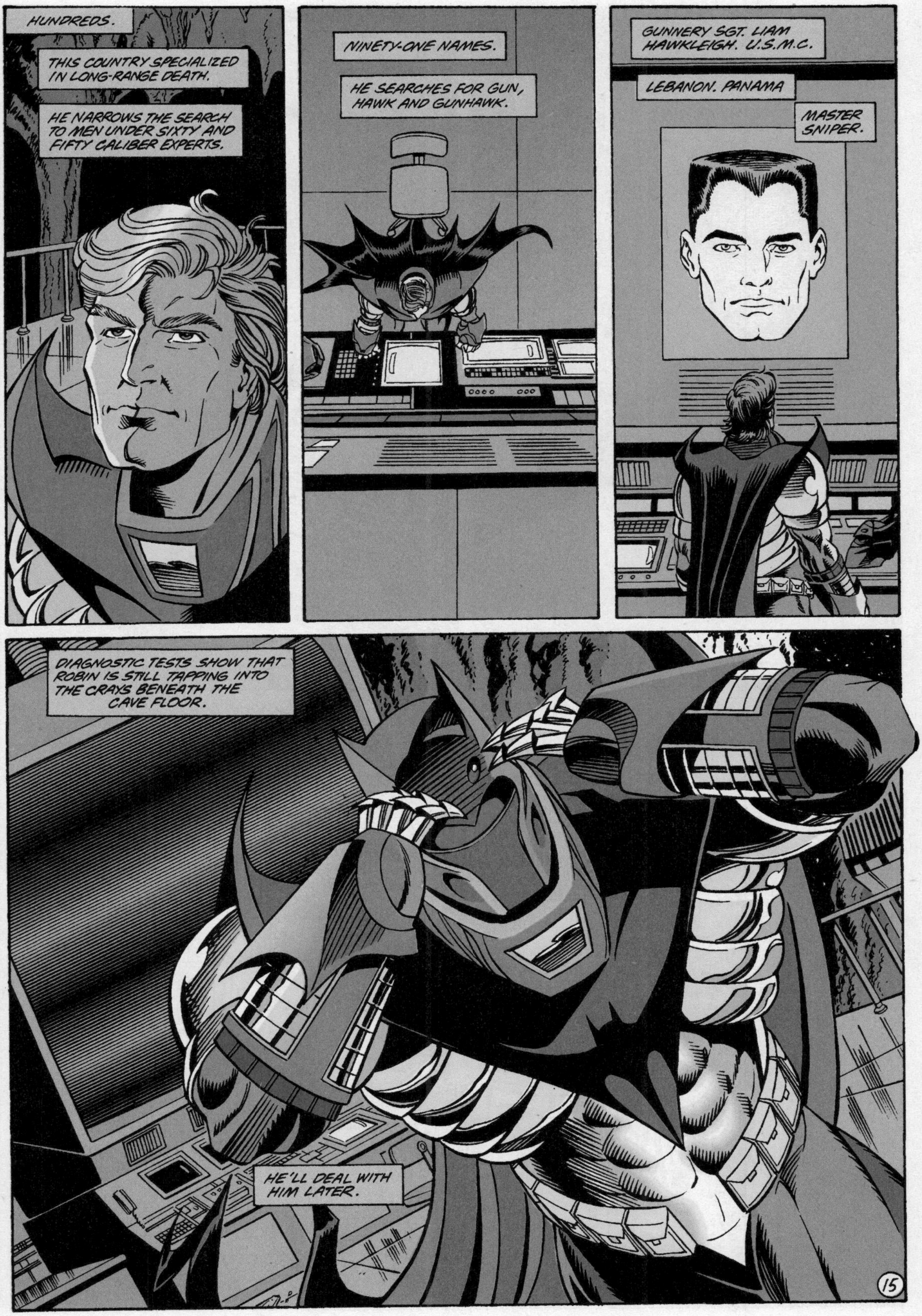
HUNDREDS.
THIS COUNTRY SPECIALIZED IN LONG-RANGE DEATH.
HE NARROWS THE SEARCH TO MEN UNDER SIXTY AND FIFTY CALIBER EXPERTS.
NINETY-ONE NAMES.
HE SEARCHES FOR GUN, HAWK AND GUNHAWK.
GUNNERY SGT. LIAM HAWKLEIGH. U.S.M.C.
LEBANON. PANAMA
MASTER SNIPER.
DIAGNOSTIC TESTS SHOW THAT ROBIN IS STILL TAPPING INTO THE CRAYS BENEATH THE CAVE FLOOR.
HE'LL DEAL WITH HIM LATER.
15

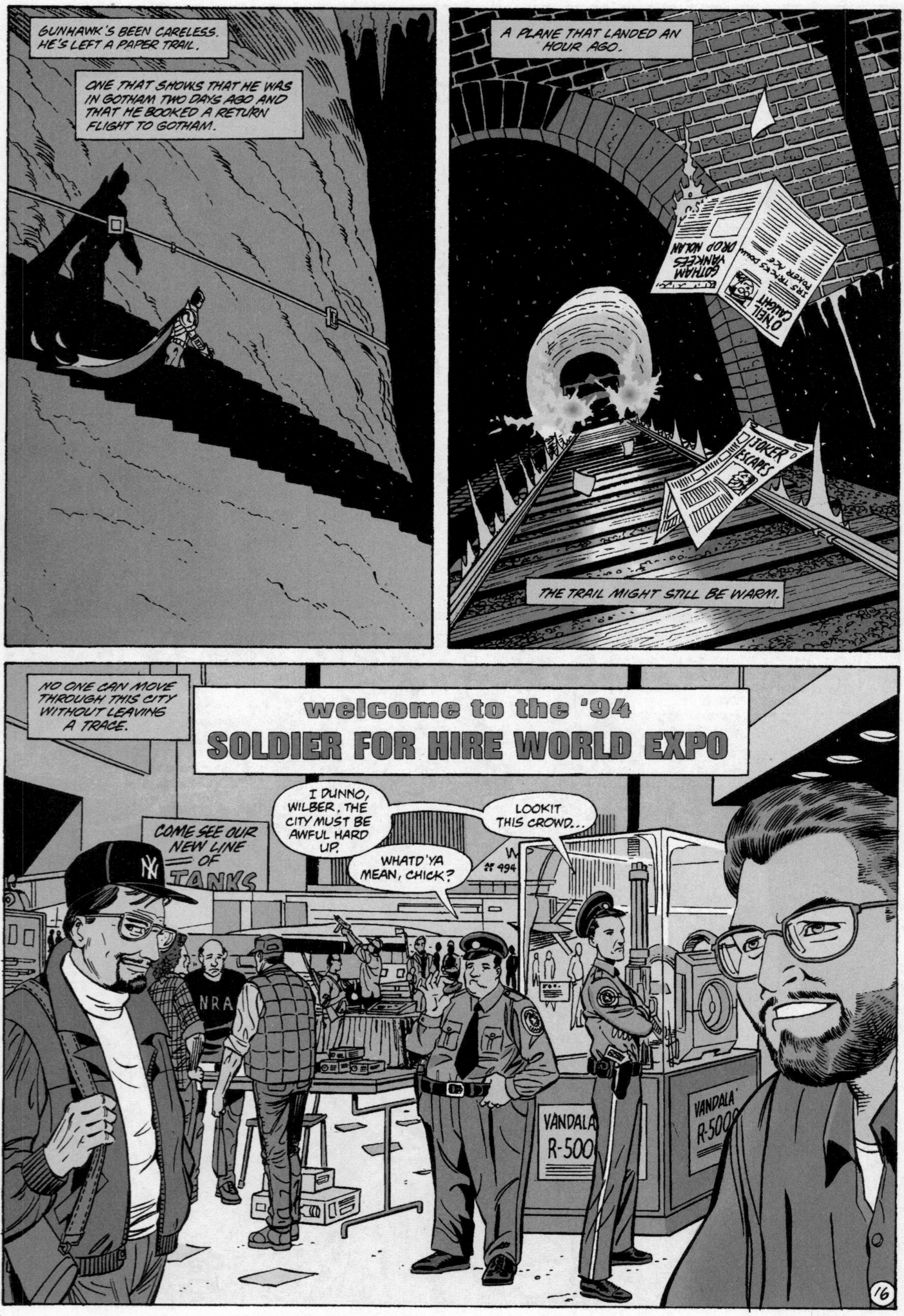
GUNHAWK'S BEEN CARELESS. HE'S LEFT A PAPER TRAIL.
ONE THAT SHOWS THAT HE WAS IN GOTHAM TWO DAYS AGO AND THAT HE BOOKED A RETURN FLIGHT TO GOTHAM.
A PLANE THAT LANDED AN HOUR AGO.
GOTHAM YANKEES DROP NOLAN
O'NEIL CAUGHT
JOKER ESCAPES
THE TRAIL MIGHT STILL BE WARM.
NO ONE CAN MOVE THROUGH THIS CITY WITHOUT LEAVING A TRACE.
welcome to the '94
SOLDIER FOR HIRE WORLD EXPO
COME SEE OUR NEW LINE OF TANKS
I DUNNO, WILBER, THE CITY MUST BE AWFUL HARD UP.
WHATD'YA MEAN, CHICK?
LOOKIT THIS CROWD...
NRA
VANDALA R-500
16

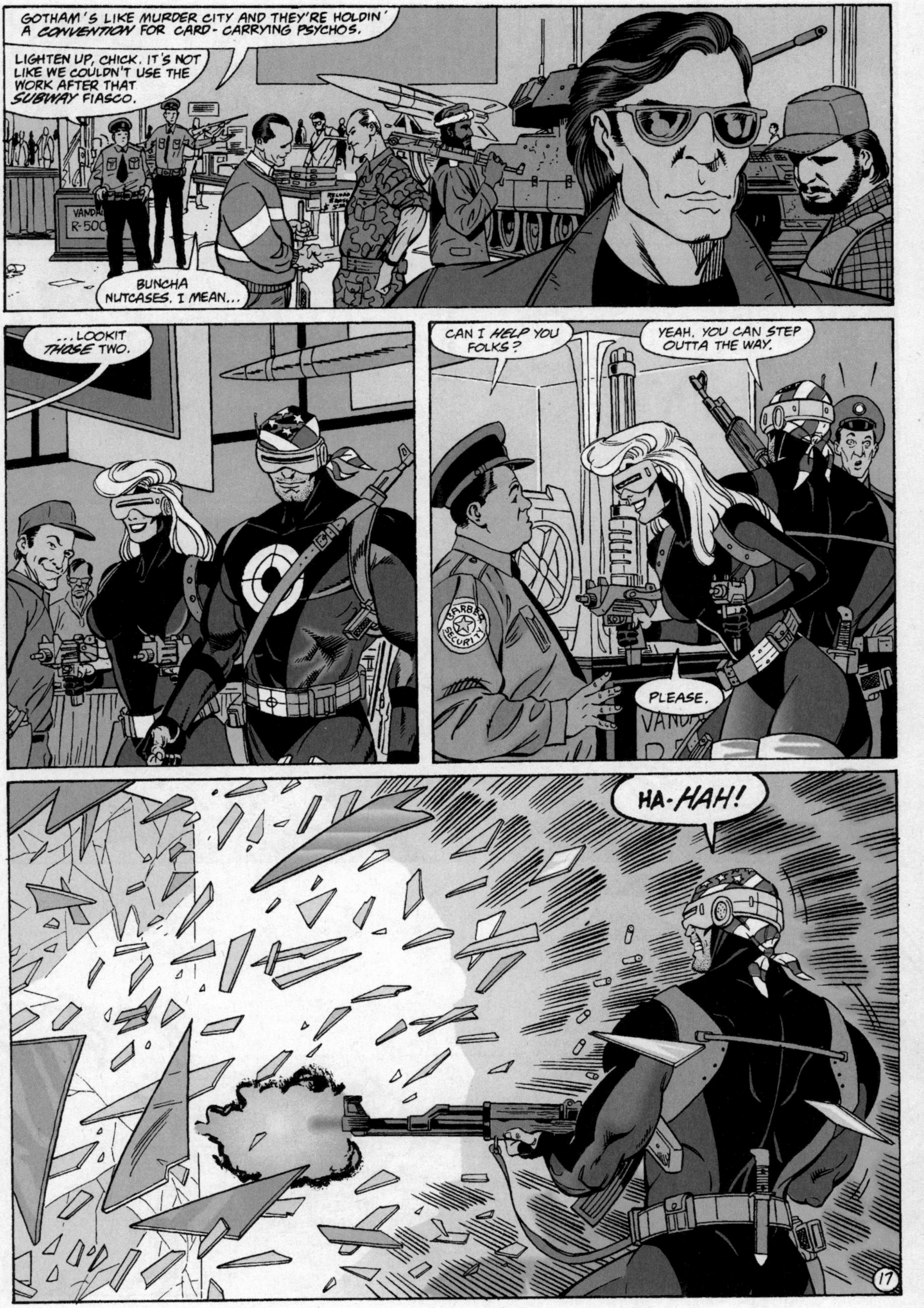
GOTHAM'S LIKE MURDER CITY AND THEY'RE HOLDIN' A CONVENTION FOR CARD-CARRYING PSYCHOS.
LIGHTEN UP, CHICK. IT'S NOT LIKE WE COULDN'T USE THE WORK AFTER THAT SUBWAY FIASCO.
BUNCHA NUTCASES. I MEAN...
...LOOKIT THOSE TWO.
CAN I HELP YOU FOLKS?
YEAH. YOU CAN STEP OUTTA THE WAY.
PLEASE.
HA-HAH!
17

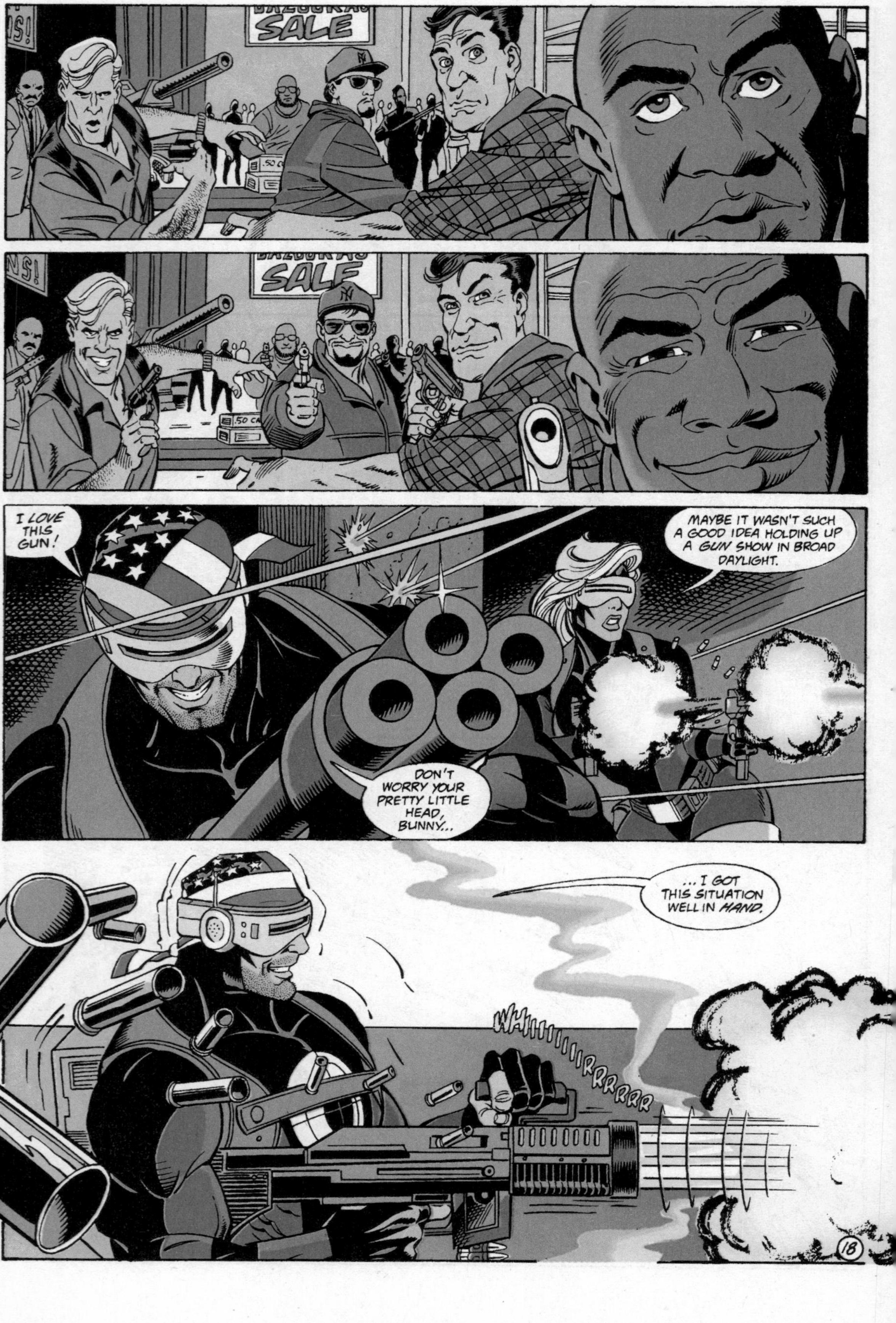
SALE
SALE
I LOVE THIS GUN!
MAYBE IT WASN'T SUCH A GOOD IDEA HOLDING UP A GUN SHOW IN BROAD DAYLIGHT.
DON'T WORRY YOUR PRETTY LITTLE HEAD, BUNNY...
...I GOT THIS SITUATION WELL IN HAND.
WHIIIIIIIRRRRRRR
18

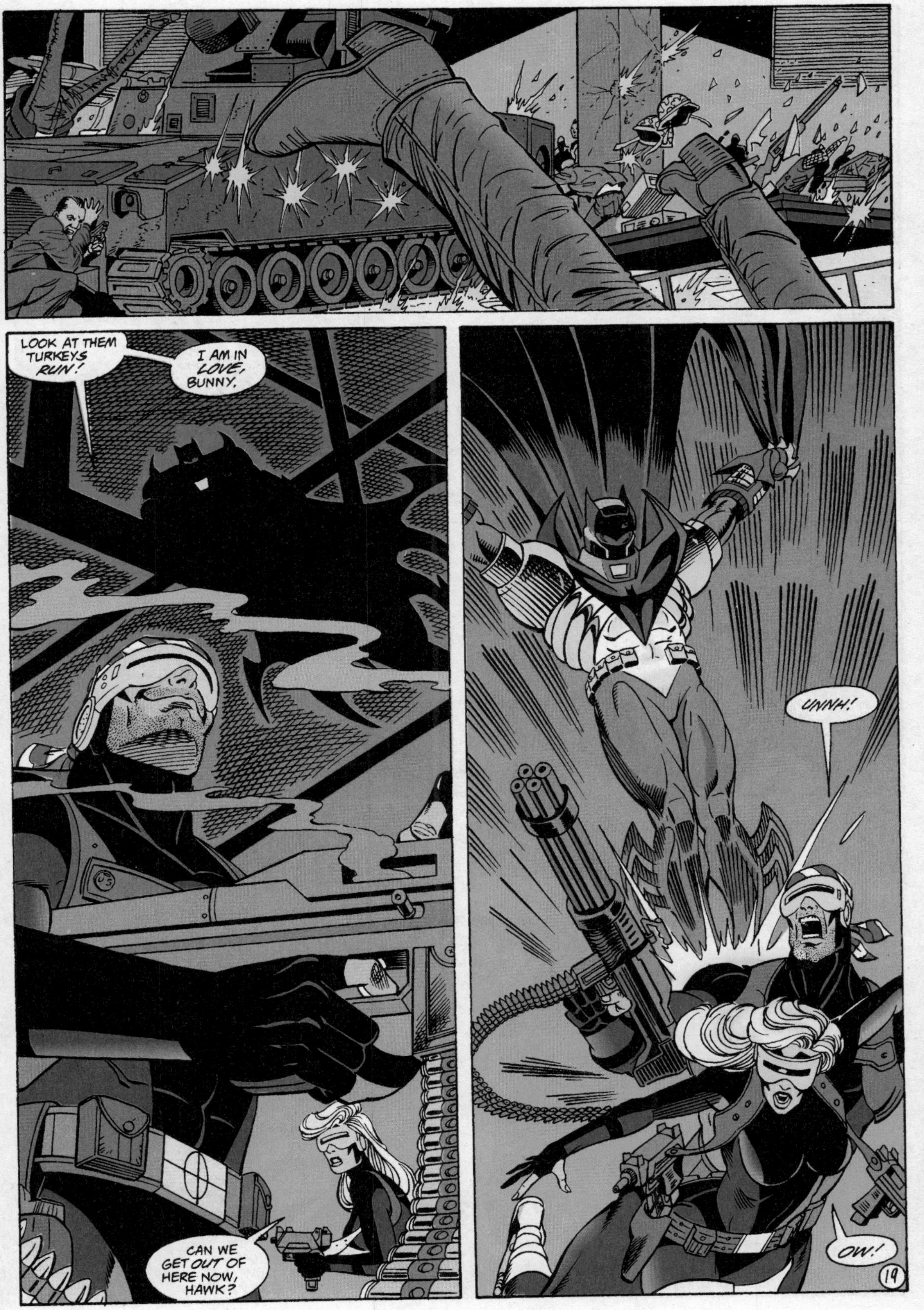
LOOK AT THEM TURKEYS RUN!
I AM IN LOVE, BUNNY.
CAN WE GET OUT OF HERE NOW, HAWK?
UNNH!
OW!
19

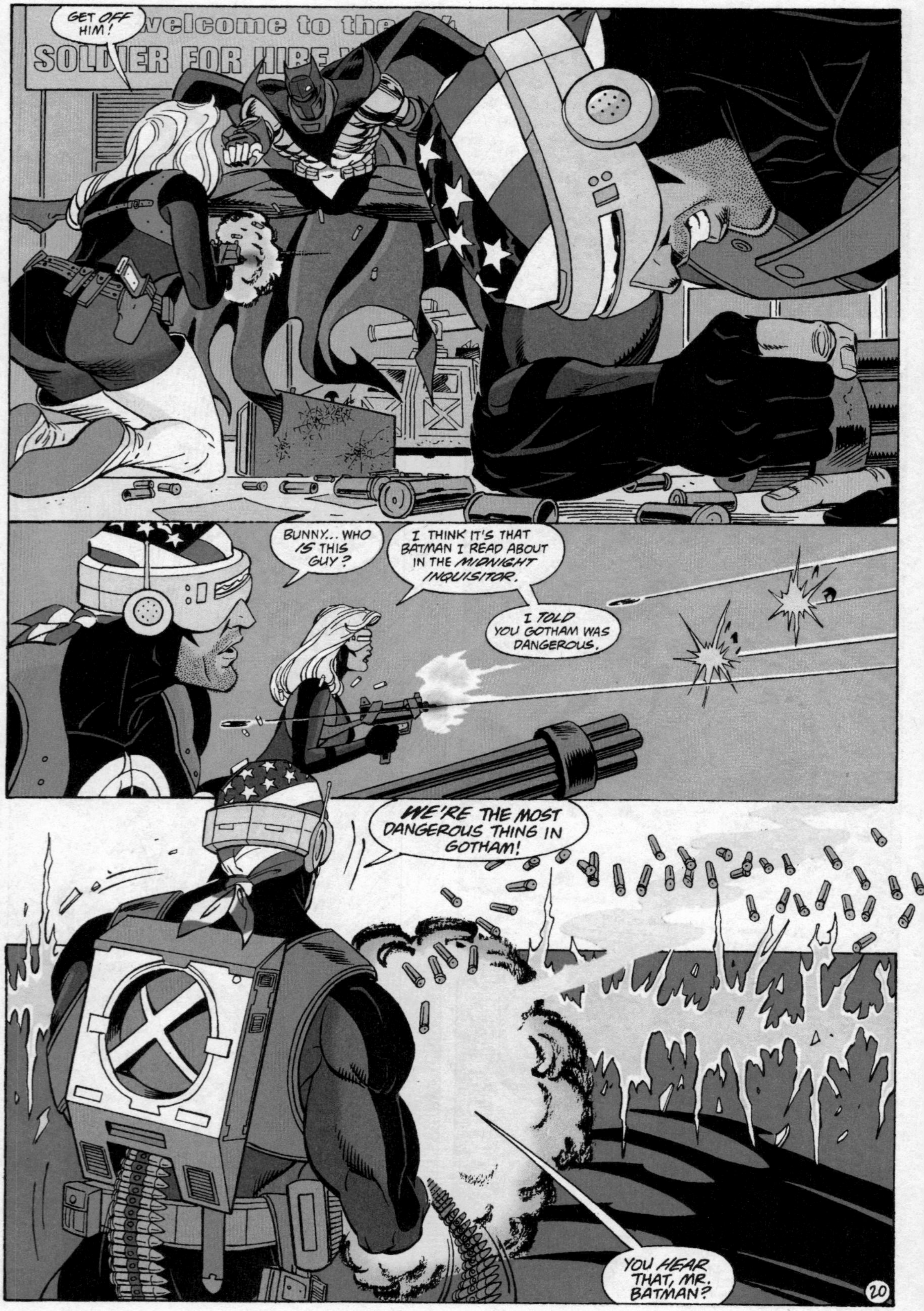
GET OFF HIM!
welcome to the
SOLDIER FOR HIRE
BUNNY... WHO IS THIS GUY?
I THINK IT'S THAT BATMAN I READ ABOUT IN THE MIDNIGHT INQUISITOR.
I TOLD YOU GOTHAM WAS DANGEROUS.
WE'RE THE MOST DANGEROUS THING IN GOTHAM!
YOU HEAR THAT, MR. BATMAN?
20

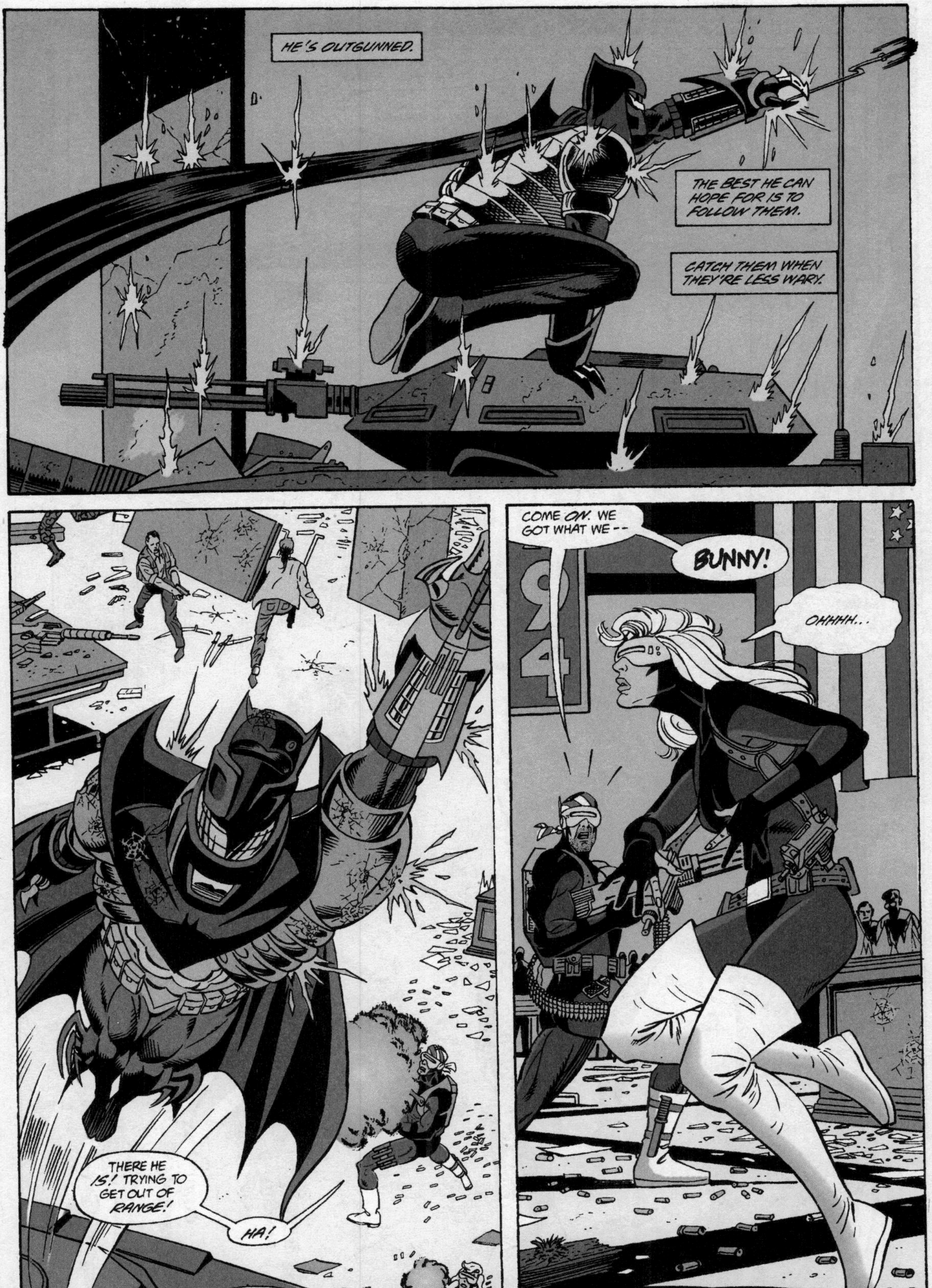
HE'S OUTGUNNED.
THE BEST HE CAN HOPE FOR IS TO FOLLOW THEM.
CATCH THEM WHEN THEY'RE LESS WARY.
THERE HE IS! TRYING TO GET OUT OF RANGE!
HA!
LEAD HIM, HAWK!
COME ON. WE GOT WHAT WE --
BUNNY!
OHHHH...
21

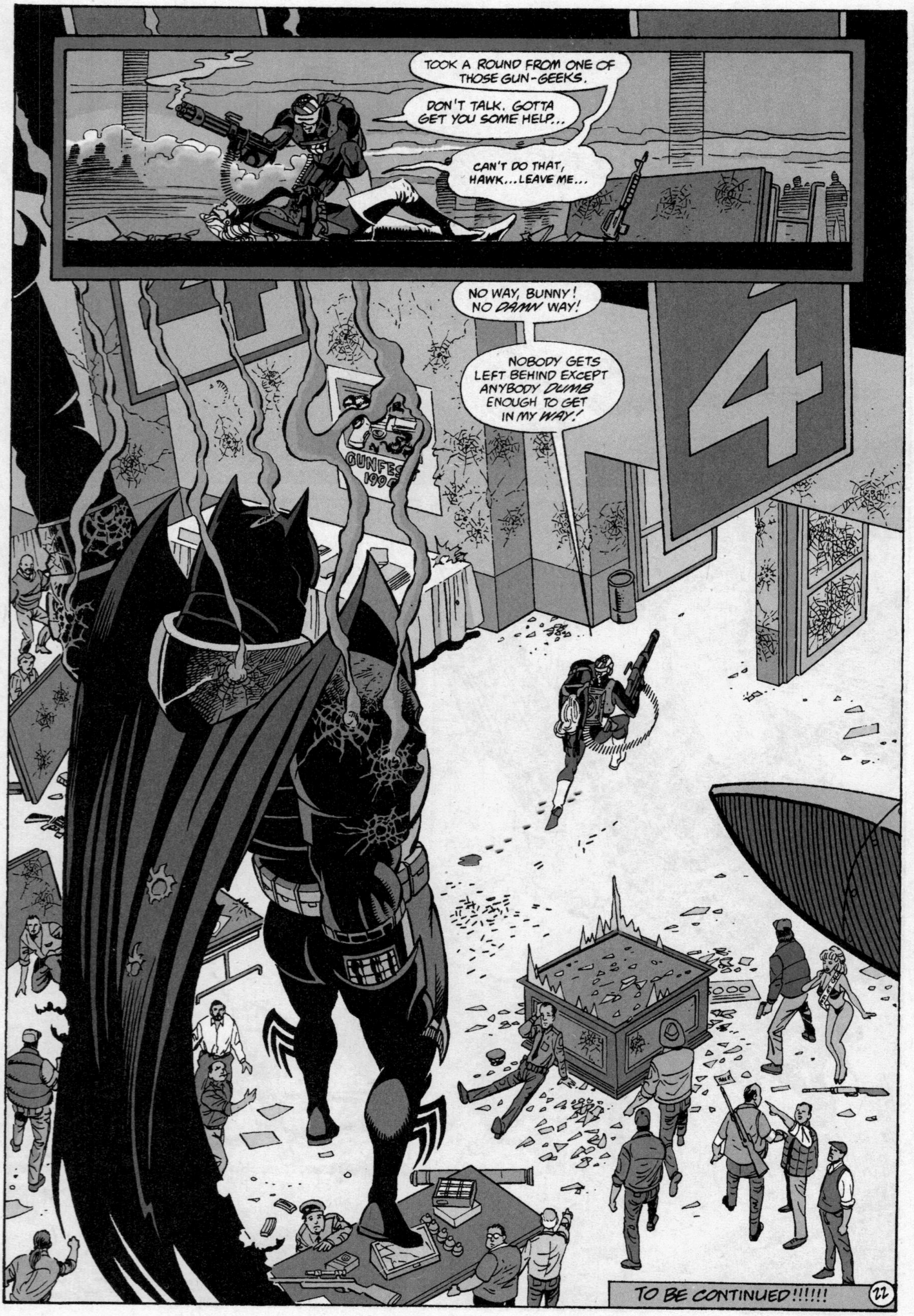
TOOK A ROUND FROM ONE OF THOSE GUN-GEEKS.
DON'T TALK. GOTTA GET YOU SOME HELP...
CAN'T DO THAT, HAWK...LEAVE ME...
NO WAY, BUNNY! NO DAMN WAY!
NOBODY GETS LEFT BEHIND EXCEPT ANYBODY DUMB ENOUGH TO GET IN MY WAY!
4
GUNFEST 1994
TO BE CONTINUED!!!!!!
22

Cover art by KELLEY JONES

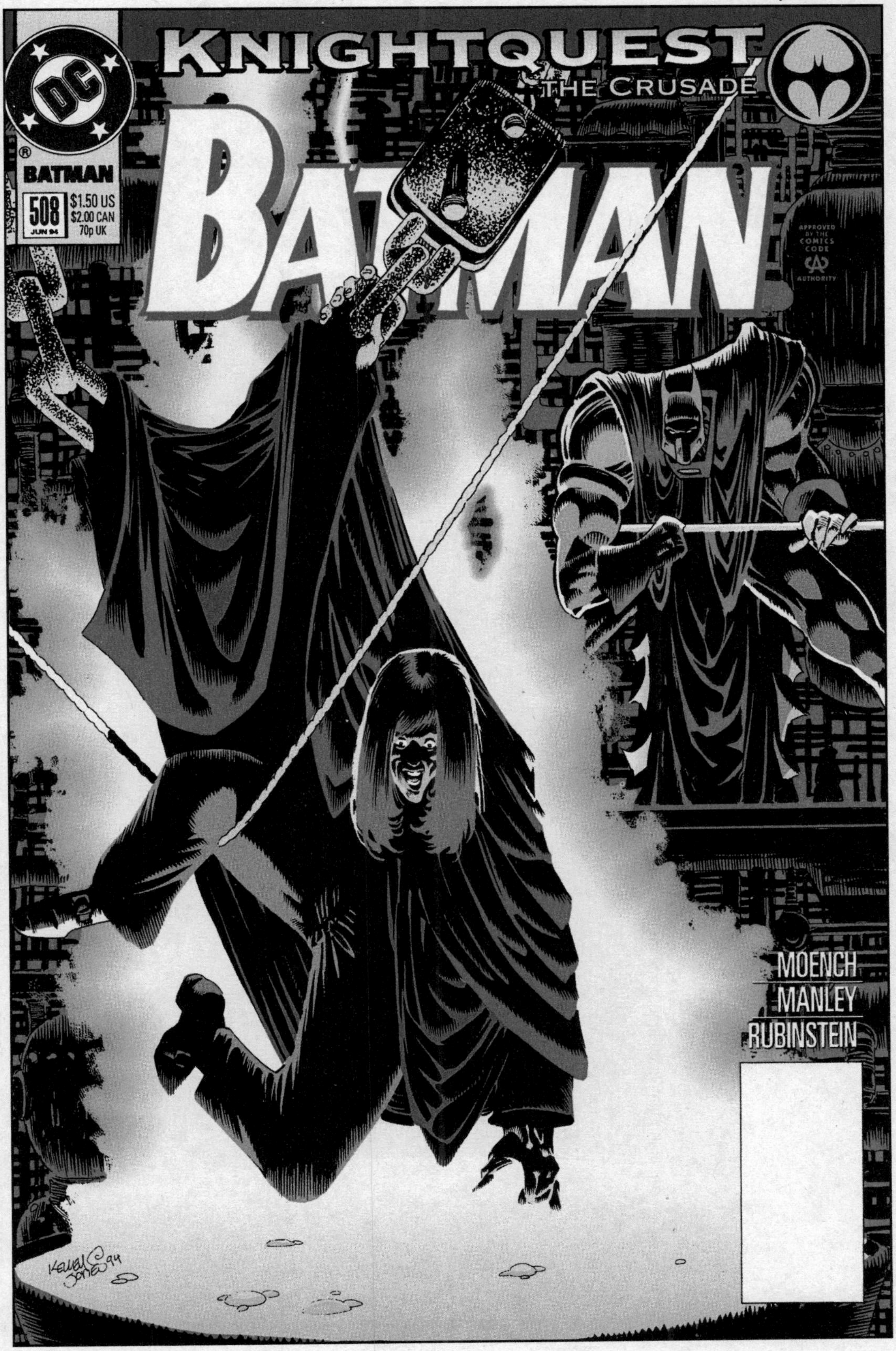
KNIGHTQUEST
THE CRUSADE
DC
BATMAN
508
JUN 94
$1.50 US
$2.00 CAN
70p UK
BATMAN
APPROVED BY THE COMICS CODE AUTHORITY
MOENCH
MANLEY
RUBINSTEIN
KELLEY JONES ©94

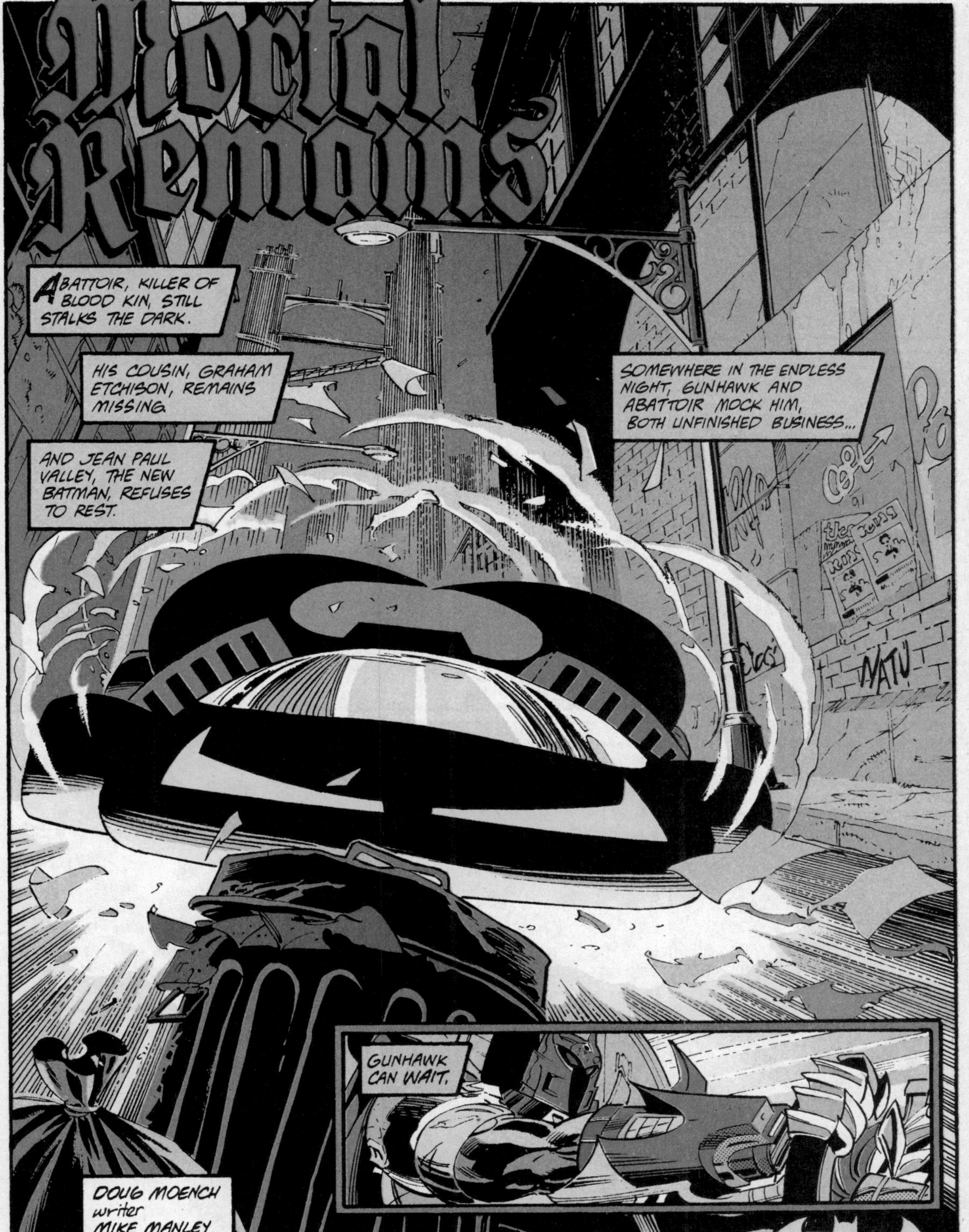
Mortal Remains
ABATTOIR, KILLER OF BLOOD KIN, STILL STALKS THE DARK.
HIS COUSIN, GRAHAM ETCHISON, REMAINS MISSING.
AND JEAN PAUL VALLEY, THE NEW BATMAN, REFUSES TO REST.
SOMEWHERE IN THE ENDLESS NIGHT, GUNHAWK AND ABATTOIR MOCK HIM, BOTH UNFINISHED BUSINESS...
NATU
GUNHAWK CAN WAIT.
DOUG MOENCH writer
MIKE MANLEY penciller
JOSEF RUBINSTEIN- guest inker
ADRIENNE ROY- colorist
KEN BRUZENAK- letterer
JORDAN B. GORFINKEL- assistant editor
DENNY O'NEIL editor
BATMAN created by BOB KANE

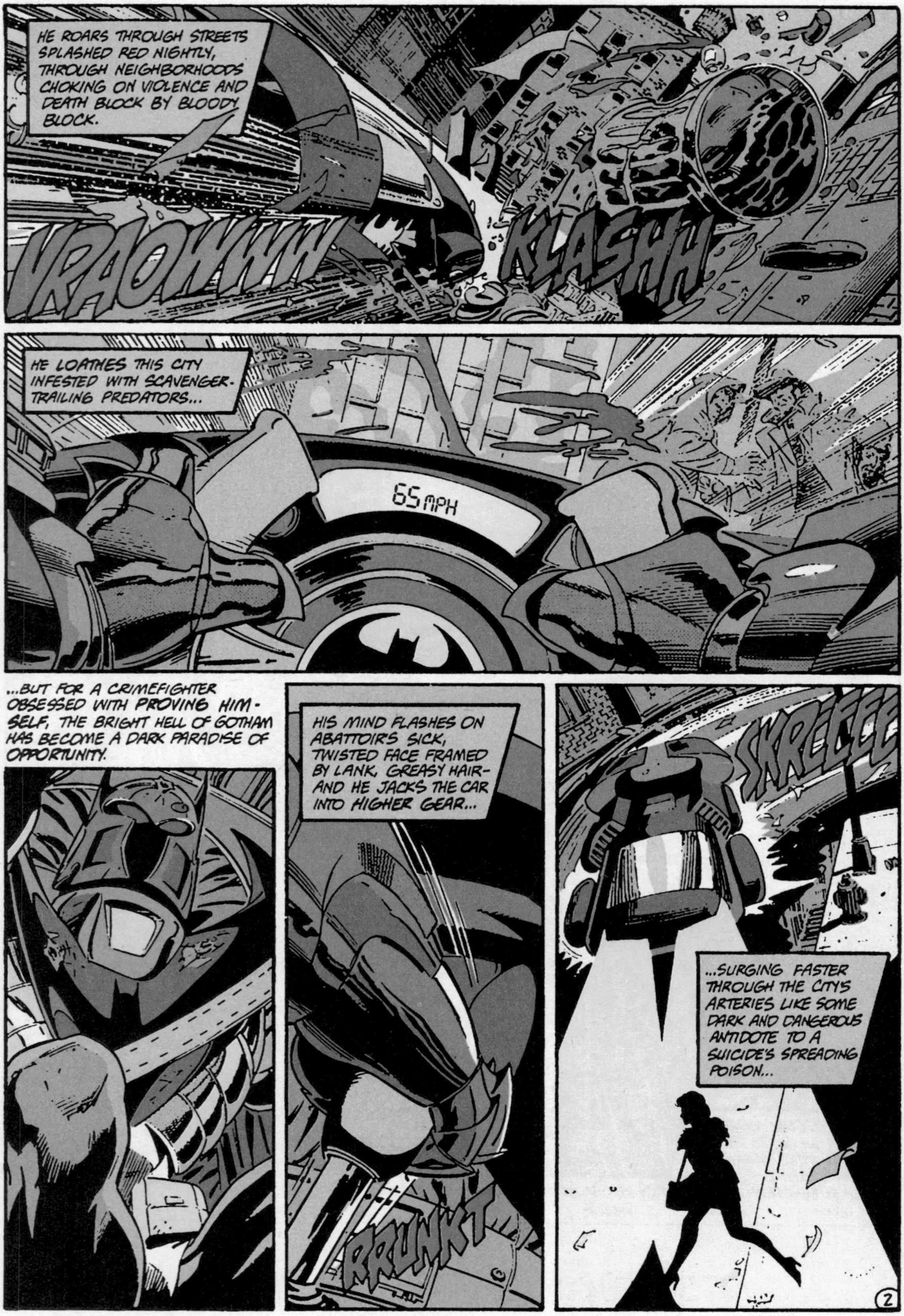
HE ROARS THROUGH STREETS SPLASHED RED NIGHTLY, THROUGH NEIGHBORHOODS CHOKING ON VIOLENCE AND DEATH BLOCK BY BLOODY BLOCK.
VRAOWWW
KLASHH
HE LOATHES THIS CITY INFESTED WITH SCAVENGER-TRAILING PREDATORS...
65 MPH
...BUT FOR A CRIMEFIGHTER OBSESSED WITH PROVING HIMSELF, THE BRIGHT HELL OF GOTHAM HAS BECOME A DARK PARADISE OF OPPORTUNITY.
HIS MIND FLASHES ON ABATTOIR'S SICK, TWISTED FACE FRAMED BY LANK, GREASY HAIR-- AND HE JACKS THE CAR INTO HIGHER GEAR...
RRUNKT
SKREEEE
...SURGING FASTER THROUGH THE CITY'S ARTERIES LIKE SOME DARK AND DANGEROUS ANTIDOTE TO A SUICIDE'S SPREADING POISON...
2

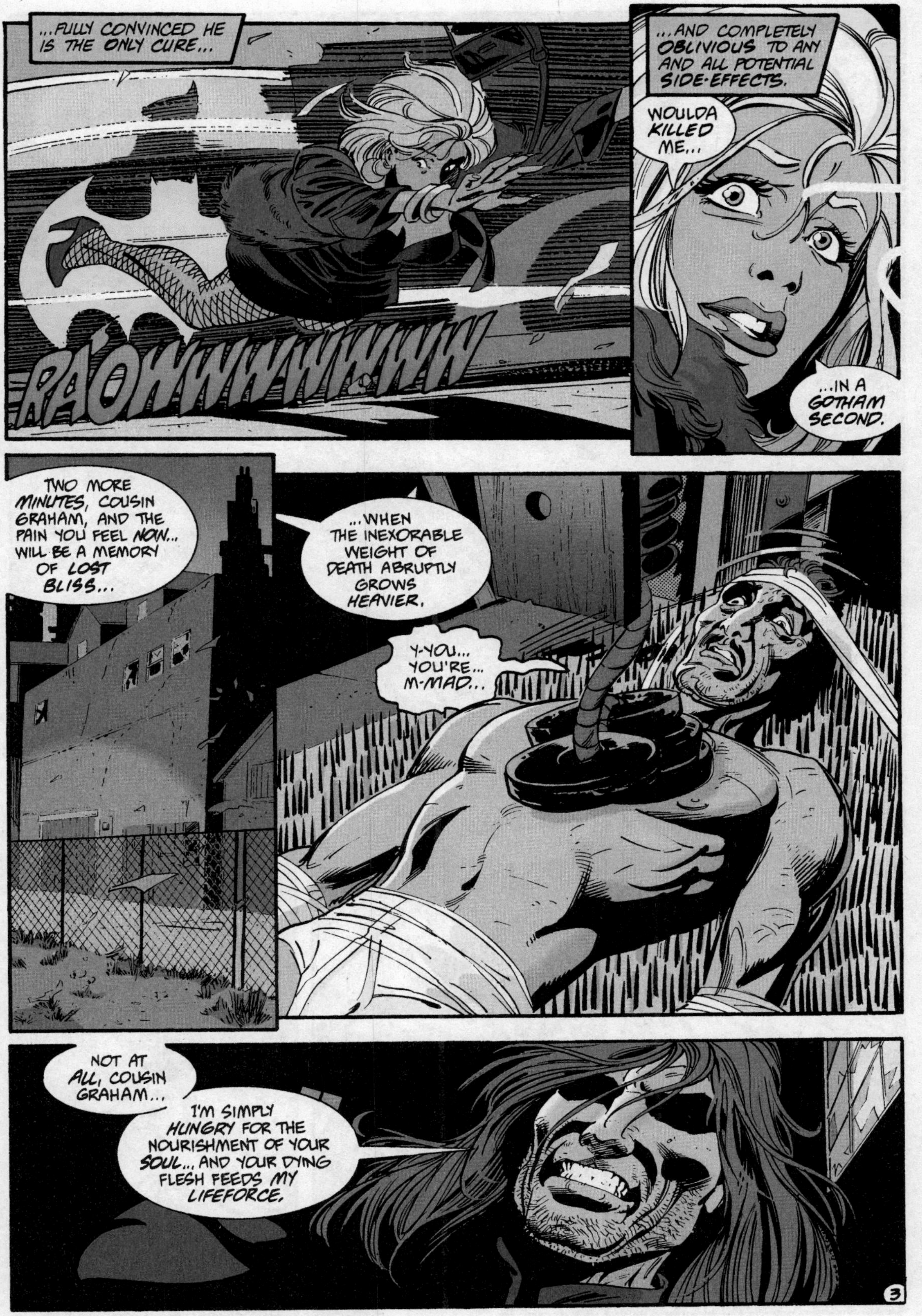

...FULLY CONVINCED HE IS THE ONLY CURE...
RA'OHWWWWWWWW
...AND COMPLETELY OBLIVIOUS TO ANY AND ALL POTENTIAL SIDE-EFFECTS.
WOULDA KILLED ME...
...IN A GOTHAM SECOND.
TWO MORE MINUTES, COUSIN GRAHAM, AND THE PAIN YOU FEEL NOW... WILL BE A MEMORY OF LOST BLISS...
...WHEN THE INEXORABLE WEIGHT OF DEATH ABRUPTLY GROWS HEAVIER.
Y-YOU... YOU'RE... M-MAD...
NOT AT ALL, COUSIN GRAHAM...
I'M SIMPLY HUNGRY FOR THE NOURISHMENT OF YOUR SOUL... AND YOUR DYING FLESH FEEDS MY LIFEFORCE.
3

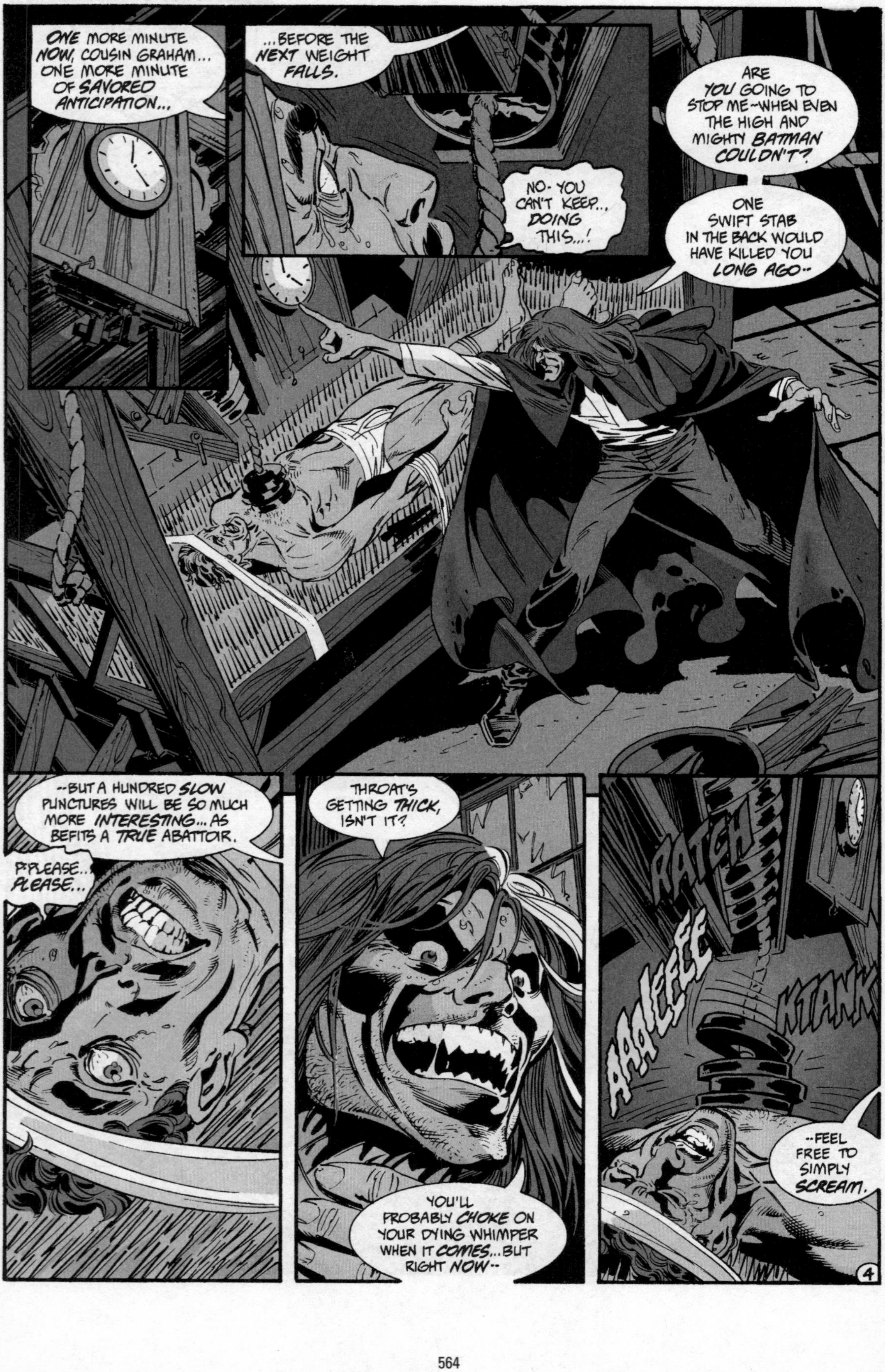
ONE MORE MINUTE NOW, COUSIN GRAHAM... ONE MORE MINUTE OF SAVORED ANTICIPATION...
...BEFORE THE NEXT WEIGHT FALLS.
NO- YOU CAN'T KEEP... DOING THIS...!
ARE YOU GOING TO STOP ME--WHEN EVEN THE HIGH AND MIGHTY BATMAN COULDN'T?
ONE SWIFT STAB IN THE BACK WOULD HAVE KILLED YOU LONG AGO--
--BUT A HUNDRED SLOW PUNCTURES WILL BE SO MUCH MORE INTERESTING... AS BEFITS A TRUE ABATTOIR.
P-PLEASE... PLEASE...
THROAT'S GETTING THICK, ISN'T IT?
YOU'LL PROBABLY CHOKE ON YOUR DYING WHIMPER WHEN IT COMES... BUT RIGHT NOW--
RATCH
AAAIEEEE
KTANK
--FEEL FREE TO SIMPLY SCREAM.
4

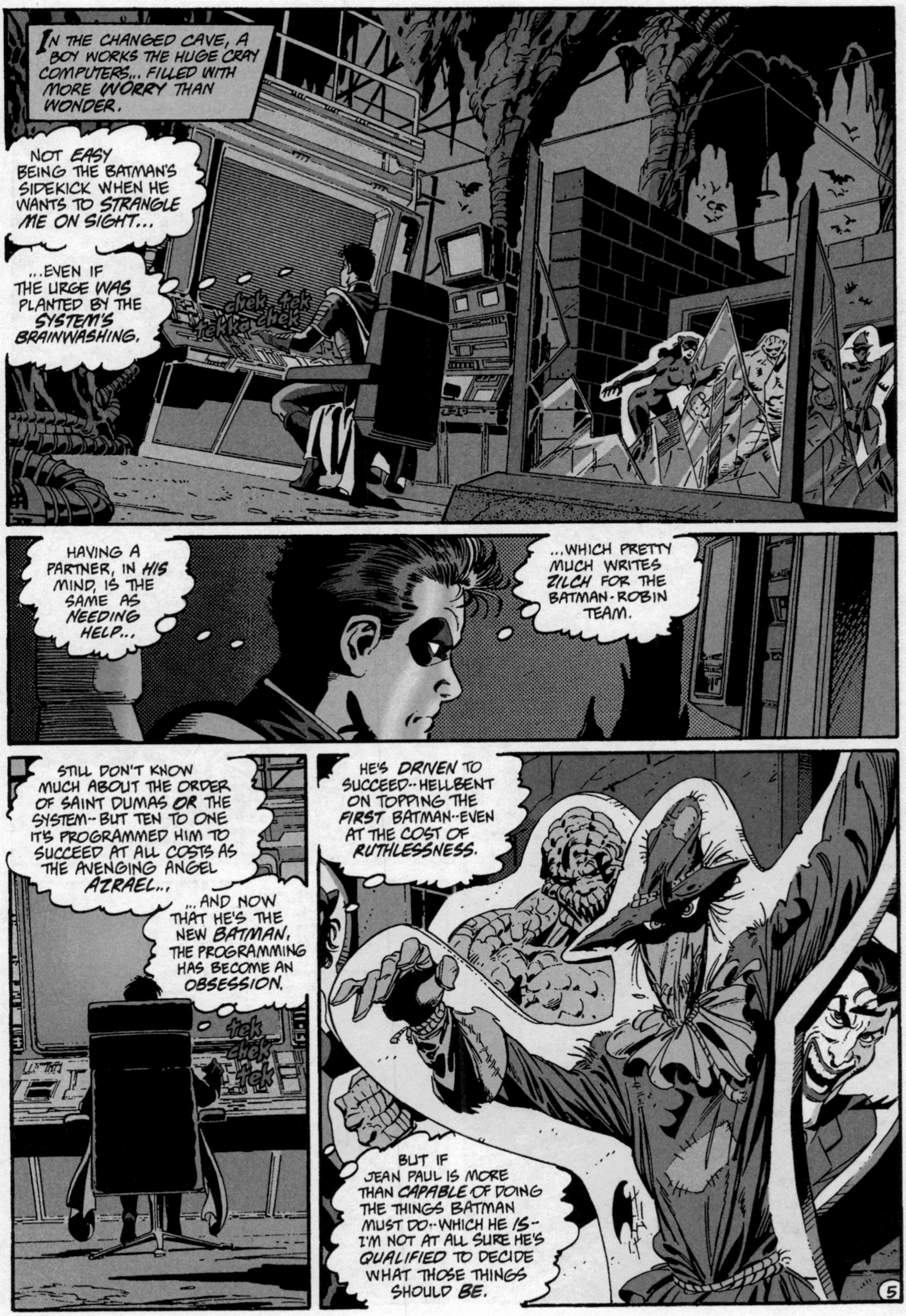
IN THE CHANGED CAVE, A BOY WORKS THE HUGE CRAY COMPUTERS... FILLED WITH MORE WORRY THAN WONDER.
NOT EASY BEING THE BATMAN'S SIDEKICK WHEN HE WANTS TO STRANGLE ME ON SIGHT...
...EVEN IF THE URGE WAS PLANTED BY THE SYSTEM'S BRAINWASHING.
chek tek tekka chek
HAVING A PARTNER, IN HIS MIND, IS THE SAME AS NEEDING HELP...
...WHICH PRETTY MUCH WRITES ZILCH FOR THE BATMAN-ROBIN TEAM.
STILL DON'T KNOW MUCH ABOUT THE ORDER OF SAINT DUMAS OR THE SYSTEM-- BUT TEN TO ONE IT'S PROGRAMMED HIM TO SUCCEED AT ALL COSTS AS THE AVENGING ANGEL AZRAEL...
...AND NOW THAT HE'S THE NEW BATMAN, THE PROGRAMMING HAS BECOME AN OBSESSION.
tek chek tek
HE'S DRIVEN TO SUCCEED-- HELLBENT ON TOPPING THE FIRST BATMAN-- EVEN AT THE COST OF RUTHLESSNESS.
BUT IF JEAN PAUL IS MORE THAN CAPABLE OF DOING THE THINGS BATMAN MUST DO-- WHICH HE IS-- I'M NOT AT ALL SURE HE'S QUALIFIED TO DECIDE WHAT THOSE THINGS SHOULD BE.
5

BEING GOOD ENOUGH *ISN'T* ENOUGH IF YOU'RE *NOT GOOD*.

LIKE THEY SAY IN HISTORY CLASS: MUSSOLINI MADE THE *TRAINS* RUN ON TIME—BUT HIS MAIN MAN HITLER WAS *USING* TRAINS TO FREIGHT PEOPLE LIKE CATTLE TO THE *SLAUGHTER*.

NOT THAT JEAN PAUL IS ANYTHING LIKE *THOSE* TWO, BUT AS LONG AS ABATTOIR REMAINS THE ONLY LEAD IN *GRAHAM ETCHISON'S* ABDUCTION, THE BATMAN'S GONNA *GET* MY HELP, WHETHER HE *WANTS* IT OR--

chek-tekka-tek

BINGO.

FINALLY HACKED INTO THE *MUNICIPAL TAX RECORDS* SYSTEM--WITH A FULL LIST OF THE *REAL ESTATE* OWNED BY *HENRY ETCHISON*...

IF HIS NEPHEW ABATTOIR IS *HIDING OUT* SOMEWHERE, THERE'S A GOOD CHANCE IT'S IN ONE OF THESE PROPERTIES...

...AND *PROBABLY* THE ONE WITH THE *LEAST CHANCE* OF DISCOVERY.

SALVAGE, 1312 TENNYSON ST.
ABANDONED WAREHOUSE 129 ON AVE.
BAY MENTS
RIVER DRIVE
AL SHORE CONDO
72 E. 23rd. ST.

6

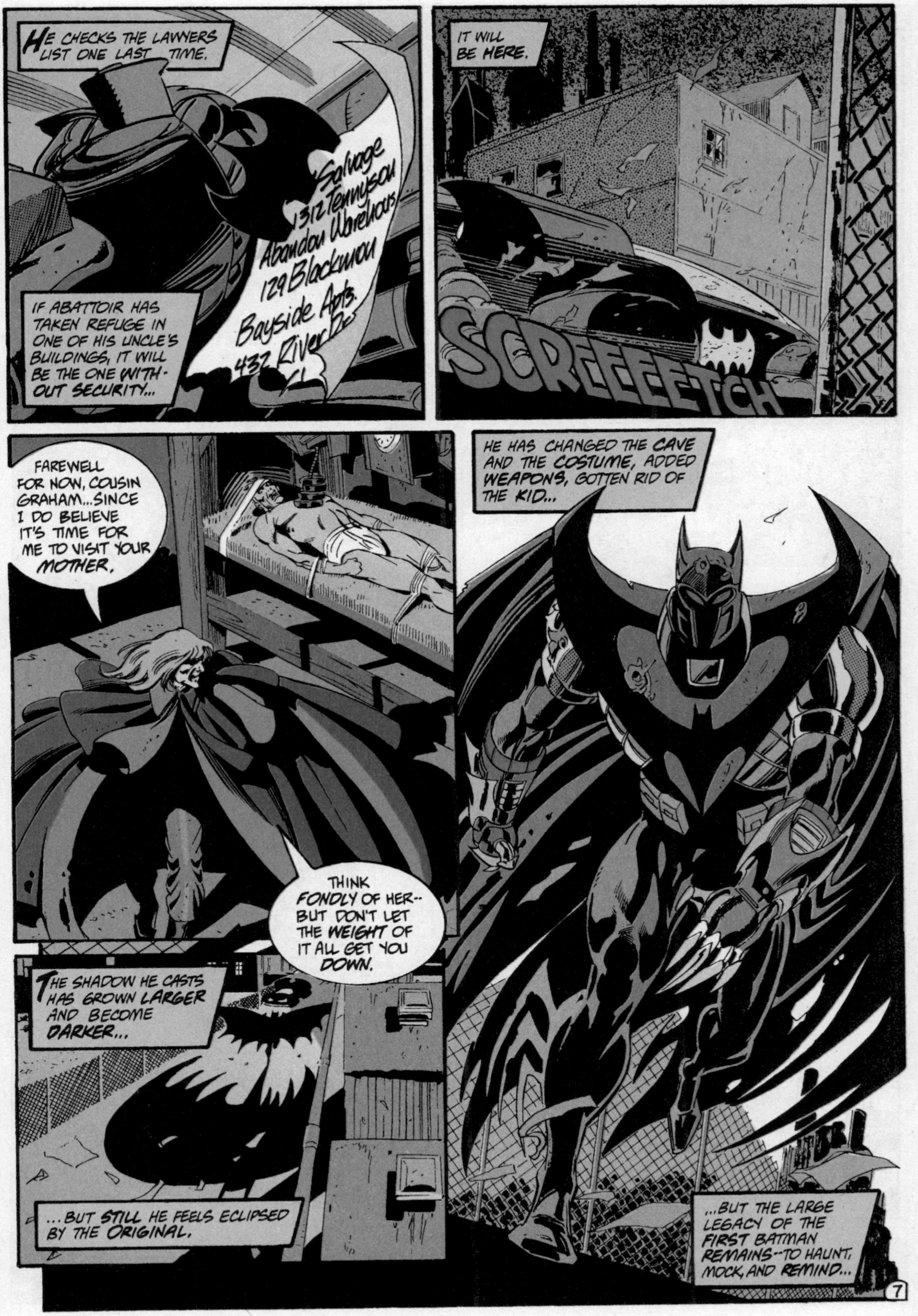
HE CHECKS THE LAWYERS LIST ONE LAST TIME.
Salvage
1312 Tennyson
Abandon Warehous
129 Blackmon
Bayside Apts.
432 River Dr.
IF ABATTOIR HAS TAKEN REFUGE IN ONE OF HIS UNCLE'S BUILDINGS, IT WILL BE THE ONE WITH-OUT SECURITY...
IT WILL BE HERE.
SCREEEETCH
FAREWELL FOR NOW, COUSIN GRAHAM...SINCE I DO BELIEVE IT'S TIME FOR ME TO VISIT YOUR MOTHER.
THINK FONDLY OF HER-- BUT DON'T LET THE WEIGHT OF IT ALL GET YOU DOWN.
HE HAS CHANGED THE CAVE AND THE COSTUME, ADDED WEAPONS, GOTTEN RID OF THE KID...
THE SHADOW HE CASTS HAS GROWN LARGER AND BECOME DARKER...
...BUT STILL HE FEELS ECLIPSED BY THE ORIGINAL.
...BUT THE LARGE LEGACY OF THE FIRST BATMAN REMAINS--TO HAUNT, MOCK, AND REMIND...
7

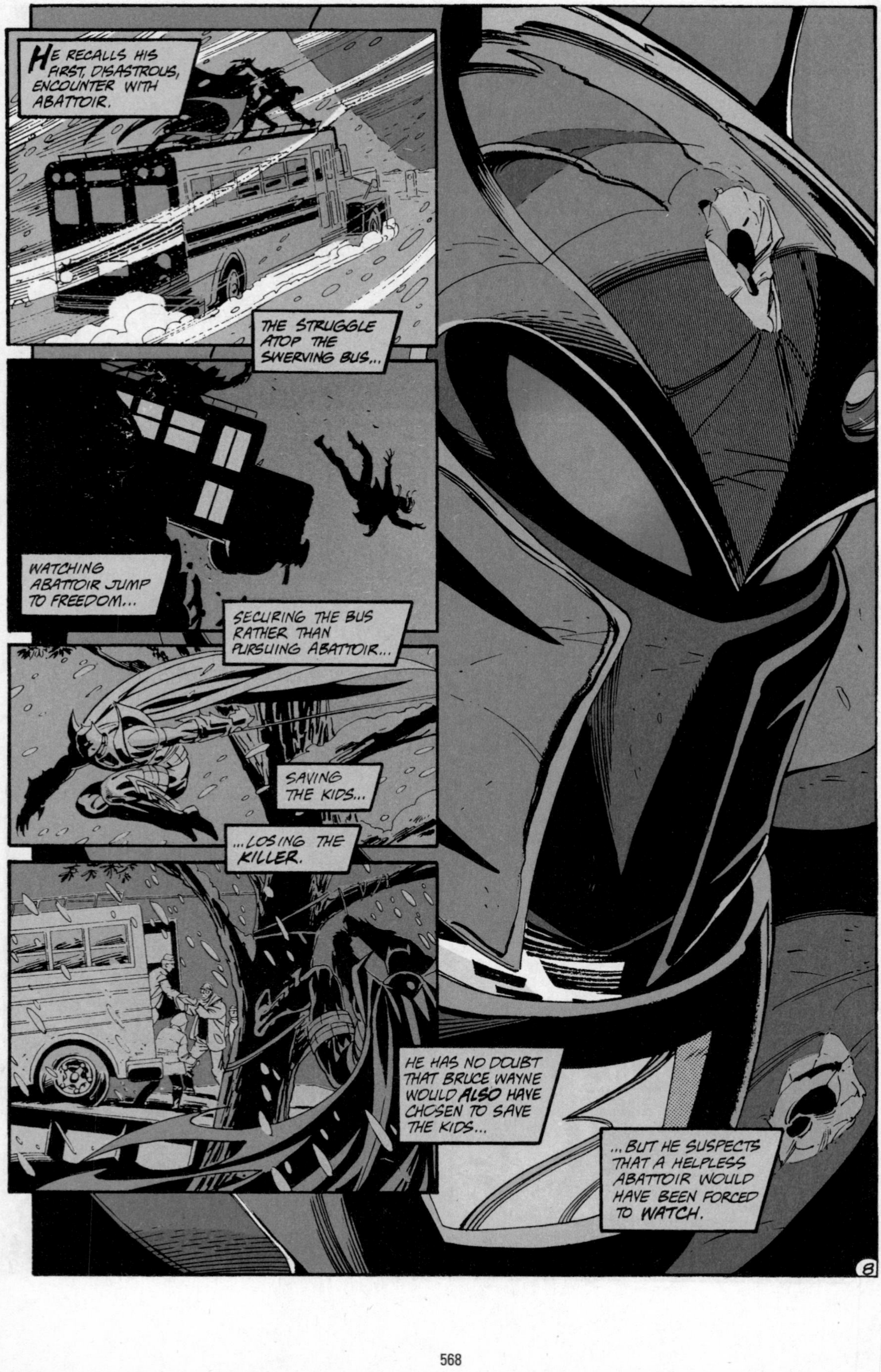
HE RECALLS HIS FIRST, DISASTROUS, ENCOUNTER WITH ABATTOIR.
THE STRUGGLE ATOP THE SWERVING BUS...
WATCHING ABATTOIR JUMP TO FREEDOM...
SECURING THE BUS RATHER THAN PURSUING ABATTOIR...
SAVING THE KIDS...
...LOSING THE KILLER.
HE HAS NO DOUBT THAT BRUCE WAYNE WOULD ALSO HAVE CHOSEN TO SAVE THE KIDS...
...BUT HE SUSPECTS THAT A HELPLESS ABATTOIR WOULD HAVE BEEN FORCED TO WATCH.
8

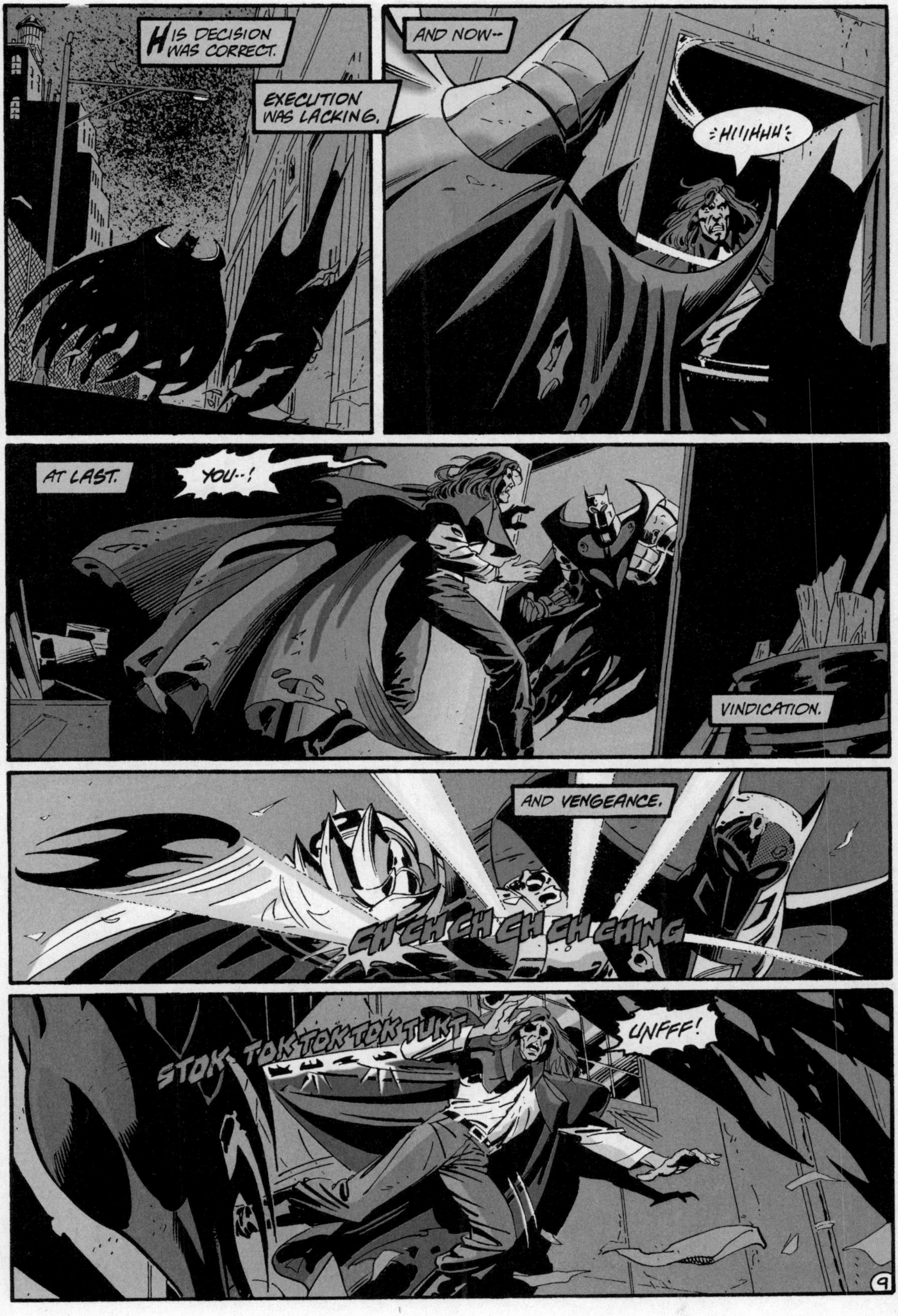
HIS DECISION WAS CORRECT.
EXECUTION WAS LACKING.
AND NOW--
HIIIHHH
AT LAST.
YOU--!
VINDICATION.
AND VENGEANCE.
CH CH CH CH CH CHING
STOK TOKTOKTOKTUKT
UNFFF!
9

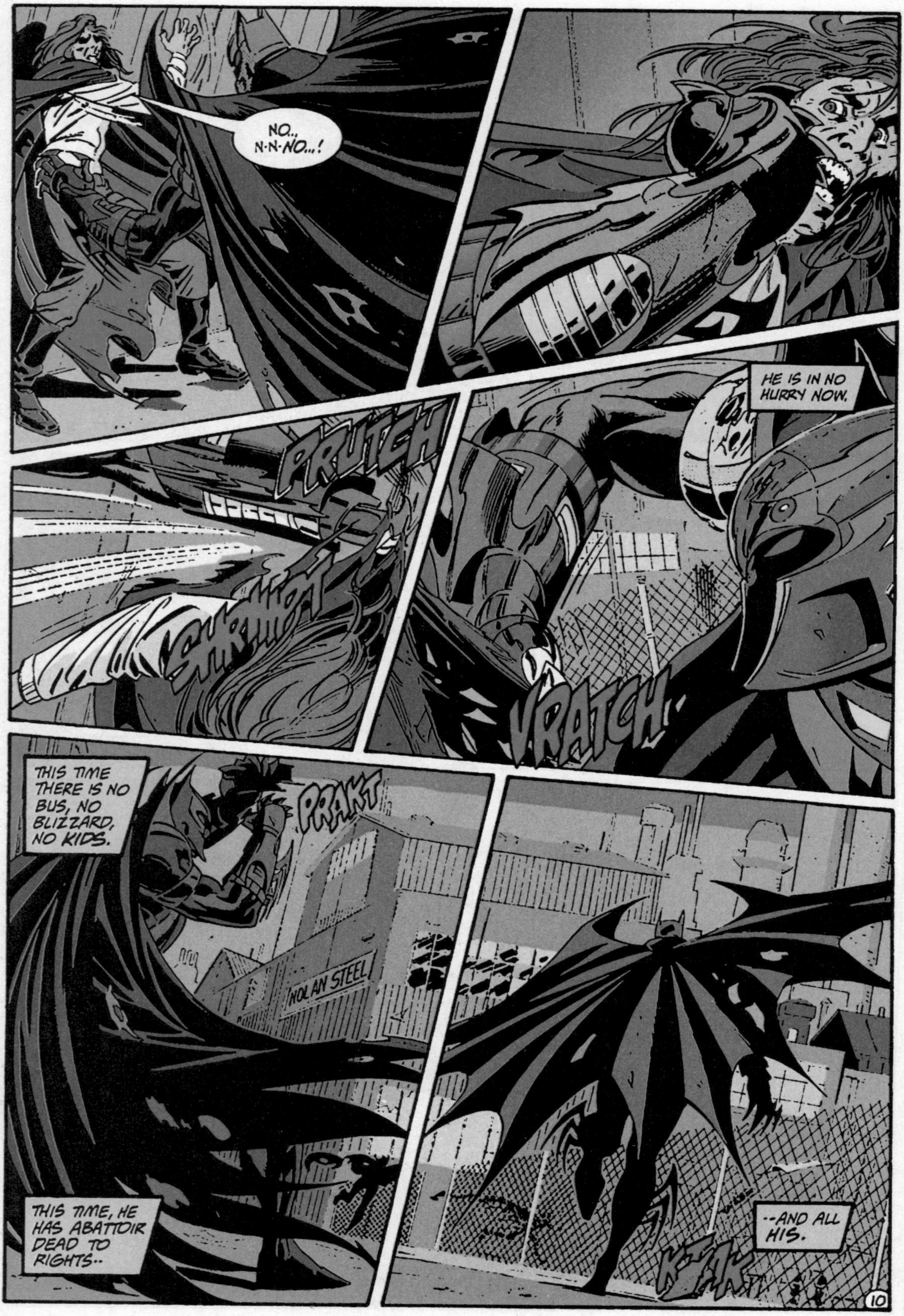
NO.. N-N-NO...!
HE IS IN NO HURRY NOW.
PRUTCH
SHRAKT
VRATCH
THIS TIME THERE IS NO BUS, NO BLIZZARD, NO KIDS.
PRAKT
NOLAN STEEL
THIS TIME, HE HAS ABATTOIR DEAD TO RIGHTS..
..AND ALL HIS.
10

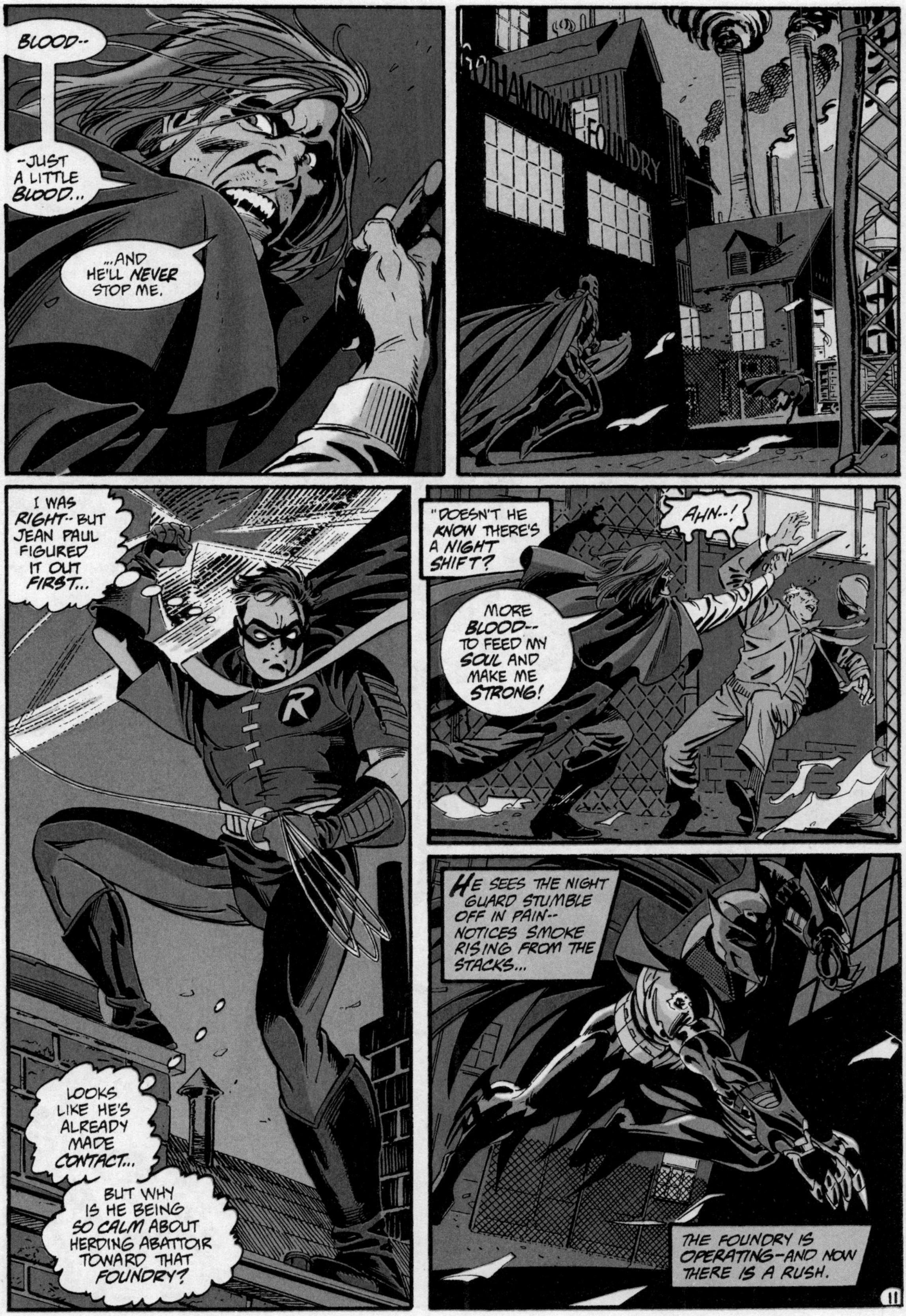

BLOOD--
-JUST A LITTLE BLOOD...
...AND HE'LL NEVER STOP ME.
GOTHAMTOWN FOUNDRY
I WAS RIGHT-- BUT JEAN PAUL FIGURED IT OUT FIRST...
LOOKS LIKE HE'S ALREADY MADE CONTACT...
BUT WHY IS HE BEING SO CALM ABOUT HERDING ABATTOIR TOWARD THAT FOUNDRY?
"DOESN'T HE KNOW THERE'S A NIGHT SHIFT?
AHN--!
MORE BLOOD-- TO FEED MY SOUL AND MAKE ME STRONG!
HE SEES THE NIGHT GUARD STUMBLE OFF IN PAIN-- NOTICES SMOKE RISING FROM THE STACKS...
THE FOUNDRY IS OPERATING--AND NOW THERE IS A RUSH.
11

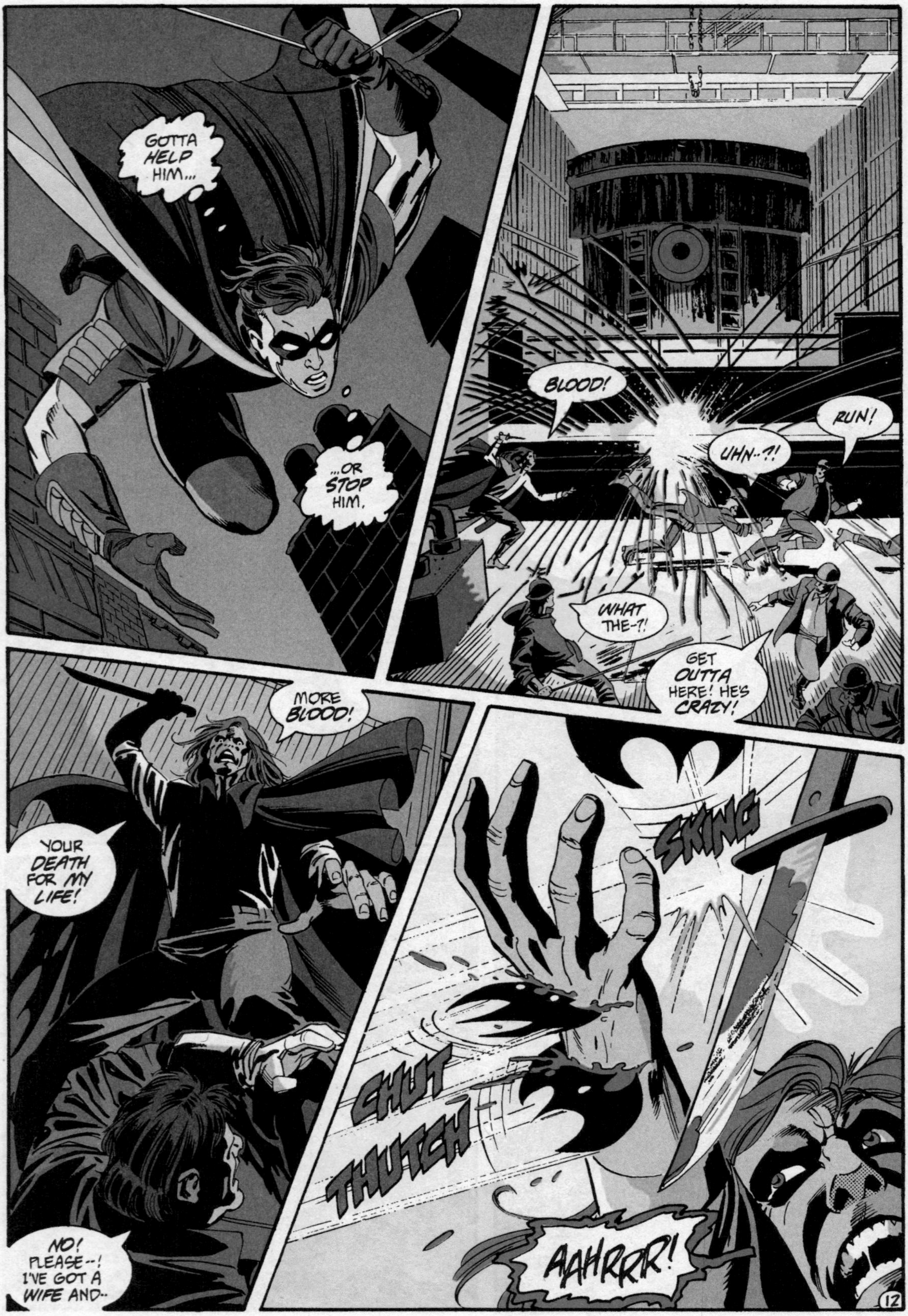
GOTTA HELP HIM...
...OR STOP HIM.
BLOOD!
UHN..?!
RUN!
WHAT THE-?!
GET OUTTA HERE! HE'S CRAZY!
MORE BLOOD!
YOUR DEATH FOR MY LIFE!
NO! PLEASE--! I'VE GOT A WIFE AND--
SKING
CHUT
THUTCH
AAHRRR!
12

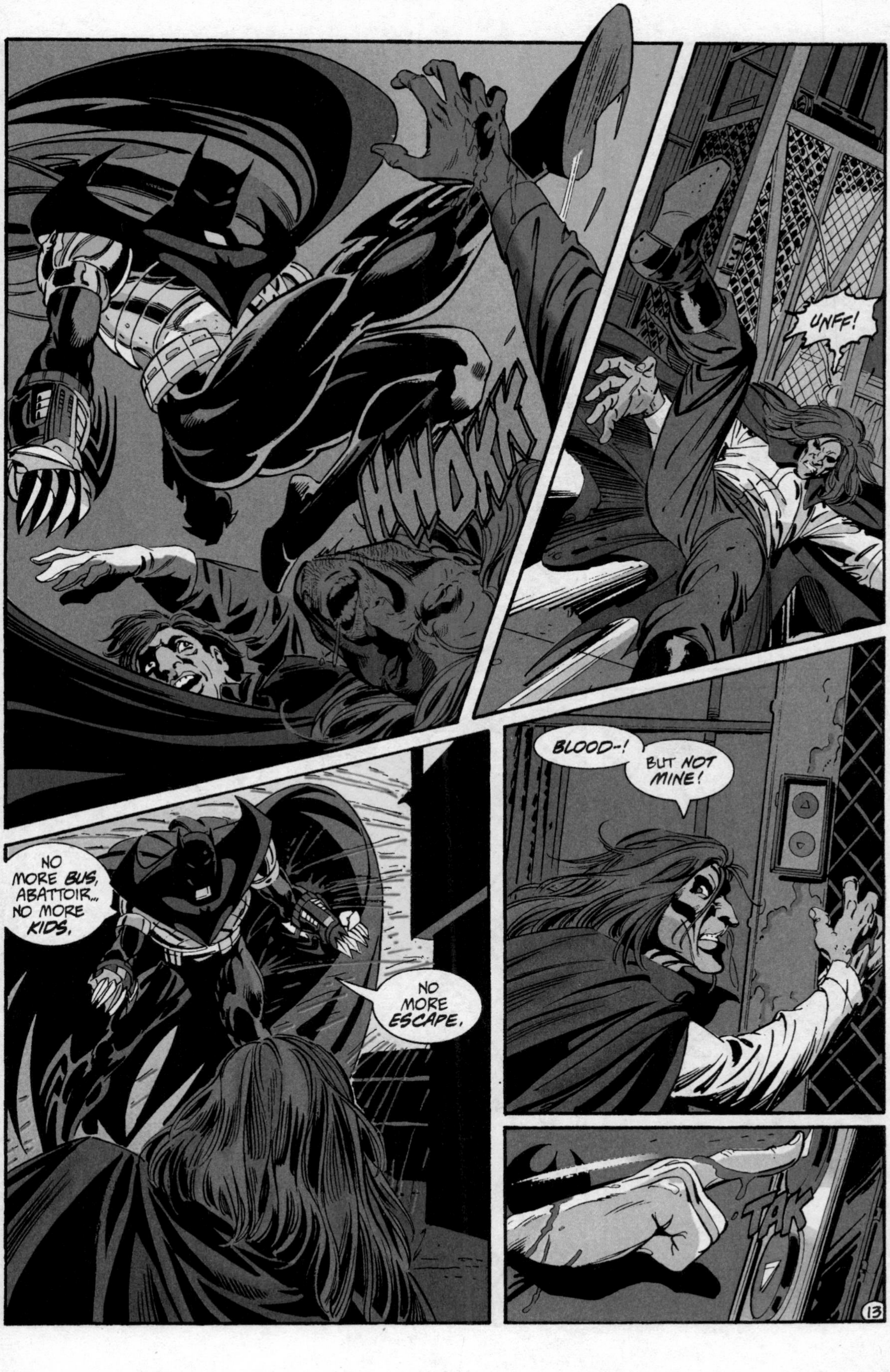
HWOKK
UNFF!
BLOOD--!
BUT NOT MINE!
NO MORE BUS, ABATTOIR... NO MORE KIDS.
NO MORE ESCAPE.
TAK
13

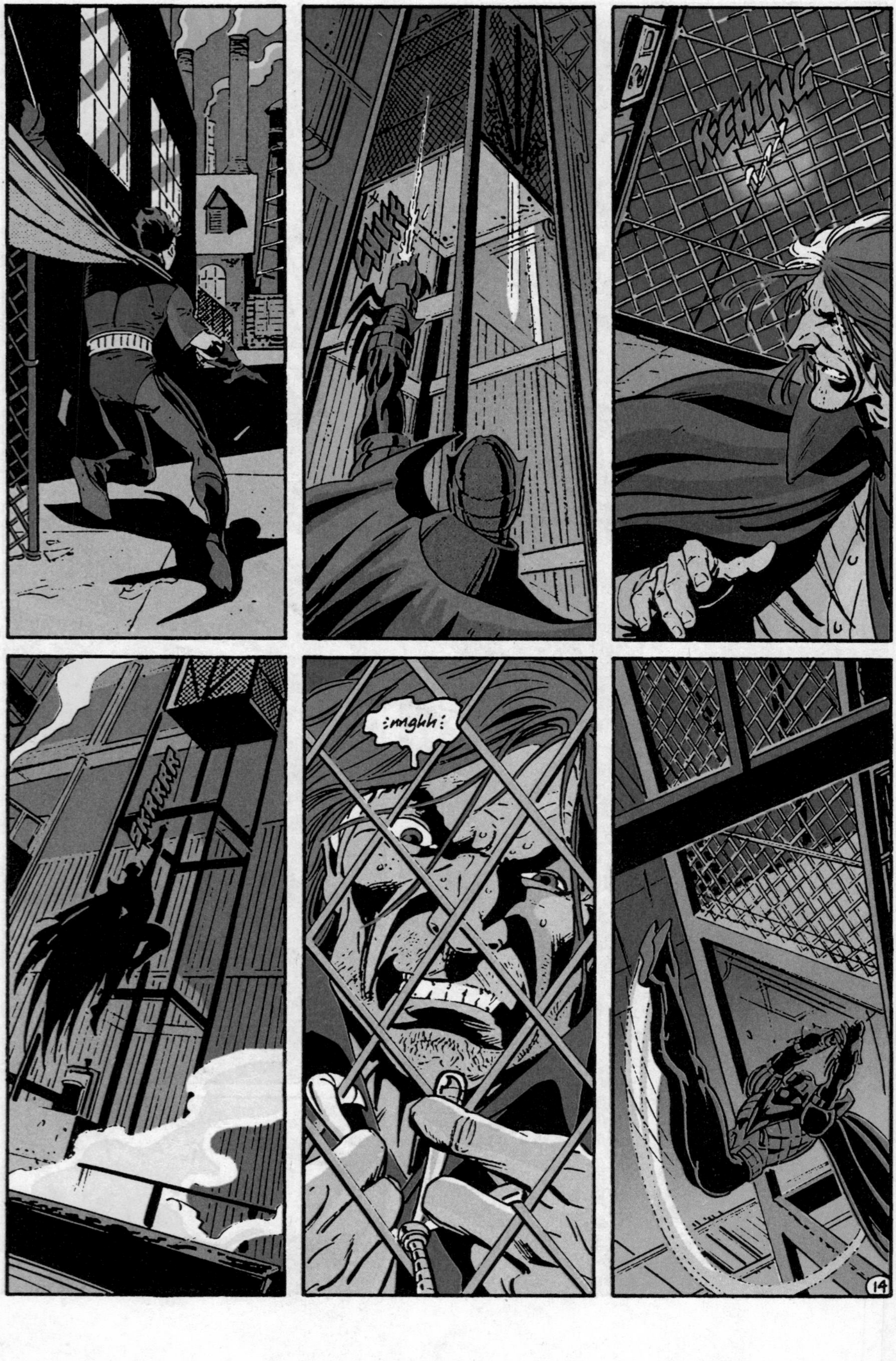
SHUFF
K-CHUNG
SKRRRR
:nnghh:
14

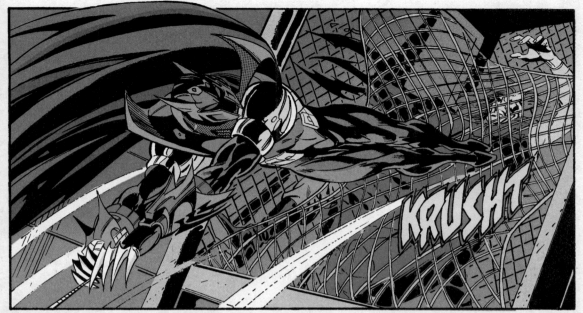

UHN~!

TERRIFIC.

JUST IN TIME FOR THE *TRAFFIC JAM.*

DO IT, ABATTOIR— TAKE YOUR *BEST* SWING.

BUT IT *WON'T* MATTER...

...YOU'RE *ALREADY DEAD.*

15

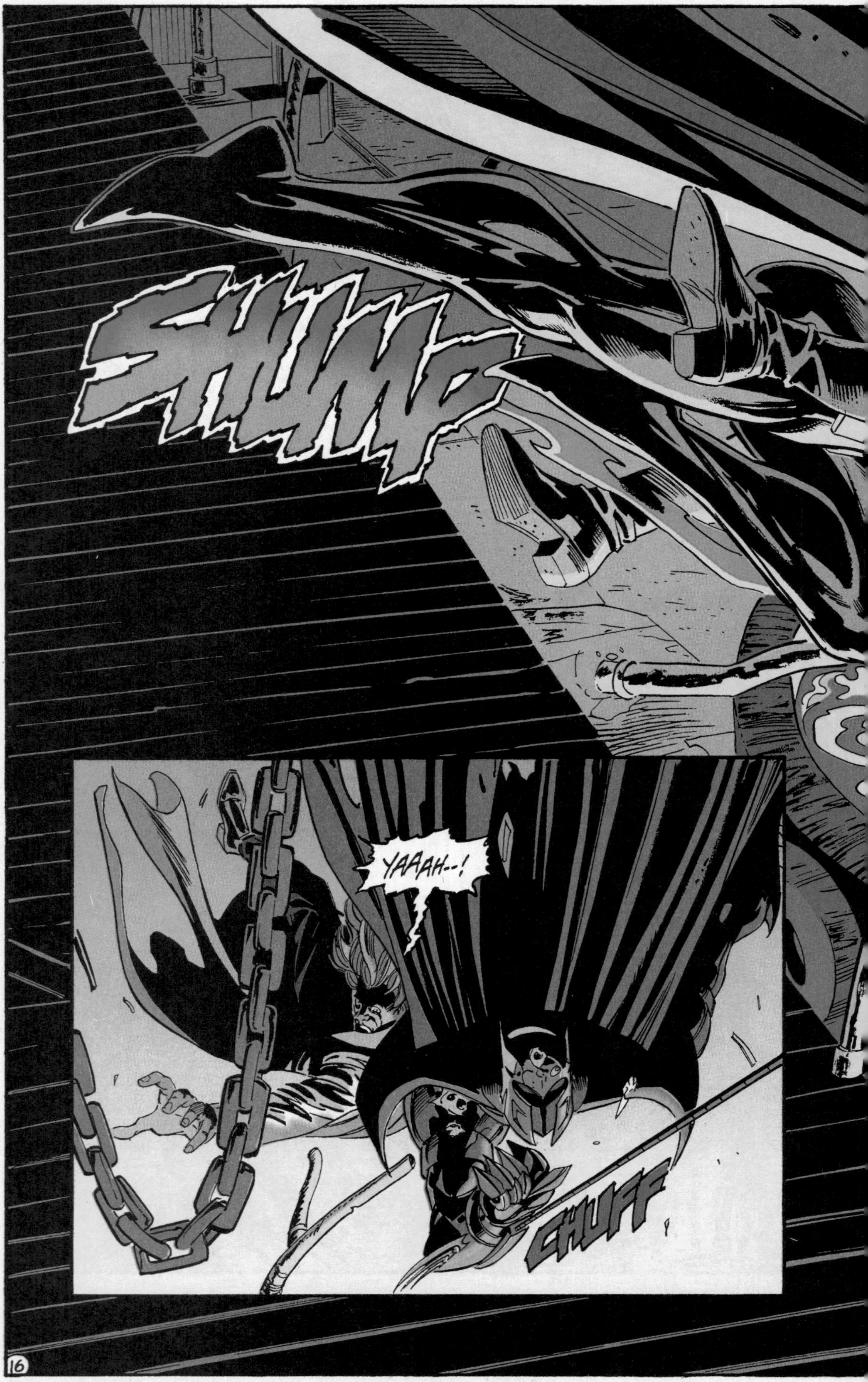
SHUMP
YAAAH--!
CHUFF

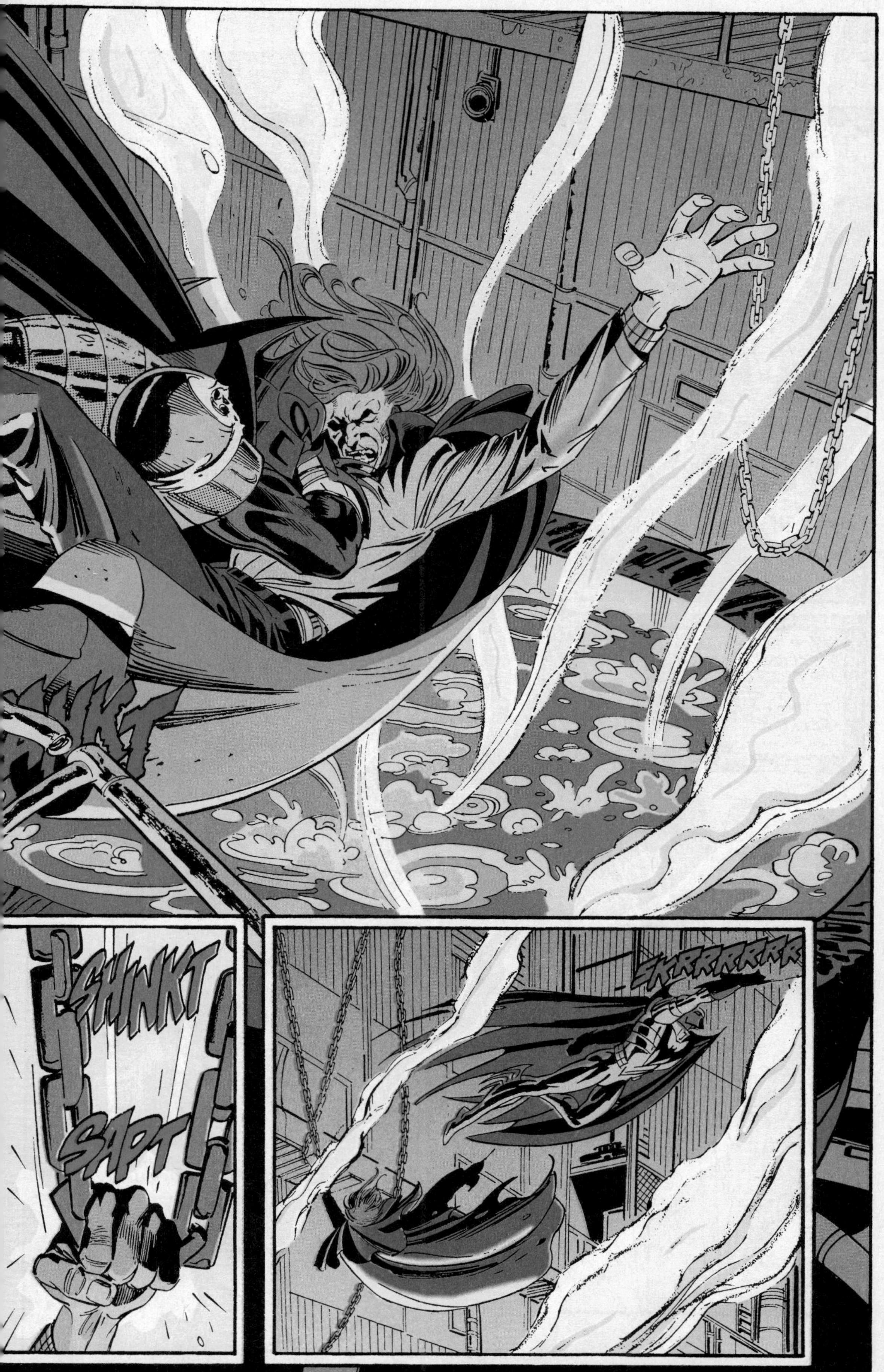
SHINKT
SAPT
SKRRRRRRR

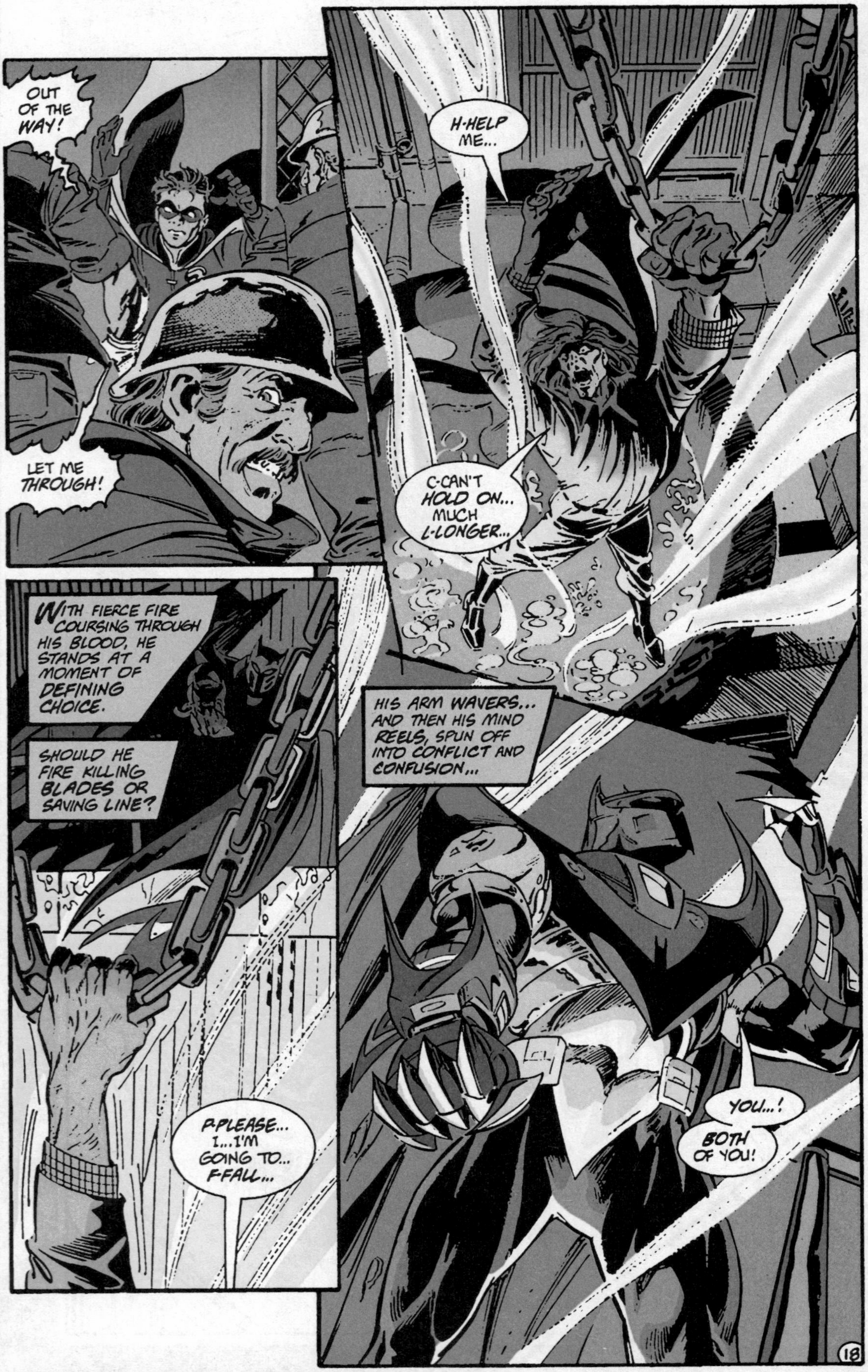
OUT OF THE WAY!
LET ME THROUGH!
H-HELP ME...
C-CAN'T HOLD ON... MUCH L-LONGER...
WITH FIERCE FIRE COURSING THROUGH HIS BLOOD, HE STANDS AT A MOMENT OF DEFINING CHOICE.
SHOULD HE FIRE KILLING BLADES OR SAVING LINE?
HIS ARM WAVERS... AND THEN HIS MIND REELS, SPUN OFF INTO CONFLICT AND CONFUSION...
P-PLEASE... I...I'M GOING TO... F-FALL...
YOU...!
BOTH OF YOU!

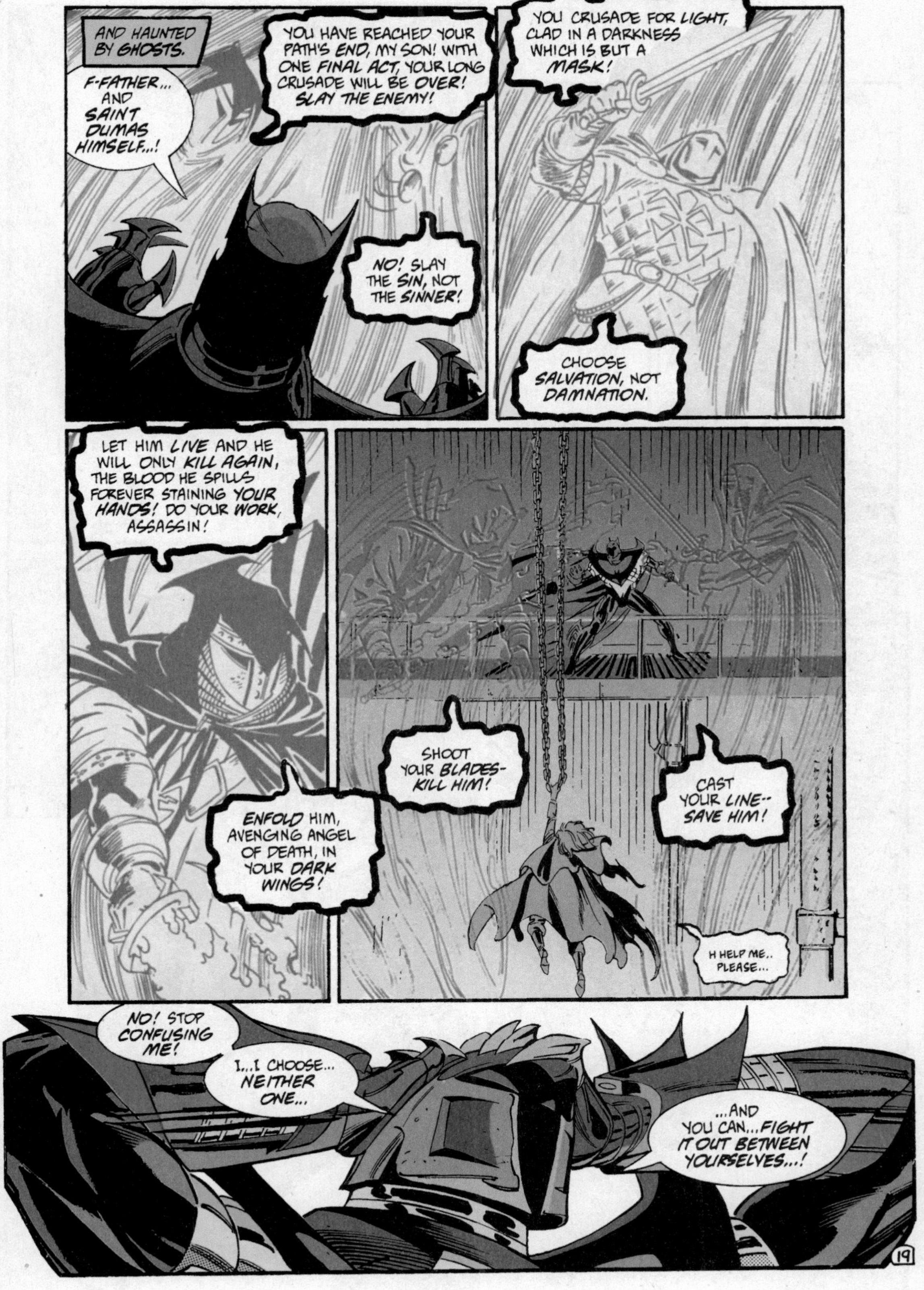
AND HAUNTED BY GHOSTS.
F-FATHER... AND SAINT DUMAS HIMSELF...!
YOU HAVE REACHED YOUR PATH'S END, MY SON! WITH ONE FINAL ACT, YOUR LONG CRUSADE WILL BE OVER! SLAY THE ENEMY!
NO! SLAY THE SIN, NOT THE SINNER!
YOU CRUSADE FOR LIGHT, CLAD IN A DARKNESS WHICH IS BUT A MASK!
CHOOSE SALVATION, NOT DAMNATION.
LET HIM LIVE AND HE WILL ONLY KILL AGAIN, THE BLOOD HE SPILLS FOREVER STAINING YOUR HANDS! DO YOUR WORK, ASSASSIN!
ENFOLD HIM, AVENGING ANGEL OF DEATH, IN YOUR DARK WINGS!
SHOOT YOUR BLADES-KILL HIM!
CAST YOUR LINE--SAVE HIM!
H HELP ME.. PLEASE...
NO! STOP CONFUSING ME!
I...I CHOOSE... NEITHER ONE...
...AND YOU CAN...FIGHT IT OUT BETWEEN YOURSELVES...!
19

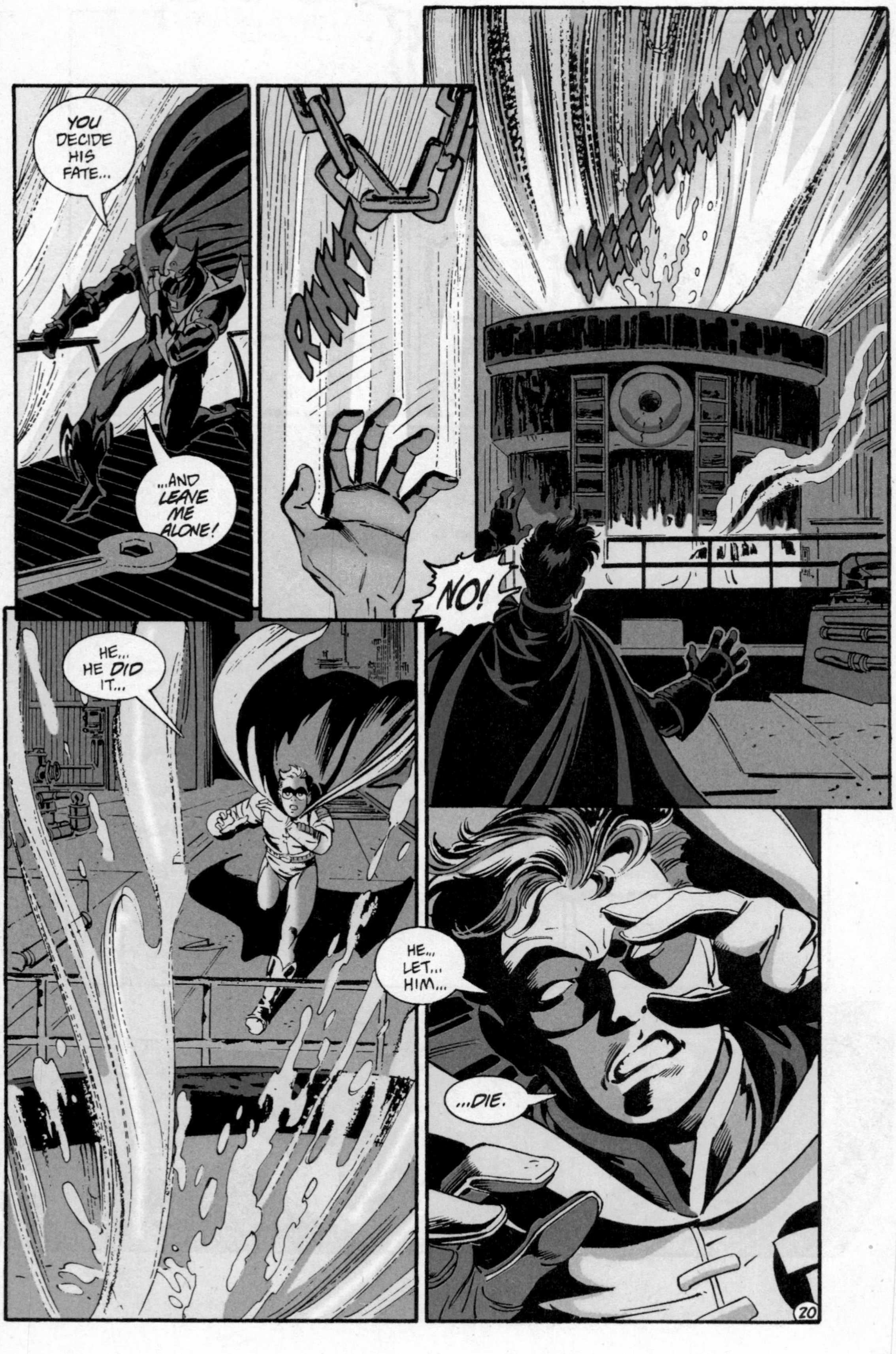
YOU DECIDE HIS FATE...
...AND LEAVE ME ALONE!
RINK!
YEEEEEAAAAAHHHHH
NO!
HE... HE DID IT...
HE... LET... HIM...
...DIE.
20

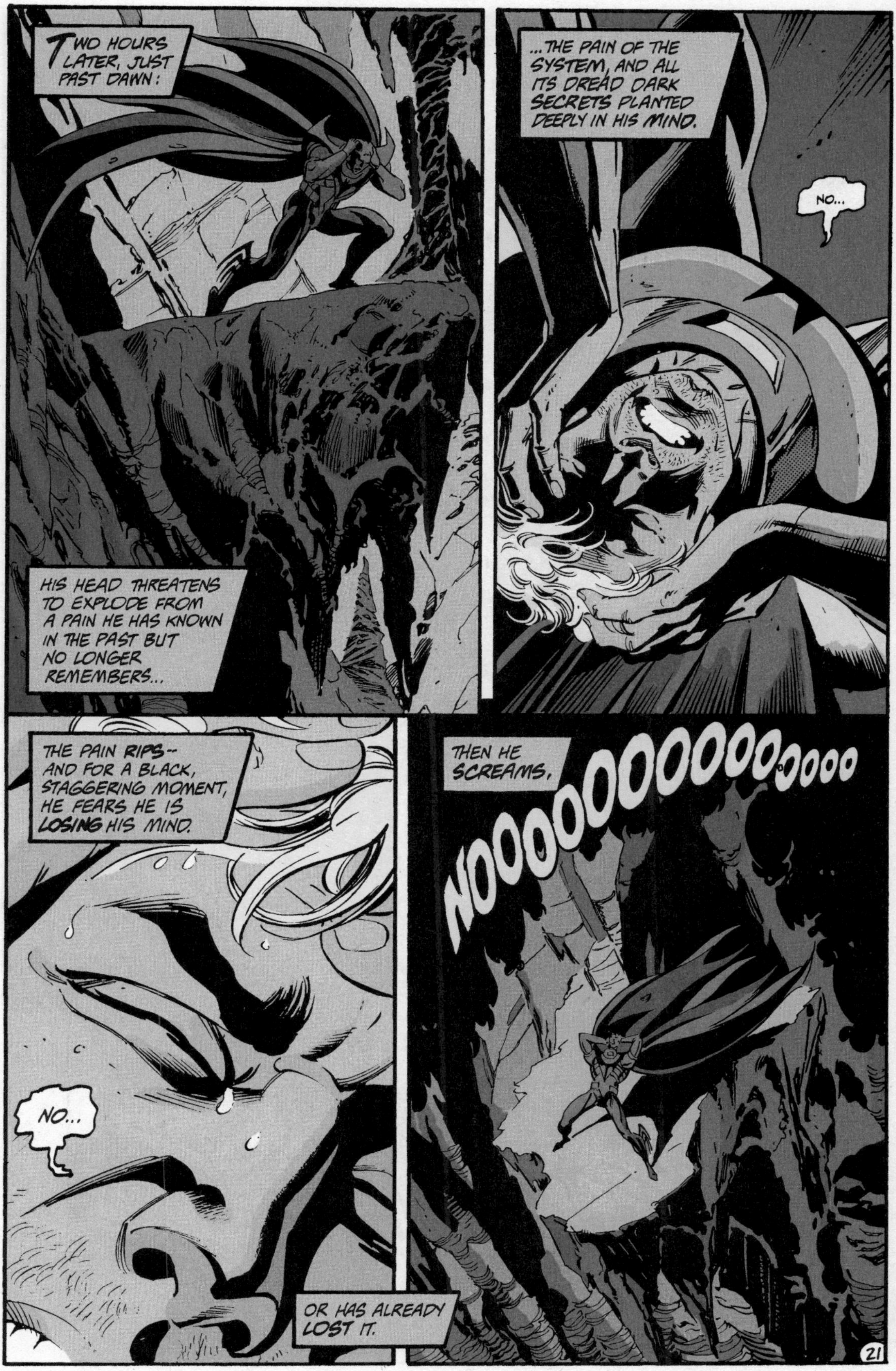

TWO HOURS LATER, JUST PAST DAWN:
HIS HEAD THREATENS TO EXPLODE FROM A PAIN HE HAS KNOWN IN THE PAST BUT NO LONGER REMEMBERS...
...THE PAIN OF THE SYSTEM, AND ALL ITS DREAD DARK SECRETS PLANTED DEEPLY IN HIS MIND.
NO...
THE PAIN RIPS-- AND FOR A BLACK, STAGGERING MOMENT, HE FEARS HE IS LOSING HIS MIND.
NO...
OR HAS ALREADY LOST IT.
THEN HE SCREAMS,
NOOOOOOOOOOOOOOOOOO
21

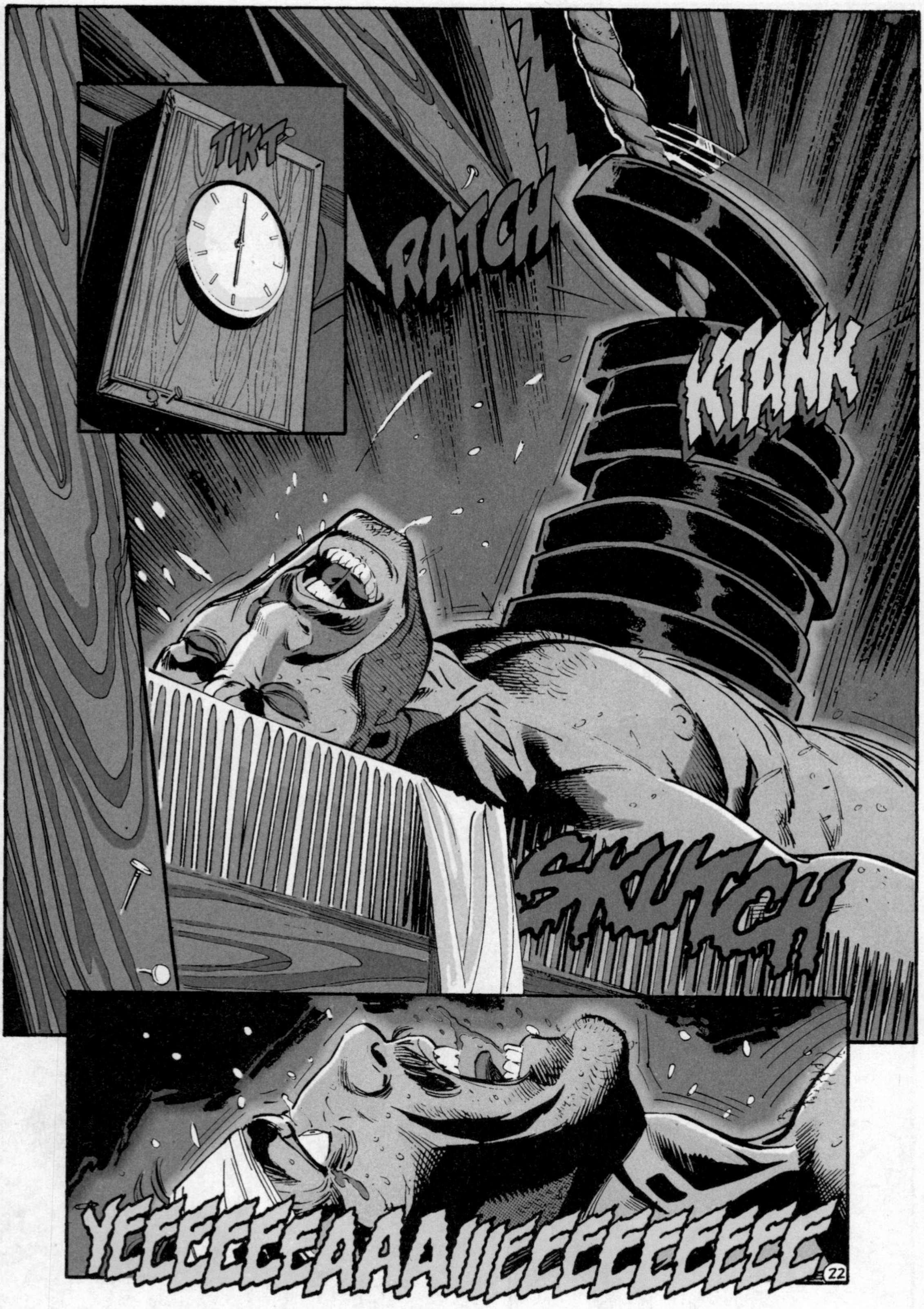
TIKT
RATCH
KTANK
SKLITCH
YEEEEEEAAAIIIEEEEEEEEEE
22

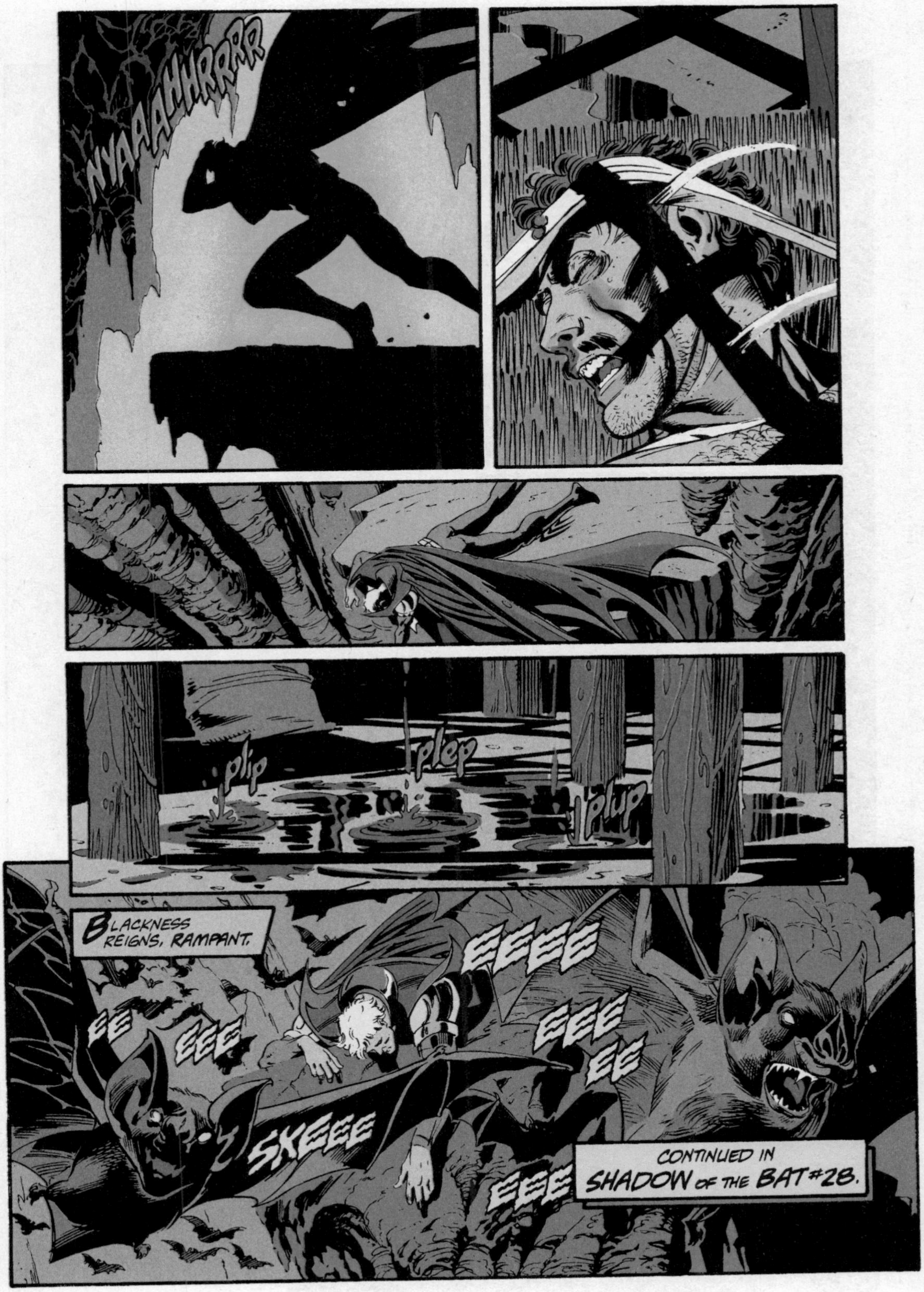
NYAAAHHRRRR
plip
plep
plup
BLACKNESS REIGNS, RAMPANT.
EEEE
EE
EEE
EEE
EE
SKEEE
EEE
CONTINUED IN SHADOW OF THE BAT #28.

Cover art by BRIAN STELFREEZE

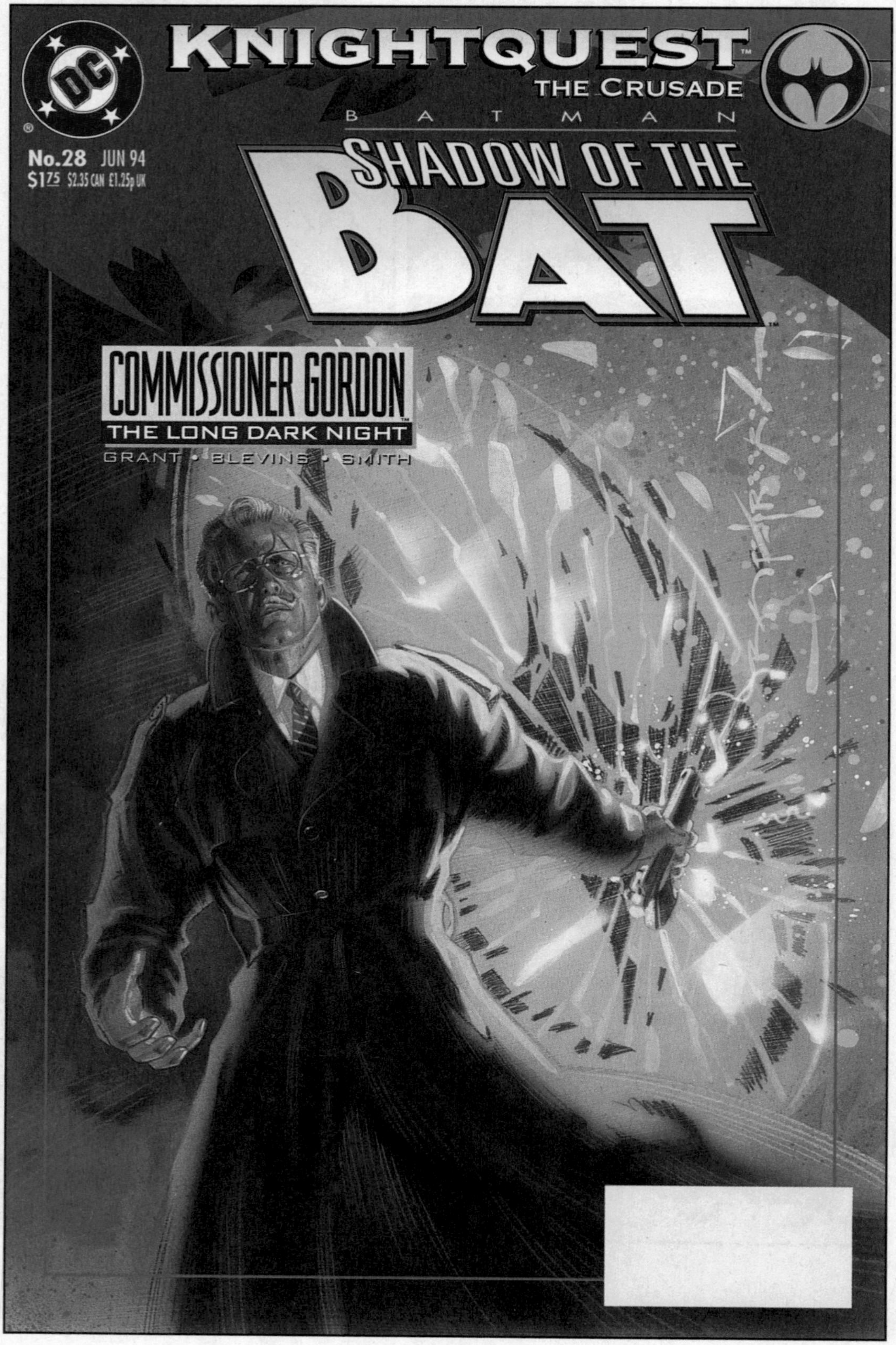
KNIGHTQUEST
THE CRUSADE
BATMAN
SHADOW OF THE BAT
No.28 JUN 94
$1.75 $2.35 CAN £1.25p UK
COMMISSIONER GORDON
THE LONG DARK NIGHT
GRANT • BLEVINS • SMITH

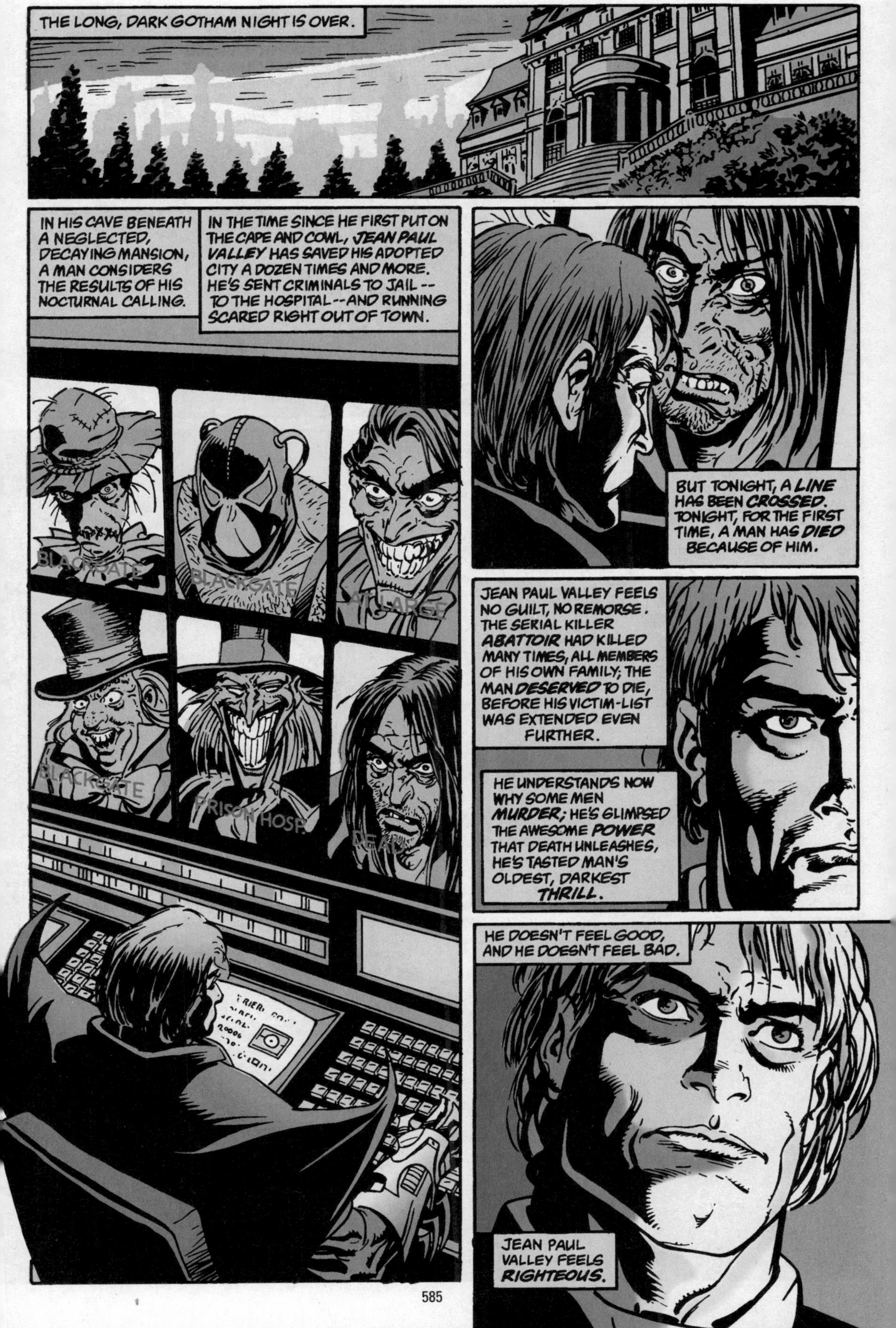
THE LONG, DARK GOTHAM NIGHT IS OVER.
IN HIS CAVE BENEATH A NEGLECTED, DECAYING MANSION, A MAN CONSIDERS THE RESULTS OF HIS NOCTURNAL CALLING.
IN THE TIME SINCE HE FIRST PUT ON THE CAPE AND COWL, JEAN PAUL VALLEY HAS SAVED HIS ADOPTED CITY A DOZEN TIMES AND MORE. HE'S SENT CRIMINALS TO JAIL -- TO THE HOSPITAL -- AND RUNNING SCARED RIGHT OUT OF TOWN.
BLACKGATE
BLACKGATE
AT LARGE
BLACKGATE
PRISON HOSP.
DEAD
BUT TONIGHT, A LINE HAS BEEN CROSSED. TONIGHT, FOR THE FIRST TIME, A MAN HAS DIED BECAUSE OF HIM.
JEAN PAUL VALLEY FEELS NO GUILT, NO REMORSE. THE SERIAL KILLER ABATTOIR HAD KILLED MANY TIMES, ALL MEMBERS OF HIS OWN FAMILY; THE MAN DESERVED TO DIE, BEFORE HIS VICTIM-LIST WAS EXTENDED EVEN FURTHER.
HE UNDERSTANDS NOW WHY SOME MEN MURDER; HE'S GLIMPSED THE AWESOME POWER THAT DEATH UNLEASHES, HE'S TASTED MAN'S OLDEST, DARKEST THRILL.
HE DOESN'T FEEL GOOD, AND HE DOESN'T FEEL BAD.
JEAN PAUL VALLEY FEELS RIGHTEOUS.

LESS THAN TEN MILES AWAY, ANOTHER MAN HAS ALSO BEEN UP ALL NIGHT--

YOU'RE ABSOLUTELY SURE?

A MAN WHO, IN HIS PRIME AND ON A TOUGH CASE, THOUGHT NOTHING OF STAYING UP 72 HOURS STRAIGHT--

NOT ONE HUNDRED PERCENT, COMMISSIONER--

--BUT THE BEST EXPLANATION SEEMS TO BE THAT BATMAN DELIBERATELY LEFT ABATTOIR TO DIE!

NO BIG LOSS, COMMISH, BELIEVE ME!

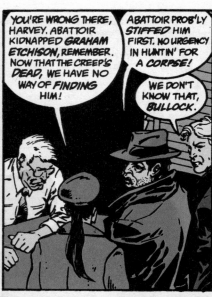

YOU'RE WRONG THERE, HARVEY. ABATTOIR KIDNAPPED GRAHAM ETCHISON, REMEMBER. NOW THAT THE CREEP'S DEAD, WE HAVE NO WAY OF FINDING HIM!

ABATTOIR PROB'LY STIFFED HIM FIRST. NO URGENCY IN HUNTIN' FOR A CORPSE!

WE DON'T KNOW THAT, BULLOCK.

WHAT WE DO KNOW IS THAT ABATTOIR'S INSANITY WAS WORSENING -- AND THAT WHERE POSSIBLE HE PREFERRED TO TORTURE HIS VICTIMS BEFORE DEATH.

IT COULD WELL BE THAT POOR WRETCH ETCHISON IS LYING. BADLY HURT SOMEPLACE!

HE'S LYIN' STIFFED, IS WHAT HE IS, KITCH!

WHAT DO YOU SAY, COMMISSIONER?

SIR?

MMM? OH--!

HE HAD ALWAYS KNOWN IT WOULD GET HARDER, THE OLDER HE BECAME--

GET EVERY SPARE UNIT ON IT--TOP PRIORITY! I WANT GRAHAM ETCHISON FOUND!

--BUT NOT EVEN IN HIS NIGHTMARES DID HE DREAM IT WOULD GET THIS HARD.

②

ONLY TEN BLOCKS FROM POLICE H.Q., A THIRD MAN HAS NOT SLEPT...

'S THE PERFECT PLAN, MAN!

NOW, IN THE PALE AFTERMATH OF A DRUG-HIGH NIGHT, *VERMIN HARNETT* HAS HAD AN IDEA THAT WILL MAKE HIM AND HIS *RAT GANG* RICH.

Y'KNOW *WILDING*, RIGHT?

WHAT *IS* THIS, MAN? A *QUIZ?* WE WILDED A *DOZEN* TIMES, VERMIN -- YOU WAS *THERE*, RIGHT? OR DID YA *DRINK* SO MUCH YA *FORGOT*...?

SO FIGURE THIS,...*ORGANIZED WILDIN'!*

MAN, IT AIN'T JUST YER *MEMORY* THE DRINK TOOK! ORGANIZED WILDIN'? IT AIN'T *LOGICAL!*

YER WRONG, *DODGE*. 'S GONNA MAKE TH' *RATS* INTA TH' *RICHEST* GANG IN GOTHAM!

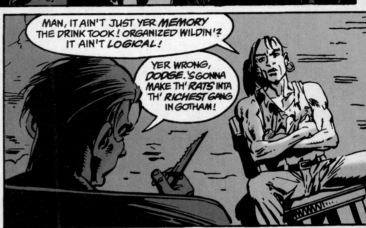

OH, AN' DODGE--

--DON'T *EVER* CALL ME ILLOGICAL, MAN!

3

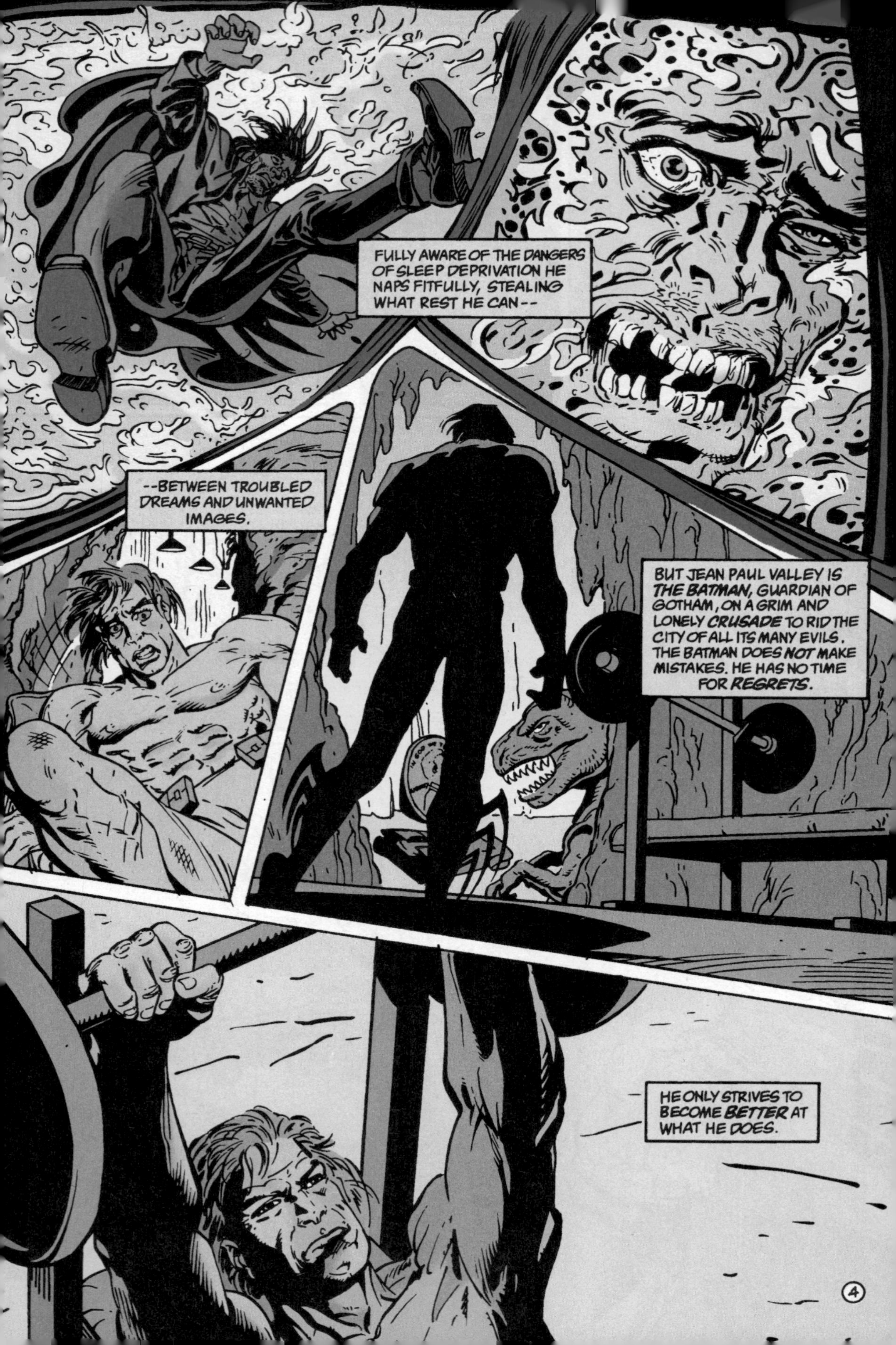

FULLY AWARE OF THE DANGERS OF SLEEP DEPRIVATION HE NAPS FITFULLY, STEALING WHAT REST HE CAN--
--BETWEEN TROUBLED DREAMS AND UNWANTED IMAGES.
BUT JEAN PAUL VALLEY IS THE BATMAN, GUARDIAN OF GOTHAM, ON A GRIM AND LONELY CRUSADE TO RID THE CITY OF ALL ITS MANY EVILS. THE BATMAN DOES NOT MAKE MISTAKES. HE HAS NO TIME FOR REGRETS.
HE ONLY STRIVES TO BECOME BETTER AT WHAT HE DOES.

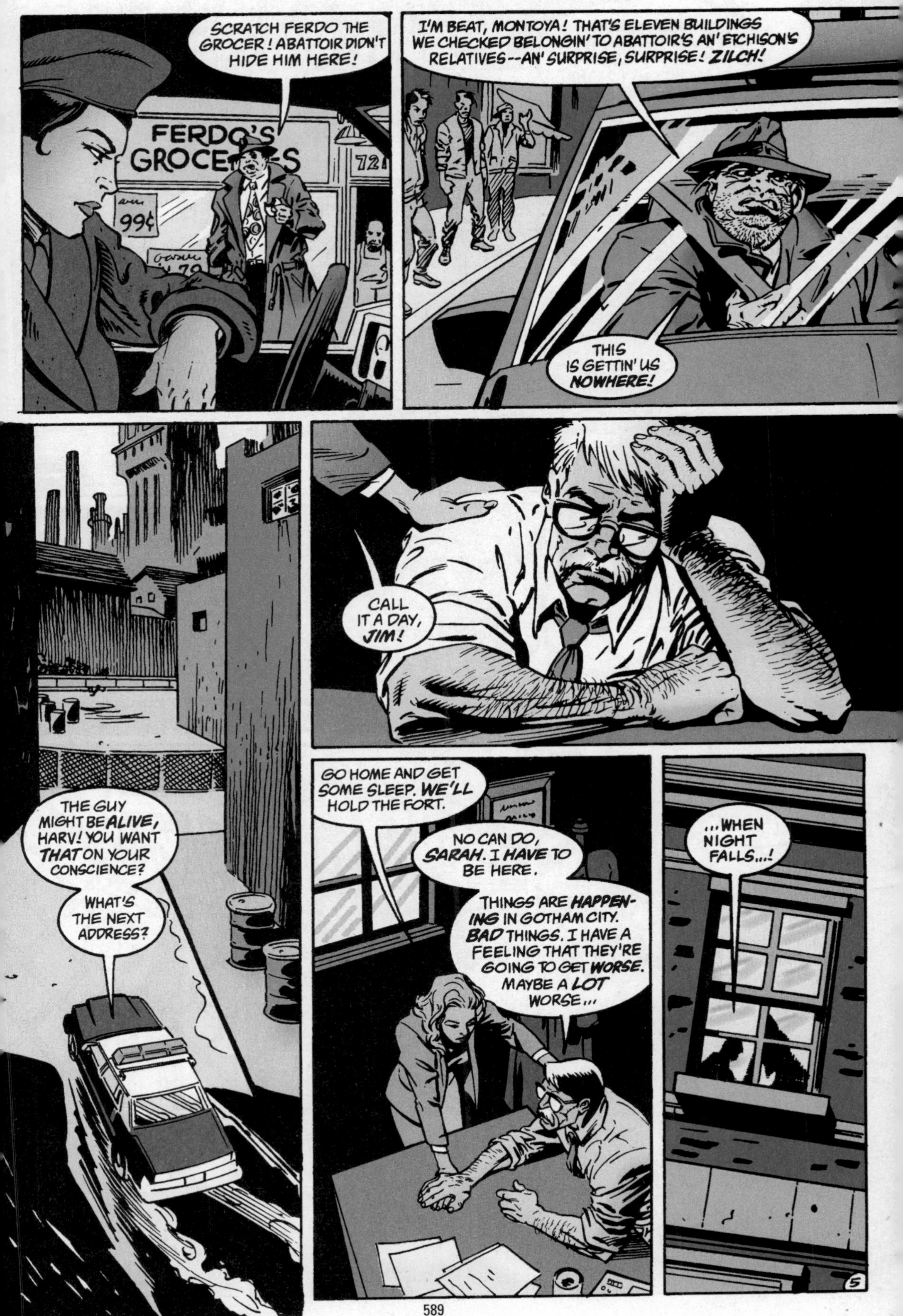
SCRATCH FERDO THE GROCER! ABATTOIR DIDN'T HIDE HIM HERE!
FERDO'S GROCE S
99¢
I'M BEAT, MONTOYA! THAT'S ELEVEN BUILDINGS WE CHECKED BELONGIN' TO ABATTOIR'S AN' ETCHISON'S RELATIVES--AN' SURPRISE, SURPRISE! ZILCH!
THIS IS GETTIN' US NOWHERE!
THE GUY MIGHT BE ALIVE, HARV! YOU WANT THAT ON YOUR CONSCIENCE?
WHAT'S THE NEXT ADDRESS?
CALL IT A DAY, JIM!
GO HOME AND GET SOME SLEEP. WE'LL HOLD THE FORT.
NO CAN DO, SARAH. I HAVE TO BE HERE.
THINGS ARE HAPPENING IN GOTHAM CITY. BAD THINGS. I HAVE A FEELING THAT THEY'RE GOING TO GET WORSE. MAYBE A LOT WORSE...
...WHEN NIGHT FALLS...!
5

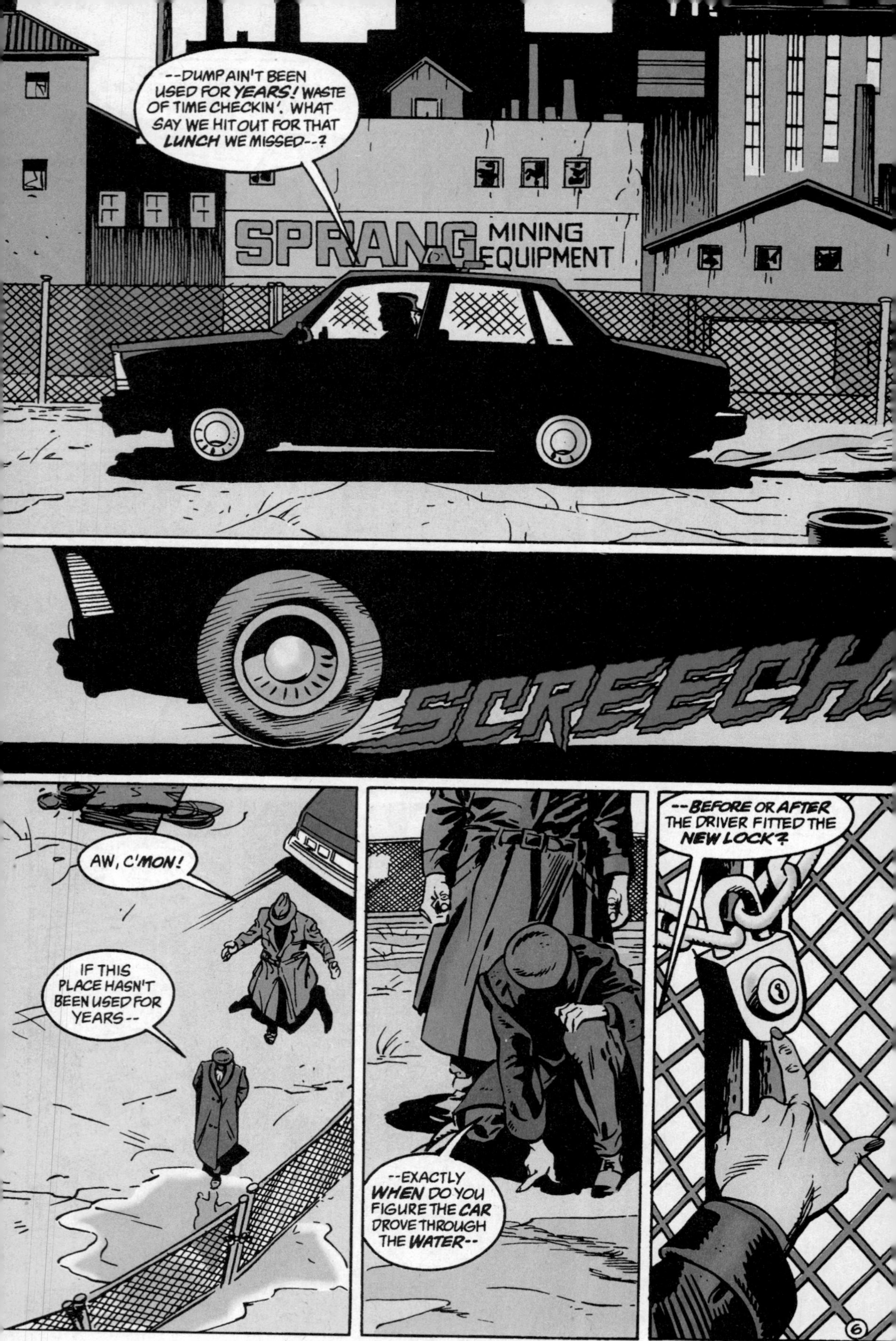
--DUMP AIN'T BEEN USED FOR YEARS! WASTE OF TIME CHECKIN'. WHAT SAY WE HIT OUT FOR THAT LUNCH WE MISSED--?
SPRANG MINING EQUIPMENT
SCREECH
AW, C'MON!
IF THIS PLACE HASN'T BEEN USED FOR YEARS--
--EXACTLY WHEN DO YOU FIGURE THE CAR DROVE THROUGH THE WATER--
--BEFORE OR AFTER THE DRIVER FITTED THE NEW LOCK?
6

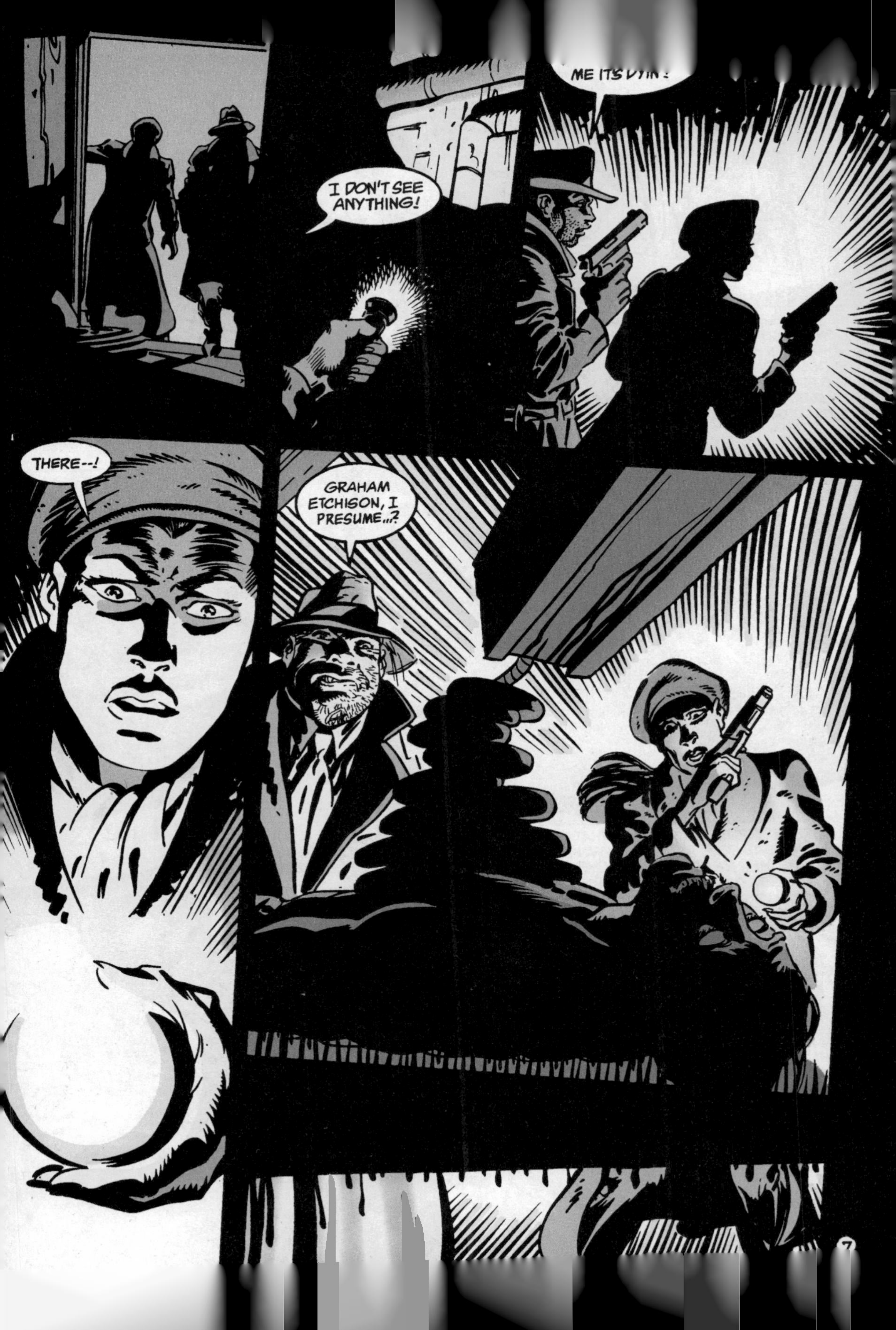
I DON'T SEE ANYTHING!
ME IT'S DYIN'!
THERE--!
GRAHAM ETCHISON, I PRESUME...?

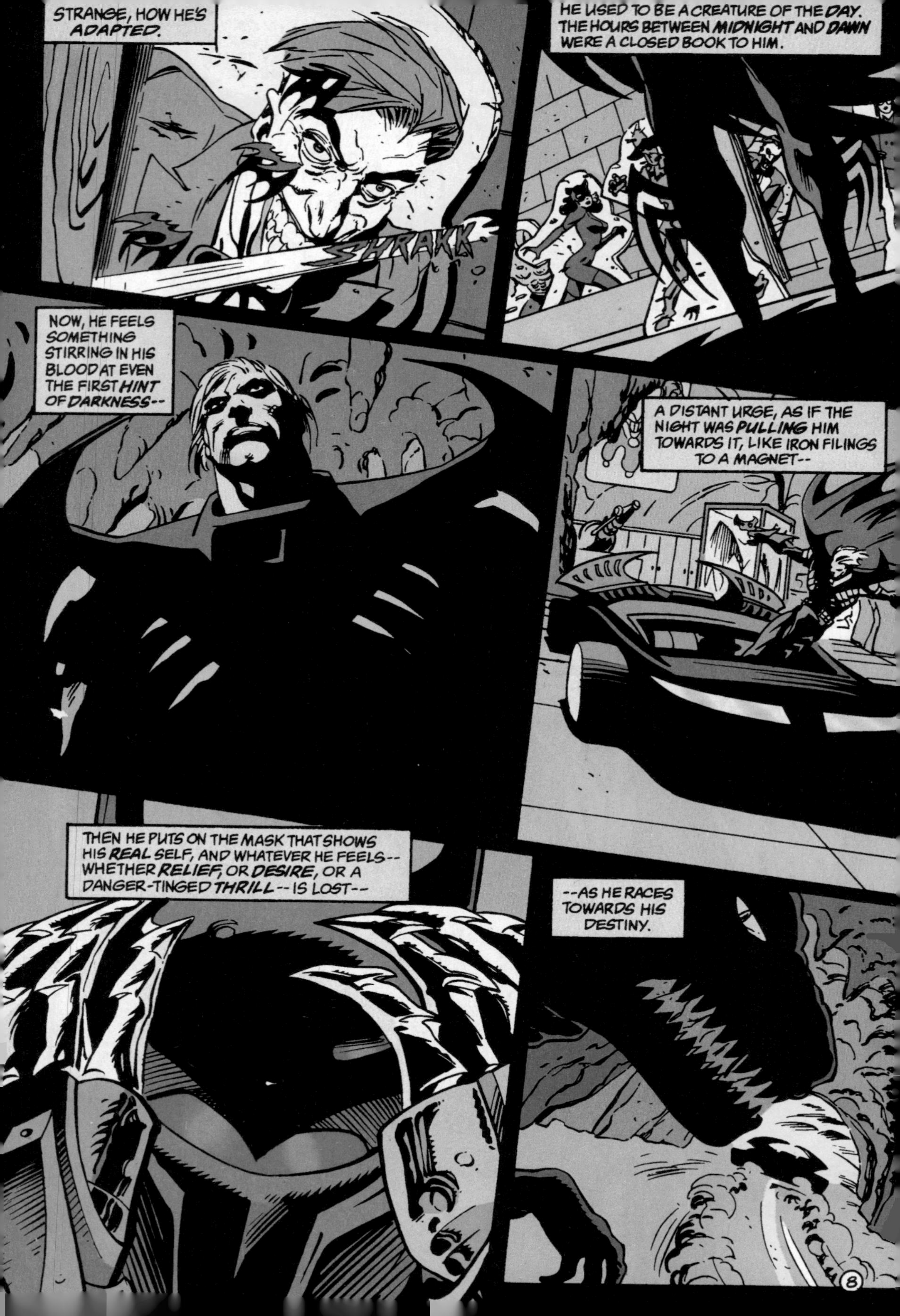

STRANGE, HOW HE'S ADAPTED.
SHRAKK
HE USED TO BE A CREATURE OF THE DAY. THE HOURS BETWEEN MIDNIGHT AND DAWN WERE A CLOSED BOOK TO HIM.
NOW, HE FEELS SOMETHING STIRRING IN HIS BLOOD AT EVEN THE FIRST HINT OF DARKNESS--
A DISTANT URGE, AS IF THE NIGHT WAS PULLING HIM TOWARDS IT, LIKE IRON FILINGS TO A MAGNET--
THEN HE PUTS ON THE MASK THAT SHOWS HIS REAL SELF, AND WHATEVER HE FEELS-- WHETHER RELIEF, OR DESIRE, OR A DANGER-TINGED THRILL -- IS LOST--
--AS HE RACES TOWARDS HIS DESTINY.
8

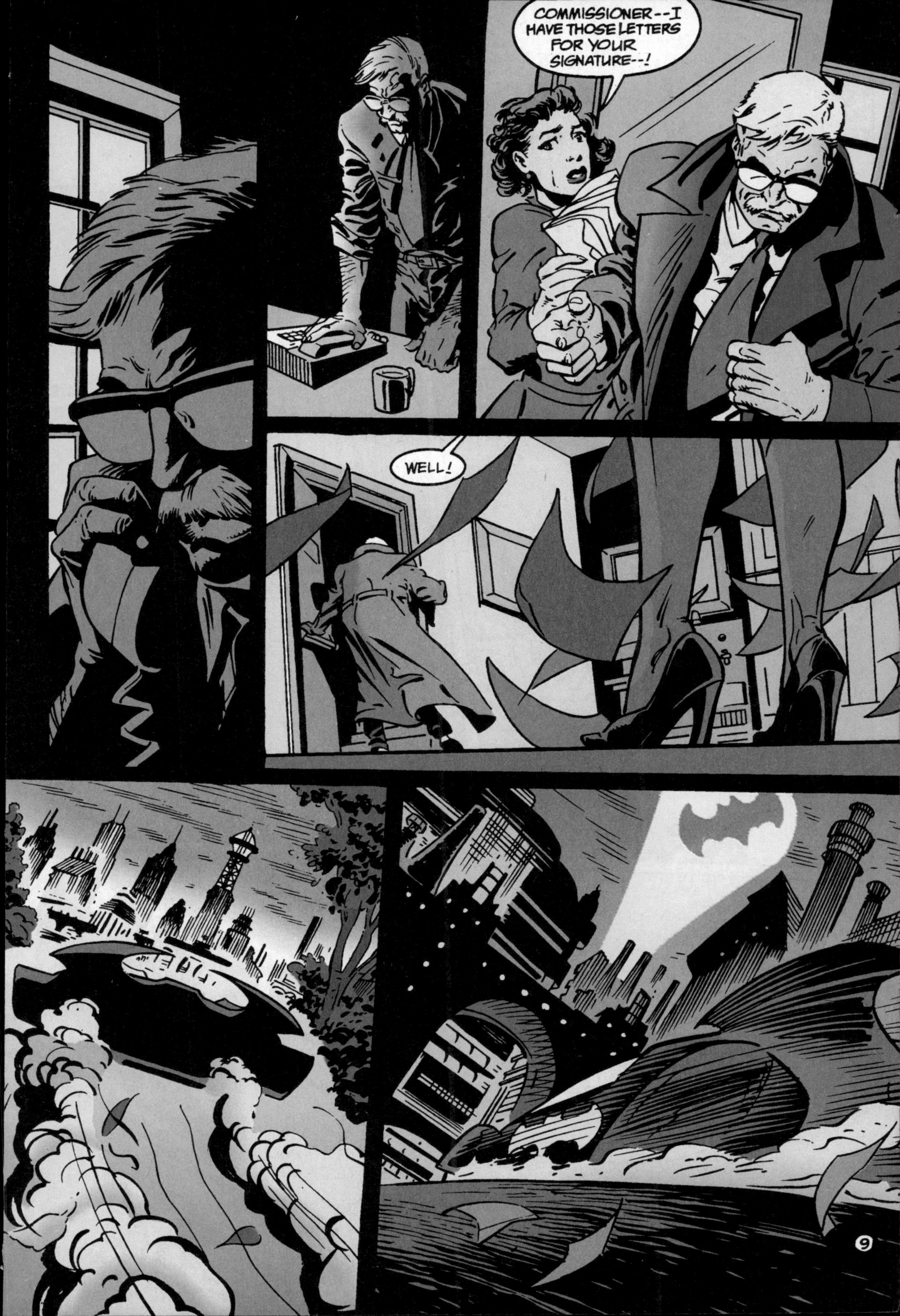
COMMISSIONER--I HAVE THOSE LETTERS FOR YOUR SIGNATURE--!
WELL!

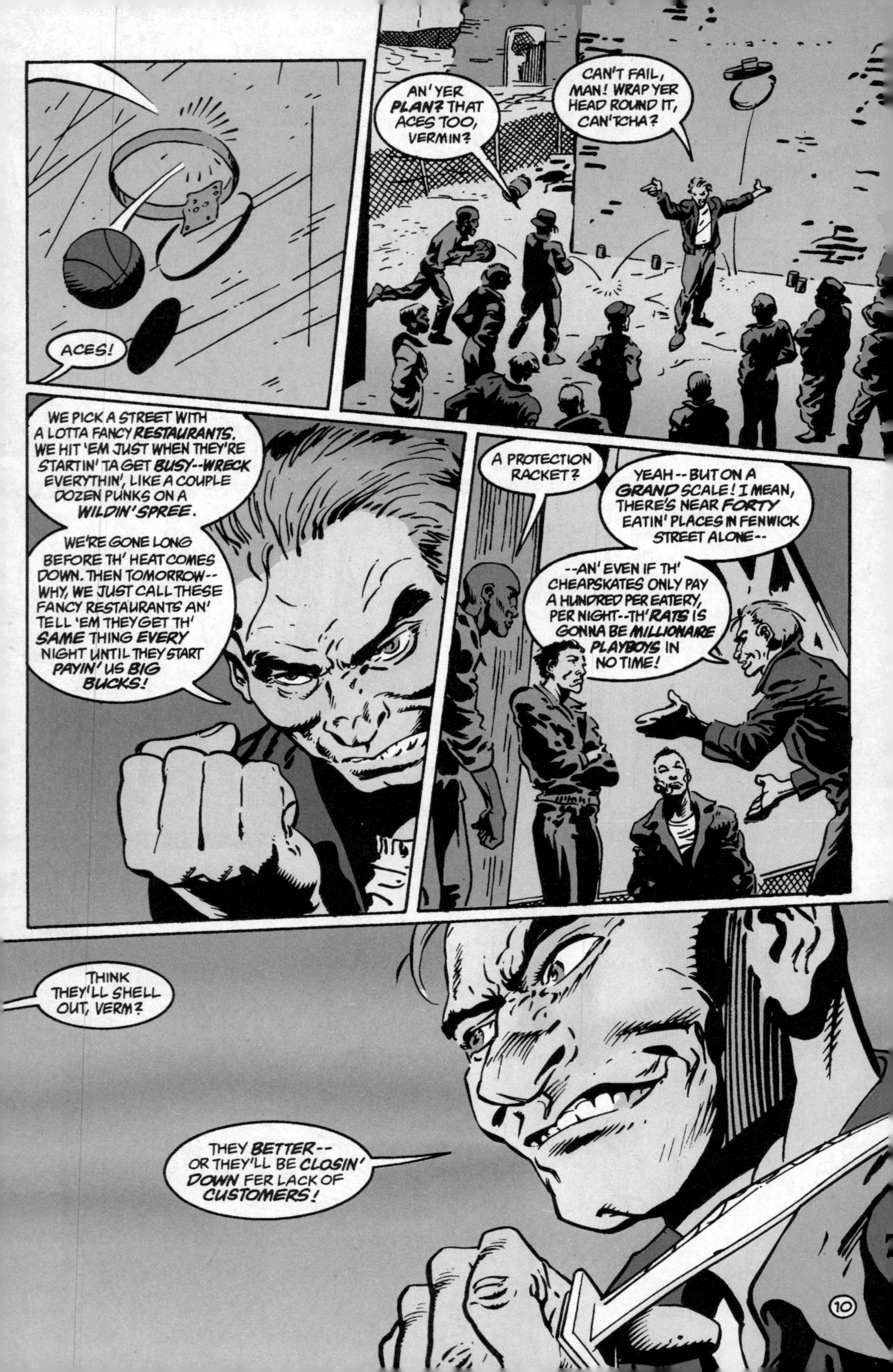
ACES!
AN' YER PLAN? THAT ACES TOO, VERMIN?
CAN'T FAIL, MAN! WRAP YER HEAD ROUND IT, CAN'TCHA?
WE PICK A STREET WITH A LOTTA FANCY RESTAURANTS. WE HIT 'EM JUST WHEN THEY'RE STARTIN' TA GET BUSY--WRECK EVERYTHIN', LIKE A COUPLE DOZEN PUNKS ON A WILDIN' SPREE.
WE'RE GONE LONG BEFORE TH' HEAT COMES DOWN. THEN TOMORROW--WHY, WE JUST CALL THESE FANCY RESTAURANTS AN' TELL 'EM THEY GET TH' SAME THING EVERY NIGHT UNTIL THEY START PAYIN' US BIG BUCKS!
A PROTECTION RACKET?
YEAH--BUT ON A GRAND SCALE! I MEAN, THERE'S NEAR FORTY EATIN' PLACES IN FENWICK STREET ALONE--
--AN' EVEN IF TH' CHEAPSKATES ONLY PAY A HUNDRED PER EATERY, PER NIGHT--TH' RATS IS GONNA BE MILLIONAIRE PLAYBOYS IN NO TIME!
THINK THEY'LL SHELL OUT, VERM?
THEY BETTER--OR THEY'LL BE CLOSIN' DOWN FER LACK OF CUSTOMERS!
10

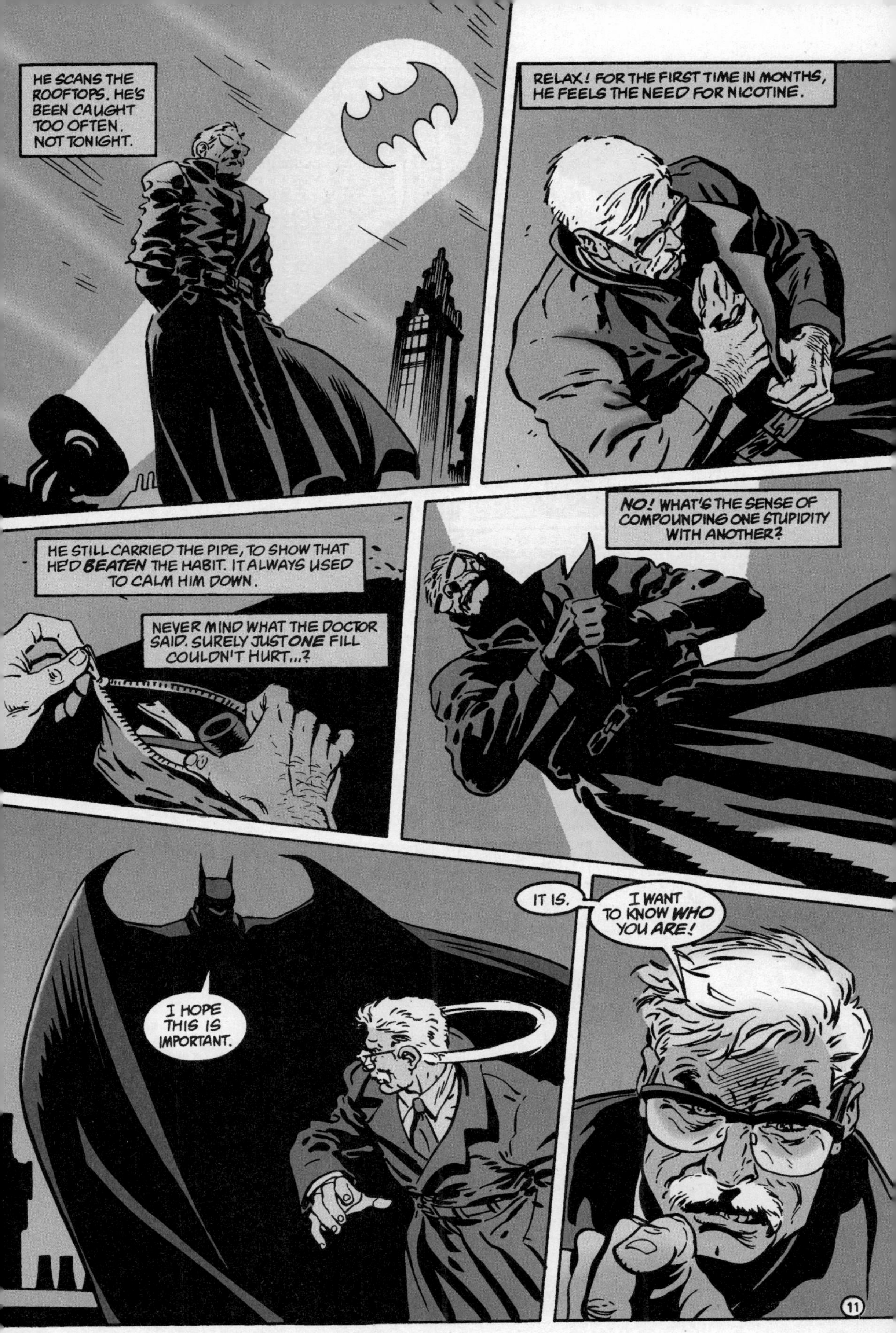

HE SCANS THE ROOFTOPS. HE'S BEEN CAUGHT TOO OFTEN. NOT TONIGHT.
RELAX! FOR THE FIRST TIME IN MONTHS, HE FEELS THE NEED FOR NICOTINE.
HE STILL CARRIED THE PIPE, TO SHOW THAT HE'D BEATEN THE HABIT. IT ALWAYS USED TO CALM HIM DOWN.
NEVER MIND WHAT THE DOCTOR SAID. SURELY JUST ONE FILL COULDN'T HURT...?
NO! WHAT'S THE SENSE OF COMPOUNDING ONE STUPIDITY WITH ANOTHER?
I HOPE THIS IS IMPORTANT.
IT IS.
I WANT TO KNOW WHO YOU ARE!
11

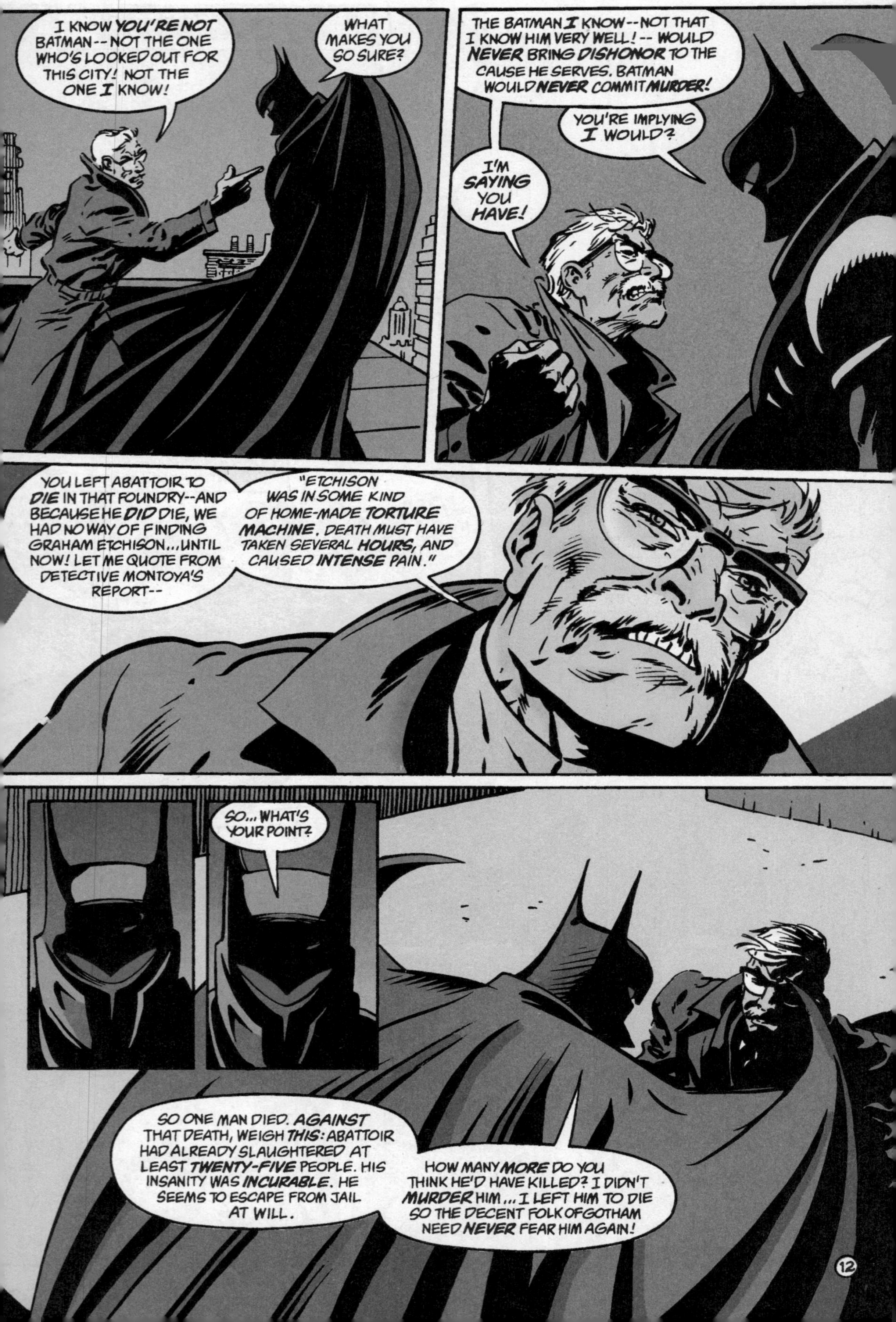

I KNOW YOU'RE NOT BATMAN--NOT THE ONE WHO'S LOOKED OUT FOR THIS CITY! NOT THE ONE I KNOW!
WHAT MAKES YOU SO SURE?
THE BATMAN I KNOW--NOT THAT I KNOW HIM VERY WELL!--WOULD NEVER BRING DISHONOR TO THE CAUSE HE SERVES. BATMAN WOULD NEVER COMMIT MURDER!
YOU'RE IMPLYING I WOULD?
I'M SAYING YOU HAVE!
YOU LEFT ABATTOIR TO DIE IN THAT FOUNDRY--AND BECAUSE HE DID DIE, WE HAD NO WAY OF FINDING GRAHAM ETCHISON...UNTIL NOW! LET ME QUOTE FROM DETECTIVE MONTOYA'S REPORT--
"ETCHISON WAS IN SOME KIND OF HOME-MADE TORTURE MACHINE. DEATH MUST HAVE TAKEN SEVERAL HOURS, AND CAUSED INTENSE PAIN."
SO...WHAT'S YOUR POINT?
SO ONE MAN DIED. AGAINST THAT DEATH, WEIGH THIS: ABATTOIR HAD ALREADY SLAUGHTERED AT LEAST TWENTY-FIVE PEOPLE. HIS INSANITY WAS INCURABLE. HE SEEMS TO ESCAPE FROM JAIL AT WILL.
HOW MANY MORE DO YOU THINK HE'D HAVE KILLED? I DIDN'T MURDER HIM...I LEFT HIM TO DIE SO THE DECENT FOLK OF GOTHAM NEED NEVER FEAR HIM AGAIN!

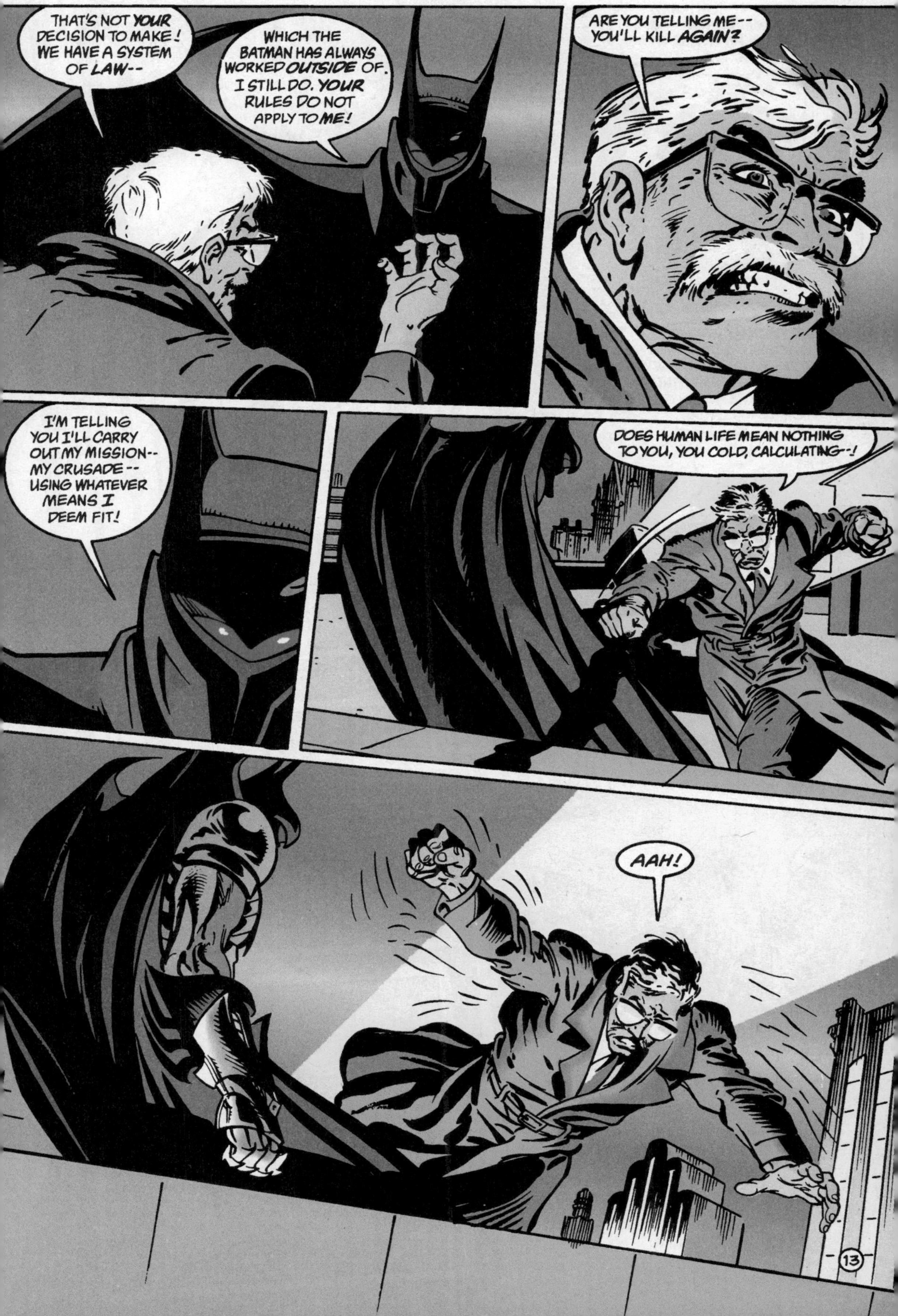
THAT'S NOT YOUR DECISION TO MAKE! WE HAVE A SYSTEM OF LAW--
WHICH THE BATMAN HAS ALWAYS WORKED OUTSIDE OF. I STILL DO. YOUR RULES DO NOT APPLY TO ME!
ARE YOU TELLING ME-- YOU'LL KILL AGAIN?
I'M TELLING YOU I'LL CARRY OUT MY MISSION-- MY CRUSADE -- USING WHATEVER MEANS I DEEM FIT!
DOES HUMAN LIFE MEAN NOTHING TO YOU, YOU COLD, CALCULATING--!
AAH!
13

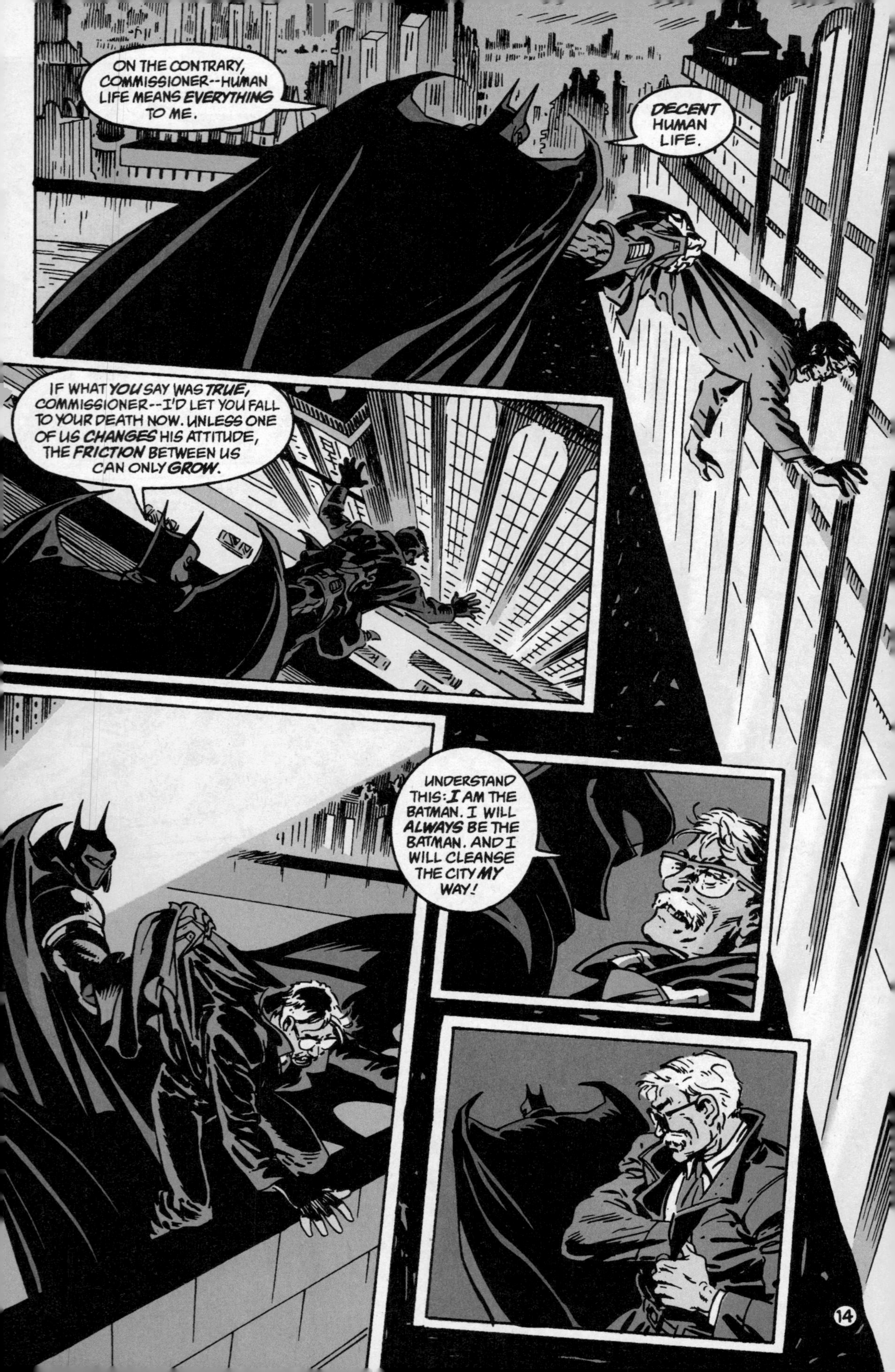
ON THE CONTRARY, COMMISSIONER--HUMAN LIFE MEANS EVERYTHING TO ME.
DECENT HUMAN LIFE.
IF WHAT YOU SAY WAS TRUE, COMMISSIONER--I'D LET YOU FALL TO YOUR DEATH NOW. UNLESS ONE OF US CHANGES HIS ATTITUDE, THE FRICTION BETWEEN US CAN ONLY GROW.
UNDERSTAND THIS: I AM THE BATMAN. I WILL ALWAYS BE THE BATMAN. AND I WILL CLEANSE THE CITY MY WAY!

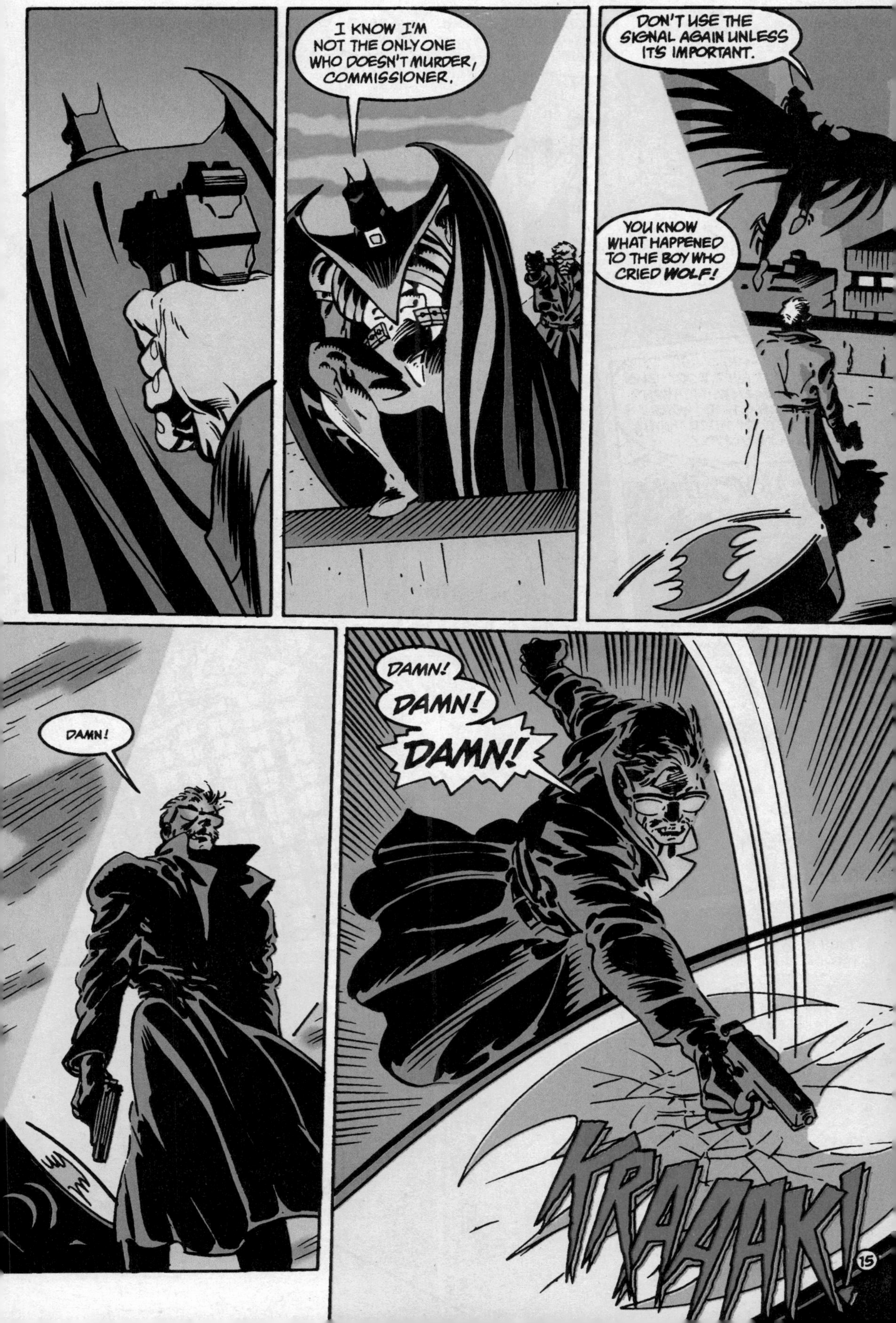
I KNOW I'M NOT THE ONLY ONE WHO DOESN'T MURDER, COMMISSIONER.
DON'T USE THE SIGNAL AGAIN UNLESS IT'S IMPORTANT.
YOU KNOW WHAT HAPPENED TO THE BOY WHO CRIED WOLF!
DAMN!
DAMN!
DAMN!
DAMN!
KRAAAK!

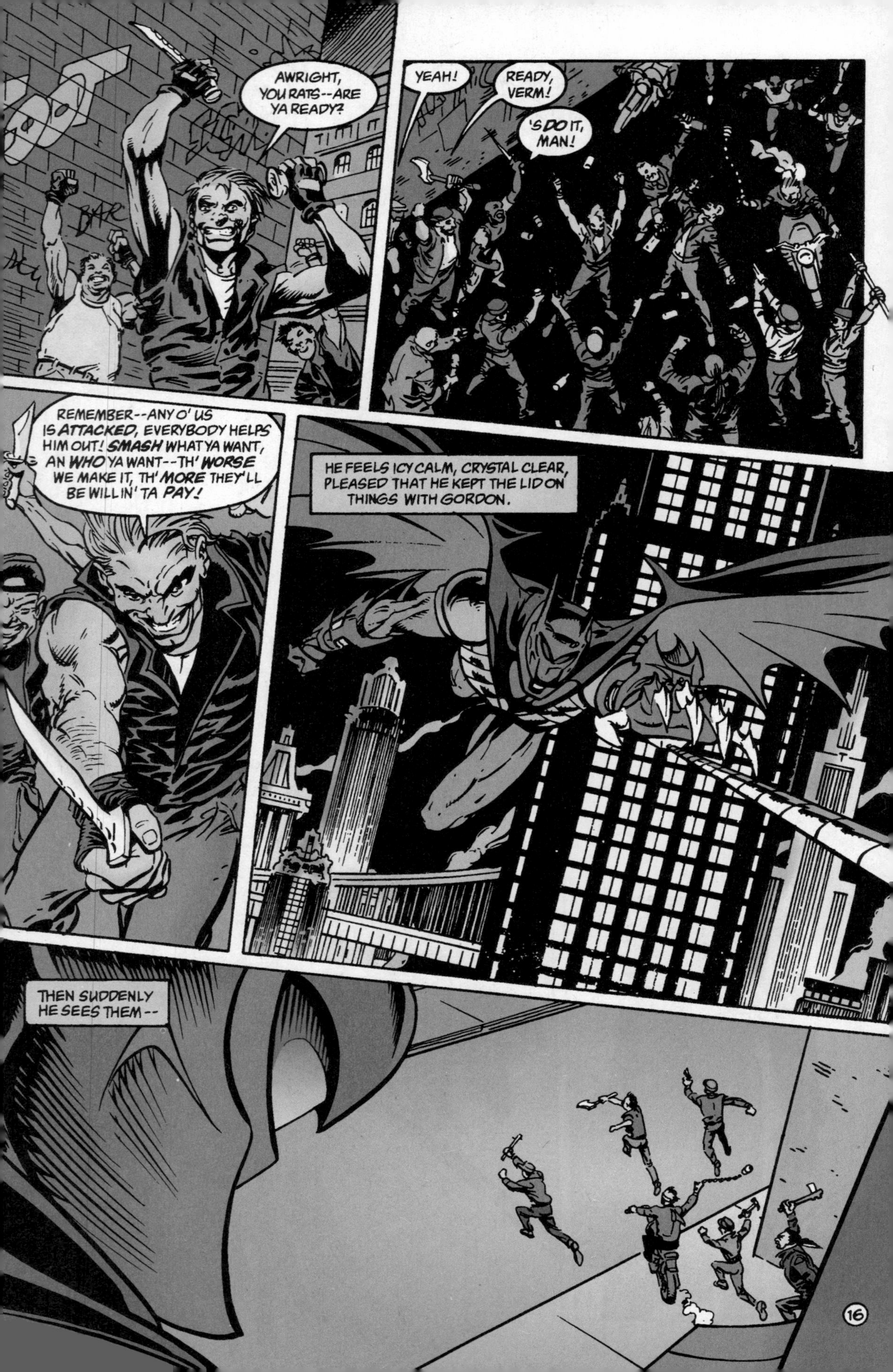
AWRIGHT, YOU RATS--ARE YA READY?
YEAH!
READY, VERM!
'S DO IT, MAN!
REMEMBER--ANY O' US IS ATTACKED, EVERYBODY HELPS HIM OUT! SMASH WHAT YA WANT, AN WHO YA WANT--TH' WORSE WE MAKE IT, TH' MORE THEY'LL BE WILLIN' TA PAY!
HE FEELS ICY CALM, CRYSTAL CLEAR, PLEASED THAT HE KEPT THE LID ON THINGS WITH GORDON.
THEN SUDDENLY HE SEES THEM--

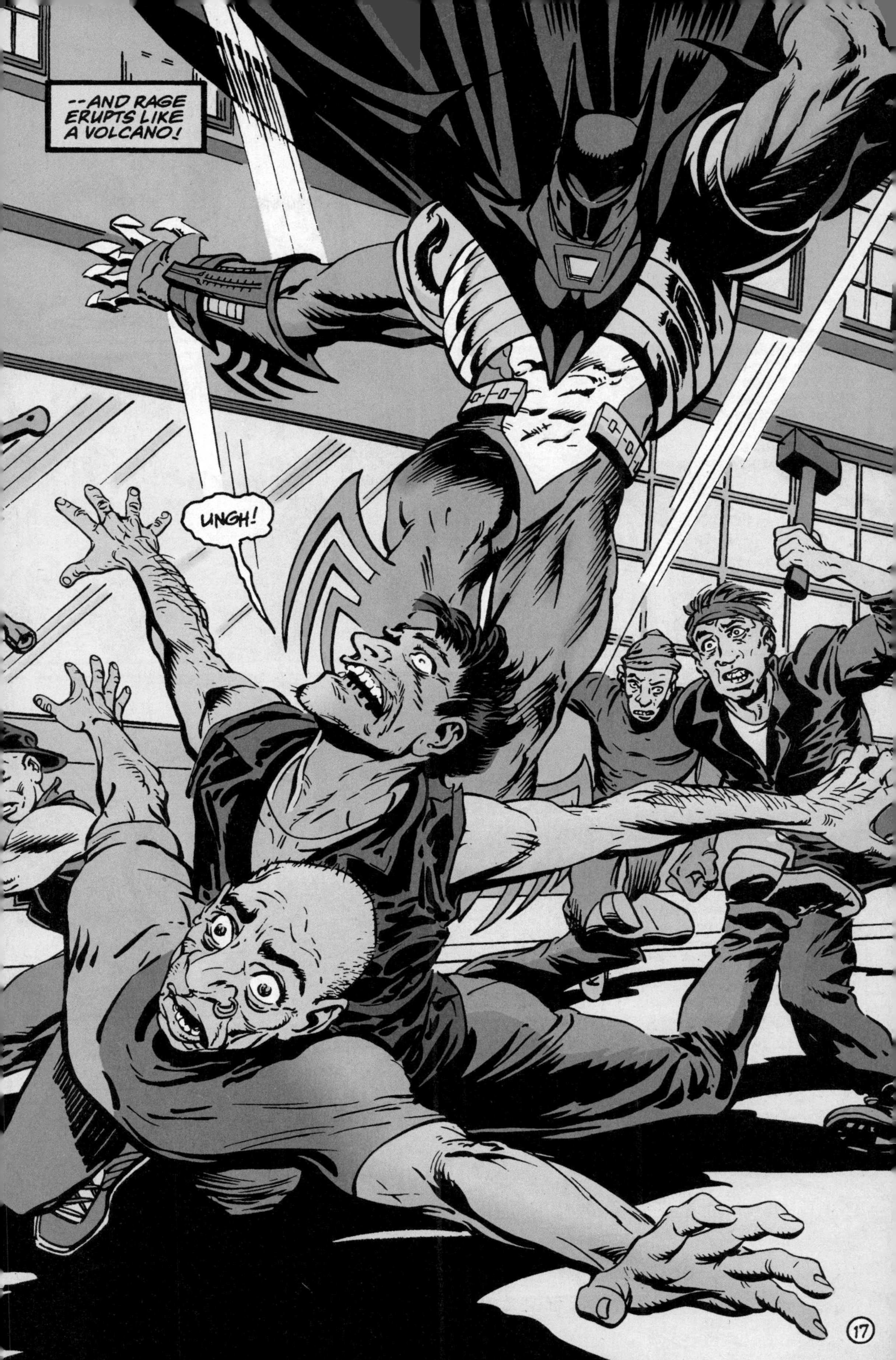
--AND RAGE ERUPTS LIKE A VOLCANO!
UNGH!

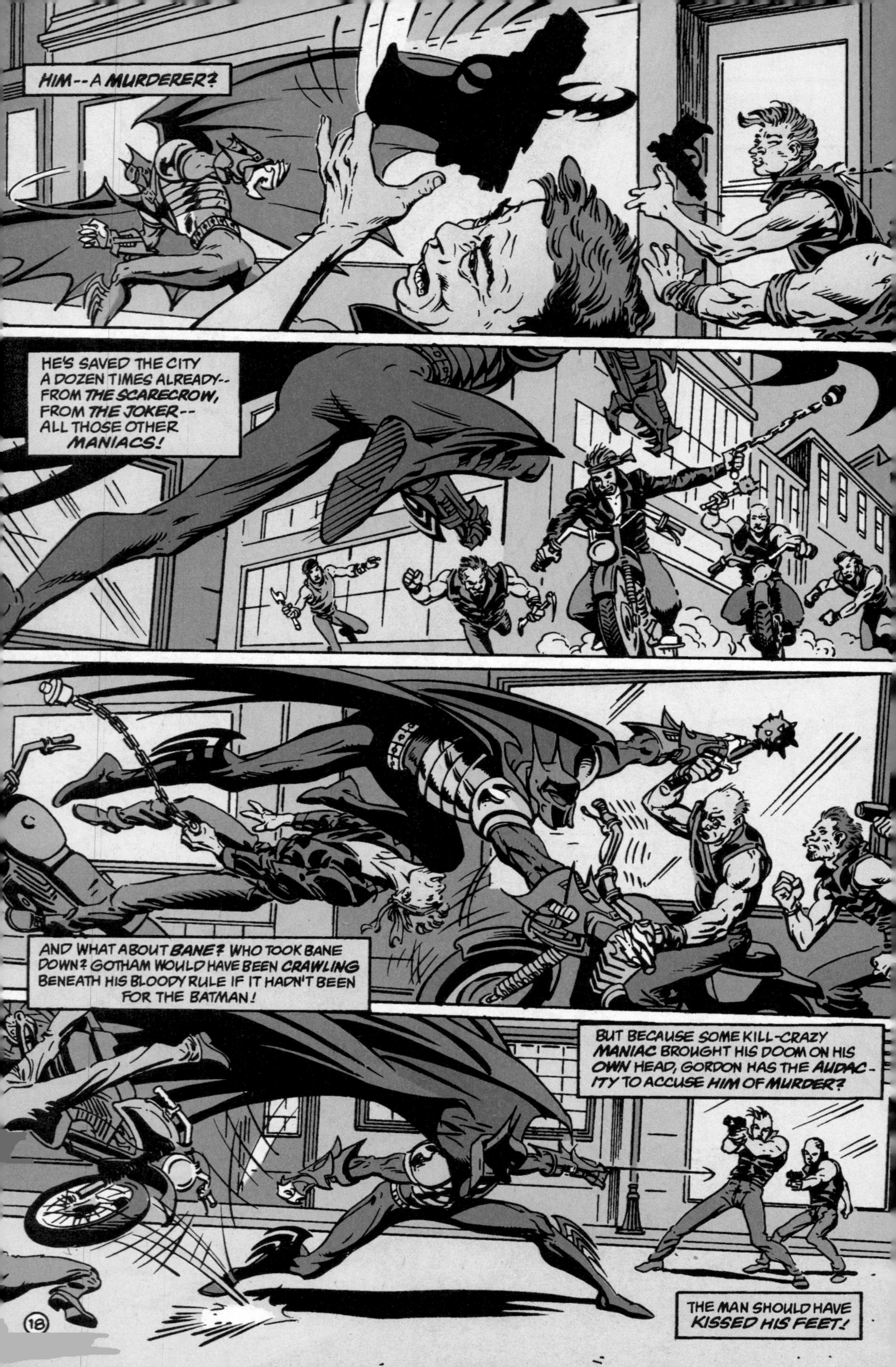
HIM--A MURDERER?
HE'S SAVED THE CITY A DOZEN TIMES ALREADY--FROM THE SCARECROW, FROM THE JOKER--ALL THOSE OTHER MANIACS!
AND WHAT ABOUT BANE? WHO TOOK BANE DOWN? GOTHAM WOULD HAVE BEEN CRAWLING BENEATH HIS BLOODY RULE IF IT HADN'T BEEN FOR THE BATMAN!
BUT BECAUSE SOME KILL-CRAZY MANIAC BROUGHT HIS DOOM ON HIS OWN HEAD, GORDON HAS THE AUDACITY TO ACCUSE HIM OF MURDER?
THE MAN SHOULD HAVE KISSED HIS FEET!
18

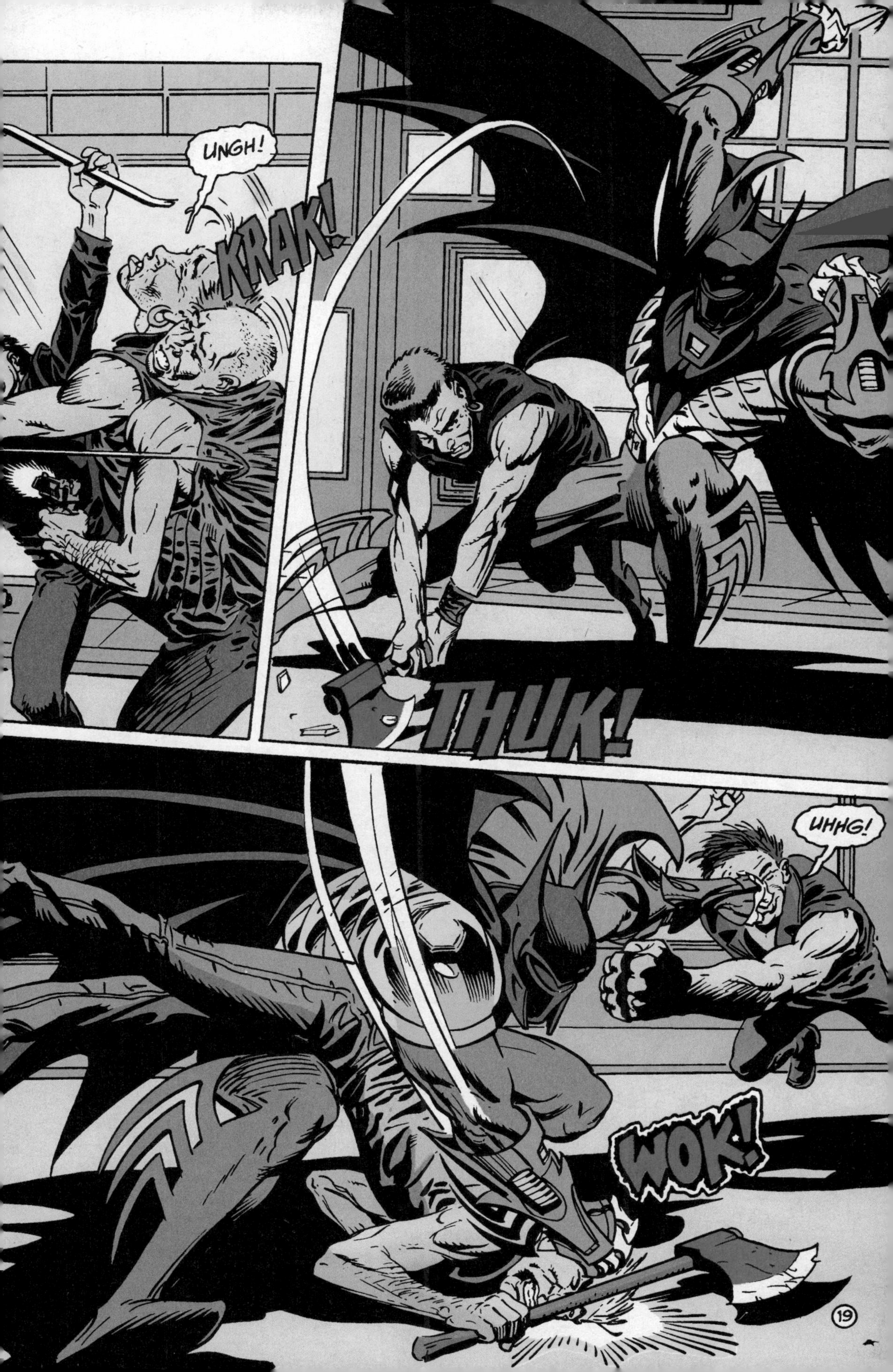
UNGH!
KRAK!
THUK!
UHHG!
WOK!
19

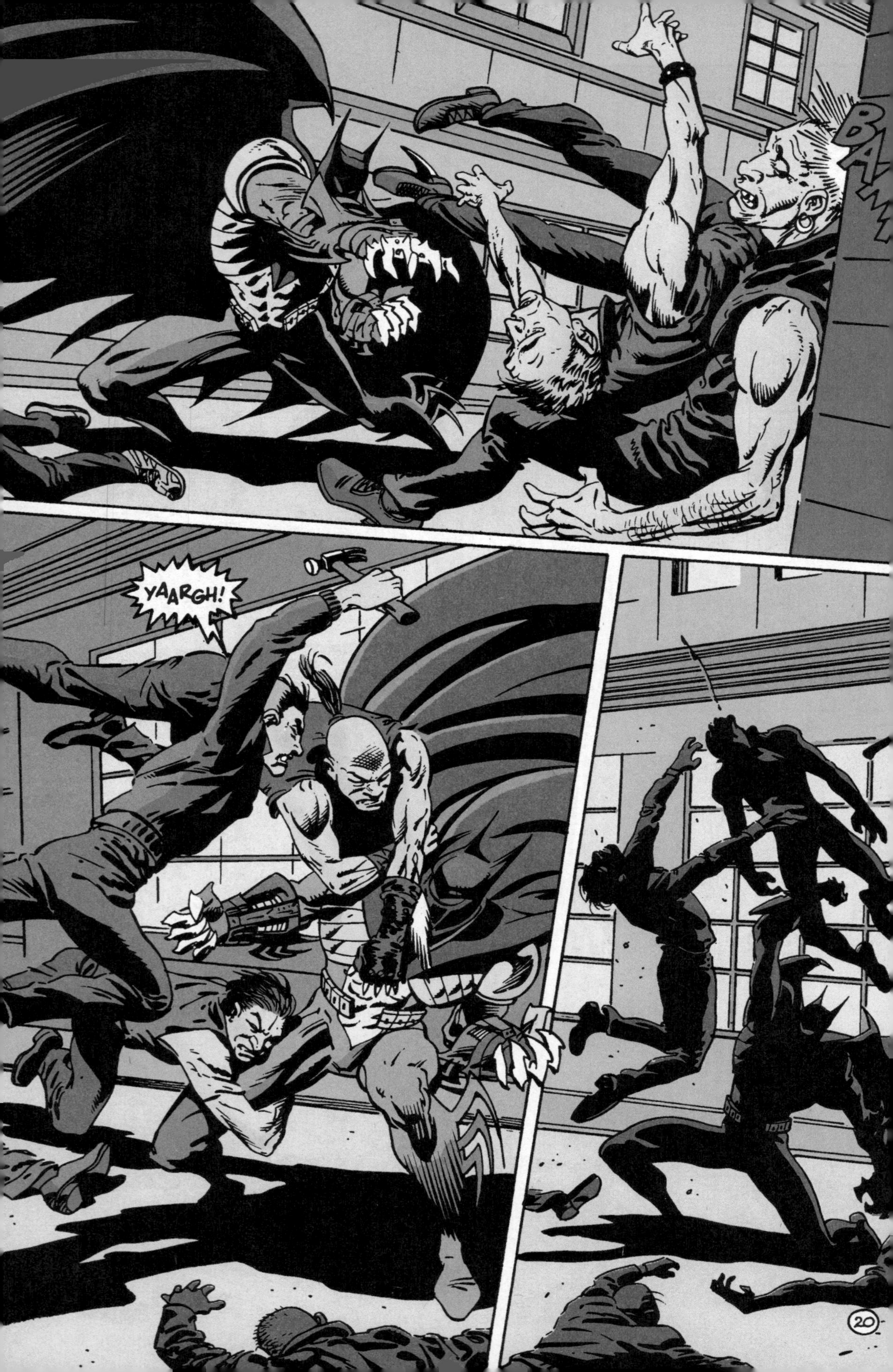
YAARGH!

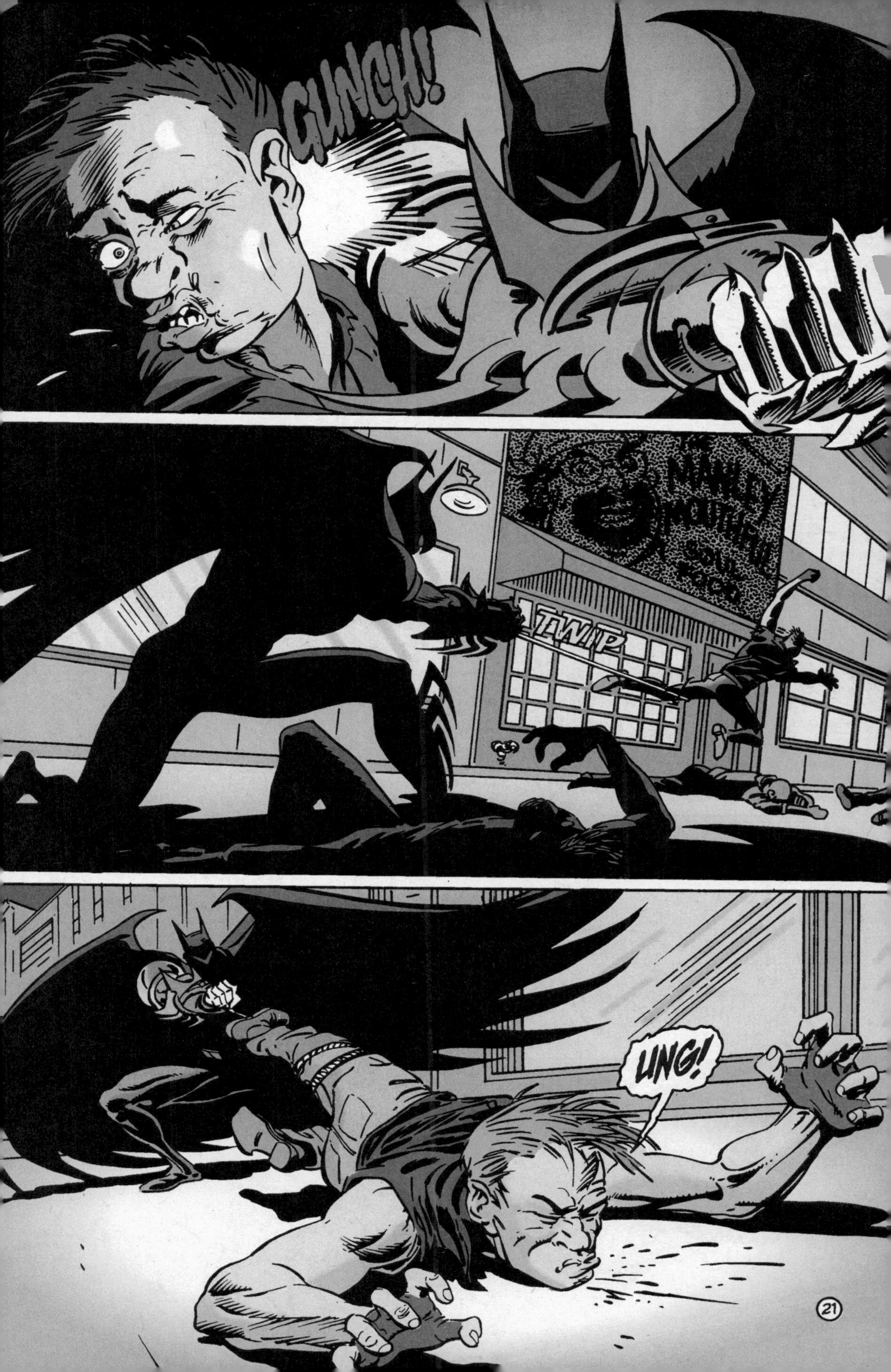
GUNCH!
TWIP
UNG!

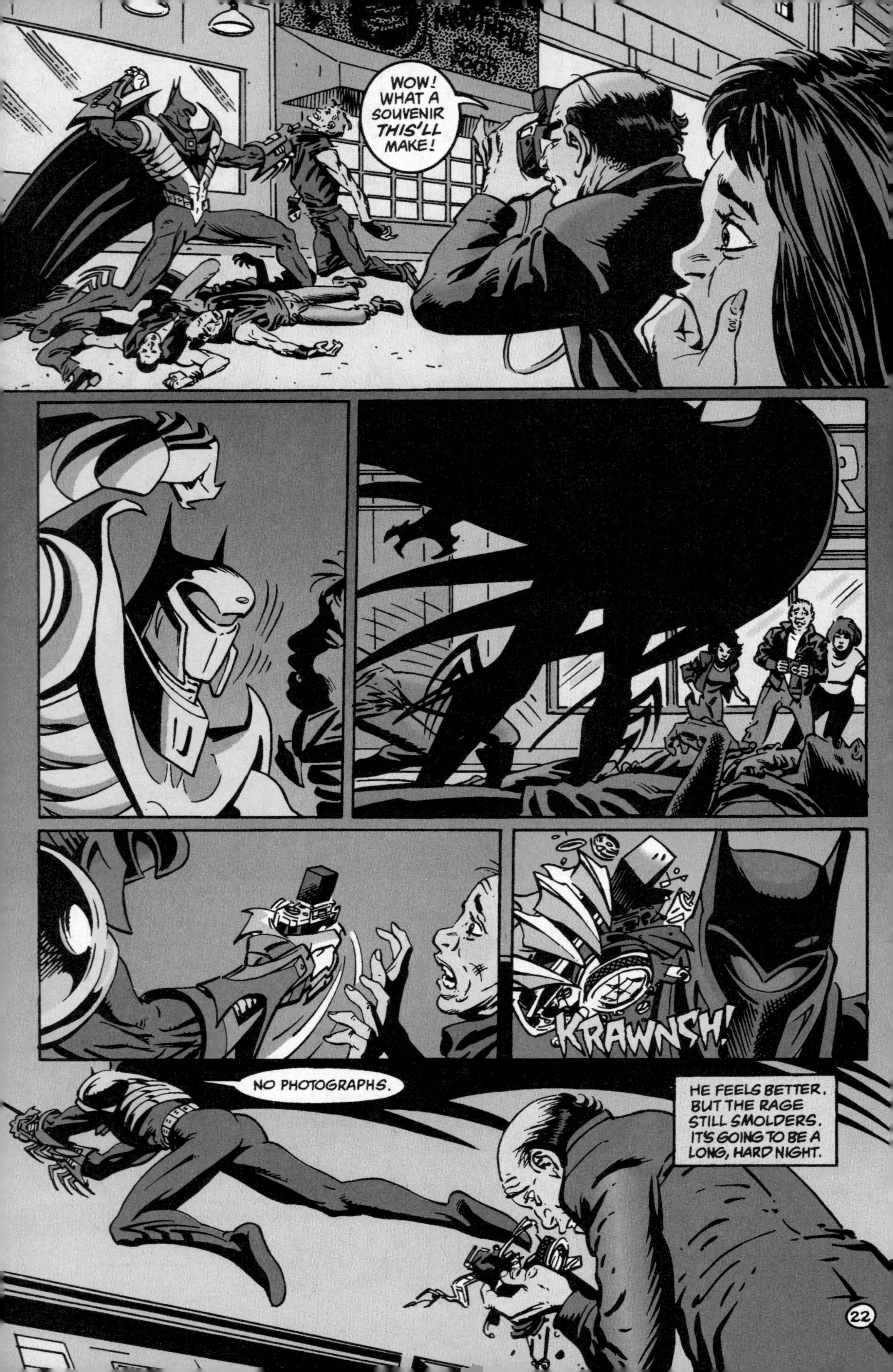
WOW! WHAT A SOUVENIR THIS'LL MAKE!
KRAWNSH!
NO PHOTOGRAPHS.
HE FEELS BETTER, BUT THE RAGE STILL SMOLDERS. IT'S GOING TO BE A LONG, HARD NIGHT.

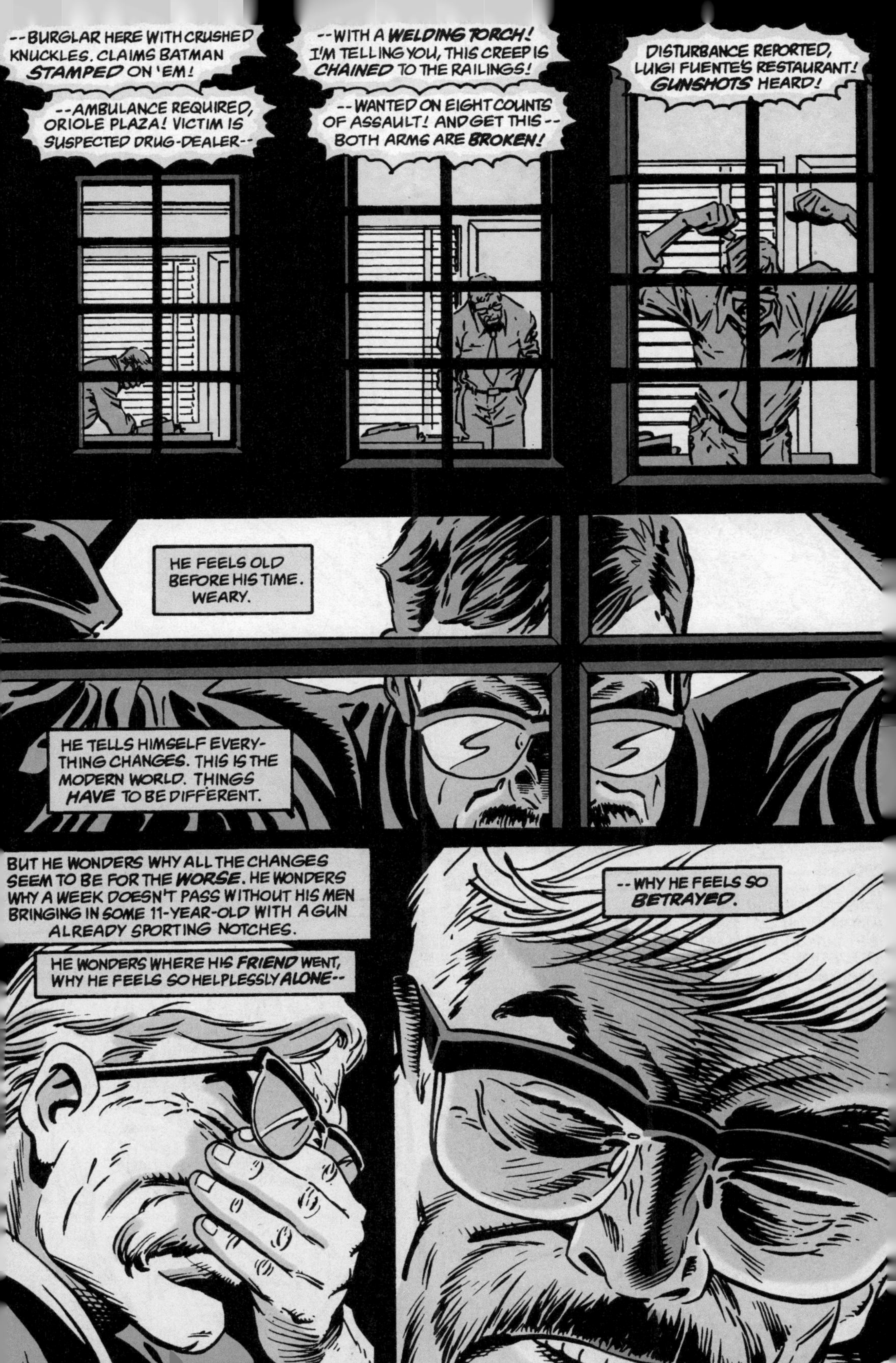
--BURGLAR HERE WITH CRUSHED KNUCKLES. CLAIMS BATMAN STAMPED ON 'EM!
--AMBULANCE REQUIRED, ORIOLE PLAZA! VICTIM IS SUSPECTED DRUG-DEALER--
--WITH A WELDING TORCH! I'M TELLING YOU, THIS CREEP IS CHAINED TO THE RAILINGS!
--WANTED ON EIGHT COUNTS OF ASSAULT! AND GET THIS-- BOTH ARMS ARE BROKEN!
DISTURBANCE REPORTED, LUIGI FUENTE'S RESTAURANT! GUNSHOTS HEARD!
HE FEELS OLD BEFORE HIS TIME. WEARY.
HE TELLS HIMSELF EVERYTHING CHANGES. THIS IS THE MODERN WORLD. THINGS HAVE TO BE DIFFERENT.
BUT HE WONDERS WHY ALL THE CHANGES SEEM TO BE FOR THE WORSE. HE WONDERS WHY A WEEK DOESN'T PASS WITHOUT HIS MEN BRINGING IN SOME 11-YEAR-OLD WITH A GUN ALREADY SPORTING NOTCHES.
HE WONDERS WHERE HIS FRIEND WENT, WHY HE FEELS SO HELPLESSLY ALONE--
--WHY HE FEELS SO BETRAYED.
2

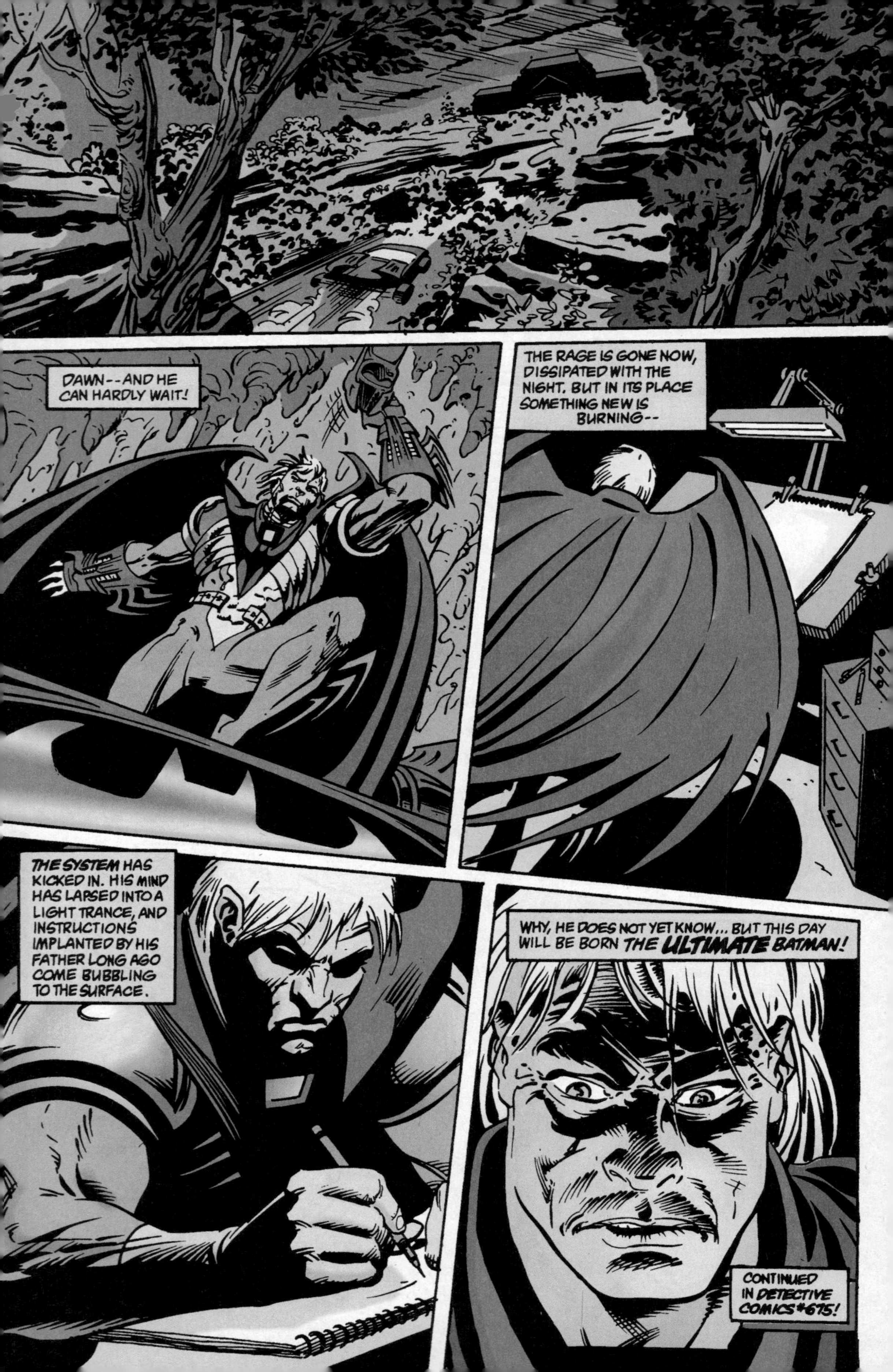
DAWN--AND HE CAN HARDLY WAIT!
THE RAGE IS GONE NOW, DISSIPATED WITH THE NIGHT. BUT IN ITS PLACE SOMETHING NEW IS BURNING--
THE SYSTEM HAS KICKED IN. HIS MIND HAS LAPSED INTO A LIGHT TRANCE, AND INSTRUCTIONS IMPLANTED BY HIS FATHER LONG AGO COME BUBBLING TO THE SURFACE.
WHY, HE DOES NOT YET KNOW... BUT THIS DAY WILL BE BORN THE ULTIMATE BATMAN!
CONTINUED IN DETECTIVE COMICS #675!

Cover art by KELLEY JONES

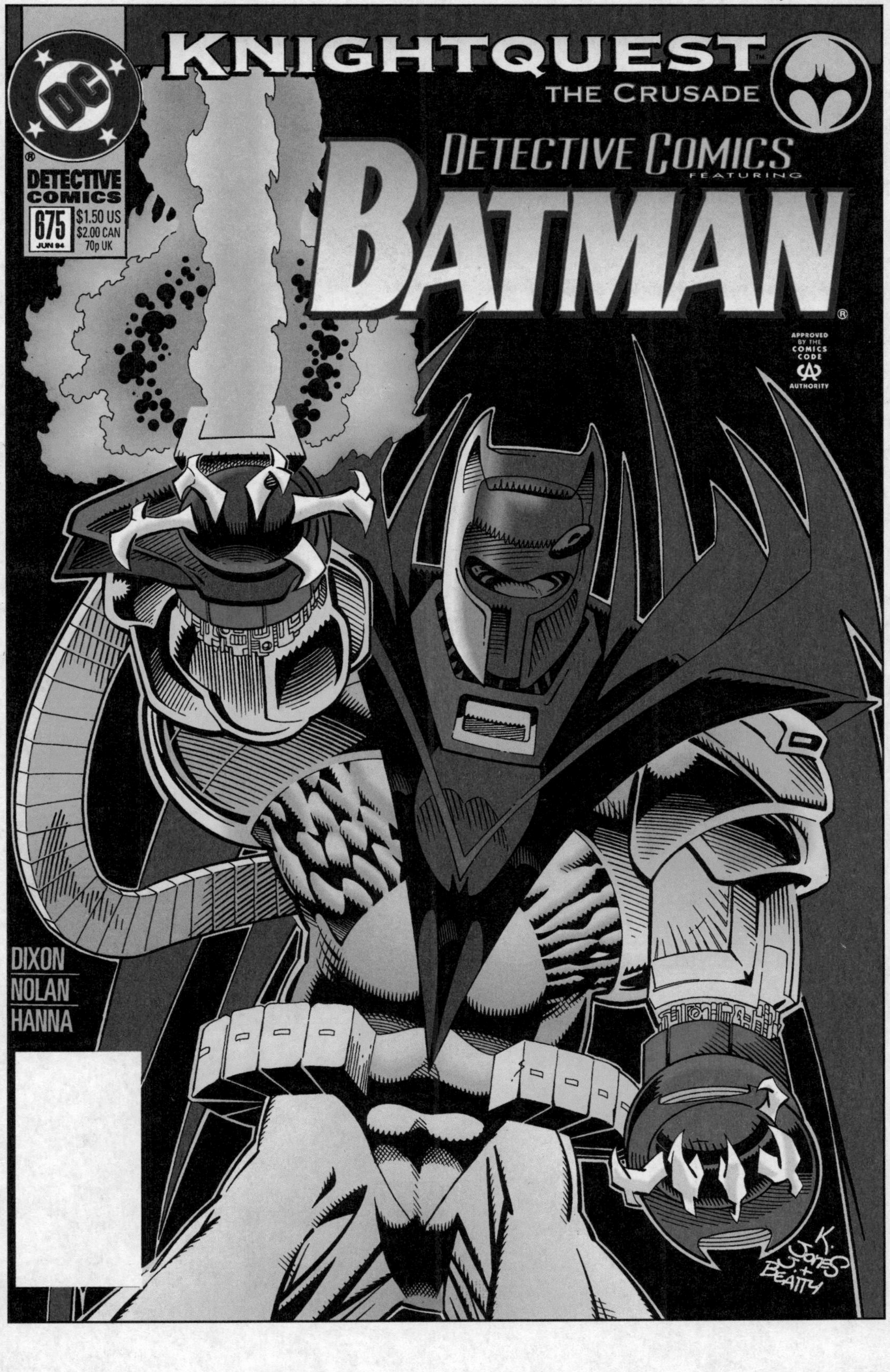
KNIGHTQUEST
THE CRUSADE
DETECTIVE COMICS
FEATURING
BATMAN
DETECTIVE COMICS
675
$1.50 US
$2.00 CAN
70p UK
JUN 94
APPROVED BY THE COMICS CODE AUTHORITY
DIXON
NOLAN
HANNA
K. JONES + BEATTY

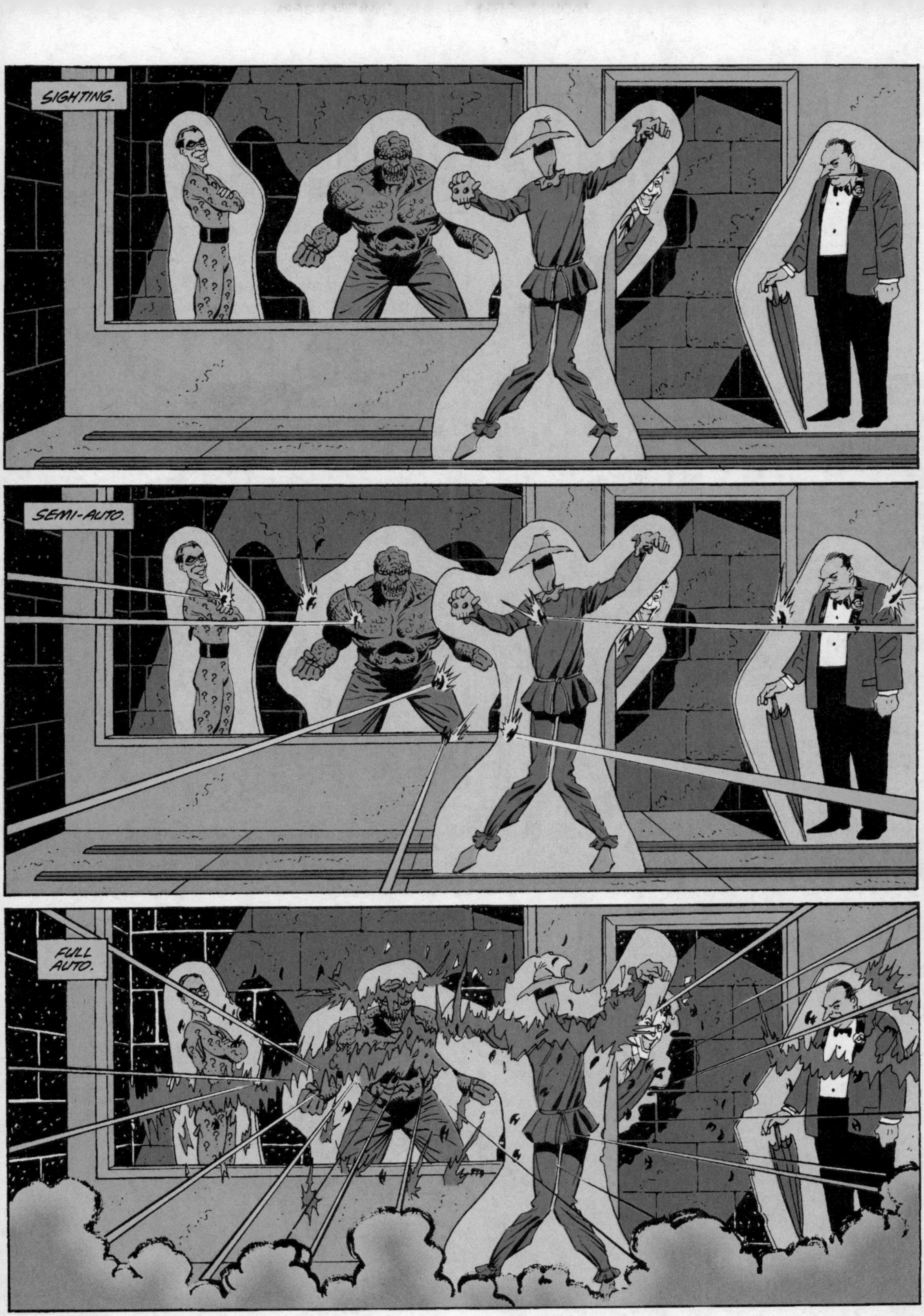
SIGHTING.
SEMI-AUTO.
FULL AUTO.

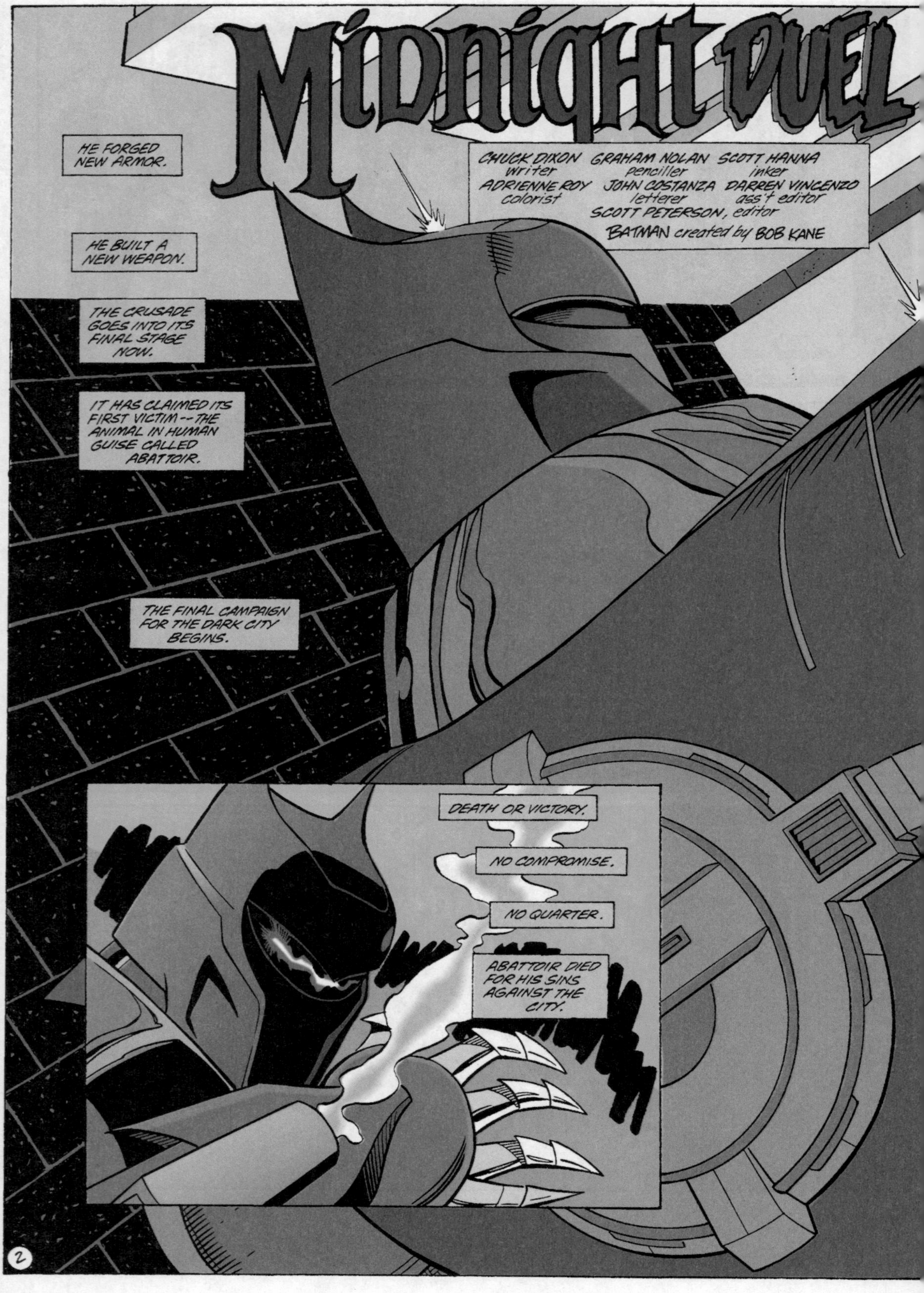
MIDNIGHT DUEL
HE FORGED NEW ARMOR.
HE BUILT A NEW WEAPON.
THE CRUSADE GOES INTO ITS FINAL STAGE NOW.
IT HAS CLAIMED ITS FIRST VICTIM -- THE ANIMAL IN HUMAN GUISE CALLED ABATTOIR.
THE FINAL CAMPAIGN FOR THE DARK CITY BEGINS.
CHUCK DIXON writer GRAHAM NOLAN penciller SCOTT HANNA inker
ADRIENNE ROY colorist JOHN COSTANZA letterer DARREN VINCENZO ass't editor
SCOTT PETERSON, editor
BATMAN created by BOB KANE
DEATH OR VICTORY.
NO COMPROMISE.
NO QUARTER.
ABATTOIR DIED FOR HIS SINS AGAINST THE CITY.
2

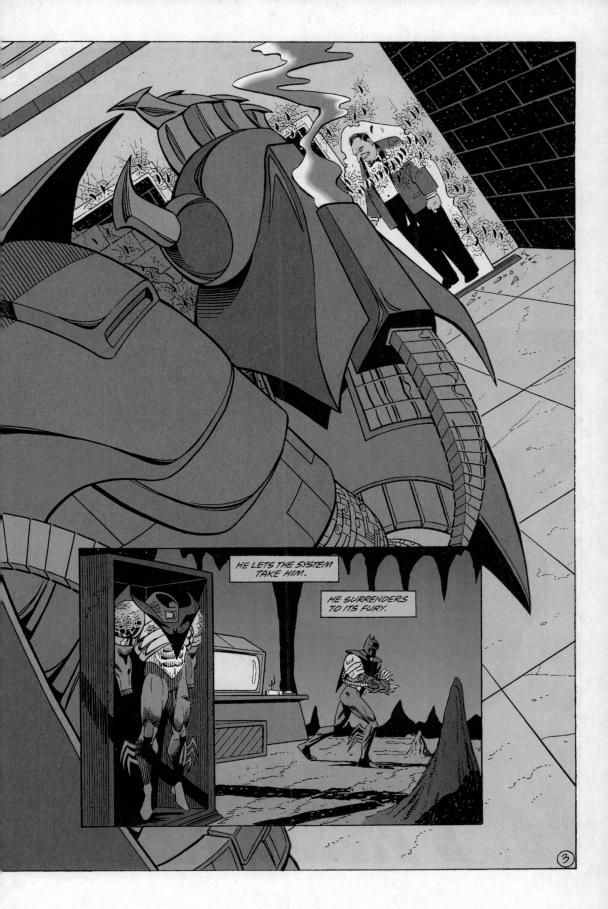

HE LETS THE SYSTEM TAKE HIM.

HE SURRENDERS TO ITS FURY.

③

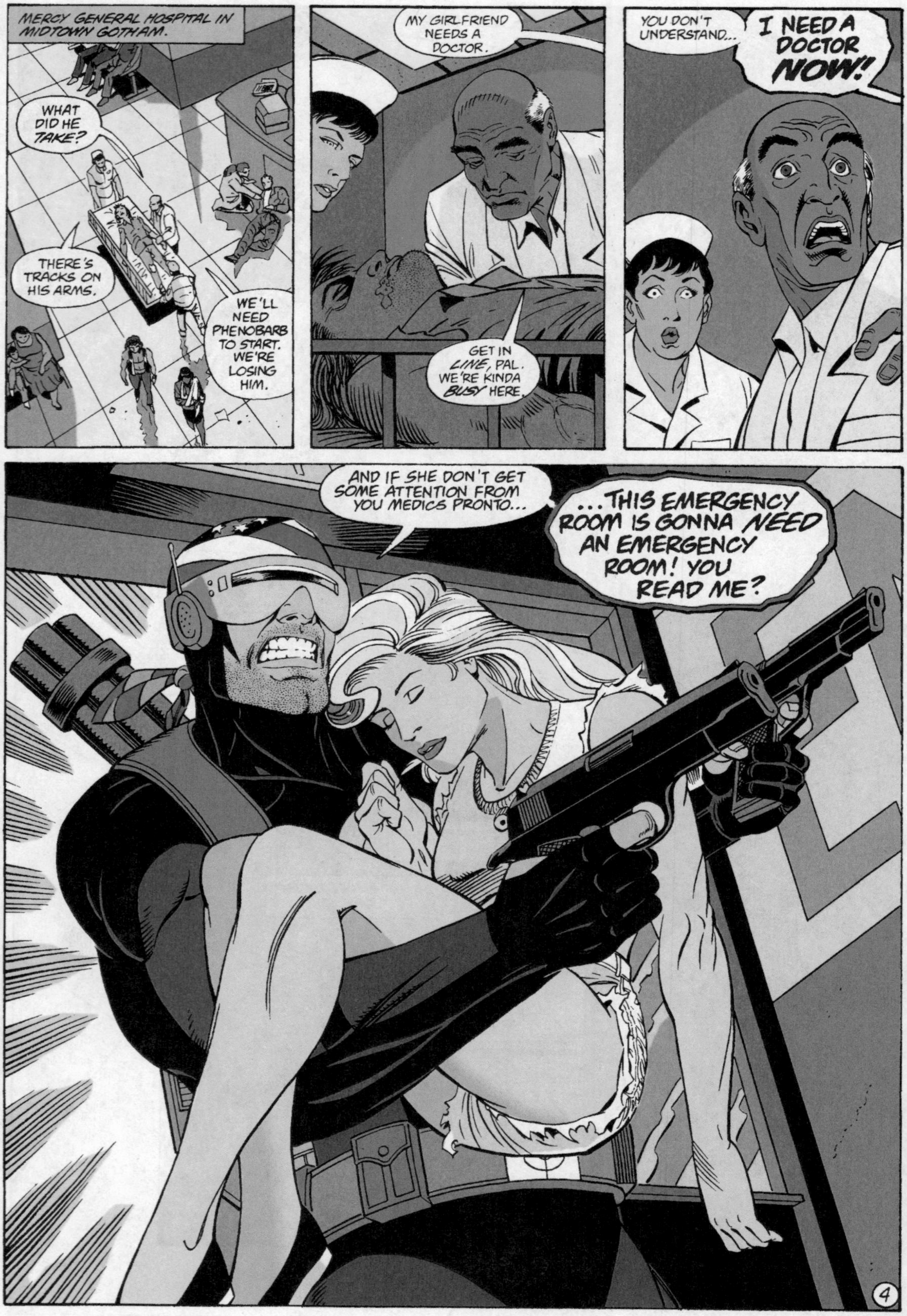
MERCY GENERAL HOSPITAL IN MIDTOWN GOTHAM.
WHAT DID HE TAKE?
THERE'S TRACKS ON HIS ARMS.
WE'LL NEED PHENOBARB TO START. WE'RE LOSING HIM.
MY GIRLFRIEND NEEDS A DOCTOR.
GET IN LINE, PAL. WE'RE KINDA BUSY HERE.
YOU DON'T UNDERSTAND...
I NEED A DOCTOR NOW!
AND IF SHE DON'T GET SOME ATTENTION FROM YOU MEDICS PRONTO...
...THIS EMERGENCY ROOM IS GONNA NEED AN EMERGENCY ROOM! YOU READ ME?
4

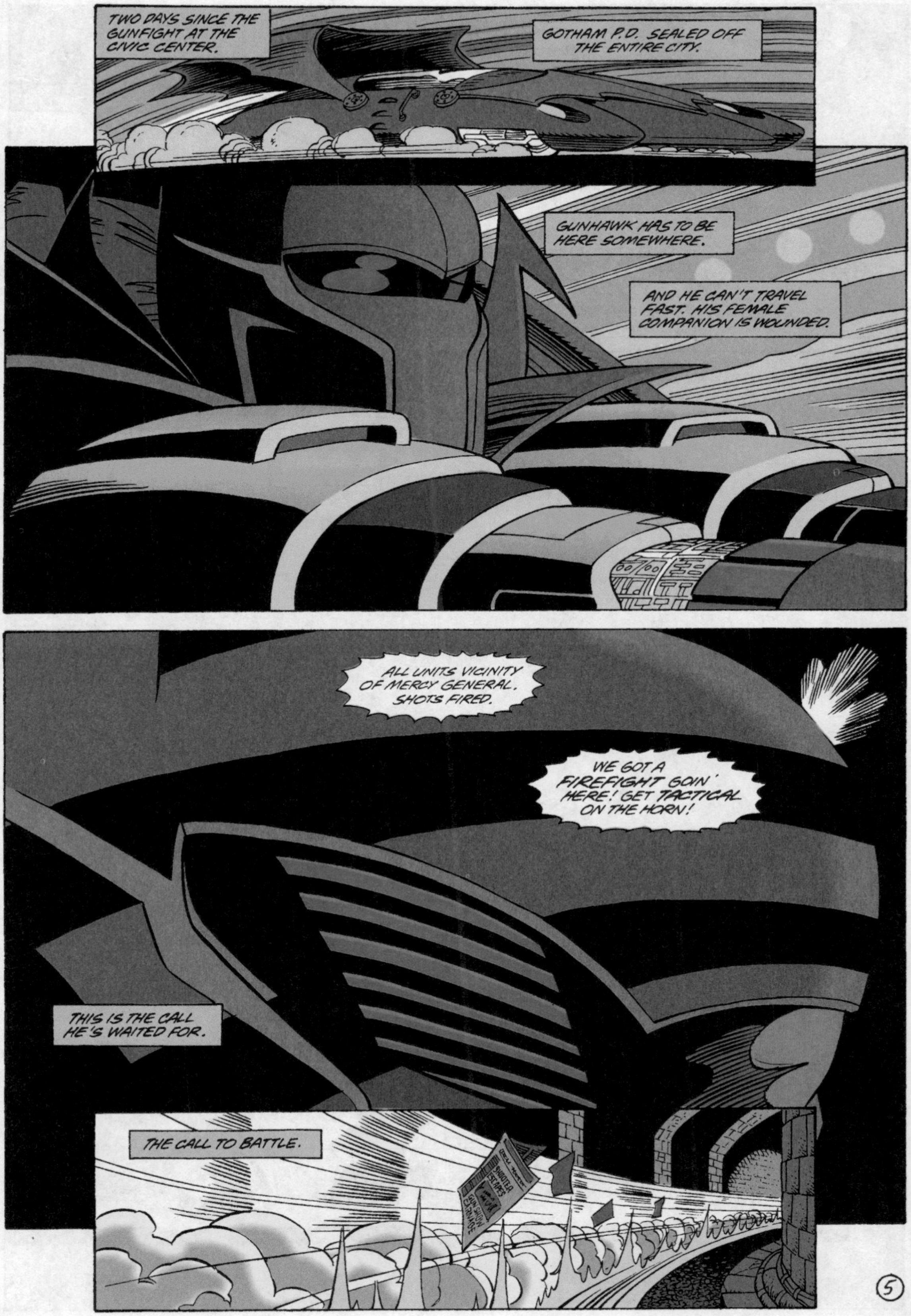
TWO DAYS SINCE THE GUNFIGHT AT THE CIVIC CENTER.
GOTHAM P.D. SEALED OFF THE ENTIRE CITY.
GUNHAWK HAS TO BE HERE SOMEWHERE.
AND HE CAN'T TRAVEL FAST. HIS FEMALE COMPANION IS WOUNDED.
ALL UNITS VICINITY OF MERCY GENERAL. SHOTS FIRED.
WE GOT A FIREFIGHT GOIN' HERE! GET TACTICAL ON THE HORN!
THIS IS THE CALL HE'S WAITED FOR.
THE CALL TO BATTLE.
5

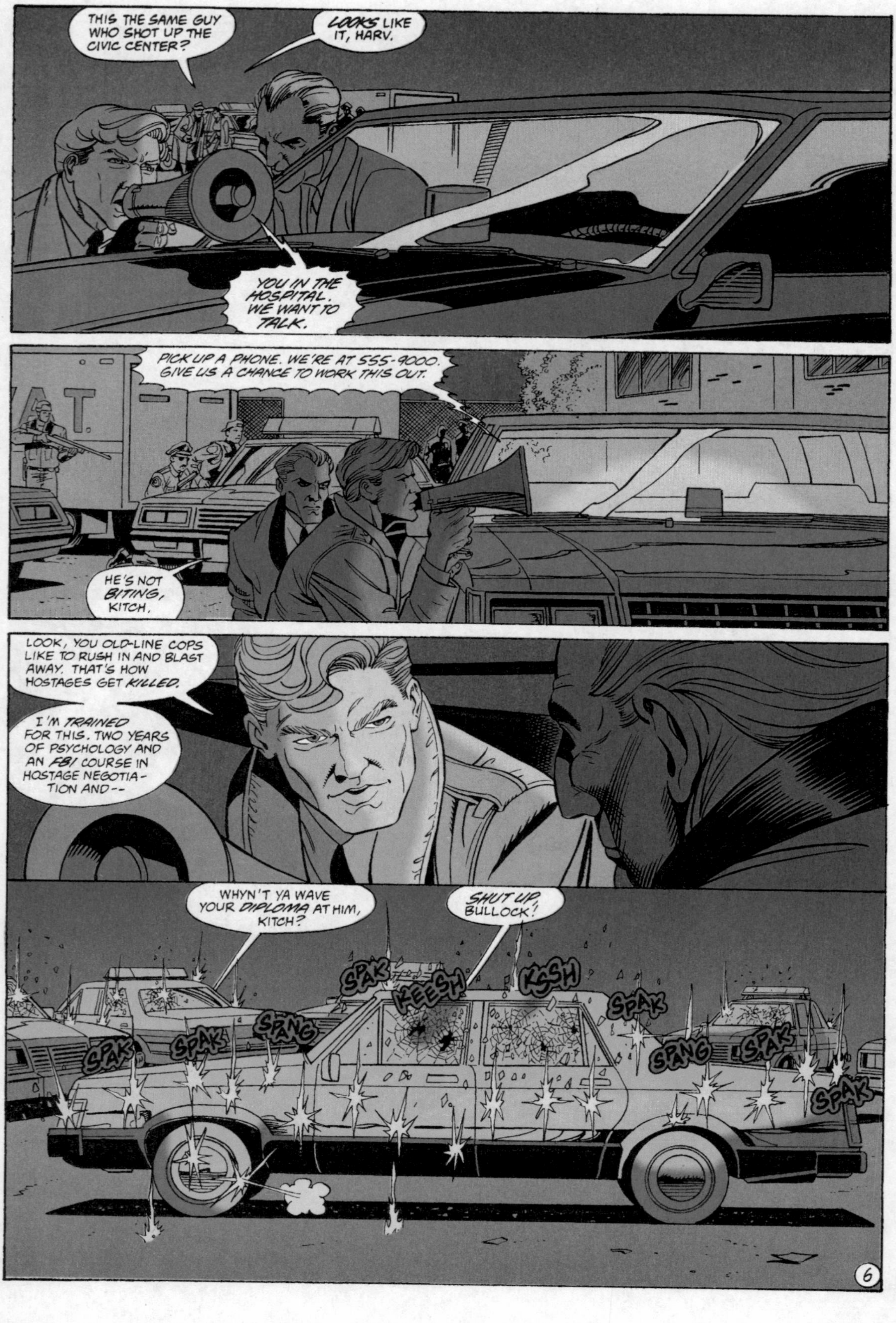
THIS THE SAME GUY WHO SHOT UP THE CIVIC CENTER?
LOOKS LIKE IT, HARV.
YOU IN THE HOSPITAL. WE WANT TO TALK.
PICK UP A PHONE. WE'RE AT 555-9000. GIVE US A CHANCE TO WORK THIS OUT.
HE'S NOT BITING, KITCH.
LOOK, YOU OLD-LINE COPS LIKE TO RUSH IN AND BLAST AWAY. THAT'S HOW HOSTAGES GET KILLED.
I'M TRAINED FOR THIS. TWO YEARS OF PSYCHOLOGY AND AN FBI COURSE IN HOSTAGE NEGOTIATION AND--
WHYN'T YA WAVE YOUR DIPLOMA AT HIM, KITCH?
SHUT UP, BULLOCK!
SPAK
KEESH
KSSH
SPAK
SPANG
SPAK
SPAK
SPANG
SPAK
SPAK
6

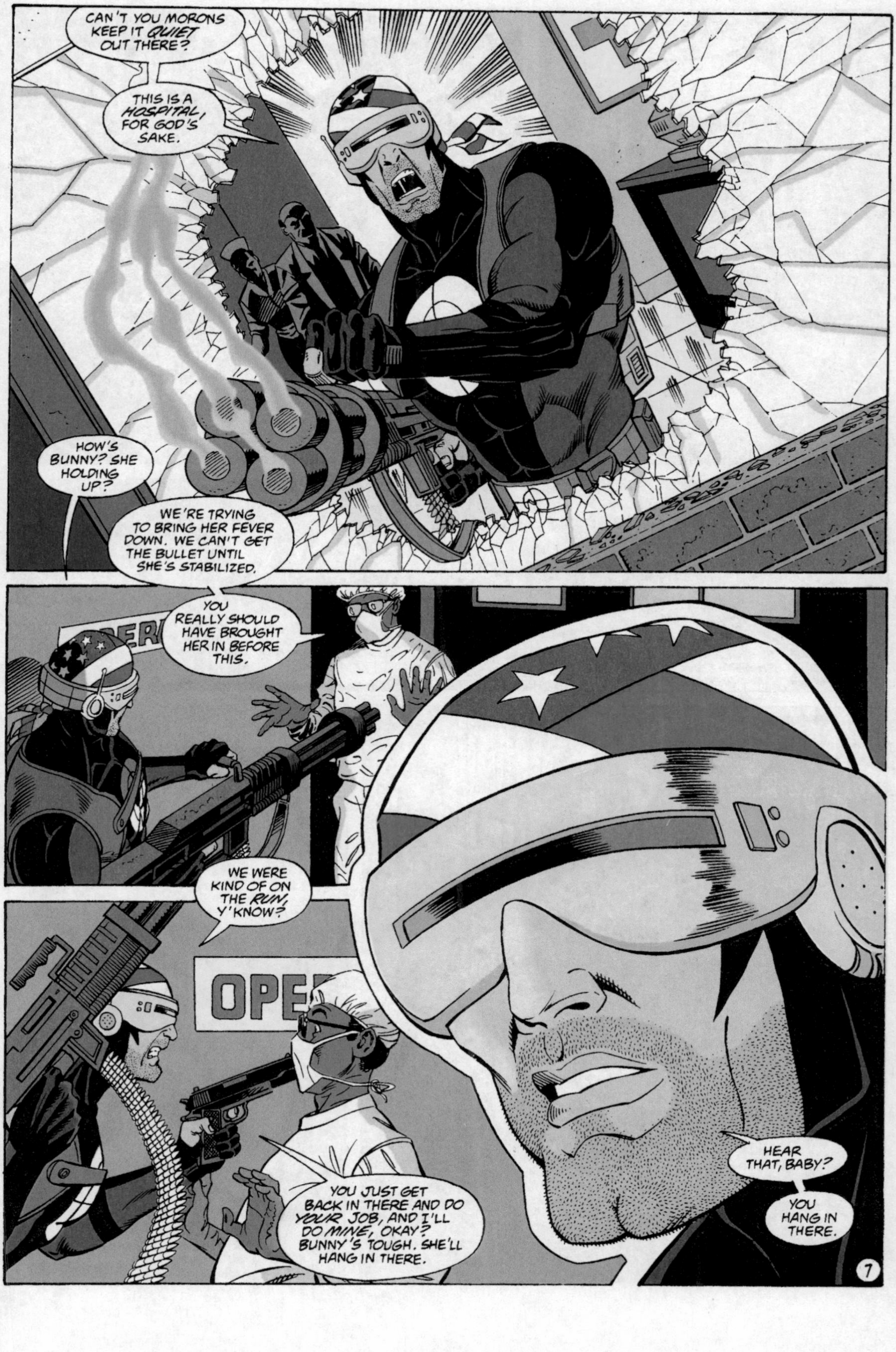

CAN'T YOU MORONS KEEP IT QUIET OUT THERE?
THIS IS A HOSPITAL, FOR GOD'S SAKE.
HOW'S BUNNY? SHE HOLDING UP?
WE'RE TRYING TO BRING HER FEVER DOWN. WE CAN'T GET THE BULLET UNTIL SHE'S STABILIZED.
YOU REALLY SHOULD HAVE BROUGHT HER IN BEFORE THIS.
WE WERE KIND OF ON THE RUN, Y'KNOW?
OPE
YOU JUST GET BACK IN THERE AND DO YOUR JOB, AND I'LL DO MINE, OKAY? BUNNY'S TOUGH. SHE'LL HANG IN THERE.
HEAR THAT, BABY?
YOU HANG IN THERE.
7

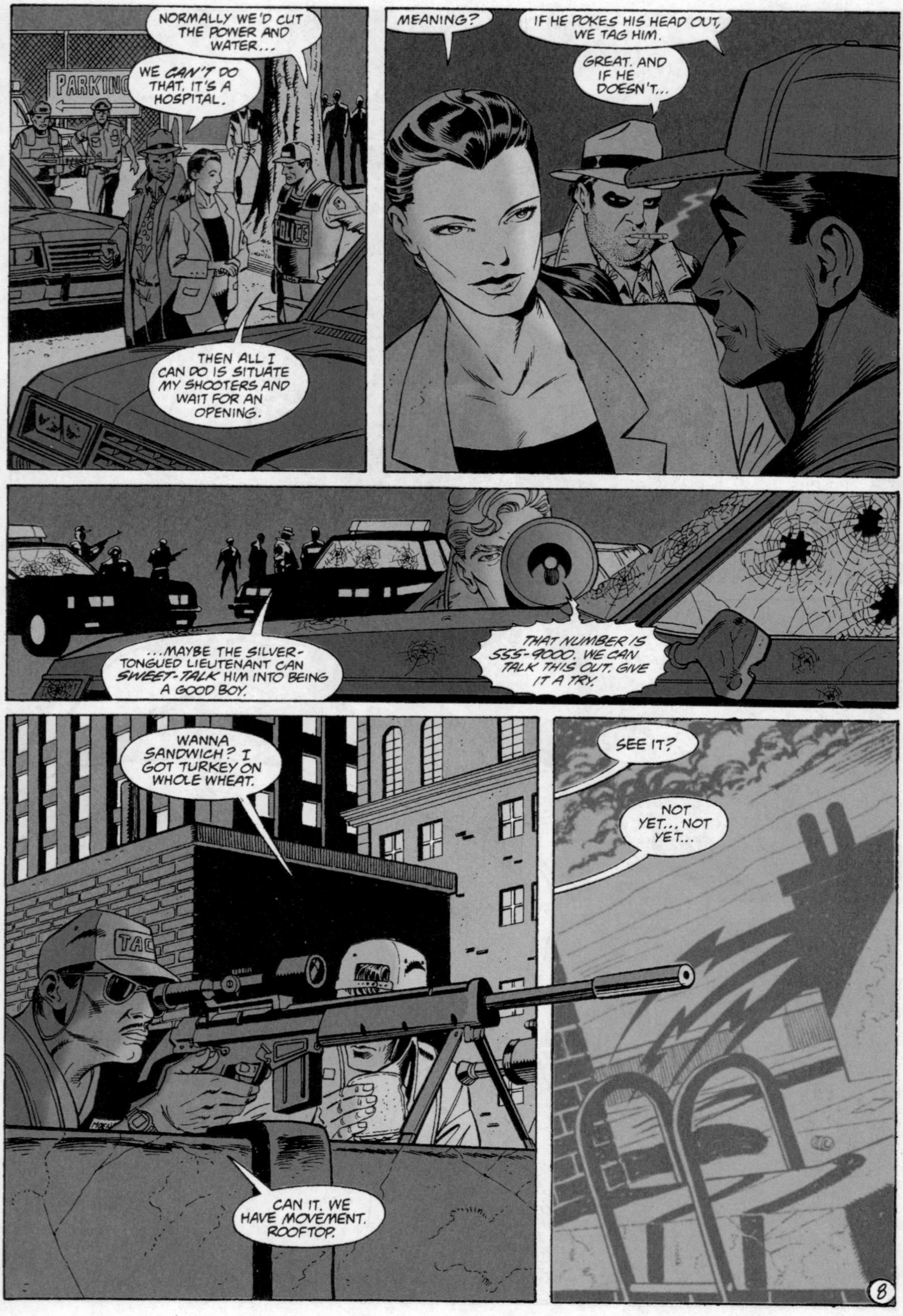
NORMALLY WE'D CUT THE POWER AND WATER...
PARKING
WE CAN'T DO THAT. IT'S A HOSPITAL.
POLICE
THEN ALL I CAN DO IS SITUATE MY SHOOTERS AND WAIT FOR AN OPENING.
MEANING?
IF HE POKES HIS HEAD OUT, WE TAG HIM.
GREAT. AND IF HE DOESN'T...
...MAYBE THE SILVER-TONGUED LIEUTENANT CAN SWEET-TALK HIM INTO BEING A GOOD BOY.
THAT NUMBER IS 555-9000. WE CAN TALK THIS OUT. GIVE IT A TRY.
WANNA SANDWICH? I GOT TURKEY ON WHOLE WHEAT.
CAN IT. WE HAVE MOVEMENT. ROOFTOP.
SEE IT?
NOT YET... NOT YET...
8

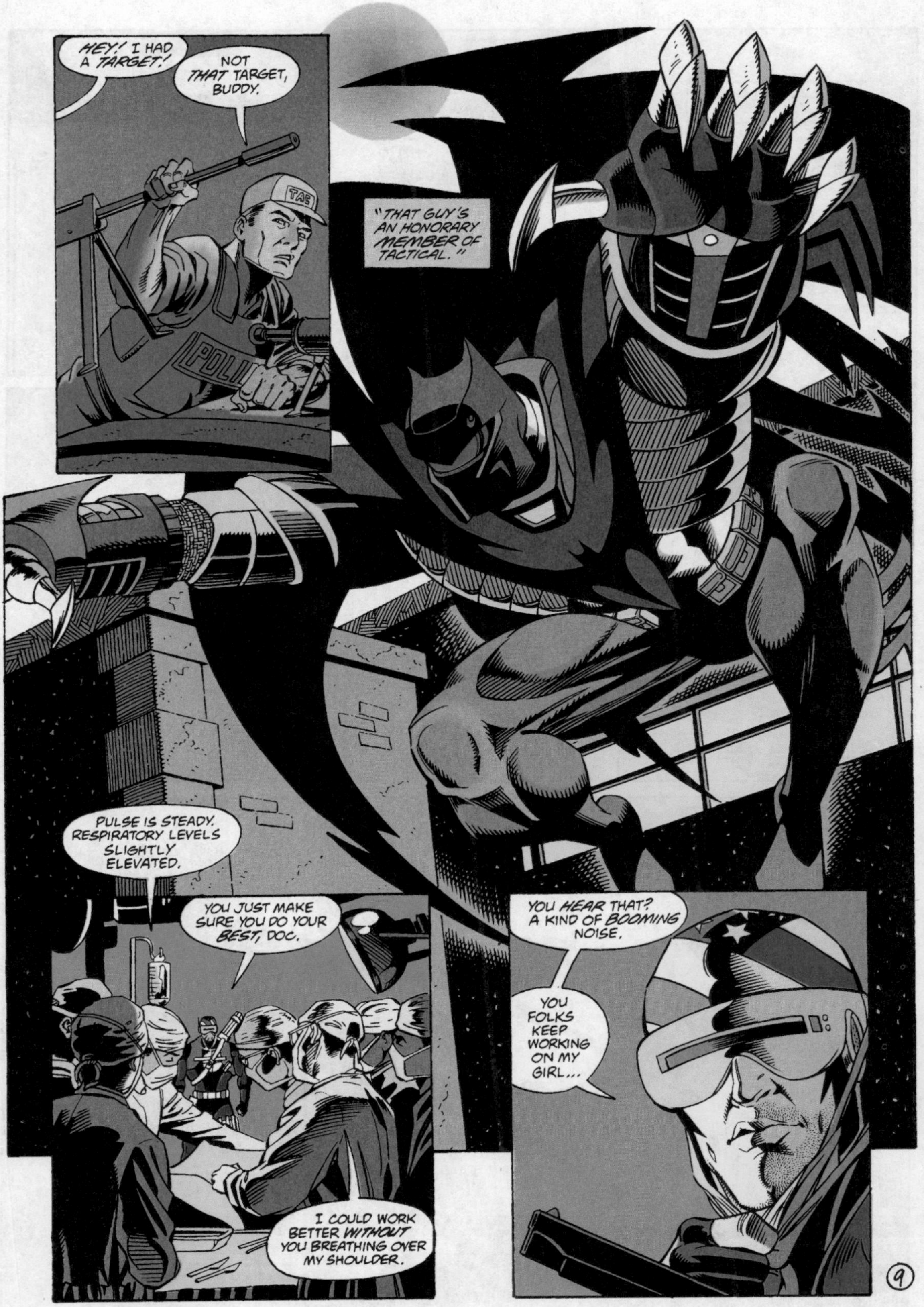
HEY! I HAD A TARGET!
NOT THAT TARGET, BUDDY.
TAB
POLI
"THAT GUY'S AN HONORARY MEMBER OF TACTICAL."
PULSE IS STEADY. RESPIRATORY LEVELS SLIGHTLY ELEVATED.
YOU JUST MAKE SURE YOU DO YOUR BEST, DOC.
I COULD WORK BETTER WITHOUT YOU BREATHING OVER MY SHOULDER.
YOU HEAR THAT? A KIND OF BOOMING NOISE.
YOU FOLKS KEEP WORKING ON MY GIRL...
9

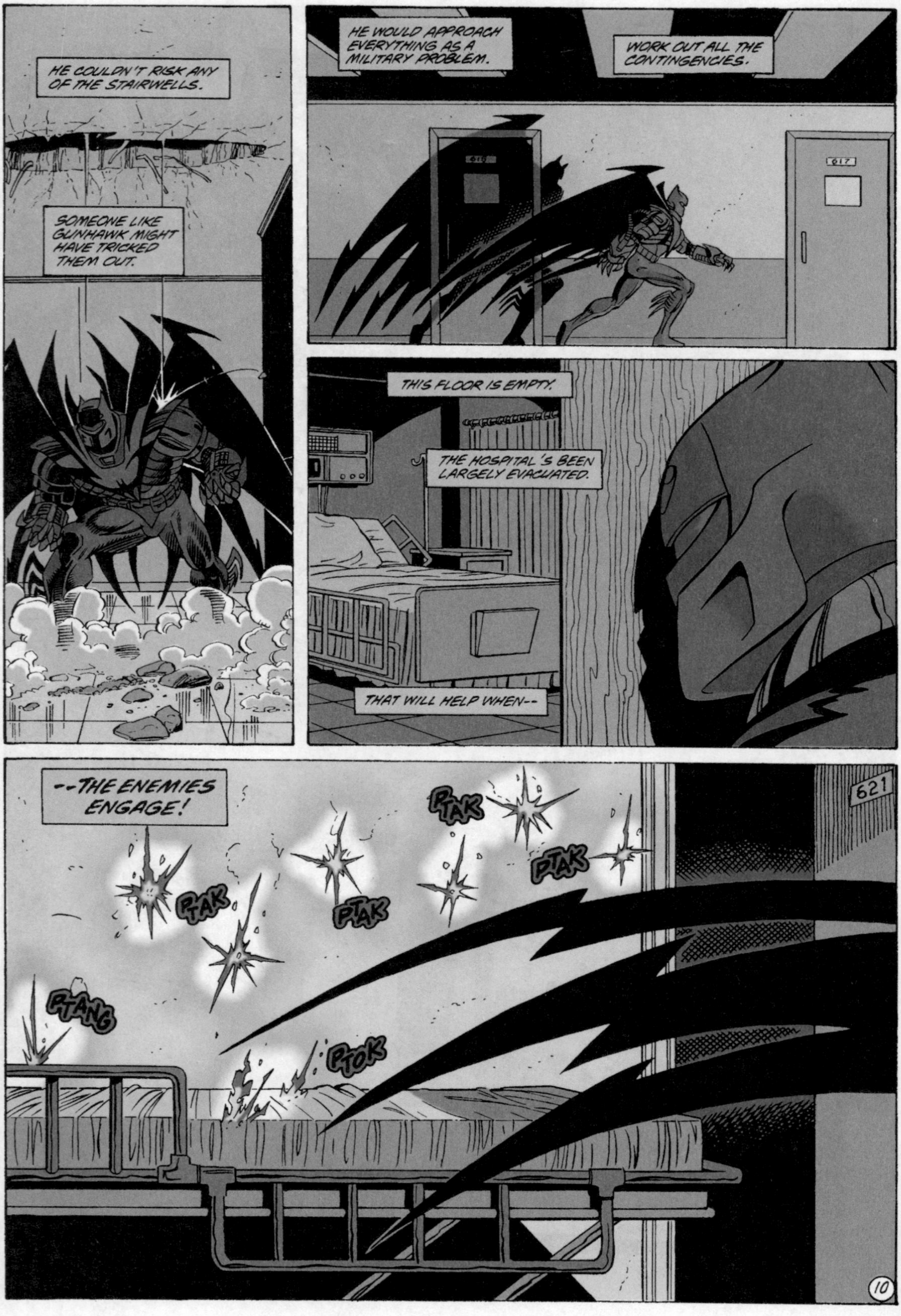
HE COULDN'T RISK ANY OF THE STAIRWELLS.
SOMEONE LIKE GUNHAWK MIGHT HAVE TRICKED THEM OUT.
HE WOULD APPROACH EVERYTHING AS A MILITARY PROBLEM.
WORK OUT ALL THE CONTINGENCIES.
617
THIS FLOOR IS EMPTY.
THE HOSPITAL'S BEEN LARGELY EVACUATED.
THAT WILL HELP WHEN--
--THE ENEMIES ENGAGE!
PTAK
PTAK
PTAK
PTAK
PTANG
PTOK
621
10

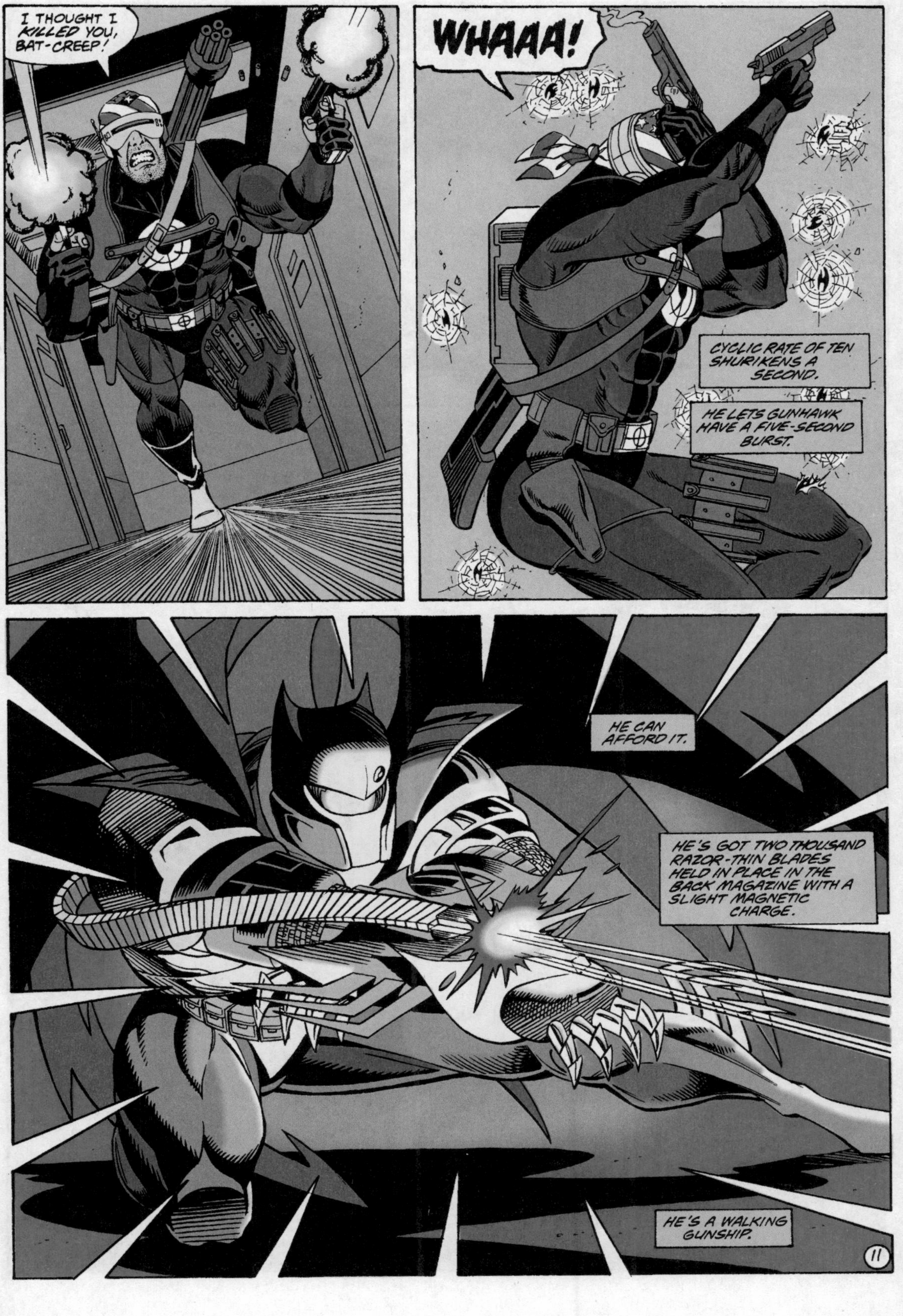
I THOUGHT I KILLED YOU, BAT-CREEP!
WHAAA!
CYCLIC RATE OF TEN SHURIKENS A SECOND.
HE LETS GUNHAWK HAVE A FIVE-SECOND BURST.
HE CAN AFFORD IT.
HE'S GOT TWO THOUSAND RAZOR-THIN BLADES HELD IN PLACE IN THE BACK MAGAZINE WITH A SLIGHT MAGNETIC CHARGE.
HE'S A WALKING GUNSHIP.
11

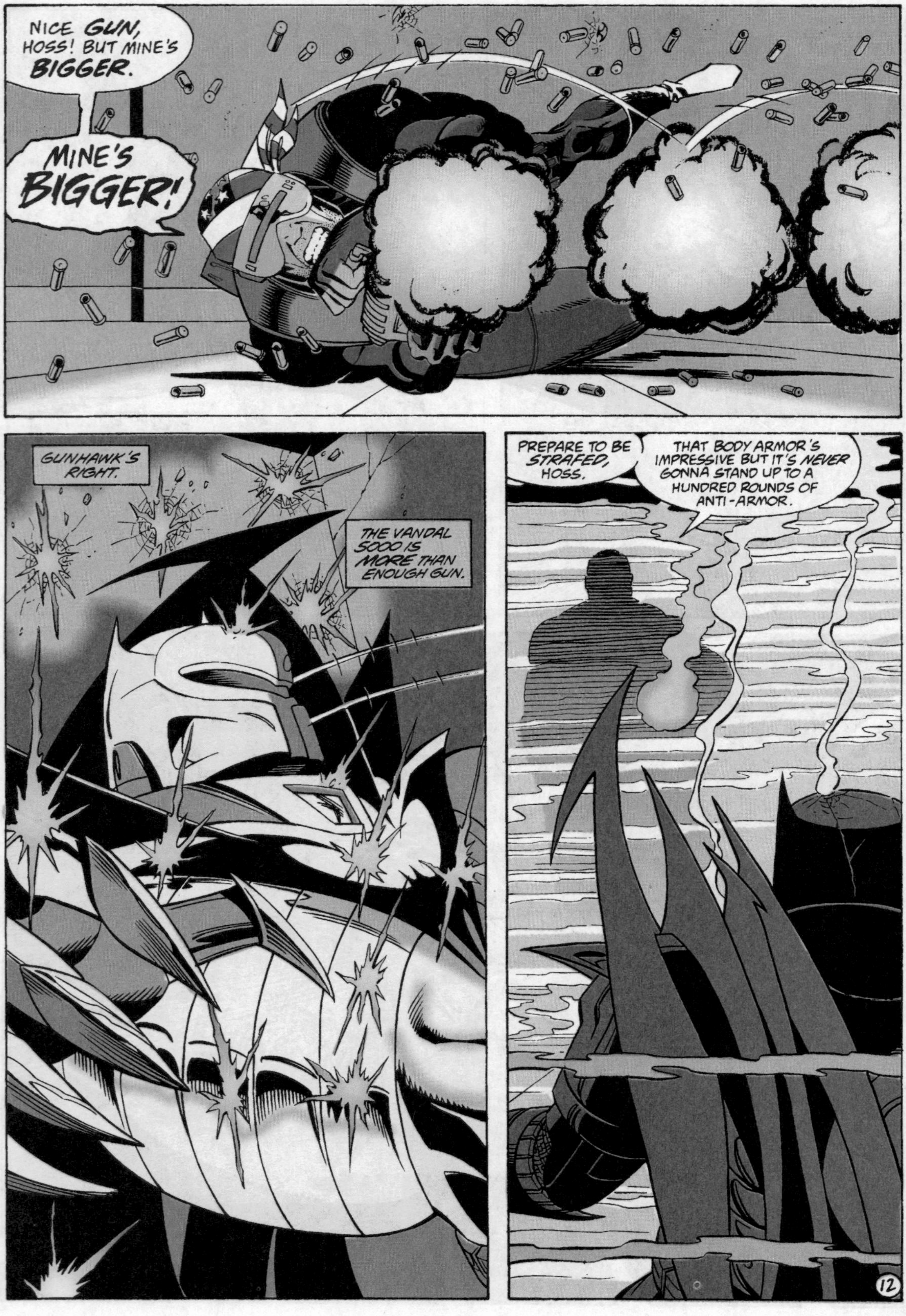
NICE GUN, HOSS! BUT MINE'S BIGGER.
MINE'S BIGGER!
GUNHAWK'S RIGHT.
THE VANDAL 5000 IS MORE THAN ENOUGH GUN.
PREPARE TO BE STRAFED, HOSS.
THAT BODY ARMOR'S IMPRESSIVE BUT IT'S NEVER GONNA STAND UP TO A HUNDRED ROUNDS OF ANTI-ARMOR.
12

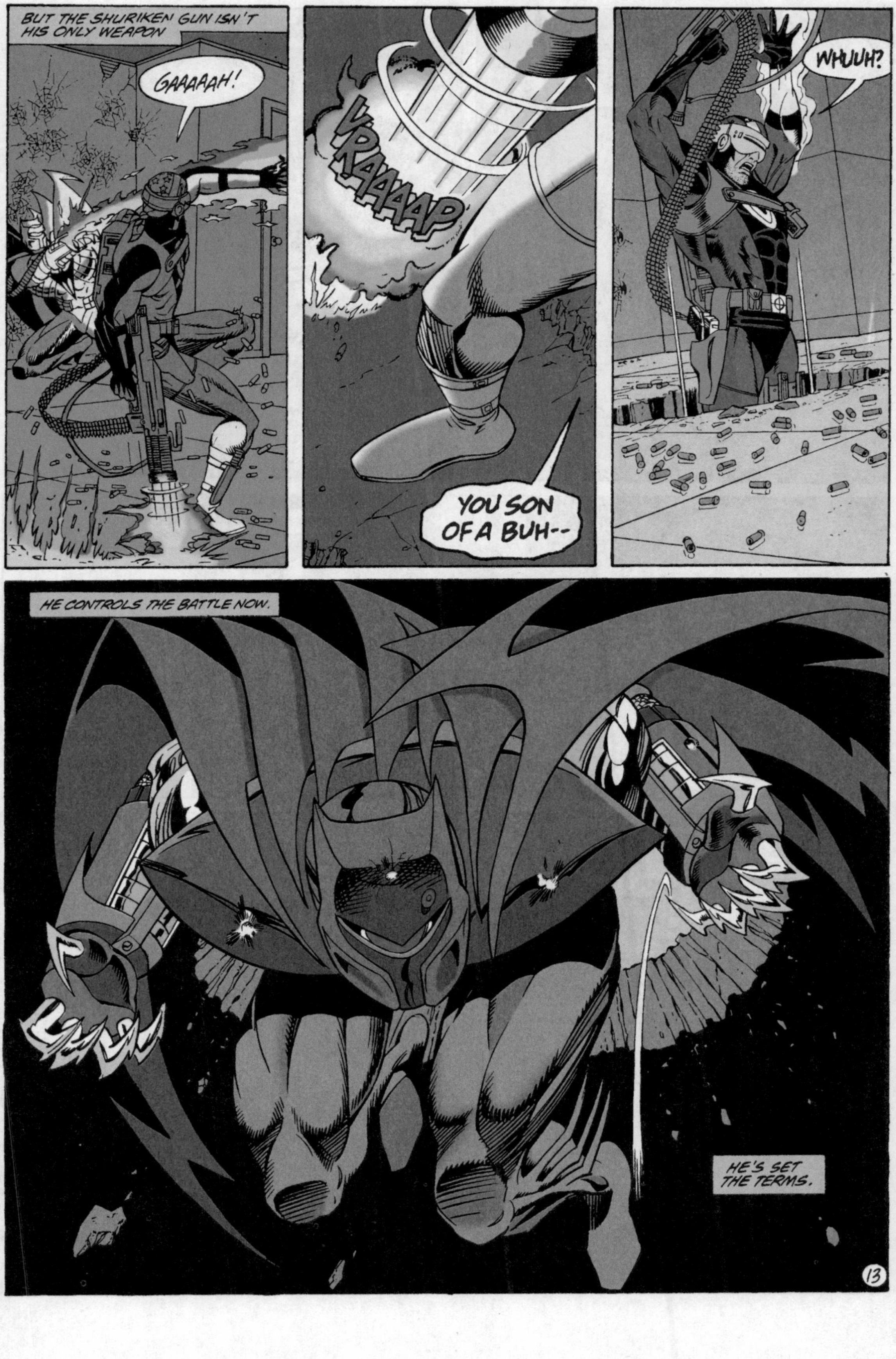
BUT THE SHURIKEN GUN ISN'T HIS ONLY WEAPON
GAAAAAH!
VRAAAAP
YOU SON OF A BUH--
WHUUH?
HE CONTROLS THE BATTLE NOW.
HE'S SET THE TERMS.
13

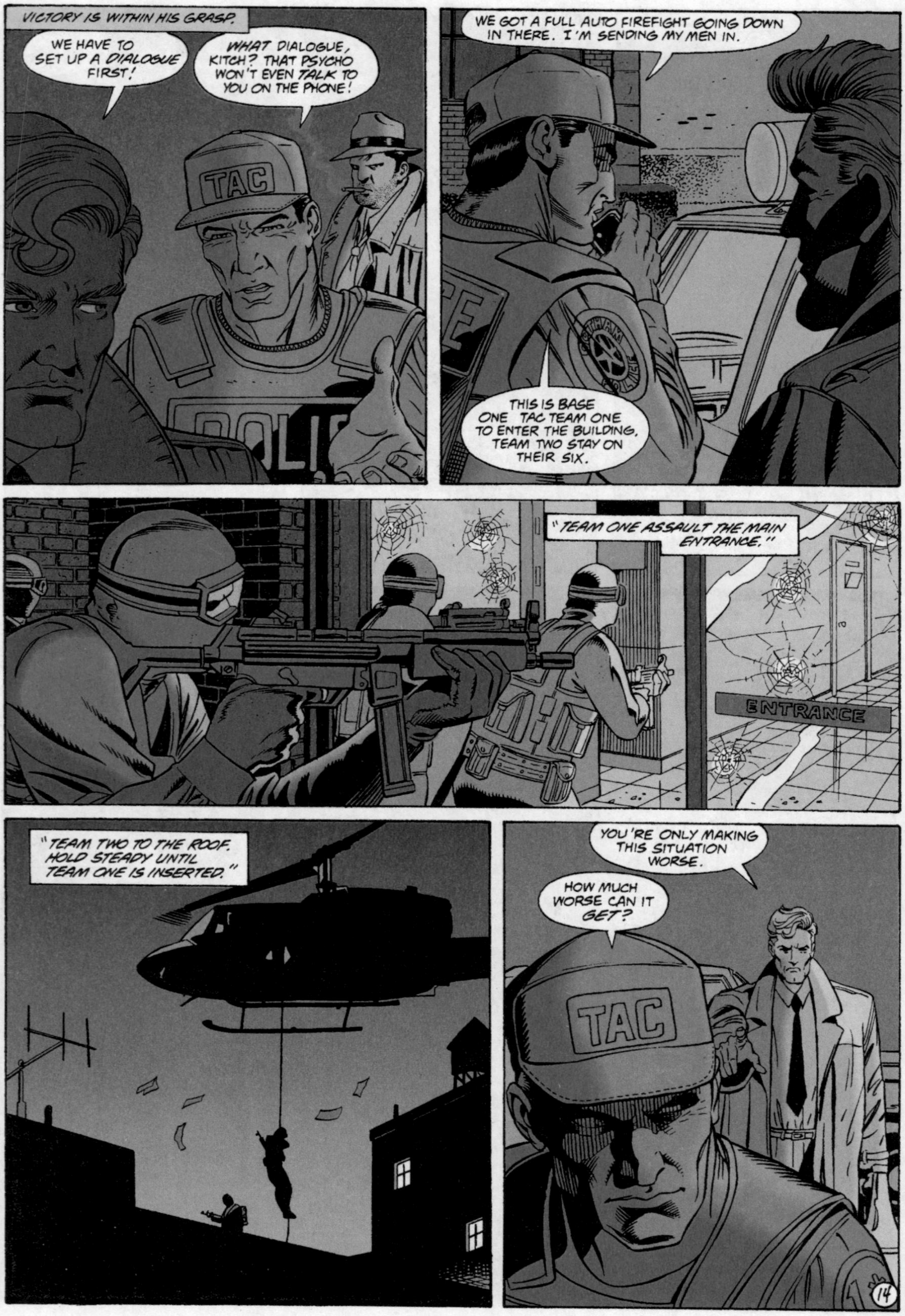
VICTORY IS WITHIN HIS GRASP.
WE HAVE TO SET UP A DIALOGUE FIRST!
WHAT DIALOGUE, KITCH? THAT PSYCHO WON'T EVEN TALK TO YOU ON THE PHONE!
TAC
WE GOT A FULL AUTO FIREFIGHT GOING DOWN IN THERE. I'M SENDING MY MEN IN.
THIS IS BASE ONE. TAC TEAM ONE TO ENTER THE BUILDING, TEAM TWO STAY ON THEIR SIX.
"TEAM ONE ASSAULT THE MAIN ENTRANCE."
ENTRANCE
"TEAM TWO TO THE ROOF. HOLD STEADY UNTIL TEAM ONE IS INSERTED."
YOU'RE ONLY MAKING THIS SITUATION WORSE.
HOW MUCH WORSE CAN IT GET?
TAC
14

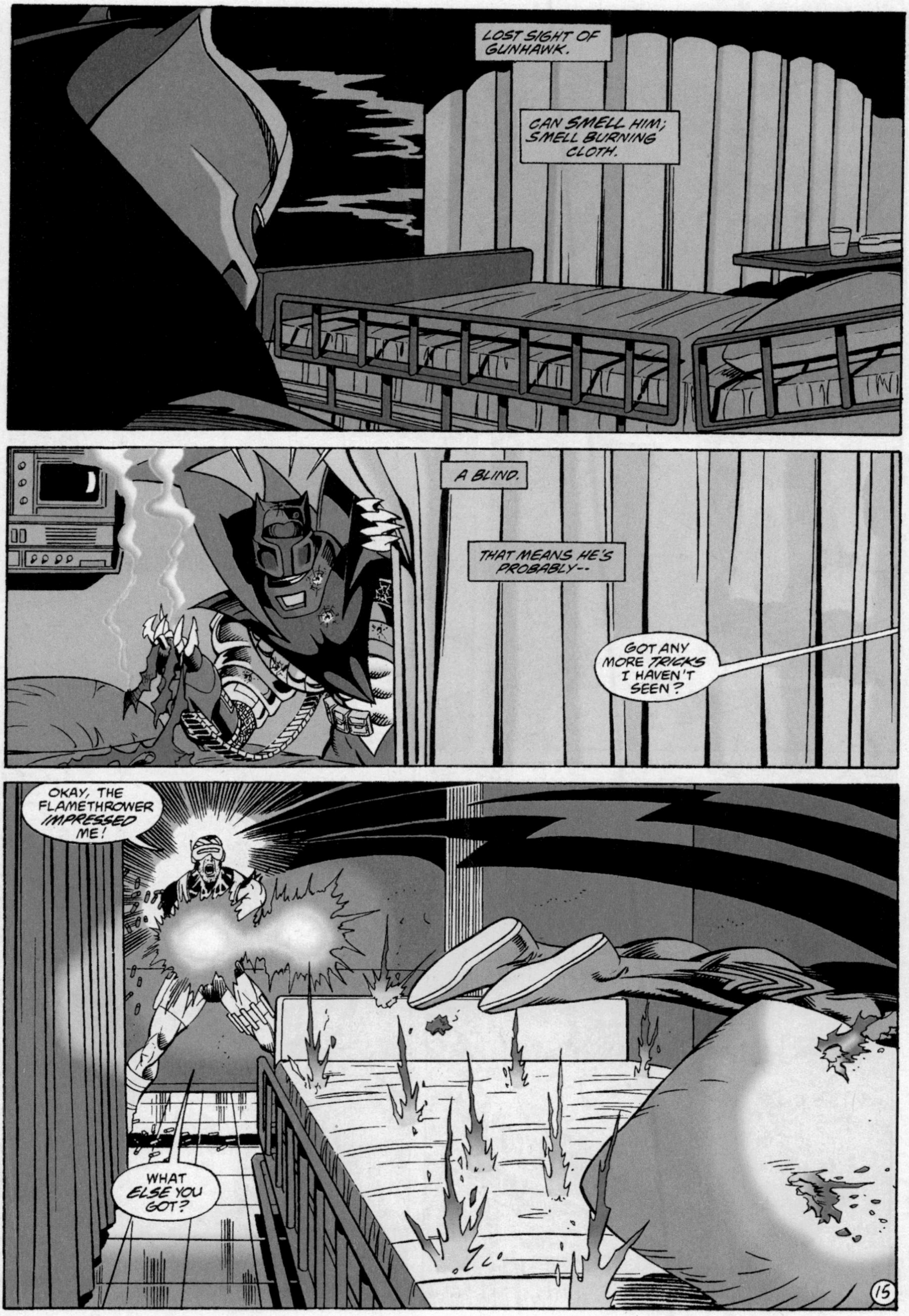
LOST SIGHT OF GUNHAWK.
CAN SMELL HIM; SMELL BURNING CLOTH.
A BLIND.
THAT MEANS HE'S PROBABLY--
GOT ANY MORE TRICKS I HAVEN'T SEEN?
OKAY, THE FLAMETHROWER IMPRESSED ME!
WHAT ELSE YOU GOT?
15

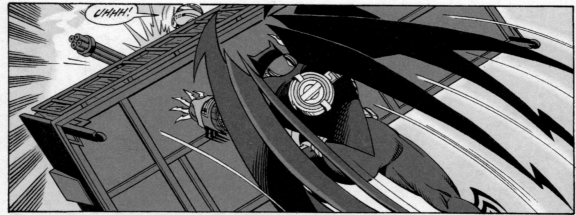

UHHH!

YOU'LL NEVER TAKE ME!

YOU'LL NEVER TAKE ME AWAY FROM BUNNY!

I'LL KILL ANYONE THAT TRIES!

ANYONE!

ONE MORE STEP AND YOU GOT HER BLOOD ON YOUR HANDS.

MORE BLOOD ON HIS HANDS.

HUH?

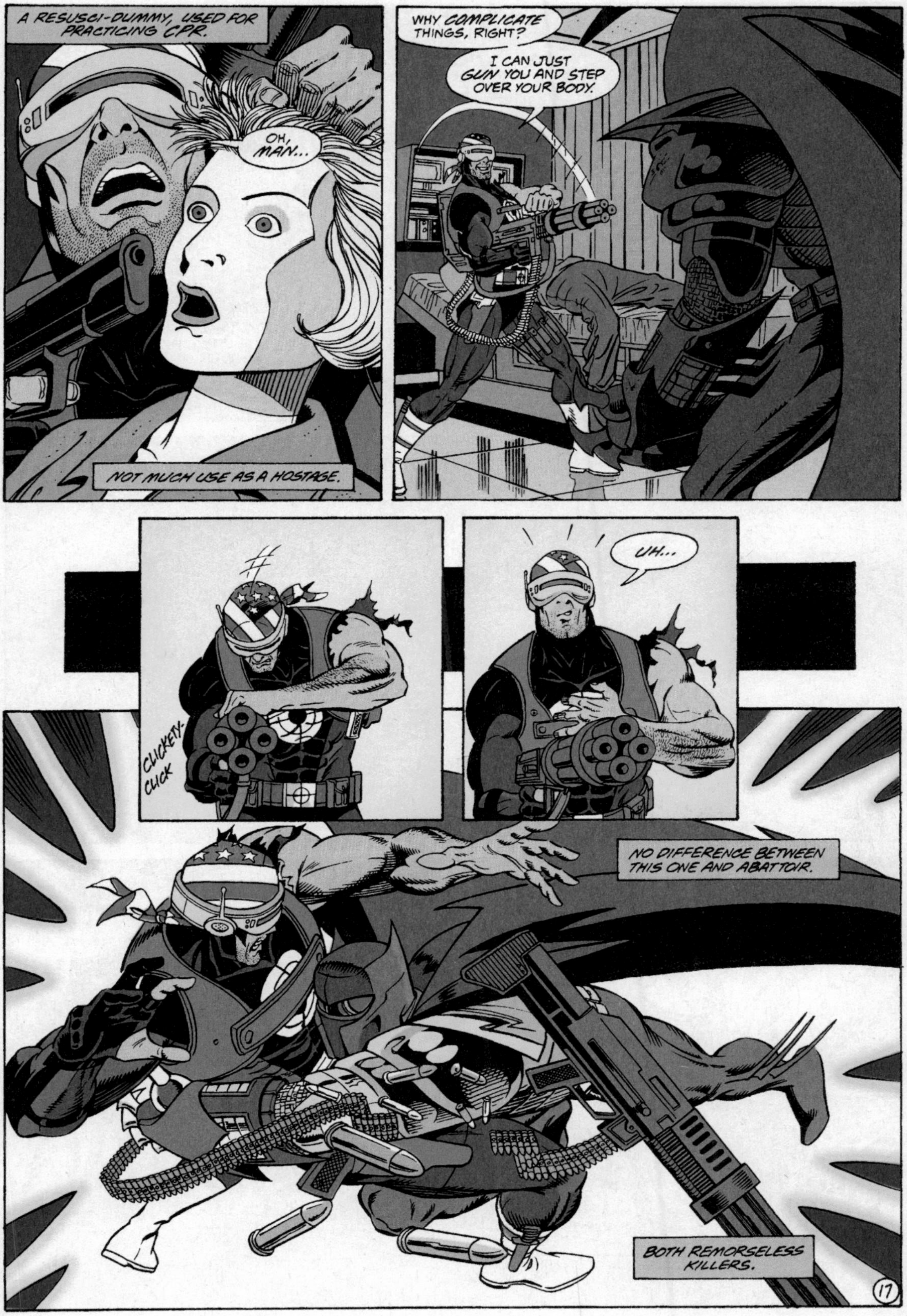
A RESUSCI-DUMMY, USED FOR PRACTICING CPR.
OH, MAN...
NOT MUCH USE AS A HOSTAGE.
WHY COMPLICATE THINGS, RIGHT?
I CAN JUST GUN YOU AND STEP OVER YOUR BODY.
CLICKETY-CLICK
UH...
NO DIFFERENCE BETWEEN THIS ONE AND ABATTOIR.
BOTH REMORSELESS KILLERS.
17

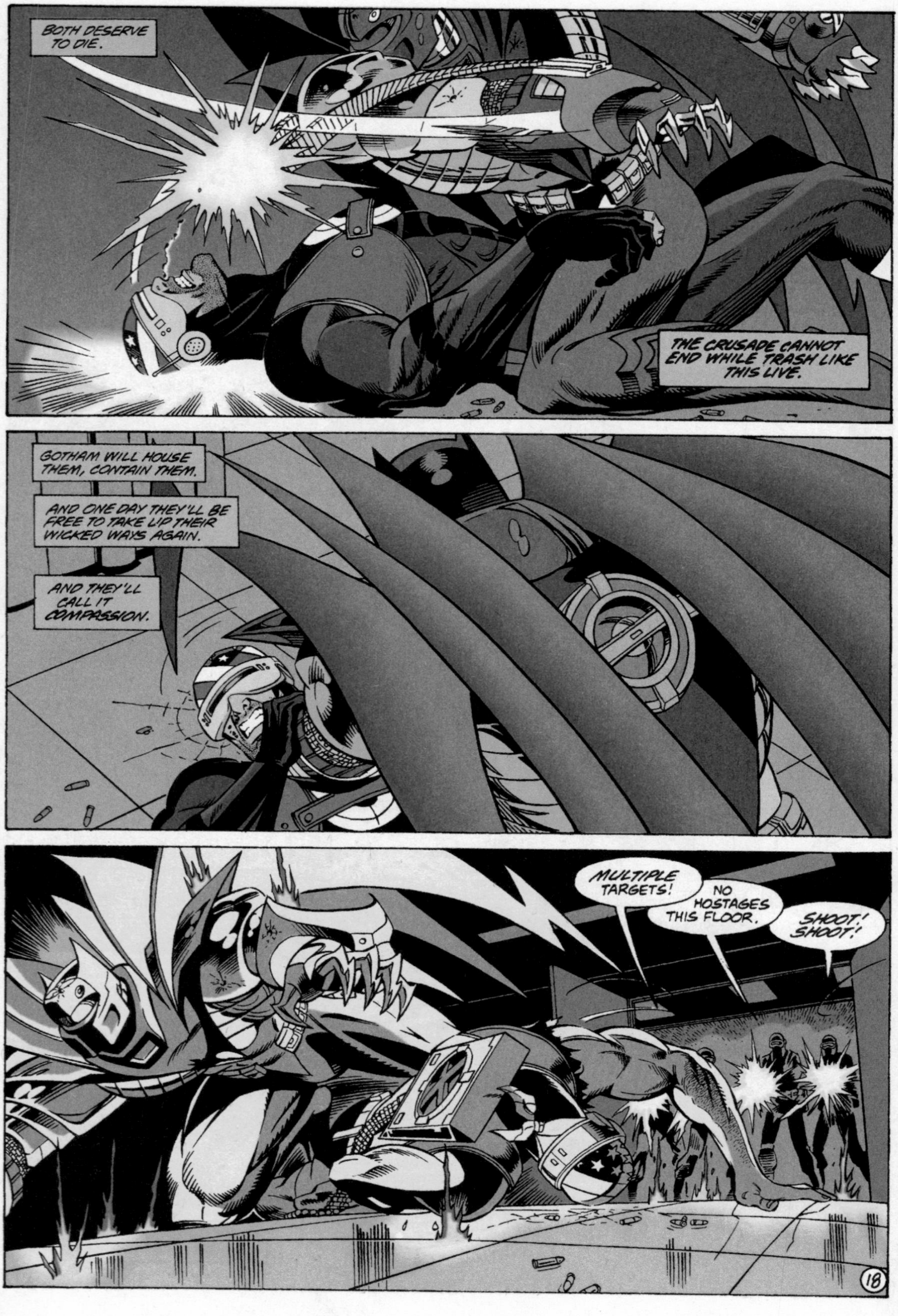
BOTH DESERVE TO DIE.
THE CRUSADE CANNOT END WHILE TRASH LIKE THIS LIVE.
GOTHAM WILL HOUSE THEM, CONTAIN THEM.
AND ONE DAY THEY'LL BE FREE TO TAKE UP THEIR WICKED WAYS AGAIN.
AND THEY'LL CALL IT COMPASSION.
MULTIPLE TARGETS!
NO HOSTAGES THIS FLOOR.
SHOOT! SHOOT!
18

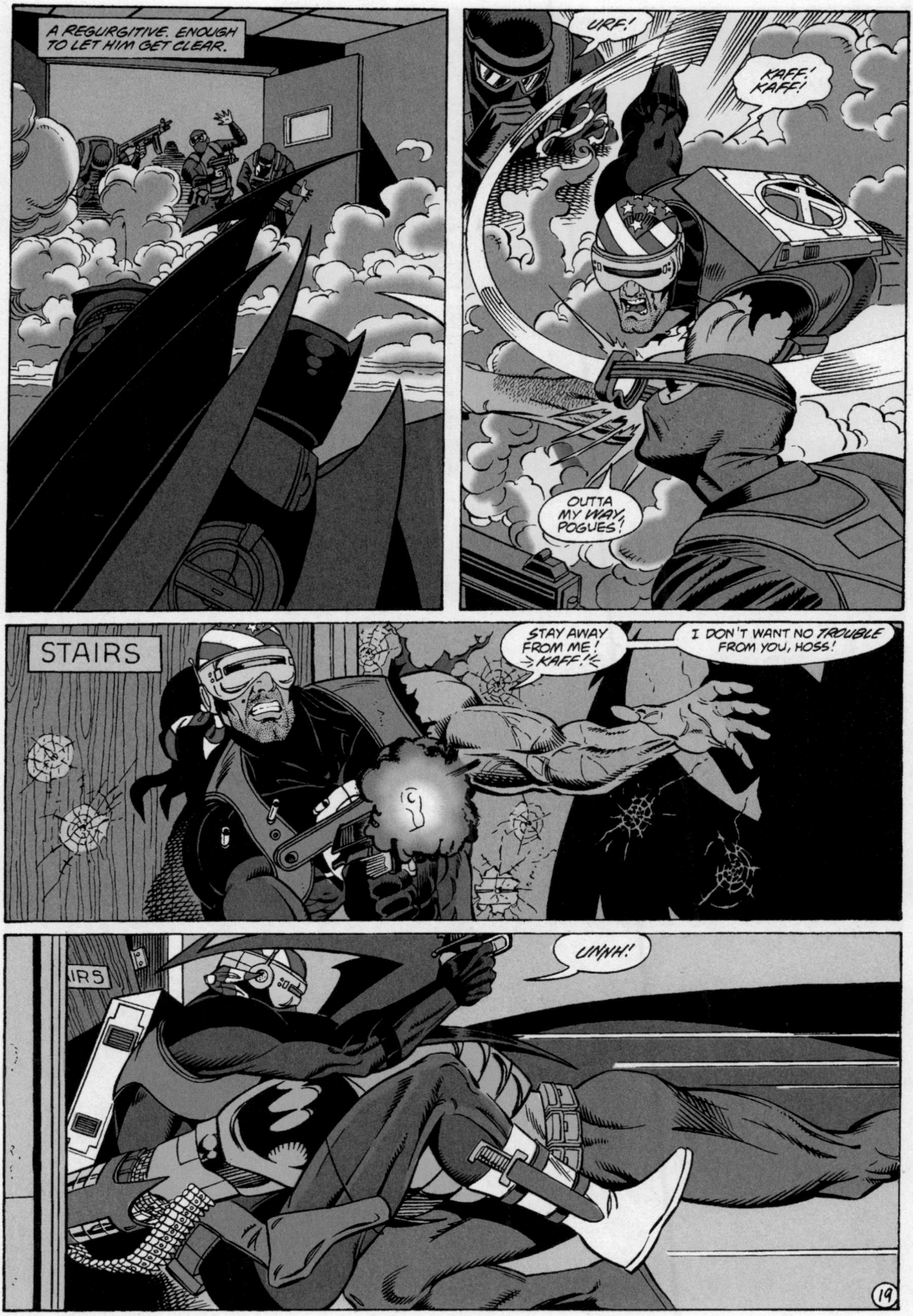
A REGURGITIVE. ENOUGH TO LET HIM GET CLEAR.
URF!
KAFF! KAFF!
OUTTA MY WAY, POGUES!
STAIRS
STAY AWAY FROM ME! KAFF!
I DON'T WANT NO TROUBLE FROM YOU, HOSS!
UNNH!
19

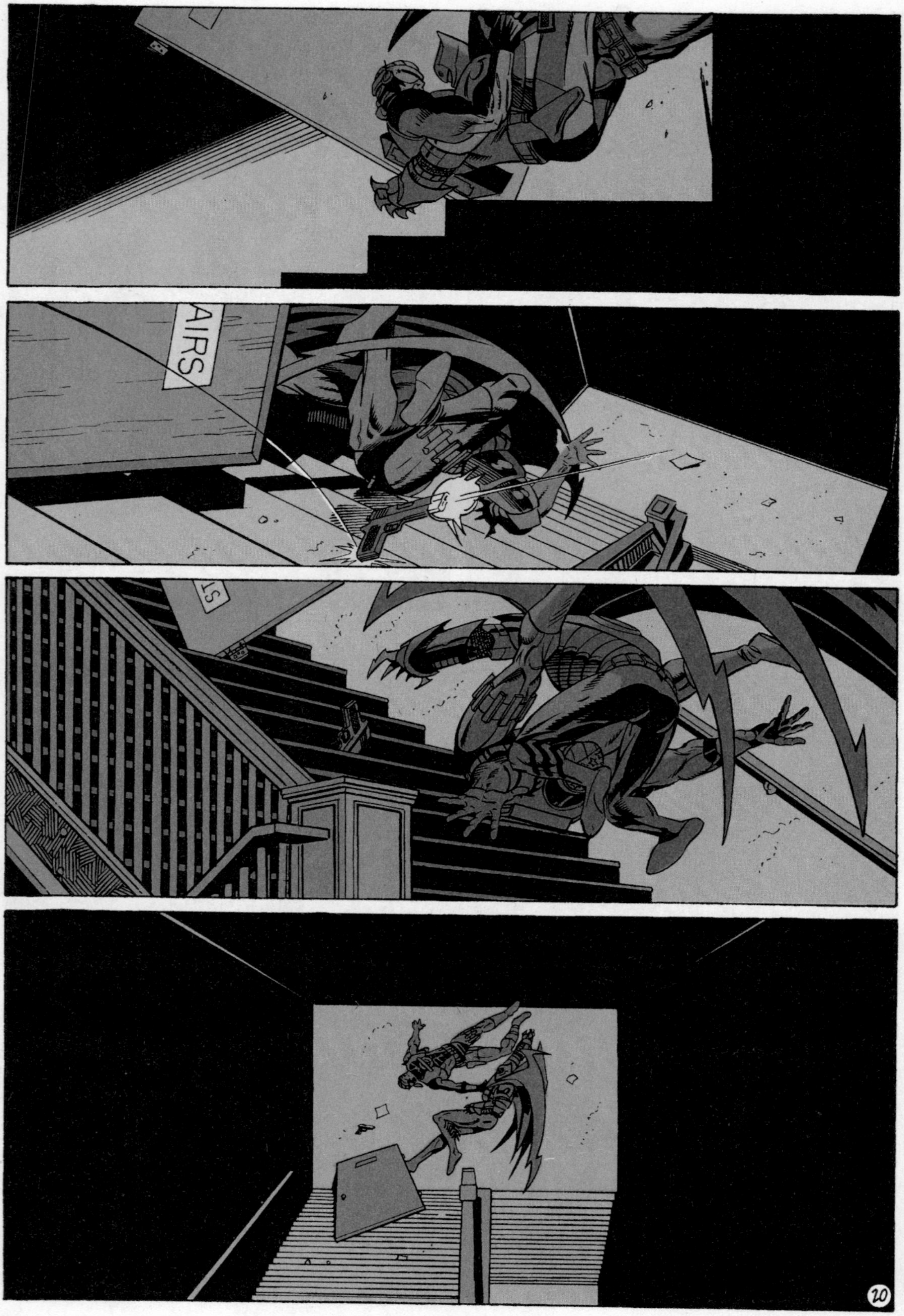
AIRS
20

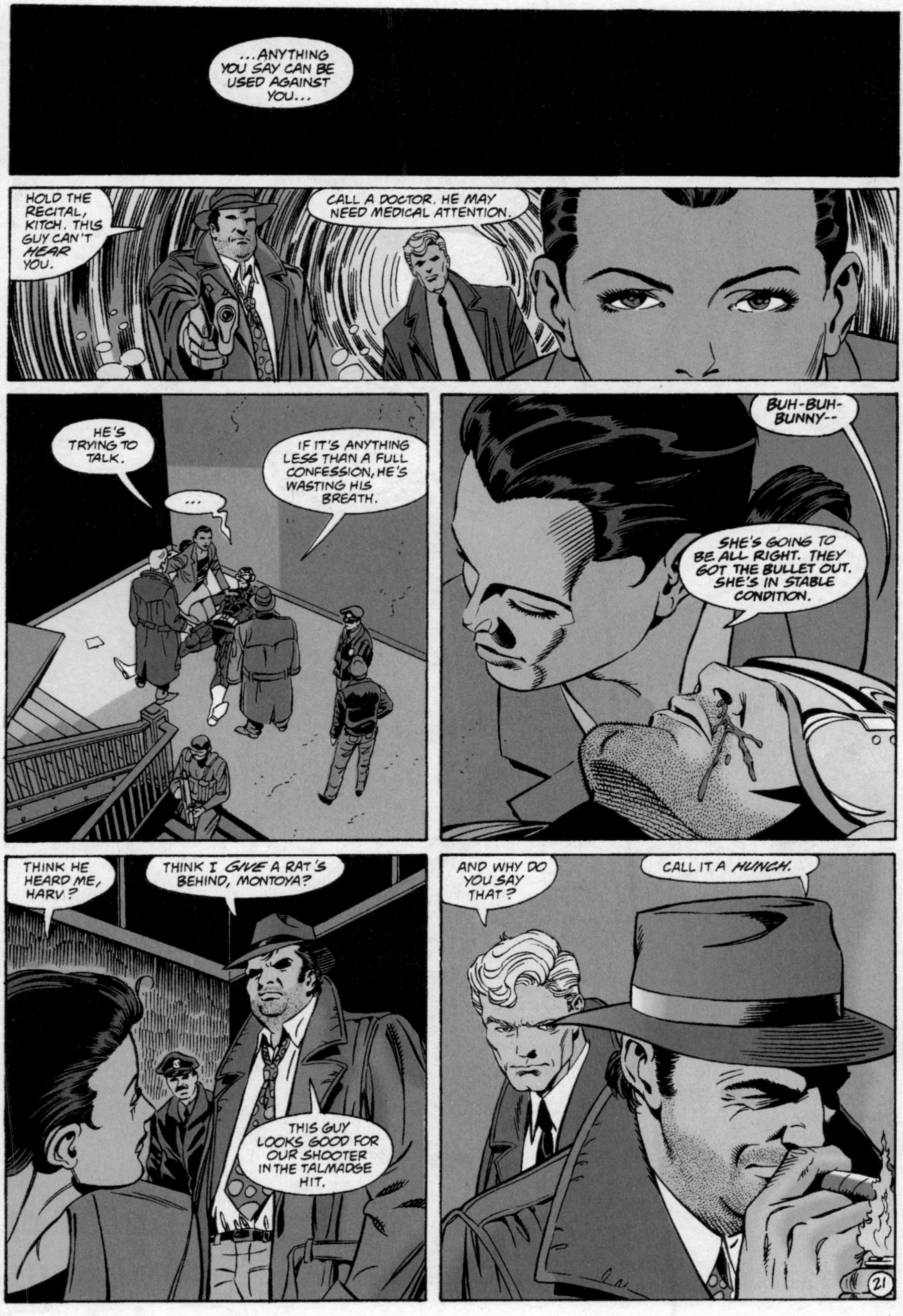
...ANYTHING YOU SAY CAN BE USED AGAINST YOU...
HOLD THE RECITAL, KITCH. THIS GUY CAN'T HEAR YOU.
CALL A DOCTOR. HE MAY NEED MEDICAL ATTENTION.
HE'S TRYING TO TALK.
...
IF IT'S ANYTHING LESS THAN A FULL CONFESSION, HE'S WASTING HIS BREATH.
BUH-BUH-BUNNY--
SHE'S GOING TO BE ALL RIGHT. THEY GOT THE BULLET OUT. SHE'S IN STABLE CONDITION.
THINK HE HEARD ME, HARV?
THINK I GIVE A RAT'S BEHIND, MONTOYA?
THIS GUY LOOKS GOOD FOR OUR SHOOTER IN THE TALMADGE HIT.
AND WHY DO YOU SAY THAT?
CALL IT A HUNCH.
21

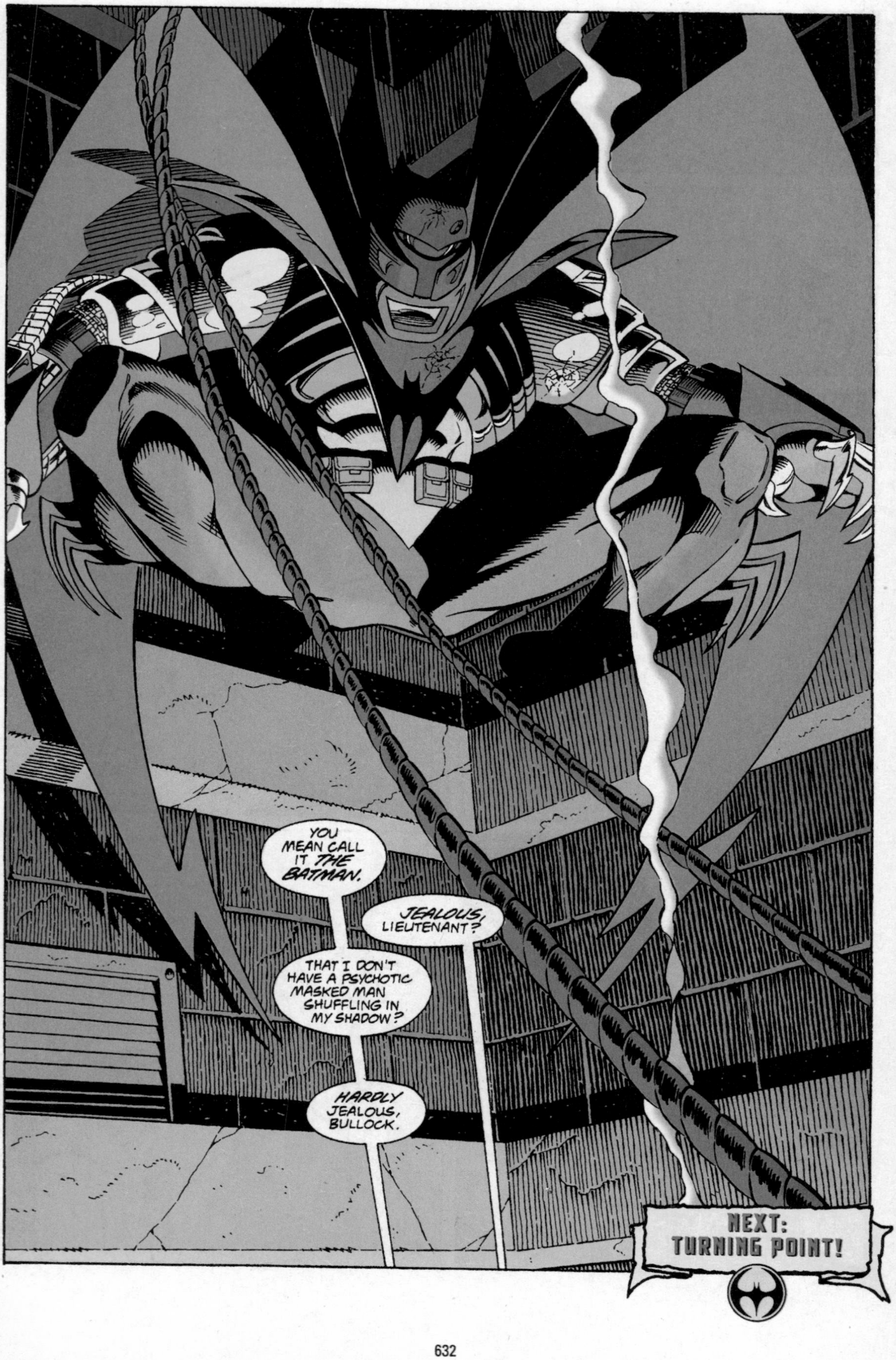
YOU MEAN CALL IT THE BATMAN.
JEALOUS, LIEUTENANT?
THAT I DON'T HAVE A PSYCHOTIC MASKED MAN SHUFFLING IN MY SHADOW?
HARDLY JEALOUS, BULLOCK.
NEXT: TURNING POINT!

Cover art by TOM GRUMMETT AND RAY KRYSSING

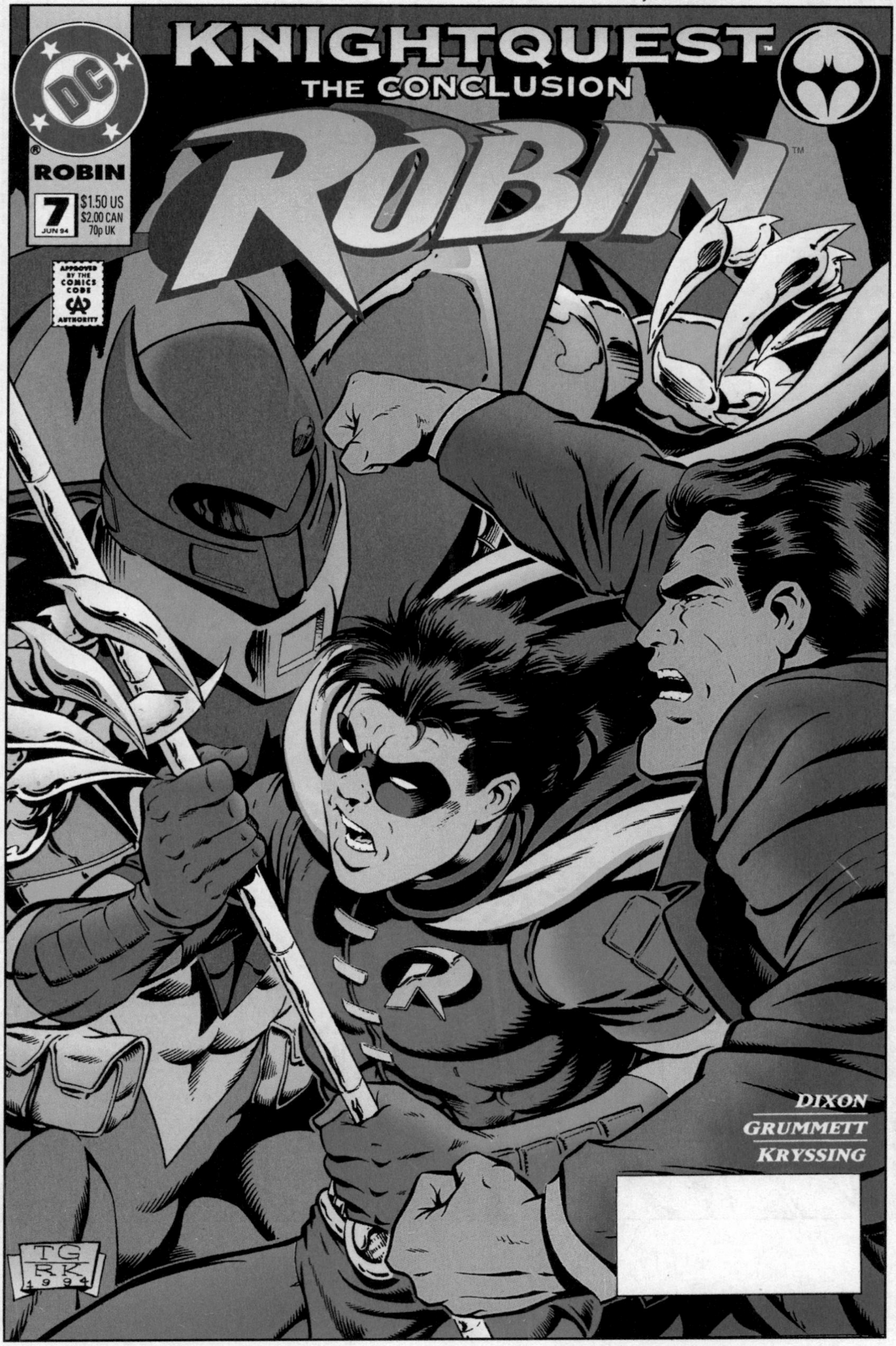
KNIGHTQUEST
THE CONCLUSION
ROBIN
DC
ROBIN
7
JUN 94
$1.50 US
$2.00 CAN
70p UK
APPROVED BY THE COMICS CODE AUTHORITY
DIXON
GRUMMETT
KRYSSING
TG RK 1994

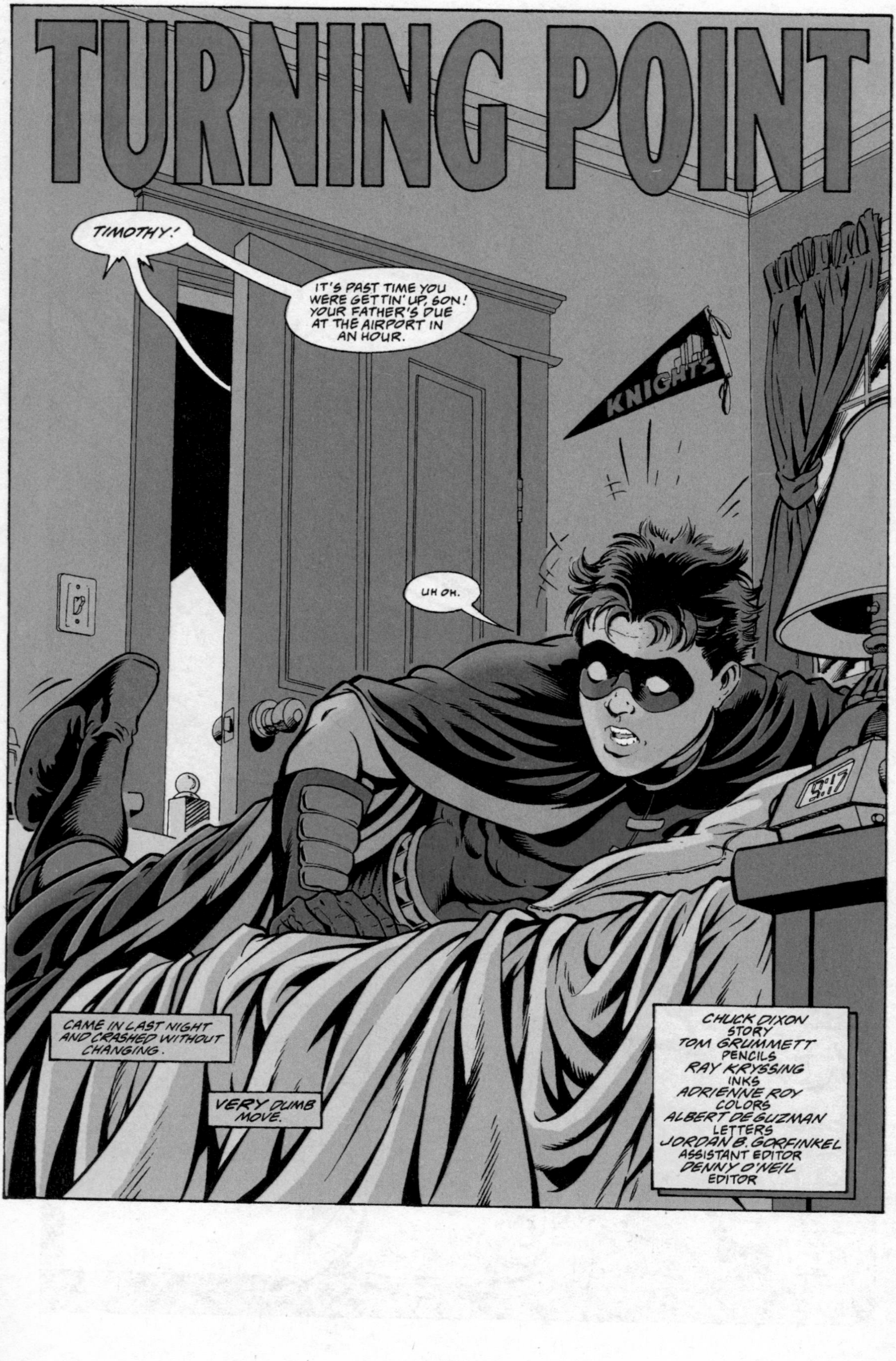
TURNING POINT
TIMOTHY!
IT'S PAST TIME YOU WERE GETTIN' UP, SON! YOUR FATHER'S DUE AT THE AIRPORT IN AN HOUR.
KNIGHTS
UH OH.
5:17
CAME IN LAST NIGHT AND CRASHED WITHOUT CHANGING.
VERY DUMB MOVE.
CHUCK DIXON STORY
TOM GRUMMETT PENCILS
RAY KRYSSING INKS
ADRIENNE ROY COLORS
ALBERT DE GUZMAN LETTERS
JORDAN B. GORFINKEL ASSISTANT EDITOR
DENNY O'NEIL EDITOR

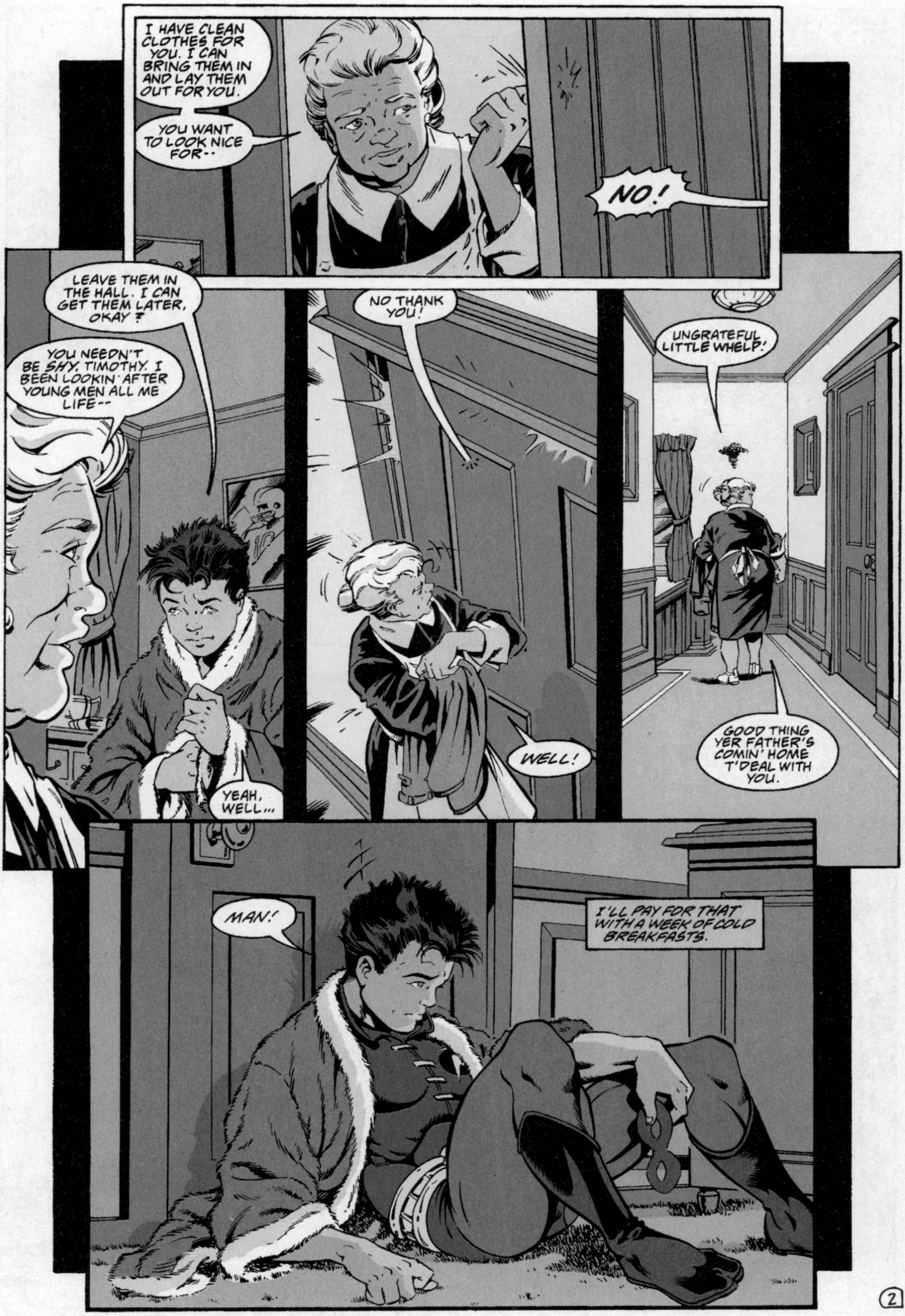
I HAVE CLEAN CLOTHES FOR YOU. I CAN BRING THEM IN AND LAY THEM OUT FOR YOU.
YOU WANT TO LOOK NICE FOR--
NO!
LEAVE THEM IN THE HALL. I CAN GET THEM LATER, OKAY?
YOU NEEDN'T BE SHY, TIMOTHY. I BEEN LOOKIN' AFTER YOUNG MEN ALL ME LIFE--
YEAH, WELL...
NO THANK YOU!
WELL!
UNGRATEFUL LITTLE WHELP!
GOOD THING YER FATHER'S COMIN' HOME T'DEAL WITH YOU.
MAN!
I'LL PAY FOR THAT WITH A WEEK OF COLD BREAKFASTS.
2

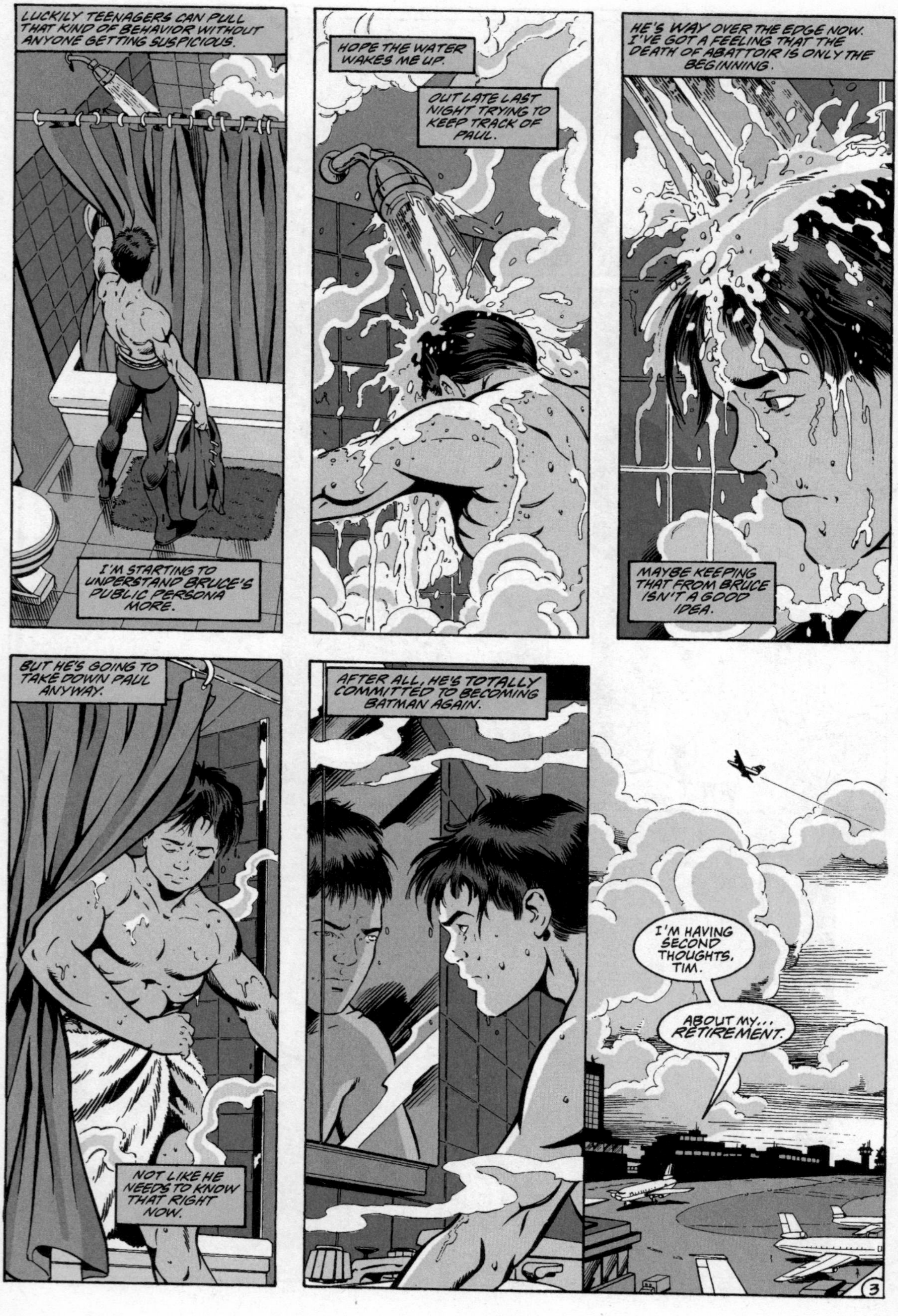
LUCKILY TEENAGERS CAN PULL THAT KIND OF BEHAVIOR WITHOUT ANYONE GETTING SUSPICIOUS.
I'M STARTING TO UNDERSTAND BRUCE'S PUBLIC PERSONA MORE.
HOPE THE WATER WAKES ME UP.
OUT LATE LAST NIGHT TRYING TO KEEP TRACK OF PAUL.
HE'S WAY OVER THE EDGE NOW. I'VE GOT A FEELING THAT THE DEATH OF ABATTOIR IS ONLY THE BEGINNING.
MAYBE KEEPING THAT FROM BRUCE ISN'T A GOOD IDEA.
BUT HE'S GOING TO TAKE DOWN PAUL ANYWAY.
NOT LIKE HE NEEDS TO KNOW THAT RIGHT NOW.
AFTER ALL, HE'S TOTALLY COMMITTED TO BECOMING BATMAN AGAIN.
I'M HAVING SECOND THOUGHTS, TIM.
ABOUT MY... RETIREMENT.
3

WHAT?

I WASN'T EXPECTING THIS REACTION.

A LITTLE DISAPPOINTMENT, MAYBE...

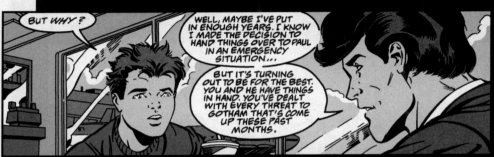

BUT WHY?

WELL, MAYBE I'VE PUT IN ENOUGH YEARS. I KNOW I MADE THE DECISION TO HAND THINGS OVER TO PAUL IN AN EMERGENCY SITUATION...

BUT IT'S TURNING OUT TO BE FOR THE BEST. YOU AND HE HAVE THINGS IN HAND. YOU'VE DEALT WITH EVERY THREAT TO GOTHAM THAT'S COME UP THESE PAST MONTHS.

I'VE NEVER SPENT MUCH TIME JUST BEING BRUCE WAYNE. IT'S NOT TOO LATE TO TRY TO HAVE A LIFE. THIS COULD BE A SECOND CHANCE FOR ME.

I'M GOING TO TAKE A SHOT AT IT. JOIN THE HUMAN RACE.

LOOK, BRUCE, THERE'S SOME THINGS I'VE GOT TO TELL YOU...

FLIGHT ONE-THREE-SEVEN FROM LONDON HEATHROW NOW ARRIVING GATE G-32.

THAT'S MY FATHER'S PLANE.

WE'LL MEET HIM AT ARRIVALS.

④

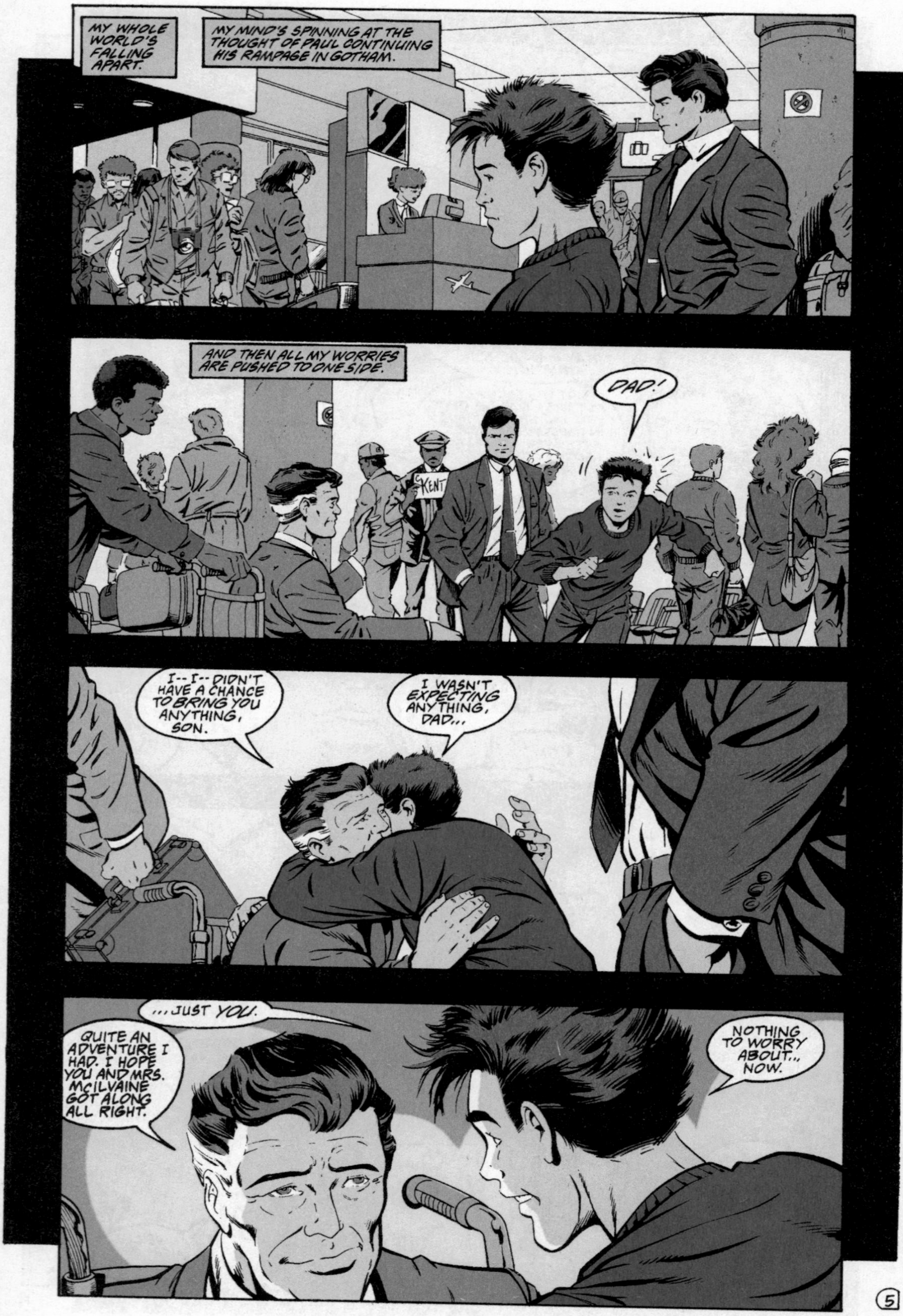
MY WHOLE WORLD'S FALLING APART.
MY MIND'S SPINNING AT THE THOUGHT OF PAUL CONTINUING HIS RAMPAGE IN GOTHAM.
AND THEN ALL MY WORRIES ARE PUSHED TO ONE SIDE.
DAD!
KENT
I-- I-- DIDN'T HAVE A CHANCE TO BRING YOU ANYTHING, SON.
I WASN'T EXPECTING ANYTHING, DAD...
...JUST YOU.
QUITE AN ADVENTURE I HAD. I HOPE YOU AND MRS. McILVAINE GOT ALONG ALL RIGHT.
NOTHING TO WORRY ABOUT... NOW.
5

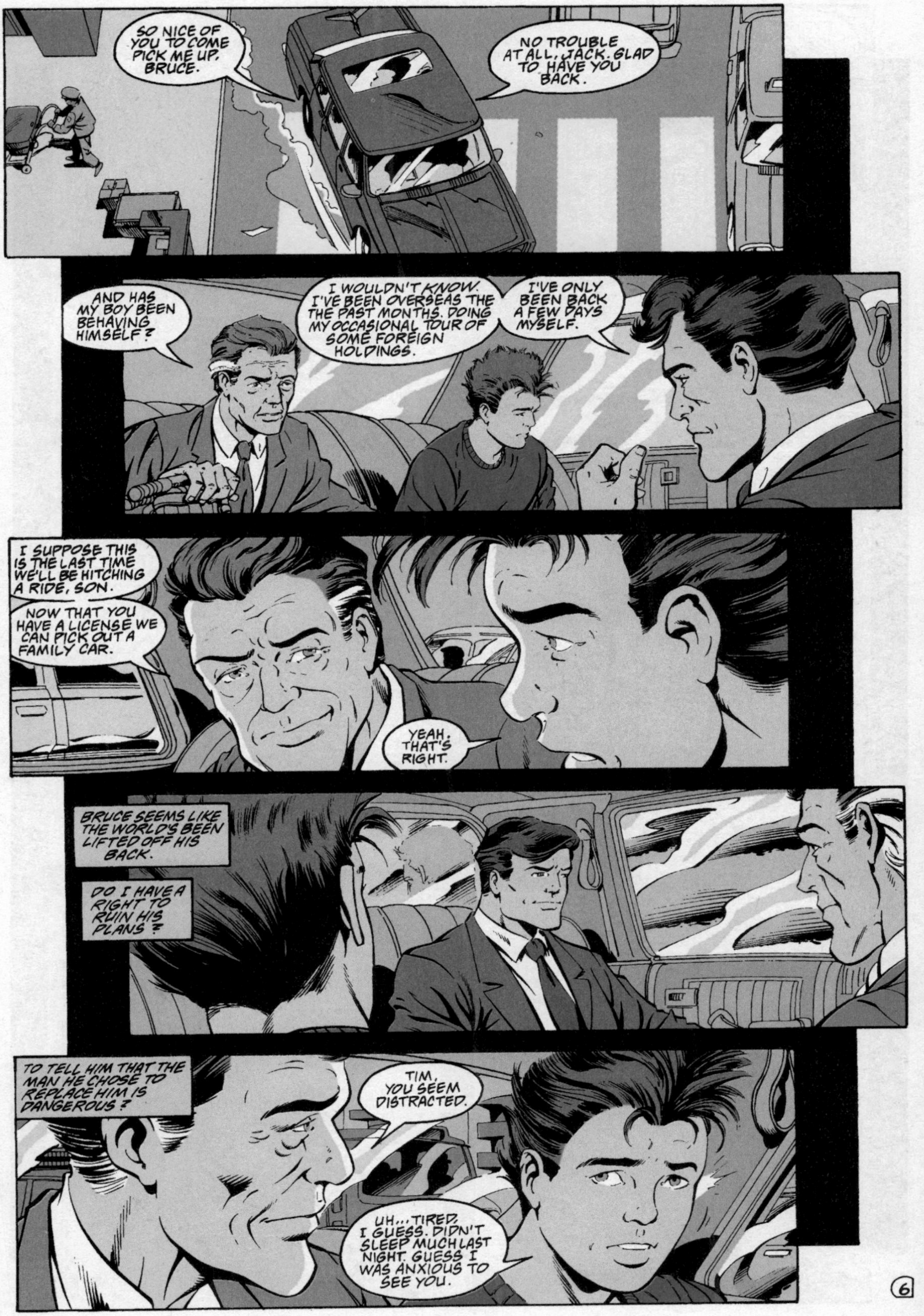
SO NICE OF YOU TO COME PICK ME UP, BRUCE.
NO TROUBLE AT ALL, JACK. GLAD TO HAVE YOU BACK.
AND HAS MY BOY BEEN BEHAVING HIMSELF?
I WOULDN'T KNOW. I'VE BEEN OVERSEAS THE THE PAST MONTHS. DOING MY OCCASIONAL TOUR OF SOME FOREIGN HOLDINGS.
I'VE ONLY BEEN BACK A FEW DAYS MYSELF.
I SUPPOSE THIS IS THE LAST TIME WE'LL BE HITCHING A RIDE, SON.
NOW THAT YOU HAVE A LICENSE WE CAN PICK OUT A FAMILY CAR.
YEAH. THAT'S RIGHT.
BRUCE SEEMS LIKE THE WORLD'S BEEN LIFTED OFF HIS BACK.
DO I HAVE A RIGHT TO RUIN HIS PLANS?
TO TELL HIM THAT THE MAN HE CHOSE TO REPLACE HIM IS DANGEROUS?
TIM, YOU SEEM DISTRACTED.
UH... TIRED, I GUESS. DIDN'T SLEEP MUCH LAST NIGHT. GUESS I WAS ANXIOUS TO SEE YOU.
6

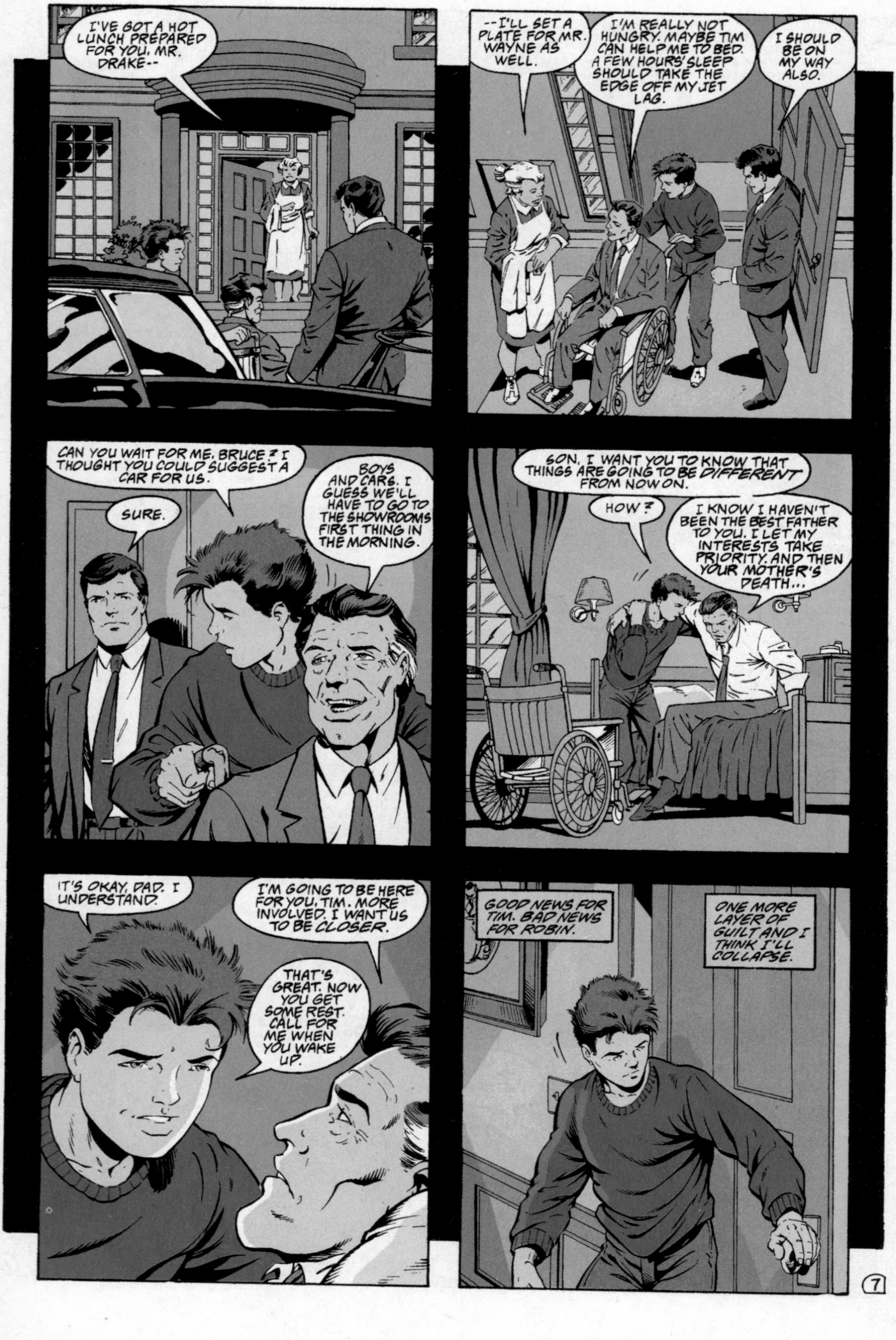
I'VE GOT A HOT LUNCH PREPARED FOR YOU, MR. DRAKE--
--I'LL SET A PLATE FOR MR. WAYNE AS WELL.
I'M REALLY NOT HUNGRY. MAYBE TIM CAN HELP ME TO BED. A FEW HOURS' SLEEP SHOULD TAKE THE EDGE OFF MY JET LAG.
I SHOULD BE ON MY WAY ALSO.
CAN YOU WAIT FOR ME, BRUCE? I THOUGHT YOU COULD SUGGEST A CAR FOR US.
SURE.
BOYS AND CARS. I GUESS WE'LL HAVE TO GO TO THE SHOWROOMS FIRST THING IN THE MORNING.
SON, I WANT YOU TO KNOW THAT THINGS ARE GOING TO BE DIFFERENT FROM NOW ON.
HOW?
I KNOW I HAVEN'T BEEN THE BEST FATHER TO YOU. I LET MY INTERESTS TAKE PRIORITY. AND THEN YOUR MOTHER'S DEATH...
IT'S OKAY, DAD. I UNDERSTAND.
I'M GOING TO BE HERE FOR YOU, TIM. MORE INVOLVED. I WANT US TO BE CLOSER.
THAT'S GREAT. NOW YOU GET SOME REST. CALL FOR ME WHEN YOU WAKE UP.
GOOD NEWS FOR TIM. BAD NEWS FOR ROBIN.
ONE MORE LAYER OF GUILT AND I THINK I'LL COLLAPSE.
7

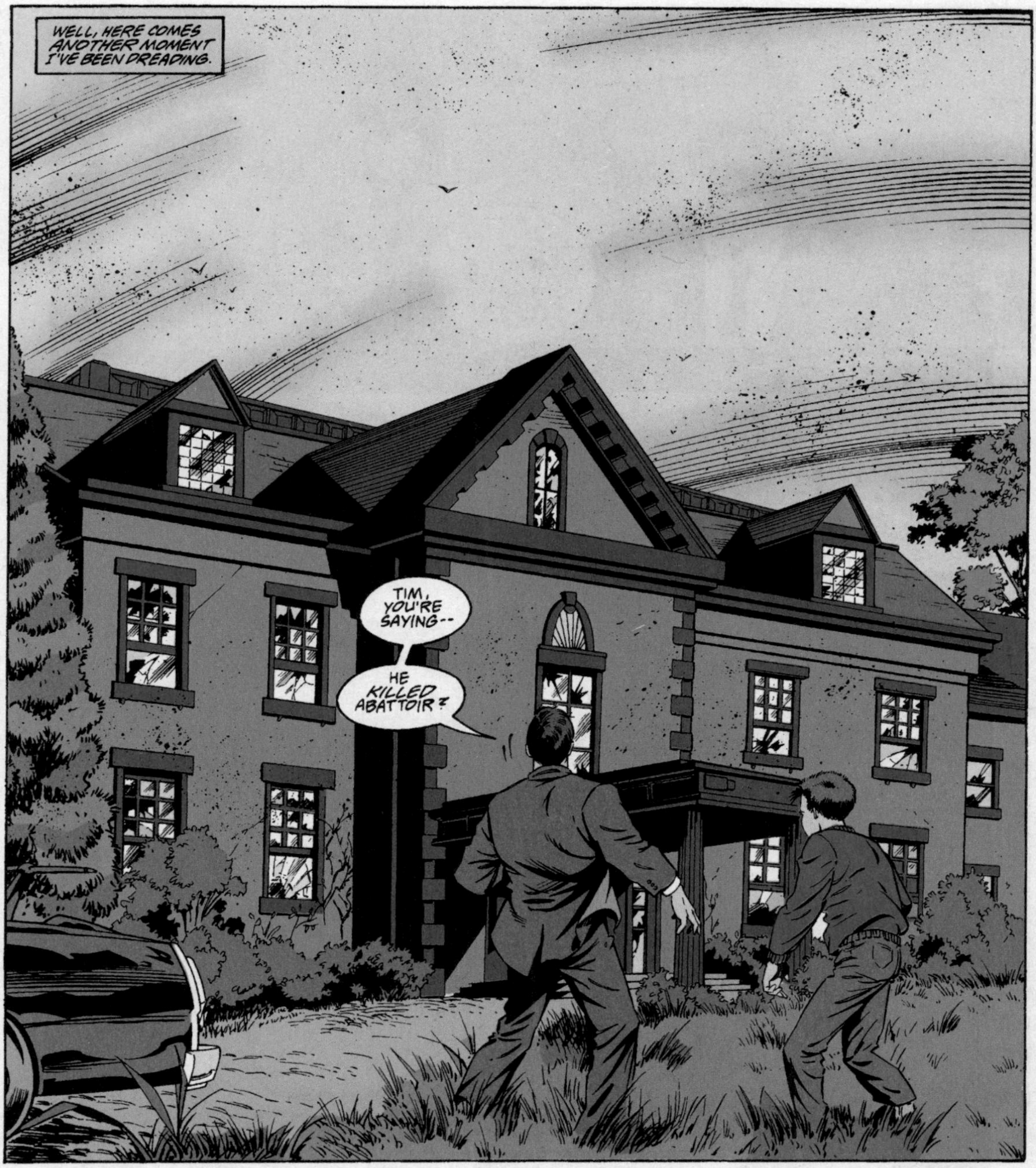
WELL, HERE COMES ANOTHER MOMENT I'VE BEEN DREADING.
TIM, YOU'RE SAYING--
HE KILLED ABATTOIR?

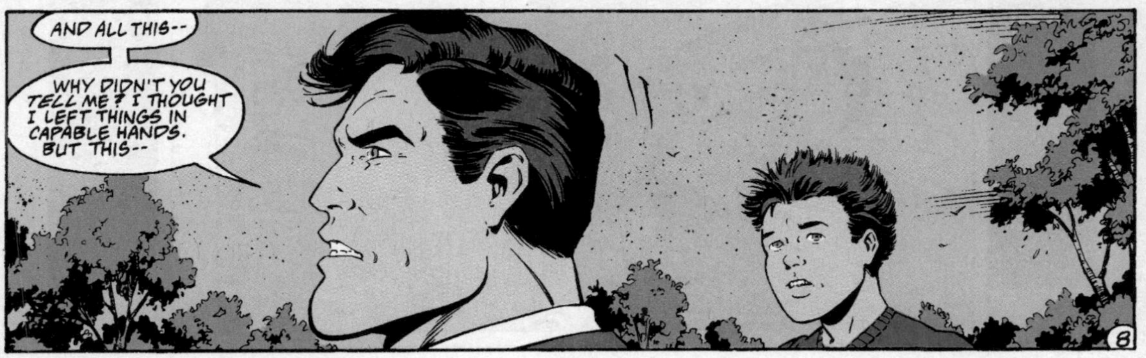
AND ALL THIS--
WHY DIDN'T YOU TELL ME? I THOUGHT I LEFT THINGS IN CAPABLE HANDS. BUT THIS--
8

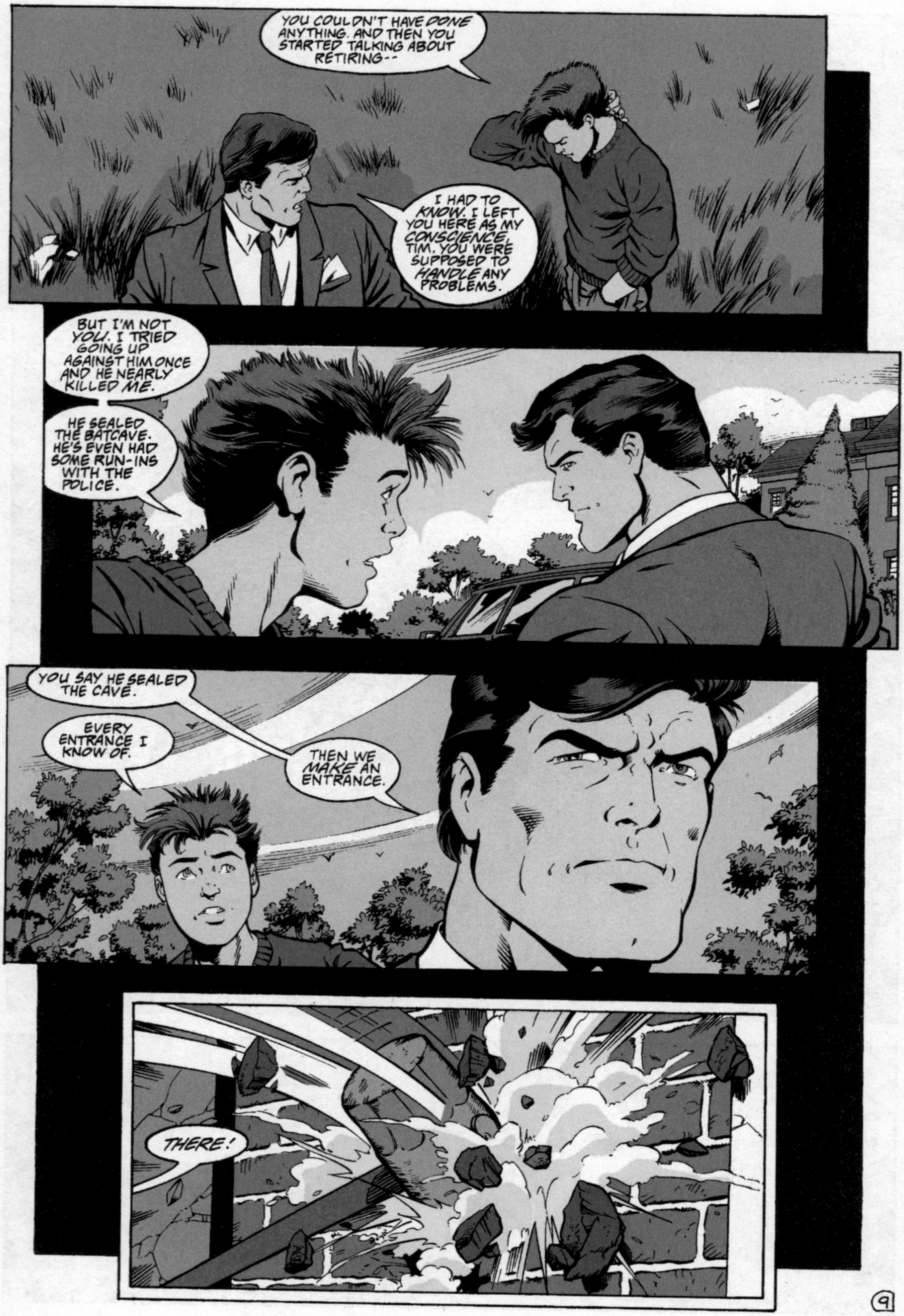
YOU COULDN'T HAVE DONE ANYTHING. AND THEN YOU STARTED TALKING ABOUT RETIRING--
I HAD TO KNOW. I LEFT YOU HERE AS MY CONSCIENCE, TIM. YOU WERE SUPPOSED TO HANDLE ANY PROBLEMS.
BUT I'M NOT YOU. I TRIED GOING UP AGAINST HIM ONCE AND HE NEARLY KILLED ME.
HE SEALED THE BATCAVE. HE'S EVEN HAD SOME RUN-INS WITH THE POLICE.
YOU SAY HE SEALED THE CAVE.
EVERY ENTRANCE I KNOW OF.
THEN WE MAKE AN ENTRANCE.
THERE!
9

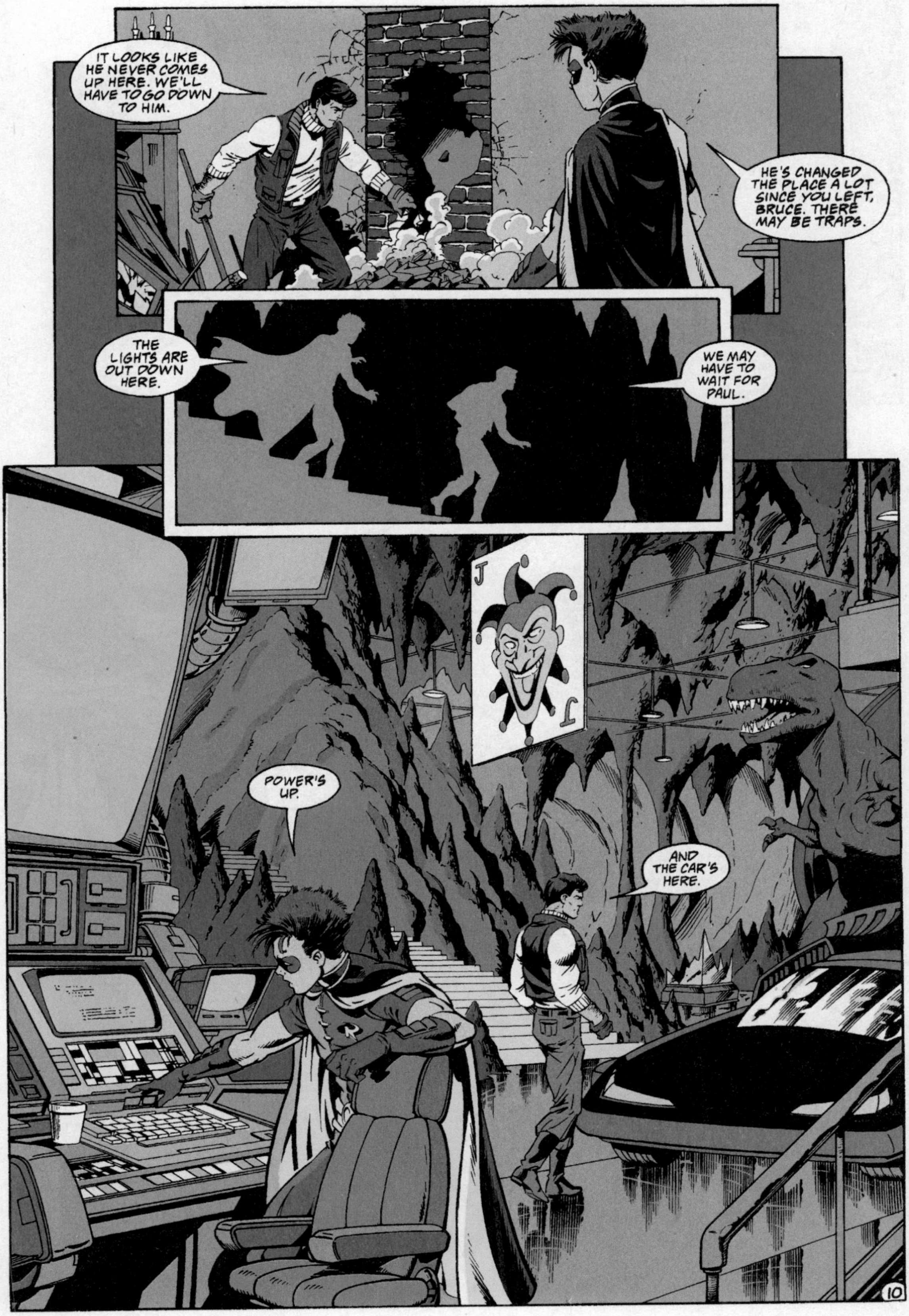
IT LOOKS LIKE HE NEVER COMES UP HERE. WE'LL HAVE TO GO DOWN TO HIM.
HE'S CHANGED THE PLACE A LOT SINCE YOU LEFT, BRUCE. THERE MAY BE TRAPS.
THE LIGHTS ARE OUT DOWN HERE.
WE MAY HAVE TO WAIT FOR PAUL.
POWER'S UP.
AND THE CAR'S HERE.
10

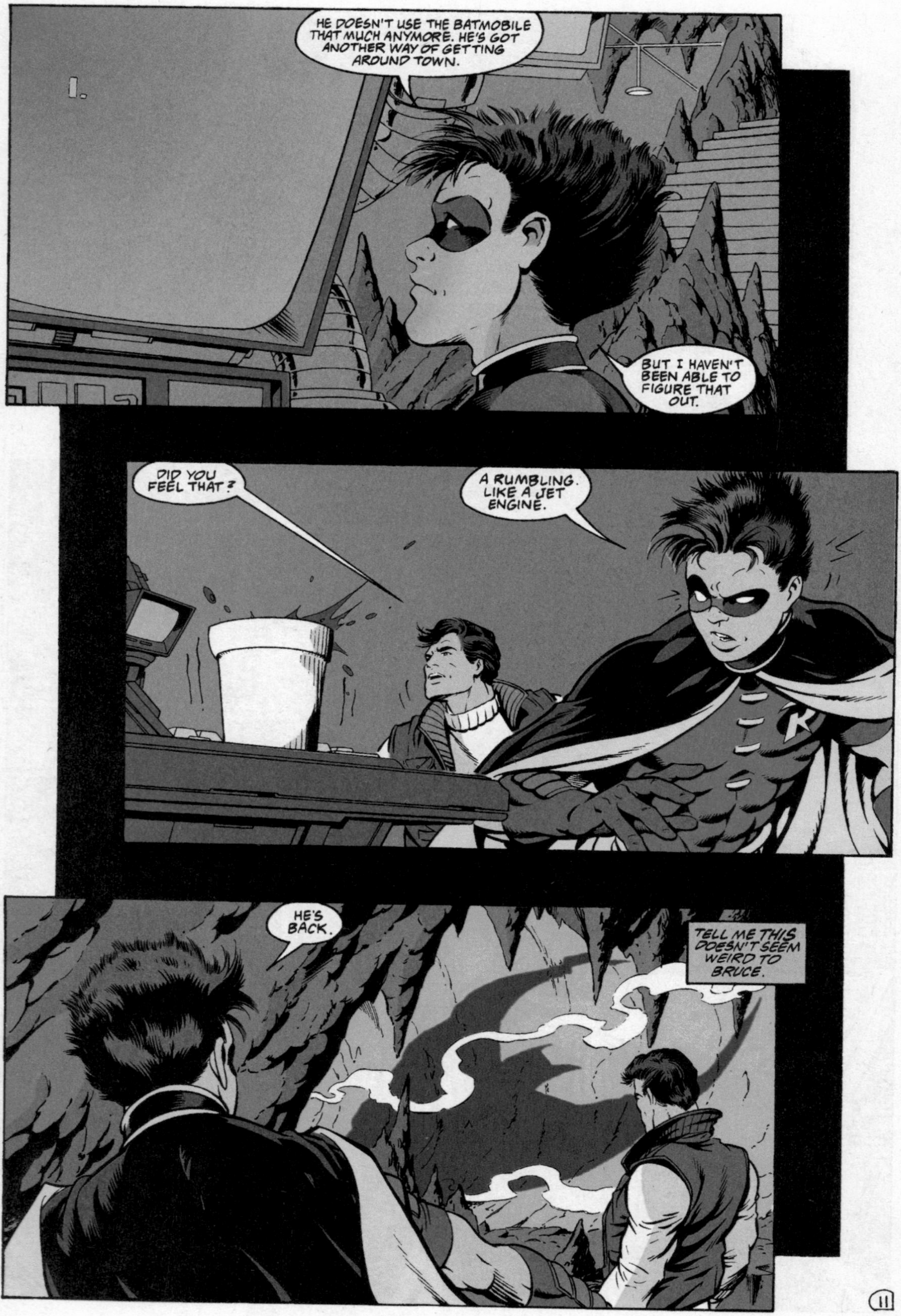
HE DOESN'T USE THE BATMOBILE THAT MUCH ANYMORE. HE'S GOT ANOTHER WAY OF GETTING AROUND TOWN.
BUT I HAVEN'T BEEN ABLE TO FIGURE THAT OUT.
DID YOU FEEL THAT?
A RUMBLING. LIKE A JET ENGINE.
HE'S BACK.
TELL ME THIS DOESN'T SEEM WEIRD TO BRUCE.
11

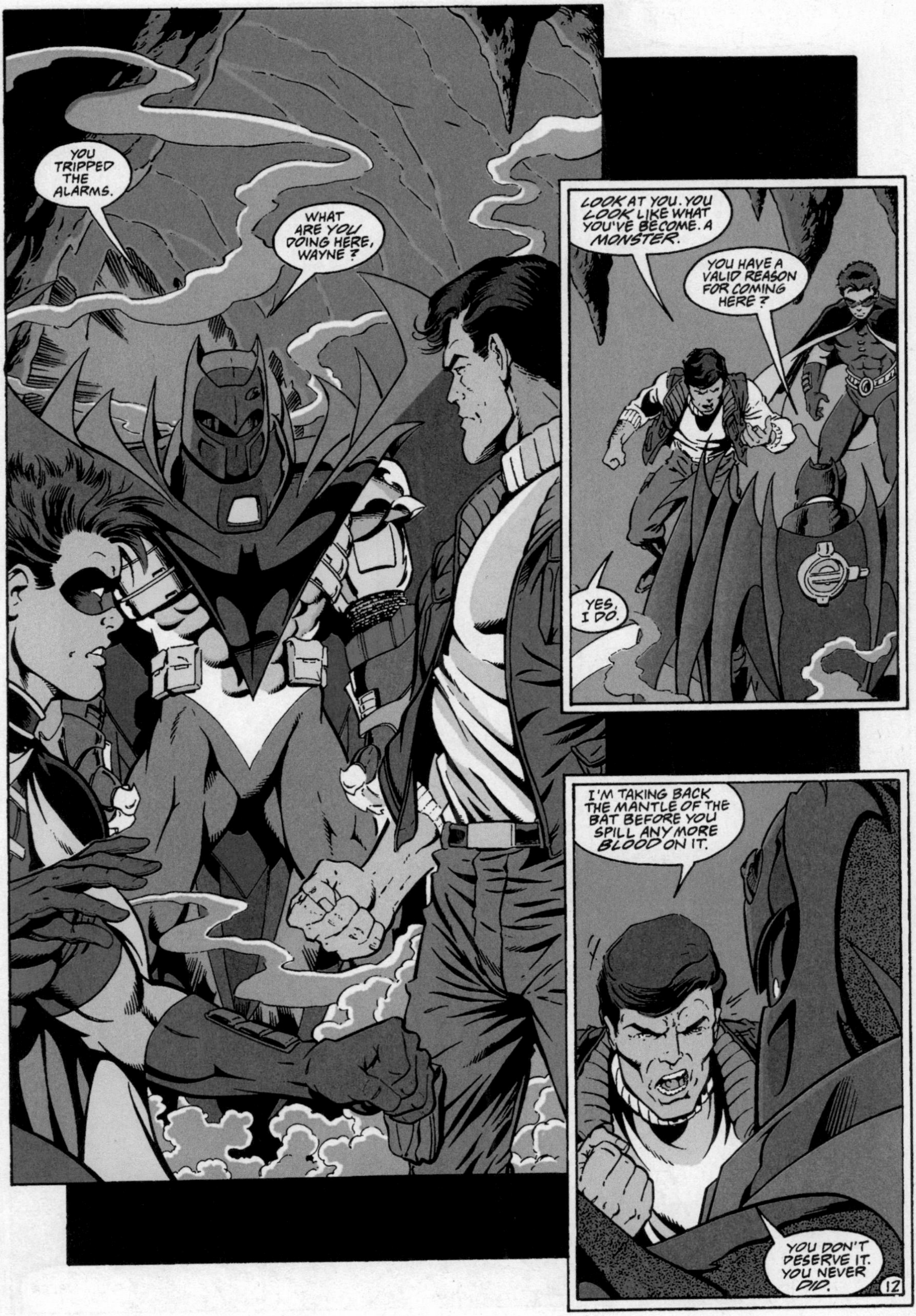
YOU TRIPPED THE ALARMS.
WHAT ARE YOU DOING HERE, WAYNE?
LOOK AT YOU. YOU LOOK LIKE WHAT YOU'VE BECOME. A MONSTER.
YOU HAVE A VALID REASON FOR COMING HERE?
YES, I DO.
I'M TAKING BACK THE MANTLE OF THE BAT BEFORE YOU SPILL ANY MORE BLOOD ON IT.
YOU DON'T DESERVE IT. YOU NEVER DID.
12

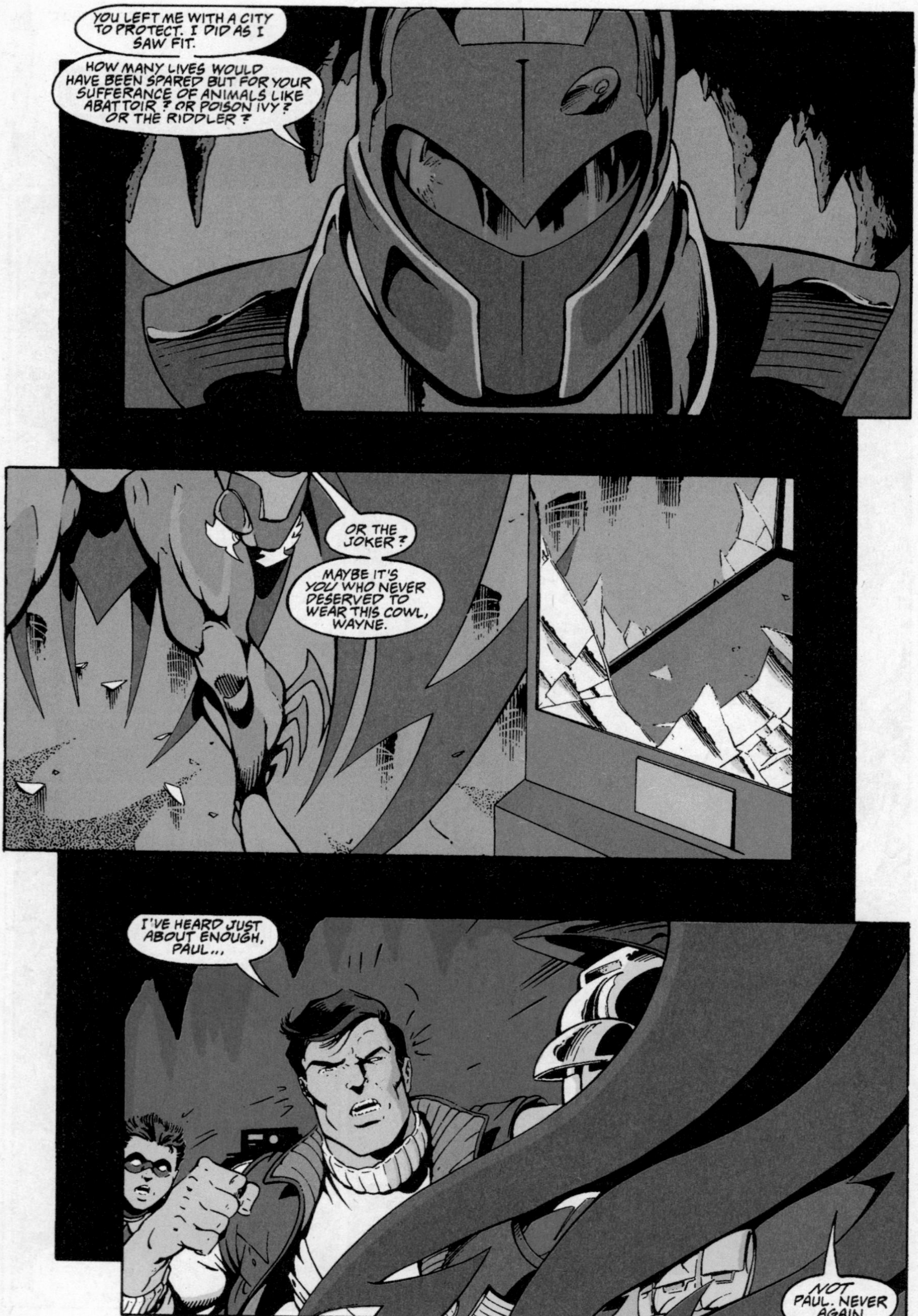
YOU LEFT ME WITH A CITY TO PROTECT. I DID AS I SAW FIT.
HOW MANY LIVES WOULD HAVE BEEN SPARED BUT FOR YOUR SUFFERANCE OF ANIMALS LIKE ABATTOIR? OR POISON IVY? OR THE RIDDLER?
OR THE JOKER?
MAYBE IT'S YOU WHO NEVER DESERVED TO WEAR THIS COWL, WAYNE.
I'VE HEARD JUST ABOUT ENOUGH, PAUL...
NOT PAUL. NEVER AGAIN.

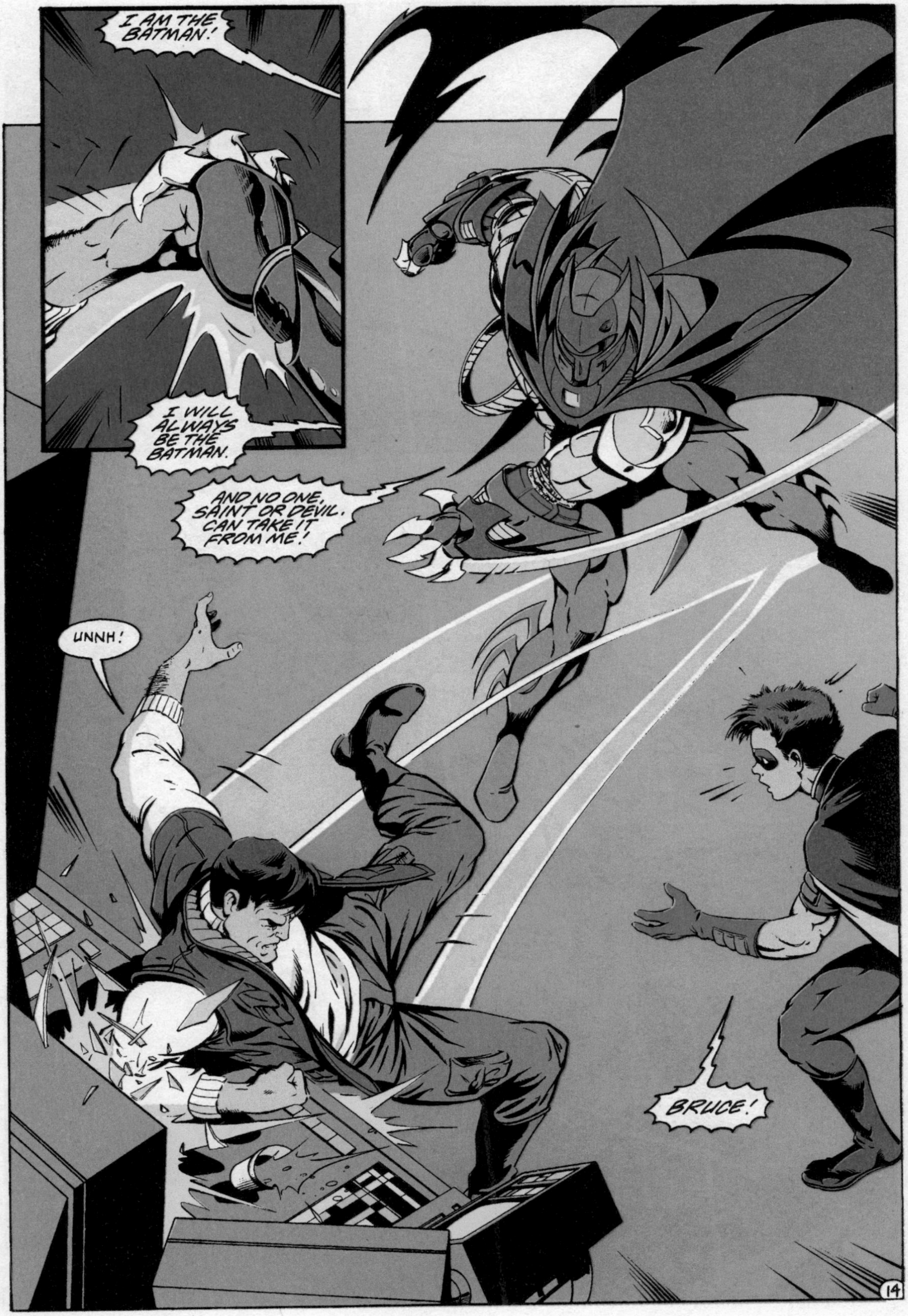
I AM THE BATMAN!
I WILL ALWAYS BE THE BATMAN.
AND NO ONE, SAINT OR DEVIL, CAN TAKE IT FROM ME!
UNNH!
BRUCE!
14

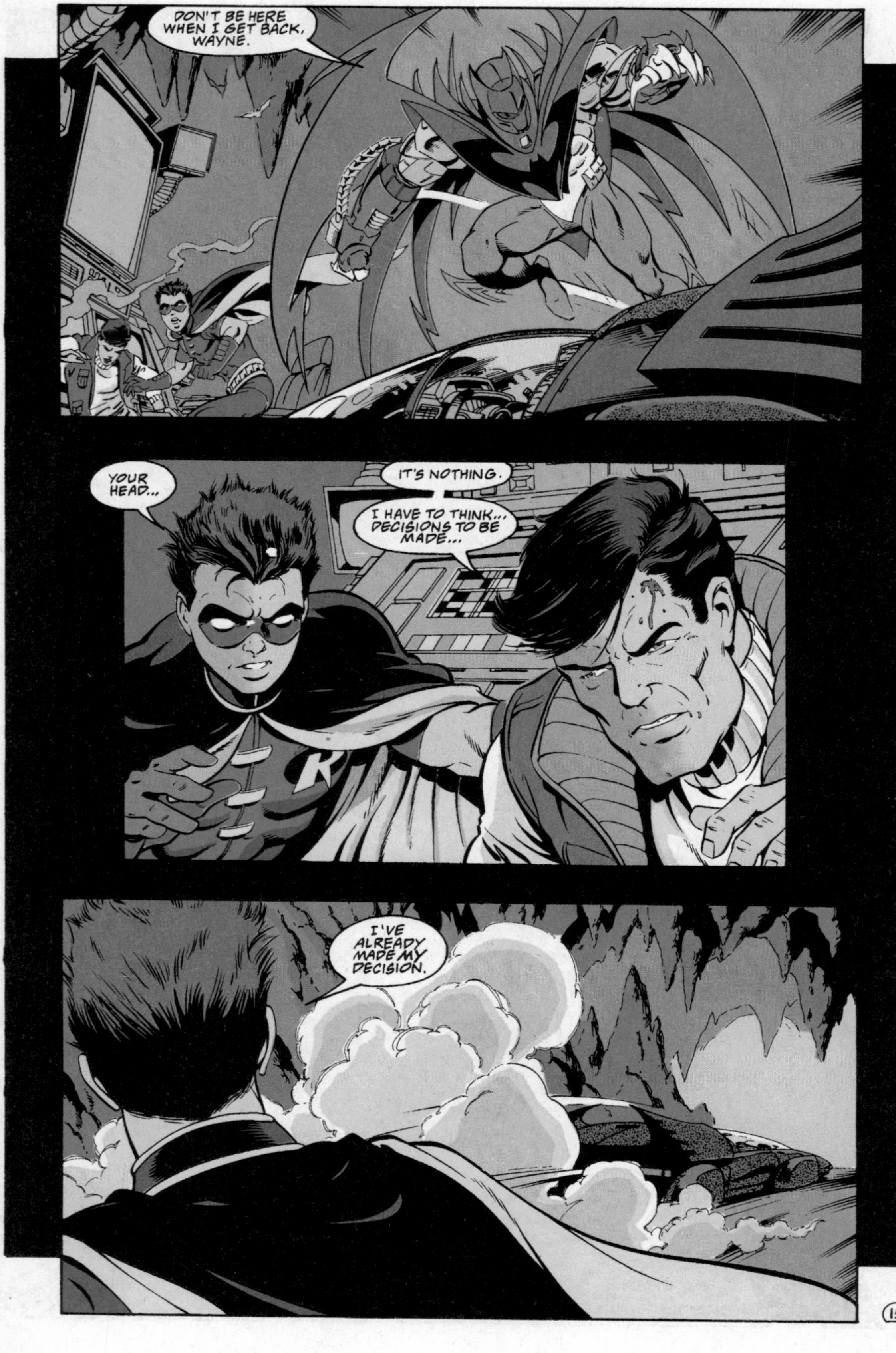
DON'T BE HERE WHEN I GET BACK, WAYNE.
YOUR HEAD...
IT'S NOTHING.
I HAVE TO THINK... DECISIONS TO BE MADE...
I'VE ALREADY MADE MY DECISION.
15

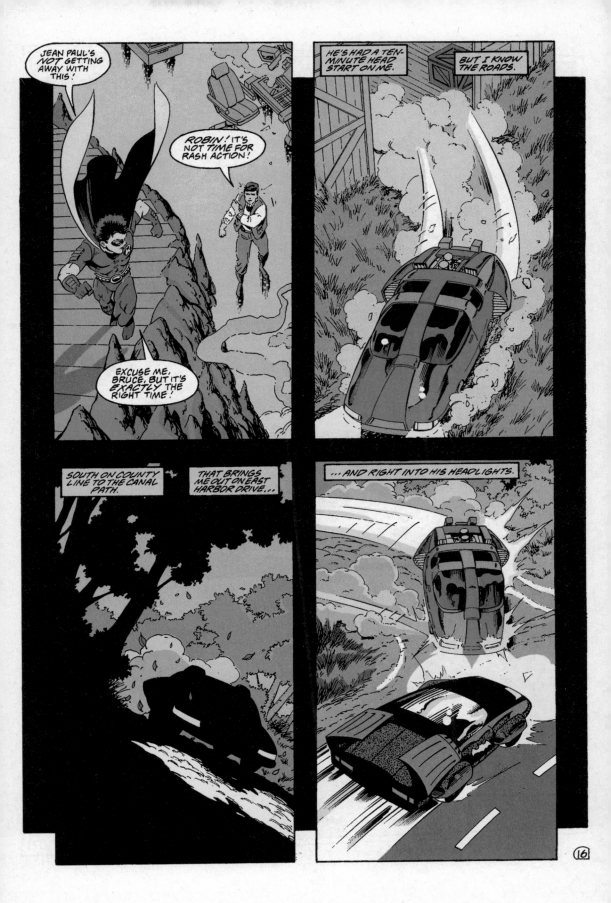

JEAN PAUL'S *NOT GETTING AWAY WITH* THIS!

ROBIN! IT'S *NOT TIME FOR RASH ACTION!*

EXCUSE ME, BRUCE, BUT IT'S *EXACTLY THE RIGHT TIME!*

HE'S HAD A *TEN-MINUTE HEAD START* ON ME.

BUT I KNOW *THE ROADS.*

SOUTH ON *COUNTY LINE* TO THE *CANAL PATH.*

THAT BRINGS ME OUT ON *EAST HARBOR DRIVE...*

...AND *RIGHT INTO HIS HEADLIGHTS.*

16

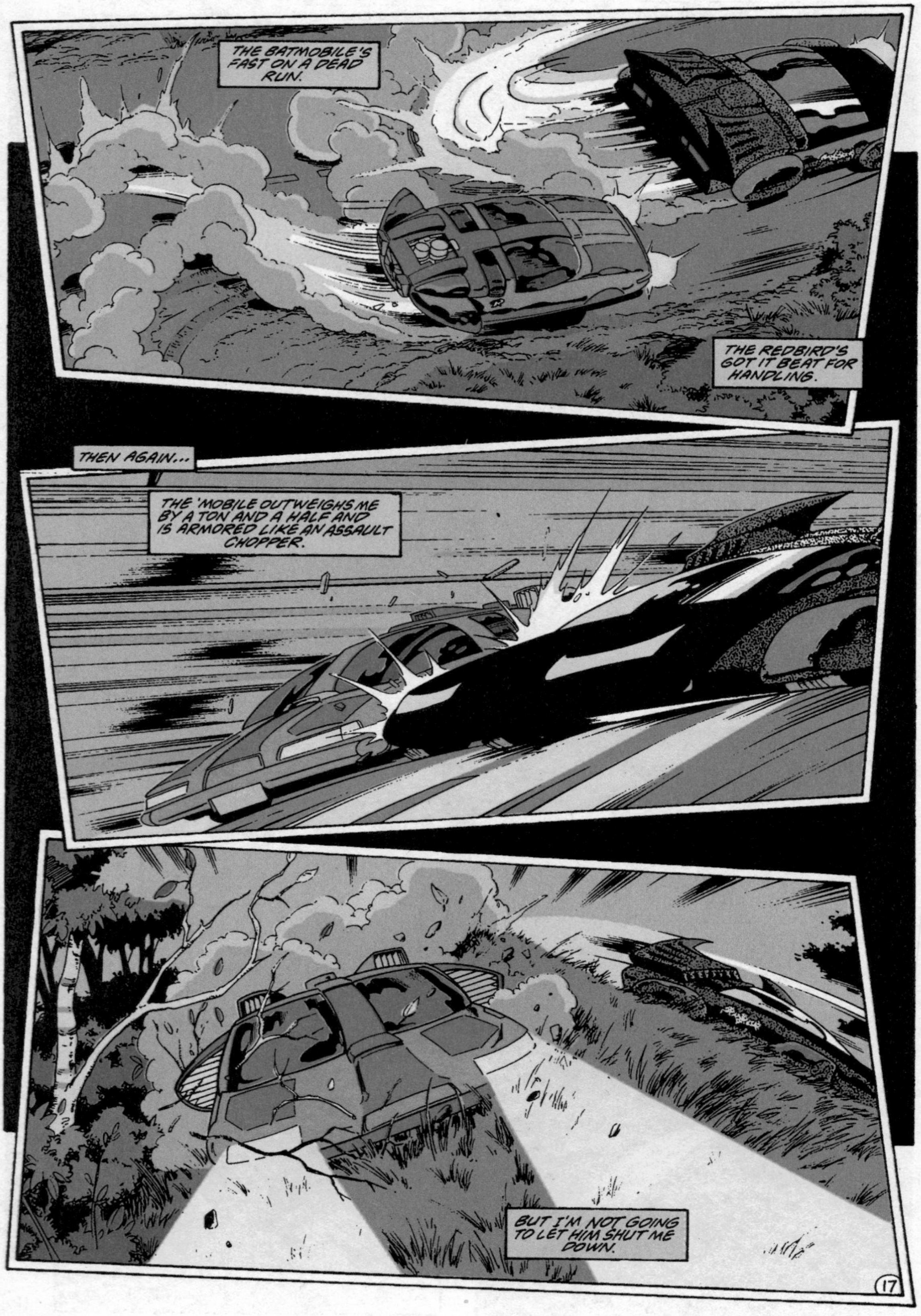

THE BATMOBILE'S FAST ON A DEAD RUN.
THE REDBIRD'S GOT IT BEAT FOR HANDLING.
THEN AGAIN...
THE 'MOBILE OUTWEIGHS ME BY A TON AND A HALF AND IS ARMORED LIKE AN ASSAULT CHOPPER.
BUT I'M NOT GOING TO LET HIM SHUT ME DOWN.
17

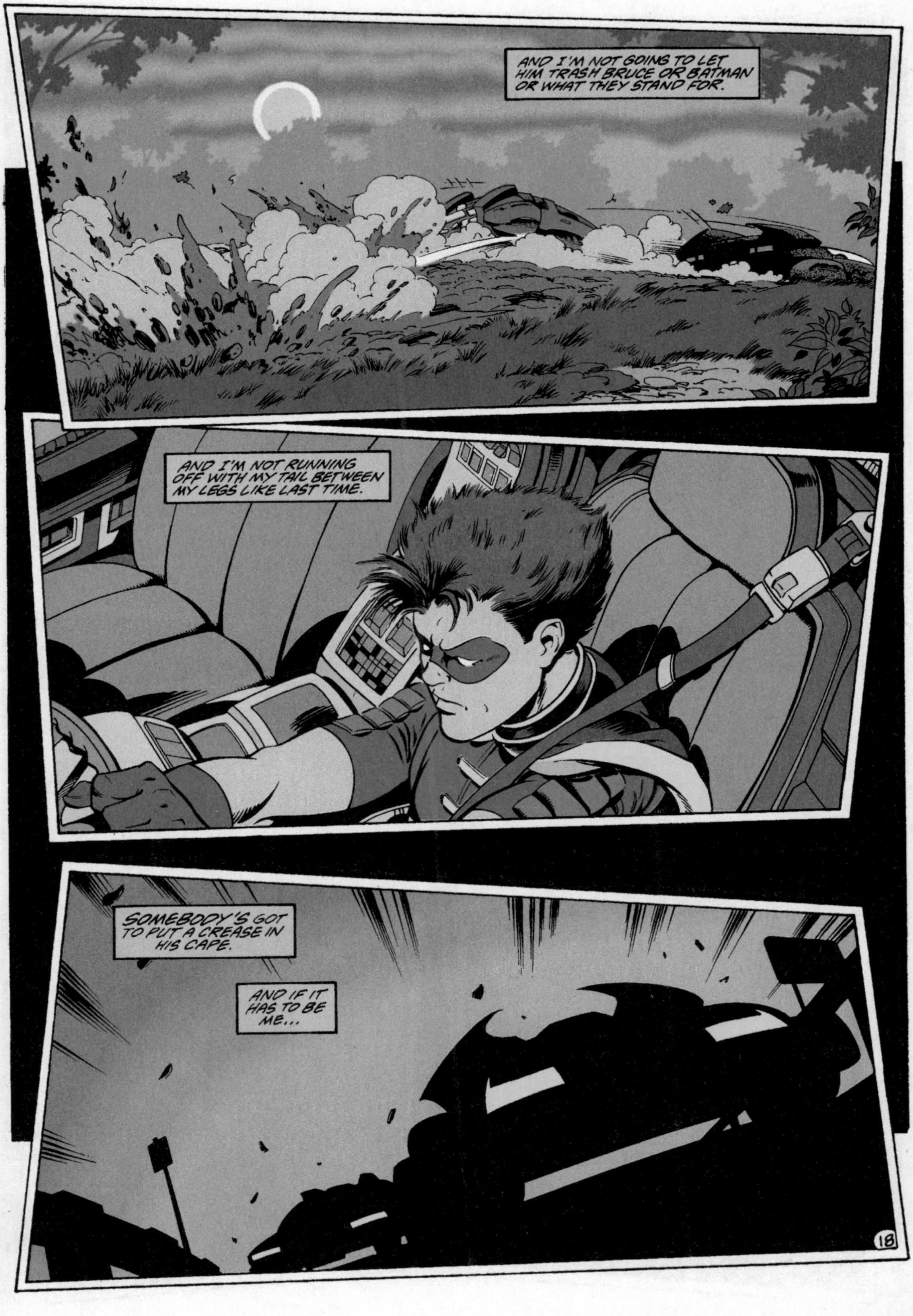
AND I'M NOT GOING TO LET HIM TRASH BRUCE OR BATMAN OR WHAT THEY STAND FOR.
AND I'M NOT RUNNING OFF WITH MY TAIL BETWEEN MY LEGS LIKE LAST TIME.
SOMEBODY'S GOT TO PUT A CREASE IN HIS CAPE.
AND IF IT HAS TO BE ME...
18

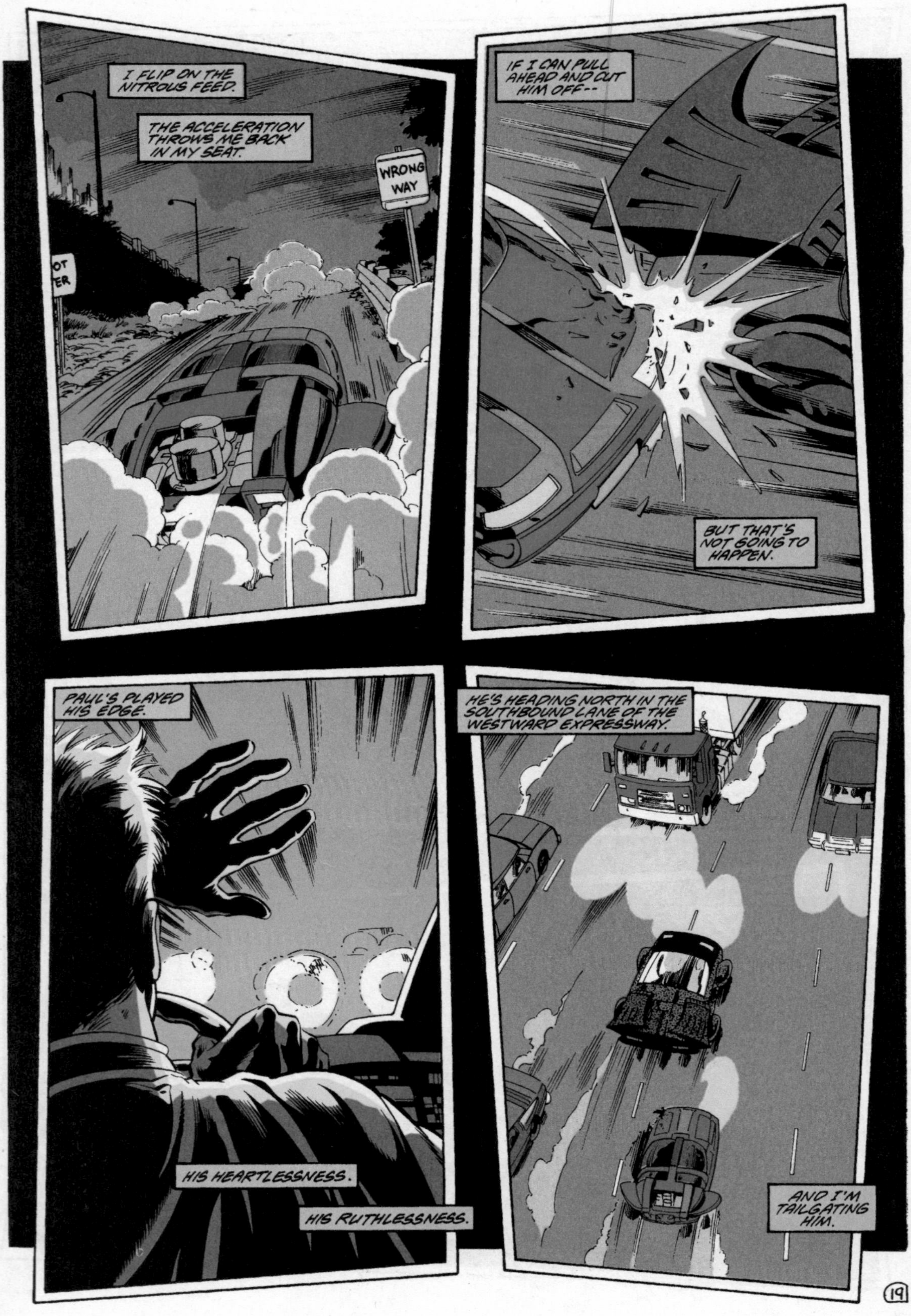
I FLIP ON THE NITROUS FEED.
THE ACCELERATION THROWS ME BACK IN MY SEAT.
WRONG WAY
IF I CAN PULL AHEAD AND CUT HIM OFF--
BUT THAT'S NOT GOING TO HAPPEN.
PAUL'S PLAYED HIS EDGE.
HIS HEARTLESSNESS.
HIS RUTHLESSNESS.
HE'S HEADING NORTH IN THE SOUTHBOUND LANE OF THE WESTWARD EXPRESSWAY.
AND I'M TAILGATING HIM.
19

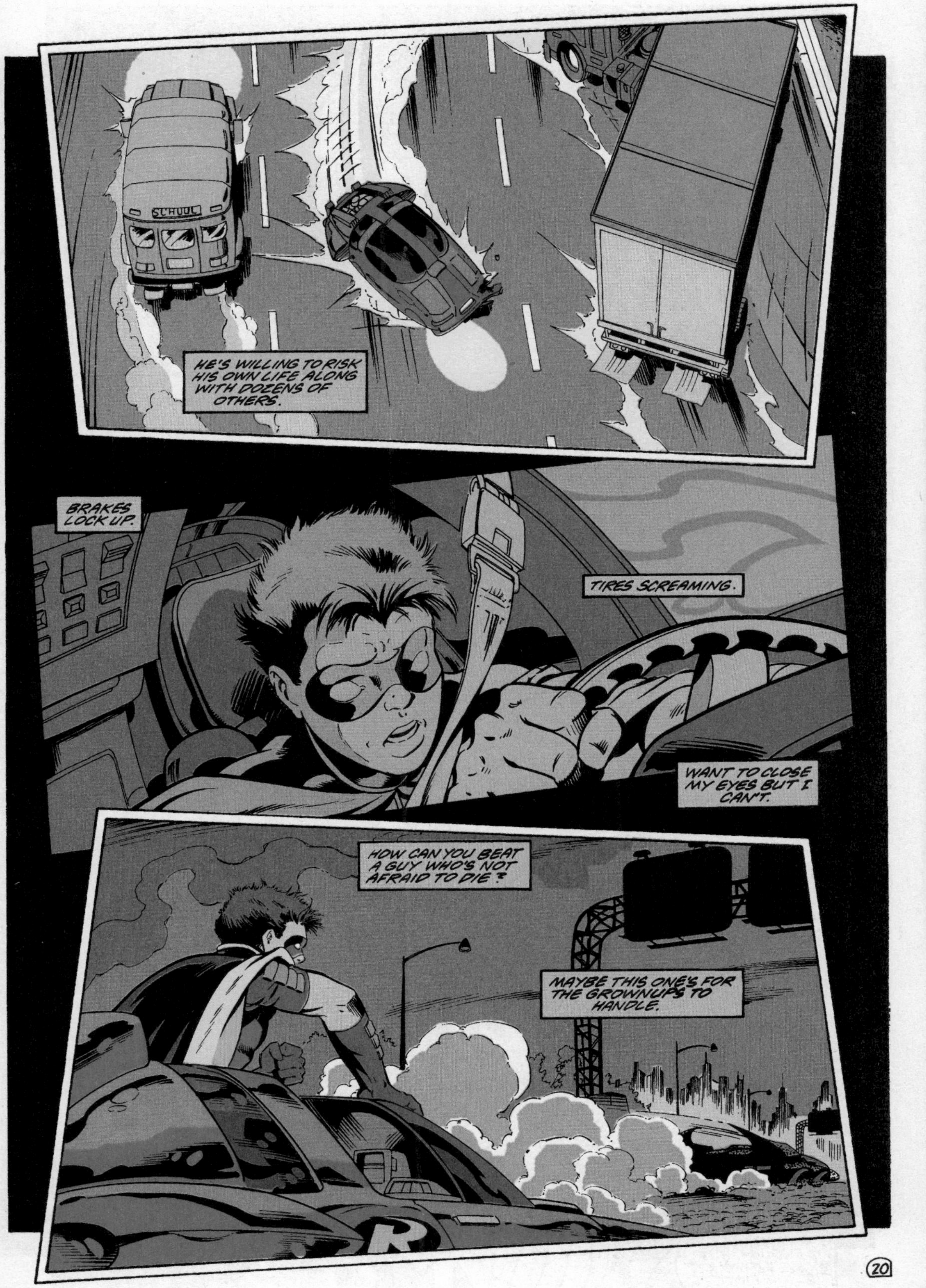
SCHOOL
HE'S WILLING TO RISK HIS OWN LIFE ALONG WITH DOZENS OF OTHERS.
BRAKES LOCK UP.
TIRES SCREAMING.
WANT TO CLOSE MY EYES BUT I CAN'T.
HOW CAN YOU BEAT A GUY WHO'S NOT AFRAID TO DIE?
MAYBE THIS ONE'S FOR THE GROWNUPS TO HANDLE.
20

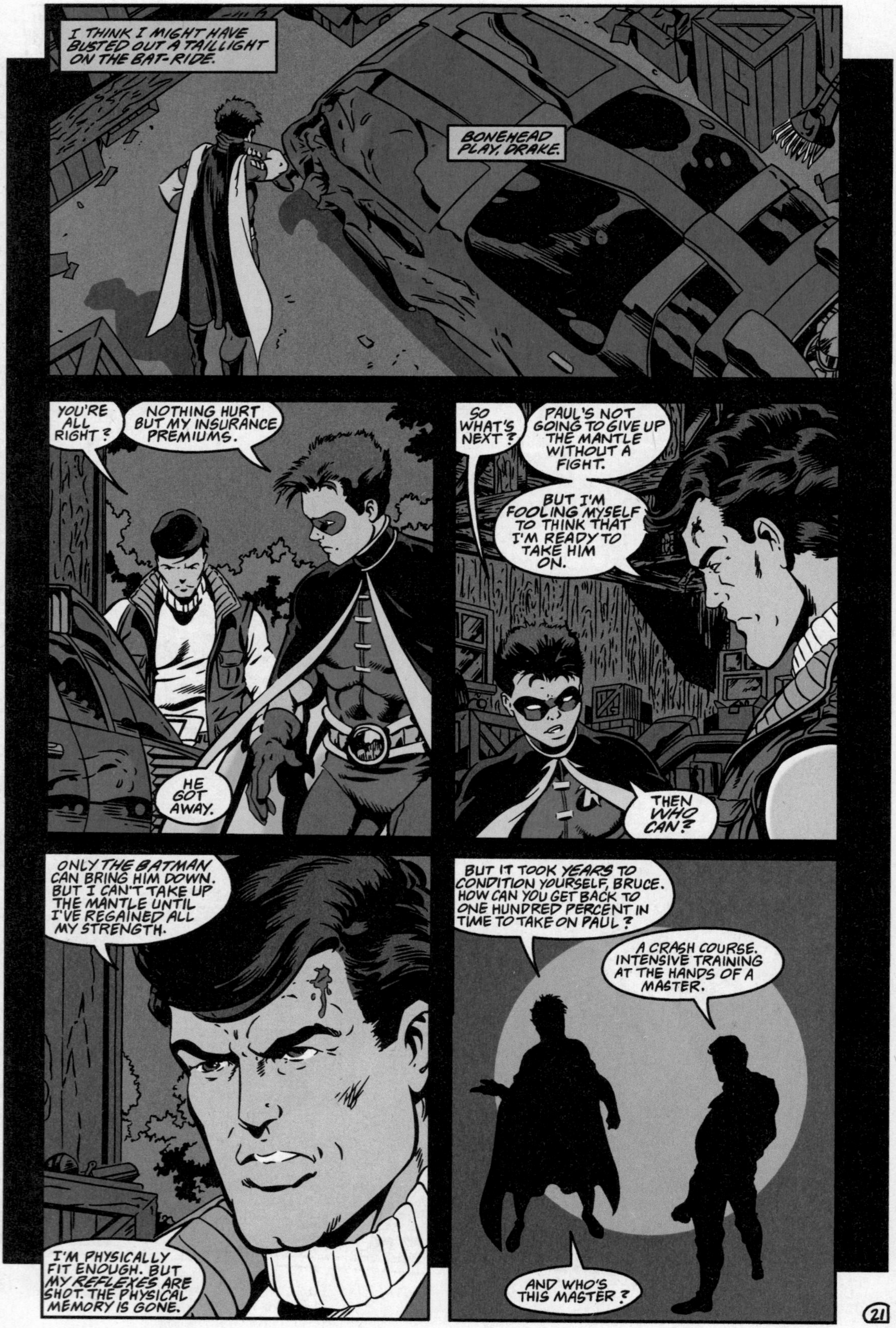
I THINK I MIGHT HAVE BUSTED OUT A TAILLIGHT ON THE BAT-RIDE.
BONEHEAD PLAY, DRAKE.
YOU'RE ALL RIGHT?
NOTHING HURT BUT MY INSURANCE PREMIUMS.
HE GOT AWAY.
SO WHAT'S NEXT?
PAUL'S NOT GOING TO GIVE UP THE MANTLE WITHOUT A FIGHT.
BUT I'M FOOLING MYSELF TO THINK THAT I'M READY TO TAKE HIM ON.
THEN WHO CAN?
ONLY THE BATMAN CAN BRING HIM DOWN. BUT I CAN'T TAKE UP THE MANTLE UNTIL I'VE REGAINED ALL MY STRENGTH.
I'M PHYSICALLY FIT ENOUGH. BUT MY REFLEXES ARE SHOT. THE PHYSICAL MEMORY IS GONE.
BUT IT TOOK YEARS TO CONDITION YOURSELF, BRUCE. HOW CAN YOU GET BACK TO ONE HUNDRED PERCENT IN TIME TO TAKE ON PAUL?
A CRASH COURSE. INTENSIVE TRAINING AT THE HANDS OF A MASTER.
AND WHO'S THIS MASTER?
21

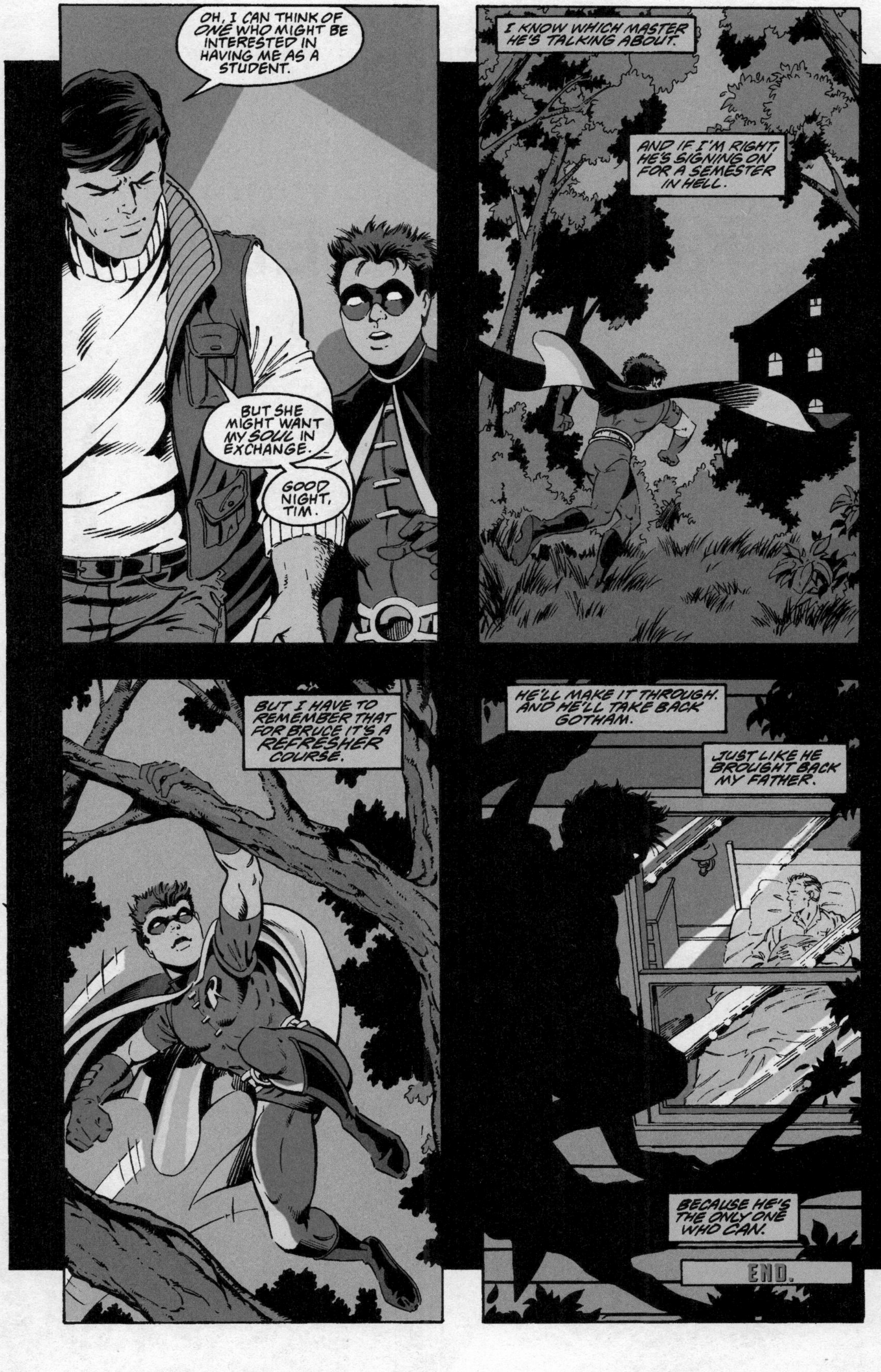
OH, I CAN THINK OF ONE WHO MIGHT BE INTERESTED IN HAVING ME AS A STUDENT.
BUT SHE MIGHT WANT MY SOUL IN EXCHANGE.
GOOD NIGHT, TIM.
I KNOW WHICH MASTER HE'S TALKING ABOUT.
AND IF I'M RIGHT, HE'S SIGNING ON FOR A SEMESTER IN HELL.
BUT I HAVE TO REMEMBER THAT FOR BRUCE IT'S A REFRESHER COURSE.
HE'LL MAKE IT THROUGH. AND HE'LL TAKE BACK GOTHAM.
JUST LIKE HE BROUGHT BACK MY FATHER.
BECAUSE HE'S THE ONLY ONE WHO CAN.
END.

Follow the adventures of Batman and his own war on crime in

BATMAN KNIGHTFALL VOLUME 3
KNIGHT'S END